BARTLETT 2017

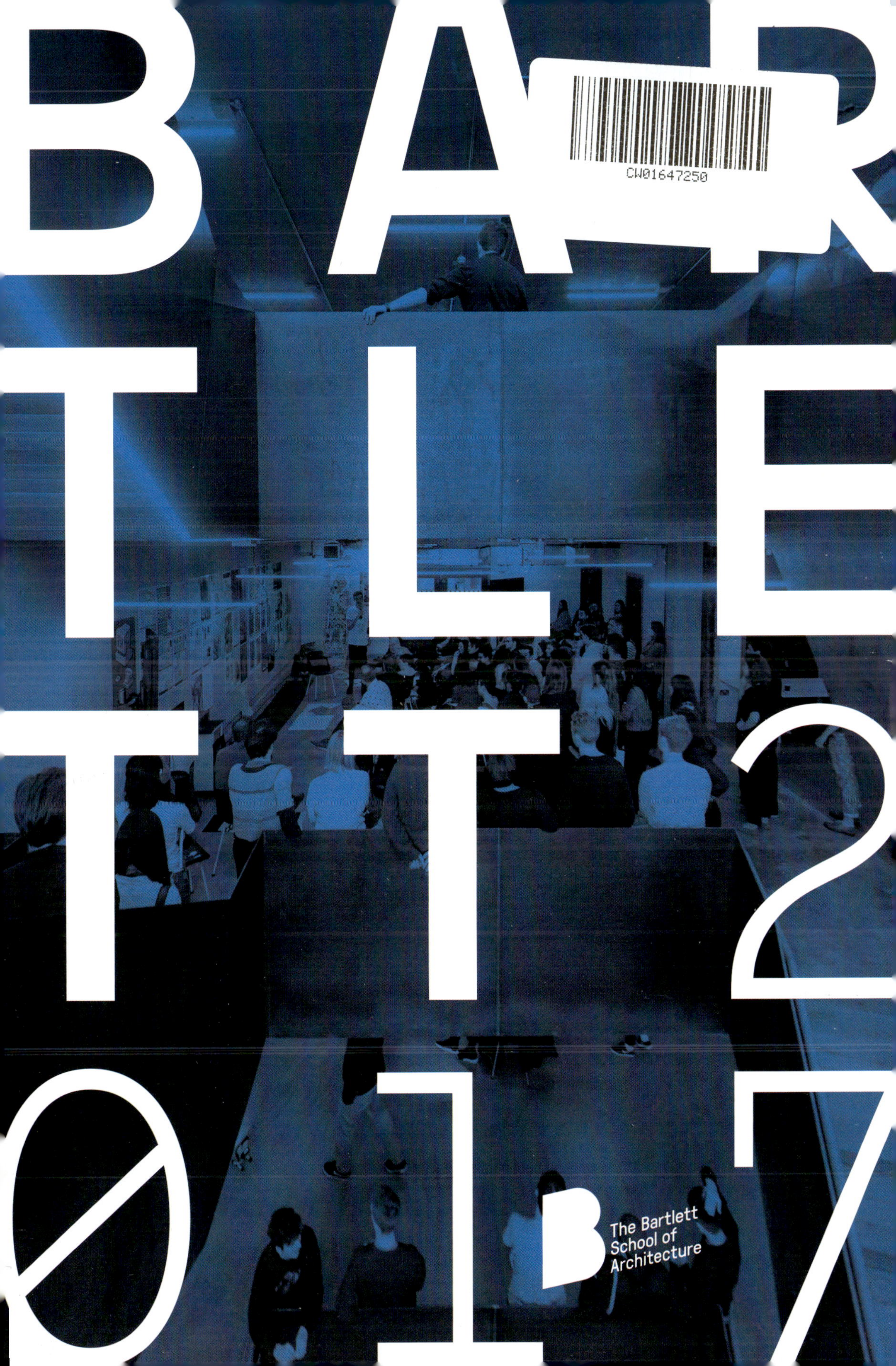

The Bartlett School of Architecture

New Scotland Yard

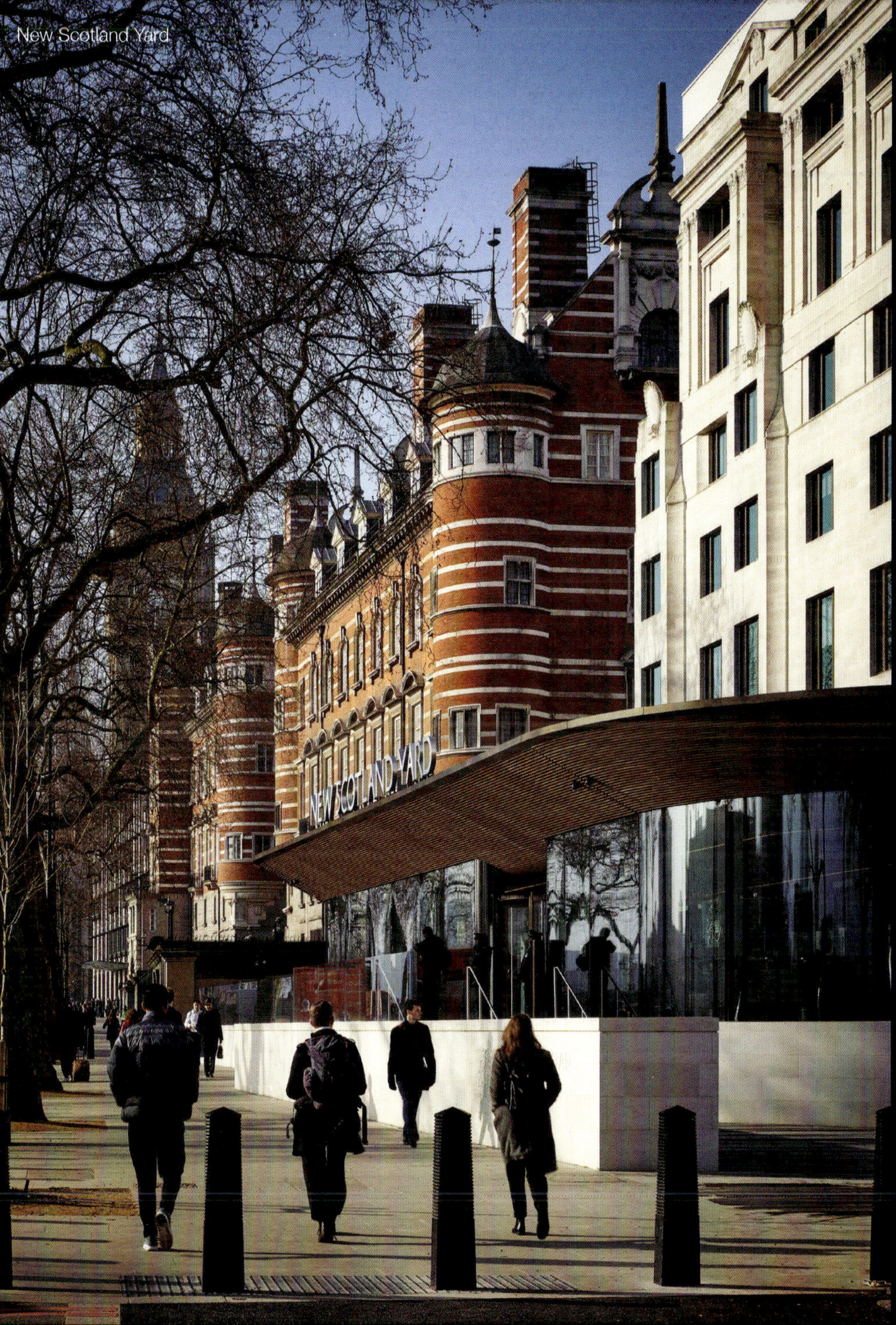

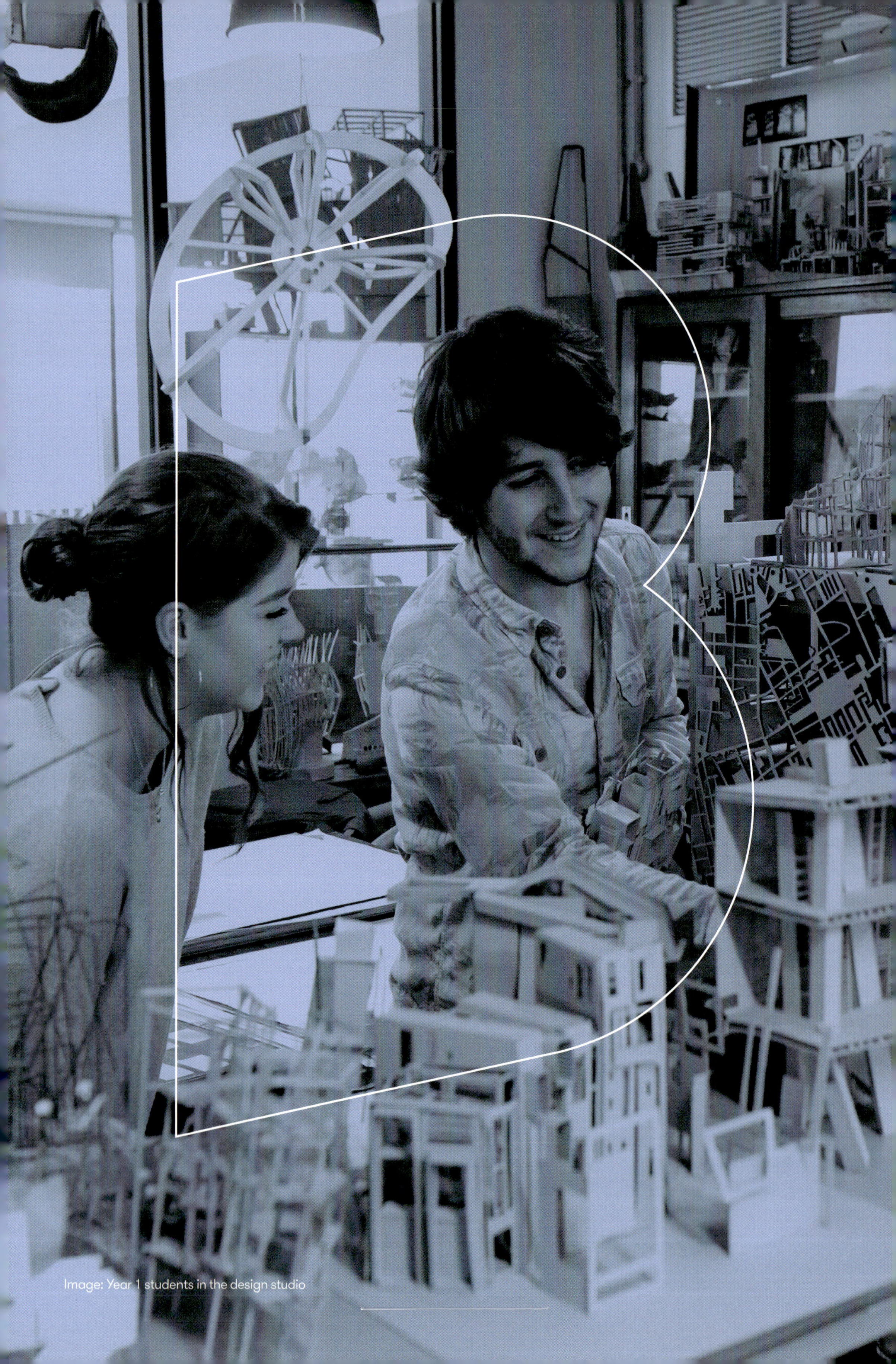

Image: Year 1 students in the design studio

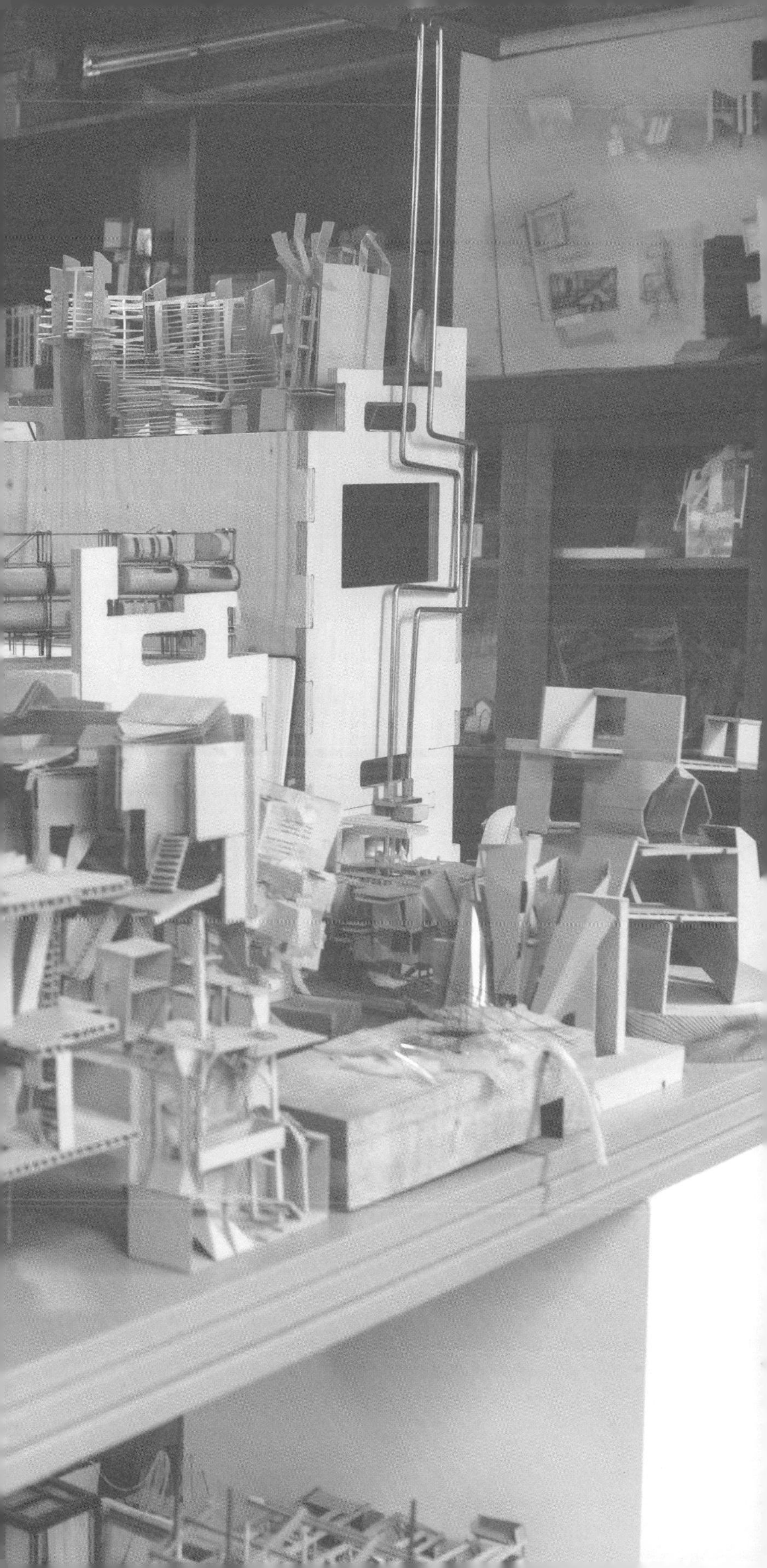

Contents

BARTLETT

SUMMER 2017

Introduction

Our annual Summer Show has been running for over 30 years, and during this time it has become a renowned and highly anticipated event in London's architecture calendar. In 1990, it was opened by Berthold Lubetkin in the cramped courtyard of Wates House, followed a year later by Enric Miralles. In subsequent years, figures such as Frank Gehry, Thom Mayne, Norman Foster, Brian Eno, Zaha Hadid, Lebbeus Woods and Richard Rogers have launched the event, which celebrates the work of our BSc Architecture, BSc Architecture and Interdisciplinary Studies and MArch Architecture students. In recent years, the show has been opened by Itsuko Hasegawa, Carme Pinós and Liz Diller – and we are delighted that our opener for 2017 is the acclaimed designer Ross Lovegrove, who has his own show running concurrently at the Centre Pompidou in Paris. We are also delighted and grateful that AHMM, the award-winning architectural practice where all four partners are Bartlett alumni, are this year's main show sponsor.

This year, our show is being held at 22 Gordon Street for the first time in sixteen years, as we have moved back into substantially refurbished and expanded premises designed for UCL by Hawkins\Brown Architects. For the past two years, we were located 'off-site' at Hampstead Road, where the show was memorably held in the basement garage of our temporary home. For the fourteen years prior to this, the show was held in the galleries of The Slade School of Fine Art, just off UCL's main quadrangle. So it's taken a while, but we're back at 22 Gordon Street – and the feeling of returning home will truly be complete once this year's show opens.

We wish therefore to thank all those who helped deliver our new building, which offers us the space in which to operate comfortably for a very long time. Our thanks also extend, of course, to all staff and students who carried out the mid-year move with efficiency and patience.

In this spirit of adventure and change, our programme directors have curated the show in a way not seen in a long time, mixing undergraduate and postgraduate spaces, rather than aligning them in blocks or housing them in separate rooms. This is more than a reflection of how our studios are laid out; it also signifies a shift that's been emerging at the School for some time now, one that recognises how units operate in association rather than isolation. It recognises how students from different units often work collaboratively and move from unit to unit over the years, and how projects and people in one unit or programme learn from projects and people in another. Our spatially porous building and the new unifying staircase also facilitate this, elevating the Summer Show – and all our annual shows – to become more than just an exhibition of parts. The space has become a collective resource that challenges how we think and operate. Like many things we do – and like everything in the show – they're an experiment, reflecting the fact that we are an experimental school.

We hope you enjoy the show and this companion publication. We are staggered by the extraordinary work of our students, and we wish them a long, bright and productive future.

Professor Frédéric Migayrou
Chair, Bartlett Professor of Architecture, The Bartlett School of Architecture

Professor Bob Sheil
Director of The Bartlett School of Architecture

Prizes 2016 – 17

Bartlett School of Architecture Medal

For students averaging 80% or higher in professional programmes

BSc Architecture
Jun Hao Chan, UG0

MArch Architecture
Christia Angelidou, Unit 12
Damien Assini, Unit 10
Paddi Benson, Unit 21
Thomas Bush, Unit 20
Clare Hawes, Unit 12
Johanna Just, Unit 11
Kai Hang Liu, Unit 10
Matthew Lucraft, Unit 24
Kirsty McMullan, Unit 25
Agostino Nickl, Unit 11
Thomas Parker, Unit 25
Jasper Stevens, Unit 24
Amani Radeef, Unit 16
Ivo Tedbury, Unit 19

BSc Architecture Year 1

Herbert Batsford Prize
Theodosia Bosy Maury

The Grocers' Company, Queen's Golden Jubilee Scholarship
Migena Hadziu

Conceptual Clarity Prize
Karl Herdersch

Tectonics, Structural and Materials Prize
Owen Mellet

Spatial Exploration Prize
Thomas Richardson

Drawing/Model Prize
Vasily Babichev

Model/Drawing Prize
Jake Williams

BSc Architecture Year 2

Victor Kite Prize for Design Technology, sponsored by AHMM
James Robinson, UG9

Professional Studies Prize
Joanna McLean, UG3
Anna O'Leary, UG10

BSc Architecture Year 3

RIBA Donaldson Medal
Jun Hao Chan, UG0

Trevor Sprott Prize for Distinguished Work in History and Theory
Ashleigh-Paige Fielding, UG12

Experimental Technology Prize
Peter Davies, UG12

Environmental Design Prize
Jun Hao Chan, UG0

Fitzroy Robinson Prize
To be announced

Making Buildings Prize
Elissavet Manou, UG8

Professional Studies Prize
James Hepper, UG12

BSc Architectural & Interdisciplinary Studies

Distinguished Work in History and Theory
Eloise Maland

MArch Architecture Year 4

History and Theory Prize
John Cruwys, Unit 24
Esha Thapar, Unit 17

Kohn Pedersen Fox Associates Bursary
Laurence Blackwell-Thale, Unit 11

Rogers Stirk Harbour + Partners Bursary
John Cruwys, Unit 24

Hawkins\Brown Bursary
Sophie Barks, Unit 12

WES Lunn Design Education Trust Scholarship
Patrick Horne, Unit 11

Saint-Gobain Innovation Award
Ryan Blackford, Unit 14
Laurence Blackwell-Thale, Unit 11
George Courtauld, Unit 14
Patrick Horne, Unit 11
Eleanor Sampson, Unit 11

MArch Architecture Year 5

Ambrose Poynter Prize
Ivo Tedbury, Unit 19

Fitzroy Robinson Drawing Prize
Thomas Parker, Unit 25

Max Fordham Environmental Design Prize
Amani Radeef, Unit 16

Brewer Smith Brewer Gulf Adaptive Technologies Prize
Thomas Bush, Unit 20

Sir Andrew Taylor Prize
Ivo Tedbury, Unit 19

Sir Banister Fletcher Medal
Agostino Nickl, Unit 11

Postgraduate Diploma in Professional Practice & Management in Architecture (ARB/RIBA Part 3)

Ross Jamieson Memorial Prize
Lilija Oblecova
Lee Jesson

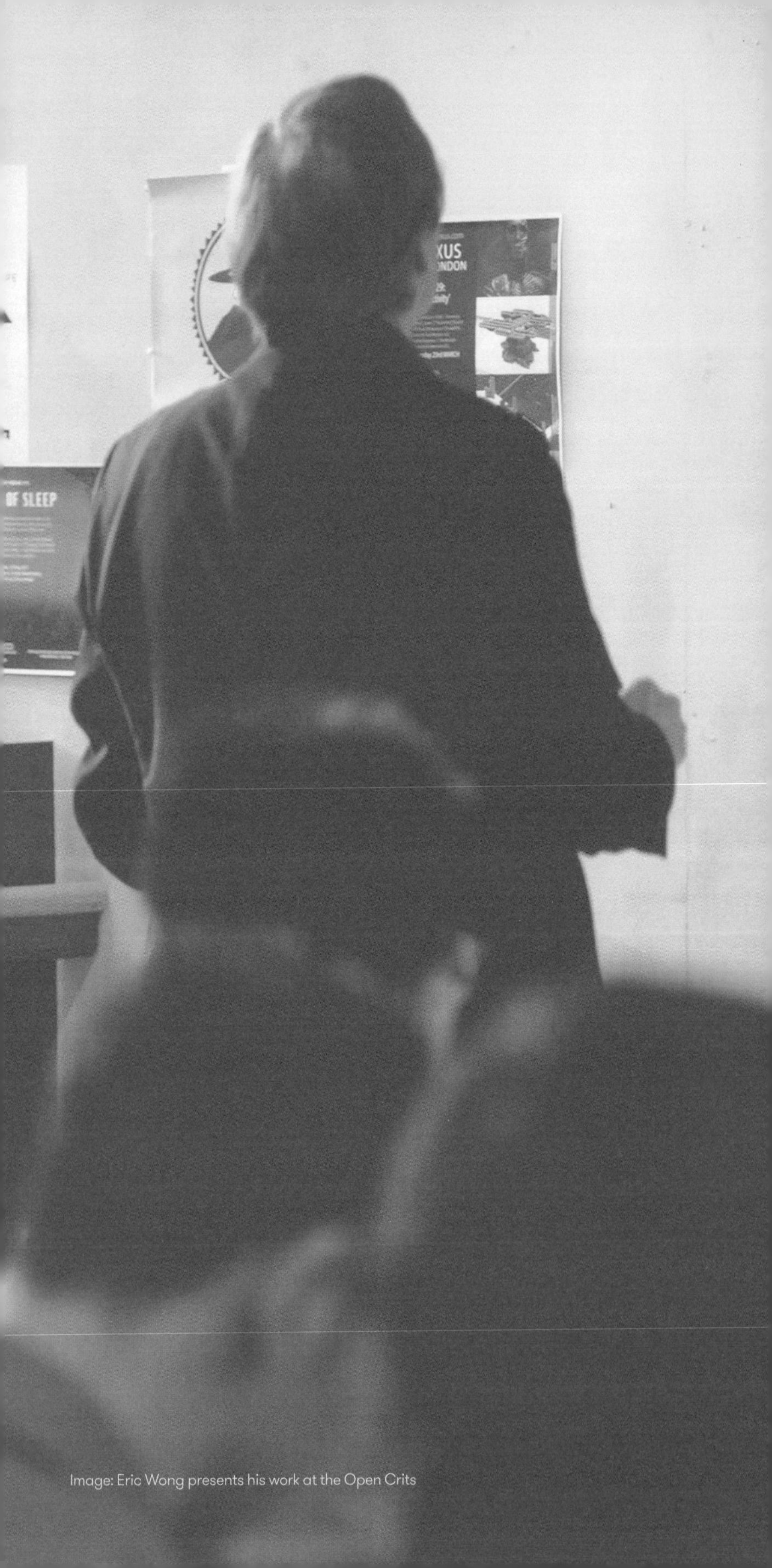

Image: Eric Wong presents his work at the Open Crits

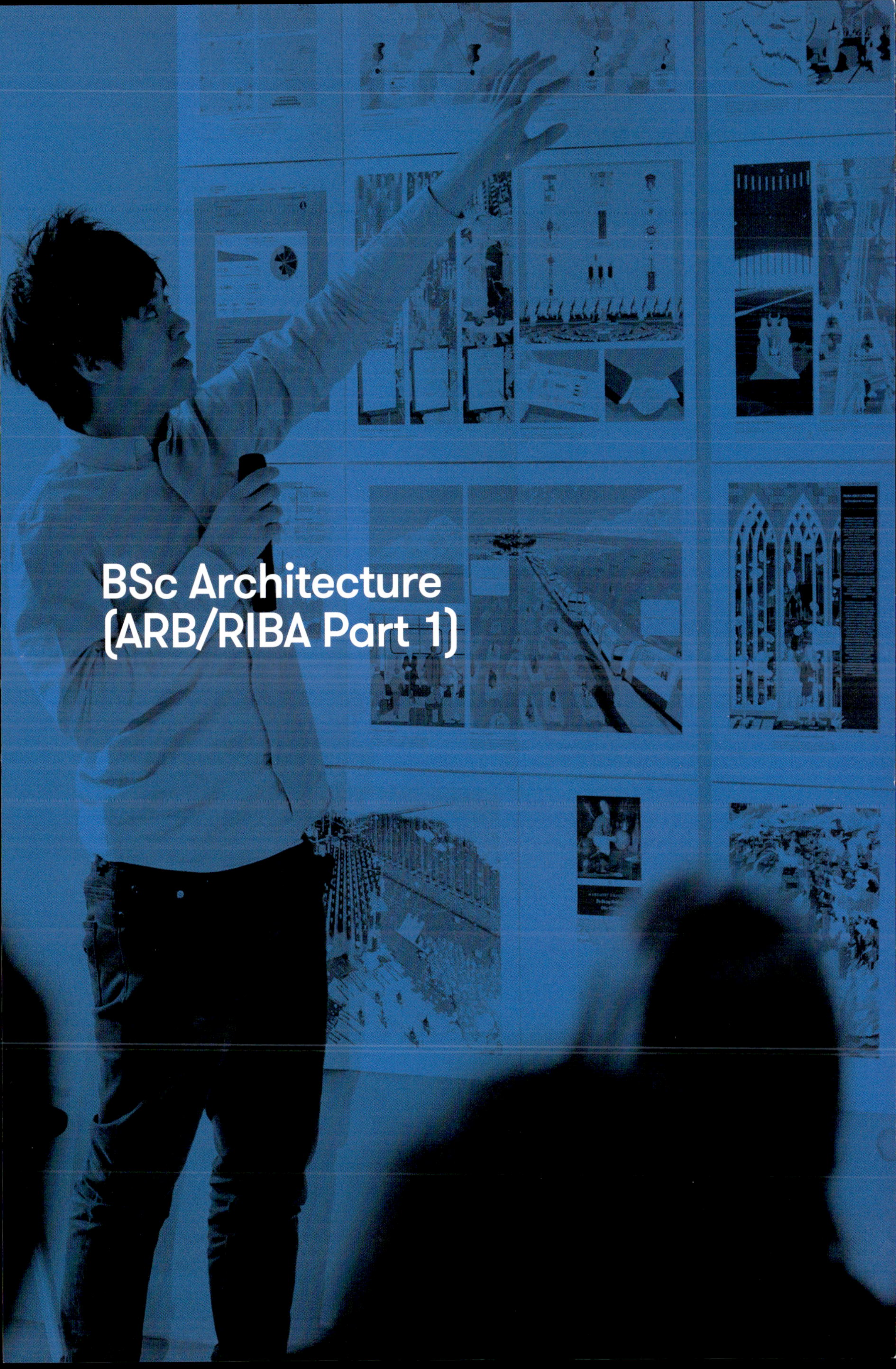

BSc Architecture (ARB/RIBA Part 1)

BSc Architecture (ARB/RIBA Part 1)

Programme Directors: Matthew Butcher, Mollie Claypool, Sara Shafiei (acting)

Year 1 Director
Frosso Pimenides

Year 1 Design Associates
Carlos Jiménez Cenamor, Gavin Robotham, Emmanouil Stavrakakis

Year 1 Tutors
Joel Cady, Fenella Coldridge, Stefan Lengen, Ifigeneia Liangi, Rebecca Loewen, Thandi Loewenson, Emma-Kate Matthews, Brian O'Reilly, Eva Ravnborg, Charlotte Reynolds, Nick Westby, Umut Yamac

Year 2 & 3 Design Tutors
UG0
Murray Fraser (on sabbatical), Tamsin Hanke, Sara Shafiei
UG1
Jon Lopez, Hikaru Nissanke
UG2
Soomeen Hahm, Aleksandrina Rizova
UG3
Luke Olsen, Graeme Williamson
UG4
Ana Monrabal-Cook, Luke Pearson
UG5
Julia Backhaus, Martin Tang
UG6
Tim Norman, Paolo Zaide
UG7
Pascal Bronner, Thomas Hillier
UG8
Colin Herperger, Thomas Pearce
UG9
Jessica In, Chee-Kit Lai
UG10
Guan Lee, Arthur Mamou-Mani
UG11
Kostas Grigoriadis, Sofia Krimizi
UG12
Johan Hybschmann, Matthew Springett

This programme concentrates on providing extensive knowledge and understanding about what architecture is as a subject, a discipline and a practice, with a distinct emphasis on architectural design through research-based education. It aims to establish the student's core knowledge, critical ability and skills through drawing and making (both analogue and digital), technology (including environmental design, sustainability and computation), history and theory and professional studies. The Year 1 cohort is organised as a single group, and a vertical unit system begins in Year 2. A core ethos of the entire BSc programme is that students relate their design projects to all other taught modules on an incremental basis. This culminates in Year 3, where design and technology are developed in synthesis, augmented by complementary self-selected themes in history and theory and professional studies.

Year 1

Year 1 is a 'contextual' year where core architectural expertise and knowledge around cities, buildings and practice is developed through diverse experimentation and exploration, including drawing, making, writing and film. The 'History of Cities and their Architecture' module is shared with fellow Bartlett BSc students of Planning, and the 'Making Cities' module is shared with fellow Bartlett BSc students of Planning, and Construction and Project Management. The final building design project evolves in parallel to separate coursework in other modules, and it finishes the year with a common springboard into Year 2. This year, we had thirteen Units in the undergraduate programme with diverse themes and agendas that included explorations into: the relationship between architecture and landscape; digital and computational design methodologies; and the role of narrative in architecture.

Year 2

Year 2 centres on 'diversity', which is exemplified by the unit system in design as well as seminar groups in history and theory. Although distinct from one another, units deliver a common set of principles that include: spatial organisation, communication, culture, critique, context, and environmental and social impact. In tandem with the final building design project, the technology module requires strategic and detailed technical investigations, including how fragments of the project could be built. This presents a tactile introduction to architectural design, its relationship to construction techniques and associated disciplines, and the challenge of making information for making buildings. Over the course of the year, students must demonstrate understanding of a selected theme in architectural history, as well as core skills in computing.

Year 3

Year 3 centres on 'synthesis' between architectural design, critical understanding, core skills, professional practice and creative exploration. Design projects evolve as an individual response to the unit brief through innovative research in tandem with a comprehensive technical dissertation. Projects are rooted in core principles of spatial and physical design, supported by an extensive network of practice-based consultants. Students are also encouraged to speculate on conventional boundaries of architectural production and architectural representation. Year 3 also includes modules in architectural history and theory, and professional practice.

Year Out

Increasingly, students are taking a further year out whilst remaining engaged with their studies. This course focuses on practice management, business and enterprise through a series of talks and seminars based on five recall days followed by informal networking events, tutorials and PEDR monitoring. Students write an end-of-year essay on a topic of interest related to contemporary practice or architectural education.

Year 1

Occupying Routes: from the City to the Valley

Director: Frosso Pimenides

Director
Frosso Pimenides

Design Associates
Carlos Jiménez Cenamor, Gavin Robotham, Emmanouil Stavrakakis

Lecture Series
Nat Chard, Peter Cook

Fabrication Consultant
Emmanuel Vercruysse

Installation Consultants
Indigo Rohrer, Nick Westby

Media Studies Tutors
Joel Cady, Danielle Hodgson

Design Tutors
Fenella Colingridge, Stefan Lengen, Ifigeneia Liangi, Rebecca Loewen, Thandi Loewenson, Emma-Kate Matthews, Brian O'Reilly, Eva Ravnborg, Farlie Reynolds, Umut Yamac

Partners
B-made workshop, CRAB studio

Thank you to:
Jenna Al-Ali, Will Armstrong, Michael Arthur (UCL President and Provost), Julia Backhaus, Blanche Cameron, Mario Carpo, Nat Chard, Peter Cook, Stewart Dodd, Emma Flynn, Adrian Forty, Christine Hawley, Daniel Howarth, Richard Jeffries, Mary Johnson, Stephen Johnson, Lilly Kudic, Saskia Lewis, CJ Lim, Phil Medowcroft, Jack Newton, Alan Penn, Jonathan Pile, Juliet Quintero, Bob Sheil, Colin Skeete, Emmanuel Vercruysse, Patrick Weber, Gwendoline Webber, Paul Wenston, Nick Westby, Nick Wood, Paolo Zaide

Initiating students into civic life and the world of architecture is the foundation of their education in the first year. Students are encouraged to develop their personality, learn skills, enter the world of ideas and cultivate creativity. Communicating ideas and expressing one's imagination through drawing and making is our main intention. A series of experiments and a group project led to an individual building project situated in East London's Lea Valley.

——The year started with a group fabrication project, 'Return and Reinstall', a celebration of a pivotal moment in the life and tradition of the School. It comprised three parts: a bonfire of old models, marking our departure from 140 Hampstead Road; a procession of 125 students transporting archived models back to our new home at 22 Gordon Street; and finally, installing these models to mark the start of a new era.

——The field trip to Northern Italy was a great source of inspiration and collective culture as students were exposed to some of the world's most influential buildings and places. By surveying a small fragment of Bologna, students immersed themselves in a different culture that they then interpreted via their own personal understanding.

——The 'Live-Work' building project, located in Lea Valley, was an opportunity to explore the importance of 'context', enclosure, spatial qualities and the materiality of a proposed vision. The project was a vehicle for students to explore their own inspirations and focus on their own interests. A series of sites were chosen adjacent to the River Lea and Olympic Park area. Each student was asked to explore and understand the character of a site and inhabit it through a proposed story (each student's personal programme) that established a dialogue with the surrounding area.

——The life of our first year students is a continuous process of testing, questioning, rethinking and visually communicating a series of design explorations over the course of a year, as part of a vibrant studio culture. It is a journey of learning skills and knowledge that give students the tools to think, experiment, make mistakes and celebrate their failures – and finally, to have fun designing.

Students
Nasra Abdullahi, Vitika Agarwal, Temilayo Ajayi, Mohammad Aldoori, Alp Amasya, Jahba Anan, Basil Babichev, Daeyong Bae, Danheng Bai, Alexander Balgarnie, Danya Barysnikov, Sadika Begum, Sheryl Beh, Victoria Blackburn, Vladyslav Bondarenko, Ted Bosy Maury, Anna Cabanlig, Maria Castello, Jason (Chun) Chan, Kelvin (Kai) Chan, Terry (Weiting) Chen, Kyrah Issariyaporn, Viktor (Hiu) Chow, Pearl (Yu) Chow, Chris Collyer, Andrew Cowie, Kasia Dabrowska, Sofya Daniltseva, Elizabeth Day, Bengisu Demir, Maria De Salvador Arnaiz, Imogen Dhesi, Amanda Dolga, Joe Douglas, Benedict Edwards, Miles Elliot, Charlotte Evans, Nanci Fairless Nicholson, Wan Feng, Georgia Green, Migena Hadziu, Bijou Harding, Eleanor Harding, Celina Harto, Holly Hatfield, Karl Herdersch, Yvonne (Yu-Wen) Huang, Abe (Zhongliang) Huang, Noriyuki Ishii, Maria Jones Delago, Peter (Yuen) Kei, Amy Kempa, Karishma Khajuria, Megan King, Sharon (Ting) Lee, Anson (Yiu) Lee, Kit Lee-Smith, Clement Le Pelley, Frances Leung, Yen (Su) Liew, Angel Lim, Jiana Lin, Jessica (Chit) Liu, Joicy (Pinyi) Liu, Hugo Loydell, Aurelia (Yixuan) Lu, Francis Magalhaes Heath, Emily Mak, Diana Marin, Kai (James) McLaughlin, Luke McMahon, Owen Mellett, Zakariya Miah, Lucy Millichamp, Indran Miranda Duraisingam, Marcus Yang Mohan, Heba Mohsen, Emilie Morrow, Nandinzul Munkhbayar, Drew Murphy, Carlota Nunez-Barranco Vallejo, Chinwe Obi, Harriet Orr, Mimi Osei-Kuffuor, Szymon Padlewski, Maria Petalidou, Muyun Qiu, Yue Ren, Joshua Richardson, Thomas Richardson, Alessandro Rognoni, Thomas Roylance, Imogen Ruthven-Taggart, Malgorzata Rutkowska, Tao Shi, Luke (Hyosub) Shin, Faustina Smolilo, Baldeep Sohal, Connie Stafford, George Stewart, Olivia (Yaqi) Su, Eugene (Wei) Tan, Hau Tang, Anabelle Tan Kai Lin, Luke Topping, Tom Ushakov, James Van Caloen, Arina Viazenkina, Benjamin Webster, Maya Whittfield, Yerkin Wilbrandt, Jake Williams, Ryan (Sung) Wong, Bill (Chuzhengnan) Xu, Venessa Yau, Simon (Zifeng) Ye, Miki (Yue) Yu, William Zeng, Moe (Mengxuan) Zhao, Yanmin Zhang

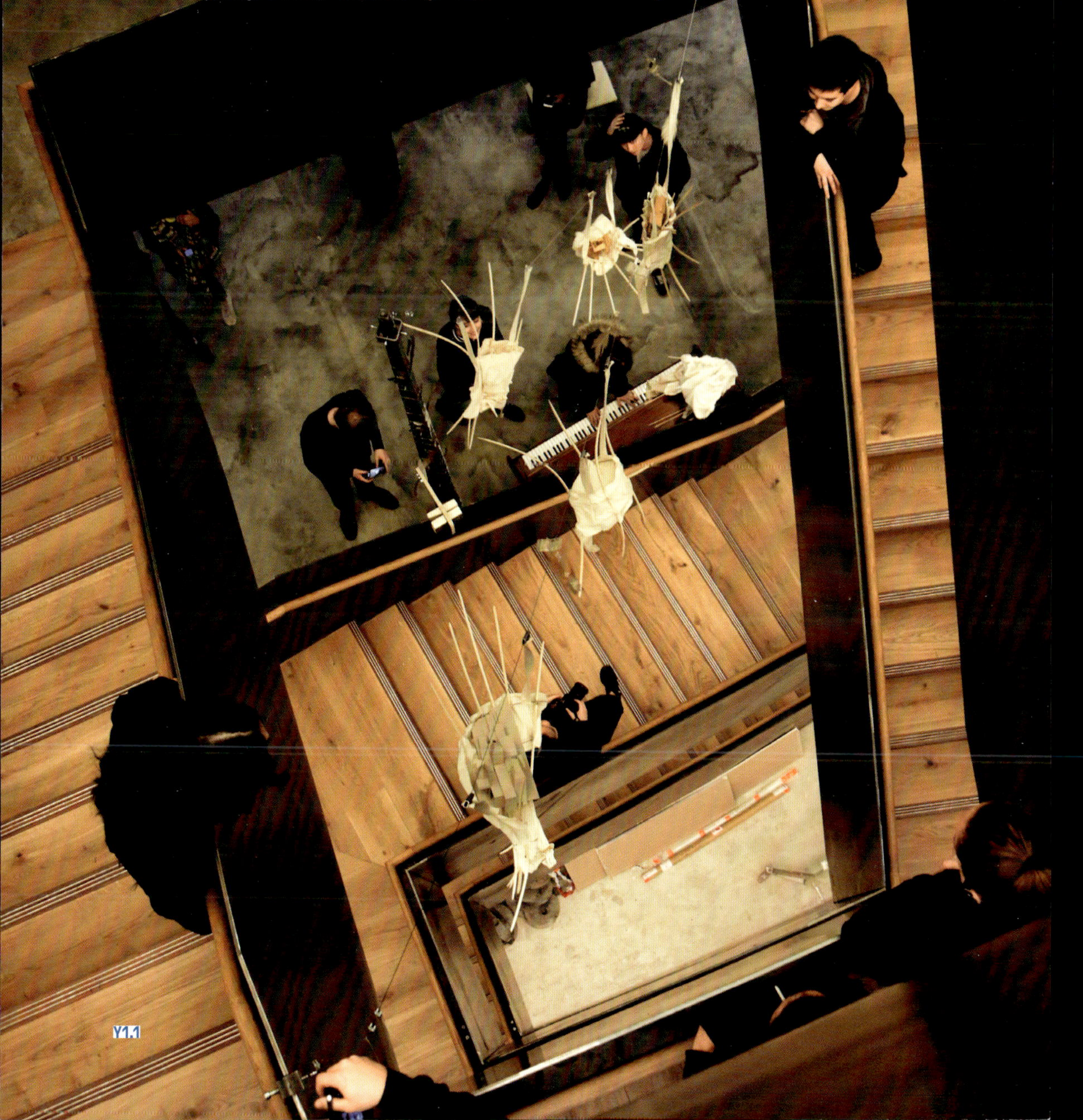

Fig. Y1.1 'RE-TURN, RE-INSTALL'. Year 1 installation project. Studios 7 and 9: A series of garments placed in the void of the stairwell, holding artefacts and relics from the past. **Fig. Y1.2** 'RE-TURN, RE-INSTALL'. Year 1 installation project. Studios 2 and 6: A landscape of boxes opens up to reveal maps from the history of the Euston area, while a series of heads interacts with the city's diversity, weather and tempestuous movement. **Fig. Y1.3** **Charlotte Evans** 'A Fish Restaurant in the Canal'. A series of tunnels disperses smells into the surrounding area and allows the movement of cats to remain separate from areas of public use. The cohabitation of the humans and the animals living at different scales initiated the design. **Fig. Y1.4** 'RE-TURN, RE-INSTALL'. Year 1 installation project. Bonfire of old relics set in the courtyard of 140 Hampstead Road to initiate the procession. **Fig. Y1.5** 'RE-TURN, RE-INSTALL'. Year 1 installation project. Studios 7 and 9: Fragment of the 'tickler' mechanism. **Fig. Y1.6** **Abe (Zhongliang) Huang**, 'Artefacts' Stories'. Mapping the story of an old model.

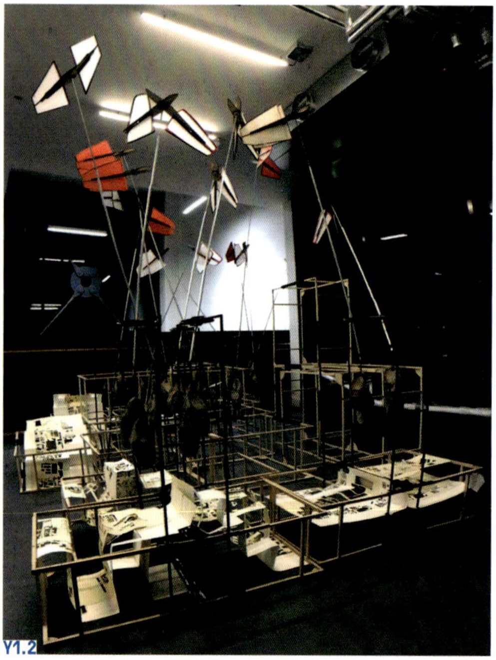

Y1.2

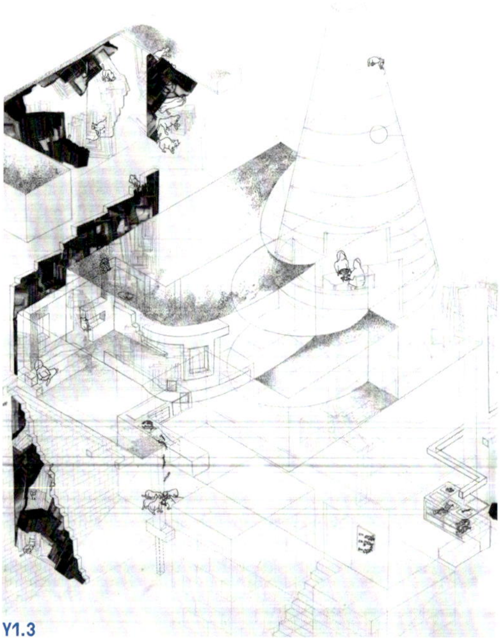

Y1.3

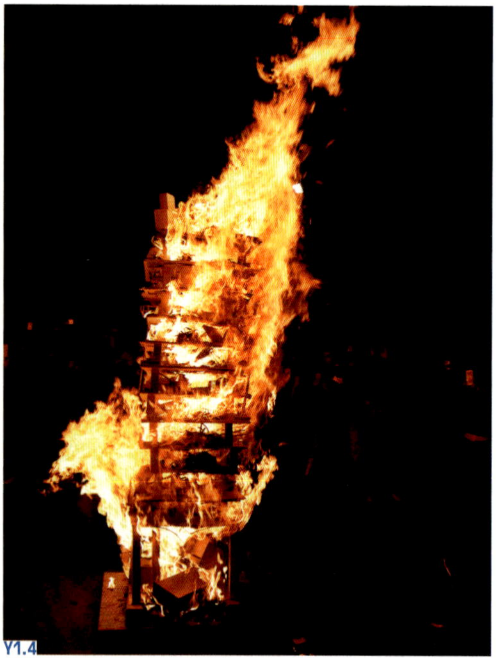

Y1.4

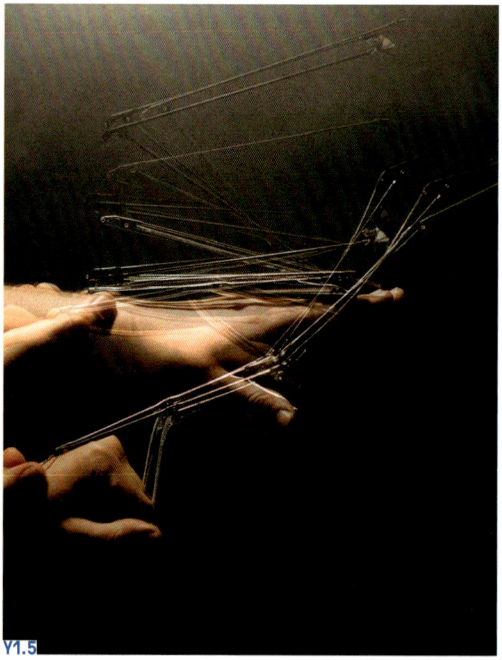

Y1.5

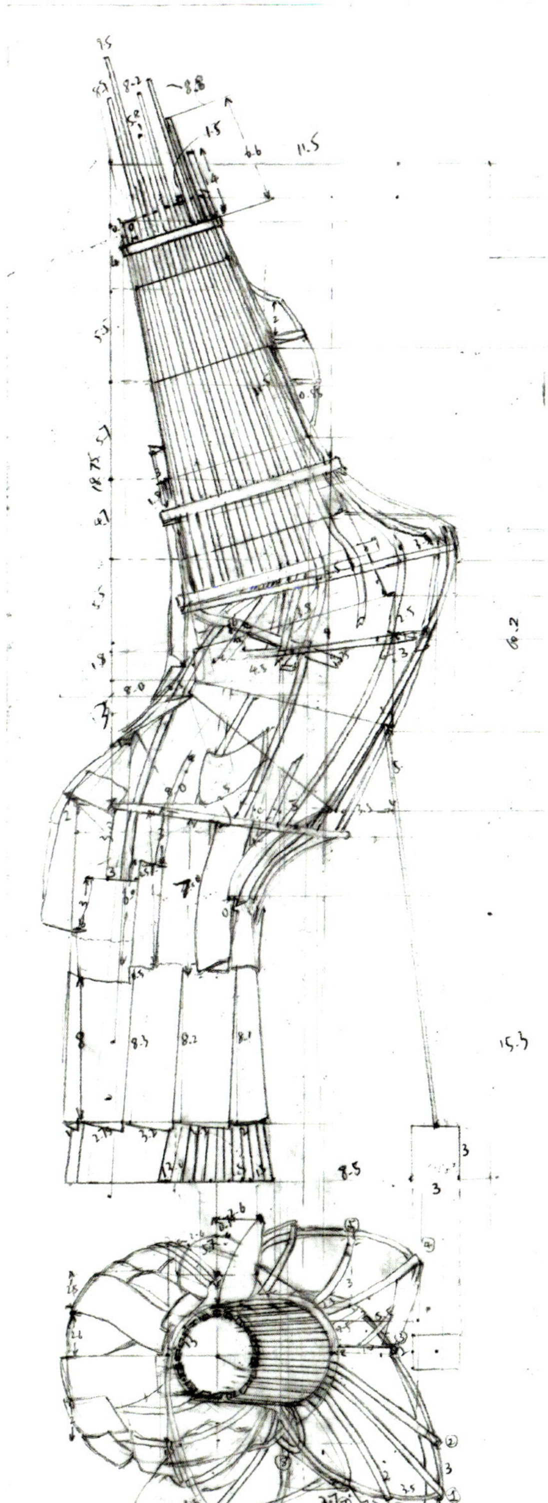

Y1.6

Fig. Y1.7 Amanda Dolgā, 'Kinetic Clock of the Watchmaker's Tower'. A combined drawing of 1:100 rotational plans and morphing elevations of the building's façade that visualises the changes over time in the exterior of the house, whilst emphasising and highlighting the shifting thresholds within the tower, thus providing different window frames which allow the resident a unique experience of the surroundings throughout the year. **Fig. Y1.8 Basil Babichev**, 'Beekeeper's Sanatorium'. The project involves bees colonising spaces beneath a bridge. Variations start as gestural models but conclude with more logic. As colonies diminish, the architecture thins from the core. Inside, wax and bee nutrients are processed and shared with the public. **Fig. Y1.9 Malgo Rutkowska**, 'Bologna Site Survey'. Shadow emphasising façade of Palazzo del Podesta in Piazzo Maggiore. **Fig. Y1.10 Jake Williams**, 'Vinyl pressing plant and record archive'. The building is composed of a series of niches that follow the ritual associated with vinyl record-pressing machines. The public observe the machines from below whilst experiencing the growth of the record archive that extends down the canal. The machines are semi-exposed, allowing the weather to affect them over time.

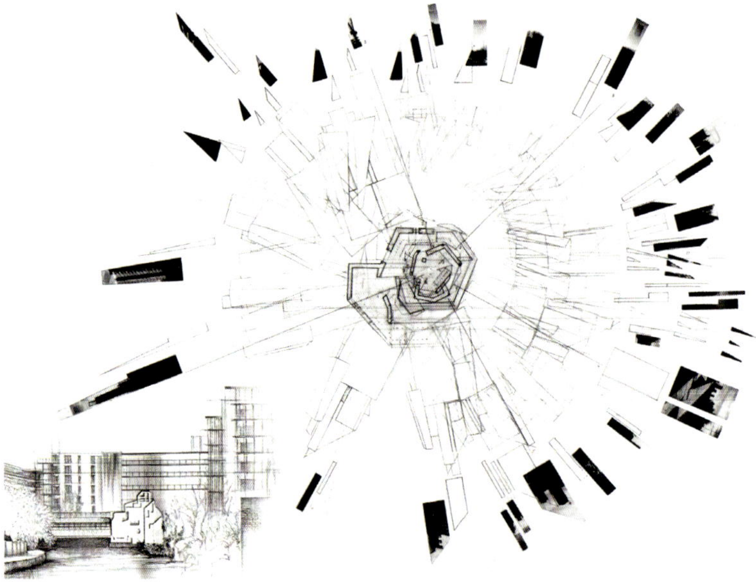

Y1.7

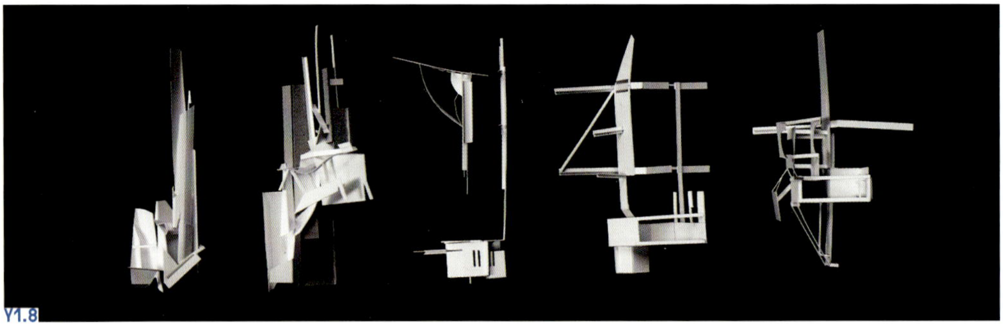

Y1.8

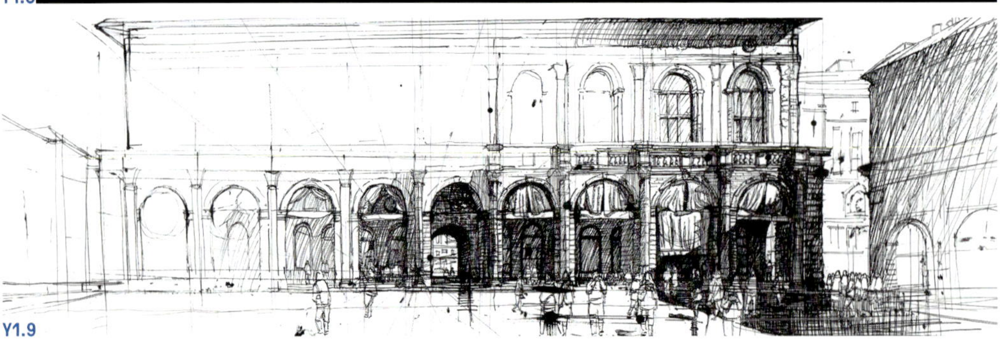

Y1.9

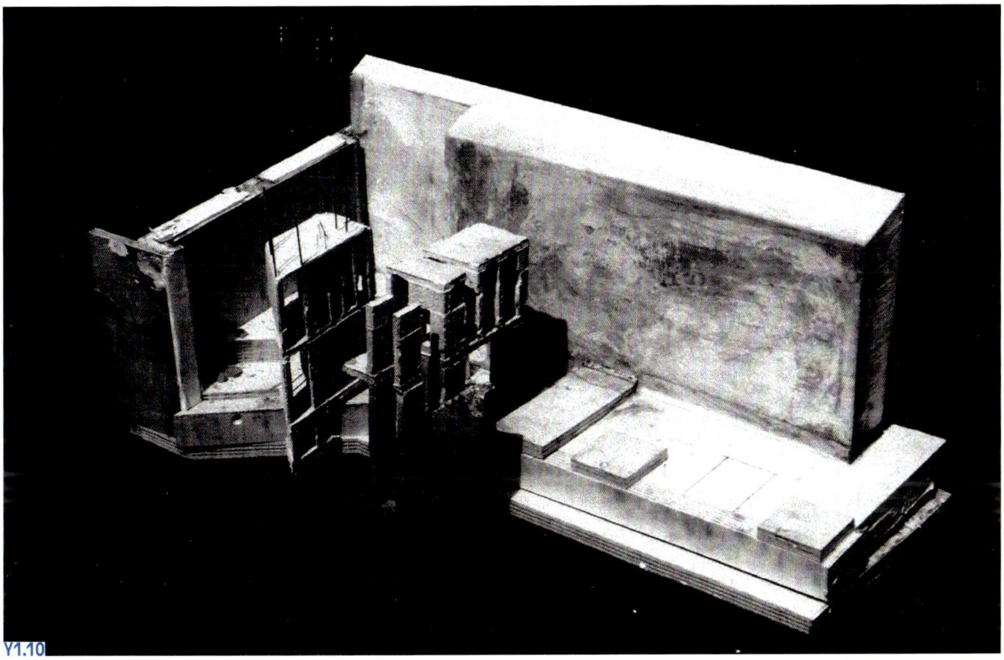

Y1.10

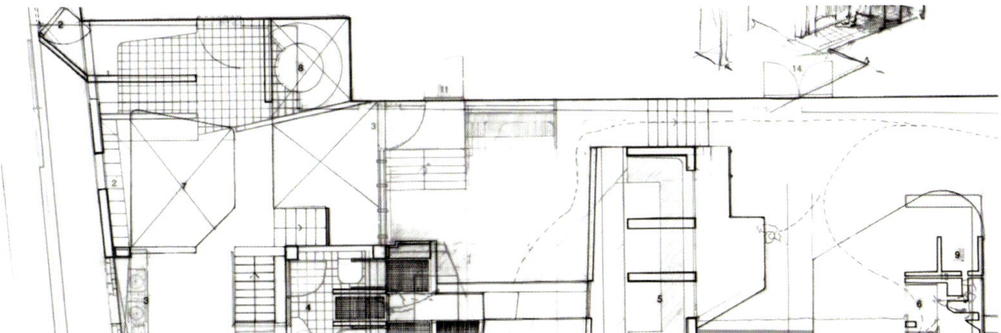

Y1.10

Fig. Y1.11 Noriyuki Ishii, 'House for Cinematographer'. Outdoor public projection space for film screenings, montage room and archive. A layered composition of screens and staircases frames the site. The living space occupies the back of the projection screen. **Fig. Y1.12 Tom Richardson**, 'House for a Fabric Dyer'. Living and working are intimately connected with each room, serving both domestic and industrial purposes. In the kitchen, plants from along the Lee Navigation are turned into natural dyes and poured into the dye baths. Rolls of fabric thread through the building into the dye pools before being dried above the canal. **Fig. Y1.13 Ted Bosy Maury**, 'Over the Edge: A House for Blue Shadows'. A series of cantilevered moving platforms above the trees form a workshop and display space for a performative cyanotype photographer and her friends, moving over the edge of the canal between land and water to come together when in use and apart when empty. Gradually, the wooden surfaces are covered with sun-exposed blueprints while changing shadows add to the shadows of trees. **Fig. Y1.14 Owen Mellett**, 'A Horticulturalist Greenhouse Home'. A house along the River Lea, which wraps around and integrates into the nature surrounding it, creating a number of interconnected microclimates in which both the owner and her plants can thrive. **Fig. Y1.15 Karl Herdersch**, 'King John's Palace/Function 1' The first of a series of public inns with self-build room extensions that sprawl across the greenway. Come celebrate its grand opening on the site where the original King John's Palace burnt down – a roller disco to the soundtrack of the demolition of Fish Island.

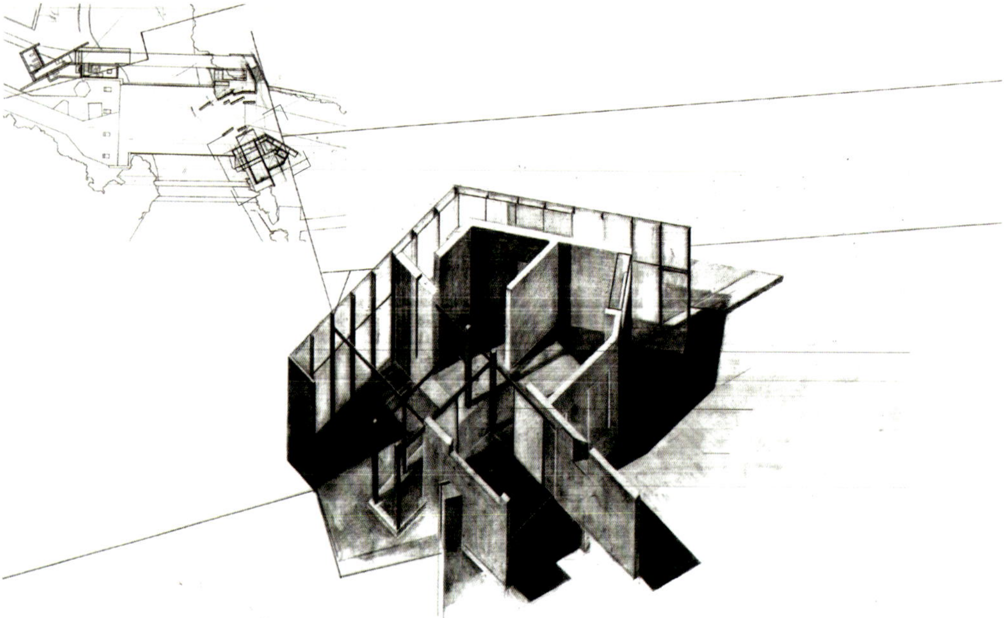

Y1.11

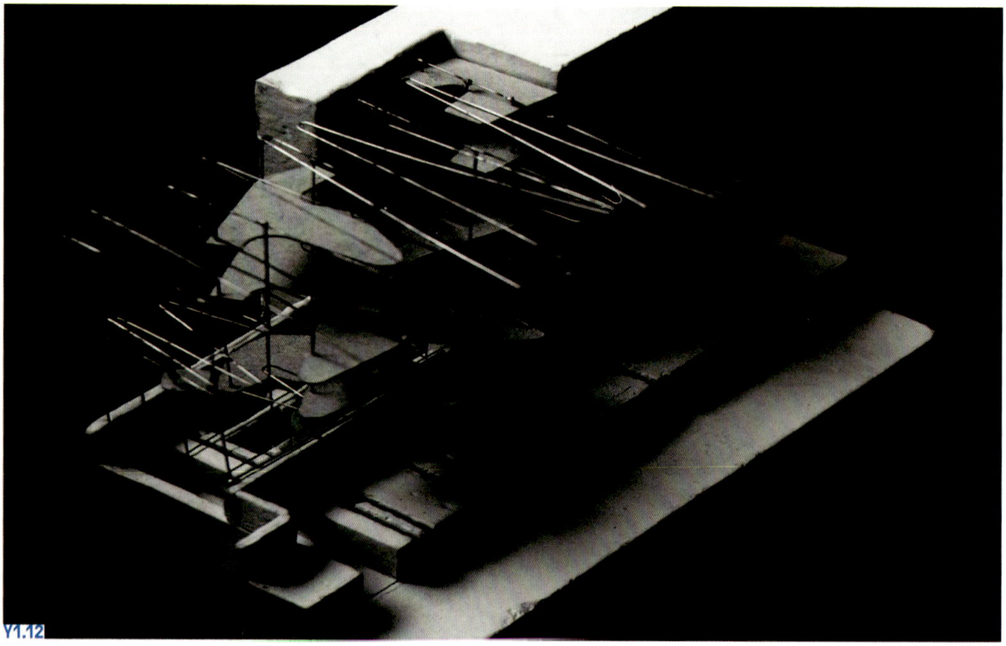

Y1.12

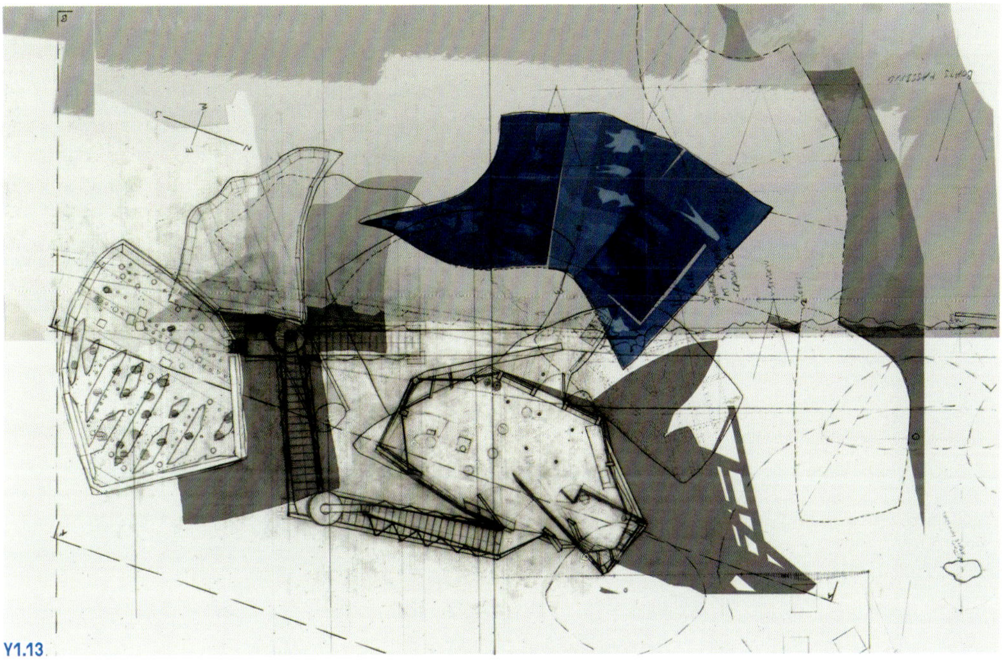

Y1.13

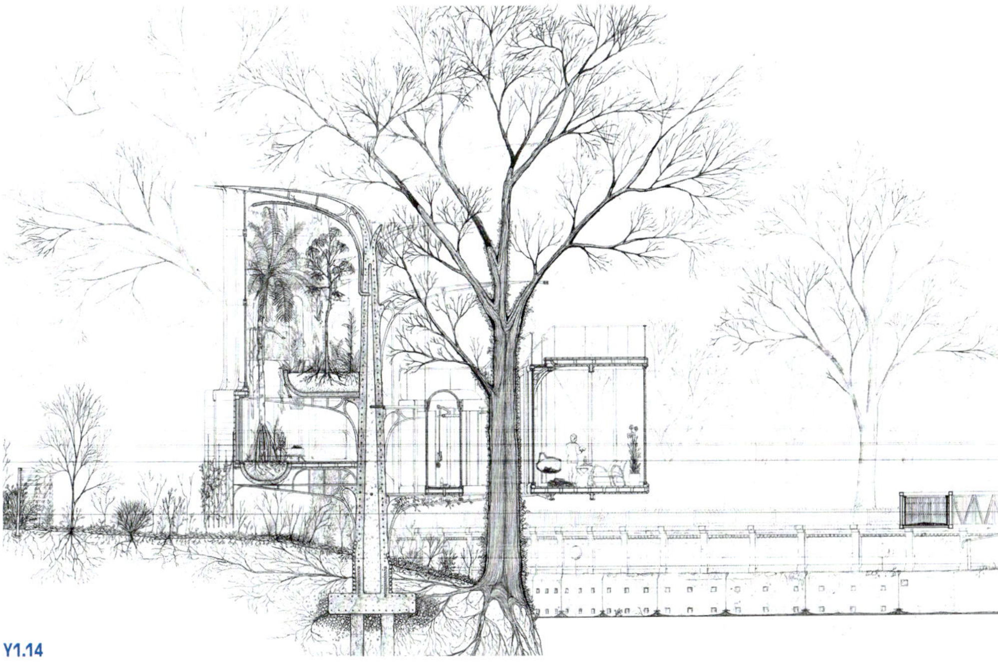

Y1.14

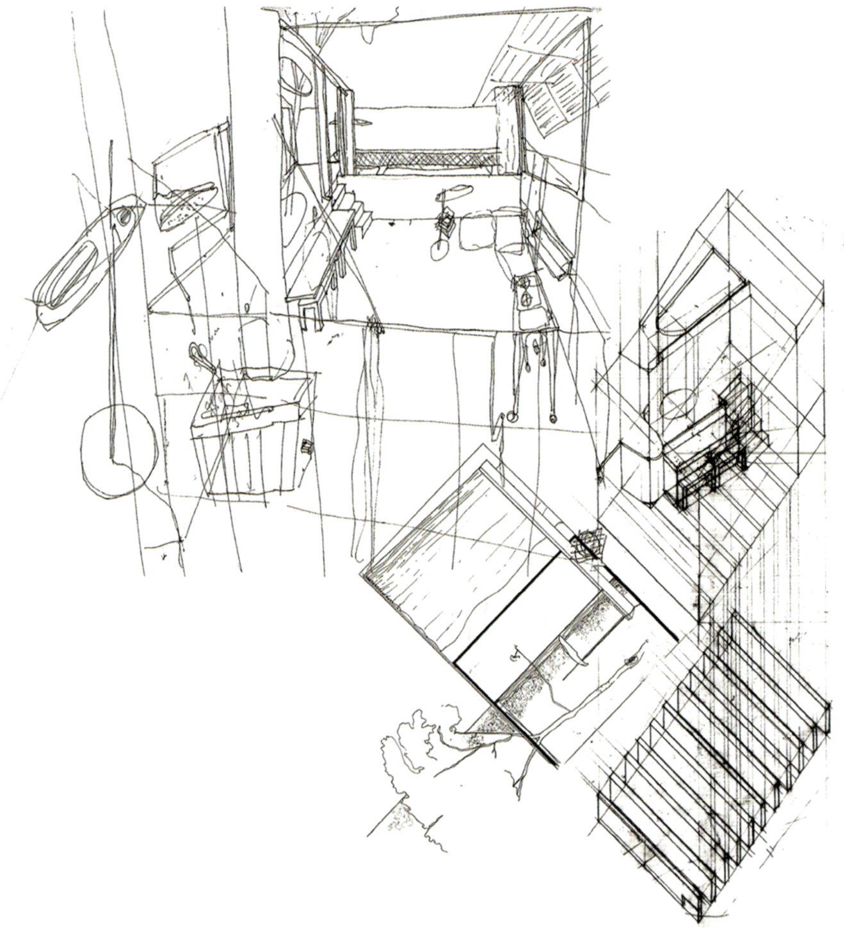

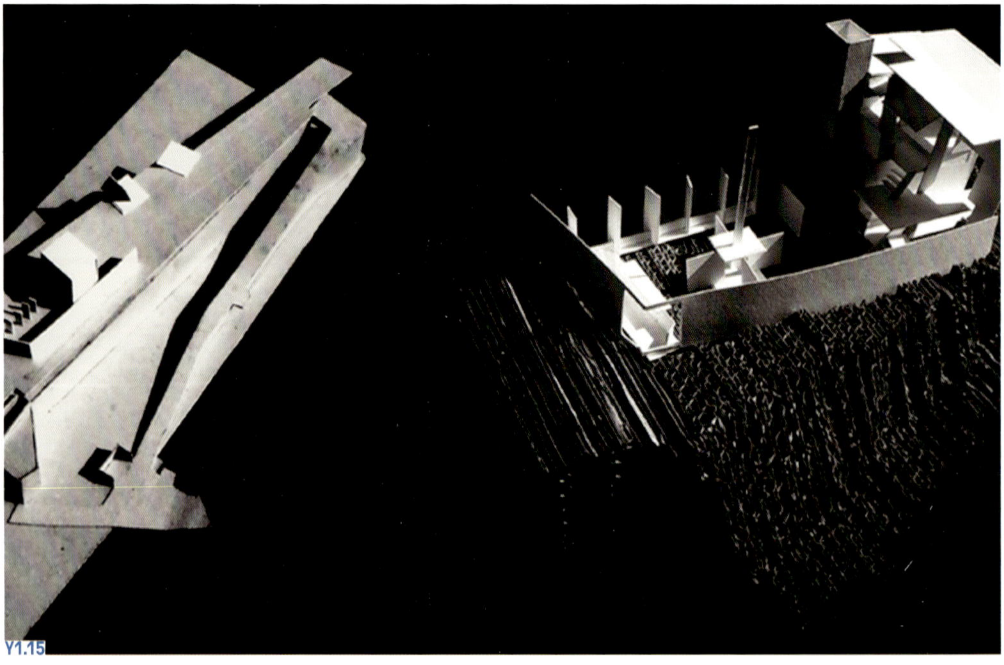

Y1.15

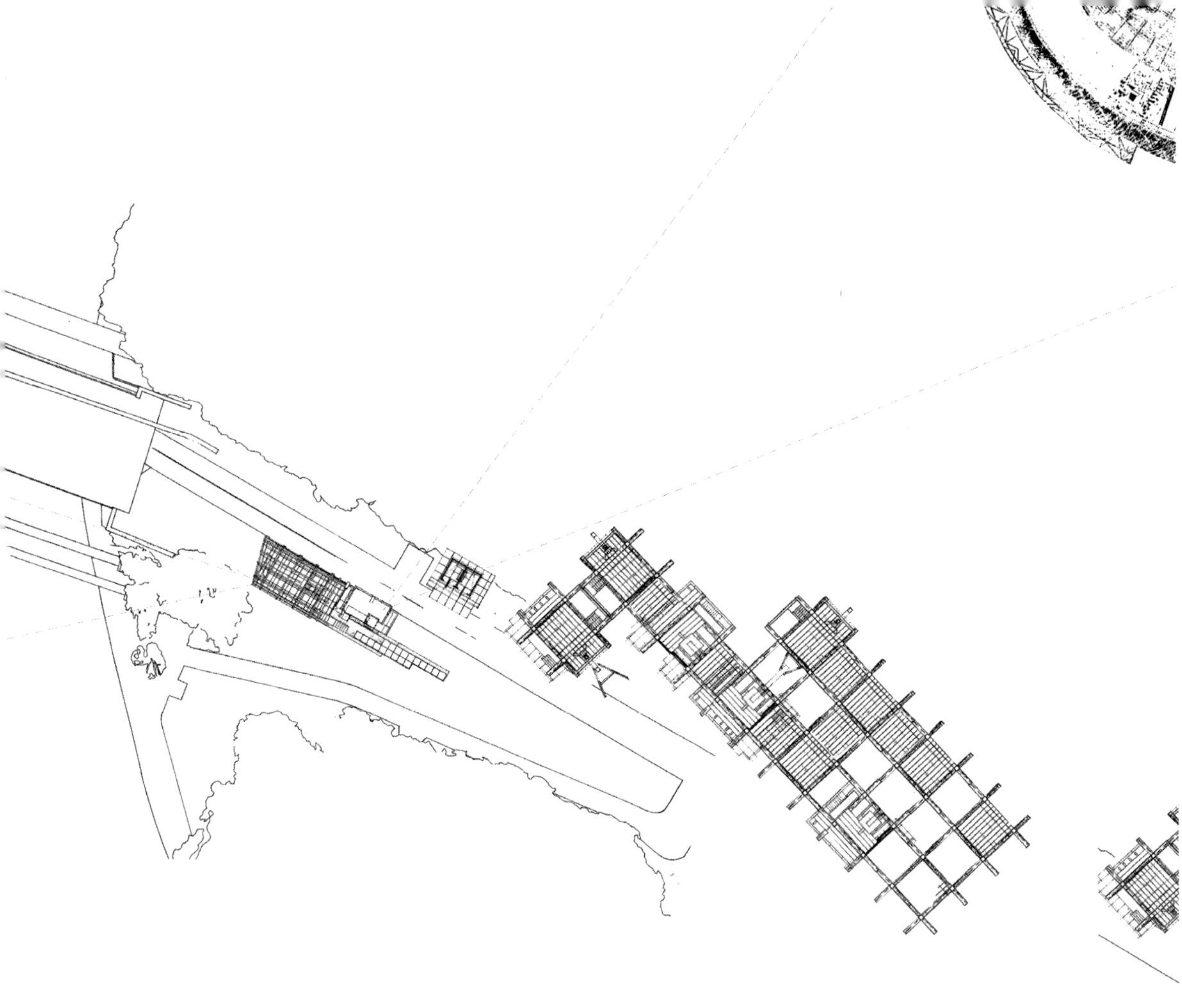

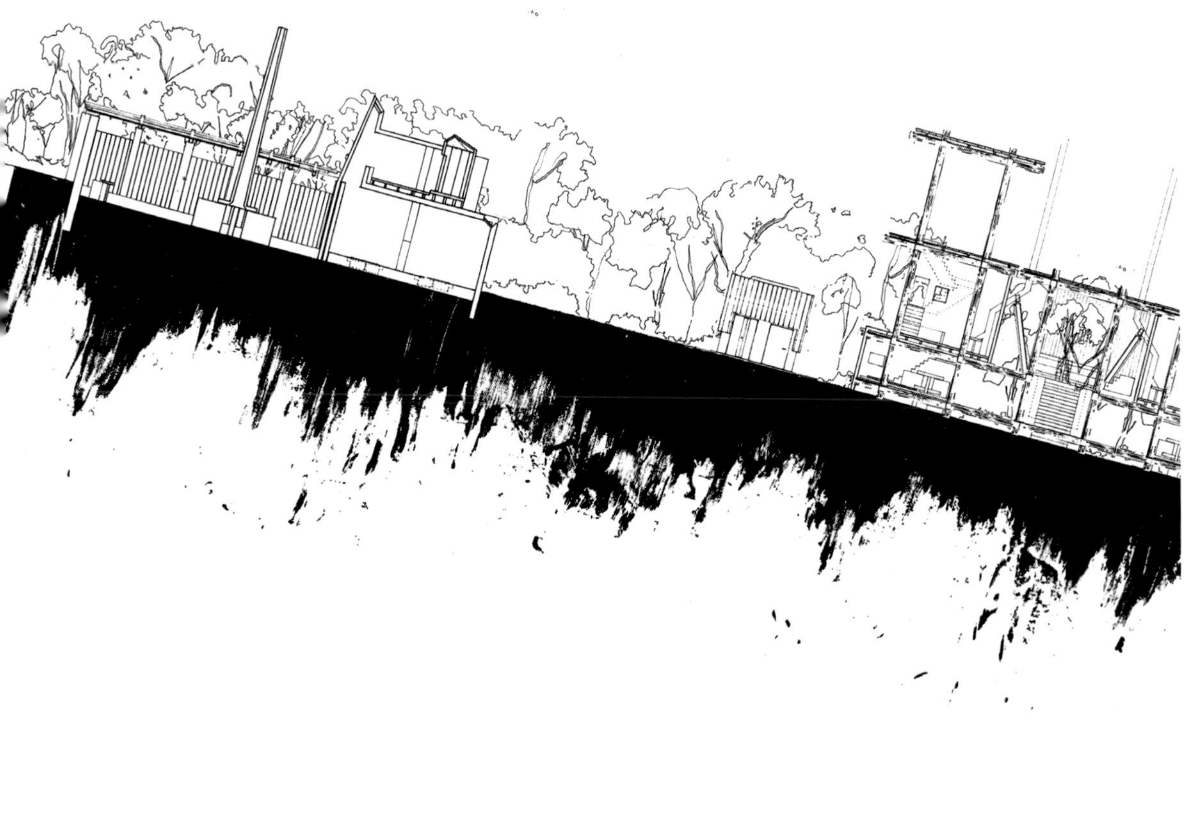

UG0

Pleasure!

Murray Fraser (on sabbatical), Tamsin Hanke, Sara Shafiei

Year 2
James Carden, Yoojin Chung, Theo Clarke, Dan Johnson, Megan Makinson, Chloe Woodhead, George Wallis

Year 3
Freya Bolton, Jun Chan, Ella Caldicott, Elliot Nash, Jimmy Liu, Dan Pope, Claudia Walton

Thank you to:
Mike Arnett, Edwina Attlee, Tim Barwell, Matthew Butcher, Joanne Chen, Max Dewdney, Stephen Gage, Ruairi Glynn, Ewa Hazla, Jessica In, Lilly Kudic, Chee Kit Lai, CJ Lim, Mads Peterson, Jonathan Pile, Richard Townend, Emmanuel Vercruysse, Patrick Weber

Sponsored by Bean Buro

Our theme for the year was pleasure. This is a complex concept, but also a deeply important one. From Ancient Greece through to more recent historical thinkers, such as Jeremy Bentham, Sigmund Freud and Henri Lefebvre, pleasure has long been one of the guiding principles of human existence. We conceived of pleasure in its widest sense, and as such, included the wide range of architectural, spatial, social and cultural discoveries that can be found in the modern city. How, then, can architects contribute to a contemporary concept of pleasure? Urban tactics for a city like London suggest a need for play, subversion, fantasy, temporariness, mobility and transgression. This year, therefore, Unit 0 students were asked to investigate and conceive projects that hinged upon ideas of urban delight.

——To start the year, students scrutinised the pleasures of everyday existence for those living in London. This involved them in rediscovering ignored, or neglected, acts of utility and function, and investigating manoeuvres and behaviours carried out instinctively. How might the process of recording these activities or things come to be seen as a moment of pleasure, perhaps by enhancing or subverting the course of the everyday, or by taking delight in silent but novel ways of capturing moments of happiness? Students imagined how the everyday might be re-read as a thing of surprise, disruption and enjoyment, thereby creating spaces or objects of delight.

——Our unit field trip in early January was to Mumbai and Ahmedabad, along with some stepwells in the Gujarat province, where we studied the conditions of pleasure to be found there in many guises. We uncovered the excitement held within ancient pieces of architecture and relived the anticipation of modernist architects as they broke ground. Students visited craftsmen who daily find inspiration and materials from the landscapes around them, and met with those in architectural schools and practices there.

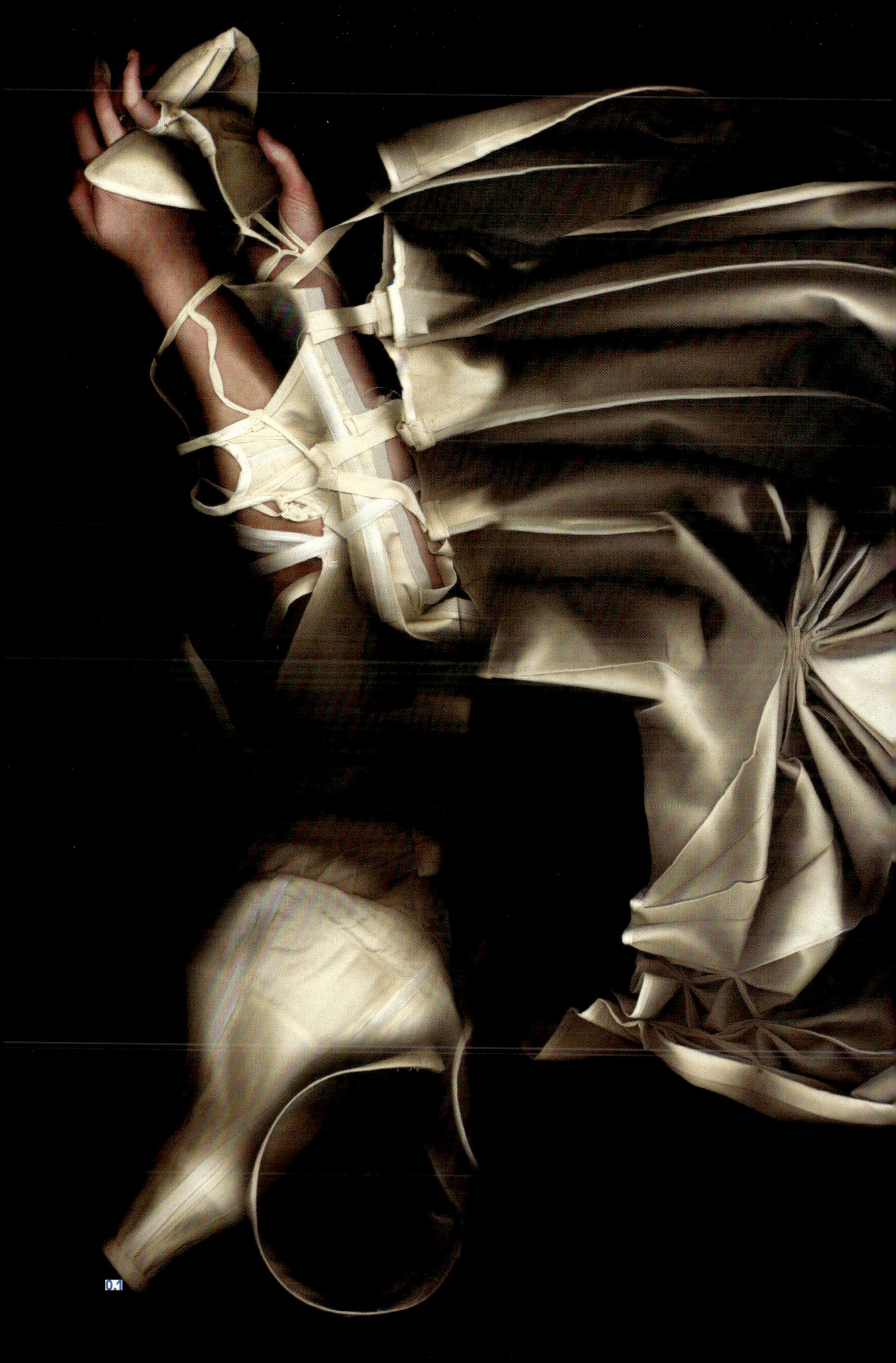

01

Fig. 0.1 Freya Bolton Y3, 'A Tailored Sanatorium', Vale of Health, Hampstead, NW3. A day-care health centre helps those affected by pollution as London's air quality becomes increasingly hostile. Conceived as a protective suit and sited in the appropriately named Vale of Health, occupants are alienated from the city around them. The breathable garment shrouds the building's body at points where the drench of rain would be felt, yet it never wholly seals the interior. Rather, the building embraces its surroundings while acting as a defensive barrier to external pollutants. **Fig. 0.2 Ella Caldicott** Y3, 'Aseptic/Administrative IV Clinic', East India Dock Basin, E14. This walk-in clinic for IV (intravenous) therapy has two halves on either side of the dock inlet: on one side is an aseptic drug preparation facility, and on the other the administration clinic – with the pharmacy acting as a 'kissing gate' between them. These elements are normally never placed together, yet here their subtle intercommunication produces its own sense of functional ornamentation. **Fig. 0.3 Jun Hao Chan Y3,** 'Capability Brown's Unfinished Landscape', Fenstanton, Cambridgeshire. The influential eighteenth-century landscape architect, Lancelot 'Capability' Brown, owned this site but never got a chance to design it. This project therefore aims to translate the uniform horizontality of the landscape into a series of rotationally cast interventions that bring out both its picturesque and its sublime qualities.

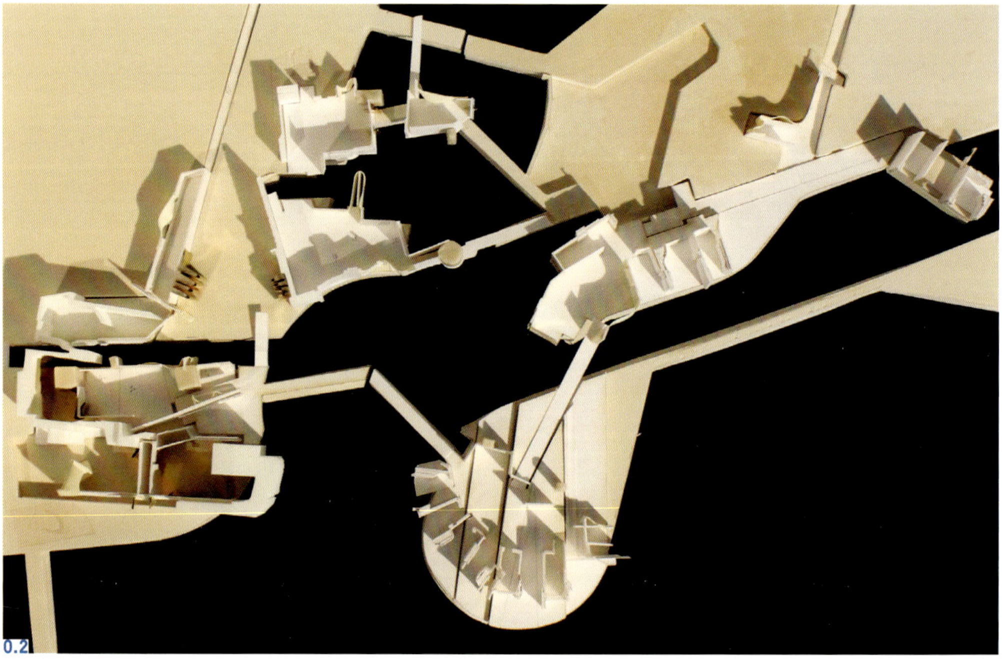

0.2

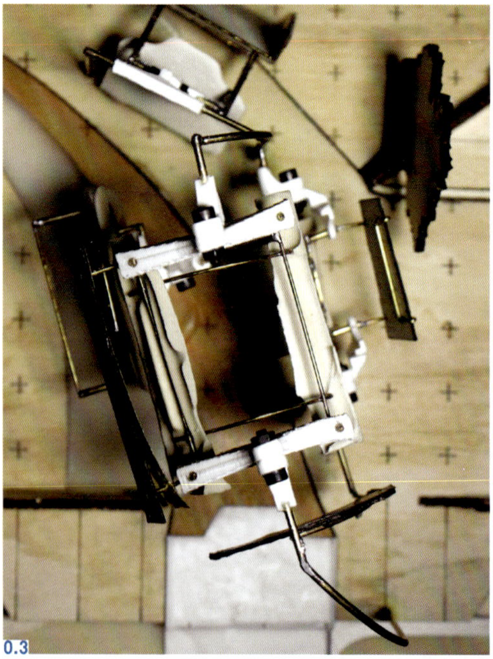

0.3

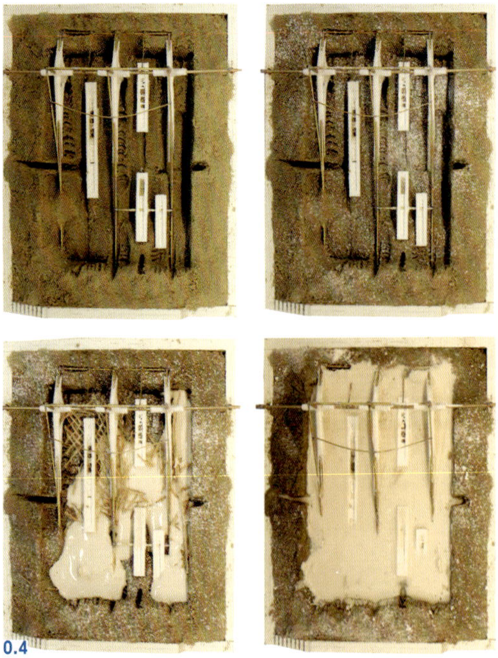

0.4

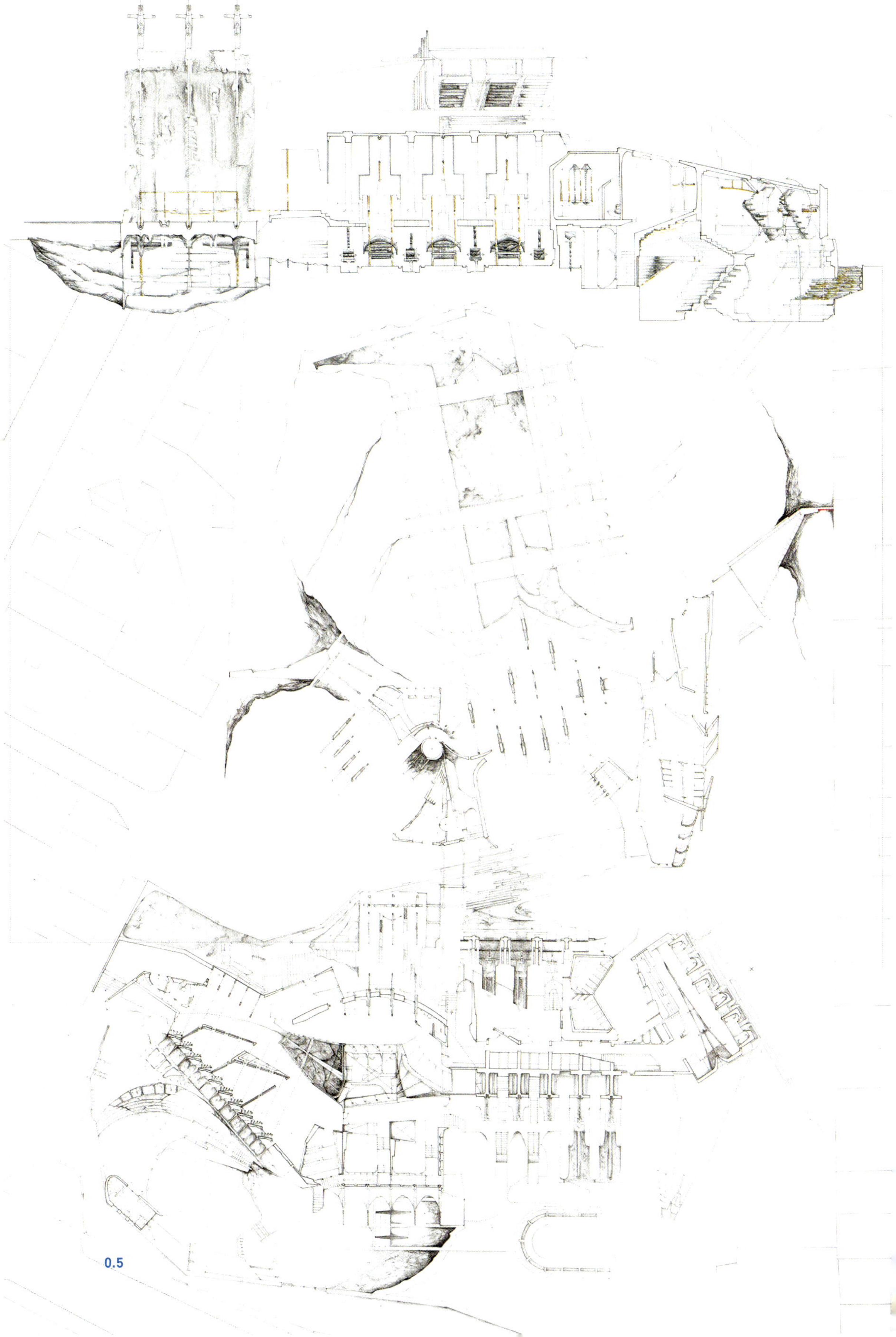

0.5

Figs. 0.4 – 0.5 Jun Hao Chan Y3, 'Institute of Geographers', Mudchute, Isle of Dogs, E14. How can the concept of horizon, as the intersection of ground and sky, be translated and challenged architecturally? Just southwest of Mudchute City Farm, a new Institute of Geographers responds to the alliance between human and physical geography caused by scientists' declaration of a new geological epoch, the Anthropocene. The building interacts directly with the site's geology through raw excavation, using special foundation techniques and the earth as formwork for concrete casting. As a result, the boundaries between earth, ground plane and inhabitable space become blurred, promoting a novel spatial experience for users. **Figs. 0.6 – 0.7 Ella Caldicott** Y3, 'Survival of the Prettiest'. Beauty and pleasure are interlinked through factors such as symmetry, thus also serving a functional purpose in evolutionary adaptation. Here a scientific study of butterflies and geometric patterns creates intense delight through slicing, folding and dissecting. **Figs. 0.8 – 0.9 Freya Bolton** Y3, 'The Pluviophile'. Encapsulating the duality of an experience when felt in two different places, London's rain – harsh drops ricocheting off concrete surfaces – stands in contrast to the immersive, atmospheric rain in the northern woods outside Preston. The culmination is a suit for a Pluviophile, someone who loves rain. When worn, the suit invokes sodden and restrictive clothing, thereby reminding its wearer of home amidst the nondescript rain in London. **Fig. 0.10 Daniel Johnston** Y2, 'The Insurance Market', St Dunstan-in-the-East, City of London, EC3. Next to a derelict City church, this project

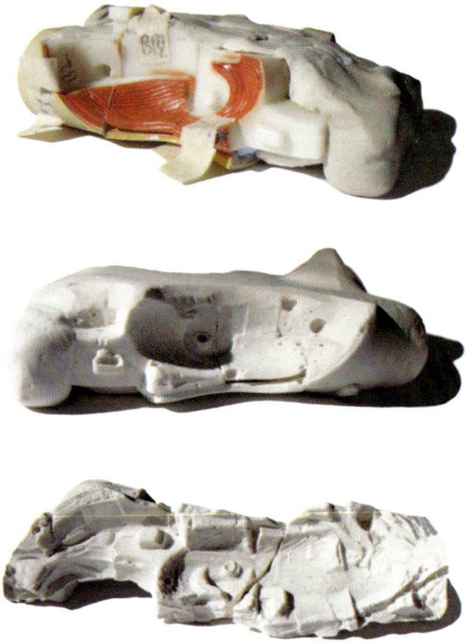

0.6

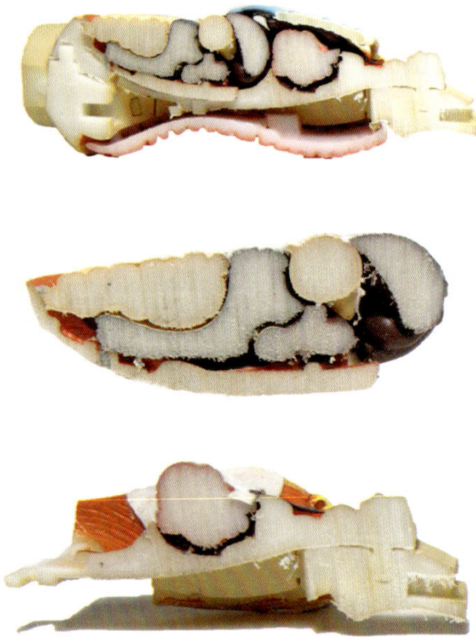

0.7

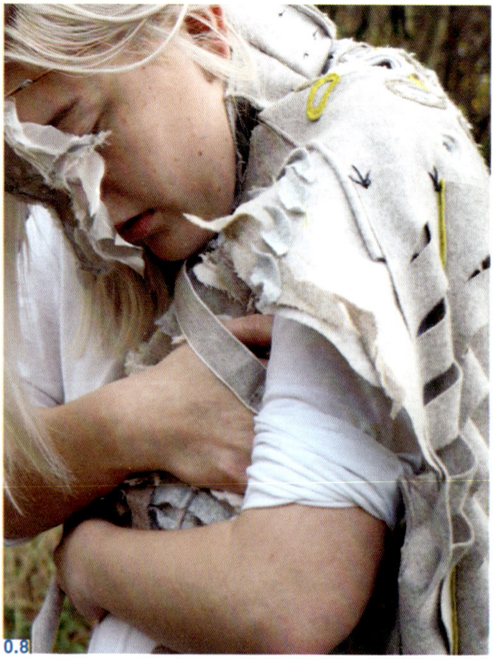

0.8

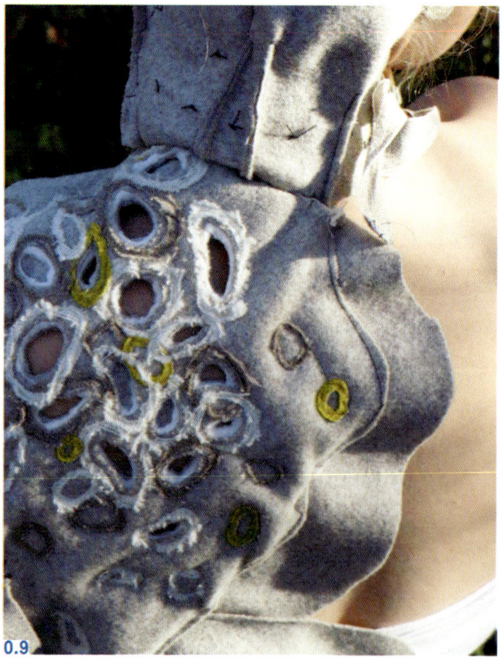

0.9

alternates between the formal space of an insurance broker and an everyday repair market where you can simply get something fixed. Suspended leather for the insurance office hints at the opulence and comfort of traditional banks, creating – perhaps – a false sense of security when buying insurance. Breaks within the stitching form pockets to file documents, stash cash, or quiet spaces to console oneself after a heavy claim. **Figs. 0.11 – 0.12** **Chloe Woodhead** Y2, 'A Natural Education', Forest Road, Dalston, E8. Amidst a square of London's dwellings, an after-school facility is buried into the soil beneath an exquisitely undulating roof – partly occupied and partly planted – to encourage 4- to 11-year-old children to immerse themselves and learn through play within the natural environment. **Fig. 0.13** **Claudia Walton** Y3, 'The Memory Theatre', Carey Street, WC2. Directly behind the Royal Courts of Justice, an innovative type of courthouse is proposed that uses theatre and set design to reconstruct the physical environment of the case being tried, so as to counteract the inaccuracies and distortions of witnesses' memory of criminal events.

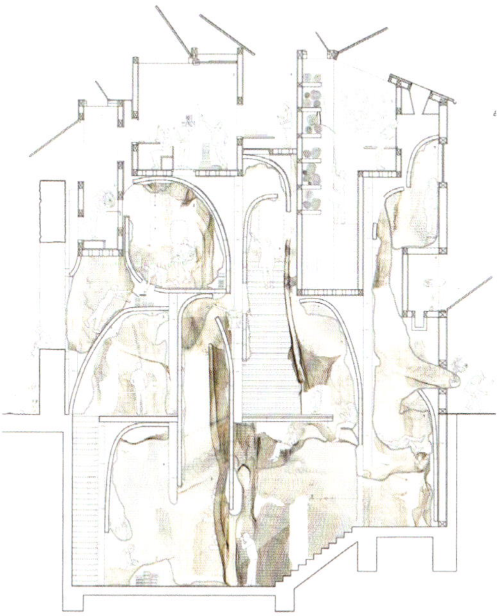

0.10

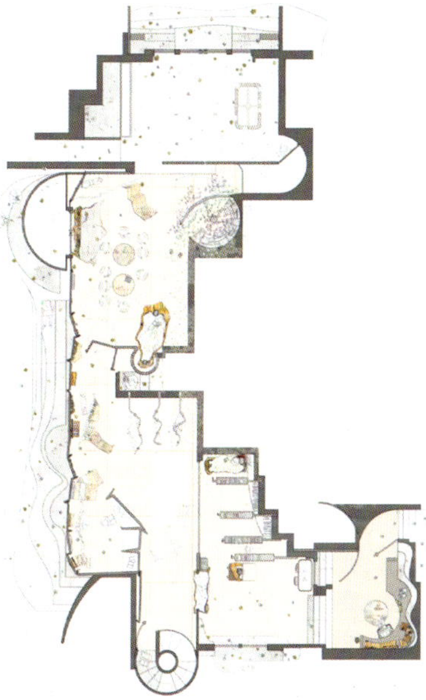

0.11

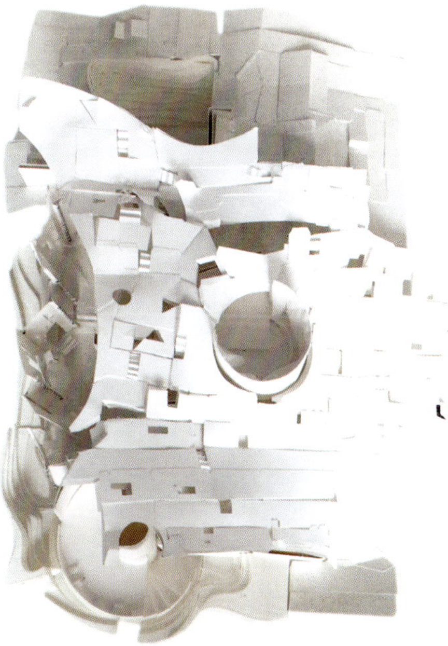

0.12

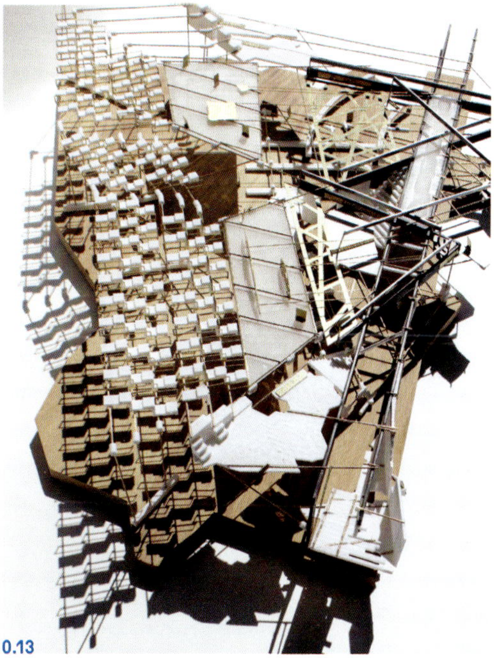

0.13

Fig. 0.14 James Carden Y2, '30 Minutes', Shoreditch High Street, E1. In an abandoned petrol station in trendy Shoreditch, a night-time observatory within a pocket urban park allows occupants to glimpse the stars and planets above. The choreographed walking route through the project takes half an hour to complete, allowing for one's eyesight to acclimatise to this microclimate of darkness in the city. **Fig. 0.15 Elliot Nash** Y3, 'Resting the Black Cab', Stoke Newington Common, N16. The iconic and nostalgic black cab is a mobile landmark within London, yet cabbies are suffering. This project forecasts change by imagining a future in which only one hundred London cabbies exist: their prices have been forced up, and they have become an exclusive service. The building serves and monumentalises the cab, welcoming back the Victorian cabmen's shelter as an exclusive place of rest. **Fig. 0.16 Megan Makinson** Y2, 'A Factory of Domesticity', Barnard Park, N1. Within a Victorian terraced street, the building provides a space for three families to inhabit and make wallpaper, thereby reviving a traditional manufacturing process. Hung paper screens act as the membrane between the domestic and the factory, allowing visitors the pleasure of peeling back a layer of wallpaper to glimpse the inhabitants' lives.

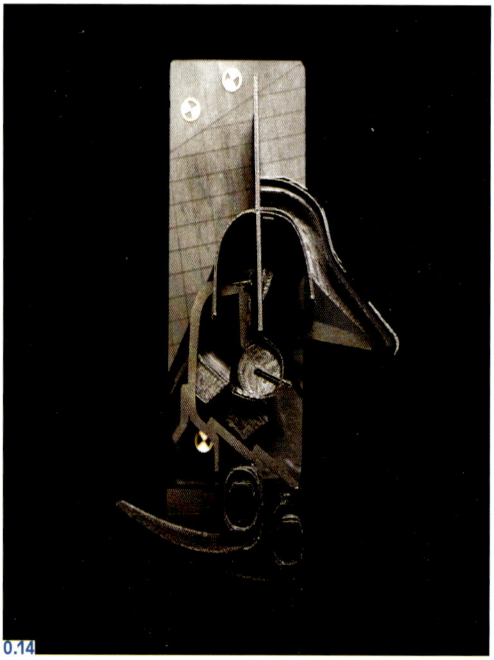
0.14

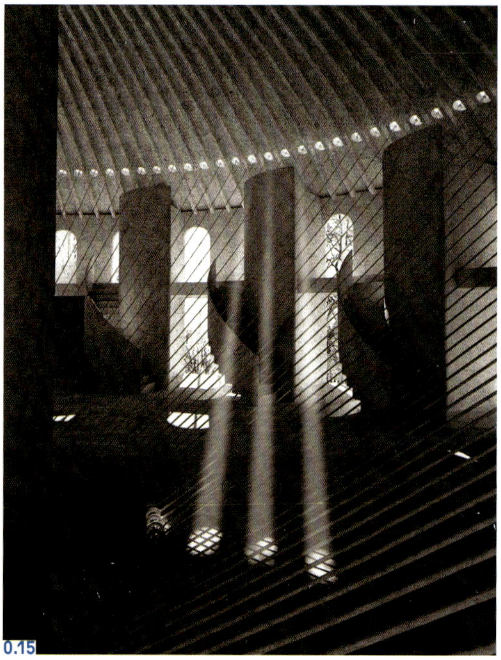
0.15

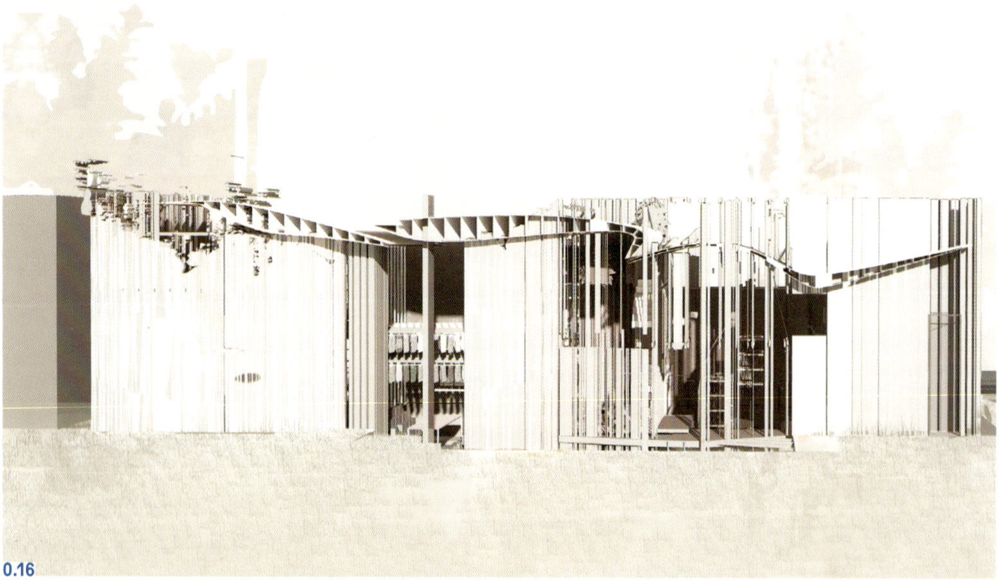
0.16

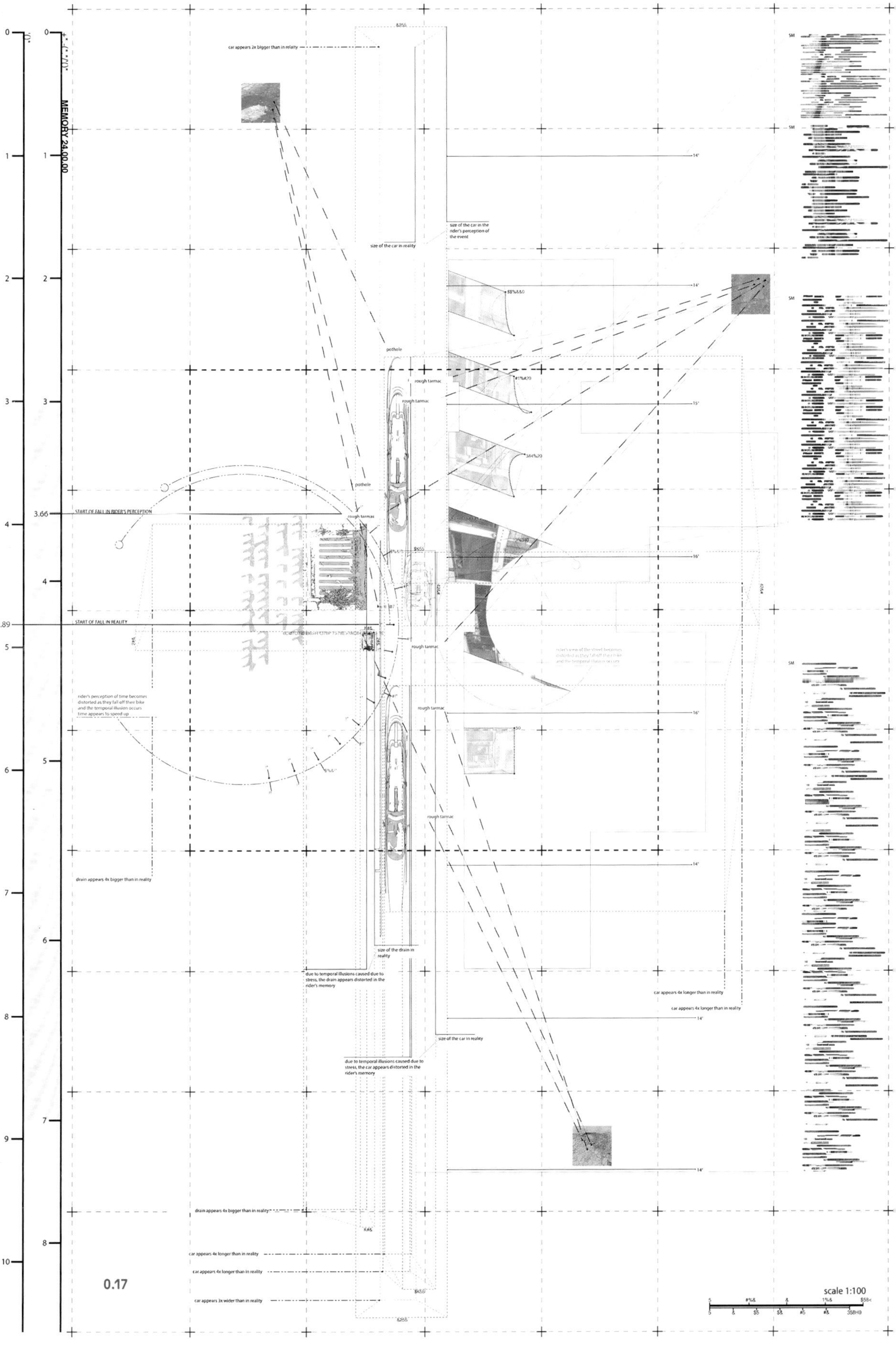
MEMORY 24.00.00
car appears 2x bigger than in reality
size of the car in the rider's perception of the event
size of the car in reality
pothole
rough tarmac
rough tarmac
pothole
rough tarmac
3.66
START OF FALL IN RIDER'S PERCEPTION
4.89
START OF FALL IN REALITY
rough tarmac
rider's perception of time becomes distorted as they fall off their bike and the temporal illusion occurs time appears to speed up
rough tarmac
rough tarmac
drain appears 4x bigger than in reality
size of the drain in reality
due to temporal illusions caused due to stress, the drain appears distorted in the rider's memory
car appears 4x longer than in reality
car appears 4x longer than in reality
size of the car in reality
due to temporal illusions caused due to stress, the car appears distorted in the rider's memory
drain appears 4x bigger than in reality
car appears 4x longer than in reality
car appears 4x longer than in reality
car appears 3x wider than in reality
0.17
scale 1:100

Fig. 0.17 Claudia Walton Y3, 'Spatialising Memory'. This is an exploration of differing perceptions of time during an event, particularly temporal illusions during moments of stress, and the effects these can then have on the space around us – such as in the personal memory of falling from a bicycle. **Fig. 0.18 Jimmy Liu** Y3, 'Kensington Cuteness', Kensington, W8. Using dwellings near to Holland Park, the project seeks to cutify London's terraced houses. Starting by deforming their front elevations through mathematical/geometrical rules, a series of structural interventions and material injections strip away Victorian conventions. **Fig. 0.19 Dan Pope** Y3, 'A Stage for Poplar', Jamestown Way, E14. A watery riverside landscape offers stages for protest in East London, as part of a broader scheme to amplify protest. Elements are conceived of as deployable interruptions within the public space, manipulating how the protests are viewed and broadcast. Strategically placed inflatable silhouette screens capture and project people's movements, whilst urinals clip together in pockets to encourage gathering. **Fig. 0.20 Dan Pope** Y3, 'What Happened to Irene?' On 18 April 1964, the body of Irene Lockwood, who had been murdered, was discovered on the Thames bank in Hammersmith. This project forensically reconstructs viewpoints from multiple witnesses through a material language that distinguishes 'known' from 'unknown'. 3D scanning technology proves an unreliable witness, as metallic surfaces in the model glitch the scanner, creating spaces of narrative ambiguity.

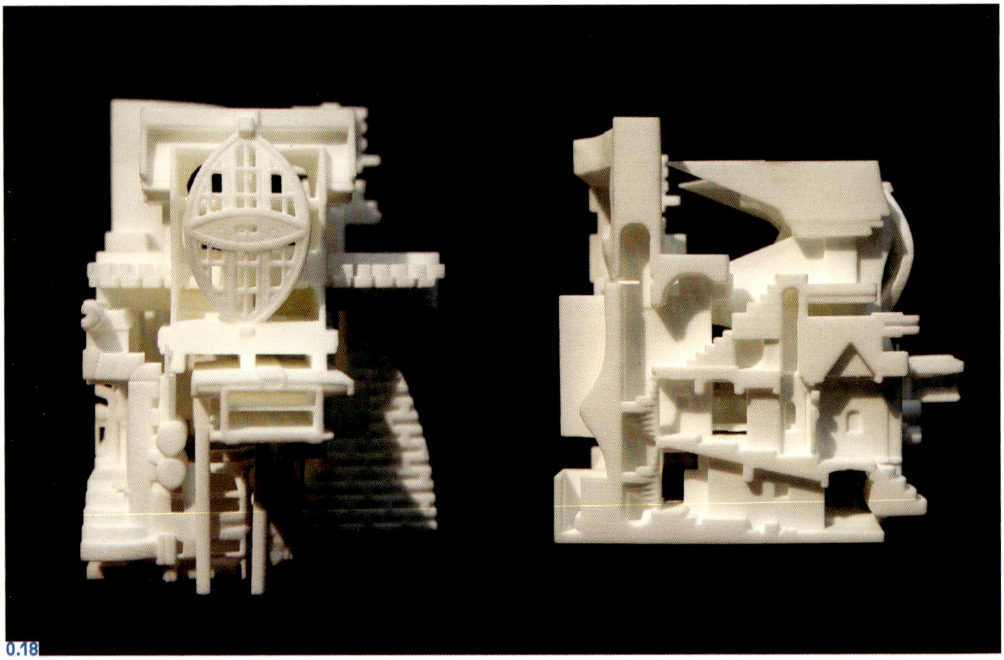

0.18

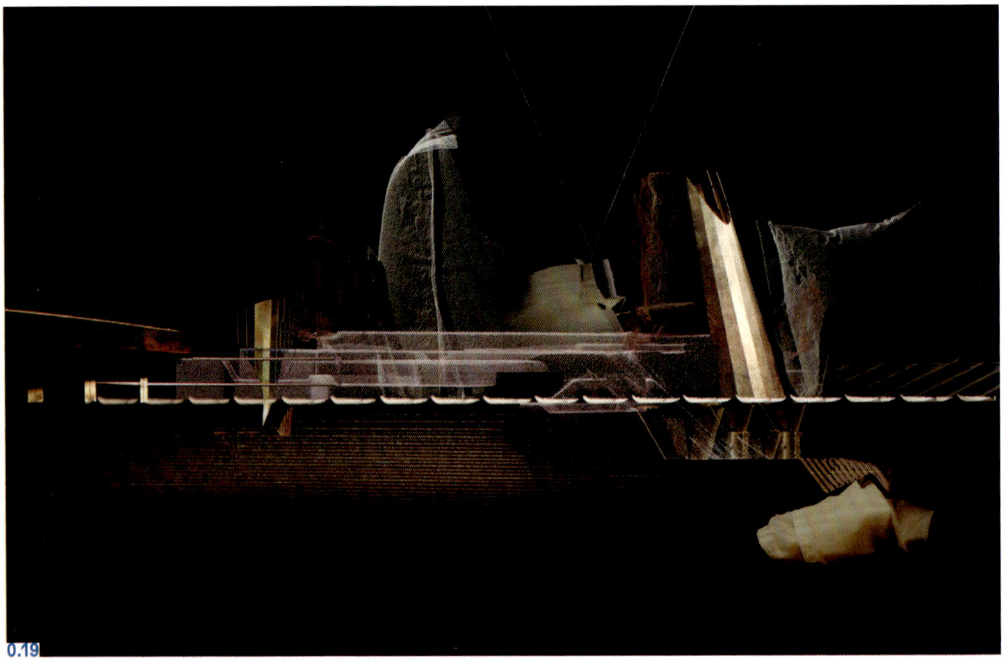

0.19

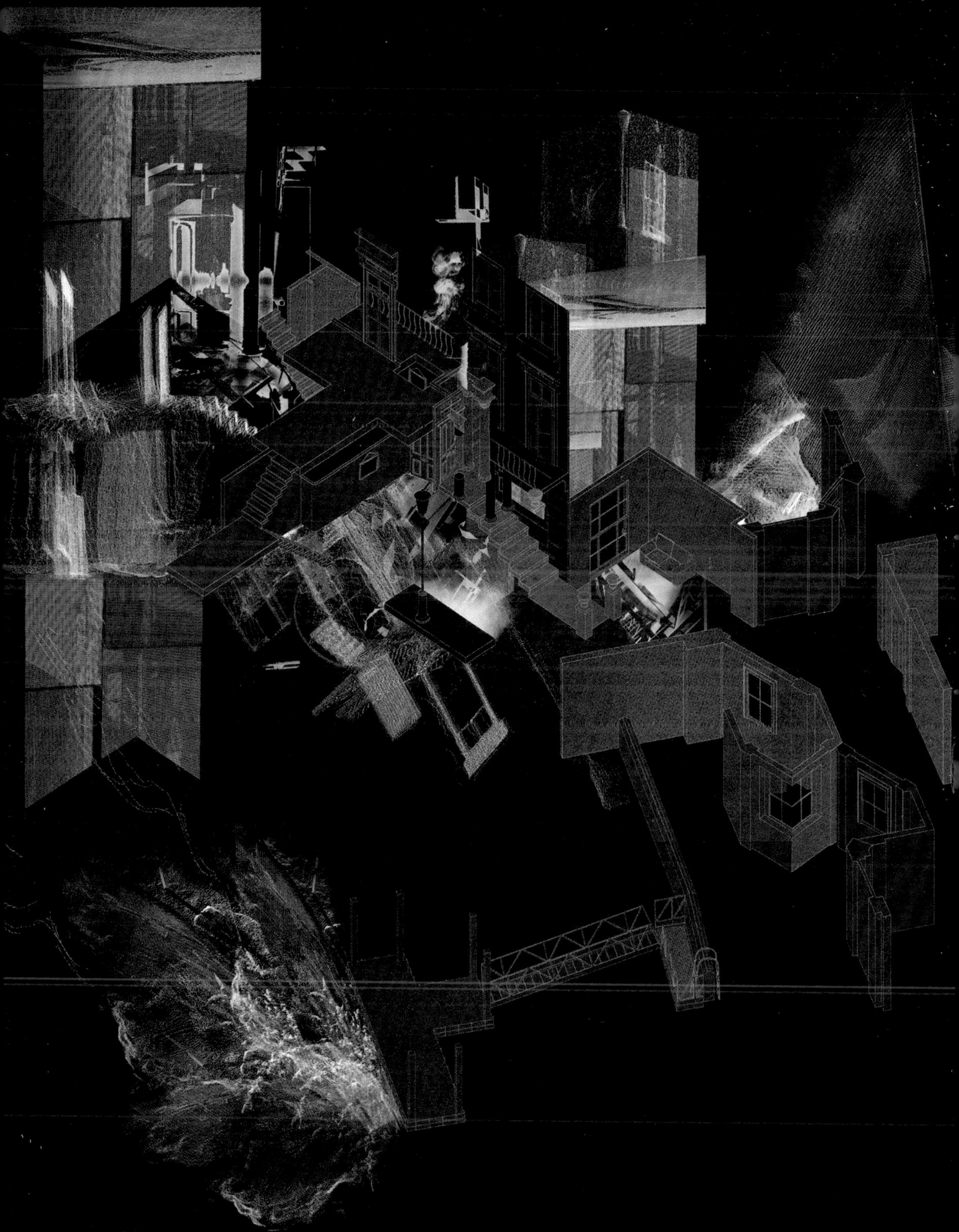

0.20

UG1

Fulfillment Centres

Jon Lopez, Hikaru Nissanke

Year 2
Gunel Aliyeva, Daniel Boran, Sarah Jones, Dagyung Lee (Eeda), Vincent Lo, Gabriella Watkins

Year 3
Ella Adu, Richard Aina, Natasha Blows, Clementine Holden, Dustin May, Edie Parfitt, Karina Tang, Connie Tang Koon Cheong

Thank you to:
Miraj Ahmed, Mick Brundle, Matthew Butcher, Paul Cowie, Pierre D'Avoine, Max Kahlen, Chee-Kit Lai, Taneli Mansikkamäki, Sabrina Morreale, Douglas Murphy, Luke Olsen, Elena Palacios Carral, Colette Sheddick, James Taylor-Foster, James Ward

A few miles east of London, where the Thames begins to snake its way out to the ocean, sits a bewilderingly banal landscape of flood plains, docklands, sheds, landfills and light industry. Our unit was interested in the relationship between all of this, with particular focus on the ties between landscape, modernity and labour.

——Students began the year in East Tilbury, an unlikely modernist utopia on the marshes of Essex. It was built by the Czech shoe maker Tomas Bata in the 1930s to provide housing and social infrastructure amongst a set of vast, hulking factory buildings. Since the factory's closure, the development and its subsequent decline is registered in the collective memory of its inhabitants and former employees. Students devised responses to the current state of the town, picking over the physical and ideological ruins of modernity. These first projects were structured around the idea of preparing and remaking the ground in anticipation of an incoming development.

——That incoming development was another bookend to the 20th-century capitalist project, the big shed. Responding to Amazon's plans to build a large distribution hub in Tilbury, the unit was interested in the shed as a representation of an immediate, untapped and unchecked ecosystem which is rapidly defining large parts of the UK. Behind their anonymous façades lies an almost endless array of objects and processes, yet decisions about their operation, use and siting has largely bypassed the architect.

——The principal project for the year was thus to confront the contemporary relationship between private enterprise and state, and between individual and community. Using the framework of a Section 106, (the mechanism through which developers and landowners are required to mitigate the impact of large development), students were asked to appraise, critique, refine, confront or wholly reimagine how such a large building might meet the context via a more humane reworking of the land. Plurality of programme was encouraged, and projects sought to express how the big shed might be stitched into the town and landscape beyond, or were considered as new, large (ex)urban interiors. The rising threat of automation loomed over many projects, as students tackled what the new routines and rituals of labour might be in this landscape. We sought to examine a non-nostalgic reading of what a relevant craft and construction might be, exploring through drawn and physical constructions a new material expression for Tilbury.

——During the year, the unit travelled to Rome in the footsteps of Piranesi. We observed and surveyed the city from antiquity onwards, to better understand its continuing ability to shape our contemporary cultural imagination.

1.1

Fig. 1.1 Edie Parfitt Y3, 'Robin Hood Gardens Ruin'. A drawing exploring the mythology of landscape and modernity, whereby an imagined section through the central mound of Alison and Peter Smithson's Robin Hood Gardens details the making of a landscape formed from the demolition and excavation of the site's previous constructions. **Figs. 1.2 – 1.5 Dustin May** Y3, 'Reconstructing the Fragment'. This project proposes the sampling of Tilbury in a non-hierarchical manner to uncover its latent beauty and potential. Situated in opposition to the idea of regeneration through a singular landmark building, the proposal seeks to encourage investment in the area by implanting pieces of social infrastructure amongst the existing housing stock. The houses are carefully surveyed, then selectively deconstructed to create a new patchwork of interiors across the town that cater for local needs. Programmatic juxtapositions are accommodated via an architectural language of cutting and fragmentation.

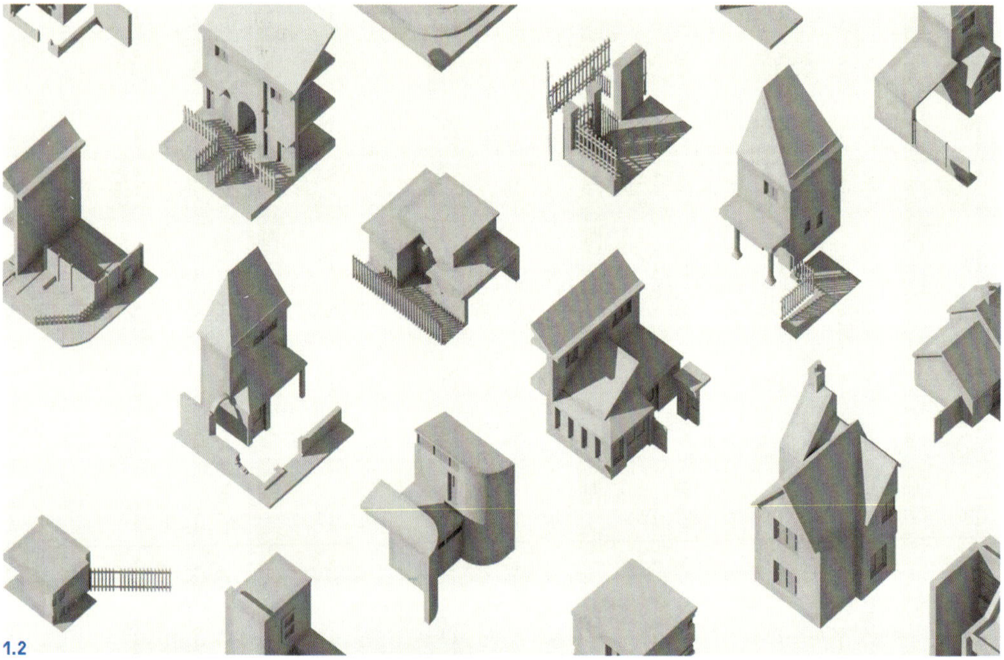

1.2

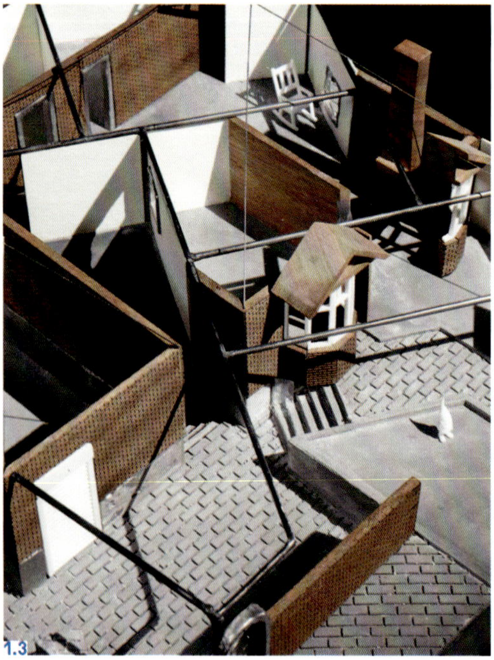

1.3

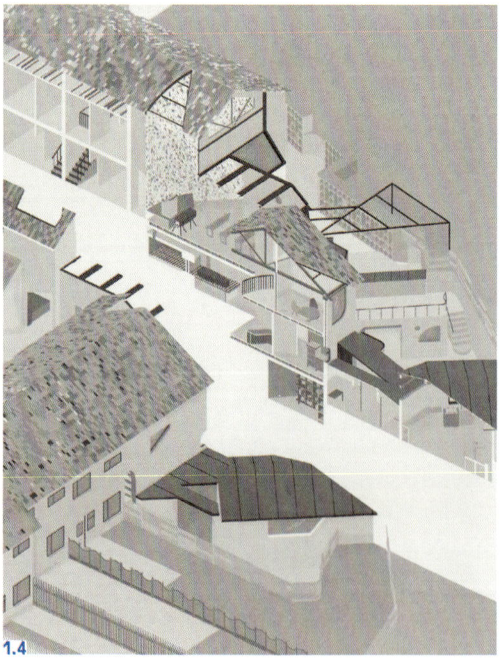

1.4

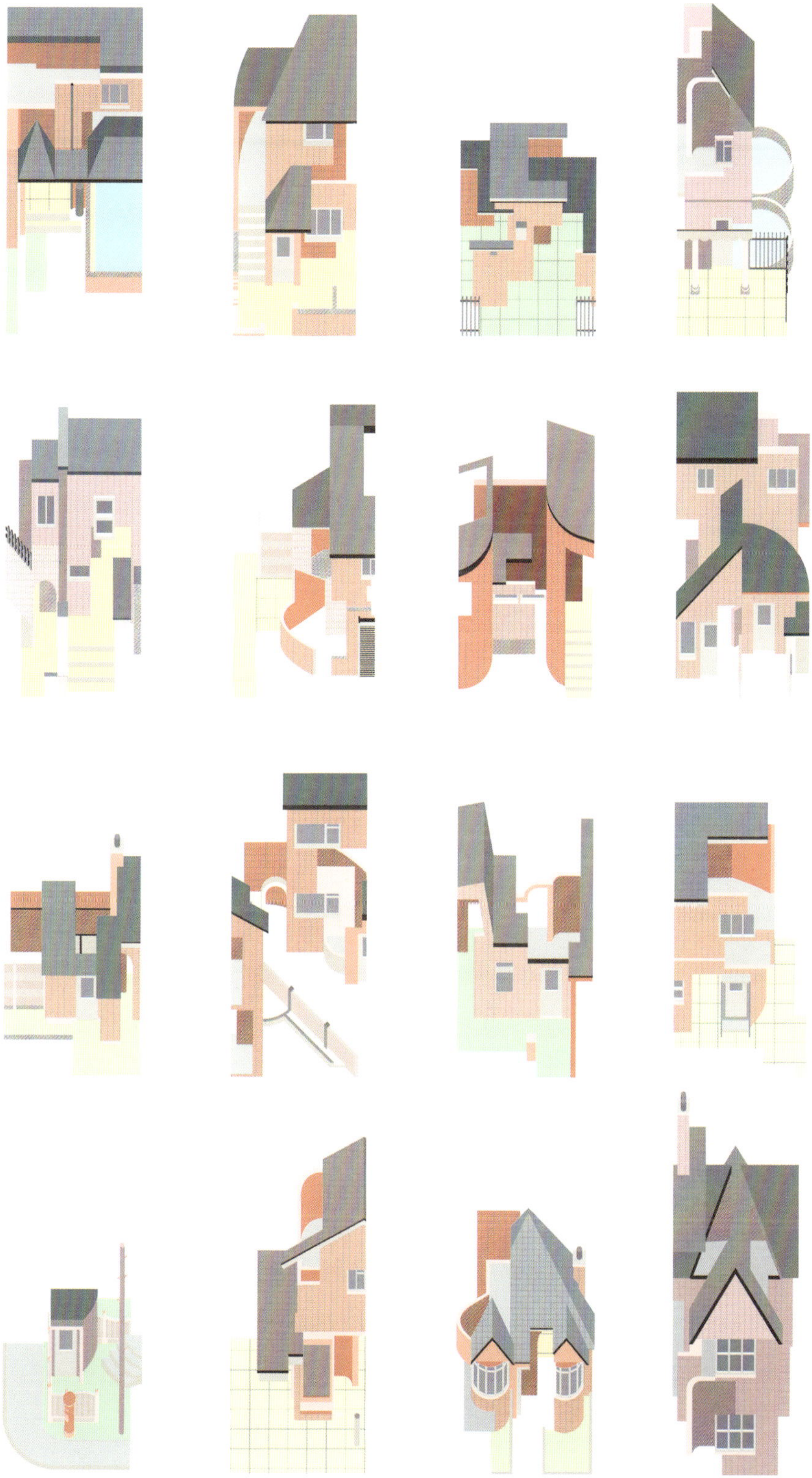

1.5

Fig. 1.6 **Richard Aina** Y3, 'Landscape, Industry and Culture'. In response to the closing of the Bata factory in 2005, the project seeks to renew two of the buildings on the site by inserting a series of performance spaces that bridge the gap between them. This new theatre extends out into a reworked marsh landscape, which anticipates potential flooding of the site by acting as a flood defence. **Figs. 1.7 - 1.9** **Edie Parfitt** Y3, 'Tilbury Civic Spine'. A new civic route is proposed along an existing A-road that separates the town of Tilbury from its port. A new town hall of sorts is imagined, strung out along the road, responding to the needs of commuters and locals alike. The existing passages of vehicles and pedestrians are augmented and intertwined to create a complex network of spaces and surreal interactions between the two. The proposal acts as a conduit for the traffic to pass freely along the road, but it also seeks to encourage lateral movement and interaction between the various 'islands' of Tilbury, with the aim of stitching the town and its inhabitants back into its surroundings.

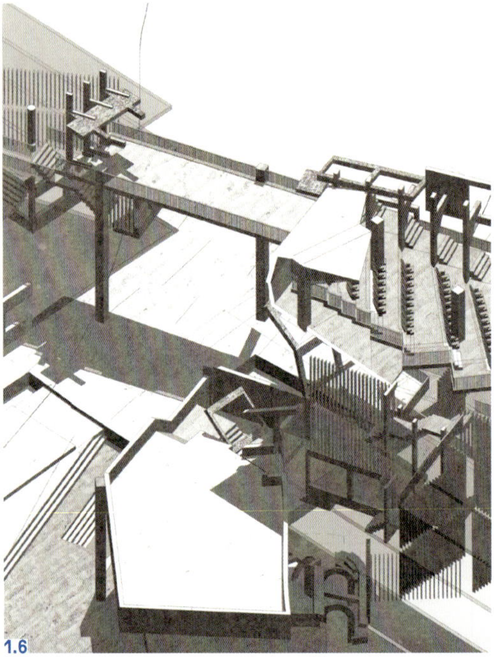

1.6

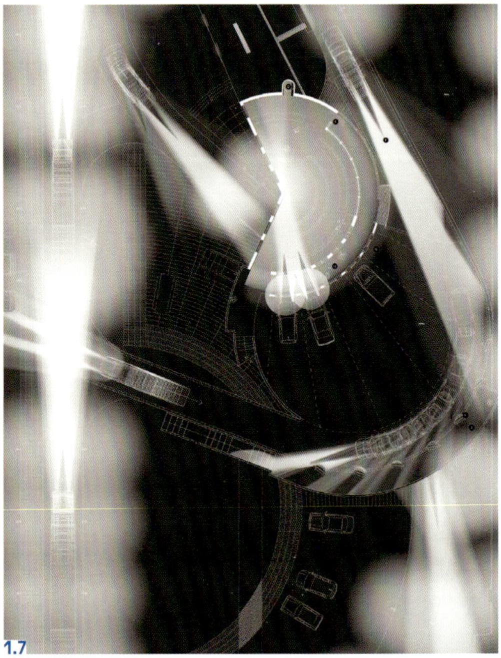

1.7

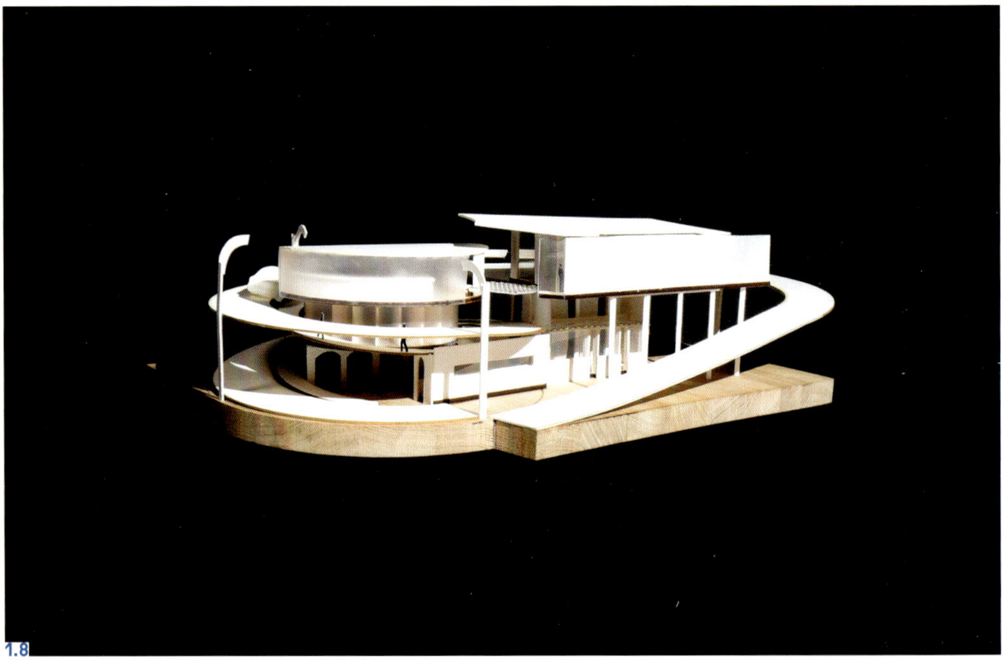

1.8

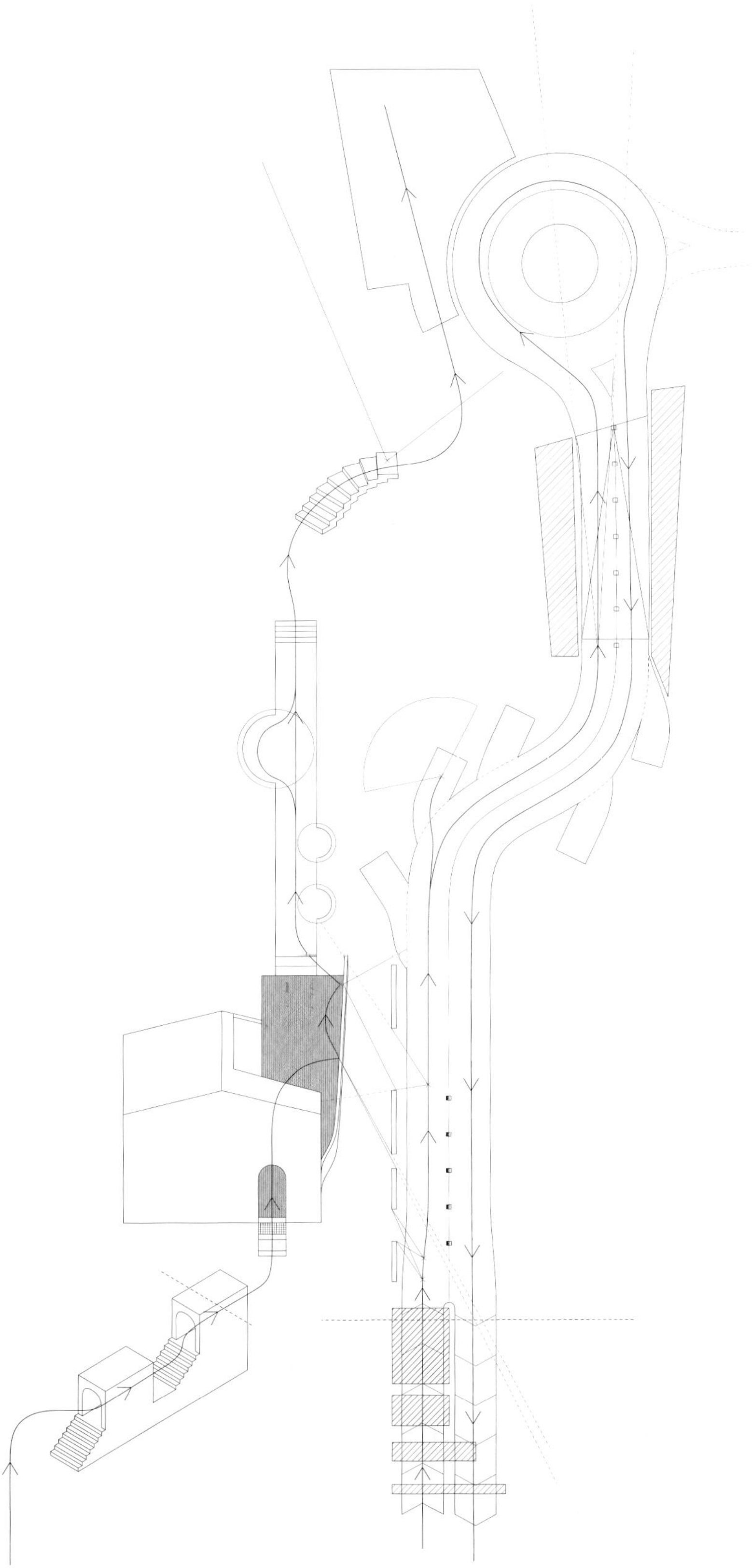

1.9

Fig. 1.10 Sarah Jones Y2, 'Thames Causeway'. Façade study for a building and landscape to collect and display the archaeology of the Thames. **Figs. 1.11 - 1.12 Gabi Watkins** Y2, 'East Tilbury Catacombs'. A new network of burial chambers forms a new ground condition for East Tilbury, connecting the former community hubs of the old factory town. These new spaces are envisaged as a series of urban interiors that accommodate both the ceremony of death as well as the routines of everyday life. Excavated earth from burial and construction is used to form the aggregate for an expanding collection of structures and rooms above ground that connect back to this subterranean world. **Fig. 1.13 Natasha Blows** Y3, 'The Institute of Copying'. Responding to regional plans to transform the Thames Estuary into a hub for creative technologies, this project proposes a meticulous copying of the most iconic of the Bata factory buildings. This notion of copying is intended as a critique of the desire to be contextual, given that the original building was such an alien imposition on the landscape. Contained within the new copy is a series of workshops, studios and public spaces for East Tilbury, which is envisaged as a new creative centre for the county.

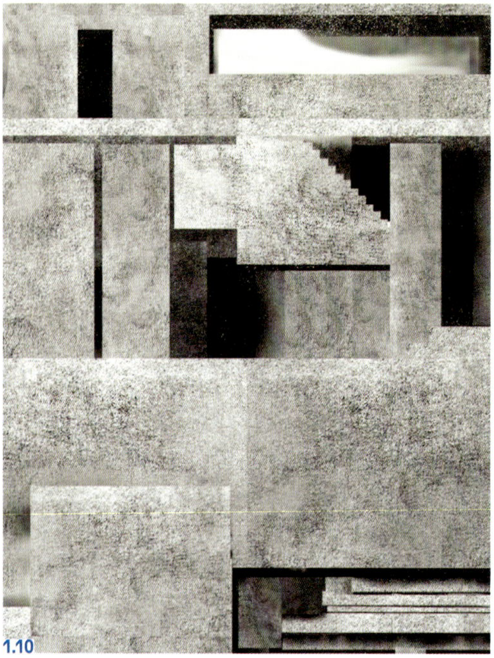
1.10

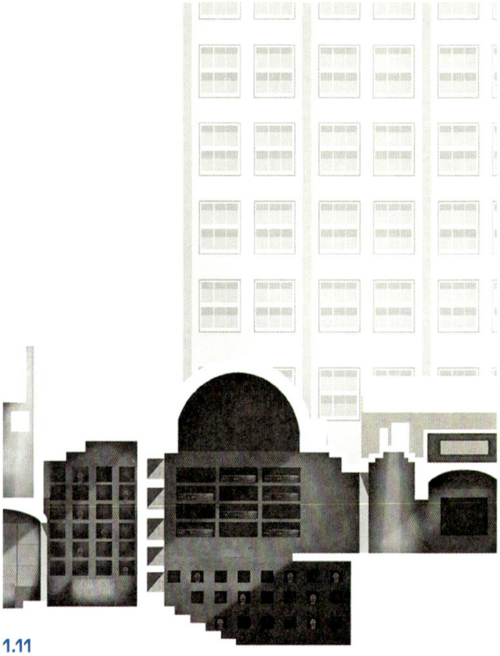
1.11

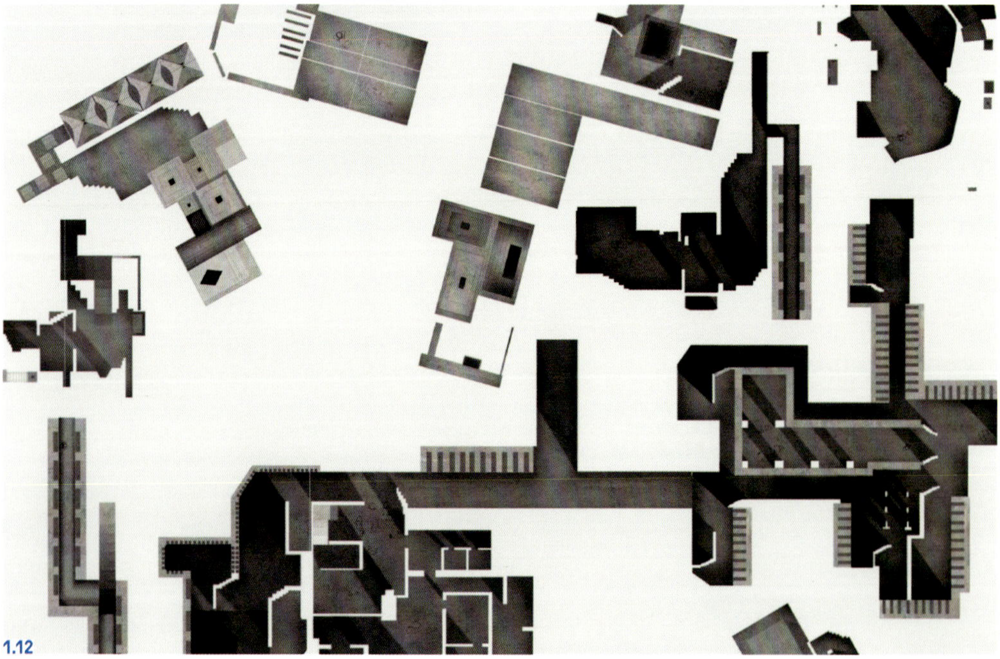
1.12

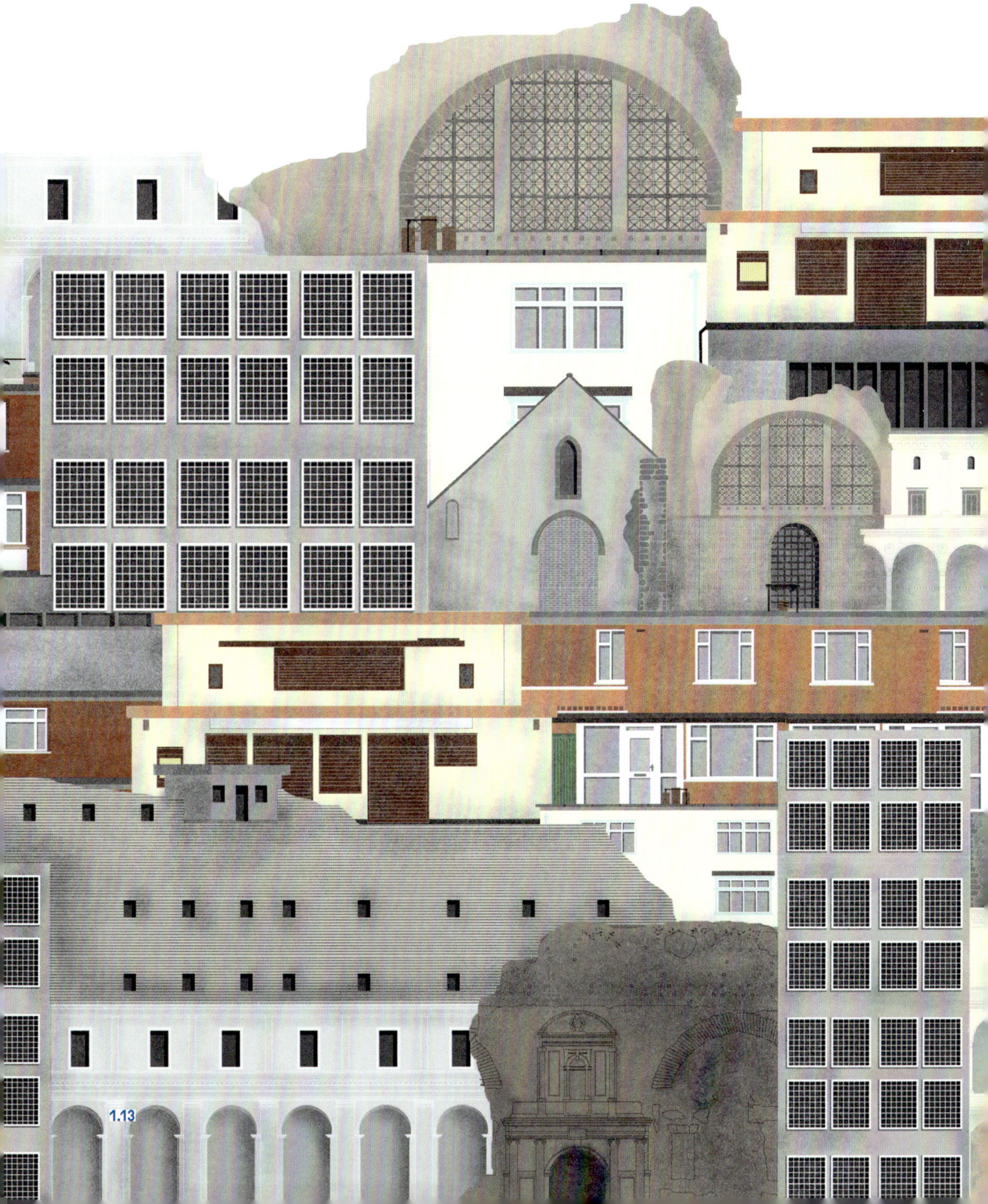
1.13

Figs. 1.14 – 1.16 Clementine Holden Y3, 'Appliance Archive'. Situated adjacent to the new Amazon fulfilment centre and conceived of as an extension to a suburban cul-de-sac, this project imagines a new archive of domestic appliances. Part museum, part landfill, the proposal aims to collect and display an ever-growing repository of material culture. Internal walls are constructed from cast in-situ expanded polystyrene blocks which function as both display niches and ornamentation.
Fig. 1.17 Karina Tang Y3, 'Knee-Deep'. A collection of minimal dwellings built on the floodplain surrounding the Amazon distribution shed to cater for seasonal shifts in the work force. To maximise profits, Amazon's labour model works on a direct relationship between number of employees and the number of things sold: the higher the demand, the more people they hire. This can mean an extra 3,500 workers are needed at peak times. During the off season, the units function as student accommodation and are clustered into small groups and communities around a collection of larger community rooms and facilities. The proposal thus responds to pertinent questions about the diminishing security of employment, the nuclear family and the 'home for life'.

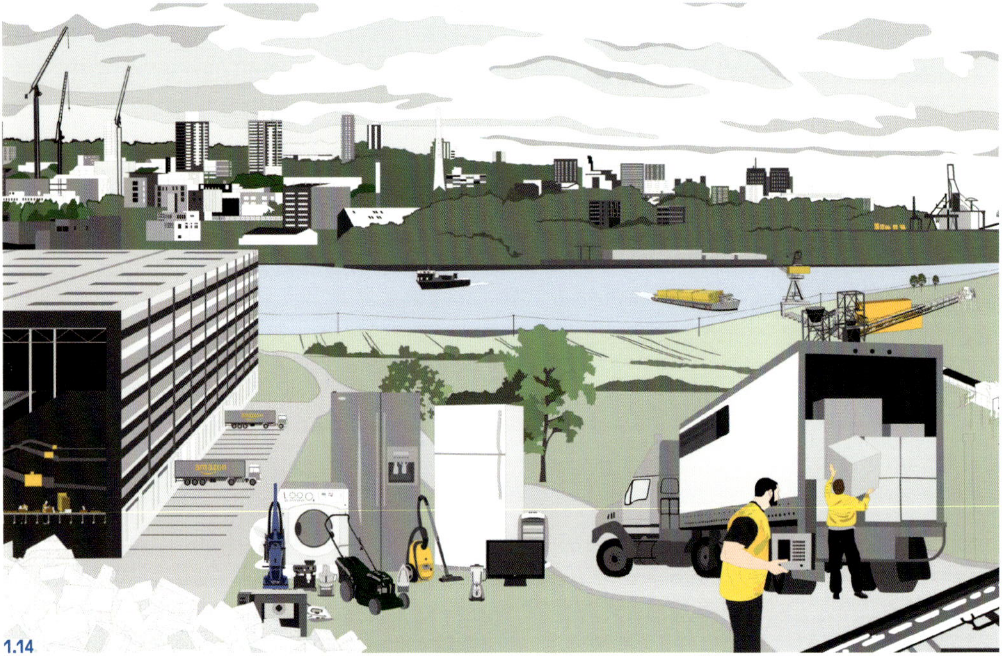

1.14

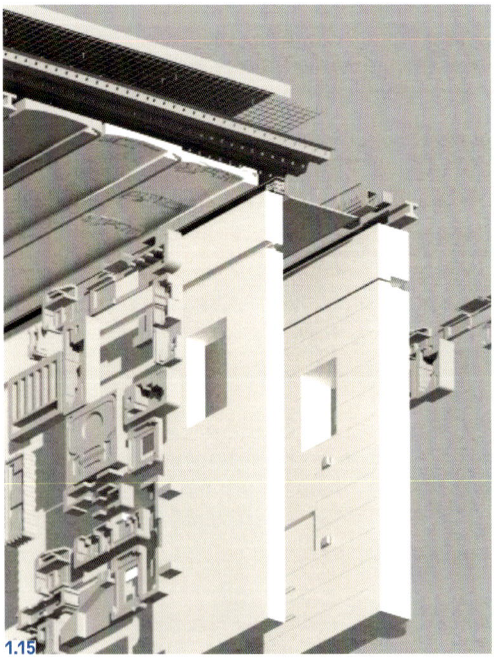

1.15

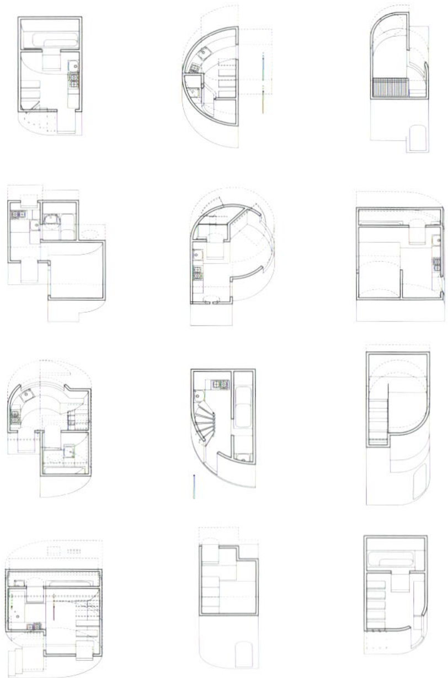

1.17

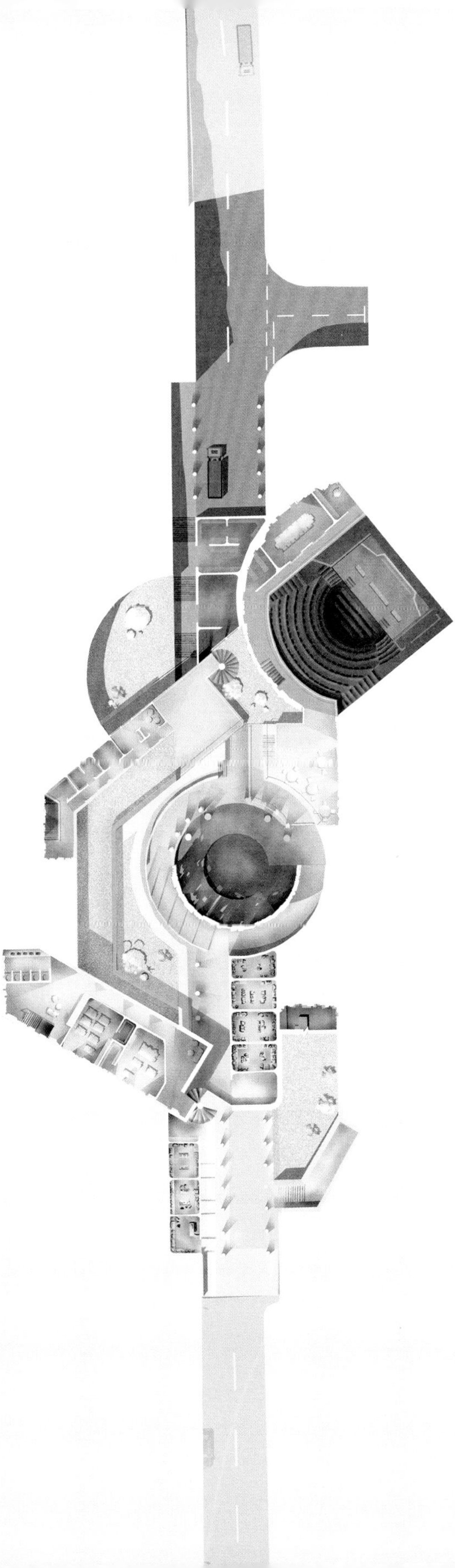

1.16

UG2

Spontaneous Procedures

Soomeen Hahm, Aleksandrina Rizova

Year 2
Paul Brooke, Yuqi Cai, Wei Ning Chung, Sebastian Fathi, Grey Grierson, Kyuri Kim, Samuel Martin

Year 3
Rupinder Gidar, Ziyu Jiang, Rachel Lee, Tung Yi Leung, Rory Noble-Turner, William Stephens, Yu Wu, Qiming Yang

Thank you to:

Consultants:
Year 3 Technical Tutor and Digital Workshops – David Edwards (Herzog & de Meuron)

Digital Workshops:
Wang Fung Chan (Heatherwick Studio), Niran Buyukkoz (Zaha Hadid Architects), Andrew Chard (Heatherwick Studio)
Guest Critics: David Edwards (Herzog & de Meuron), Konstantinos Chalaris (Chelsea College of Art), Aleksandar Bursac (Soomeen Hahm Design), Pereen d'Avoine (Russian for Fish), Nilesh Mahendra Shah (Russian for Fish), Serena Croxson, Manuel Jiménez García (The Bartlett, UCL), Caroline Lundin (Sundae Creative), Igor Pantic (Zaha Hadid Architects)

Guest Critics:
David Edwards (Herzog & de Meuron), Konstantinos Chalaris (Chelsea College of Art), Aleksandar Bursac (Soomeen Hahm Design), Pereen d'Avoine (Russian for Fish), Nilesh Mahendra Shah (Russian for Fish), Serena Croxson, Manuel Jiménez García (The Bartlett, UCL), Caroline Lundin (Sundae Creative), Igor Pantic (Zaha Hadid Architects)

In Unit 2, we develop ideas through digital simulations, analogue prototypes, material tests and digital fabrication. We encourage digital and analogue making, shifting quickly between the hand and the computer. We are inspired by local materials, textures, architectural and urban typologies and local context.

——Our students' projects this year are situated in Mexico City, a large metropolis with an ever-growing population. Our theme focused on the notion of spontaneous procedures on an architectural and urban scale. Through an understanding of algorithmic design methodology, we asked the students to juxtapose organised and spontaneous systems – could we design through transformation, adaptation, re-organisation? We looked at the interfaces between stasis and flux, local and global, bottom-up and top-down, natural and artificial. Throughout the year, students developed highly spatial and architectural individual approaches informed by sophisticated urban, spatial and material research.

——The year commenced with a short research project where students developed a range of analogue and physical prototypes informed by a procedure – a making technique. These initial constructs were then developed into architectural spatial systems, resulting in intricate structures, elaborate skins and integrated inhabited spaces. Students were encouraged to combine a range of design techniques in order to achieve highly articulated spatial hybrid constructs.

——After the field trip in January, students chose individual sites and developed building projects in Mexico City. We were fascinated by the Mayan ruins still visible in the city, Louis Barragan's beautiful use of colour and texture and the urban mix of various programmes, rituals, and ornament and building styles. We drew inspiration from the growing urban patterns in the city, the naturally occurring slum areas and defined modernist city blocks, and the interaction between natural and urban landscapes. We explored Mexico City as a spontaneous urban system and asked students to respond to its emerging contradictions. The projects are contextually sensitive while being contemporary and innovative in their architectural agenda. They vary in scale – from a secluded nunnery to a large infrastructural hub in the historic centre – with each responding to the cultural and urban diversities we found in the city.

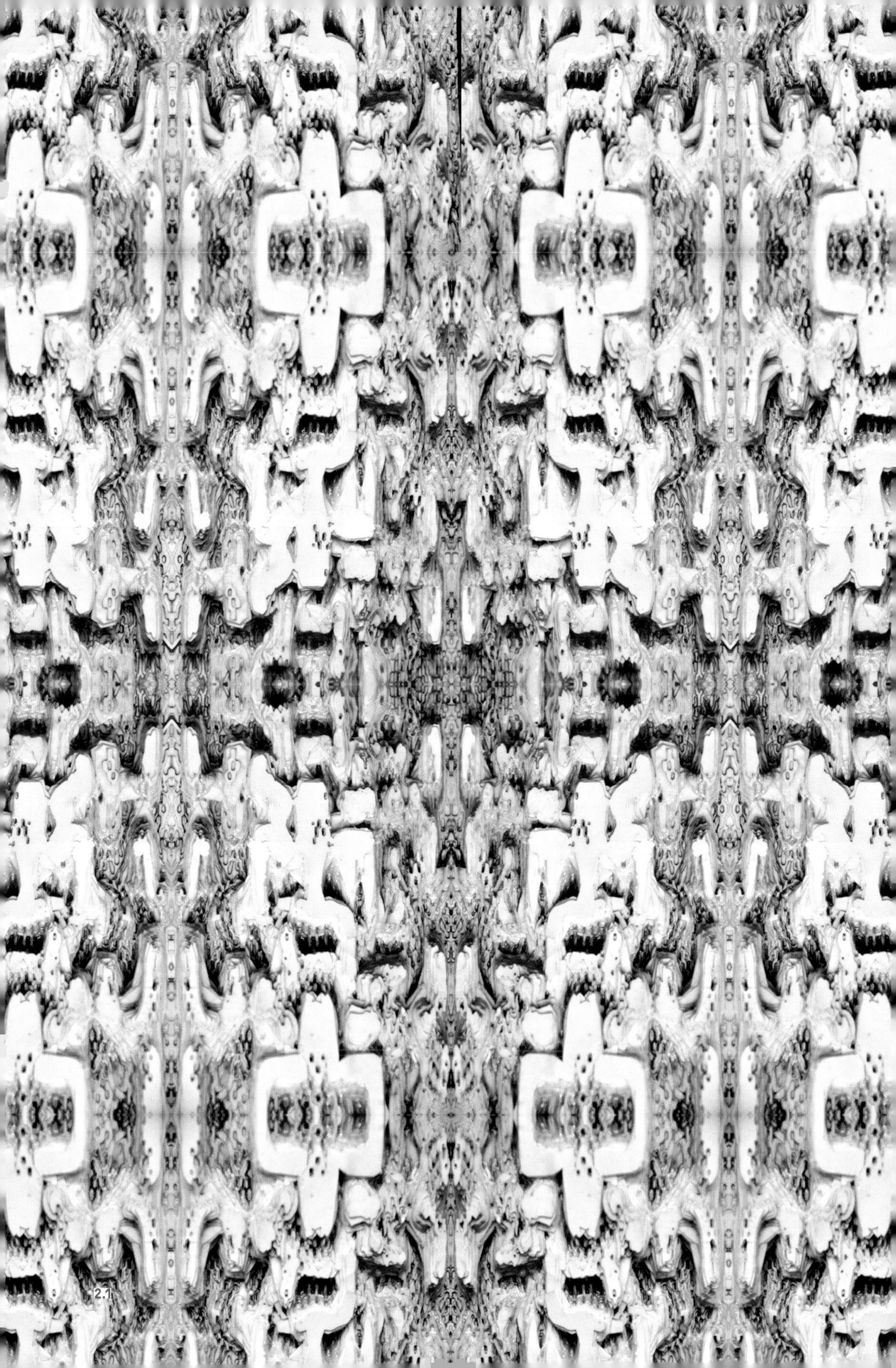

2.1

Fig. 2.1 Tung Yi Leung Y3, 'Reconstructing Mayan Architecture'. Based in the heart of Mexico City, the aim of the project is to reinterpret and reconstruct Mayan relief patterns with modern digital technology. Inspired by the geometric architectural decorations on the ornamental zoomorphic entrance from the Rio Bec, Chenes and Puuc regions from the 7th to 10th centuries, the building consists of a reusable building fabric that constantly changes according to the reconstruction that is taking place. **Fig. 2.2 Rupinder Gidar** Y3, 'Reconfigurable Laminated Structures'. The building project is a new factory typology where flexible surfaces control visibility and light. **Fig. 2.3 Kyuri Kim** Y2, 'Woven Structure'. The project studies the behaviour of woven strands through large-scale physical prototypes of foam and concrete. **Fig. 2.4 Rachel Lee** Y3, 'Liquid Formations'. A particular interest in fluid dynamics and substances interaction was tested through a series of casts and moulds. These initial tests informed the notion of generating unique spaces using simulation in the building project later on. **Fig. 2.5 Paul Brooke** Y2, 'OsteoFabricate'. The project focused on the transformation of fluid, free-forming material such as expanding foam into a structured and controlled architectural proposal. The resulting porosity and opacity gradients allow for varying quality of light. The material was tested using a bespoke apparatus in order to create a family of structural joints.

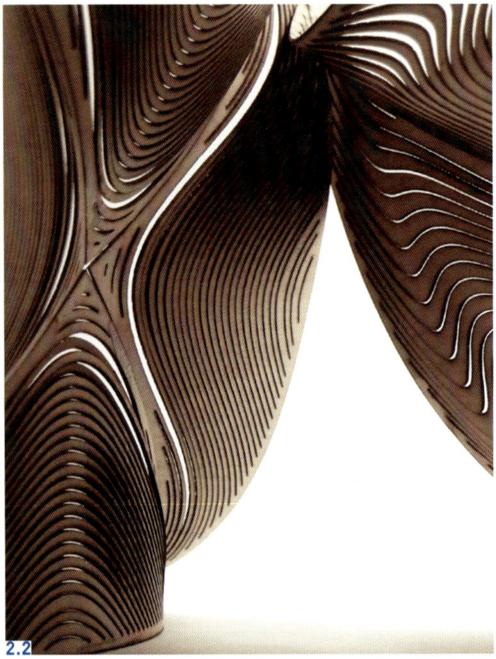
2.2

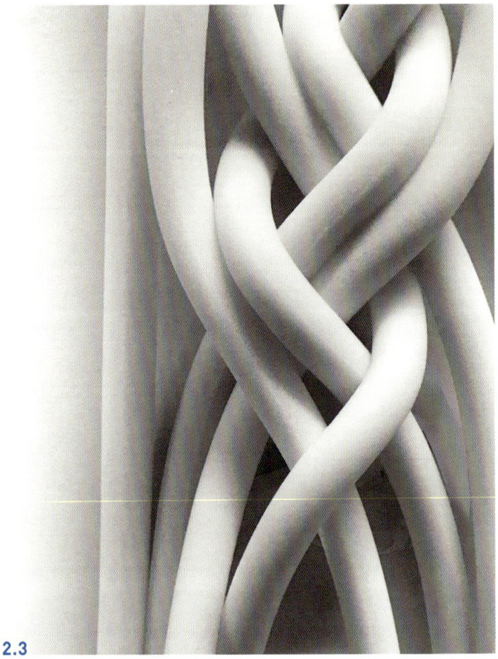
2.3

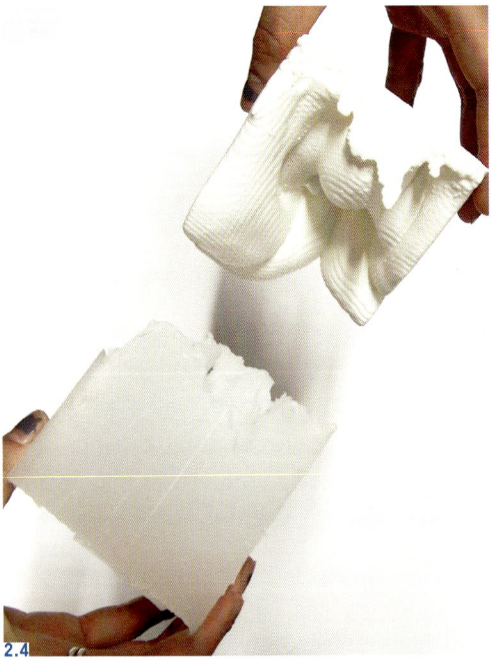
2.4

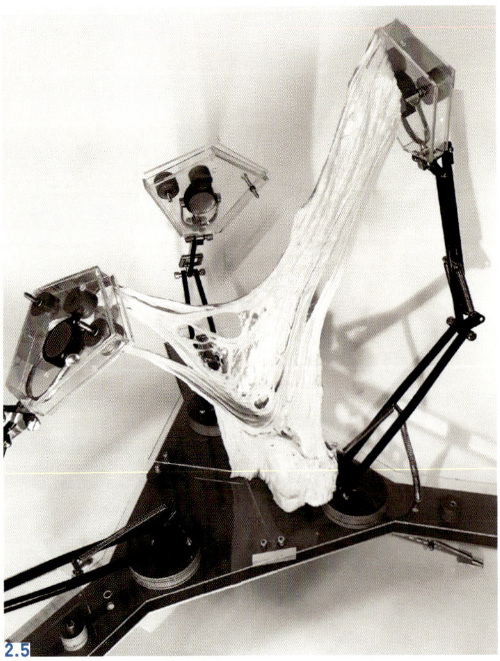
2.5

Fig. 2.6 Wei Ning Chung Y2, 'Mexican Pottery Workshop'. The building consists of modular timber-frame components which can be adapted for various uses – housing market stalls, or creating stairs and roof platforms. The structures plug into the existing market street, creating a dialogue with the context and existing activities. **Fig. 2.7 Samuel Martin** Y2, 'Cinema Complex'. The project is located in a residential area in Mexico City. Dynamic façade patterns are used as projection devices, creating an ever-changing building skin. The building skin also guides visitors through the building, creating a smooth transition between inside and outside. **Fig. 2.8 Yu Wu** Y3, 'Dancing School'. The design is inspired by traditional Mexican dresses with their rich layers of patterns and materials. Studies into the movement of a Mexican dress led to the development of a complex hyperbolic roof structure. The roof folds create shading for the outdoor performance area and also establish a highly spatial experience for the dancers inside. **Fig. 2.9 Sebastian Fathi** Y2, 'Glimpses into a Political Symbiosis'. The site in Mexico City is adjacent to Bazar El Oro which is a local 'tianguis' (temporary market). The proposal plays with a very particular political idiom in the city – the exchange between the market union leaders and the political delegate of the borough. The building provides a hostel for the tianguis market vendors between their nomadic trips across the city visiting other markets, office space for the local delegate and the vendors, and in addition, it augments the existing tianguis by introducing a new through-route.

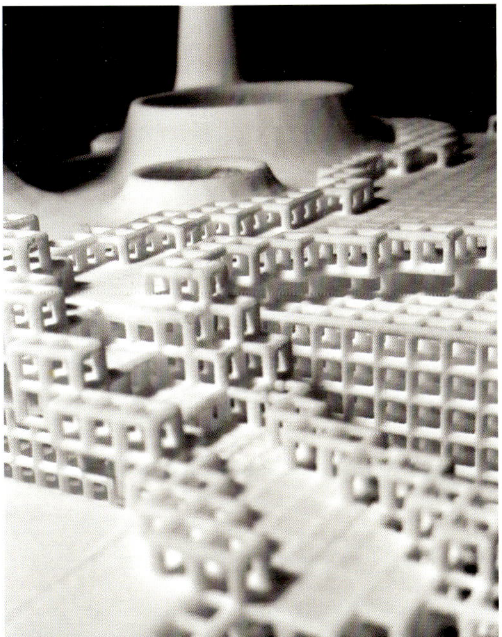

2.6

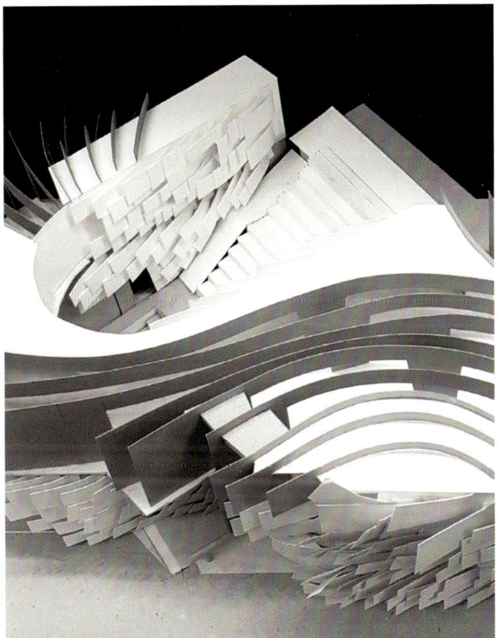

2.7

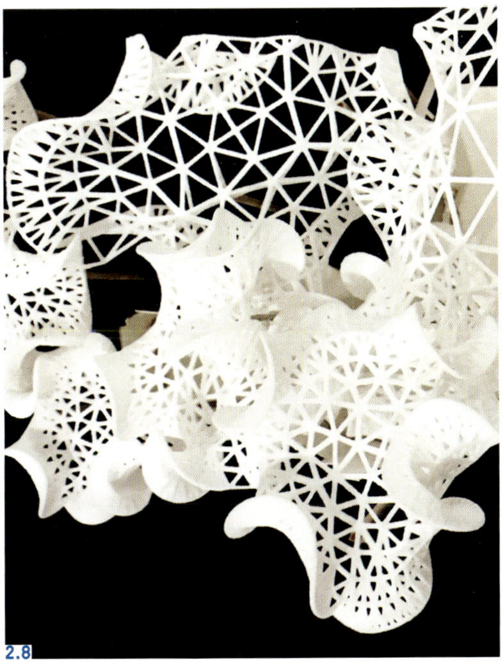

2.8

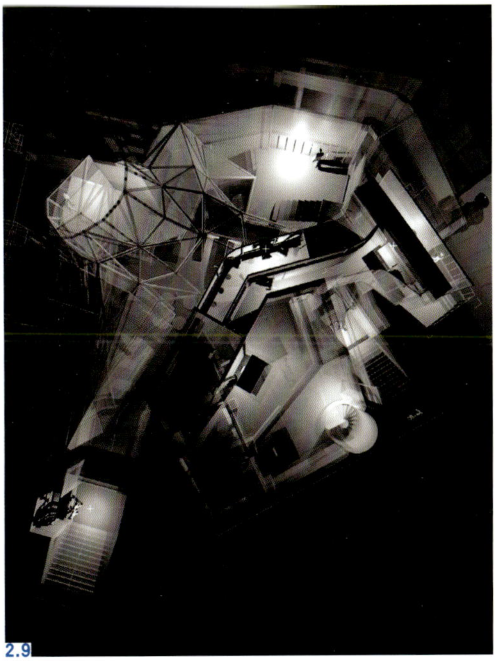

2.9

Figs. 2.10 – 2.11 Grey Grierson Y2, 'Student Housing'. The project reinterprets the traditional 'Vecidade' model (collective housing) for Mexico City's student population. The angular outer geometry of the building is designed to draw away from the noise of the busy traffic on the adjacent motorway. The idea of the fold is taken from the entrance through to the communal courtyard landscape and the student rooms. The doors of the student units are able to fold across, allowing the students to create a highly social atmosphere. The skin is inspired by the geometric nature of traditional Mexican textiles which blend patterns of various geometries and sizes into one another. **Figs. 2.12 – 2.14 Qiming Yang** Y3, 'Piñata Children's Workshop'. Piñata plays an important social role in Mexican's festival culture. The building provides space for children to design, make and showcase their own piñatas. The content of the building would eventually attract both locals and tourists so that they could experience the palace of piñatas as well as the nearby park. A series of study models reveals a deep façade with inhabited pockets and intricate structures, allowing for views and light to penetrate the building.

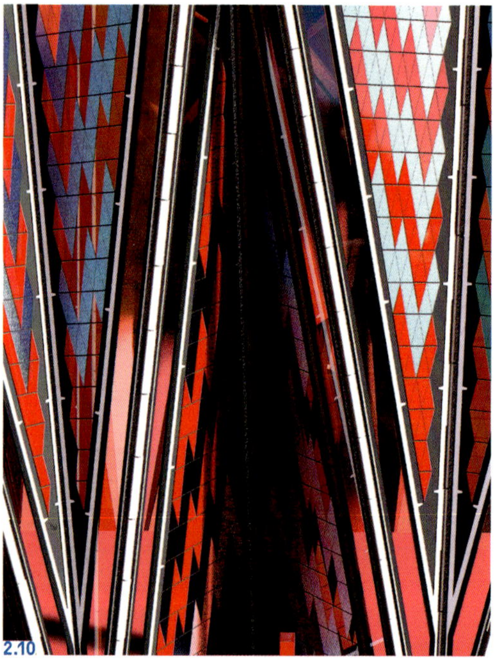

2.10

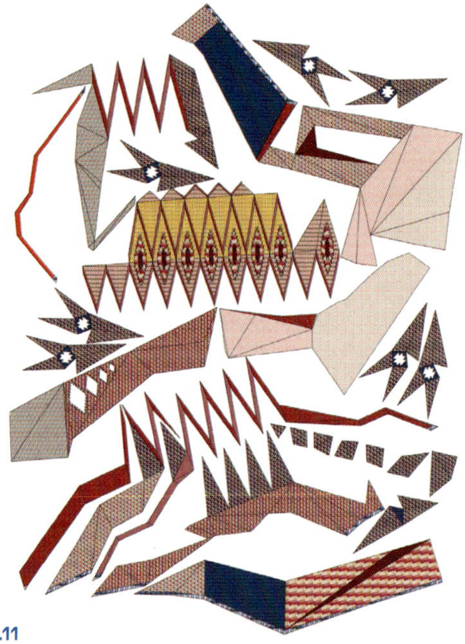

2.11

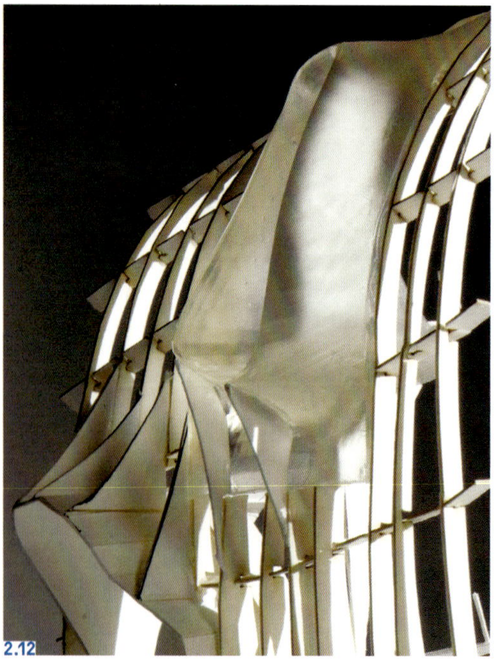

2.12

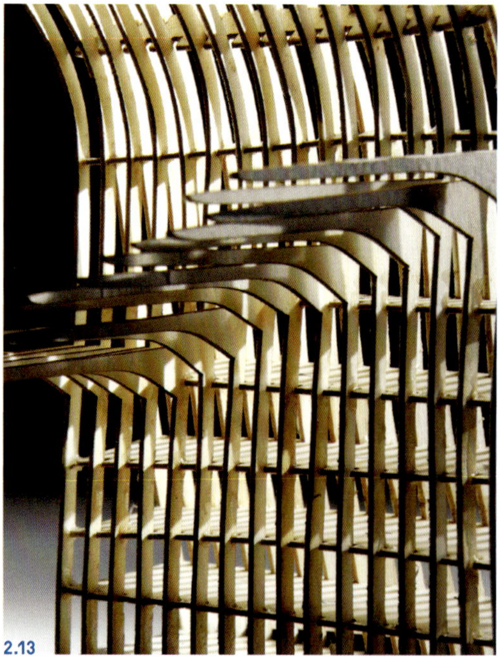

2.13

FOUNDATION

Director Saskia Lewis
Studio Masters Umberto Bellardi Ricci, Juliet Haysom
Tutor Sylvie Taher
Students Mia Aoun, Kerem Edmonds, Anthony Flouty, Danya Gittler, Joseph Hellman, Solvieg Jappy, Laetitia Khachwajian, Barbara Koch, Ferial Massoud, Julia Pawlowska, Linden Seddon, Zuzanna Sienczyk, Aude Tollo, Celine Topsakal, Marine Zovighian
Thanks Sue Barr, Maria Brewster, Mark Campbell, Fenella Collingridge, Charlie Corry Wright, Georgie Corry Wright, Caroline Esclapez, Trevor Flynn, Chiyan Ho, Michael Ho, Antoni Malinowski, Anya Martsenko, George Massoud, Flora McLean, Cassidy Moses, Sara Muzio, Francesco Neri, Joel Newman, Luca Nostri, Jessica Pappalardo, Claire Potter, Daniela Puga, Nabil Randeree, Matthew Rice, Adrian Taylor, Trys Smith, Camiel Van Noten

FIRST YEAR

Head of First Year Monia De Marchi
Studio Staff Delfina Bocca, Pol Esteve, Costandis Kizis, Nacho Marti, Patricia Mato Mora, John Ng, Thomas Randall Page, Sara Saleh, Alexandra Vougia
Sonia Syed, Vang Anh Tran, Tommaso Tugnoli, Carlos Uribe, Mariana Valenzuela Lombera, Kelly Elizabeth Van Homrigh, James Wallis, Ruoning Wu, Tzu-shuo Wu, Qian Yang, Mohamad Riad Yassine, Ron-fu Yeh, Yasemin Yesilipek, Peixuan Zhang, Yan Ying Zhang
Acknowledgements Stefan Jovanovic, Adam Kaasa, Sofia Krimizi, Douglas John Miller, John Philip Sage, Pablo Zamorano
Thanks Atelier Deshaus, Foster + Partners, Heatherwick Studio, Steven Holl Architects, Zaha Hadid Architects, and to our guests and critics.

INTERMEDIATE 1

Unit Masters Lara Lesmes, Carl Fredrik, Valdemar Hellberg
Students Anne-Lise Agossa, Isabel Castro, Charlotte Jia Qing Chan, Ludvig Holmen, Kyungjoo Min, Mira Oktay, Anushri Patel, Peter Yimyung Roh, Bulat Safaev, Maša Tatalovič, Daniel Tayar-Watson, Zixin Ye
Thanks Miraj Ahmed, Edward Bottoms, Timothy Brittain Catlin, Ricardo de Ostos, Max Dewdney, Ryan Dillon, Oliver Domiesen, Maria Fedorchenko, Kenny Fraser, Gonzalo Herrero Delicado, Carlos Jimenez Cenamor, Amandine Kastler, David Kohn, Tyen Masten, Gili Merin, Aram Mooradian, Sabrina Morreale, Mark Morris, Shaun Murray, Jiachen Cui, Chi Yan Matthew Mark Ho, Gréta Tekla Gedeon, Caterina Pereira, Haya Morowa, Thomas Faulkner, Mamoru Hoshi, Taiki Takemura, Efe Gole, Shlok Soni
Thanks Nathan Su, Nicholas Zembashi, Assaf Kimmel, Graeme Wallace, Nina McCallion, Wolfgang Frese, Sarah Handelman, Theodore Spyropoulos, Nerma Cridge, David Hutama, Yeena Yoon, Song Jie, Karsten Huneck, Barbara-Ann Campbell-Lange, Nat Chard, Oliver Domeisen, Jennifer Chen, Alma Wang, Mark Morris, Javier Castanon, Haaris Ramzan, Nate Kolbe, Theodore Spyropoulos and DRL students, Nathan Su, Anis Kamaruddin, Alice Labourel, Nina McCallion, Tom Clewlow

INTERMEDIATE 4

Unit Tutors Arantza Ozaeta, Álvaro M Fidalgo
Students Zhaniya Alimzhanova, Luciana Bondio, Liwei Cheng, Dariya Cheremisina, Zhehao Hong, Bour Chiang Huang, Sooyeon Lim, Ziyad Louis Mourad, Athena Erato Thrasyvoulou, Zi Min Ting, Dana Wazni, Cuicheng Zhang, Yuting Zhang
Lecturers & Workshop Collaborators Sue Barr, Brendan Cormier, Charlie Corry-Wright, Simon Dickens, Kenneth Fraiser, Pablo Gugel, Angel Lara, Nina McCallion, Paula Rodríguez, Pablo Saiz, Manolis Stavrakakis, Nathan Su

EXHIBITION 2018 GUIDE

Students Bolurin Michael Adedipe, Andrea Agostini, Youngchae Ahn, Polina Aleshkina, Malek Pierre Arif, Ishita Arora, Ammara Asdar, Armaan Bansal, Alice Baseian, Tsolmon Bat-Enkh, Emre Bekisoglu, Carmen Bisono Turull, Beatrice Boselli, Thanida Buranasujja, Jiaxin Cao, Xiaotian Cao, Oz Caspi, Defne Cengic, Yi Hin Chan, Laetitia Chauveau, Siying Chen, Tung-Hua Chen, Brian Joseph Hok Man Chung, Jean-Baptiste Coulomb, Anna Soonchil Dei, Judi Diab, Isabollo Doumet, Gaetano Drago, Kamal El Kharrat, Anastasia Fedotova, Lap Ming, Norman Fong, Nika Galkina, Nethra Ganesan, Vasundhara Goyal, Seongsoo Han, Yu-fu Huang, Elsa Jacob, Altynay Jakisheva, Yue Jiang, Edouard Joiris De Caussin, Hosung Joo, Cesar Jucker, Igne Jurgaityte, Dongki Kang, Vedika Kapur, Kah Ling Kong, Olga Kostur, Sofia Krivashina, Hoi Ching Lee, Zhi Wee Lee, Weiqing Liang, Emma Magnusson, Jumana Mahrous, Tara Malek Gilani, Marina Matinopoulou, Patrick McGraw, Nicolaos Moustroufis, Su Yeon Mun, Rojan Nekourouymotlagh, Chia Cheng Ng, Lana Atef Nsouli, Joana Oliviera Tavira, Deniz Ozcan, Logan Paine, Vian Rasool, Noah Robinson-Stanier, Sapolachet Sankosik, William Keaton Seddon, Sherif Shehata, Daniel Leo Swarovski, Adam Nathaniel Furman, John Ng, Nandi Nobell, Lorenzo Perri, Christopher Pierce, Caroline Rabourdin, Yael Reiser, Theodore Spyropoulos, Sylvie Taher, Carlos Villanueva Brandt, John Walter, Michael Weinstock, Mark Cousins, Sergio Irigoyen, James Taylor Foster

INTERMEDIATE 2

Unit Master Ana Araujo
Students Edoardo Albertini Petroni, Sebastian Cheng Ge Cornwell, Ellie Cullen, Clara Dahan, Rashad Fakhouri, Philip Nazih Gharios, Anna Glik, Frida Ostby Hansen, Salomé Hirsch, Darya Naumchenko, Ainhoa Tamara Schapira Perez, Mu Zhang
Acknowledgements Isabel Allen, Anouk Ahlborn, Simon Beames, Barbara-Ann Campbell-Lange, Ryan Dillon, Susie Dowding, Christiane Felber, Sarah Handelman, Juliet Haysom, Jonathan Hill, Niall Hobhouse, Aidan Hodgkinson, Nuria Alvarez Lombardero, Patricia Mato-Mora, Helen Mallinson, Christopher Pierce, Celia Scott, Ro Spankie, Christian Spencer-Davies

INTERMEDIATE 3

Unit Staff Ricardo de Ostos, Nannette Jackowski, Nathan Su
Students Tomiris Batalova, Kwang Yi Goh, Thanks Aitor Almaraz, Christina Argyros, Nerea Calvillo, Javier Castañón, Monia de Marchi, Alex de Rijke, Ryan Dillon, Georgios Eftaxiopoulos, Carlos Jiménez Cenamor, Fredrik Hellberg, Costandis Kizis, Sofia Krimizi, CJ Lim, Theo Lorenz, Zachary Mollica, Mark Morris, John Ng, Christopher Pierce, Sabrina Puddu, Eduardo Rico, Tanja Siems, Eva Sopeoglou, Sylvie Taher, Antoine Vaxelaire, Alvaro Velasco, Manijeh Verghese, Andrea Zanderigo

INTERMEDIATE 5

Staff Ryan Dillon, David Greene
Students Matis Barollier, Jumana Bawazir, Camille Bongard, Audrey Kai Qing Chan, Gabrielle Eglen, Wei Xuan Sean Gwee, Sensy Mania, Quentin Martin, Caspar Anne Schols, Ezgi Terzioglu, Taek Gyun Won, Alexander Zikanov
Friends Jeroen van Ameijde, Ana Araujo, Valentin Bontjes van Beek, Ed Bottoms, Barbara-Ann Campbell-Lange, Brendon Carlin, Mark Cousins, Charlie Corry-Wright, Georgie Corry-Wright, Arantza Ozaeta Cortázar, Kate Davies Francesca Dell'Aglio, Monia De Marchi, Shin Egashira, Liza Fior, Winston Hampel, Samantha Hardingham, Christine Hawley, Fredrik Hellberg, Kenneth Fraser, Francisco Gonzales de Canales,

Kostas Grigoriadis, Costandis Kizis, Lara Lesmes, Nuria Alvarez Lombardero, Tyen Masten, Inigo Minns, Mark Morris, Christopher Pierce, Theodore Spyropoulos, Silvana Taher, Max Turnheim, Emmanuel Vercruysse, Manijeh Verghese, Alexandra Vougia, Thomas Weaver
A special thank you to Eddie Farrell for his time throughout the year

INTERMEDIATE6

Unit Masters Jeroen van Ameijde, Brendon Carlin
Unit Tutor Norine Chu
Students Nena Naima Olga Aru, Muqing Bai, Carlo Alberto Campolo, Niccoló Cesaris, Jia Long Feng, Hangyul Jeong, Lito Karamitsou, Marko Krackovic, Alexandru Octavian Mitea, Nuragiyanti Dewi Permatasari, Pranav Vakharia
Thanks Maria Fedorchenko, Ryan Dillon, Soomeen Hahm, Alexandros Kallegias, Mizue Katayama, Angel Fernando Lara Moreira, Ricardo de Ostos, Lukas Pauer, Ioanna Pin, Ingrid Schröder, Sylvie Taher, Stan Turcon, Jerome Tsui, Suzan Ucmaklioglu, Carlos Villanueva Brandt, Astrid Klein (Klein Dytham Architects), Fusako Ishikawa (Shimizu Corporation), Rafael A. Balboa (The University of Tokyo), Takeshi Yamamura (Waseda University)

INTERMEDIATE 7

Unit Staff Marco Vanucci, Anna Muzychak
Students Kanoo Almoayyed, Hau Yan Gordon Chan, Napat Chayochaichana, Nata Dzhmukhadze, Igor Bartlomiej Gola, Yewen Jin, Kin Yat Uno Lam, Karolina Anna Leszkowicz, Ka Shut Leung, Yu Lian, Leonard Liao-Briere, Khun Wong, Allister Low
Thanks Manuel Orazi, Francis McCloskey, Marko Gligorov, Carlos Villanueva Brandt, Sylvie Taher, Francesca Romana D'Aglio, Stefan Popa, Eleni Axioti, Mark Morris, Jeroen Van Ameijde, Julian Siravo, Simon Rowe, Claudia Pasquero, Yona Friedman, Alexandros Kallegias, Silan Yip, Annarita Papeschi, John Ng, Soomeen Hahm, Elif Erdine, Davide Sacconi, Klaus Platzgummer, Simon Withers, Kenny Fraser, Gramazio Kohler Group (ETH), Block Research Group (ETH)

INTERMEDIATE 8

Unit Staff Francisco González de Canales, Nuria Álvarez Lombardero
Students Aleksanda Aksentijevic, Farah Bizrah, Marina Isabella Gubbins Uccelli, Dara Nerweyi, Chu Ying Ng, Natacha Palomeque Coll, Tamara Husam Rasoul, Romain Bernard Christian Rihouet, Zahra Sheikh Sarbuland, Zaina Sweidan, Maroussia Georgia Chiara Tasiaux, Maciej Jerzy Tomaka
Workshop tutors Matej Hosek, Mattia Santi
Thanks Sylvie Taher, Nacho Martí, Adam Kaasa, Alicia Nahmad, Taneli Mansikkama, Douglas Spencer, Mark Morris, Kenny Fraser, Amar Mehta, Fang Lee, Catalin Crina, Angel Lara-Moreira, Pierandrea Angius, Naiara Vegara, Costandis Kizis, Alexandra Vougia, Harikleia Karamali, Arturo Revilla, Alexandros Kallegias, Conrad Koslowsky, Sara Saleh, Diego Ricalde in the Universidad Iberoamericana Ciudad de México, Catalina Corcuera in the Casa-Museo Barragán, and the architects Gabriela Etchegaray, Jorge Ambrosi, Manuel Cervantes Céspedes, Oscar Rodriguez, Francisco Pardo, Fernando Polidura and Tatiana Bilbao in Mexico City, Iulia Statica, Tao Sule, Pol Esteve, Yota Adilenidou, John Ng, Kostas Grigoriadis, Rodolfo Rodriguez, Manuel Collado, Sylvie Taher, Nacho Martí, Adam Kaasa, Alicia Nahmad, Taneli Mansikkama, Douglas Spencer, Mark Morris, Samantha Hardigham, Kenny Fraser, Amar Mehta, Fang Lee, Catalin Crina, Angel Lara-Moreira, Pierandrea Angius, Naiara Vegara, Costandis Kizis, Alexandra Vougia, Harikleia Karamali, Arturo Revilla, Alexandros Kallegias, Conrad Koslowsky, Sofia Krimizi, James Khamsi and Sara Saleh

INTERMEDIATE 9

Tutors Amandine Kastler, Christopher Pierce, Christopher Matthews
Students Victoria Abel, Jasmine Abu-Hamdan, Sinan Asdar, Ran Ben-Shaya, Alessia Broggini, Daniel Hambly, Woojin Kim, Jean Kouassi, Nicholas Lin, Daria Nepop, Shaha Raphael, Talya Yigitbasi

INTERMEDIATE 10

Tutors Valentin Bontjes van Beek, Winston Hampel
Students Farida Aliyeva, Valeria Armendáriz Pedrero, Esther Brizard, Phillip Chee Fai Chung, Ylam Deme, Amalia Gîscă-Chițac, Jun Wei Koh, Si Jing Lai, Lior Ramon, Shaeron Santosa, Andreea Vasilcin, Paul Vecsei
Thanks Nuria Alvarez Lombardero, Sue Barr, Florian Busch, Nerea Calvillo, Barbara-Ann Campbell-Lange, Angharad Davies, Monia De Marchi, Ryan Dillon, Shin Egashira, Pol Esteve, Kenny Fraser, Francisco Gonzalez de Canales, Kostas Grigoriadis, Sarah Handelman, Samantha Hardingham, William Hutchins Orr, Max Kahlen, Costandis Kizis, Marina Lathouri Hwa Jeong Lee, Hye Rim Lee, Lara Lesmes, Aram Mooradian, Timothy O'Hare, Rory Sherlock, Hiroe Shigemitsu, Mike Tonkin, Max Turnheim, Manijeh Verghese, Carlos Villanueva Brandt, Owen Watson, Thomas Weaver, Simon Withers

INTERMEDIATE 11

Unit Staff Nerea Calvillo, Manuel Collado
Consultant Nacho Martín
Students Maite Garcia-Lascurain Fernandez, Gian Francesco Brivio Sforza, Yee Fei Tan, YoungBin Shin, Neill In, Yu Wei Cong, WonYoung Jeong, Leo Xiangyu Sun, May Slaoui, Chiao Yang, Rohzana Bahzoon, Iris Meng
Thanks Miau, Javier Peña, Yee Thong Chai
And all the jurors that have contributed to our reviews

INTERMEDIATE 12

Tutors Taneli Mansikkamäki, Max Turnheim
Students Amy Glover, Emma Voisin Isdahl, Sarochinee Wongchotsathit, Elisa Commanay, Tamir Cohen Aharoni, Romain Conti-Granteral, Wenyi Hu, Maya Kleiman, Christopher Ioannou, Julian Morisset, Simon Glemser,Sofia Tabet-aoul
Visiting Critics Umberto Bellardi Ricci, Winston Hampel, Max Kahlen, Martti Kalliala, Sofia Krimizi, Jon Lopez, Dan Meththananda, Elena Paca, Christopher Pierce, Sari Räthel, Jenna Sutela, Sylvie Taher, Tuomas Toivonen, Antoine Vaxelaire, Ricarda Wolf

INTERMEDIATE 13

Unit Master Soomeen Hahm
Students Dalal Itani, Luisa Pires, Vivian Olawepo, Louisa Wong, Davide Apolloni, Weina Zhang, Falah Al-Rashidi
Technical Support Saenawee Chatameteewong, Suchart Ouypornchaisakul, Chloe Hjentiens, Hanjun Kim
External Crits Jeroen van Ameijde, Daniel Kohler, Kostas Grioriadis, Alexandros Kallegias, Kwanphil Cho, Alvaro Lopez, Stefan Bassing, Angel Moreira, Ryan Dillon

INTERMEDIATE 14

Unit Masters Shaun Murray, Simon Withers
Students Miles Hudson Mahdavi, Camille Puech, Gemma Raad, Ifeoluwasimi Somefun, Khaled Al-Bashir, Luke Decker, Jin Ho Yim, Ele How Yan Mun, Sergey Nadtochiy, Frank Quek Yu Hong, Kellin Wang
Thanks Mark Morris, Tim Waterman, Ed Wall, Ed Bottoms, Theo Spyropolous, Nat Chard, Barbara-Ann Campbell-Lange, Thomas Pearce, Kate Davies, Simon Winters, Yorgos Loizos, Bastien Glaessner, Eddie Farrell, David Greene, Gary Woodley, Robin Wilson, Neil Spiller

INTERMEDIATE 15

Tutor Ryan Neiheiser, Xristina Argyros
Students Aijie Xiong, Altan Jurca Avci, Amaya Hernandez, Atiehsadat Naghavi, Georgia Kestekoglou, Jonas Popp, Kevin Larson, Maria Nefeli Stamatari, Phillip Zhao Jie Tsang, Theodora Giovanazzi, Vic Shengya Huang, Zhao Qiuyu

INTERMEDIATE 16

Unit Master Silvana Taher
Unit Tutor Rodolfo Rodriquez
Students Hsiang Kuo, Yin Ning Lee, Jingyeong Ryu, Theo Sykes, Shutian Zhou, Anna Aleshkina, Sung Vin Cho, Oussama Garti, Sorana-Ștefana Mazilu, Rin Seo, Yu-Cheng Su, Estelle Tan

DIPLOMA 1

Unit Staff Miraj Ahmed, Martin Jameson
Students Mu-Jung Chiu, Ryan Cook, Ali El-Hashimi, David Flook, Mikolaj Karczewski, Julia Kubisty, Christoph Lenhart, Molly Mummery, Raya Shaban, Yu-Hsiang Wang, Zhongtian Yuan, Yu Zhou
Guests Pierre d'Avoine, Leon Chew, Barbara Campbell-Lange, Nicolas Feldmeyer, Fredrik Hellberg, Joseph Halligan, David Harley, Nicholas Lobo-Brenan, Jon Lopez, Bethan James, Chris Johnson, David McAlmont, James Mak, Mark Morris, Joel Newman, Hikaru Nissanke, Francois Penz, Gregory Ross, Carlos Sanchez, Colette Sheddick, Takero Shimazaki, Helene Solvay, Patrick Usborne

DIPLOMA 2

Unit Staff Kostas Grigoriadis
Students Matteo Agnoletto, Alex Chan, Michael Cheung, Marco Chui, Raphael Fogel, Chung Kim, Adi Krainer, Jonathan Law, Li Loh, Natalie Ow, Laura Vitzthum, Enshen Wang, Carolyn Wong
Thanks Valentin Bontjes van Beek, Carlos Villanueva Brandt, Barbara-Ann Campbell-Lange, José Navarrete Deza, Ryan Dillon, Sam Esses, Maria Fedorchenko, Marc Fornes, David Greene, Soomeen Hahm, Harriet Harriss, Michael Herrmann, Mitchell Joachim, Vicky Lai, Theo Lalis, Philipp Längst, Lambros Malafouris, Monia De Marchi, Nacho Marti, Leah Meisterlin, Mark Morris, Chris Pierce, Elliott Sclar, Theodore Spyropoulos, Silvana Taher, Naiara Vegara, Andrew Yau, Jonathan Wong

DIPLOMA 4

Unit Masters John Palmesino, Ann-Sofi Rönnskog
Students Olukoye Akinkugbe, Seungah Choi, Lola Conte, Eva Ibáñez Fuertes, Oskar Johanson, Sihyun Kim, Sandra Kolacz, Sahir Patel, Vaclav Pechan, Rebecca Ploj, Stanislas Turcon, Kai Hang Yau
Thanks Andy Lowe, Stavros Papavassiliou, Eleni Tzavellou Gavalla, Maria Radjenovic, Maximilian Schob, Mark Morris, Samantha Hardingham, Adam Lowe, Irit Rogoff, Carlos Villanueva-Brandt, Elena Pascolo, Marina Lathouri, Jan Zalasiewicz, Anthropocene Working Group, James Anicich, Van Phung Hieu Minh, Byron Blakeley, Roberta Jenkins, Susan Schuppli, Centre for Research Architecture—Goldsmiths, Angela Pomaro, CNR—ISMAR Istituto Scienze del Mare Venezia, European Commission Joint Research, European Commission Joint Research Centre JRC, Ispra

DIPLOMA 5

Unit Staff Cristina Díaz Moreno, Efrén Garcia Grinda, Benjamin Reynolds
Students Yang Yang Chen, Mads Bjorn Christiansen, Isotta Cornacchia Biasion, Liam Denhamer, Federico Fauli, Ronghua Lei, Kevin See-Yat Leung, Zi Shan Lim, Zsuzsa Peter, Simone Tchonova, Brandon Whitwell-Mak

DIPLOMA 8

Unit Master Maria Fedorchenko
Students Francesco Maria Bozzerla, Pui Quan Choi, Shereen Maria Doummar, Luca Gamberini, Iris Florence Francesca Gramegna, Olivier Jauniaux, Sukgyo Lloyd Lee, Katarzyna Lengiewicz, Alessandro Magliani, Olimpia Presutti, Gleb Sheykin, Ruoming Song, Tan Ao
Key Workshops Nabila Mahdi, Sabrina Morreale, Lorenzo Perri
Acknowledgements Miraj Ahmed, Bozar Ben-Zeev, Lawrence Barth, Javier Castanon, Barbara-Ann Campbell-Lange, Brendon Carlin, Monia De Marchi, Richard Difford, Minh Duc Le, Shin Egashira, María Álvarez García, Angela Gigliotti, Kostas Grigoriadis, Penelope Haralambidou, Samantha Hardingham, Brian Hatton, Fredrik Hellberg, Inigo Minns, Mark Morris, Christopher Pierce, Olympia Simopoulou, Manolis Stavrakakis, Antoine Vaxelaire, Carlos Villanueva Brandt
+ former Dip 8 and Inter 7 students, and all of our critics and guests

DIPLOMA 9

Tutors Antoine Vaxelaire, Stefan Laxness
Students Sophia Alami, Kishan San, Yee Thong Chai, Petro El Hage, Etienne Gilly, Ema Hana Kacar, Assaf Kimmel, Jie Hao Lau, Efim Leonov,

Foundation

FIRST FLOOR

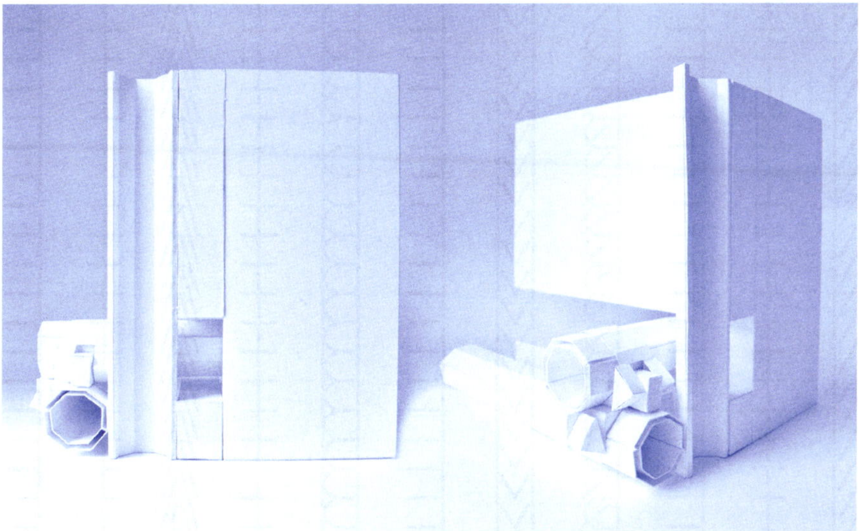

Aude Tollo, still from a stop-frame animation of a figure clothed in a white protective suit inhabiting a snowy landscape

The studio-based AA Foundation introduces students who are new to the disciplines of architecture and design to a range of skills alongside discussions of context, content, scale and materiality. Through drawing, 3D model-making and media-based projects, students identify their own territories of interest and then make a series of experiments and explorations to extrapolate lines of enquiry. This year the studio took trips to Italy and the AA campus at Hooke Park in Dorset.

First Year

FIRST FLOOR

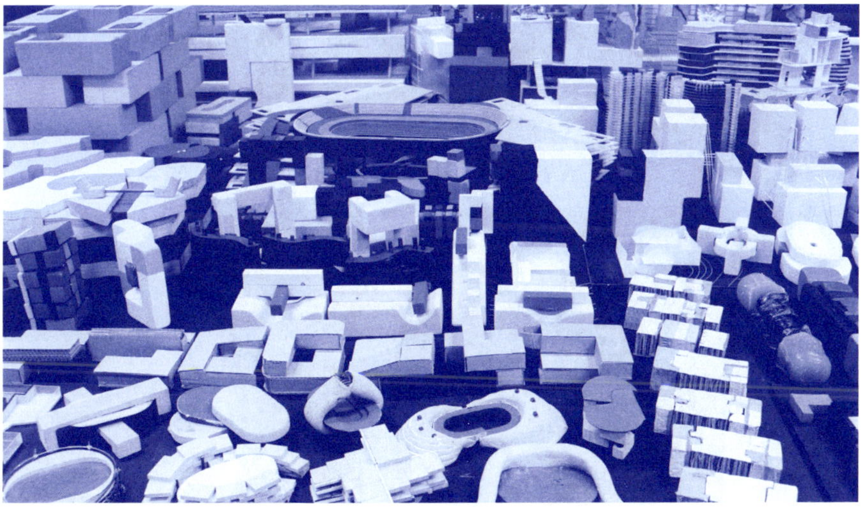

Models in the First Year studio

As the first of three years of architectural studies at the AA (resulting in the professional RIBA Part 1), First Year focuses on the starting points for architectural briefs and projects. Our testing ground this year was the built environment. Fieldwork, visits to buildings and construction sites in the UK and China, and physical contexts were the starting points for three briefs that challenged the tectonic and technology, programme and space, typology and spatial organisation.

Intermediate 1

GROUND FLOOR

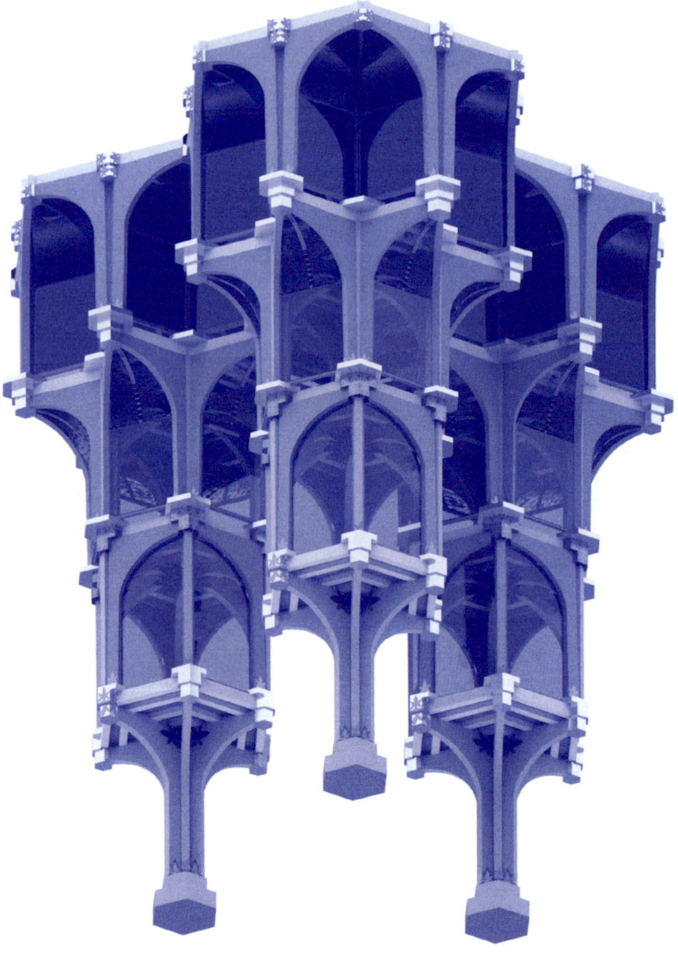

Anushri Patel, Accretion of Intricacies: Fractalisation of two-dimensional squinches

Q: How do we develop a criteria for designing experience-driven building systems?
A: In the form of questions from students this year: Can texture become furniture and construct a holistic architecture that comes in contact with the body? What will you call a society that lives and develops in a DIY reef-like favela? What would happen if my body becomes your home? Will you let me hold your roof, brace your walls? Is humanity collectively building a new dataist way of seeing the world? Can we make architecture move around us rather than us move through it? How does seeing and being seen influence our behaviour and our sense of privacy or lack thereof? How do we design spaces that offer simultaneously prospect and refuge? What constitutes immersive environments? How can detail and ornamentation be designed to reveal itself in stages as we move through and spend time in space? How are fragmented spaces mentally reconstructed when being explored? Can the formal strategy of a building be learned through inhabitation? Is there a role for monumentality in contemporary society? Can space have the power to elevate the previously mundane? Can we freeze a moment in the growth of the ornamental creature over the architectural body? Do architectural languages get along, argue, love or hate each other? Are there ways to confine volumes without walls? Can we define new kinds of boundaries that allow rooms to overlap and be inhabited simultaneously? What happens on the dark side of the rib-vault? How do edges influence our experience of space? What does seamless inhabitation mean?

Intermediate 2

FIRST FLOOR

Mu Zhang, site model

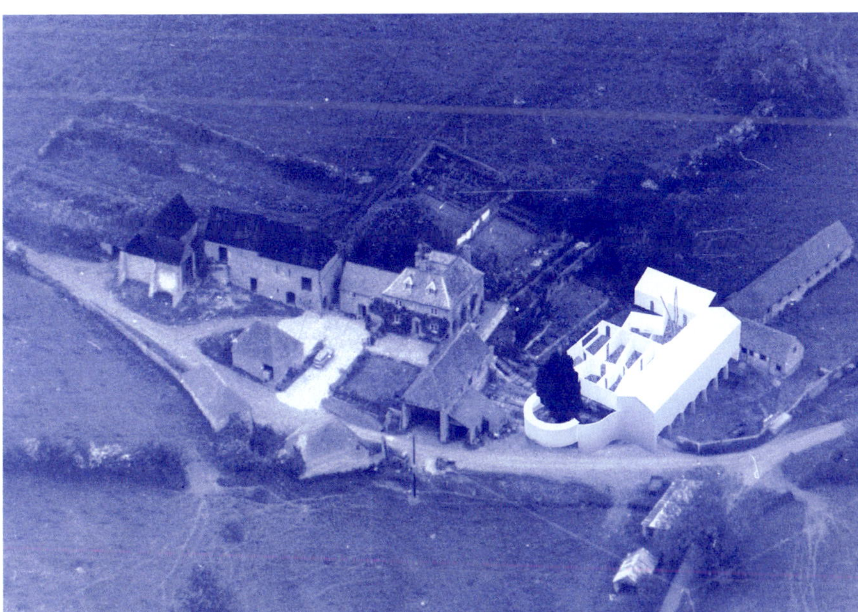

This year we worked with Drawing Matter, a trust established by English art collector Niall Hobhouse, which over the last 30 years has put together a remarkable collection of architectural drawings and models spanning from the sixteenth century to the present moment. Our brief sited us at the collection's home – Shatwell Farm, in Somerset – as we set out to design a gallery for the display of architectural drawings, as well as places to eat, shop and learn. Students developed their own interpretations based on observations of the site, programme and interactions with the Drawing Matter team.

Intermediate 3

GROUND FLOOR

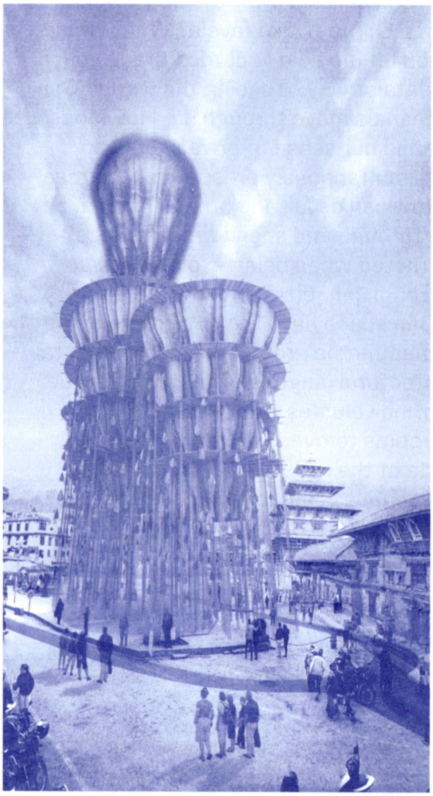

Mamoru Hoshi. Breathing Kathmandu – a hovering creature that reacts to the thick layer of smog in Kathmandu

We are interested in how myth and storytelling interweave with technological developments in cities and forests today. Although often treated as distinct in academic endeavour, these entities can in fact be found together, co-evolving in urban environments today. Take Nepal as an example – our unit trip destination and research field testing site. While many of its vernacular languages are connected to the religious and ritual heritage of Hindu and Buddhist traditions, its big cities face crises of pollution and bad waste management. Nepal additionally suffers the legacy of the 2015 earthquake which devastated large parts of the country's built heritage. But instead of using existing infrastructural solutions to address the relation between modernisation and contemporary urban problems, the students of Intermediate 3 sought inspiration from culture and social behaviour. While our work is often imaginative, it is never myopic in its reading of contemporary problems. To doubt productively is perhaps the best way to colour a dream.

Intermediate 4

SECOND FLOOR

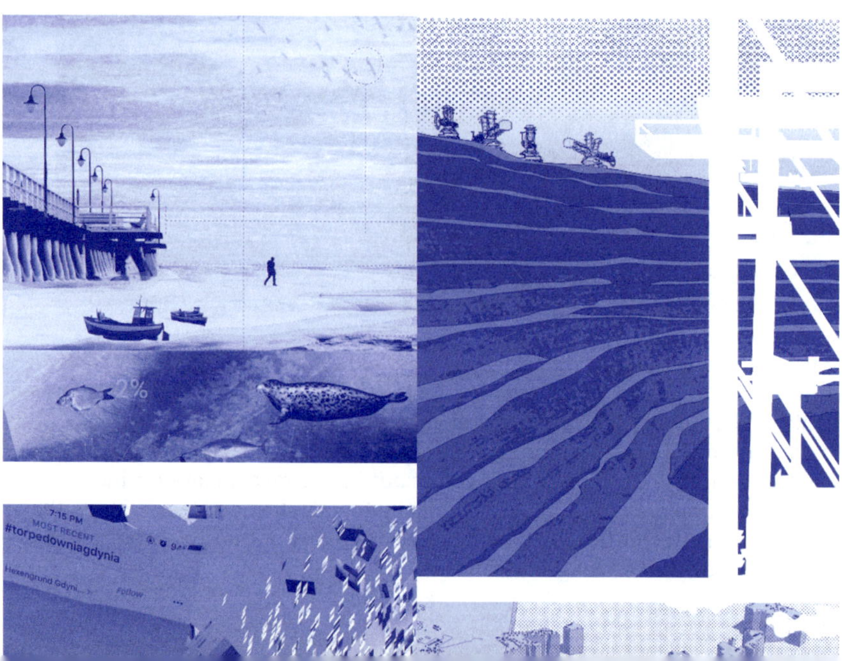

Bour Chiang Huang. Torpedownia Island: and Zhaniya Alimzhanova. Blue Monster Village

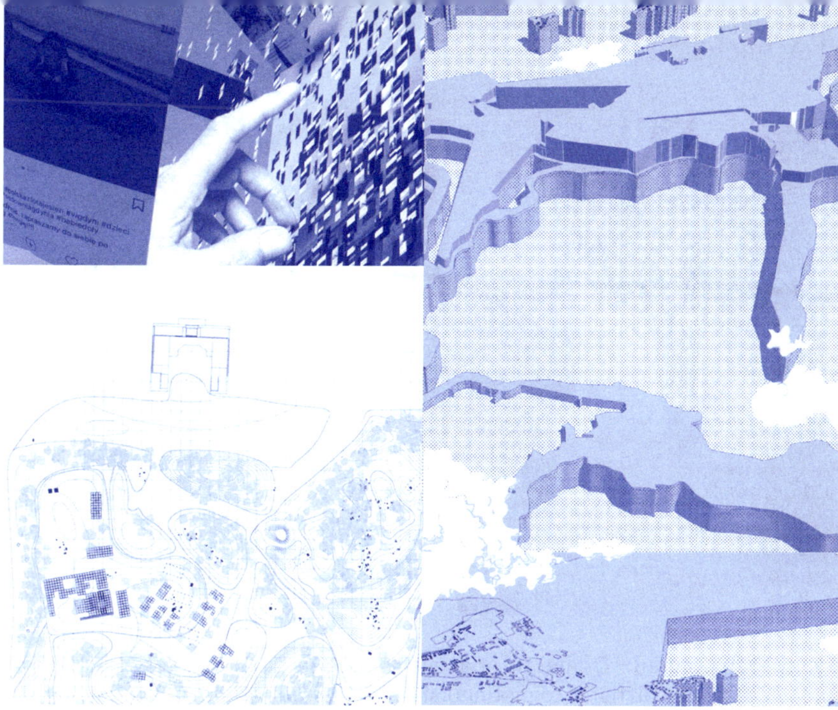

Intermediate 4 detects areas of opportunity within a constantly changing European environment and develops tools to respond to it through fantasy, innovation and precision. This year the unit looked to the architecture of past occupation, the new logics of post-production and the ecologies of post-vacancy. We travelled throughout Europe, exploring infrastructural architectures that have been rendered obsolete – stopped, abandoned or rejected – due to shifts in our environmental, economic, sociopolitical and ideological models. These spaces shaped a framework for projects, enabling students to interrogate the line between protection and destruction, preservation and progress, growth and shrinkage.

The resulting work proposes unique architectures that understand a site as both a biogeography (alive and evolutionary, inhabited by humans and non-humans) and a building as a system (adaptable and reactive). Projects assert that inhabiting involves not only construction but also adaptation; not only enlargement but also dismantlement; not only discarding but also reusing, reducing and refurbishing.

Intermediate 5

FIRST FLOOR

The unit 5 uses the fourth dimension – time – as a line of demarcation within the built environment, optimistically altering our perception of everyday life by splintering the status quo into oblivion. As part of an ongoing exploration of time and space, the local and the global, Intermediate 5 walked the 1851 Prime Meridian (0°'00'05.3101"), drove along the 1767 Mason-Dixon Line (39°'43'0"N, 75° 47'0"W) and set sail down the 1884 International Date Line (0°'0'0"N, 180°'0'0"W). With time as our guide these examinations offered a series of social, technological, time-based and sometimes playfully random constraints as catalysts for generating the central aim of each unit project - a material architectural intervention to question the mechanisms that govern our existence.

Intermediate 6

FIRST FLOOR

Agi Permatasari, 'Self Domestication Device'

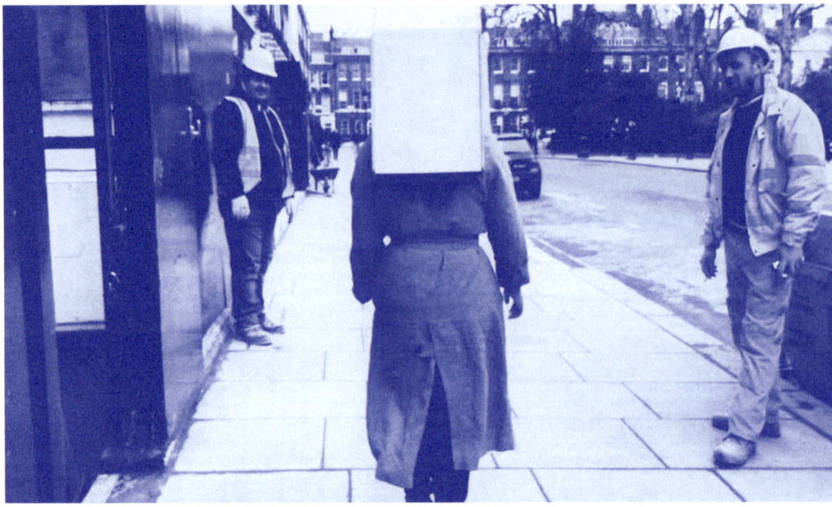

The Everyday Transfigured Domestic space is an architectural category that is becoming increasingly difficult to distinguish from the rest of the metropolis as a separate sphere of life. The workplace and the entirety of the city increasingly take on features once associated with the private domestic realm. It is no coincidence that this tendency unfolds in parallel to extended hours and increasing self-identification through work, greater social isolation, falling birth rates and rising ratios of living-to-earning costs. It has also led to the emergence of a desperate desire to be in close proximity to others. We feel a need to 'share'.

Nowhere are these tendencies and their consequences more apparent than in the emergence of the corporations profiting from the 'sharing-economy' with offerings of 'homey' co-working environments and intimate and personal 'networking' opportunities. This year Intermediate 6 has sought to develop research and projects that analyse, expose and question the architecture of these developments and their cultural-political and socio-economic features.

Intermediate 7

SECOND FLOOR

Kin Yat Uno Lam

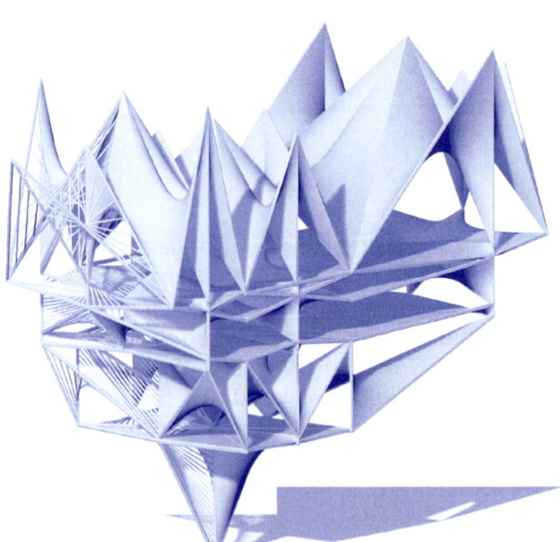

Material Life III – Tabula Automata Intermediate 7 embarked on a year-long study of how automation and AI will reshape the fabric of our cities. We studied material organisational and building systems to look at new forms of organisation where automated processes have been implemented.

Placing our projects and speculations in the future – year 2050 – we have imagined a scenario where new hybrid building types emerge out of the integration of intelligent and automated systems into the fabric of architecture. In both London and Zurich we have studied the role of architectural organisation as engines to construct architecture. Through this we have developed a range of hybrid architectural typologies: from infrastructural hubs to on-demands co-living housing blocks, from hospital to fast-deploying structures, co-working and academic institutions.

Intermediate 8

FIRST FLOOR

Natacha Palomeque Coll, Horizontal Densification: Appropriation of Leftover Spaces across Mexico City Colonia Condesa

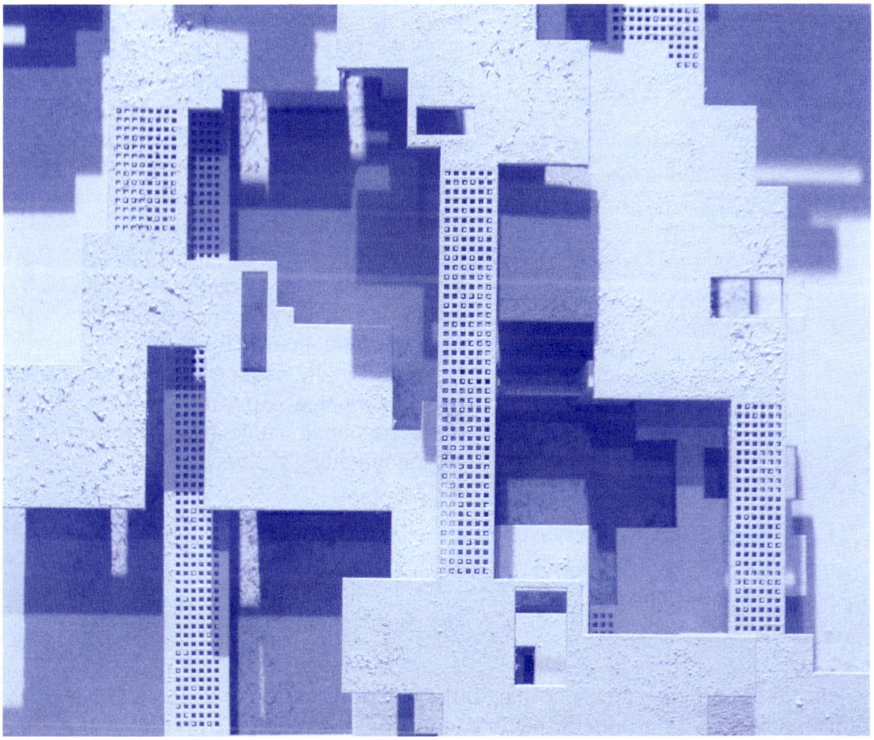

Politics of the Hyperwall: Snaky Lines of Densification in Mexico City
Most densification plans in Latin American metropolises heavily rely on the high-rise typology, but in Mexico City dominated by its own informal qualities Intermediate 8 proposes an alternative: lines of densification for in the form of a hyperwall that exploits existing infrastructural, natural and socio-spatial conditions to break through the barriers that hijack this unmanageable megalopolis. Following the unit's strong interest in form, each student has investigated the articulation of relations that these hyperwalls formally regenerate both as an internal structure and as an element of mediation with the existing city.

Intermediate 9

SECOND FLOOR

Shaha Raphael, Koji micro-connections

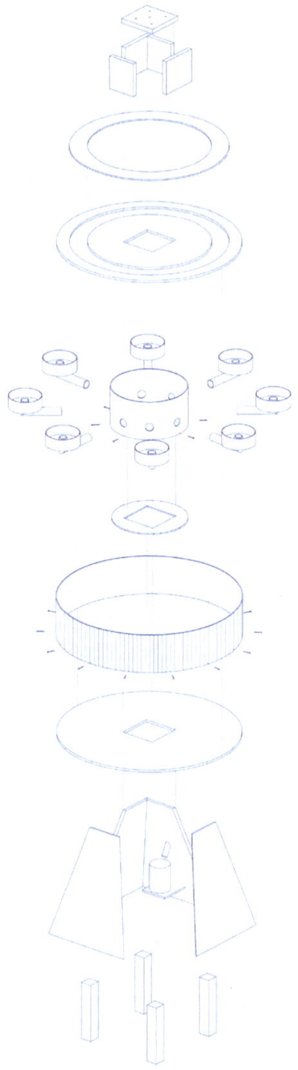

In and Out of the Swamp
Ingredients: 12 students, three tutors, one teaching assistant, one collaborator, one site

Step 1 Start with rice, fish, soya beans and wheat flour. Design and build four low-cost environments, one for each ingredient, add the catalyst and ferment for the required time. This will produce a variation of koji, garum, tempeh and bread (to go on the side). The result will, in all likelihood, be inedible, but it will produce notes, experiments and inspiration.

Step 2 Add a three-star Michelin restaurant and its quixotic range of suppliers to the mix. For the filling start by preparing a surreal site survey of Ekebergparken – a slice of Norwegian landscape in the centre of Oslo.

Step 3 The number and amount of remaining ingredients are unspecified, but they should be foraged from Oslo and Lyngør Islands. At this point, notice that much of the landscape, traditions and history of Norway have been absorbed in the mix.

Step 4 Pass mixture through a fine-grade sieve to extract only the most interesting and original pieces (architectural concepts).

Step 5 Finally, season with Norse myths, technical experiments and a variety of incalculable accidents that happened along the way.

Intermediate 10

SECOND FLOOR

The belief that the ordinary needs nothing but close observation to become extraordinary makes up the core of the unit. How does one charge something, or give it presence and quality? Cut it. After a conference where we exchanged positions on the cut and cutting, we went to Seoul, Busan, Teshima, Kyoto and eventually Tokyo. There we were confronted with the impossibility of the metropolis. Back in London, we built a 1:1 interface between ourselves and our sites – perhaps to ease the transition from the proposal to the actual realities of the place. Propositions began to take shape, seeking to charge, reinvent or even possess existing conditions – cuts – in London: a water treatment plant; an inhabitable periscope under and over the Westway; the insertion of a botanical archive into a secret garden in Harringay; housing above and under the Bermondsey railway tracks; a new kindergarten in the airplane crash zone at Silvertown; a trust and a community centre placed in an (un)attractively inaccessible plot to recover a Brixton offcut.

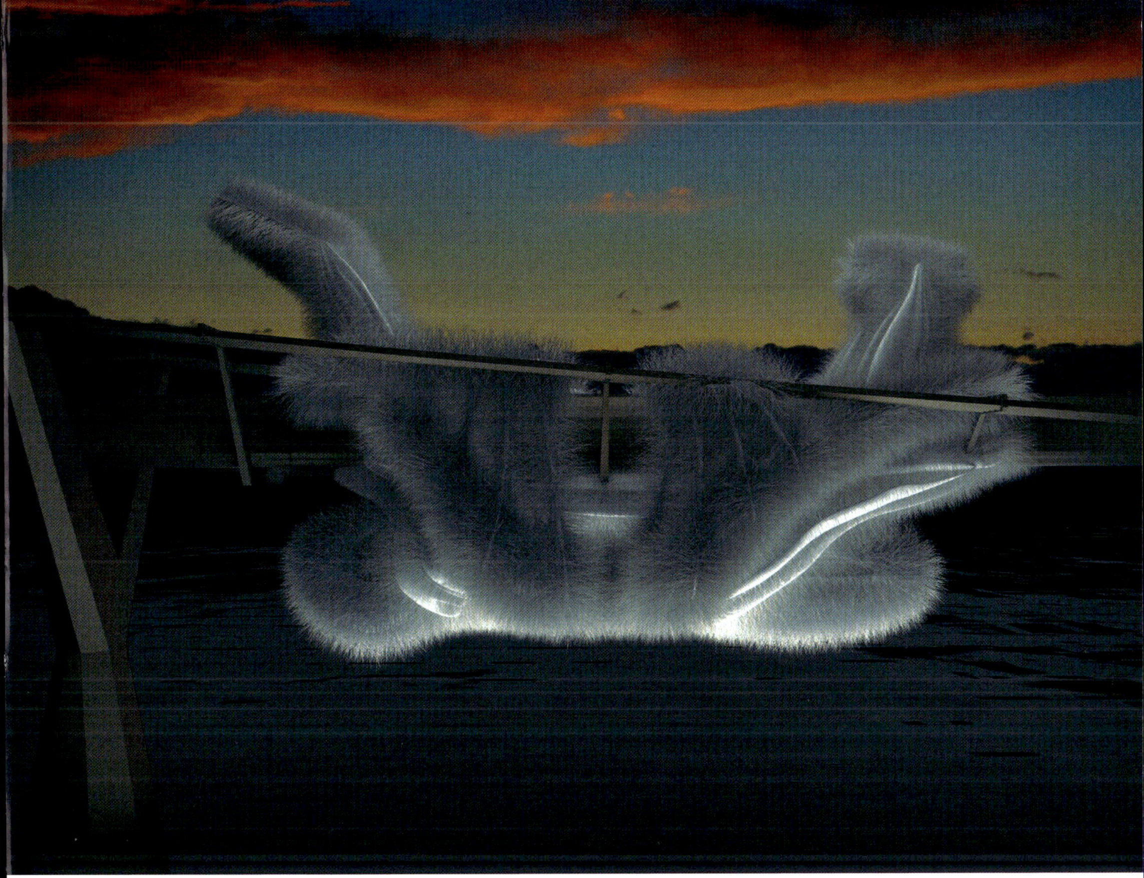

Work of Intermediate 5

Andrea and Lior – interface of a generic chair and Tajik (sic!) sock: a sock inverter (Intermediate 10)

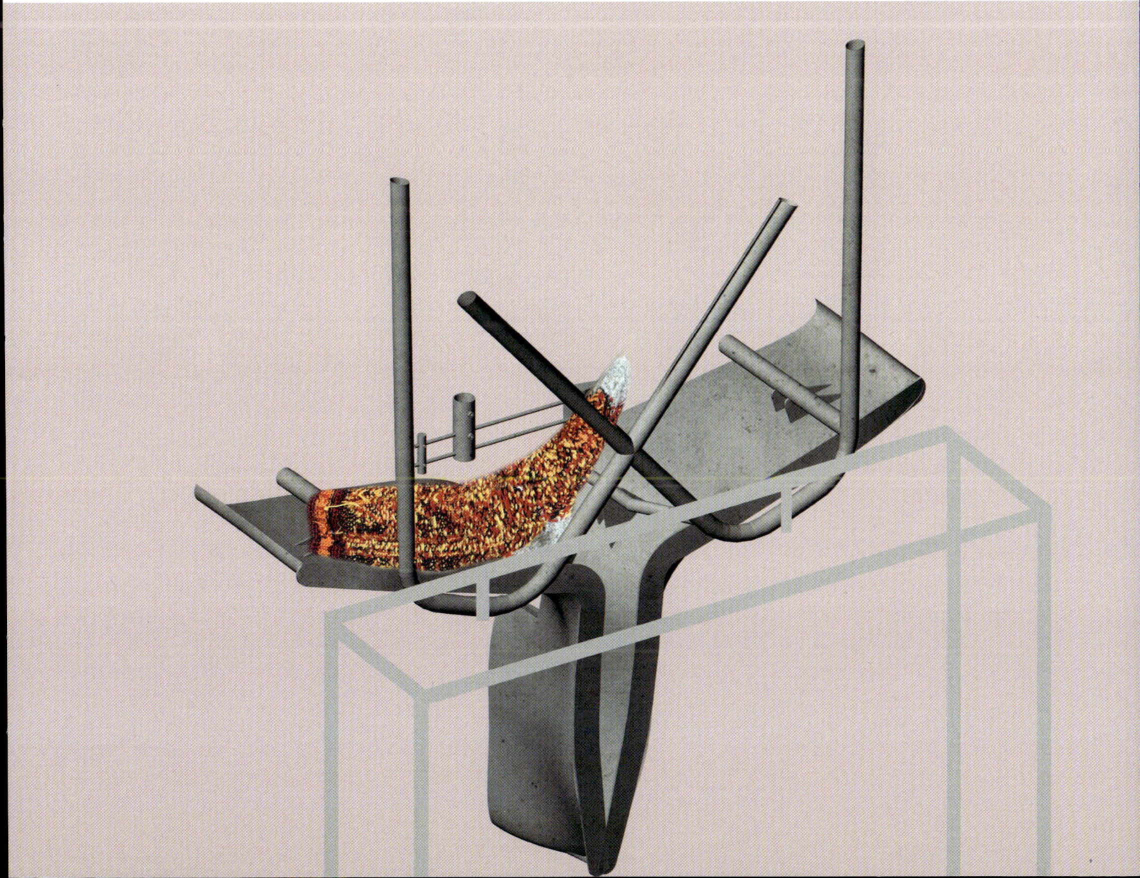

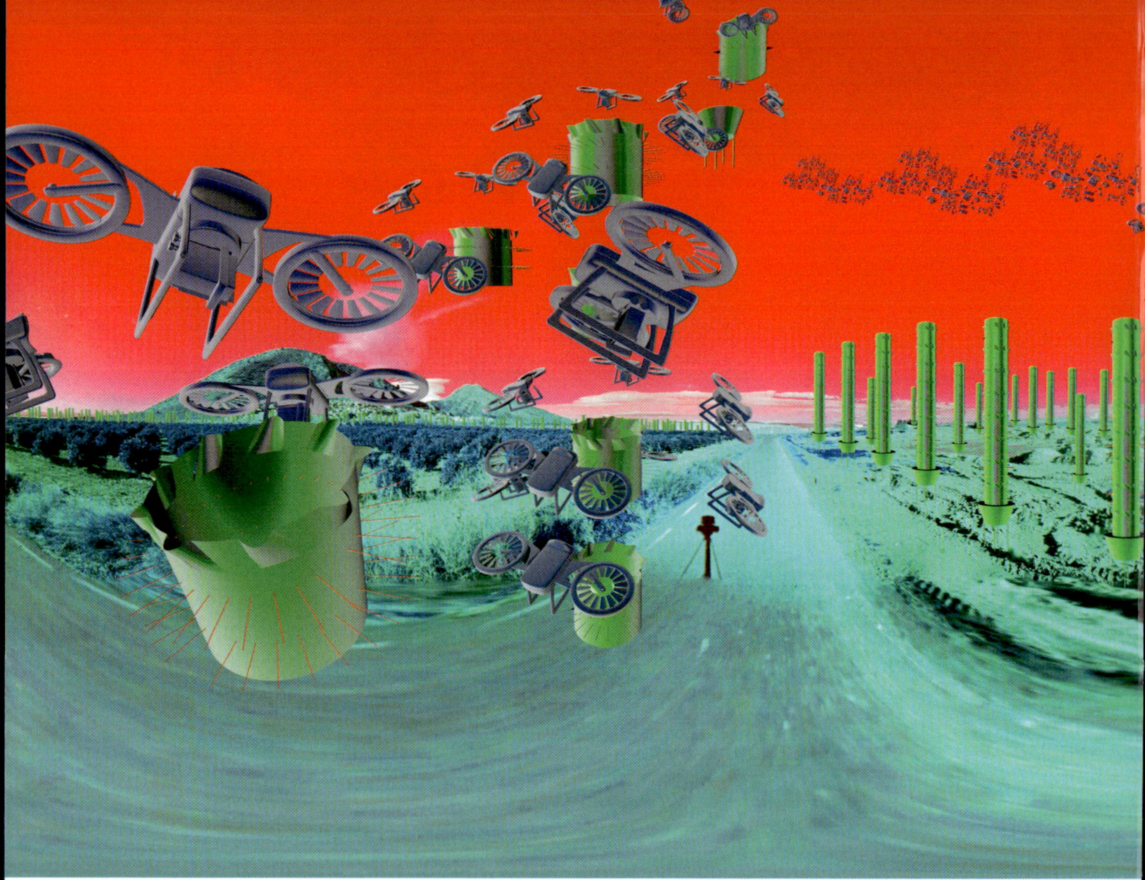

Neill In, Hydroponic is the Answer, so what was the Question? (Intermediate 11)

Luke Decker (Intermediate 14)

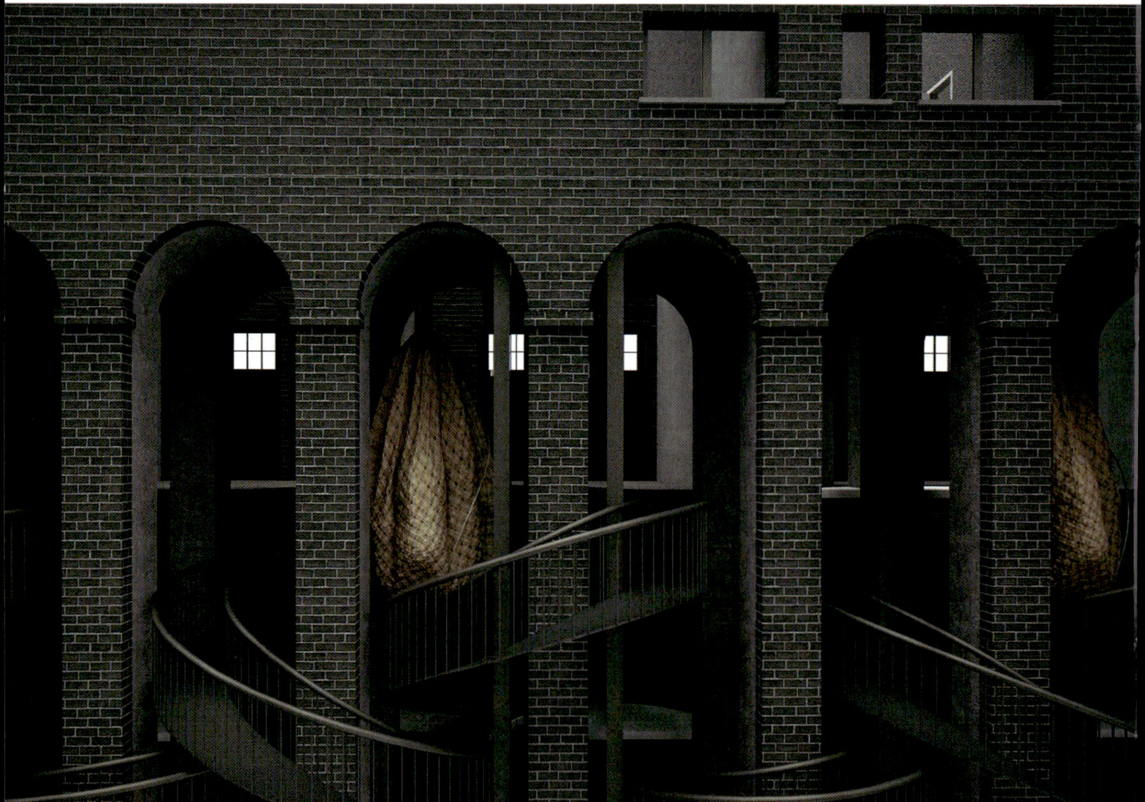

Intermediate 11

FIRST FLOOR

<u>Black Toxic</u> One of the biggest ecological disasters in Europe, a mining spill in the Portman Bay in the south of Spain, has defined the unit's site and agenda. Its toxic consequences and intense touristic ecosystem have provided the architectural framework for the unit's proposals, which look at alternative tourist spaces, reflect on the temporal and nomadic conditions of these new forms of inhabitation and bring together material, social, cultural, spiritual and environmental aspects of the site and beyond. These new touristic spaces – what we call stations – are designed to put travellers into direct physical contact with polluted landscapes.

The unit also explores immersion through virtual reality. All physical interventions, together with their virtual kits, explore how these new scenarios, including their toxic data can be hybridised to define new architectural versions of future tourism.

Intermediate 12

SECOND FLOOR

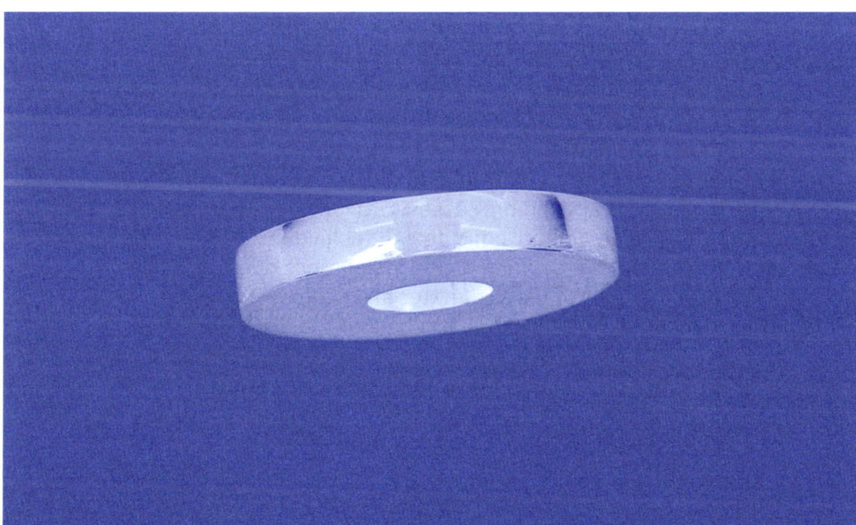

Amy Glover, The Perfect Washer, Go d plated brass, 12 × 5mm

<u>Doubling Fiskars</u> Intermediate 12 looks at how to build through simple means while maintaining quality and improving efficiency. This year our site was the centuries-old ironworking village of Fiskars, located 100km west of Helsinki. Although home to Finland's first workshop, the existing factories have since relocated to a nearby village and the demographics have changed; Fiskars now is not only a town but a global corporation. The village itself is no longer populated by factory workers but by a cooperative of about 100 artists, designers and their families. The Fiskars corporation still owns the 15,000 hectares of land and the adjacent 100 lakes, which makes it the sole decision maker in allocating housing in the village. It is believed that the village can keep attracting new tenants and aims double its creative population from 480 tenants to 960. Intermediate 12 attempted to fulfil the company's objective to double the population. However, after our visit to the village, the general approach opened up unexpected economic and social models as answers to the company's brief.

Intermediate 13

GROUND FLOOR

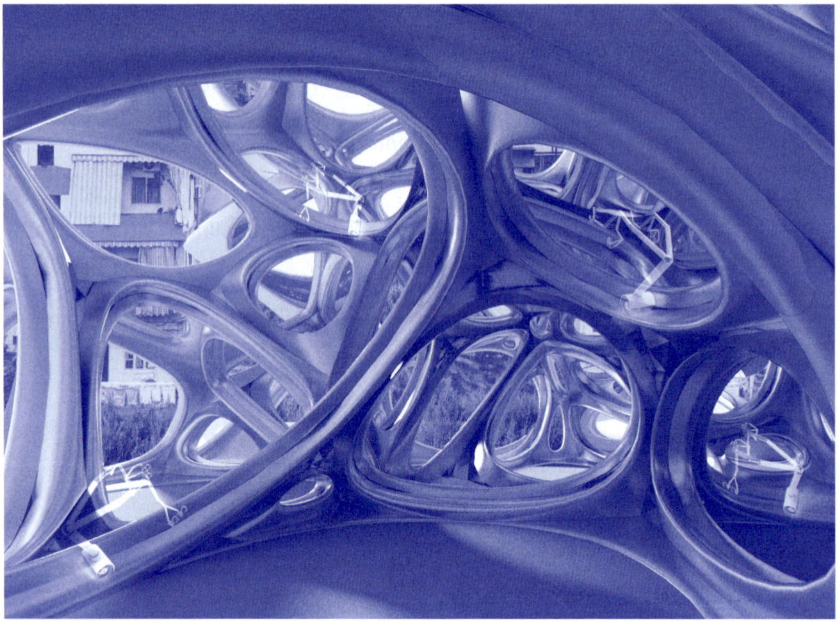

Dala Itani – 3D printed cellular spaces dealing with existing building refurbishment through machine learning

Computational Ornamentation – Proto-Building Our methodology is informed by computational design thinking. Through a series of 1:1 prototypes, the unit investigates a number of design and fabrication techniques, driven by material behaviour as well as by specific crafting techniques, both digital and analogue.

We focus on geometry and materiality, and we constantly look to pursue unique spatial formations where both internal and external experiences are informed by the specificity of applied processes. Students this year have achieved this through computational and algorithmic design techniques, each corresponding to a unique material system. The resulting digital simulations operate in constant feedback with the development of parallel material systems – allowing computational techniques to be a fundamental part of the design process.

Intermediate 14

SECOND FLOOR

Radical Foundations in Bloomsbury Radical Foundations in Bloomsbury is the first section of Intermediate 14's projected three-year close study of Bloomsbury. In a world confronted by unknown political, social and technological distortions, the time has come for a fundamental realignment. What is at stake is nothing less than the opportunity for world-making, in which the role of architect is paramount. Taking cues from the uniquely fertile culture that both spawns and develops great schools of art, students designed new foundations – a new art school in Bloomsbury. The intention was not so much to develop a school per se, but to devise a complex set of ingenious spatial interrelationships that form a full-blown notational system for a building. Parts of the building might twitch, hum or sing you a lullaby. Beginning with the design of an aedicule composed of nine architectural elements – threshold, foundation, wall, floor, ceiling, aperture, stair, ramp and corridor – extraordinary and radical orchestrations of elements ensued.

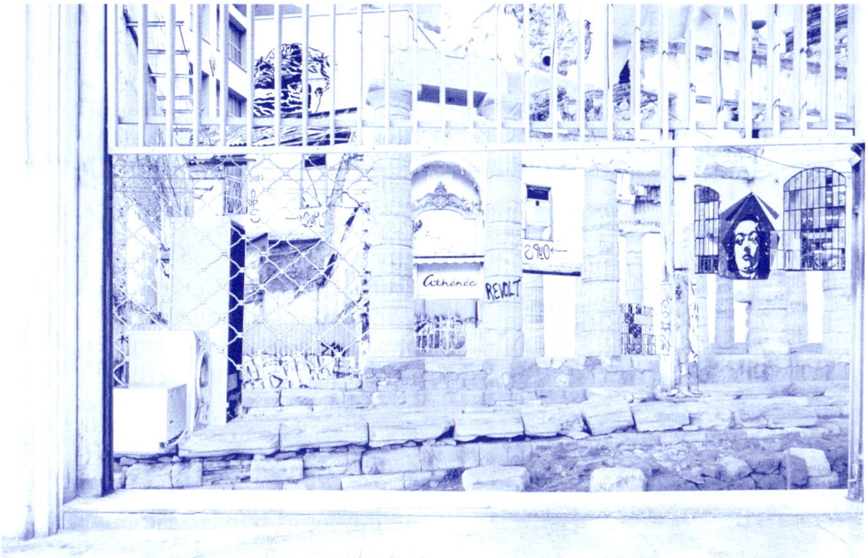

Dala Itani – 3D printed cellular spaces dealing with existing building refurbishment through machine learning

<u>The School of Athens</u> Athens is a city of contradictions: a city at the centre of European identity and at the edge of the 'western' world; a city with massive influxes of voluntary tourists and involuntary immigrants; a new city that thinks it is old; a city defined as much by its amorphous sea of generic white buildings as by its perfect monuments of architecture. Above all Athens is in crisis, but creating more 'public space' alone isn't enough. The challenge of Athens is best approached by rethinking its civic institutions, the monuments and voids which orient us in the isotropic fabric of the city.

This year Intermediate 15 has rethought the institution of the university, starting from the hypothesis that the architecture of academic institutions is uniquely able to reorganise and reinvigorate the city. Our work examines how these institutions are currently manifested in Athens, identifies and critiques emerging models and historical precedents, and imagines radical new propositions at both the urban and architectural scale. Only by reinventing these institutions – both their logics and their forms – can we reinvent the future of the city.

Oussama Garti

Archaeology of the Future: Exploring Tangiers The Moroccan city of Tangier sits at a crossroads of civilisations. As the closest African city to Europe, it has supported a mixture of cultures from the Phoenicians and Romans, to the English and French. The result is a city both mesmerising and fragmented. Intermediate 16 engages this condition, asking students to question how a city might embrace its past, without formfitting its future. Proposals address subjects as far-reaching as alternative routes through the city, water as a driver for social gathering, the questioning of cultural norms through cultural institutions, and traditional food and craft. What we propose in this year's work is a complex, changeable city, one that is not defined by its past but instead driven forward by it.

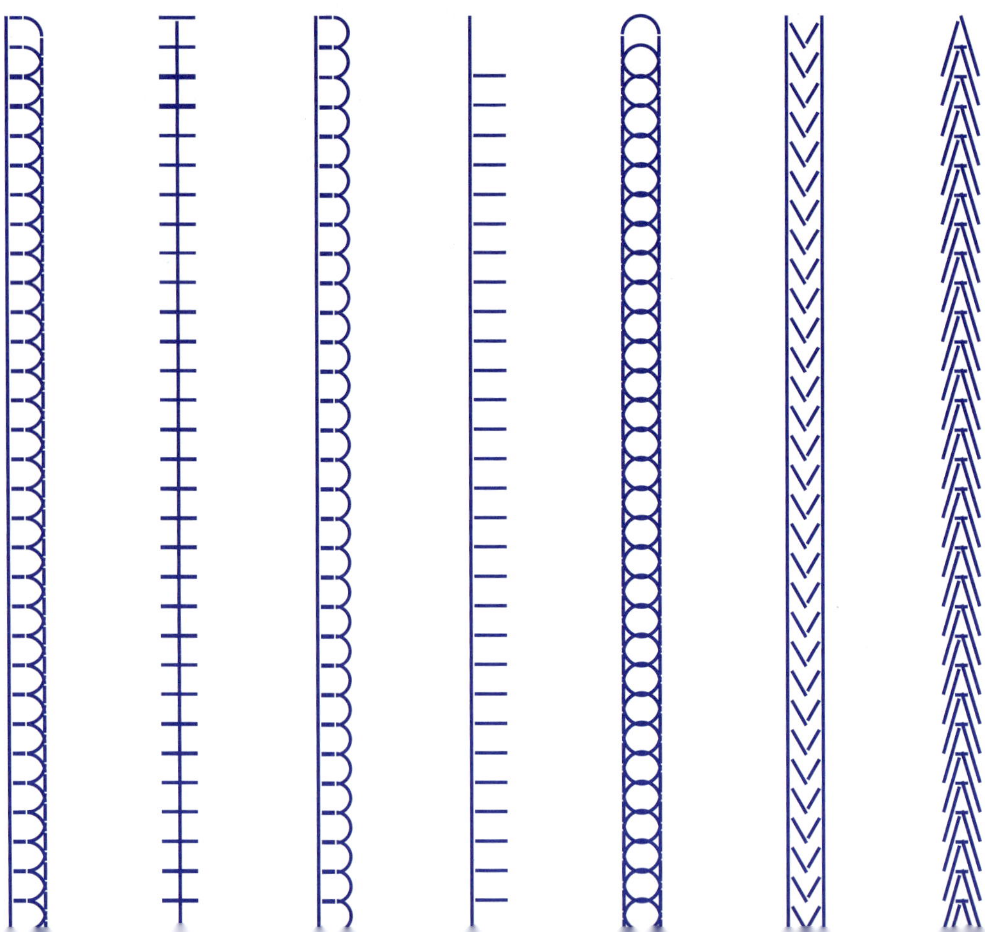

Ali El Hashimi – a motel for suburban transient populations referencing the film noir atmosphere of the Thames Estuary

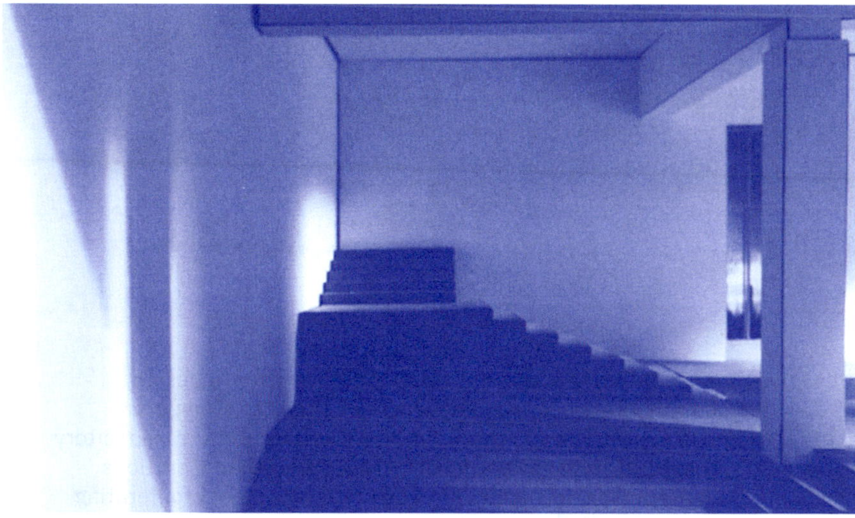

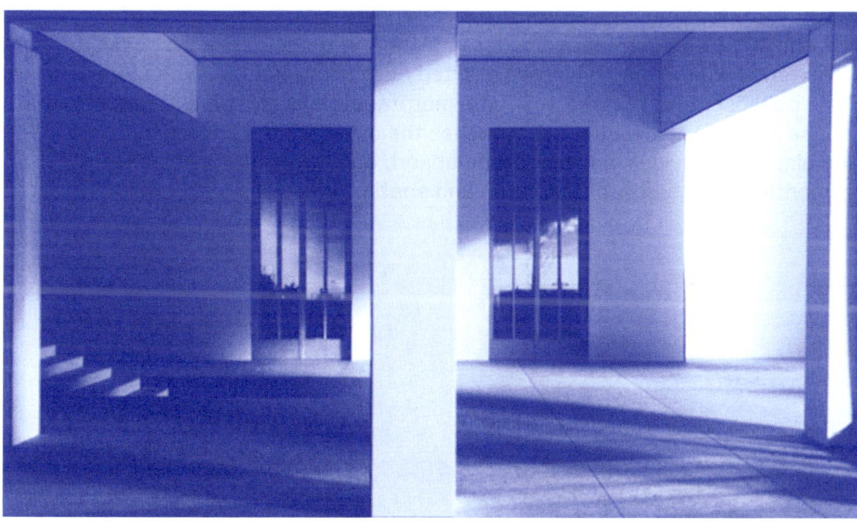

Film City: Dagenham The work of Diploma 1 explores the role of the poetic imagination and artistic methodologies in the development of London city planning and architecture. This year we focused on the cinematic as a generative tool using the GLA-backed plans for new East London film studios as our catalyst. With the decline of both the docks and of car manufacturing, this part of the Thames estuary has been the target of regeneration efforts for the past 20 years – the film studio initiative is part of this series of economic efforts. Against this background, the unit has questioned regeneration based on meeting financial targets and has instead explored the potential of cultural and artistic considerations as ends in themselves.

One group of propositions has used cinema as a direct inspiration. The second group of propositions looks more broadly at the cinematic potential of the streetscape.

Diplomа 2

FIRST FLOOR

Carolyn Wong, Where is the Facade

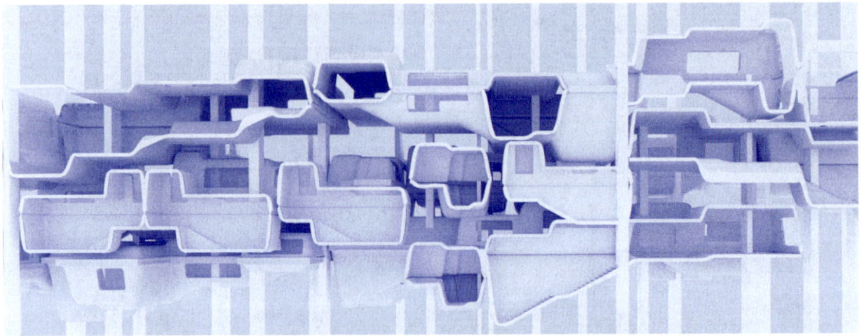

The unit's main preoccupation this year has been to rethink, from a design point of view, the contemporary building facade. Operating in contemporary Manhattan, which in many ways forms the quintessential architectural repository of styles and historically radical takes on the envelope, our design operations have included inflating, opening up, distorting, instrumentalising or proliferating in three dimensions the conventionally neutral and flat architectural skin. Most importantly, the intent has been to re-establish the long-lost connection of the external boundary to its corresponding internal inhabitation. From a proposed a series of external walkway connections grafted onto Stuyvesant Town's modernist blocks to a publicscraper that draws on the multifaceted nature of contemporary public space in New York, each project pushes the envelope to be more than just a surface plane that divides, and to instead absorb and negotiate the clashes between conflicting urban, programmatic and spatial conditions.

Diploma 4

FIRST FLOOR

Oskar Johanson – boundaries of contemporary logistical spaces and automatic protocols of separation and exclusion

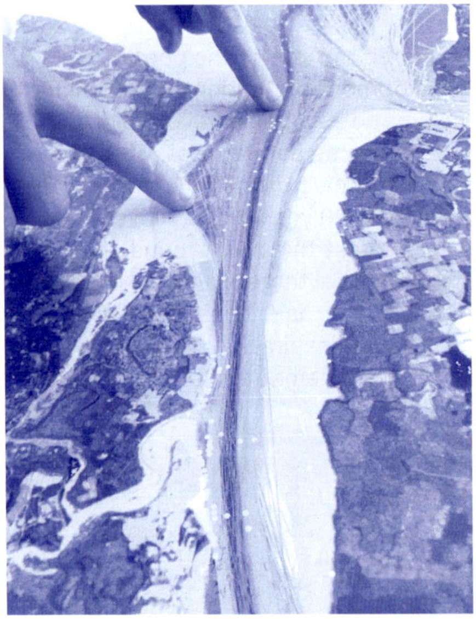

The Coast of Europe—Technosphere
An emerging figure, a system yet to come whose outlines and contours are beginning to reshape the grounds of the Earth: we investigate the Anthropocene and the rise of the technosphere.
The technosphere baffles architecture: from within it appears as the result of the multiple projects, designs, actions and processes of humans. From the outset humans are only a component of it, drawn into its functioning and endeavouring for its sustainment.
We start with a simple question: how heavy is a city? The complex answers are activated in conversations with scientists, activists, artists, architects and theorists student projects and then tested throught..

Yang Yang Chen, New Domesticity in Bangalore

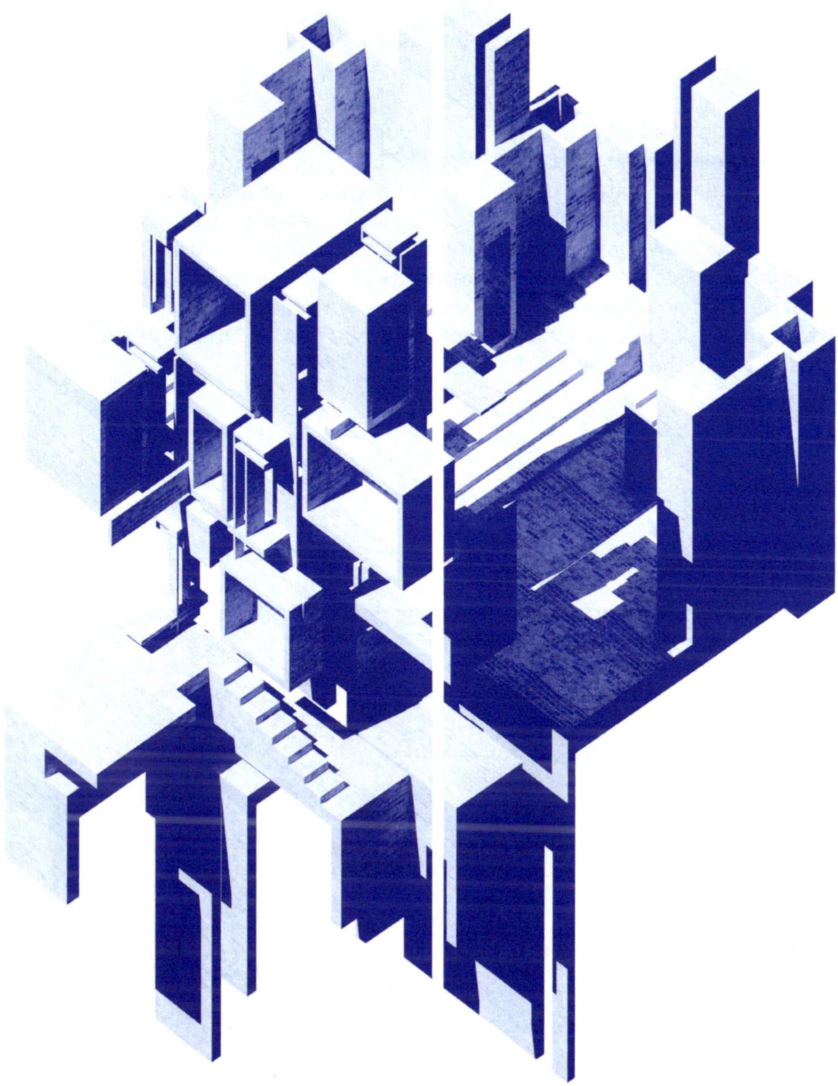

This year the renunciation of an initial brief expanded on the unit's methodology, which embraces the complexity of the problems of our day, to develop concrete and specific methodologies related to the special nature of each situation. This abandonment reinforces the responsibility and emancipation of the student as an intellectually independent and productive individual, and accepts the recognition of one's own ignorance and the epistemological anarchism as indispensable tools in the heuristic resolution of conflicts or situations.

The course began with a twofold question: first, what are the alternative forms that living together with others in a broad sense can trigger? And second, how to examine the silent ways in which the forms of business based on digital technologies have invaded, distorted and abused the ways in which we share, obtain information and negotiate our subjectivities? Ultimately the contemporary project proposed filters and orders to the ocean of information, data and knowledge that we have access to through digital networks. Our work bulds a propositional and critical ways to modify our environment with the new brutality that emerges from digital networks and processes.

Diploma 8

FIRST FLOOR

Meta-Elements and Integrated Morphologies The unit pursues an engaged disciplinary project on the European city, mediating between urban and architectural, imaginary and real, conceptual and formal domains. This year, we correlated multiple levels of work on dis-continuity, focusing on urban meta-elements as integrated diagrams and morphologies. We constructed our briefs in relation to disciplinary and urban contexts, explored hybrid methods and processes and curated expanded cultural projects. Our shared quests took us on mythical and spatial 'journeys' across imaginary landscapes, inter-connecting the transitions of cultural, urban and environmental archetypes. These shifts meant that we had to incorporate multiple contexts into thicker conceptual frameworks and also engage with creative agency and process. As a collective, we aimed to assert architecture's ability to revitalise from within, to redirect the project on architectural object and form, and to revive the urban-visionary spirit.

Diploma 9

FIRST FLOOR

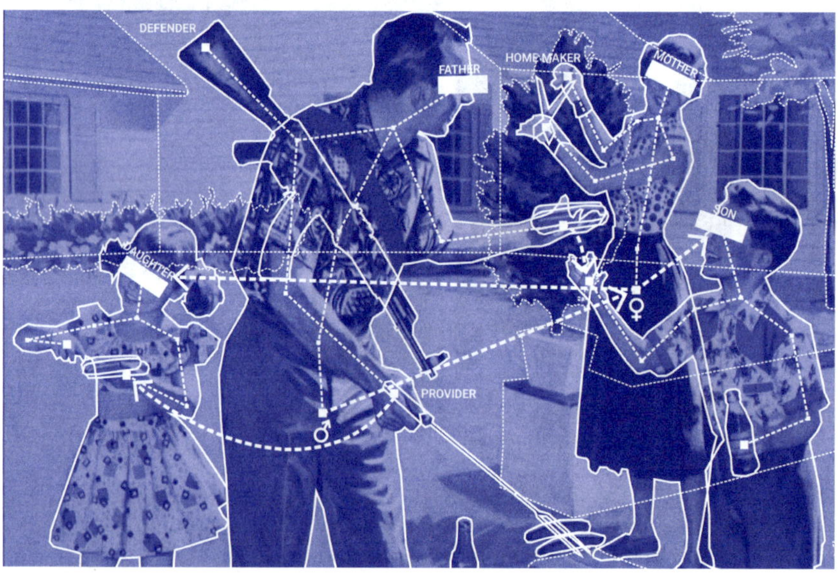

Yee Thong Chai, Shallow Ecotones

P2P: Panning to Pantopia Diploma 9's year-long quest was to voyage to Pantopia, a not-so-far-away place of speculation, built from the processes of world sourcing, building and inhabitation. Our near-realities are simultaneously utopian, dystopian and protopian; they optimistically embrace the unrelenting onslaught of technology on our cultures. Each student explored his or her version of Pantopia, defining its scale, its machines – to aid navigation and operation within it and ultimately the possible individual that might inhabit our new terrain.

As a unit, we are dedicated to panning, as a way to both design and explore our Pantopian Landscapes. Panning is a technique born on the internet, native of contemporary network culture and heavily reliant on collective intelligence, open-endedness, extreme diffusivity and constant world-sourcing. By relentlessly panning over every piece of land and every byte of information, the students have designed built environments that assimilate all of Pantopia's incredible volume, velocity and variety.

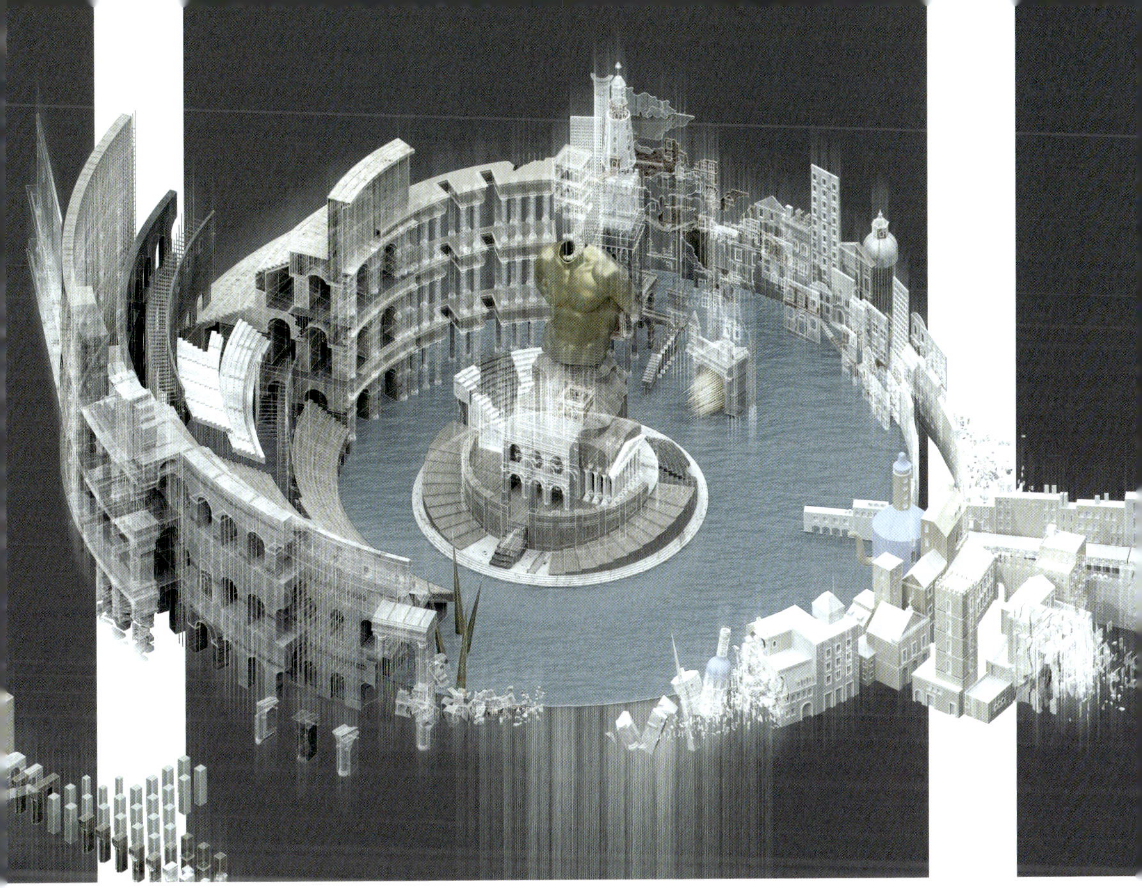

Luca Gamberini, Temporal Condensers (Diploma 8)

Timothy O'Hare, South Bermondsey Loop (Diploma 11)

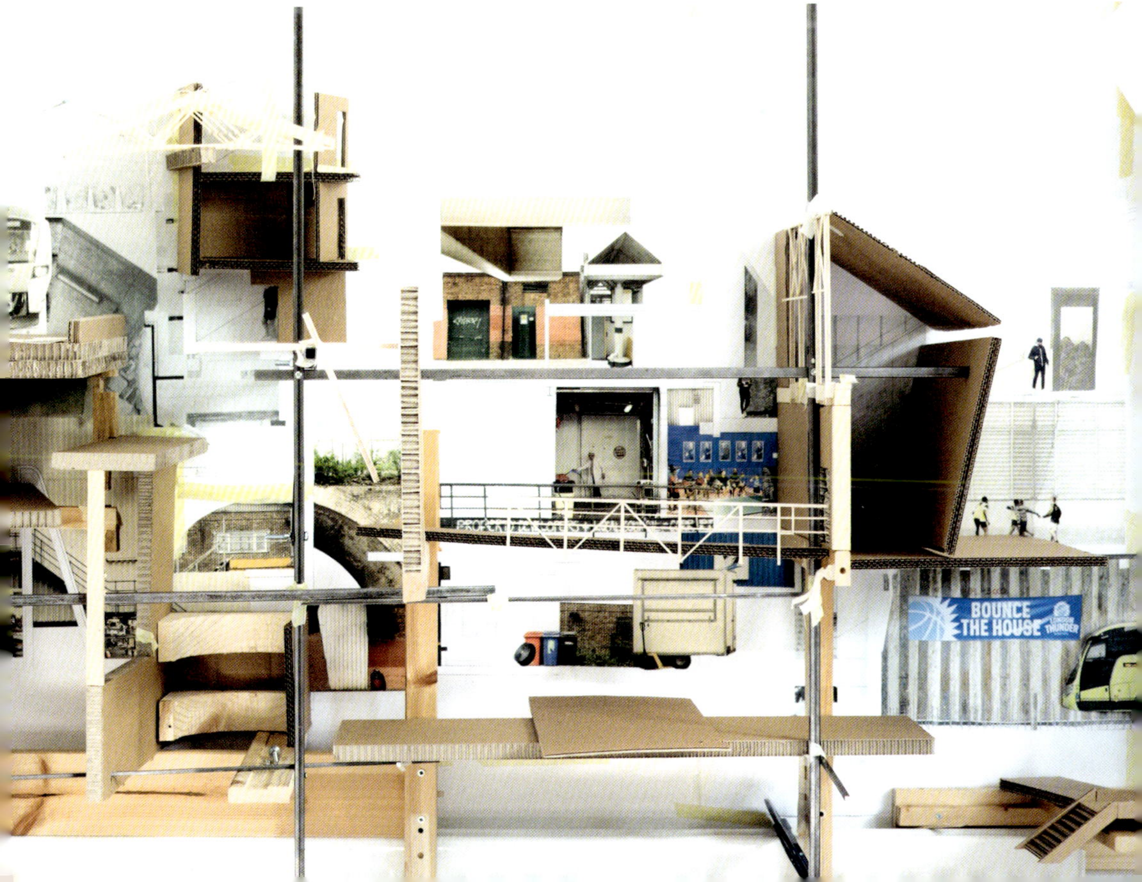

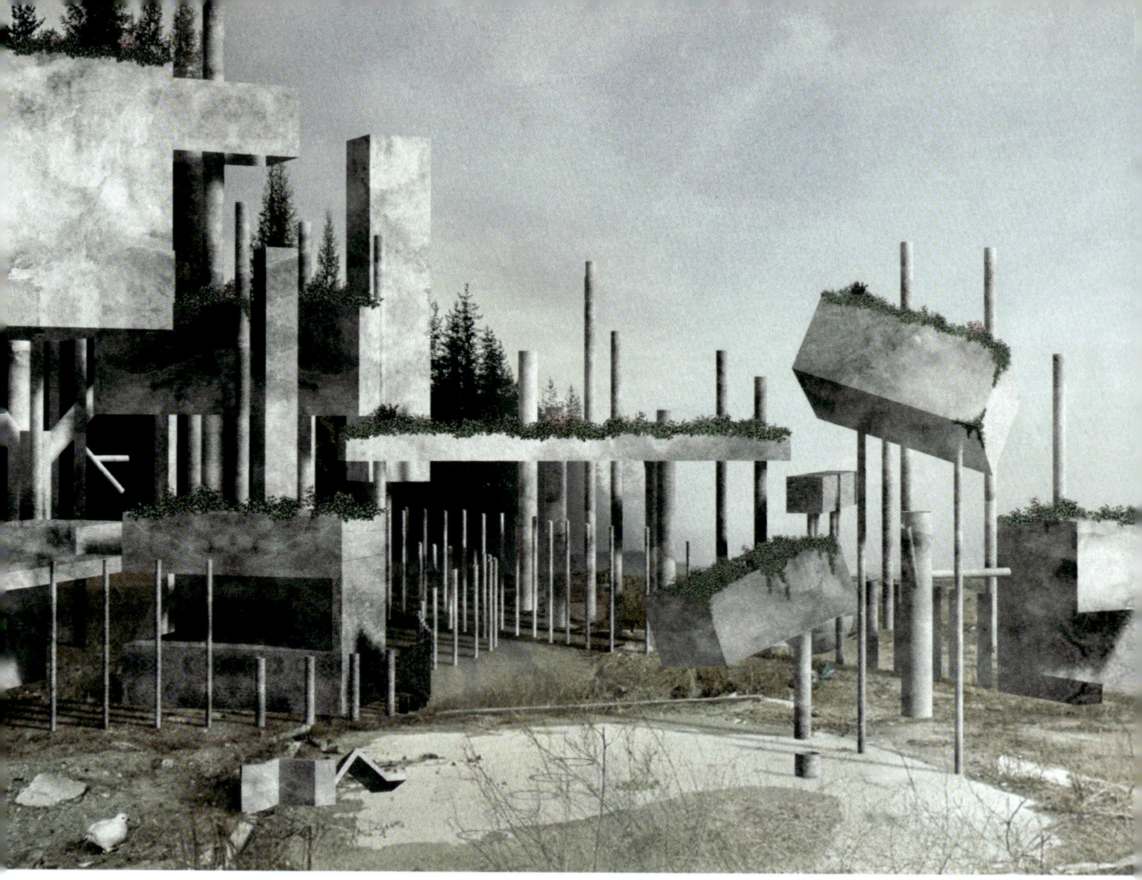

Roman Lovegrove, Radioactive remediation in Fukushima (Diploma 13)

May Ibentoumert – exploring friction of digital precision and material indeterminacy (Diploma 17)

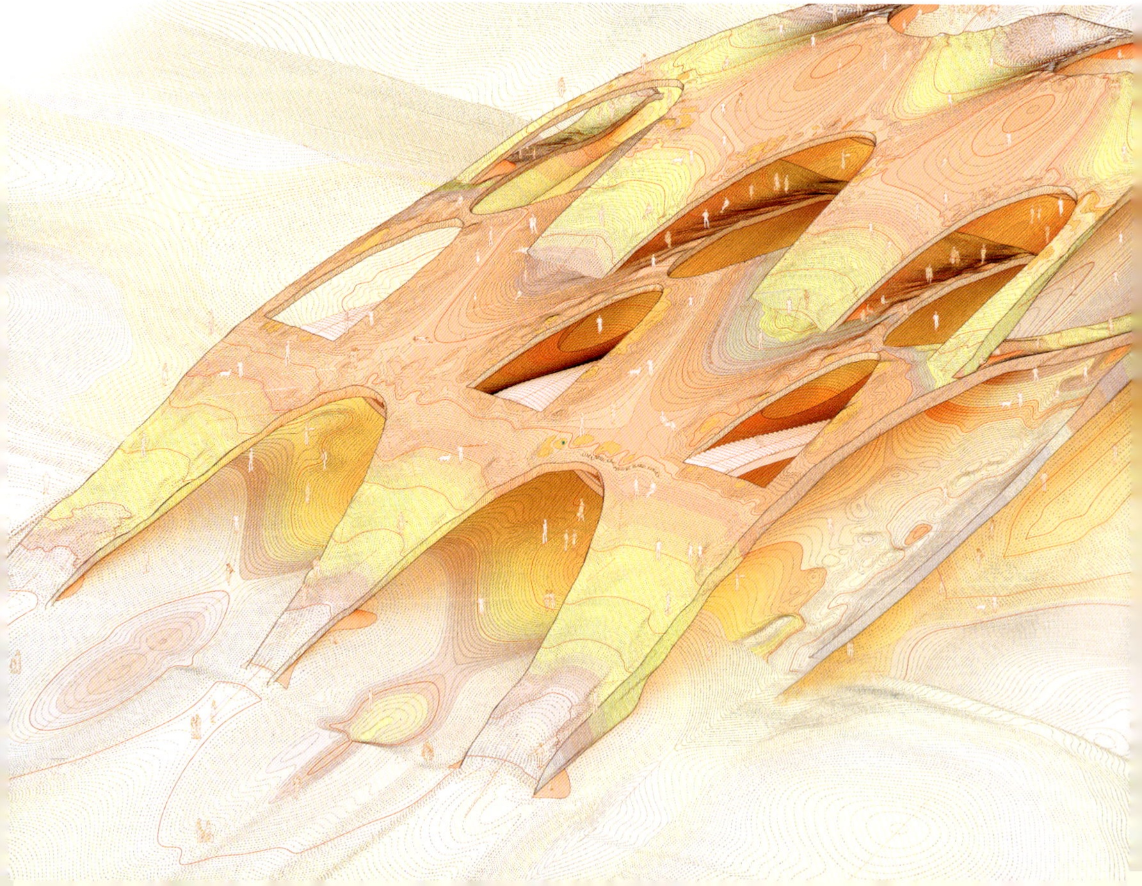

Fang Lee, Porous Cloud (Diploma 16)

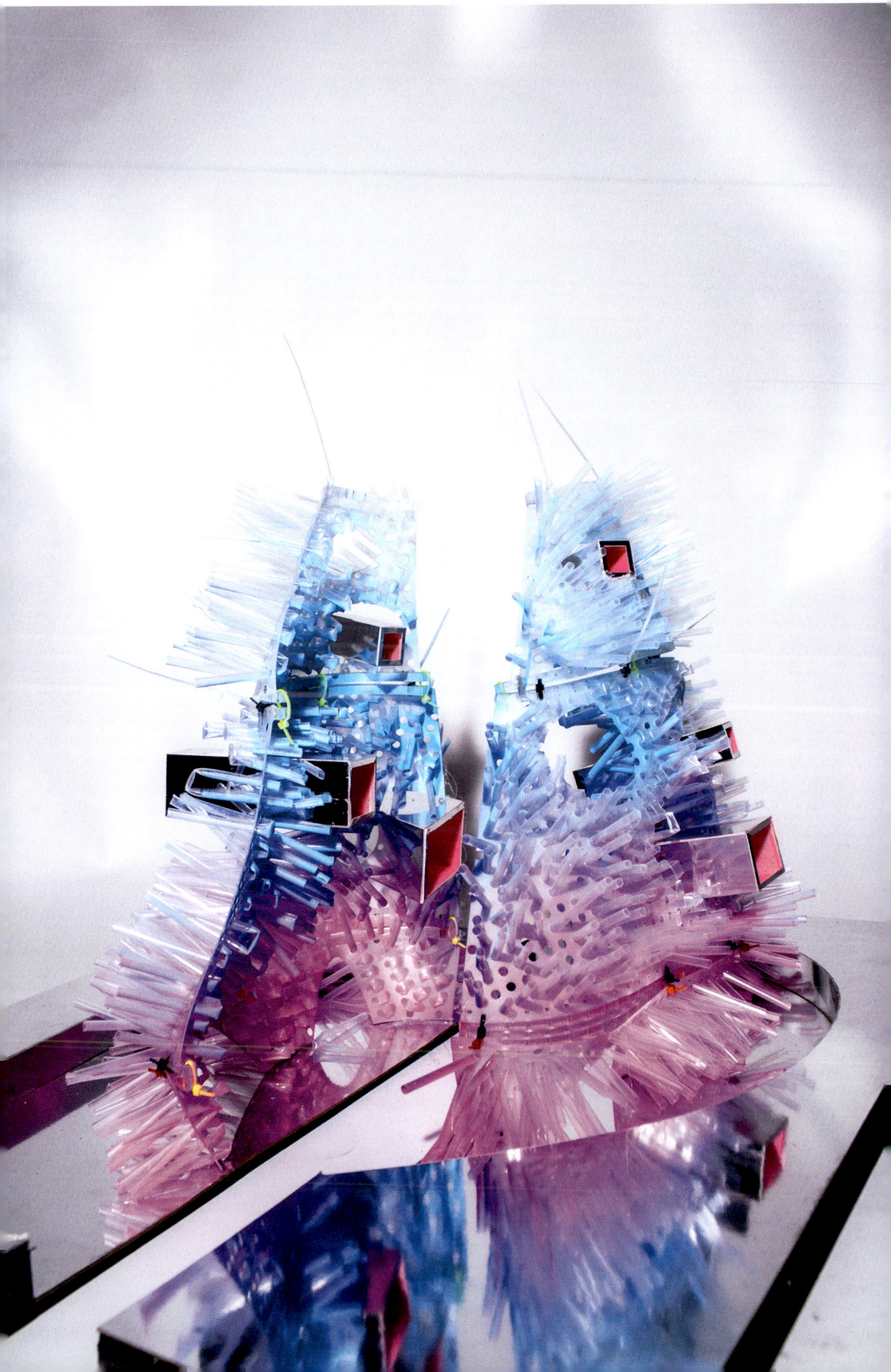

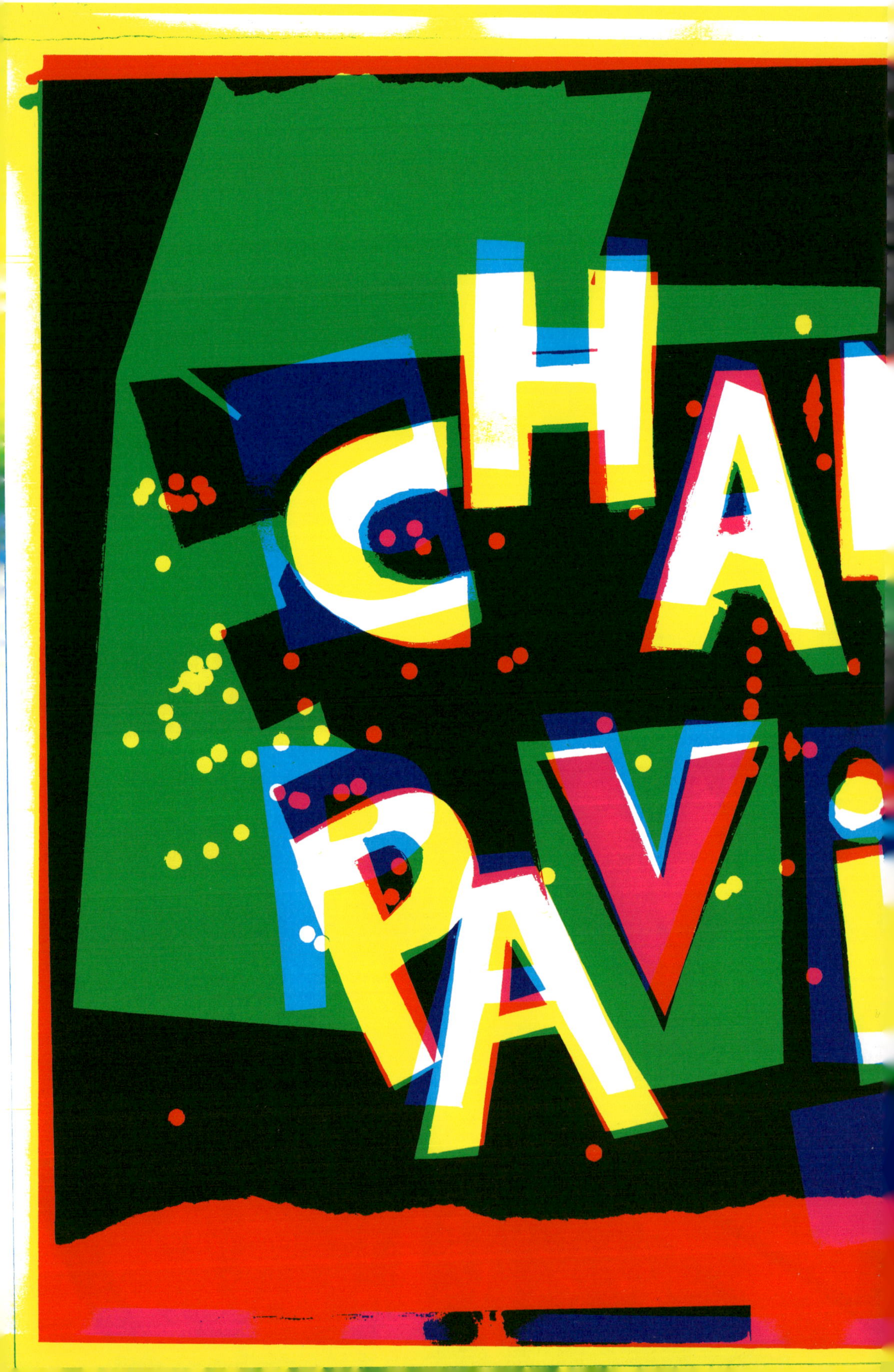
CHA
PAVI

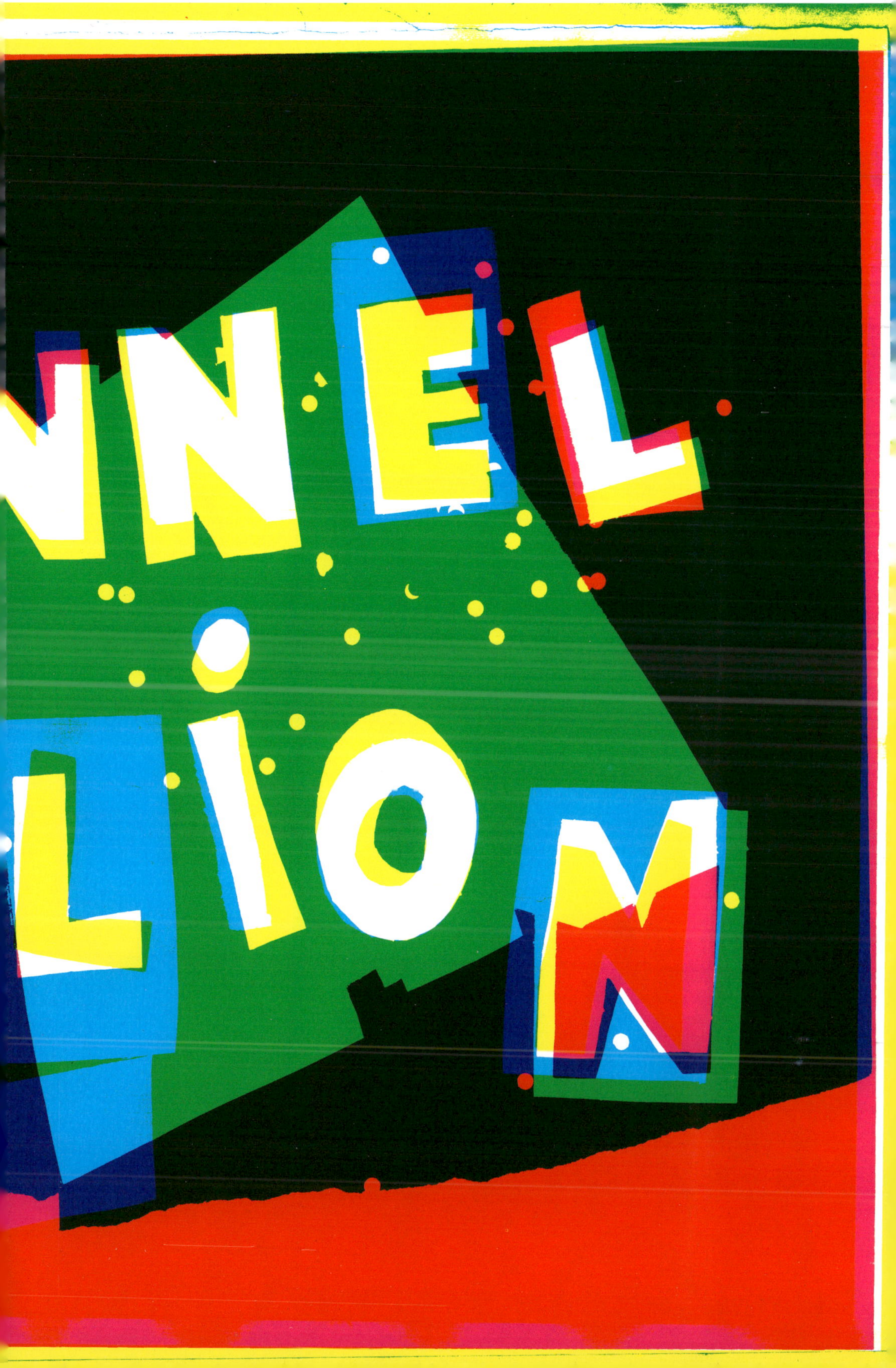
NNEL
LION

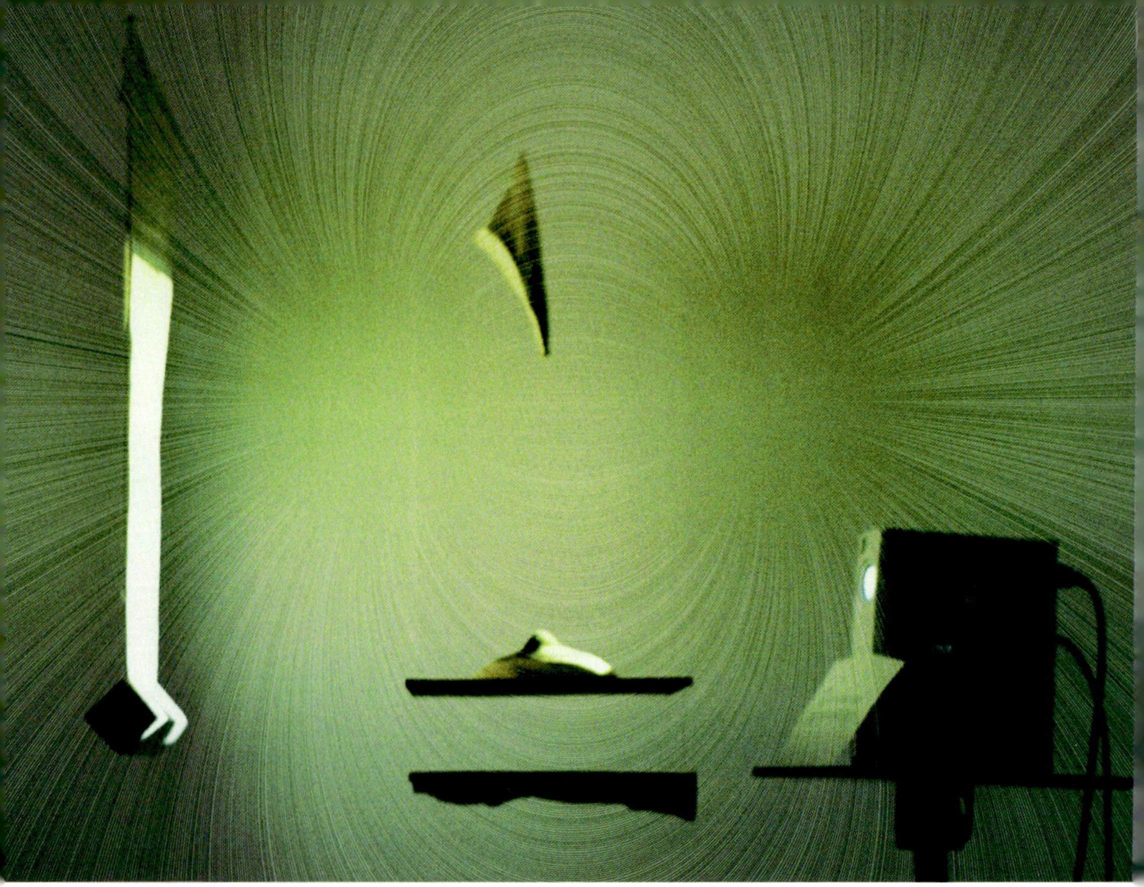

Gianfrancesco Brivio Sforza, Field Operations with Kate Davies (Media Studies)

Dangi Kang, Ordinary Domesticity with Flavien Menu (Media Studies)

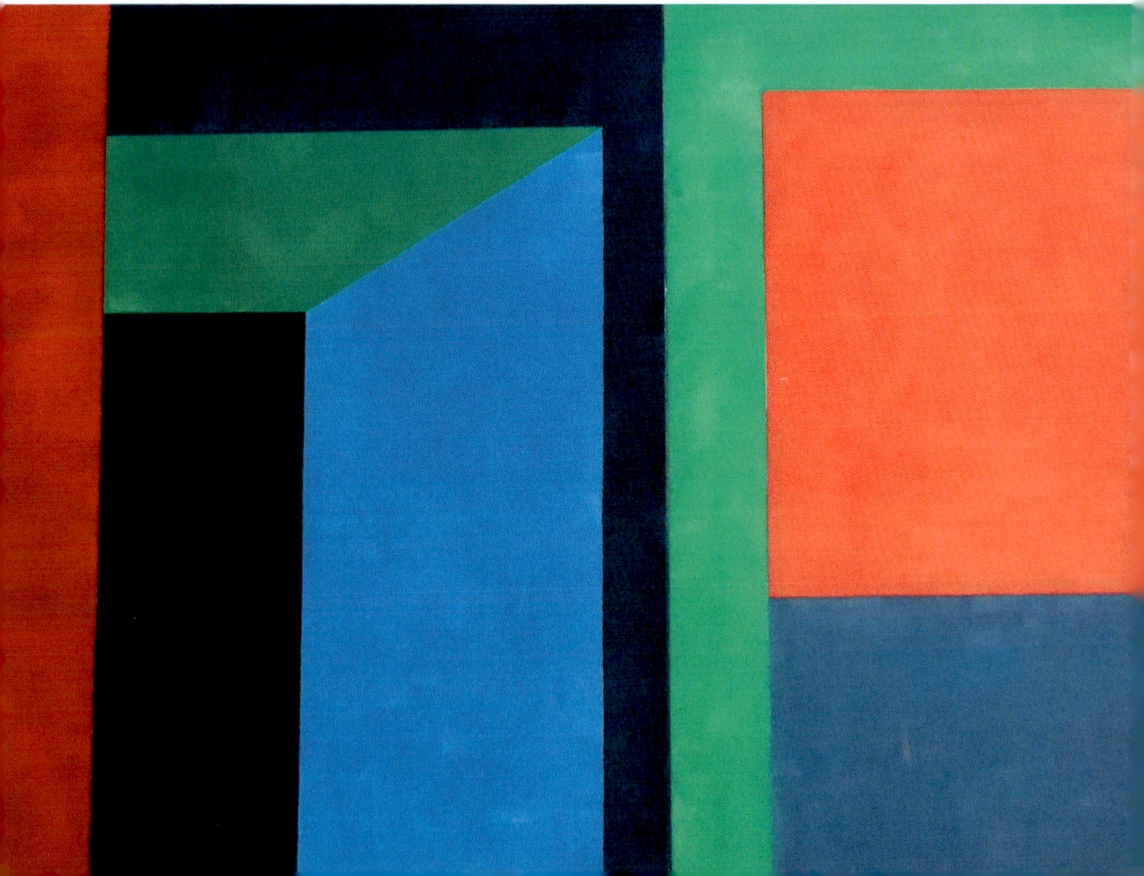

Dalia Frontini Matsuura, Prajapati's Painted Bodhi, 5th Year Technical Studies High Pass with Distinction (Diploma 16)

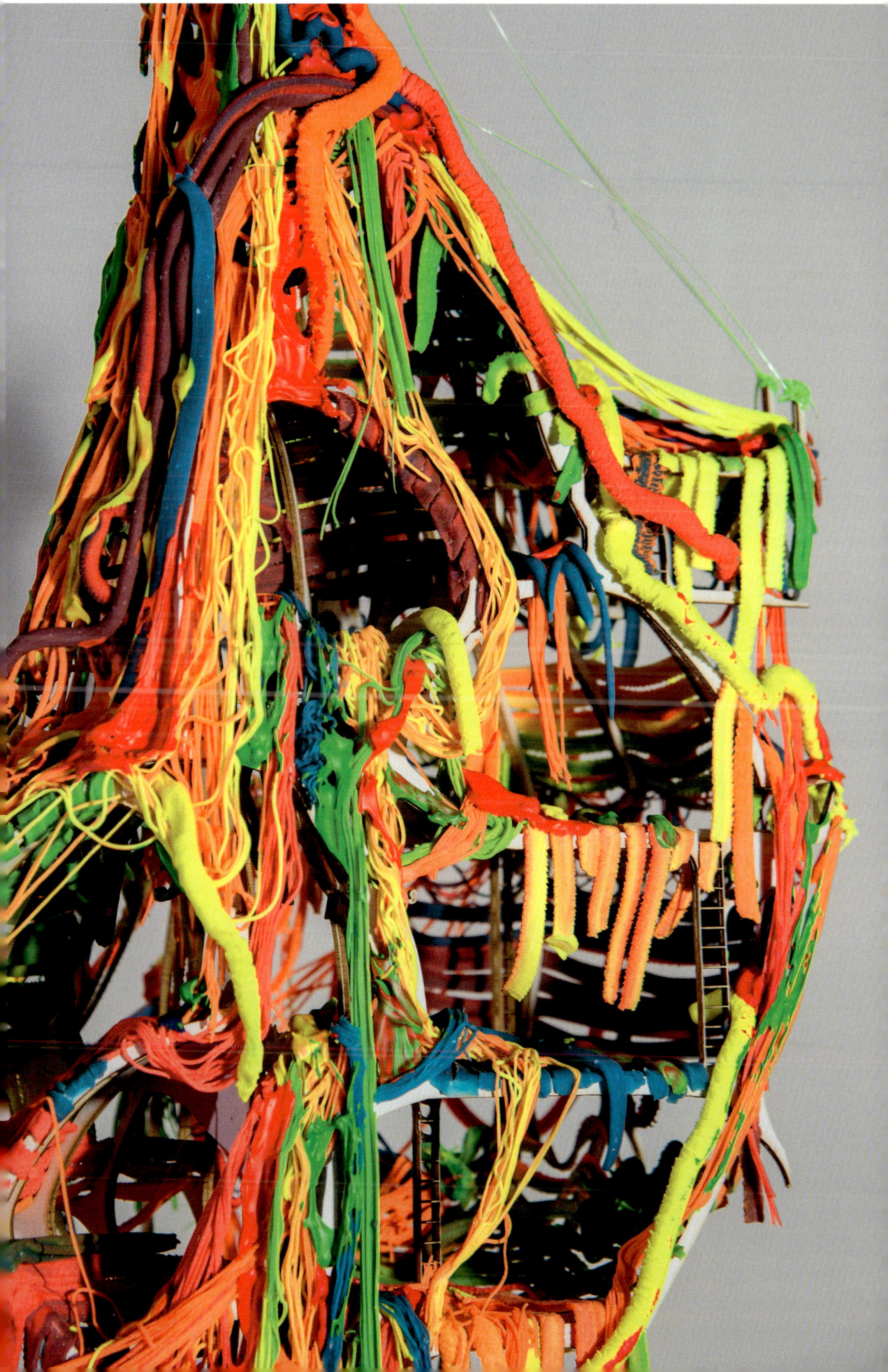

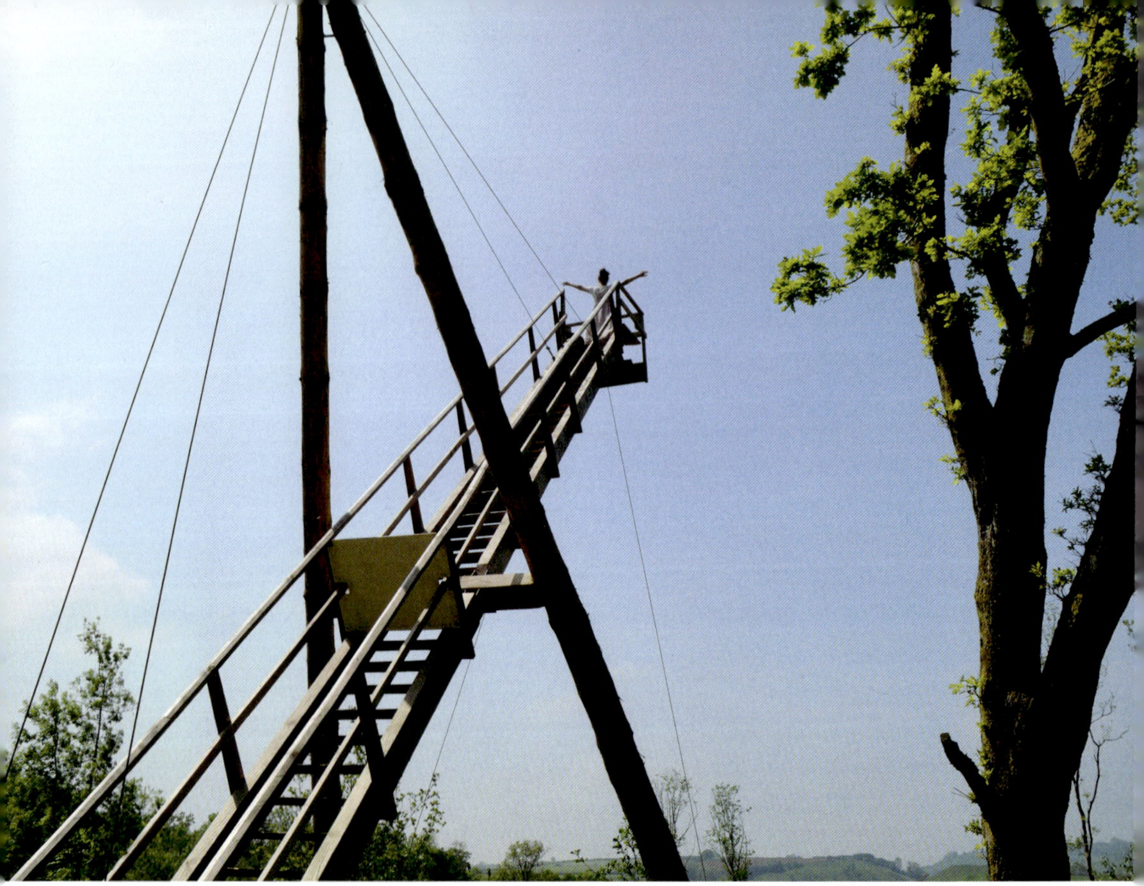

Exploring Hooke Park, collaboration with Arup

El Alto AA Visiting School, Final Jury

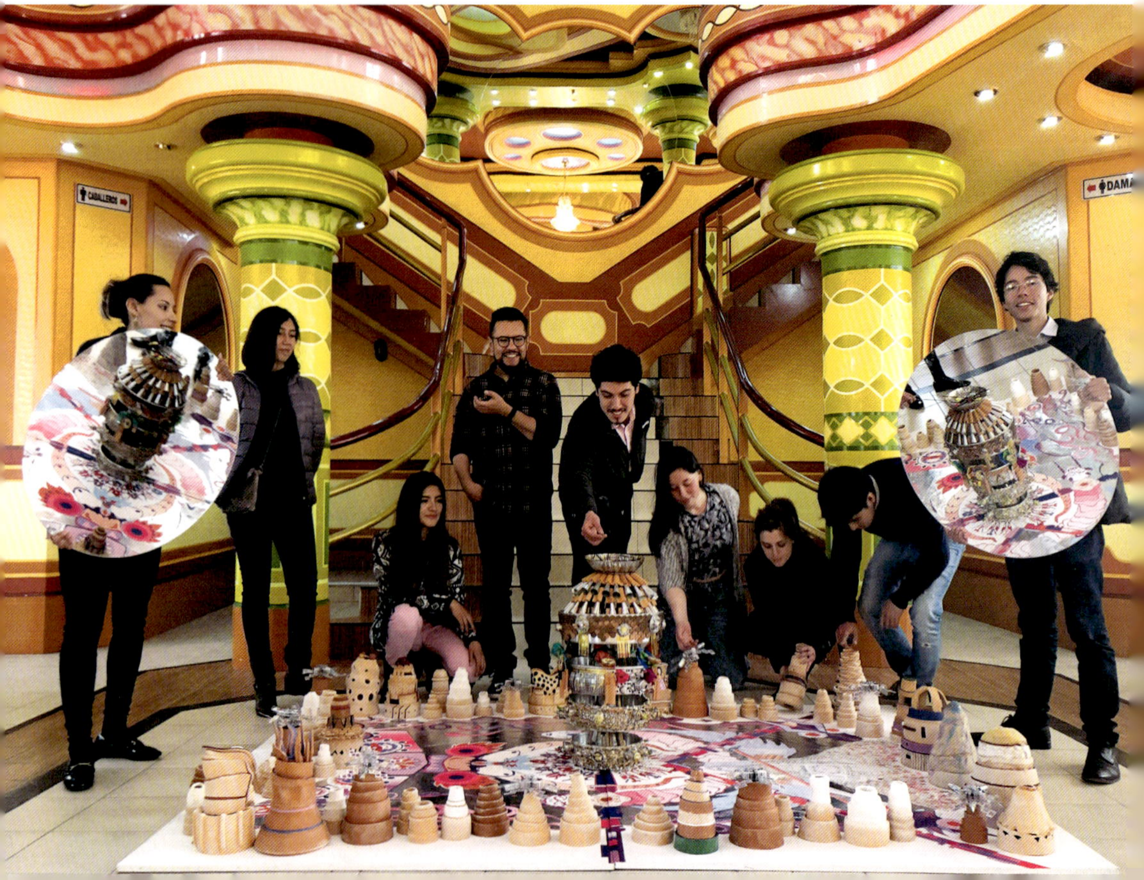

Diploma 10

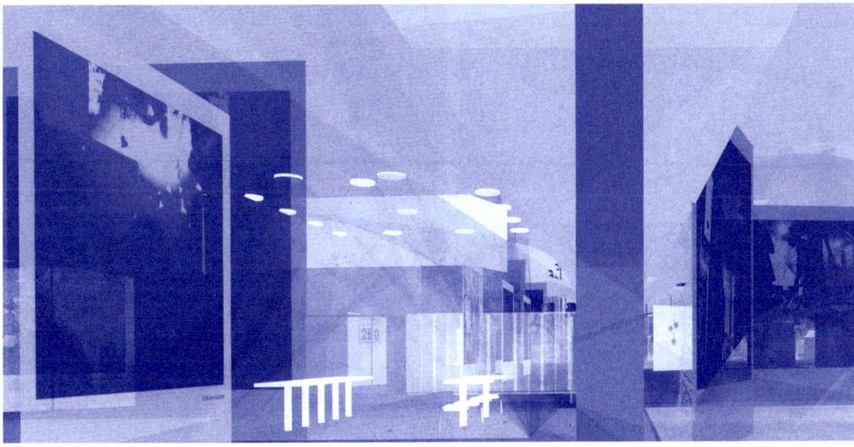

Nabil Randeree, Pleasure Garden, sectional view

Turning Clockwise to Lambeth   What role will the 32 London Boroughs play in the future of London?

Learning from the city, we experimented with the representation and inclusion of the city's more imponderable factors – trends, terrorism, crime, groups and religion. We reassessed and redefined context, and then found ways to work with it. Focusing on arbitrary territories within the south London borough of Lambeth, we worked with some of the area's variables to create new types of civic insertions. Through a scanning process, a spatial construct, situations, sections, architectural insertions and direct strategies, we experimented with complex spatial interventions that directly affect the live realm of the city and transform Lambeth's urban fabric. Work this year has interrogated the architect's role in reclaiming and activating public spaces, the narratives that generate social space, market structures, surveillance, alternative high streets and the idea of community.

Diploma 11

The creases and fault lines that once safeguarded historical layers and anomalies in London are slowly being ironed out. Following the seamlessness of the urban fabric, we arrive at a 5km-long railway viaduct between London Bridge and New Cross where the tide of development has yet to find a way in. This line became the datum for our exploration. We gathered the city's contents found along the railway: objects, textures, events and derelict spaces. Our aim was to de-collage the city by reassembling its parts, loosening up its architecture and deconstructing its boundaries. We took our interests to Shanghai – proposing an alternative urban renewal strategy to the favoured scrap and build block development – and Tokyo – compacting the city into one collage to be read and misread. The projects of the unit are informed by London's generosity to cultivate objects, knowledge and expression that make the city beautifully incomplete and dynamically dysfunctional.

Patricia de Souza Leaõ Müller, Holy Fool Studio

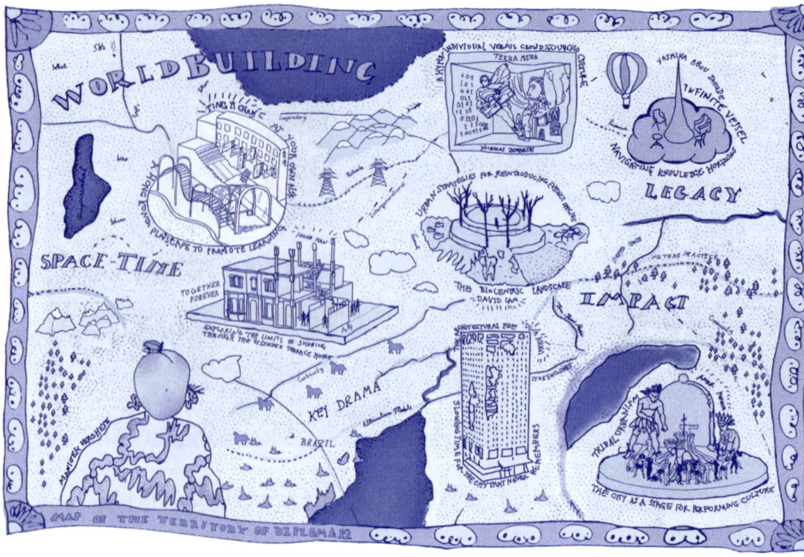

<u>World Building: Scripting Spaces</u> In our search for diverse forms of practice, Diploma 12 asks what alternative methods and outputs architecture could adopt to bring about change. To expand traditional models we have visited visionary architectural projects, taken part in cross-unit knowledge exchanges, experienced ancient time-travelling techniques and virtual reality journeys with otherworldly creatures. On our trip to Brazil, we traversed worlds within worlds: from the sculptural concrete of Lina Bo Bardi to Oscar Niemeyer's modernist vision for Brasília. On our return, the projects evolved from the utopian to the real and manifest. We worked with time-based media to define clear architectural and social strategies and developed technical elements to help refine precise architectural languages. In this way, we invented new and more clearly defined roles for the architect to intervene and shape the future.

Diploma 13

FIRST FLOOR

<u>Sick City Rehab</u> Following three years of research into the NHS, the unit has widened its scope beyond the UK to research health in other parts of the world. We act inside other cultures as we review the wide-reaching histories, rituals, policies, laws, infrastructures, institutions, economies and typologies of healthcare systems elsewhere. Rather than focusing on points of treatment such as hospitals, clinics and surgeries, our sites of interest are spaces of preventative care – networked through the city and countryside these care infrastructures create a family of types that promote health in the city in unexpected ways, and equation-exiting relationships between bodies and public space. Using the lens of the body each student has developed a sensuous and witty materiality in the architectural detail, emphasising its atmospheric effects. All of our drawings are performed, with a 3D element unfolding spatially and a 4D interactivity engaging with time.

The health of our civilisation is defined by how we institutionalise care and look after those in need. Diploma 13 calls for the urgent application of both formal, clinical abstraction and pleasurable, bodily atmosphere in architecture to interrogate the relationship between the body and the institution, and resuscitate our democracies.

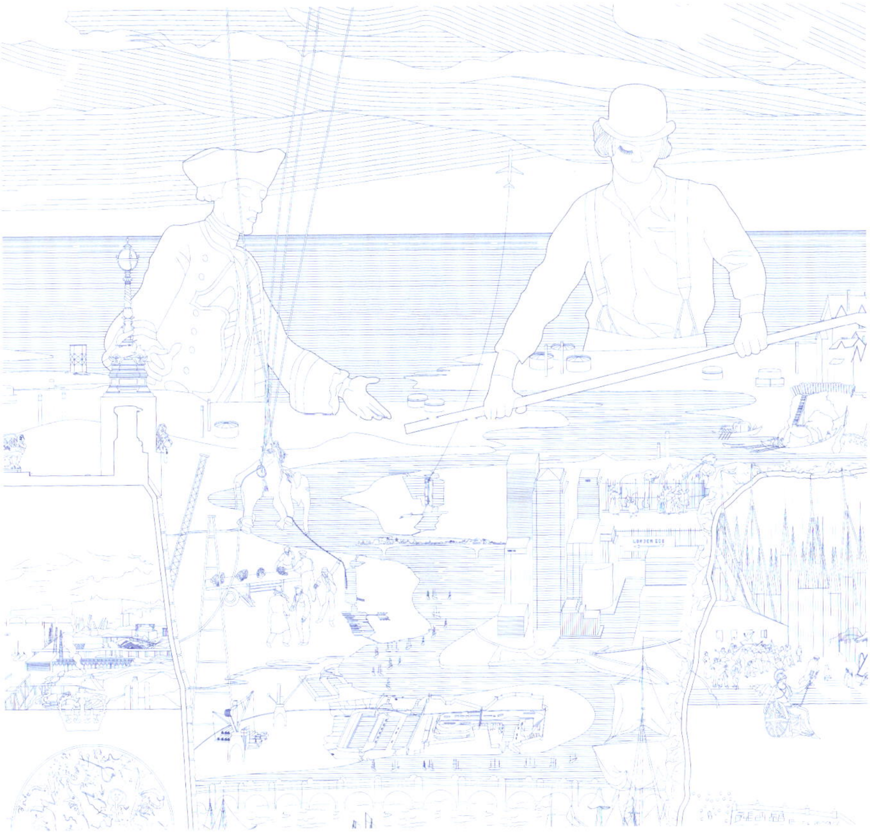

Emily Priest, Taming the Thames: The Enclosure of a River

This year Diploma 14 focused on the project of the 'void'. Far from being empty, the void is everything that is not occupied by buildings or other forms of built density, and it appears to us as a 'natural' reservoir. This void can exist inside or outside the city, and it is often a contested territory where the tendency to enclose space for the sake of profit meets the resistance of the citizens' desire to use it freely. The urban 'void' is therefore a site of struggle, between processes of exploitation and reappropriation, and perhaps the most direct testimony to the enclosure of resources that marked the beginning of capitalism.

Our projects addressed this condition by defining strategies of de-commodification that can be made visible and tangible through specific architectural interventions. In order to advance this idea we used the concept of the park as our starting point. As one of urban modernism's most problematic figures, the park has been used to naturalise the conflictual history of urban territories. Within the modern city it has played the role of the 'jungle' – a piece of wilderness enclosed by the artificiality of the city. Yet the more this the 'jungle' celebrates a primordial return to nature, the more it casts a shadow on the city as an (un)governable place in which order and disorder are no longer opposing forces but, two faces of the same coin. Indeed, the image of the park as pastoral retreat is often used to hide the violence of dispossession that has produced the contemporary city. The question of the studio has therefore been how to use the park not as an idealisation of nature and rurality, but as a territorial system that allows the reappropriation of resources and makes legible the forces and conflicts that produce our own urban condition.

Diploma 15

FIRST FLOOR

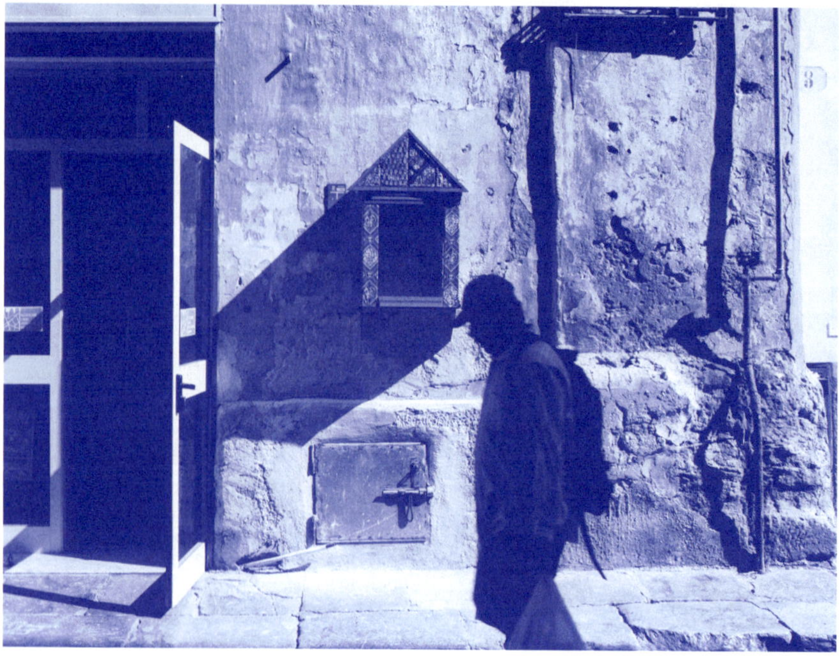

AA Museum Lab – The Manifesta Edition This year Diploma 15 – the AA Museum Lab – has participated as an exhibitor in the 12th edition the Manifesta art biennial to investigate the complexities of Palermo's formal and informal cultural scene. The ambition of the AA Museum Lab is to examine, unveil and instrumentalise such a condition by proposing curatorial strategies that allow each site to enjoy a renewed value. Dispersed across the city as site-specific installations, student projects will be presented to the Manifesta audience in the format of a collective exhibition held within the complex of Sant'Antonio. Relying heavily on close collaborations with local actors, the projects contest gentrification, respond to EU political imperatives, unveil the historic layering of areas of the city, question preservation paradigms and curate a progressive demolition of abandoned houses of the infamous *Pizzo Sella* by accelerating a re-naturalisation process of destructive local pioneer species.

Diploma 16

GROUND FLOOR

The Ecological Revolution I: Buildings as Architecture Diploma 16 engages with the evolution of building design and the speculation on an ecological future of architecture. We explore how the material processes deployed in the creation of design models, digital or analogue, could reintroduce an agile element of surprise and discovery necessitated by the current top-down BIM-centric building design process currently favoured by the industry at large. Diploma 16 challenged students to design and construct a series of models of a building complex situated in an intense and expanding urban environment at the present or in the near future. Due to recent technical development of new super polymers and carbon-based materials, the self-weight of materials is no longer a deciding factor for what and at which scale we can build – a situation addressed by these projects. The ensuing building models possess a particular formal, spatial, material and experiential character integrated with a positive ecological footprint in order for the building to be discussed as a serious piece of architecture. The outcome is a series of design models based around digital and analogue material processes addressing basic design parameters such as ground, sky, enclosure and tectonic resulting in the design and production of a building model that can be construed as building, as well as ecological architecture with an element of ignorance and surprise.

Diploma 17

GROUND FLOOR

Maximum Comfort Diploma 17 is interested in the socio-political role of architectural form. This year we continued our investigation into the implications of information and communication technologies on occupancy, and we explored tactics of destabilising the body as a way of employing the haptic qualities of architecture. The work expresses a critical position towards architecture's capacity to enact and affect participation, stimulate the corporeal experience of space and provide a framework for public life.

We developed urban proposals through research and design experimentation – compositing material tests, prototyping, photography, film and virtual reality to negotiate our ideas with the real. The production of architecture, and to a large extent our creativity, is increasingly conditioned by the industrialisation of architectural elements and the automation of the design tools we use. Over the last few years, the unit has searched for greater corporeality in the production and communication of architecture – mixing the use of physical and virtual media, and challenging a culture of the flat in favour of new materiality nested within digital practice.

Diploma 18

GROUND FLOOR

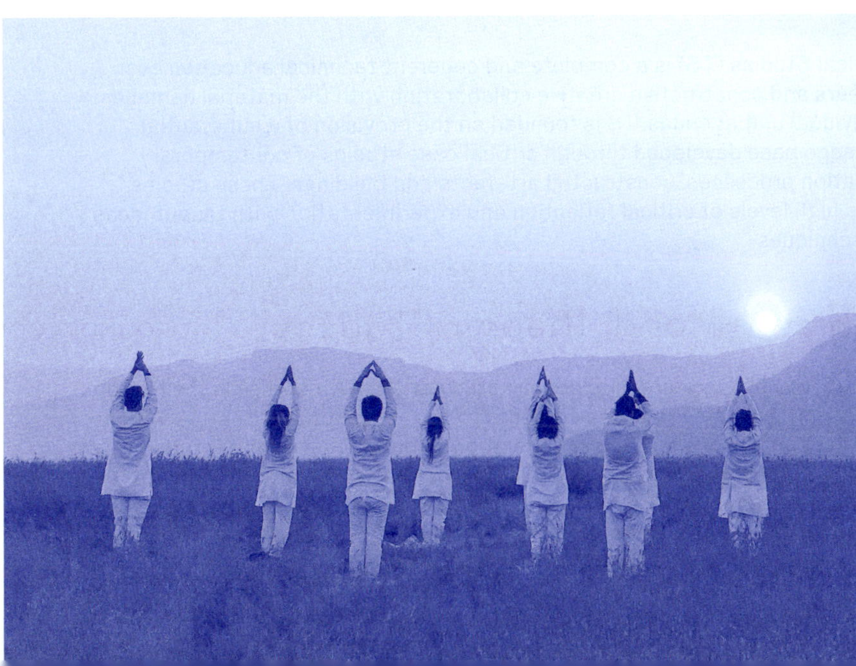

Diploma 18, Performance 9

The Home of Performance Diploma 18 looks at the idea of home and what it means in the context of global warming. The unit explores our relationship to the grid and local, national and international forms of infrastructure. We reflect on the challenging paradoxes that arise when we examine an alternative off-grid scenario. Architecture is an incubator for global warming, but it is also a possibility for a solution. Home is a stage for our daily performance and where identity emerges in its most decisive form. This year Diploma 18 travelled to India as guests of the Shillim Foundation – an organisation dedicated to rebuilding a more harmonious relationship between land and occupancy, and which aims to return a modest area of country back to its natural state to re-establish a connection to the environment. The architect as activist underpins the unit ethos, with each member of our tribe developing how their own kind of activism manifests.

COMPLEMENTARY

Media Studies

FIRST FLOOR

AA Media is a testing ground for exploring the processes and interrogating the tools involved in making architecture – the tools with which we speculate, manipulate and play; compute and control; communicate, seduce and provoke. The department operates a diverse multidisciplinary programme where unexpected collisions and obsessive attention to detail expose rich seams of creative potential. By actively testing modes of production through focused acts of doing and making, students gain a range of opportunities to develop individual practice and hone dexterity with both established and progressive media.

Technical Studies

GROUND FLOOR

Technical Studies (TS) is a complete and coherent technical education over five years and constructs a creative collaboration with the material demands of individual unit agendas. TS is founded on the provision of a substantial knowledge base developed through critical case studies of contemporary fabrication processes, constructed artefacts and buildings. These studies involve high levels of critical reflection and experimentation with taught ideas and techniques.

History and Theory Studies

GROUND FLOOR

Running over all five years of academic study at the AA, courses in the History & Theory programme introduce students to the nature of architecture within the larger context of the discipline's relation to past, present and future cultures. Students learn that architectural projects exist not as isolated fragments, but as the impetus, symptom or result of social, political, cultural and economic contexts. Writing plays a crucial role in coursework, with each year culminating in a competition for outstanding writing at the AA.

AA Interprofessional Studio

GROUND FLOOR

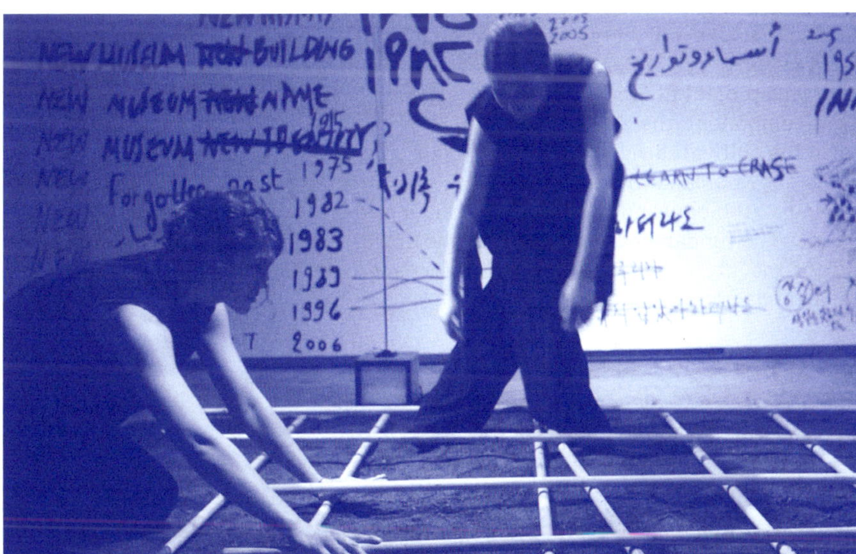

Jeehyeon Rosa Wang and Thourayya Kreidieh, Even Though We Didn't Go Through It

The Interprofessional Studio (AAIS) explores alternative forms of collaboration between multiple creative professions. Our work demonstrates a wide field that stretches beyond architecture and the established professions to an 'in between' space of disciplines. Each year AAIS designs, curates and constructs events that include a range of creative disciplines such as dance, movement, performance, sound, theatre, in multiple exhibitions, festivals and academic events.

This year we entered a season of events and shows that were exhibited across the world, from the UK to Spain and to China. Curated and created by the students of the programme, the events reached a broad audience of more than 2,500.

Design + Make

FIRST FLOOR

Wakeford Hall Assembly

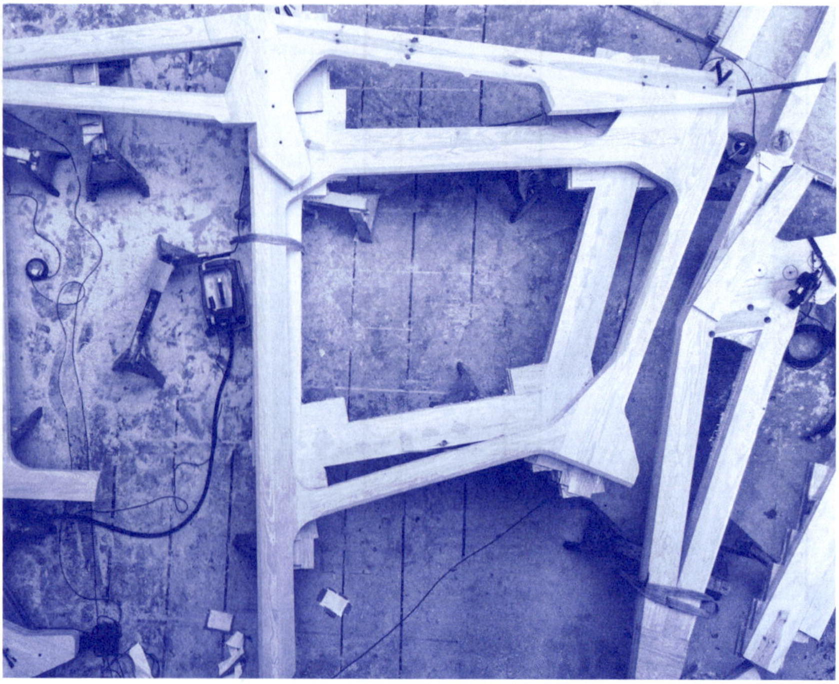

Design + Make investigates and generates new protocols, operations and attitudes within the realm of experimental constructs. We foster a deep interest in traditional fabrication principles and merge this knowledge with advanced digital tools, creating hybrid and bespoke system operations. Recently we embarked on the multi-layered Wakeford Hall project at Hooke Park, Dorset, focusing on the design and manufacture of its first component: the library. This temple of knowledge occupies a strategic position in the cultivated wilderness of Hooke Park. As a highly charged vessel it negotiates our woodland (the site of our material library – governed by cycles, wildlife, mystery and mythology) and our architectural laboratory (the space of our fabrication experiment). The fundamental concepts of the structural skeleton, the inhabitation of the skin and the internal workings, form the fertile ground for our most recent aim to produce an audacious architecture.

Design Research Laboratory

FIRST FLOOR

Experimentation and Innovation (v20) The AADRL is a work-in-progress. In method and practice the lab challenges the orthodoxies of convention in how we discuss, design, fabricate and live within architecture and urbanism. Participation is at the heart of this continuous project in which self-organised teams of international students bring their knowledge to the lab while engaging with the latest technologies that are reinventing our society. The attempt is to offer more – to treat architecture as a mode of enquiry that extends from material behaviour and artificial intelligence, to the challenges of infrastructure and urbanism. Our work examines the future of work, living and culture and proposes design research that examines the means to enable this through three-dimensional printed structures, self-aware and structured robotic agents, multi-authored designed urbanism, and swarms of drone printing.

Pete Qiang, Fragment of ADMCP VR Research Environment (Media Practices)

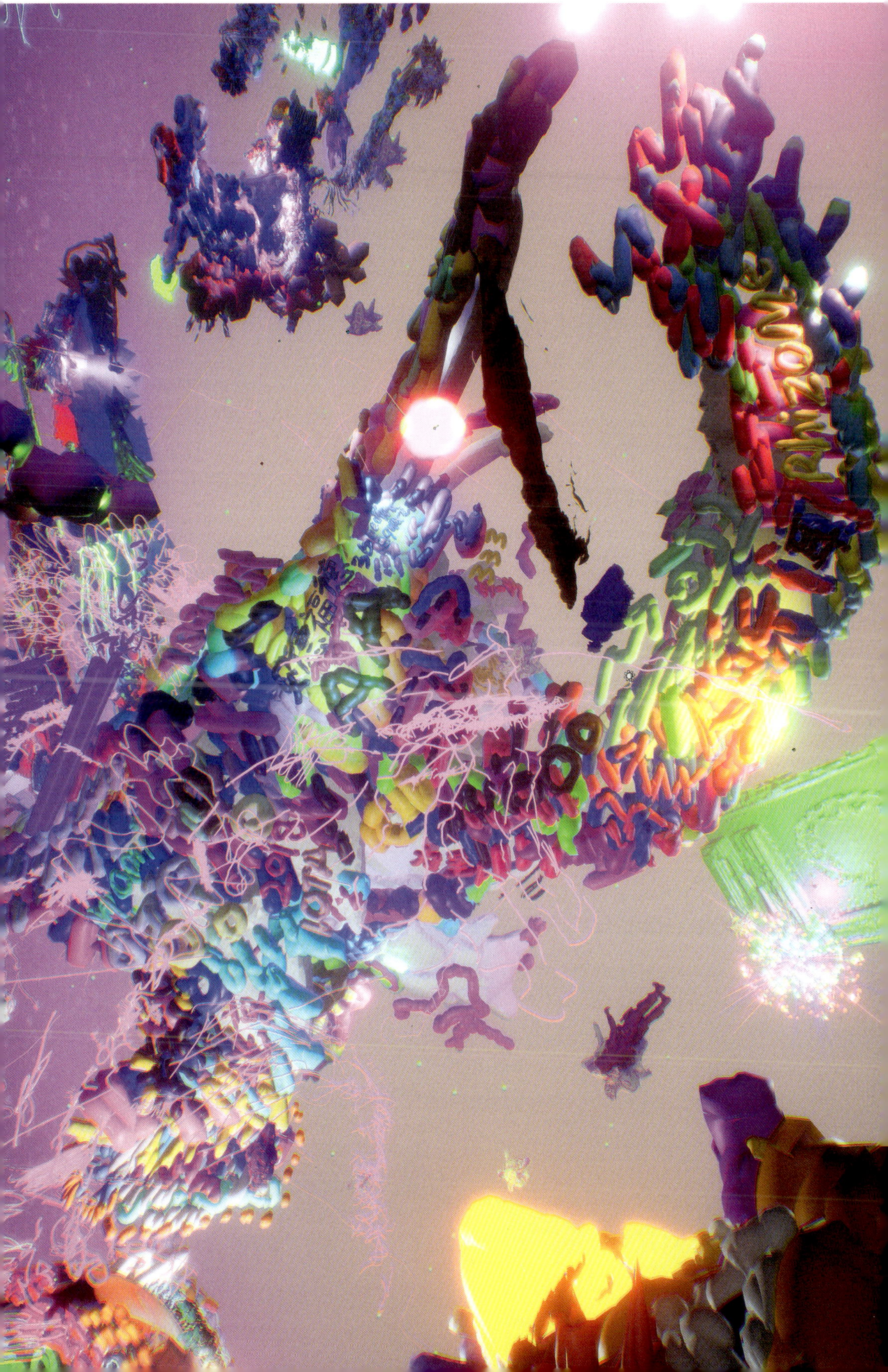

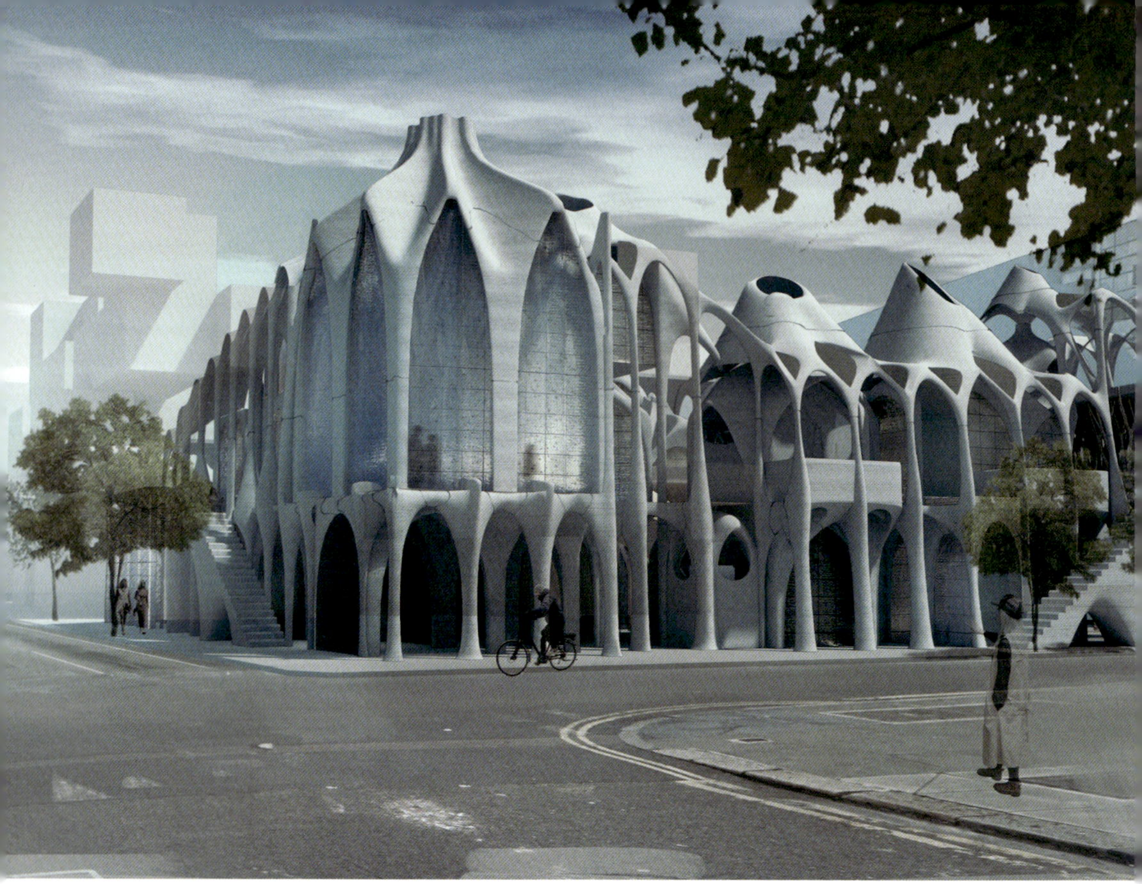

Networks Studio: Suchart Ouypornchaisakul, Jeffrey Widjaja, Taole Chen (AADRL)

Swati Bhargava, Environmental Strategies for Workspaces in Hot-Dry Regions of India (SED)

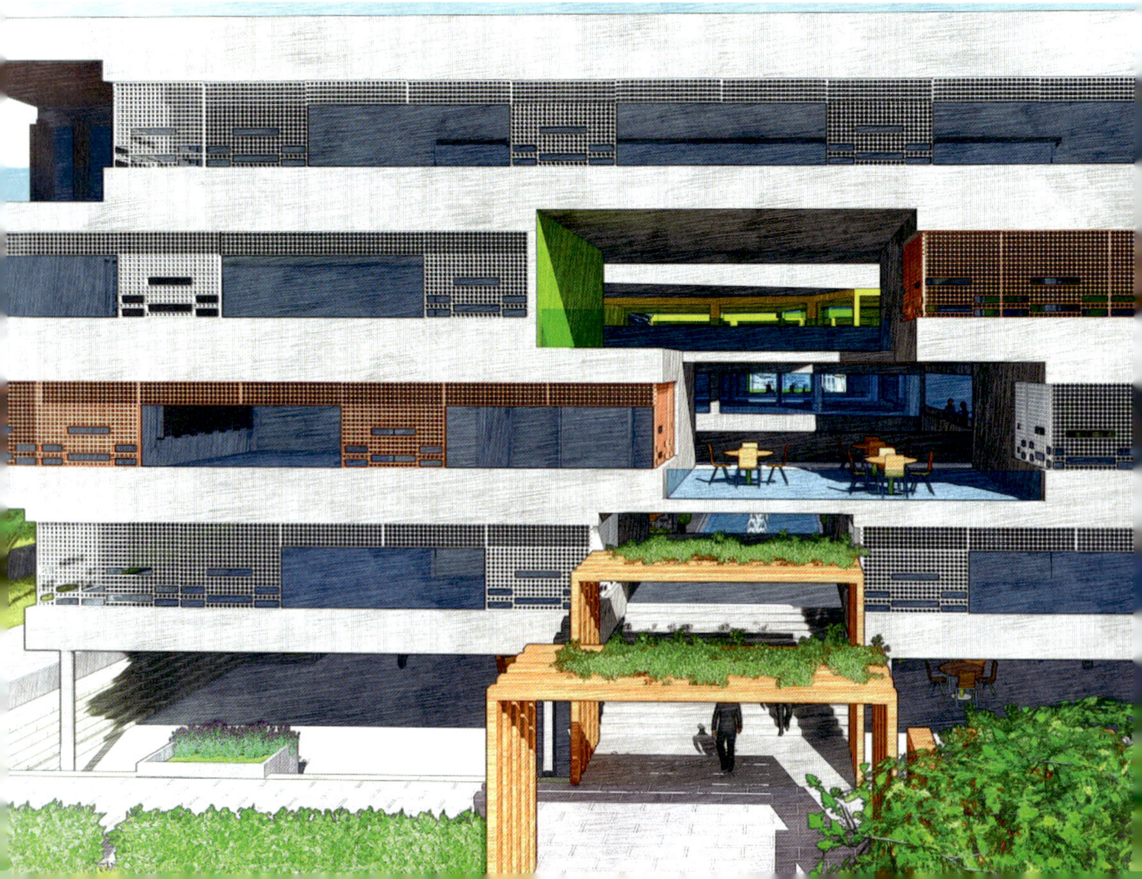

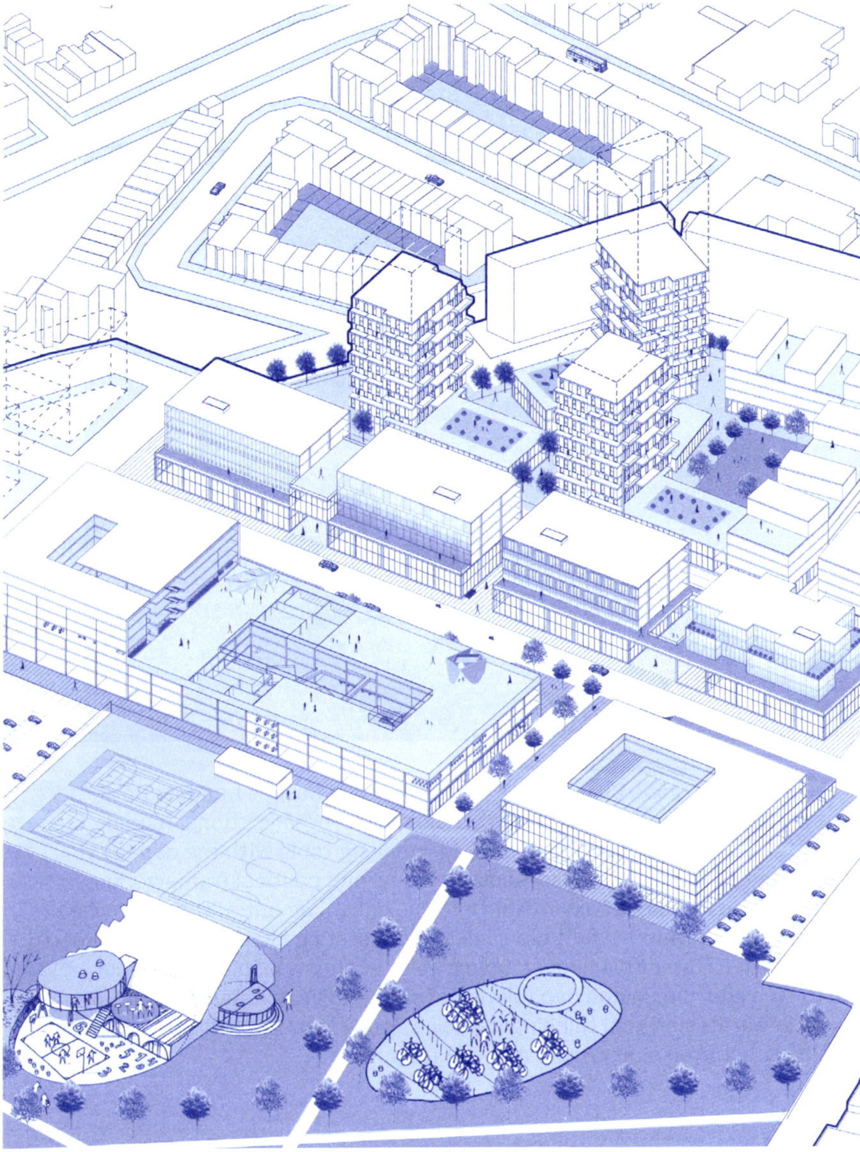

Enhanced services and the intensification of urban neighbourhoods in London and Bangkok

Housing and Urbanism focuses on the drivers of urban change across multiple scales – from the dwelling to the metropolitan region – and gives students (through a 12-month MA or 16-month MArch) the opportunity to integrate their project work with a well founded understanding of the urban process and contemporary international practice. Our primary urban laboratory is London, whose tremendous energy and diversity allow faculty and students to explore the broadest range of urban conditions. Our study trip to Berlin included a symposium organised together with the University of Nottingham and the TU Berlin on the topic, 'Building Knowledge Neighbourhoods', and our urban explorations emphasised close study of the architecture of the well-integrated and adaptive city. Our second trip each year brings us together with a host government and university in a knowledge exchange programme structured around an intensive workshop. This past year, in Bogotá with the city government and the Universidad de Los Andes, our theme was to link future mobility with heightened services and the pursuit of more robust and successful networks of production.

Landscape Urbanism

BARREL VAULT

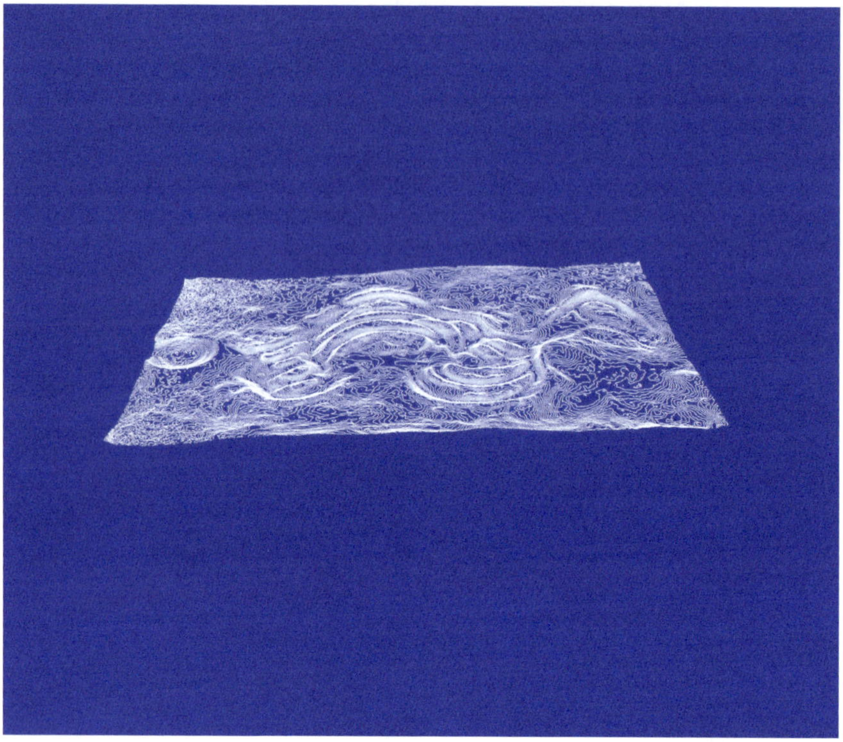

Simulation of riverine landscape with physical tank

Beyond the design of single buildings or pieces of urban design, Landscape Urbanism is interested in the design of spatial policies, organisational models, innovative regulatory plans and visual decision-making tools with the capacity to integrate design within economic, social, cultural and political frameworks. The aim of the programme is to contribute to the enhancement of the discipline by making it more relevant at multiple scales and fostering closer dialogues and debates with different disciplines (geography, economy, ecology, political science), to highlight the unique capabilities of design. The constantly evolving programme integrates critical thinking as well as practices such as cartographic representation, scripted simulations and GIS mapping.

Media Practices

GROUND FLOOR

In an era defined by the instant transmission of information, the MPhil in Media Practices questions how various media can inform a reading of architecture, a discipline characterised by the laborious speed at which it is often produced. The course stems from the argument that the conventional techniques of making and understanding architecture – drawing, modelling, talking and writing – now require augmenting in the contemporary world.

Work this year considered how alternative practices might elicit an expanded investigation of contemporary architecture. Historical and traditional modes of representing architecture were studied in advance of investigations into alternative and expanded practices.

EmTech

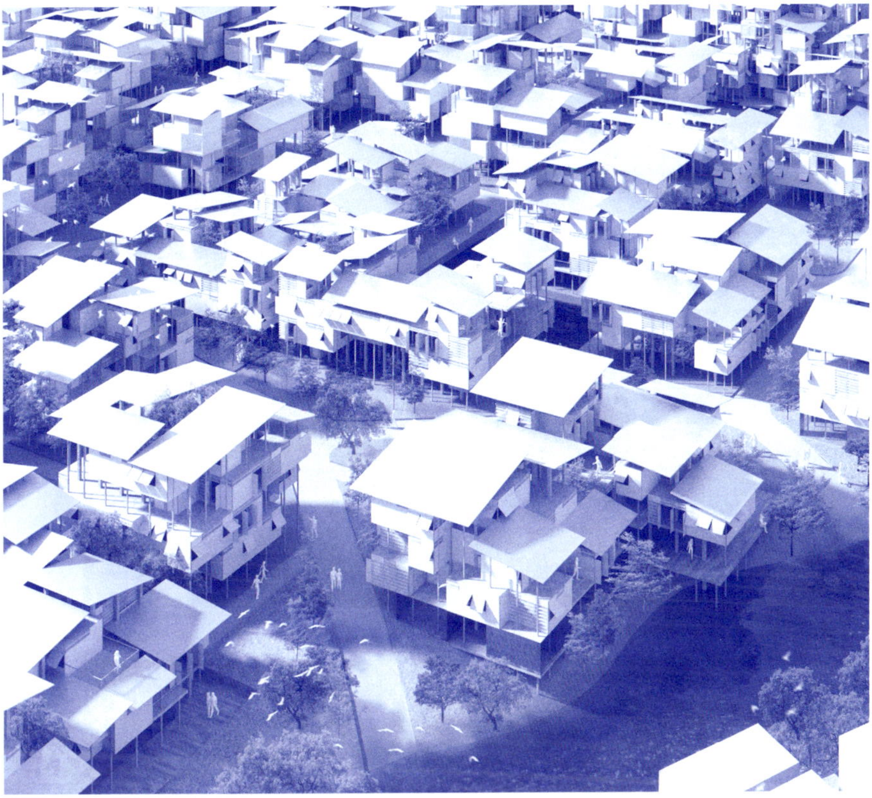

Song Jie Lim, Shih Hsin Wuu, Varvara Vasilatou, Tectonics of Informality

AA Emergent Technologies & Design (EmTech) investigates new synergies of architecture and ecology through the critical intersection of computational design and fabrication. The programme (offered as an MArch or MSc) stimulates thinking through research-driven design projects that are developed in an intellectually rigorous and creative studio environment. Projects are pursued in multiple iterations through hypothesis, material and computational experimentation, robotic fabrication and evaluation. They are further examined in presentations and documented in analytical and scientific papers. The programme is made up of two phases: studio and dissertation. Both are supported by the expertise of the programme team, AA alumni and research colleagues in practice.

Sustainable Environmental Design

BARREL VAULT

Sustainable Environmental Design (SED) engages with real-life problems that affect buildings and cities across the world. Design research is driven by evidence-based performance criteria following a process of adaptive architecturing, which proceeds from inside to outside, attuning built form and users to natural rhythms and occupant activities. Key objectives of all SED projects are to improve environmental quality in cities, achieve independence from non-renewable energy sources and to foster an environmentally sustainable architecture that is capable of adapting to changing climates and urban environments.

Urban Design: Projective Cities

GROUND FLOOR

Ricardo Palma Prieto, Community-Led Housing in London: The Case of StART

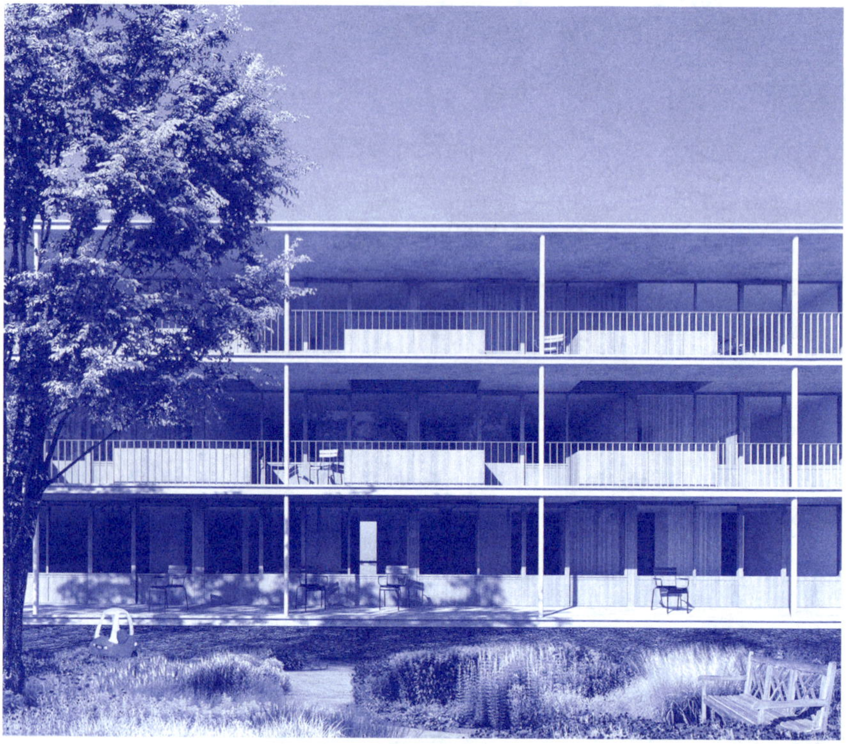

The MPhil in Architecture and Urban Design: Projective Cities supports original enquiries into the city within diverse political, economic, social, historical and cultural contexts. Research is motivated by two fundamental enquiries: first, to develop the methods, objectives and means of design research. And second, to develop architectural urbanism as an approach to design crossing conventional disciplinary separations. This year, projects have examined public services and education in migration cities such as Tijuana, the provision and procurement of public housing in Barcelona, the need for community-led housing in London, the Church of England as a new urban institution, and the English Garden Town.

History and Critical Thinking

GROUND FLOOR

'In my practice I work towards the photograph as opposed to the set-up of this exercise where I am starting from the photograph and mutability of the image in the mind is fixed onto paper. I have begun by writing descriptions of each image – to try and explicate the images through text – but the task to use language to replicate the logic of the images is incomplete.' - Collette Sheddick, 'Five Memos'

The MA History and Critical Thinking is a postgraduate platform for engaging with contemporary architecture and city cultures through history - its writings, conceptual assumptions and methodologies. The programme's ambition is threefold: to connect contemporary debates and projects to a wider historical, cultural and political context; to explore historical writing and the ways in which social, political and cultural agendas become effective arguments in particular accounts of architectural and urban modernity; to investigate forms of research, communication and practice technologies in the context of recent cultural and geopolitical developments to produce knowledge that relates to practices and public cultures in architecture.

PhD

GROUND FLOOR

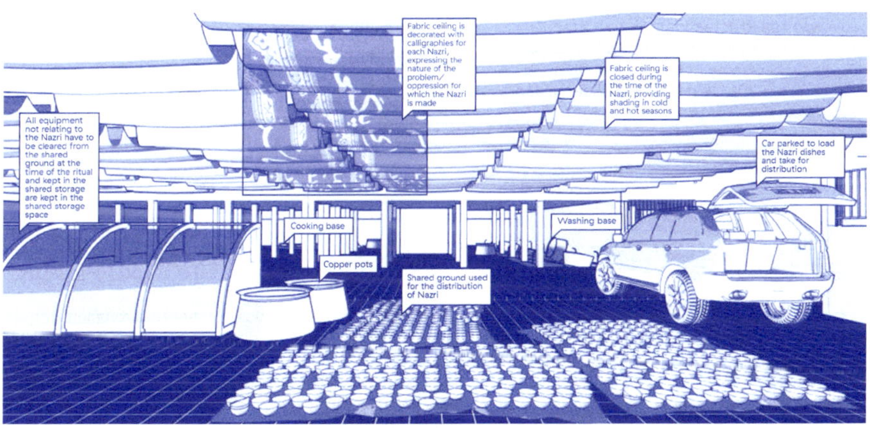

Samaneh Moafi, Domestic Architecture, Governance and Conflict in Iran

Doctoral studies at the AA combine advanced research with a broader educational agenda, preparing graduates for practice in global academic and professional environments. Architectural history and theory research is directed by Mark Cousins and Marina Lathouri. Research addressing urban and housing issues, policy and spatial design is supported by Lawrence Barth, Jorge Fiori and Hugo Hinsley. Research in emergent technologies in architectural design is directed by Michael Weinstock and George Jeronimidis, architectural research on sustainable environmental design is directed by Simos Yannas and Paula Cadima. 'City-Architecture', a collective design research agenda, is directed by Pier Vittorio Aureli and Maria Giudici. PhD candidates in any of these areas may follow either the traditional route of the written dissertation or combine writing with design research for the studio-based PhD in architectural design. Regular Term 1 and 2 seminar series were followed by a PhD by Design Symposium in January, presentations by new and completing PhD research students in May and a symposium organised by continuing PhD candidates in June. Outside the AA PhD students took part in international conferences in countries including the CAADRIA 2018 in Beijing, the Society of Architectural Historians 71st Conference in St Paul, Minnesota and the AHRA Conference in Helsinki. Papers were published in the *International Journal of Architectural Computing*, *Thresholds 46: Scatter!* and *Kårk*.

Visiting School

AA SALON

The AA Visiting School (AAVS) is held on five continents in dozens of cities, territories and remote regions. The diverse courses that make up the AAVS programme provide teaching and learning opportunities for students, professionals and international participants to engage with the world's most pressing architectural, technological, cultural, urban and social issues. Short-course offerings in the Visiting School are open to visiting students enrolled at schools throughout the world, currently enrolled AA students, recent graduates, architects and creative individuals and professionals who wish to further their knowledge, practice and skills in architecture.

Director Christopher Pierce

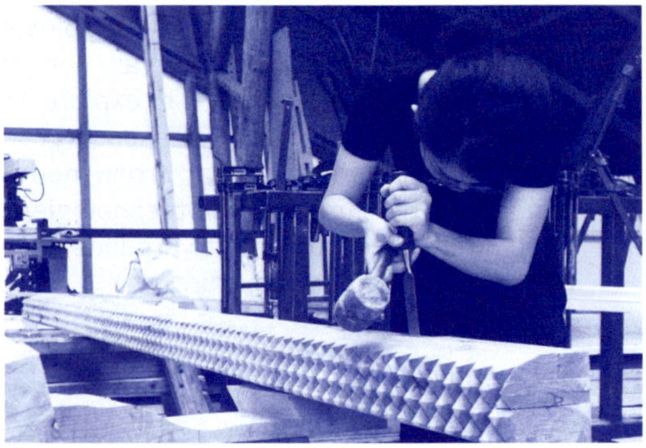

AA Visiting School Robotic Fabrications at Hooke Park, Dorset

Hooke Park

FIRST FLOOR

Hooke Park is the AA's woodland campus and is located on a 350-acre working forest in an area of outstanding natural beauty in Dorset, southwest England. This year we commenced construction of the Wakeford Hall project, which is being designed and built by the Dorset-based Design + Make masters students. The first phase – the library wing adjacent to the future lecture hall – will be completed later in 2018. On a smaller scale, a new Darkroom cabin was constructed for the photographic processing equipment previously housed in Bedford Square and makes use of part of the timber frame of the Maison Dom-ino exhibited by the AA in Venice in 2014. A mix of AA students and local volunteers also took part in Landscape Weekends, which involve hands-on forest maintenance activities. A series of public evening talks was held through Spring 2018 in collaboration with art-environment charity Common Ground. This year the new Kingcombe Visiting School programme started a design-build project at the neighbouring Kingcombe Wildlife Centre to deliver an outdoor classroom, while the Robotics Fabrications Visiting School ran its second course with a focus on new robotic band-saw tooling.

Head Martin Self

AA Collections

GROUND FLOOR

This year the AA Archives, Library and Photo Library have joined forces to showcase the unique research resources available within the AA's own collections.
Displayed in the entrance hallway of No 34 is a selection of newly acquired material, including drawings for 'Giant-Sized Baby Town', a Diploma 10 project from 1982 by Neil Porter (of the award-winning landscape architecture practice Gustafson Porter + Bowman). Also from the Archive is a series of works by the legendary hand of Amarjit Kali – who became a director at Richard Rogers Partnership at the age of 30, just seven years after graduating from the AA. From the AA Photo Library is a set of photographs selected from the archives of Denys Lasdun and Reyner Banham, while the AA Library presents some of the highlights of the 1000+ titles purchased throughout the last year. In the entrance hallway and staircase of No 33 research material from across the AA Collections reveals the variety of approaches taken within the AA over the last 100 years, regarding the question of social housing provision. From rare publications to student proposals and photographic essays, the exhibition aims to demonstrate the richness of the original research material held within the AA's remarkable historic collections.

AA Collections Eleanor Gawne, Aileen SMith, Edward Bottoms, Beatriz Flora, Simine Marine, Martina Babetto, Byron Blackely

Membership

The Architectural Association was formed as a learned society in 1847, and today the AA is made up of over 7,000 Members across the world. AA Members are a community of professionals, alumni, students, researchers and academics from many fields who share architecture as a common interest. Members are involved in the life of the AA in many ways through volunteering time, expertise, and supporting students in need, as well as receiving the many benefits of Membership including access to the AA Library, Photolibrary and Archives, organising and enjoying Members' Events such as talks, building visits, guided walks, film screenings, private views and more, plus an annual subscription to *AA Files*. AA Membership is open to anyone with a genuine interest in architecture and we are keen to hear from people looking to join, visit aaschool.ac.uk/members.

Membership Staff Alex Lorente, Guy Norton, Eva Shannan

Digital Platforms

A Digital Platforms enables the AA's online presence across the web and social media and works to support the life at the AA through different online channels. The department's primary focus remains on aaschool.ac.uk, which provides a window to the AA's worlds. With the AA Public Programme, we have continued to reach tens of thousands of viewers across the globe. The new AA Research section highlights outstanding work of staff and forms the school's first research repository.
This year Digital Platforms launched AA Live, an app that puts our architectural culture of lectures, exhibitions, Member events, news, AA Conversations and social media channels in one place. Digital communication including AA Weekly, AA Sporadical and AA Visiting School Communique now provide better communication with our Members and Alumni. In our ongoing work with AA Visiting School, we helped design and build more than 20 microsites, offering in-depth information about workshops around the world. This year we also opened up our social media channels to students and staff, with take-over initiatives producing a presence that mirrored the diversity of the school. §Each year Digital Platforms produces the annual Projects Review website, which gives the AA's units, programmes and students a high-profile online presence. Projects Review 2018 is online at pr2018.aaschool.ac.uk.

Digital Platforms Staff — Zeynep Carozza, Simeon Simeonov

AA Publications

The Architectural Association publishes titles that explore developments in architecture, engineering, landscape and urbanism, as well as the fields that touch on them – philosophy, history, art and photography. Founded as a means of examining influential contemporary projects and opening up ideas to debate, AA Publications has a long tradition of publishing architects, artists and theorists early in their careers. New titles in 2017–18 featured work of the AA's units, as seen in Scavengers and Other Creatures in Promised Lands, a 10-year survey of the globally focused research of Intermediate 3, led by Ricardo de Ostos and Nannette Jackowski. And as part of the centenary celebrations of AA Women in Architecture, an eponymously titled book explored the past, present and future of the women alumni and tutors who have helped shape the institution. In December AA Publications released AA Files 75, and this summer sees the release of AA Files X, an issue that looks back on 75 issues of the long-running journal, co-edited by four AA Diploma students. In addition to AA Book 2018, the anthology of student work at the AA, this summer AA Publications will release An Anatomy of Influence, by Thomas Daniell, which explores postwar Japanese architecture through the lives of 12 distinct architects.

AA Print Studio — Sarah Handelman, Boris Meister, Michela Zoppi, Angela Denney

Public Programme

AA SALON

The AA Public Programme brings together personalities, projects and audiences for lectures, conversations, symposia, open workshops and performances throughout the year. All of these events seek to connect the AA to the wider, global culture of architecture and its associated disciplines. This past autumn, the AA XX 100 project marked a centenary of women at the AA with a lecture series, a new publication, an exhibition and an international conference. And as part of the search for our new director, we hosted five conversations on education, inviting practitioners, critics and collaborators from all over the world to discuss different models of architectural pedagogy and the future of the AA. In the spring, we celebrated another anniversary – 30 years of Mark Cousins' Friday Evening Lectures, with the final lecture paying tribute to the lectern itself. Last winter, Studio CE's exhibition Mudun, Urban Cultures in Transit focused on the architecture and design of the Middle East and North African region, and was supported by a lecture series that invited architects, artists and curators to speak about their work in a non-Western context. This summer, we will host the second Bedford Square Festival, which brings together cultural institutions around the square for a four-day festival of talks, performances and walking tours. FORMAT also returns as our summer series curated by Shumon Basar, questioning the role of the individual in the worlds of art, architecture, theory, media and more.

Head of Lectures & Public Programme Curator — Manijeh Verghese

Student Forum

AA SALON

The Student Forum consists of a group of AA student volunteers representing all years of study. Throughout the academic calendar the Student Forum organises activities and addresses issues and concerns raised within the school. It operates through various committees responsible for student concerns, student projects, travel bursaries, parties/events and networking. The overarching aim of the Student Forum is to facilitate conversations across programmes and schools.

AA LAWuN

AA SALON

Led by David Greene and Eddie Farrell, and conceived as part-thinktank and part-unit, LAWuN challenges the conventions of architectural education to imagine something new. Events and worshops this year included a flower show, sports day, ' On the Carpet' crits and pub quiz in our newly restored Barrel Vault – together offering an opportunity for different kinds of exchanges about architecture at the AA.

Staff — David Greene, Eddie Farrell

FORMAT Issue 8

ORGANISED BY
Shumon Basar

AA SALON

All events take place in
the AA Gallery at 6.30 pm
Entrance is free and
open to the public

SELF

Format is a live magazine looking at the shapes that discourse takes. The eighth issue focuses on Self Format. Is the individual being reinvented and redefined in our age of data capitalism? How much intimacy can be surrendered to surveillance? Is the opposite of the individual still the crowd, or is it something else? And would you mind being cloned? Invited guests, from the worlds of art, design, literature, theory, media and more, share their Self Formats.

Wednesday 4 July
Shumon Basar and Sophia Al Maria

Friday 6 July
Douglas Coupland and Hans Ulrich Obrist

Wednesday 11 July
Jack Self and Adam Thirlwell

Friday 13 July
Brendan McGetrick and Olivia Sudjic

format.aaschool.ac.uk

Patricia Moericke, Hana Shokr, Elias Tamer, York Tsing Yeung

DIPLOMA 10

Unit Master Carlos Villanueva Brandt
Students So Jae An, Thanas Apilikitsmai (Ing), Caroline Esclapez, Elizabeth Hardie, Juana Horcajo Rubi (Jane), Mizue Katayama, Hye Rim Lee, Nabil Randeree, Nathalie Reifschneider, Palita Rompotiyoke (Sandy), Irene Squilloni
Situation Workshops Nichola Barrington-Leach, Nick Green
Technical Workshop Nick Green
Tokyo Workshop Tom Heneghan, Tamao Hashimoto

DIPLOMA 11

Students Eyal Elyahu Amsili Giovannetti, Tiffany Elodie Attali, Carolin Adele Bongartz, Nga Fong Lisa Chan, Alison Cheuk Yee Cheng, My Yen Dang, Daria Igorevna Gavrilova, Chiyan Ho, Michael Ho, Jinah Kim, Vasilisa Lucic, Henry Ngo, Timothy James O'Hare, Paolo Emilio Pisano
Thanks Peter Thomas, Mike Morris,Nicholas Boyarsky, David Greene, Kate Darby, Kate Davies, Takero Shimazaki, George Legendre, Maria Fedorchenko, Carlos Villanueva-Brandt, Tom Heneghan, Kanto Iwamura, Tamao Hashimoto, Yusuke Obuchi, Yuko Odaira, Shintaro Tsuruoka, Akira Suzuki, Keisuke Oka, Shigeru Aoki, Rie Azuma, Kazuio Shejima, Mitshuhiro Kanada, Maeda Corporation, David Schwitzke, Charlie Corry Wright, Javier Castañon, David Grahame Shane, Reem Charif, Lena Emanuelsen, Silvana Taher, Florian Bagel, Philip Christou, Fred Scott, Valentin Bontjes van Beek, Hua Li, Susan Chai, Summer Islam, Kei Machida
A special thank you to Hugo Hinsley, an endless source of inspiration and knowledge for Dip 11 throughout the years. He will be missed

DIPLOMA 12

Tutors Inigo Minns, Manijeh Verghese
Students Amar Mehta, David Lam, Dina Khaki, Fabienne Tjia, Ioana Man, Julien Sebban, Lingge Yang, Nicholas Zembashi, Patricia de Souza Leao, Roy Coupland, Sebastian Tiew, Ting-Yi Chan, Yasmina Abou Jaoude
Thanks ADS4 at the RCA, Alexandra Daisy Ginsberg, Amandine Kastler, Analog Studio, Andre Spicer, Aram Mooradian, Arantza Ozaeta Cortazar, Belinda Flaherty (our muse), Camila Bechelany, Camila Soares, Chee-Kit Lai, Chris Pierce, Danielle Hewitt, Dash Macdonald, David Greene, Eddie Farrell, Edward Bottoms, Eleanor Dodman, Elena Palacios Carral, Ernesto Cruz, Fabio Zuker, Finn Wilkie, Francesca Hughes, Francesco Anselmo, Giles Bruce, Gili Merin, Gonzalo Herrero Delicado, J&K (Janne Schäfer and Kristine Agergaard), Jack Hardy, Javier Castanon, Jessica In, Jessica Reynolds, Juan Hermida, Kate Davies, Kenny Fraser, Lara Lesmes, Laura de Azcarate, Ligia Nobre, Lily Jencks, Maria Fedorchenko, Mariana Pestana, Mark Morris, Max Dewdney, Miraj Ahmed, Monia de Marchi, Nacho Marti, Nathan Su, O Grupo Inteiro, Pablo Leon de la Barra, Paulo Soares, Rubens Azevedo, Ryan Dillon, Samantha Hardingham, Samantha Lee, Sahra Hersi, Sebastien Noel, Sofia Krimizi, Sol Camacho, Sylvie Taher, Tyen Masten

DIPLOMA 13

Unit Tutors Lily Jencks, Jessica Reynolds
Students Roman Lovegrove, Georgi Delyanov, HyunJun Kim, Arvind Roy, Min Jung, Seunghun Lee, James Deru, James Pulman, Martina Contento, Andrew Yuen, Anna Wahlsten, Judy El Hajjar
Thanks Charles Jencks, Manijeh Verghese, Mark Morris, Miraj Ahmed, Sylvie Taher, Hannah Lawson, Nick Hornby, Catherine Pease, Marina Lathouri, Barbara-Ann Campbell-Lange, Ana Araujo, John Ng, Jen Gutteridge, Megan Burke, Korbinian Kainz, Liam Ashmore, Ingrid Schroeder, Owen Hopkins, Eddie Blake, Robin Farmer, Ema Hau, Rosemary Jenssen, Carole Crane, Inigo Minns

DIPLOMA 14

Unit Masters Pier Vittorio Aureli, Maria Shéhérazade Giudici
Students Ana Maria Nicolaescu, Anya Martsenko, Avery Jiehui Chen, Bodo Neuss, Emily Priest, Ines Tazi, Jacek Rewiński, Joshua Harskamp, Love Di Marco, Moad Musbahi, Quentin Dauvergne, Roberto Boettger, Sam Little, Shaan Patel
Thanks Fabrizio Ballabio, David Burns, Platon Issaias, Jeremy Lecomte, Gili Merin, Gabriele Mastrigli

DIPLOMA 15

Unit Master Giulia Foscari
Unit Tutors Harikleia Karamali, Giacomo Ardesio
Students Vidhi Goel, William Himpe, Andrew Kwok, Linxin Li, Mingyi Lim, David Lin I-Chun, Sadia Rahman, Alexandra Savtchenko-Belskaia, Zhan Su, Jane Wong
Thanks Barbara-Ann Campbell-Lange

DIPLOMA 16

Unit Staff Andrew Yau, Jonas Lundberg
Thanks Réne Peralta, Alex Santander, Denise Luna, Woodbury University School of Architecture San Diego, Enrique González-Silva, Escuela Libre de Arquitectura Tijuana, Stefan Svedberg, Hseng Tai Ja Reng Lintner, Marcelo Spina, Peter Testa, Maxi Spina, Florencia Pita, Marcelyn Gow, Dwayne Oyler
Guest Critics Ashkan Sadeghi, Maciej Woroniecki, Emily Thurlow, Duncan Berntsen, Nathan Kolbe, Iseki Takehiko, Elliot Krause, Anat Stern, Kostas Grigoriadis, Michael Kloihofer, Arya Safavi, Rebecca Spencer, Jin Ho Kim, Natasha Tariq, Adam Holloway, Kerry Dickenson, Claudia White, Jerry KK Lam

DIPLOMA 17

Unit Staff Dora Sweijd, Theodore Sarantoglou Lalis
Students Jocelyn Arnold, Alvaro Calle Moreno, Matthew Hepburn, May Ibentoumert, Berkin Islam, John Kanakas, Cheryl Lim, Bea Melli, Calle Pettersson, Zineb Sentissi, Pierre Vaubourg, Emily Watts, Yuan Zhai
Thanks Miraj Ahmed, Jonathan Cheng, Elif Erdine, Philippe Block, Benjamin Dillenburger, Di Zhan, Michael Herrmann, Naida Iljasovic, Angel Lara Moreira, Valentine Kozin, Mateus Seco, Leonardo Lattavo, Ivan Abreu, Franklin Lee, Anne Save de Beaurecueil, Raz Keltsh, Jonas Lundberg, Harikleia Karamali, Andrew Porter, Christopher Pierce, Kenny Frazer, Simon Taylor, Jeff Turko, Alexis Kallegias, Mike Weinstock, Oscar Niemeyer

DIPLOMA 18

Tutors Enric Ruiz Geli, Simon Taylor
Teaching assistants Bianca Moldoveanu, Patricia de Osma, Mila Moskalenko
Students Daisy Adebiyi, Arslan Arkallayev, Shu-Wei Chang, Gian Andrea Diana, Omer Hadar, Oren Karev, Vittoria Lenzi, Sixuan Li, Ali Mirzaei, Serwan Saleme, Milivoje Sestovic, Ke Bo Tsai, Konrad Weka
Diploma 18 had the pleasure to collaborate in 2017-18 with Shillim Foundation, Chandigarh City, Fondation Le Corbusier, IAAC, Rmit Europe, El Bulli Foundation, The Byrd Hoffman Water Mill Foundation, Disfrutar, Royal National Institute of Blind People, Carys Staton, Bradbury Oak House
Thanks Margie Ruddick, Denzil de Souza, Karen de Souza and Gavin de Souza
CHANDIGARH Sangeeta Bagga Megta (Headmistress of Chandigarh, College of Architecture, CCA), Disha Singh (CCA), Kapil Setia (Chief Architect of Chandigarh), Ms. Deepika Gandhi (Director of Le Corbusier Centre of Chandigarh)
SHILLIM Sasha (Shillim – AA Collaboration Assistance), Aditya (Dipendar and Bebe (Helpers at Shillim Foundation), Shubhendu Kadam (Executive Chef of Shillim Foundation), Tejaswini Sharma (Ceramic Atelier of Shillim Foundation)
Shillim online and on-site jurors at the 'jungle' jury Denzil De Souza, Karen De Souza, Gavin De Souza, Margie Ruddick, Aaron Mendonca, Martin Brody, Tom Zook, Cecil Howell, Erin Gee, Vicky Colombet, Simon Taylor, Oswald Pereira (Architect from Pune), Anilkumar J Hatkar (Architect & President of AUM LAI Chapter, Maharashtra), Raviraj Soman (Wildlife Specialist), Jeevan (Helper at Shillim Foundation)
AA Samantha Hardingham, Mark Morris, John Palmesino
IAAC Areti Markopoulou, Mireia Luzárraga, The Tribe at Self Sufficient Buildings Studio, Barcelona
RMIT Martyn Hook, Marta Fernandez
Long-time collaborators Michael Horsham, Ibrahim Muasher
Very special thanks The Bolli Family
no FAMILIES no HOMES

AAIS

Studio Director Theo Lorenz
Studio Master Tanja Siems
Tutors Andrew Dean, David McAlmont, Heiko Kalmbach, Joel Newman, Malgorzata Dzierzon, Mauricio Pauly, Renaud Wiser, Steve Webb, Joel Newman
Student Mona Camille, Lumia Shurong Liu, Jonghyun Tom Park, Noa Segev, Hila Shemer, Tuo Lin, Miranda Orozco, Jeehyeon Rosa Wang, Thourayya Kreidieh
Thanks Christian Küsters, Tony Thatcher, Miraj Ahmed, Victor Wang, Mark Morris, Paul Cosby, Edward Farrel, Peter Szots, Javier Peña Ibanéz, Irene Fernandez Garijo, Rebeca Castellano, Gonzalo Herrero Delicado, Gabriel Hernandez, Eryck Brahmania, Meng Zhang, Dia, Nakia Shuhong Hao, Zhuolong Yu, Qiuyu Yu, Binwei Lu, Linxin Li, Margret Schuetz, Ping Ping Lu, Lucía Blanco Vega, Emilio Anaya Acosta, Jimena Ochoa, James Greenhalgh, Argyris Angeli, Kyriaki Nasioula, Qiuyu Yu, Arantza Ozaeta Cortázar, Álvaro Martín Fidalga, Kelly Chorpening, Andi Hu, Ania Straczynska, Mohamed Lamine Camara, Roman Baca, Eva Linyingchi, Paula Malgorzata Jankowska, Elena Kolia Kalliopi
Venues p21 Gallery, China exchange, CHK design, Concéntrico Festival, Rambert Gallery

DESIGN+MAKE

Directors Emmanuel Vercruysse, Martin Self
Tutor Zachary Mollica
Make Tutor Jack Draper
Thesis Tutor Mark Campbell
Students Aitor Almaraz, Veda Barath, Kevin Kim, Pedro Bran Redondo, Mariela Reyes, Xin Tu, Yanxiu Chen, Mengyun Mao, Kheng Hock Oh, Tudor Tenea, Laura Welsh, Francisco Adriasola, Unha Park, Florencia Rodriguez Aranda, Thomas Dawson, Jack Fogel, Lucas Wilson
Visiting lecturers and jurors Sue Barr, James Binning, Clementine Blakemore, Charley Brentnall, Nat Chard, Tim Crabtree, Harry Cursham, Kate Davies, Fran Edgerley, Shin Egashira, Will Gowland, Samantha Hardingham, Richard Harris, Anderson Inge, Phil Leary, Chris Leung, Sophie Le Bourva, Melissa Mean, William Moorwood, Mark Morris, Nozomi Nakabayaskhi, Thomas Parker, Caroline Rabourdin, Jeremy Ralph, Thomas Randall-Page, Bob Sheil, Jeroen van Ameijde
Wakeford Hall Advisory Group Joanna Chambers, Michael Dickson, Samantha Hardingham, William Moorwood, Mark Morris, Christine Price, Carlos Villanueva Brandt
Engineering Support Arup (Francis Archer, Adam Buchanan, Tara Clinton)

HOOKE PARK STAFF

Director Martin Self
Workshop Manager Charlie Corry Wright
Head Forester Christopher Sadd
Administrator Laura Kaddey
Technical Coordinator Edward Coo
Robotics Developer Michael Arnett
Kitchen Manager Georgie Corry Wright
Thanks Lyme Regis Boatbuilding Academy, Millimetre, Flimwell Woodland Enterprise Centre, Longleat Estate

DRL

Director Theodore Spyropoulos
Founder Patrik Schumacher
Course Masters Shajay Bhooshan, David Greene
Programme Coordinator Ryan Dillon
Course Tutors Pierandrea Angius, Apostolos Despotidis, Mostafa El-Sayed, Alicia Nahmad Vasquez, Klaus Platzgummer, Alexandra Vougia
Technical Tutors Albert Taylor, Edward Moseley, Camilla Bartolucci

Software Tutors Torsten Broeder, Paul Jeffries, Evangelia Magnisali, Octavian Mihai Gheorghiu
External examiners Stephen Gage
Invited Critics Ariane Koek, Alberto Alessi, Mario Carpo, Mark Cousins, Reinier de Graaf, Yan Gao, Samantha Hardingham, Tom Kovac, Philippe Morel, Robert R Neumayr, Davide Quayola
Students Aseem Ahmed, Alaa A K Ikbarieh, Prabhat Arora, Cho-long Baek, Caleb Baldwin, Irfan Abdul Bhakrani, Yuet Sum Samantha Chai, Sie-Jhih Chen, Taizhong Chen, Tian Chen, Jianfei Chu, Ece Bahar Elmaci Badanoz, César Fragachán, Pengfei Gao, Pendar Golfeshan, Chenlong Gu, Otrebor Jean Francois Lavado, Omar Kaddourah, Casiana Kennedy, Dahyun Kim, Taeyoon Kim, Melis Küçüktunç, Bhavatarini Kumaravel, Suyang Li, Qiquan Lu, Ali Rais, Simon Rosa Perez, Didem Sahin, Ogulcan Sulucay, Zhongya Sun, Atahan Topçu, Nicholas Rawitscher Torres, Lara Vartziotis, Dingming Wang, Xiujing Wang, Yuzhi Xu, Yuxuan Zhao, Rohit Ahuja, Leo Claudius Bieling, Valentina Cerrone, Weihan Chang, Saenawee Chatameteewong, Taole Chen, Basant Alaa Ali Elshimy, Emre Erdoğan Arash Firouzi, Anri Gyuloyan, Heidi Eunha Han, Neha Kalokhe, Ariadna Lopez, Yuki Matsuda, Sareh Mirseyednazari, Suchart Ouypornchaisakul, Ripple Shantilal Patel, Sooraj Poojari, Elena Puchkova, Rajat Sanghvi, Cherylene Marbaniang Shangpliang, Genci Sulo, Konstantina Stella Tsagkaratou, Angelica Maria Videla Cardenas, Lei Wang, Ziqian Wang, Jeffrey Valentino Widjaja, Yihui Wu, Yanling Xu, Ruilin Yang, Fei Zheng

HOUSING AND URBANISM

H&U Staff Jorge Fiori, Hugo Hinsley, Lawrence Barth, Elad Eisenstein, Dominic Papa, Elena Pascolo, Anna Shapiro, Naiara Vegara, Francesco Zuddas
Students Santiago Benenati, Polina Gladova, Kamil Hafeez, Zainab Javed, Farhana Khaleda Khan, Priyanka Sharad Kulkarni, Sebastian Montalvo Millet, Charlotte Lin Pedersen, Ayca Gulben Sapaz, Ahaladini Sridharan, Jierong Tan, Meenaal Fatma, Tanvi Grover, Wentao Hou, Prakhar Jain, Xueli Jiang, Naina Vishnu Kunta, Shukti Sahni, Bhavishya, Tara Saripalli, Amreen Riaz Shaikh, Simran Singh, Khanittha Torchareon, Wei Wen, Wenyi Zhang, Zhiwen Bian, Mariana Cesar Chaves, Lea Haddad Hyo Eon Kim, Zak Michael Lawson, Jinxin Ma, Mansi Mehta, Madelyn Pena, Giulia Sarmenghi, Selin Tosun, Preeyanan Vanichchokij, Marco Veneri, Siwat Wittayalertpanya
Special thanks to those who helped make our study this year particularly rich
LONDON Pablo Benetti, Katharina Borsi, Florian Dirschedl, Louise Duggan, Maria Fedorchenko, Nick Ffoulkes, Juliana Martins, Rodrigo O'Malley, Christos Passas, Patrik Schumacher, Dan Stubbergaard, Carlos Villanueva Brandt
BERLIN Katharina Borsi, Prof. Dr.-Ing.habil. Jörg H. Gleiter, Christoph Heinemann, Florian Köhl, Christoph Roedig
BOGOTÁ Elesban Anadon Vargas, Laura Caicedo Lopez, Juanita Fonseca, Mariana Moro, Carlos Nuñez Davila, Diana Rodriguez, Claudio Rossi

LANDSCAPE URBANISM

Directors José Alfredo Ramírez, Eduardo Rico
Studio Master Clara Oloriz
Seminar Staff Douglas Spencer
Technical Tutors Claudio Campanile, Gustavo Romanillos
Students Raul Bielsa Perez, Rimjhim Chauhan, Hao Huang, Shivani Kotecha, Seyedeh Majedeh Mohammad Syyedi, Camila Ocejo Domenge, Pafun Palwatwichai, Shobhana Parameswaran, Tao Sun, Jimmy Khanh Ta, Tianyi Zhao, Yaxin Zhao, Kai Zhu
Visiting Lecturers Fernada Balata, New Economics Foundation, Joe Beswick, New Economics Foundation, Andrew Barkwith, British Geological Survey, Elena Longhin, IUAV, Venice School of Architecture, Elise Hunchuck , Dubravka Sekulic

MEDIA PRACTICES

Director Mark Campbell
Staff Pier Vittorio Aureli, Yoni Bentovim, Polly Braden, Mark Cousins, Reuben de Lautour, Eva Stenram, Laura Tunbridge
Students Ana Olmedo Alguacil, Pete Qiang

EMTECH

Director Michael Weinstock
Studio Master Elif Erdine
Studio Tutors Lidia Badarnah, Antiopi Koronaki, Alican Sungur
Distinguished Professor George Jeronimidis
Visiting Lecturers Jens Pedersen, Aalborg University, Kostas Grigoriadis, AA, UCL Bartlett Axel Koerner, ITKE Institute of Building Structures and Structural Design, University of Stuttgart, Suryansh Chandra, Automata Technologies, Henrik Jeldtoft Jensen, Centre for Complexity Science, Imperial College London, Murat Erkurt, Centre for Complexity Science, Imperial College London, Anand Sahasranaman, Centre for Complexity Science, Imperial College London
Guest Critics Andrei Martin, PLP Architecture Lars Hesselgren, PLP Architecture, Camila Rock De Luigi, Grimshaw, Yassaman Mousavi, Grimshaw, Spyros Efthymiou, AKT II, Nicolò Bencini, Buro Happold Engineering, Mike Cook, Buro Happold Engineering, Eduardo Rico, AA
Students Itamar Amrany, Claudio Campanile, Carlos Palomera Gonzalez, Mo Liu, Maria-Christina Manousaki, Eleni Polychronaki, Varvara Vasilatou, Maria Aceytuno Poch, Theofano Antonakou, Massimiliano Battisti, Kavya Chandrasekar, Song Jie Lim, Mithuna Keshav Murugesh, Giovanna Carolina Perea Ore, Gili Ron, Sara Mohamed Adnan Shalaby, Elena Shilova, Mihirkumar Madhubhai Vasani, Shih Hsin Wuu, Shivani Akar, Abhinav Ranjan Chaudhary, Brittney Leigh Dillon, Miguel Escallon, Ti Long Fu, Neil Deep Singh Grewal, Alina Hramyka, Kutay Mert Kilcioglu, Carmen Cristiana Matiz, Heather McMenomy, Ekaterina Ostrogradskaya, Elisabeth Riederer, Rita Stella Roesch Diaz, Maritza Regina Rubio Martin, Anuradha Naresh Suryavanshi, Yufeng Zhai
Partners and Sponsors Buro Happold, Hanson Plywood, Media 10, Timber Research and Development Association (TRADA)

SED

Staff Simos Yannas, Paula Cadima, Jorge Rodriguez Alvarez, Nick Baker, Gustavo Brunelli, Klaus Bode, Herman Calleja, Mariam Kapsali, Byron Mardas
Students Bálint Bakos, Eftychia Chatzistefanou, Mana Fana, Sawant Goswami, Rupashi Govindarajulu, Nur Kayali, Deepak Maurya, Ioannis Politis, Ka Po Yung, Tony Lahoud, Khayati Mitra, Maria Andrée Osoy Escobar, Bilkay Begüm Peker, Melissa Romo Serrano, Xiaonan Zhang, Mohannad Abu Suhaiban, Maria Luisa Arze, Swati Bhargava, Kanishk Bhatt, Georgina Di Gironimo, Deep Kiran Gala, Tingting Gao, Daniel Ibarra Flores, Karthica Kalyanasundaram, Anupa Ria Kurian, Pavithra Lakshmi, Naitikkumar Patel, Poonam Sachdev Kaur, Gunveer Singh, Anjana Suresh
Contributors Rafael Alonso Candau, Ron Bakker, Patrick Bellew, Jason Cornish, Anneloes de Koff, Christian Dimbleby, Kimmy El-Dash, Peter Fisher, Brian Ford, Irene Giglio, Joana Gonçalves, Pablo Gugel, Sara Cansın Güngör, Vidhi Gupta, Alan Harries, Catherine Harrington, Richard Hawkes, Dean Hawkes Hooke Park Staff, Daniel Ibarra Flores, Massimo Imparato, Dimitra Kyrkou, Mathilde Landgren, Chris Mackey, Simine Marine, MCA Architects, Kim Morgan, Maria Chiara Multari, Fergus Nicol,Mileni Pamfili, Craig Robertson, Andrea Rossi, Harald Røstvik, Mostapha Sadeghipour Roudsari, Tomas Swett, Juan Vallejo, ZED Factory

PROJECTIVE CITIES

Programme Staff Sam Jacoby, Platon Issaias, Mark Campbell, Spyros Efthymiou
Guest Lecturers David Madden, Jingru Cyan Cheng, Josep Bohigas
Students Lucia Alonso Aranda, Raül Avilla Royo, Ricardo Palma Prieto, Susana Rojas Savinon, Vasav Vakilna, Gianna Bottema, Huajing Wen
We thank all our reviewers and guests!

HISTORY AND CRITICAL THINKING

Director Marina Lathouri
Programme Staff Brian Hatton, John Palmesino, Caroline Rabourdin, Douglas Spencer
Visiting Tutors Tim Benton, Tina di Carlo, Fabrizio Gallanti
Students Olivier Bellflamme, Maria Brewster, Angharad Davies, Stephanie Delgado, Chandni Joshi, Sophie Lanigan, Nicolas Rivera, Colette Sheddick, Roshanak Sheikh, Marko Skoblar
Guest Speakers Shumon Bazar, Tim Benton, Smadar Dreyfus, Helene Frichot, Yve Lomax, Lucie Mercier, Mark Morris, Emmanouil Stavrakakis, Georgios Tsagdis, Thanos Zartaloudis

PHD

Director Simos Yannas
Current Supervisors Pier Vittorio Aureli, Paula Cadima, Mark Campbell, Chittawadi Chitrabongs, Mark Cousins, Jorge Fiori, Murray Fraser, Fabrizio Gallanti, Maria Giudici, Sam Jacoby, George Jeronimidis, Marina Lathouri, Adrian Lahoud, Joan Ockman, Nina Power, Emmanuel Vercruysse, Anthony Vidler, Alexandra Vougia, Michael Weinstock, Thanos Zartaloudis
Students Nihal Al Sabbagh, Eleni Axioti, Brendon Carlin, Jingru Cyan Cheng, Tatjana Crossley, Georgios Eftaxiopoulos, Gabriel Felmer Plominsky, Shu Hui Andrea Goh, Naina Gupta, David Hutama, Serena Jarvis, Kornkamon Kaewprasert, Kanyaphorn Kaewprasert, Sofia Krimizi, Mohammed Makki, Olivia Marra, Gili Merin, Samaneh Moafi, Hyun-Jae Nam, William Hutchins Orr, Elena Palacios Carral, Lukas Pauer, Ioanna Piniara, Stefan Popa, Arturo Revilla, Ricardo Ruivo Pereira, Davide Sacconi, Milad Showkatbakhsh, Thiago de Soveral, Aiman Tabony, Ayse Aylin Tarlan, Damnoen Techamai, Aldo Urbinati, Alvaro Velasco Perez

Coinciding with the Projects Review 2018 exhibition are this year's *AA Book* and website pr2018.aaschool.ac.uk. Both provide a comprehensive record of the work produced by AA students this year.

AA Projects Review 2018
pr2018.aaschool.ac.uk

Exhibition guide produced by
AA Print Studio
Art Direction: Boris Meister
Design: Michela Zoppi
Printed in England by Push

Exhibition produced by
AA Director's Office with
AA Student Design Forum.

Published by the
Architectural Association
36 Bedford Square,
London WC1B 3ES
T +44 (0)20 7887 4000
F +44 (0)20 7414 0782

AA Members can access a black and white and /or larger print version of print material by going to the AA website at www.aaschool.ac.uk
Alternatively, contact the AA Membership Office by email on membership@aaschool.ac.uk or on +44 (0)20 7887 4076
For the audio infoline, please call +44 (0)20 7887 4111

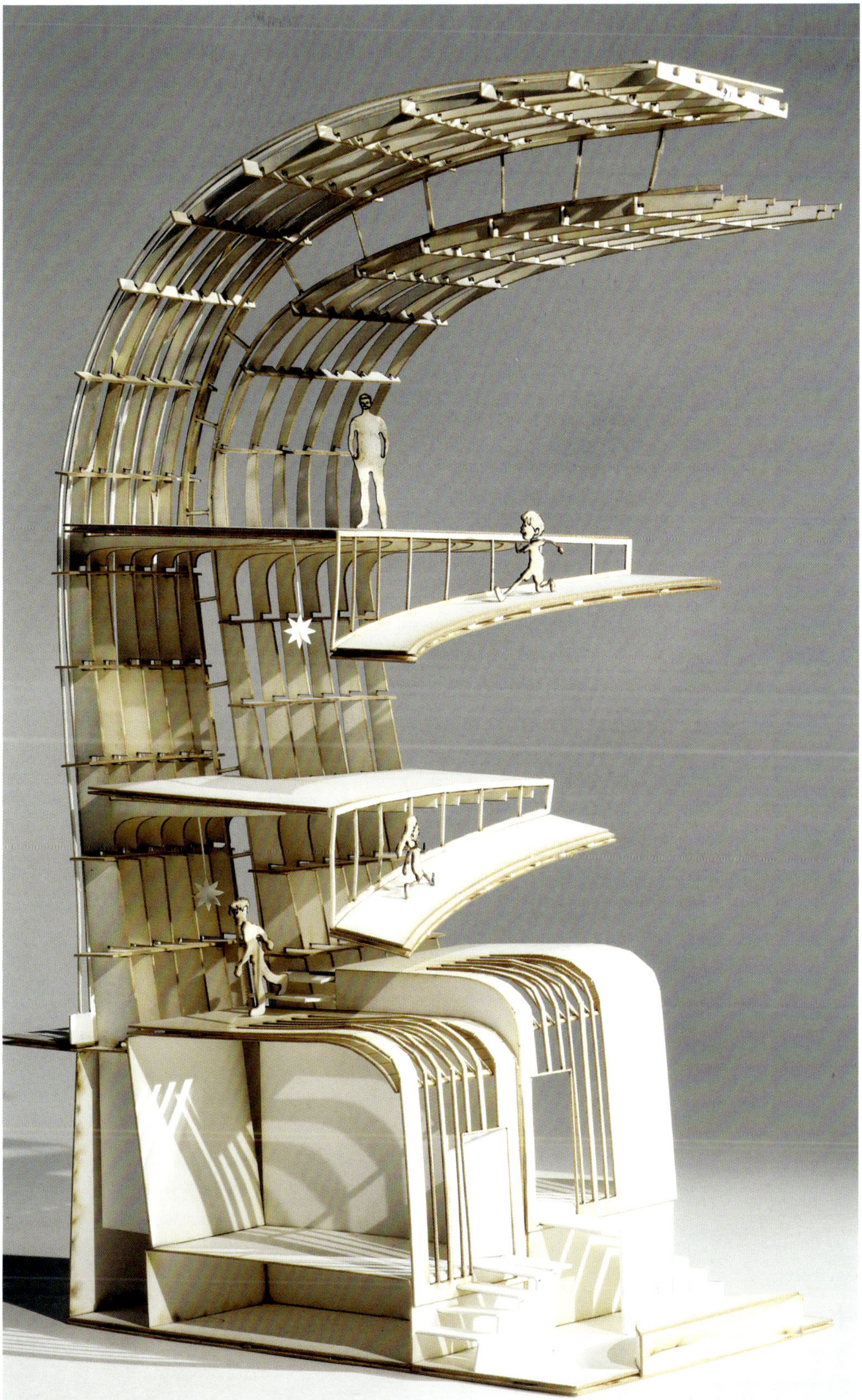

2.14

Figs. 2.15 – 2.19 Rory Noble-Turner Y3, 'A Descent into Hallowed Strata'. Located in the historic centre of Mexico City, the scheme proposes to rejuvenate the existing Pino Suárez public plaza to provide a new transportation hub and market space within a deep-excavated landscape. The project proposes an architecture of continuous excavation – a space that is constantly growing whilst adapting to ever-changing programmatic, structural and geological conditions. It was on this site, half a millennium ago, that magnificent architecture once stood, its passages and cooling channels built in honour of the flow of wind and rain. Today, all that remains of this historic place of worship is the crown jewel of the once-great complex, the central shrine to Ehecatl. The shrine's moment of resurrection has finally arrived, its position of power rightfully restored upon a new celebratory pedestal, seated at the heart of this proposed scheme. One could argue that today's modern cathedrals take the form of transportation hubs, an architecture in honour of the flow of people, cultures and ideas. This scheme aims to become just that, a future monument to a city densely layered in history and culture. A constructed ruin, where the boundary between architecture and landscape becomes blurred. This four-dimensional, inhabited excavation occurs in stages, after one year, 10 years, 25 years, perhaps even 50 years; with the architecture constantly adapting to unpredictable geological conditions, the unforeseen unearthing of Aztec remains, and the rapidly evolving programmatic and infrastructural requirements.

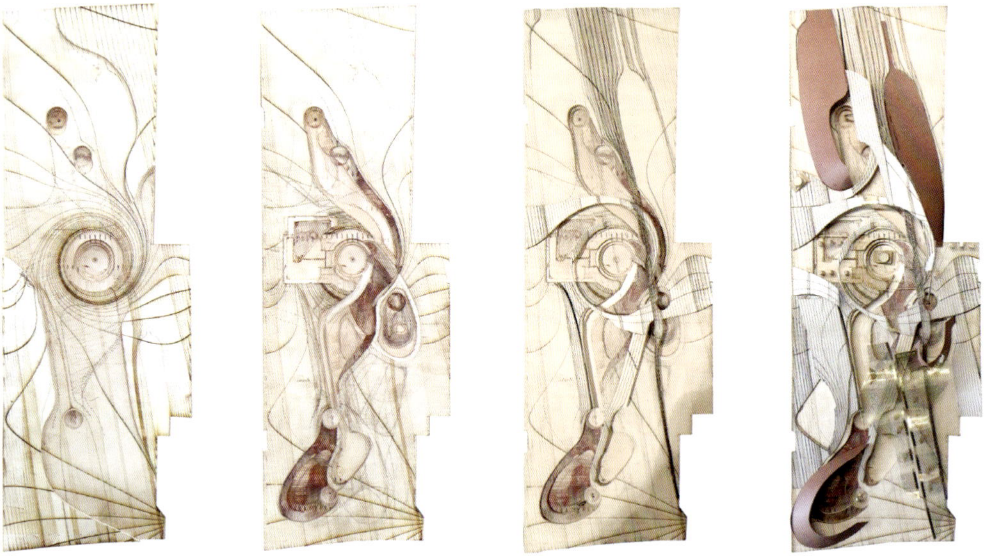

2.15

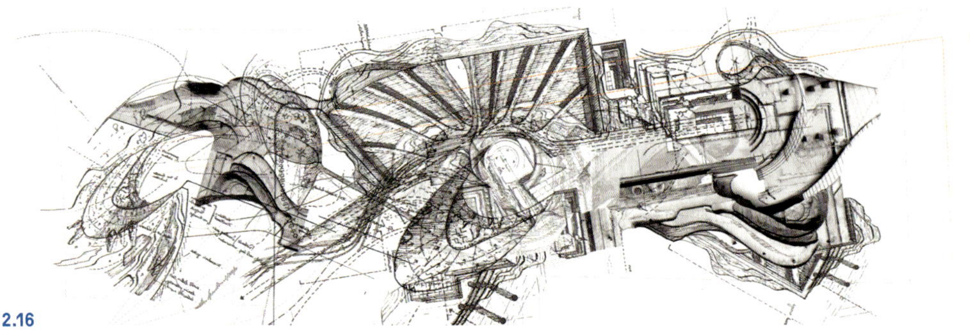

2.16

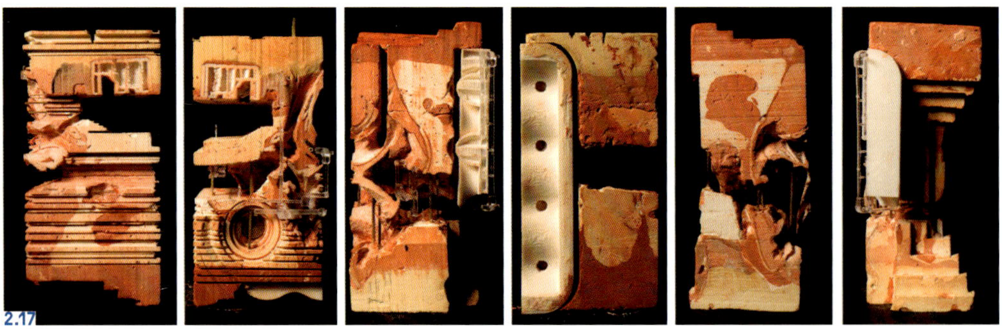

2.17

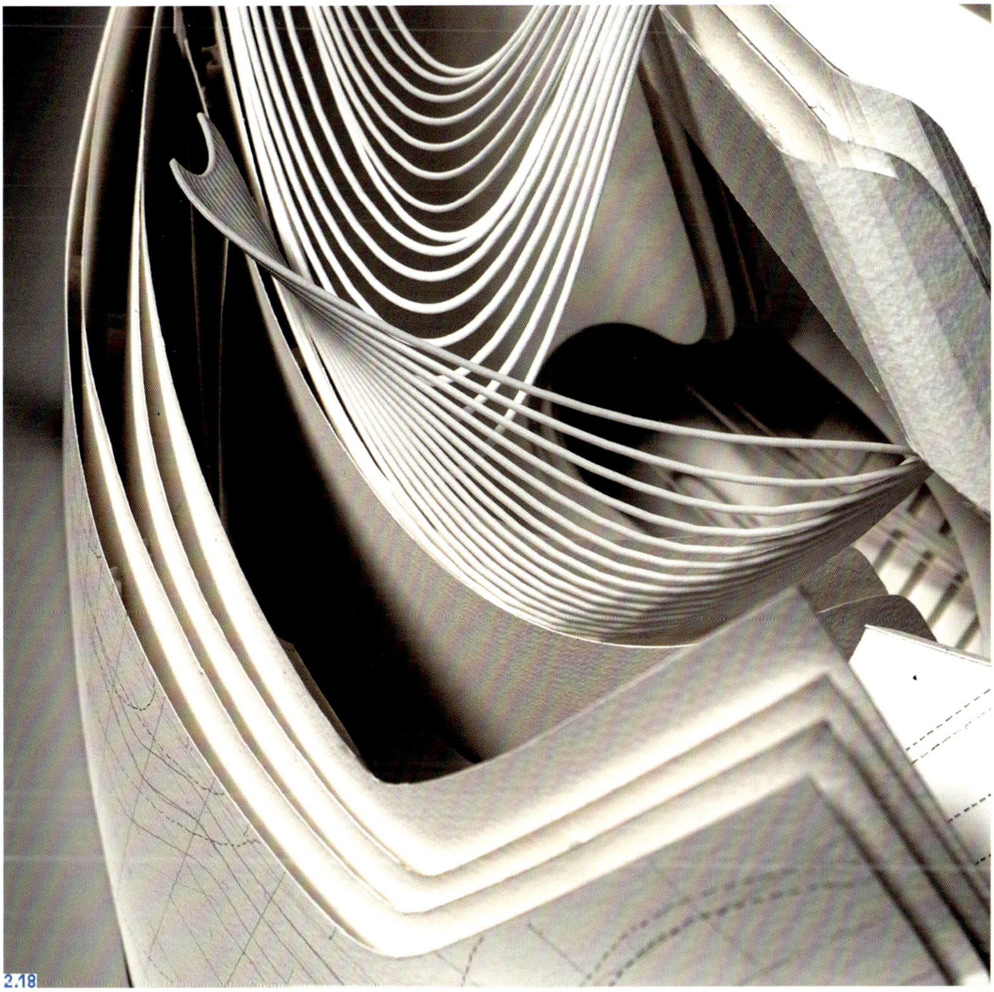
2.18

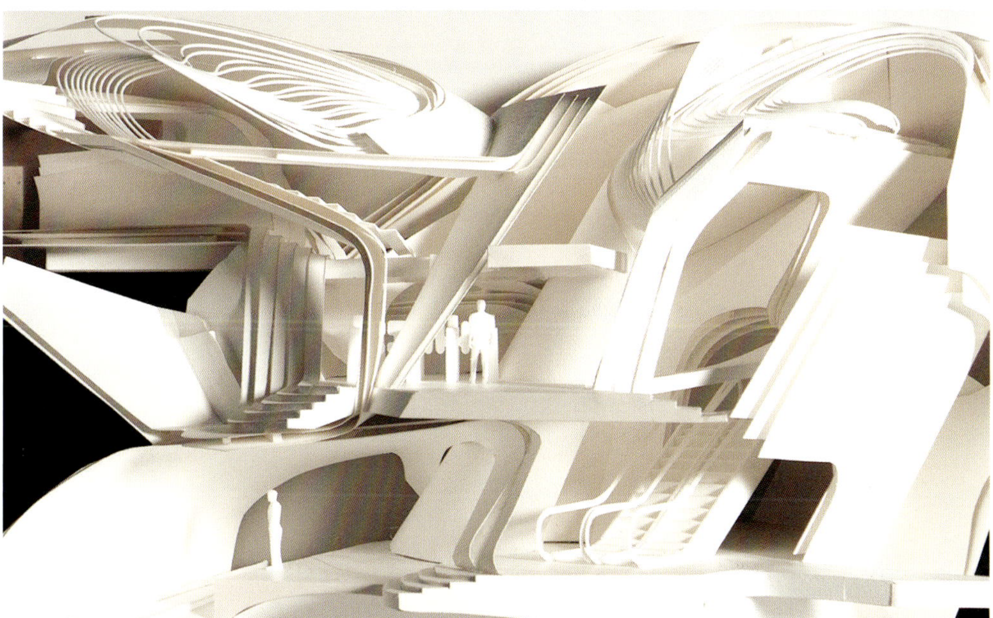
2.19

Fig. 2.20 Yuqi Cai Y2, 'Tacubaya Ceramic Gallery'. The site sits next to the 'Triangle of Tacubaya', a cultural destination consisting of two art galleries and Luis Barragan House and Studio. The programme is a ceramic artist residence. The building exhibits ceramic artworks and also provides a residence for national and international ceramic artists to stay in temporarily. **Fig. 2.21 William Stephens** Y3, 'Permeating the Gated School'. Hanging tensile structures create an upside-down school, allowing for existing archaeological heritage and public space to exist below. Intricate structural skin allows light to penetrate deep into the classrooms and ground plane. **Figs. 2.22 – 2.24 Ziyu Jiang** Y3, 'Monastic Centre'. Inspired by early studies into water flow and corrosion, the project exploits the potential of entropic design in the form of a nunnery in Mexico City. The general arrangement of water, trees and public circulation through the building forms a symbiotic system. The skin and roof are designed to absorb and collect water through porous concrete panels which gradually degrade over time. Spaces are naturally uncovered over the 100-year lifespan of the building, colours bloom over time due to the corrosion of copper panelling, light enters through increasingly porous external walls, and water is allowed to flow via its natural path through the site, as if to converse with the delicate and fragile relationship between time and architecture.

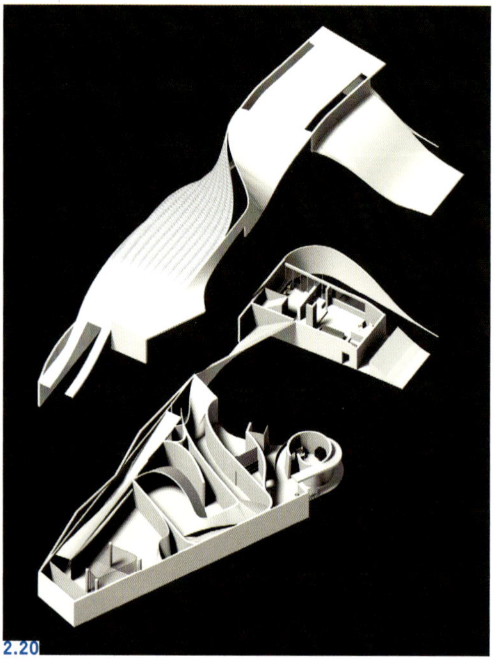

2.20

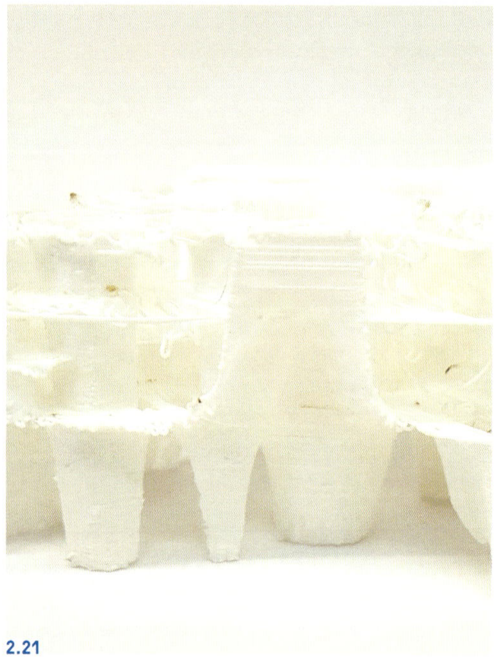

2.21

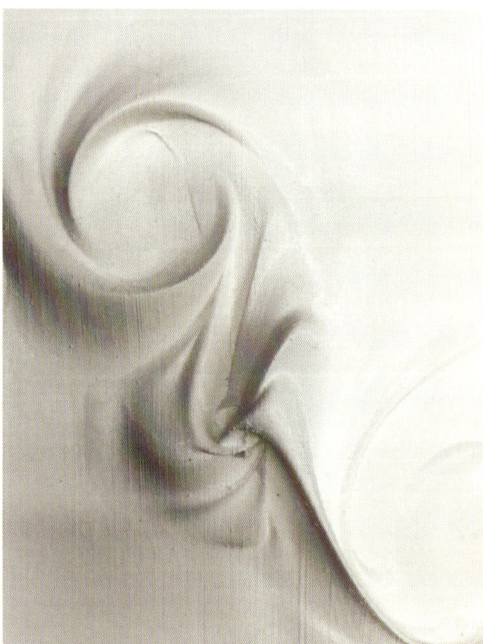

2.22

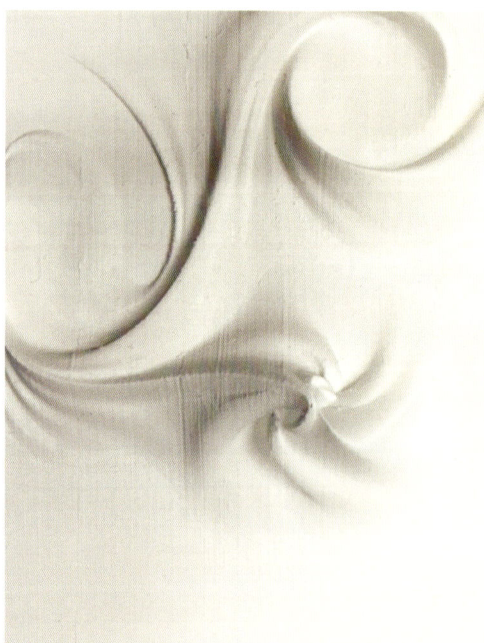

2.23

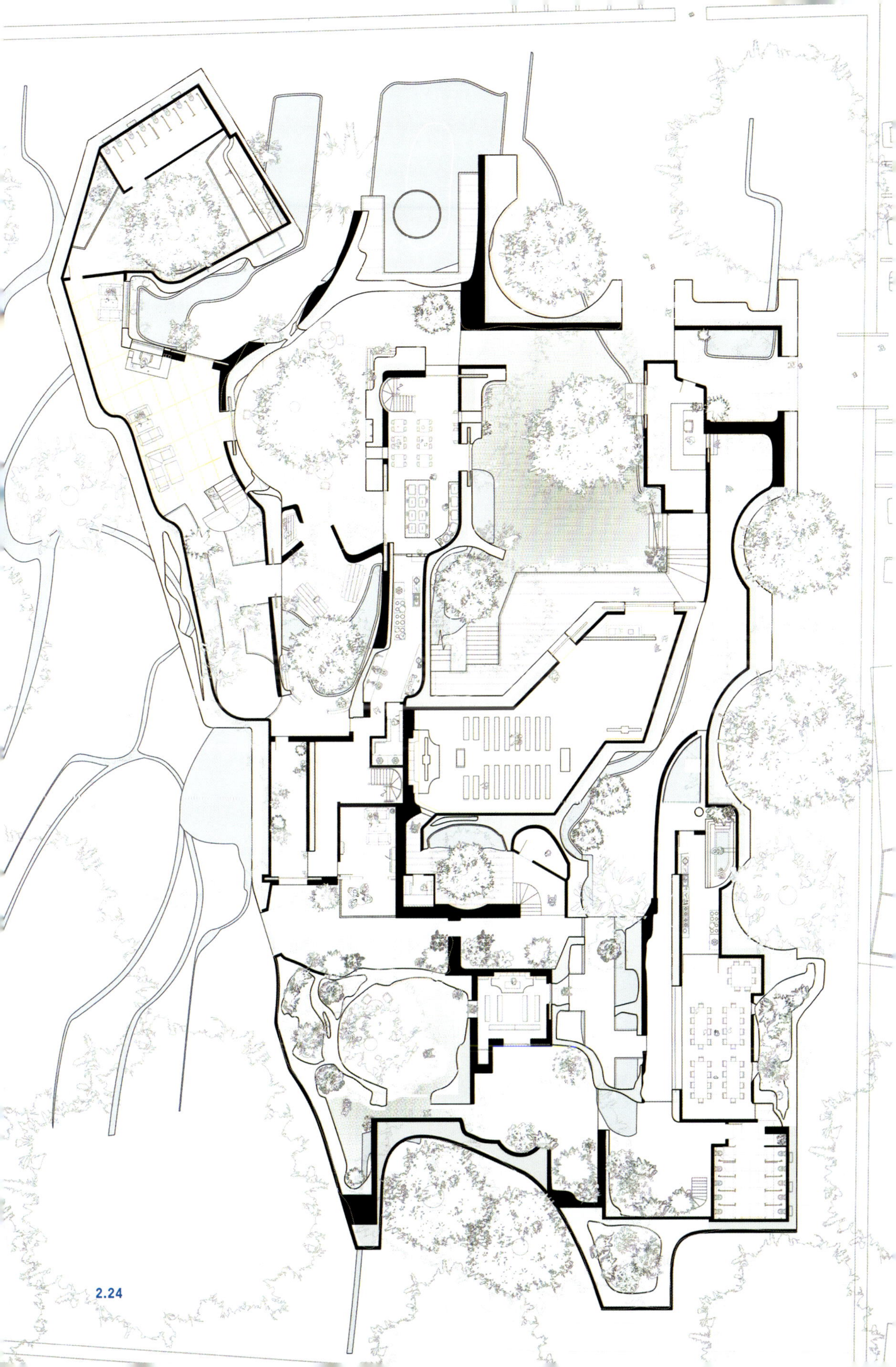

2.24

UG3

Energy Mass Light

Luke Olsen, Graeme Williamson

Year 2
Elizabeth Atherton, Liana Buttigieg, Bryn Davies, Ela Gok, Katarina Krajciova, Joanna McLean, Maya Patel, Giselle Thong

Year 3
Una Haran, Nnenna Itanyi, Divesh Mayaramani, Samuel Napleton, Luke Sanders, Ella Wragg

Thank you to: Gabby Shawcross (SOCA and U26, Tutor), Leon Chew (Modern Parallax, Cinematography), Jason Brooks (Opticalism, Visual post-production), Wayne Urqhart (Studio Archetype, Audio and Atmos)

Thank you to our critics: Roz Barr, Maria Brewster, Rebecca Feiner, Stephen Gage, Penelope Harambidou, Christine Hawley, Jack Hosea, Murray Kerr, Chris Leung, James O'Leary, Chris Roberts, Bob Sheil, Tim Sloan

"If you want to find the secrets of the universe, think in terms of energy, frequency and vibration," Nikola Tesla

Ideology
Unit 3 explores the parallel worlds of the physical (made) and the illusory (cinematic). Students' work exists between the made and imagined, the prop and the portrayal, the artefact and the dream.

Theme
We investigate ideas of energy, mass, light, duration, acceleration, the kinetic, potential, entropy, resonance, half-life, after-life, state change, transcendence and glow.

Brief
This year we considered energy, light, mass and the architectures that house power, reimagining the mute monoliths and glittering citadels that proliferate within our cities and landscapes. We explore buildings that, despite their economic, social and political might, are largely invisible and uncelebrated – as highlighted by recent politically-driven projects such as the architectless Hinckley Point Plant. Yet London has a gilded history of architect-led powerhouses, such as the iconic Bankside and Battersea Power Stations, now cultural and social hotspots. We sought to establish new terms of reference in the creation of architectures that flux, aura, shimmer and hum.

Resonant Dissipation
In Project 1, students made 1:1 objects, props and/or entities in an atmospheric, disused warehouse in East London. The interventions explore the idea of energy as light to form the basis of short films which premiered at a public cinema, The Institute of Light.

Field Trip : Reykjavik, Iceland
Energy is free in Iceland thanks to its abundant natural geothermal activity. Due to its climatic extremes, beguiling landscape, spectacular light and unique culture, Iceland delivered a tantalising test bed for this year's unit.

Powerhouse
This major building programme explicitly and openly explores the full range of ideas that a powerhouse suggests. We are interested in the interconnection between energy mass and light as contained, resonant and motivational elements within a creative design process.

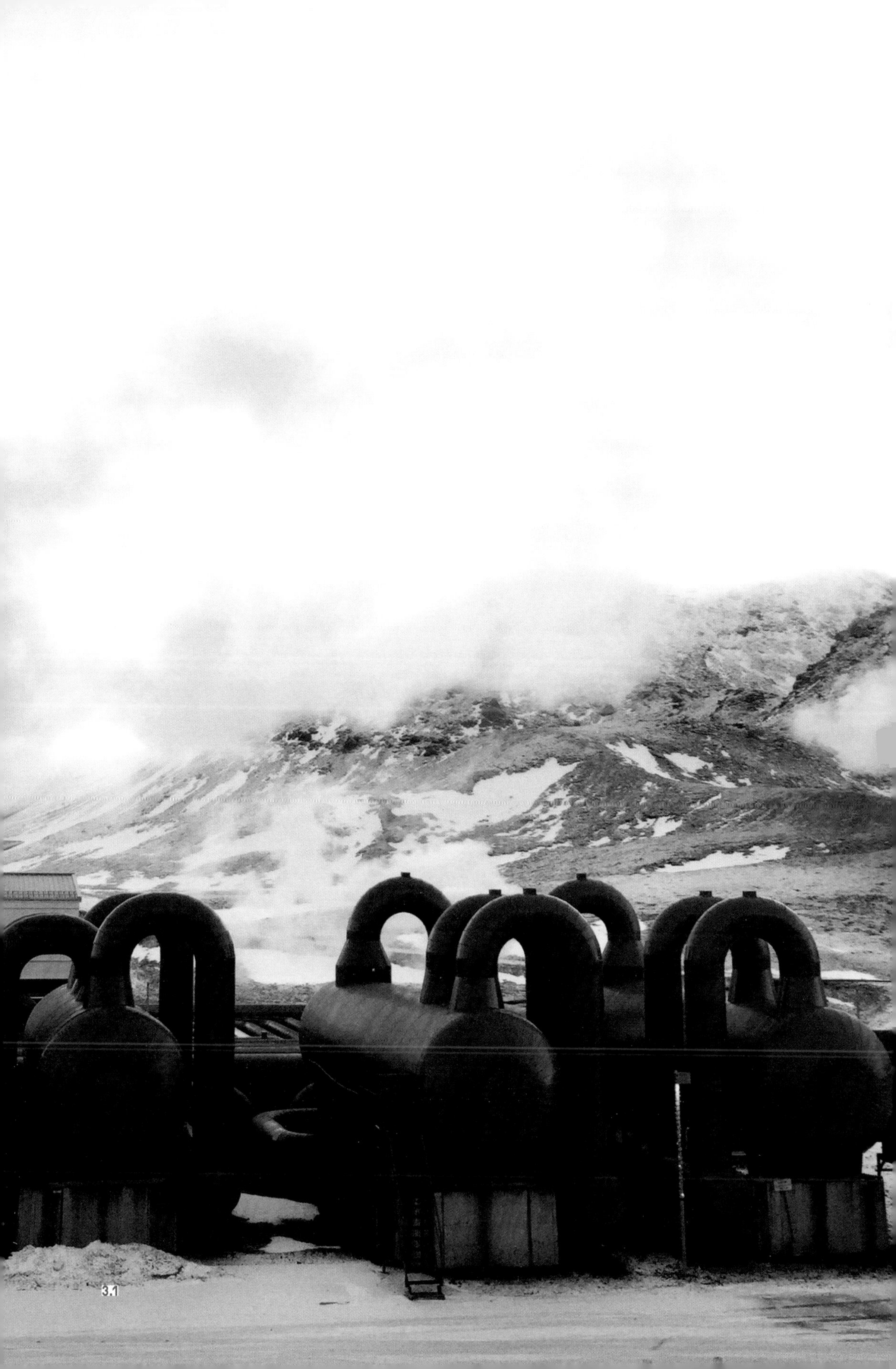

3.1

Fig 3.1 Geothermal Power Station, Iceland. **Fig 3.2 Giselle Thong** Y2, 'Nebula'. Giselle created the impossibility of a cloud floating within a disused warehouse space. The illusion is generated through the manufactured prop – in this case a framing armature holding an array of atomisers. The temporary relationships between built object, water vapour, background space, lighting and filmic sequence or photography are the parameters within which the illusion is generated.

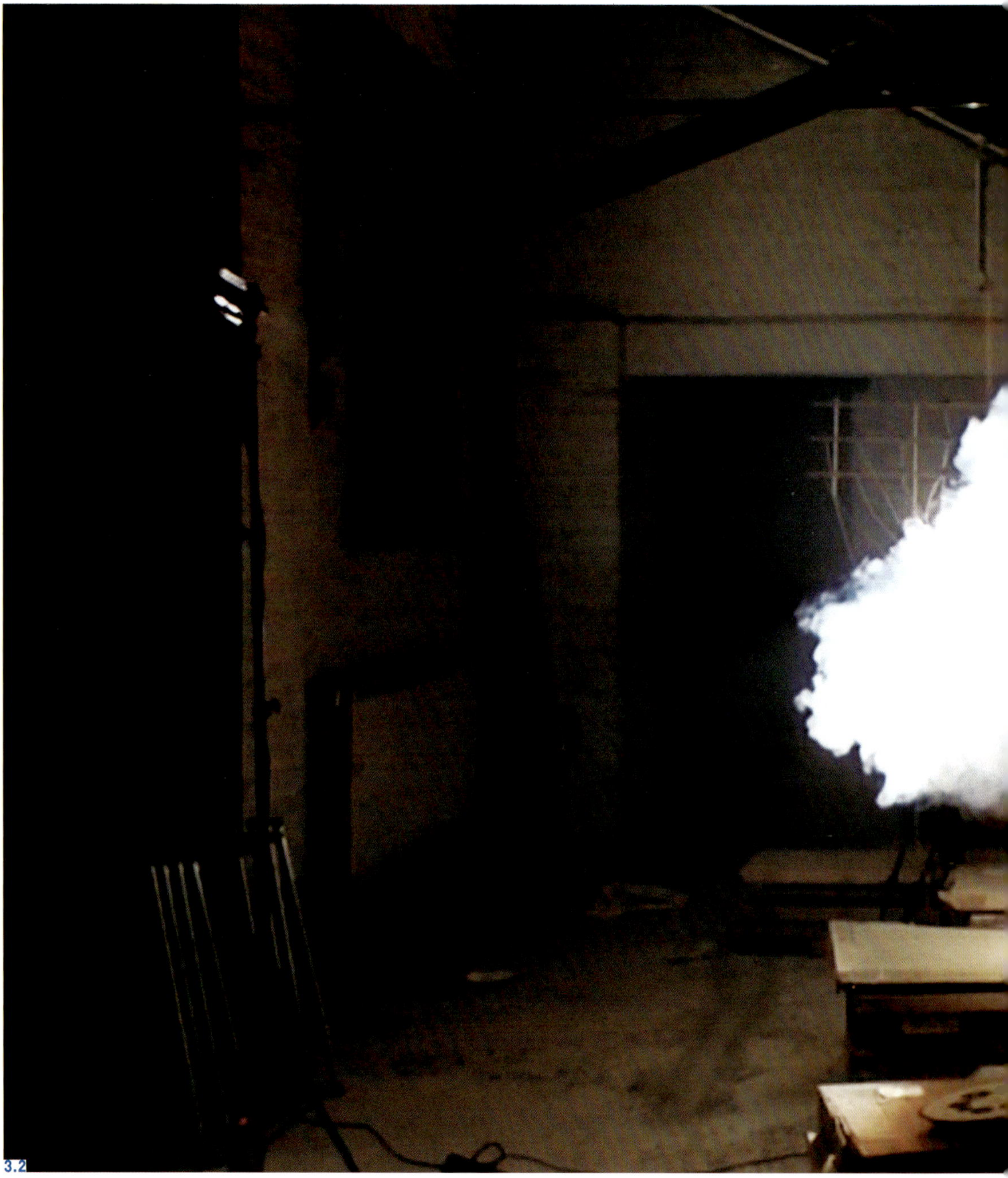

3.2

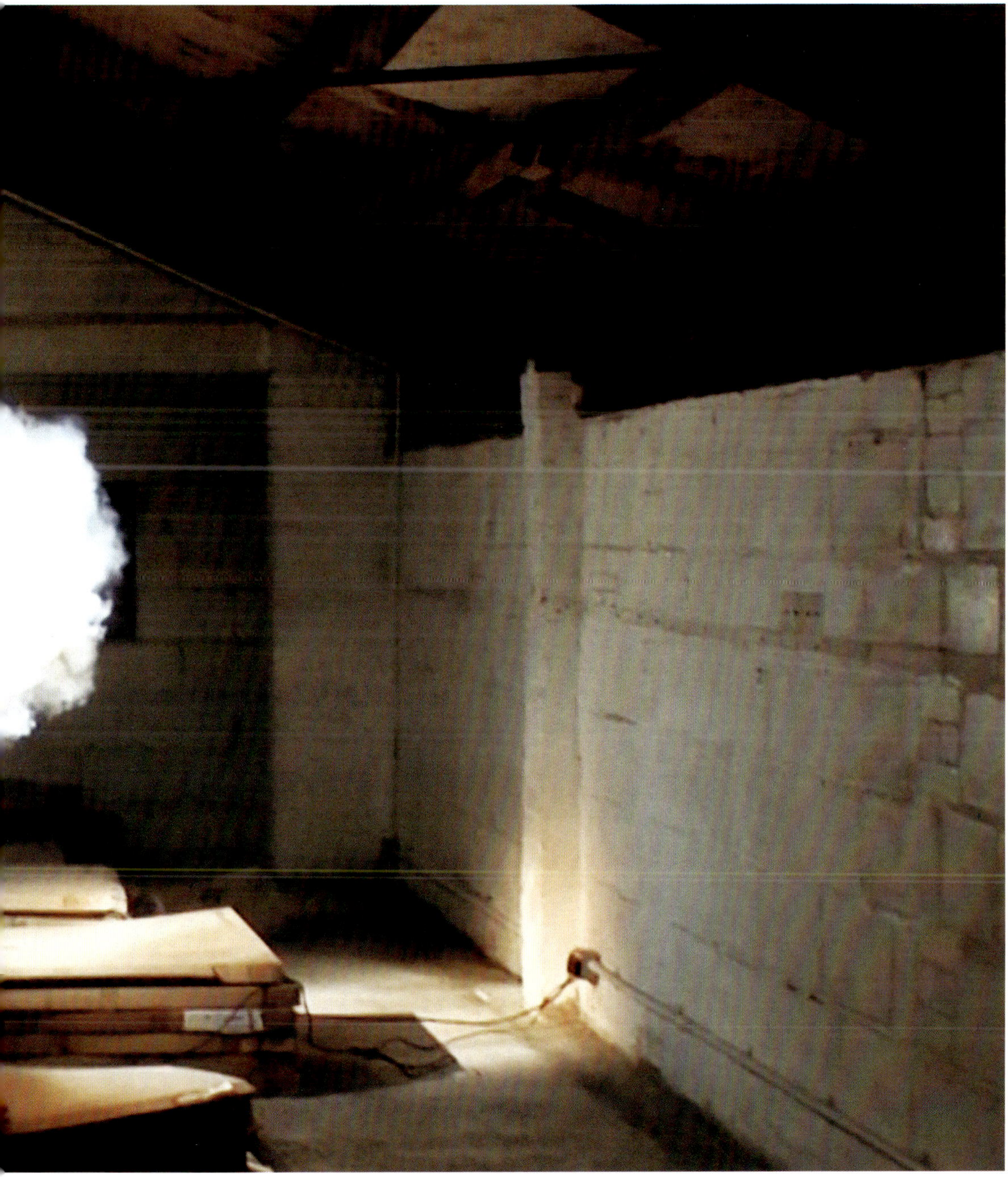

Fig. 3.3 Ela Gok Y2, 'Reconstituted Sleep'. Film still showing a series of 100 x 100mm carved wooden blocks laid out on a stainless steel mortuary table. The eight blocks, representing eight hours of sleep, were manufactured from EEG information gathered from the student's alpha-wave brain activity over the course of a single night. An animated datastream is projected from above, following the aesthetic principles of a clinical scanner. **Figs. 3.4 - 3.5 Joanna McLean** Y2, 'Crematorium, Fludir'. Charred timber cladding - building fragment test and carved timber façade study. **Fig. 3.6 Giselle Thong** Y2, 'Dance School, Reykjavik'. Modulated façade study in timber fins. **Fig. 3.7 Maya Patel**, Y2, 'Recovery In Weightlessness – Hydrotherapy Treatment Centre, Fludir'. Component study for bathing areas.

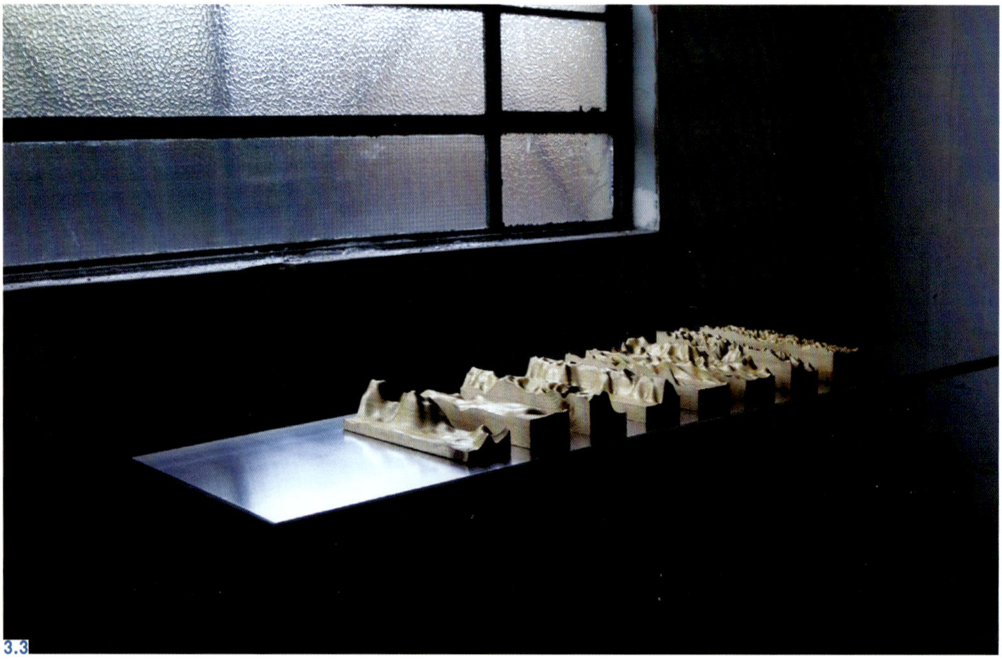
3.3

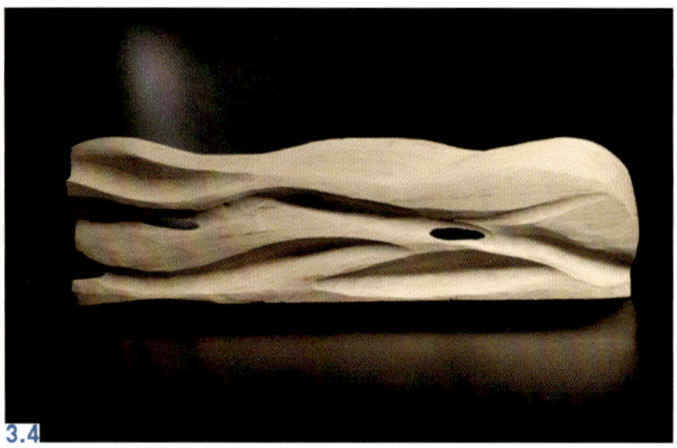
3.4

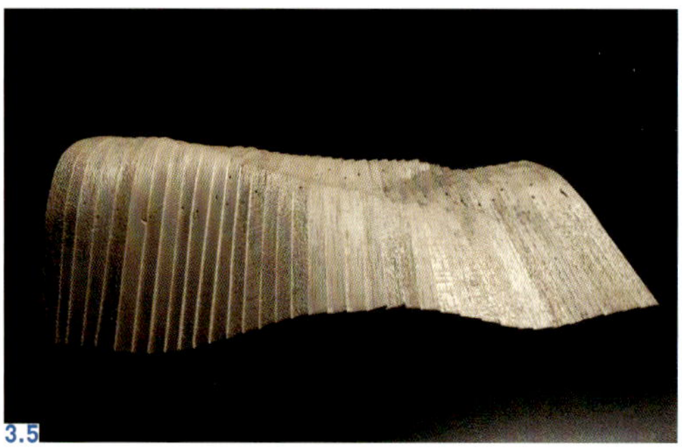
3.5

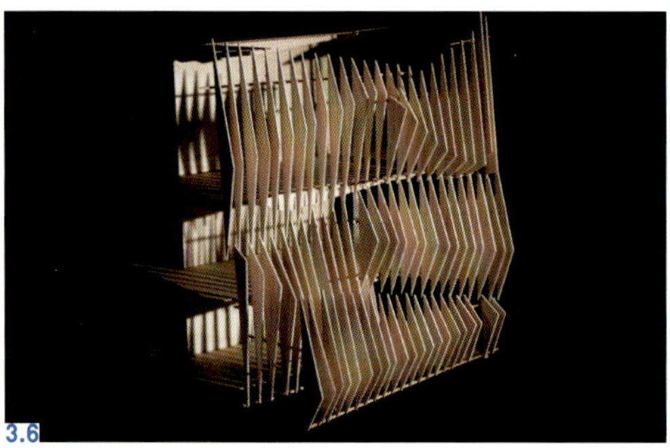
3.6

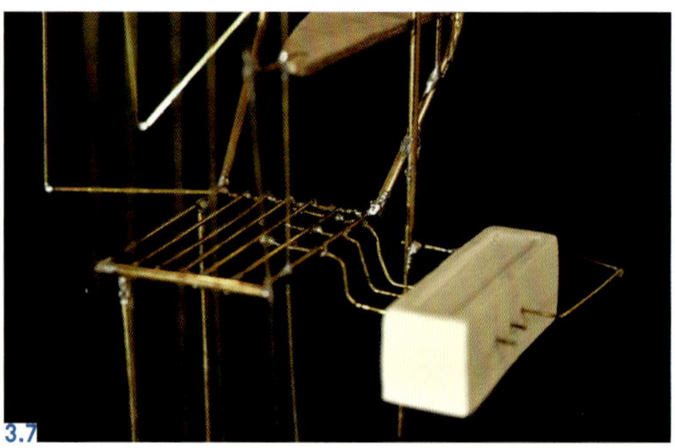
3.7

Figs. 3.8 – 3.9 Elizabeth Atherton Y2, 'Deployable Planning Consultation Unit (For Elves)', Reykjavik. Installed on new developments across Iceland as a community outreach. Adaptable structure fragment study and deployable container drawing. **Fig. 3.10 Maya Patel,** Y2. 'Recovery In Weightlessness - Hydrotherapy Treatment Centre, Fludir'. Sited in a remote geothermal location, the centre contains an array of heated pools set within the landscape.

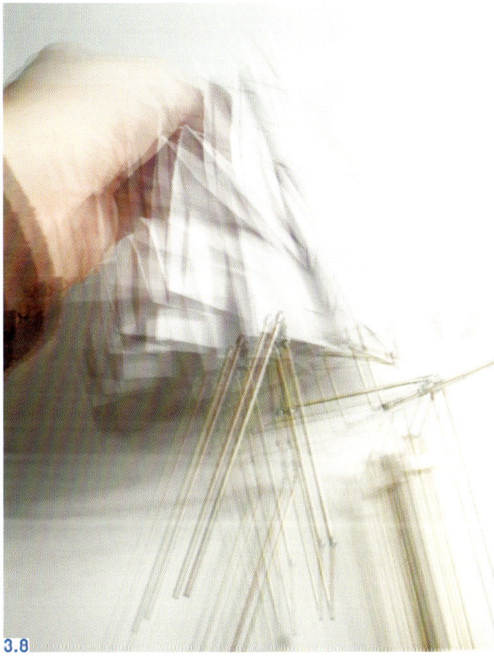

3.8

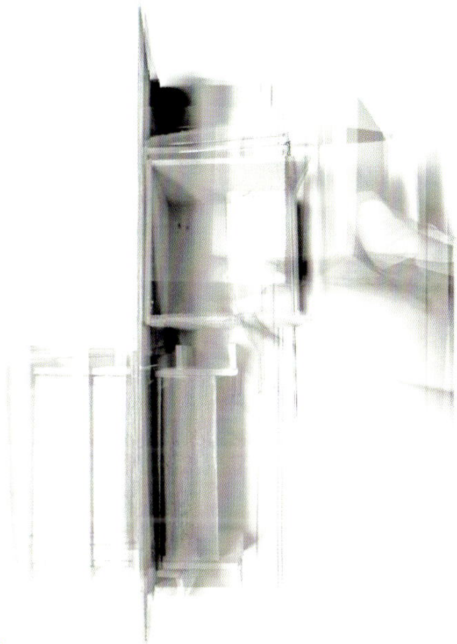

3.9

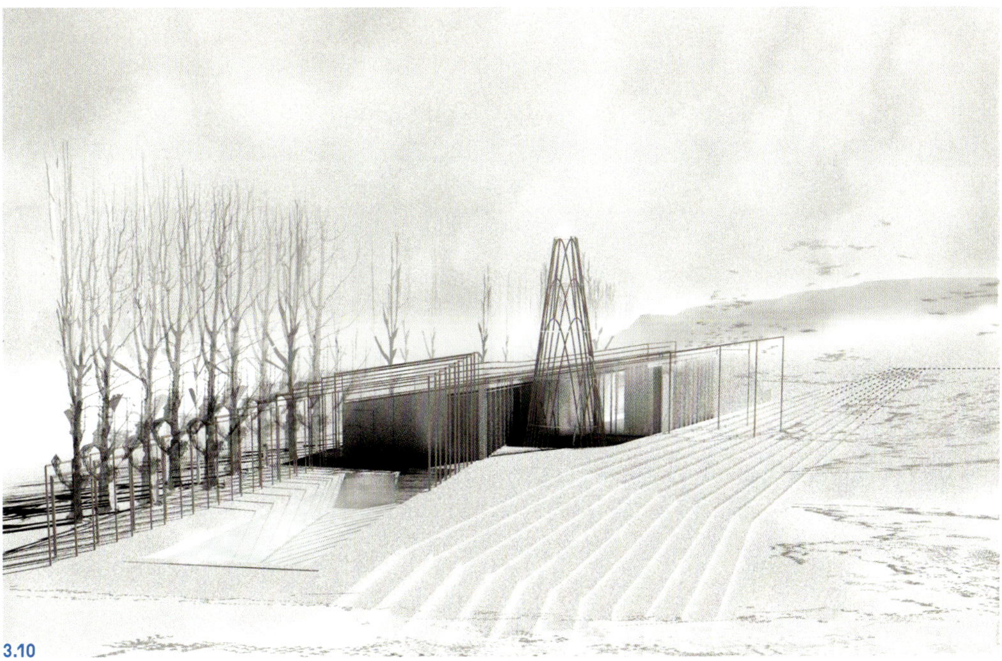

3.10

Fig. 3.11 **Nnenna Itanyi** Y3, 'Perfume Factory', Fludir. Exploded component drawing for glasshouse roof structures. Iceland is populated with glasshouses to sustain its population, and the project sought to evolve this language through the brief.
Figs. 3.12 – 3.14 **Ella Wragg** Y3, 'Prepper's Paradise', Fludir. A model of the Kvoldvaka Chapel set within a defensible compound. Both projects are located within the same remote geothermal site and adopt this free energy in equally unique ways – as light and heating for the mass production of rose petals and as limitless power source to sustain a post-apocalyptic community.

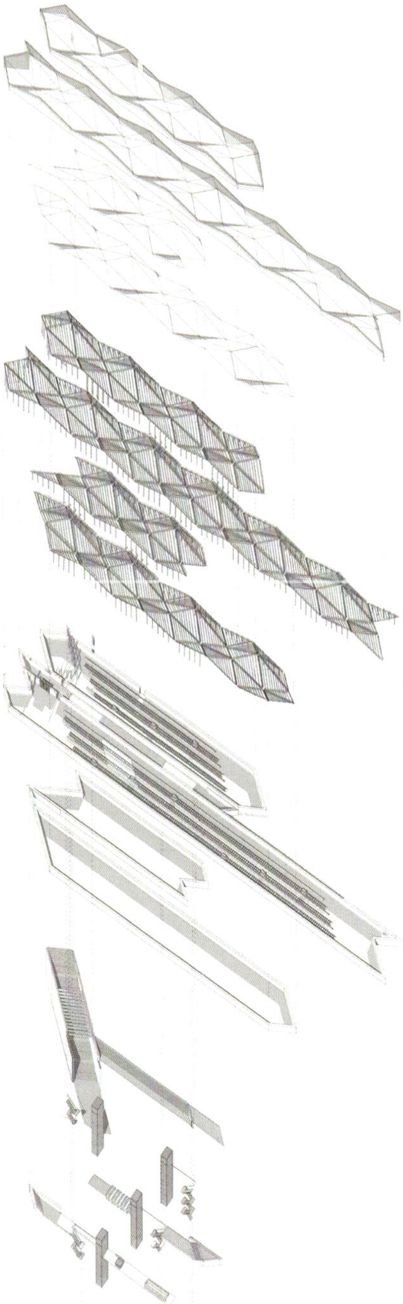

3.11

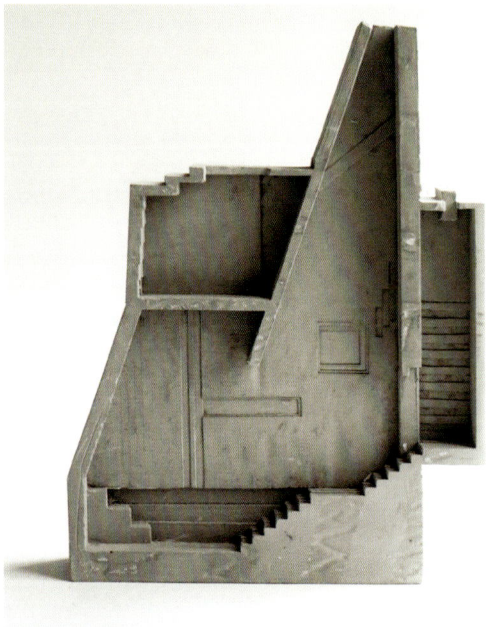

3.12

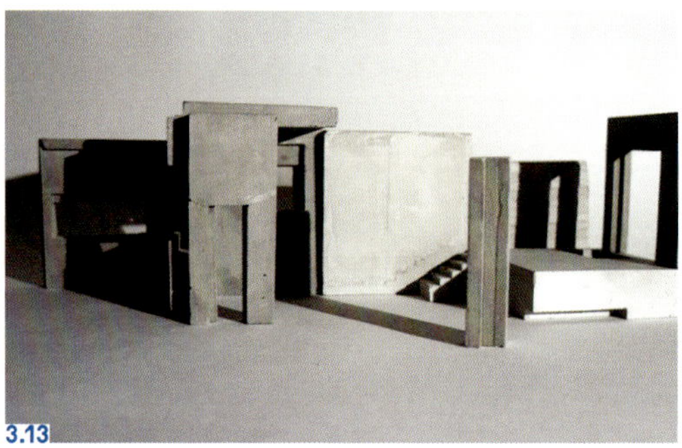

3.13

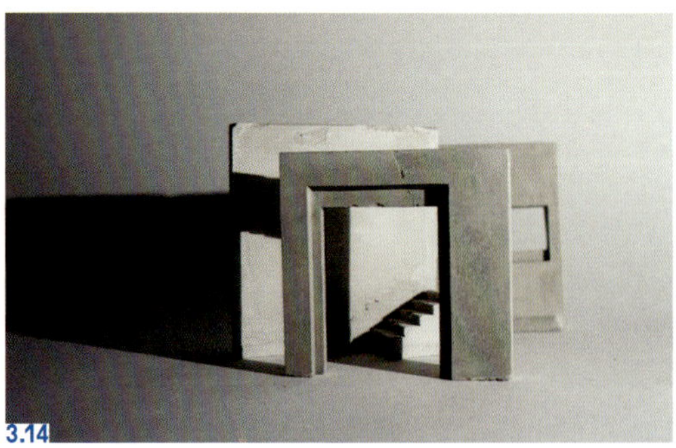

3.14

Fig. 3.15 **Luke Sanders** Y3, 'Dead Star Mausoleum and New Star Fusion Reactor', Geldinganes Island, Rekjavik. The duality of the brief sought to memorialise both the implosion of stars and the creation of energy through nuclear fusion. This is a building fragment for Dark Adaptive Corridor, which prepares visitors for night sky vision. **Fig. 3.16** **Katarina Krajciova** Y2, 'Institute of Icelandic Poetry', Geldinganes Island, Reykjavik. Projects illustrated on this page and overleaf were sited within the rough-hewn landscape of an abandoned quarry.

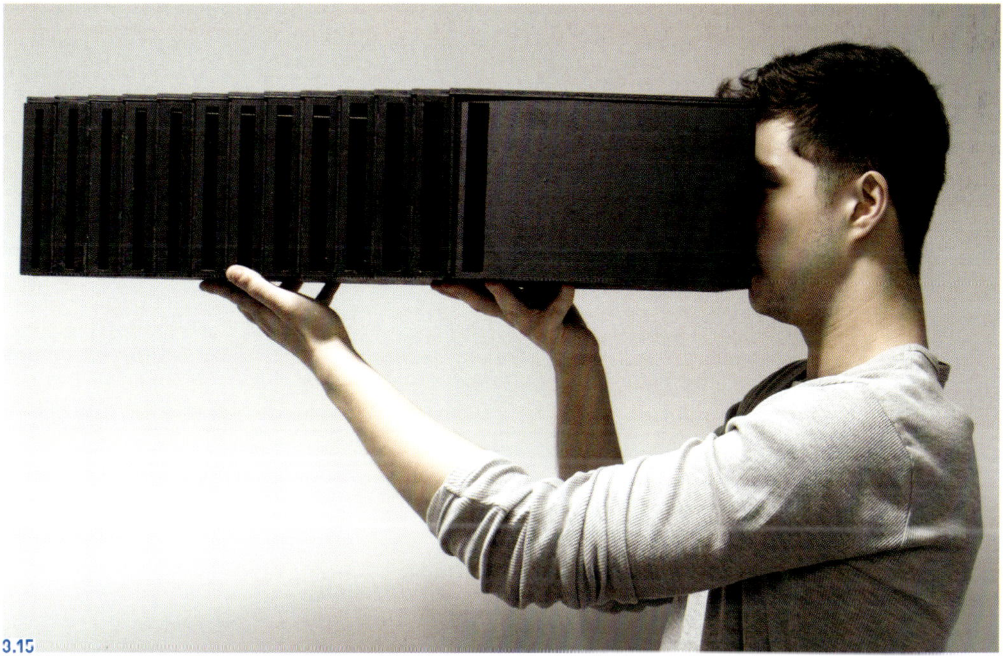
3.15

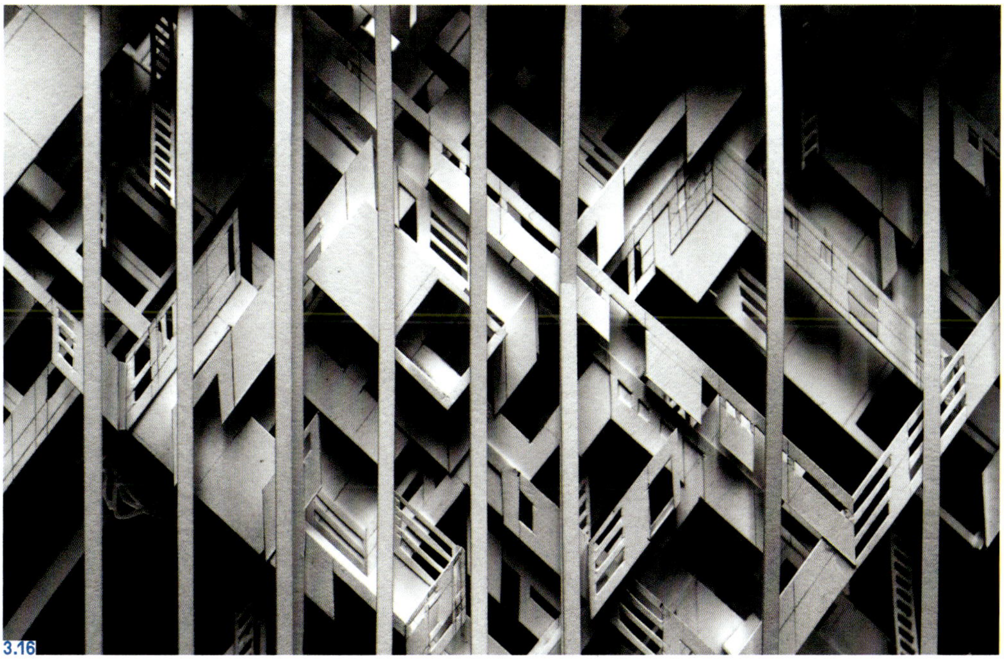
3.16

Figs. 3.17 – 19 Divesh Mayaramani Y3, 'Solarium & SAD. Treatment Centre,' Geldinganes, Reykjavik. The building adopts a solar array and supplementary lighting to capture and recreate a Valencian dusk in the form of an extended Golden Hour. The premise of the solarium brief is one of transcendence during the dark months with residents bathing in light for therapeutic benefit.

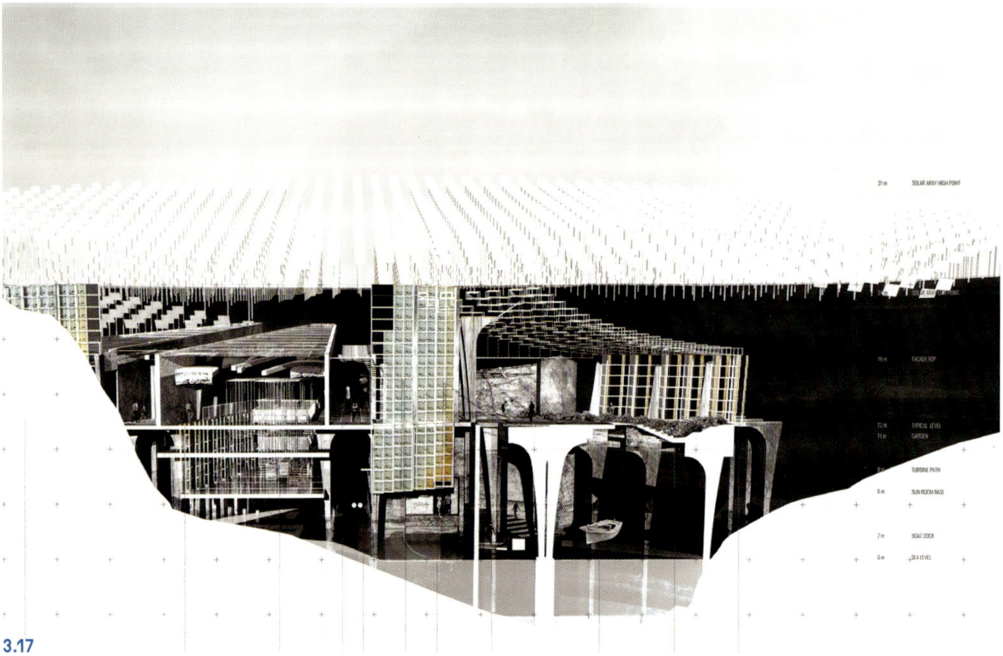

3.17

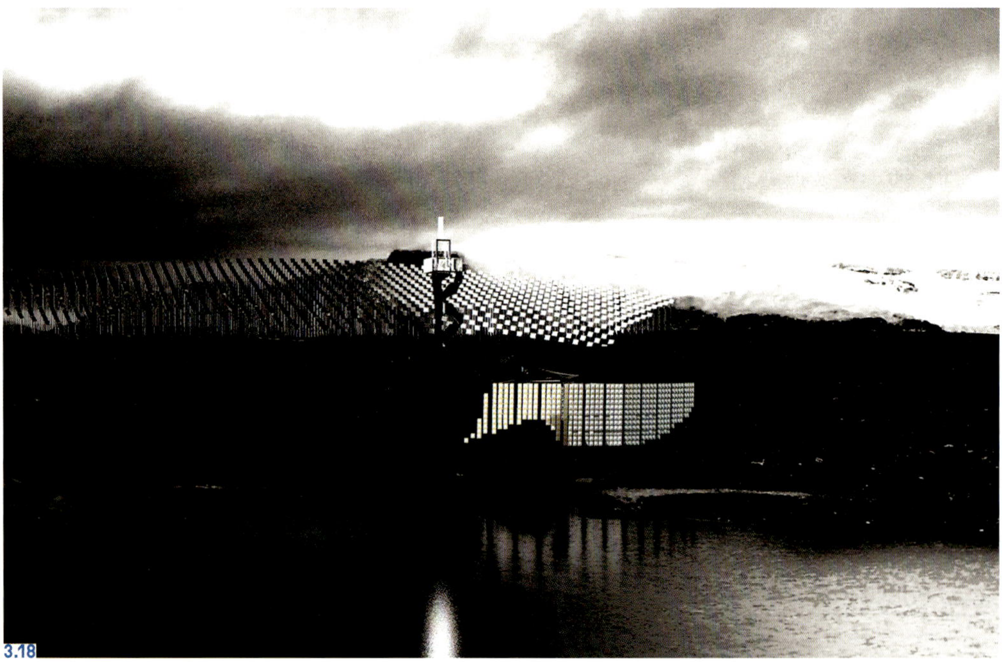

3.18

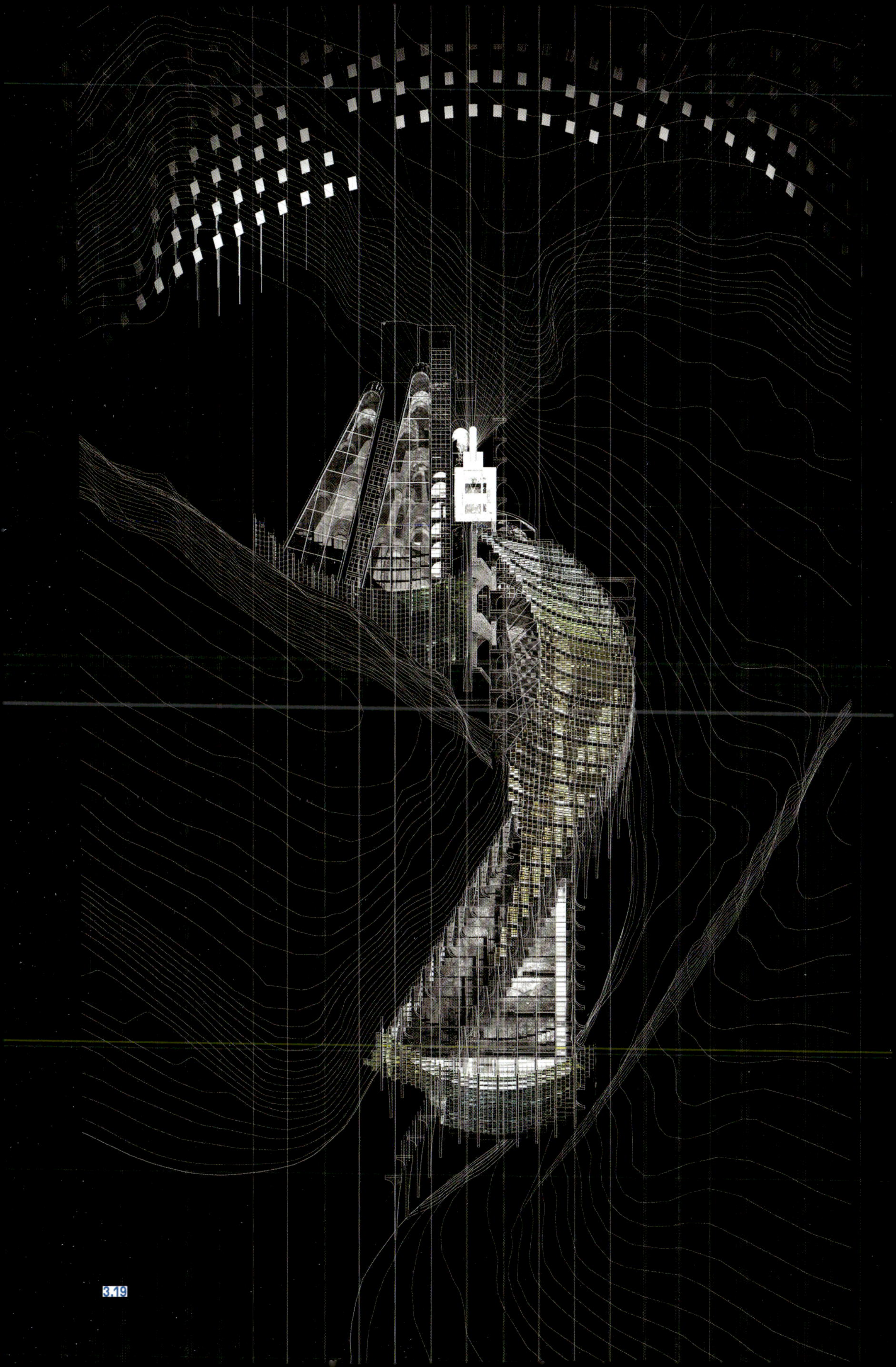
3.19

UG4

Supersaturators

Ana Monrabal-Cook, Luke Pearson

Year 2
Jack Barnett, Caitlin Davies, Aleksy Dojnow, Lingyun (Lynn) Qian, Kenji Tang, Jarron Tham, Rupert Woods

Year 3
Gabriel Beard, Se (Elva) Choi, Alex Desov, Yidong (Isabel) Li, Jack Spence, Tze-Chuan (Roger) Tung, Ryan Walsh, Hyun (Kevin) Yoon

Many thanks to Gavin Hutchison for his continued help and advice as our technical tutor. Thanks also to Sam McGill and Dan Scoulding (Studio Archetype) for their media workshops, computing tutorials and support

Thank you to our critics: Laura Allen, Abigail Ashton, Iain Borden, Matthew Butcher, Ian Chalk, Pierre D'Avoine, Oliver Houchell, Gavin Hutchison, Will Jefferies, Ifi Liangi, Jon Lopez, Shneel Malik, Adrian Massidda, Sam McGill, Hikaru Nissanke, Dan Scoulding, Stamatis Zografos

UG4 explores architectures that embody character, challenge stereotypes and engage with the public through the new media that contemporary designers have available to them. We are intrigued by the ability to tell stories and create experiences through combinations of craft and new technologies that challenge architecture by pushing the experiential boundaries of place and space. We propose architectures of communication that challenge and enhance the spatial art. Our students design events, attractors and virtual spaces as a counterpart to physical designs. We fold new technologies into making drawings, crafting models and synthesising stories into the buildings we design. Our projects strive to challenge architecture in a supersaturated world.

——This year we researched the city that provoked studies into saturation over 40 years ago – Las Vegas. The archetypal city of desire, and a mythical destination summoned from the desert by the money of gambling institutions, Las Vegas is a city borne out of the technological event, a synonym for packaged pleasure and excess. In 1972, Robert Venturi and Denise Scott-Brown produced their seminal and controversial book 'Learning from Las Vegas', which studied the ways in which Las Vegas communicated with its visitors. They perceptively foresaw architecture as a multimedia discipline. The book used the study of symbolism in Las Vegas to call on architects to appreciate pop culture rather than only designing 'heroic' monuments to themselves. But contemporary Las Vegas seems weirdly 'heroic' itself – a city of extravagance and escapism sitting alone in the desert, churning out fantasy as real tensions grow in the America that surrounds it.

——This year, our projects drew from the energy, irony and saturation of The Strip, channelling this into buildings that gazed down upon the lights from a giant man-made land formation on the outskirts of the city. VR and videogame technologies embellished structures and challenged boundaries between the digital and the real in architectural space; encrypted furniture and algorithmically generated terrazzo patterns formed the key to unlocking the *safest safe* in Vegas; new conceptions of the retreat revived the cosmic landscapes of the Native Americans and made worlds for casino carpet obsessives, while the material limits of steel created architectural mirages – buildings becoming bodies of water in times of drought.

——Throughout the year our students developed unique ways of drawing, modelling, simulating and playing as part of a design process that 'desaturated' the qualities of Las Vegas, re-injecting it into speculative projects that emerged as our architectural Supersaturators.

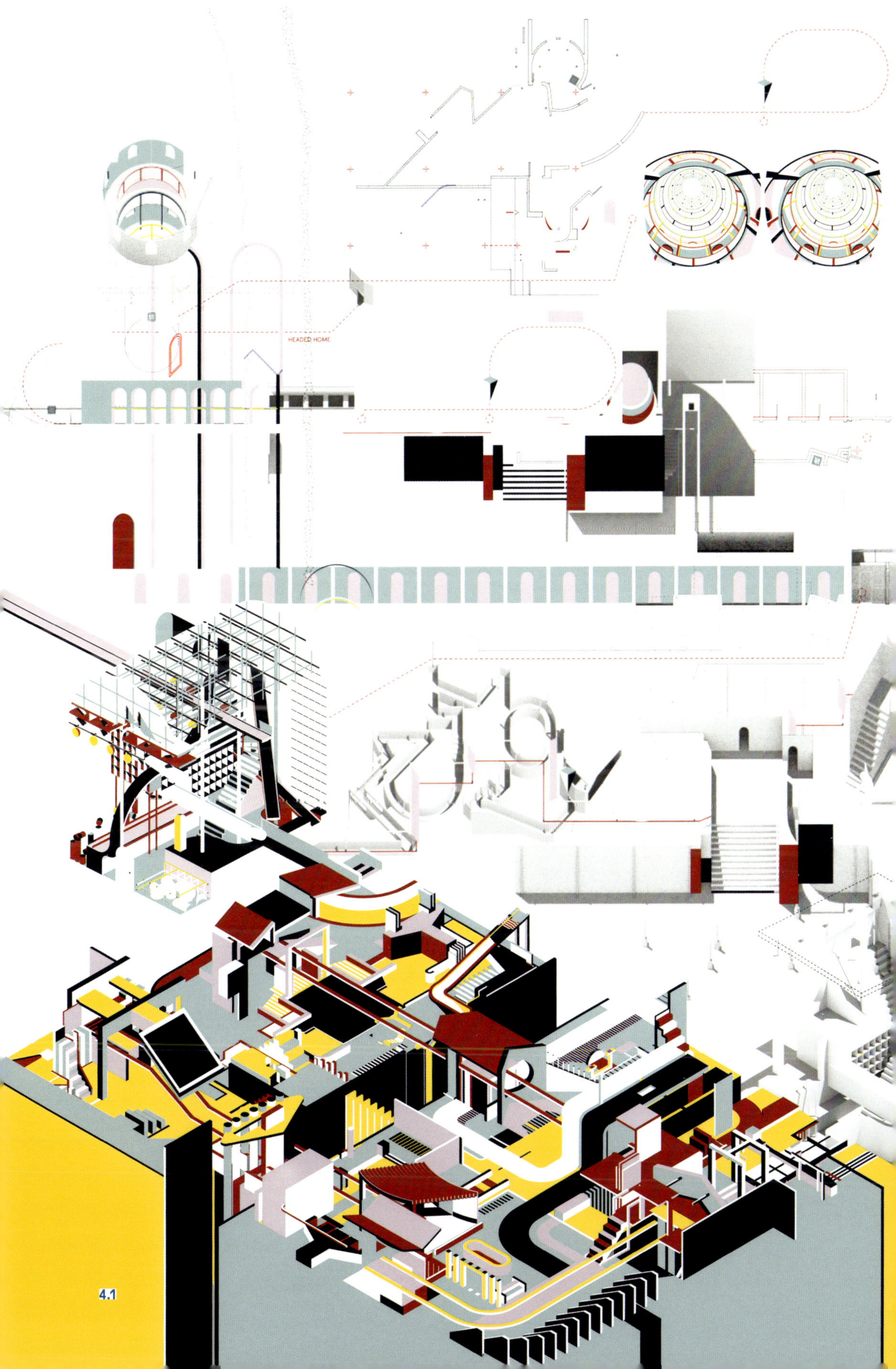
HEADED HOME
4.1

Fig. 4.1 Gabriel Beard Y3, 'Ascaya City Hall VR'. The Ascaya City Hall is the civic hub for a gated community just outside Las Vegas, which is experienced as both a physical building and virtual reality videogame space. Playing on the history of exaggerated neoclassical architecture used in American municipal buildings, the project extends this language via VR technologies. Building upon a playable architectural videogame that examines the plight of the pedestrian on the Las Vegas Strip, the project explores how virtual worlds can be used to satisfy the symbolic portion of American civic architecture. The research explored architecture in relation to videogame space, and the direct use of game-engine technologies such as Unity in architectural design. Inspired by Lev Manovich's comparison between the image-space of historical murals and contemporary VR, the architecture takes advantage of VR positional tracking technologies and research into 'redirected walking' to give the user an impression of a physically extendible architecture where space and image merge together. **Fig. 4.2 Aleksy Dojnow** Y2, 'The Almost Legal Water Hub'. The project is a centre for rest and relaxation but additionally acts as an undercover water collection and storage facility. Due to Nevada's legal restrictions on collecting rain water, the building plays with water flows both overtly and covertly. Existing as a cavern in the landscape, water becomes a priceless resource in the face of worldwide desertification. **Fig. 4.3 Caitlin Davies** Y2, 'Endangered Species'. Las Vegas is the city of the endangered. Unprofitable casinos are exploded, out-of-fashion entertainers are sidelined to the off-strip and

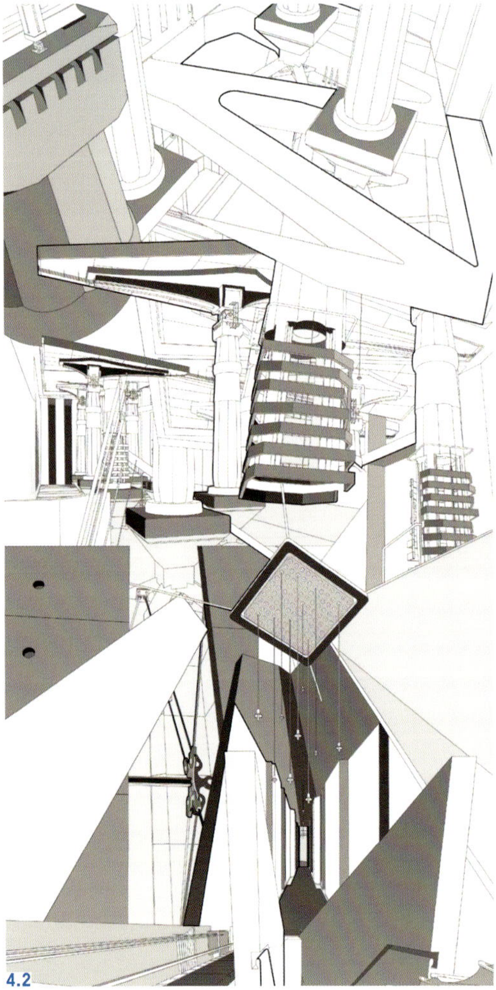
4.2

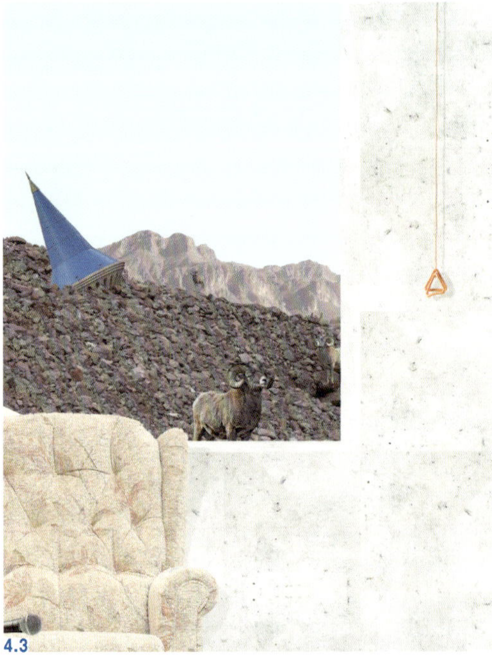
4.3

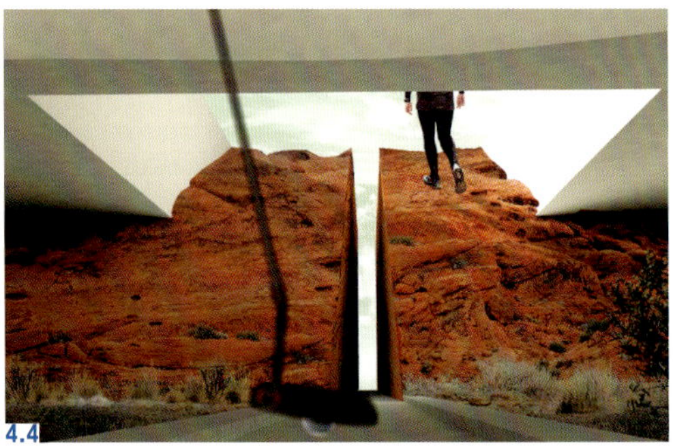
4.4

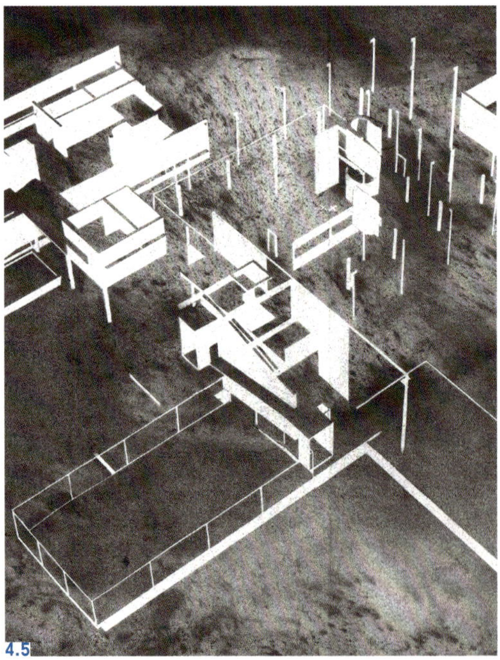
4.5

local wildlife is constantly threatened by new building works. This project preserves all three. Geriatric performers sing amongst the pens of endangered lizards which scuttle around the luminous turrets of the latest casino to be demolished, in a landscape of surreal pathos. **Fig. 4.4 Kenji Tang** Y2, 'Crazy Golf Decompression'. A crazy golf course where players de-stress from the rigours of life on the strip by pitching and putting their way through a strange Martian landscape. **Fig. 4.5 Jack Barnett** Y2, 'Modern Caricature'. The project explores Las Vegas' relationship to architectural caricature and applies it to modernism. Drawing from Gombrich's writings on the 'truth' of caricature, the project frames modernism in the window of Vegas' abstractions. By means of a series of conceptual and theoretical studies, the project explores the distillation of modernist characteristics into a series of tropes and symbols appropriate for dissemination on the Strip. **Fig. 4.6 Se (Elva) Choi** Y3, 'The Red Carpet Treatment'. Do you see carpet as 'a floor-covering made from thick woven fabric'? Do you see it as something that changes the atmosphere of the entire space, as in the casinos of Las Vegas or Gottfried Semper's origin of architectural creation? Carpet could be something more. The project proposes an enclosed resort for lovers of carpet in Las Vegas. The building includes a carpet-weaving workshop and a relaxation area amongst carpet spa and saunas. Sited on the top of a hill overlooking Vegas, the project becomes almost a site of religious revelation, a monastery for those devoted to the aesthetics and haptics of carpet.

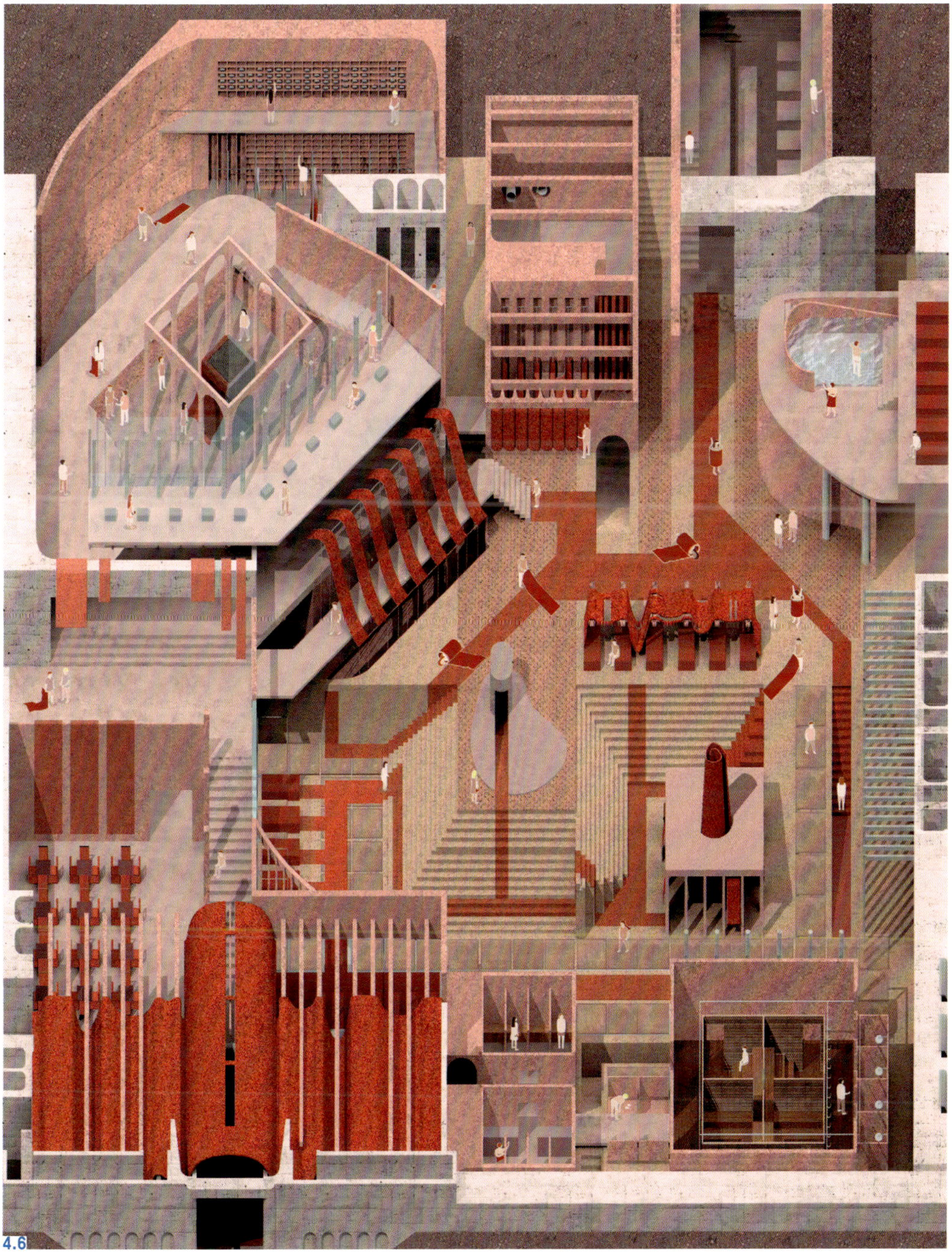

4.6

Fig. 4.7 Rupert Woods Y2, 'Title of Project'. Following research into 'growing' drawings and landscapes using Conway's 'Game of Life', the project establishes a facility for generating and distributing digitally derived replicas of the environments and architectural styles that Nevada's 'McMansions' regularly take their inspiration from. Clients watch as facsimile environments are grown from their algorithmic DNA and become architectural-scale souvenirs delivered direct to their door. **Fig. 4.8 Jack Spence** Y3, 'Ascaya Warden and Police Department'. The project plays on the fine line between America's police and the ubiquitous private security forces that patrol the inumerable gated communities surrounding Las Vegas. The building leads a double life, presenting a carefully cultivated face to the residents while also appearing pumped-up and fortified to any potential trespasser. Through the careful use of lighting, inflatable structures and light-catching meshes, the building bulks itself up by night while appearing permeable by day – an architecture that places layer upon layer of armour on itself. Here we see the building as it appears to the resident, the police officer and the criminal. **Fig. 4.9 Ling Yun (Lynn) Qian** Y2, 'The Gold Mining Museum of Nevada'. Inspired by Nevada's rich history of gold-mining, the proejct establishes an architecture that draws from the gold geography of the state and turns it into a symbolic landscape. A series of symbolic grids are overlaid onto the site, into which a series of follies – inspired by gold-mining and refining procedures – are inserted, which structure the visitor's experience as they follow a golden path through the building.

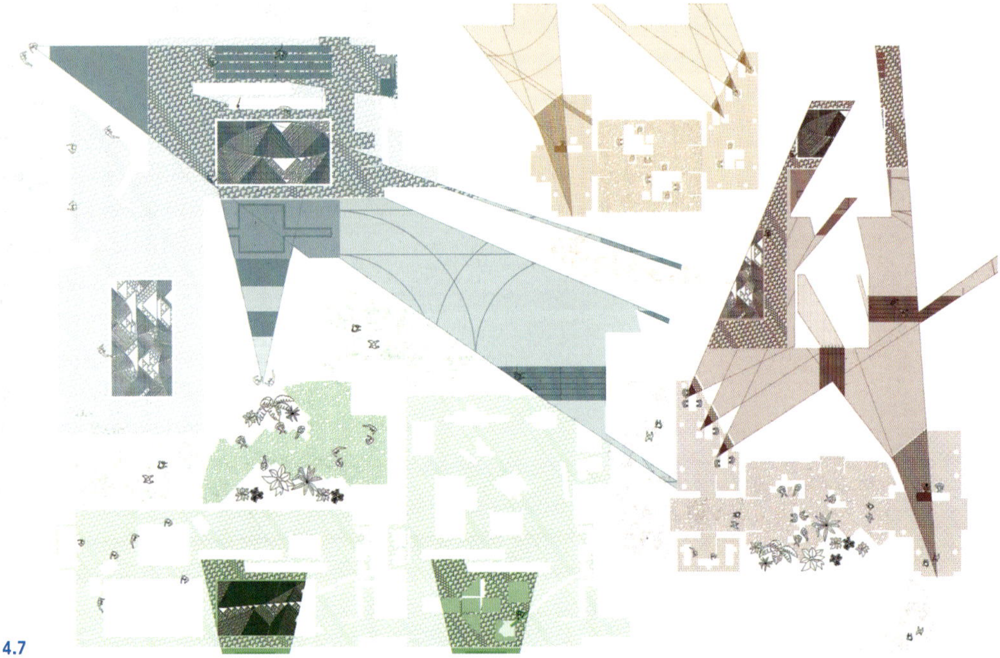

4.7

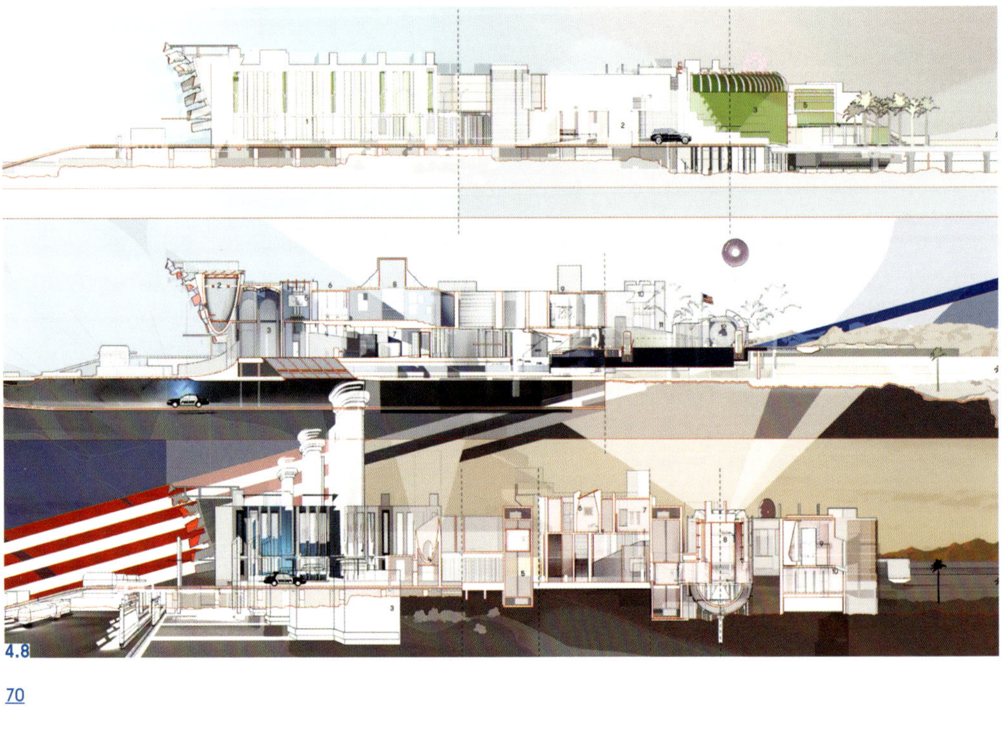

4.8

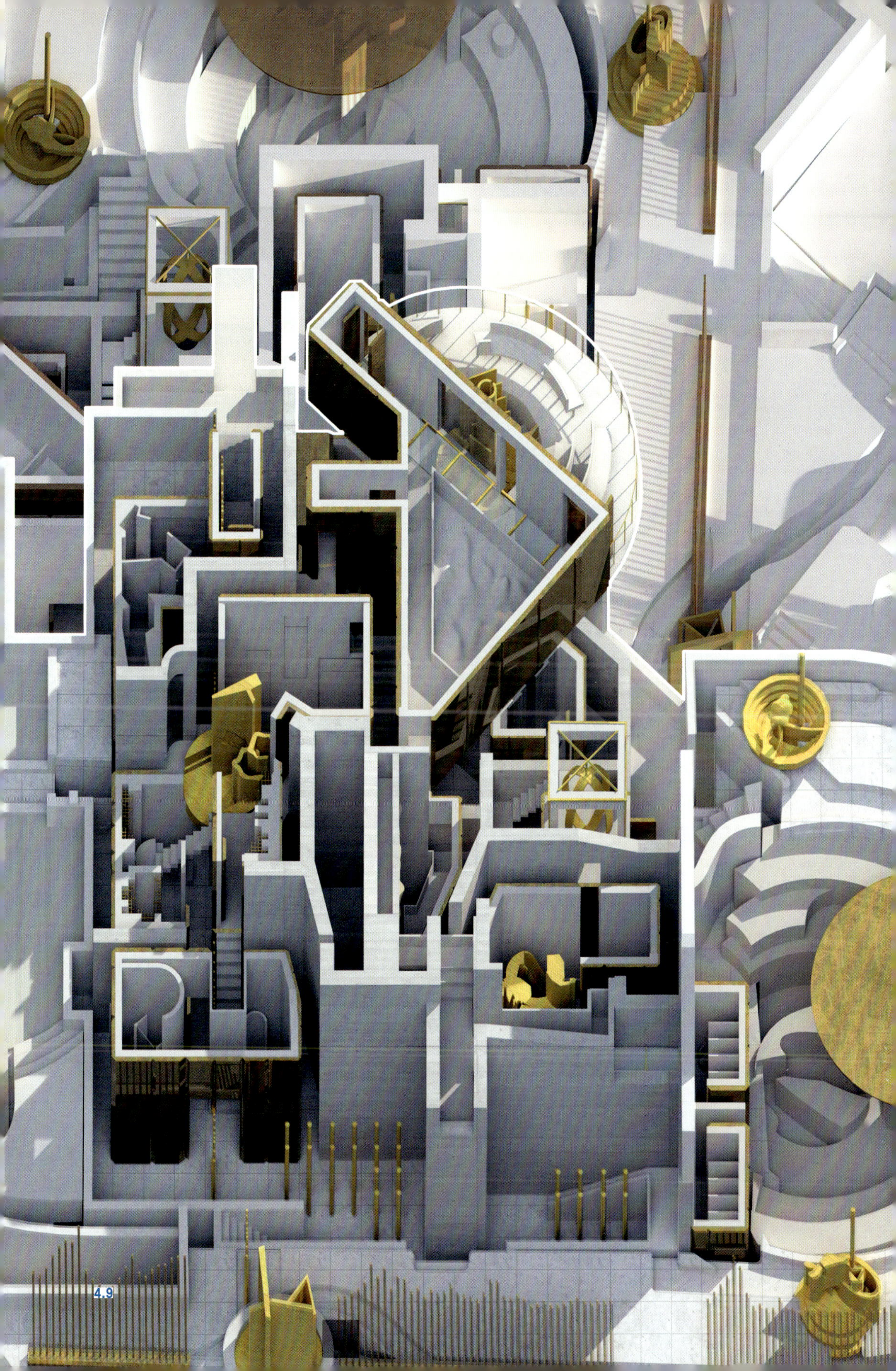
4.9

Fig. 4.10 Alex Desov Y3, 'The Maintenance Oasis'. The project was designed in response to the huge amount of cultivated landscapes within Las Vegas, and the armies of staff required to maintain them. It takes the form of a housing scheme built around an artificial oasis that uses collected water to drive a series of algae systems that turn the building into a readout of environmental conditions. By providing market stalls and community spaces, the building offers the maintenance workers of the Vegas Strip their own private paradise. **Fig. 4.11 Jarron Tham** Y2, 'UNKind: Chindustrial Aesthetics'. Inspired by Donald Trump's famed disinterest in renewable energy sources, the project also explores the vagaries of the American immigration system, where green cards can be obtained by foreign nationals bringing a certain amount of money and jobs to the US. Under this guise, the project proposes that what ostensibly appears to be a solar energy plant is in fact a private club and holiday home for rich Chinese investors attracted by these visa loopholes. Developing an architectural language, 'Chindustrial', the building, plays on recognisable forms, drawing from traditional Chinese architecture and aesthetics, combining them with industrial 'functionality.' Industrial building materials meet the protocols of Feng Shui, and Chinese characters inform the shape and appearance of spaces. Read by a US factory inspector, the building appears to be a working industrial facility, yet through the eyes of a Chinese speaker, an entire other architectural landscape unfolds. **Fig. 4.12 Tze-Chuan (Roger) Tung** Y3, 'Laser Safari'. Taking inspiration from the American desire

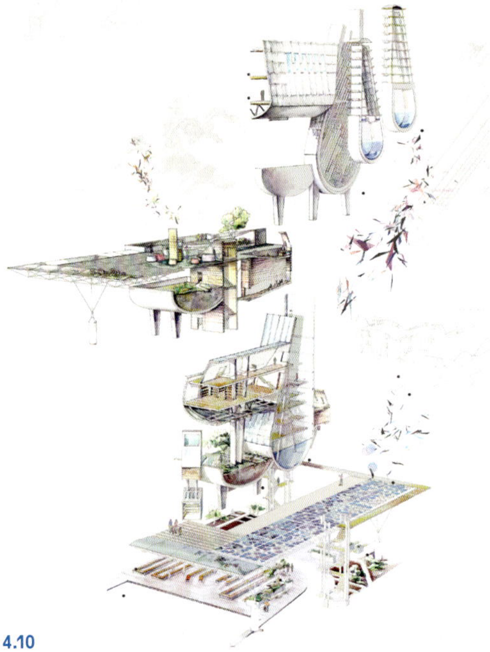

4.10

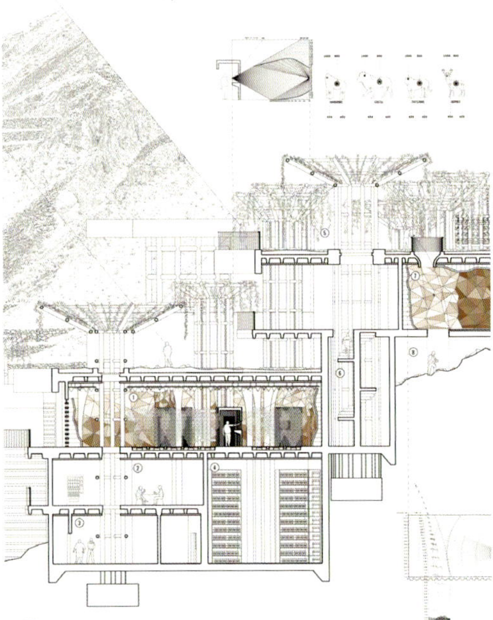

4.12

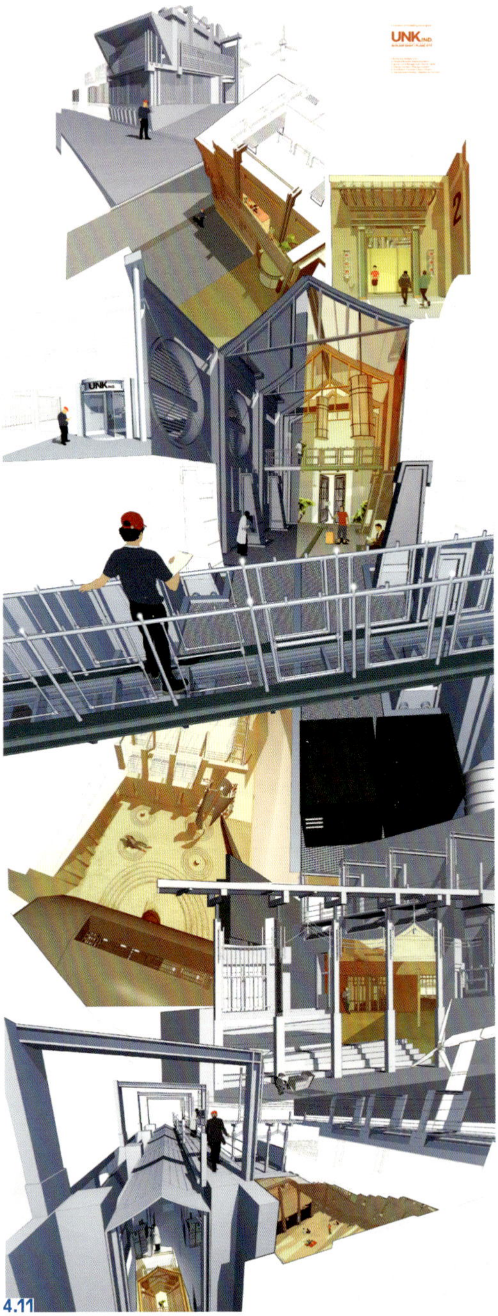

4.11

for the hunt, and the plight of Cecil the Lion, the project creates a series of facsimile environments where visitors can track and pursue animals in a supernatural landscape. Low-poly, videogame-like geometries and replica animals mix with intrepid hunters in a game with only one winner. Evoking the safari-hunter paying thousands of dollars to have their perfect shot lined up by local trackers, the building provides a satirical environment that mediates between the simulated and the absurd. **Fig. 4.13 Yidong (Isabel) Li** Y3, 'Endangered Species'. Engaging with the Native American culture of Nevada, the project transcribes the landscapes from a number of reservations across the state into an architecture that is cut into the surrounding site. Taking in Native American conceptions of the sky and the ground, the building sits as part of their cosmic sphere, connecting to above through views and to the ground through materiality. A series of sweat lodges and other vernacular spaces are woven into the building, where gentle transitions in materiality and climate demarcate the move from one landscape to another. Together, these become a microcosm of the indigenous lands that responds to the overbearing cultural appropriation of the Las Vegas Strip by proposing an architectural counterpoint that draws from the spirit of its sources rather than becoming a parody of it.

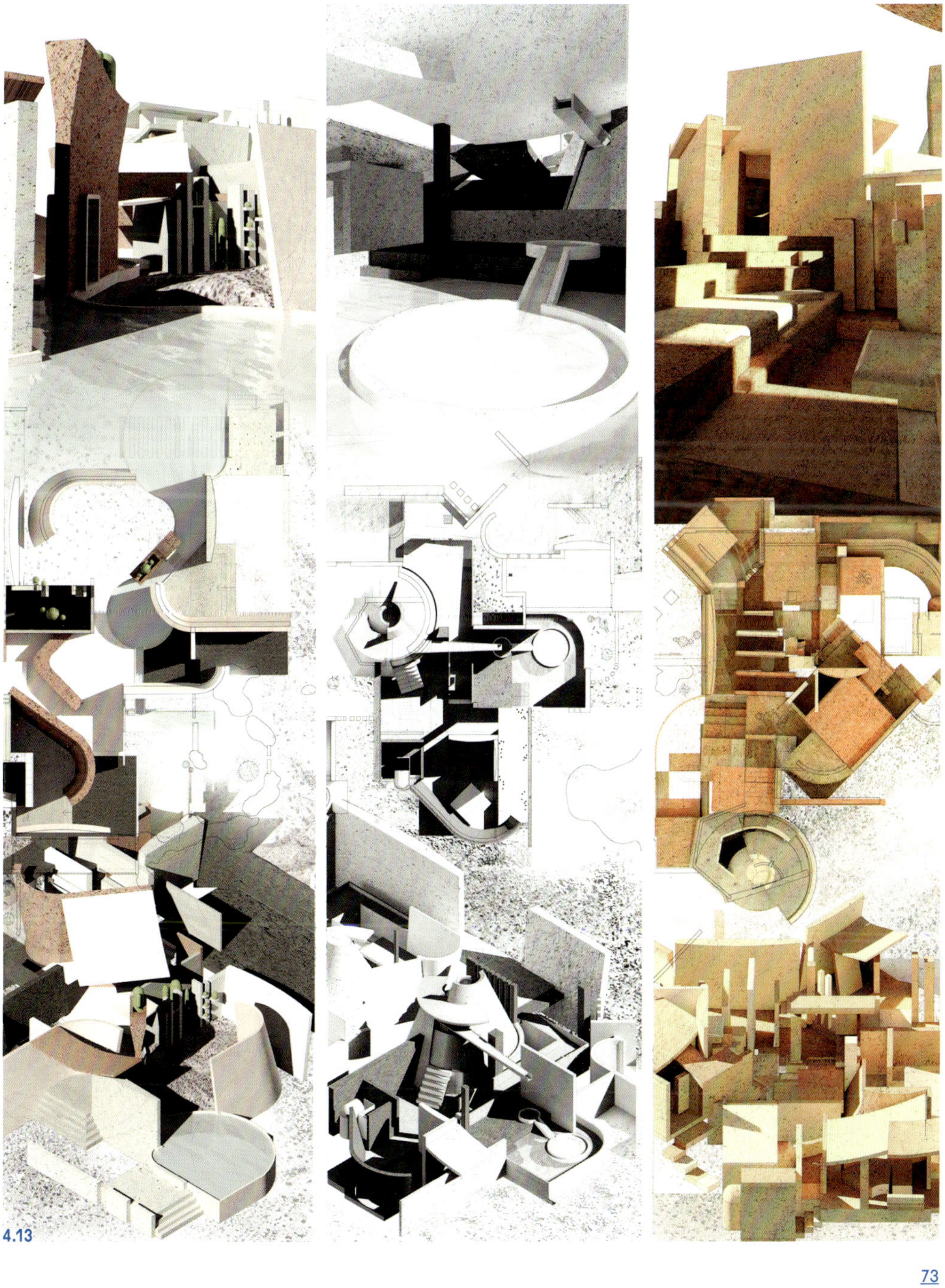

4.13

Figs. 4.14 – 4.16 Ryan Walsh Y3, 'Creating a Mirage'. Given its climate, Las Vegas and its surroundings are prime mirage country. Yet on the few rainy Nevada days, rapid plant growth raises the risks of wildfire. Water leads to fire. In response, the project, a local fire station, attempts to create a water-like architectural mirage by means of a treated blue steel roof that nestles into the site to be superheated by the sun. Underneath, a well-insulated engine bay holds the fire engines and a series of training spaces for firemen that emerge onto the roof, turning the heated surface into part of their regular fire simulations. On the hottest days, the building will appear to hover in the air like a film of liquid in an ironic nod to the dangers of rainfall in Nevada. **Fig. 4.17 Hyun (Kevin) Yoon** Y3, 'The Metamorphosing Bank'. Drawing from first term research into the protocols of augmented reality technologies, and how to manipulate them in physical space through architectural models, the project questions how an architecture itself may act as a 'lock'. Proposing the 'Safest Safe' in Las Vegas, the building unfolds through an augmented choreography carried out by the clients. Elements of the built fabric push, slide and lock into place causing the building to respond. Algorithmically designed terrazzo surfaces combine ornamentation with advanced security features that explore how contemporary digital encryption techniques could be applied to architecture. Finally, a series of augmented reality drawings built in the Unity game engine, seen through the Vuforia AR app, show the spatial effect of these systems, updating to reflect the viewer's interaction with them in real time.

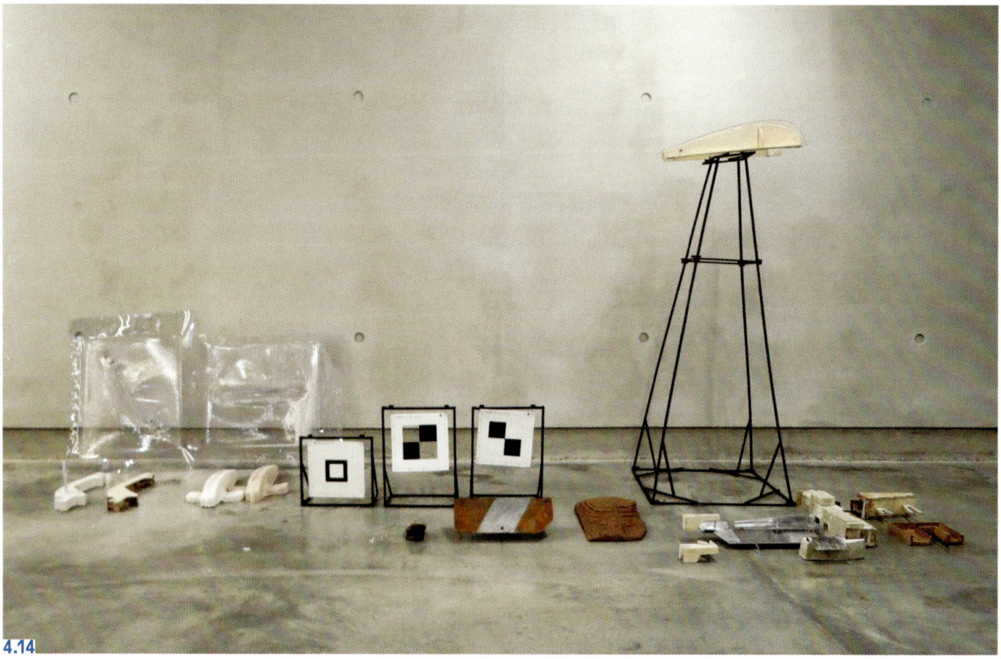

4.14

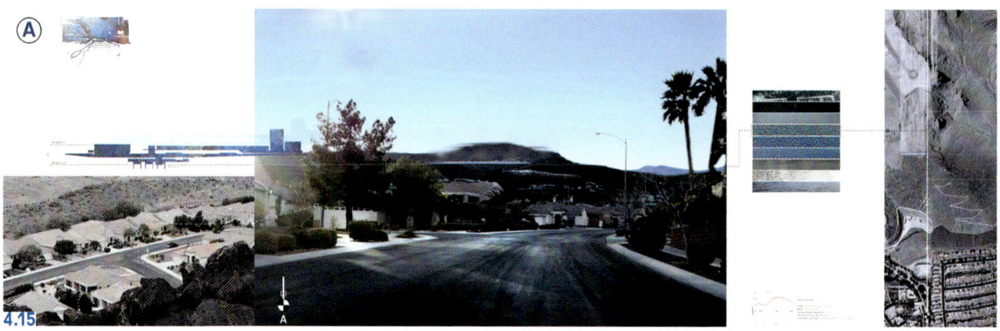

4.15

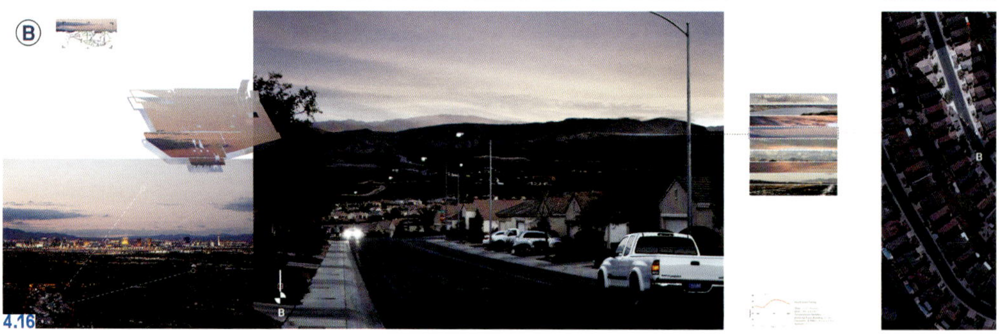

4.16

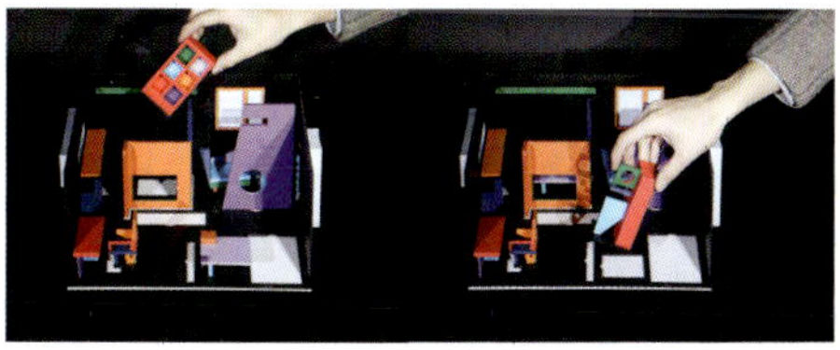

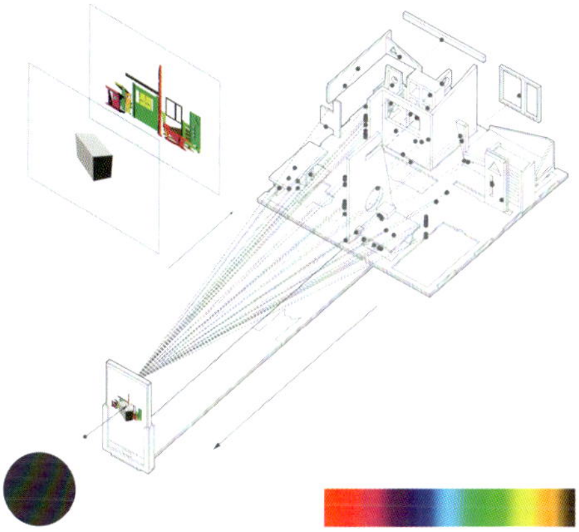

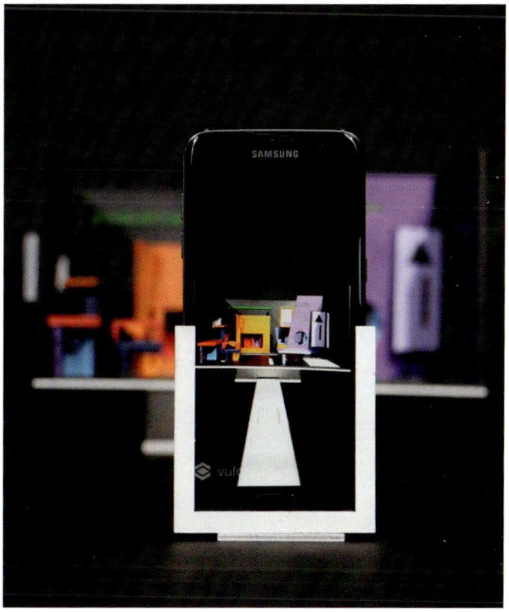

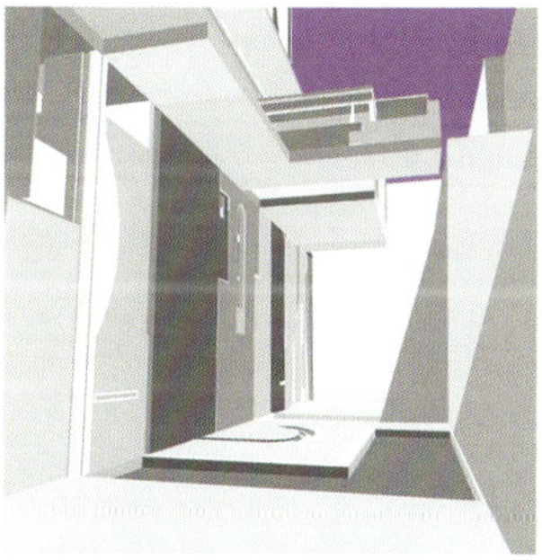

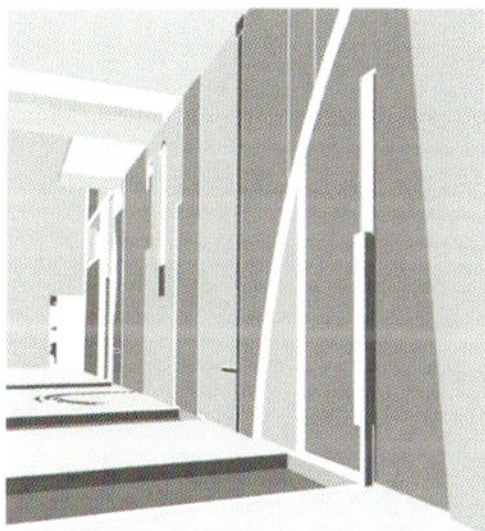

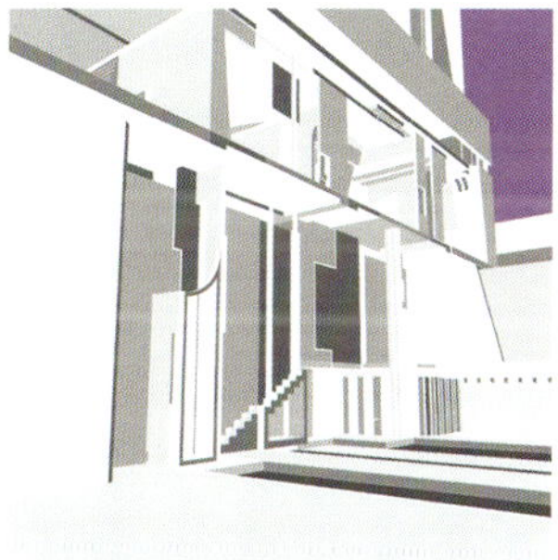

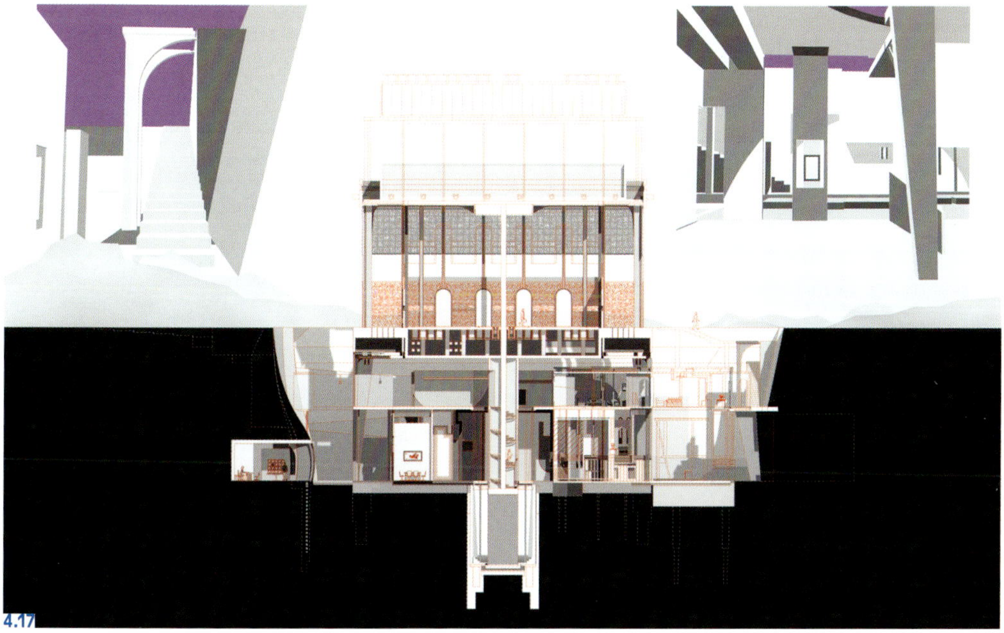

4.17

UG5

Local Quarantines

Julia Backhaus, Martin Tang

Year 2
Annette Choy de Leon, Zachariah Harper le Roux, Victor (Tsz) Leung, Nur Mohamad Adzlee, Chandni Patel, Katherine Ramchand, Chun (Derek)Wong

Year 3
Aya Ataya, Nur (Sabrina) Azman, Lap (Justin) Chow, Nicholas Chrysostomou, Joanna Hobbs, Ka Chi Law, Alvin Lim, Ziyuan (Oliver) Zhu

Thank you to:
Barbara-Ann Campbell-Lange, Pedro Font Alba, Bruce Irwin, Frosso Piminedes, Stephen Gage, CJ Lim, Sabine Storp, Carlos Jiménez Cenamor, Matthew Butcher, Sarah Shafiei, Thandie Loewenson, Daniel Koo, Lucas Alperi, Bob Sheil, Matt Springett, Johan Hybschmann, Sofia Krimizi, James Hampton, Kaowen Ho, David Roberts

This year our unit started with an experimental investigation into the practice of quarantine as a strategic spatial tool. In medical terms, quarantine is described as a state of isolation imposed to prevent the spread of disease. However, we didn't limit our exploration to disease control. We explored quarantines in a much broader sense: as a strategy of containment, encapsulation or preservation; a spatial separation for the purpose of protecting one thing from exposure to the other; a self-contained micro-cosmos that sustains a delicate balance with its surroundings.

——China became the test bed for our investigations. China today seems omnipresent – in the news, in our workplaces and in every trip to the shops. Its growth seems unprecedented and unending. Economic expansion and relocation to China's cities are radically altering China's urban and rural infrastructure and built environment, rapidly taking on a Western veneer. Our appetite for consumption and our concern for the health of our planet creates an uneasy contradiction: it feeds the tension between the pure and the polluted, the local and the foreign, the healthy and the sick, the fake and the original. What architectures can we propose for those uncertain and fragile relationships?

——Term one was research-based and propositional at the same time, studying China's culture and Shanghai from afar. We explored various scales of quarantines and our investigations reached from everyday spatial interventions to the great firewall of China. From smog, dust and pollution control to isolated Santa Claus production villages; from 'Chinawood', the world's largest film studio and camera-ready version of Chinese history to hermetically sealed greenhouses.

——In early January, we travelled to Shanghai and Hangzhou. In our search for sites, we found a fast-moving and muscular city. With over 4,000 high-rise buildings having sprouted out of its ground since the mid-1980s, Shanghai's skyline has become a strangely exuberant version of a *Blade Runner* aesthetic, with simple geometries and sharp lines cutting into the sky. Its architecture contains a permanent tension between the past and the future. In contrast, Hangzhou's dreamy West Lake panoramas and hilly backdrop lured us into believing it was almost a classical Chinese watercolour.

——The main brief challenged the unit to site the research from their project within a real context.

——Briefs ranged from an urban clay quarry to a G20 summit guesthouse, from a wildlife research center in the strangely illuminated forest of Hangzhou to a bone china pet cemetery. The propositions that emerged this year were firmly set in China's future – where they explored their own definitions of quarantines in the context of China and an architecture that is fictional yet possible, ironic yet critical, and affirmative yet progressive.

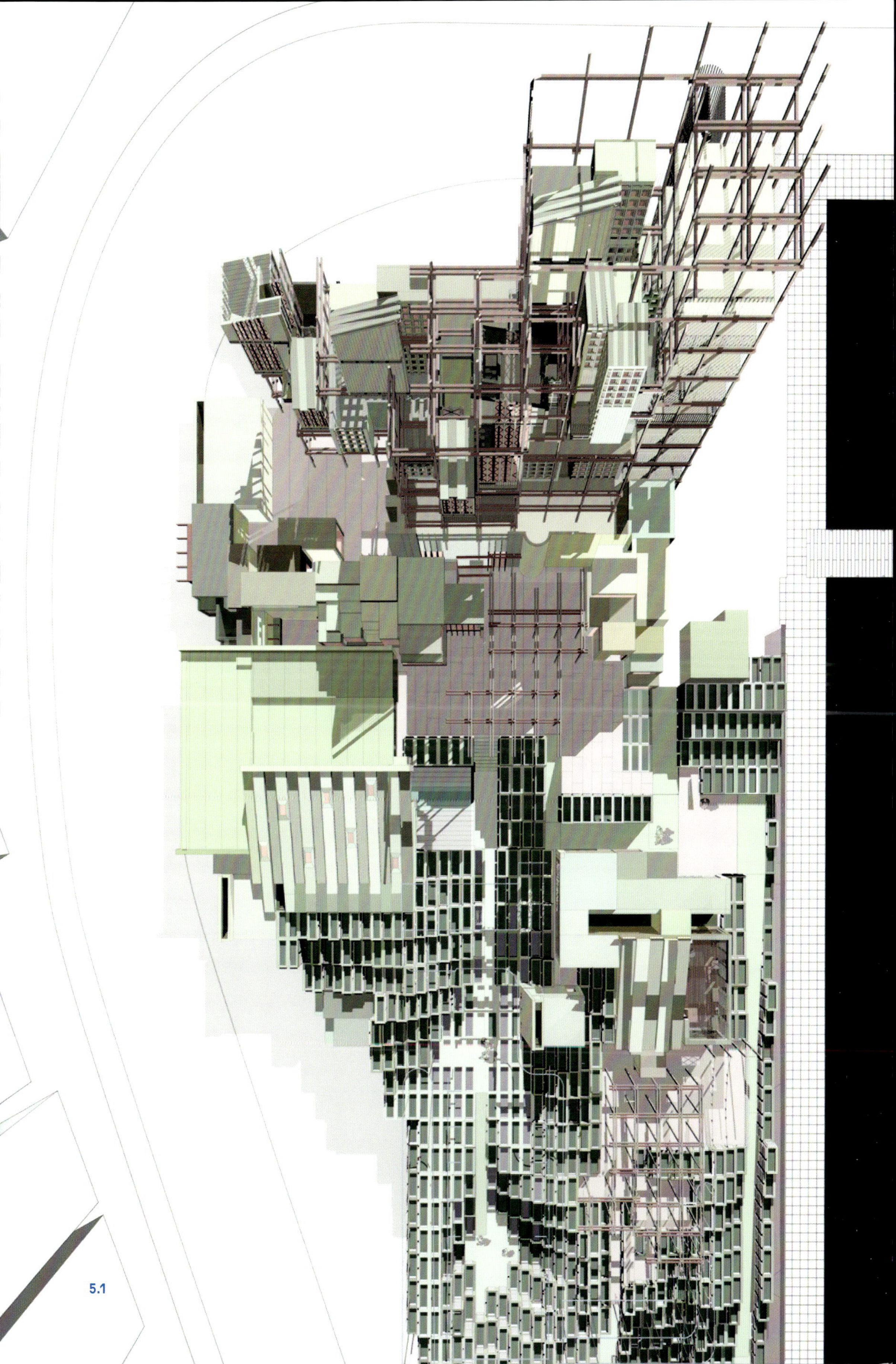

5.1

Fig. 5.1 Nicholas Chrysostomou Y3, 'Ex-Farmer's Clubhouse'. The current legislation of the Hukou system limits internal migration and only provides healthcare and education to nationals if they remain within the constraints of their Hukou passport. The Shanghai Ex-Farmers' Clubhouse is based on the philanthropy of those ex-farmers who 'made it' in the city, and triggers memories of a lost rural landscape within its context, as well as offering services such as healthcare and education. **Figs. 5.2 – 5.4 Lap (Justin) Chow** Y3, 'The G20 Village'. Sited in Hangzhou's West Lake, the sustainable fishing village hosts a number of G20 meetings throughout the year. A modular diaphragm roof hybridises vernacular construction with high-tech, serving as a barometer and litmus test for the city whilst recording and displaying pollution levels. Floating plug-in modules allow for the complex dual occupancy of the building. **Fig. 5.5 Ziyuan (Oliver) Zhu** Y3, 'Archiving Live Views'. Situated on the Su Causeway on the West Lake, the project is based on the proposal for an urban planning and broadcasting centre that has the ability to alter the backdrop of the recording studios and the 'chameleon skin' on its façade. It aims to create virtual scenarios that speculate about the future and the past of the city of Hangzhou and its natural surroundings.

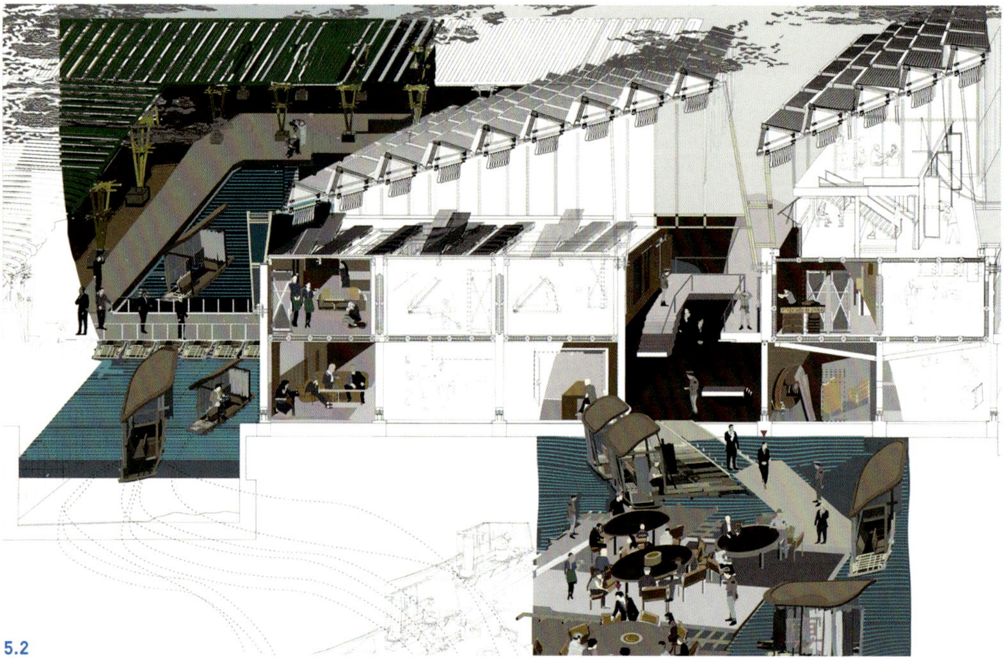

5.2

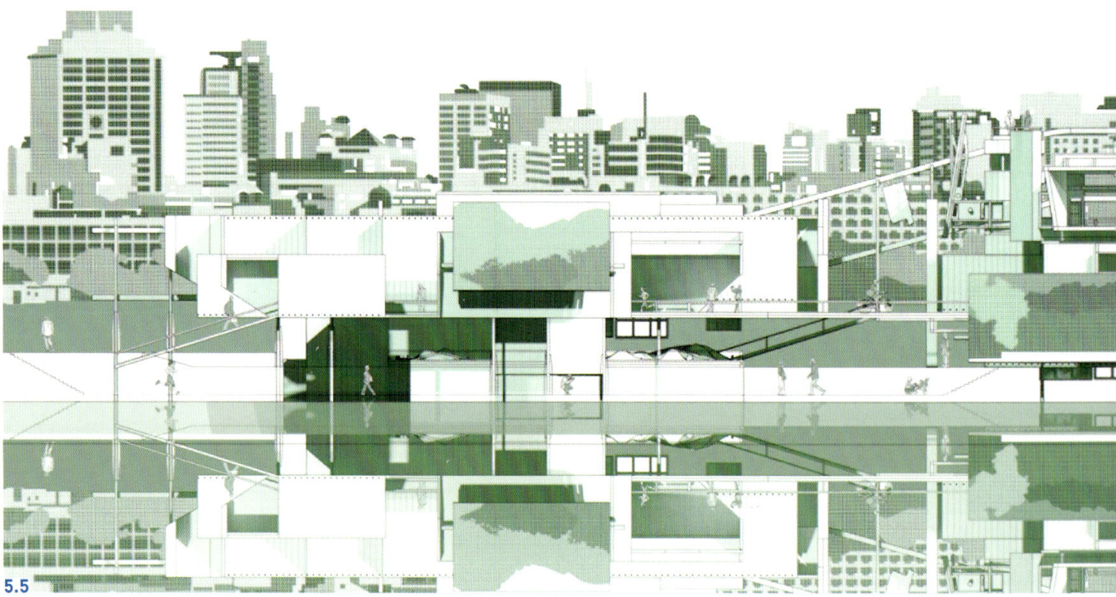

5.5

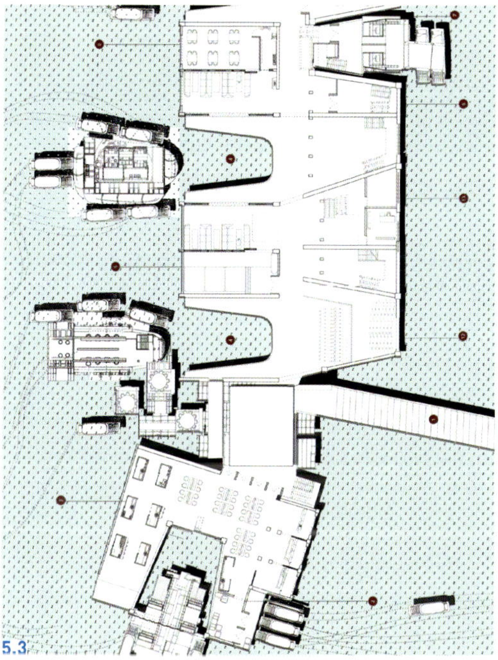
5.3

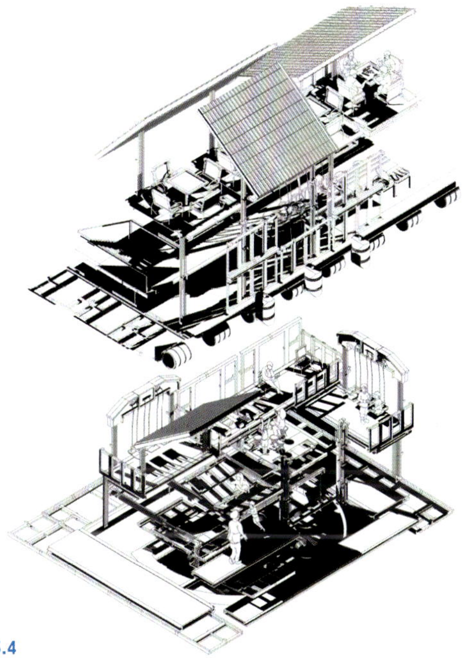
5.4

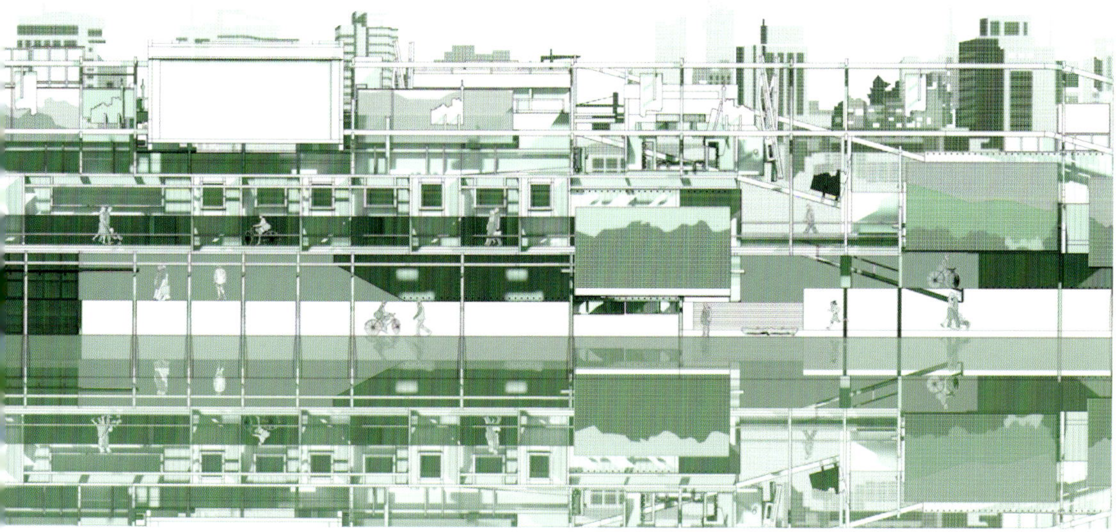

Figs. 5.6 – 5.7 Nur (Sabrina) Azman Y3, 'The Yangtze Dolphin Sanctuary'. The building acts as a safe haven for injured and sick dolphins along the Yangtze River. Dolphins that require extra care and attention will be temporarily relocated to the sanctuary, where they recover, and gradually helped to return to the wild. The building negotiates the unpredictable behaviours of flood water, which is celebrated and welcomed into the building in order to optimise the use of the facility and recalibrates the shifting boundary between water and land. **Fig. 5.8 Nur Mohamad Adzlee** Y2, 'Elderly Community Centre and Antique Marketplace'. The scheme proposes a new dating spot for the elderly, where modular buildings contains unfolding market stalls that maximise productivity and provide a socialising platform. **Fig. 5.9 Chandni Patel** Y2, 'Made in China: Shanghai Arbitration Institute'. Proposed from the phenomenon of Shanzhai, the project creates an arbitration institute in the Free Trade Zone of Shanghai to protect the legal rights of abused factory workers in China. Using a typology of the anti-monumental to entice migrant workers to a usually intimidating legal environment, owners of factories are coaxed into legal conversations and covert transactions with their factory workers. **Figs. 5.10 – 5.11 Zachariah Harper Le Roux** Y2, 'Airpocalypse Archive'. Set in Shanghai's 2010 Expo Park, the project reflects critical opinions about the environmental legacy of the event. It was portrayed in the media as a symbol of China's commitment to sustainable development, where technology enables the imagined harmonious reconciliation of urban and rural development. The project serves as the

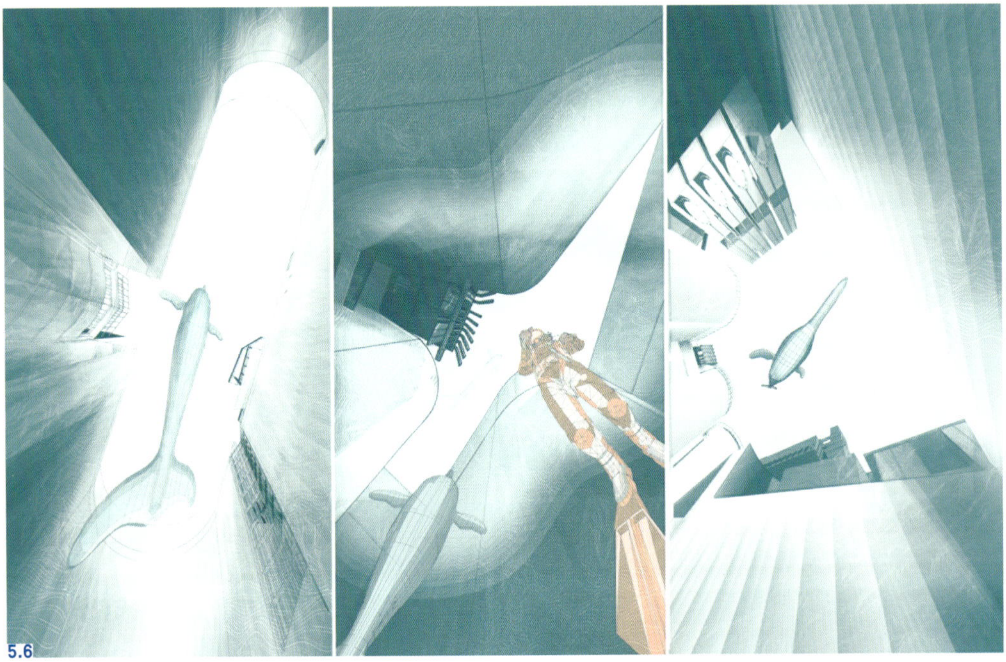

5.6

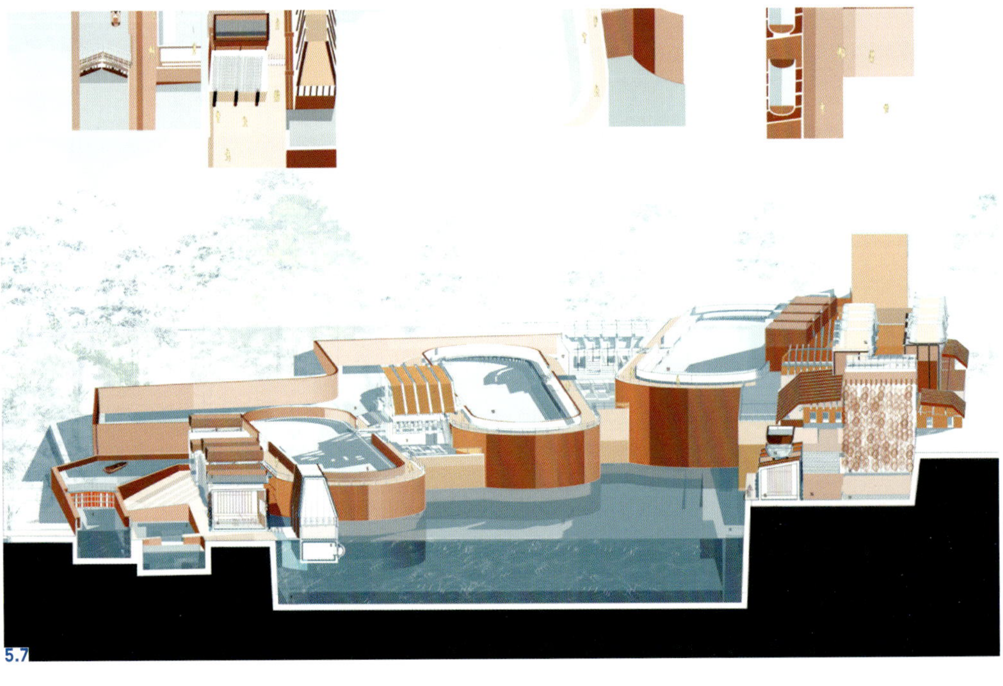

5.7

'mothership' for the collection of environmental data and takes samples from monitoring stations throughout the city, acting as an archive and lab for testing these samples, highlighting the problem and challenges of air pollution.

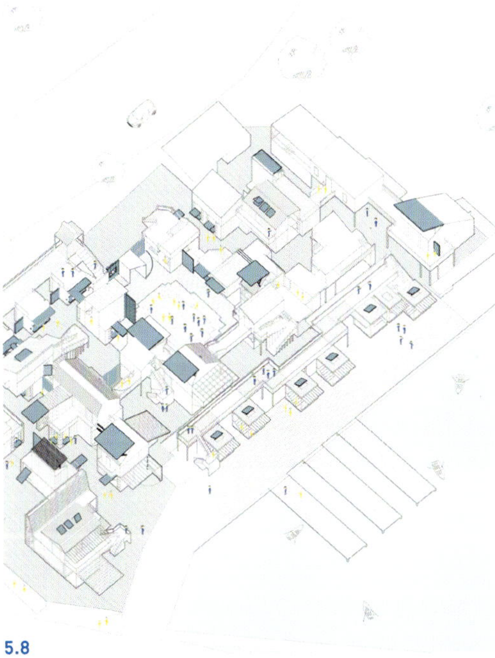

5.8

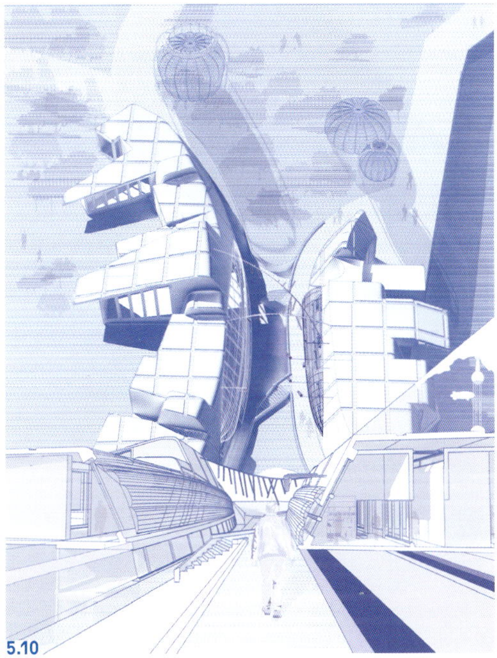

5.10

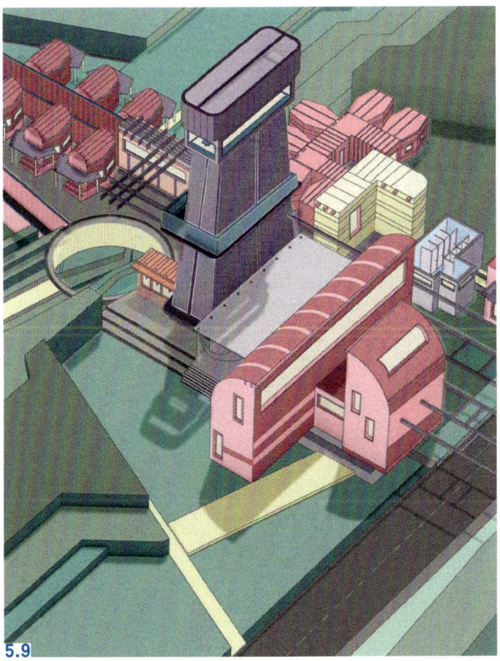

5.9

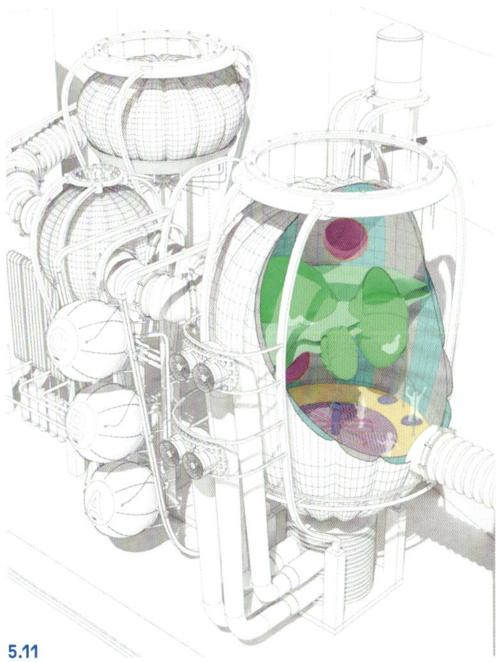

5.11

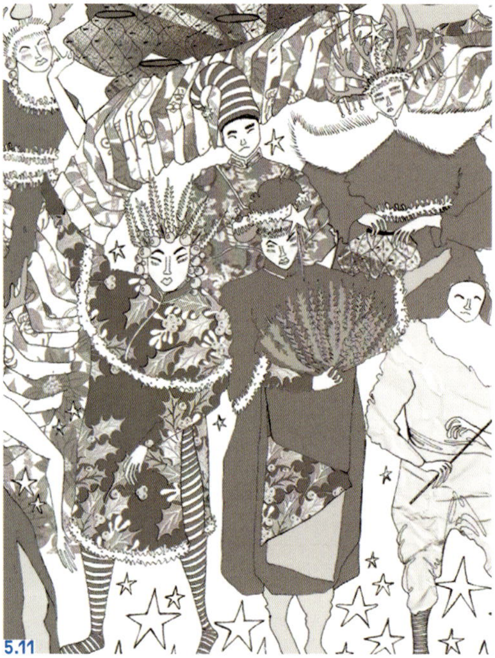

5.11

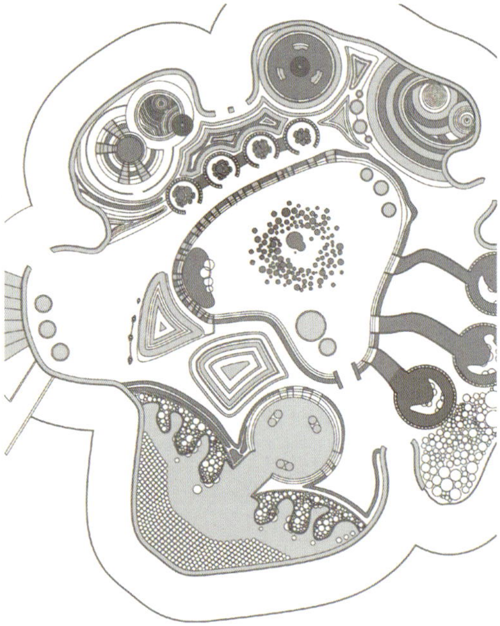

5.12

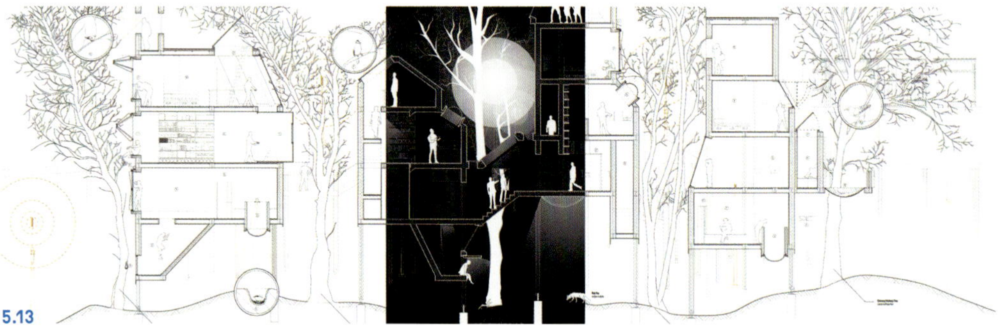

5.13

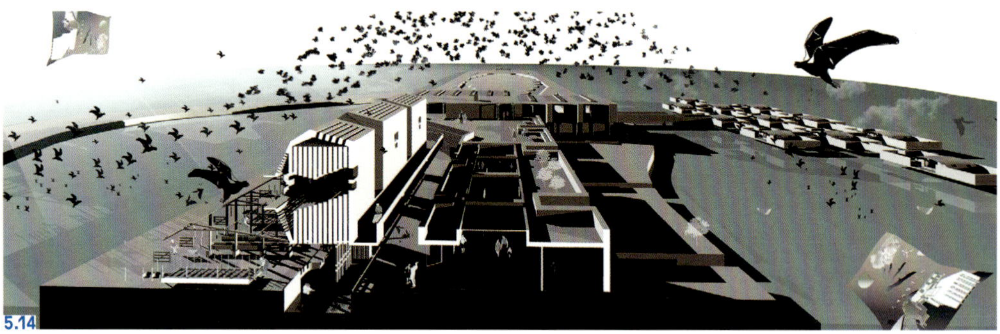

5.14

Fig. 5.11 Katherine Ramchand Y2, 'The New Santa Claus Production Village' is a critique of the Christmas village of Yiwu. Yiwu is home to 600 factories who collectively churn out over 60% of all the world's Christmas decorations. The proposal uses phytoremediation to transform its toxic red landscape into China's royal colour yellow. **Fig. 5.12 Annette Choy De Leon** Y2, 'The Travelling Medical Centre'. Sited in the water village Zhujiajiao, Shanghai, the complex provides visitors with a healing, organic and overall green experience as plants are cultivated for herbal medicines and broths. **Fig. 5.13 Victor (Tsz) Leung** Y2, 'Nocturnal Forest'. In response to the addition of lampposts throughout the forests surrounding China's West Lake, the building is a nocturnal forest research centre designed to sit lightly between the trees of the forest. Observation of the effects of prolonged artificial illumination on the area's famous biodiversity is therefore made possible. **Fig. 5.14 Chun (Derek) Wong** Y2, 'Organic Firework Factory'. Located in Dishui Lake, bat droppings are a key renewable component for material processes in the factory. The building's display of fireworks showcases the lost colour and excitement in the Shanghai sky. **Figs 5.15 – 5.16 Alvin Lim** Y3, 'Houtan Pet Cemetery'. Deep within Houtan Park, a forest on the border of Huangpu River, lies Houtan Pet Cemetery, an isolated landscape for deceased pets. The building is designed around a ritual that reflects the mourners' stages of grief. Upon cremation, the pet is immortalised from its ashes as bone china memorabilia that celebrates man's best friend.

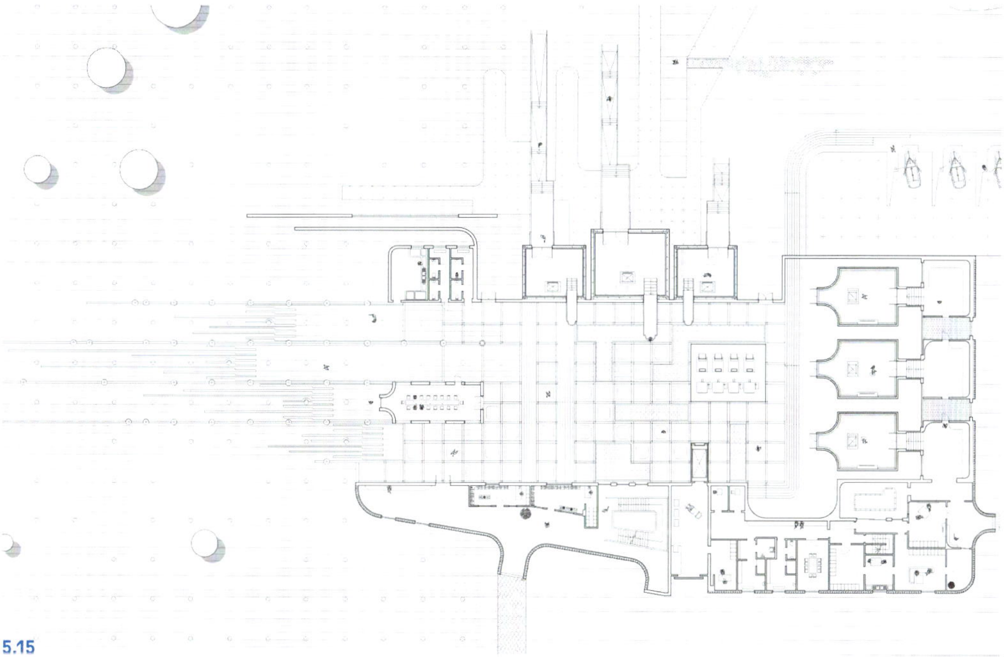

5.15

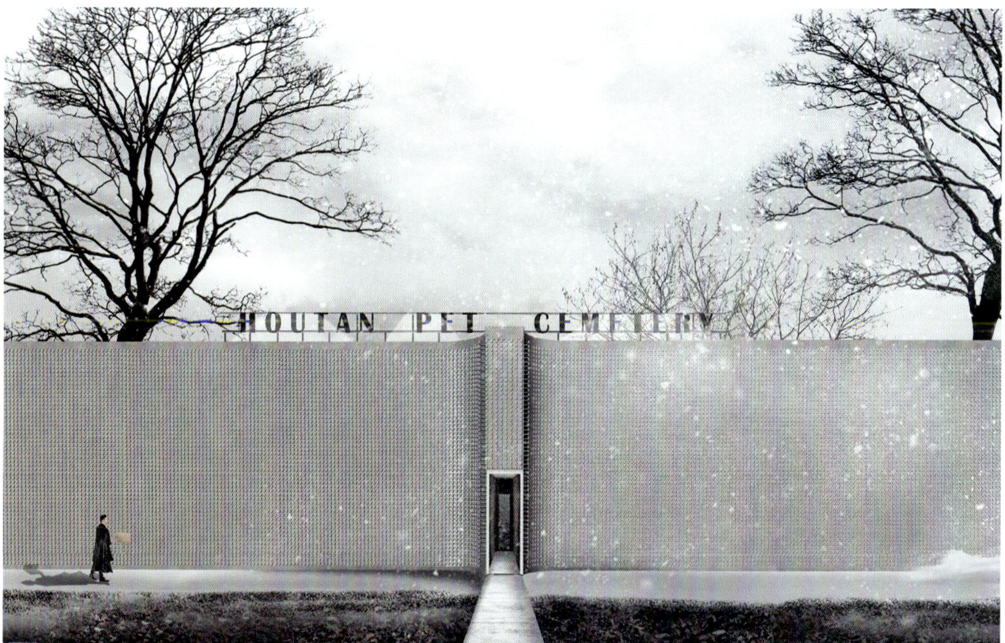

5.16

Figs. 5.17 – 5.18 Joanna Hobbs Y3, 'Orchestra of Crickets'. An arena dedicated to the sport of cricket fighting. Located at the centre of the ghost city of Rushan, the arena amplifies the crickets' activities and regenerates the surrounding city. Fighter crickets require specific diets, exercise and environments which are incorporated into both the human and cricket spaces within the building, creating a constant fluctuation between cricket and human scales. **Fig. 5.19 Aya Ataya** Y3, 'Carving Conversation'. The project is a deconstruction of a censored government building to provide democratic space for the exchange of uncensored information and freedom of speech. The target is the National Museum of China in Beijing, where a new landscape is being carved and designed. The nature of the architecture is to be open and accessible, which is essential in order to enable and enrich free speech within the structure, with enclosed spaces forming a study-focused Cultural Centre. **Figs. 5.20 – 5.21 Ka Chi Law** Y3, 'The Shanghai Urban Quarry' proposes an excavation strategy to refurbish the endangered Shanghai lane houses, whilst creating an experimental urban housing scheme situated in the environmental microcosm of the carved-out space. The 'down-rise' architecture consists of prefabricated living pods bolted to the trenches of the clay pit, and clad with terracotta tiles fired in-situ. The clusters of pods and lower-ground spaces is reminiscent of Shanghainese communal living culture, and opposes the mass construction of residential high-rises.

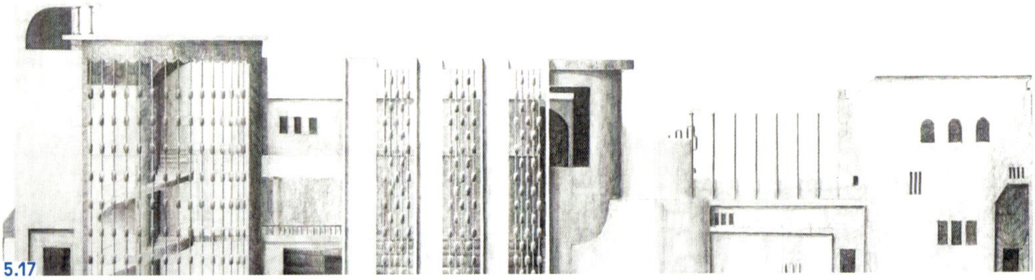
5.17

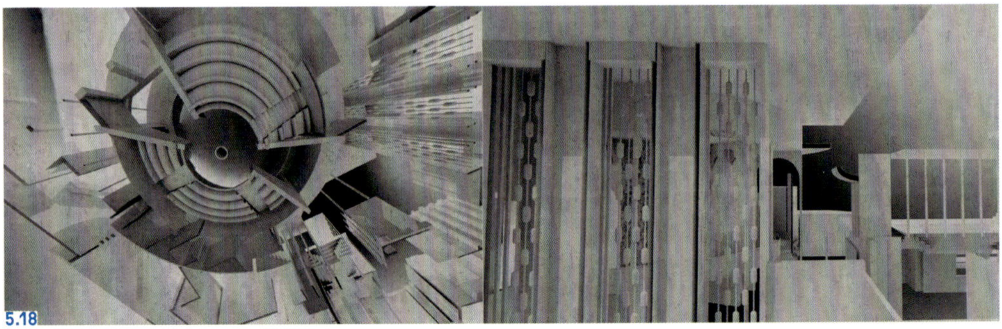
5.18

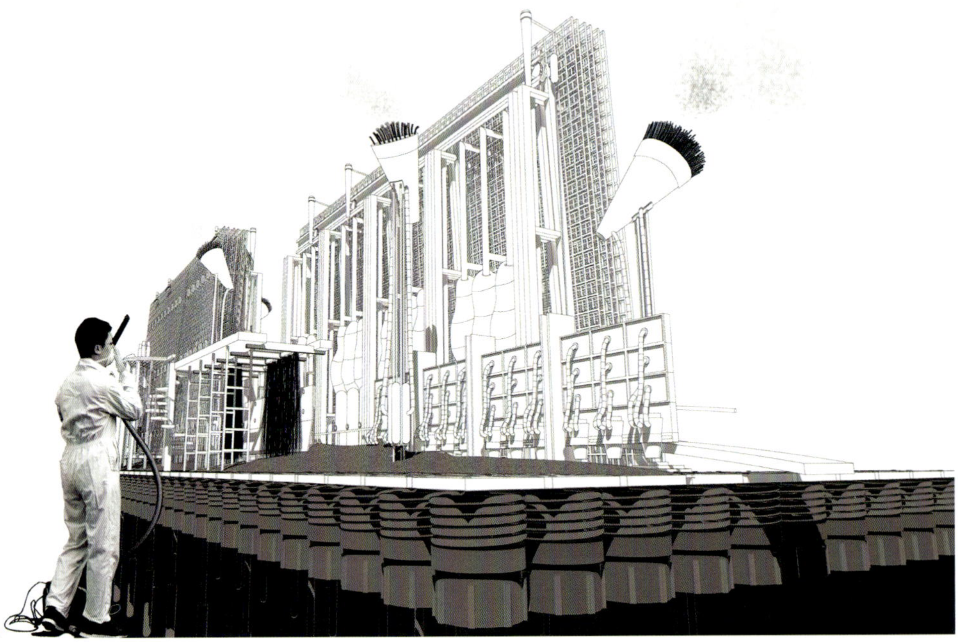
5.20

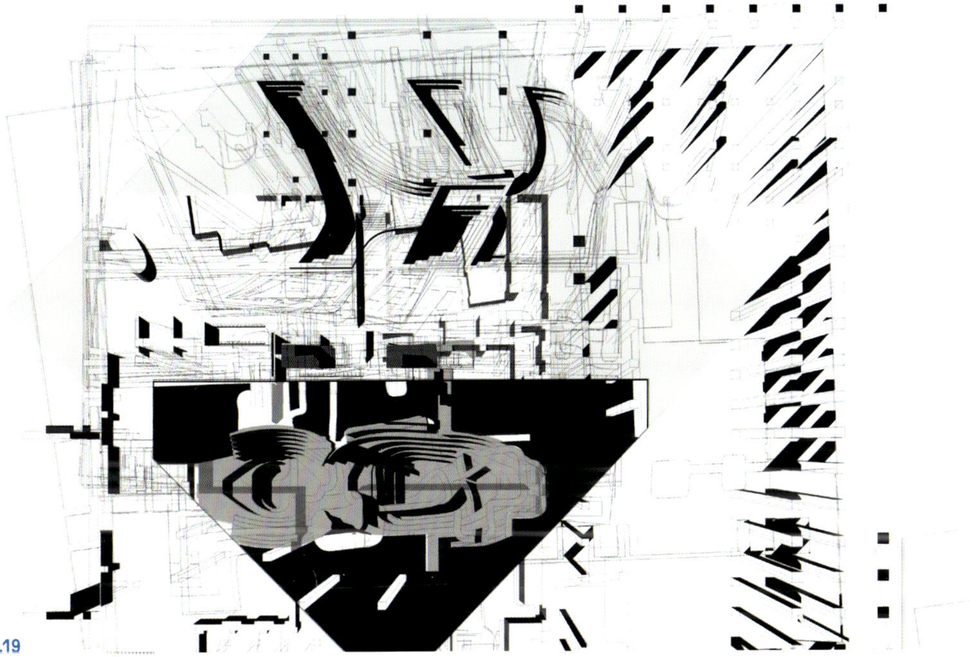

5.19

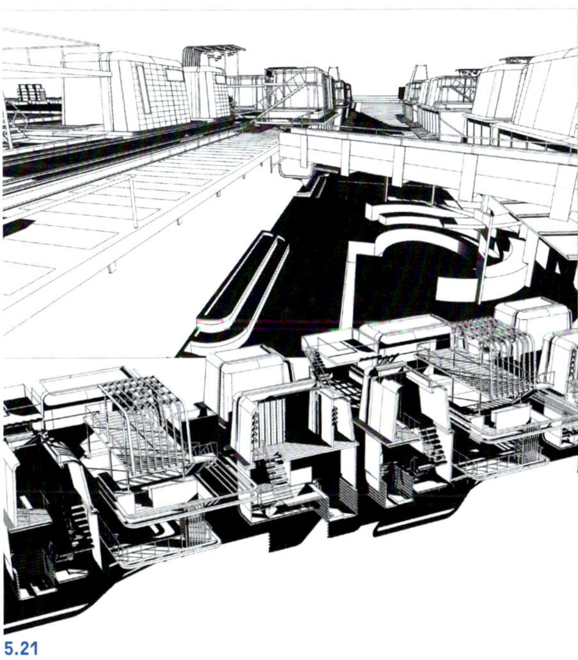

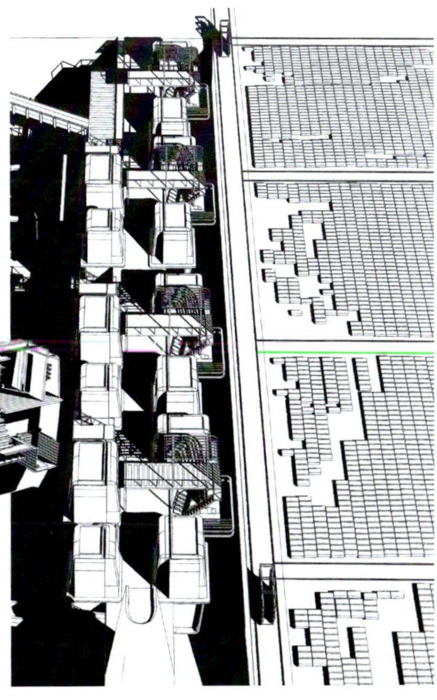

5.21

UG6

Drifting Cityscapes

Tim Norman, Paolo Zaide

Year 2
Xavier De La Roche, Yee (Enoch) Liang, Gabriel Pavlides, Max Hanmo Shen, Negar Taatizadeh, Olivia Trinder, Gordon Yuk Yips

Year 3
Nikhil (Isaac) Cherian, Wing (Melody) Chu, Nichole Qi Ho, Kaizer Hud, Shi Yin Ling, Carolina Mondragon-Bayarri, Rosie Murphy, Fola-Sade (Victoria) Oshinusi

Thank you to:
Christine Hawley, CJ Lim, David Roberts, Mike Tite, Patrick Weber, Peter Bishop, Sabine Storp, Stephen Gage, as well as friends of the unit: Emily Priest, George Courtauld, Ivan Hung, Jin Kuo, Joe Travers-Jones, Max Butler, Sam Tan, Yiki Liong, Yip-Wing Siu

Thank you also to our computing tutors Jack Holmes and Joerg Majer and our technical tutors Clyde Watson and Dimitris Argyros

With today's fragile borders being redrawn by identity politics, migration-related challenges are increasingly something architects must understand and respond to. Just last summer, we watched Rio de Janeiro open the 31st Summer Olympics to welcome athletes from across 207 nations. While the Games presented an opportunity to celebrate the coming together of the global community, other forms of migration today present far greater challenges: in the Mediterranean, the unfolding refugee crisis continues to strain both political and race relations across Europe, while in the US, the newly elected 45th president leads a populist campaign that promises to build an 3,100 kilometre-long "impenetrable, physical, tall, powerful, beautiful, southern border wall" to separate Mexico from the Land of the Free. Back in Britain, after a vote to leave the European Union, businesses begin to relax, as the grey-cloud prophecies of the end to free movement of labour have not yet come true – Brexit, of course, is still to come.

The question of migration might be a complex one, but this year's theme was an invitation for our imagination to drift and to speculate. This century will see a dramatic rise in different types of migration, from communities escaping from the political or environmental conditions of their home to mobile people who choose to live in other parts of the world simply because they can. With the question of how future migrants will integrate, live and operate in their new host environments the unit continued to consider the organisation of communities, and to explore the architectural design of the individual and shared programmes, spaces and infrastructures. This year's brief took the optimistic tone of Doug Sanders' 'Arrival City', in which migration, and its inherent goal of resettling people, is presented as one of the great opportunities of our time. The brief was an invitation to explore this theme from the abstract to the poetic – and from the pragmatic to the fantastic. Where do these journeys begin? How do they unfold? Do they end, propagate or simply continue to drift?

The main brief for the year was a challenge to consider the Arrival City beyond the merely pragmatic – what is desirable? What levels of functionality would actually improve the quality of living in our city in fifty years' time? And how do we integrate qualities of transience, flexibility and adaptation? In a cityscape with shifting territories and ecologies, mobile and settling communities, how do we design spaces that have practical, social and cultural value? What stories can future communities share? The work from the unit is filled equally with optimism, provocation and wonder.

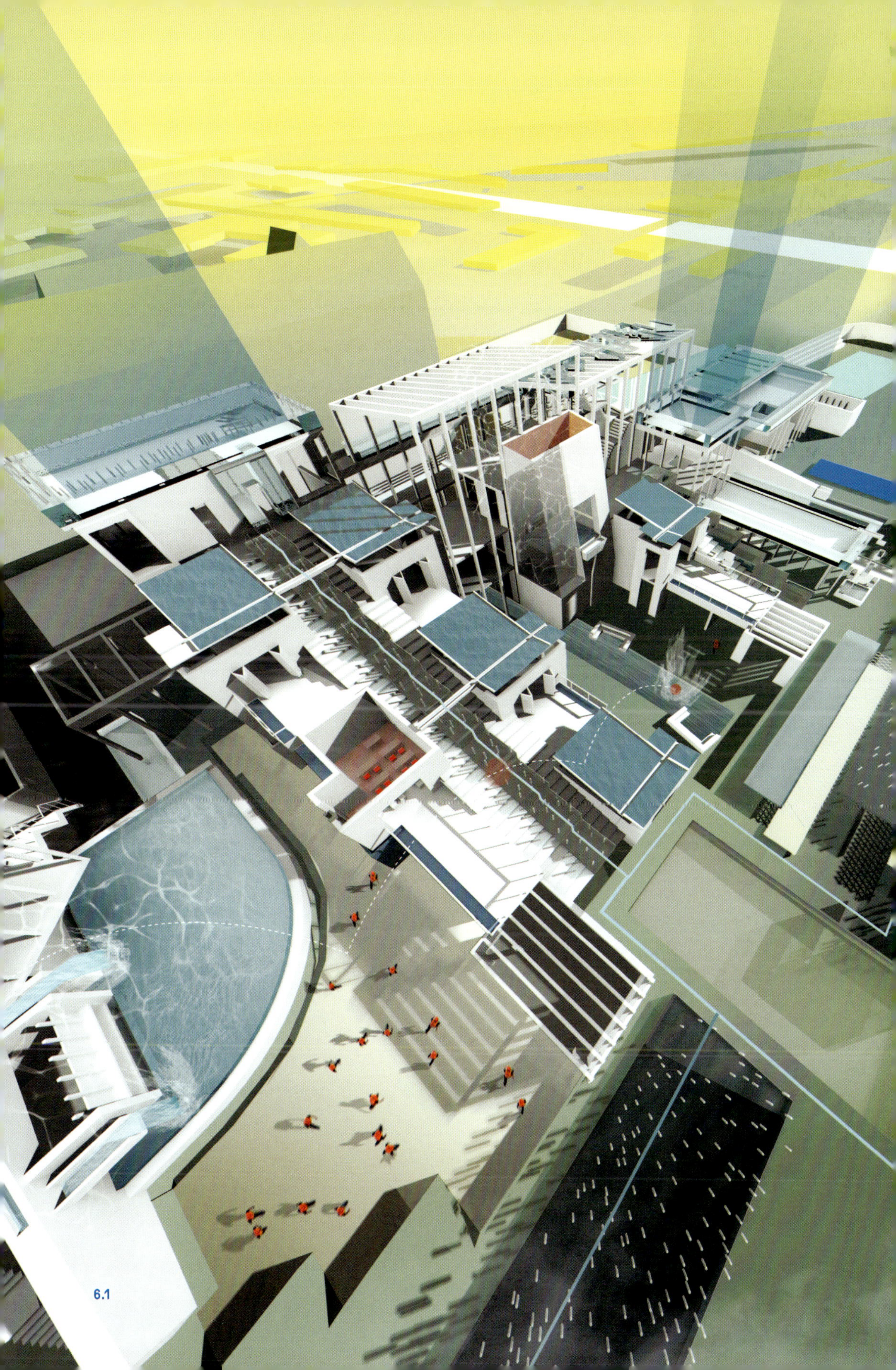

6.1

Fig. 6.1 Kaizer Hud Y3, 'Stepney Hydrosensitive School'. The school aims to stimulate urban water sensitivity by positioning itself as a water recycling interface. Taking cues from Islamic architecture via the local Bangladeshi population, the water system is exposed to incite students' curiosity. Captured rainwater and grey water from surrounding houses is filtered and used as a resource for play, learning and spiritual reflection. **Fig. 6.2 Gabriel Pavlides** Y2, 'School of Landscape Design'. By placing the building along the canal in Mile End Park, students are encouraged to interact with gardens and greenhouses to influence the way people experience nature. **Fig. 6.3 Olivia Trinder** Y2, 'East End Azulejos'. With old Arts and Crafts techniques re-emerging, the project encourages local communities to come together in artisan workshops and studios for the production of glazed ceramic tiles. **Fig. 6.4 Wing (Melody) Chu** Y3, 'The Dunstan Elderly Centre'. The project redevelops two Victorian dwellings in Stepney Green into a mixed-use centre for the elderly, serving the existing residents in the context of the ageing population of 50 years' time. **Fig. 6.5 Nikhil (Isaac) Cherian** Y3, 'Whitechapel Craft Arcade'. As the Whitechapel Bell Foundry announces its departure, the project rejuvenates the future of craft by housing workshop spaces and yearly fairs as a twist on London's affluent arcade shopping experience. **Fig. 6.6 Nichole Qi Ho** Y3, 'Theatre for Storytellers'. A community theatre created as a space for stories to be told through performances and conversations, providing a shared experience to empower the voices of both immigrants and

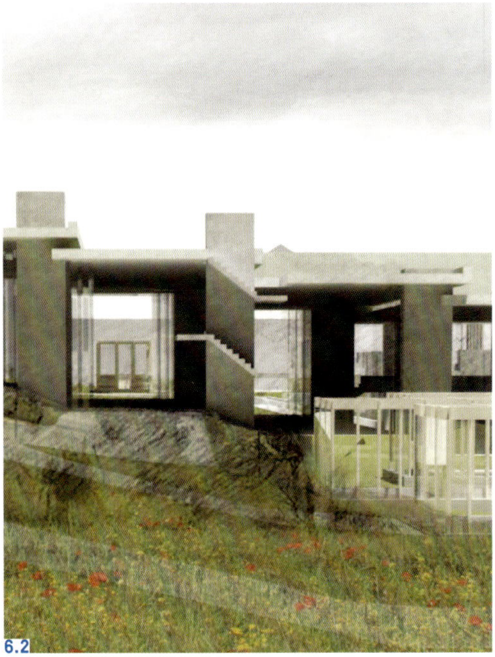

6.2

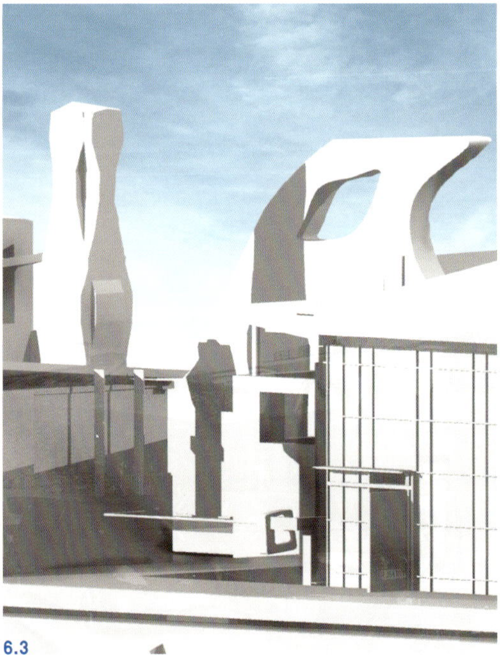

6.3

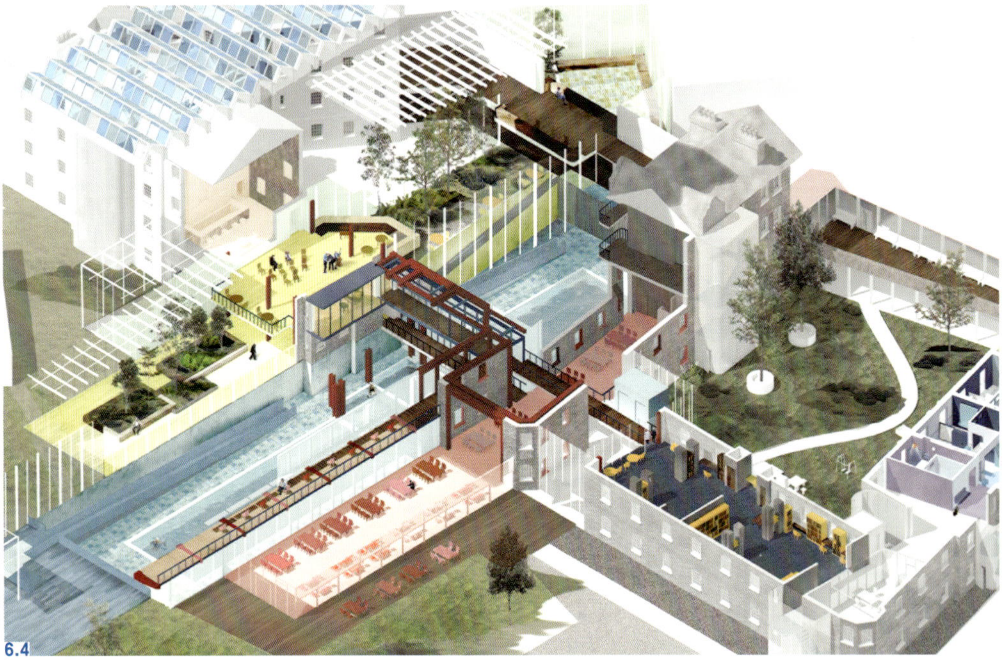

6.4

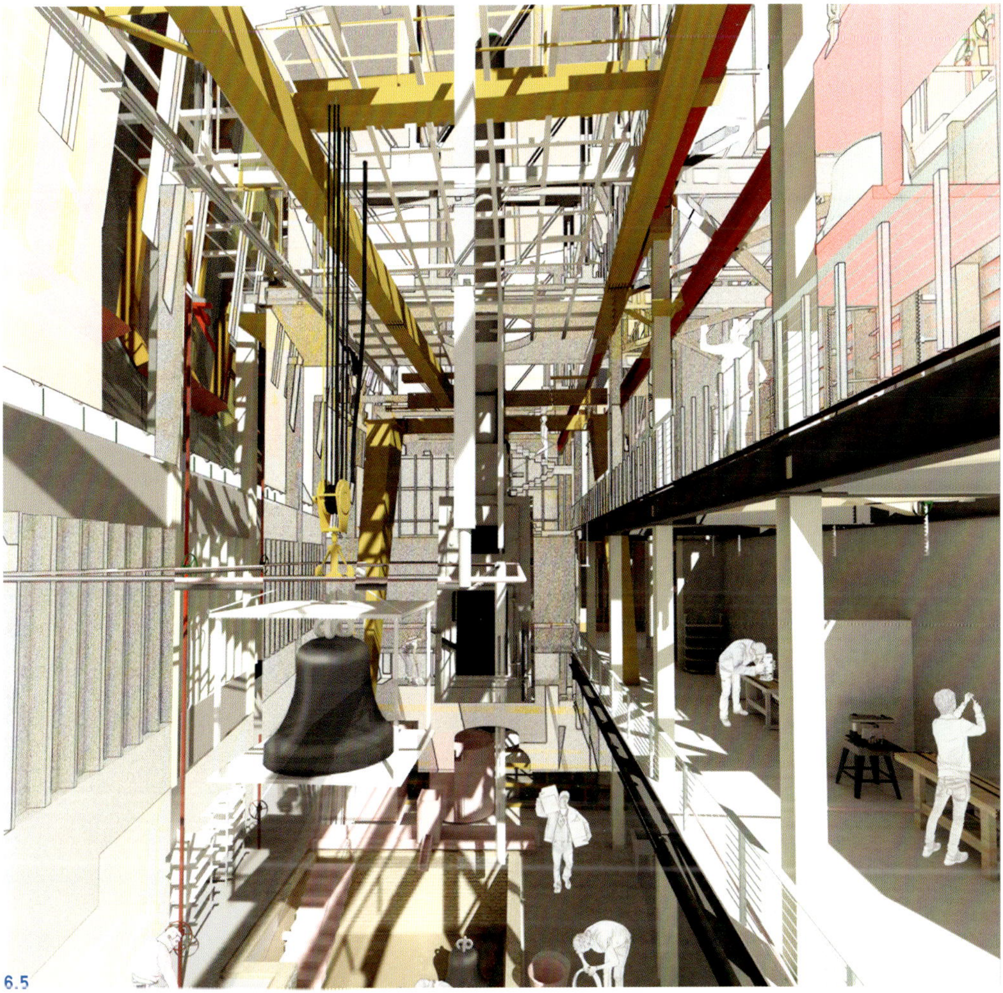
6.5

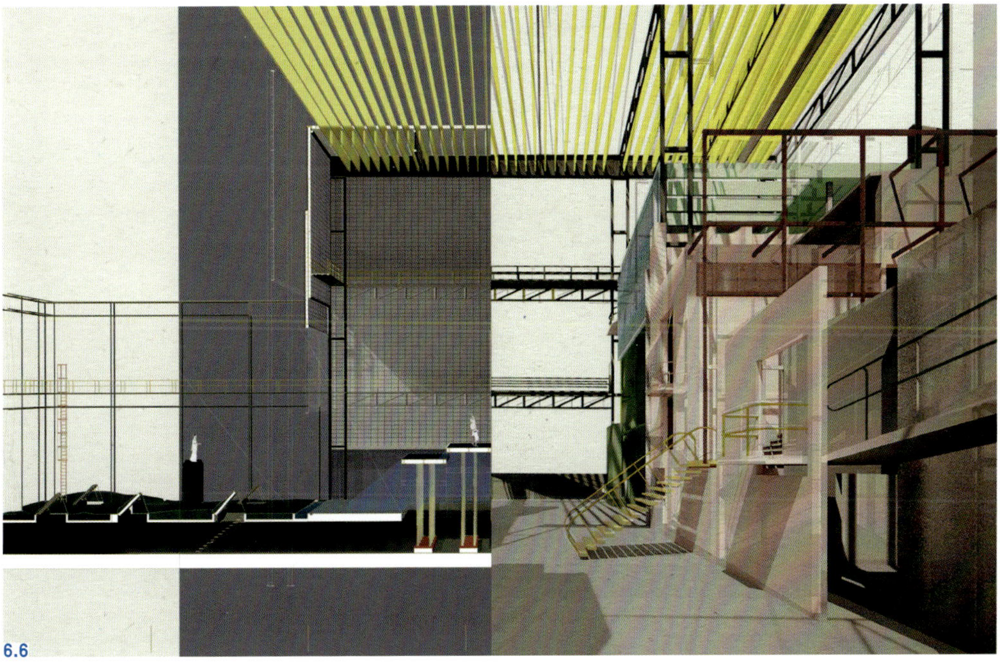
6.6

Fig. 6.7 Carolina Mondragon-Bayarri Y3, 'Women's Refuge'. An urban secret garden that assists newly-immigrated women to integrate into their new environment through blurring exterior and interior boundaries by manipulating light, sound and views. **Fig. 6.8 Negar Taatizadeh** Y2, 'Theatre and Performance Spaces'. The project investigates the concept of the building acting as a theatre stage itself, creating surprising moments for visitors as they become part of the act. **Fig. 6.9 Xavier De La Roche** Y2, 'Trading Archive'. Reoccupation of a 17th-century almshouse originally built for travelling seamen, and redefining its interior as a network of highly sculptural spaces to provoke a critique of the East India Company's controversial history. **Fig. 6.10 Max Hanmo Shen** Y2, 'City Farm of the Future'. An alternative city farm typology which also functions as a market and a playscape that is woven through the stepped pastures of the market roof. **Figs. 6.11 – 6.12 Fola-Sade (Victoria) Oshinusi** Y3, 'The Stepney Green Landscape of Transient Accommodation'. Providing three guest accommodation typologies existing alongside current residents, this project focuses on the spatial requirements needed to accommodate residents who will be staying on different timescales: from the long-term comfort and adaptability of existing residents to the short-term needs of overnight residents.

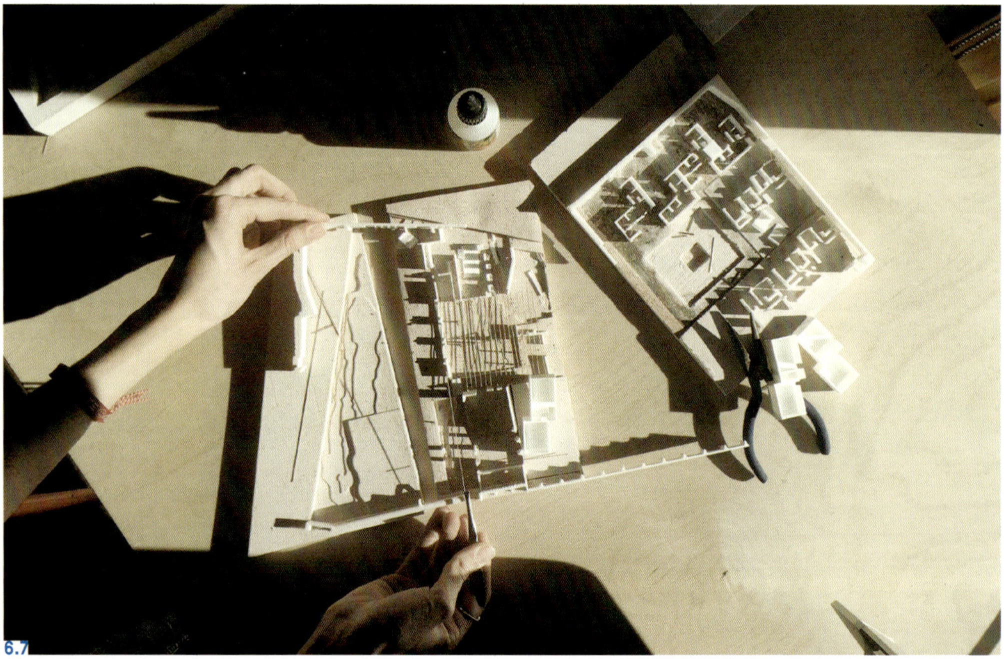

6.7

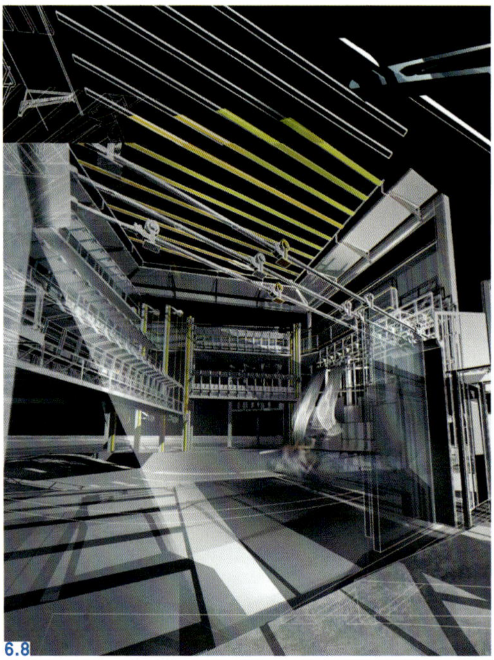

6.8

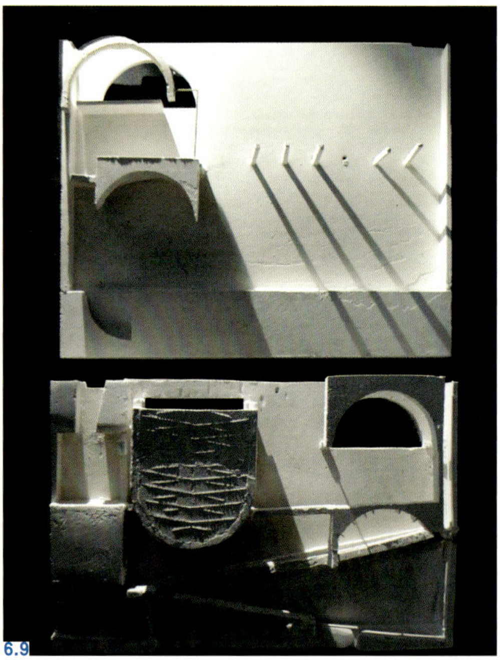

6.9

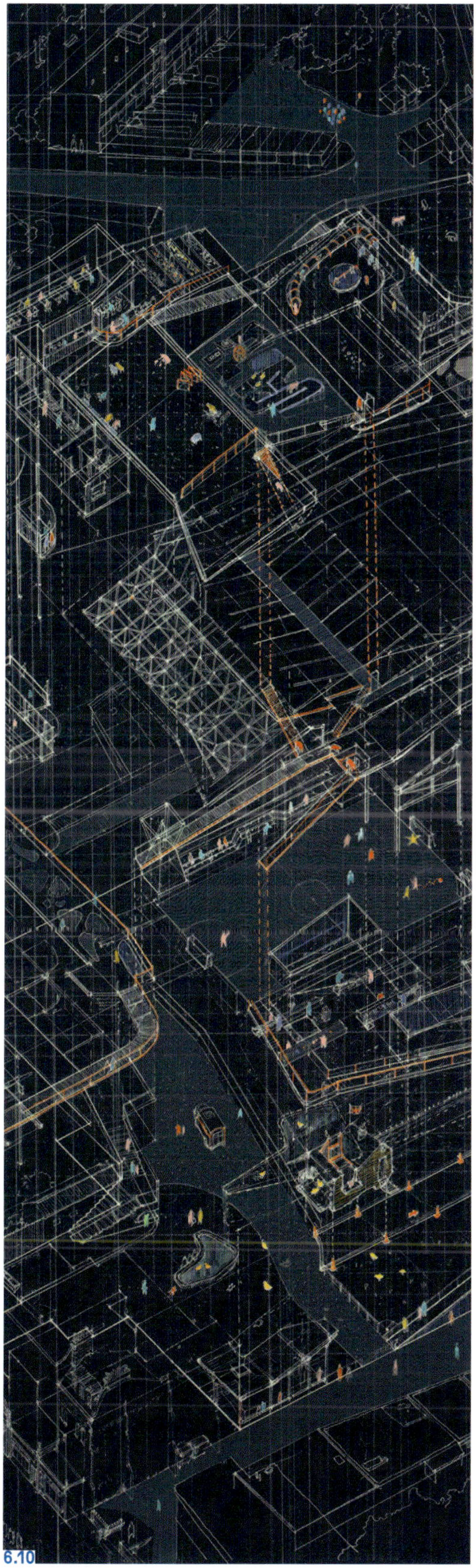
6.10

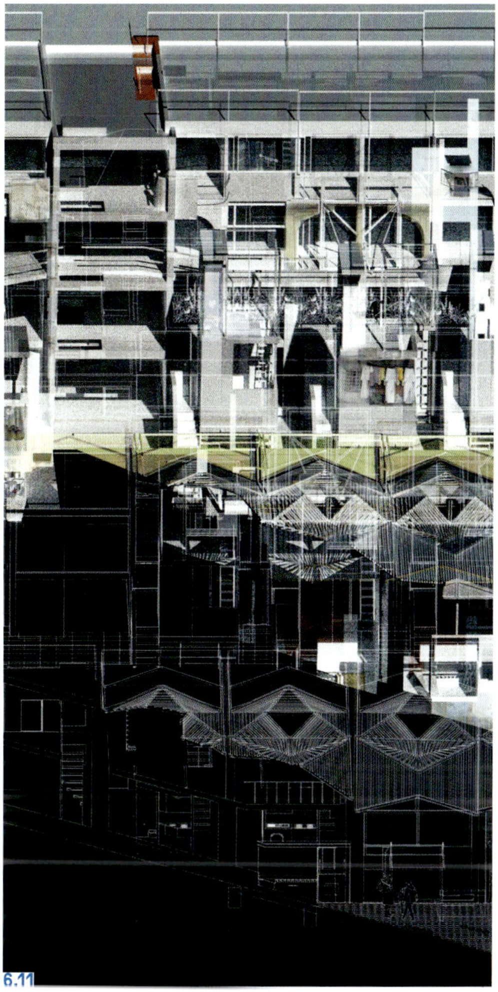
6.11

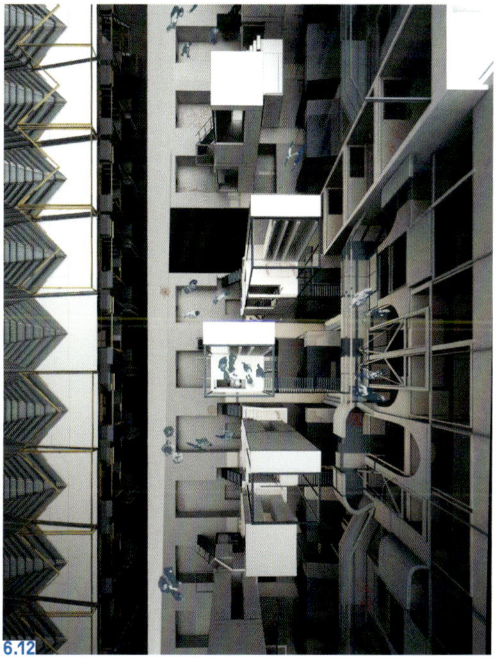
6.12

Figs. 6.13 – 6.14 **Shi Yin Ling** Y3, 'Anchor Park Mixed Development'. The issue of migration pushes the city of London to grow outwards and upwards. The project instead proposes a low-rise, high-density residential development that integrates ecological density through an interweave of green courtyards and pockets. **Fig. 6.15** **Rosie Murphy** Y3, 'Intergenerational Agri(Culture)'. The project nurtures the passing on of traditions and knowledge of different cultures, and encourages intergenerational connections by incorporating greenhouses of varying climates that celebrate universally significant activities of growing, cooking and eating. **Fig. 6.16** **Yee (Enoch) Liang** Y2, 'Whitechapel Carpentry Guild'. The Whitechapel Carpentry Guild looks to revive the fading crafting culture by providing a testing ground for woodwork that will eventually be constructed around London. **Fig. 6.17** **Gordon Yip** Y2, 'Adaptive Communal Housing'. A housing scheme focusing on adaptability for individual and communal interests.

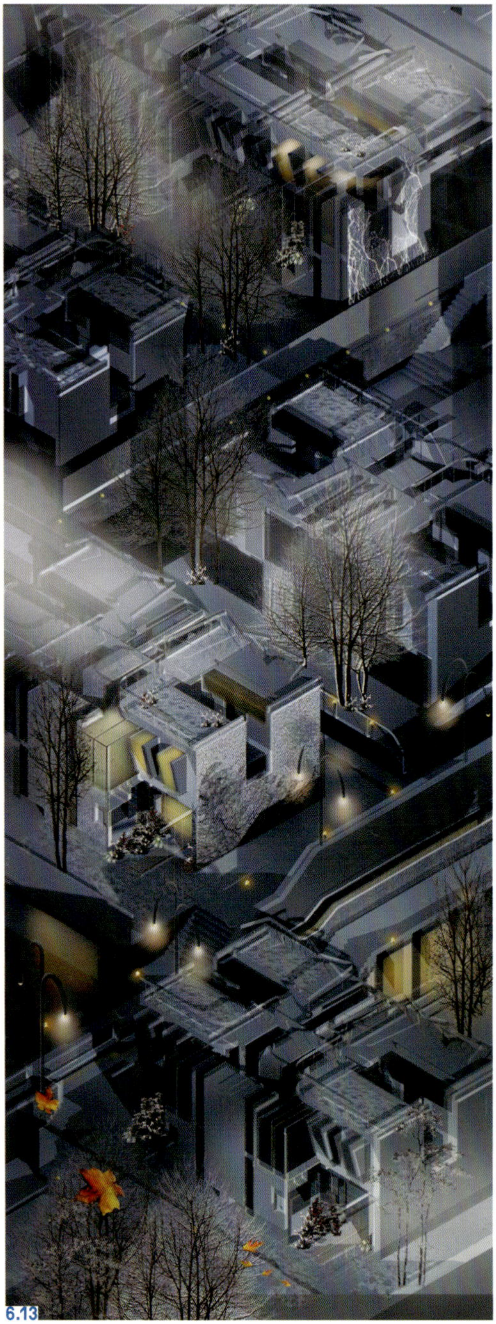

6.13

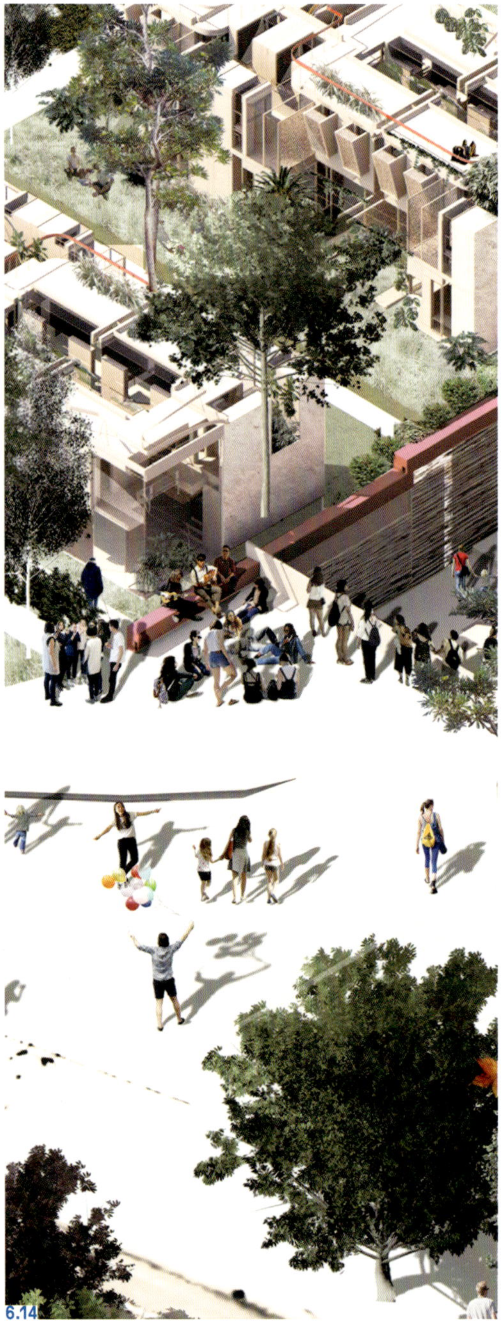

6.14

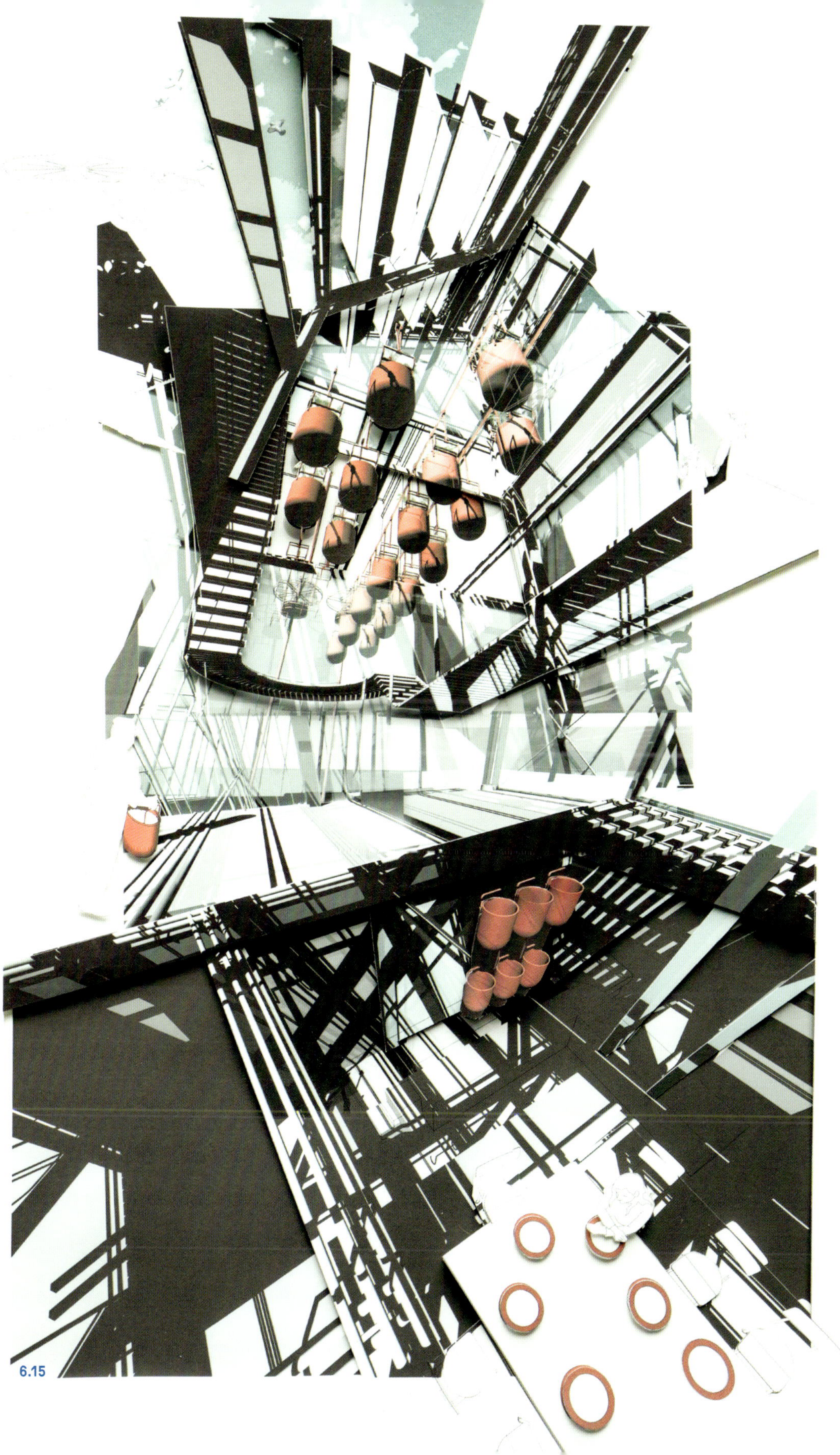

6.15

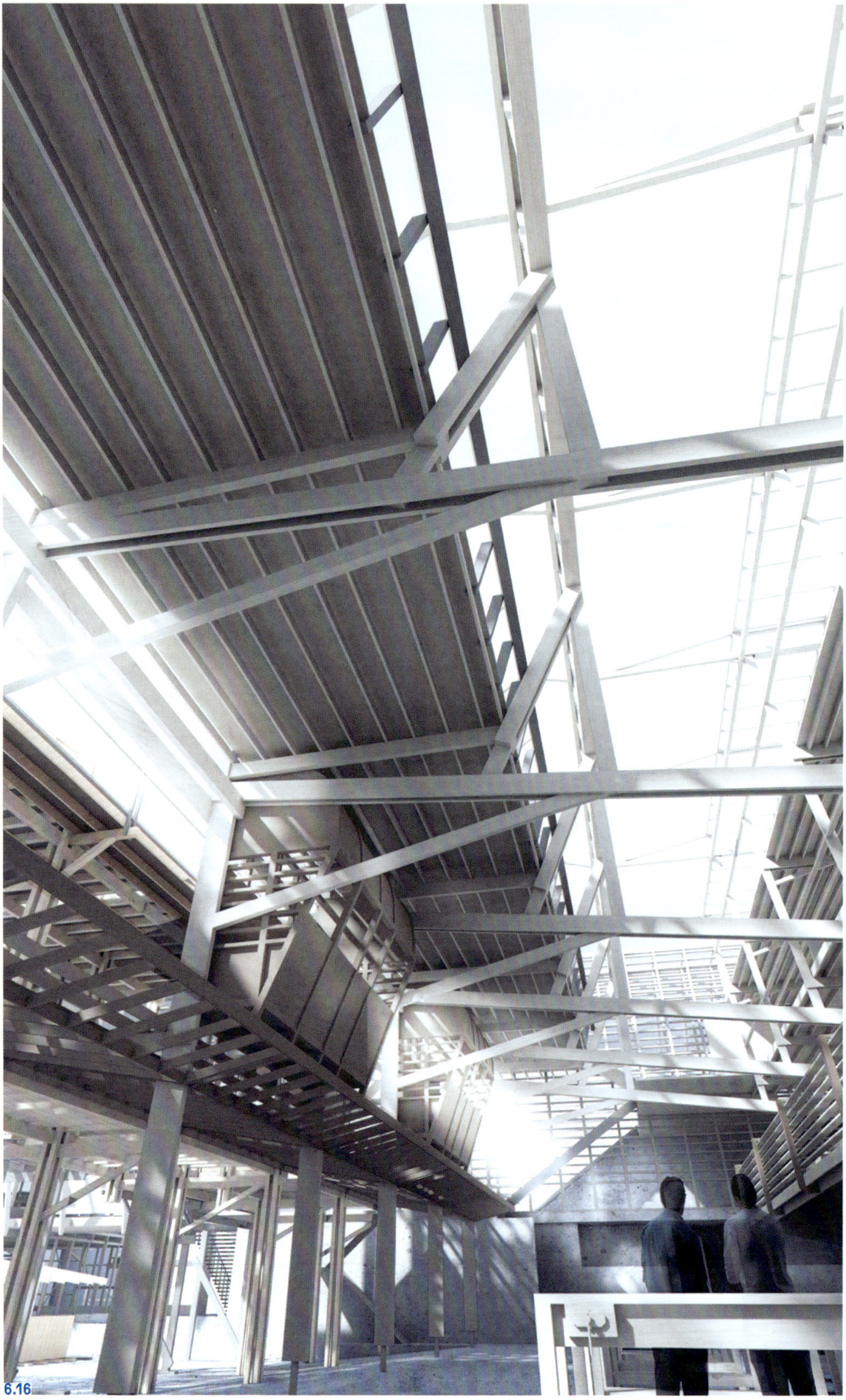

6.16

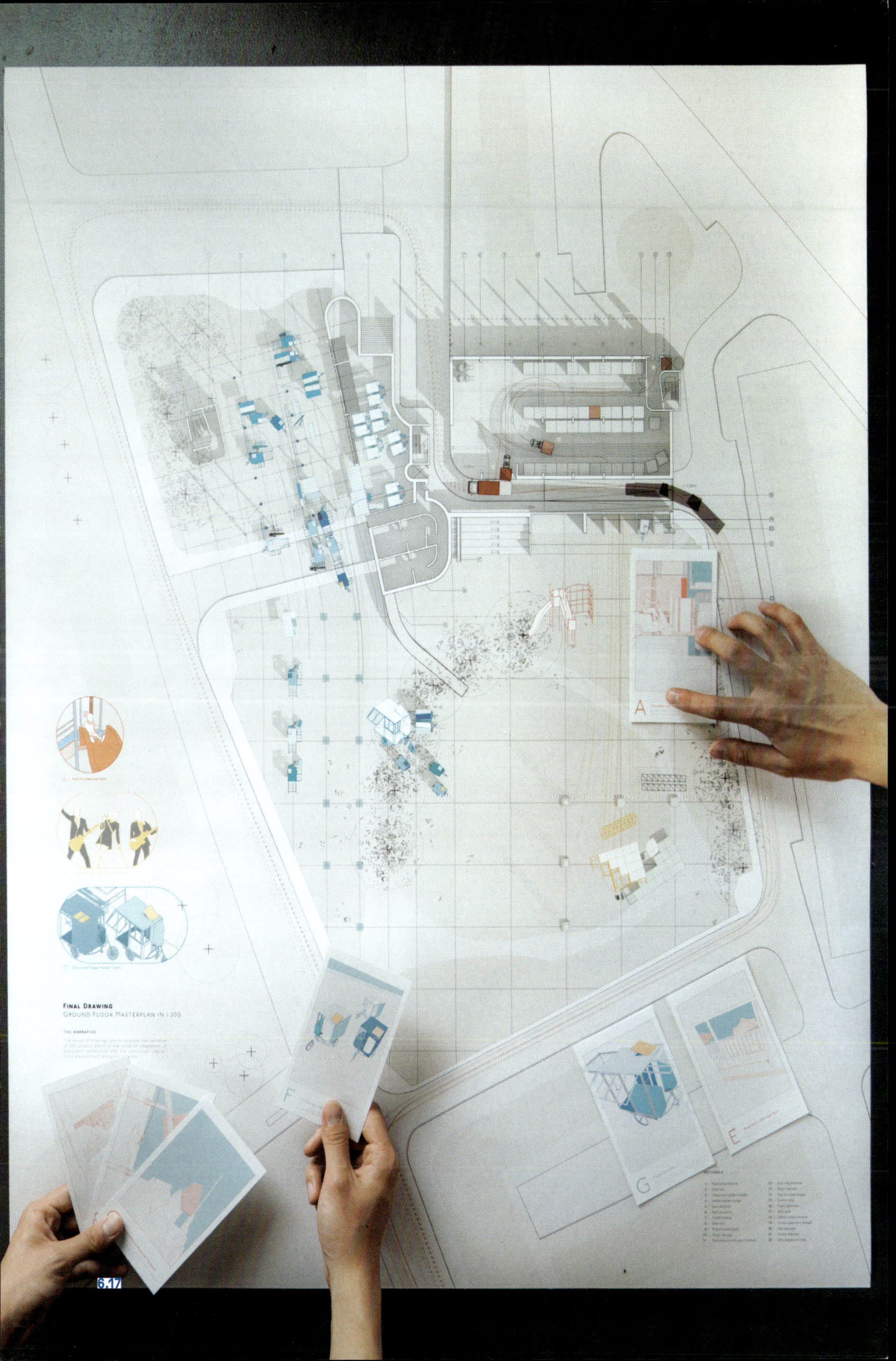
Final Drawing
Ground Floor Masterplan in 1:200
The narrative
A
F
G
E

6.17

UG7

The Drowning Crescent

Pascal Bronner, Thomas Hillier

Year 2
Oliver Ansell, Grant Beaumont, Lauren Childs, James Cook, Mengzi Fu, Margarita Marsheva, Cherie Wong, Arthur Wong

Year 3
Alexandra Campbell, Glen Heng, Hanna Idziak, Harry Johnson, Hannah Lewis, Harry Pizzey, Fei Yen Waller, Lisa Fan Wu

Thank you to our technical tutor David Storring and computing tutor Sean Allen

Thank you to our critics: Jenna Al-Ali, Peter Bishop, Matthew Butcher, David Edwards, Stephen Gage, Soomeen Hahm, CJ Lim, Shaun Murray, Justin Nicholls, Alan Penn, Aleksandrina Rizova, Joshua Scott, Alistair Shaw

Humankind's relationship with water has always been a fascinating one, one that has shaped civilisations, sculpted cities, inspired writers, artists, and captivated architects. But today the fundamental relationship between water and human habitation is being transformed in the wake of an escalating global crisis. To explore this, the unit travelled to New Orleans, a city virtually surrounded by water. Built on thousands of feet of soft sand, silt and clay on the banks of the Mississippi, the city actually sits within a bowl, surrounded by protection levees and floodwalls, with half of the city located eight feet below sea level.

——Paradoxically, these man-made levees reduced the threat of the great Mississippi River's seasonal flooding, allowing New Orleanians to expand their metropolis over generations. But that same infrastructure also set in motion environmental shifts that made the city more vulnerable to storms. Today, the Mississippi Delta is sinking a centimetre a year, whilst sea levels are rising at an accelerating rate, and are predicted to be two metres higher by the year 2100, submerging most of New Orleans. Over the next 15 years scientists believe that, if nothing is done, over 300 square miles of Louisiana will disappear, with many fearing New Orleans might become one of the first cities of the modern age to face extinction, creating a modern-day Atlantis, lost to the sea.

——It is this ever-changing relationship between water and human habitation that we wanted our students to investigate, but before we set foot in the Crescent City, they were tasked with exploring, researching and (re)interpreting the specific effects of water on New Orleans in an attempt to understand its history, masterplan, neighbourhoods and most importantly, inhabitants. By extrapolating these findings they began to design their own drawn, modelled or collaged urban water narrative that culminated in an architectural or infrastructural innovation, allegorical or real in nature.

——These macro-scale interventions were, in some form, taken to New Orleans where they were applied as a strategic compass to discover their future programme and site for the main building project, the only requisite being that the building in some form dealt with water. New Orleans is a unique city and the students' architecture had to be equally as bespoke, specific and tailor-made. As always, their work embodied the unit's agenda of craft, speculation, experimentation, wonder and delight – with the only limit being their imaginations.

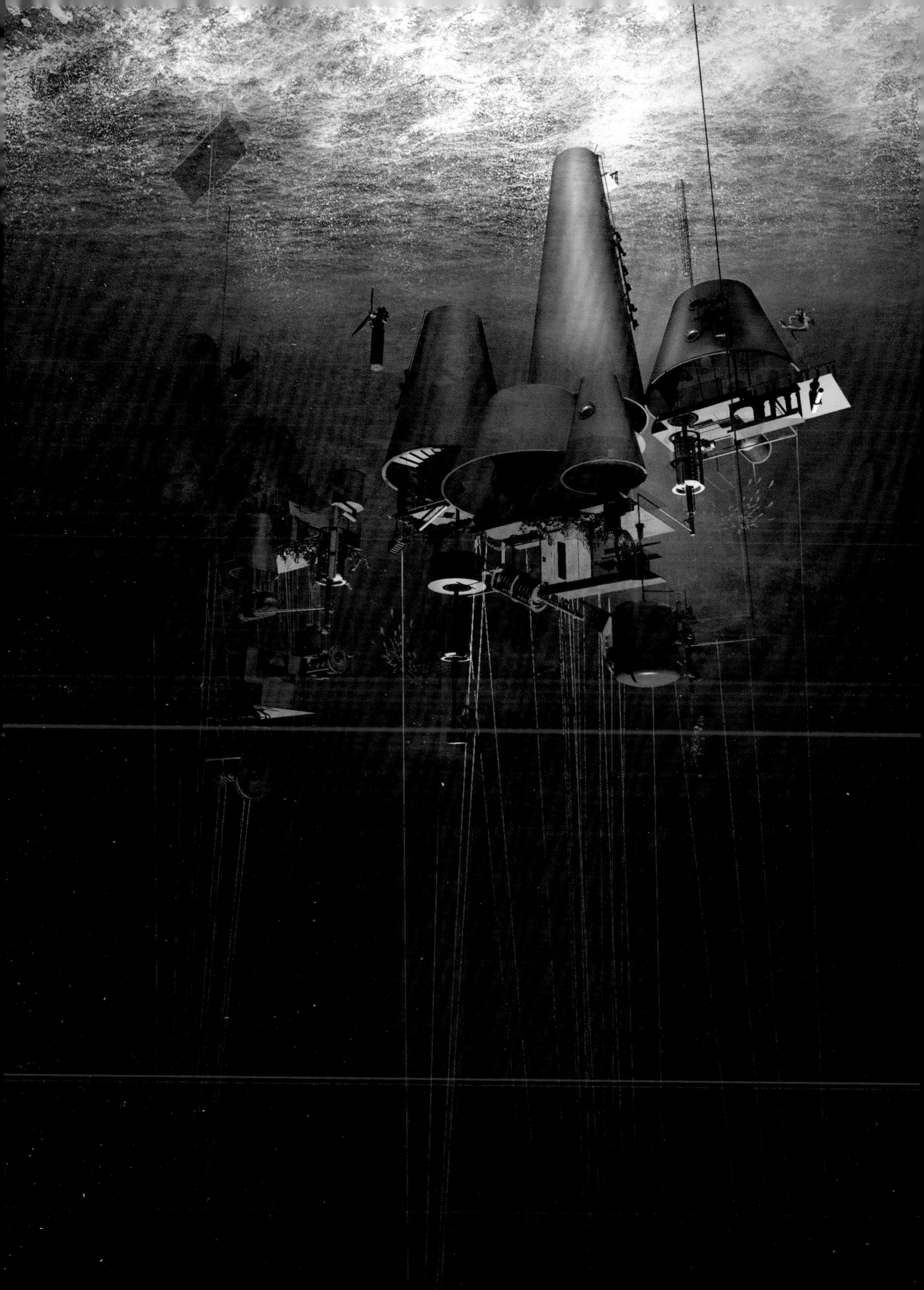

7.1

Fig. 7.1 **Hannah Lewis** Y3, '20 Leagues Under the Sea'. This proposed underwater settlement posits a world where sea levels have risen above the protection levees of New Orleans, forcing American suburbia to retreat into the ocean, creating a new form of wet living. **Fig. 7.2** **Oliver Ansell** Y2, 'The Prolonging of Pilottown'. With a population of zero, Pilottown, located at the mouth of the Mississippi River, has become a ghost town lost to the floods. This proposed retreat, for six elderly and original residents of the town, aims to prolong – through a communal form of architecture – the lifespan of Pilottown before it is altogether consumed by rising waters. **Figs. 7.3 – 7.4** **Cherie Wong** Y2, 'St. Louis Voodoo Temple'. This new home for the voodoo practitioners of New Orleans sits within the famed St. Louis Cemetery, where Marie Laveau, the first voodoo queen of Louisiana, is buried. Controlled by sunlight and moonlight, the building is activated incrementally at particular times across the day to allow its inhabitants to follow the very specific voodoo calendar of rituals. **Fig. 7.5** **Alexandra Campbell** Y3, 'The Ninth Ward Floodwall'. Based on the festival Anba Dlo ('beneath the waters'), the building is both scientific and spiritual in nature, with the pragmatism of science setting with the sun, and the ethereality of spirit taking over with the appearance of the moon. Situated along, and being intrinsically linked to, a new floodwall along the Lower Ninth Ward, this institute for flood research and spiritual enlightenment inhabits the boundary between sanctuary and threat. The architecture aims to create a new sacrificial symbol of safety for New Orleans.

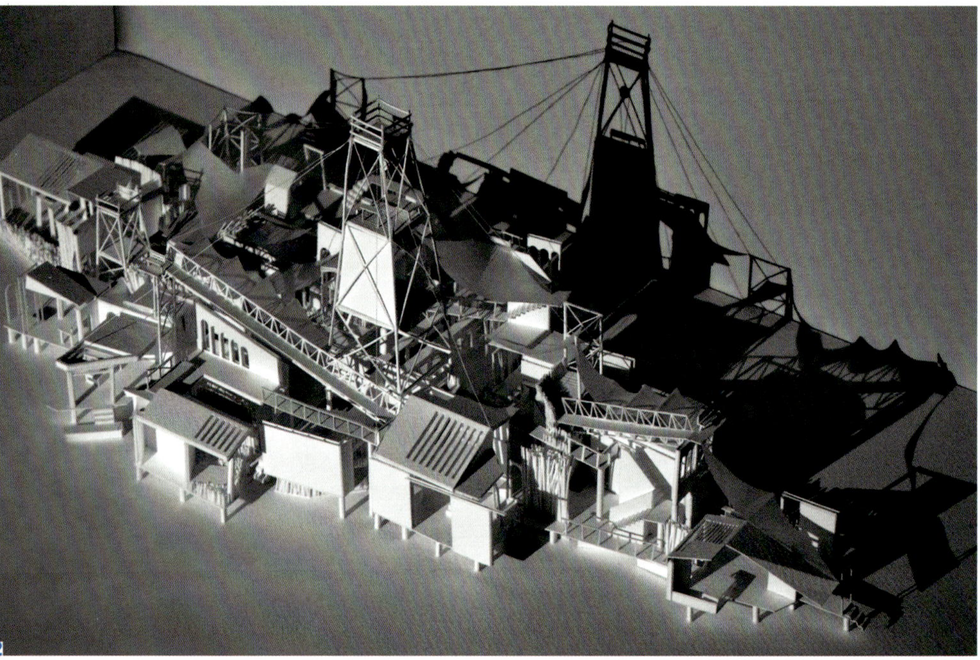

7.2

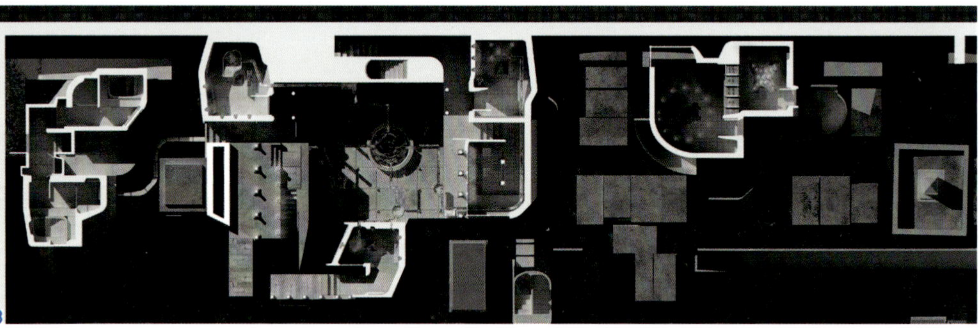

7.3

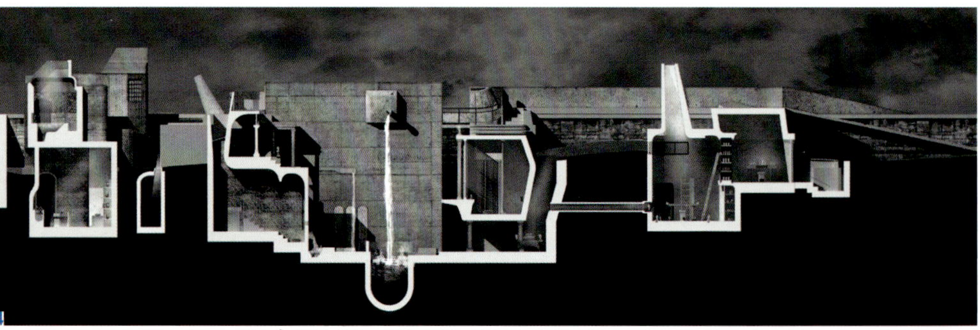

7.4

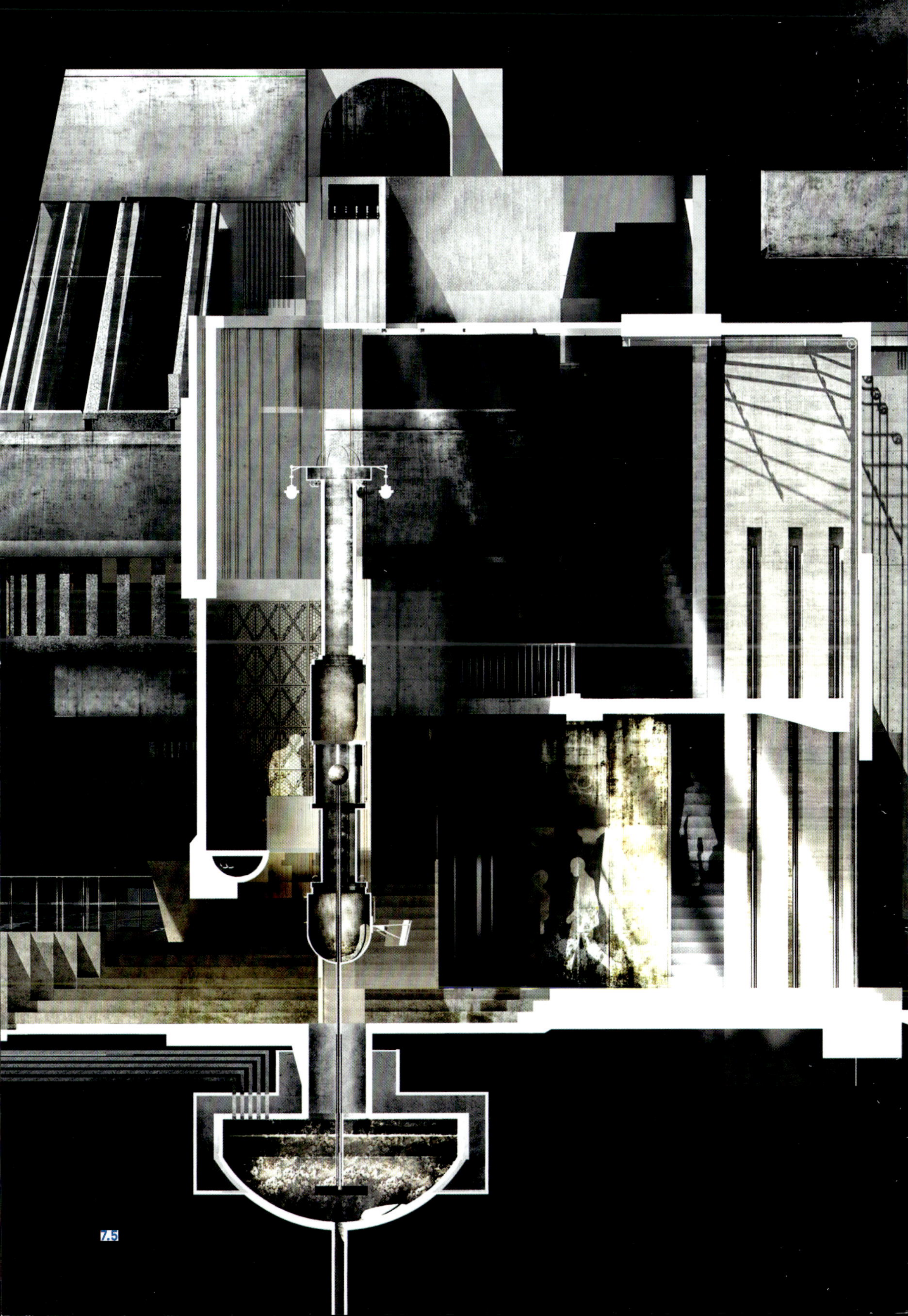
7.5

Fig. 7.6 **Lauren Childs** Y2, 'The Iron Lace Ladies'. New Orleans is characterised by its ornate ironwork that decorates otherwise sober building façades. Located on the famed Royal Street, the building is an ironwork foundry that restores and replaces ironwork in disrepair. Alongside this, the building is a refuge for woman during and after a flood, containing enough water, food and beds to ensure a safe haven for anyone who enters. **Fig. 7.7** **Grant Beaumont** Y2, 'Imaging Usonia'. This investigation creates, measures and occupies unseen spaces. A series of concocted material samples underwent an overlaid scanning process through a bespoke device to develop visible and invisible data points. Each of these points became a peak or trough marker creating a visual, spatial map that is both macro and micro in scale. **Fig. 7.8** **Mengzi Fu** Y2, 'The Thin House'. Inspired by Italo Calvino's 'Invisible Cities', the Thin House explores the notion of living in a building where piped services are not hidden within walls or under floorboards, but exposed and reconfigured to create a complex, interlaced world of inhabitable space. **Fig. 7.9** **Harry Johnson** Y3, 'The Folk Craft Guild of New Orleans'. In its 50th year, The Smithsonian Institution has commissioned a Guild to present and preserve the indigenous crafts of Louisiana. Located on Royal Street, alongside a succession of craft and antique outlets, folk craft practitioners work side by side, exploring local traditions such as steam bending and Bousillage. Crafted entirely from the bald cypress tree, the official state tree of Louisiana, the Guild aims to promote both local traditions and the use of locally sourced materials.

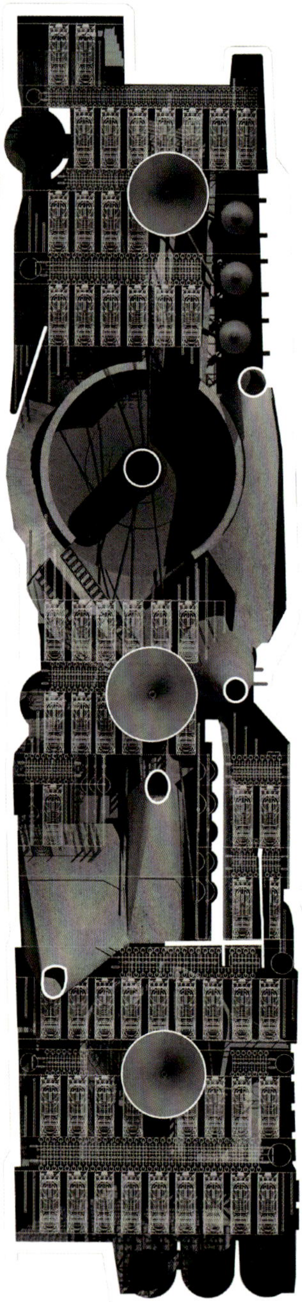

7.6

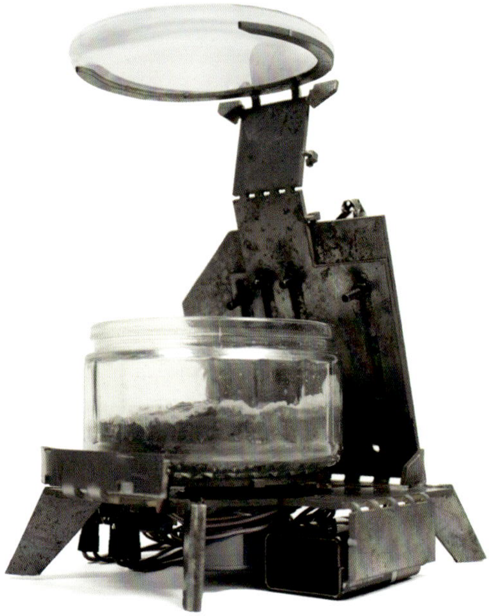

7.7

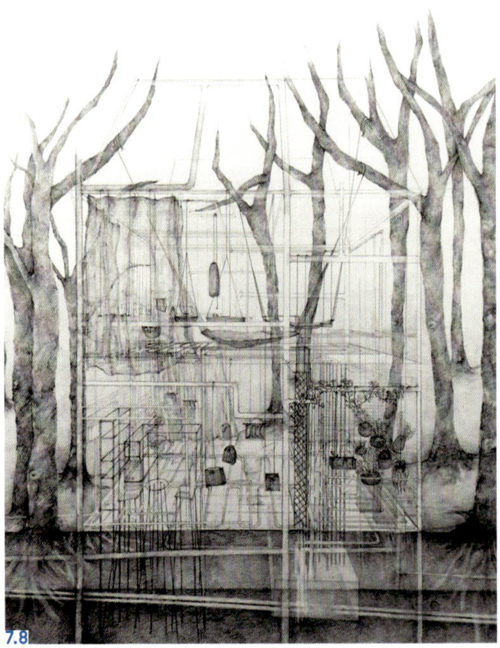

7.8

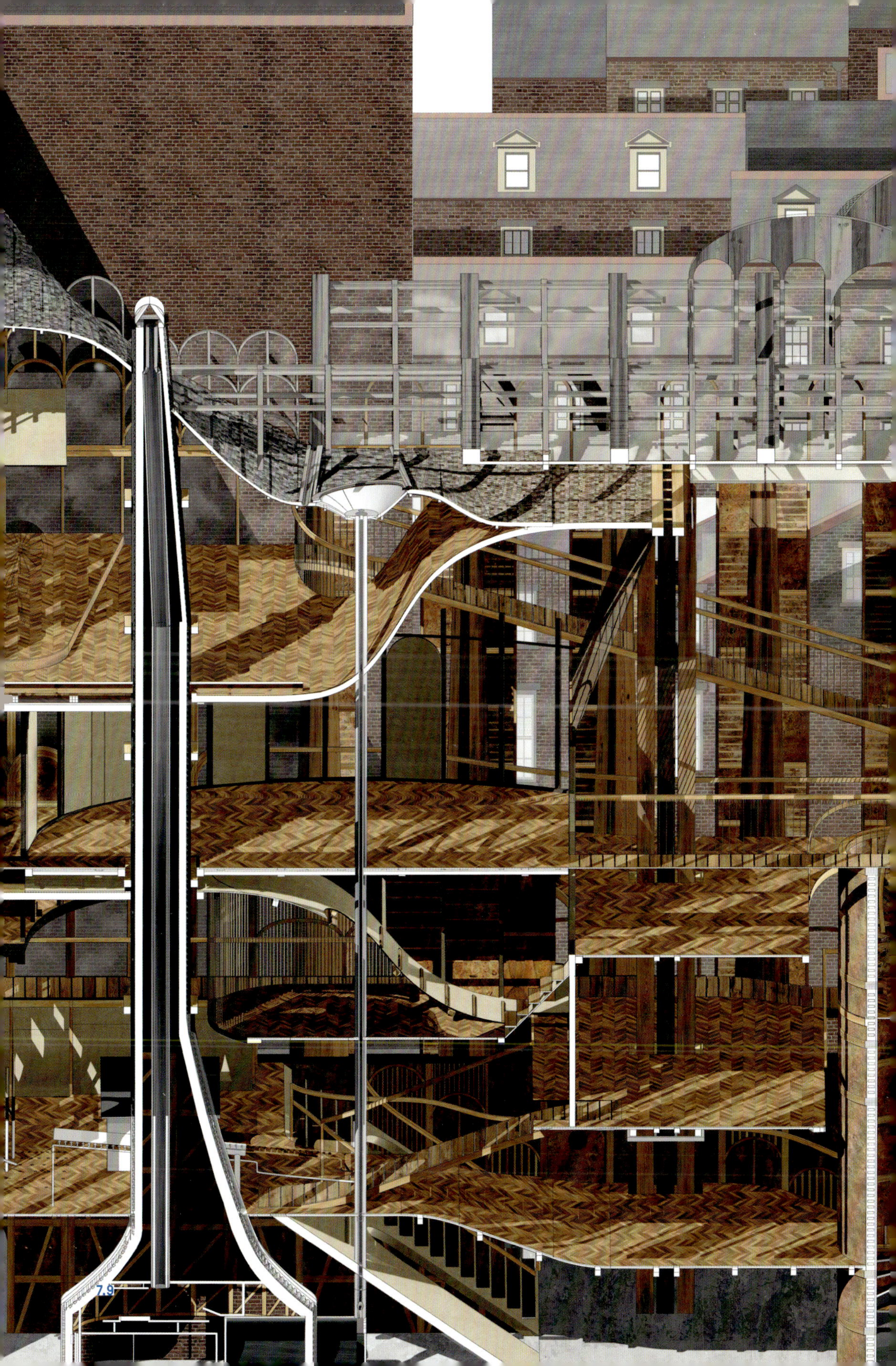
7.9

Fig. 7.10 Glen Heng Y3, 'The Dixon Street Mercedes – Columbarium'. Sitting at the heart of New Orleans' Business District, adjacent to the famous Mercedes Superdome, floats a stone landscape that becomes the next in a long line of famous cemeteries to drape this city. The columbarium, set above the existing concrete landscape, is built to lift the curse (believed to have begun when the Girod Street Cemetery was demolished to make way for the Superdome) that created the longest losing streak the New Orleans Saints have ever seen. **Fig. 7.11 Lisa Fan Wu** Y3, 'The Breakwater Yacht Club'. During Hurricane Katrina, New Orleans' only yacht club, the famous Breakwater Park yacht club, was completely destroyed. This project proposes the creation of a new yacht club that is also a specialised water film studio, bringing a new industry to New Orleans, capitalising on what famously surrounds this city – water. The new yacht club sits within a carved landscape that forms a giant, open air water tank for filming. When full, and being used for a film, the club itself is completely submerged in water and it is not until the tank is drained that the architecture is revealed. **Fig. 7.12 Hanna Idziak** Y3, 'New Isle de Jean Charles'. For over 170 years, the Isle de Jean Charles to the southwest of New Orleans has been the historical homeland and burial ground of the Native American Biloxi-Chitimacha-Choctaw tribe. Coastal erosion and rising sea levels have forced the tribe to move. This government-funded proposal creates a new permanent homeland for the tribe that is self-sustainable, flood-resistant and revives lost traditions, allowing the people to live off the land once again.

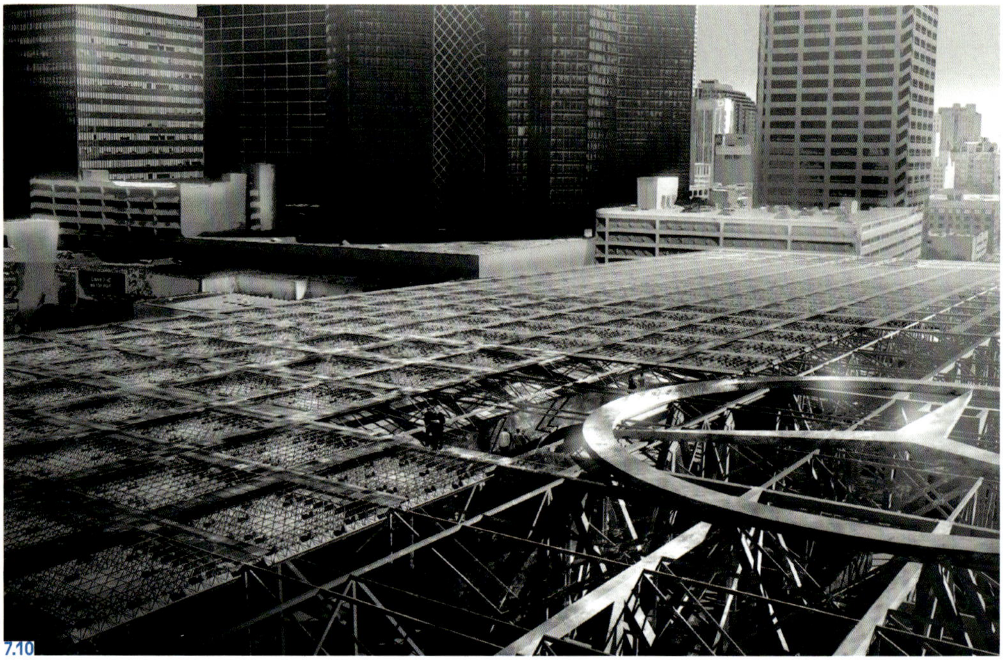

7.10

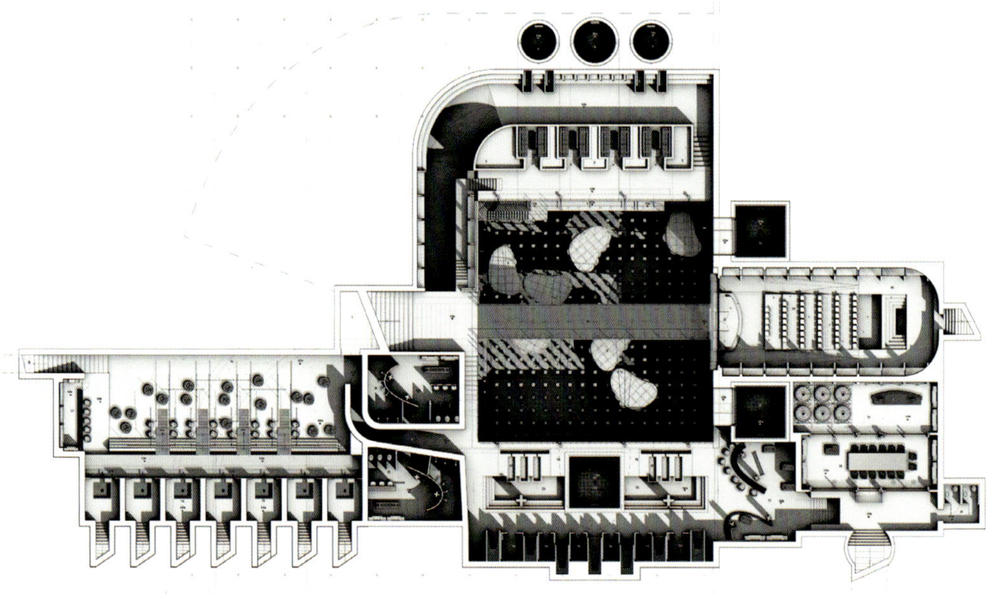

7.11

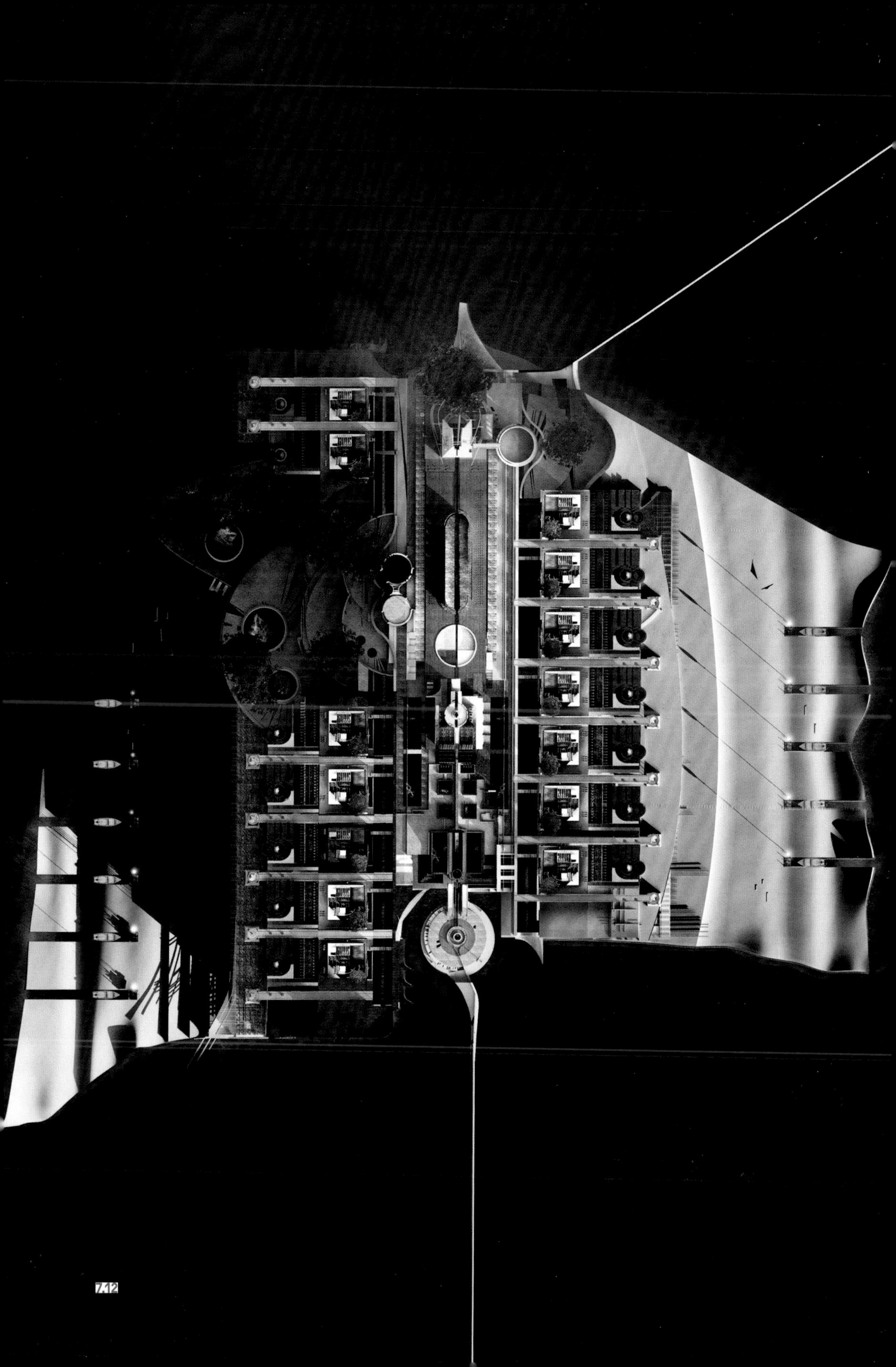

7.12

Fig. 7.13 Arthur Wong Y2, 'The Water Keeper's House'. Inspired by a fascination with water and its ability to create surreal conditions, alongside the unique geography of New Orleans, the Water Keeper's House becomes the all-seeing eye at the edge of a water recharge and retention reservoir. Sited in an area destroyed by Hurricane Katrina, domestic rooms are scattered around this liquid landscape, each embracing a characteristic and phenomenon of water. **Fig. 7.14 James Cook** Y2, 'The Hoffman Triangle Melodic Assembly Building'. In the Hoffman Neighbourhood at the centre of the Seventh Ward, an area severely hit during the catastrophic events of Katrina, lies this new gospel performance building. Funded by local entrepreneur and long-time resident of the Triangle, Troy Jackson, this new communal building – dedicated to re-housing the African American gospel community – is constructed using remnants of the former Saint Francis de Sales Church that it now replaces. **Fig. 7.15 Harry Pizzey** Y3, 'The Ninth Ward Safe Houses'. This new street square in the heart of the Ninth Ward aims to protect the traditional vernacular and way of life of the residents hardest hit by Hurricane Katrina. This sculpted concrete and tile landscape, inspired by the ghostly foundations of the building lost to the flood, accepts that future floods will occur so prepares its inhabitants through an architecture of disassembly. In the event of a flood, the shotgun house, a common typology of New Orleans, can be dismantled in a matter of hours and stored in a concrete appendage located within the square, which also acts as a retreat for the residents for the duration of the flood.

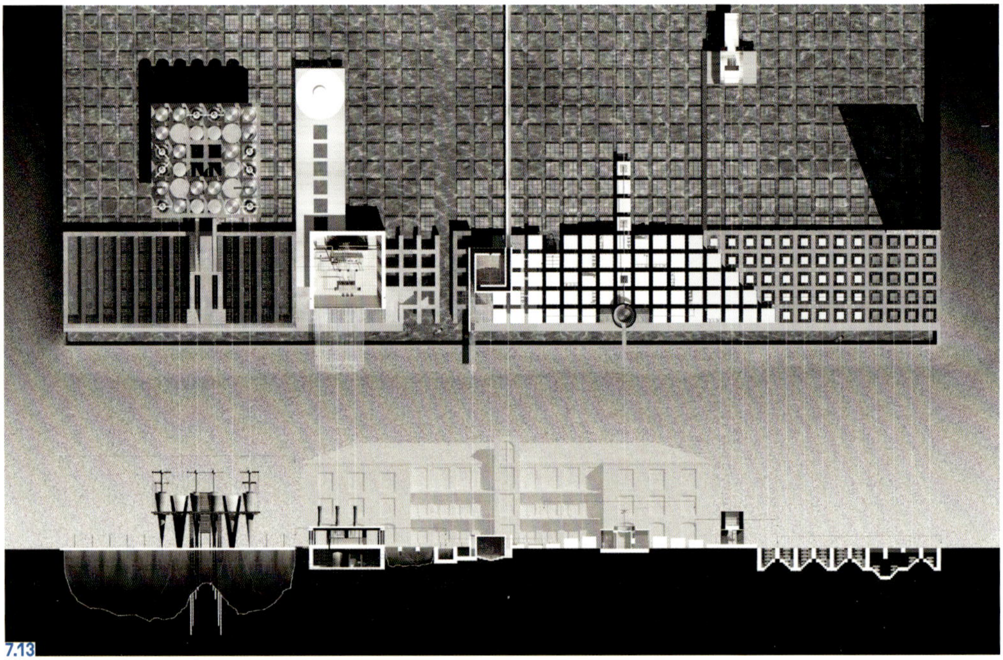

7.13

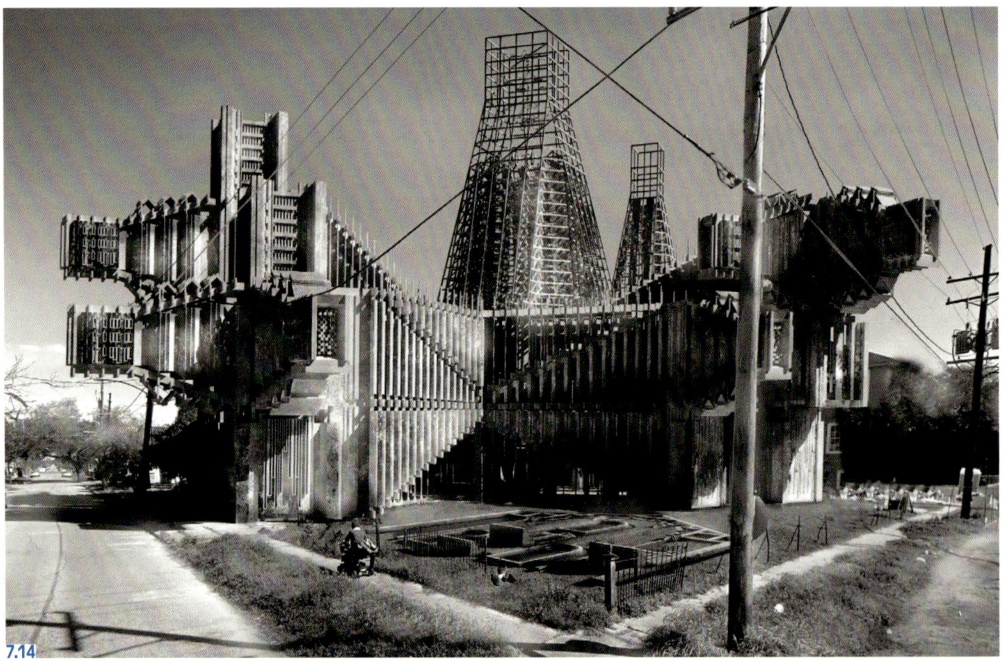

7.14

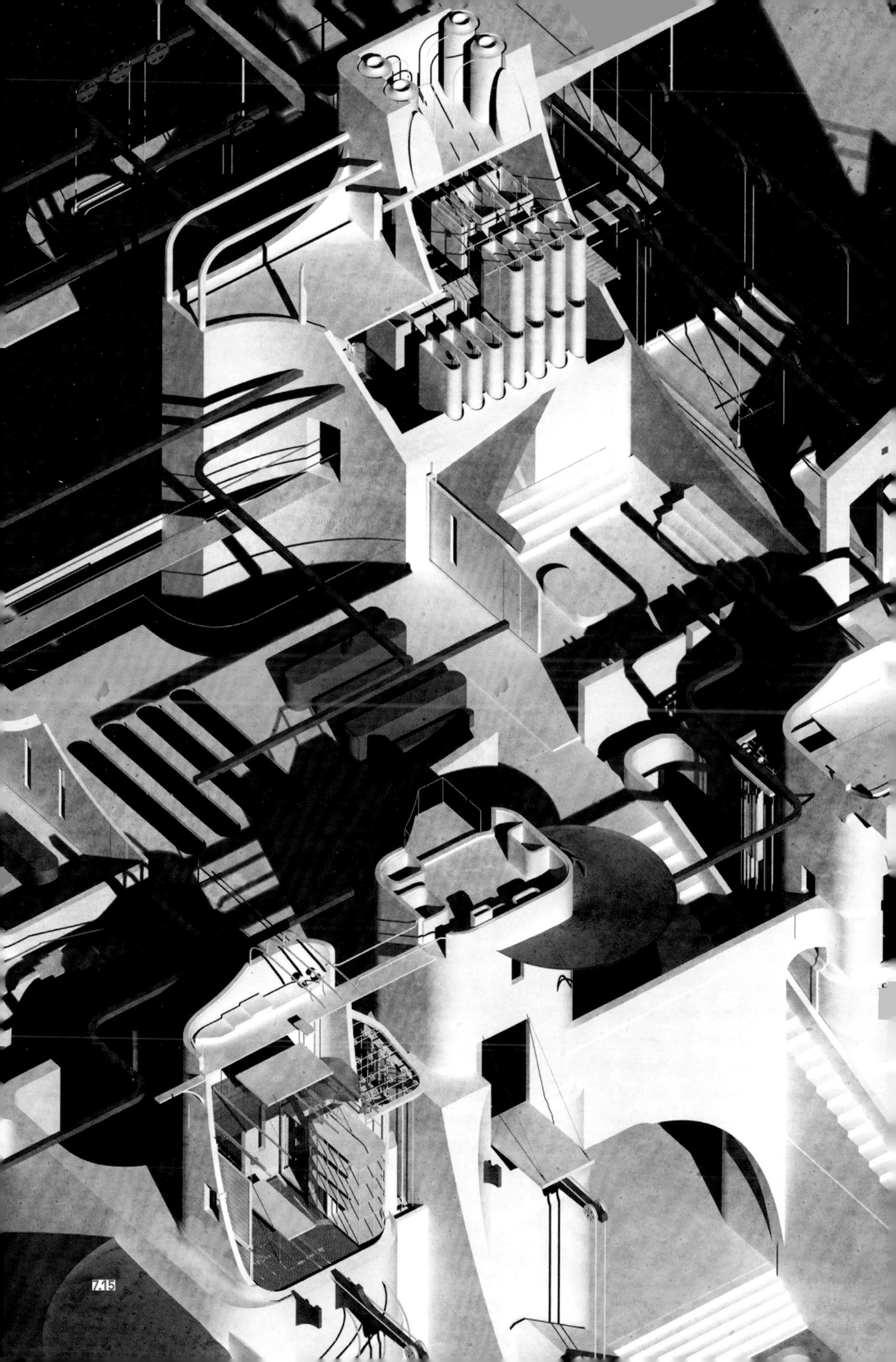

7.15

UG8

Precise Disasters: A Laboratory at the Edge of Failure

Colin Herperger, Thomas Pearce

Year 2
Maxim Goldau, Millicent Green, Lola Haines, Florence Hemmings, Joe Johnson, Ying-Ying Lou (Iris), Oscar Maguire

Year 3
Hohgun Choi, Thomas Chu, Christina Garbi, Georgia Jaeckle, Carmen Kong, Aleksandra Kugacka, Elissavet Manou, Felix Sagar

Special thanks to our technical tutor Jerry Tate

Thank you to our critics, speakers and supporters: Charles Arsene-Henry, Alastair Browning, Nat Chard, Ricardo de Ostos, Max Dewdney, Gary Edwards, Jurgis Gecys, Jack Holmes, Jessica Inn, Bálint Kádár, Korbinian Kainz, Luke Lupton, Mara Kanthak, Gergely Kovacs, Ifigeneia Liangi, Thandi Loewenson, Dora Mathe, Emma-Kate Matthews, Inigo Minns, Shaun Murray, Thomas Parker, Frederik Petersen, Caroline Rabourdin, Soma Sato, Peter Scully, Bob Sheil, Greg Storrar, Anna Tripamer, William Trossell, Athanasios Varnavas, Simon Withers

Thank you to our sponsors: FABberz, ScanLAB Projects, Tate Harmer & Ultimaker

"If I fail, I will fail so hard that I can never recover." Werner Herzog, before beginning his first feature film, *Herakles*

The lifeblood of any experiment in science or design is its potential to fail. Progress is all about being wrong. Searching for the horizon, we must be ready to find the edge of collapse as a place of excitement. To try is to fail and to fail is to discover.

——This year, Unit 8 sets out to explore the fringes of failure as a space of seduction and a vehicle for creative opportunity. In architectural education most are scared of the very idea of failure. Why? Perhaps it could be considered the point where learning begins – a liberated escape from the shadow of rehearsal.

——In our Laboratory at the Edge of Failure, we chased the subtle delights of this nimble edge, tempting us beyond assumption into the world of the unexpected. To do so, we operated with a sense of poetry and tenacity, but also with utmost precision, producing well-crafted failures on the edge of perception, collapse or consciousness. We hunted the boundaries of structural and material performance, chased the seduction of the glitch, the misaligned and mistranslated, the shadows of knowledge and common sense, the technological blind-spots and slippages of control.

——On our field trip from Vienna to Budapest and through the wild countryside in between, we tracked the experiments of a series of architectural and artistic misfits, outsiders venturing to the edges of failure, consciousness and supposed good taste: Adolf Loos' notoriously 'unfashionable' buildings, Egon Schiele's perverse character of line within figure drawing, Fritz Wotruba's controversial sculpture-turned-architecture, Coop Himmelb(l)au's technical challenge of a religious adherence to an intoxicated sketch, Imre Makovecz's politically and structurally subversive architectural inventions, as well as the difficult material and conceptual junctions in the sculpture and architecture of Walter Pichler, created at his farm.

——The building projects continued our research into strategies of disturbance and failure by translating ideas into inventive architecture. Our projects were situated along the Danube trajectory in difficult topographies and various cultural conditions, in order to serve up a range of possibility and resistance to spatial ideas.

——In Unit 8 we like to make disobedient things and find curiosity within challenging ideas. This is delightfully hard but is nurtured within the studio through creative practice – a focused learning of architectural craft and technique through repeated prediction, attempt, reflection and iteration. This allows for the development of an intuitive ability to become precise in a manner that holds no responsibility to prove, but, more importantly, does have the will to find out. We seek pleasure in the precision of the unresolved.

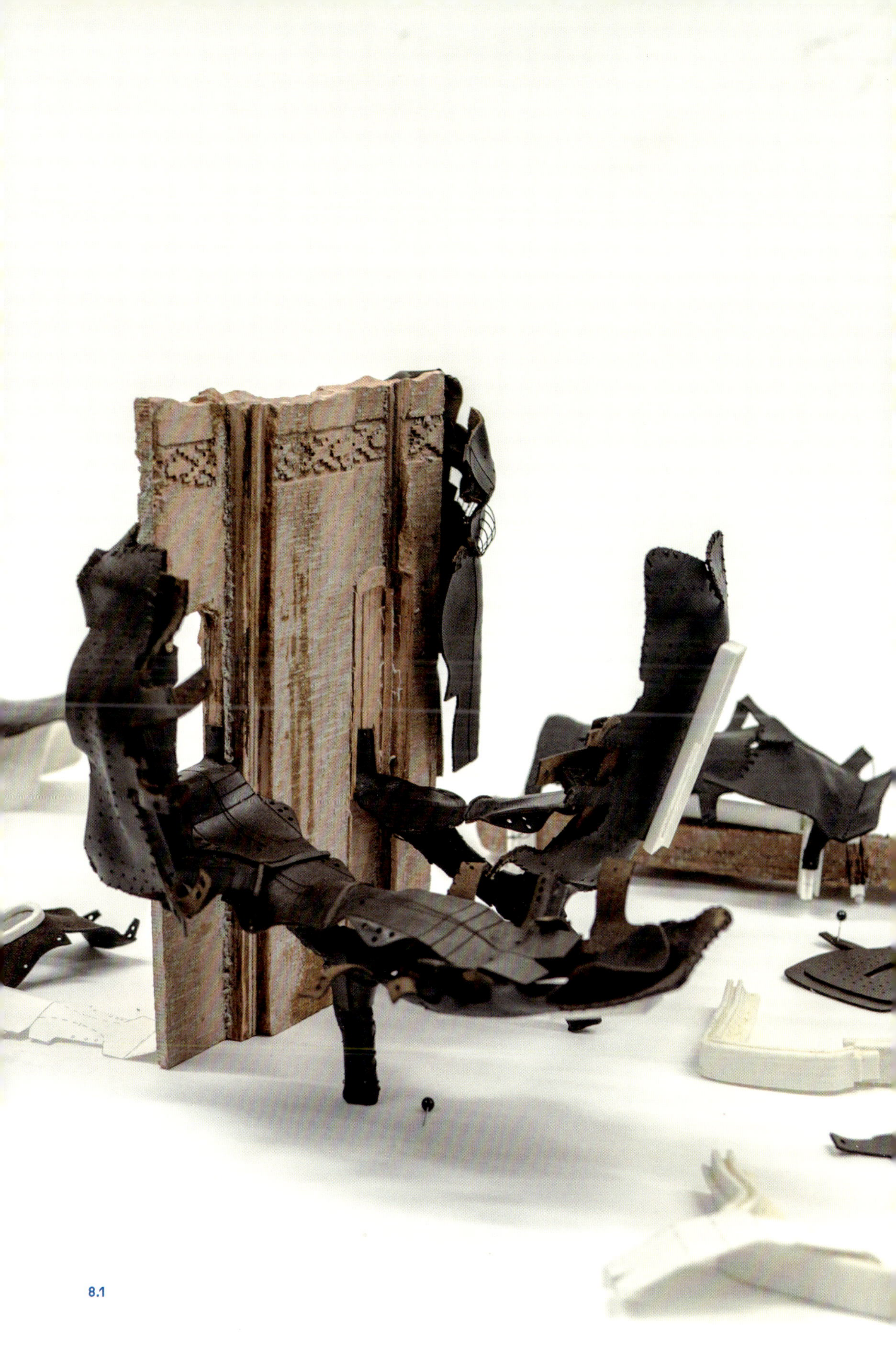

8.1

Figs. 8.1 – 8.2 Elissavet Manou Y3, 'Wearing Out-Wearing In'. Nested within the Gül Baba ruins on the hills of Budapest, this Academy of Method Acting is completely fabricated via Hungarian saddlemaking techniques. Through an intimate architectural dialogue between the ruin and the leather structures, notions of performance and reality, and between artifice and authenticity, are blurred and dissolved. **Fig. 8.3 Joe Johnson** Y2, 'Rhythmicised soundscapes'. A Viennese café transforms into a nightclub by amplifying, distorting and tuning the café's native soundscape through a series of automated sound nests. The project operates through the simultaneous simulation, scripting and actuation of hybrid physical and digital, architectural and acoustic models. **Figs. 8.4 – 8.6 Hohgun Choi** Y3, 'Part-time Art Time'. An underground art gallery and bank challenging Vienna's obsession with the ornate and opulent, and the current trend towards art-as-commodity. The vaults store secrets instead of money. This programmatic duality is explored through a kinetic shift in the building that changes the bank into a publicly accessible art gallery and pavilion.

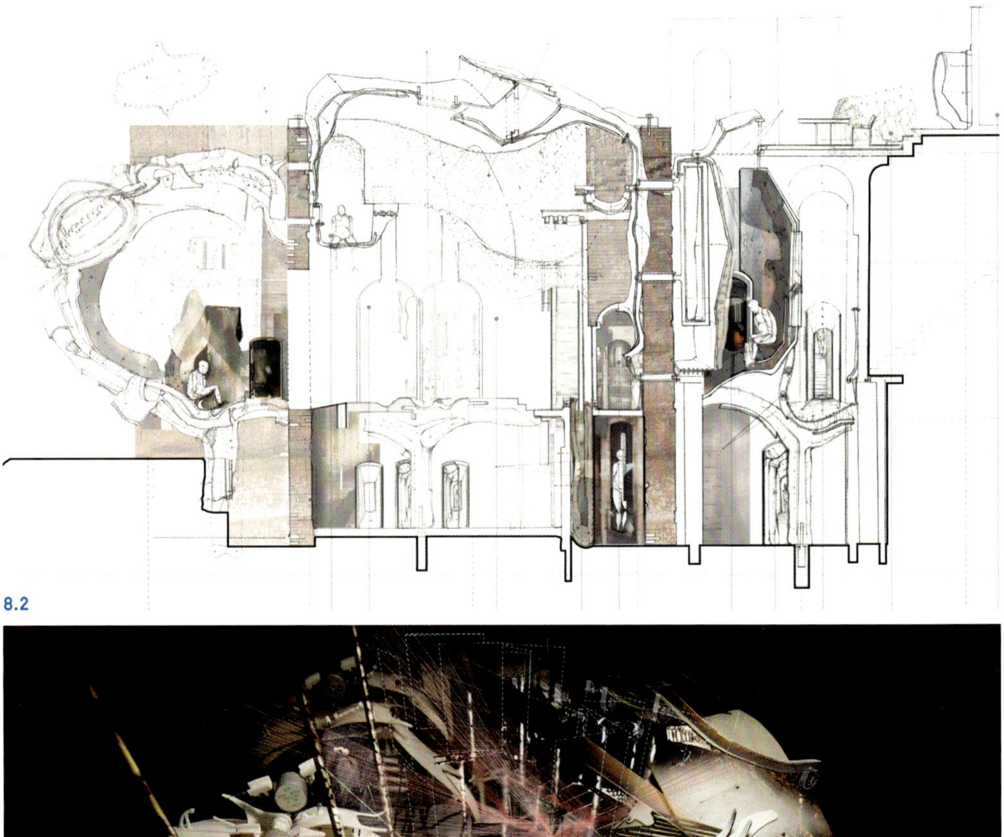

8.2

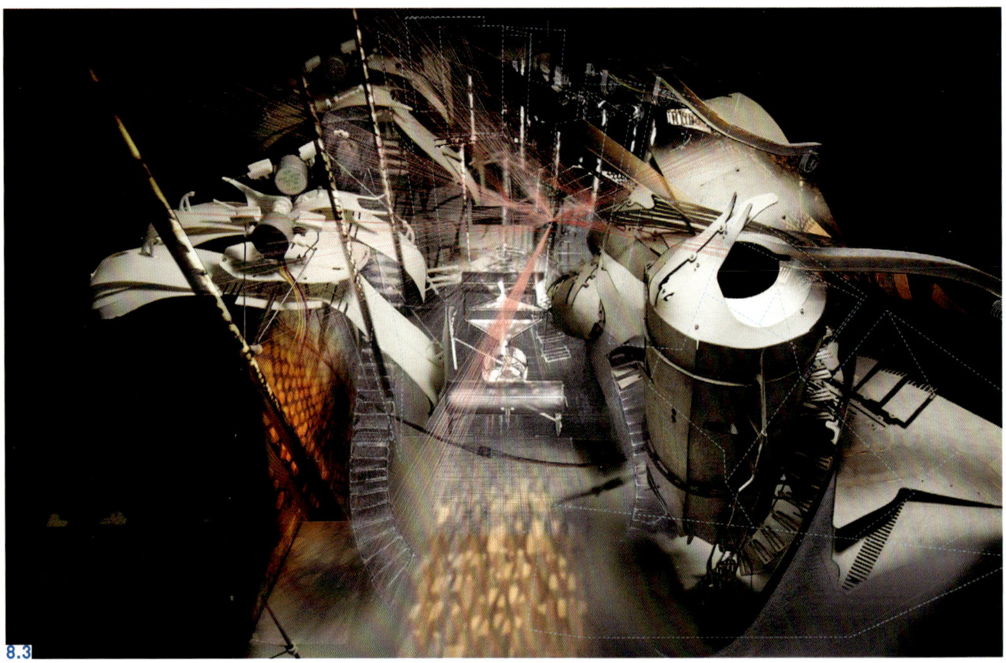

8.3

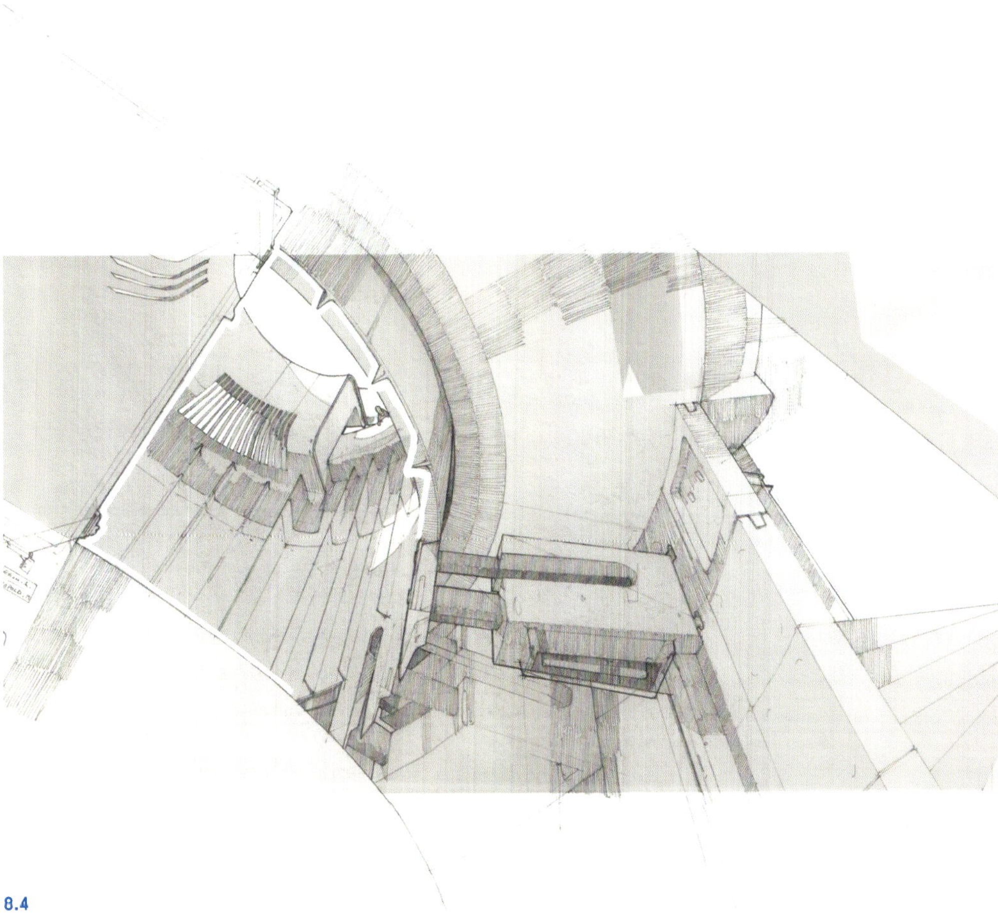

8.4

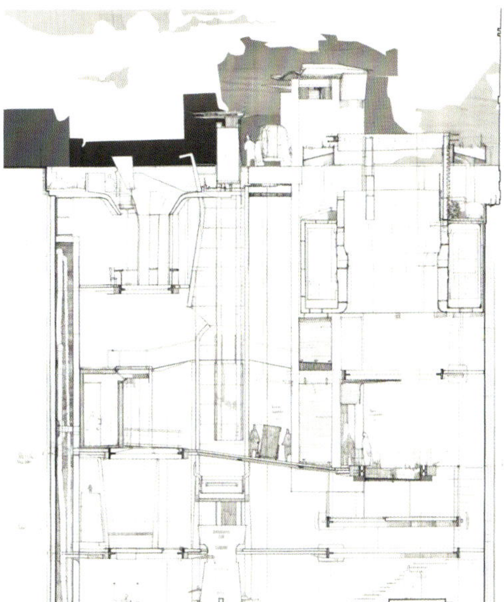

8.5

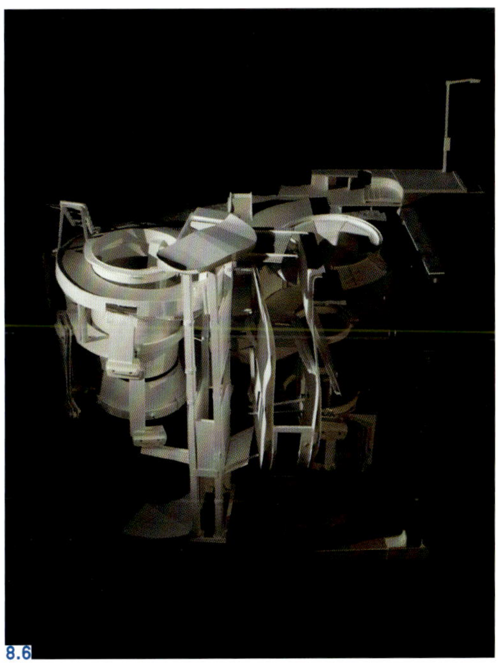

8.6

Figs. 8.7 – 8.8 Florence Hemmings Y2, 'Unfurling Subjects, Inverted Objects'. A tailoring shop in central Vienna uses strategies of material and programmatic inversion on the scales of the body, the garment and the building. This plays host to a sequence of displays, initially treating display windows as an observed object, and then becoming the subject of/subject to the shop. **Fig. 8.9 Lola Haines** Y2, 'Museum of Baroque Theatre'. A gallery situated in Vienna to house a permanent theatre exhibition capturing the magic of stage and illusion. The project merges intuitive analogue figure-modelling and digital fabrication to bridge the boundaries between sculpture and architecture, and building and exhibit. **Fig. 8.10 Maxim Goldau** Y2, 'When Chi Chi Met Semper'. This is a conceptual arts faculty for the Viennese Academy, emerging from an imaginative misreading of the Semperdepot as well as from an illusionistic ceiling painting and an ongoing genealogy of mistranslated panda light drawings. It seeks to manifest the expectation and interpretation of the designer into an architectural form.

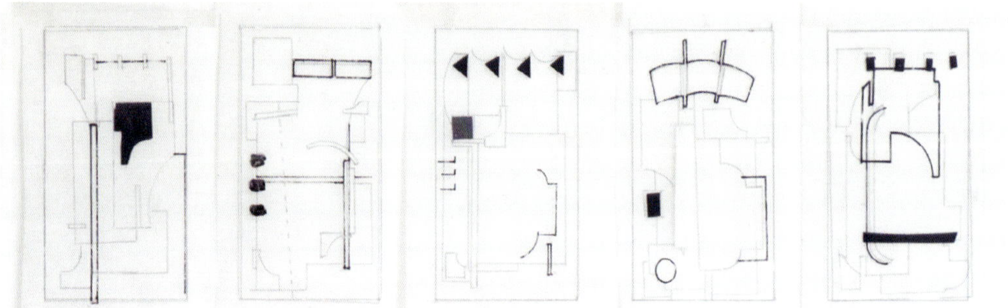

8.7

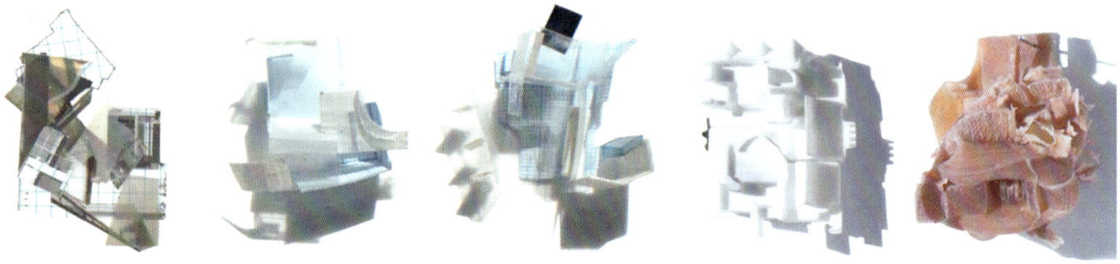

8.8

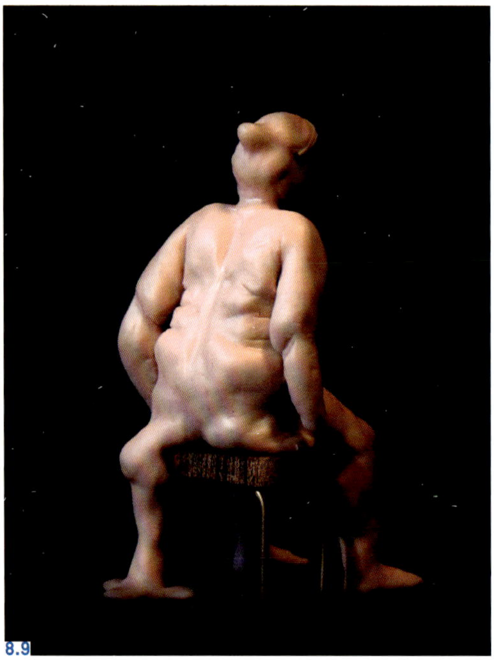

8.9

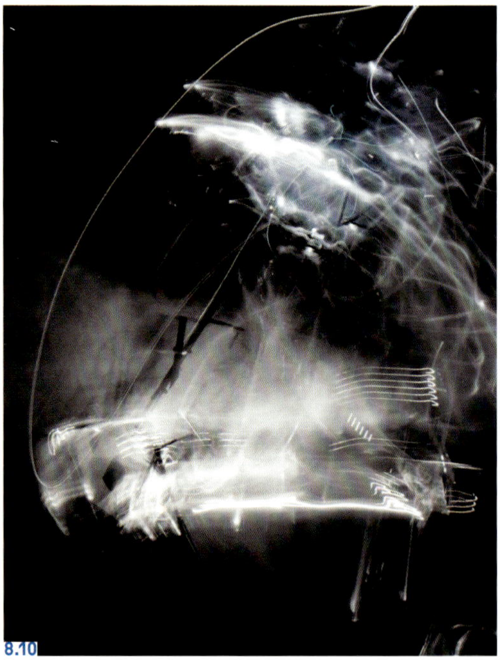

8.10

Figs. 8.11 – 8.12 Felix Sagar Y3, 'Object Hallucinations'. Through practicing object-triggered 'free association', the project questions whether the flickering-up and passing-away of consciousness during object perception can be used as a tool in architectural design. The visitor unexpectedly comes face-to-face with the creatures that now inhabit six of Sigmund Freud's objects, re-imagined and re-composed as a Reptile House.

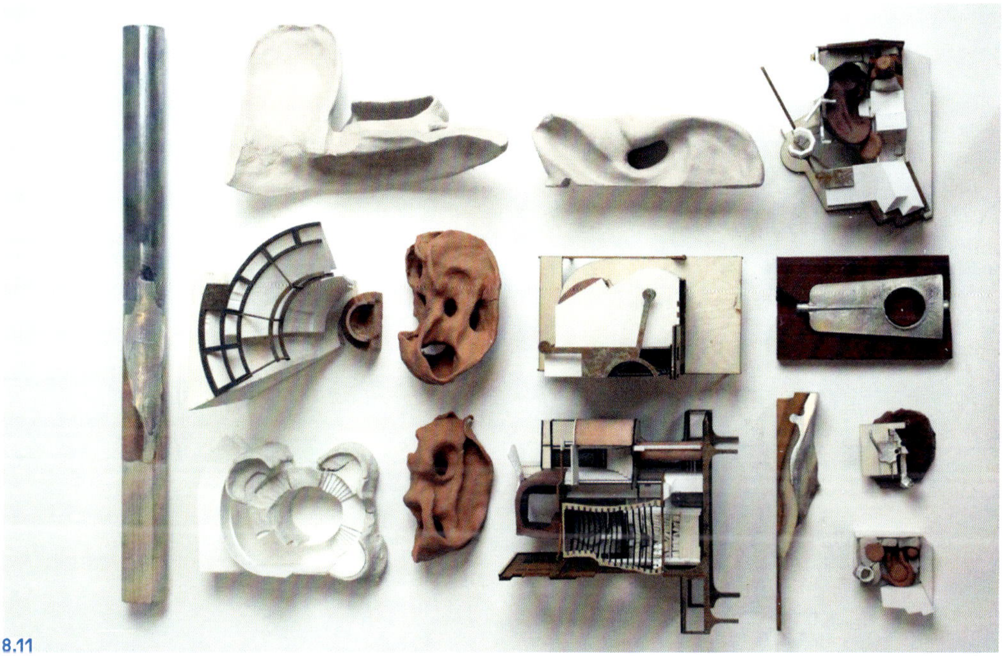

8.11

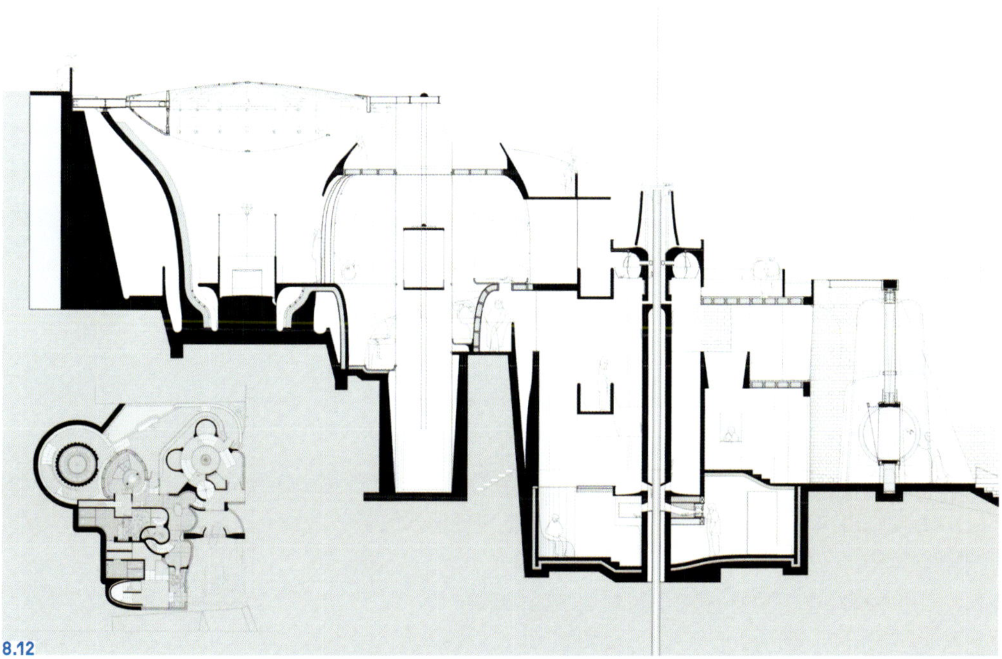

8.12

Fig. 8.13 Millie Green Y2, 'The Climbing Library'. The project aims to explore aspects of climbing: tension, counterbalance and the equilibrium between the heavy and the light. A cantilevering lightweight chassis, in the form of a library, supports a mass of counterbalancing books, only achieving its equilibrium by its symbiotic relationship with an out-of-balance climbing wall. **Fig. 8.14 Carmen Kong** Y3, 'Palinka Hotel'. A micro-distillery and hotel exploring the interaction between a tasting experience and the perception of colour. Carved out of the hills of Buda, it uses discreet materials to blend into Budapest's landscape during the day – but at night, it comes alive in saturated brightness, and guests enjoy palinka in special tasting rooms located around the hotel. **Fig. 8.15 Christina Garbi** Y3, 'A Cathedral of Water'. A bath house on the banks of the Danube that uses inflatable casting techniques to create an architecture of thin fragile shells. The perfect geometries of the computationally designed inflatables are distorted when tailored and cast, creating shells of collapsing curved surfaces with traces of deflation.

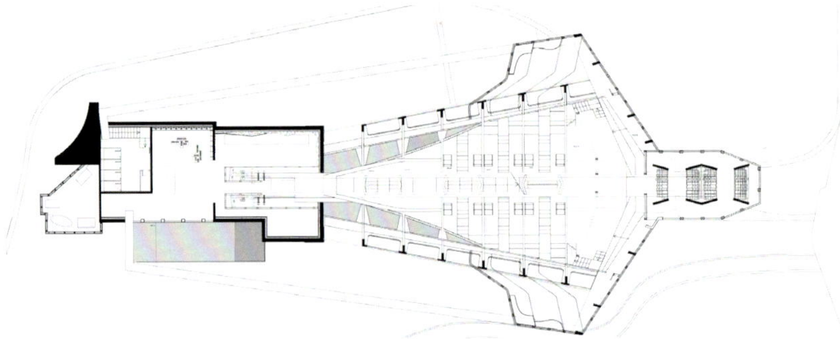

8.13

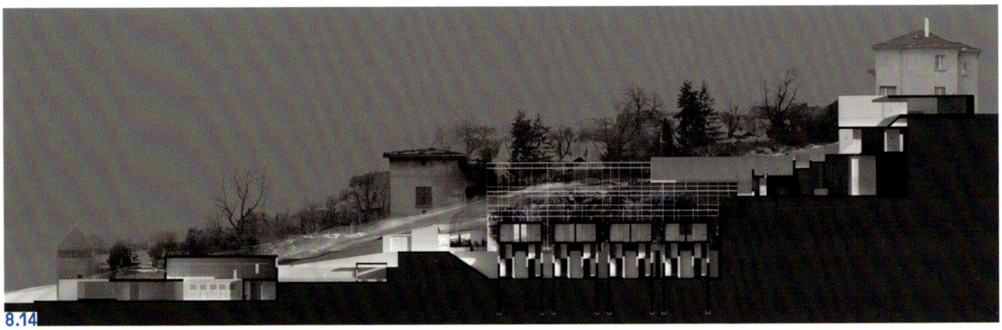

8.14

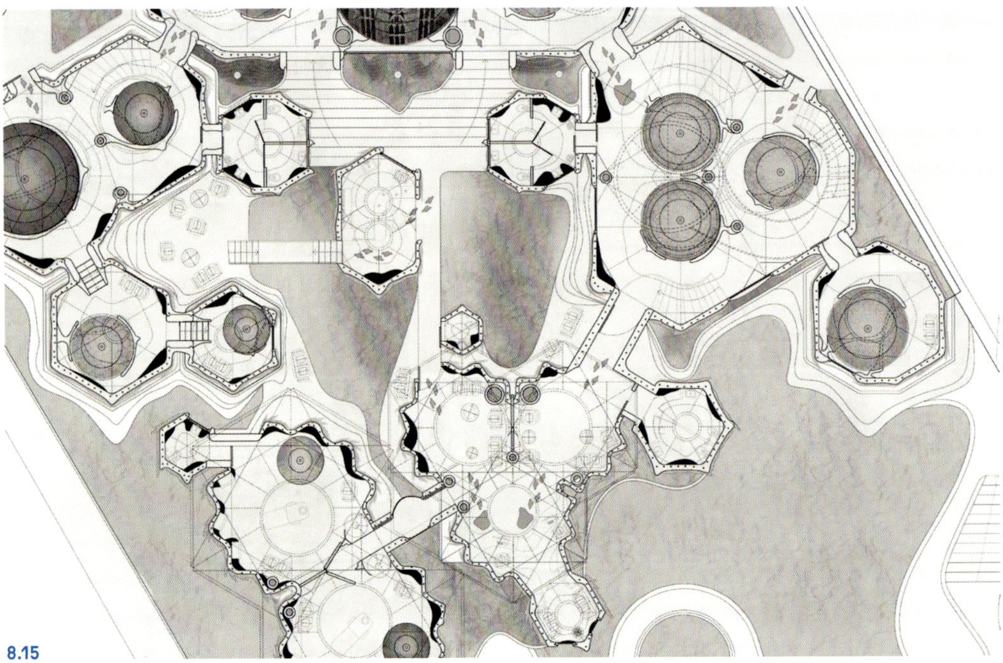

8.15

Fig. 8.16 Thomas Chu Y3, 'House for a Conductor'. The house explores the manipulation of sound and light through an architecture of thin, layered translucent screens made using the Baroque technique of scagliola. Enveloping a central auditorium, these form a sequence of structurally independent layers that create acoustic and atmospheric buffers between the city of Budapest and the inhabitants and functions on the house. **Figs. 8.17 – 8.18 Georgia May Jaeckle** Y3, 'Between the Haptic and the Optic'. A 35mm film museum in Vienna which, through the hand-crafted alchemy of celluloid, seeks to spatially compose an internal landscape and architectural binary of positive and negative. It negotiates the discrepancy between the projected flicker and the fall of natural light on textured plaster through a curated architectural aperture.

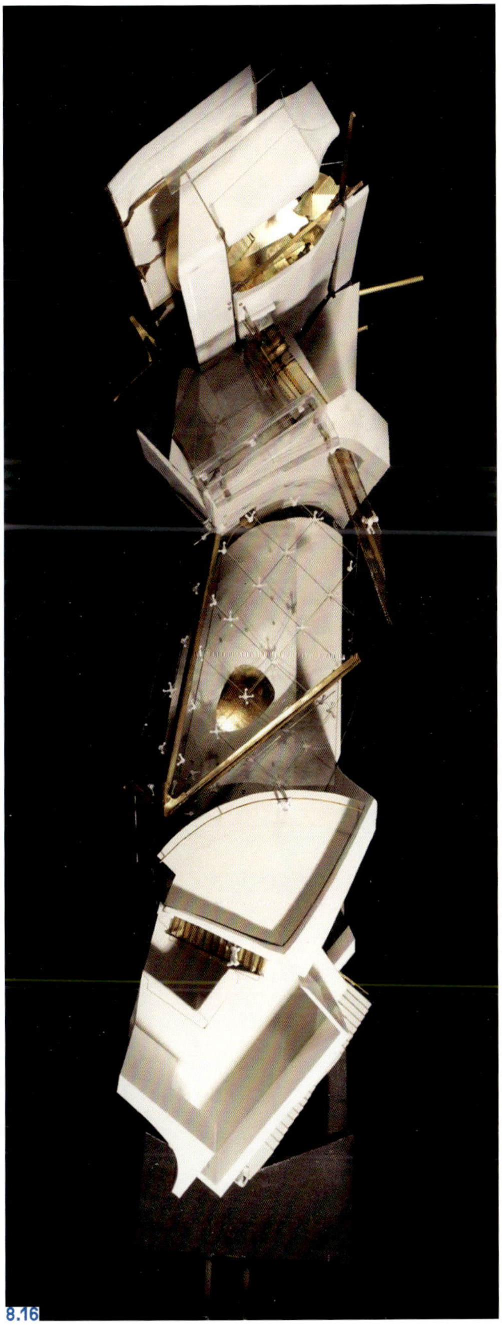
8.16

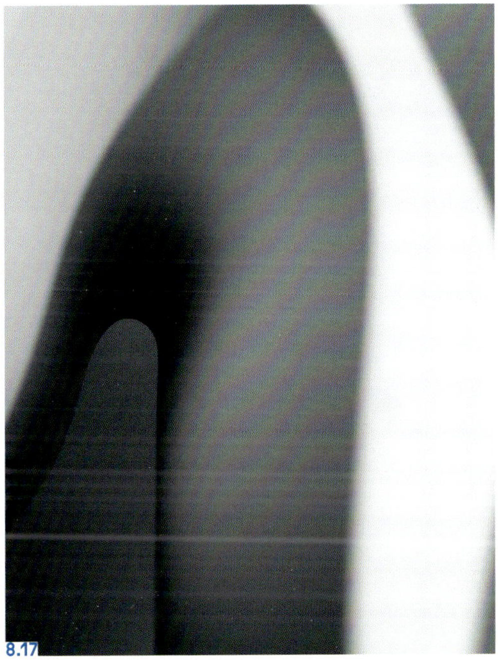
8.17

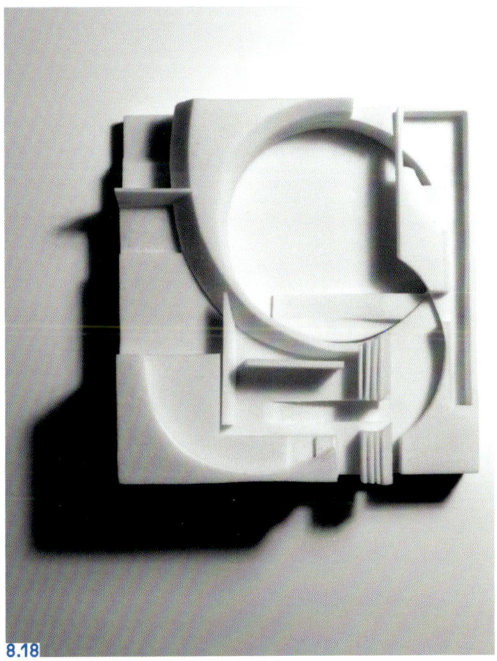
8.18

Fig. 8.19 **Joe Johnson** Y2, 'Rhythmicised soundscapes'. A 1:25 kinetic model exploring how the wall planes move in response to spontaneous events in a simulation. **Figs. 8.20 – 8.22** **Aleksandra Kugacka** Y3, 'Hotel Unheimlich'. Secret mechanisms, out-of-sight ornaments, strangely familiar shadows - these things are uncanny: they ought to have remained hidden, yet they have come to light. The back of the building emerges, the entrance is lost in darkness. Crafted nooks and passages seduce and bewitch the occupants. The memory of home blurs as the architectural uncanny materialises. **Fig. 8.23** **Oscar Maguire** Y2, 'Twisting, Turning and the Dance of Learning'. A language school in Vienna considers learning as a performative act: building understanding on top of the sediment of successes, failures and fruity glitches laid down by enacting certain actions again and again. It translates performances into landscaped ceramic floors, sculptural cores and baroque revolving doors.

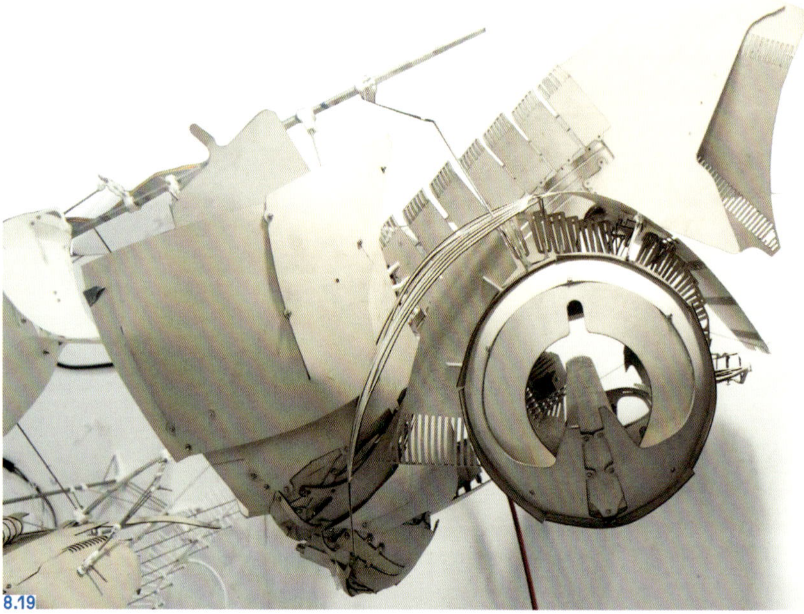

8.19

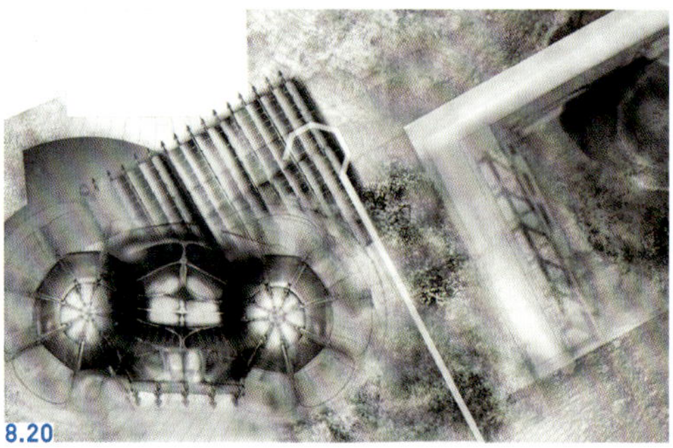

8.20

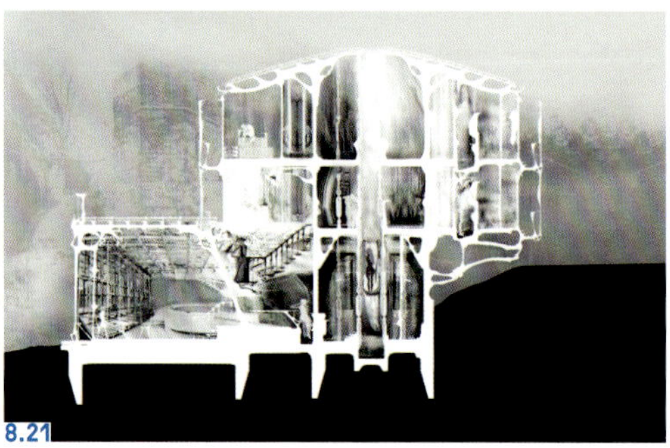

8.21

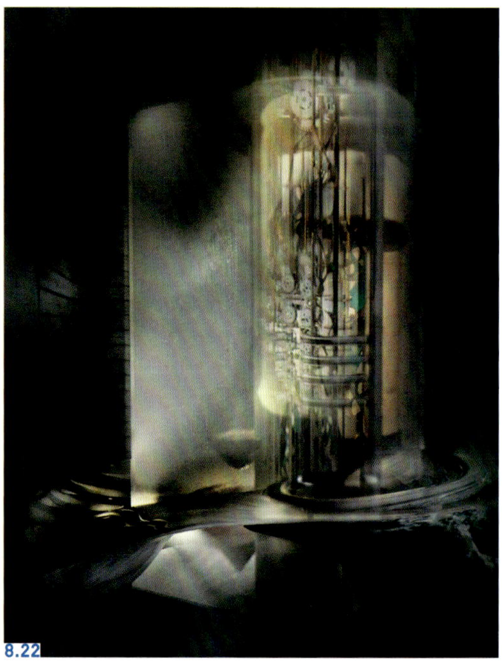

8.22

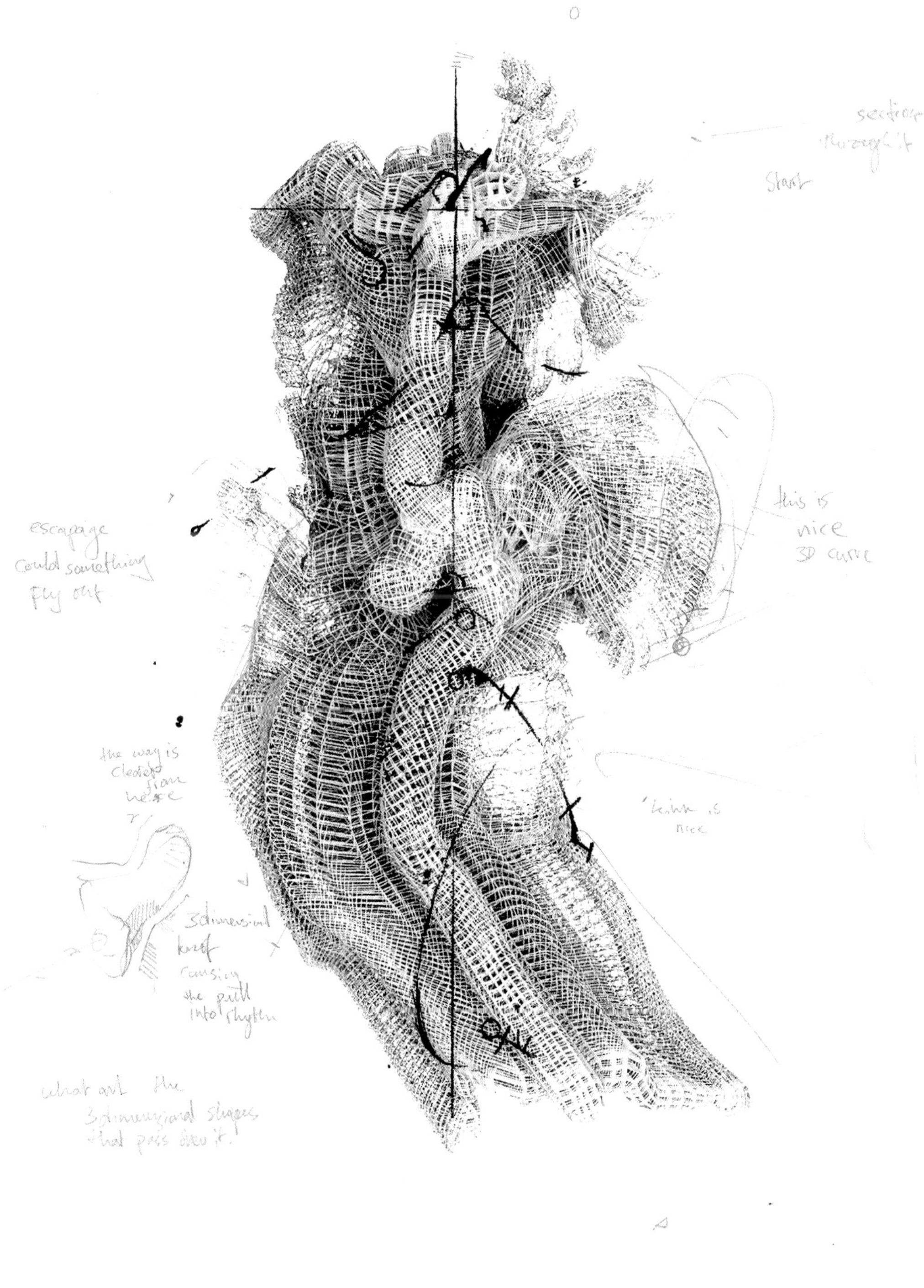
section through it
Start
this is nice 3D curve
escapage could something fly out
3dimensional knot causing the path into rhythm
what are the 3dimensional shapes that pass over it.

8.23

UG9

The Ephemeral City

Jessica In, Chee-Kit Lai

Year 2
Assankhan Amirov, Theo Brader-Tan, Eleanor Evason, Gabriele Grassi, Thomas Leggatt, Patrycja Panek, James Robinson

Year 3
Krina Christopoulou, Morgan Hamel de Monchenault, Arthur Harmsworth, Janis Ho, Jaejun Kim, Minghan (Tom) Lin, Xiao Ma, Samuel Price, Niraj Shah

Unit 9 also continues an ongoing collaboration with Denis Vlieghe, who runs a Physical Computing Workshop as part of Project 1 (Interactive Device)

Thank you to our critics: Sam Aitkenhead, Edwina Attlee, Paul Bavister, Alastair Browning, Nat Chard, Kacper Chmielewski, Richard Difford, Elizabeth Dow, Murray Fraser, Ruairi Glynn, Penelope Haralambidou, Jonathan Hill, Lilly Kudic, Constance Lau, Jamie Lilley, CJ Lim, Emma-Kate Matthews, James O'Leary, Jonathan Pile, Sophia Psarra, Arturo Revilla, Farlie Reynolds, Don Shillingburg, Andrew Slack, Giles Smith, Eva Sopeoglou, Ivo Tedbury, Manijeh Verghese, Denis Vlieghe, Patrick Weber, Nick Westby, Dan Wilkinson, Simon Withers, Fiona Zisch

Special thanks for photography workshop by Soma Sato

Special thanks for computing workshops by Steven Howson and Denis Vlieghe

"The difference between a piece of architecture and an image is that people can move through architecture, meaning that the element of time is the crucial difference. Architecture is the opposite of an image. Architecture is not about space, but about time," Vito Acconci

This year, our investigations began by considering the concept of dimension beyond physical objects, negotiating between different planes of time to create the architecture of the Ephemeral City. Our early studies explored Mexican culture from afar, to design and create a time-based, spatially embedded device. Speculative in nature, these design explorations are nonetheless bound by determined roles and relationships and form the basis of an architectural analysis – measuring geographically defined qualities of space such as rhythm, tempo and speed, creating kinematic representations of place closely related to the performance of its inhabitants.

——Our field trip led us to Mexico City, where we considered Mexican culture across multiple planes of time – the modern-day capital, the Spanish-colonial influence, and the ancient sites of the Aztecs – the combination of which creates the vibrant, complex and overflowing metropolis that is Mexico City today. Our main project is a complex building for a public programme that speculates on and suggests new forms of the Ephemeral City. The projects propose a new urban typology for an architecture that could act as a generator for future change, or as a resource for forgotten communities. The proposals are led by students' initial curiosities, then are developed and driven by considering inhabitants not as passive receptors, but instead as active elements in the definition of our architecture.

——Unit 9 is interested in an architecture that mediates between matter and form, and the relation between design and occupation. We are interested in the celebratory, the continually reconfiguring and reinvented. We see performance as intrinsically linked to the development of technology beyond the discipline of architecture. We are critical of the passive consumption of technology and instead support rigorous investigations into its application to design processes. We continually question the conventions of the production of architecture, pushing the boundaries of drawing, making and interactivity to actively promote both analogue and digital craftsmanship.

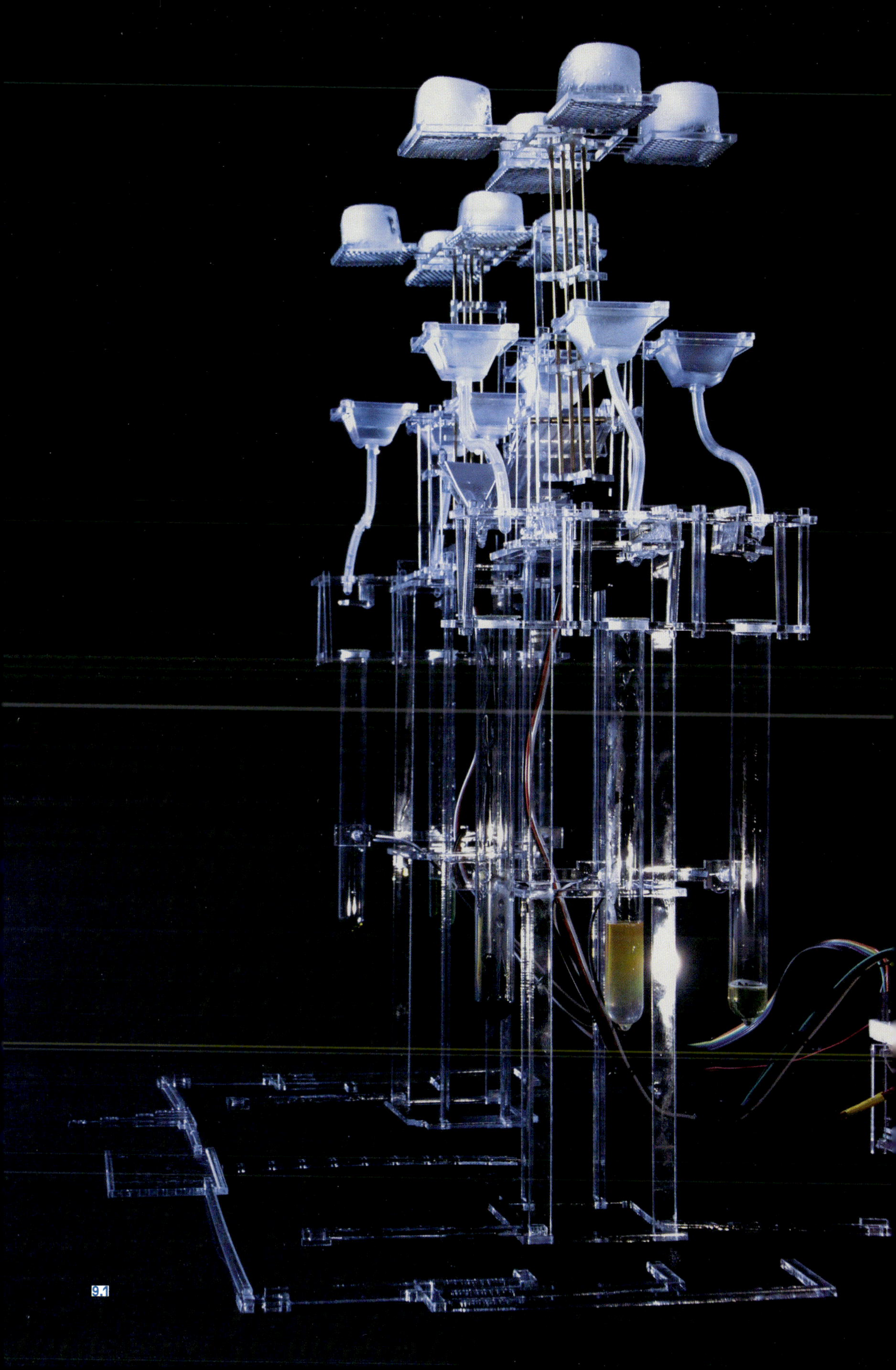

9.1

Fig. 9.1 **James Robinson** Y2, 'One Drop at a Time'. The device is a micro-archive of different water samples found in Mexico City. It reveals apparently unnoticeable changes within the water system (of waste and pollutants, etc), allowing viewers a glimpse into Mexico City's complex relationship with water and the environment over time. Fig. 9.2 **Jaejun Kim** Y3, 'Flight Club', interactive model with remote control and laser lights. The building is a proposal for a nighttime hand-gliding club. Located on an archaeological landscape northeast of Mexico City, the club offers visitors a different experience of viewing the Pre-Hispanic city of Teotihuacan (a UNESCO World Heritage site). The proposal consists of an indoor training section which allows beginners to practice, as well as multiple runways for more advanced users and viewing platforms for visitors. Whilst gliders can also visit during the day, night-gliding is the main attraction and the architecture sets the backdrop for the ephemeral performance of light and flight after sunset. Fig. 9.3 **Minghan (Tom) Lin** Y3, 'Drug Rehabilitation Centre'. This proposal is for a drug rehabilitation centre in Mexico City. The architecture of the building consists of a series of carefully choreographed waterscapes that create soft barriers. This is juxtaposed against the rigid daily routine of the programme. Using only natural light, users are directed around the building throughout the day. Sunlight falling onto the different surfaces of the building, together with the presence of flowing water, creates moments in which matte concrete walls become mirrors of their context, and shallow ponds not only reflect the sky, but also create moving rainbows. Fig. 9.4 **Janis Ho** Y3,

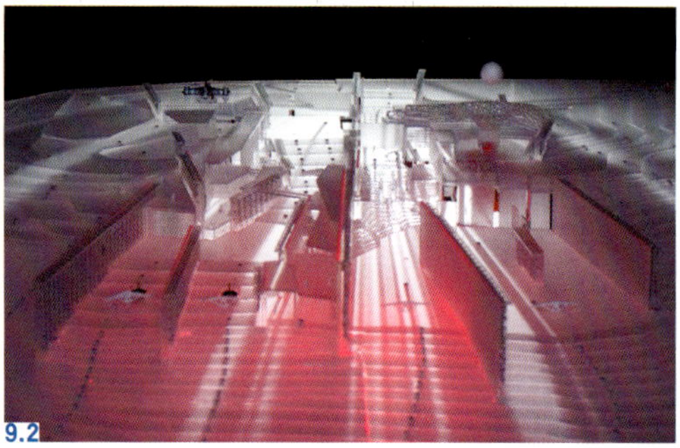

9.2

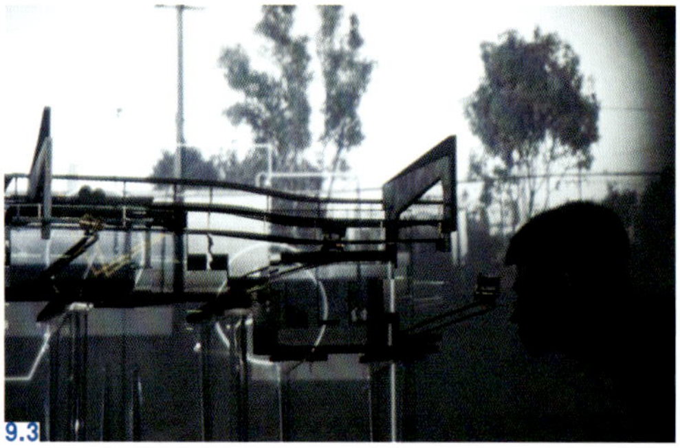

9.3

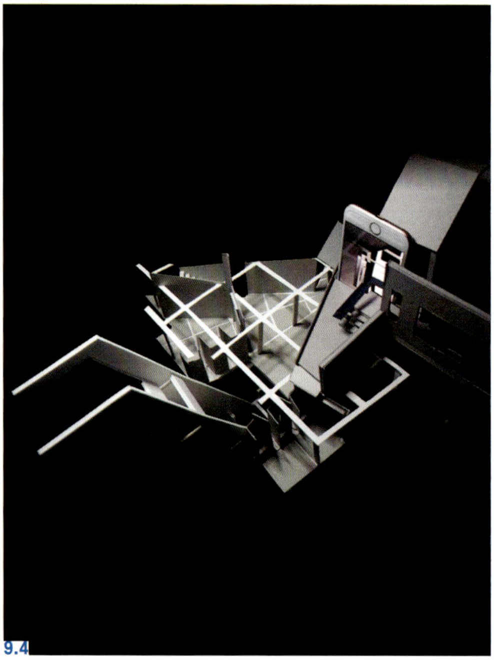

9.4

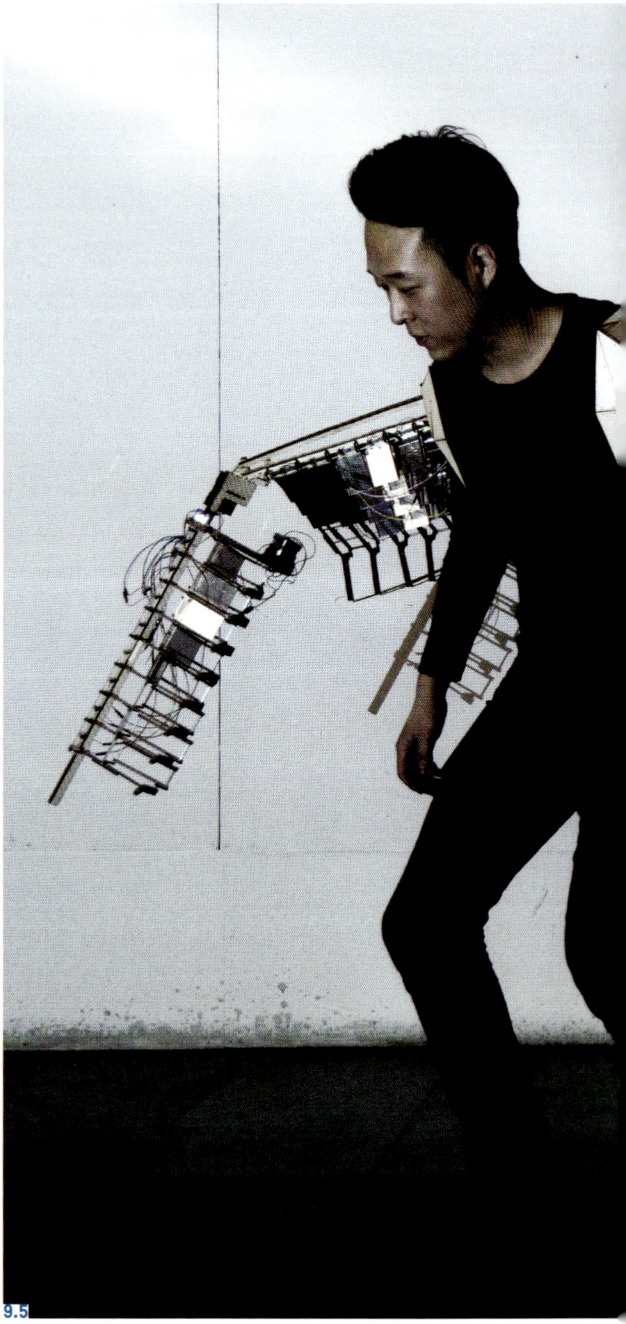

9.5

'Cinematic Courthouse'. The proposal is for a cinematic courthouse in Mexico City. The building openly engages in filming courtroom proceedings in an attempt to open up the country's judicial system to a public which has arguably lost faith in it. The architecture intentionally dramatises key figures moving through spaces, by using cinematic lighting and moving cameras. Viewers attending court proceedings or viewing remotely via smart devices are fed live footage of the events, with all key figures portrayed as equals. It is hoped that justice can be served without prejudice. **Fig. 9.5 Jaejun Kim** Y3, 'Flight'. Throughout history, people have had the desire to fly. The interactive device captures the essence of the ritualistic Mexican 'Hopi' run. Using Arduino, the device shows the basic gestures of the eagle's wings, including the intricate change of the direction of feathers, all in one smooth movement. The performance of the device allows viewers a sense of flight. Essential elements to the 'Hopi' tribe, such as rainwater, cloud and lightning, are represented with lasers, mirrors and fog.

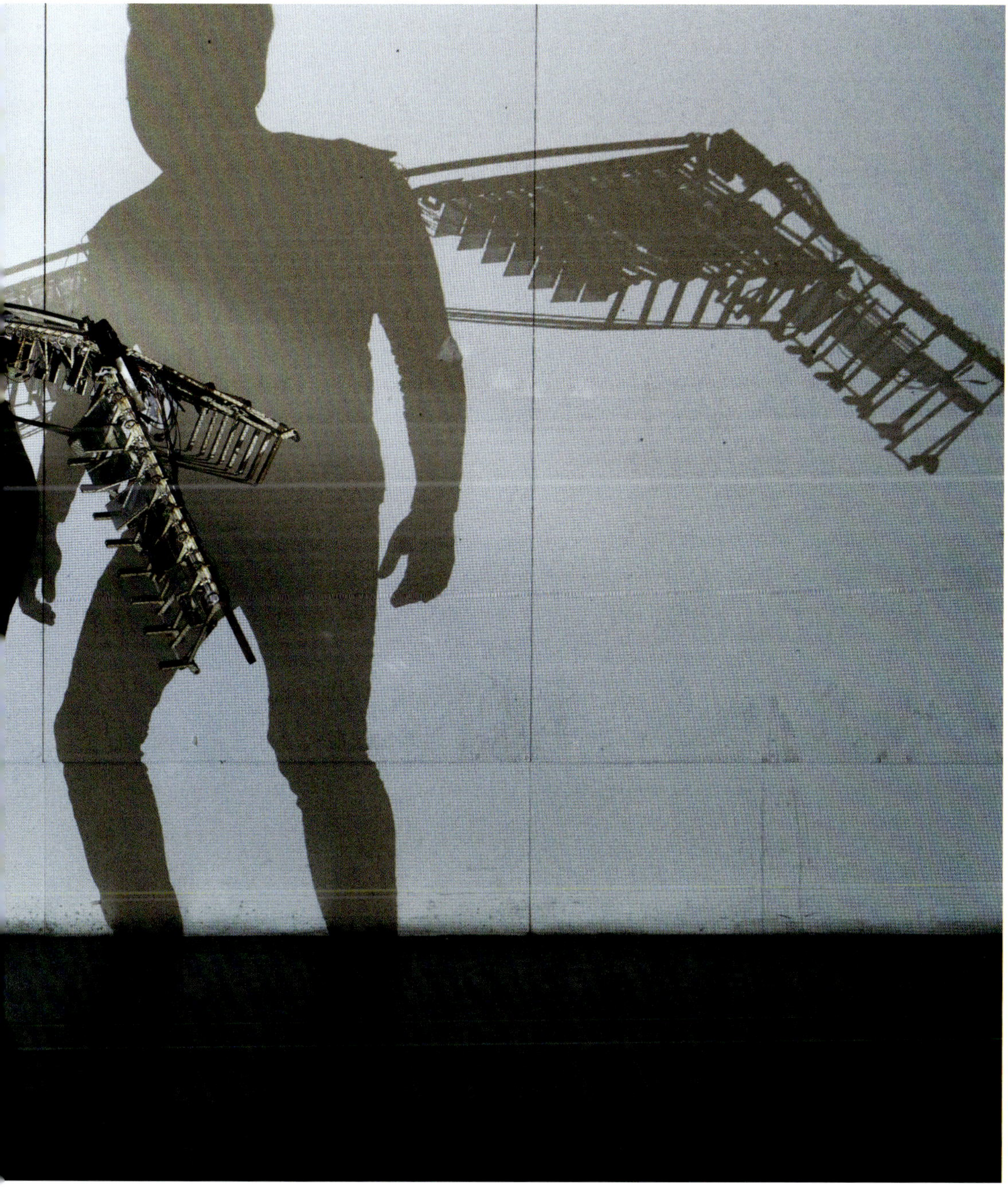

Figs. 9.6 – 9.7 James Robinson Y2, 'Hydrodynamic Landscape and Water Archive'. The building captures the lost lakes of Mexico City. The proposal includes private laboratories, a water archive, a public park, and nutrient-emitting cranes hovering above open lakes. Different parts of the building are allowed to be flooded as the landscape fluctuates with the seasons. The architecture is a cross between a building and a scenographic landscape. **Fig. 9.8 Thomas Leggatt** Y2, 'Equilibrium Weather Device'. The device looks to engage an audience to question the balance between man-made environmental issues and the human intervention required to reduce their impact. It requires constant human interaction to create equilibrium, by way of interventions that allude to man's misuse of water and nature's way of replenishing such natural resources. The design questions how man balances out these forces. **Fig. 9.9 Thomas Leggatt** Y2, 'The Sound Archive'. Sited in Centro Historico, The Sound Archive uses an architectural language to act as instruments for rainwater during the wet season. The sounds created are recorded as an archive for future reference. During the dry season, the archive sounds are replayed to create a folly-esque representation of water flowing through the design. The experience of the architecture juxtaposes live and mediated soundscapes.

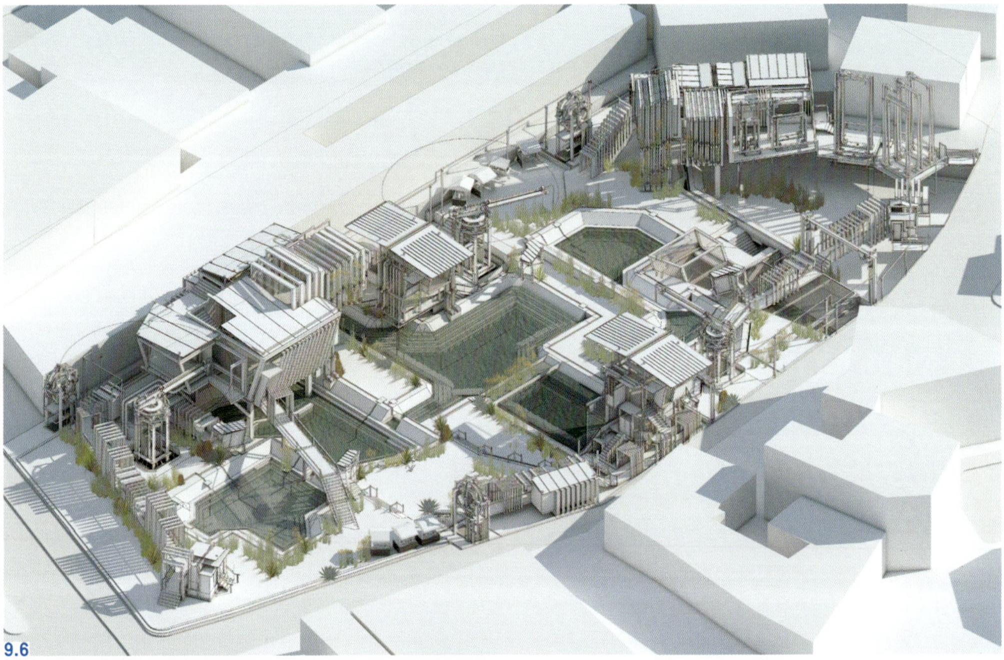

9.6

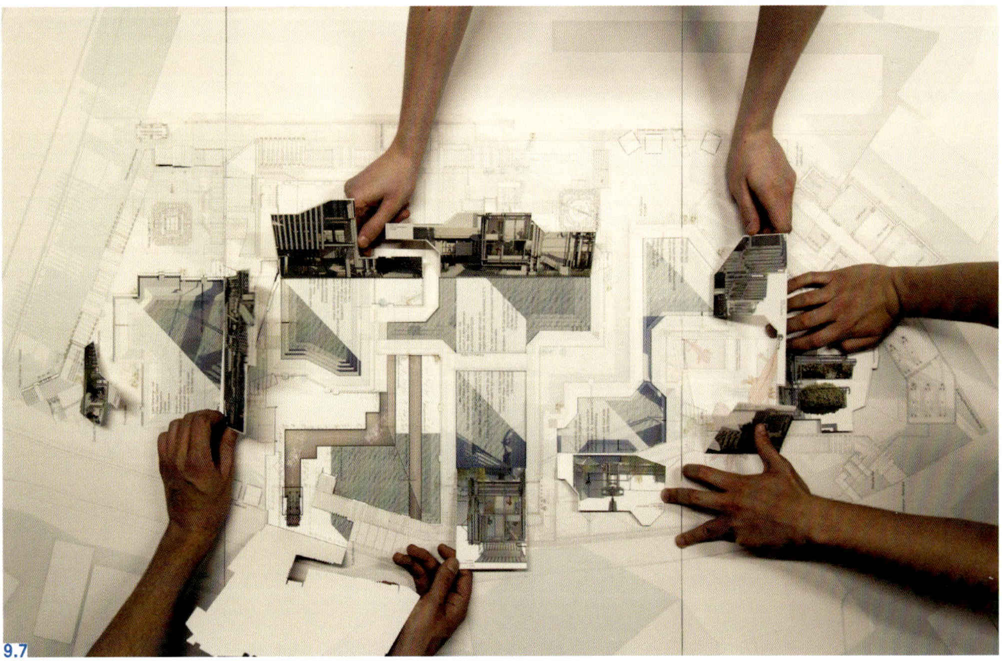

9.7

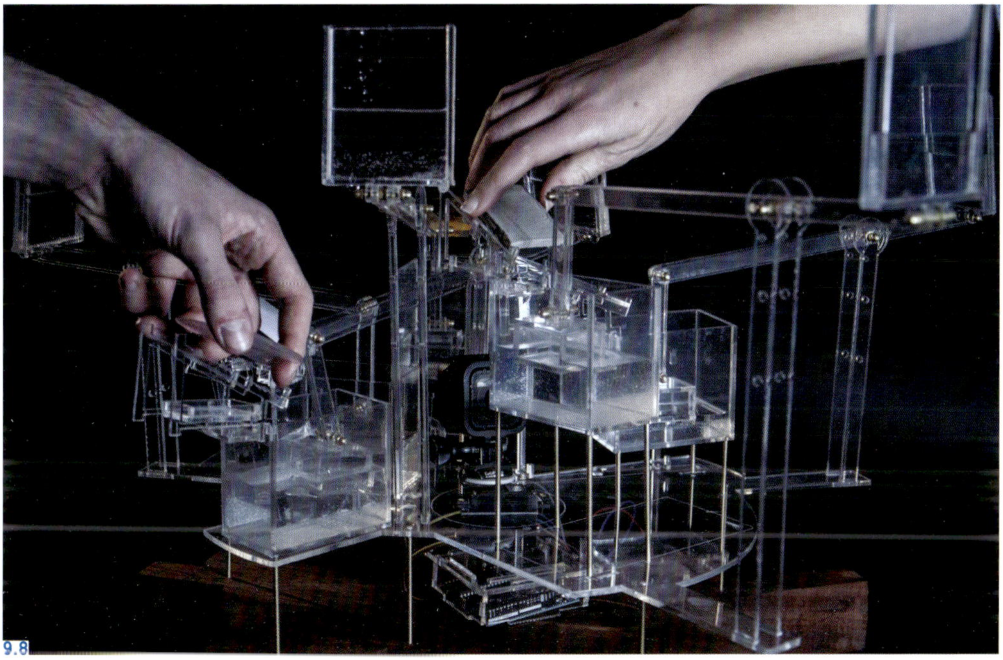

9.8

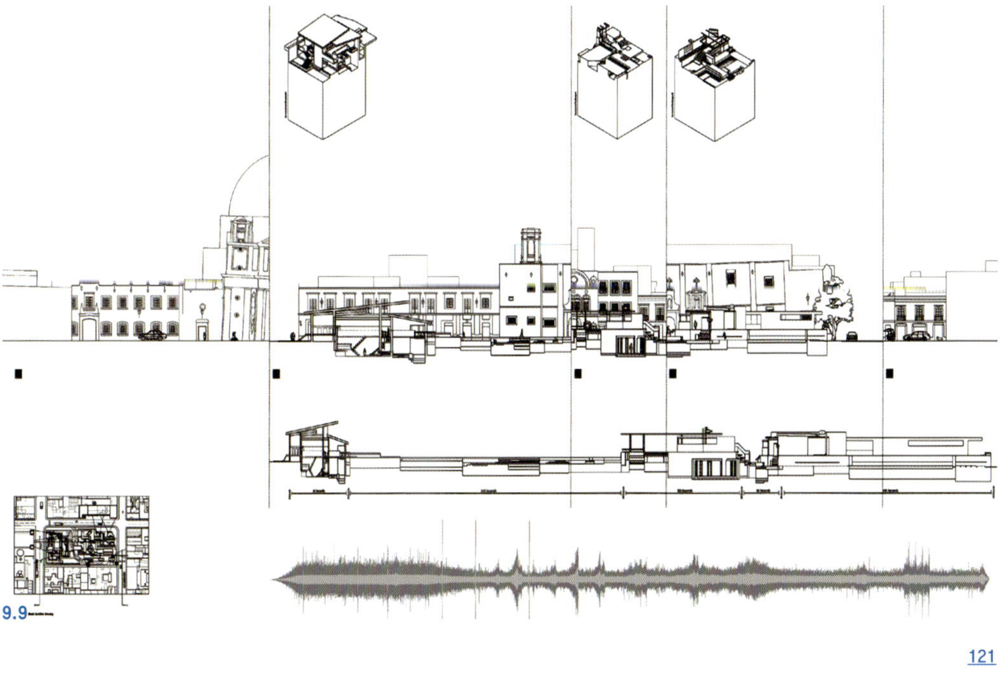

9.9

Fig. 9.10 Assankhan Amirov Y2, 'Mercado de Niño Jesús'. The building is for a vertical market to accommodate the production of the much-loved baby Jesus dolls. Sited in Centro Historico, the programme also includes bars, restaurants, museums and platforms, which offer stunning views across the city centre. Much of the building is made up of large exposed ramps and stairs, which encourage informal trading and community life, all of which are visible to the public at street level. There are also plug-in pods for more permanent activities and back-of-house spaces. The façade is made of recycled tarpaulin salvaged from old market stalls and street vendors. **Fig. 9.11 Gabriele Grassi** Y2, 'Ghost Recon Gaming Centre'. Situated in Roma Norte in Mexico City, the building is a labyrinth for gamers, developers and viewers. The proposal offers a series of pixellated spaces that weave public and private, indoor and outdoor. To gamers on VR headsets, the spaces they occupy have the ability to appear bigger than their physical presence, thereby creating infinite possibilities within the game. To viewers, they are simply running around the same reconfigured spaces using sliding and rotating elements within the architecture. There is a park in front of the building, and the building sits on an island site with a front-facing public park. The blank façade act as a screen for the projection of gaming activities. **Fig. 9.12 Eleanor Evason** Y2, 'Language Centre for the Indigenous People of Mexico City'. Here, the digital language of code is an allegory for verbal language. This project is an experiment in generative design which uses the cellular structure of the Voronoi mesh for the subdivision

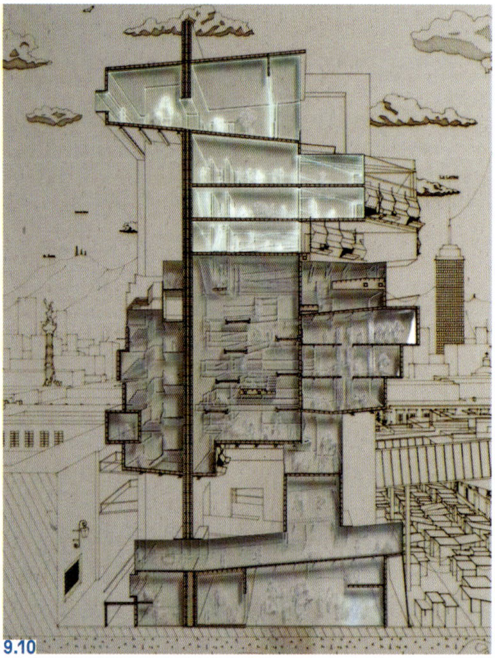

9.10

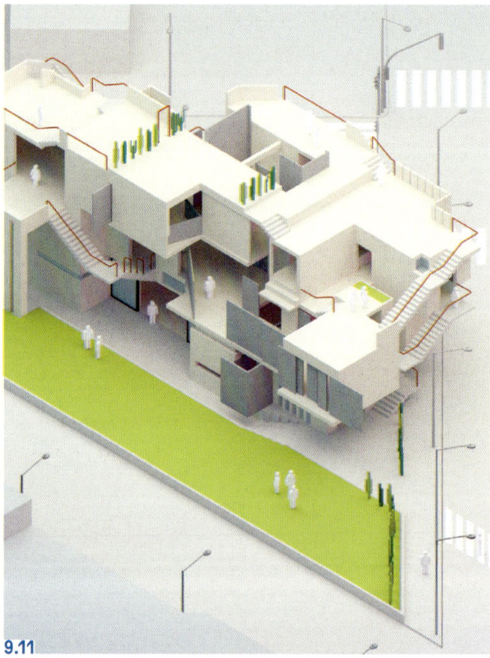

9.11

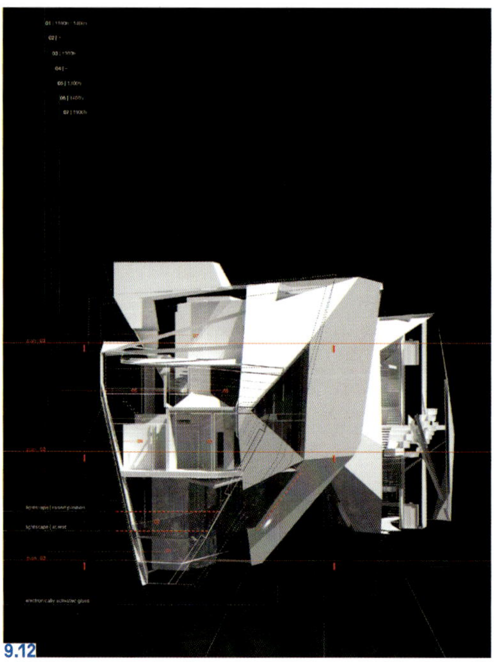

9.12

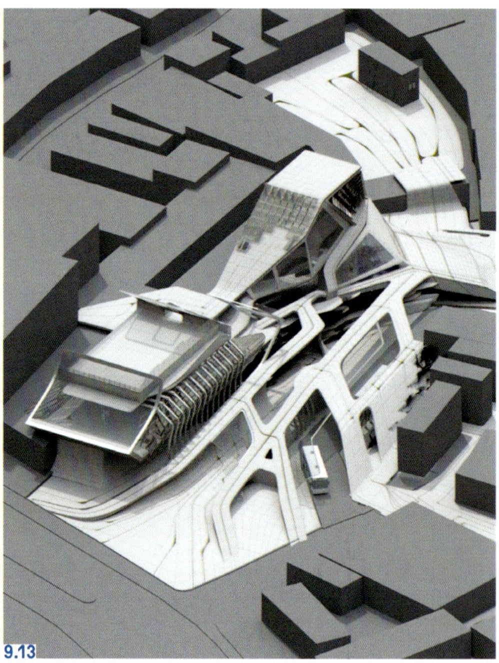

9.13

of space as a result of pointcloud glitches. The building uses light, both natural and artificial, to choreograph the user experience of the spaces. Planar surfaces are used to reflect light and create moments of clarity throughout the building, echoing the visitor's progression through a language. **Fig. 9.13** **Niraj Shah** Y3, 'Complejo Deportivo'. The building is a combination of sports complex, public park and bus stop. Made from concrete panels of different bounce tolerance, occupiers are free to use its surfaces for impromptu sporting activities – thereby encouraging visitors from afar who have travelled there by bus, and local residents, to interact with it in a playful way. There is also a dedicated sports complex for more formal activities such as basketball, mini-football, squash and swimming. **Fig. 9.14** **Theo Brader-Tan** Y2, 'Street Vendor Hub'. By day, the building deploys vendor carts across the local neighbourhood to sell street food popular with local residents and tourists. By night, the carts dock at the main building to create a large kitchen, turning the building into a series of restaurants and bars, housed in inflatable structures. The architecture is visually open in order to preserve the tradition of street food and aims to provide a more sustainable approach for the future.

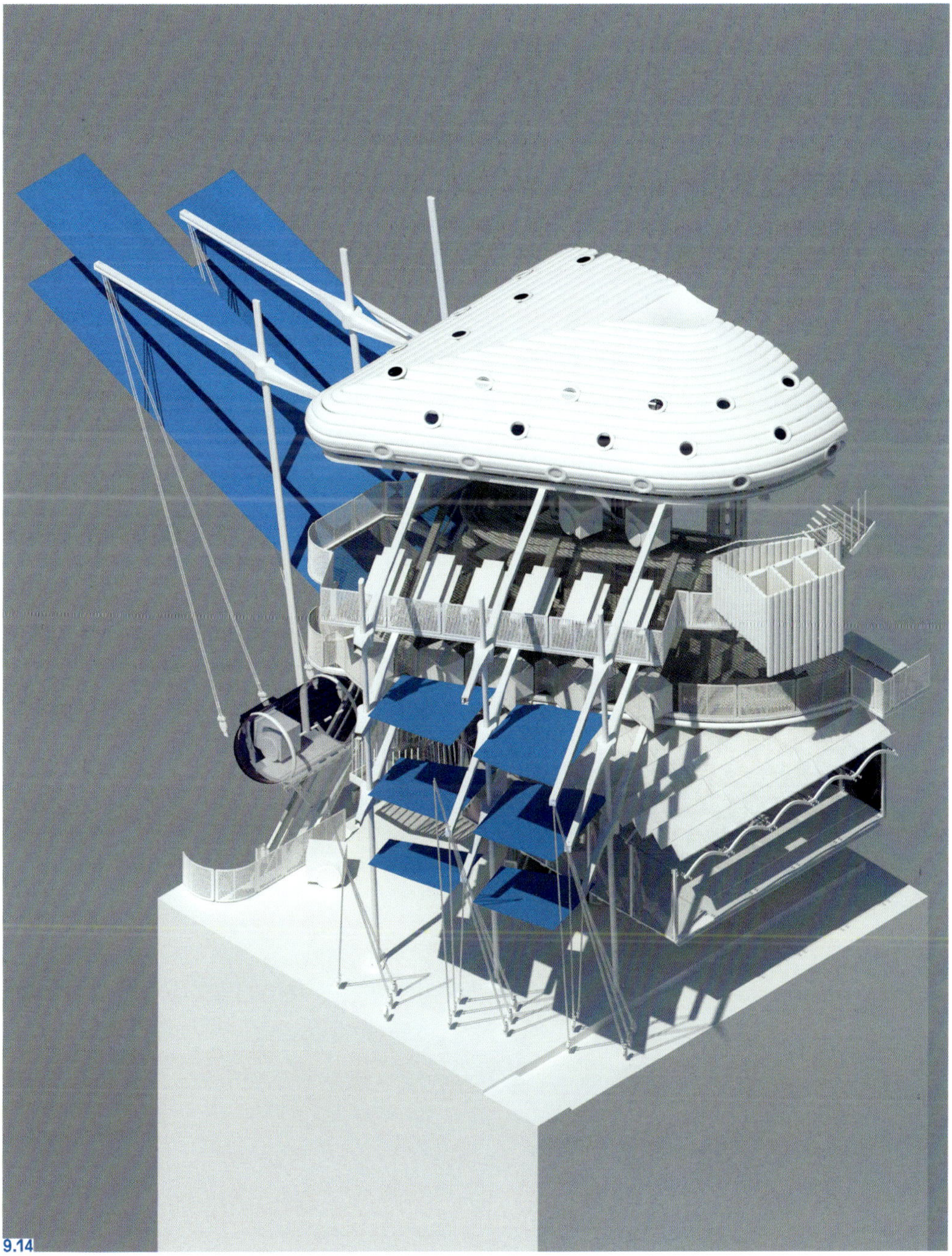

9.14

Figs. 9.15 – 9.18 Krina Christopoulou Y3, 'Digital Wonderland'. Located on the island of the Lago Mayor in Mexico City, the Cartographic Library houses maps of places that never existed. The proposed library archive is built underground, and upon retrieving a map with an augmented reality interface, the laser infrastructure on the roof recreates the phantom place through a triangulated laser-scape of the map's topographic character. Upon arriving at the library, visitors may enter the underground archives of the physical maps. Scanning the maps with a smartphone reveals an augmented reality interface with which visitors can select the maps they wish to view on the roof's laser-scape. The underground spaces are designed following principles of landscaping, and assuming arrangements that combine central nodes of activity with smaller, more intricate connecting routes. Conceptually, the architectural experience of the building is structured around the concept of deja-vu, created by the duplication of experiences. This creates an stereoscopy of similar experiences, whose similarity questions the memory of the past, the integrity of the present and the assumption of the future. The library is built underground, assimilating the island's topography, resurfacing on the site with its extensive roof.

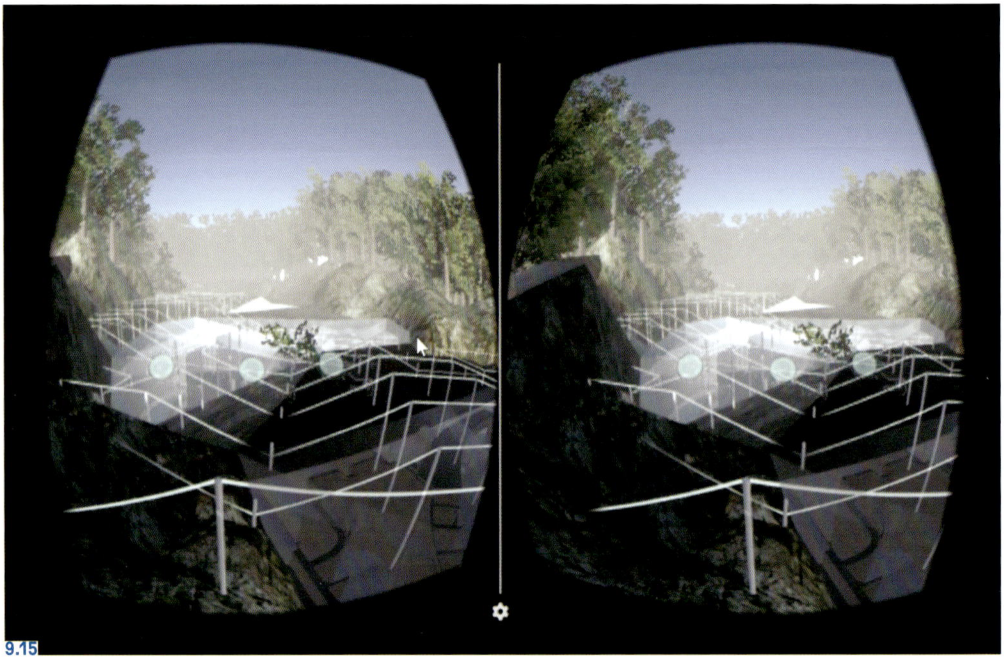

9.15

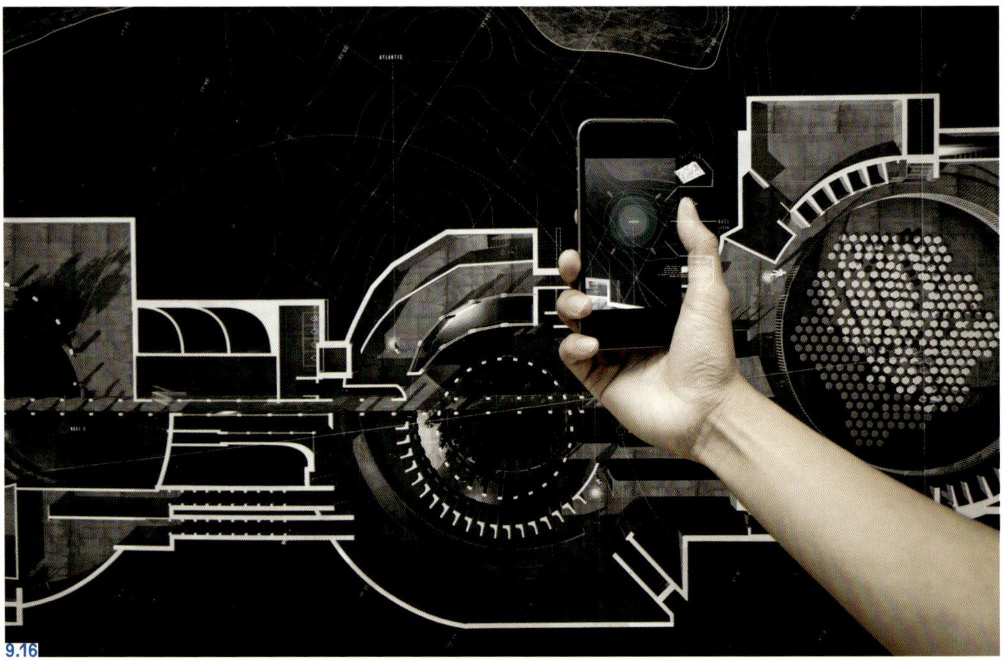

9.16

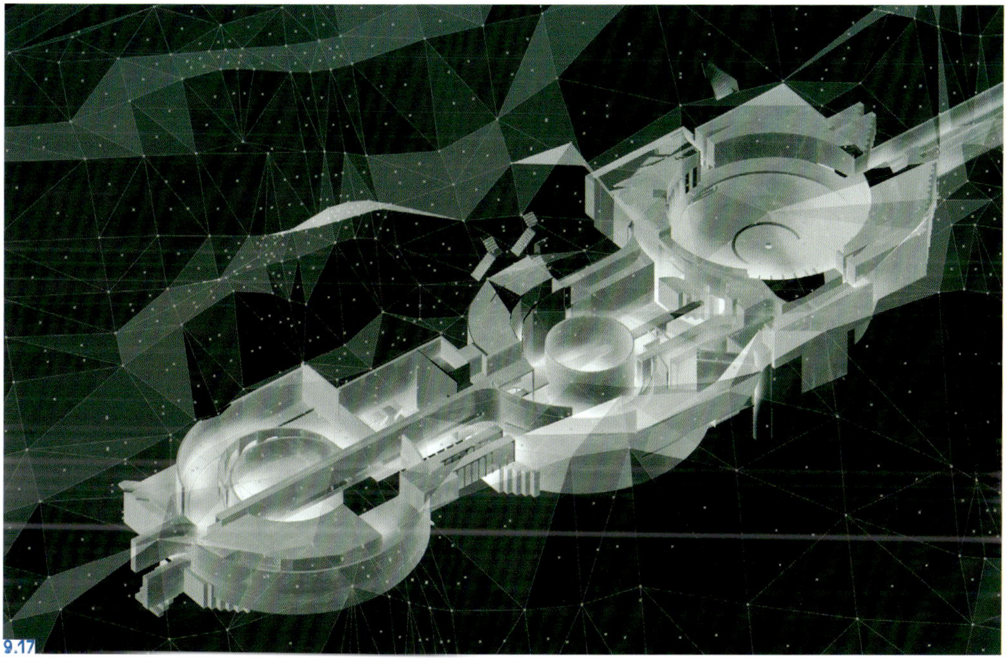
9.17

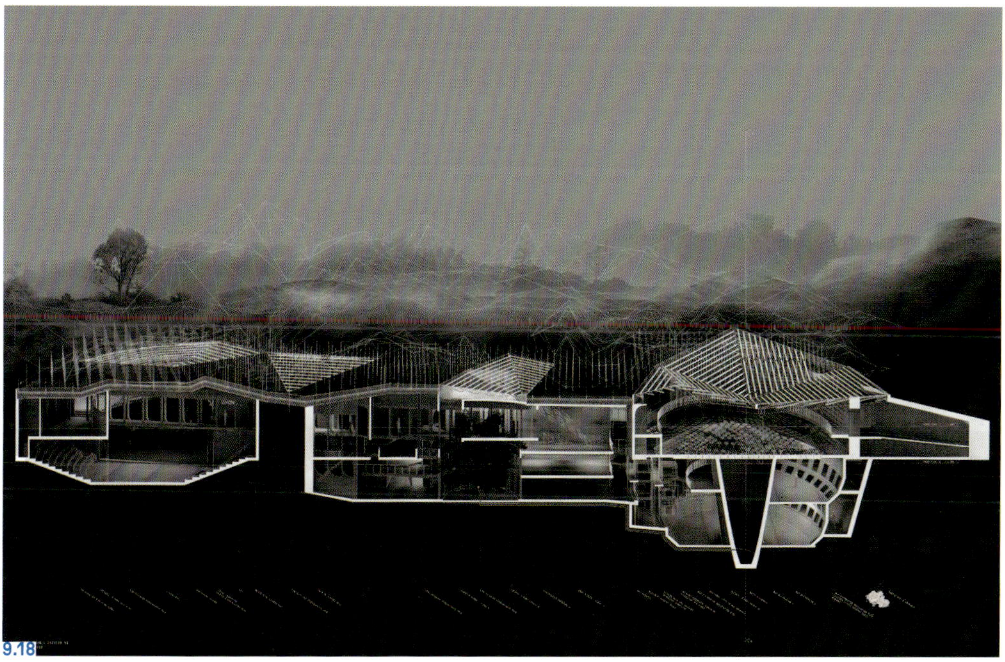
9.18

UG10 Vital Forces in Architecture

Guan Lee, Arthur Mamou-Mani

Year 2
Poppy Becke, George Brazier, Young To (Toby) Chan, Camille Dunlop, Linggezi (Yuki) Man, John Mathers, Anna O'Leary, Edward Taft

Year 3
Nour Al Ahmad, Yin Zara Chen, Wai Nam (Tiffany) Chong, Hanadi Izzuddin, Holy Moore, Ke Yang

Thank you to our guest critics: Robert Aish, Alisa Andrasek, Francis Archer, Anthony Boulanger, Andy Edge, Michael Hadi, Colin Herperger, Steve Johnson, Constance Lau, Mike Lim, Thomas Pearce, Stuart Piercy, James Pockson, Mike Tonkin, Mario Tsiliakos, Ben Sweeting, Toby Burgess

Special thanks to: Riyad Joucka (SHoP Architects), Dewitt Godfrey, Gustav Fagerström (Walter P Moore), Michael DiCarlo (Associated Fabrication)

Thank you to: Mike Lim and James Pockson (drawing workshop), Pamela Casey and Ralph Ghoche (archive visit at Avery, Columbia University), Paul Jeffries (technical tutor)

The 'Maker Movement' is enabling young designers to learn how to collaborate with other designers and work with machines directly to materialise their ideas. Open-source and parametric online platforms are accelerating this process, turning each contributor into an active node of a much larger and ever-growing system. Design, engineering and fabrication processes are merging, giving birth to a new kind of digital polymath role which replaces the different related professions. Creative studios, mini-factories and open workshops, dotted around the London boroughs of Tower Hamlets and Hackney, form an energetic and dynamic part of East London, an area of London declared by *Time Out* as the 'maker's new breeding ground'. More than one year on, a lot has happened, but most importantly in this context the UK has voted to leave the European Union. The question of how London's local economies can adapt has emerged as a critical issue.

——Students started the year by considering 'What is parametric design?' They proposed a small architectural intervention based on simple digital scripts and material constraints. Methods of design moved between digital intentions and physical modelling in order to test the nature of materials alongside computational logic. The building projects that followed ask the same question at a larger scale, with the added challenge of programmatic considerations. Some students gravitated towards the design of construction systems, while others focused on the potential of formal possibilities. Questions were raised about the economic future of small craft-based practices in the East London area and how a community can work more collaboratively. This changing landscape of small industries has provided inspiration for students to rethink how we design and make.

——With the rise of digital fabrication technology, architecture is evolving into an ecosystem of codes. These codes can be interlinked to inform each other through the use of structural and environmental simulation as well as material behaviour. Similar to the empirical process that was key to the evolution of cathedrals, the design of building components can optimise itself via an accelerated digital process. If buildings become self-optimising codes and cranes become 3D printers, what will be the role of the client, architect, engineers, quantity surveyors, project managers and the contractor in the near future? Which vital forces will drive and infuse the humanless codes? In relation to questions of aesthetic and tradition, will these forces be naturally implicit within the systems?

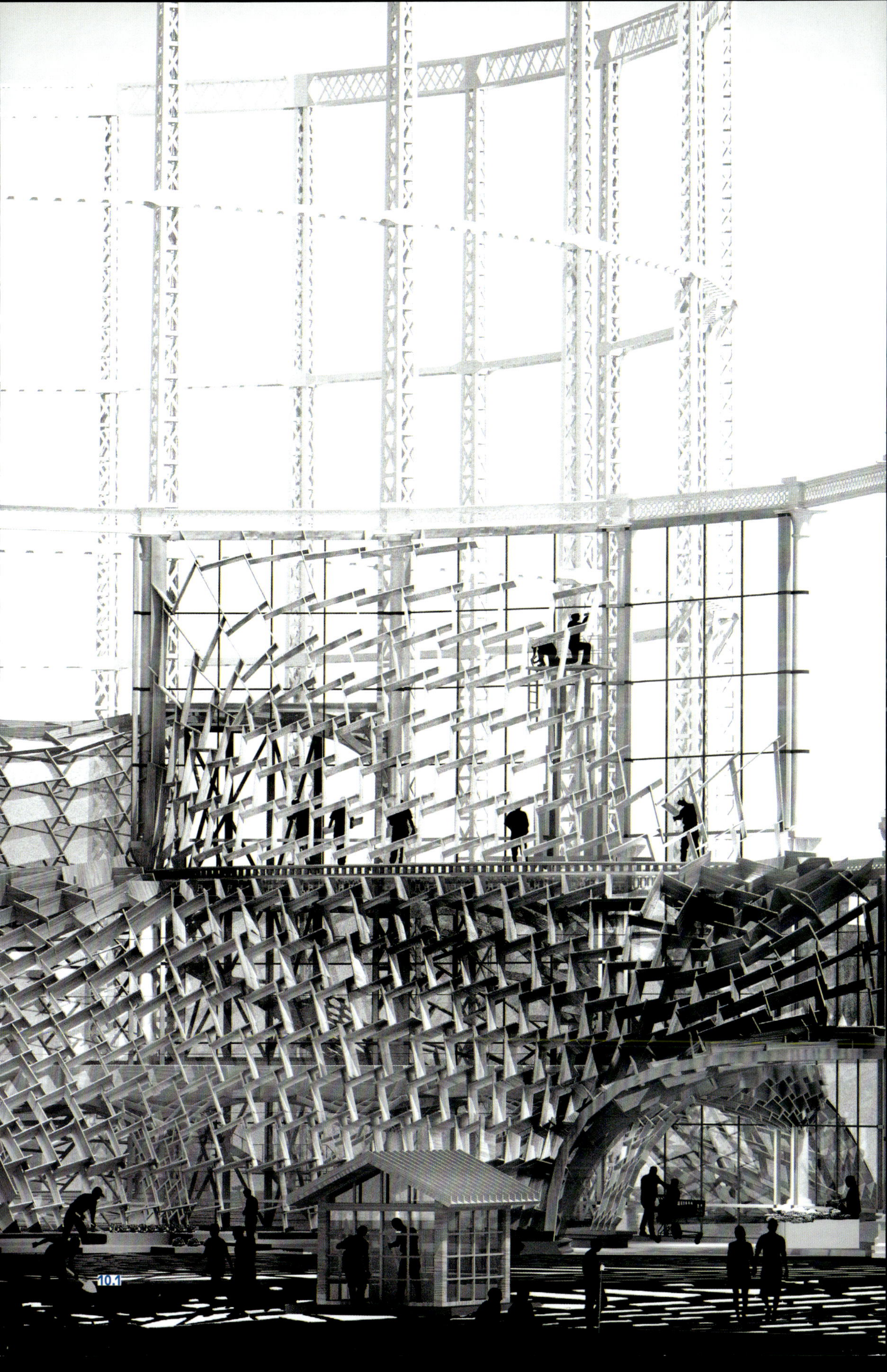

10.1

Fig. 10.1 Ke Yang Y3, '(re)Store'. This is a project about humanising parametric architecture. It is a series of self-build timber structures that create an urban agricultural landscape. The aim is to create a structure that can resonate with the existing Victorian gas-holders while restoring the contaminated site. **Fig. 10.2 Hanadi Izzuddin** Y3, 'Through The Roof'. This is a project using gridshell morphologies to unite 'makers' on Vyner Street in Hackney across its existing flat roofscape. This project envisions cheap, lightweight, deployable structures to create a school of making as a rooftop extension to the street's existing maker spaces. Various kerf-cut incisions on a triangular lattice hinge component investigate how a two-dimensional pattern can modulate three-dimensional space both structurally and environmentally – in other words, how it can become a functional ornament. **Fig. 10.3 Linggezi (Yuki) Man** Y2, 'Hackney Hydros'. A learning and communication centre with indoor greenhouses and leisure spaces for visitors to participate in the processes of growing vegetables, idea sharing and enjoying their produce as a community.

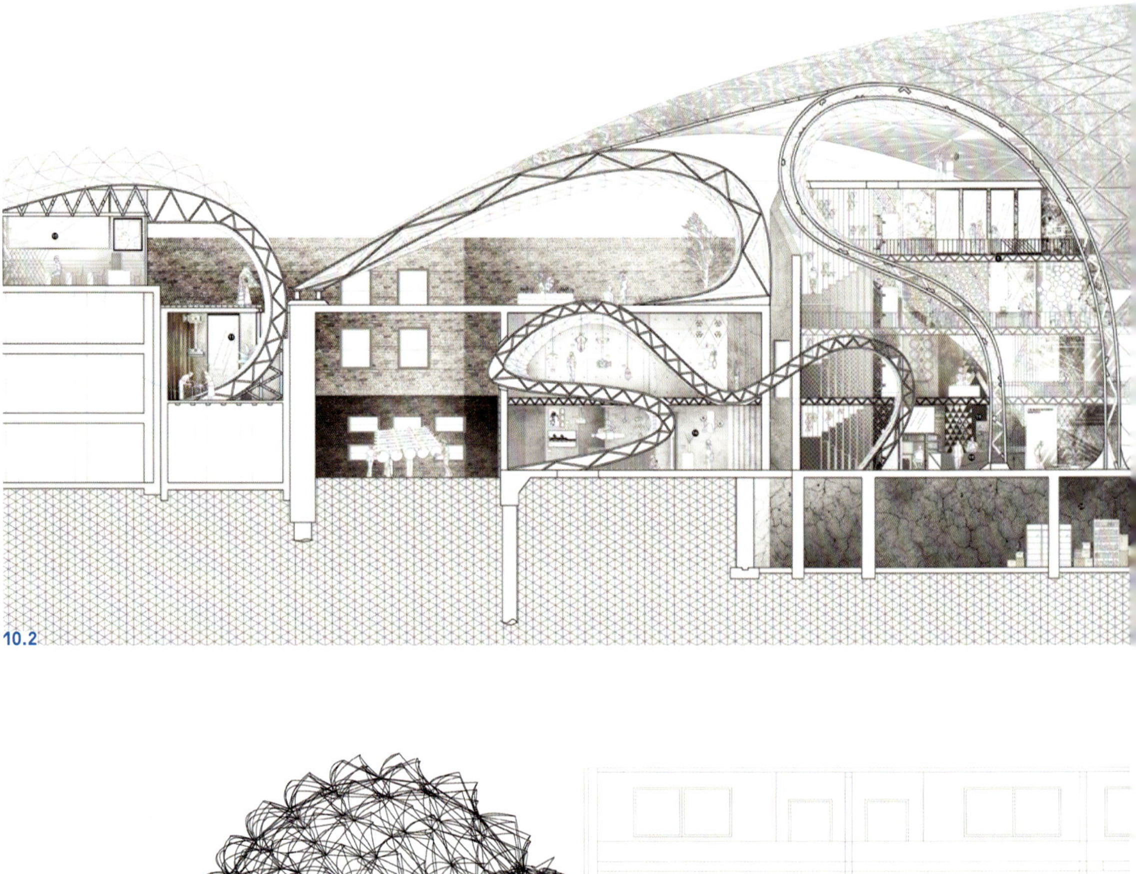

10.2

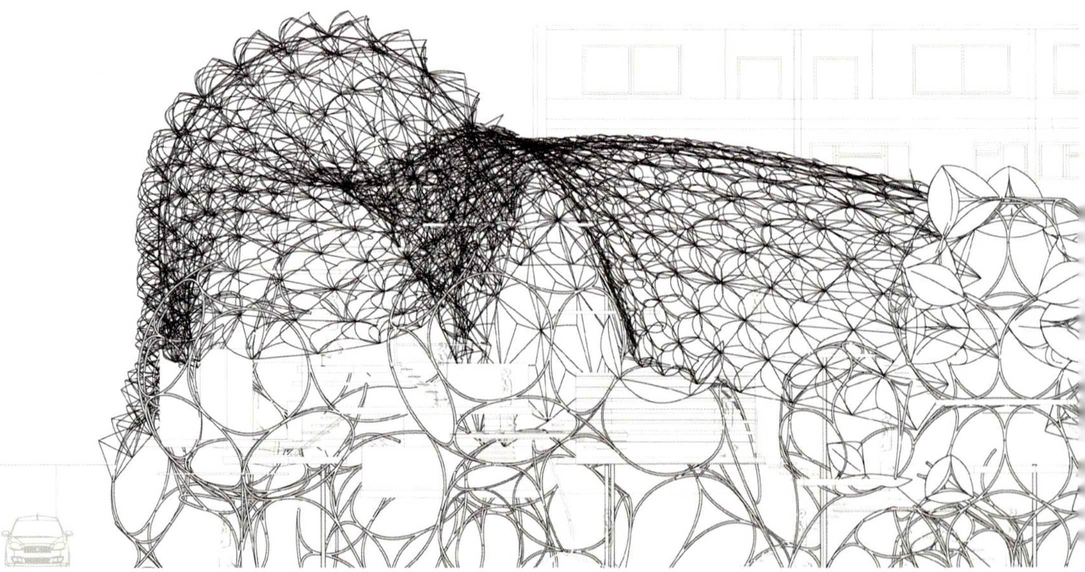

10.3

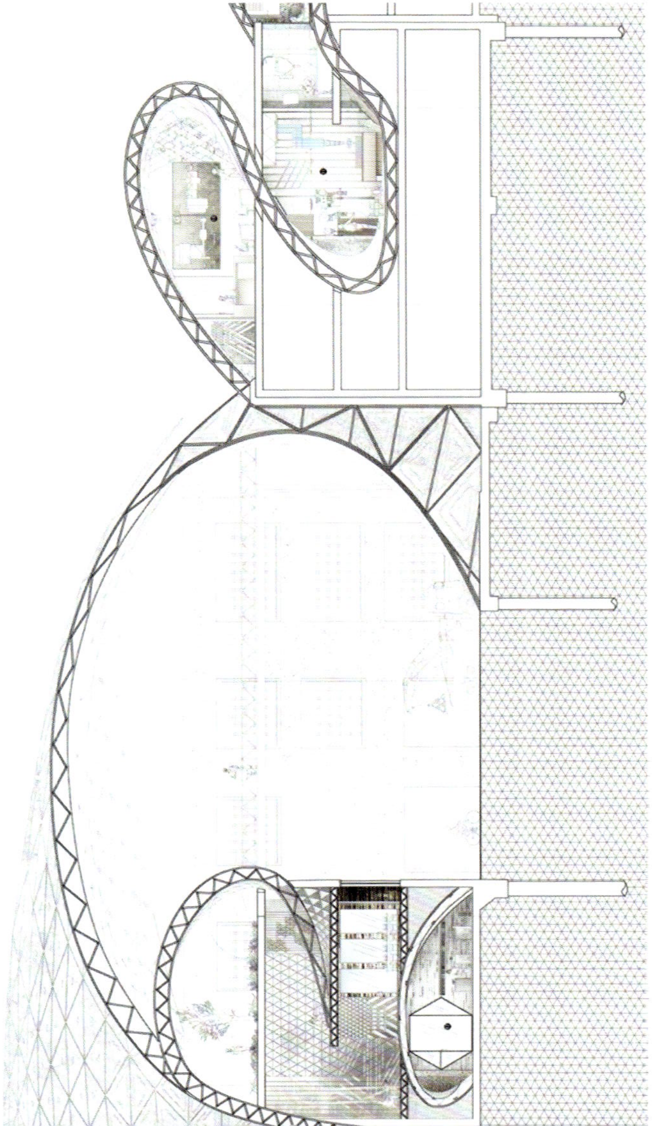

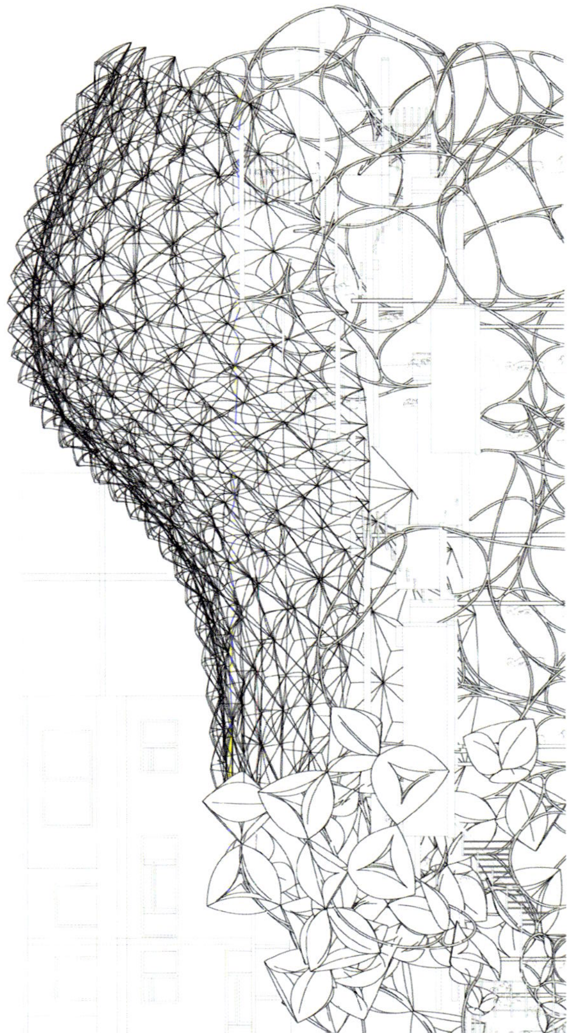

Fig. 10.4 **Wai Nam (Tiffany) Chong** Y3, 'Institute of Process'. A museum where local artists in Hackney Wick use the principle of Process Art to respond to the pollution of the River Lea, which has arisen due to the area's over-development. The project focuses on the materiality of plaster and its ability to translate pollution into art. **Fig. 10.5** **Anna O'Leary** Y2, 'Disruptive Innovation: A Contemporary Workspace'. This project explores disruptive innovation and how this can be encouraged in a workspace. The building encourages disruption through maximum interconnectivity: it connects to local creative companies in the Oval through a series of walkways, which allows unexpected interactions and communications to occur. Within the building, there are unconventional suspended spaces, both static and moveable, in which these unexpected and creative interactions can take place. **Figs. 10.6 – 10.7** **Holly Moore** Y3, 'Museum of Making'. A museum of making that questions how art is made and how it is displayed by proposing ordered maker spaces and disordered exhibition spaces that challenge convention. A 1:50 model was made using CNC machining techniques to explore the creation of two contrasting spaces using digital form-finding tools and traditional tile-vaulting as a method of construction. Combining maker spaces with exhibition spaces, this created a building that celebrates the entire making process from concept to completion.

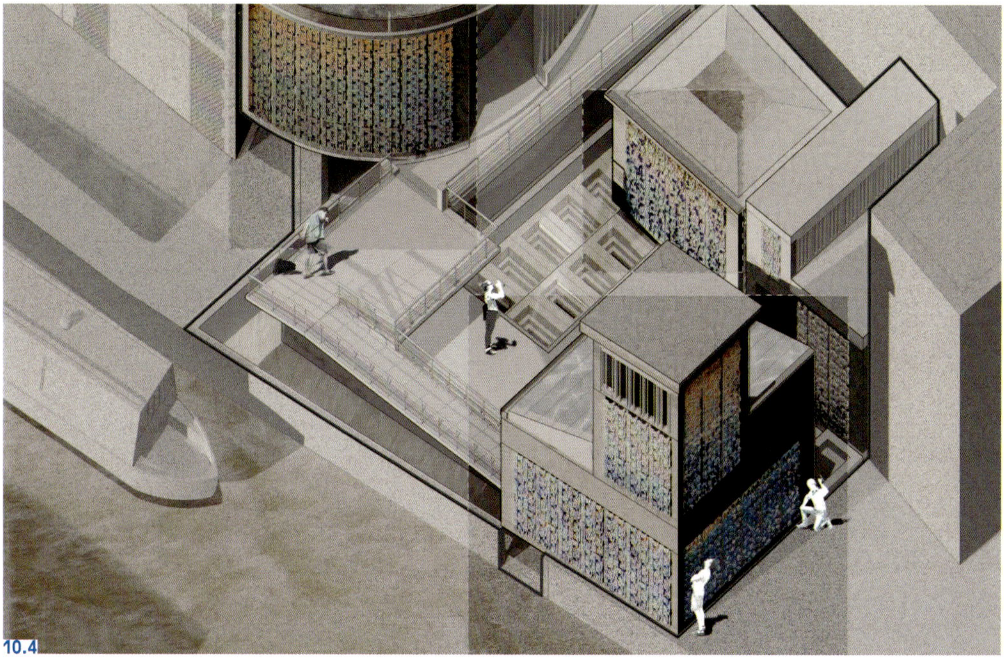

10.4

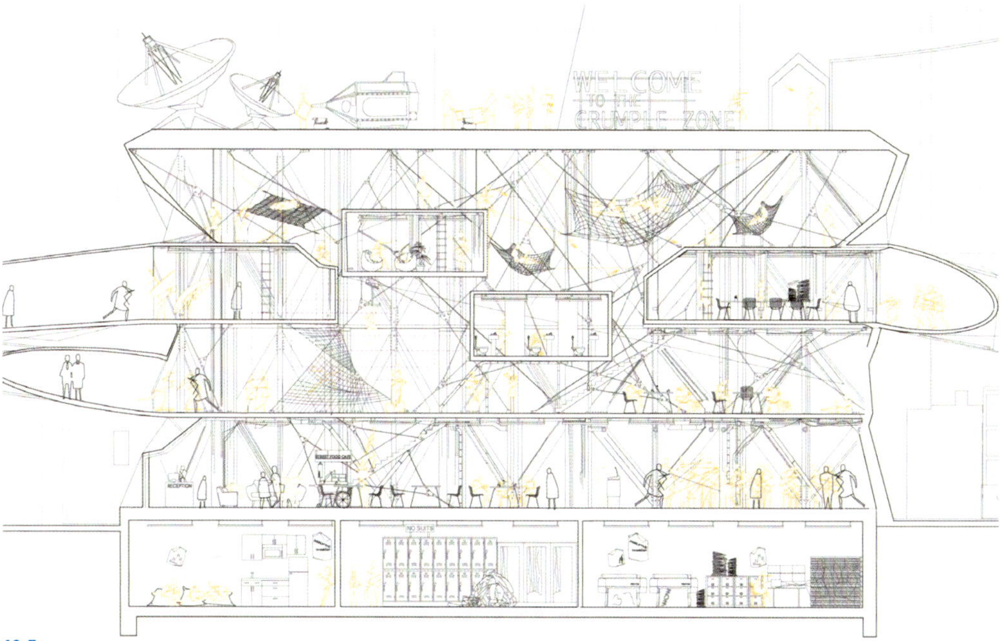

10.5

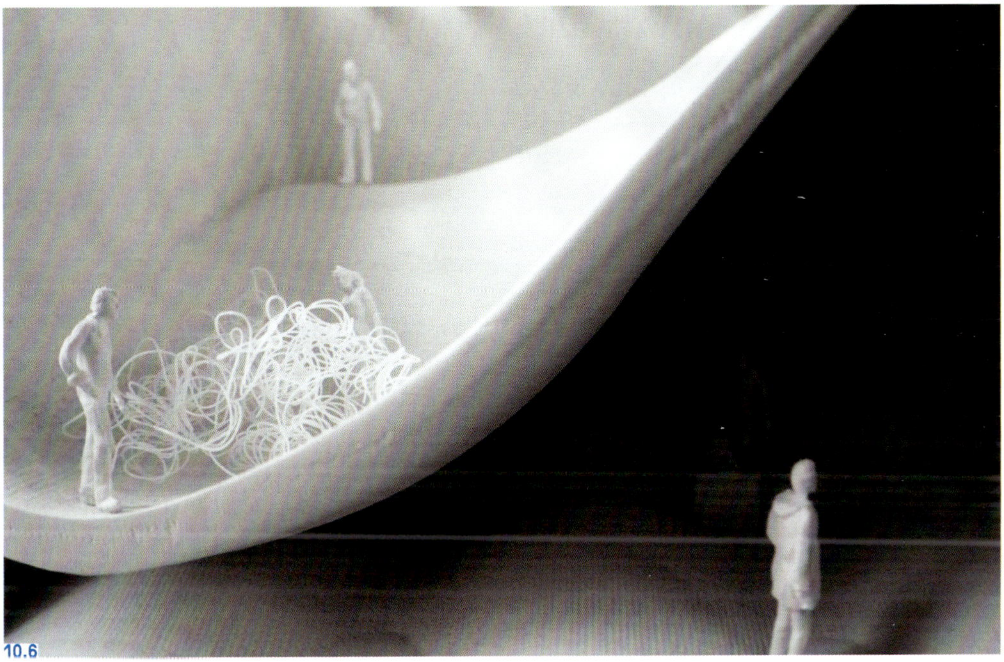
10.6

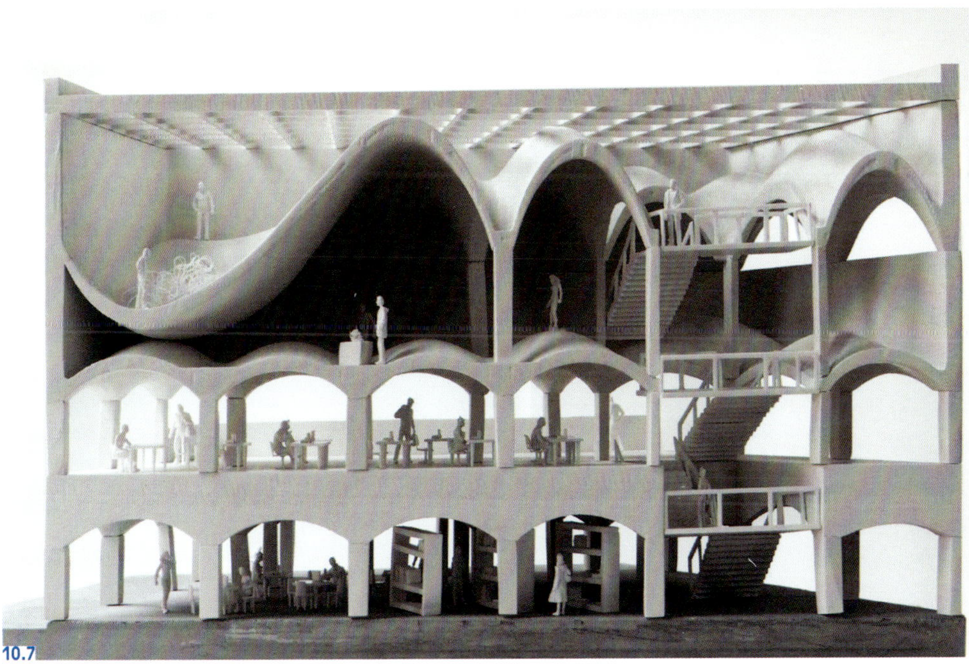
10.7

Figs. 10.8 – 10.9 Camille Dunlop Y2, 'Progressive Extraction and Corruption of the Traditional: a Contemporary Dance Centre'. This series of renders travels through spaces that are progressively corrupted as dance studios. This is a sectional render of the vertical progression in corrupted dance studios.
Fig. 10.10 Yung To (Toby) Chan Y2, 'London Tube Playground'. The project refurbishes Bow Road Underground Station by replacing the existing roof structure with a playground to serve the family-based communities of Bow. The playground features pockets of intensities which borrow from the rules and strategies in the game 'Hide and Seek'. The project celebrates the act of waiting, and questions accessibility and visibility in public space.

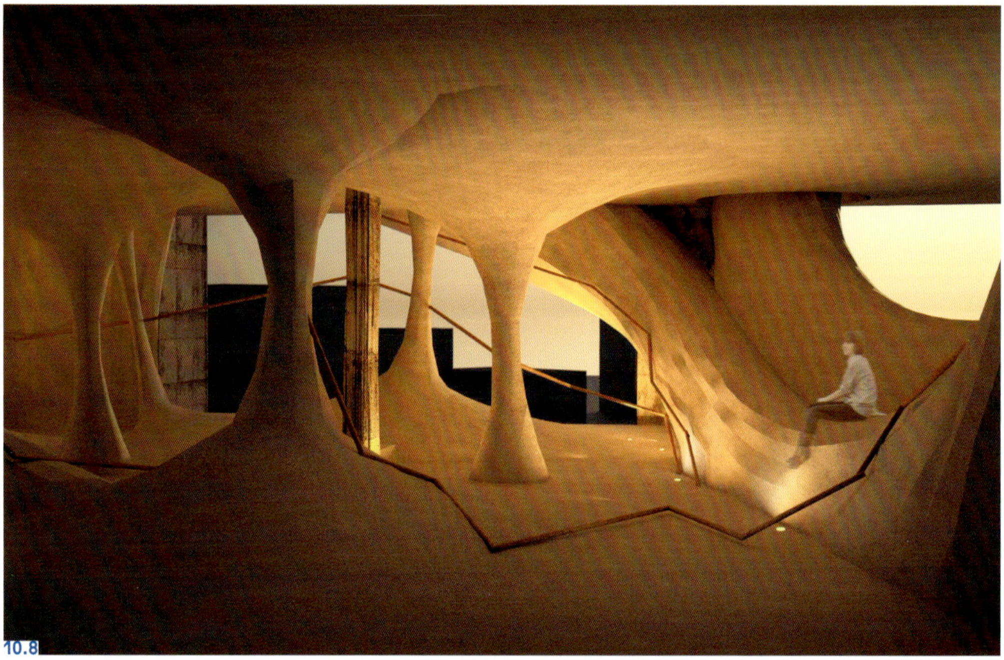

10.8

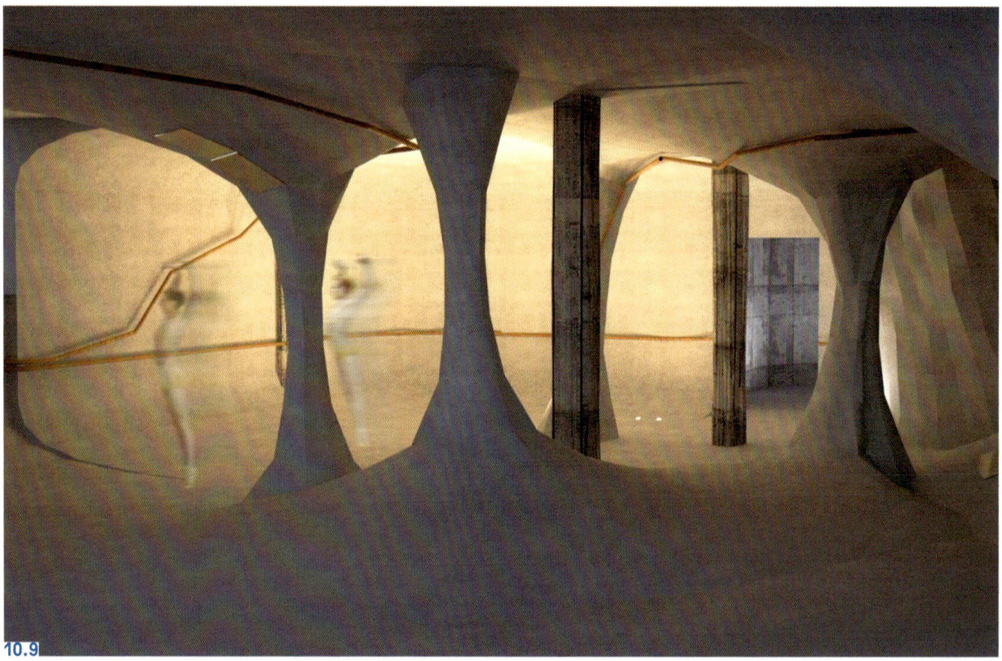

10.9

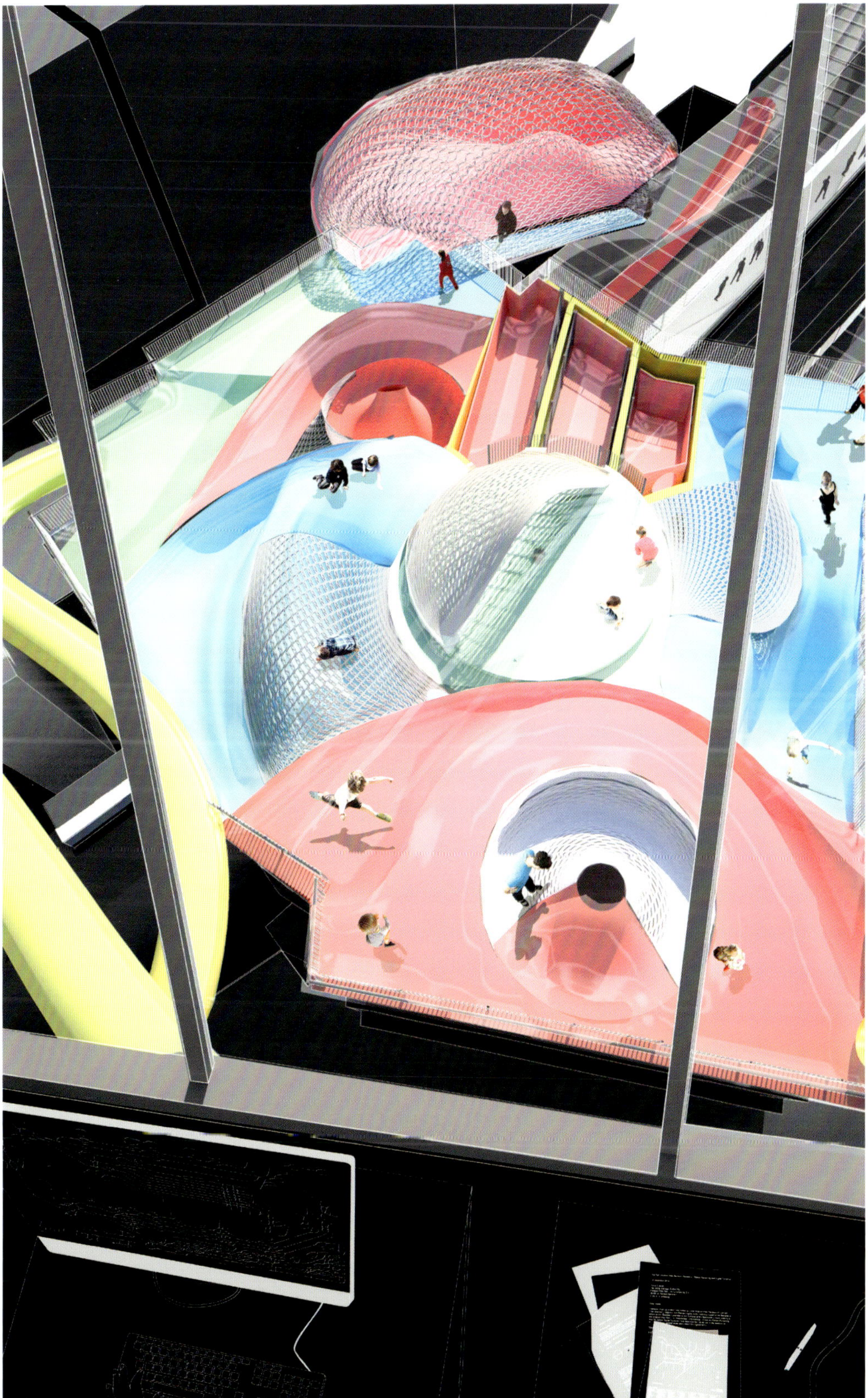

10.10

Figs. 10.11 – Fig. 10.12 George Brazier Y2, 'Hackney Wick YMCA: Harmonising Religion with Mind, Body and Spirit'. This project proposes a faith-led community YMCA, combining physical fitness, spirituality and accommodation. Its aim is to illuminate a polluted void in Hackney, located under the A12. **Fig. 10.13 Edward Taft** Y2, 'CLT Futures'. This project uses algorithmic systems to explore the capabilities of CLT and give expressive form to a typically uniform construction material. This sectional drawing shows a mixed programme factory and innovation centre within an algorithmically generated structure.

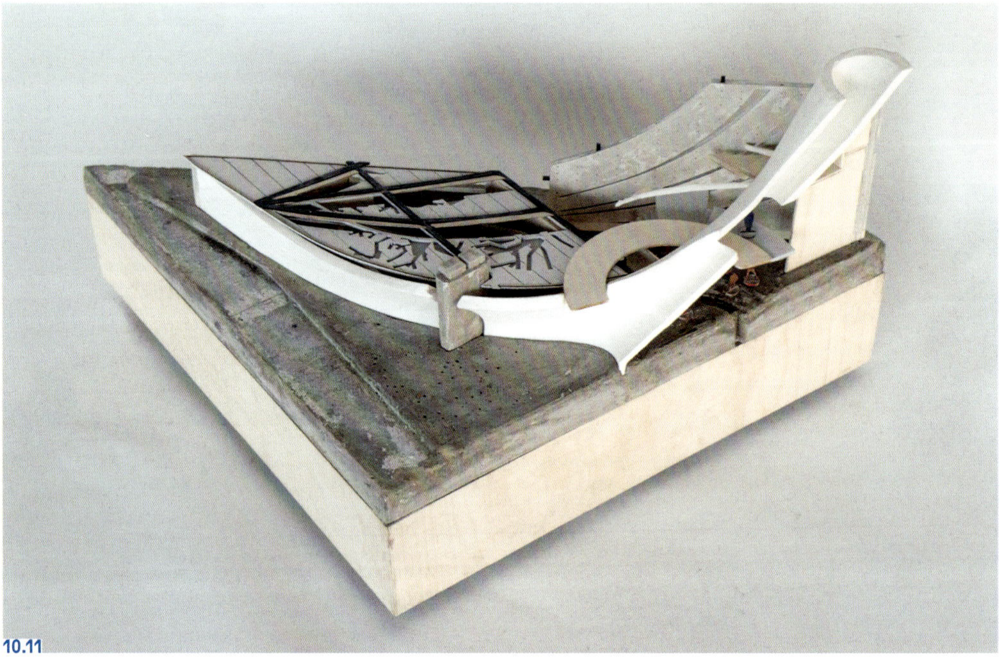

10.11

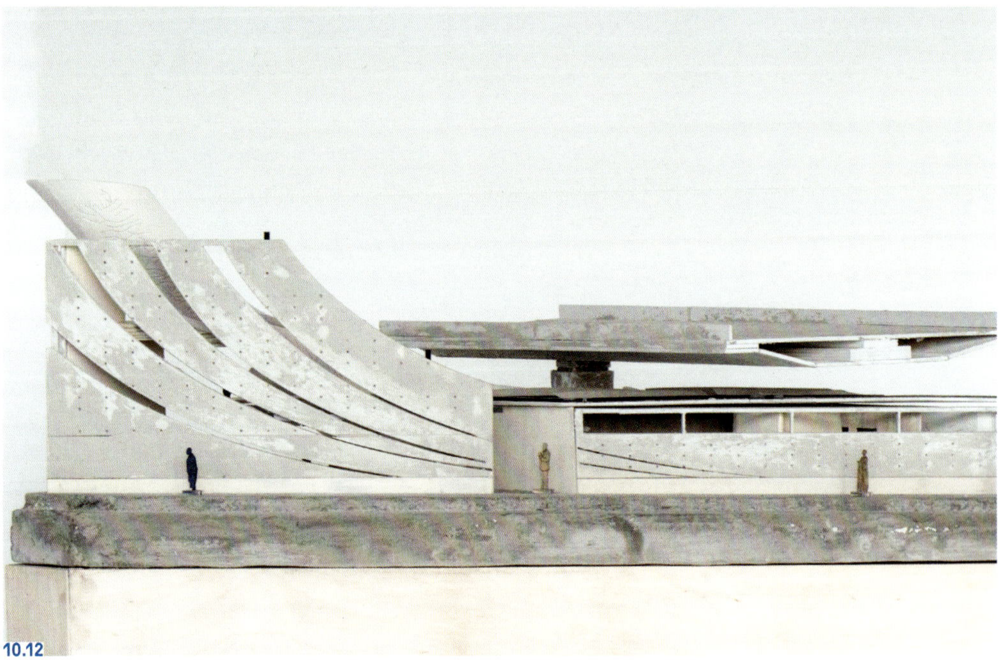

10.12

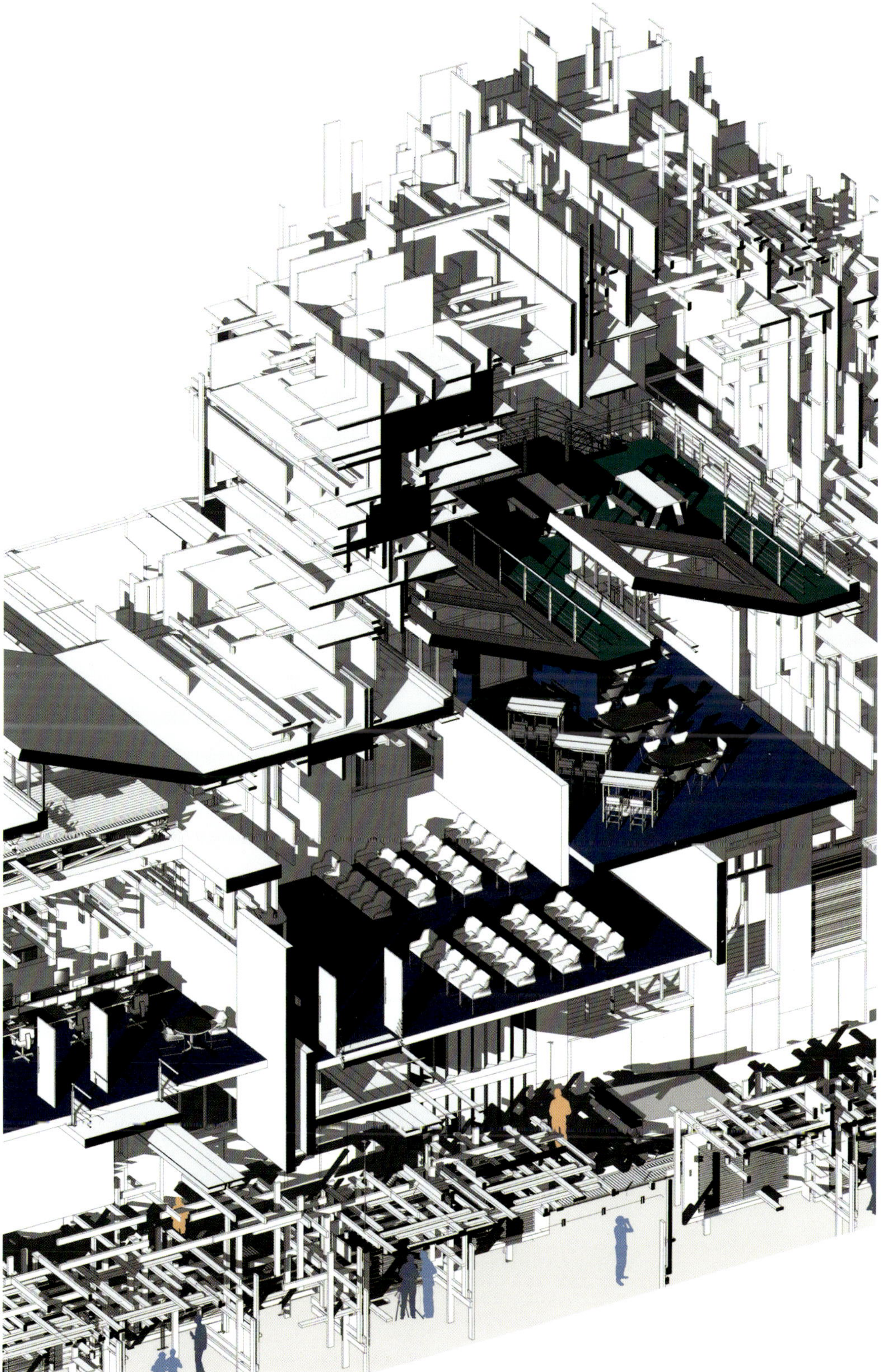

10.13

UG11

Process Matters

Kostas Grigoriadis, Sofia Krimiz

Year 2
Teresa Carmelita, Du Hao, Michelle Hoe, Jie Kuek, Jiyoon Lee, Zhi Tam, Jun Yap, Renzhi Zeng

Year 3
Kelly Au, Samuel Grice, Ana-Maria Ilusca, Olga Karchevska

Thank you to:
Sean-Paul von Ancken, Biayna Bogosian, Ivi Diamandopoulou, Natalia Hayes, Michael Herrmann, Alvin Huang, Francesca Hughes, Rick Joy Architects, Claudia Kappl, Hanne Sue Kirsch, Costandis Kizis, Colby Ritter, Sylvie Taher, Roger Tomalty

In the beginning of the 20th century, the art historian Alois Riegl wrote of a decisive change that took place at the time – namely the transition from the valuation of old materials to the valuation of new ones. This reflected the shift in early modern Europe towards a preoccupation with newness, which eventually paved the way for the constant invention of new materials that could be easily manufactured via mechanised mass production, as opposed to artisanal making. This shift effectively also triggered the modernist collapse of the links between design, form and materiality.

——More than a century later, the material invention paradigm that Riegl once witnessed is now happening at an exponentially fast rate, with new materials and production methods being concocted each and every day. In architecture, on the other hand, the age-old separation of the types of construction in tectonics and stereotomics are – surprisingly – still valid, illustrating quite clearly the fact that architecture, and the way it is designed and built, has yet to catch up with the exponentially advancing material innovations of today.

——In this context, the objective of the studio is to align with these developments, and to attempt to generate a new architecture in sync with contemporaneous material advances. Rethinking the ways in which space is conceived and designed, buildings are constructed, and architecture is inhabited generates for us an unprecedented opportunity for spatial and architectural innovation, informed by twenty-first century materials and materialisms.

——In pursuit of this, we initially looked into materiality in its malleable, liquid state. We explored different ways in which liquid materials can be physically admixed and cast, and their rheological properties – with flow and coagulation simulated digitally. In parallel with this, we pursued unconventional fabrication techniques that explored the reciprocal relationship between mould and cast, pushing the solidified materials to breaking point, and understanding both the inherent and unexpected properties of our admixtures.

——We then travelled to Los Angeles and Phoenix. In this land of extreme juxtapositions and odd notions of architectural normality, the truth in materials was whatever we decided it to be. Our search explored the banal, weird and wonderful ways that cast materials can be produced. The metropolitan architecture of LA was effectively juxtaposed with the utopic character of Paolo Soleri's Arcosanti and his concept of 'Arcology'. Our aim was to formulate a firm architectural position through recursive readings of the habitat and instil some of these observations into the urban context of LA, where our buildings were situated. In this process of architectural transplantation, we aspired to rebuild the modernist collapse of the relationship between form, design, materiality and process in order to generate a new type of architecture, or a 21st-century Arcology that has finally caught up with the future.

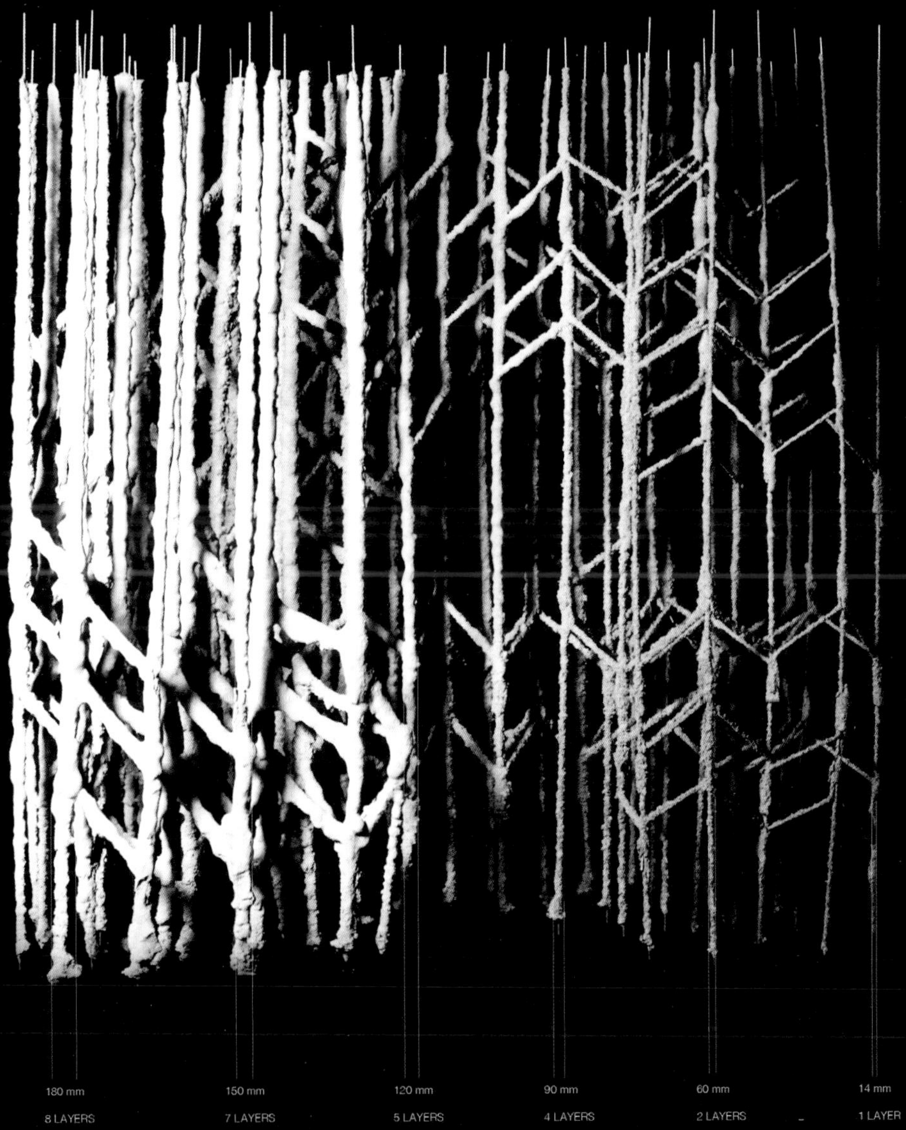
180 mm
8 LAYERS
150 mm
7 LAYERS
120 mm
5 LAYERS
90 mm
4 LAYERS
60 mm
2 LAYERS
14 mm
1 LAYER

11.1

Fig. 11.1 Michelle Hoe Y2, 'After the Earthquake'. Gradient concrete-spraying study model of the inhabitable scaffolding module. **Figs. 11.2 – 11.4 Renzhi Zeng** Y2, 'Homeless City'. A 3D-printed framework designed through liquid material simulations is openly inhabited by homeless people currently occupying large parts of Skid Row in Los Angeles. The main spaces consist of a central communal area that is designed to provide basic sanitary facilities and specialised areas that enhance the interactions of the occupants. In addition, the open-cellular organisation of the living units aims to strengthen the micro-social relationship of homeless people. **Fig. 11.5 Jiyoon Lee** Y2, 'Truck Hotel and People's Highway'. Forming an oasis in the endless desert of the interstate highways complex, the project consists of an automated parking system and living and communal spaces for large vehicle drivers, who are otherwise not allowed to exit the highways. The individual habitation modules can be customised in number and size in order to fit into various freeway intersections in key locations across the main east-to-west truck routes.

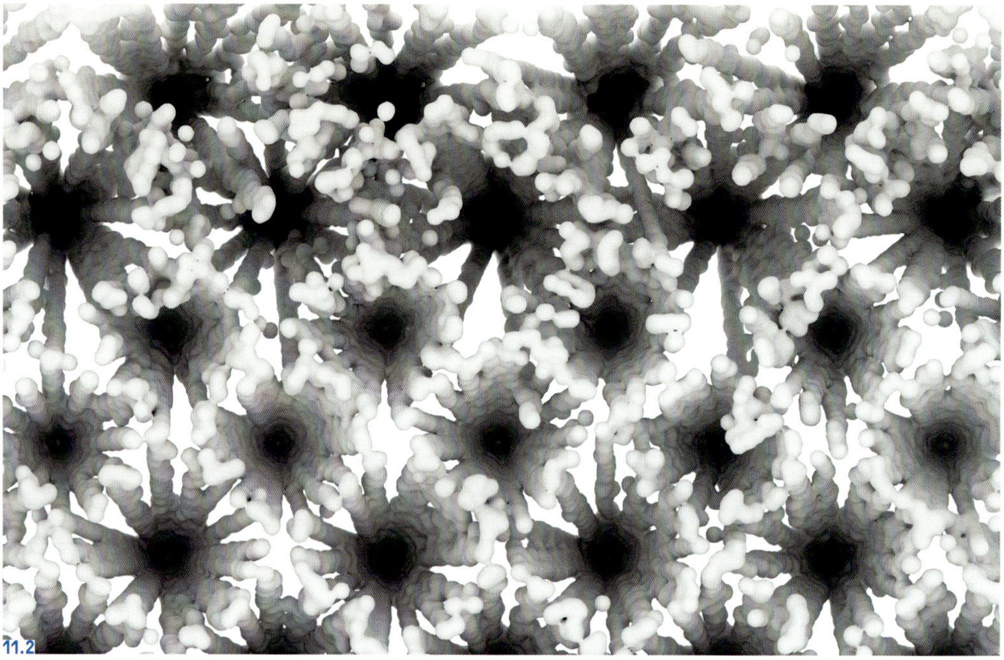

11.2

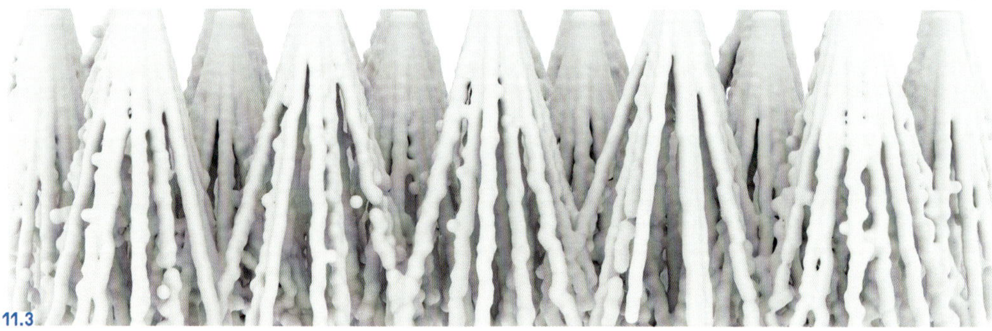

11.3

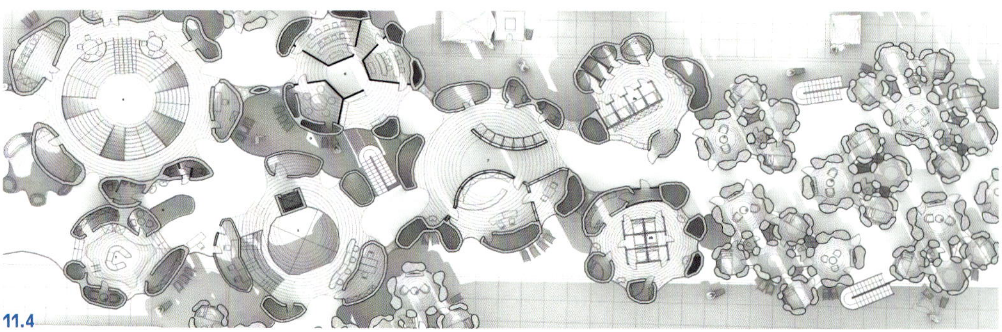

11.4

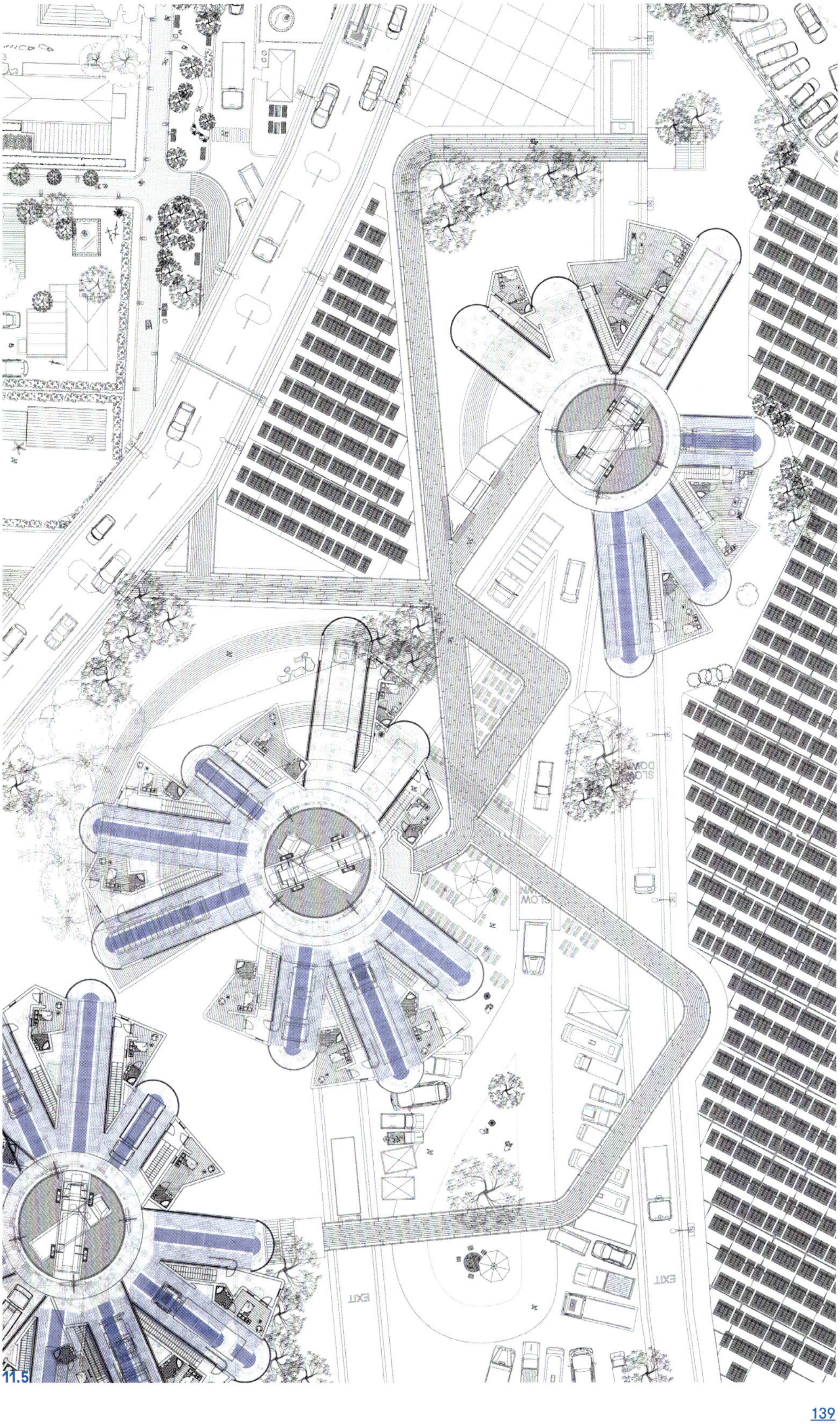

11.5

Figs. 11.6 – 11.7 Teresa Carmelita Y2, 'Foam Aggregations'. A series of study models exploring the relationship between top-down control imposed by the model maker and the material's intrinsic bottom-up behaviour. Here, the s-shaped foam blueprint ends up in a fractal-like series of folds that are generated as a result of this negotiation between design and materiality. **Figs. 11.8 – 11.9 Michelle Hoe** Y2, 'After the Earthquake'. Anticipating the next big earthquake to strike Los Angeles, the proposal consists of a series of inhabitable scaffolding modules that act as bracing systems when placed in between earthquake-affected historical buildings. Dwellings, utility and social spaces within the scaffolding allow users of the adjacent buildings to go about their daily activities – and for habitation to carry on – despite the disaster.

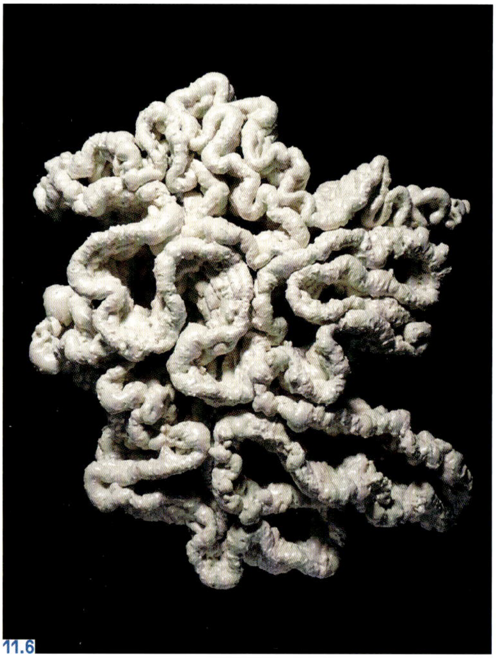

11.6

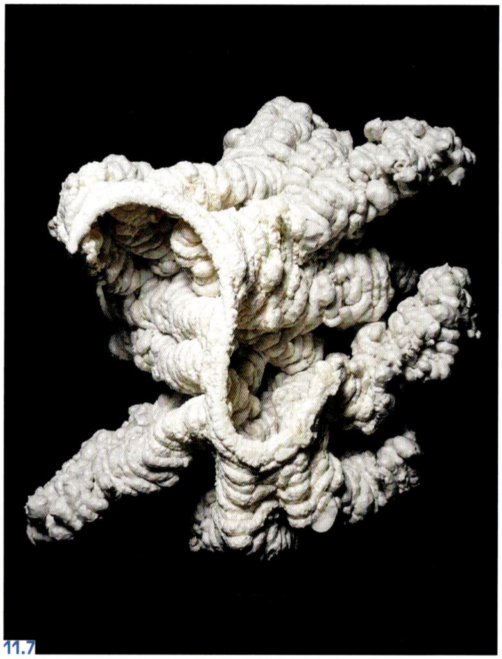

11.7

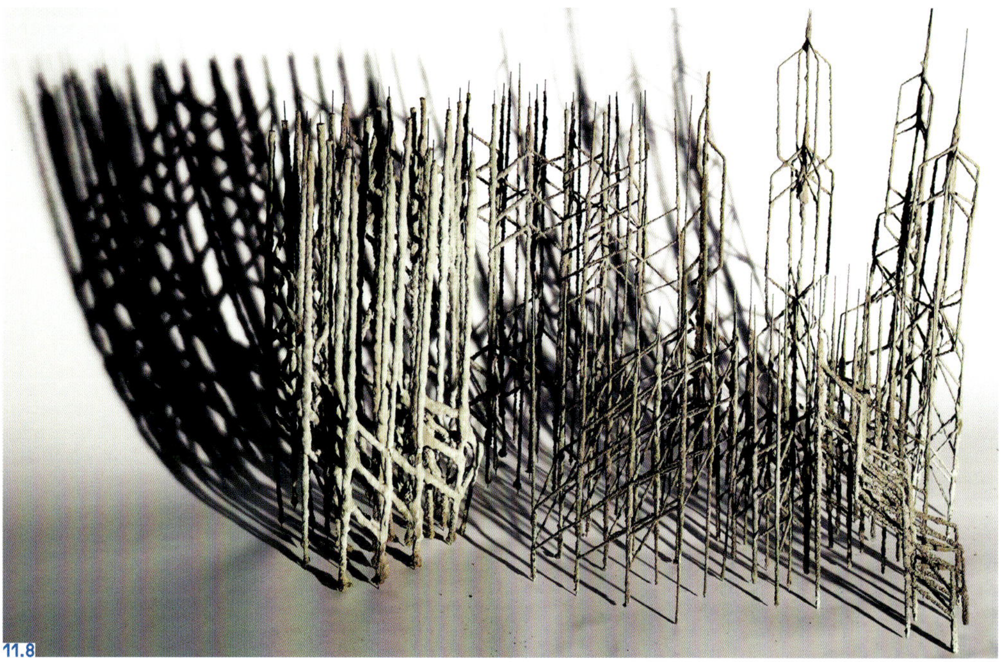

11.8

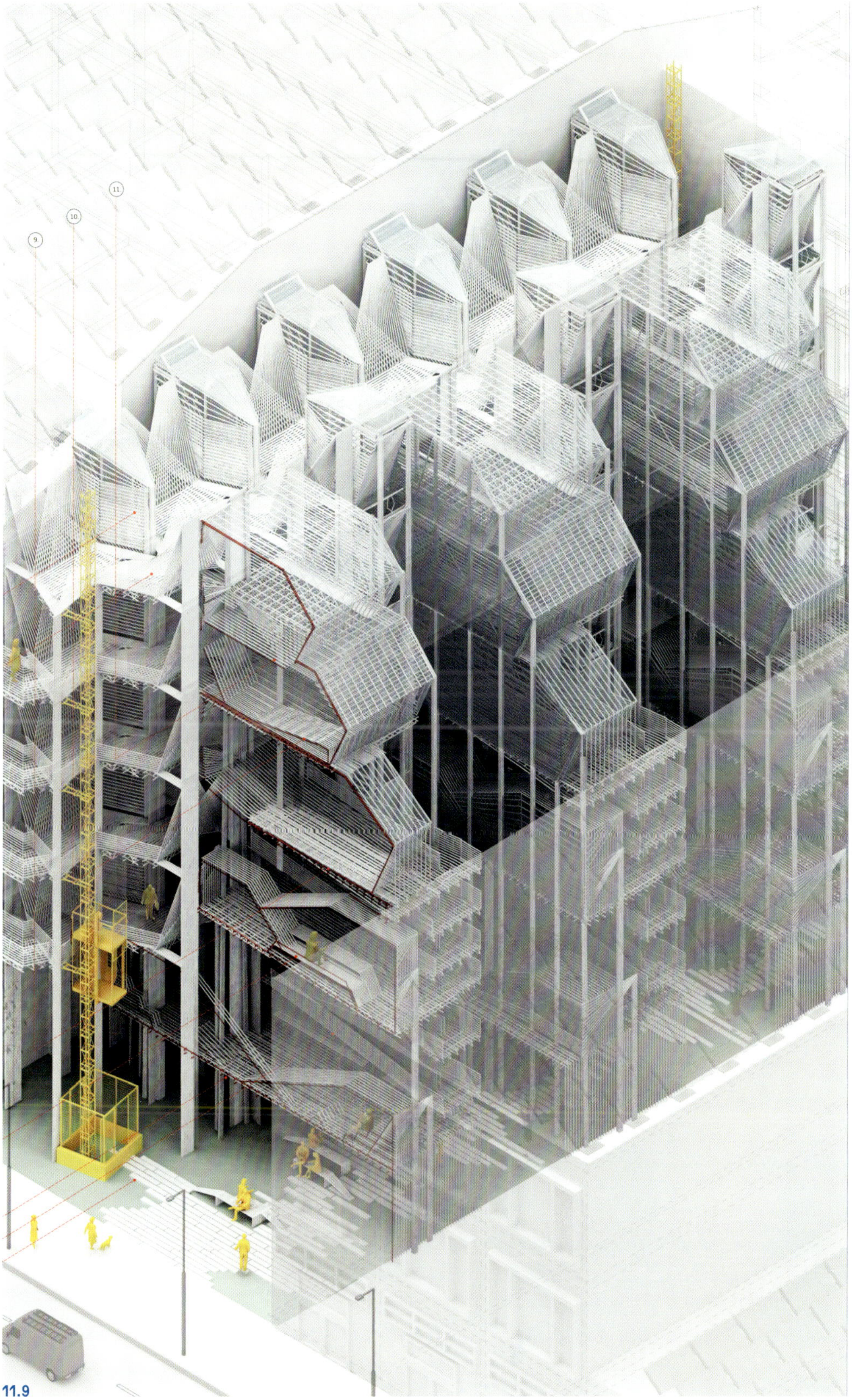

11.9

Figs. 11.10 – 11.11 Du Hao Y2, 'LA Actors' Homestage'. The project is a hybrid of living spaces and stages for struggling actors in Los Angeles, located on top of the disused Regent Theatre in downtown LA. A series of catenary arches, made up of steel tubes sprayed with concrete, forms an easily deployable building system that organises the plan and structures the distribution of acting and living spaces below. **Figs. 11.12 – 11.13 Ana-Maria Ilusca** Y3, 'The Museum of Light'. The project looks at the evolution of light and colour in the cinematic industry and proposes a series of spaces that capture the stylistic, visual and spatial qualities of film noir. Here, a series of Hele-Shaw cell experiments are tested out as a technique for recreating the stark contrasts between light and shadow found in this particular genre.

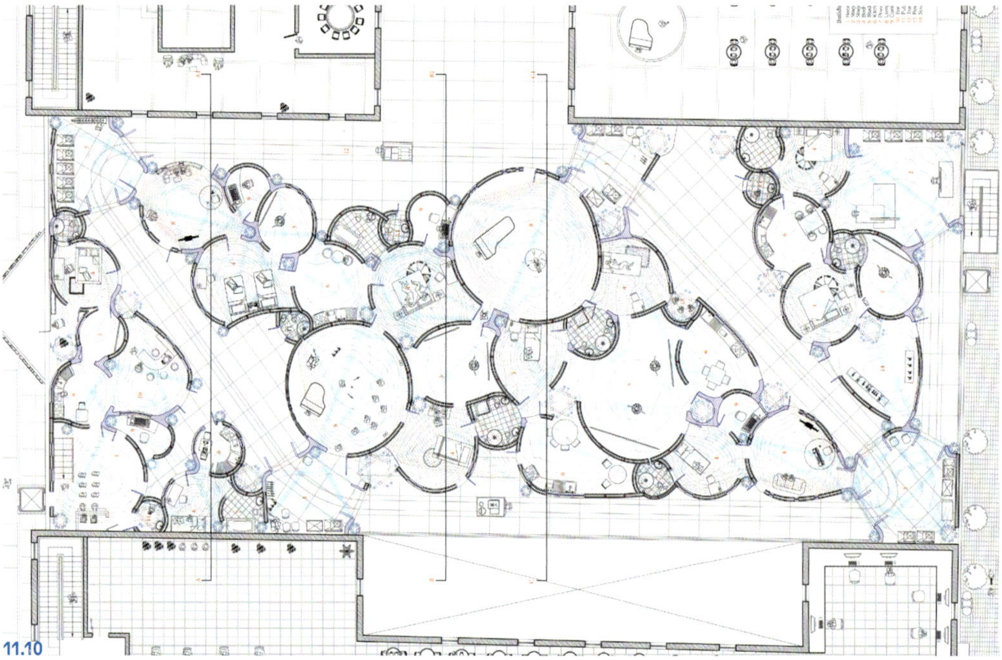

11.10

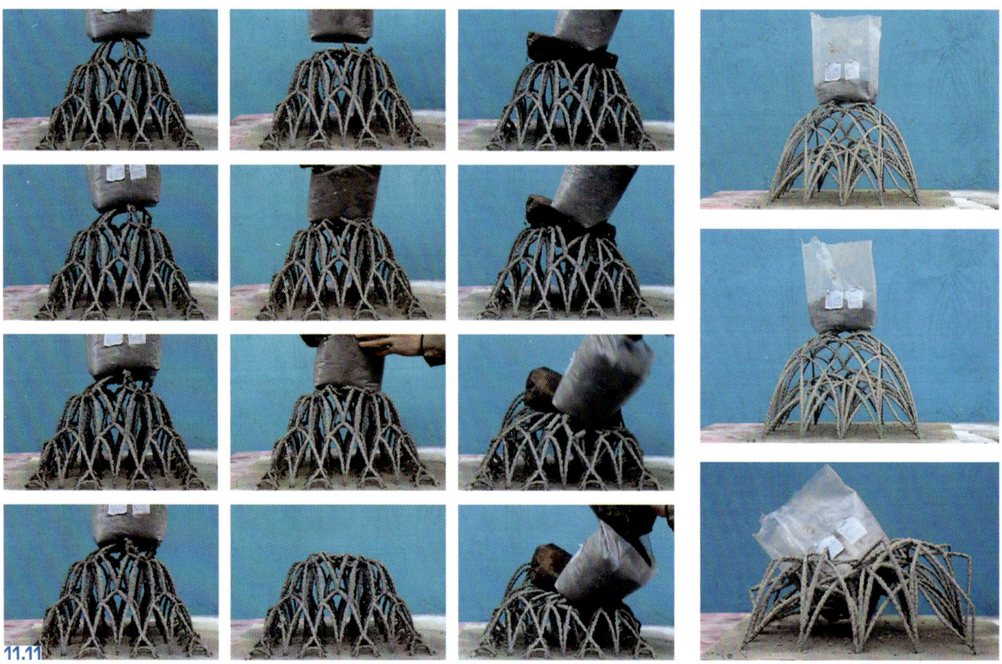

11.11

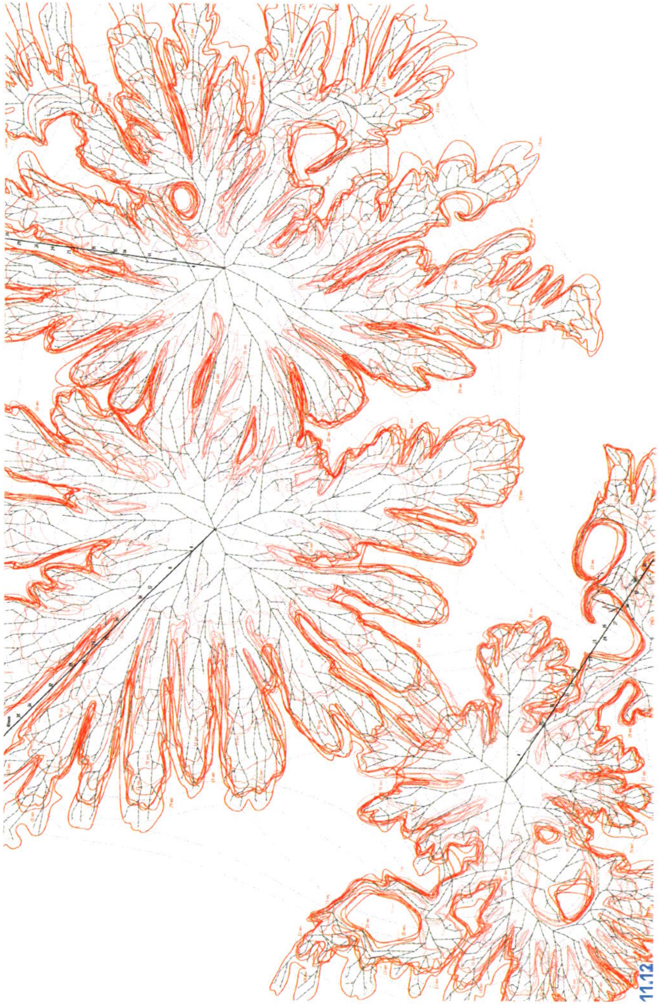

11.12

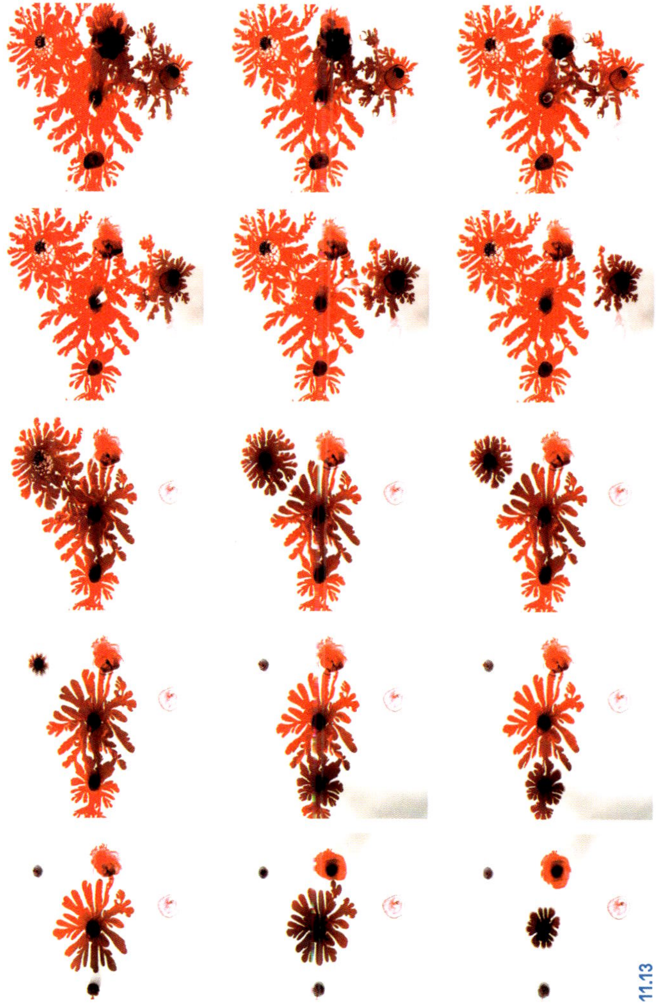

11.13

Figs. 11.14 – 11.15 Zhi Tam Y2, 'LA 2024'. One of the decommissioned Astronaut Islands off the Long Beach coast in LA is redesigned to accommodate diving and swimming events during the 2024 Olympics. The scheme is designed around a series of elevated vistas that frame strategic views of the city, generating a multi-layered and multiple set of pictures, experienced via television as well as other media interfaces. **Figs. 11.16 – 11.17 Kelly Au** Y3, 'Lungs of LA'. Inspired by Biosphere 2 in Arizona, the project consists of a prototypical learning environment designed to filter and clean the polluted LA air, as a response to the increasing number of children with respiratory problems in the city. Providing these controlled-air environments are a series of tensegrity structures made of a latex skin held in tension by wooden members, with all the materials that make up the proposal locally sourced from native Californian rubber trees.

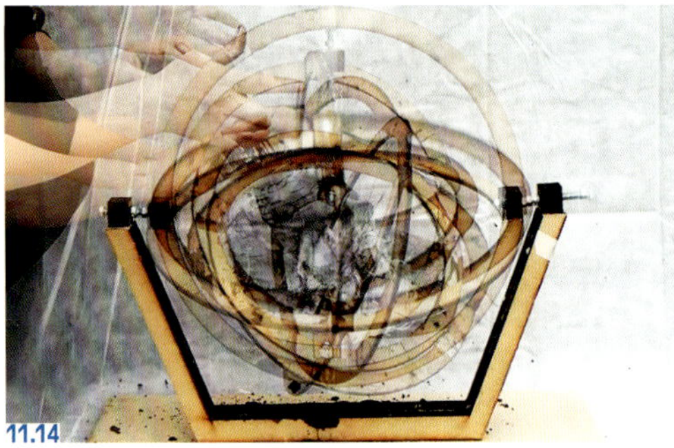
11.14

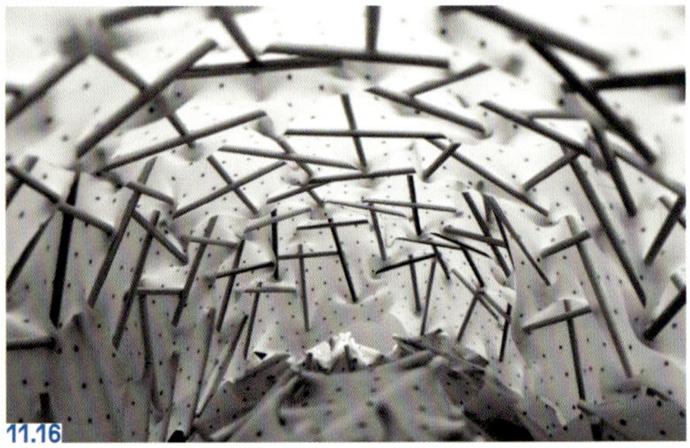
11.16

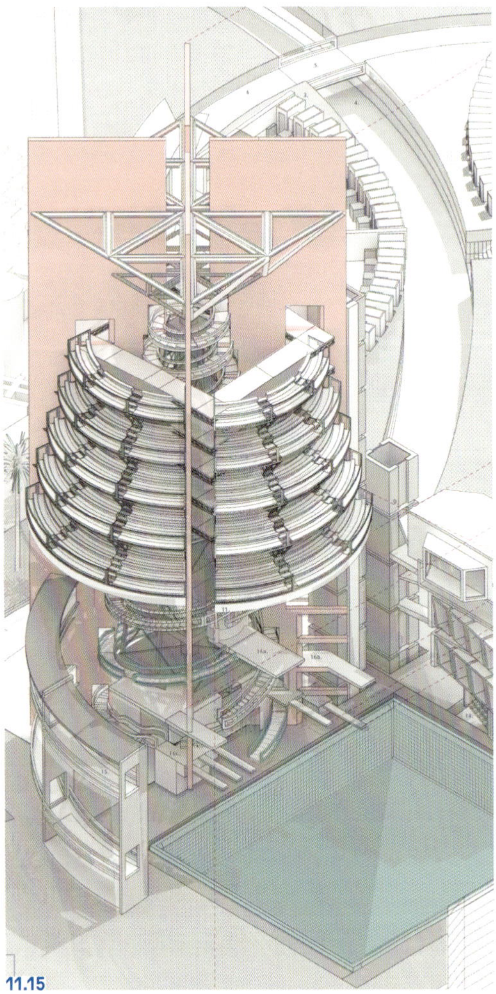
11.15

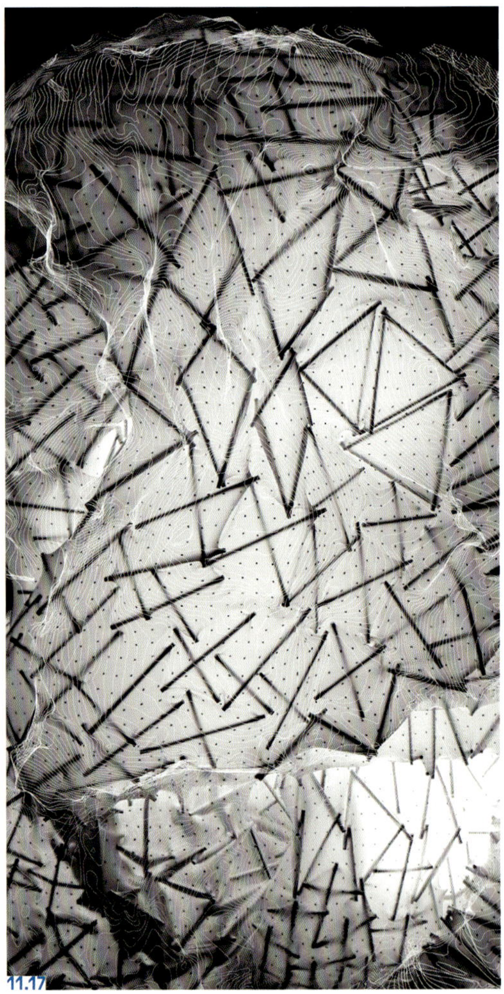
11.17

Fig. 11.18 Jie Kuek Y2, 'Depolluted Learning - Filtering Wall Study'. The Maywood area in south Los Angeles is suffering from air pollution, a long-existing problem in the city, as well as from soil contamination caused by the discharge of exide lead during the processing of industrial waste. The project attempts to address these issues through a series of tectonic elements that filter the air and clean up the soil, minimising site pollution and providing a clean environment in which local children play and learn. **Figs. 11.19 – 11.20 Jun Yap** Y2, 'Mould and Moulded'. This process consists of the recording of traces generated and left over by a solvent acting on dissolvable substances and the casting of concrete within these partially dissolved moulds. The aim is to effectively obtain a moulded structure, observe the negative spaces formed by the solvent and translate these into spatial elements. **Fig. 11.21 Jiyoon Lee** Y2, 'Angle of Repose'. The project explores the self-forming behaviour of sand under the mere influence of gravity.

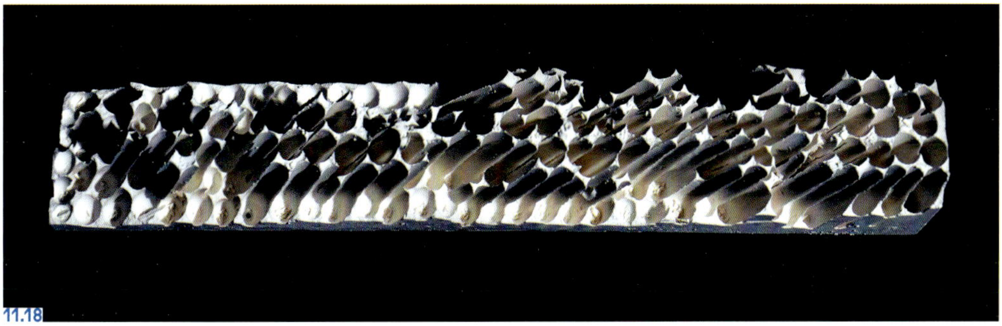

11.18

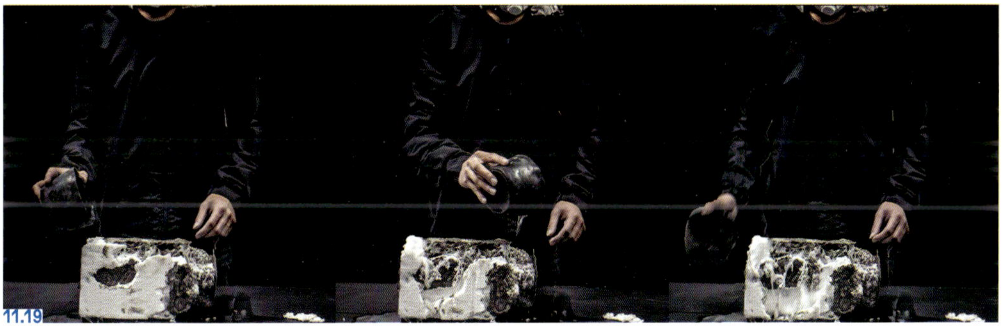

11.19

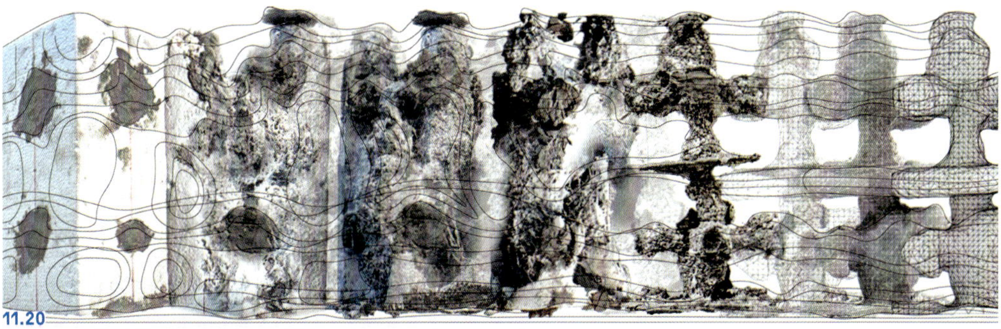

11.20

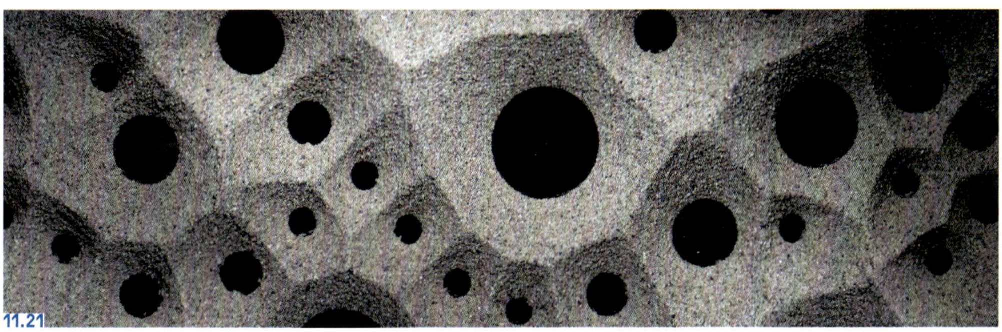

11.21

UG12 The 'Embassy'

Johan Hybschmann, Matthew Springett

Year 2
Alys Hargreaves, Yo Hosoyamada, Lauren McNicoll, Agnes Parker, Jolanta Piotrowska, Justine Shirley, An-Ni Teng

Year 3
Peter Davies, Ashleigh-Paige Fielding, James Hepper, Subin Koo, Simina Marin, Hoi (Aikawa) Mok, Elena Real-Davies, Edward Sear, Sarmad Suhail

Thank you to our technical tutor, Stephen Foster and to Bill Hodgson, computing tutor

Thank you to our critics: Laura Allen, Margaret Bursa, Patrick Weber, Jonathan Pile, Sabine Storp, Colin Smith, Nikolas Travasaros, Frosso Pimenides

Thank you to our partners: Beam Center, NYC; UASDC, NYC

Thank you to our sponsor: Architecture Project Funds

Our unit aims to focus on the extraordinary nature of the ordinary brief. We enjoy the richness that can come from a simple programme skillfully executed. We prioritise spatial inventiveness and imaginative making over complexity of programme. We believe that extraordinary architecture can be developed from simple briefs (exquisitely considered and refined) through an instrumental design process where drawings, models, installations and other techniques are used to test and enhance a site's coding.

——Fabrication is key to the studio and production is seen as a vital bridge between an architectural intention and reality. Making something physical (drawing, cast, model, collection, instrument etc.) enables a dialogue to develop, both in the context of the studio, and in the context of making architecture. Students will be encouraged to design by spatial experience – and fabrication is a vital tool in transforming this experience into architecture.

——We started the year by exploring how we belong to London. We analysed and explored places to which we felt connected: be it the familiarity of a known context or a social or cultural belonging, and described these spaces in a document representing our important London moments. From these studies we created a small building which reflected our preoccupations. In doing so we thought about neighbourhoods and communities that had strong identities and, with other earlier findings in mind, we developed a brief that bridged, protected or was a conduit to the local community.

——Our field trip took us to New York City: the location for siting our major building project. New York has a remarkable history of immigration and constitutional settlement, not to mention being the now politically loaded hometown of President Trump. It remains one of the most diverse cities on the planet, with defined areas of ethnic and cultural specificity. Many other cities depend on the economic climate of this great metropolis and therefore, despite not being a capital, it always mediates and finds other nations/entities represented within its boundaries.

——During our stay we researched and refined our area of interest for the building brief and worked closely, through a number of hands-on model making workshops, with BEAM in Brooklyn and UASDC in Manhattan. Drawing on the theme of 'Embassy', the building briefs all developed notions of representing, protecting, inviting or concealing a specific community in the city. We encouraged simple programmes which are explored inventively.

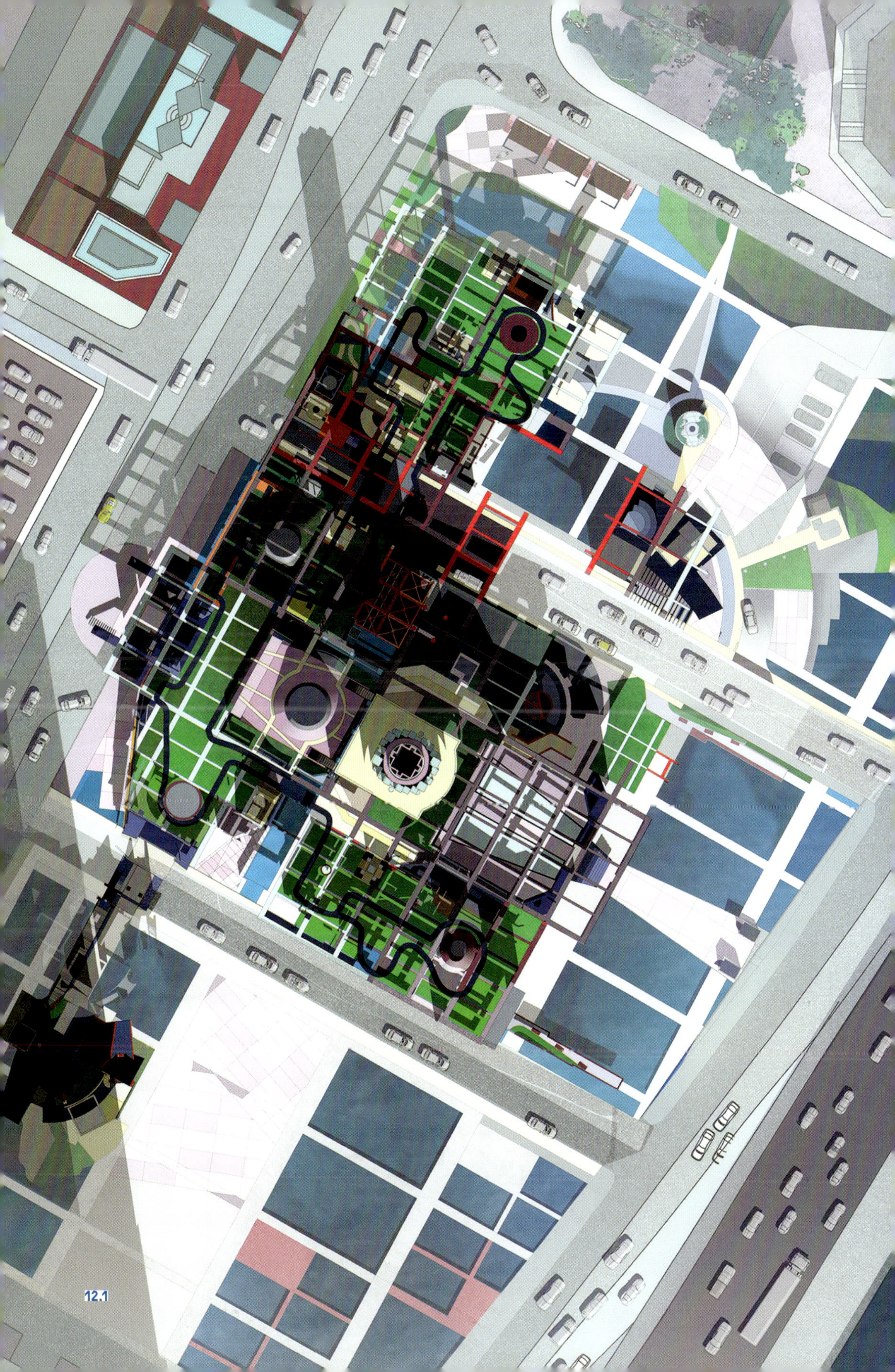

12.1

Fig. 12.1 **Sarmad Suhail** Y3, 'United New York Building'. A new, publicly accessible city hall that encodes the typologies of the five boroughs into spaces for greater inter-district collaboration. **Figs. 12.2 – 12.3 Peter Davies** Y3, 'NYC White House Presidential Offices'. A library, media pavilions and gardens located on the secluded Ellis Island.

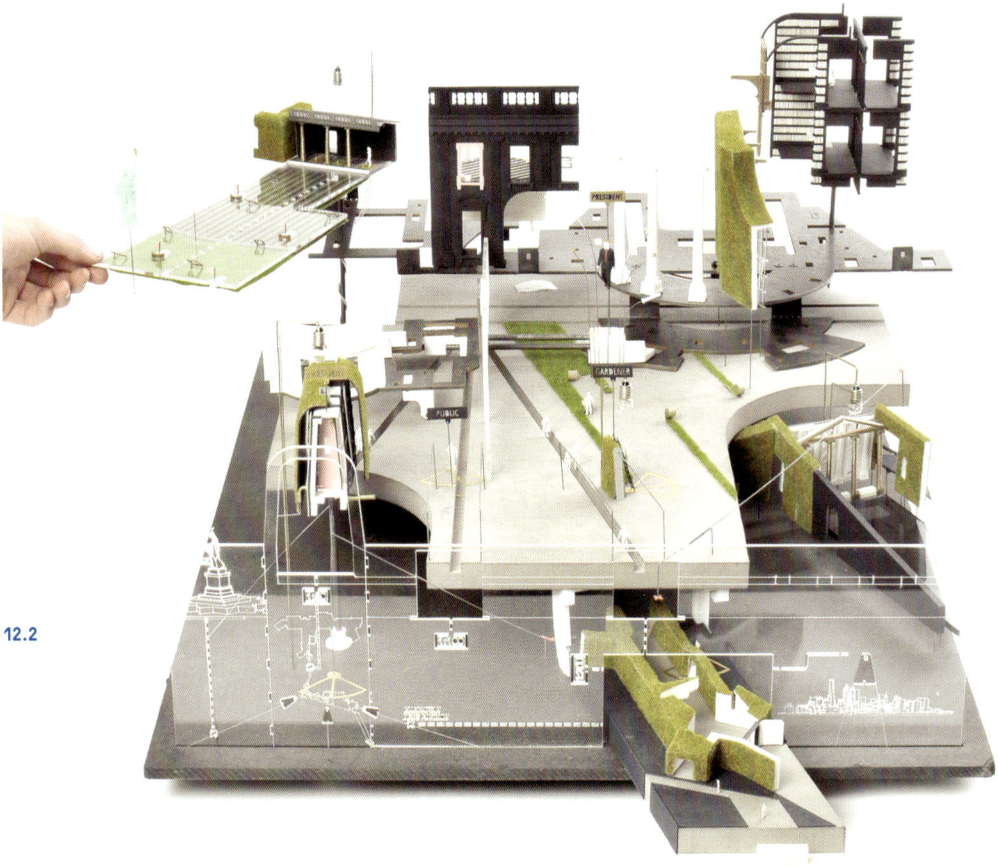

12.2

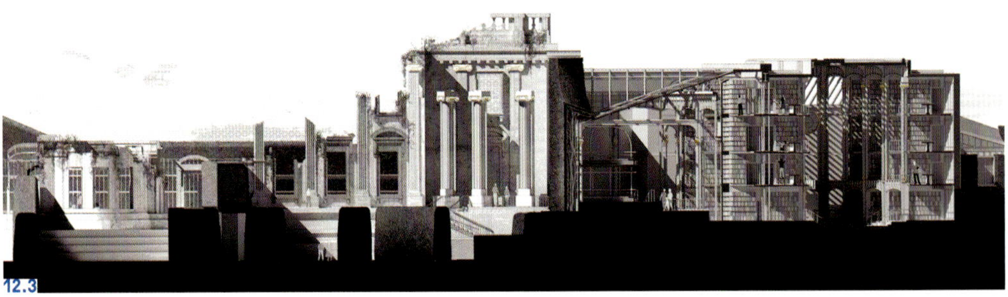

12.3

Figs. 12.4 – 12.6 Ashleigh-Paige Fielding Y3, 'Curate-able'. A proposal for a curateable artists housing community in the East Village, NYC, including social housing, studio spaces and public cultural/leisure amenities.

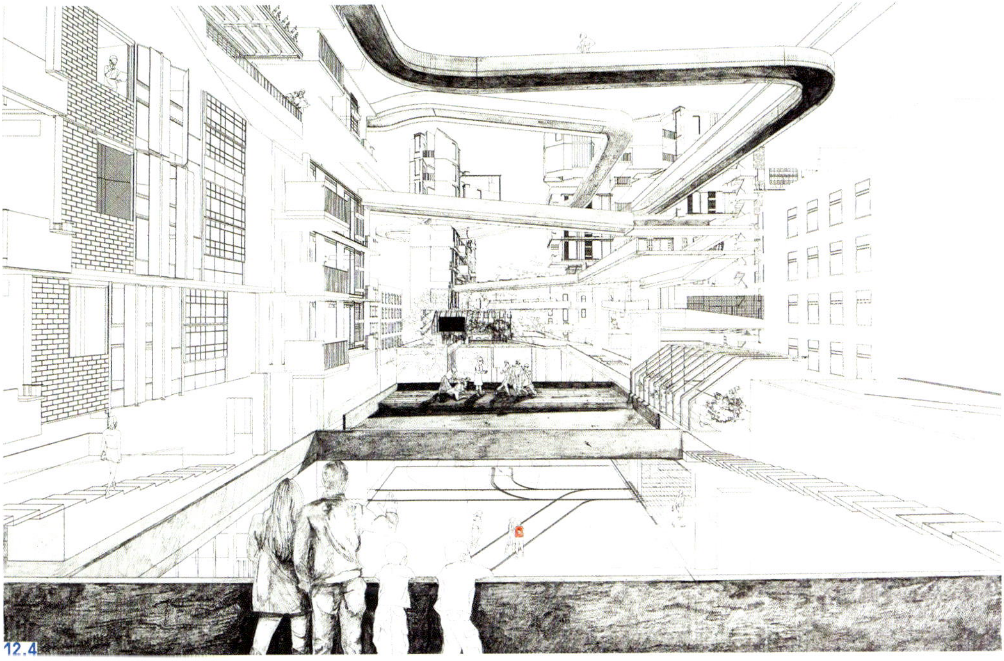

12.4

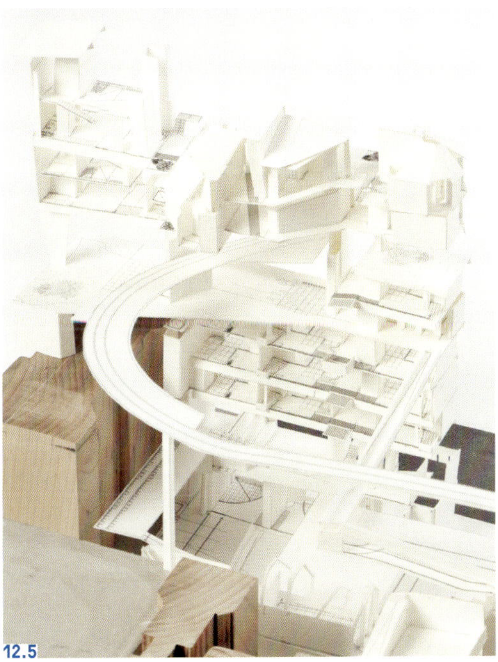

12.5

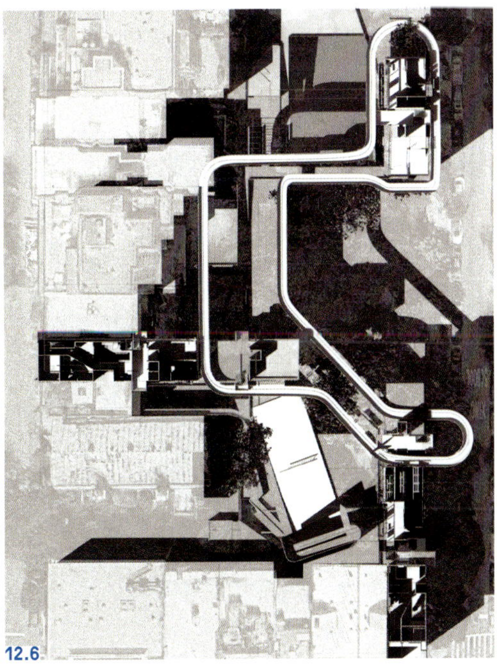

12.6

Figs. 12.7 – 12.9 Edward Sear Y3, 'Centre for City Planning'. A public building in the heart of NYC providing offices, archives and a publicly accessible demonstration planning theatre. **Fig. 12.10 Lauren McNicoll** Y2, 'Embassy of Craft'. A model demonstrating a transition through the spaces of a nightworkers café in London that leads to a project which anchors making to Williamsburg, Brooklyn, creating an embassy of craft.

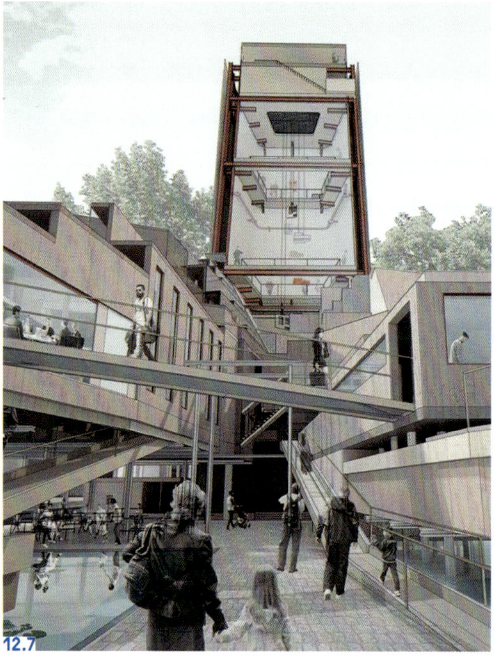

12.7

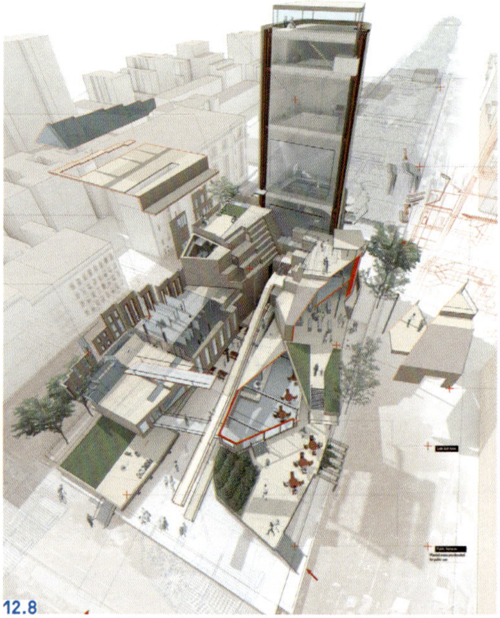

12.8

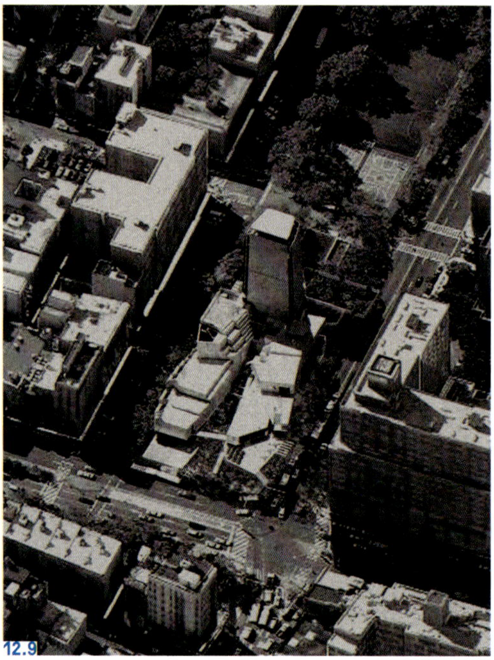

12.9

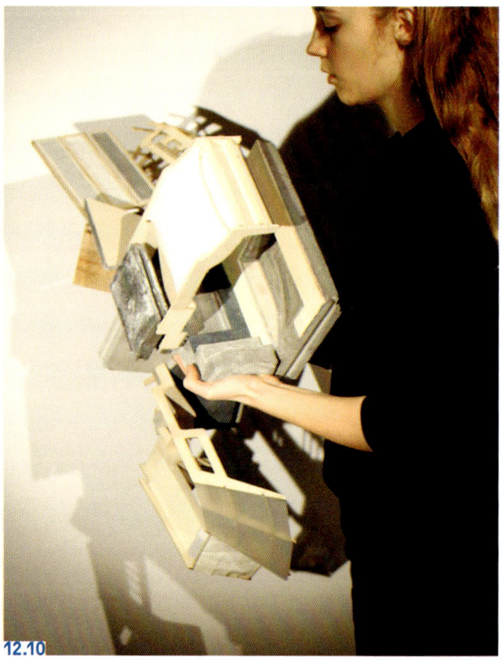

12.10

Figs. 12.11 – 12.14 Hoi (Aikawa) Mok Y3, 'Wall Street Extension'. A new international conference hall and negotiation centre merged with a public-sector financial library and intertidal landscape.

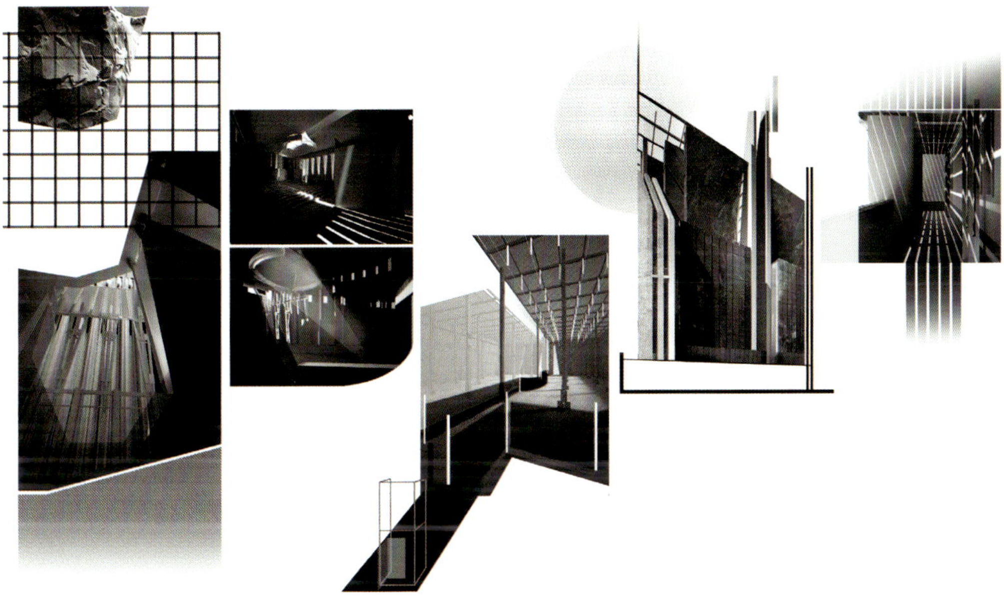

12.11

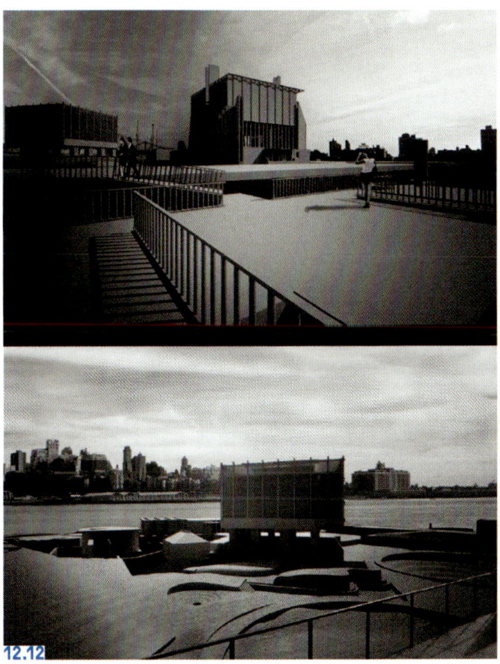

12.12

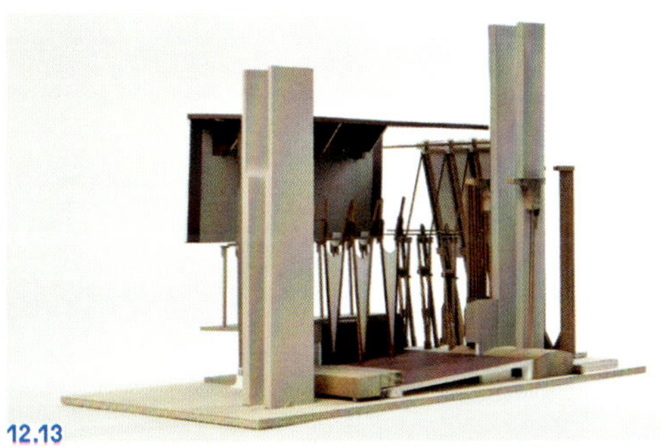

12.13

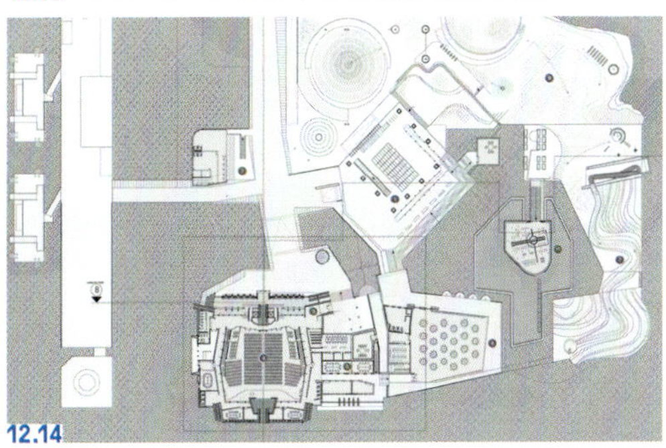

12.14

Figs. 12.15 – 12.17 Elena Real-Davies Y3, 'Space of Birth'. A pioneering birthing centre in New York for the population of Queens; sculpting an aquatic landscape in which women and new families can feel safe and at home. **Fig. 12.18 Yo Hosoyamada** Y2, 'Sunset Park Community Centre and Library'. A proposal for a Mexican community and legal advice centre in the heart of Sunset Park, Brooklyn.

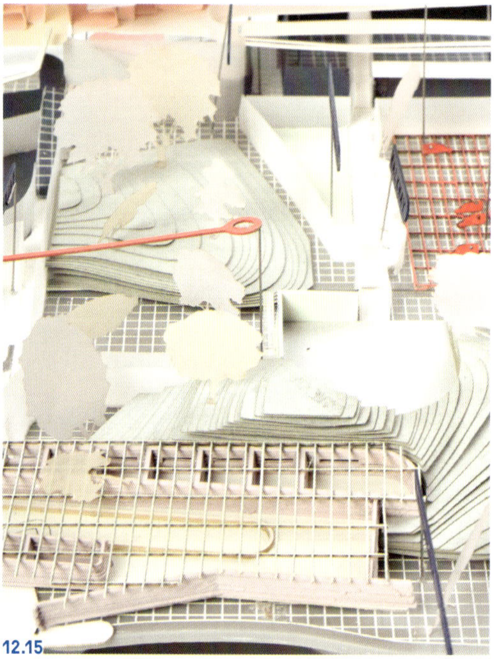

12.15

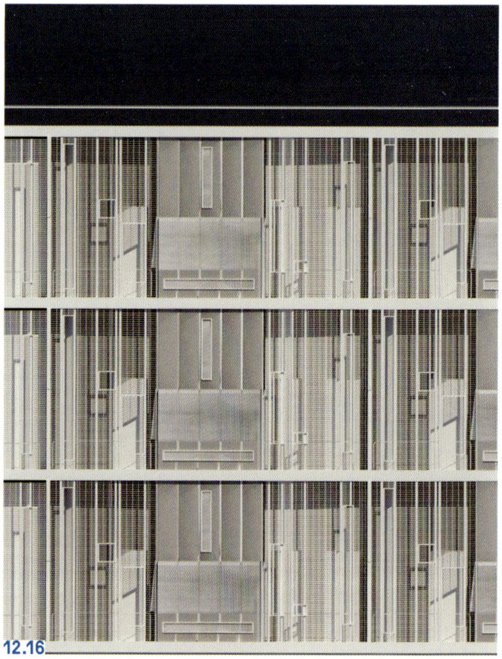

12.16

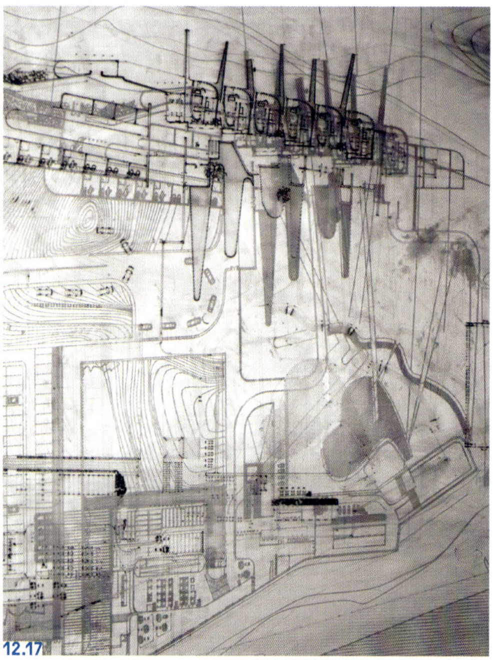

12.17

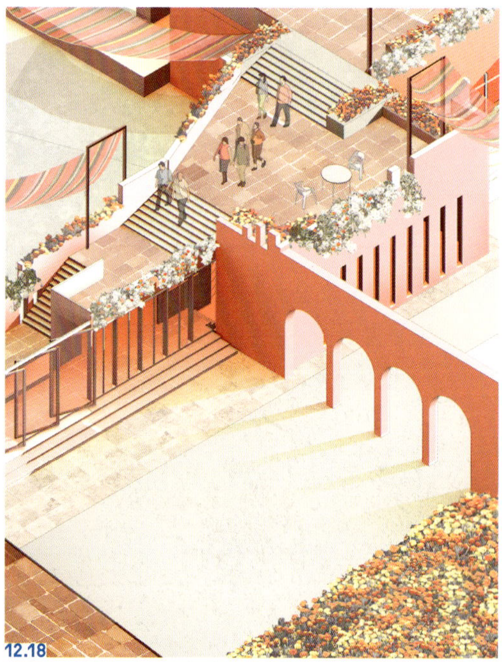

12.18

Figs. 12.19 – 12.20 Simina Marin Y3, 'Torre'. A proposal for a Mexican consulate and community centre on 57th Street based on the notion of an inhabited wall. The building becomes a metaphor for a secret garden, highly inaccessible and desirable, with a liberating internal space of celebration.
Fig. 12.21 An-Ni Teng Y2, 'Spanish Consulate and Community Centre'. Image showing meeting spaces for overseas students at UCL, exploring the notions of ambiguity and identity that arise when embarking on a new life in a foreign city. These ideas were taken forward to a Spanish community centre in Central Manhattan.

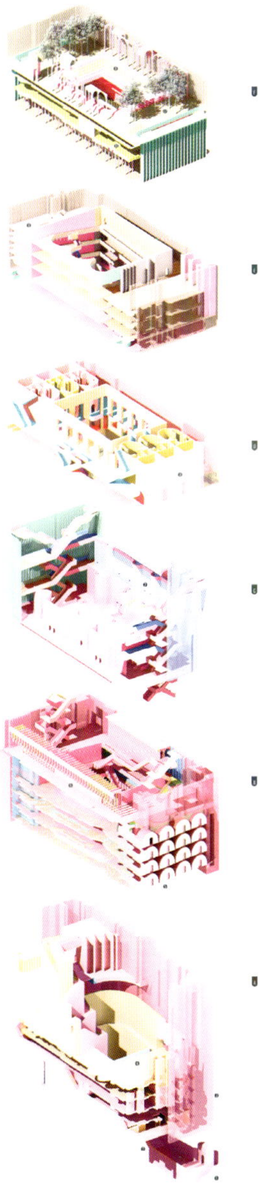

12.19

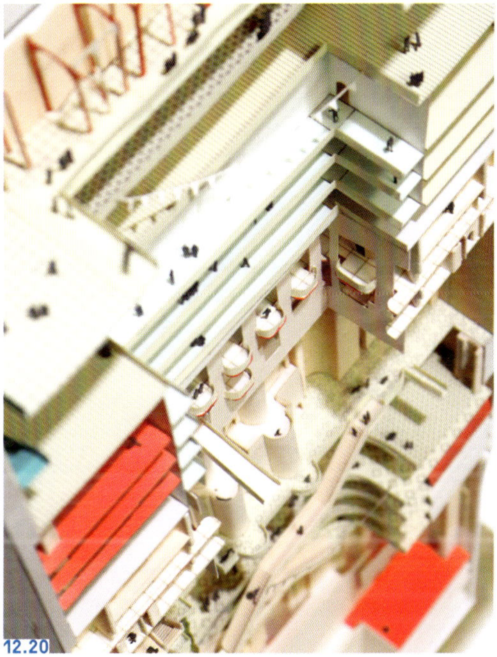

12.20

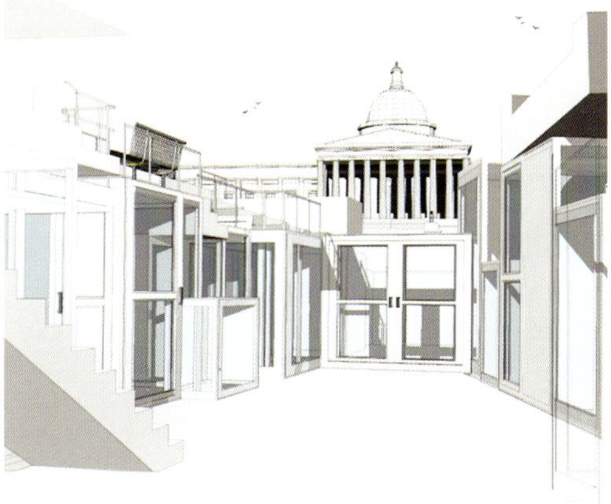

12.21

Figs. 12.22 – 12.23 James Hepper Y3, 'Mott Street General Store'. A re-imagining of the historic hybrid programme of a market street and Buddhist temples in Chinatown, NYC. **Figs. 12.24 – 25 Jolanta Piotrowska** Y2, 'NYC Syrian Refugee Centre'. A building that creates a safe community for Syrian refugees. It aims to support people suffering from PTSD during their transition to life in America. **12.26 Sarmad Suhail** Y3, 'United New York Building'. Sketch explorations for a new, publicly accessible city hall that encodes the typologies of the city's five boroughs.

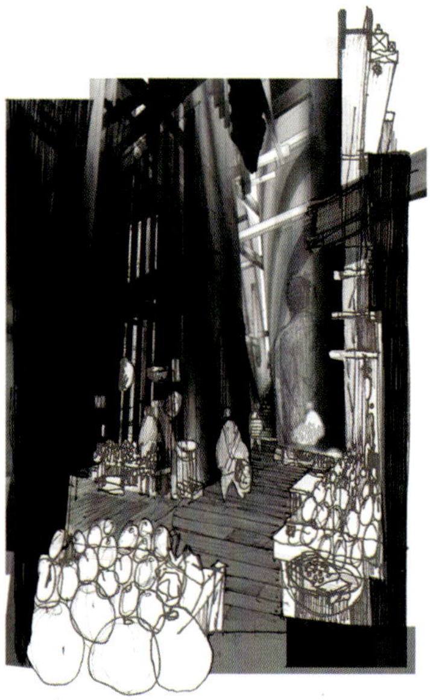

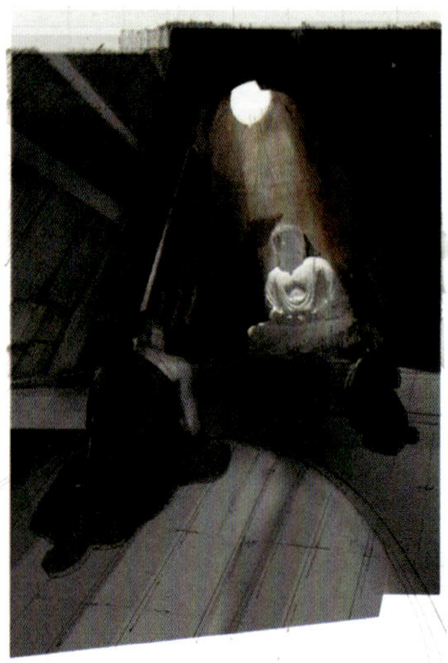

12.22

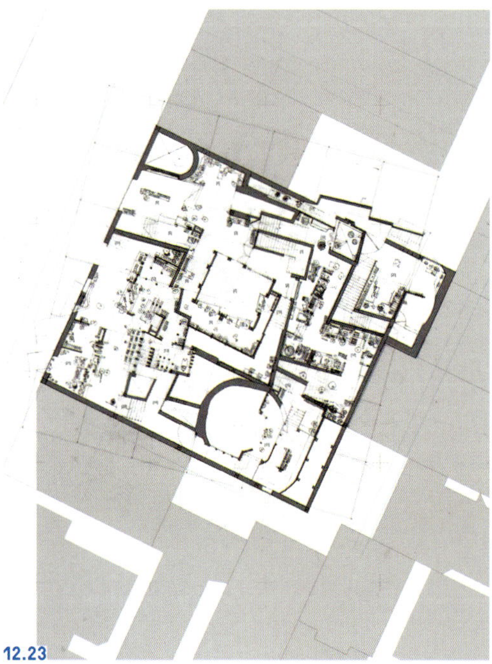

12.23

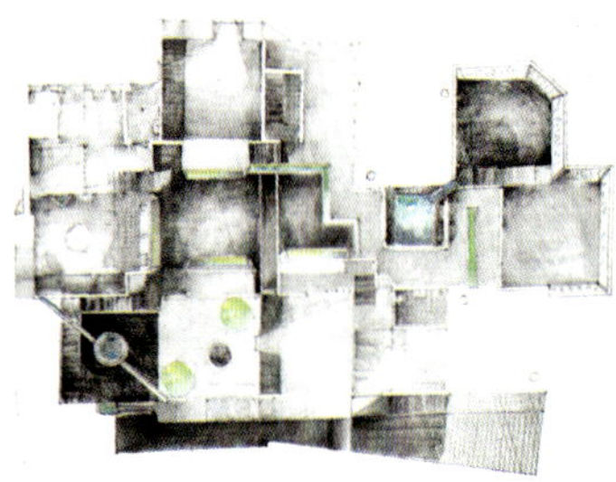

12.24

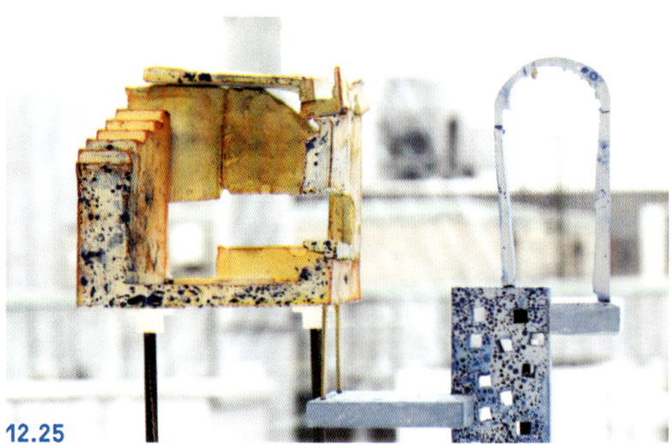

12.25

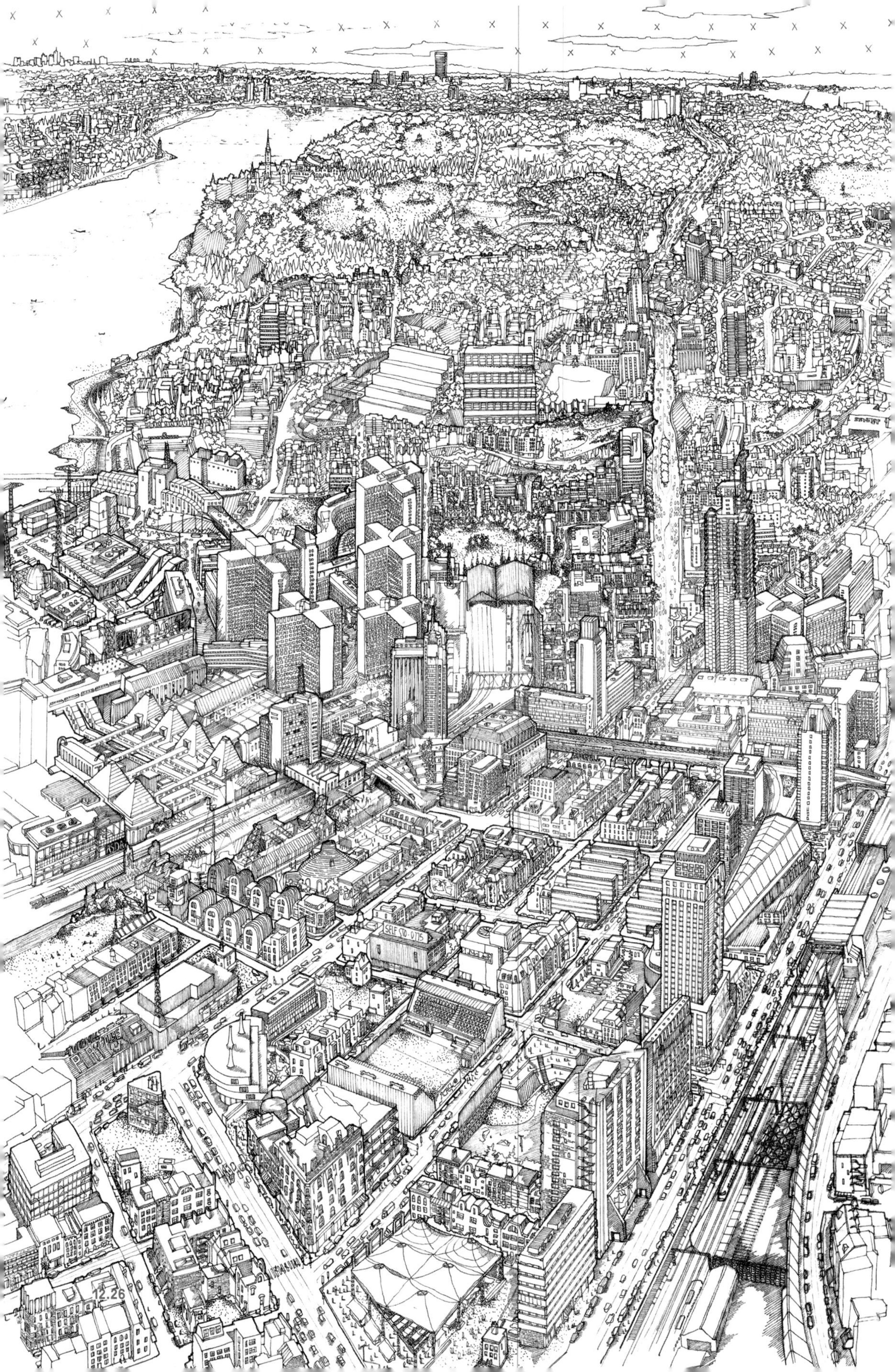
SELF STO-0775

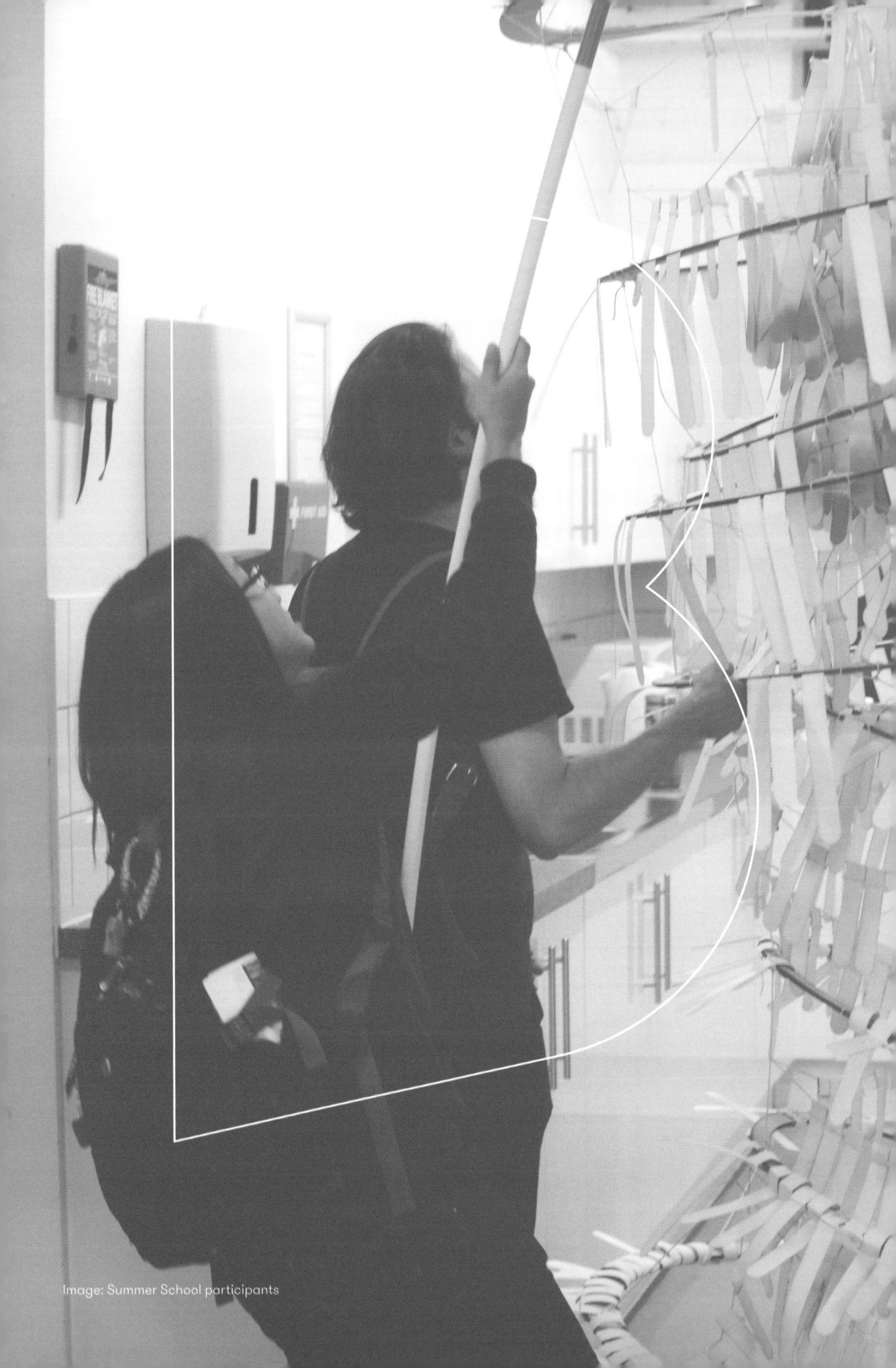

Image: Summer School participants

BSc Architectural & Interdisciplinary Studies

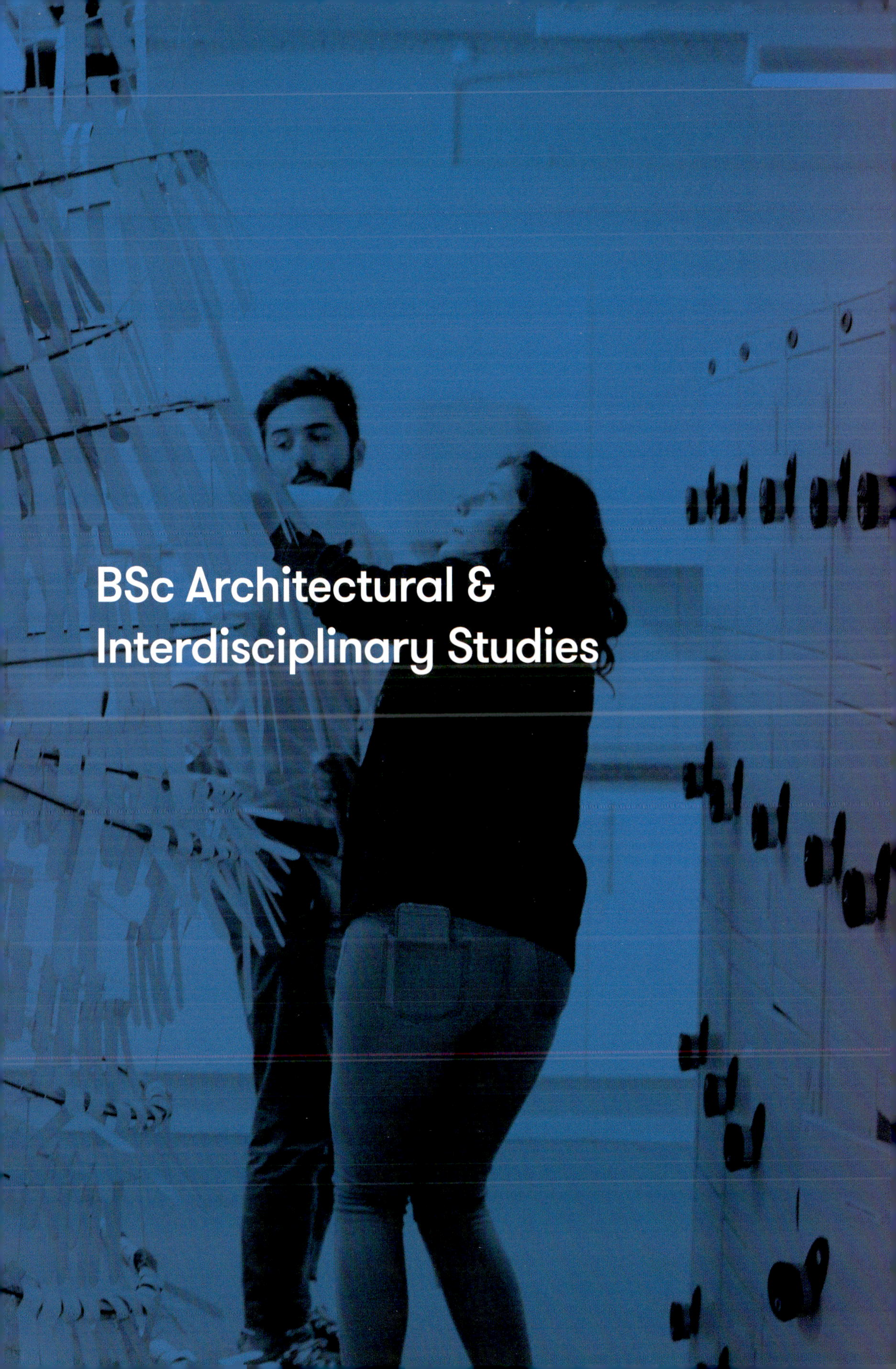

BSc Architectural & Interdisciplinary Studies

Programme Director: Elizabeth Dow

Architectural Research I & II
Barbara Penner, Sophie Read, Nina Vollenbroker

Dissertation in Advanced Architectural Studies
Brent Carnell, David Roberts

Project X – Design & Creative Practice
Elizabeth Dow, Kevin Green, Mara Kanthak, Chee-Kit Lai, Emma-Kate Matthews, Freddy Tuppen, Michelle Young

Architectural culture has never been exclusively a product certified by architects, but now, more than ever, there are many other people working in related fields (film, media, curation, design and creative practice) who shape debate and ideas around architecture in significant ways. In bringing together architectural research and design and creative practice courses, BSc Architecture and Interdisciplinary Studies develops independent-minded graduates who are equipped to participate in these complex debates.

——This unique programme allows students to follow modules within the Bartlett as well as in other UCL departments. Graduates have gone on to postgraduate studies and professional careers in a wide variety of fields including journalism, landscape design, sustainable design consultancy, lighting design, international development, fine arts, photography, print-making, arts education and management, events management, urban planning, law, accounting, property valuation and construction management. They have pursued graduate studies at universities such as the Royal College of Art, Central Saint Martins, Brunel, Imperial College, the London School of Economics and ETH in Zurich as well as at UCL.

——The great strength of the programme is its interdisciplinarity: students are able to tailor their own course of study to suit their particular interests and future postgraduate and career plans. The course suits highly motivated, independent students who are interested in architecture, design and urban studies, but who also wish to take advantage of electives on offer elsewhere in UCL. Popular choices are art history, management, languages, economics, psychology, history, mathematics, anthropology, law, archaeology and geography.

——There are two specially tailored module streams for BSc AIS students within The Bartlett: our Design and Creative Practice modules, Project X 1, 2 & 3, and our Architectural Research I & II and Dissertation modules.

The Dissertation

Module Coordinator: Brent Carnell
Module Tutor: David Roberts

The Dissertation in Architectural & Interdisciplinary Studies enables students to undertake an independent research project of 10,000 words. The emphasis in this course is on conducting original research and producing an investigative, in-depth written piece, supported by appropriate visual and textual documentation. This module is taught through individual and small group tutorials, supplemented by occasional seminars and group meetings.

Year 2
Ged Ribas Goody

Year 3
Jade Chao, Jinyu (Sandy) Chen, Iona Farrar-Bell, Sandhya Gulsin, Yufan Jin, Yashika Kerai, Lau (Kelly) Shuen, Eloise Maland, Natalie Newsome, Imogen Newton, Rattan Sehra, Anna Livia Vorsel, Velvet Young

Eloise Maland
The Architecture of Violence
Repression and Resistance in Pontecorvo's The Battle of Algiers

The Battle of Algiers, made in 1966 by Italian director Gillo Pontecorvo, is set during the Algerian War of Independence. The film narrates the anti-colonial struggle and the escalating fight between the Algerian Front de Libération National (FLN) and the French army as the Algerians attempt to liberate themselves from colonial rule.

——The film is constructed around the theme of violence, a concept intrinsic to the colonial system. This violence surrounds us within *The Battle of Algiers*; shaping, reflecting and fighting against the architecture and spaces we confront. Set in the city of Algiers itself, the film moves between the Algerian part of the city, the Casbah, and its European quarters, built soon after the French occupation in 1830. The architecture of the city is highly politicised, with the spaces reflecting the power dynamics of the colonial relationship.

——This dissertation brings together film studies, postcolonialism and postcolonial architectural theory to dissect *The Battle of Algiers* in order to examine and question the violent negotiation of power that is inherent to decolonisation and embedded within the architecture of the colonial city.

——Using postcolonial architectural theory to read *The Battle of Algiers* allows for a more nuanced understanding of the experience of decolonisation. Architecture, through the camera lens, becomes a language to be read, understood and questioned as the spaces we encounter are used to demonstrate the violent and shifting relationship between the coloniser and the colonised. By understanding how architecture can be used to manipulate, control and enforce the dominance of the coloniser, the spaces in the film become active as they become sites of repression and sites of resistance. At the same time, film makes postcolonial architectural theory visceral. Film allows the audience to imagine and feel the architecture of the city, making visible how it shapes and segregates people and illustrating how it can be used to enact power.

——This analysis of *The Battle of Algiers* highlights the importance of architecture in shaping our lives and also of film in interrogating the consequences of architecture and urban design. *The Battle of Algiers* demonstrates how the camera can be used to identify, reveal and question the power dynamics enacted in the spaces that surround us: how they can repress and how they can be resisted.

Ged Ribas Goody

A gentle crash: on the movement of queer bodies and the eroticism of non-linear belonging

Our bodies and our identities shape, and in turn are shaped by, the spaces we move through as well as the 'world of objects' found within and beyond these spaces. For Ballard (1971), the car represents the culmination of human desire and technological advancement. In its design can be found the stylised forms of the body. Movement and the ability to travel are central to the hegemonic notion of the body. A 'legitimate' body can perform both with ease (Amoore 2006: 339). Hegemonic forms of belonging heavily rely on the conflation of physical proximity with kinship and of distance with difference, and thus force people to rely on the prostheses of travel and of movement to fulfil their desire to belong, even after displacement.

——The privilege of travel is one afforded to those bodies seen as safe, or ideal. The bonds enforced on the movement of non-linear (queer, migrant, disabled, etc.) bodies, whether in airports or on the street, are incredibly debilitating. If there is a restricted notion of movement (i.e. purely physical) then there is a restricted notion of the body (i.e. purely physical). Ambiguous bodies that are perceived to be 'risky', and who can therefore be restricted from travelling on international flights, are being distinguished from the safe 'travelable' population in a way that limits them to their physicality and denies them of the possibility, or desire, to belong through conventional means.

——Non-linear belonging describes a frayed orientation between multiple objects/spaces/bodies. There is no subject at its heart, but it is instead an act of navigation of belonging itself, of bodies, objects and spaces: the boundaries between what is external and what is internal to the body break down: the body is projected, in all its desires, identities and pains, onto external landscapes, which then become internal, and conversely the body's anatomy becomes externalised through this projection. Whereas the seduction of hegemonic belongings rests in the enticement of the subject, the eroticism of non-linear belongings rests in the act of exploration: the mutual exploration of the body and of the spaces it moves through.

——Acknowledging the reflexivity between and multiplicity of spaces/objects and the body is important, as it allows the unrestrained movement, or oscillation, between and beyond the constructed boundaries of form, object and subject for bodies whose physical movement may be restricted in a number of other ways. Belonging, and the body, are mediated through orientations that are at once sexual and spatial. In order to truly dissect the body we must dissect the spatial and erotic nature of movement itself, and acknowledge the possibilities of movement that acts along non-linear orientations that challenge the conventional lines of how bodies are expected to move through architectural space.

——Sara Ahmed (Ahmed 2006: 7) suggests that "'getting lost' still takes us somewhere; and being lost is a way of inhabiting space by registering what is not familiar: being lost can in its turn become a familiar feeling".

——To reclaim the stasis normally imposed on queer bodies by an external hand and to embrace it as a spatial as well as erotic exploration is an act of disorientation. The mutually imposed physical stasis that is experienced during the act of bondage breaks down the boundaries between our internal desires and the spaces we are occupying, between stasis and being lost in the prostheses of our vehicle.

Project X: Design and Creative Practice 1, 2 & 3

——Project X: Design and Creative Practice aims to help students build a creative and reflective practice of their own, undertaking a mode of working that particularly interests them and an independent practice-based project in which they can research and pursue a subject of their preference. Students are asked to think of architecture in interdisciplinary ways, explore alternative approaches to design and situate their work within a broader cultural context. The work is developed in conjunction with a short written piece. A series of key questions confront students at different stages of the year concerning the nature of their practice, the contribution of their work to the broader field of architecture, the originality of their project, and the selection of appropriate media for the ideas pursued.

——Based on the assumption that there is no such thing as a 'finished' piece of work, Year 1's Project X brief was titled 'Exercises in Appropriation'. Students explored iteration and repetition as productive and reflective design methods. The initial project, the 'Oulipo Marathon', took Raymond Queneau's novel 'Exercises in Style' as a precedent, handing every student out a series of words or phrases related to the broad topic of the year paired with different methods of working. Through these quick and intuitive works, each student developed an individual interest that led to further explorations throughout the course. They developed documentary films, games, magazines, 1:1 devices, haptic collections, audio installations, immersive experimental set-ups or speculative objects.

——Year 2 Project X students worked on three different projects this year. The first was a three-month interactive group projects to create site-specific installations for the UCL Bloomsbury campus. The group endeavour, entitled 'Replacing Realities', explored the re-reading of the architecture of college buildings to provide a series of new immersive interventions. The second, entitled 'Reinterpreting Agency' was a personal project, with students developing their own unique creative spatial practice, drawing inspiration from Project 1. Project 3, entitled 'Curating New Worlds', was a collective effort to set up the conceptual framework for the end-of-year exhibition to showcase the diversity of work across the programme.

——The Year 3 Project X brief was 'The Happiness Project'. Initiated by three short projects to encourage engagement with a wider public outside The Bartlett, the projects investigated how notions of happiness in contemporary society are affected by automation, increased leisure time and experience-based consumerism. These developed into individual projects examining a broad range of themes. As final year students, about to embark on their own individual creative practice journeys, students were encouraged to develop strategies for collaborative practice, peer review, public engagement and exhibition presentation. Additionally, the students inspired and co-curated a programme of workshops, inviting practitioners into The Bartlett from a wide range of disciplines, from publishing to film-making to curating.

Year 1
Isabelle Arusilor, Hannah Averbeck, Marius Balan, Esme Chong, Isabel Dorn, Roxanne Gonzales, Nyima Murry, Eva Tisnikar, Yasmine Zein El Abdeen, Camilla Romano

Year 2
Lucy Brown, Jasmine Ceccarelli-Drewry, Sharon Chang, Li'Er Chen, James Curtis, Luofei Dong, Lillie Hall, Julia Millang, Oliver Mitchell, Vikrim Nagra, Tanzim Naser, Ryuhei Oishi, Ged Ribas Goody, Grace Simmonds, Andreea Vihristencu, Jonathan Whitfield, Yolanda Ye, Yurou Zhang

Year 3
Jade Chao, Sandy Chen, Rickie Cheuk, Iona Farrar-Bell, Chloe Gould, Sandhya Gulsin, Yufan Jin, Yashika Kerai, Kelly Lau, Eloise Maland, Natalie Newsome, Imogen Newton, Anna Livia Vorsel, Rattan Sehra, Velvet Young

Thank you to: Sarah Aulombard, Alfonso Borragán, Jos Boys, Dr Eva Branscome, Rob Crosse, Robin Farmer, Nicolas Feldmeyer, Holly Fisher, Daisy Froud, Jessica In, Tobias Jones, Thomas Kendall, Ifigenia Liangi, Rebecca Loewen, Anders Luhr, Yeoryia Manolopoulou, Alan McQuillan, Emily Norman, Theo Games Petrohilos, Peg Rawes, Hannah Regel, Harriet Richardson, Luke Scott, Ned Scott, Tania Sengupta, David Shanks, James Shaw, Zofia Trafas White, Nina Shen Poblete, Sayan Skandarajah, Gabriel Warshafsky, Richard Wentworth, Tom Wilkinson

Fig. X.1 & X.4 **Yasmine Zein El Abdeen** Y1. This project takes an ironic approach to ways of dealing with social awkwardness. It materialises hypothetical solutions that often come to mind when one is stuck in a socially awkward or uncomfortable situation. It poses a 'what if?' question intended to open a discussion about the consequences of the commodification of modern-day social interaction. Today, social media encourages us to use the simplest forms of communication (for example, in the shape of an emoji), narrowing language down to its barest bones and perhaps preventing us from strengthening our communication skills in the real world. **Fig. X.2** **Nyima Murry** Y1, 'Uncomfortable'. This project led to the creation of an alter ego, known as Cecilia, whose rainbow hair and flamboyant style pushed Nyima out of her comfort zone. Her excess led to her own destruction in the symbolic act of shaving the rainbow hair off. This act was a chance to destroy Cecilia, whilst simultaneously pushing others into feeling uncomfortable. **Fig. X.3** **Eva Tisnikar** Y1, 'Communication & Translation'. This project explores the different definitions of translation and communication. The metal backpiece aims to discover whether it is possible to translate a nation and its culture into an object.

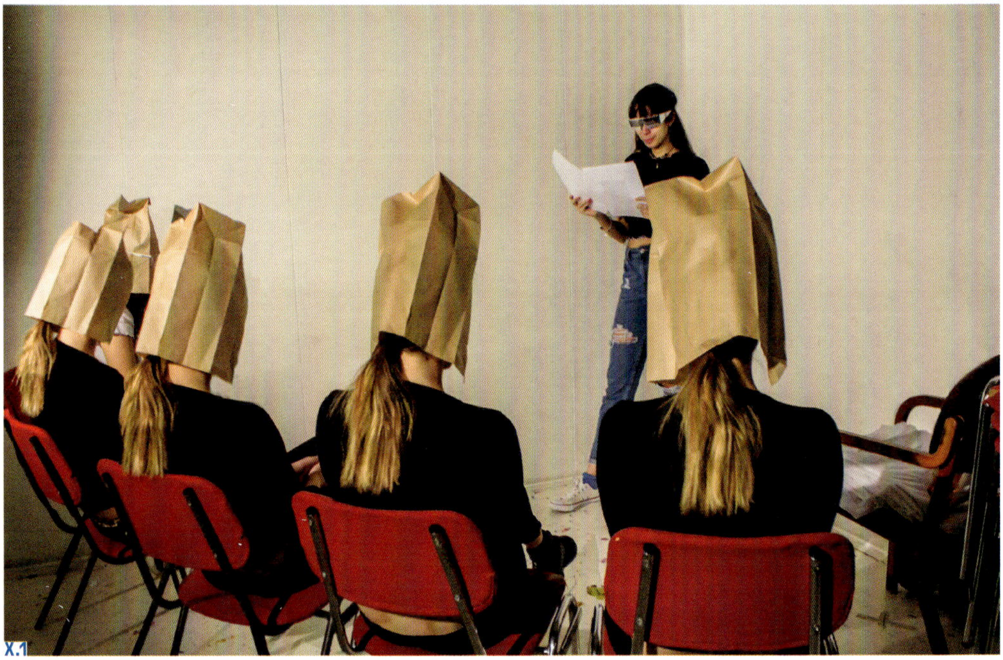

X.1

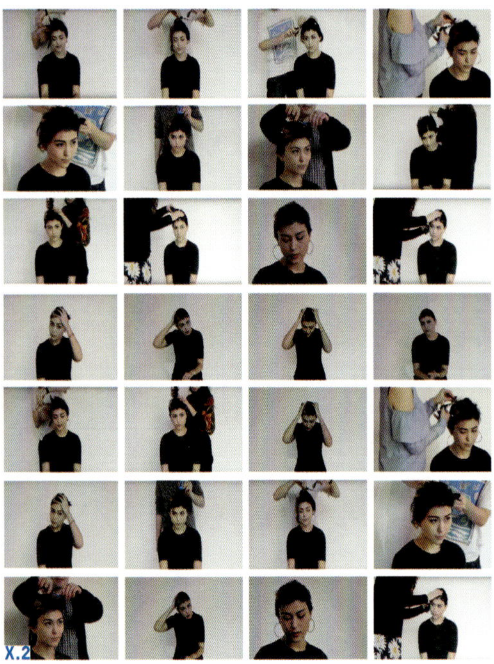

X.2

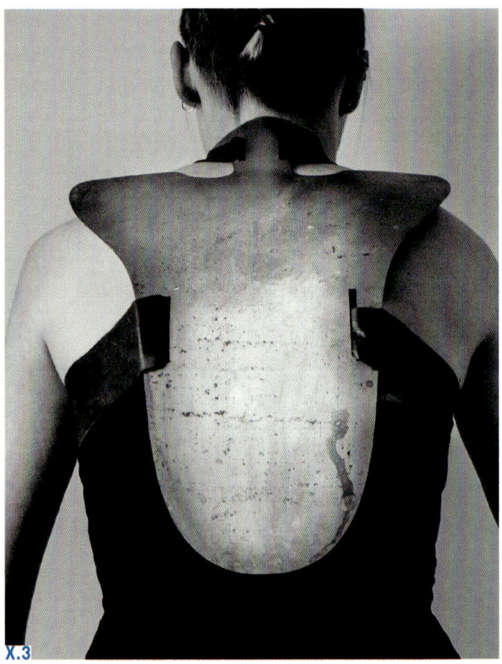

X.3

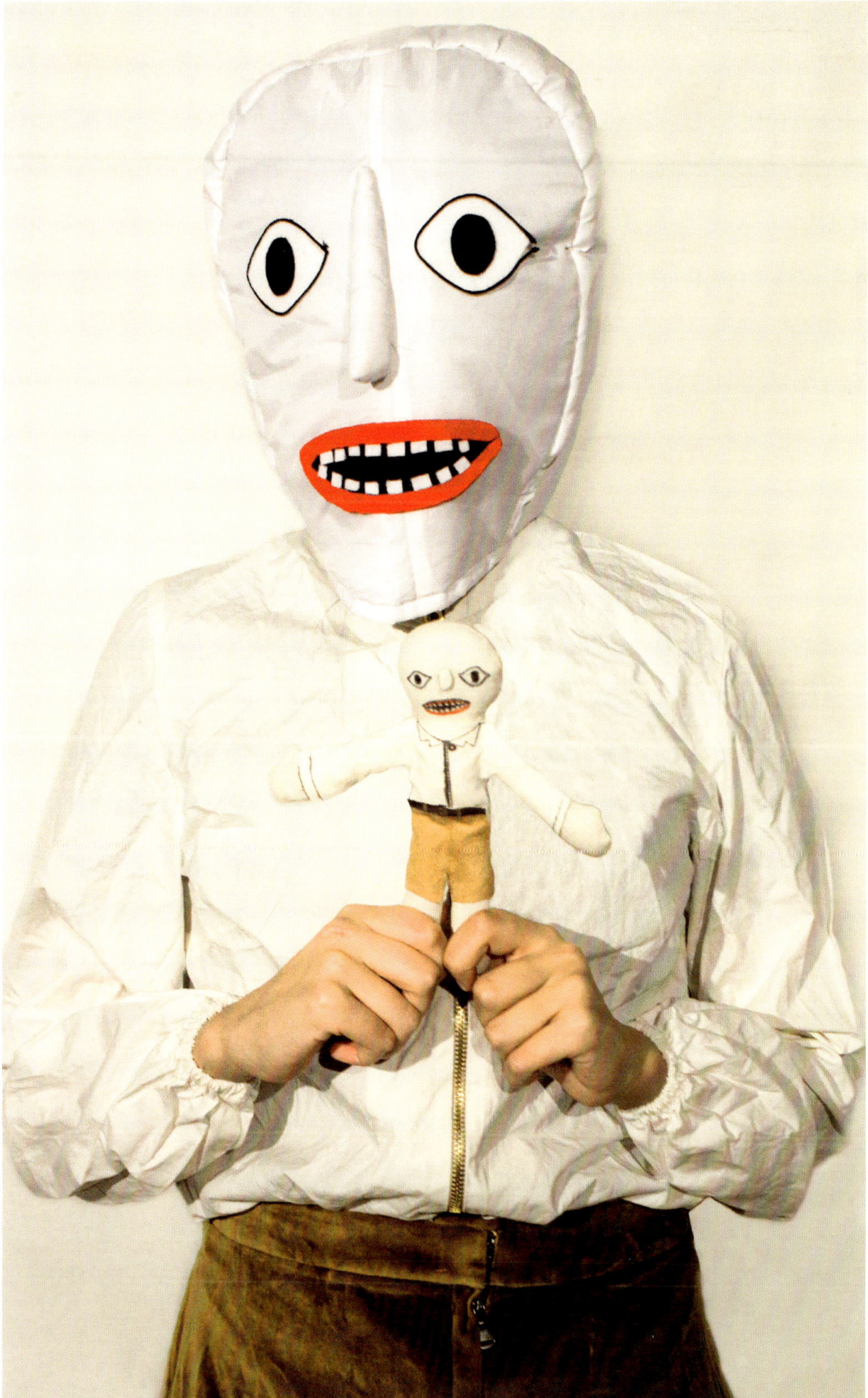

X.4

Fig. X.5 Luofei Dong Y2, 'Dictionary of Smell'. The project explores the possibilities and impossibilities of olfactory description through both written and visual languages. This captured image is composed of ten three-dimensional models, each derived from hand-drawings and digitised using computer software. Each form represents a single smell from a single object, which is personal and relatable to Luofei's identity/experience, e.g. 'damp cigarette stub' or 'worn leather shoes'. **Fig. X.6 Ryuhei Oishi** Y2, 'In the Sea'. "I made a stool with driftwood, without using any electrical tools, nails nor screws. I feel machinery deprives natural beings of their vitality. To preserve the vitality, it is essential to stick to nature. By the way, I know what is natural and unnatural a priori. Anyway, why do I believe in nature so much? The answer is simple. I have never seen anything more sublime than nature. I'm not talking about a dichotomy between nature and humans, but instead, about the simple oneness of nature." **Fig. X.7 Grace Simmonds** Y2, 'Kite Surveillance'. A still from the film 'Kite Surveillance' of Sir Denys Lasdun's student accommodation at UEA. A commentary on modern-day dystopian surveillance systems.

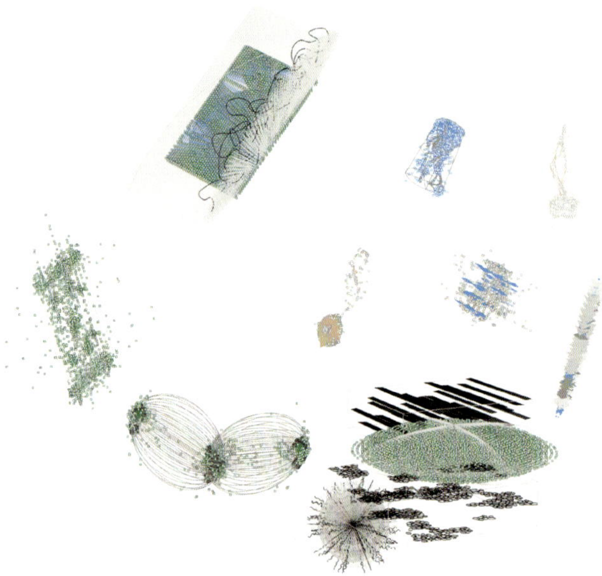

X.5

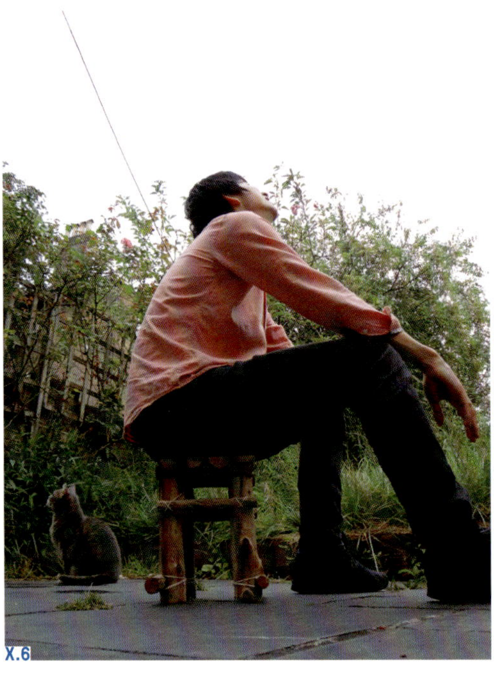

X.6

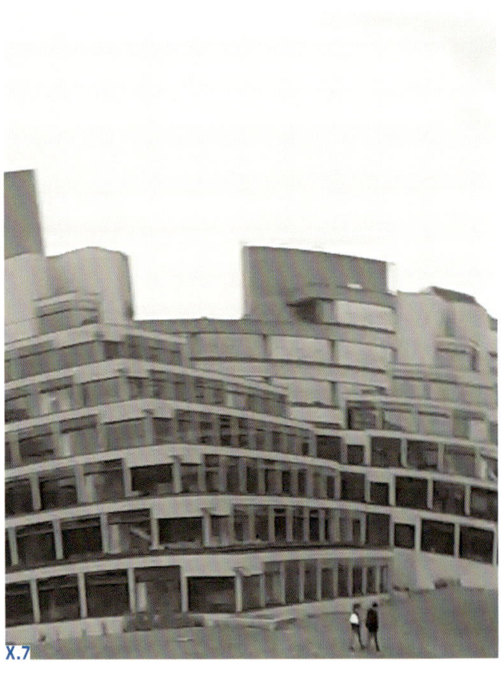

X.7

Fig. X.8 **Jonathan Whitfield** Y2, 'EXCR / EAT'. This project explored the inherent but taboo relationship between the processes of eating and excreting, and our common, innate sense of cleanliness and hygiene. Taking the form of a sound piece, we placed users in an audio environment where an 'alternate reality' of the toilet could be unearthed, using recorded sounds of the body and digestion as a medium to explore this. The sound piece was partly constructed using audio recorded with a contact microphone placed on the body - this image illustrates the noises produced by the throat during peristalsis whilst swallowing. Fig. X.9 **Grace Simmonds** Y3, 'Untitled'. Interactive audio installation concept for the Grant Museum of Zoology. A wooden speaker houses sounds of specimens only activated and heard via a stethoscope. Figs. X.10, X.11, X.17 & X.18 **Eloise Maland** Y3, 'Seeing / Dementia'. Re-imagining the landscape and the physical to re-imagine the mind. Exploring and examining the notion of identity and how we can negotiate, re-learn and re-define our identity in the context of dementia.

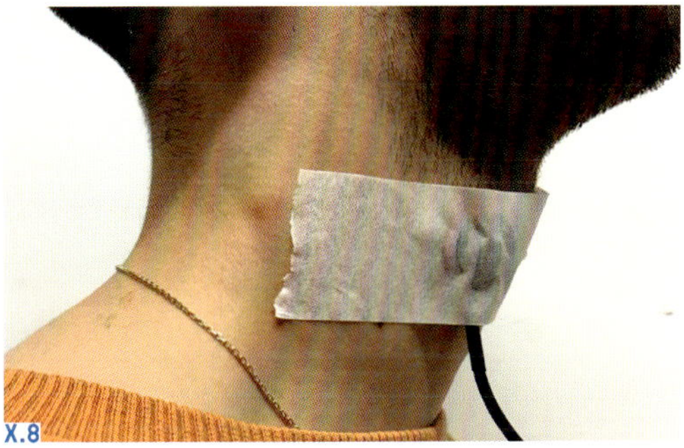

X.8

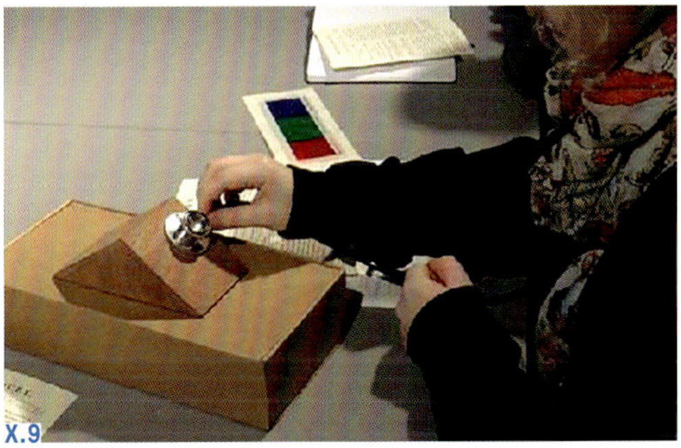

X.9

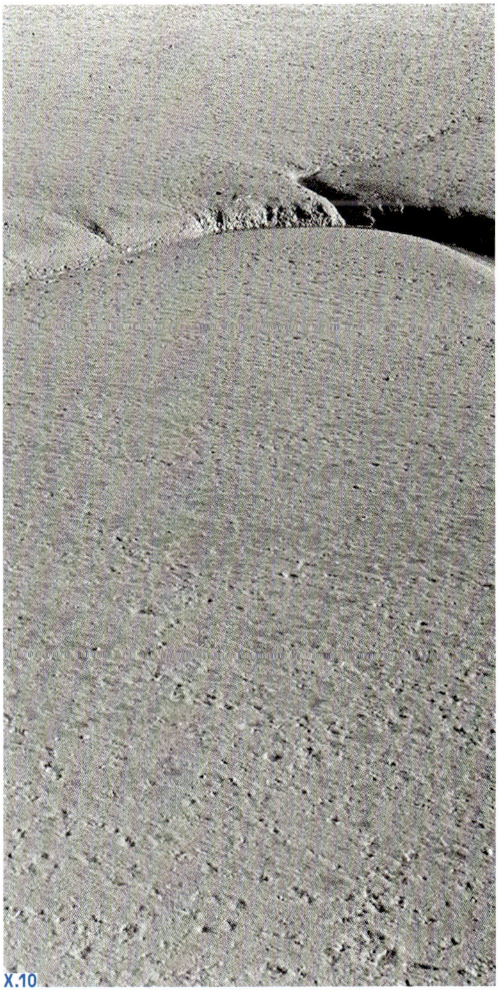

X.10

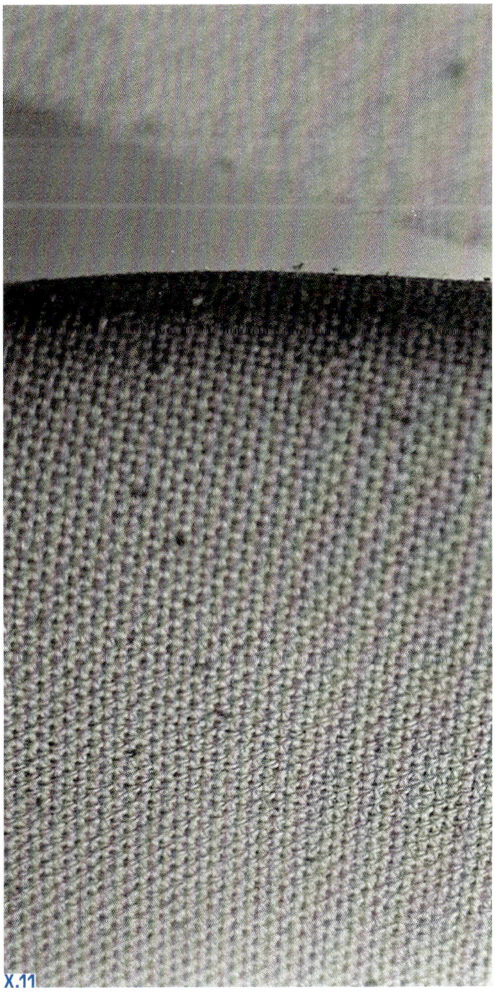

X.11

Fig. X.12 Rickie Cheuk Y3, 'Waste?'. Why do we let stuff go to waste and fill the world with pollution when we can develop it into useful products? We should constantly remake the way we make and discover new possibilities of doing more with less in order to minimise damage to the environment. **Fig. X.13 Anna Vorsel & Alina Hackett** Y3, 'Nails'. Through the medium of film, the project maps the positions of power, and the physical movements within, a nail salon. It juxtaposes the processes of reward, luxury and female beautification in the act of the 'manicure' with the conditions of the nail technicians. **Fig. X.14 Elvira Hojberg** Y3, 'Post-Human Archive'. A lexicon-archive, creating a linguistic framework for the theoretical concept of 'post-humanism'. Its aim is to explore the role of language in allowing for new discourses.

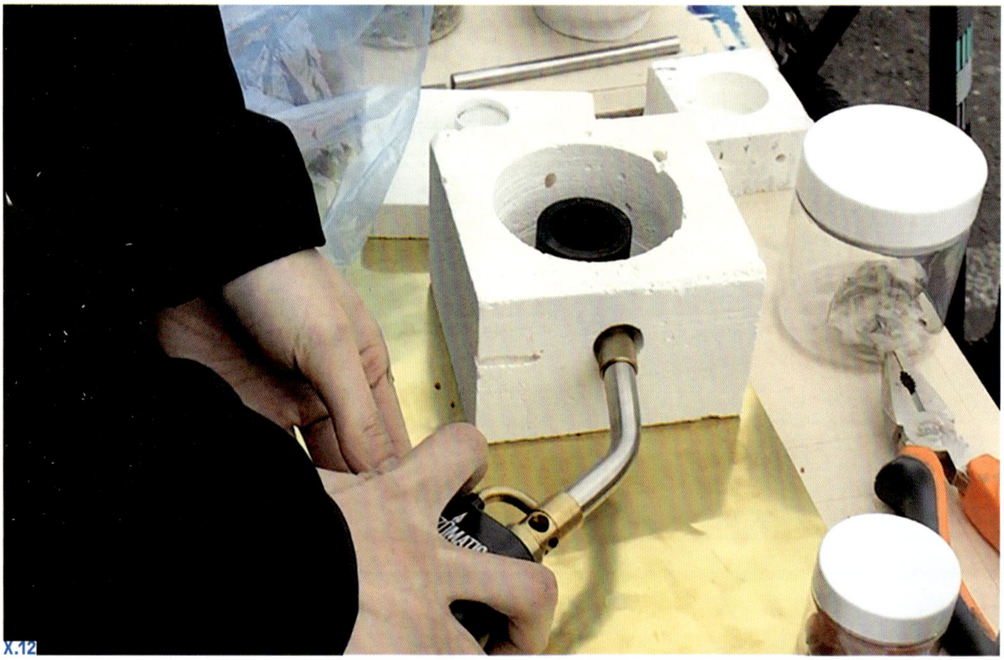
X.12

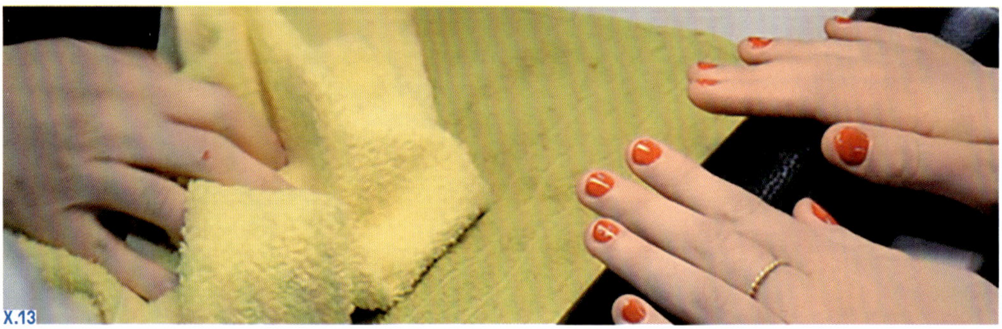
X.13

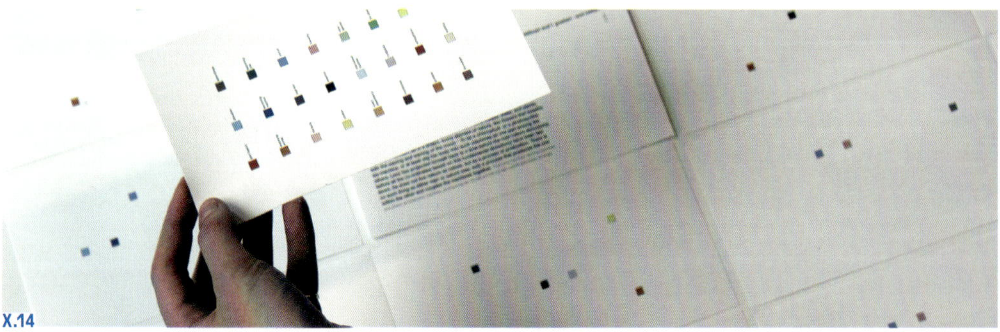
X.14

Figs. X.15 – X.16 Natalie Newsome Y3, 'Narrating Perception'. This project examines the relationship between image and reality through a variety of different media. By identifying a journey as the gap between image and reality, the project concludes in a film installation and book that explore the way in which journeys manipulate our own preconceptions of a place.

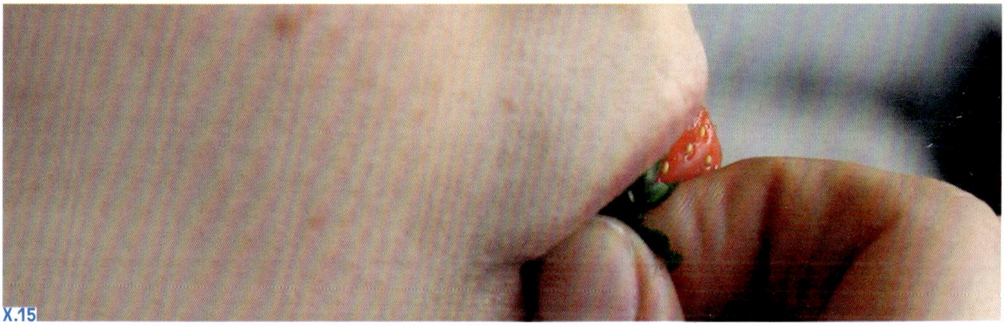
X.15

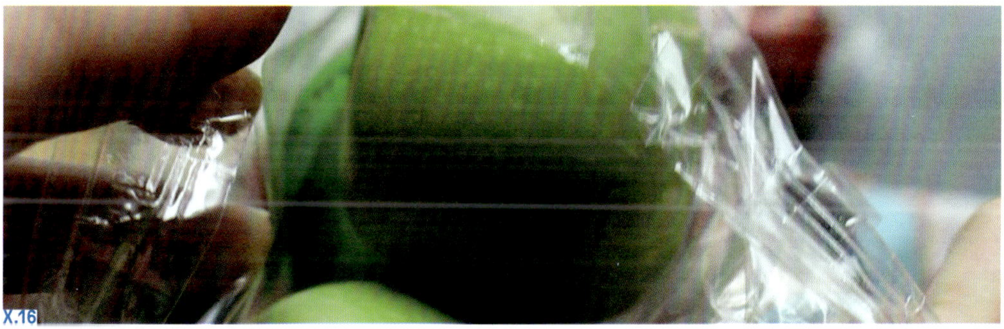
X.16

X.17

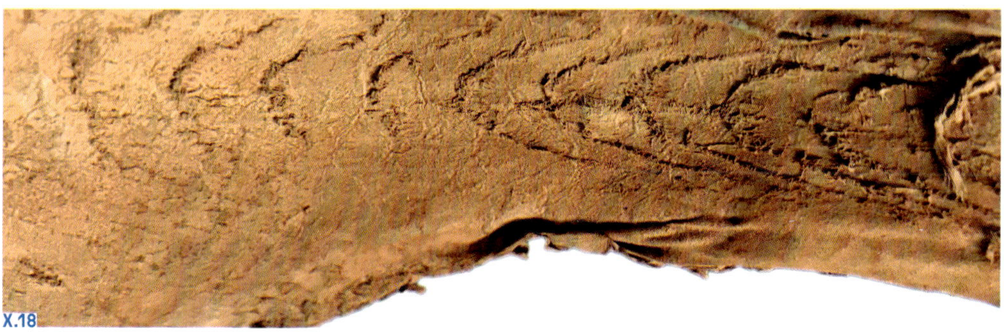
X.18

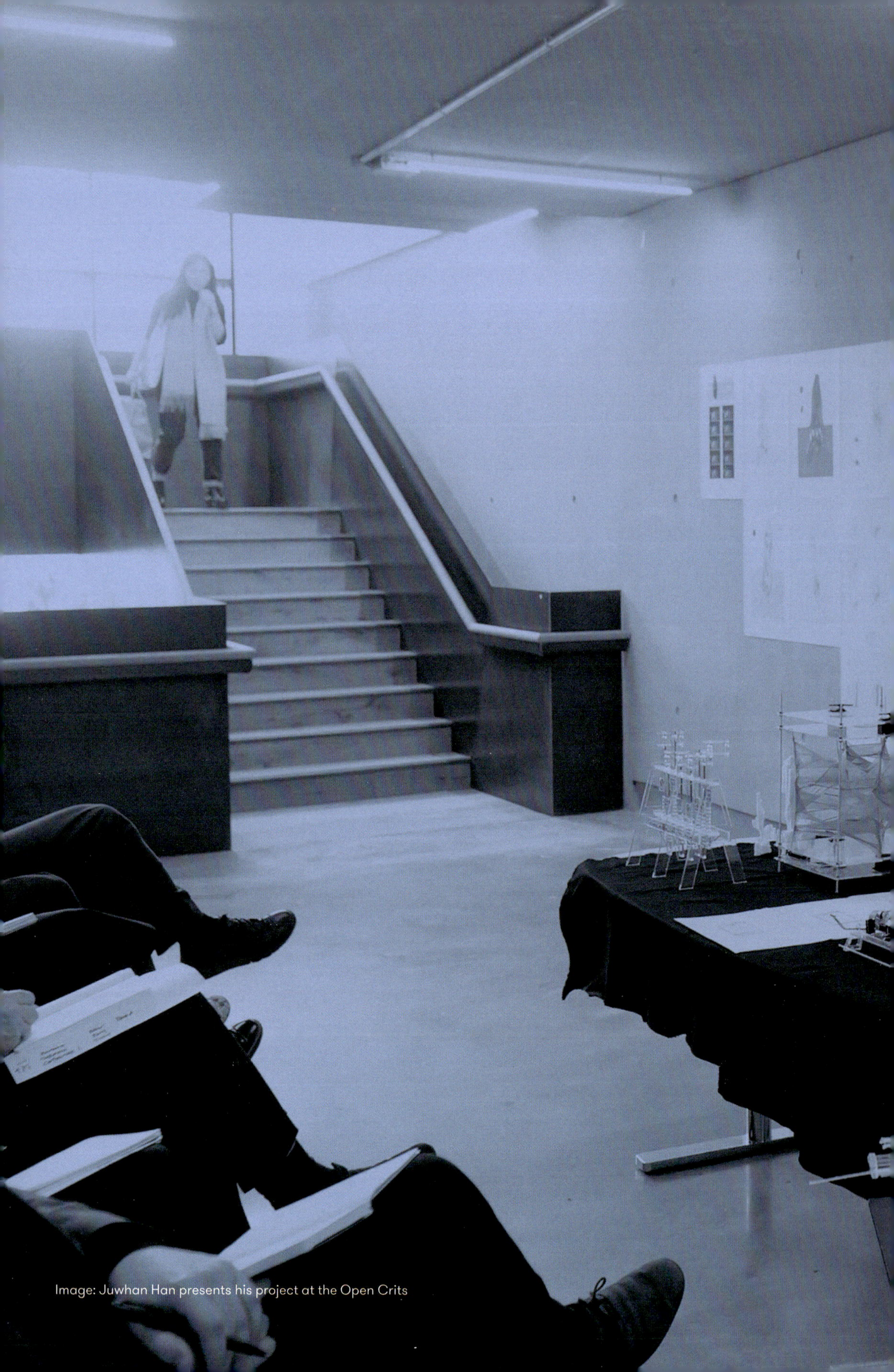

Image: Juwhan Han presents his project at the Open Crits

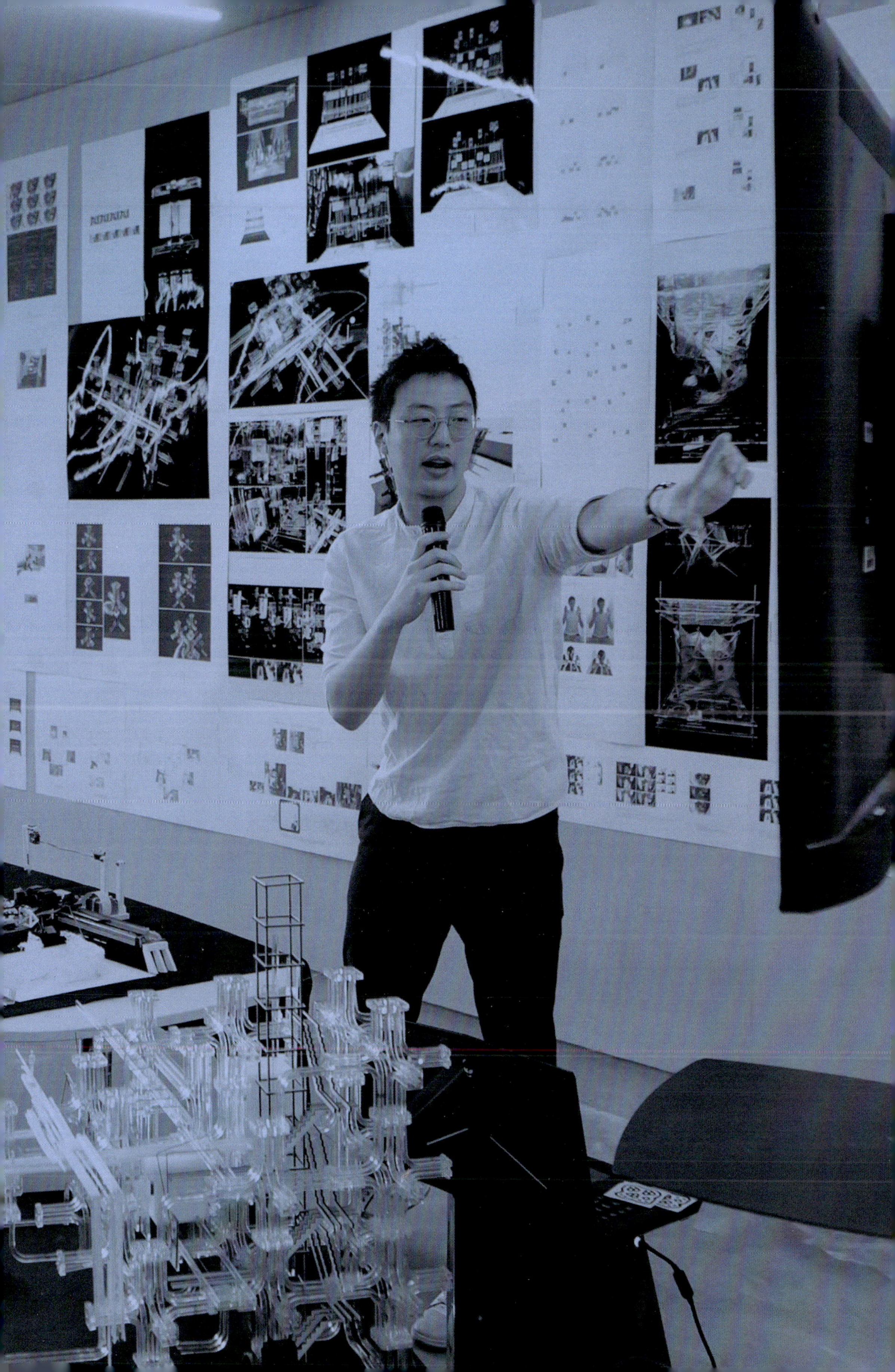

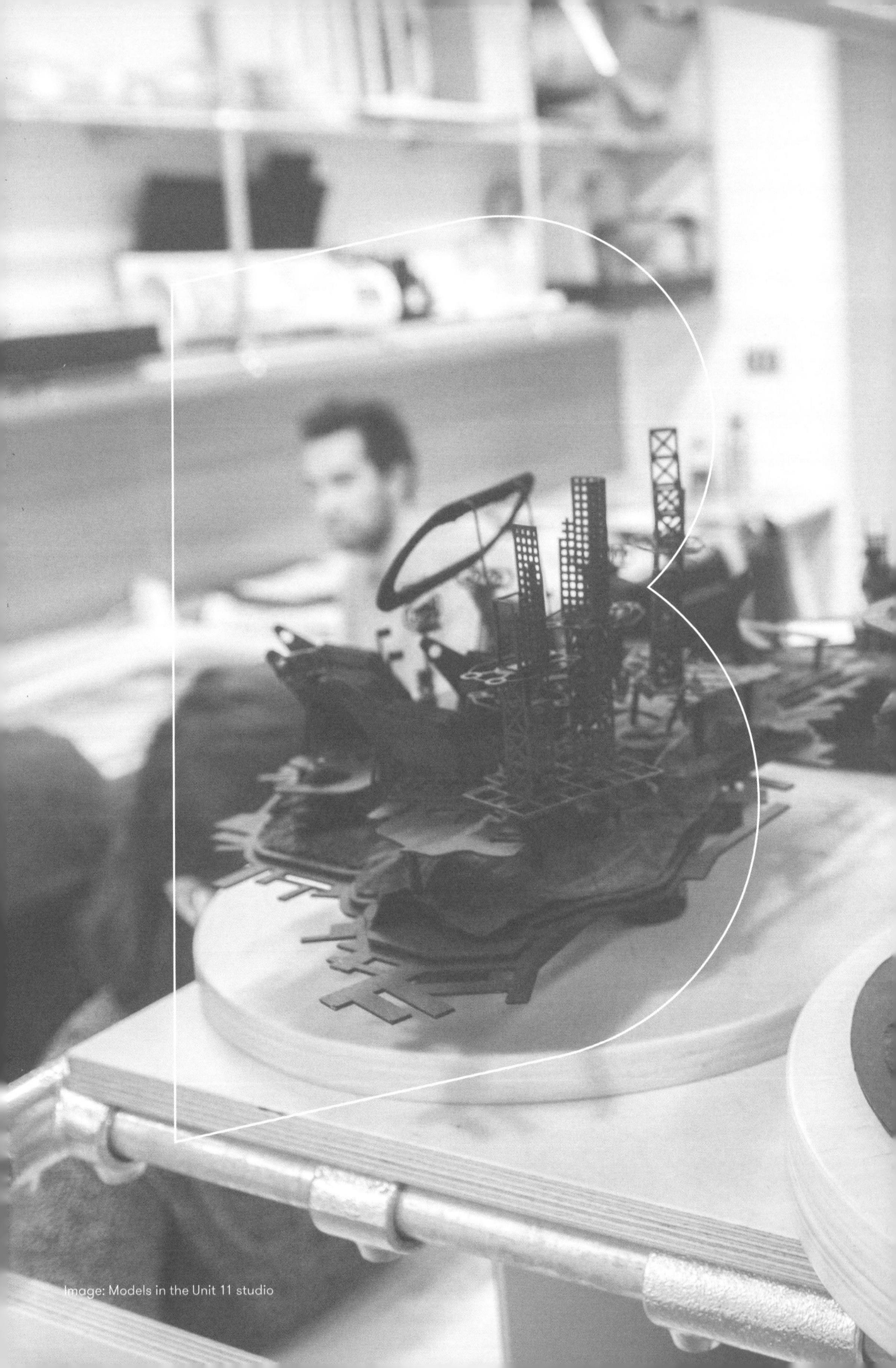

Image: Models in the Unit 11 studio

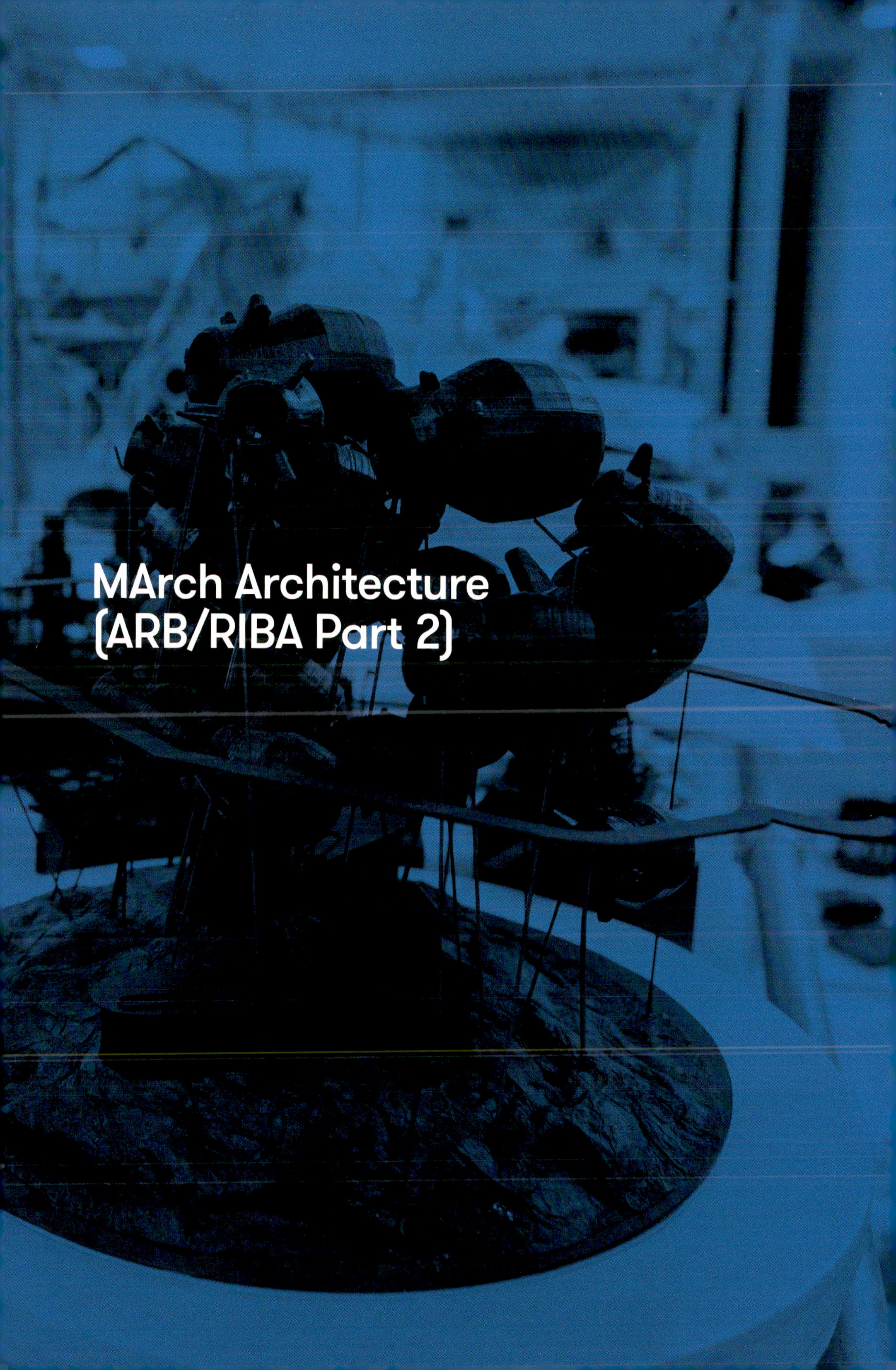

MArch Architecture (ARB/RIBA Part 2)

MArch Architecture (ARB/RIBA Part 2)

Programme Directors: Julia Backhaus, Professor Marjan Colletti

Advanced Architectural Studies (History & Theory)
Tania Sengupta

Design Realisation (Technology & Professional Studies)
James O'Leary, Dirk Krolikowski

Thesis
Edward Denison, Robin Wilson, Oliver Wilton

Design Unit Tutors
Unit 10
Simon Dickens, CJ Lim
Unit 11
Laura Allen, Mark Smout
Unit 12
Matthew Butcher, Jonathan Hill
Unit 14
Evan Greenberg, Dirk Krolikowski
Unit 15
Maximiliano Arrocet, Alice Dietsch, Amanda Levete, Ho-Yin Ng, Raffael Petrovic
Unit 16
Johan Berglund, Colin Herperger
Unit 17
Yeoryia Manolopoulou, Níall McLaughlin, Michiko Sumi
Unit 18
Isaïe Bloch, Ricardo de Ostos
Unit 19
Mollie Claypool, Manuel Jimenez García, Gilles Retsin
Unit 20
Marjan Colletti, Marcos Cruz, Javier Ruiz Rodriguez
Unit 21
Abigail Ashton, Tom Holberton, Andrew Porter
Unit 22
Carlos Jiménez Cenamor, Izaskun Chinchilla
Unit 24
Penelope Haralambidou, Michael Tite
Unit 25
Nat Chard, Emma-Kate Matthews
Unit 26
Simon Kennedy, Gabby Shawcross

The diversity of students' prior experience underpins the programme's core appetite for curiosity, invention and renewal. The programme allows students to develop a position of deep understanding about what architecture is – and what it could be – as a subject, discipline, practice and domain in which they can already contribute. It aims to strengthen their core skills in design (through drawing and making, both analogue and digital), technology (including environmental design, sustainability and computation), history and theory and professional studies. Half the degree is delivered through design modules. Both years of the programme operate a vertical unit system, with 15 units operating this year. Students may switch units after Year 4, though most stay in the same unit for both years. Although distinct from one another, units deliver a common set of principles that include communication, culture, critique, context, social impact and both design and research methods.

Year 4

Year 4 is structured around the notions of constraint and creativity, with the programme working as a sequence in two phases. The first phase extends from the start of term one in Year 4 to the start of term three in Year 4. In this phase, and consistently across all units, every student must develop and resolve a comprehensive building design project. This phase builds on the momentum students have gained from practice on their year (or two years) out, and allows us to coordinate an intense sequence of associated lectures, cross-unit crits and practice-based seminars. It allows students from different backgrounds, and different prior educational and practical experience, to phase into The Bartlett School of Architecture unit system through an initial common challenge that each unit approaches in its own way. Key to delivering this phase is the support of a dedicated practice-based tutor for every unit, whose involvement is fully integrated in the operations of the unit for the majority of the year. The second phase begins in term three of Year 4, when students are encouraged to identify areas of research that they will develop in their final year (Year 5). This phasing allows students to establish a bridge over the summer between both years, so that when they return in the autumn they already have a strong sense of direction for Year 5.

Year 5

Year 5 is driven by rigour, freedom and excellence and is understood as the School's pinnacle in research-based professional architectural education. Underpinned by the intensity and comprehensiveness of Year 4 – which provides a platform for our students' professional confidence – Year 5 offers an entire academic year to develop a complex design proposition in synthesis with a comprehensive thesis. Seen very much as paired works, thesis and portfolio evolve in parallel through diverse forms of experimentation and research, leading to a sophisticated and skilled resolution. Students are encouraged to take speculative risks with their projects in order to test the boundaries of how architecture is defined, understood, practiced and researched. Final projects take many forms, including entirely drawn work, entirely made work, films, prototypes, digital artefacts or systems, performance, models, structures and interdisciplinary collaborations.

Unit 10

Relocation: The Making of Utopia

Simon Dickens, CJ Lim

Year 4
Anna Andronova, Qaisyfullah Bin Jaslenda Mohamad, Jason Ho, Gintare Kapociute, Kannawat Limratepong, Alfie Stephenson-Boyles, Tristan Taylor, Yui Wong

Year 5
Damien Assini, LiJia Bao, Nathan Fairbrother, Isabelle Lam, Kai Hang Liu, Zhang Wen

Thank you to Jon Kaminsky for his teaching of the Design Realisation module

"Arrival of the Floating Pool after 40 years of crossing the Atlantic, the architects/lifeguards reach their destination. They have to swim toward what they want to get away from and away from where they want to go," Rem Koolhaas, 'The Story of the Pool', 1977.

In Koolhaas' 'Delirious New York', in the tradition of the science fiction tropes of Jonathan Swift and Jules Verne, Russian Modernist architects used a portable pool infrastructure to escape Soviet oppression and make it to the United States of America. Meanwhile, the architects of the 'Wandering Turtle', Brodsky and Utkin, opted instead to remain in Russia to produce "an escape into the realm of the imagination that ended as a visual commentary on what was wrong with social and physical reality, and how its ills might be remedied". The decisions to relocate or to remain are both basic human rights, and can be applied as strategies for the making of utopia. According to the 2006 Stern Review, around 200 million people will be permanently displaced by 2050, through an amalgamation of complex economic, social and political drivers, exacerbated by increasingly unpredictable environmental conditions. Rather than 'fighting', governments, together with planners and architects, need to envision built environments that embrace the enemy.

——Relocation of capital cities is not uncommon. The ancient Egyptians, Romans and Chinese changed their capitals frequently. Some countries choose new capitals that are more easily defended in a time of invasion or war; others build in undeveloped areas to spur unity, security and prosperity. The decision to relocate the Brazilian capital from Rio de Janeiro to Brasilia was intended not only to relocate the seat of national power symbolically but also to shift the demographic and economic focus away from the country's European colonial powers and towards the vast hinterland.

——Can the appropriation of fiction and narrative inform the shaping of an urban and architectural vision, while addressing real and urgent sociopolitical, economy and environmental concerns? In PROJECT 1, students will speculate, prioritise and redefine the poetics of 'relocation' and 'utopia'. The interpretations and identified issues will provide a speculative framework and programme for the year. In PROJECT 2, utopia has to be located at a place of 'undesired'. Does 'utopia' occupy the territory of 'urban', 'suburban' or 'landscape'? We encourage expressions of personal ideology, scale and working methods in search of visionary and innovative architectural proposals.

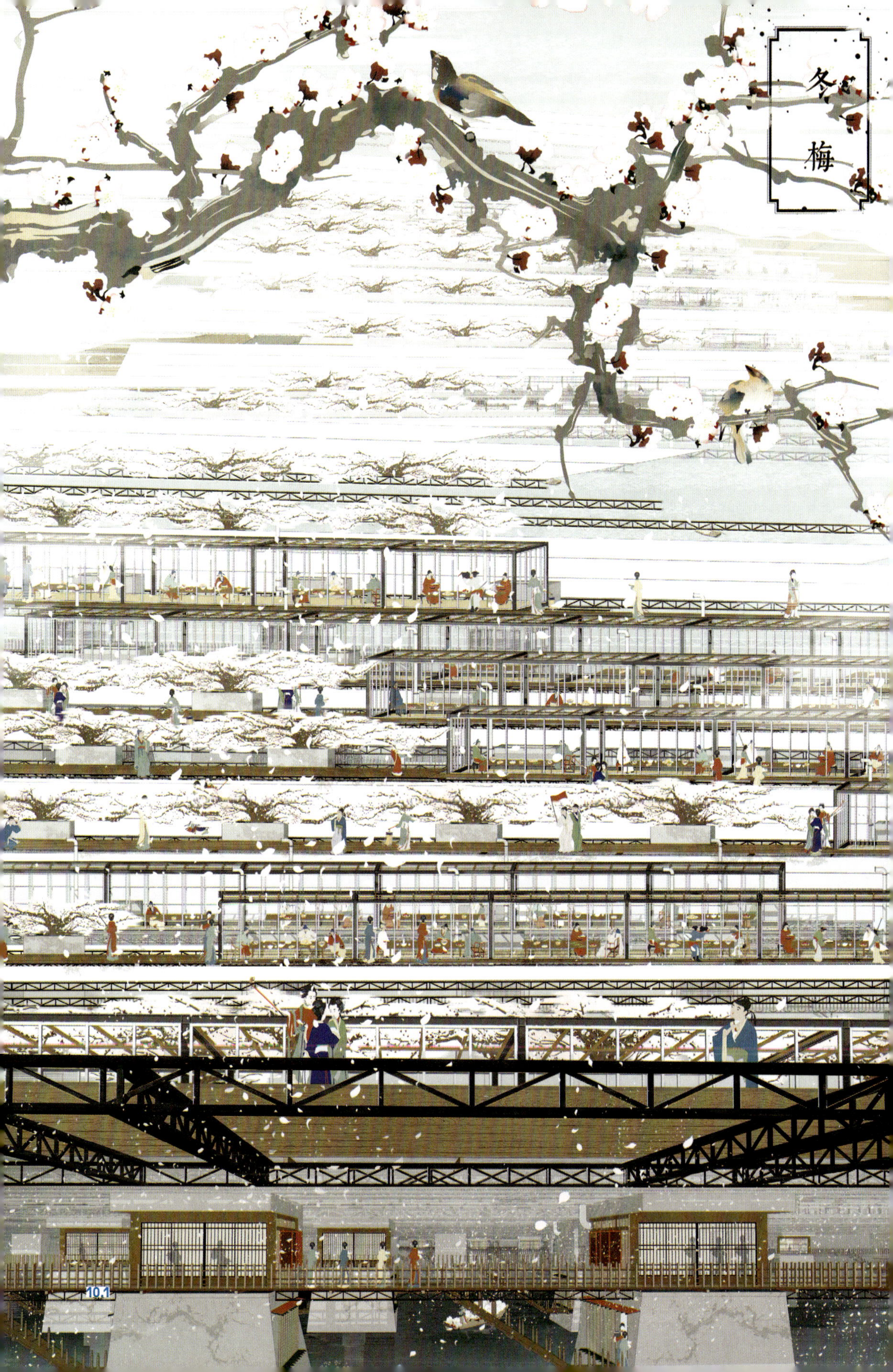
冬梅
10.1

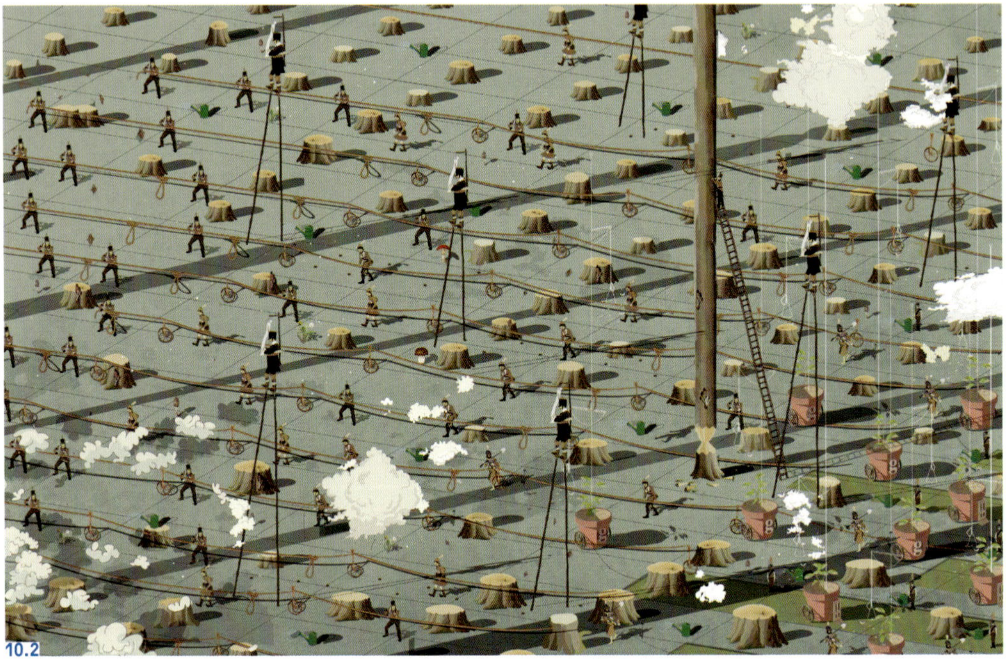

10.2

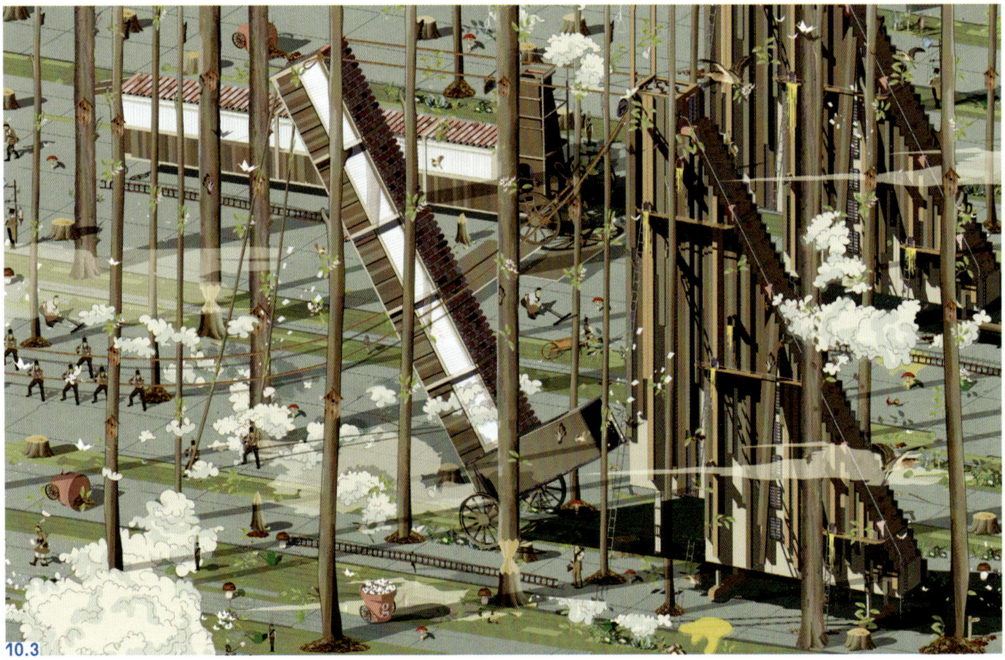

10.3

Fig. 10.1 LiJia Bao Y5, 'Splendour: The Eastern Cultural Capital'. An attempt to rebrand its political image, China relocates its cultural investments to the disputed territories in the South China Sea. Splendour aims to be the 'open' pilgrimage destination for all Chinese-speaking global citizens. **Figs. 10.2 – 10.4 Damien Assini** Y5, 'The Re-Imagination of HS2'. The UK government claims that the high-speed rail that links London with the Midlands will boost productivity. Through the socioeconomic lens of the Guardian newspaper, the project speculates what the urban alternatives might have been instead of the transport link. **Fig. 10.5 Zhang Wen** Y5, 'The Liquid Gold Odyssey'. China exploits Greece's financial woes to gain an economic and investment foothold in Europe, and relocates the Port of Shanghai to the Cyclades. Inspired by Homer's 'Odyssey', the new development provides a strategic trading outpost for Chinese merchants to source high-grade 'liquid gold' – olive oil for the ever-growing market in the East. **Fig. 10.6 Isabelle Lam** Y5, 'Moonrise Kingdom'. The alternative Legislative Council of Hong Kong is a network of recycling centres and prefabricated temporary floating homes, and implements policies of anti-consumerism, pro-democracy and philanthropy.

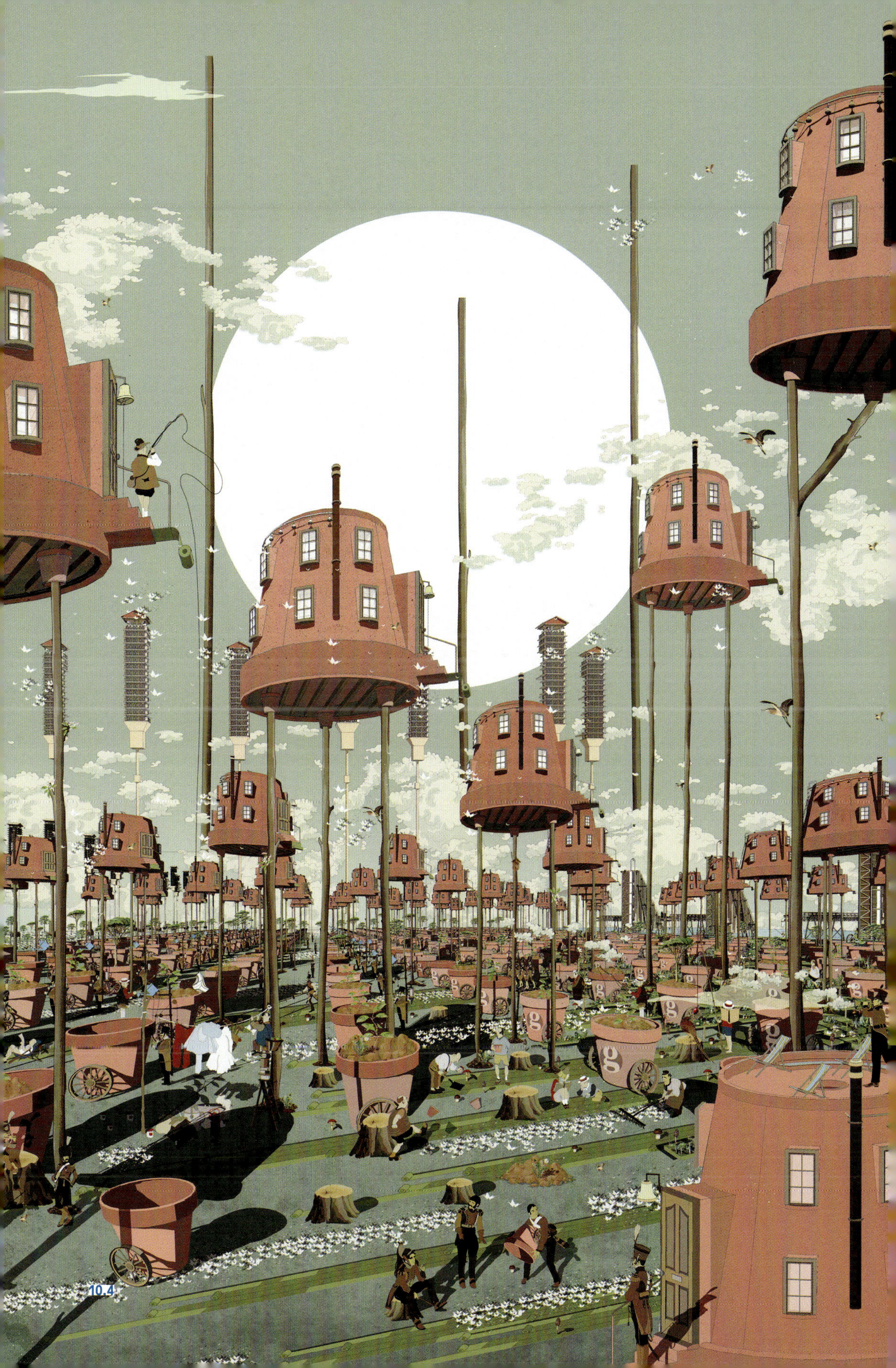

10.4

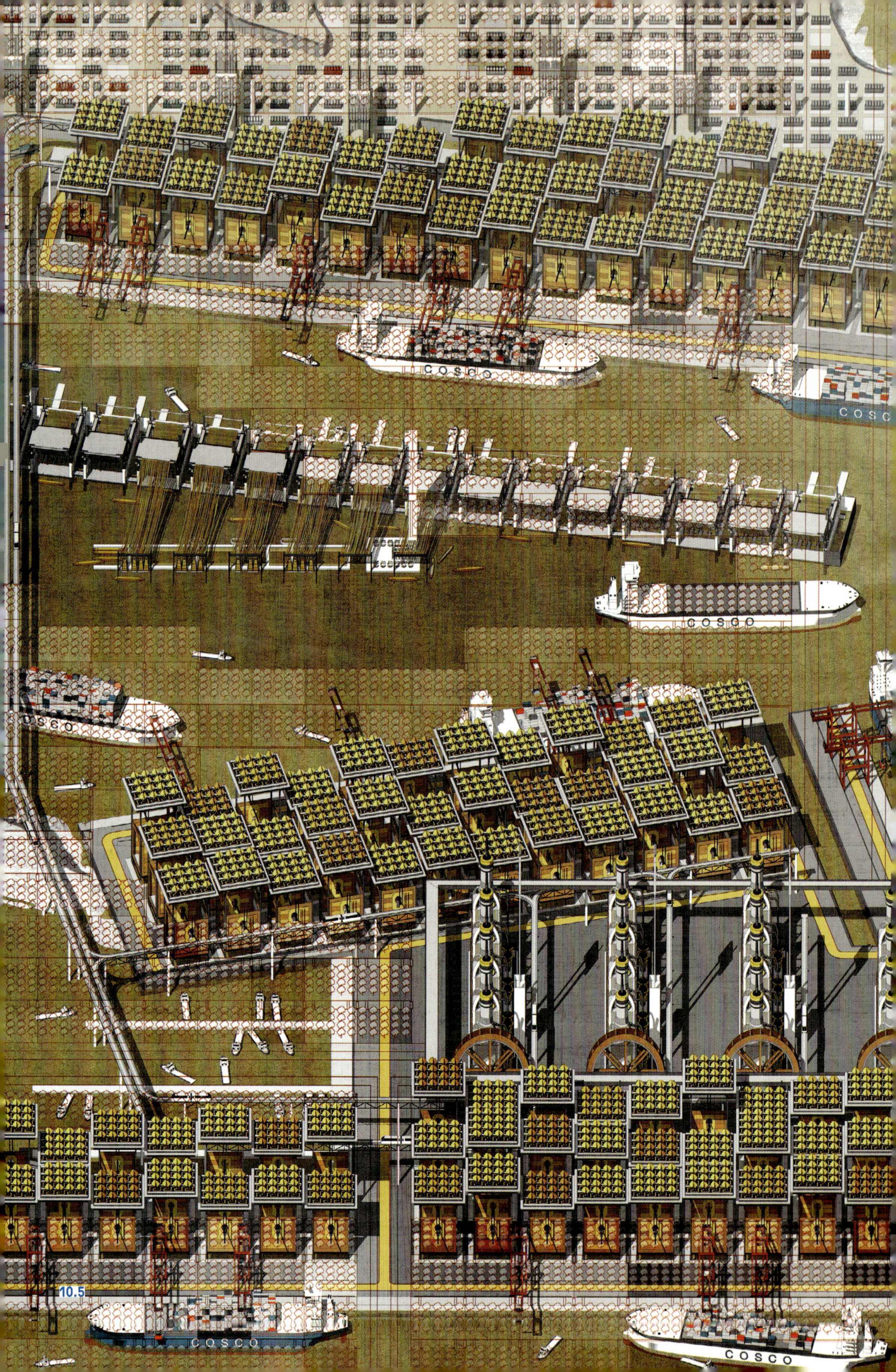

10.5

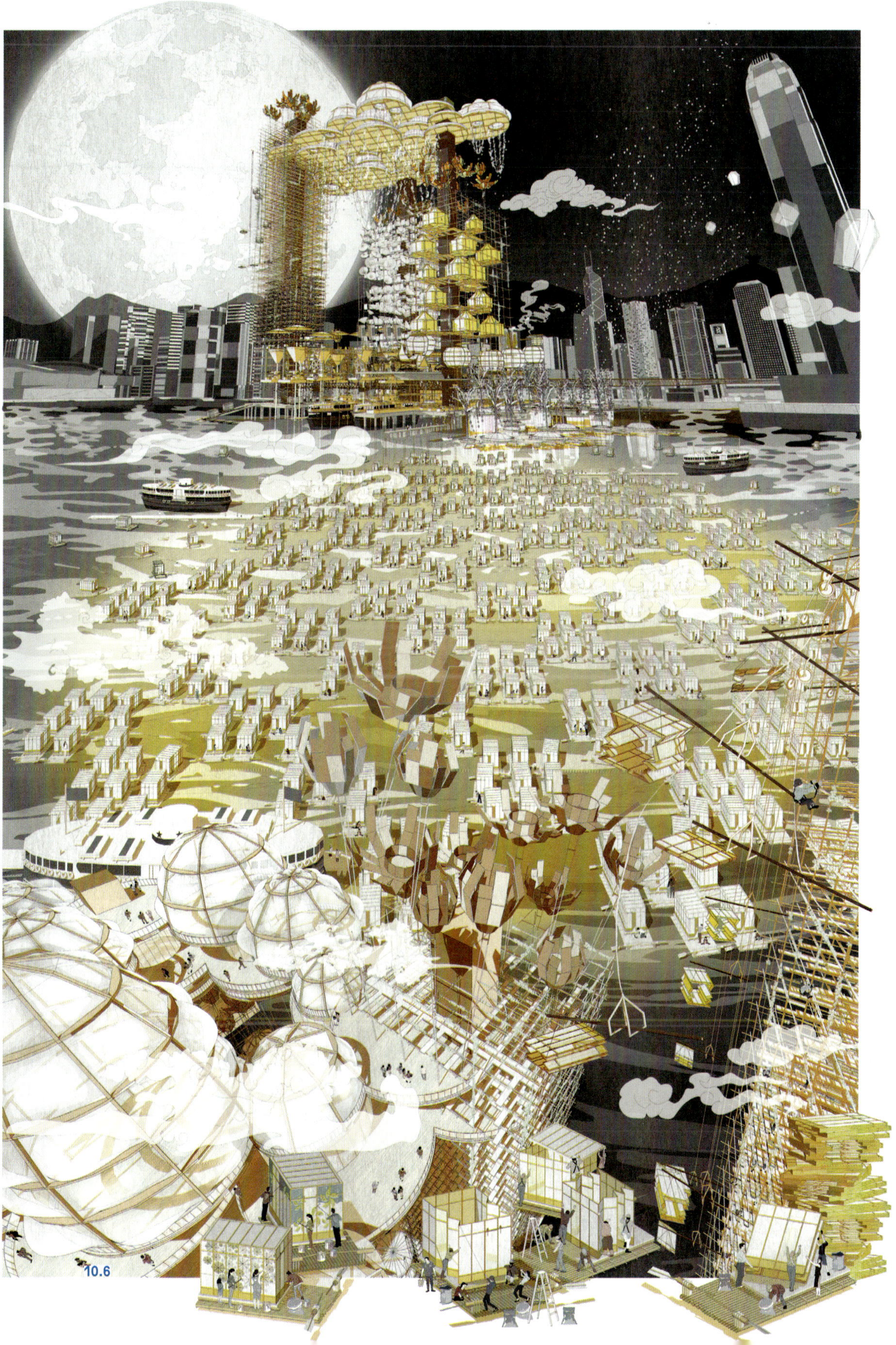

10.6

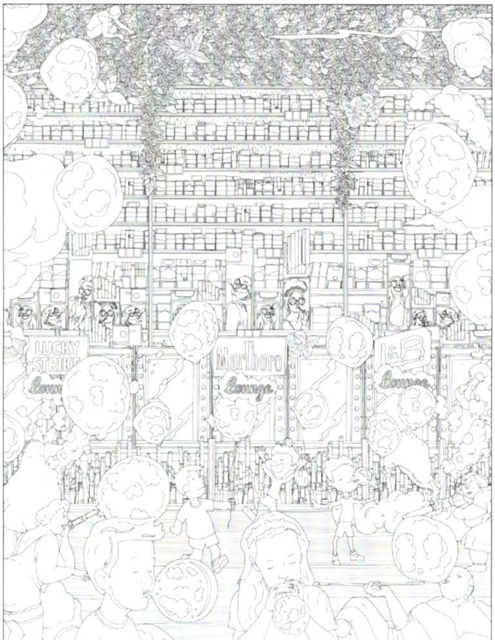

10.7

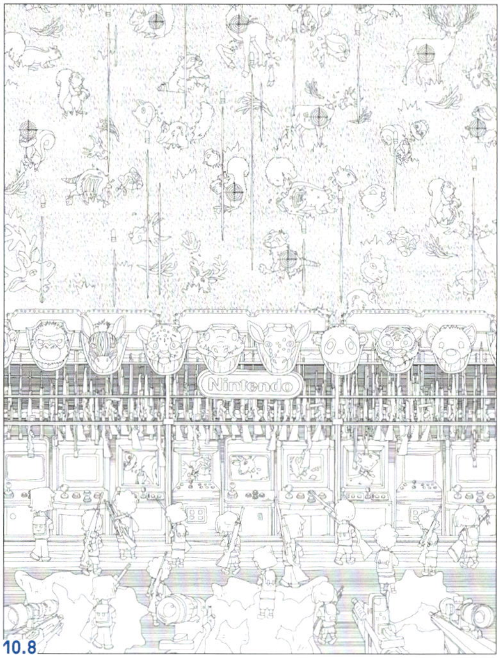

10.8

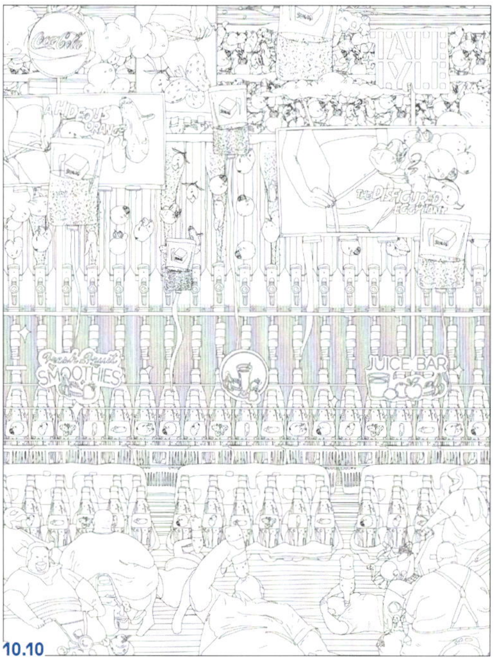

10.10

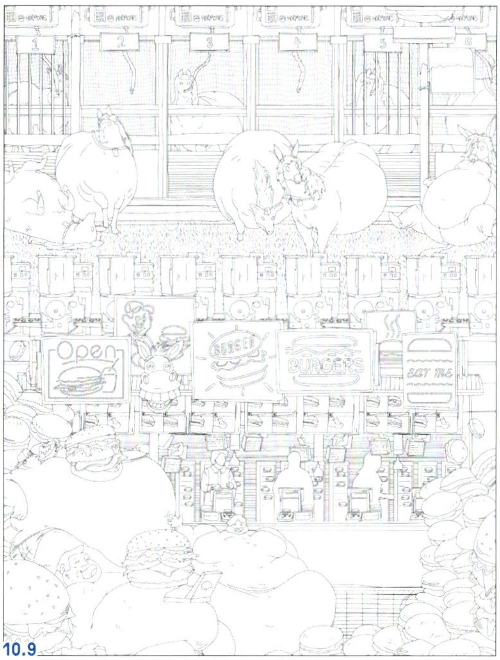

10.9

Figs. 10.7 – 10.11 Kai Hang Liu Y5, 'Sin City'. Seven DC comic supervillains metaphorically strategise the urban redevelopment of Boston in Lincolnshire. The project demonstrates a hard post-Brexit scenario where sins question the traditional canon of building typologies, and vice facilitates socioeconomic programmes through anti-EU legislation. Immortality, greed and envy can be celebrated without consequence. **Figs. 10.12 – 10.13 Nathan Fairbrother** Y5, 'A Festival of Brexit'. The urban regeneration of Wolverhampton celebrates the metaphors and imagination of 'Mary Poppins' by P.L. Travers. By empowering local people to take back control over employment, health and education, the project aims to provide a hopeful and positive vision for Brexit.

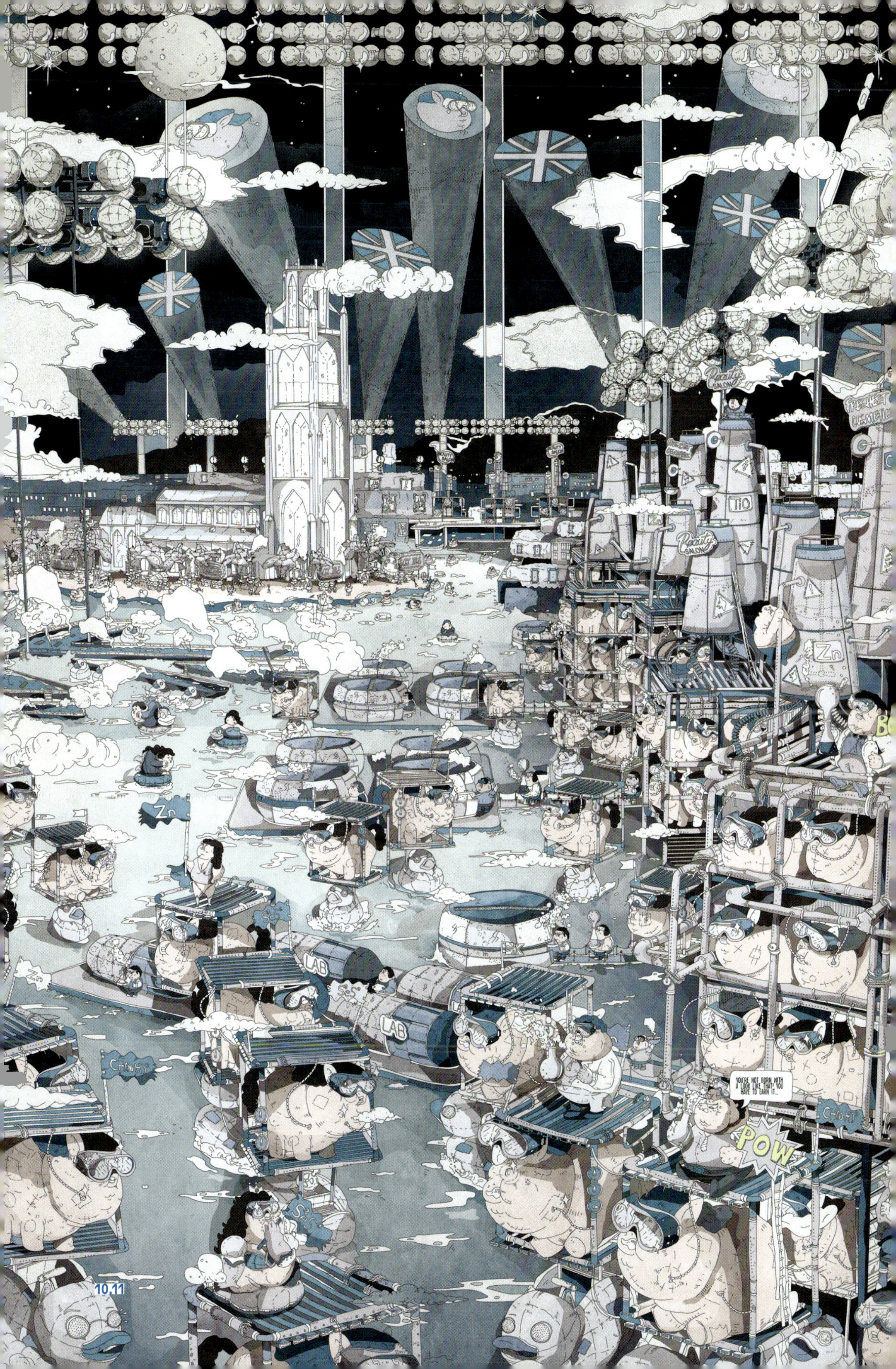
TIO
Zn
Zn
LAB
LAB
YOU'RE NOT BORN WITH A LOOK LIKE THAT! YOU HAVE TO EARN IT...
POW

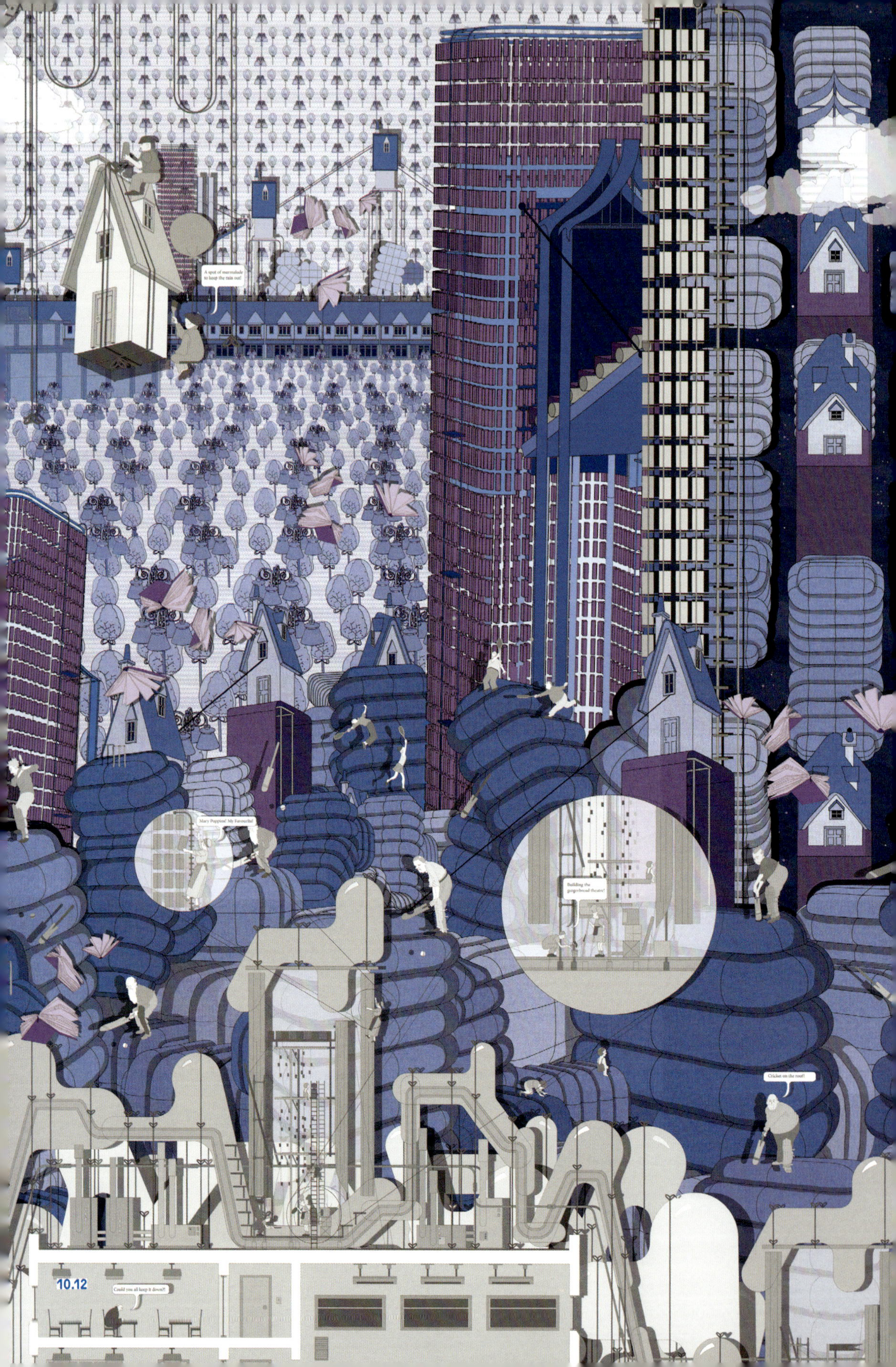
A spot of marmalade
to keep the rain out!
Mary Poppins! My Favourite!
Building the
gingerbread theatre!
Cricket on the roof!
Could you all keep it down?!

10.12

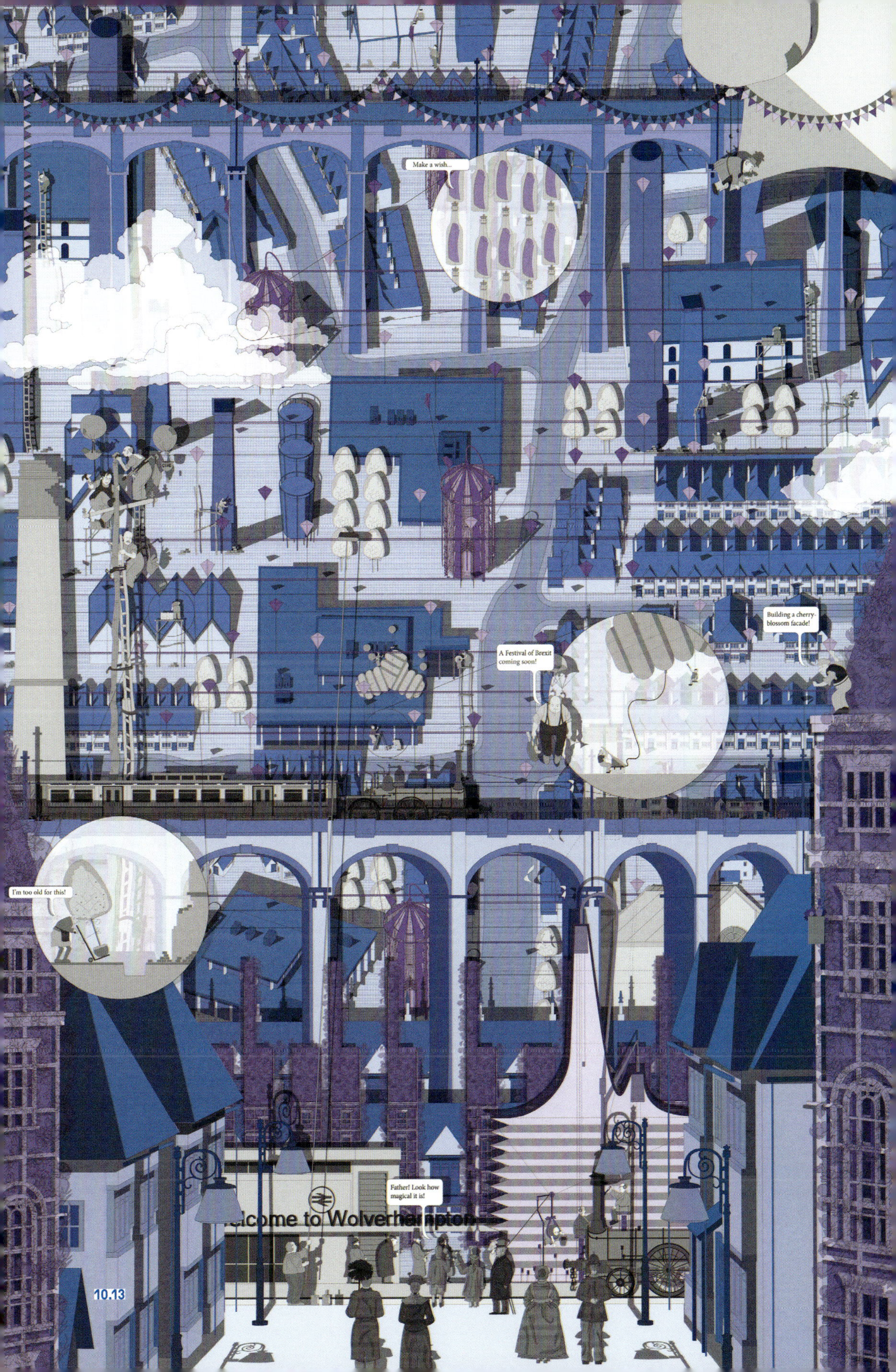
Make a wish...
Building a cherry-blossom facade!
A Festival of Brexit coming soon!
I'm too old for this!
Father! Look how magical it is!
lcome to Wolverhampton
10.13

Unit 11 Back to the Future

Laura Allen, Mark Smout

Year 4
Bethany Bird, Laurence Blackwell-Thale, Emma Colthurst, Patrick Horne, Lex Liew, Joe Roberts, Ellie Sampson

Year 5
Alexander Chapman, Chris Delahunt, Johanna Just, Anthony Ko, Ness Lafoy, Milo de Luca, Agostino Nickl

Thanks to our Design Realisation tutor Rhys Cannon

Thank you to:
Steven Foster Engineers, Ali Shaw at Max Fordham and to our critics Brendan Cormier, Edward Denison, Stephen Gage, Dan Hill, Joseph Grima, Rory Hyde, Zoe Laughlin, Holly Lewis, Peter Liversidge, Luke Pearson, Tania Sengupta, Tomas Stokke, Gwen Webber, Patrick Weber, Elly Ward Morris

This year, we dreamt of future pasts. The natural tensions and antithetical relationships characterised by the struggle between preservation and progress provide lessons, opportunities and limits for the continuum of landscape and urban histories and, more importantly, determine their emerging futures.

——The zenith of preservation is the UNESCO World Heritage List for natural, built and cultural landscapes, cities and monuments. It seeks to record and preserve cities and landscapes, making them, to an extent, 'future-proof' – and at the same time inadvertently fossilised in their current states. The UNESCO list is diverse and wide-ranging, and includes Easter Island, 17 works by Le Corbusier, the Statue of Liberty and the industrial ruins of an Argentinian Fray Bentos Factory. Listing provides protection through international law, however, it has also been described as a lethal weapon deployed in the act of preservation's crimes against cities.

——The Venetian Lagoon (the journey's end of our European trip this year) is striving to maintain its inclusion on the World Heritage List, despite a developing battle between tourism and culture. The city hosts over 600 cruise ships and 20 million visitors per year, which, as well as pumping tourist money into the city, also endangers its physical fabric and cultural integrity under the terms of its UNESCO listing.

——Could the construction of replica cities and pseudo-landscapes, relocated across the world, be an alternative to the museumification of listed cities such as Venice? These embodiments of Umberto Eco's concept of 'Uffiziland', such as the unfeasibly blue and chlorinated Grand Canal at the Venetian hotel-casino in Las Vegas, are designed to improve on the touristic rather than the authentic 'experience'.

——The opportunity for the retelling and recasting of histories through copies, and their significance in preservation, is given credence via museum collections such as the Cast Courts at the V&A, which contain collections of historic plaster and wax replicas of monumental sculptural and architectural fragments collected in the 19th century. Their collection also reveals the contemporary role of copies in the preservation of cultural artifacts and global heritage threatened by war, climate change and societal pressures. The emergence of new technologies such as 3D scanning and digital printing mean that copies can now be 'dematerialised' to the hard-drive rather than to the museum gallery. One can imagine a future reprinting, like a Jurassic Park style recreation of cultural artifacts, cut off from their context and meaning, reanimated nowhere and everywhere, even at an urban or landscape scale.

——In attempt to recast 'Wonderland' and to create instant histories, inspiration for our year's work included UNESCO's list of intangible Cultural and World Heritage, model villages, alternative preservation manifestos, fakery, architectural graveyards, demonstration landscapes, cultural migration, monuments and their doppelgängers.

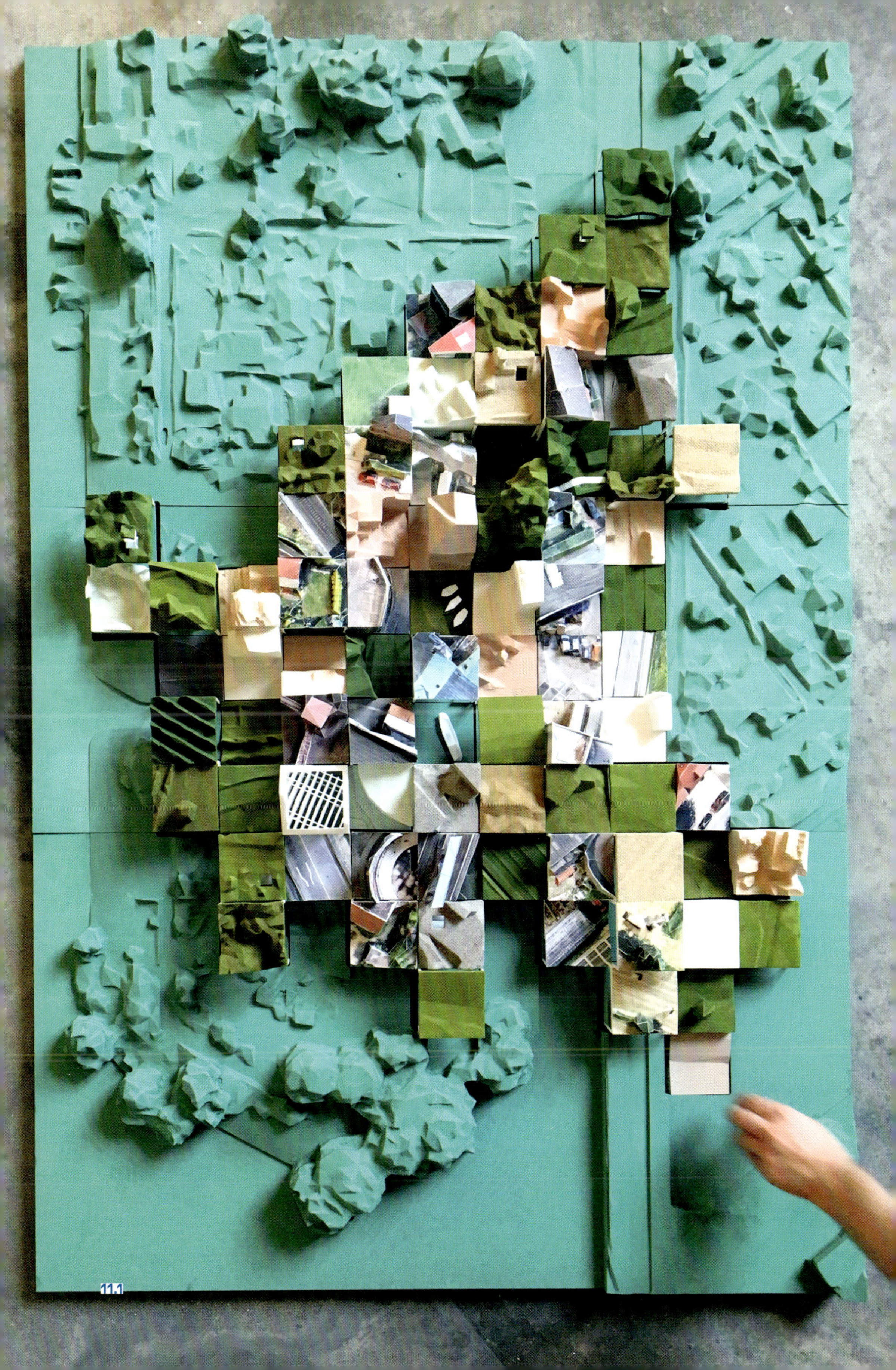

11.1

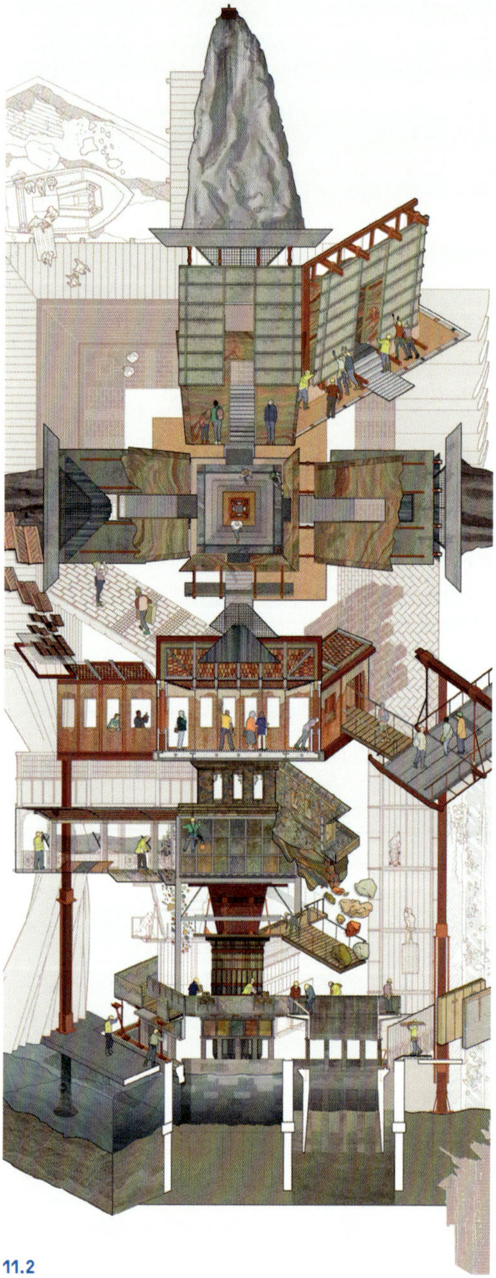

11.2

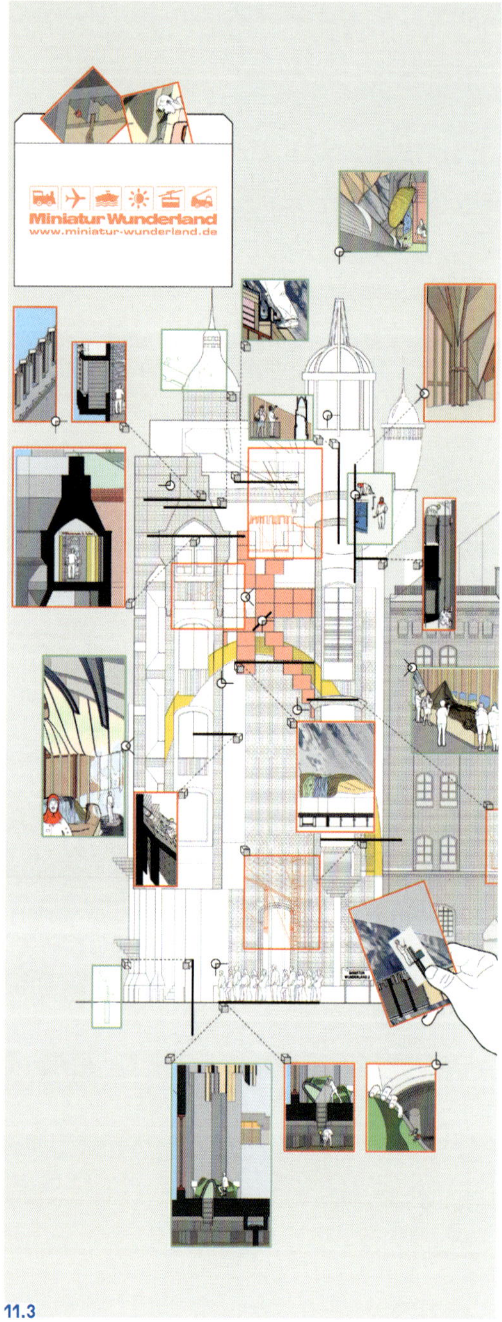

11.3

Fig. 11.1 Agostino Nickl Y5, 'Low-res City'. Using photogrammetric data, Hamburg is compressed into 80 specimens mined from across the city. These low-res samples become true representatives of the urban fabric containing extracts of fields, the Autobahn, a brutalist warehouse, a church and an airplane, amongst others. They serve as testbeds for newly developed and existing fabrication techniques. **Fig. 11.2 Ellie Sampson** Y4, 'The Torcello Typology Repository'. Composite drawing. An elevated island in the marshy landscape towards the north of the lagoon, the repository uses channelled water, limestone-lined vessels and purposefully eroding walls to recreate and intensify the processes attacking Venice's unique infrastructure. **Fig. 11.3 Laurence Blackwell-Thale** Y4, 'Miniatur Wunderland Extension'. Positioned as a critique of a flawed UNESCO listing, the 1:87 model museum's sets, including a 35m-tall Mount Everest, have internal environments that mimic real climates with scale adjusted. **Fig. 11.4 Ness Lafoy** Y5, 'A New Alpine Convention'. The project imagines an alternative future for French ski resorts which combines luxury tourism with the Alpine Convention's mission to protect the natural heritage of the region. Pine forest test-beds, curated to 'romantic alpine landscape' principles, are cultivated and configured as a temporary backdrop for the resort. They are subsequently distributed to sites across the region and permanently grafted into the landscape, in order to help reconnect fragmented habitats.

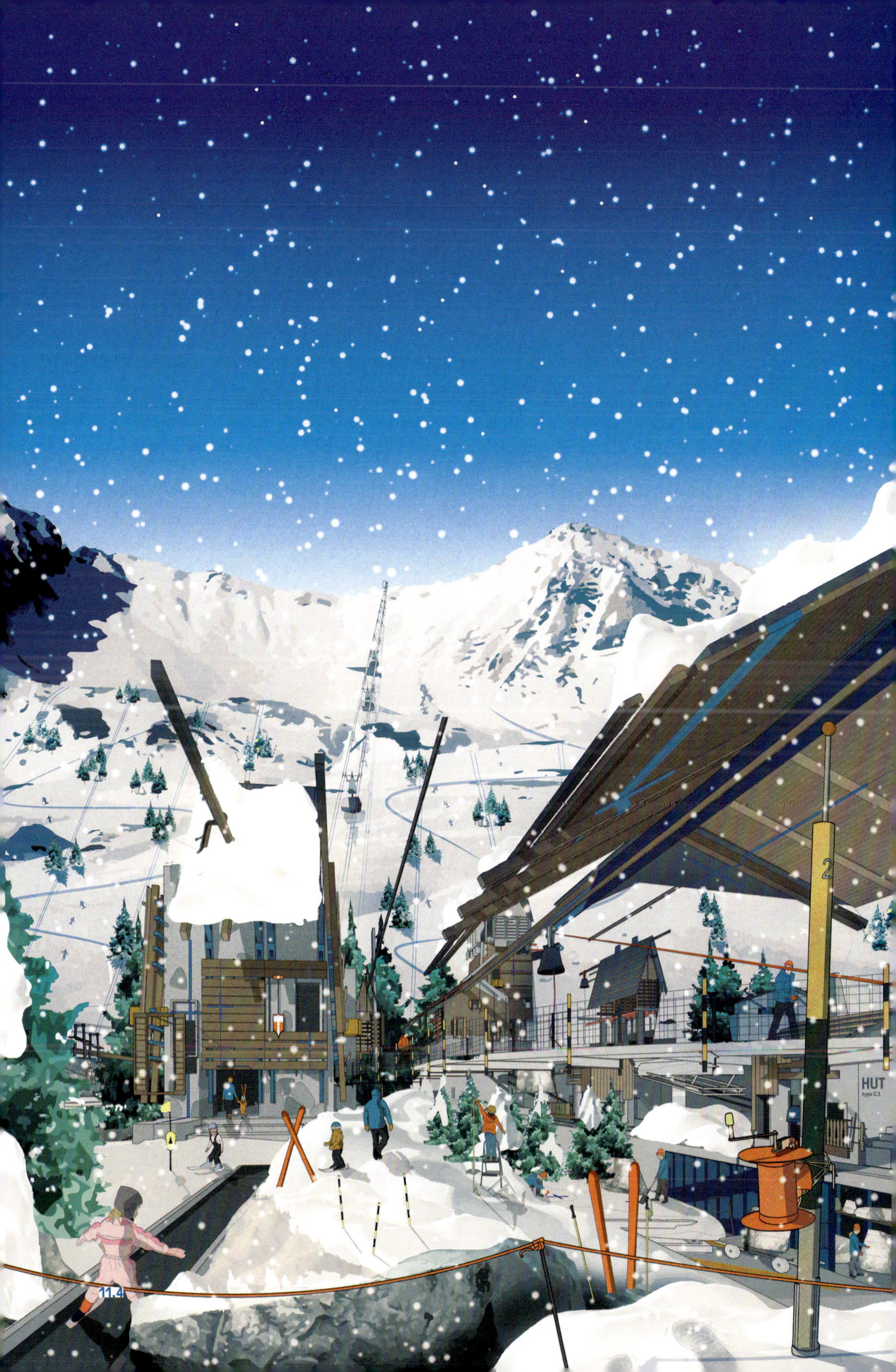
2
HUT
type C.1
11.4

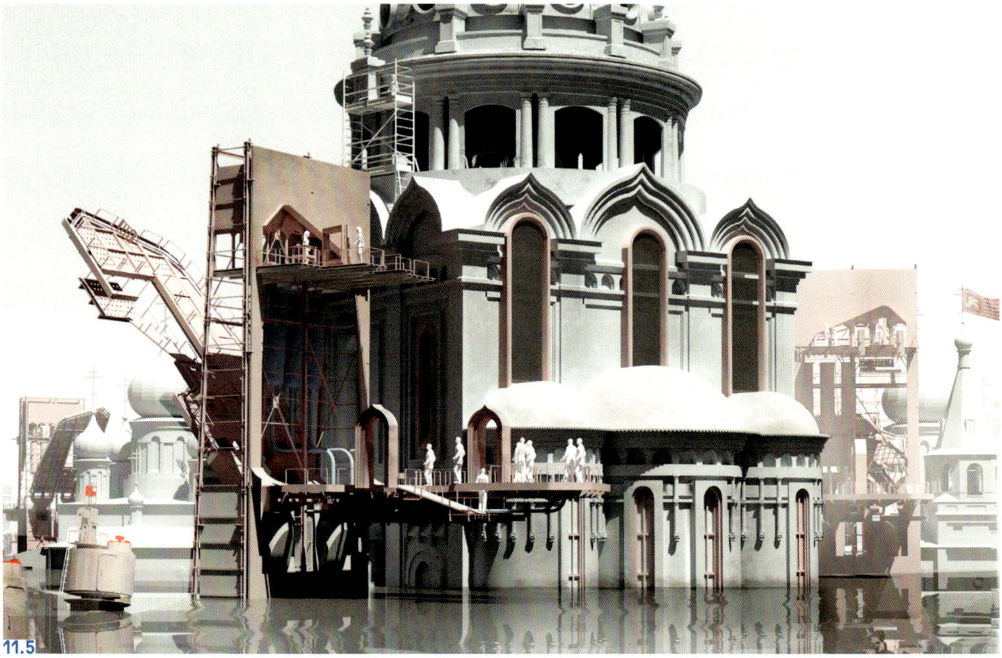

11.5

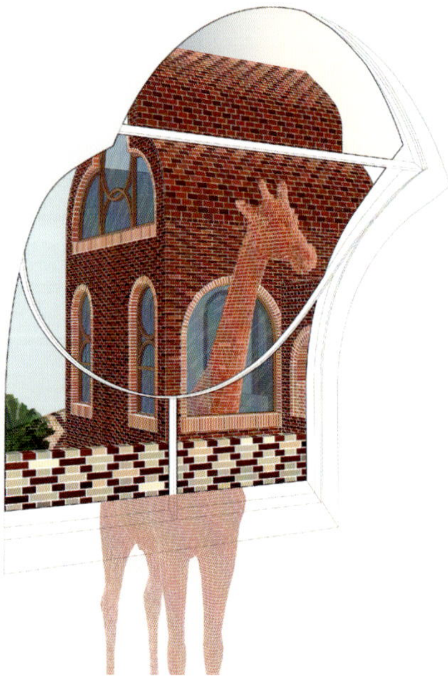

11.6

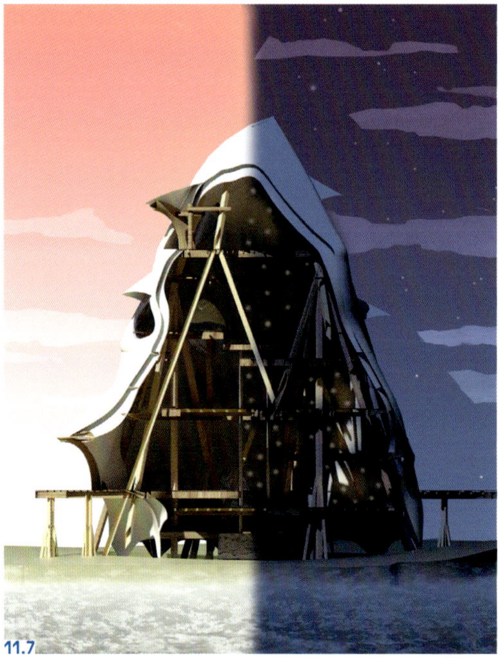

11.7

Fig. 11.5 Lex Lieu Y4, 'Auctioning Venice'. As the sea-level rises, the physical sovereignty of Venice is drowned, but a sense of cultural preservation can be retained through the distribution of Venice's architectural relics. The auction house commemorates the fragile city and prepares it for a future elsewhere. **Fig. 11.6 Emma Colthurst** Y4, 'The Sant'Alvise Children's Hospital'. This healthcare extension reimagines the Italian Renaissance garden as a series of joyful community spaces. Allegorical creatures emerge through the scheme to delight and lead visitors through the centre, which aims to reconnect the youngest generations of Venice back to its community, history and urban fabric. **Fig. 11.7 Bethany Bird** Y4, 'Studio Plastica'. A recycling centre, located in the Venetian Lagoon, for waste plastic and a workshop for crafted plastic products, glimmers in the day and lights up at night as a lantern, showcasing the possible applications of plastic waste. **Fig. 11.8 Johanna Just** Y5, 'Palazzo Pubblico – Disrupting the Lagoon Loop'. Palazzo Pubblico aims to disrupt the Venetian 'set' to help the city break free from the self-referential loop it is stuck in. The building offers infrastructure for cultural exchange and serves as a test-piece for a new, association-based design method, challenging existing preservation concepts that let the city become a static museum.

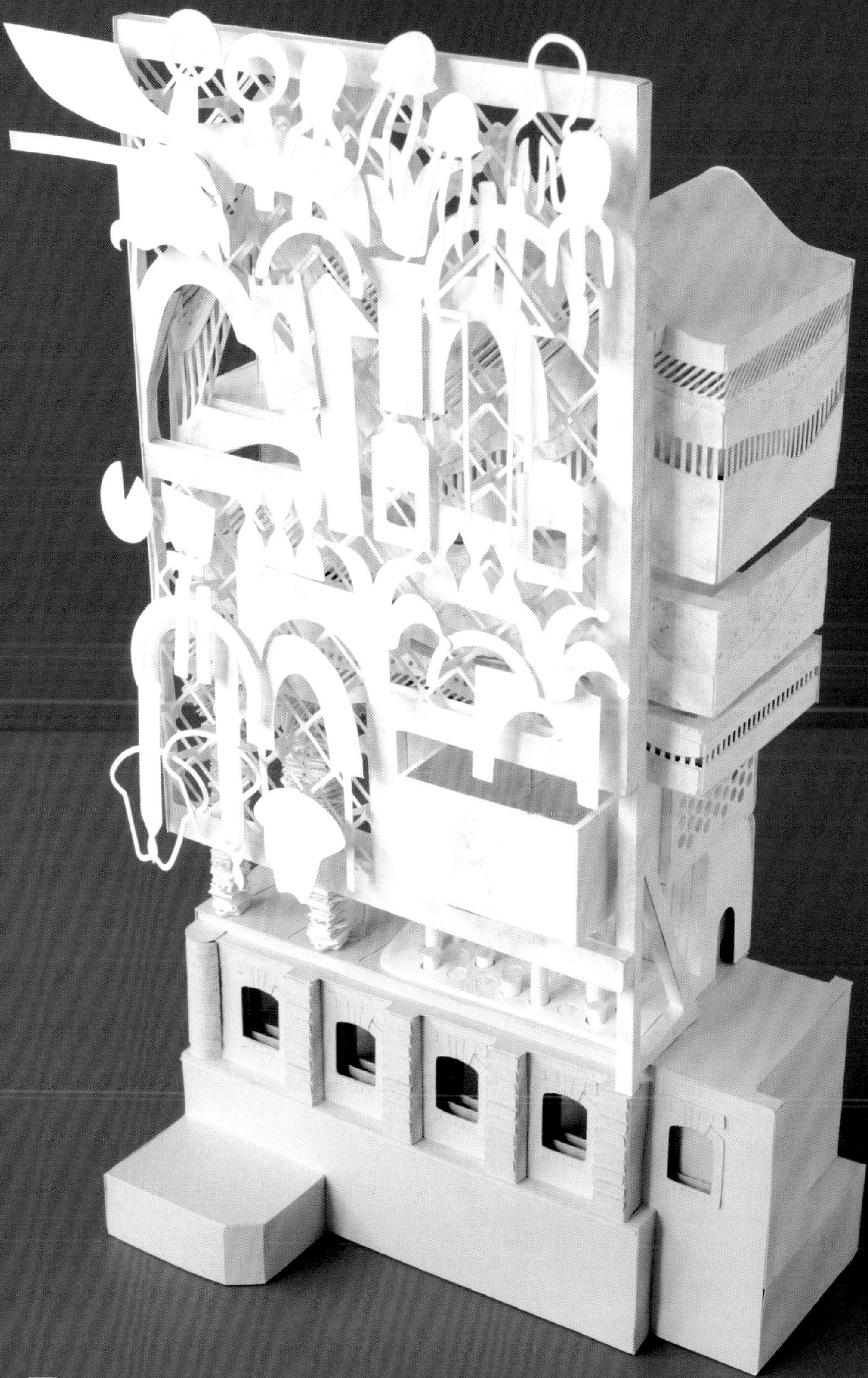

11.8

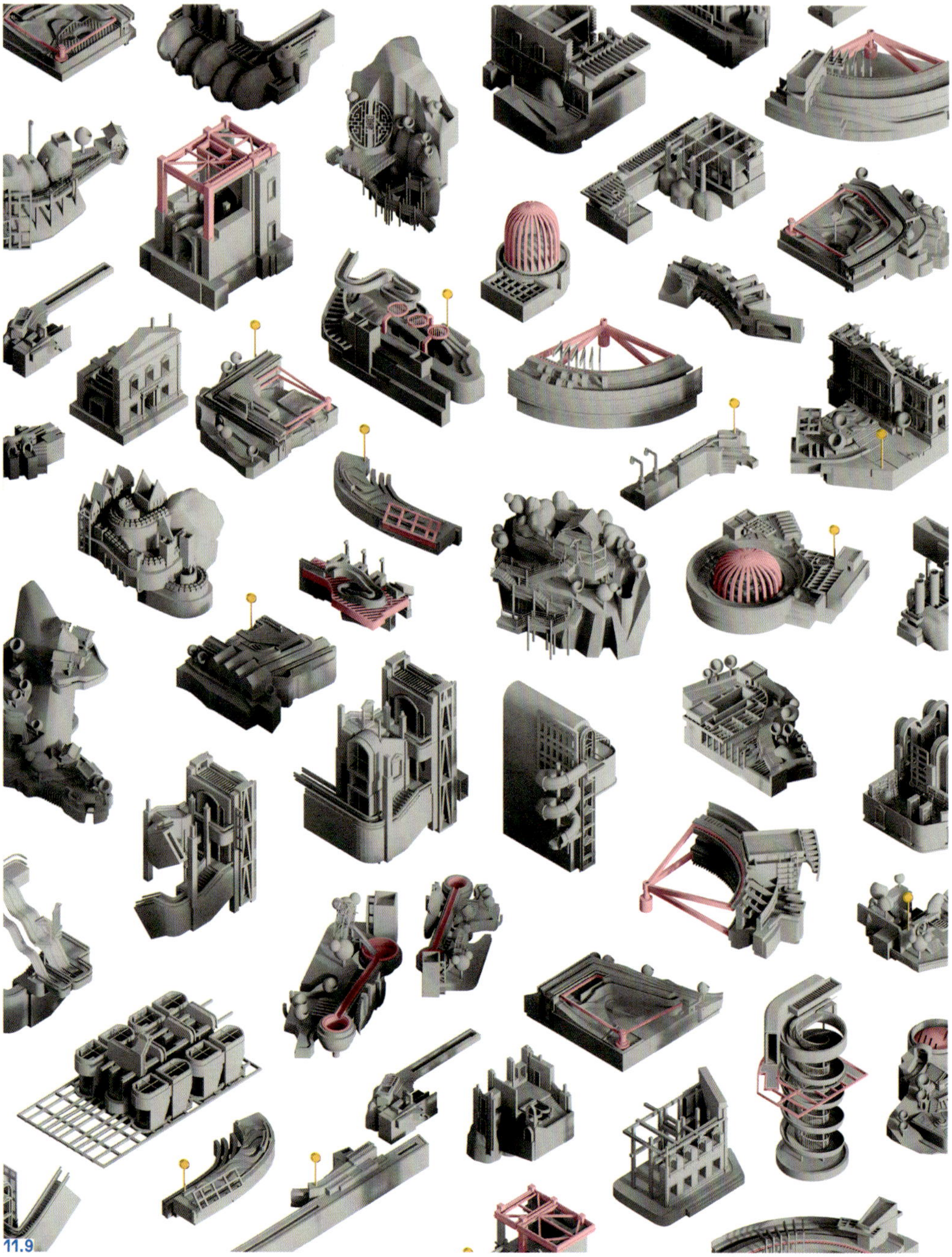

11.9

Fig. 11.9 Alexander Chapman Y5, 'Macau's Euraserie'. This project creates an exportable series of architectural extensions to the UNESCO monuments in Macau's historic centre, a contemporary reversal of Chinoiserie. On the one hand it deals with the damage caused by an overzealous, cultural tourism and on the other, it creates a platform for Macau's heritage to rival the casino skyline. **Fig. 11.10 Chris Delahunt** Y5, 'Google Venice'. The Google-sponsored internet physicalisation factory creates physical back-ups of digital cultural heritage in tapestry format. Sited on the origin of a re-emerging global trade route coined 'The Silicon Road', data becomes the main traded commodity of a Venetian Internet Port.

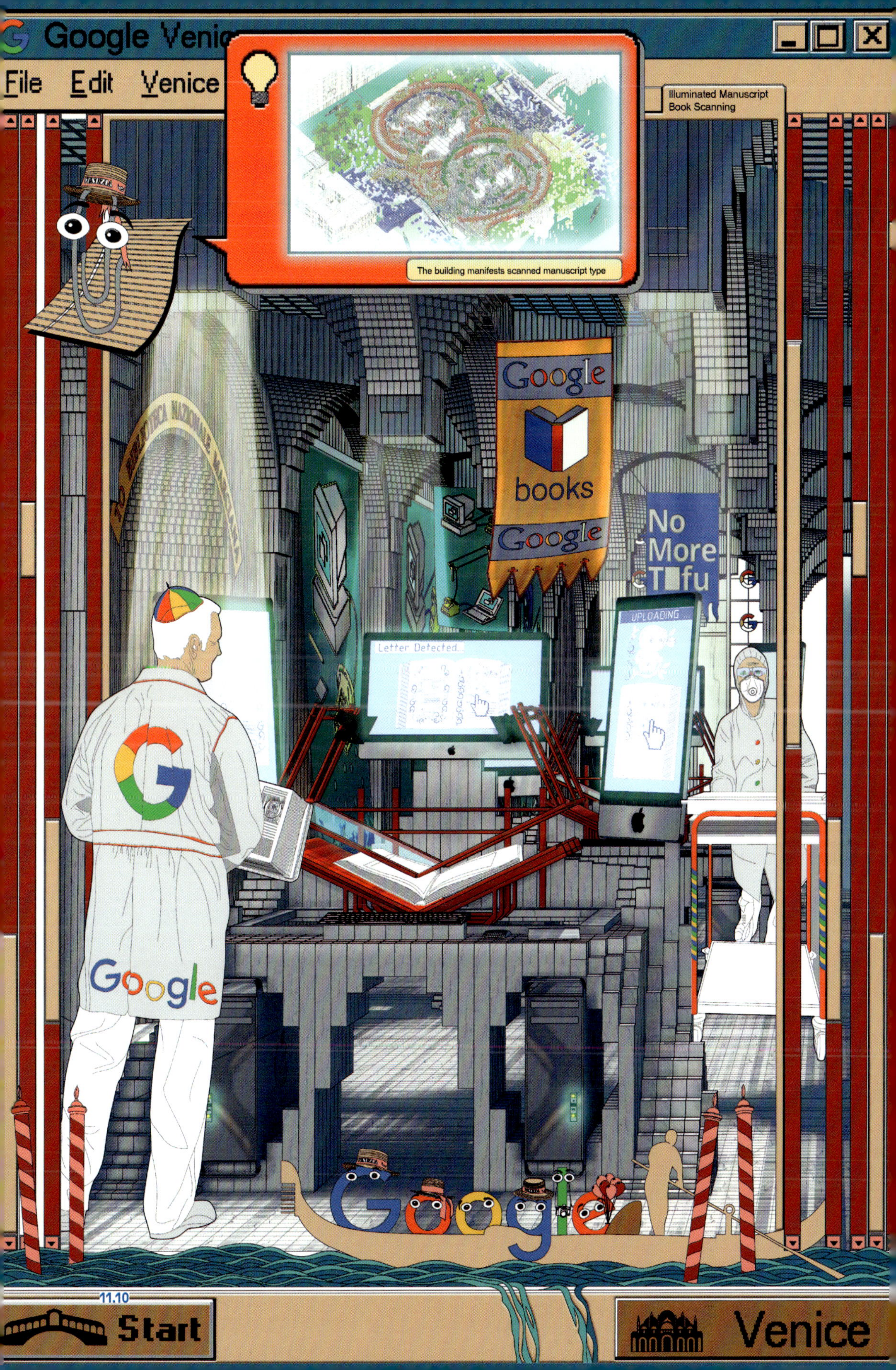

Google Venic
File Edit Venice
The building manifests scanned manuscript type
Illuminated Manuscript
Book Scanning
Google
books
Google
No
More
T fu
UPLOADING
Letter Detected
Google
Google
11.10
Start
Venice

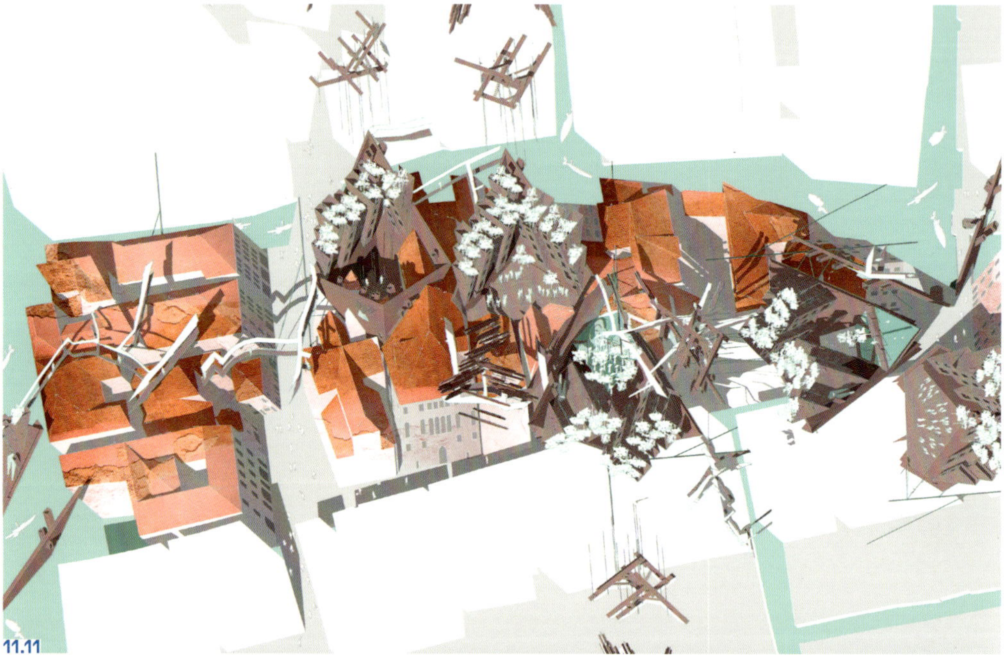

11.11

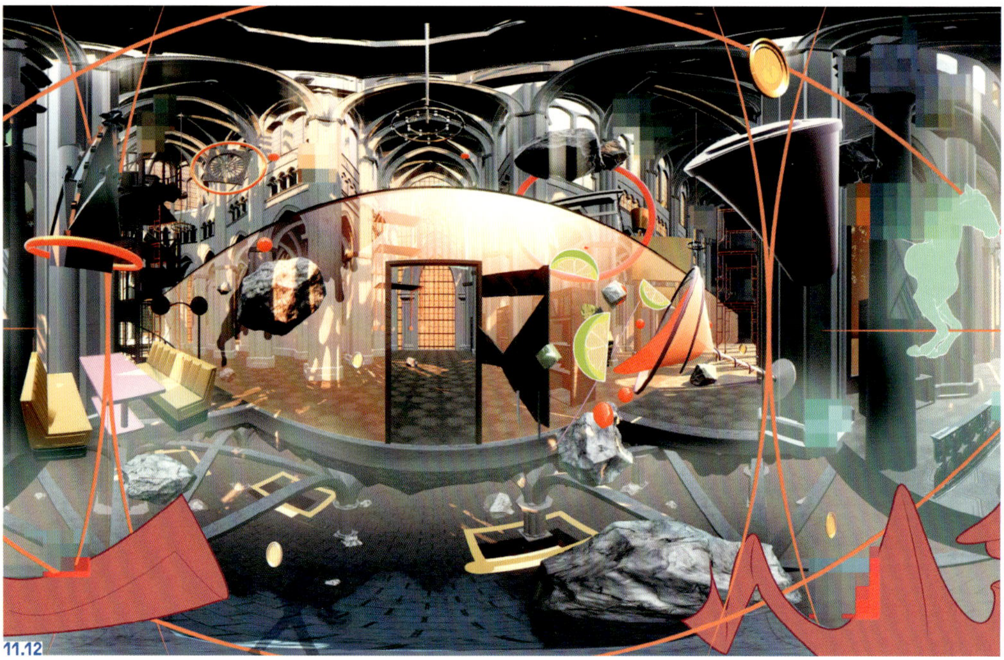

11.12

Fig. 11.11 Milo de Luca Y5, 'New Venice: Fragments of an Ideal City for Residents'. New Venice is a response to Venice's increasing physical and social decay. Saturating the stratifications of the decaying urban landscape via its insertion within the existing city's rooftops, bridges and canals, the architectural 'fragments' provide residential and social improvement, implementing an ideal vision of a city with the housing, community spaces and amenities required for the Venetians who serve the existing city. **Fig. 11.12 Patrick Horne** Y4, 'Travels in Cyber Reality' speculates upon the role of the architect in our increasing inhabitation of digital space. The project culminates in an exploration of the panorama as a new form of experiential drawing technique, whereby two-dimensional illustrations are spatially translated and tested through Virtual Reality technologies. **Fig. 11.13 Anthony Ko** Y5, 'An Activist Artifact'. The Sino-British declaration of 1997 aimed to ensure fifty years of stability for Hong Kong. However, the Chinese communists didn't keep their promises and have long been initiating changes to Hong Kong's freedoms. Hong Kong's historic defensive environments, such as the Frontier Controlled Area and Macintosh Forts, are reimagined together with Hong Kong's artwork, photographs and totems, to formulate a collage city of activistic architecture. An art auction house and artist settlement rebel against China and defend its heterotopic identities from eradication through the trade of politically charged Hong Kong art.

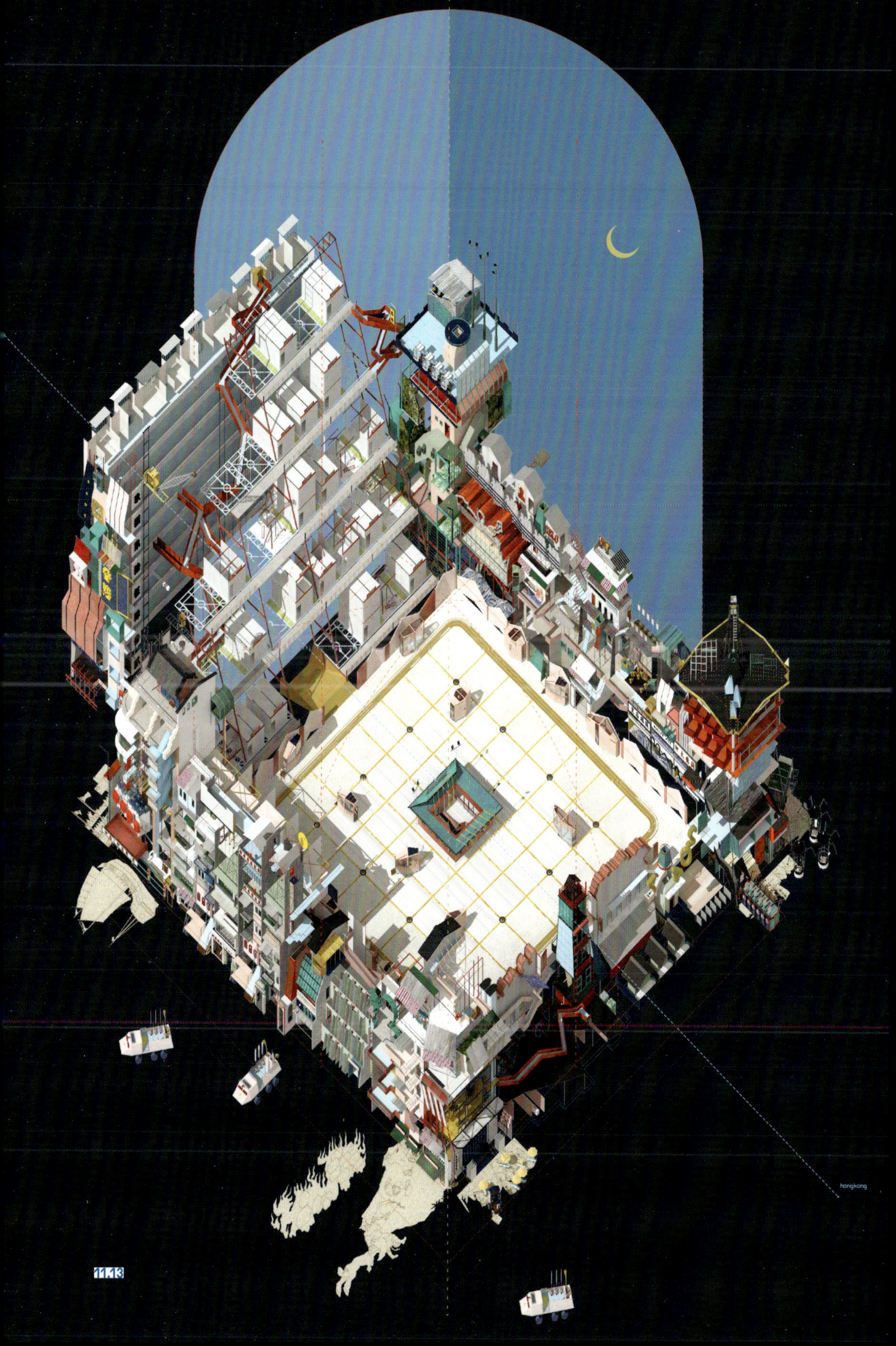

11.13

Unit 12 What is New?

Matthew Butcher, Jonathan Hill

Year 4
Sophie Barks, Boon Yik Chung, Samuel Coulton, Iga Martynow, Dan Meredith, Elin Soderberg

Year 5
Christia Angelidou, Mariya Badeva, Emma De Haan, Mihail Dinu, Clare Hawes, Rawan Hussin, Raphae Memon, Meya Tazi, Ioana Vierita

Thank you to our Design Realisation tutor James Hampton of Periscope, and DR structural consultant James Nevin of Blue Engineering

Thank you to Ben Clement and Sebastian de la Cour of benandsebastian

Thank you to our critics: Ana Araujo, Alessandro Ayuso, Shumi Bose, Eva Branscome, Barbara-Ann Campbell-Lange, Tom Coward, Oliver Domeisen, Ben Ferns, Paul Fineberg, Omar Ghazal, Sean Griffiths, Jessica In, Chee-Kit Lai, Constance Lau, Lesley McFadyen, Tom Noonan, Luke Pearson, Peg Rawes, Gilles Retsin, Tania Sengupta, Ana Vale, Nina Vollenbröker, Dan Wilkinson

The desire for the new is seen in our need to consume the latest fashions, technologies, artworks and ideas. The promise of the new stimulates the recurring cycles of production and obsolescence that feed consumption in a capitalist society. But it is also a creative and critical stimulus to cultural, social and technological innovation. This year, our aim is to explore how this informs the ways we conceive and produce architecture.

——Often, what is presented as new is not new at all, but a revival of an earlier form, idea or practice. To ask 'What is new?' involves other questions: why is it new, how is it new, and where is it new? Alongside cultural and social investigations into notions of newness, we ask what is really new in any subject that concerns us.

——The 20th century avant-garde were the quintessential advocates of the new. They sought to discover art forms that would question bourgeois traditions and transform society culturally, socially and politically. Their influence was profound even though they were assimilated into the cultural establishment. To explore the possibilities for a better world, we ask what is a new avant-garde today, what should it propose, what values and systems should it question and why.

——To understand what is new, we investigate the present, the past and the future: we think historically. Defining something as new is an inherently historical act because it requires an awareness of what is old. We are not interested in unquestioning newness for its own sake, and we do not wish to reject the past or negate its value. Sometimes the old is even more radical than the new. Rather than the modernist *tabula rasa* in which the new destroys the old, we propose an evolving dialogue between the new and the old in which one informs the other.

——Thomas More's *Utopia* celebrated its 500-year anniversary in 2016, reviving questions of its present relevance. One possible translation of its full title 'De optimo rei publicae deque nova insula Utopia' is 'Of a republic's best state and of the new island Utopia'. More was reputed to have refused to translate his Utopia from Latin, but we look at translation as a means to imagine the new.

——Our site is Berlin. More than any other European city, Berlin offers a cavalcade of buildings that were once really new. Continually reinventing itself, Berlin offers a historically and politically fecund environment in which our students proposed a state, an island or a quarter of considered newness. Initially this new state was remotely imagined from London. In Berlin we set its foundations, and on our return to London this 'city within a city' was brought to fruition.

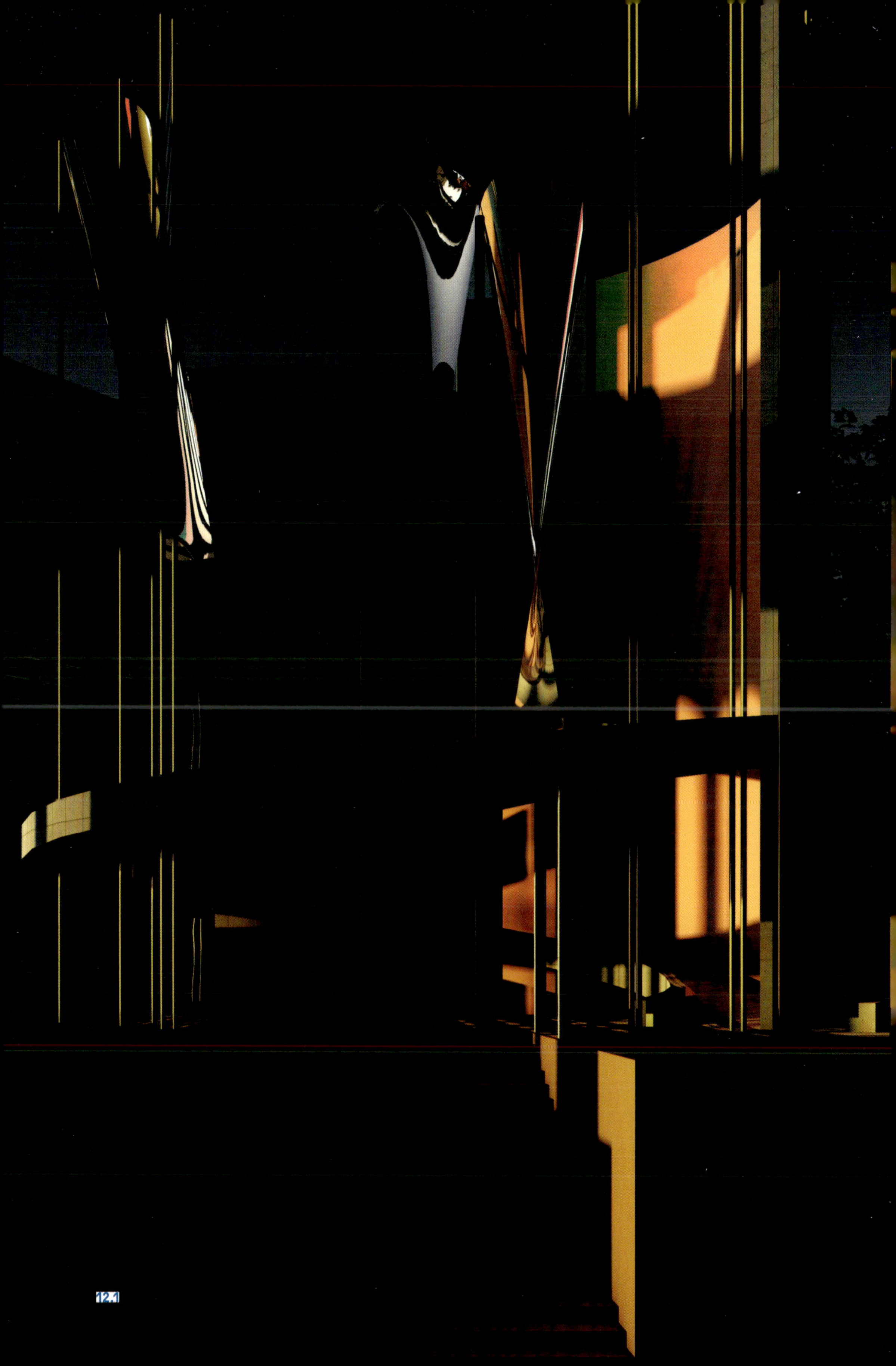

12.1

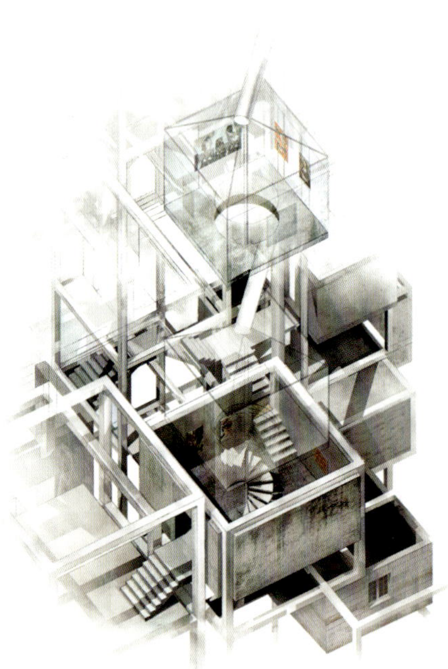

12.2

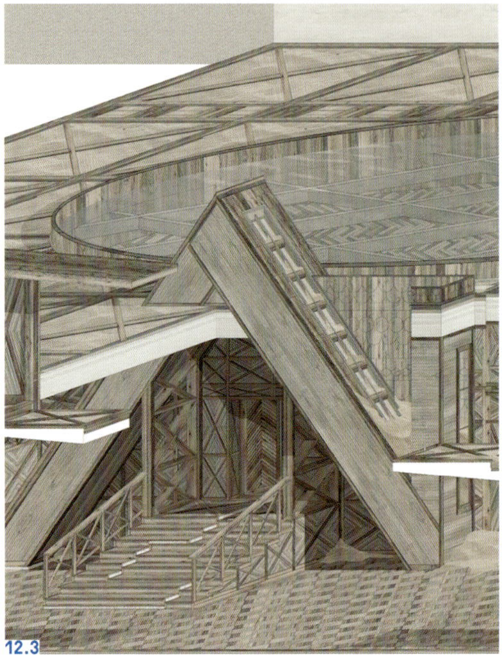

12.3

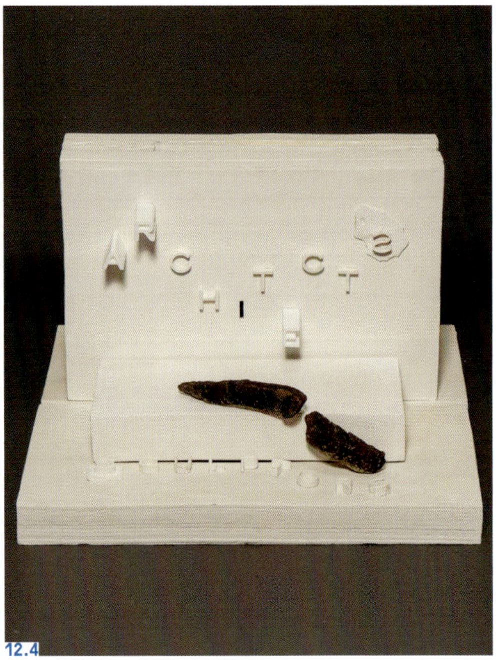

12.4

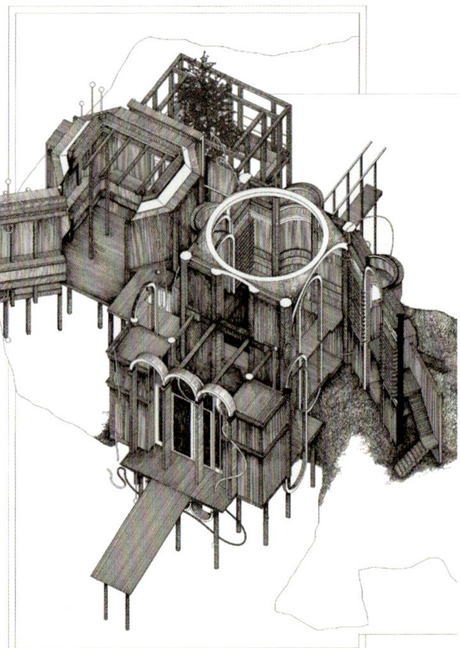

12.5

Fig. 12.1 Raphae Memon Y5, 'Tierwald: Berlin's City-Architect-Scenographer'. The project is a landscape of buildings-as-public-squares, deep in a constructed forest within Berlin's Tiergarten. In the centre is the city-architect-scenographer, a yearly appointed artistic director of the city who coordinates the fragmented architectures so that they transform during the interstices between sunrise and sunset. The design facilitates scenographic proposals for the city, which are designed, built, tested, performed and stored. Light creates perceptive conditions of darkness and provokes scenographic occupations for the future. **Fig 12.2 Iga Martynow** Y4, 'Museum for Dada Art'. The museum is located on the exact site of a 1920s exhibition. It plays on ideas of the nonsensical and absurd, recreating the original gallery as a labyrinth of interconnected rooms, inhabiting the spaces between the white, superfluous grid. **Fig. 12.3 Elin Soderberg** Y4, 'The New Friedrichshain Bank'. Addressing themes of financial speculation and time, the project positions itself within the recurring property cycle. Set within a geological and seasonal timescale, it discusses the possibility of a new model for slow banking. **Fig. 12.4 Boon Yik Chung** Y4, 'Museum for 20th Century Arts'. A fix for Herzog & de Meuron's botched attempt, the project employs creative strategies associated with artistic practice in the synthesis of idea and physical production of architecture, to create gallery spaces truly representative of 20th century arts: radical, humorous and subversive. The alternative proposal tests the limit of architecture as a creative practice, and personal and societal

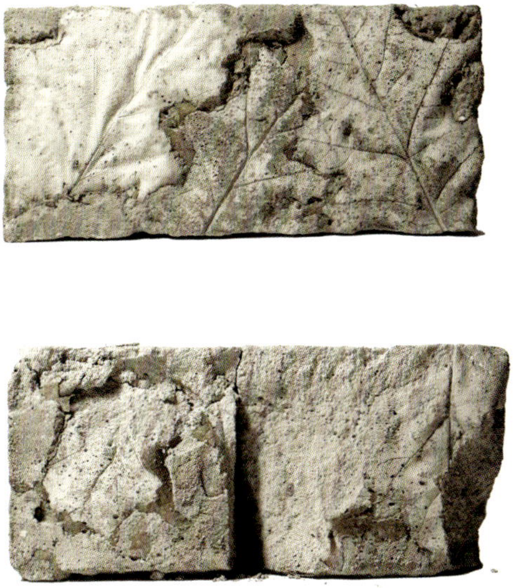

12.6

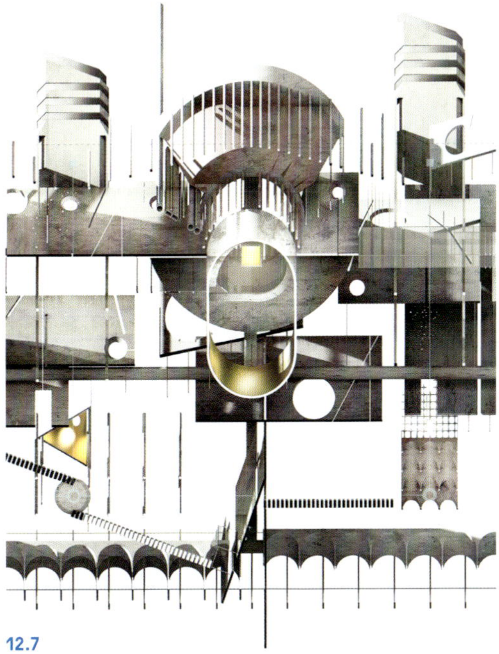

12.7

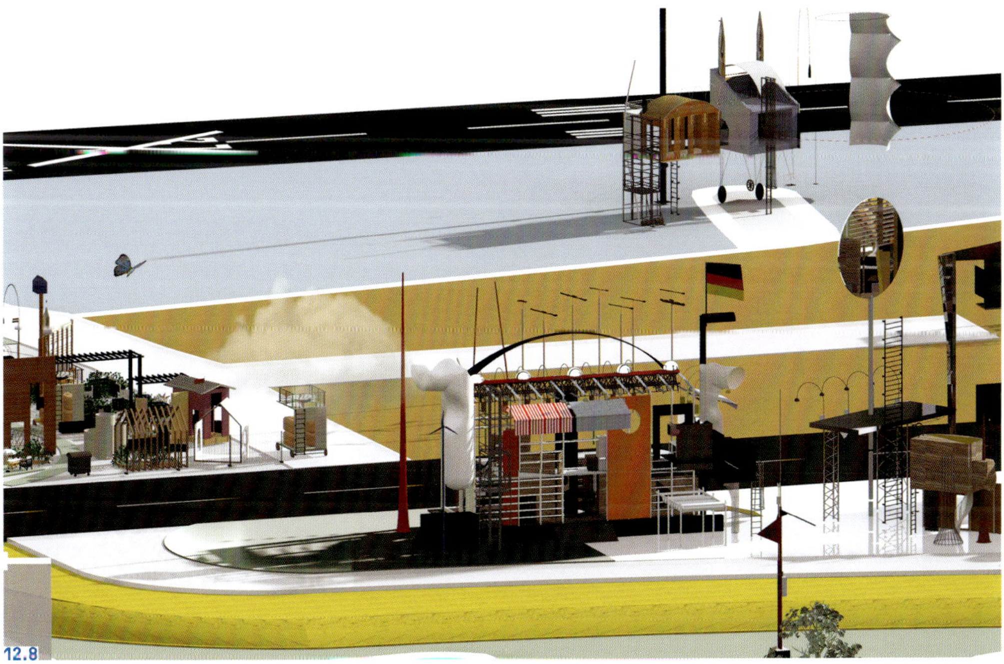

12.8

expression. **Fig. 12.5 Sophie Barks** Y4, 'Kriminalgericht Totschlag; Law Court, Berlin'. The project responds to the constructed, complex environments of dreams that feature a directory of architectural elements both familiar and unfamiliar, assembling these fragments and juxtaposing them together. It also embodies the liminal transition theories of ritual and its place within our society. **Fig. 12.6 Dan Meredith** Y4, 'The Cuvry Brache Memory Health Clinic'. The project proposes that in a society obsessed with information and data collection, the things we remember are new. Forgetting is made spatial and experiential through degradation – symbolic of the decay of human memory. **Fig. 12.7 Samuel Coulton** Y4, 'Berlin School of Environmental Policy'. Climatic conditions are recorded and celebrated as the occupants and architect enjoy 'submitting to the seasons.' Timescales at the micro and macro levels are exhibited, through tracking of the sun across a room, bleaching of cladding over a year, or gradual change in how the building can be used. **Fig. 12.8 Mariya Badeva** Y5, 'Eastern Objects, Western Fields: The Architecture of the New Berlin Quarter'. Situated in Berlin's biggest void, the former Tempelhof airport, the project explores newness and nostalgia, utopia and heterotopia, emptiness and possibility, event and appropriation. An island within a city, the proposal conceives of a new quarter in the heart of Berlin, established by the users of the field. A dispersed assemblage of unexpected individual buildings, the dynamic space is put to the creativity of the new non-architect, allowed on the field not simply as a visitor but also as a creator.

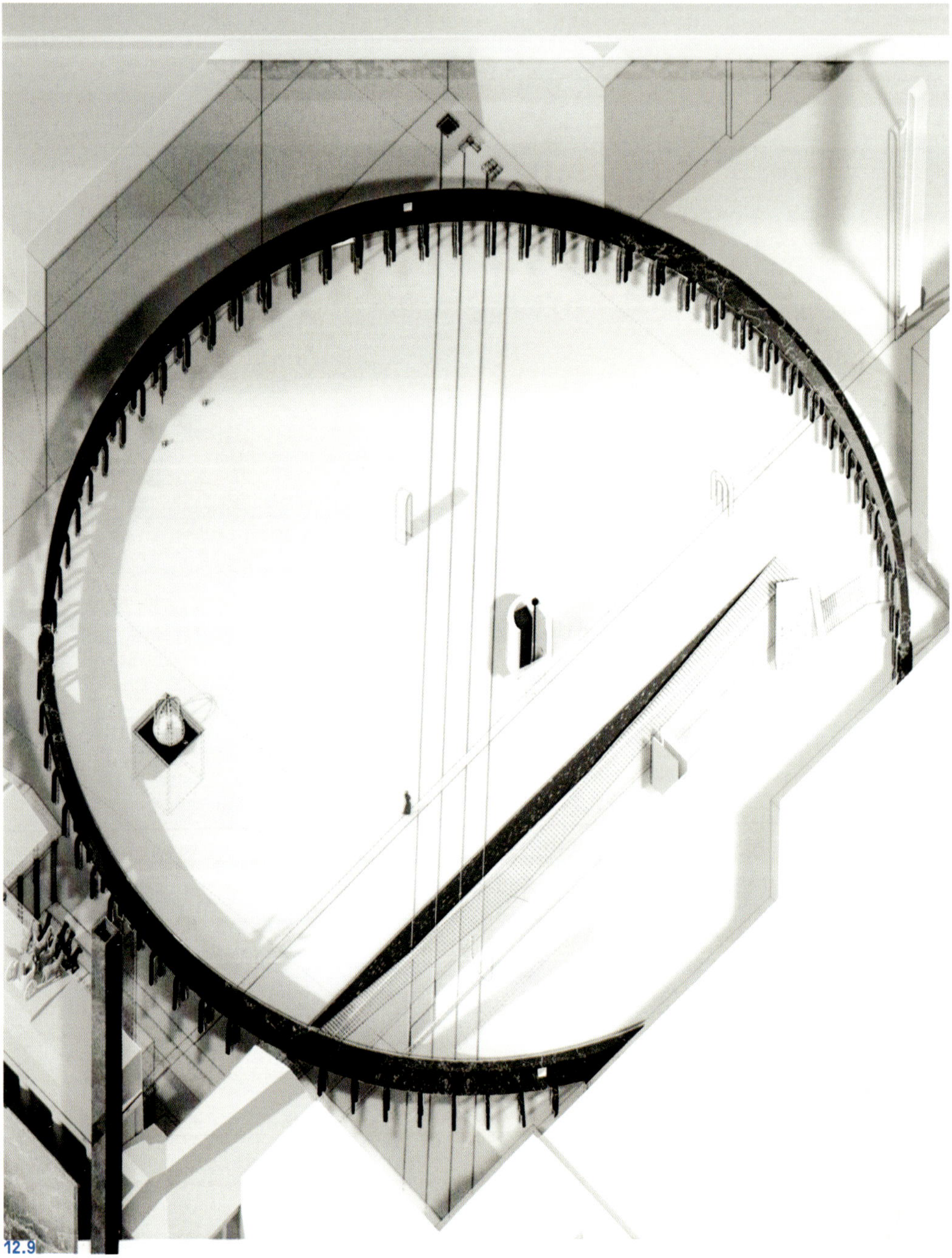

12.9

Fig. 12.9 Emma de Haan Y5, 'New Architecture of Romance'. We are at a moment in history where political relationships between countries, governments, politicians and subjects are turning sour. As a reaction, this project proposes a New Architecture of Romance for Berlin. Applied to a Ministry for Foreign Reunification affairs, the building facilitates the long and intimate discussion needed for diplomats to decide whether to divorce, marry or reunite. Its language challenges our flippant visualisation of romance, reinstating its fundamental importance with a material palette that is also a relational cross-section.

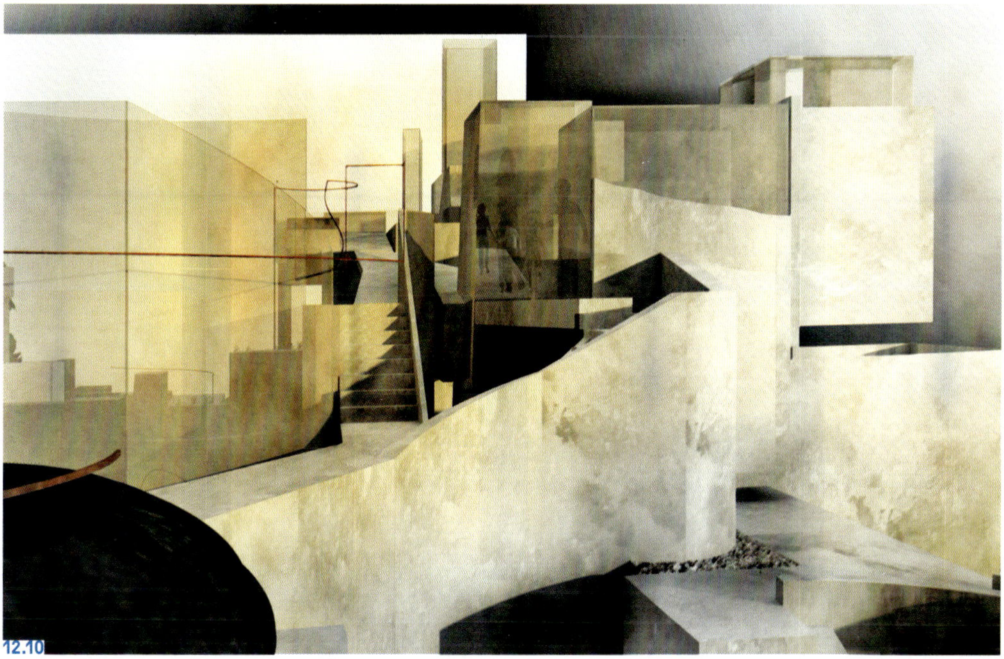

12.10

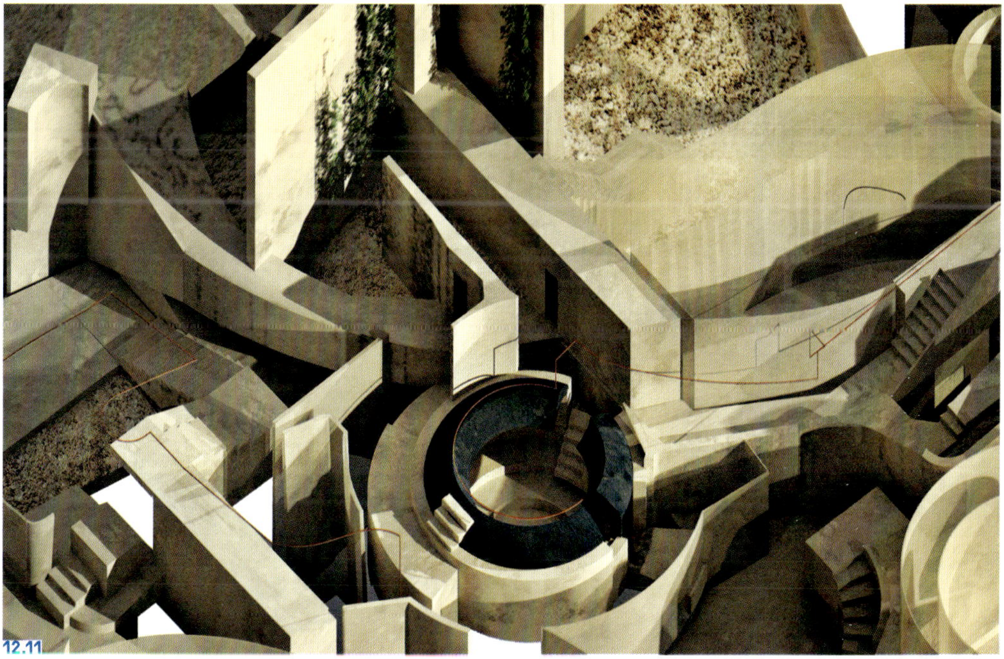

12.11

Figs. 12.10 – 12.11 Ioana Vierita Y5, 'Under the Linden-Tree, a Nursery and an Elderly Care Home in Berlin'. This project proposes a new urban model for a future intergenerational city as a new typology for urban space. It seeks to unite generations that have become estranged from one another, or who are generally displaced outside the city centre, by offering them a habitat in the city. Continuing the tradition of German Romanticism's desire for a harmony between the creative genius and the rational world, public space is represented as a dreamy part-paper, part-papercrete ambiguous space, which stirs the visual imagination.

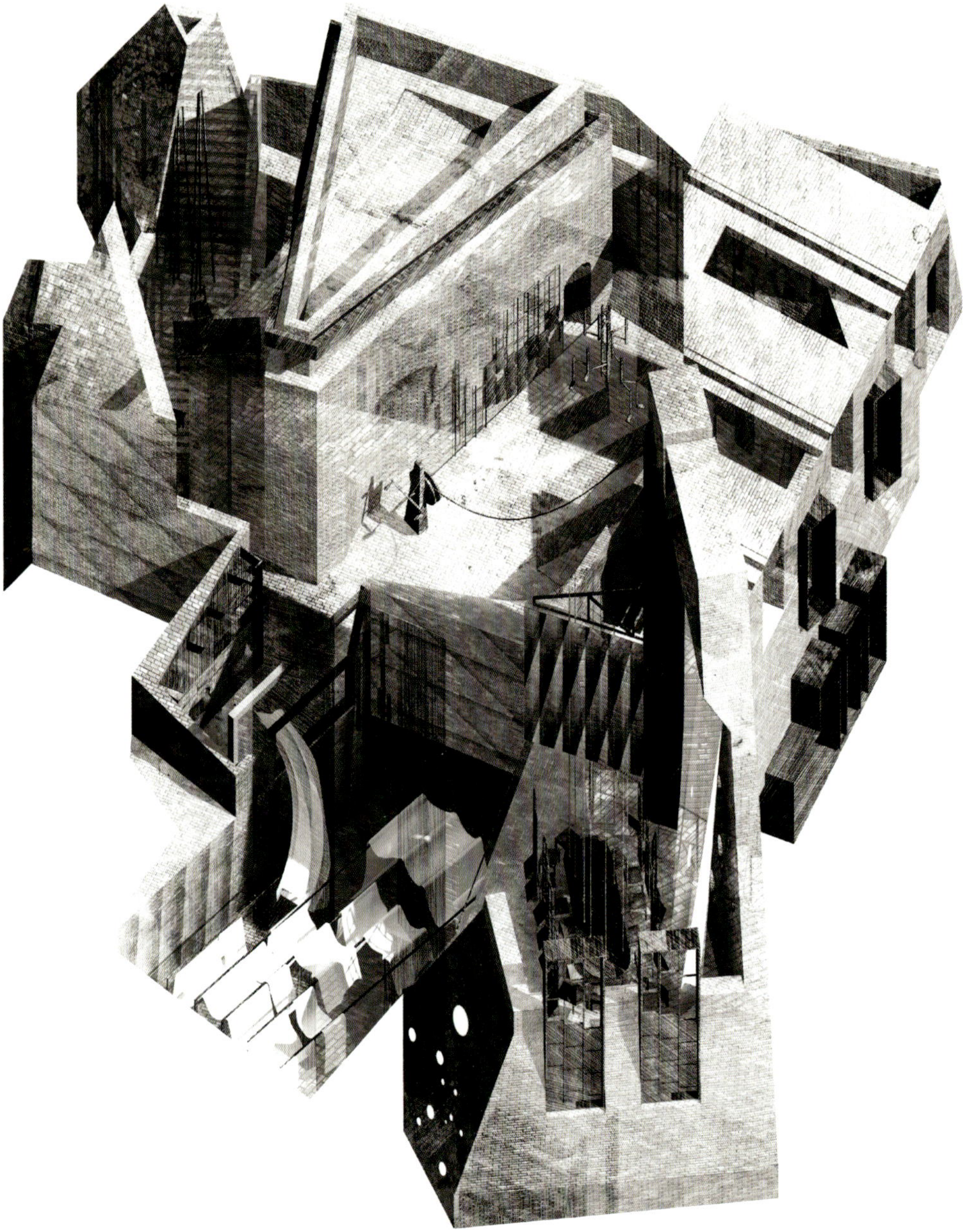

12.12

Fig. 12.12 Mihail Dinu Y5, 'EU Renegotiations Institute'. This project is concerned with the Union's Extended Process of Self-Inquiry initiated in the aftermath of the British EU Referendum. Its functions are housed within a parastatal architecture which manifests critical distancing through its campus layout. Material unity and the stereotomics of the fragments washed ashore by the flexing and convoluting of the Spree create an architecture of multiple localities within the city of Berlin.

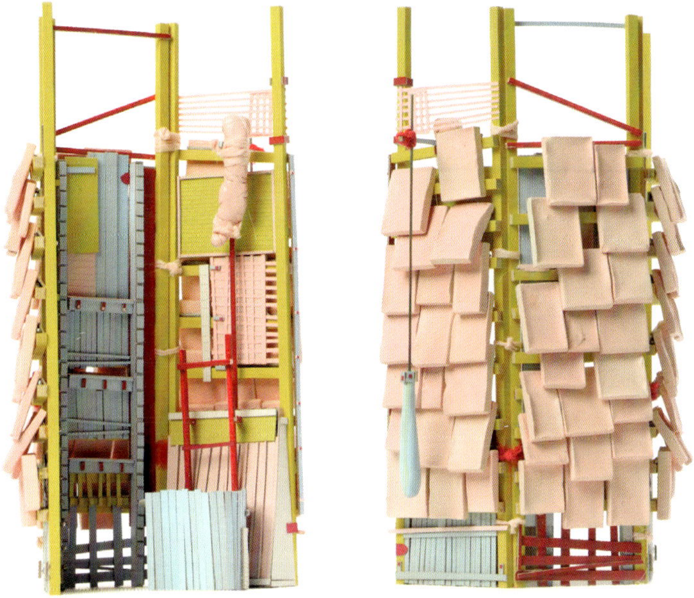

12.13

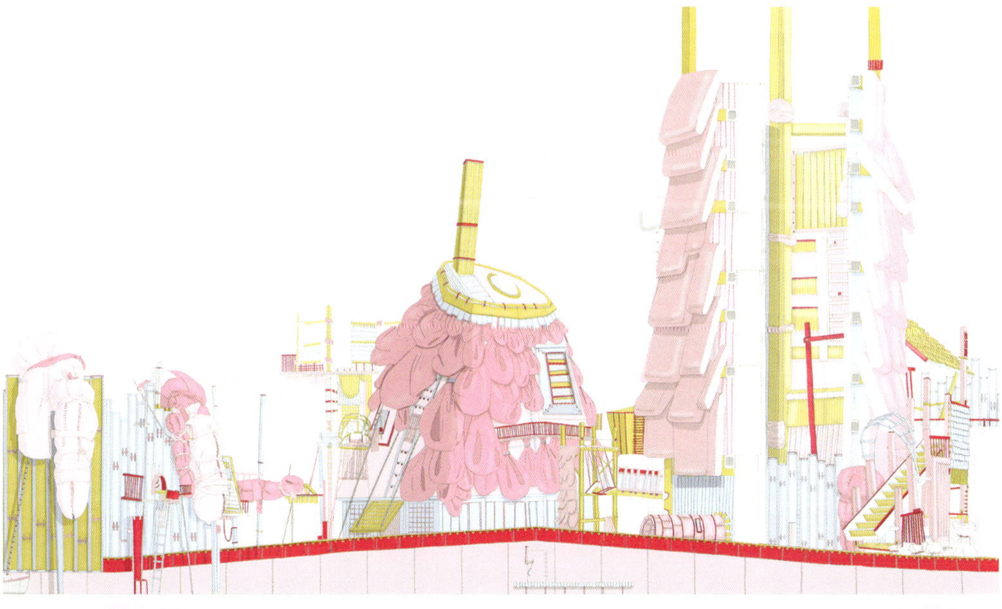

12.14

Figs. 12.13 – 12.14 Clare Hawes Y5, 'In the Pink: A New Headquarters for the United Nations'. Following the election of Donald Trump in November 2016, the future status of the United States within the United Nations has become uncertain. The project speculates on the relocation of the UN Headquarters from its existing location in New York to Lustgarten, Berlin. The project is an investigation into where the new headquarters should be located, what it should look like and how it might function.

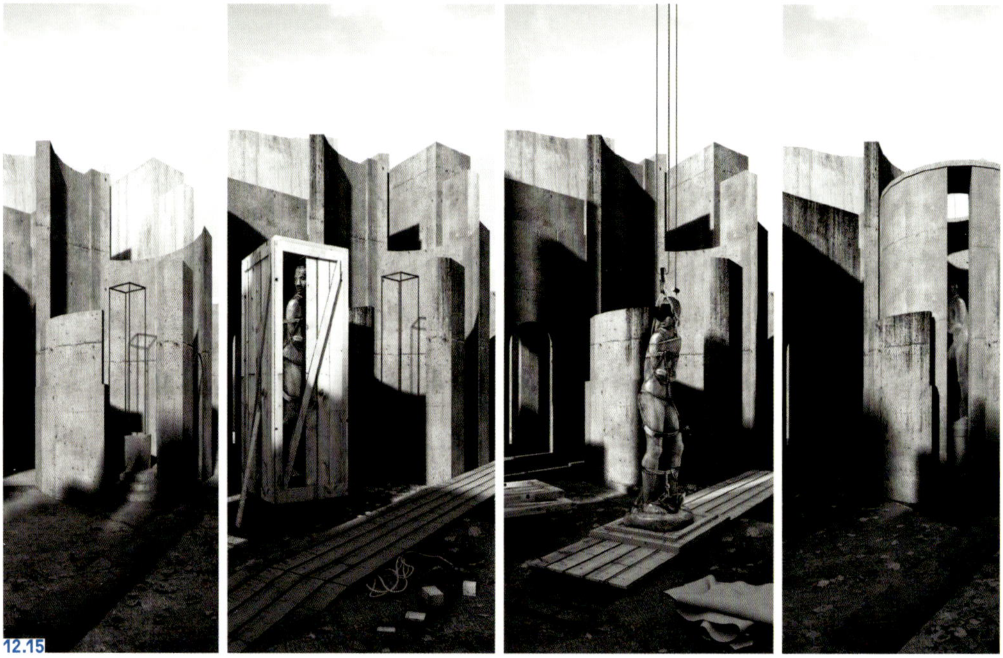

12.15

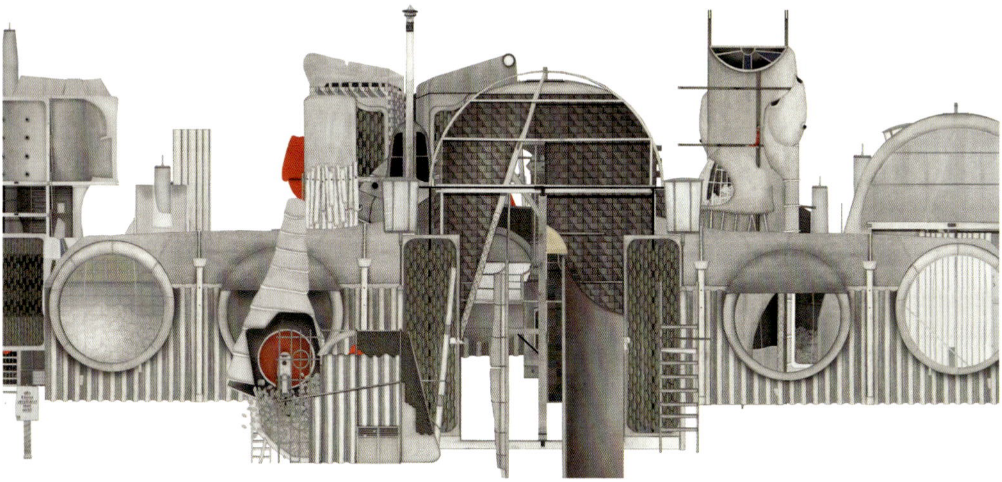

12.16

Fig. 12.15 Rawan Hussin Y5, 'The International Commission for Nazi-Looted Art'. The proposal is a response to the looting of art in Germany by Soviet forces after World War II, and its hardness is an analogue for its fleshy history. A new advisory body is responsible for investigating the war-related removal of cultural property under Soviet occupation, while housing a collection of objects that have been subject to illegal trafficking and destruction. **Fig. 12.16 Meya Tazi** Y5, 'Kreuzberg is Not Babylon: The Civil Defence Community of Kreuzberg'. The project becomes the symbol of its resilient and insurgent communities, a prototype of resistance against gentrification. An alternative ecological typology uses waste to counter the urban and anthropogenic crisis. An architecture of assemblage, as a barometer to the changing environment of Kreuzberg, destabilises the entrenched imagery of individualistic mastery and control of the mogul system. Kreuzberg's waste becomes its resource reservoir and resists its full domestication. **Fig. 12.17 Christia Angelidou** Y5, 'Four Journeys to 'New Hope', a School for Cypriot Peace Culture Education, in the Last Divided Capital: Nicosia, Cyprus'. The project attempts to restore peace in the island of Cyprus, by inviting people from both Greek and Turkish Cypriot communities to recognize their shared connections to existing places of division. Four journeys through four different parts of the school unfold temporal and physical locations of the past as a crucial means of creating understanding between the different groups of people.

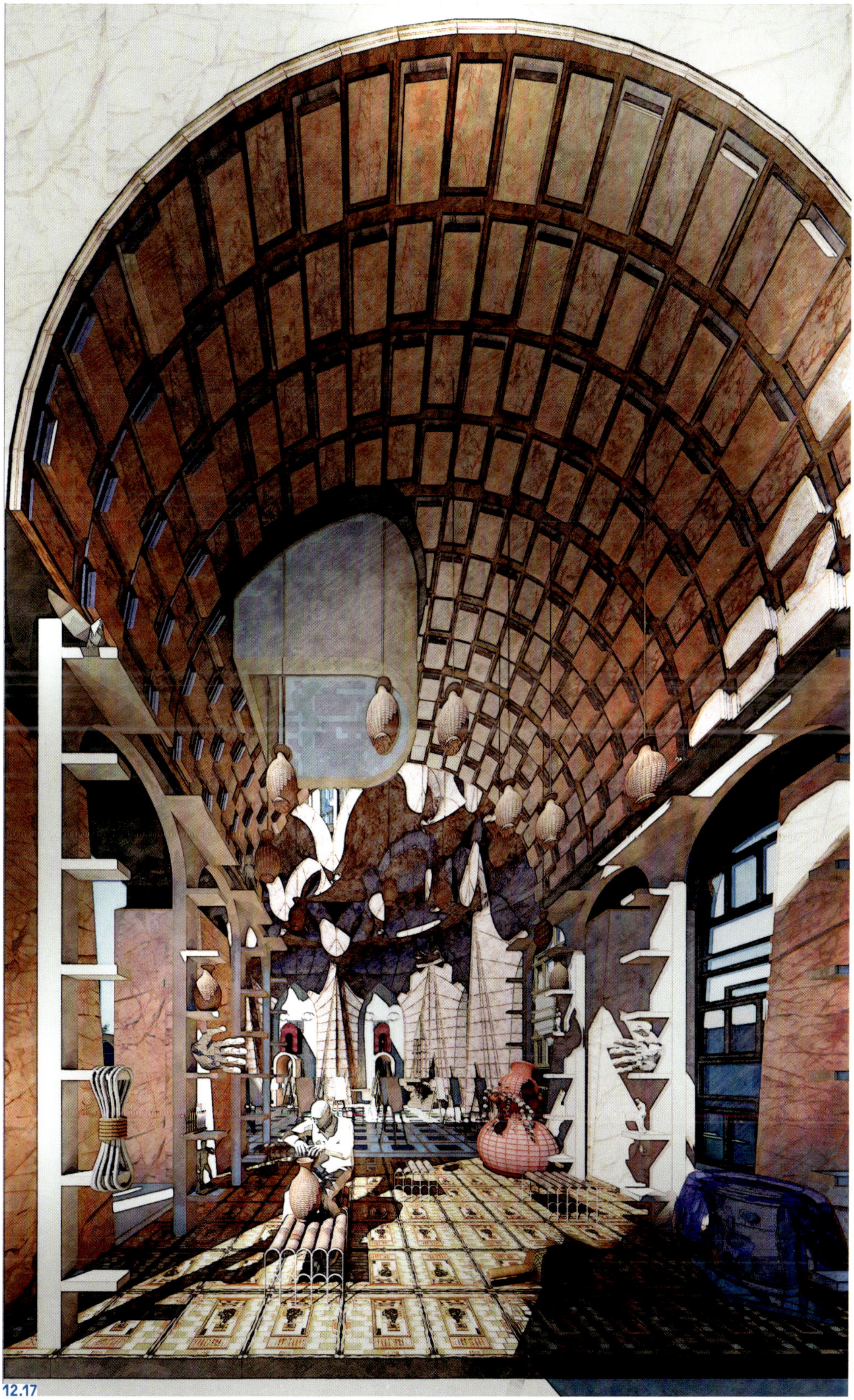

12.17

Unit 14 Disruptive Technology

Evan Greenberg, Dirk Krolikowski

Year 4
Ryan Blackford, Alexander Bramhill, George Courtauld, Maggie Lan, Natasha Marks, Christopher Singh, Yan Kee (Adrian) Siu, Thomas Smith, Joshua Thomson, Simon Wimble

Year 5
Joshua Honeysett, Yi Lu, Cassidy Reid, Anthony Williams, Jonathan Wren

Thank you to:
Andrew Abdulezer (Seth Stein Architects), Julia Backhaus (BSA), Barbara-Ann Campbell-Lange (Campbell-Lange Workshop), Mike Davies (Rogers Stirk Harbour + Partners), Xavier de Kestelier (Foster + Partners), Ryan Dillon (AA), Elif Erdine (AA), Damian Eley (ARUP), Ashley Fridd (BSA), Fernanda Fiuza (Rogers Stirk Harbour + Partners), Stephen Gage (BSA), Jan Güell (NIKKEN SEKKEI), Laura Hannigan (AKTII), Will Jefferies (Rogers Stirk Harbour + Partners), Alexandros Kallegias (Zaha Hadid Architects), Antiopi Koronaki (University of Bath), Guan Lee (BSA), Nacho Martí (AA), Jack Newton (Rogers Stirk Harbour + Partners), Mario Pirwitz (JSWD), Bob Sheil (BSA), Falko Schmitt (DKFS Architects), Alican Sungur (Pattern Architects), Marco Vanucci (AA), Michael Weinstock (AA)

Unit 14 is a test bed for exploration and innovation, examining the role of the architect in an environment of continuous change. We are in search of the new, leveraging technologies, workflows and modes of production seen in disciplines outside our own. We test ideas systematically by means of digital as well as physical drawings, models and prototypes. Our work evolves around technological speculation with a research-driven core, generating momentum through astute synthesis.

——Our propositions are ultimately made through the design of buildings and through the in-depth consideration of structural formation and tectonic constituents. This, coupled with a strong research ethos, has generated new proposals which are both viable and spectacular.

——This year, Unit 14 examined the way in which culture relates to technology and how technology is a constituent part as well as a driver for radical cultural change. As a laboratory for these investigations, Unit 14 situated itself within Europe and its rich and diverse cultural context. It is shaped by separation, unification and deformation as well as reformation – and at its core, humanist Renaissance thinking is embedded in its architecture, traditions and progress. Thriving on competent research, the rich cultural environment of Europe, as well as speculation and vision, we accept that technology changes the way we think, live and work.

——To probe Europe's rich cultural legacy, we travelled to Vienna, the heart of Central Europe and what was once the capital of the Austro-Hungarian Empire. From Vienna's central station, we departed late at night via a sleeper train, riding through the Czech Republic and Slovakia to wake up in Krakow, the intellectual centre of Poland, deeply embedded within the continent, in search of the wild and wonderful, the scientific and science fictional.

——While we dream of the unexpected we pursue innovation as part of our culture, and in doing so we create architectures which have the potential to disrupt and augment what we think we know about Europe.

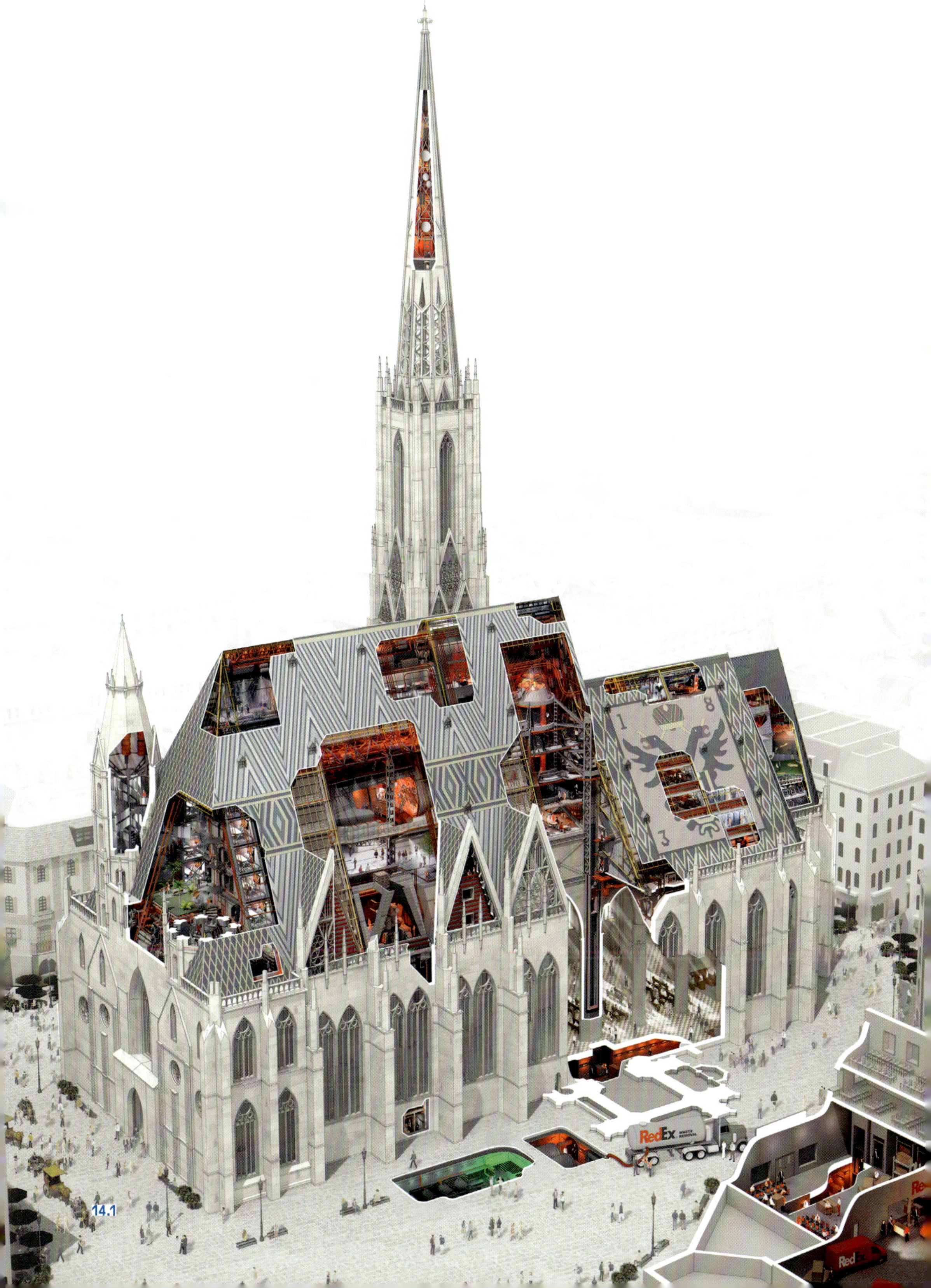
14.1
RedEx

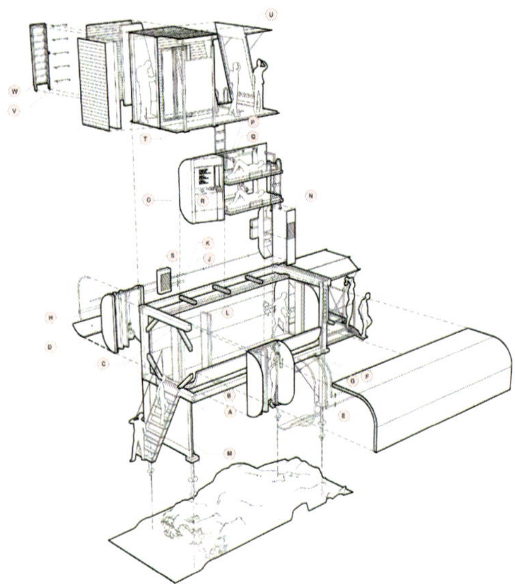

14.2

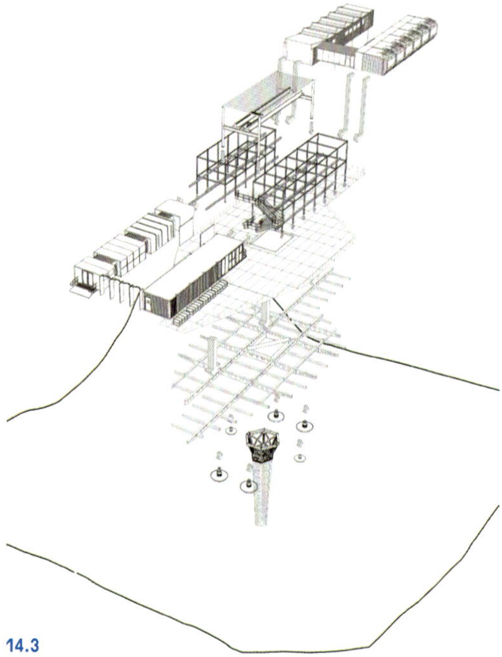

14.3

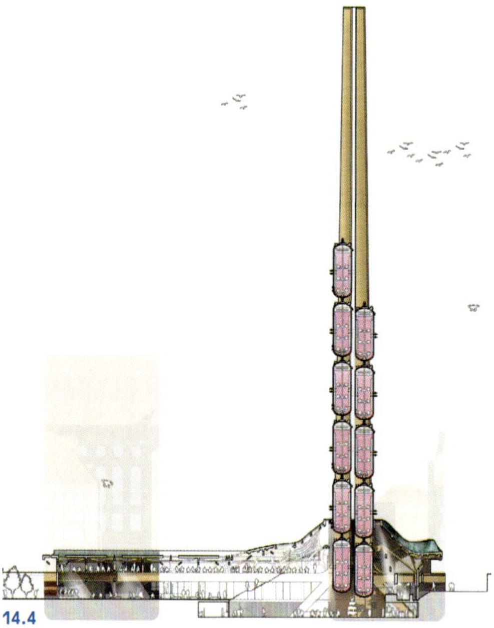

14.4

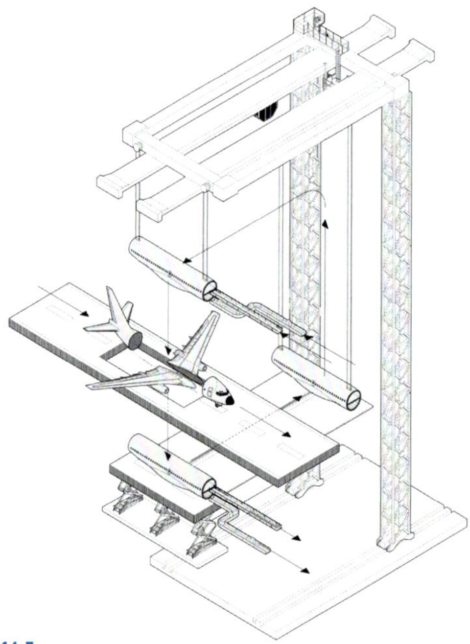

14.5

Fig. 14.1 **Ryan Blackford** Y4, 'Motherboard Russia'. A proposal for a Russian state-sponsored cyber operations centre, tasked with disrupting Europe's political landscape through fake news, hack attacks and phishing scams on an unprecedented scale. Through a covert occupation of Vienna's most iconic landmark, the operation combines the notion of 'hacking' as a contemporary political strategy with 'hacking' as a spatial strategy for architectural intervention. **Fig. 14.2** **Natasha Marks** Y4, 'High Altitude Training Basecamp'. Located at 3,700m in the Sierra Nevada mountains of Spain, the Civil Guards use the camp to increase their fitness through a series of hypoxic (low oxygen) environments. Each of these is serviced by a robotic care compartment to assist and monitor the Guards in this extreme location. **Fig. 14.3** **Maggie Lan** Y4, 'Swiss Glaciology Base Station'. Situated on the fastest retreating glacier in Switzerland, the Great Aletsch Glacier. The building will work in conjunction with GLAMOS to better understand the connections between glaciers and the global climate system by analysing ice core samples and investigating the interactions between the glacial ice and the glacier bed. **Fig. 14.4** **Anthony Williams** Y5, 'Cultured [Meat]ropolis'. The project embraces and celebrates a widespread overconsumption of meat by integrating the innovative and sustainable technology of biofabrication into our urban centres. Using Munich as a prototype, we will redefine regional food production through the introduction of a new urban meat-producing typology: the 'Brathaus'. **Fig. 14.5** **Thomas Smith** Y4, 'Oslo City Airport'. The project proposes a new type of airport for Oslo city centre.

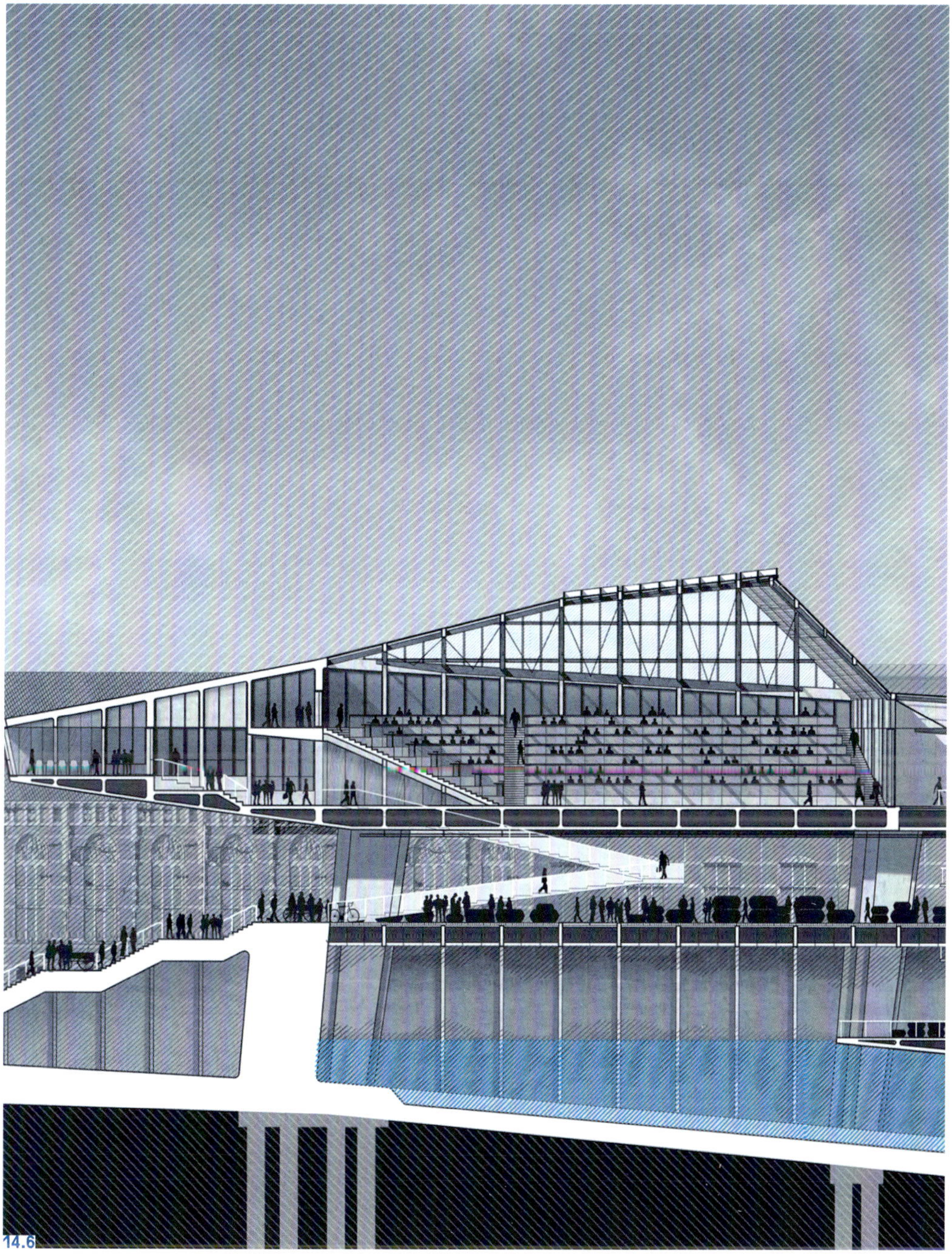

14.6

The airport is based on speculations around two patents released by Boeing in 2016, which allow the airport to move into Oslo city centre and become part of the public realm. **Fig. 14.6 Simon Wimble** Y4, 'Water from Amsterdam'. Desalinating sea water in a context of fresh water scarcity is an opportunity for the Dutch to utilise a new agricultural landscape when 55% of their land is lost to the rise in sea levels. This commodity is traded in the Amsterdam Watermarkt, where the Dutch cultural traditions of markets and commerce define the architectural intervention.

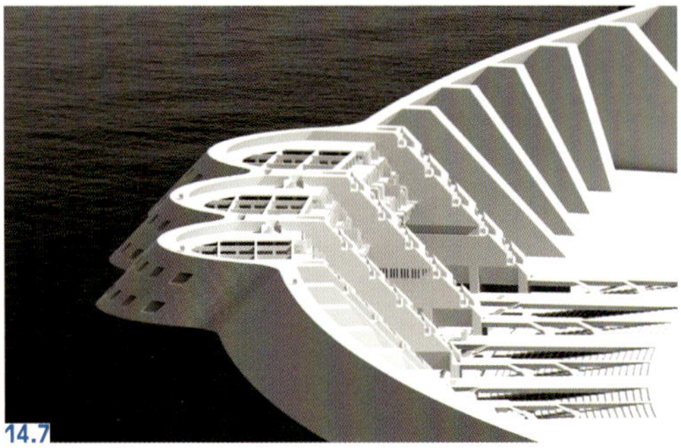

14.7

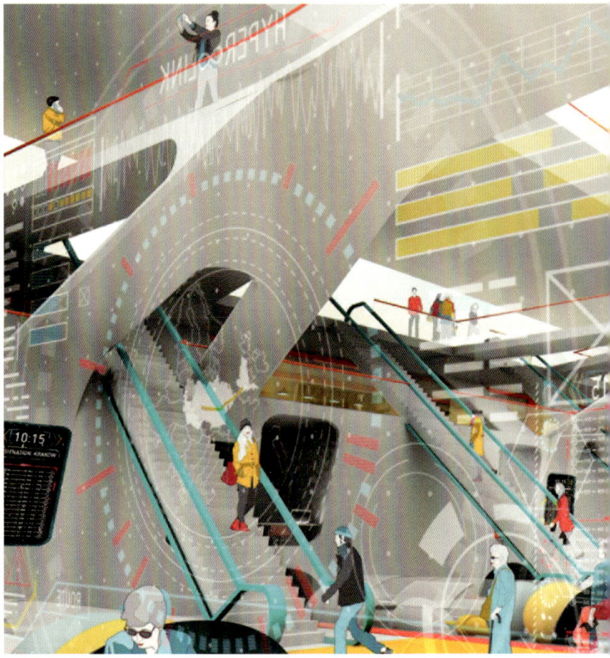

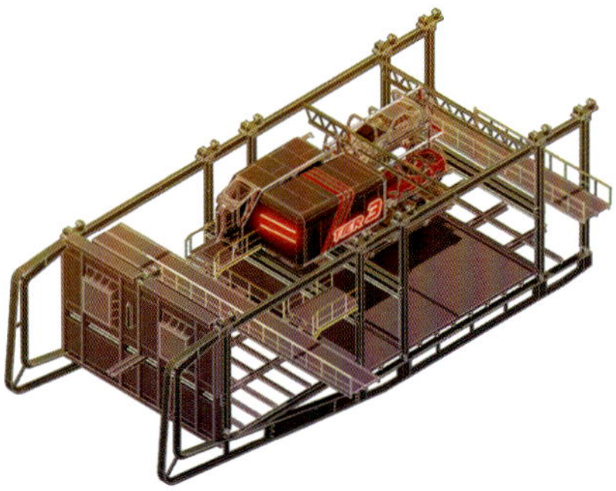

14.8

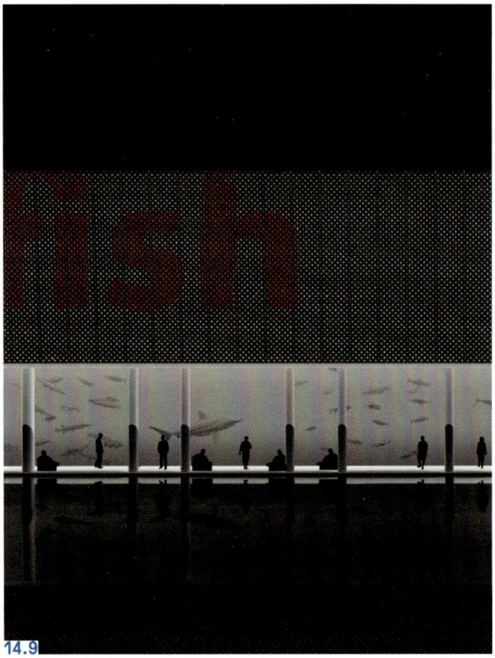

14.9

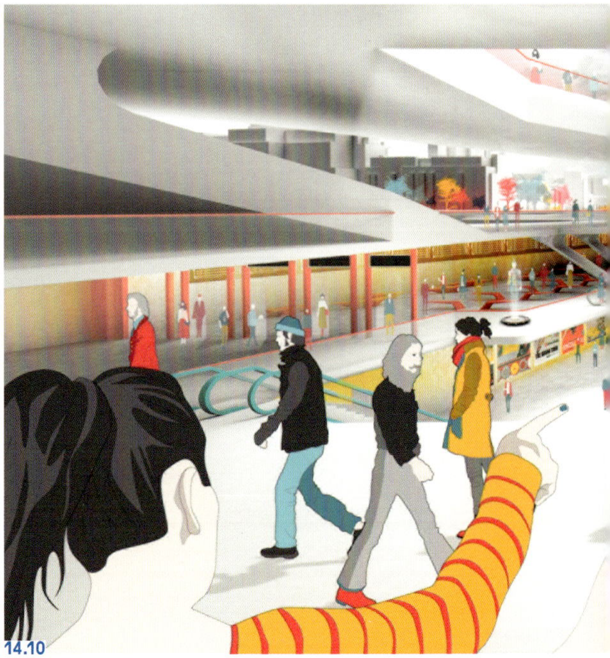

14.10

Fig. 14.7 Joshua Thomson Y4, 'Doggerbank: Le Grand Projet'. A 'Grand Project' for Europe to reveal the historic lost land of Doggerbank and provide the home for a newly reformed and united EU. **Fig. 14.8 Yan Kee (Adrian) Siu** Y4, 'Autonomous Anonymous: Sanctuary for the Petrolheads'. Under the dominance of autonomous vehicles in 2030, petrolheads in Cologne hijack the proposed carport as their secret sanctuary to worship petrol automobiles and rebel against the ban of combustion engines in Germany. **Fig. 14.9 Jonathan Wren** Y5, 'Swissfish'. Swissfish is an Alpine fishery and genebank, responding to uniquely Swiss environmental conditions, such as water security and fish altitude migration. The dismantable building aims to ensure sustainable and economic methods of food production, whilst using Switzerland's waterways for fish distribution and building relocation. **Fig. 14.10 Cassidy Reid** Y5, 'Pan-European Corridor'. The design proposal aims to uncover and enhance Europe's cultural corridor. By leveraging highly efficient technology, the Hyperloop will enable this corridor to become easily accessible. This route will in turn have the potential to become Europe's backbone of free trade and free movement.

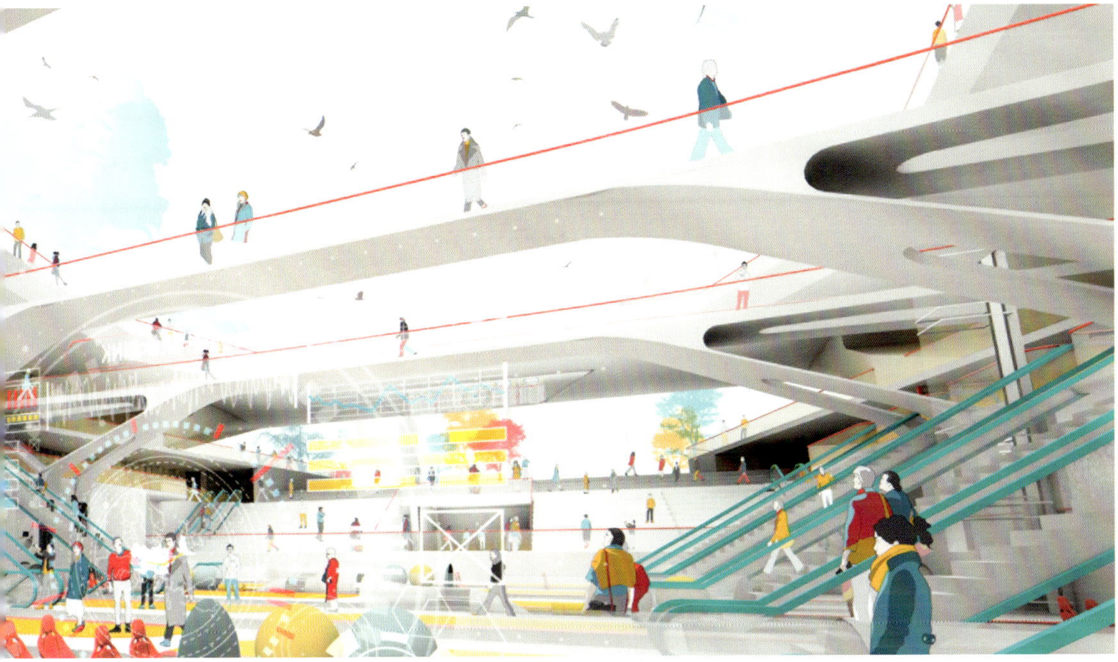

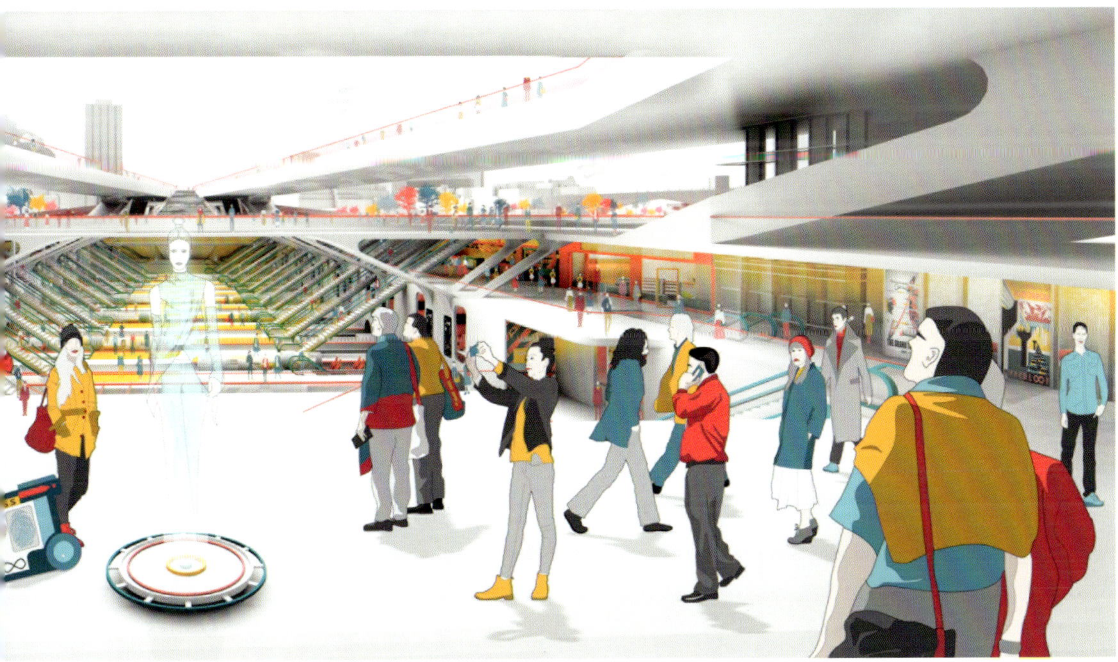

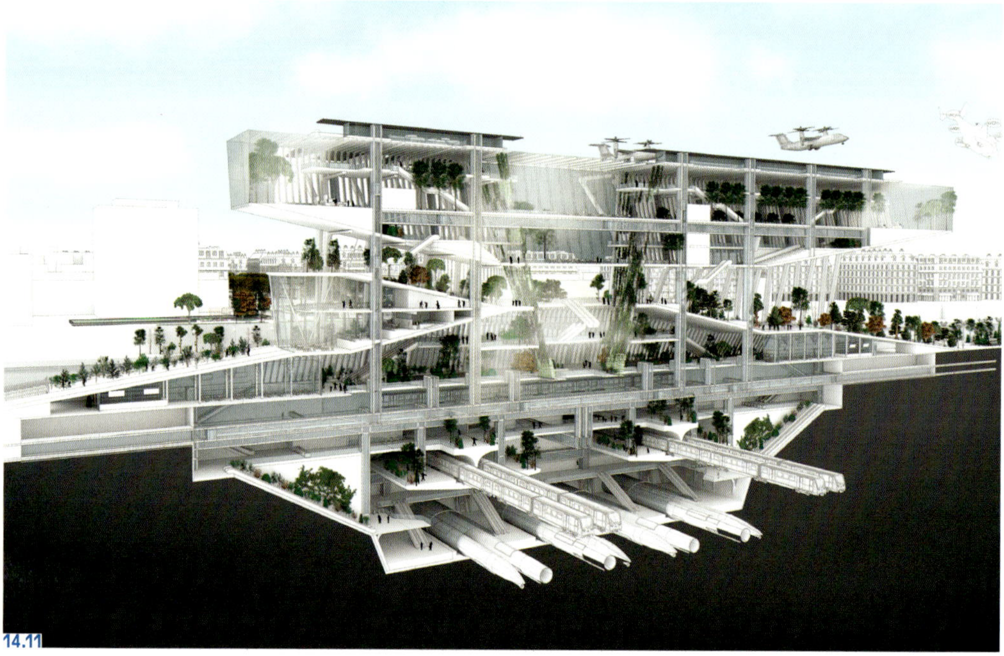

14.11

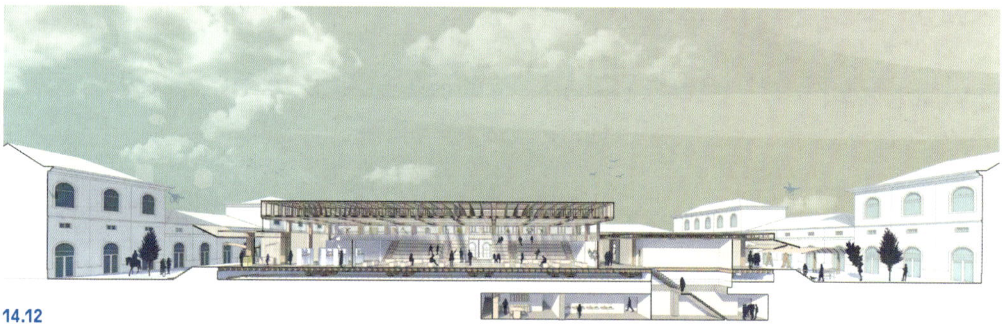

14.12

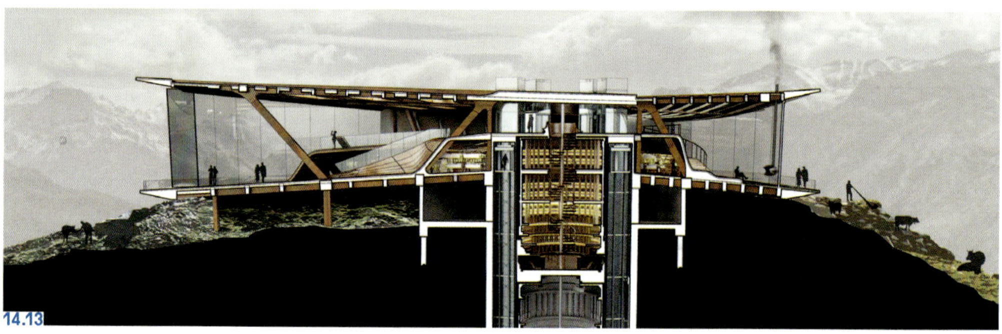

14.13

Fig. 14.11 Joshua Honeysett Y5, 'Paris Interchange, 2054'. The project speculates on a radical future for urban transportation in Paris. It envisions a world where cars and elevators have become streamlined into a singular multi-directional elevator network, VTOL aircrafts have become commercially viable, and the Hyperloop has been realised. The extensive transport network is housed underground, freeing the streets of Paris to become landscaped public space/parks. **Fig. 14.12 Alex Bramhill** Y4, 'Il Viaggio Nella Democrazia (The Journey Into Democracy)'. 'The Journey into Democracy' explores the reformation of the corrupt Italian political system through the creation of a mobile political vessel. This new travelling 'direct democracy' vessel places power into the hands of the populace, addressing how to retain Italy's national identity whilst undergoing political devolution. **Fig. 14.13 Christopher Singh** Y4, 'The Porta Alpina Revival'. A prototype transport hub as part of a wider sub-Alpine transportation network, made possible by advanced excavation technologies – a vehicle for the democratisation of the Alps.

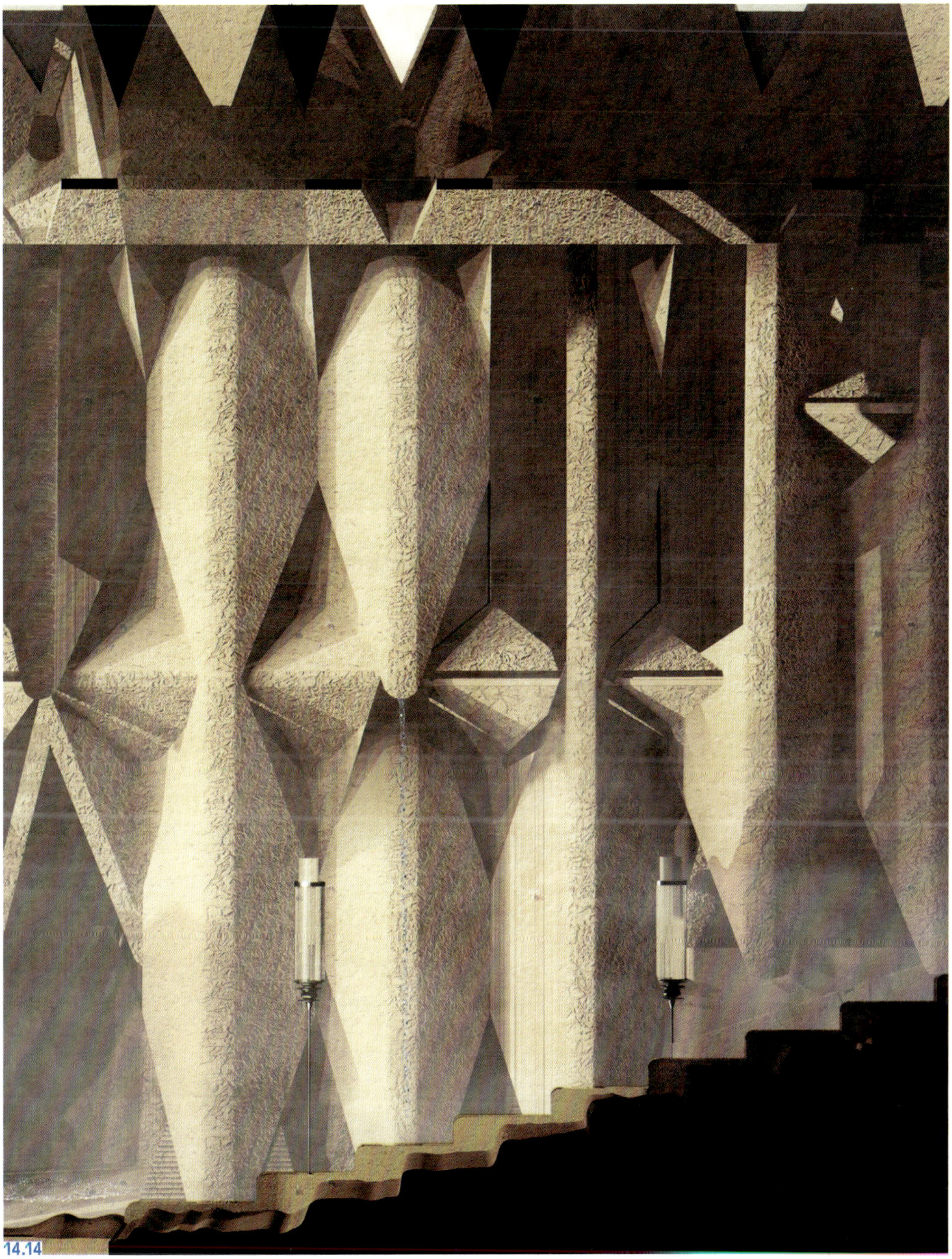

14.14

Fig. 14.14 Yi Lu Y5, 'Prototype for a Clay Village'. Using clay through innovative folding techniques, 'Prototype for a Clay Village', situated in Valencia, Spain, challenges the image of traditional clay building and introduces architecture through innovative form and environmental performance. **Fig. 14.15 George Courtauld** Y4, 'Opera / Night Club'. Music has always been about the communal act of sharing ideas and experiences. In a time when we are losing cultural infrastructure, this project aims to tap into the democratisation of music, culture and our city streets through technology.

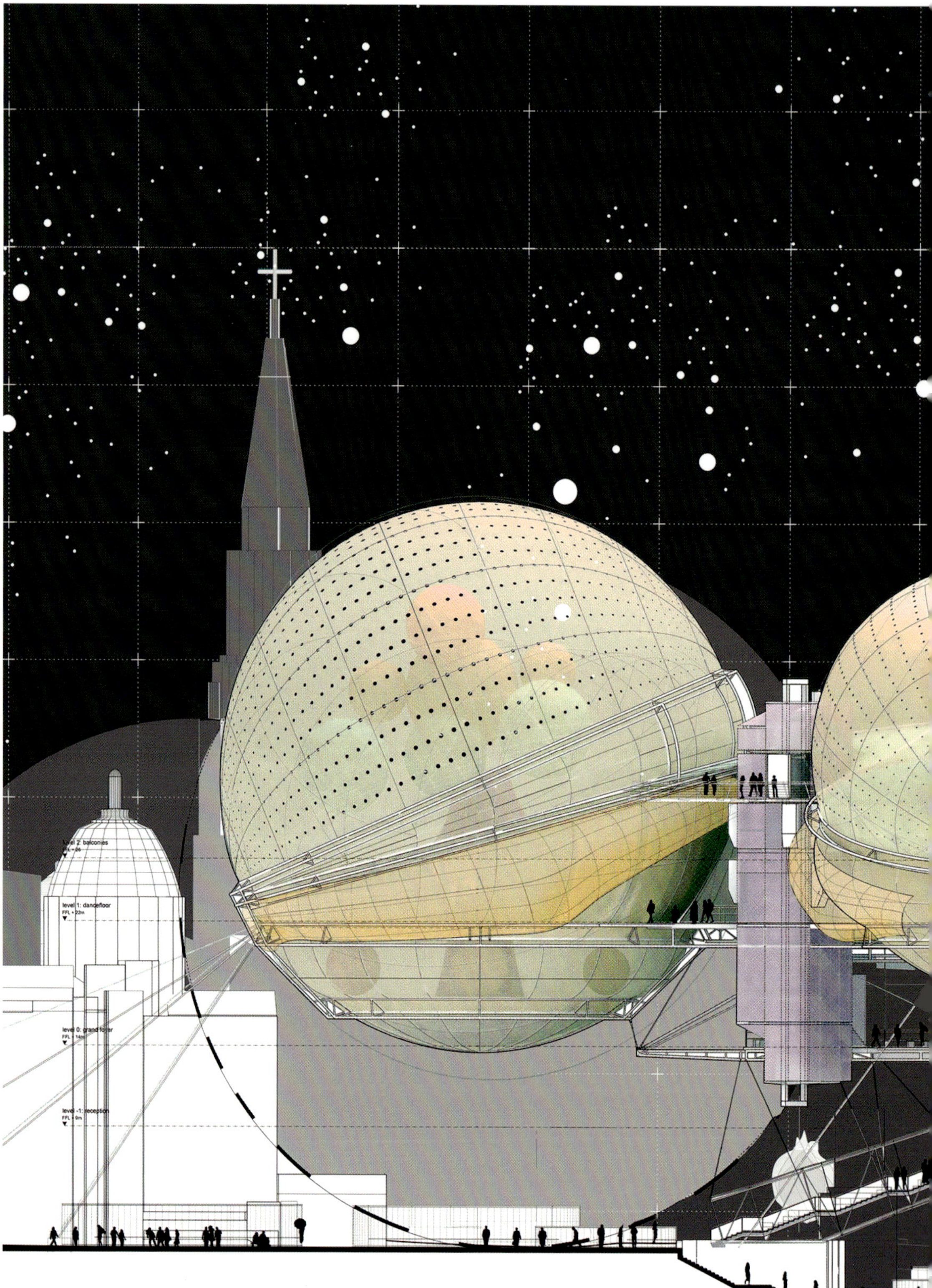
level 2: balconies
level 1: dancefloor
FFL + 22m
level 0: grand foyer
level -1: reception
FFL + 9m

14.15

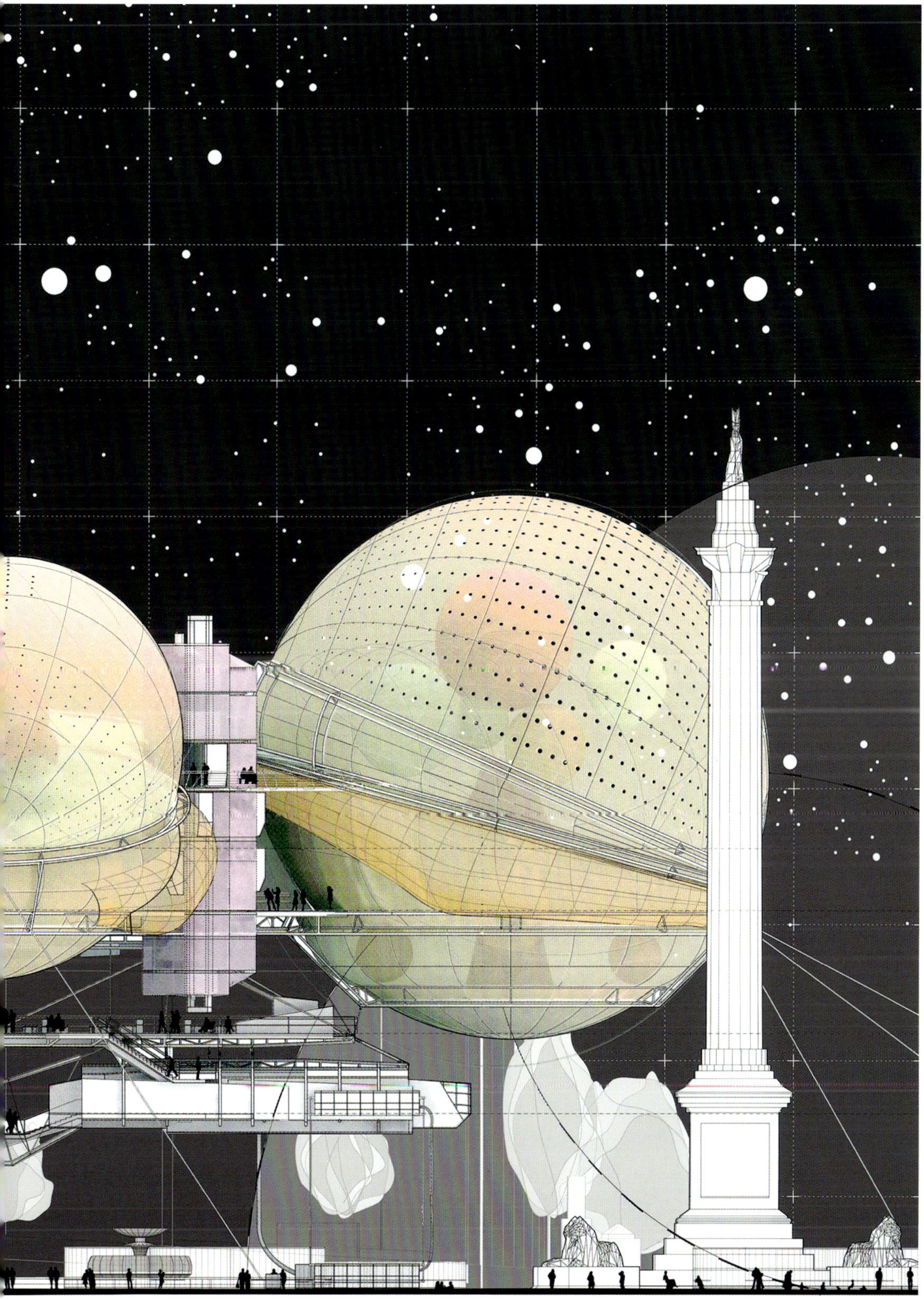

Unit 15 On the Edge

Maximiliano Arrocet, Alice Dietsch, Amanda Levete, Ho-Yin Ng, Raffael Petrovic

Year 4
Josh Corfield, Paddy Fernandez, Stefan Necula, Katriona Eleni Pillay, Wonseok Woo

Year 5
Qiuling Guan, Jiatong Hu, Yue Ma, Sachi Oberoi, Bethany Penman, Henry Schofield, Zuzana Sojkova

Thank you to Ed Clark

Unit 15 explores the identity of places and how the transformation of a piece of city can be brought about by buildings that are rooted in their place. Our projects are driven by research into geographical, cultural and economic contexts in order to create a sense of place and community. We investigate the intersections between craftsmanship, volume production and innovative digital design tools, alongside the role narrative plays in designing a building.

——This year's projects are set in Lisbon. The city's geography is beguiling: seven hills reveal dramatic vistas at every street corner, the Tagus estuary promises so much and the line at which river becomes ocean is palpable. Lisbon's position on the edge of Europe has shaped its identity, its architecture and the civic sensibilities of Lisboetas. Rather than being mired in European affairs, Lisbon has always looked outwards, towards the sea - towards Africa, South America and Asia. The city is an expression of its inhabitants and their relationship not only to the sea but also to history and craft: from *calçada* pavements to the *azulejos*, the predominantly blue-and-white ceramic tiles that decorate countless walls of everything from churches to bars. Lisbon is both high-octane and relaxed; it is young and diverse, tolerant and affordable, and washed in a sublime light.

——Today, the riverside edges of Lisbon, from where the great explorers set off, are disconnected from the city and its hills. We propose buildings that reconnect the city to its riverfront. The projects are located along Lisbon's Arco Ribeirinho, stretching from the EXPO '98 site in the north to the Torre de Belém in the southeast.

——On our field trip, we travelled from Porto to Lisbon, investigating both cities' distinct relationships with their respective rivers, the Douro and the Tagus. We visited key buildings along our journey including the Leça Swimming Pools by Alvaro Siza, the Casa da Musica by OMA and the recently completed MAAT museum. We exchanged ideas with Afaconsult, the engineers behind Eduardo Souto de Moura's Braga stadium, and Aires Mateus, the architects who designed EDP's Lisbon headquarters.

——Students conceived their individual projects through an intensive exploration of Lisbon's cultural, historical and physical topography. Proposals vary in scale from urban projects that look at larger parts of the city down to individual buildings which are tightly integrated into their surroundings. Together, they create a vision for a Lisbon newly reconnected to its waterfront and redefine a city's 21st-century relationship to its river.

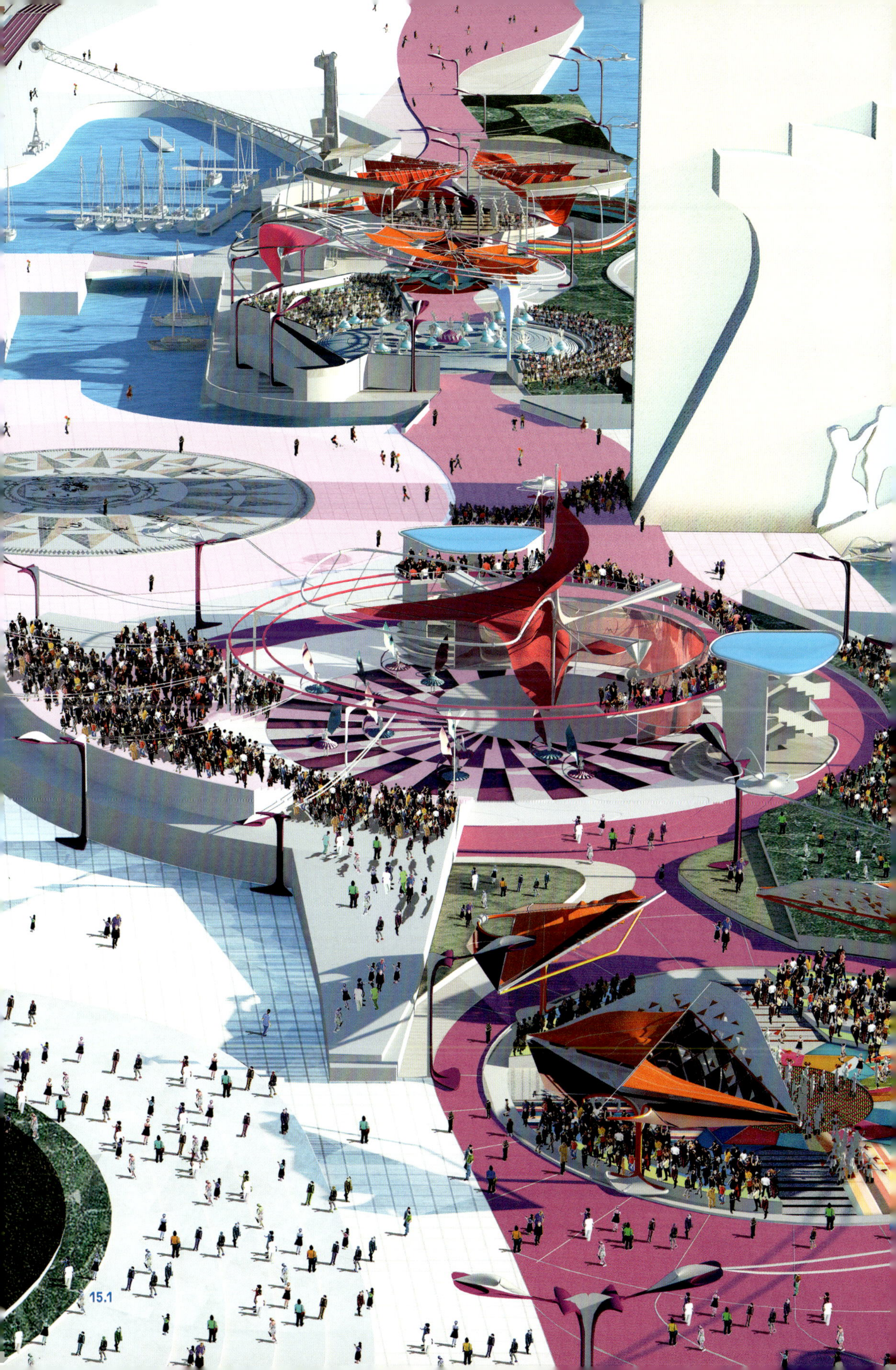
15.1

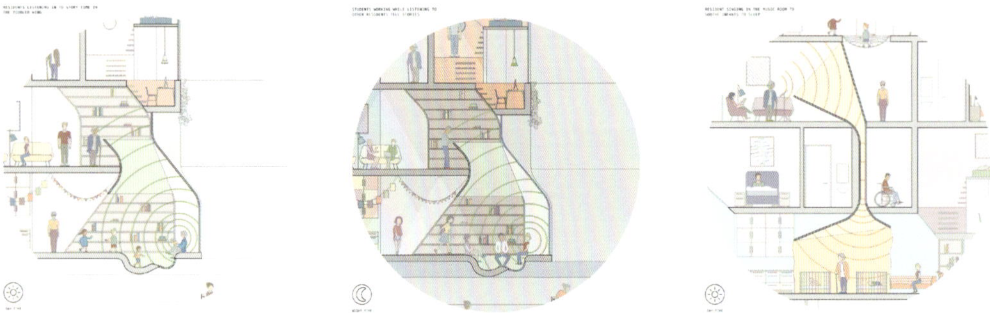

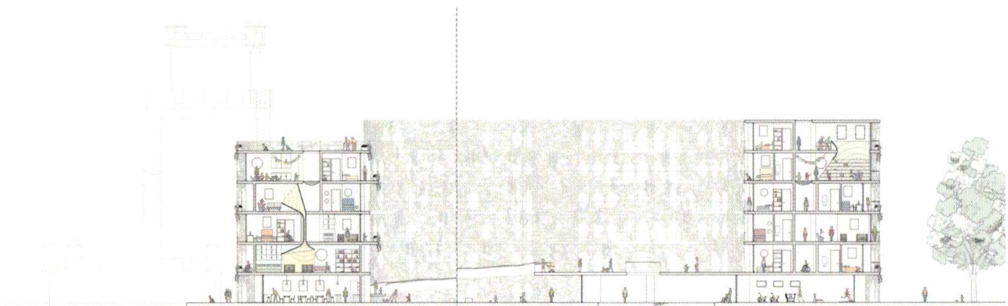

15.2

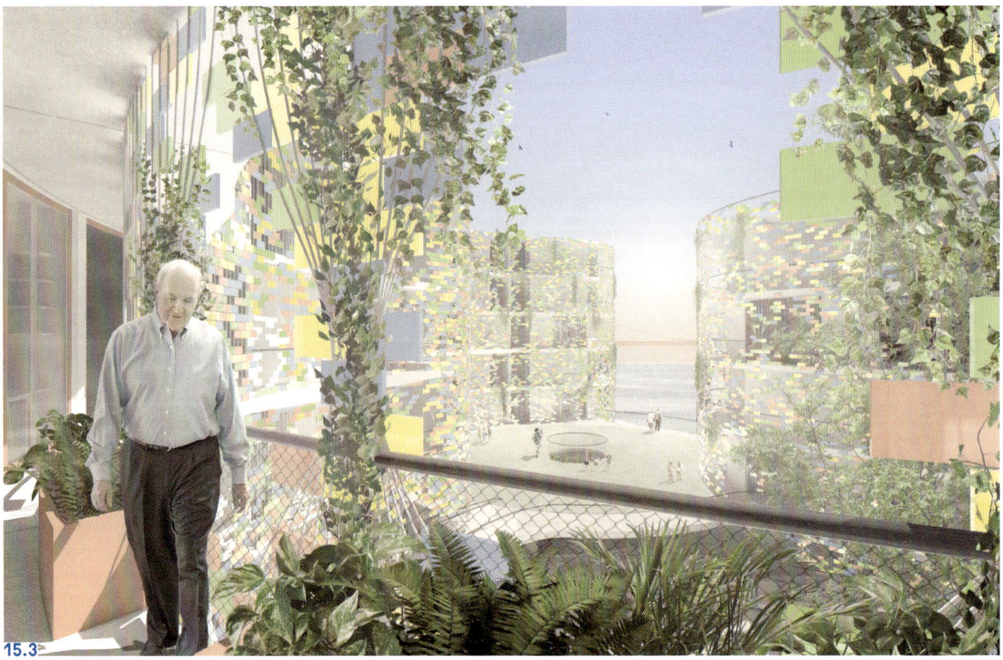

15.3

Fig. 15.1 Henry Schofield Y5, Lisbon's 'Belem Four Dances' masterplan acknowledges the existence of three of the city's most prominent former colonies: Brazil, Angola and Mozambique, which all share exquisite carnival, theatrical and dance heritages. The masterplan creates a new common ground in Lisbon within which performance art becomes the daily programme of the site and a place of expression for marginalised Africans and Brazilians who have been displaced by postcolonial Portuguese society. The masterplan is a series of four pavilions, meeting spaces or carnival arenas amassed within an urban project which speaks of the typological nature of each country's national dance. The scheme aims to regenerate Belem's waterfront promenade by reconciling the divide created by an eight-lane road and railway line.

Figs. 15.2 – 15.3 Bethany Penman Y5, The 'Belem Intergenerational Residence and Pre-School' socially integrates generations. The project aims to address the needs of an ageing population while also addressing the care concerns of the elderly and the young. The building combines three typologies: a nursing home, a student halls of residence and a pre-school, to form a new typology. During the day, the pre-school provides opportunities for the elderly residents to interact with young children. At night, student residents socialise with their elderly neighbours. There are many recognised health and social benefits of intergenerational programmes, such as increased self-worth and a decline in depression. Engaging spatial layouts and circulation routes aim to highlight and encourage the mingling of these three groups.

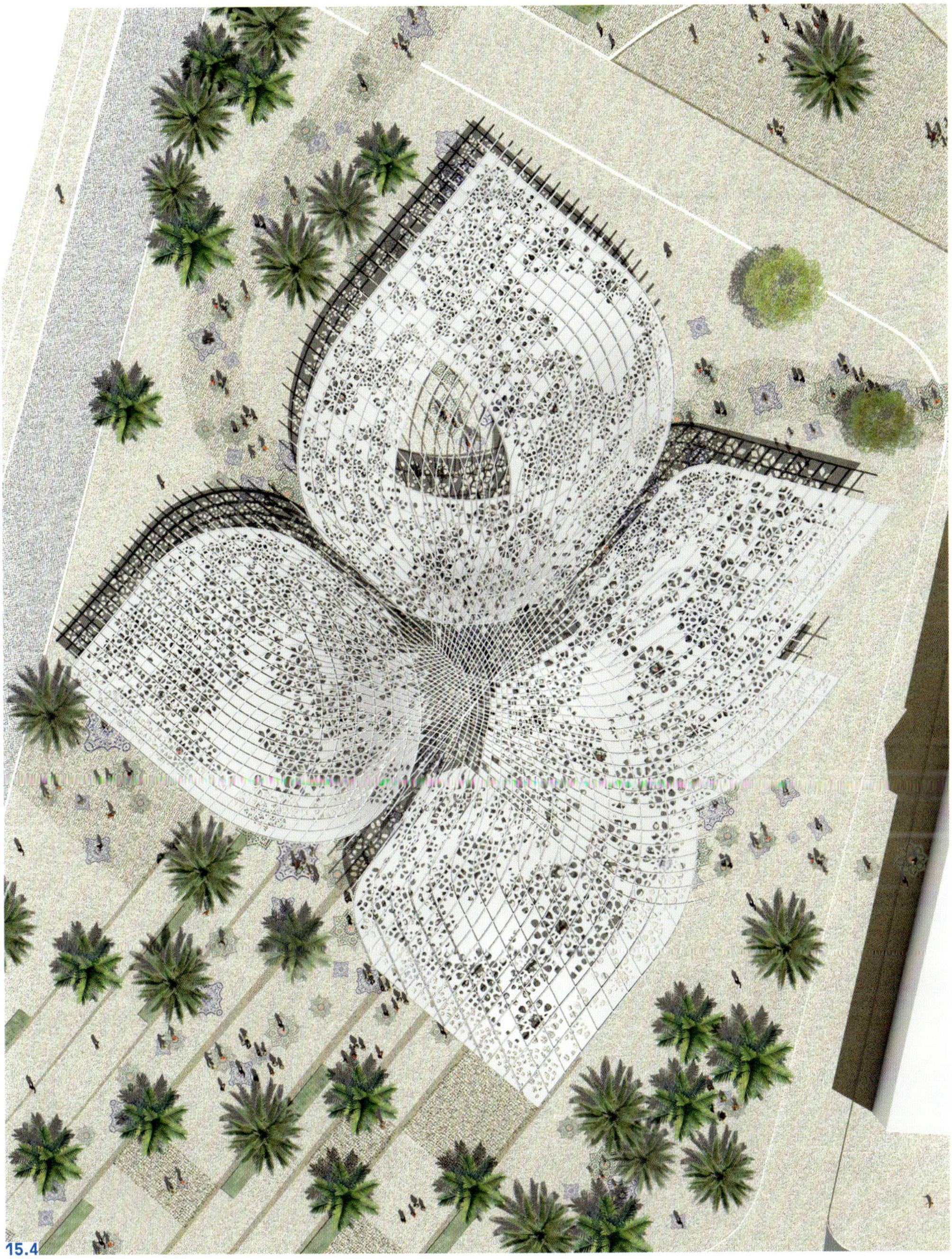

15.4

Fig. 15.4 Josh Corfield Y4, 'Cultural Exchange'. The Cultural Exchange represents a new chapter in Lisbon's rich history of multiculturalism and outward acceptance. United beneath an overarching roof that reveals a canvas where interaction and integration can happen below, a non-verbal exchange between two cultures is promoted through key cultural platforms that epitomise a national identity – dance, food, music and craft. The roof represents a social catalyst that aims to ignite and foster understanding between different nations, playing an active role in establishing new relationships and cultural awareness. The proposal is an extension of Lisbon's urban realm, delineating a vibrant new public centre in the city.
Fig. 15.5 Paddy Fernandez Y4, 'The Entrepreneurs' City'. The project rethinks the relationship between a workplace and the city in the age of digital technology. The proposed space is dynamic and energetic. Each work cluster is staggered to provide unique sightlines throughout the building and out to the city and the Tagus River. The project explores how an architecture can influence behaviour and how the delicate mechanics of the city already contribute to the patterns and interactions of its users.

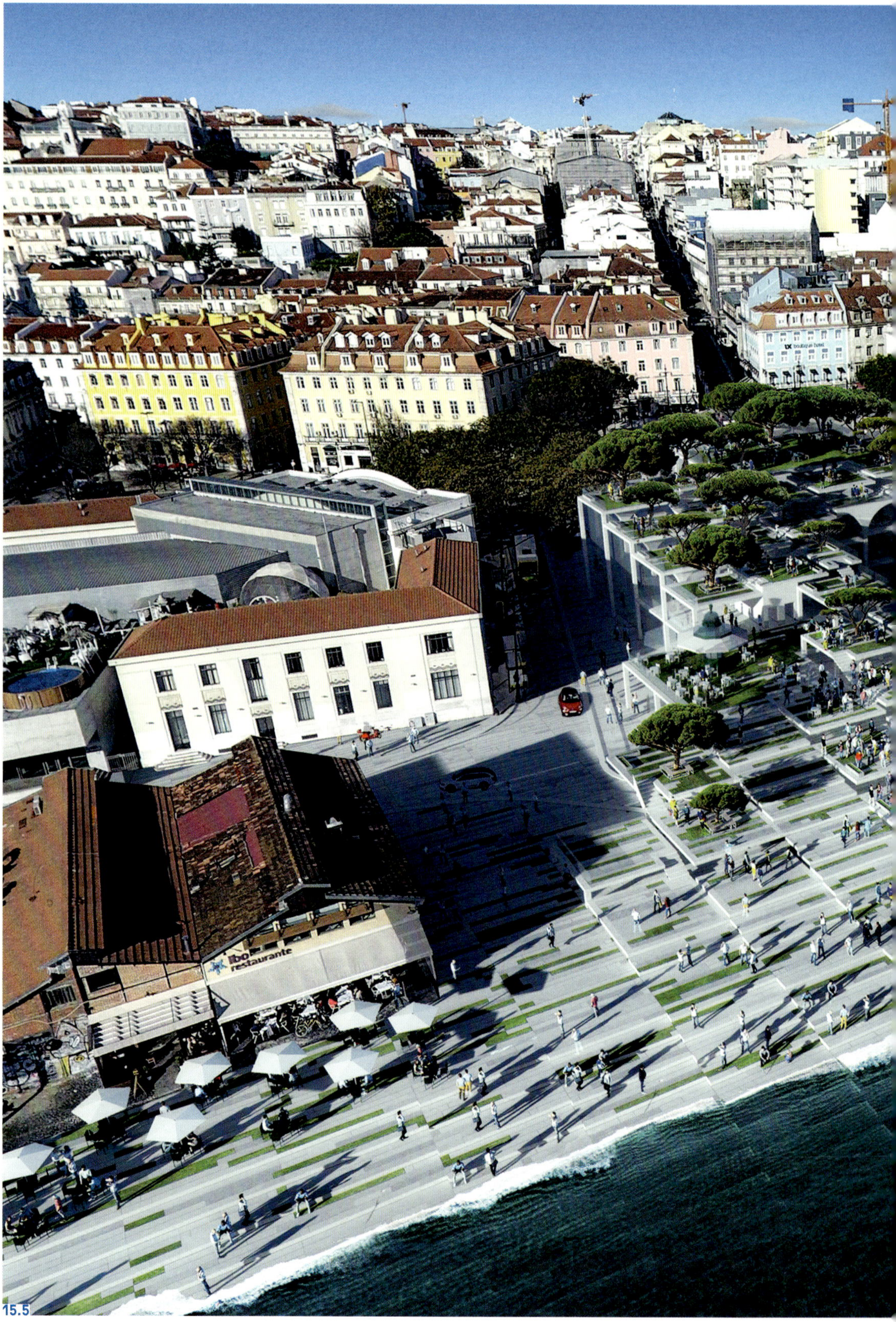

15.5

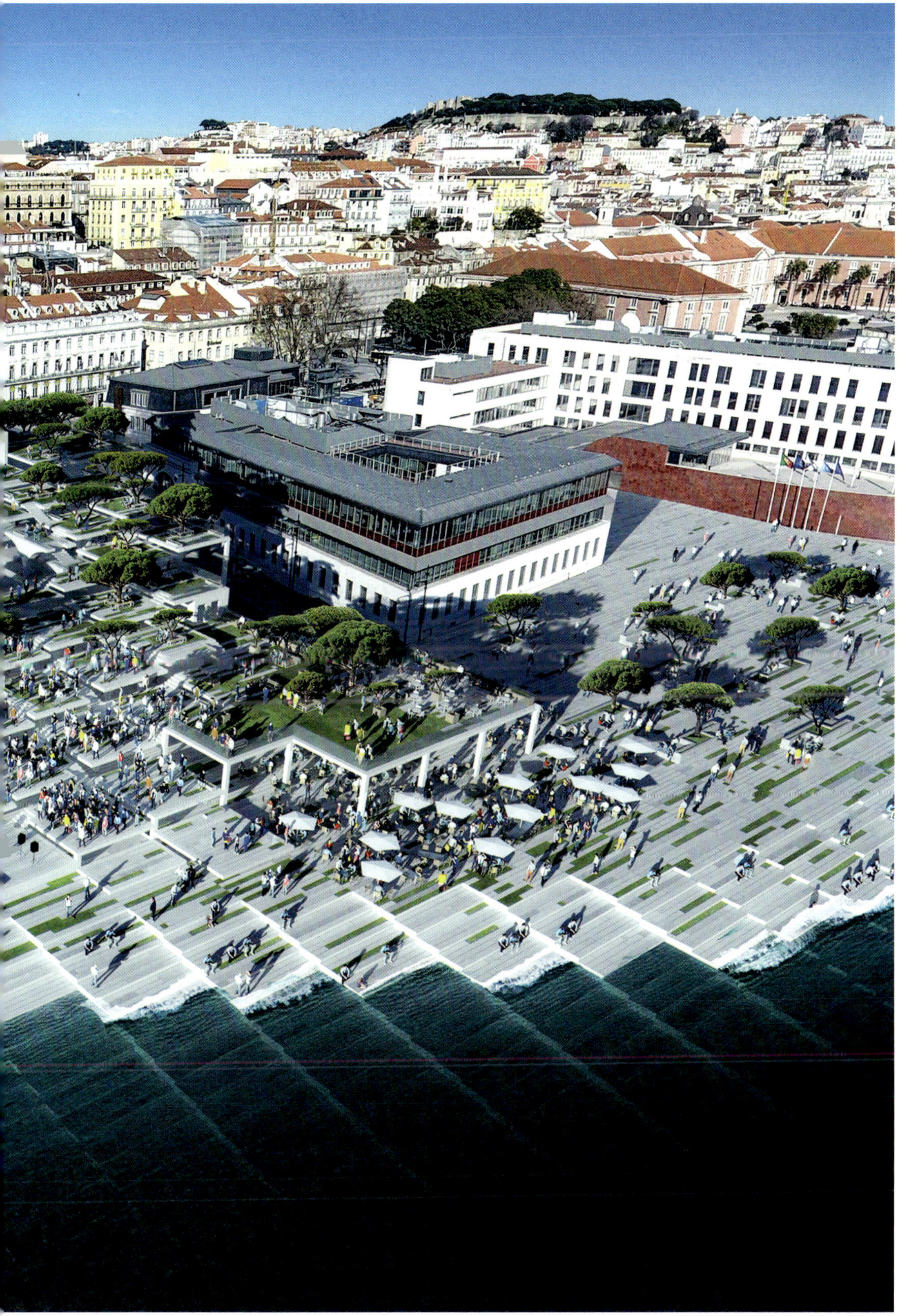

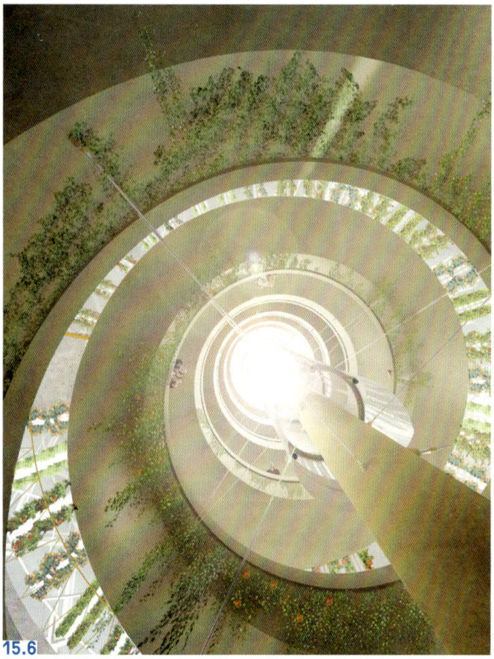

15.6

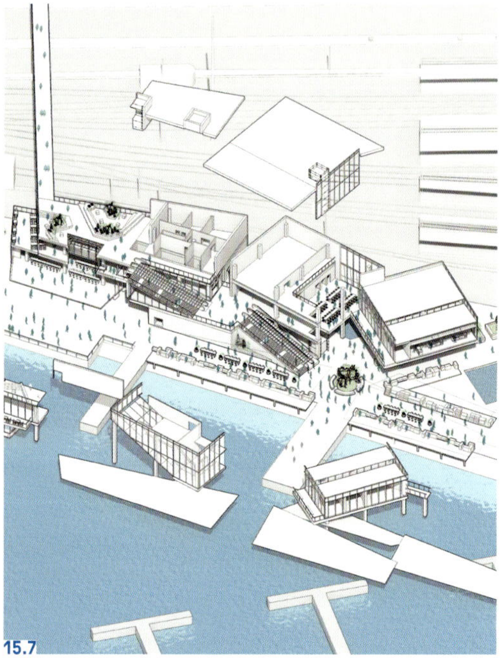

15.7

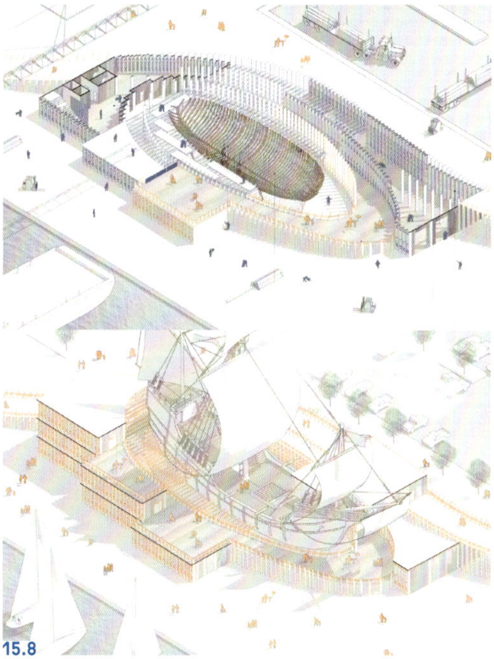

15.8

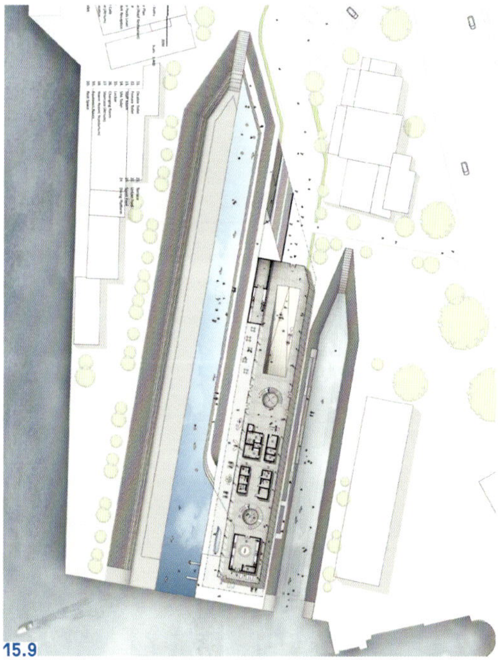

15.9

Fig. 15.6 Stefan Necula Y4, 'Silo Vivo'. One of Lisbon's most striking features is its southern light, which results in a pleasant climate all year long. The project aims to harness these natural elements as a design driver. It proposes to convert an existing industrial silo into a hydroponic farm which houses a seafood restaurant on its ground floor. The building's internal ecosystem is designed to maximise yield while keeping waste production and energy consumption to a minimum. Thus, the 1,200m² of growing area can produce the ingredients for 350 restaurant meals a day. **Fig. 15.7 Jiatong Hu** Y5, 'Lisbon School of Seafood'. Fishing has always been a major part of the Portuguese economy. Lisbon's coastline used to be populated with docks for fisheries and offshore seafood markets. Today, all memory of Lisbon's former fishing industry is lost. This project aims to bring Portuguese seafood culture back into the heart of Lisbon. An amalgamation of a fish market, a cooking school, a restaurant and public spaces re-engages Lisboetas with their maritime past. **Fig. 15. 8 Wonseok Woo** Y4, 'Growing Discovery Museum'. **Fig. 15.9 Qiuling Guan** Y5, 'Tagus Baths'. An extensive beach once defined the waterfront and image of Lisbon. The growth of the port, accelerated by industrialisation, reshaped the riverfront into an embankment of concrete. The project proposes an urban bath located in an abandoned dry dock close to the centre of Lisbon. It seeks to bring the lost tradition of bathing in the river back to life. The dry docks are converted into a large pool and an urban beach connected to the tides of the Tagus.

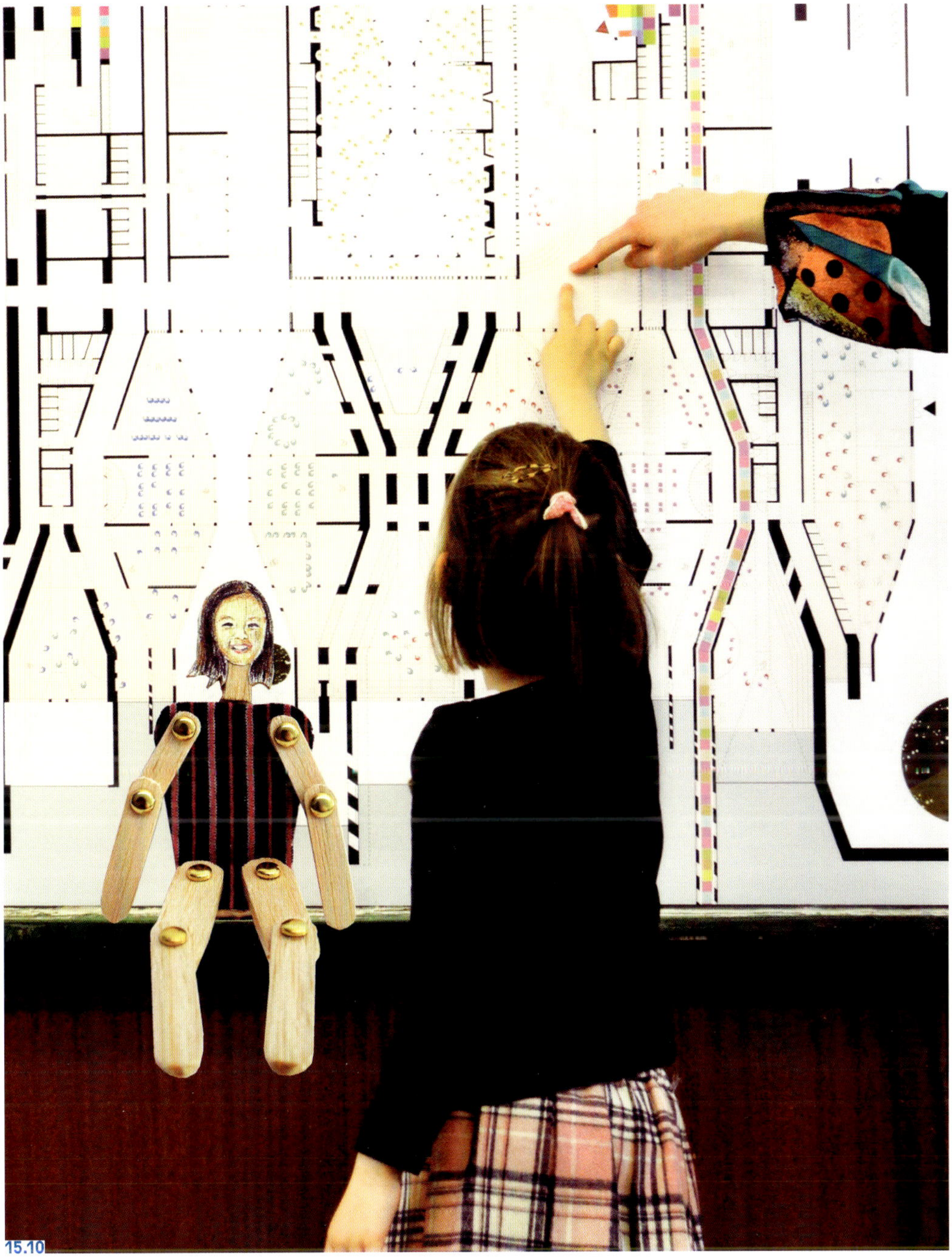

15.10

Fig. 15.10 Zuzana Sojkova Y5, 'Intercultural School'. The project aims to explore the possibilities of incorporating theatrical principles into education design in order to provide a common world for children from all corners of the planet, while fostering mutual understanding and respect. Such educational space should spark creativity, spatial awareness and courage, resulting in experimentation and an environment which produces flexible individuals who accept life as ongoing and in constant flux. In order to test the findings and filter the research question through children's minds, drawing tasks were assigned to pupils from Zuzana's former primary school during the project's development. Findings from that workshop further informed the design project.

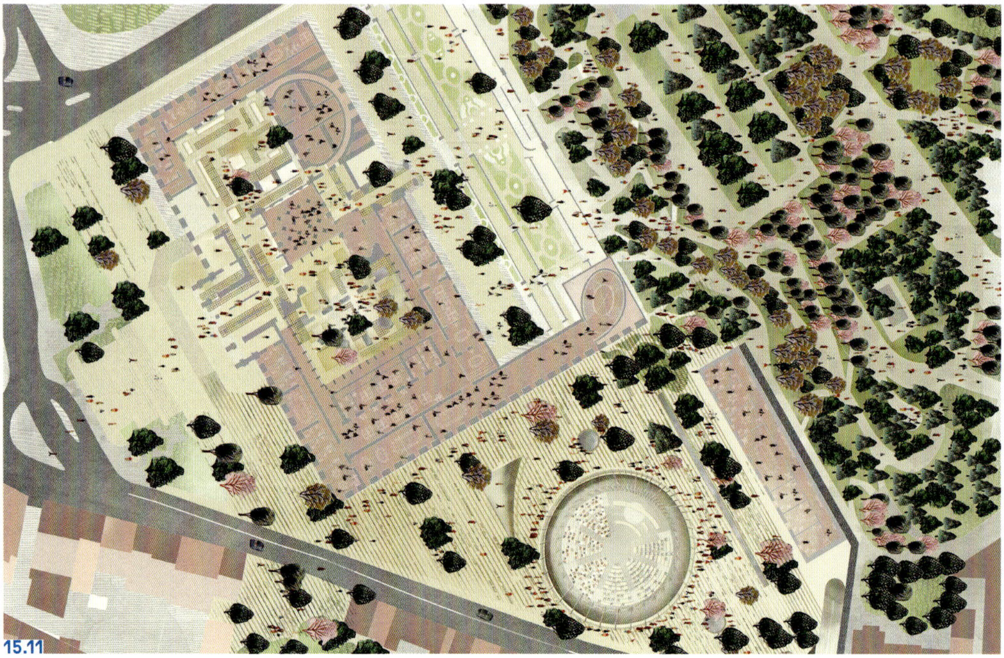
15.11

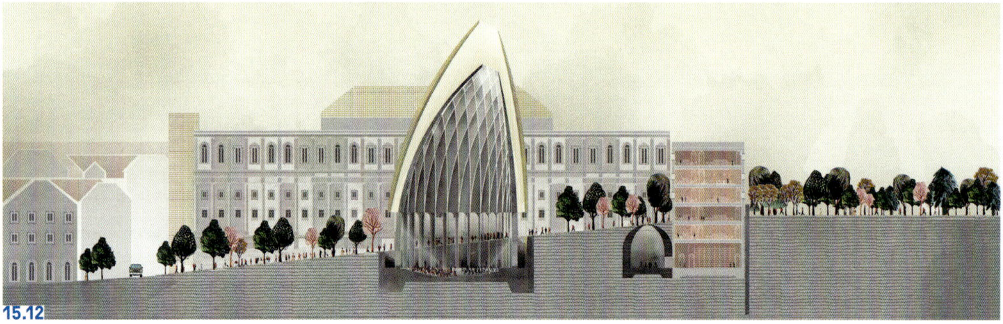
15.12

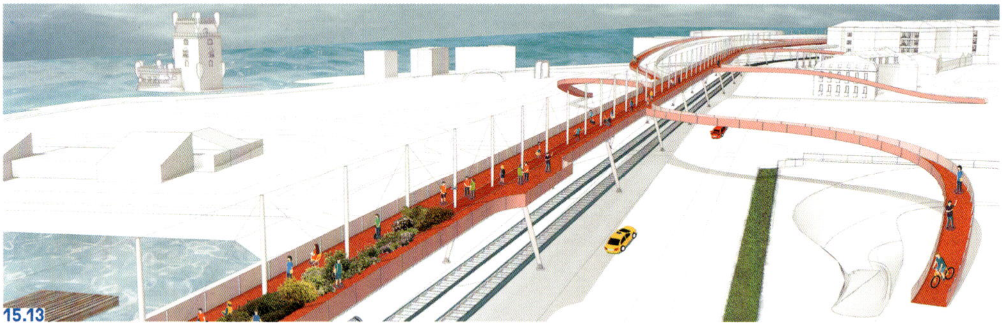
15.13

Figs. 15.11 – 15.12 Sachi Oberoi Y5, 'The People's Chamber'. The project questions the lack of transparency between politicians and the public, and the role of parliament today. In Lisbon, the debating chamber – where essential decisions affecting the country are made – is actually tucked away, hidden from public view, in an imposing neoclassical structure. My proposal removes the debating chamber from the cloister of the São Bento palace and places it next to the palace, in order to create transparency between the politicians and the public. In addition, rather than being shrouded with ancient and intimidating symbols of ornamentation, the architecture of the new debating chamber celebrates the two key eternal elements of the city: the golden light of Lisbon and its people.
Fig. 15.13 Yue Ma Y5, 'Linear Park'. Lisbon's waterfront is separated from its urban fabric by a continuous 'wall': the transportation network developed on the edge of the water to serve the industrial port over the past two centuries. These important infrastructure settlements, which have brought enormous wealth to the city, have become an obstacle in the way of its citizens' enjoyment of the sea. The project proposes a 7.5km linear park raised above the existing transportation artery in order to create a multitude of connections between the waterfront and the city.

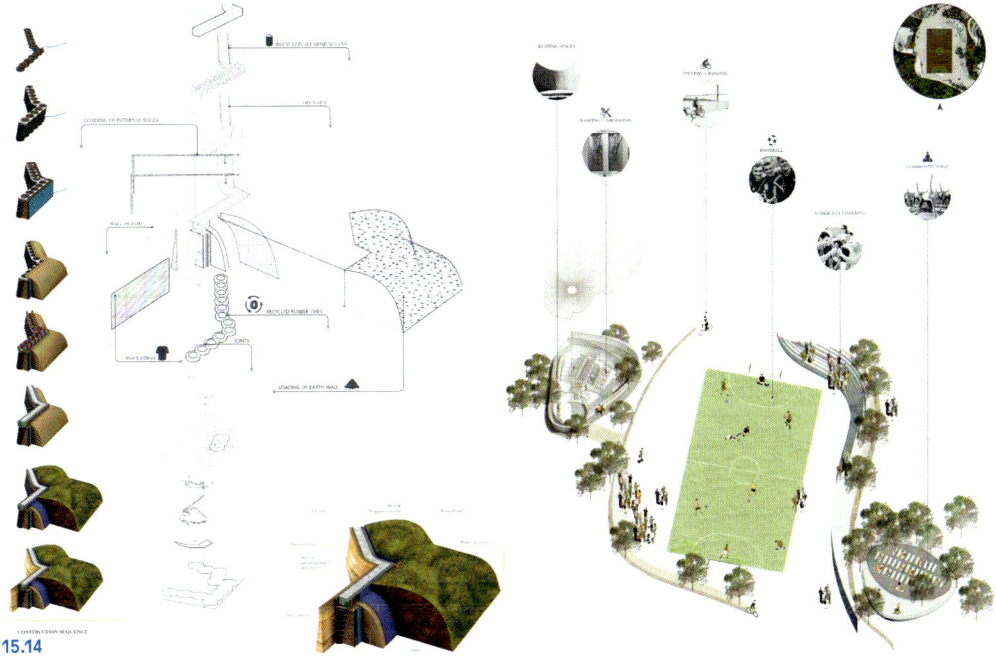

15.14

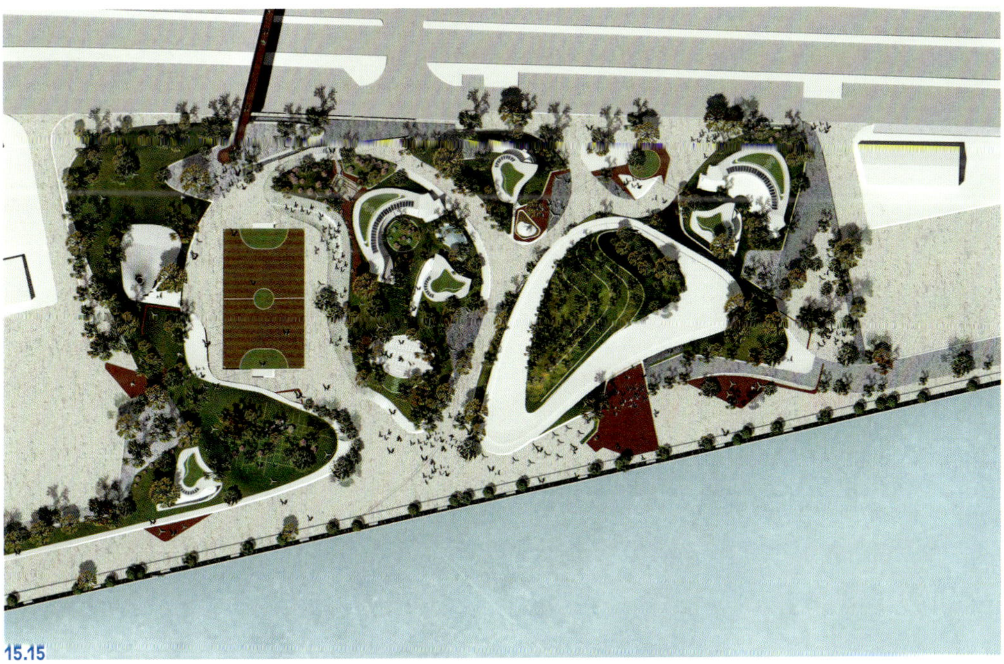

15.15

Figs. 15.14 – 15.15 Katriona Eleni Pillay Y4, 'Lisbon Community Garden of Social Reintegration'. This project celebrates the raising of a new self-sustaining garden hub housing a programme that aims to reintegrate Lisbon's displaced people back into society. As part of a wider national 'Community Garden Project', working alongside 'Serve the City Lisboa', the project – which approaches the Tagus as a green belt – is a knowledge-sharing base and inclusive platform that roots an integrated place of exchange with a socially driven programme, encompassing principles of integrity, kindness, respect and collaboration.

Unit 16 An Architecture of the Wild

Johan Berglund, Colin Herperger

Year 4
Tom Budd, Charlotte Carless, Jarrell Goh, Karen Ko, Sonia Magdziarz, Rebecca Sturgess, Sarah Stone

Year 5
Jaspal Channa, Dean Hedman, Ian Ng, Amani Radeef, Simran Sidhu, Joshua Toh, Ozan Toksoz-Blauel, Richard Tsang

Thank you to Ralph Parker for teaching the DR module, Andrew Best and Nikul Vadgama from BuroHappold for technical input, all thesis tutors who have given valuable input to the Y5 projects, and all our critics for their immensely valuable input throughout the year

Unit 16 enjoys the challenge of making difficult things. We seek to generate work and ideas that have the confidence to find their own language of expression and invention. There is a strong emphasis on exploration through a range of made and drawn physical production. We are not afraid to go rogue with an idea and encourage work that has the tenacity to take risks, or to rigorously chase a hunch into the unknown. Ultimately, we are interested in creating a learning environment where a variety of approaches to creative production help each student to work in a manner that both draws out and challenges their personal character and preferred approach.

——This year, we took an interest in finite and infinite processes, and the exploration of the edge of the remote. To find this edge we ventured deep into the Icelandic wilderness to explore and work inventively over immense scales of time, in places that were very much alive. We considered how one might activate remote territories rich with aggressive natural phenomena, bursting bellies of thermal heat, and a stretching of time from the appearance of the midnight sun to full days of darkness.

——The focus of the unit has been to notice the strange, often harder to find nuances of a place, and to react with inventive curiosity. How is architecture able to work with the environment and draw from its immense scale, strangeness and power? Lead by discovery but tested through invention, our design projects have sought to imagine new and unapologetic architectures that engage directly within the natural forces at the perceived edge of the civilized world.

——When thinking about and working with landscapes, we need to be aware of the shift in timescale from the fast and relentless pace of 21st century life to a slower, deeper timescale. What if your architecture needs to last for centuries, or millennia?

——We also wanted to understand how a sense of curiosity is developed within remote territories over longer periods, even decades, or perhaps a lifetime. How does one develop a self-sufficiency to excite one's own imagination? Living in a place that is on the edge of the remote, one can kindle curiosity in a range of ways. Both remoteness and emptiness signify a place of potential – and most importantly, an adventure that has to be made rather than given.

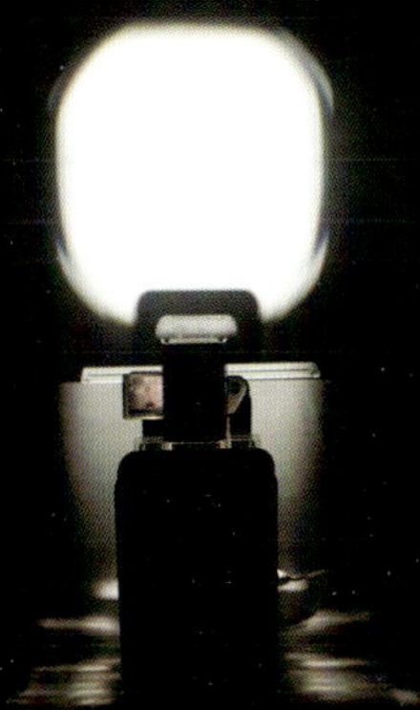

Projection 1
Source to Receptor - 1.5m

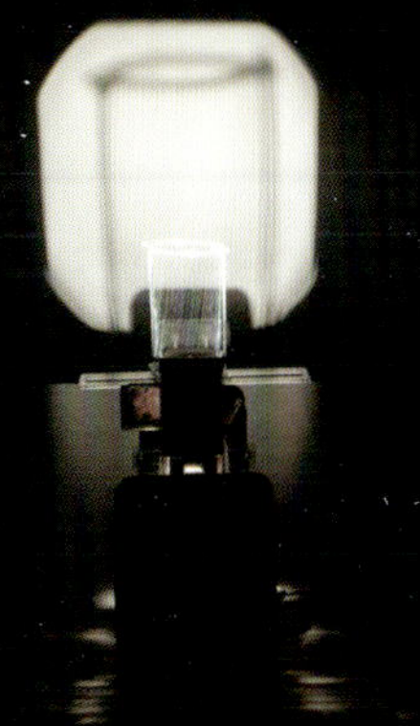

Projection 2
Source to Receptor - 1.5m
Twisted nylon string screen - 0.80m

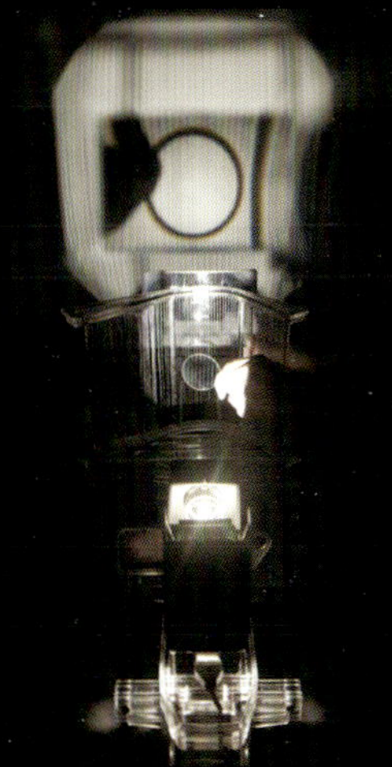

Projection 3
Source to Receptor - 1.9m
Double Convex lense (50cm) - 1.2m
Curved nylon string screen (Curve) - 0.90m
Fresnel Lense (A5) (Unbent) - 0.8m

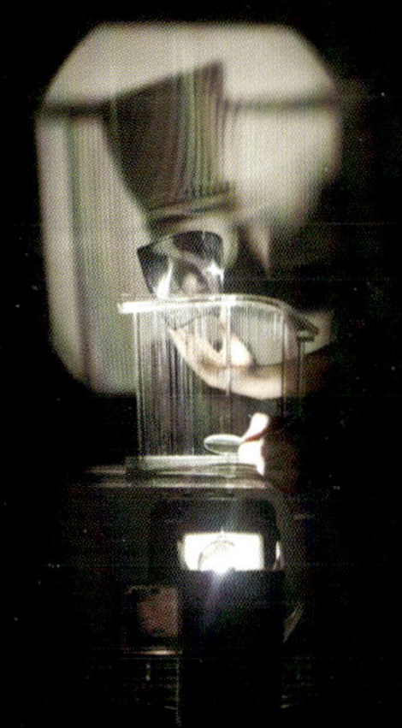

Projection 4
Source to Receptor - 2.0m
Double Convex lense (50cm) (Angled) - 1.5m
Curved nylon string screen (Straight) - 1.2m
Fresnel Lense (A5) (Bent) - 1.1m

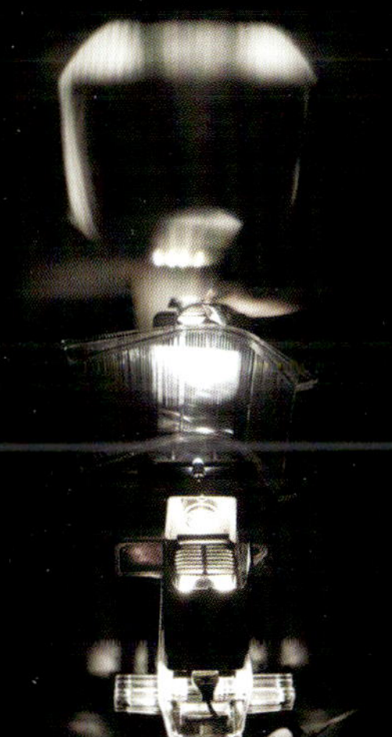

Projection 5
Source to Receptor - 1.5m
Curved nylon string screen (Curve) - 1.3m
Fresnel Lense (A5) (Straight) - 1.2m
Double Concave lense (50cm) - 1.0m

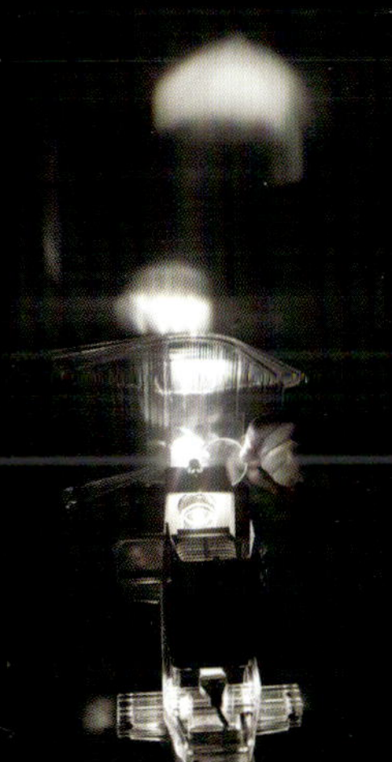

Projection 6
Source to Receptor - 1.8m
Double Concave lense (50cm) - 1.75m
Fresnel Lense (pocket size) (Unbent) - 1.7m
Curved nylon string screen (Curve) - 1.3m
Fresnel Lense (A5) (Unbent) - 1.2m

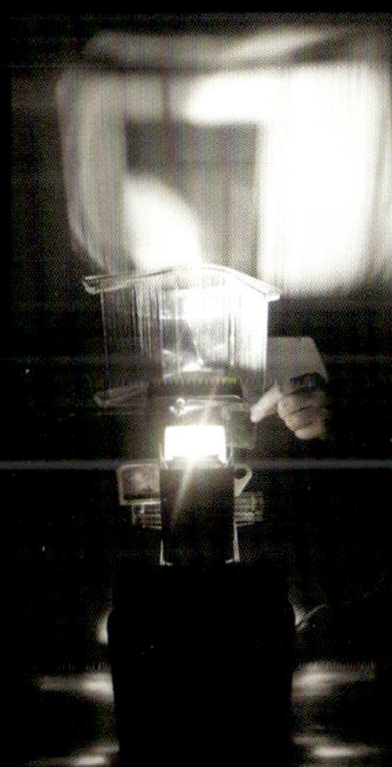

Projection 7
Source to Receptor - 2.0m
Fresnel Lense (pocket size) (Unbent) - 1.8m
Curved nylon string screen (Curve) - 1.0m
Fresnel Lense (A5) (Unbent) - 0.8m

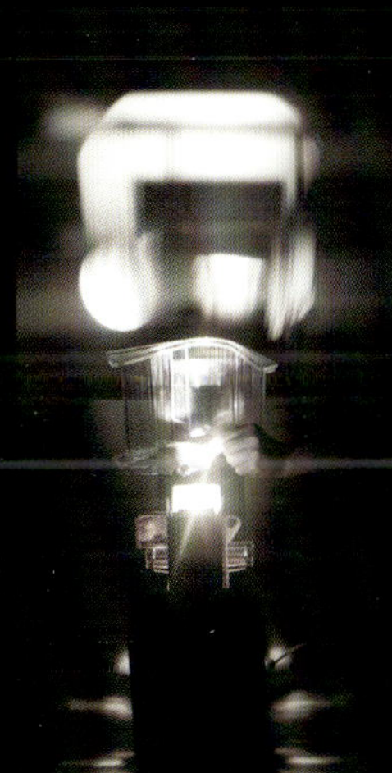

Projection 8
Source to Receptor - 2.0m
Fresnel Lense (pocket size) (Unbent) - 1.7m
Curved nylon string screen (Straight) - 1.4m
Fresnel Lense (A5) (Unbent) - 1.2m

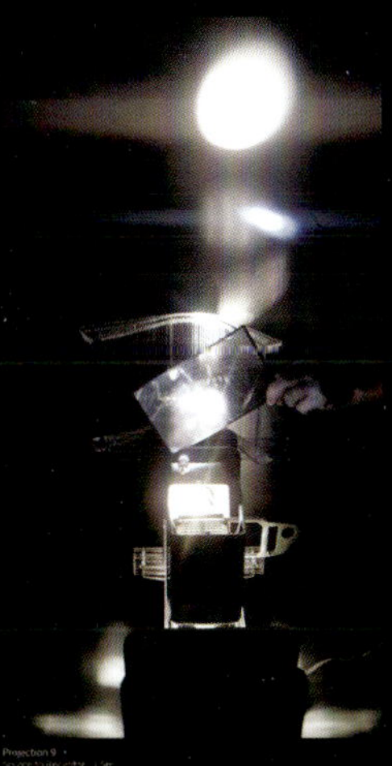

Projection 9
Source to Receptor - 1.5m
Fresnel Lense (A5) (unbent/rotated) - 1.2m
Curved nylon string screen (Curve) - 1.0m
Double Concave lense (50cm) - 0.9m

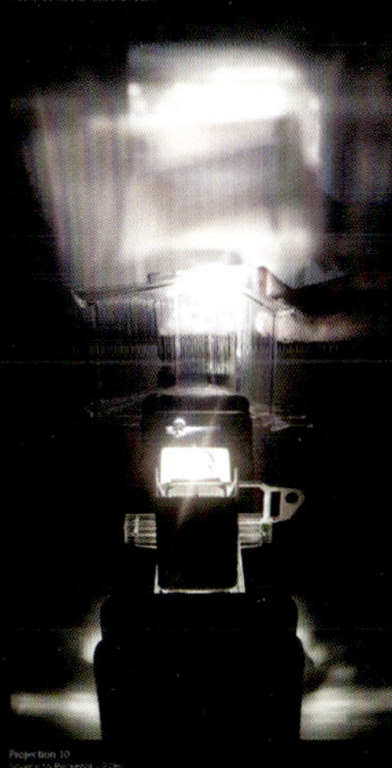

Projection 10
Source to Receptor - 2.0m
Curved nylon string screen (Curve) - 1.8m
Fresnel Lense (A5) (Unbent) - 1.5m
Fresnel Lense (pocket size) (Unbent) - 1.1m

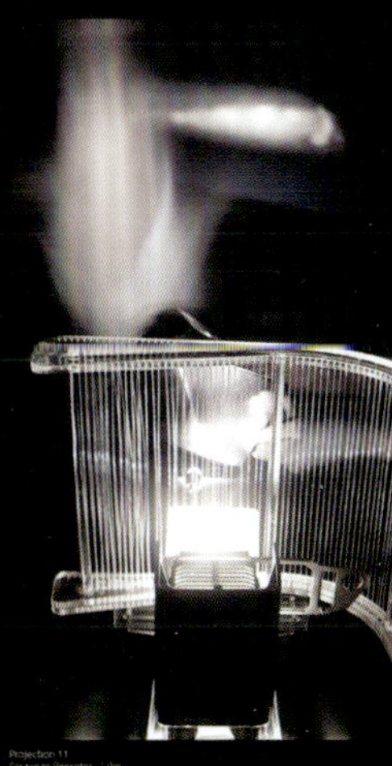

Projection 11
Source to Receptor - 1.0m
Curved nylon string screen (Curve) - 0.9m
Fresnel Lense (A5) (Unbent) - 0.6m

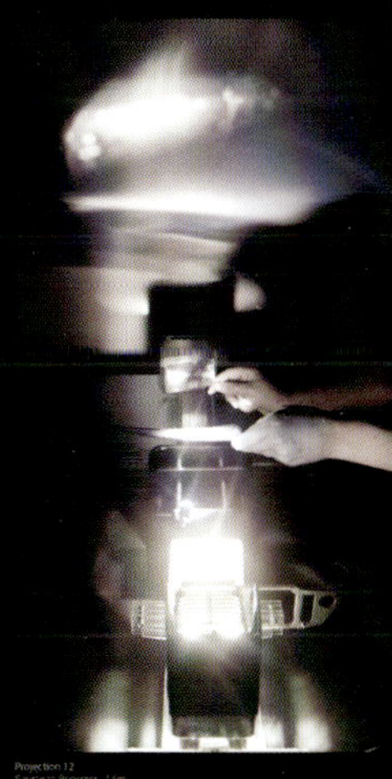

Projection 12
Source to Receptor - 1.6m
Fresnel Lense (A5) (unbent/rotated) - 1.1m
Fresnel Lense (pocket size) (Unbent) - 0.8m

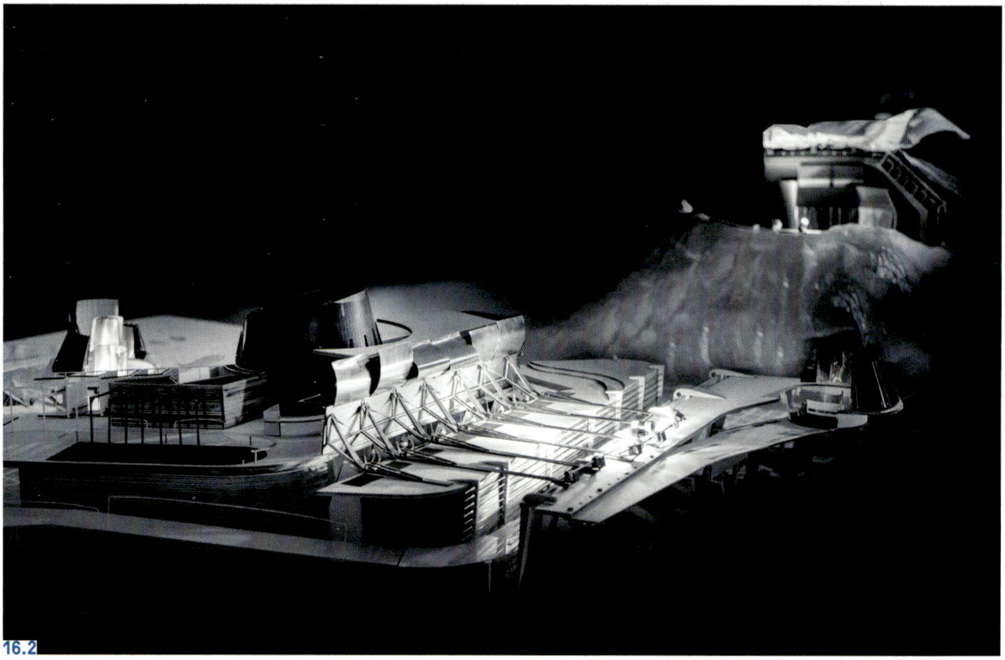
16.2

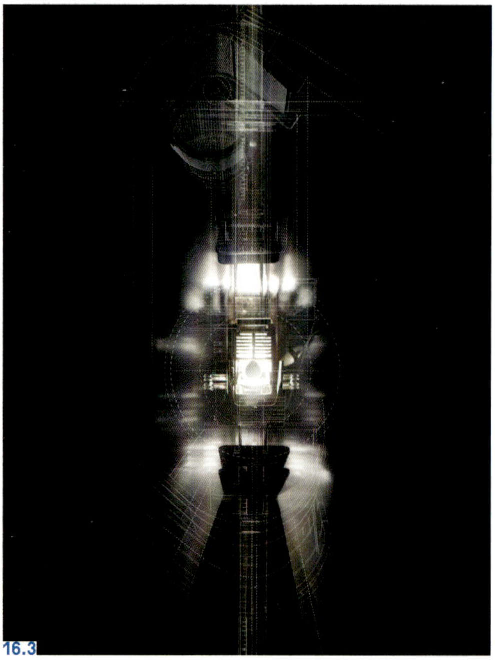
16.3

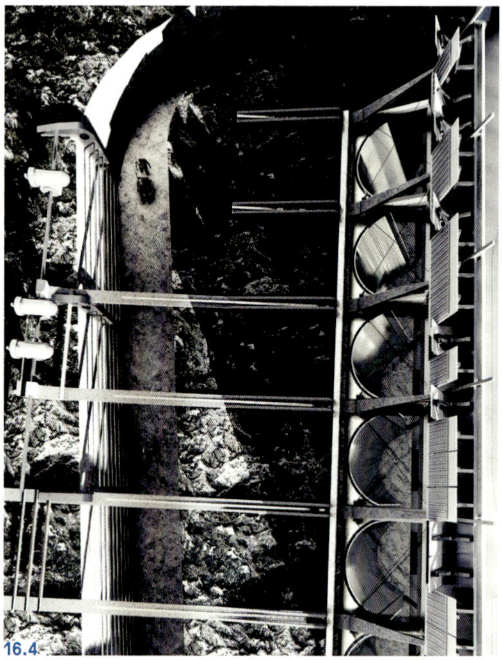
16.4

Figs. 16.1 – 16.4 **Amani Radeef** Y5, 'An Architecture of Darkness – Lighting Lake Myvatn'. An architecture of darkness reveals the heterotopic nature of spatial constructs relative to our vision activated by light, or by the lack of it. This heightens our sensations and makes us more sensitive to our environments. The project re-imagines a Viking longhouse as a Town Hall and archives centre for Lake Myvatn, where, through materiality and formal language, the manipulation of light would also occur. **Fig. 16.5** **Joshua Toh** Y5, 'A Strange Thing in the Sky'. How would one create an architectural dress for the wilderness of Iceland? The Nostromo is an attempt to answer this question, a tailored airship for the skies, a piece of couture defining the sensory experience of its occupants as it floats above the Icelandic landscape.

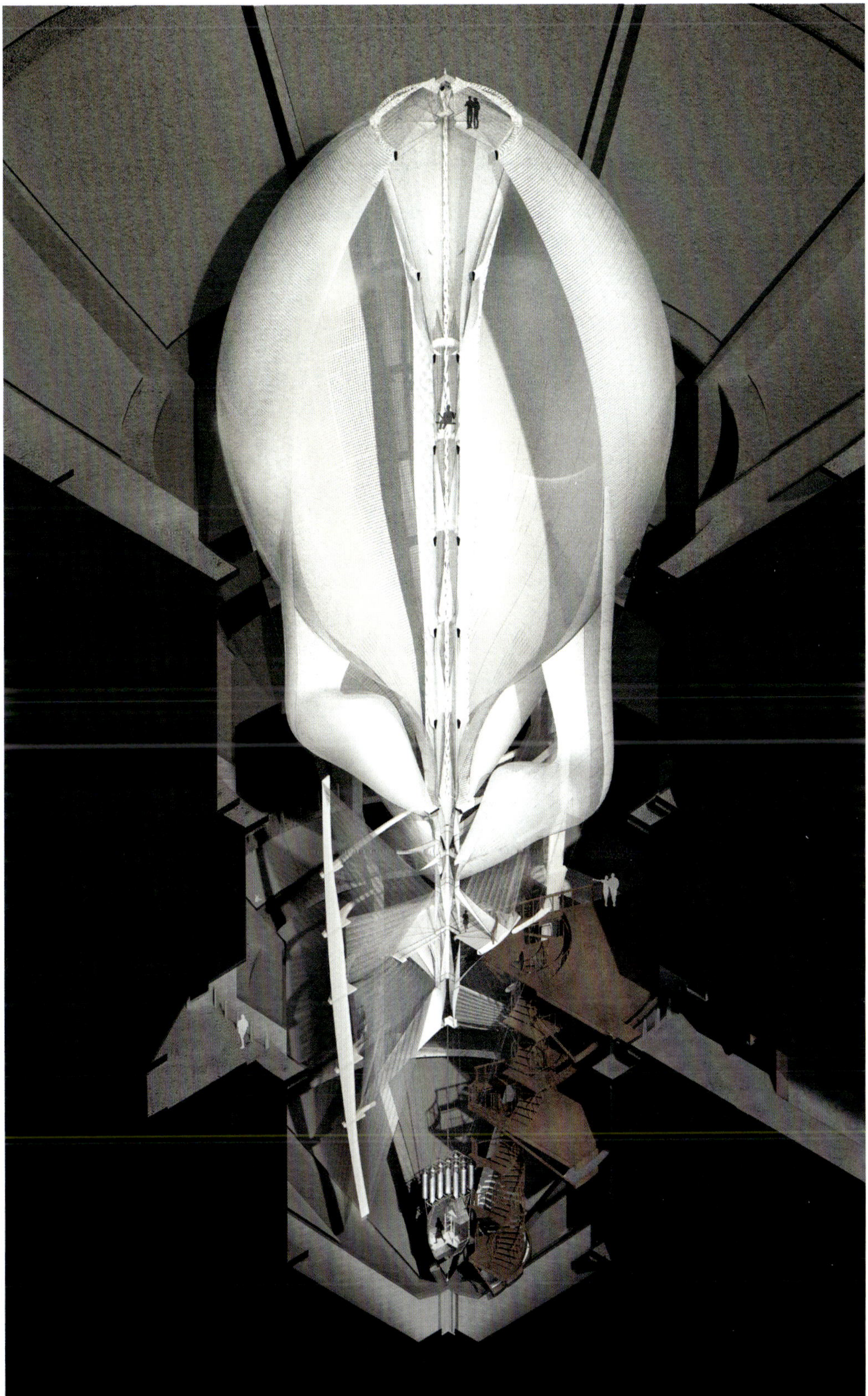

16.5

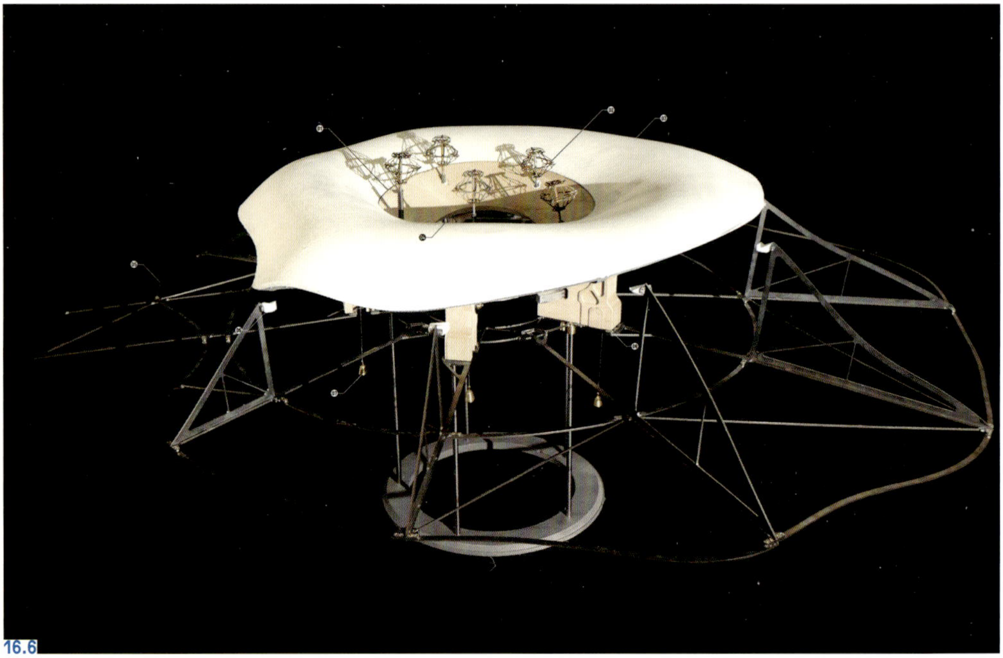

16.6

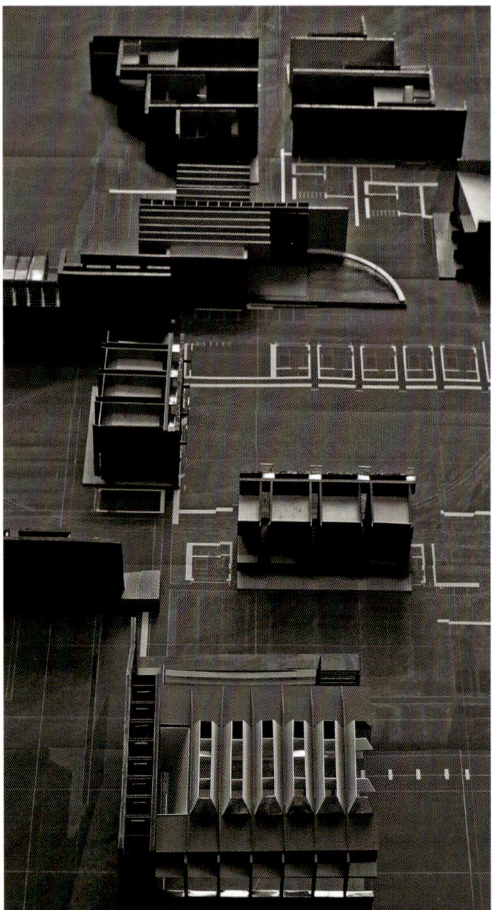

16.7

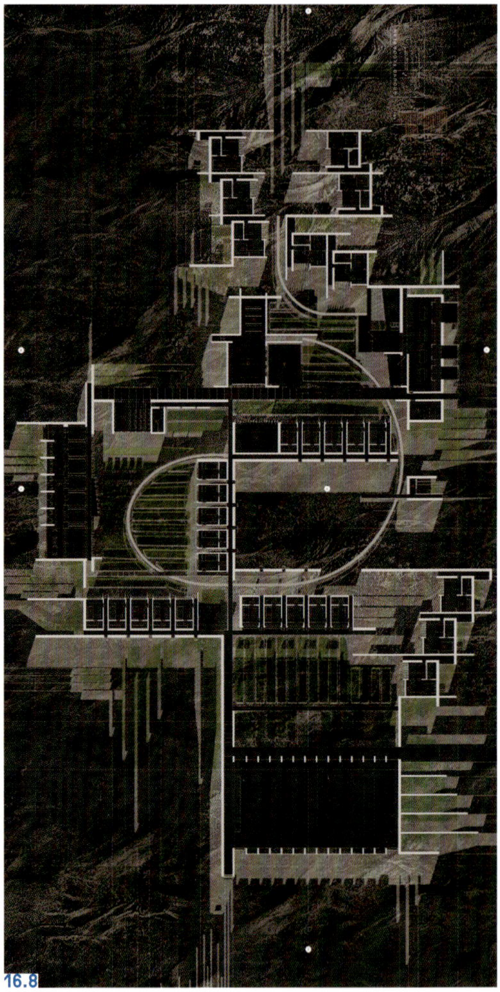

16.8

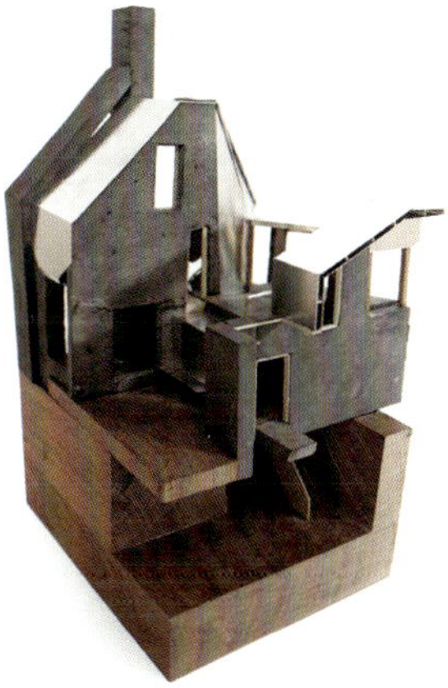

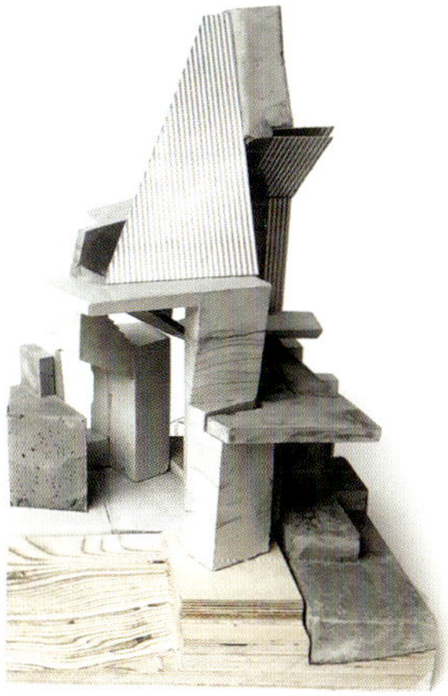

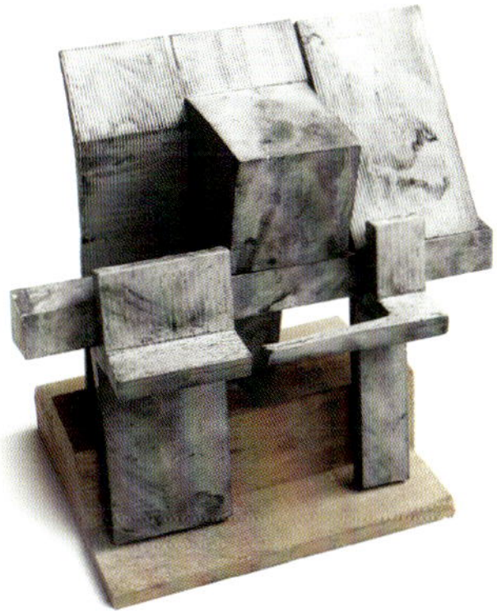

16.9

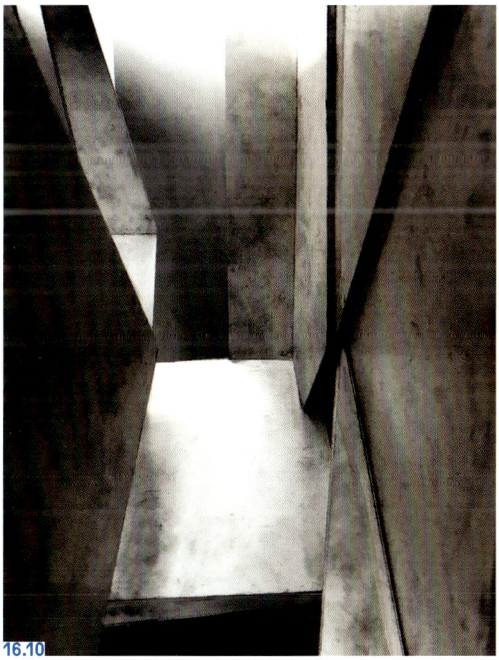

16.10

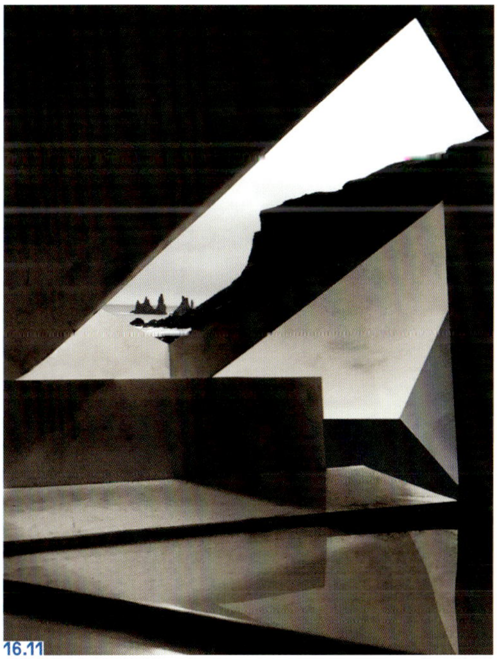

16.11

Fig. 16.6 Ian Ng Y5, 'Invisible Infrastructure: An Ice Lens for Skutustadir'. Harnessing the natural climatology of Lake Myvatn, an ice lens 60m in diameter is formed annually within the negative space of a pseudocrater – both of which are geological formations unique to the area. The ice lens forms with different aberrations as an indicator of the year's conditions, and the space within it changes and adapts according to the shrinking mass of the ice through a system of counterweights. **Fig. 16.7 Ozan Toksoz-Blauel** Y5, 'The School of Land Restoration in Alftaver'. Situated between shrinking farmland and an expanding black sand desert, this project proposes to preserve a remnant of the man-made farmland landscape within a school campus. **Figs. 16.9 – 16.11 Rebecca Sturgess** Y4, 'Vik Cultural Hub'. Situated in a country defined by its strange and dramatic landscapes, the focus on mass and void creates a strangeness of the 'in-between'. This encourages random interactions and meetings between refugees and tourists, as they transition into the peculiarity of life in Icelandic society.

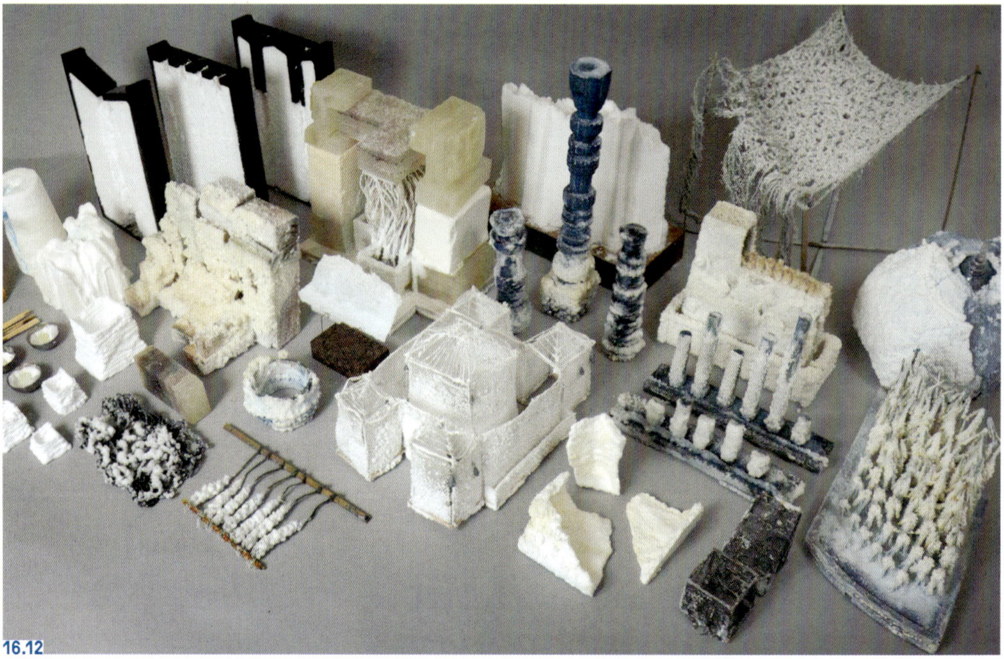

16.12

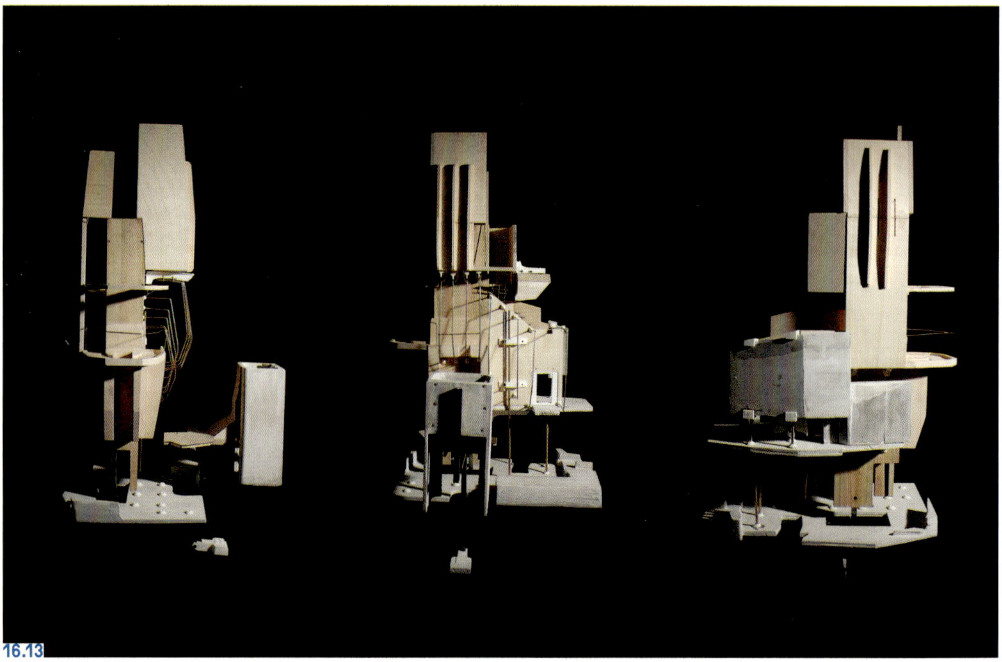

16.13

Fig. 16.12 Jarrell Goh Y4, 'The Nordur Saltworks'. The project imagines the expansion of a sea salt factory in the shallow shoals of the Icelandic Westfjords. The design was led by material tests that discovered the architectural potential of the crystals - creating a building which was making, and was made of, salt. **Fig. 16.13 Jaspal Channa** Y5, 'The Wayward Observatory'. This project negotiates the anticipated realm of the mountain ridge, moving between clarity and discovery whilst investigating the spatial potential of waywardness. The employment of spontaneity in the design method encouraged this condition to emerge. **Fig. 16.14 Charlotte Carless** Y4, 'Jarðskjálfti Seismic Station: Earth Moves'. The project explores a supernature – an ancient volcanic, seismic site – and proposes an architecture carved into the rock face it inhabits. This has a closeness with the earth around it, in particular, with the ancient lava fields at the foothills of two sub-glacial volcanoes. **Fig. 16.15 Sonia Magdziarz** Y4, 'Hús Is'. Hús Is explores what happens when you fuse a building with its landscape, creating a co-existence in which neither is sacrificed at the expense of the other. The house, carved into basalt rock, tries to domesticate the scale of the landscape. It is a poetic search for ways of engraving the memory of the changing climate into the fabric of the building. **Fig. 16.16 Richard Tsang** Y5, 'Reykjavik Film School'. The project sets out to embody the feelings of nostalgia and desolation, which are often hallmarks of Icelandic cinema. Played out in a carved-out basalt quarry, the spaces unfold into a rich and atmospheric space for study and contemplation.

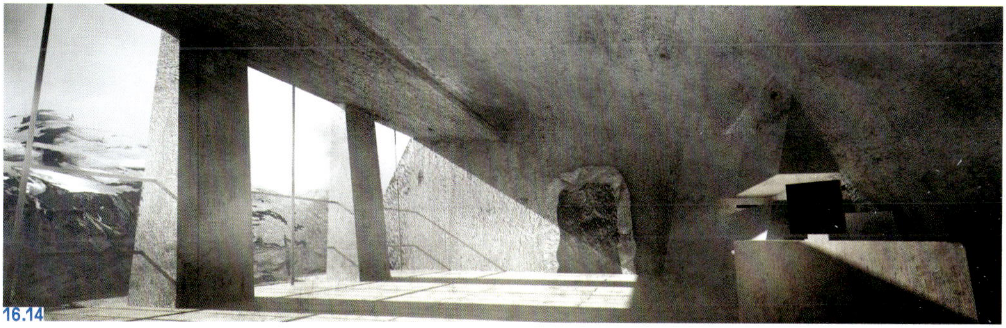
16.14

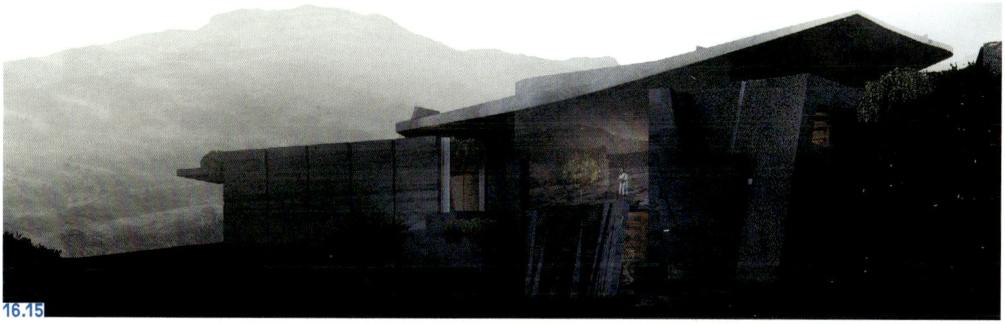
16.15

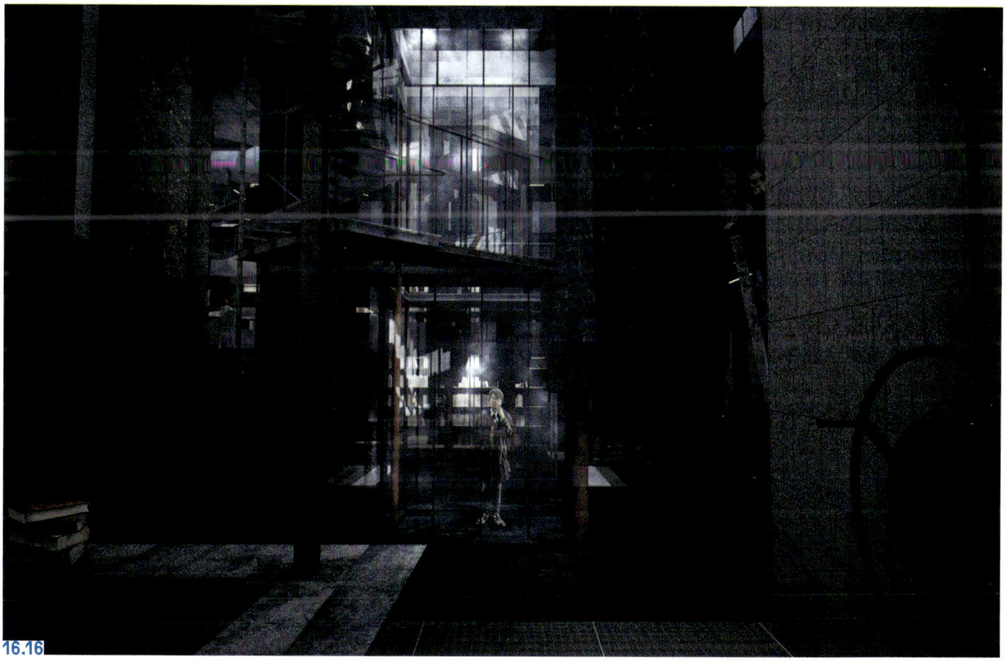
16.16

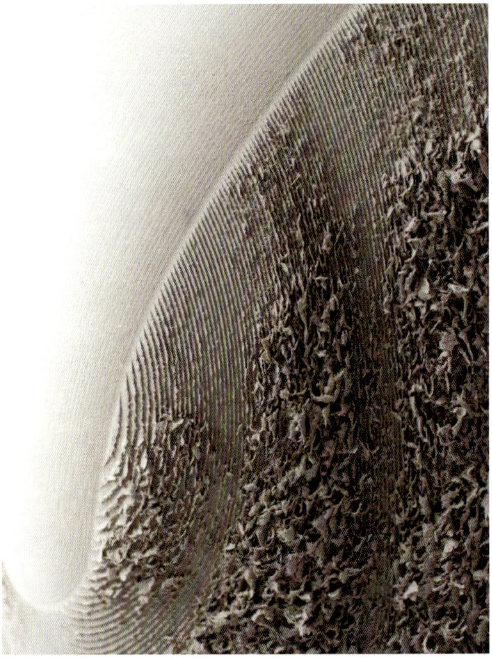

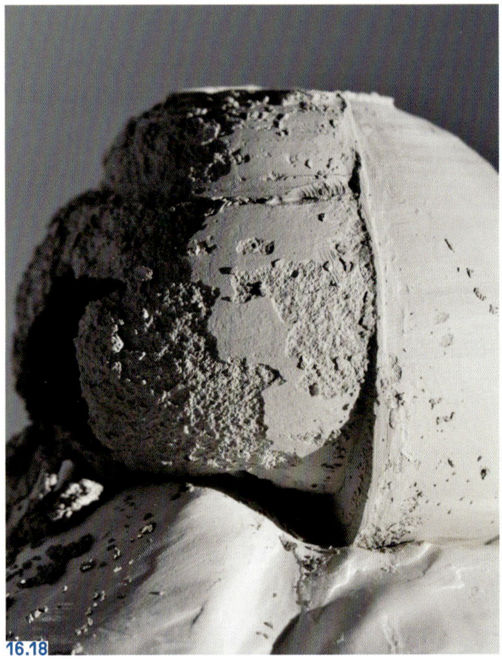

16.18

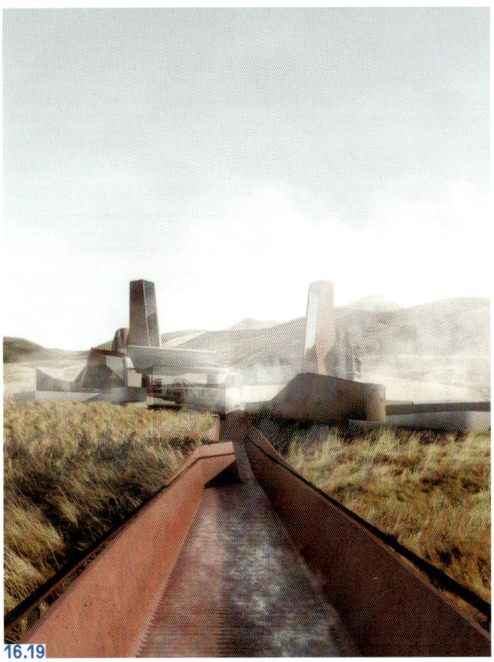

16.19

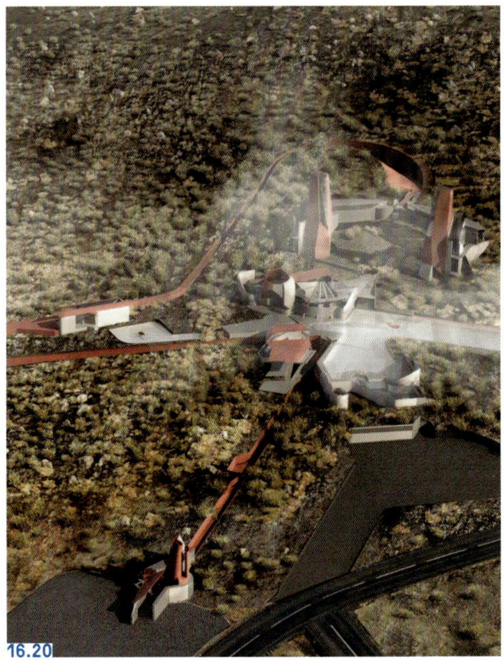

16.20

Fig. 16.17 Sonia Magdziarz Y4, 'Hús Is'. **Fig. 16.18 Karen Ko** Y4, 'Earth and Fire'. By digging into and shaping the ground, investigating clay and geological expressions inherent to their location, an outcome becomes synonymous with the setting in which it is made. **Figs. 16.19 - 16.20 Tom Budd** Y4, 'Creating Intimacy within the Inhospitable'. This project focuses on the design of a space for social interaction within the remote landscape of Iceland. Through the study of swimming pool culture in the country, the project seeks to explore and draw out these distinctly Icelandic experiences whilst designing a new swimming pool and assembly halls in Reykjahlíð, a small town in the north of the country. **Fig. 16.21 Simran Sidhu** Y5, 'StitchScape'. Examining the body as landscape, and the landscape as a body to be dressed, the work attempts to find a middle ground where the spaces are read as both architectural space and garment.

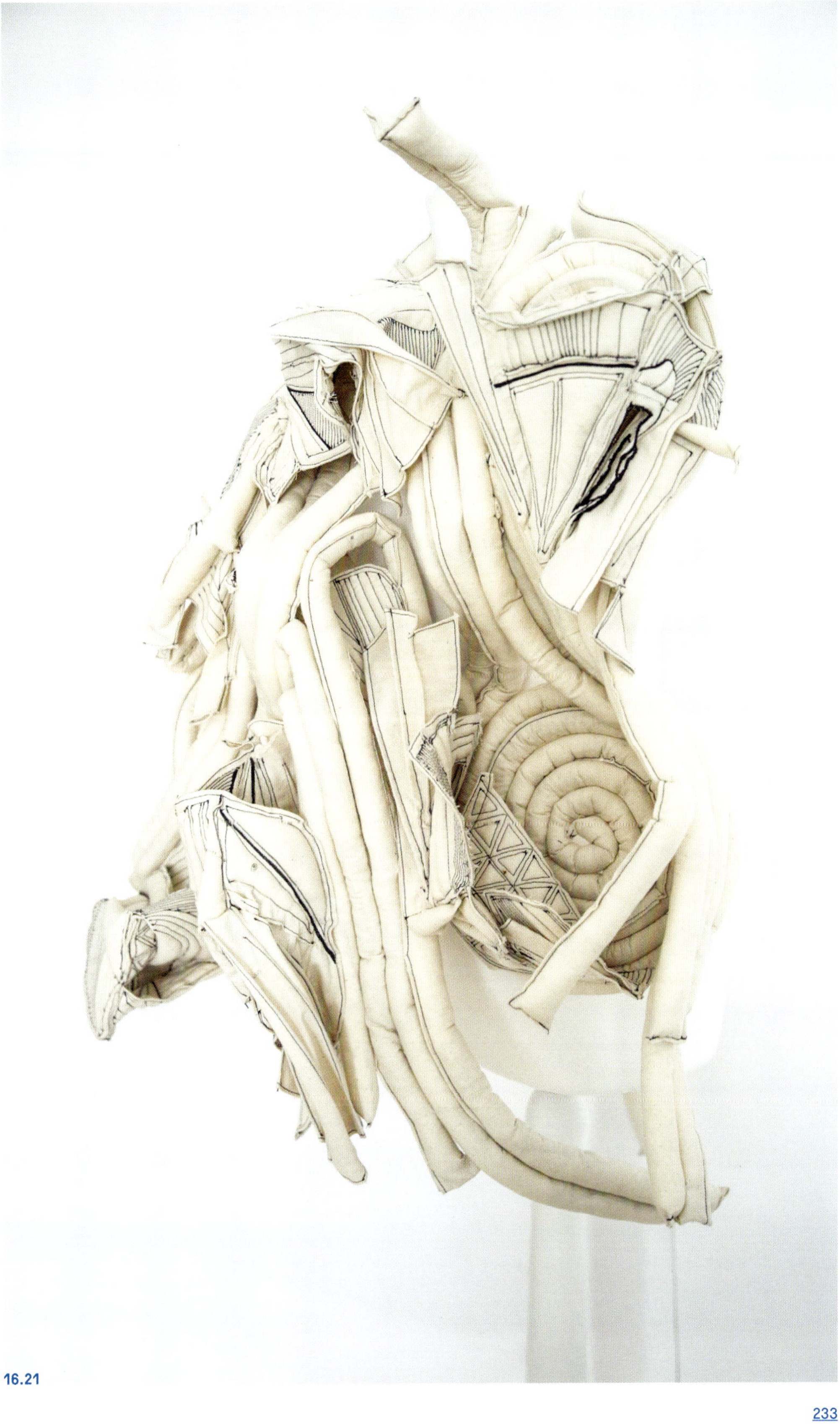

16.21

Unit 17 2 3 5 7 11 13 17

Yeoryia Manolopoulou, Níall McLaughlin, Michiko Sumi

Year 4
Naomi Au, Jinman Choi, James Greig, Julia Scheutz, Mai Que Ta, Sam Tan, Esha Thapar, Krystal Tsai Ting, Torris Kaul Varoystrand, Alexander Wood, Eleni Zygogianni

Year 5
Malina Dabrowska, Juwhan Han, Carl Inder, Vasilis Marcou Ilchuck, Oscar Plastow, Henry Svendsen, Christie Yeung

Thank you to our Design Realisation Tutors James Daykin and Simon Tonks

Thank you to our invited speakers who introduced us to mathematical concepts related to philosophy, design and computation: Adam Beck, Mario Carpo, Sean Hanna

Thank you to Maciej Czarnecki, Edward Denison, Joanna Leman and Gdynia's Foreign Relations Department for their support during our field trip in Poland

Thank you to our critics: Alessandro Ayuso, Julia Backhaus, Anthony Boulanger, Gillian Brady, Barbara-Ann Campbell-Lange, Nat Chard, Claire Chawke, Sophie Cole, Marjan Colletti, James Daykin, Lily Jencks, Anna Liu, Jack Newton, Jessica Reynolds, Henning Stummel, Peter Thomas, Mike Tite, Simon Tonks, St John Walsh, Victoria Watson, Mika Zacharias.

Consultants:
William Whitby (ARUP), Hareth Pochee (Max Fordham)

Unit 17 takes a progressive and experimental approach to architecture that is specific to place and culture. Our work develops through open inquiry. It is founded on the recognition that the architect works both as scientist and poet, being equally engaged in empirical analysis, abstraction, speculation and invention.

——Last year, our theme was time, linked with place and history. This year we took a different take on the same subject to explore its more mathematical aspects: periodic and cyclical rhythms, simultaneity, chance and alternating systems in the fabric of our landscapes and urban environments. We explored the spatiality of some of the most fascinating mathematical ideas embedded in nature, inside our bodies, and in the multitude of networks that condition our cities and daily lives.

——Mathematical concepts have shaped our perception of the universe and the evolution of the cosmos since the Babylonian era. They influence and explain how animals, landscape, people and politics interact. They model contemporary global systems, commodification, finances, communications, data and workflows, climate, the human brain, social infrastructures, health and population statistics. They condition nature, governance, economy and human experience.

——Contrary to the view that sees mathematics exclusively as abstract and the basis of science, we were interested in the role that mathematical structures can play in shaping everyday experiences and the spectrum of human creativity across fields: from natural philosophy, biology and quantum physics to architecture, literature, painting and music. Think about Bach, Theo van Doesburg, Jorge Luis Borges and Ryoji Ikeda; and architects from the Ancient Egyptians to Palladio and Xenakis. Can a contemporary study of mathematics that is not reductive, utilitarian or sacred push architecture to novel directions? One of our questions was to understand architecture's association with digital mathematics. Avoiding the simplistic acceptance of parametricism on the one hand and its severe criticism on the other, we searched for the spatial, social and aesthetic consequences of mathematical ideas in deeply performative and experiential projects.

Mathematical Forms: During term 1 students produced drawing notations, performative models and large-scale installations exploring mathematical forms influenced by: the Transfinite, PvNP, Calculus, Chaos Theory, Prime Numbers, Combinatorics, Rhythmanalysis, Klein Bottle, Stochastic Processes, the I Ching, Game Theory, weather forecasting and Epigenetics.

Nested Rhythms: We travelled from Cracow, the Tatras Mountains and Warsaw to Szczecin, Gdynia and Gdansk on the Baltic Sea. Students recorded rhythms, whether embedded in urban or rural areas, rivers or social media platforms. They chose sites for their building projects, shifting their attention from mathematical abstraction to architectural proposition.

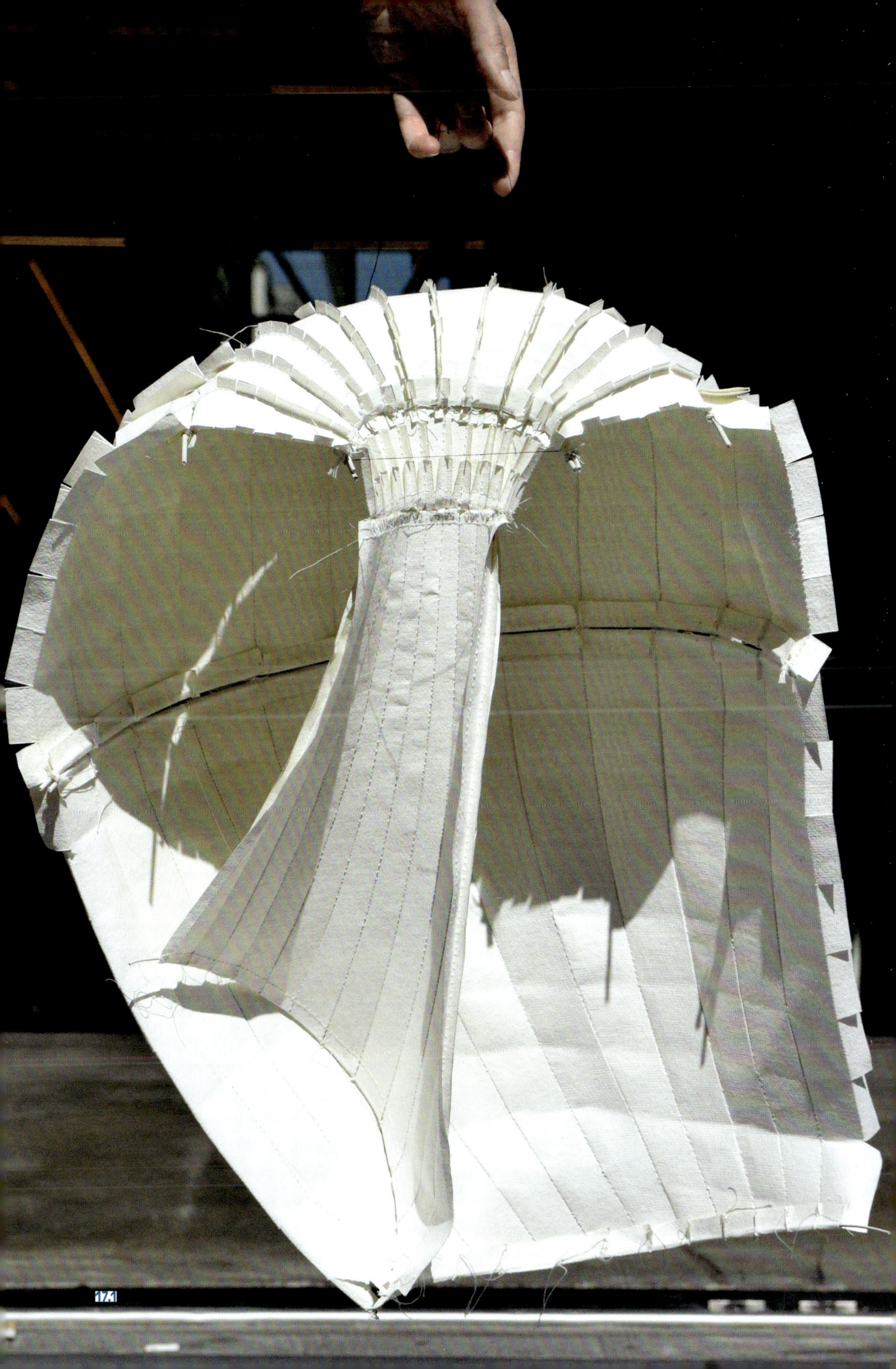

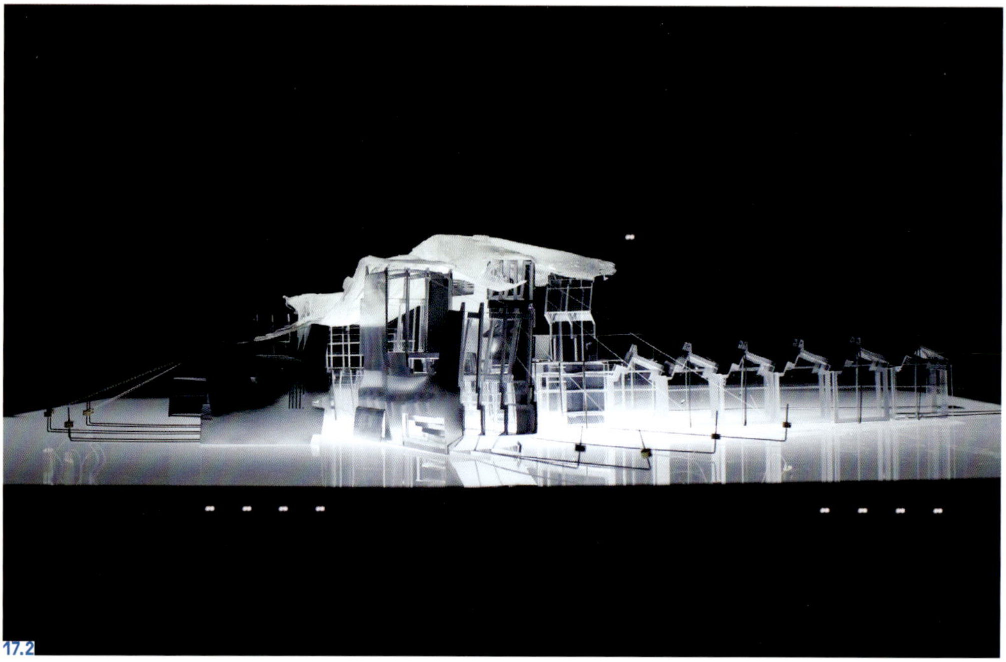

17.2

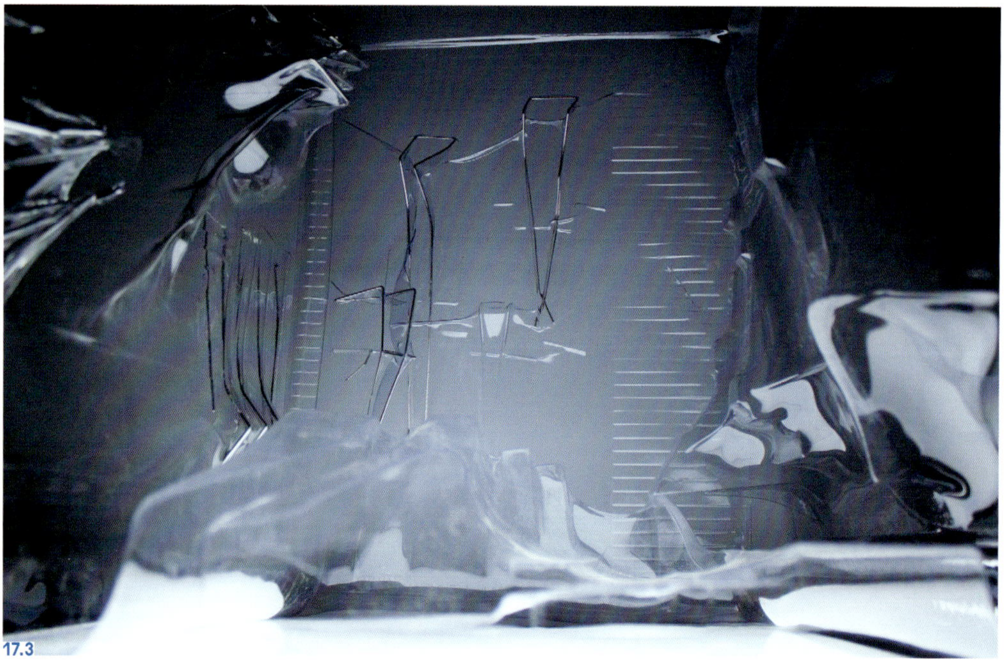

17.3

Fig. 17.1 Malina Dabrowska Y5, 'Klein Earth Sciences Gallery', Wieliczka Salt Mine, Poland. An investigation of the mathematical surfaces of a Klein bottle led to analogous constructions using paper-sewn models. The building proposal for a gallery and conference centre, sited at the UNESCO Heritage Site of Wieliczka Salt Mine in Poland, suggests intersecting volumes made of salt-impregnated plywood strips and dichroic glass, expressing the intricacy of the double-sided Klein topological surface. The two main chambers of the building interlock with each other and the ground, forming a space which draws the visitor in, blurring the boundaries between the external and internal elements of the structure. The project has been explored through physical models, which test its spatial and light-based qualities in a variety of scales and typologies of the double-sided geometric surfaces. **Figs. 17.2 – 17.3 Henry Svendsen** Y5, 'WaterDATA Centre', Delta of the Vistula River, Poland. Processing and archiving hidden data that reveals environmental and sociological conditions of the river, the building provides administrative offices for the water management of Gdańsk. Sited on an outlet artificially created to reduce ice jams, the proposal introduces a flood prevention scheme of water reservoirs. During cold conditions, this excess water is misted throughout the building, allowing ice to form around the steel, glass and cable structures. This not only stores excess flood water in a solid form that slowly melts during the year, but also becomes a heraldic physical representation of the river.

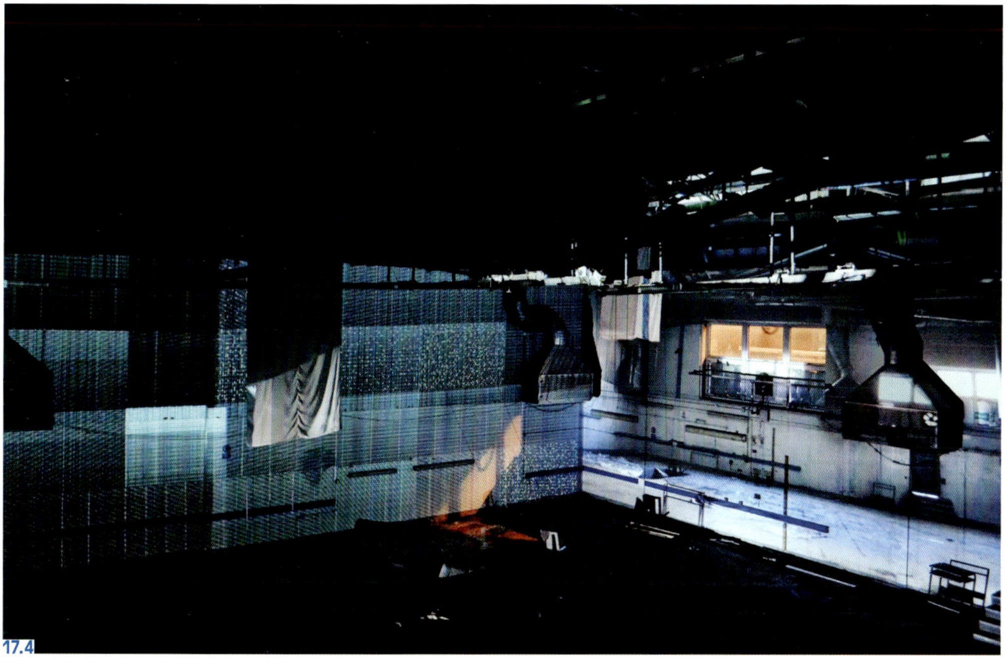

17.4

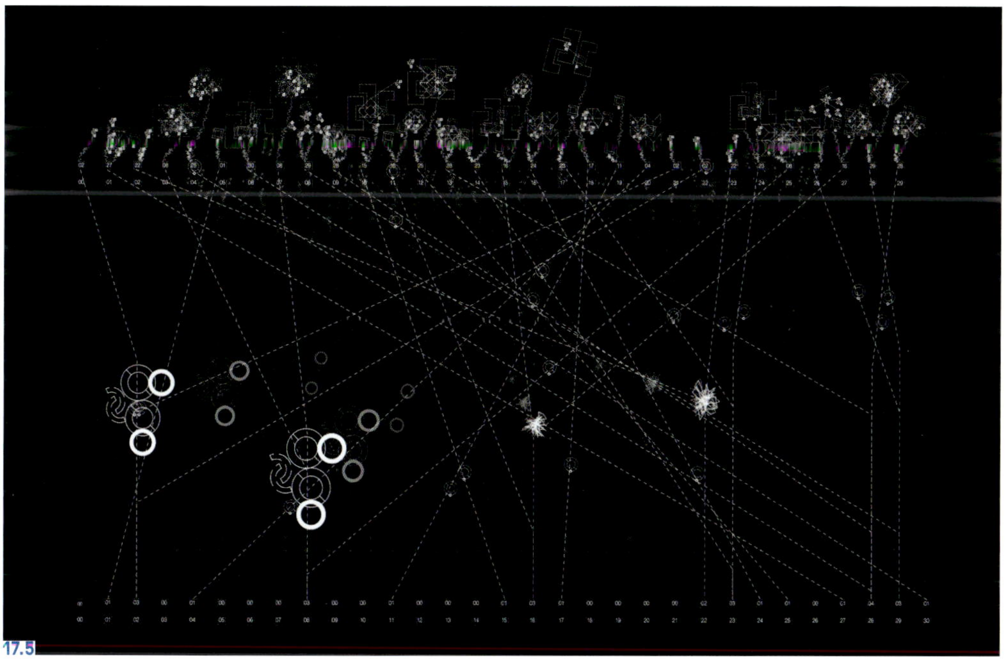

17.5

Fig. 17.4 Sam Tan Y4, 'The People's Square of Manifestations', Parade Square, Warsaw. The project begins by exploring the phenomena of chaos theory, which is intrinsic to weather changes, and the notion of a constructed language of digitality as the perceived finite truth of reality. A range of animated configurations of predictive weather data form part of various large-scale immersive installations. The experiential qualities of these initial pieces go on to inform an architectural proposition: a physical display of public opinion across the second largest public square in Europe, overlooked by the Palace of Culture and Science in Warsaw. This uses the chaotic societal impetus of contemporary political public opinion as the driver of its transitory spatiality. **Fig. 17.5 Krystal Tsai Ting** Y4, 'Data-Driven Train Station', Warszawa Miedzeszyn Station, Poland. The architecture of this data-driven station is inspired by a spatial mathematical language developed through iterative models, drawings and films with 'reactions' between numbers. Numbers determine everyday life, in our patterns of movement, commerce, telecommunications, financial and digital transactions. In this project, each number is individually designed while larger numbers are assembled as complex composites of smaller units. The architecture of the station responds when deployable kite-like roofs are thrust upwards as commuters enjoy vertically moving seats. This performative structure is generated by the temporal logic of the station, particularly the time announcements of arrivals and departures of trains.

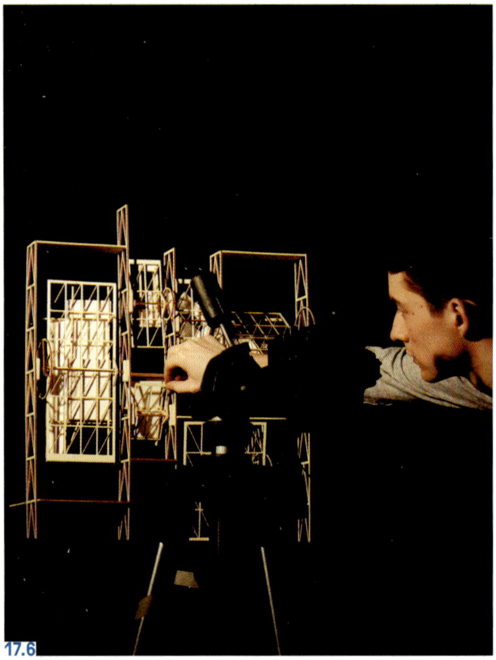

17.6

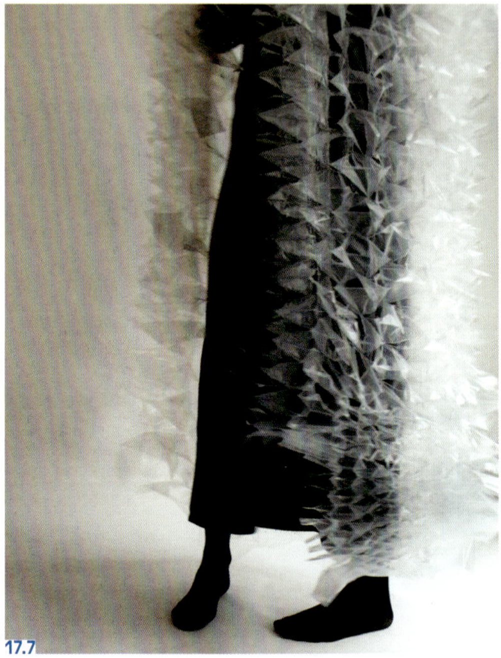

17.7

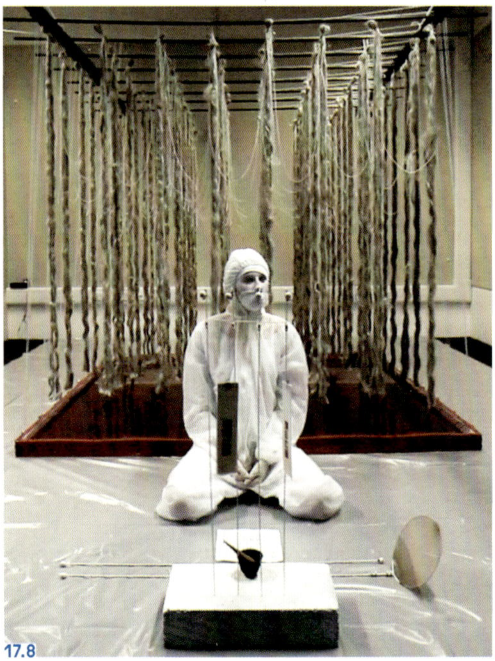

17.8

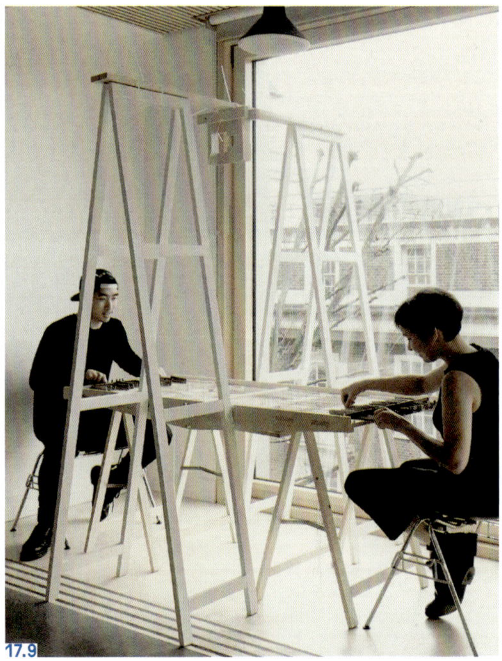

17.9

Fig. 17.6 James Greig Y4, 'Permitted Impermanence', Gdyńia Planning Department. A temporary planning workshop plays host to the cyclical, rhythmic creation of fictional versions of the city in an urban site of disputed ownership. The edge interface of the building becomes an instrument through which these rhythms become writ large in the city. **Fig. 17.7 Mai Que Ta** Y4, 'Oxygen; Stratifying the Blanket'. The piece communicates the rhythms of the human body. Space becomes an extension of the membrane beyond the edges of an individual. **Fig. 17.8 Julia Scheutz** Y4, 'Public Baths', Gdańsk. The I Ching was explored as a medium of communication and a system developed to act as a carrier of meaning. This investigation led to a change in understanding mathematics and language, drawing further parallels to genetics and epigenetics, developing the notion of chance-invoked change. **Fig. 17.9 Torris Kaul Varoystrand** Y4, ' Sand Drawing'. The project researches stochastic processes in music and architecture. A series of scores and time-based performative instruments gradually lead to the design of a seasonal hotel and shared public facilities in Gdańsk. **Fig. 17.10 Juwhan Han** Y5, 'Towards [Human] Responsive Architecture: The Haunted House', King's Cross, London. Starting from a personal experience of being separated from one's family, the project investigates a real-time design system between Seoul and London where spaces respond to behaviours of people in both places. Through live telecommunication experiments between the two locations, it orchestrates a highly responsive home, away from home.

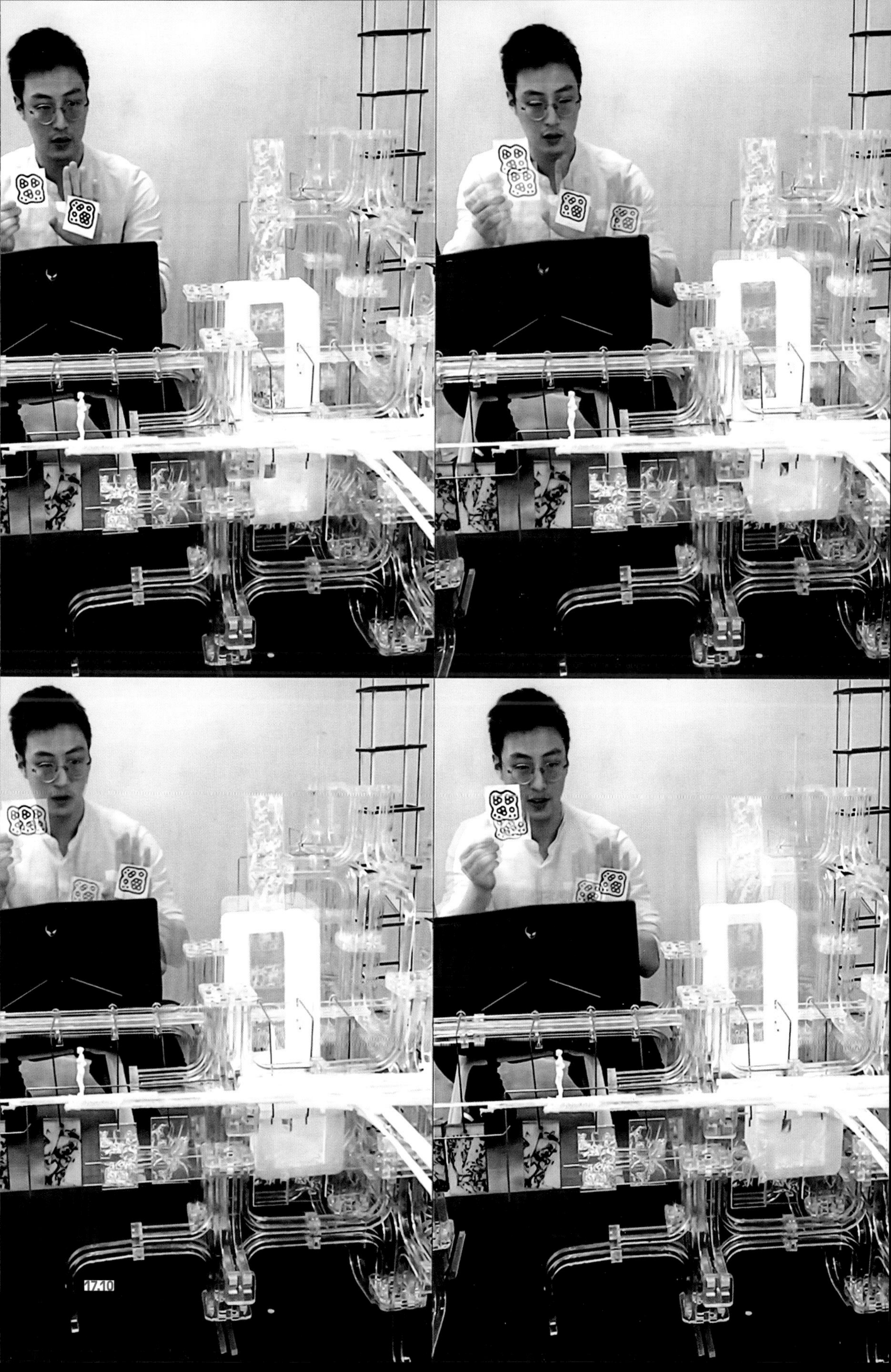
17:10

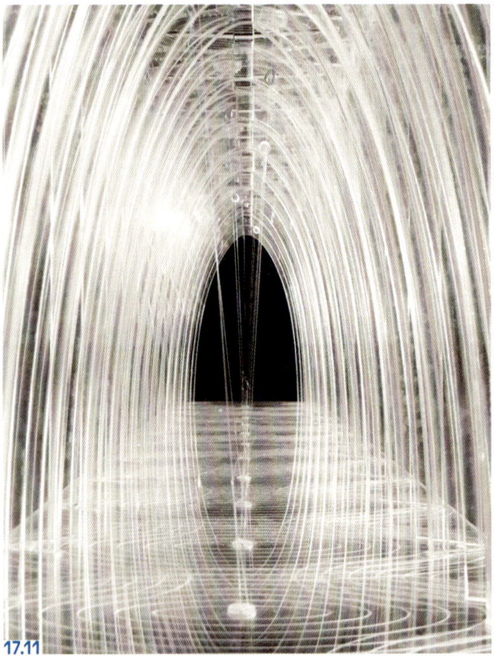
17.11

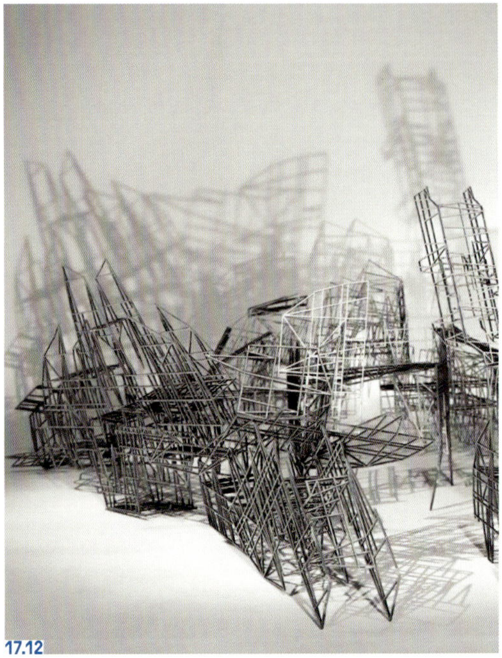
17.12

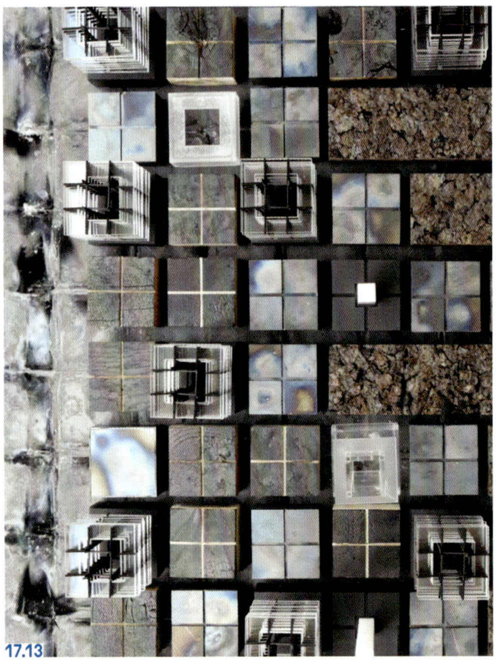
17.13

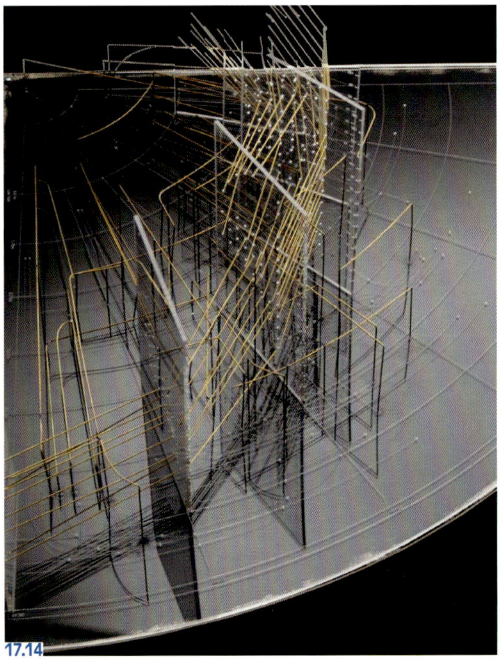
17.14

Fig. 17.11 Jinman Choi Y4, 'Shared Theatre', Dunajec River. This experimental theatre, located at the border of Poland and Slovakia on the Dunajec River, is based on structural, spatial and social oscillations that are made possible through its performative architecture. Non-linear movements generated by the audience's activities on either side of the riverbank activate a moveable floating stage in the middle of the river. **Fig. 17.12 Esha Thapar** Y4, 'Baltic Amber Institute', Gdańsk. This project explores the precise spatiality of human movement, including the residues and remains of a dancer's movements throughout time. In the building proposal, the ruined walls of Granary Island, Gdańsk, become a place for everyday choreographies, housing workshops, public events and festivals. **Fig. 17.13 Alexander Wood** Y4, 'Co-Operative Agraria', Malopolska. A collective farming initiative, structured as a new project for the charity Oxfam, provides an architecture for promoting rural agronomy in the Malopolska region of Southern Poland. As land is cultivated for the production of food, the site is modified and constructed to generate its own architecture. **Fig 17.14 Carl Inder** Y5, 'FABULA: The Baltic Children's Story Park'. Informed by the concept of 'magic realism' as manifested in 'The Tin Drum', the project speculates how similar tactics might be developed architecturally to convert the monumental 'U-Boat Hall' and rehabilitate the site by challenging and exploring ideas about space, history and cultural identity through storytelling.

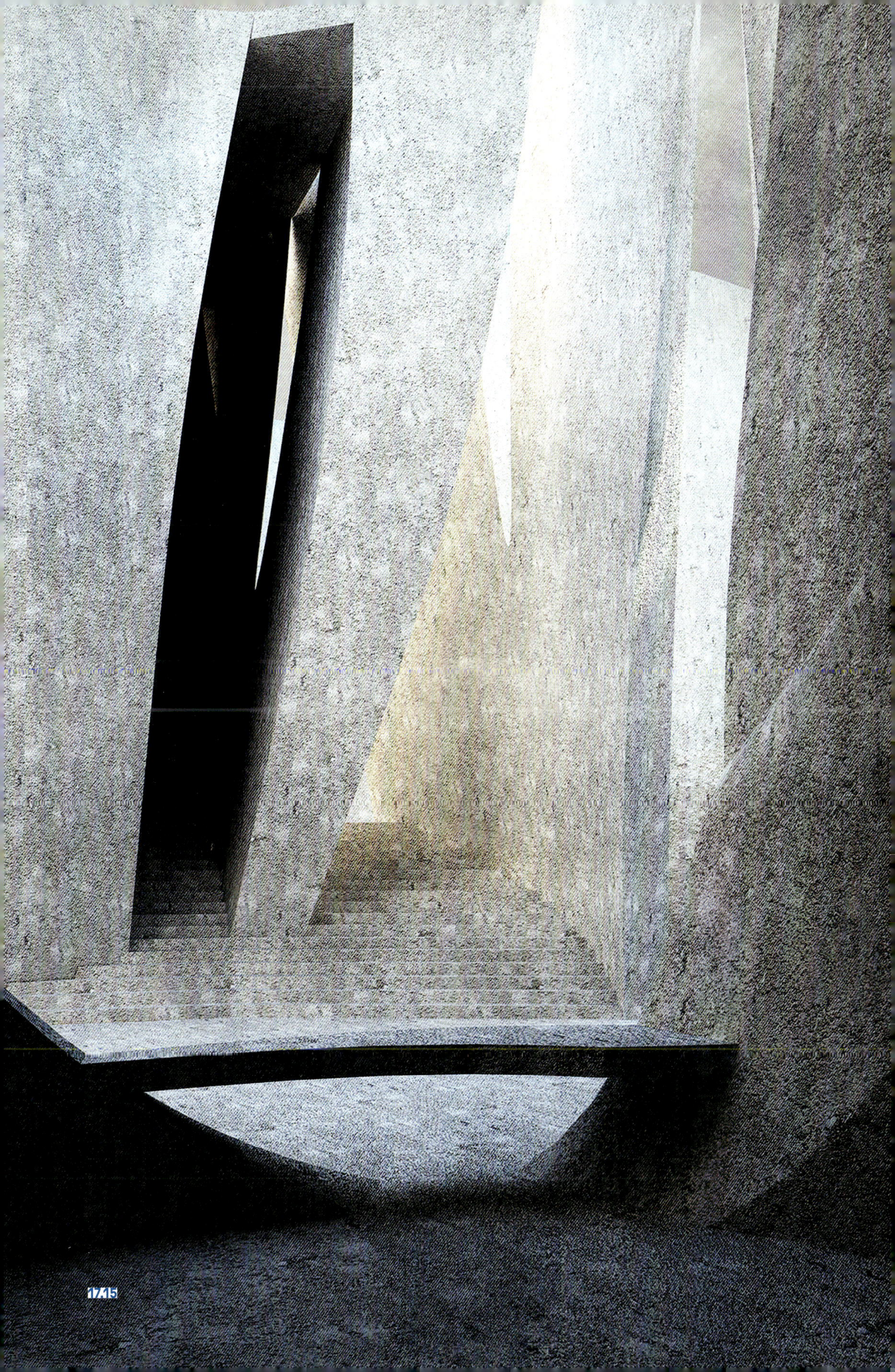

17.15

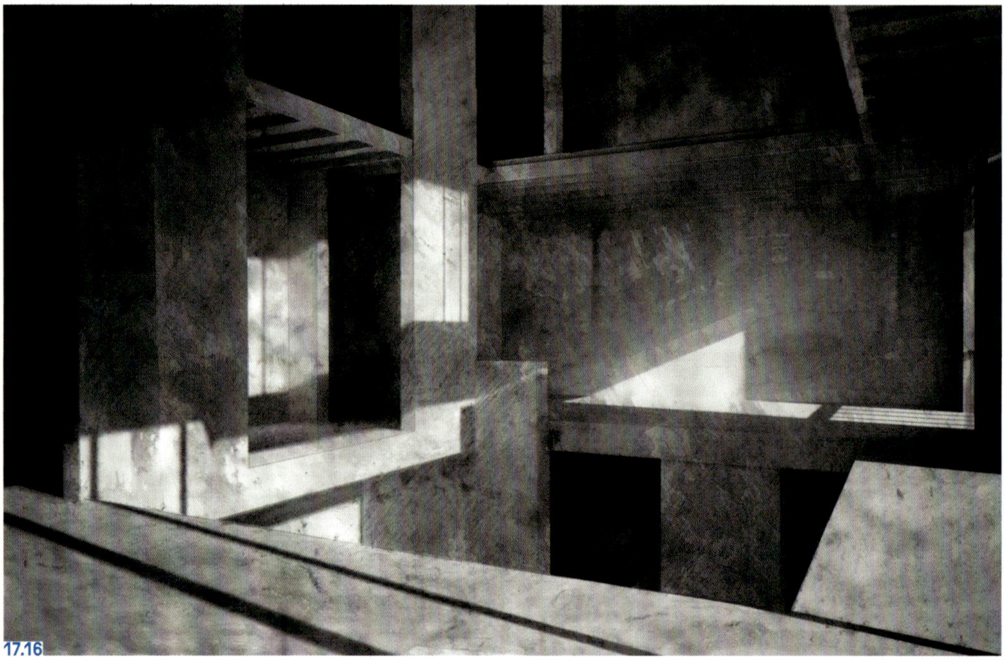

17.16

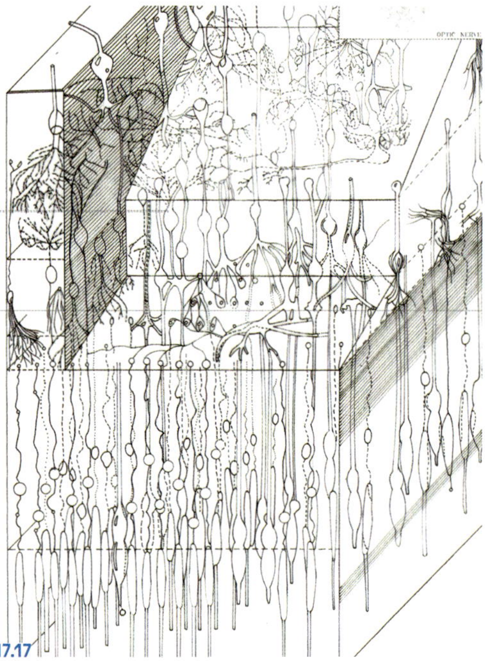

17.17

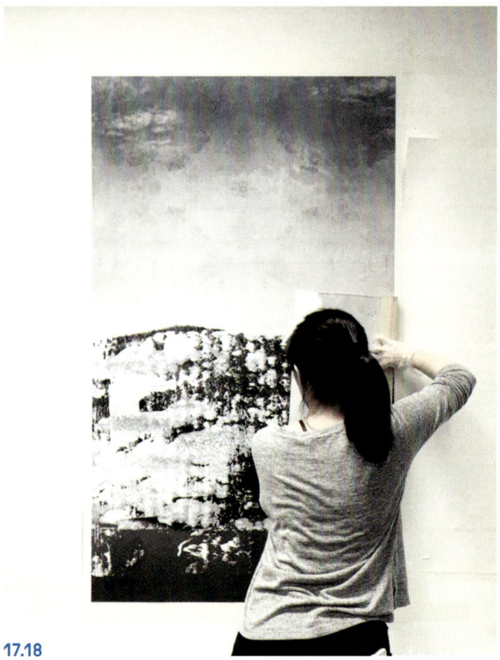

17.18

Fig. 17.15 **Vasilis Marcou Ilchuck** Y5, 'Chrono–Spaces', Famagusta, Cyprus. The project explores 'lived spaces' as described in the recorded memories of the old inhabitants of Famagusta who have been displaced from their homes since 1974. Collective and individual memories are transformed into spaces to be inhabited by both Turkish and Greek-speaking Cypriots, enhancing their relation with nature, their land and the daily and annual cycles of the seasons. 'Chrono–Spaces' explores how an unprogrammed and anticipatory architecture within this 'ghost' city may become a new environment for future social and political events. The design is carved into the ground, made by limestone. It evolves from the study of temporal and structural formations of tree rings (dendrochronology), seeking to find analogous manifestations in the vernacular arrangements of settlements. **Fig. 17.6** **Oscar Plastow** Y5, 'Sculpting Void: The Allure of Mountains', Zakopane, Poland. Inspired by the brutalist work of Walter Förderer and the experimental, chance and spontaneity-based methodologies of avant-garde art, this work develops through iterative physical models and a set of sequential drawings that explore interiority and light. The proposal sees an existing mountain hut in Zakopane enveloped by a new building which both has a more contemporary use, yet manages to retain the unique character and political history of the location. Driven by Townscape Principles, the project proposes a sequence of interiors that are in direct dialogue with the surrounding landscape.

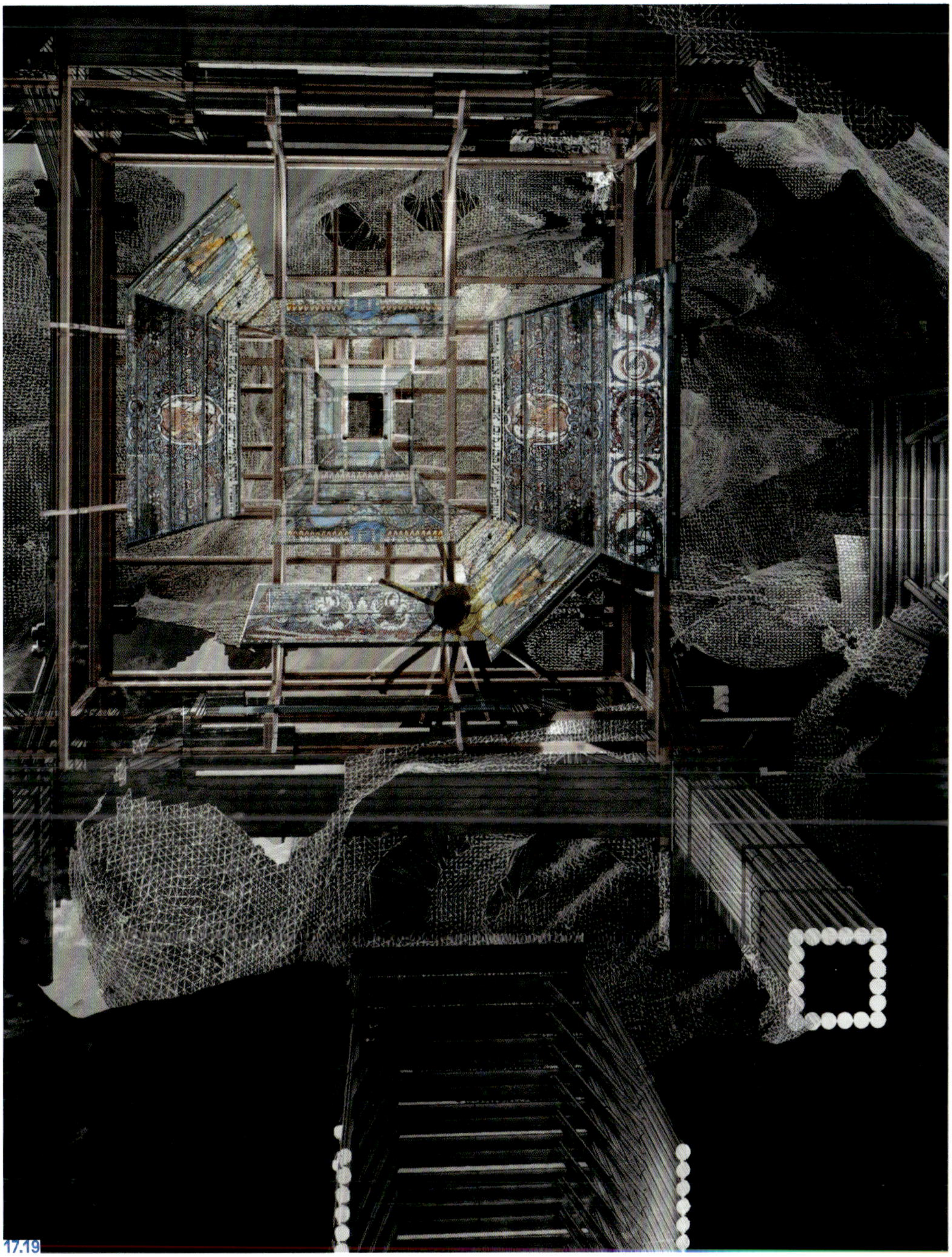

17.19

Fig. 17.17 Eleni Zygogianni Y4, 'The New Ministry of Education of Poland', Warsaw, Poland. The proposed Government Institution for Education is structured as a labyrinthine journey through the pages of a book. The project starts with a series of anatomical drawings that investigate the cognitive functions of the brain, and attempts to find equivalent complex intersections in the plan of the proposed building. **Fig. 17.18 Naomi Au** Y4, 'On-Stream Casino', Niedzica, Poland. Inspired by the puzzling nature of particle behaviour at the quantum scale, the proposed online gambling data centre embodies the ambiguous nature of quantum theory through its ever-changing states. Dependent on the steam generated by the gambling activities and the surrounding landscape near Niedzica's water power station, the building transforms throughout the seasons. **Fig. 17.19 Christie Kwan Yeung** Y5, 'Salt Galleries', Wieliczka, Poland. The project examines the architectural and social character of the lost wooden Synagogues in Poland, built during the Polish-Lithuanian Commonwealth period and destroyed during World War II. Timber fragments of the synagogues are preserved and displayed in the purifying environment of the magnificent underground salt mines, particularly in the cavities of salt rock layers abundant beneath the town of Wieliczka. This allows for a new form of inhabitation of the precious fragments of these timber synagogues, which were built during the 16th and 17th centuries.

Unit 18

Generational Phantoms/ Re-de-constructing Ecology

Isaïe Bloch, Ricardo de Ostos

Year 4
James Joseph Bashford, Matthew James Rogers, Alisa Silanteva, Tatiana Rocio Southey-Bassols, Ren Yang Tan, Arturs Tols

Year 5
Arti Braude, Anjie Gu, Man Jia, Nikolaos Koutroulos, Matteo Mauro, Nicholas Stamford, Risa Tadauchi, Samuel Whiting, Chan Sze (Maisie) Yan

Thank you to:
Sir Peter Cook, Manuel Jimenez García, Jakub Klaska, Daniel Kohler, Claudia Palma, Igor Pantic, Yael Reisner, Javier Ruiz, Harald Trapp, Daniel Widrig, Yeena Yoon

Up close, no one is normal. In architecture and cultural studies, a similar saying can also apply. It is easy to conceive of an image about general contextual characteristics, national styles, local mannerisms or regional patterns. However, when exploring those elements in design, it becomes clear that form follows culture. But what are the opportunities for cultural studies in architectural design?

——This year we travelled to Peru to investigate how the Andean landscape shaped architecture and its many lifestyles, villages and cities. Home to the Inca civilization, we visited multiple urban and natural sites at different altitudes, from the ancient ruins of Machu Picchu to Peru's capital city of Lima, with its modern and colonial architecture; from the Pacific Ocean climate to the dry deserts of Pachacamac. For many students, it was their first visit to South America, and that precise feeling of strangeness and contemplation generated many discussions. Cheerful conversations with our many hosts varied from gender-based houses, mystic landscapes, desert-dwelling adaptation, altitude sickness, and how Peruvian food and its cities are incredibly rich and deeply flavoured. The return to London meant great memories, but also the challenge to mediate critically between cultural references and design ambitions.

——If experimentation in design is about taking risks, testing out techniques and exploring the unknown, our students have been highly experimental. Mixing contemporary design strategies and older crafts, projects were developed as a response to both the context of Peru, and also to the context of making itself. From concrete casting, wood and metal carving, nylon 3D-printed moulds to jelly blobs and furry upholstering, we experimented how to think via design.

——Matteo Mauro recreates the ongoing airport masterplan for the city of Cuzco as a sacred geoglyph. By understanding the Inca tradition of city-building and contrasting it with colonial and contemporary commercial built practices, he re-imagines parts of the site as semi-figurative enclosures, built as long-term negotiations between the community and the city. Nicholas Stamford proposes a decomposing community centre, tying together the problematic of mining towns and village resilience. As parts of the factory building erode in time, new spaces appear to be appropriated by the community, and also by local fauna and flora.

——This year we learnt about the beauty of contextualising architecture and also the necessity to be – and feel – alien in the emerging landscapes of spatial politics.

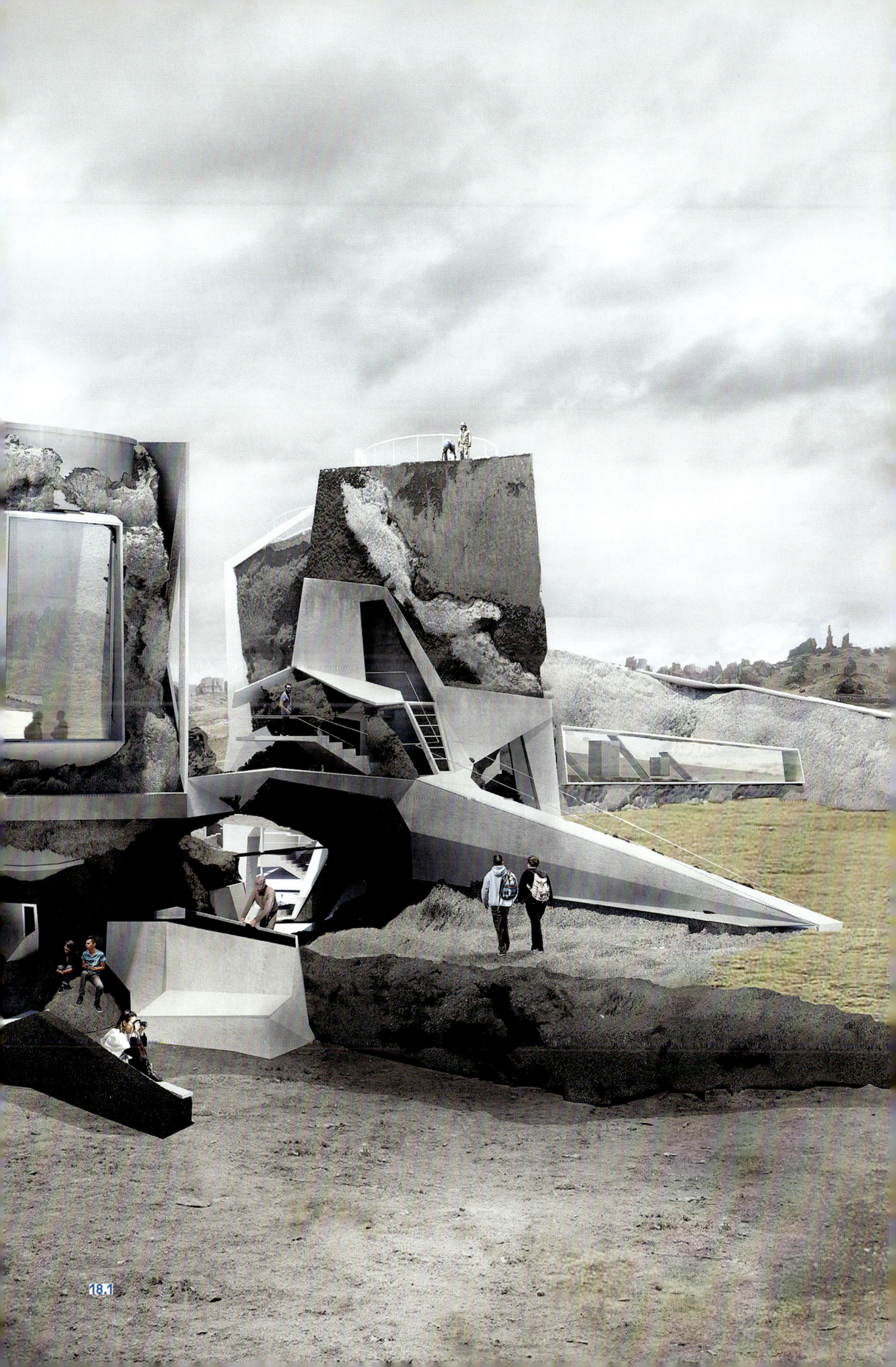

18.1

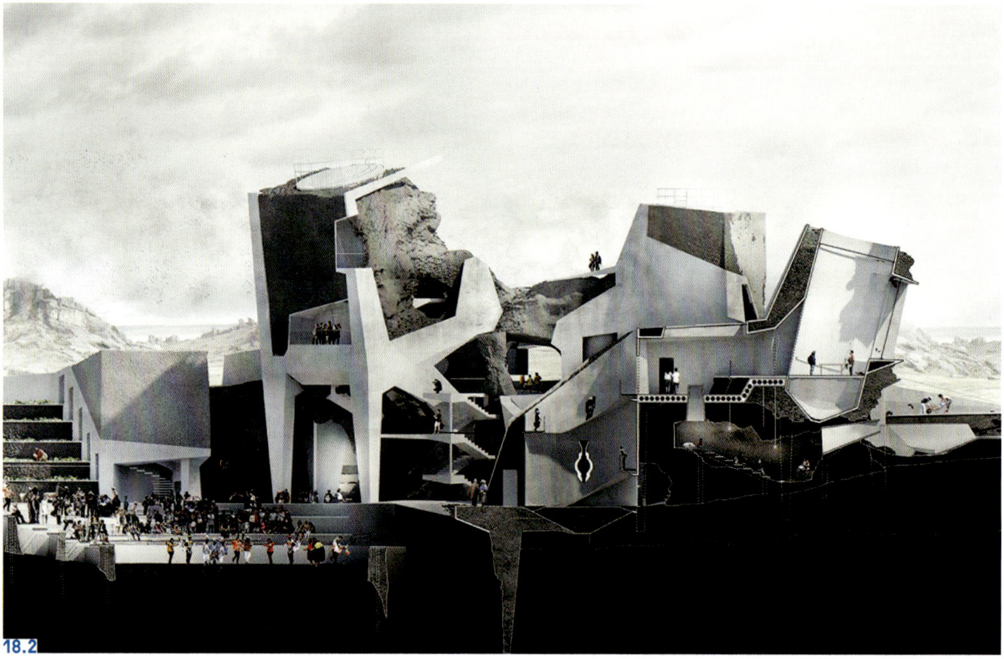

18.2

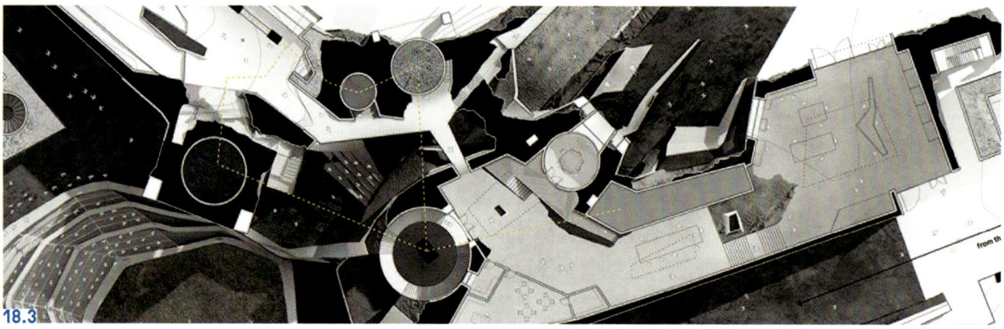

18.3

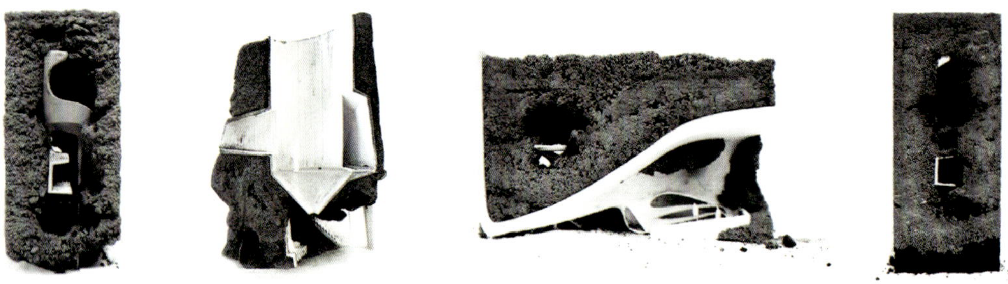

18.4

Figs. 18.1 – 18.4 Nicholas Stamford Y5. 'A Resilient Landscape'. In Huayllay, 4,300m above sea level in the Andes, the project mediates the eroding materiality of the landscape, creating cycles of formal shift based on material consistency and village ritual cycles. The section illustrates the forum area and farming terraces. Through years of usage and landscape metamorphosing, the area behind the main building-mass exposes its material decomposition and renewal. The plan exhibits the infrastructural concrete masses and user circulation zones. By mixing existing local mining waste and sustainable local practices, the building articulates both industrial and indigenous traditions in a project of interiors and vast panoramic views. A series of physical models test material consistency between concrete, sand, earth and volcanic ash, as well as triggering different cycles of formal decomposition in response to local wind patterns and usage.

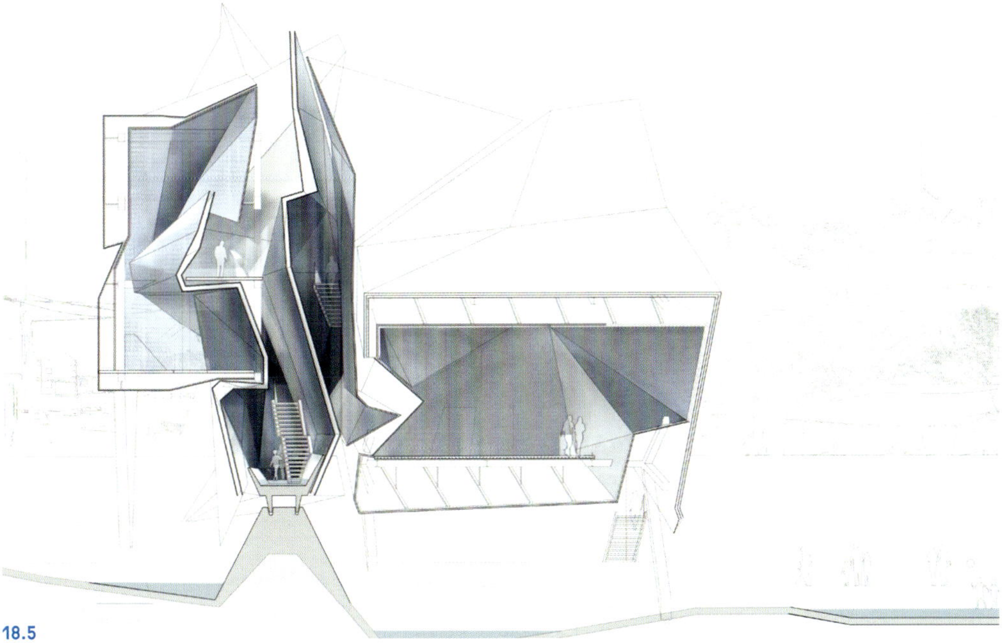

18.5

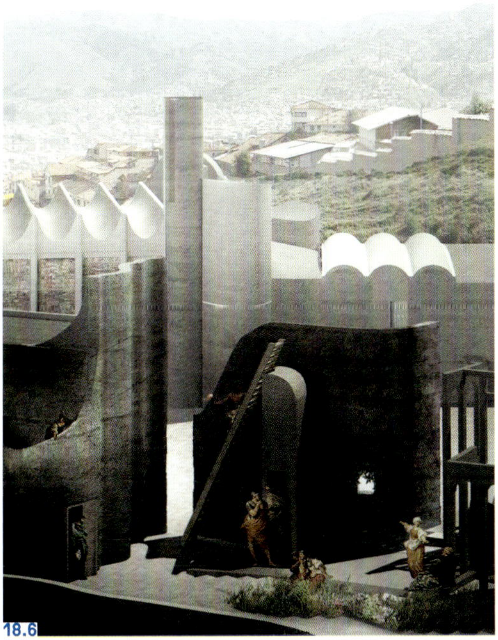

18.6

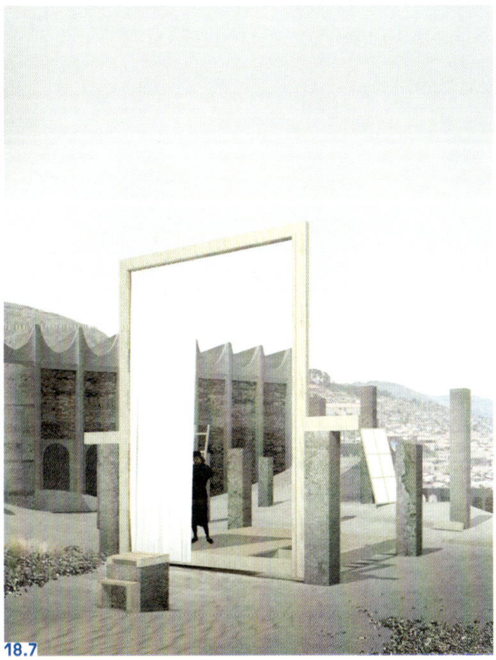

18.7

Fig. 18.5 Alisa Silanteva Y4, 'Waterscapes'. Section through a proposal for an educational centre located in Lima, where surface delaminations result in spatial permeability. By bringing water in and around the building, the scheme allows light reflection and cooling to counterpoint the surrounding dry urbanscape. **Figs. 18.6 – 18.7 Artur Tols** Y4, 'Cusco Landscape Theatre'. Both illustrations represent an alternative way of engaging with theatre space and performance. The landscape surrounding the theatre enclosure is overlaid with a residue of theatre props and other architectural elements, which by themselves act as a more spontaneous form of play. Users can reappropriate those elements and congregate around them for a vast range of activities.

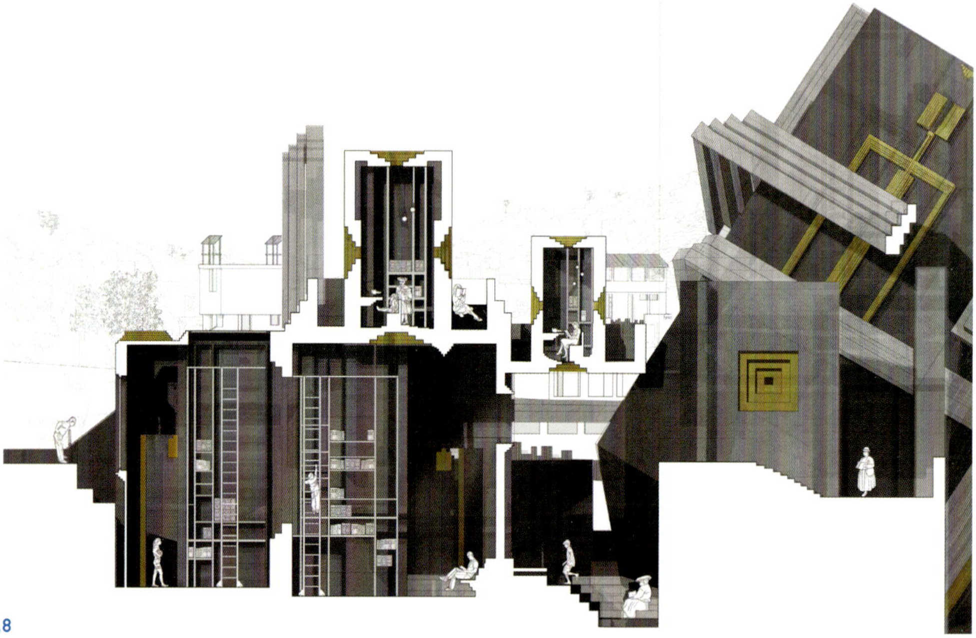

18.8

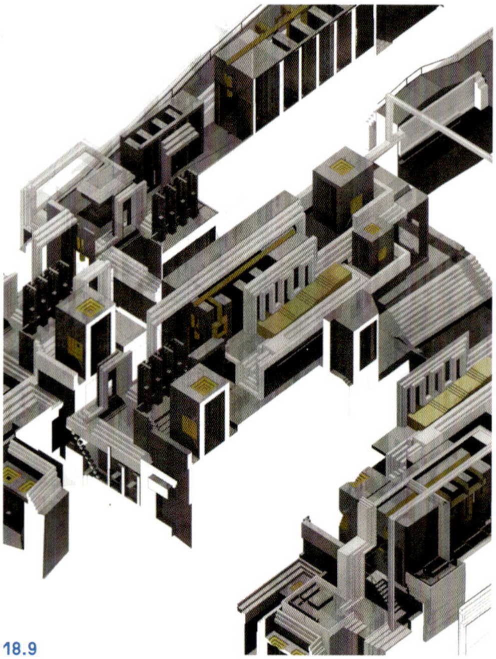

18.9

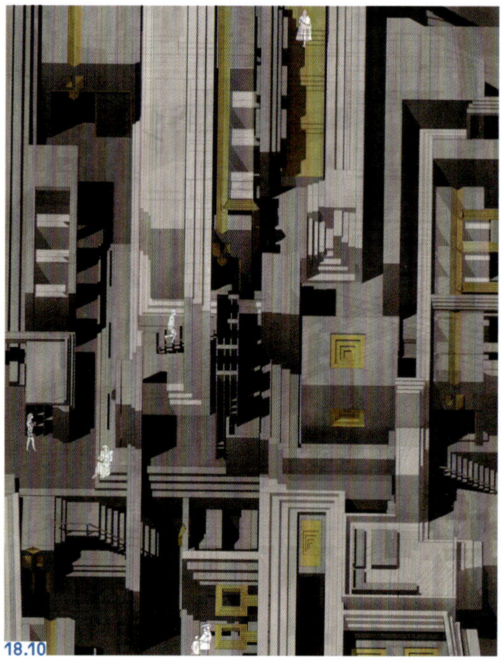

18.10

Figs. 18.8 – 18.10 Samuel Whiting Y5, 'Aymara Archive'. The project facilitates the continuous growing of the archive by providing rooms for locals to record their oral stories. By doing so, this establishes a new cycle of inclusion for the Aymara culture. Located in the city of Juli in Peru, the project references the research of cognitive scientist Rafael Nuñez to create a language of spatial framing, linear pattern, motive repetition and non-linear paths. The overall circulation through the archive uses a system of Aymara gestures and patterns. Users of the archive must pass through specific signifiers (such as a golden marker) a certain number of times in order fully to understand the complexities of the archive and decipher the relationship between its elements in relation to the information stored.

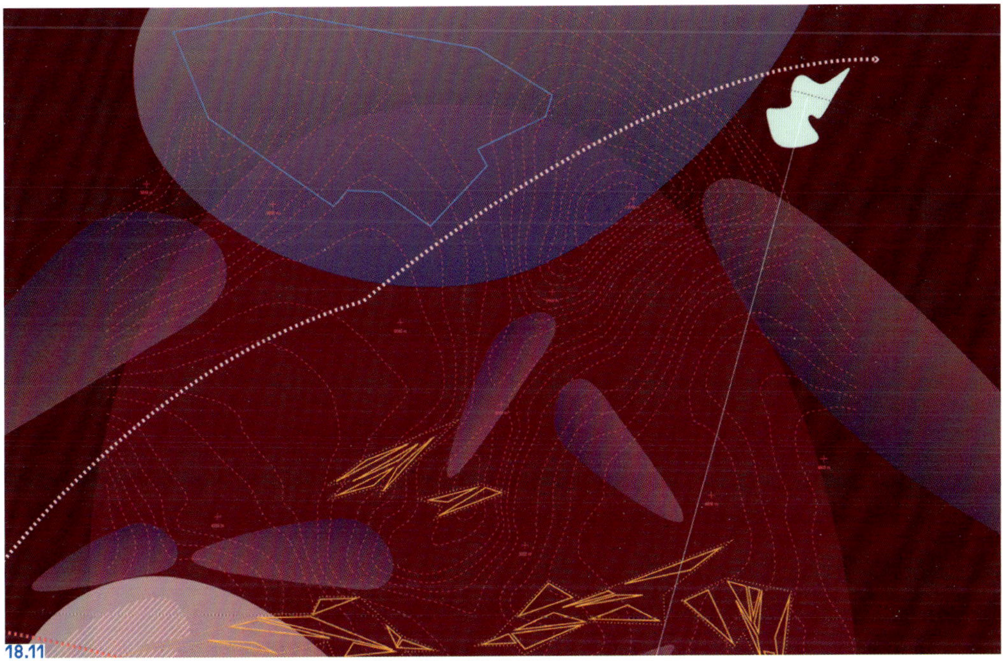

18.11

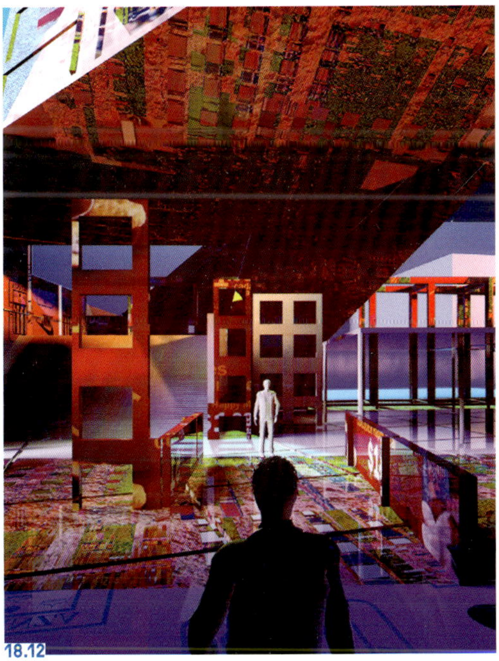

18.12

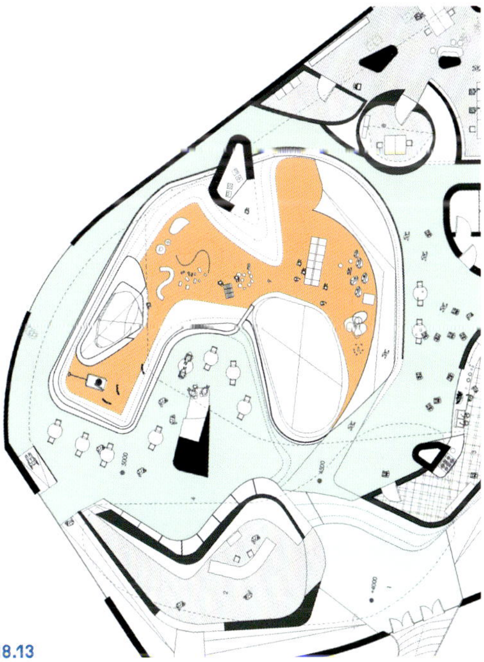

18.13

Fig. 18.11 Risa Tadauchi Y5, 'Landscape Intimacy'. Located in the Rainbow Mountains in Peru, a series of lodges explore the notion of comfort and intimacy in a unique environmental setting. The project explores material malleability and the threshold between soft and hard surfaces in a high-altitude terrain. **Fig. 18.12 Nikolaos Koutroulos** Y5, 'Lima 2019 Screens'. The project proposes to redesign a partially existing sports site in the city of Lima in order to host the 2019 Pan American Games, which will be held in the city. Based on Chicha, a local street culture and visual signage in Lima, the design speculates about a hyper-intense blend of sports and popular imagery. It mixes both screens and physical infographics to mediate different uses. **Fig. 18.13 Tatiana Rocio Southey-Bassols** Y4 'A Vendor's Retreat'. Speculating on female empowerment and the effects of displacement on the everyday life of a street-vending community in Lima. The proposal articulates mass, atmosphere and ground extension to create an inclusive architecture of practical hope.

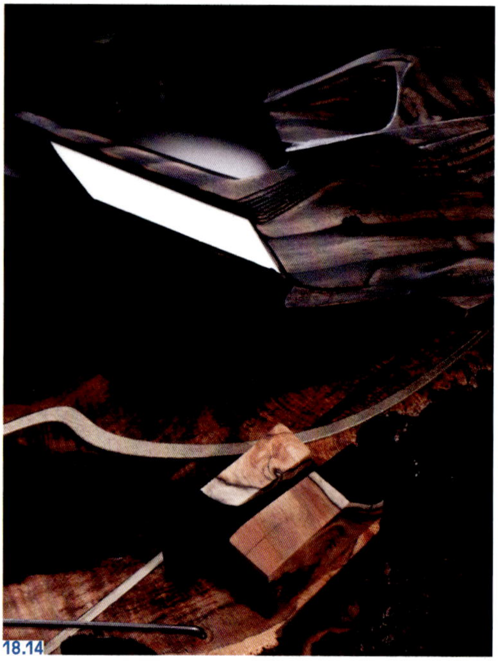

18.14

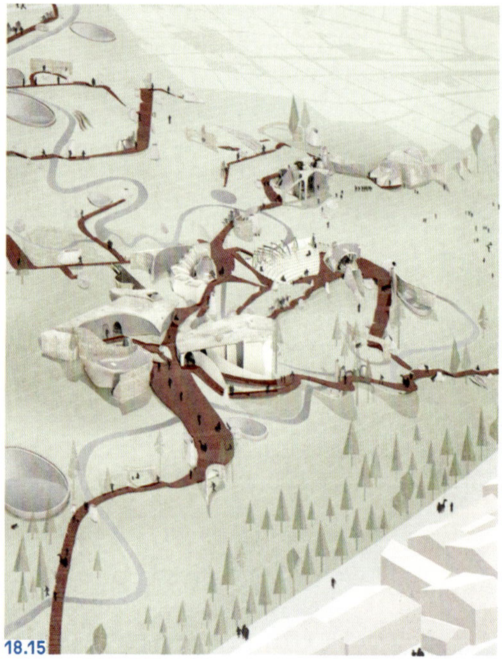

18.15

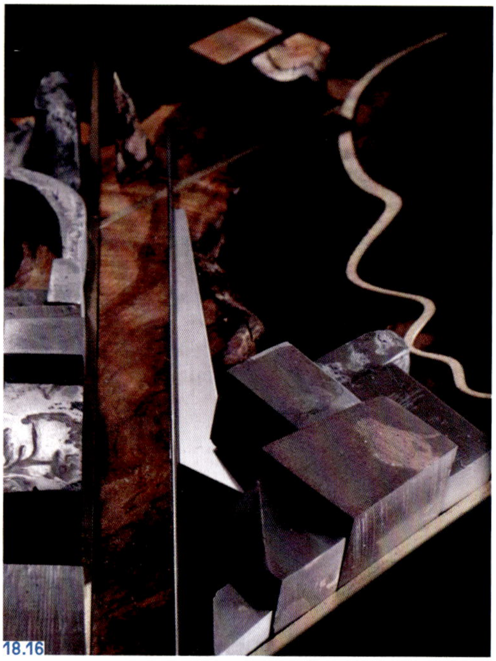

18.16

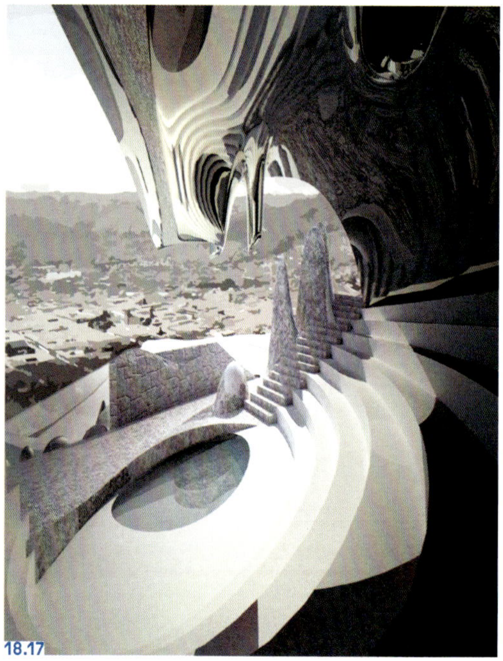

18.17

Figs. 18.14, 18.16 & 18.18 Matteo Mauro Y5, 'MicroMegalic DeJavu'. Physical model exploring a more hands-on/crafted way of engaging with city planning, thus suggesting and relating to a non-western form of urban organisation. Investigating a contemporary way of using large-scale figural elements in order to dissolve an even larger-scale infrastructural geoglyph within the city of Cusco. **Fig. 18.15 Man Jia** Y5, 'Land Speaks Identity'. Section through the landscape, Quechua Language School. By designing a rule set for the position, forms, openings and materials of the schools, a journey of discovery ensues. Allowing Quechua language, identity and landscape to encounter each other within a steep mountainous topography. **Fig. 18.17 Man Jia** Y5, 'Land Speaks Identity'. Mixing chromatic and stone materials, the design develops a formal language that recreates native navigation methods using contemporary undertones and laminations. Through a series of semi-open spaces and plateaus along an ascending route, the project intends to produce a public space in which Quechua language students, locals and tourists can interact and engage in sharing knowledge.

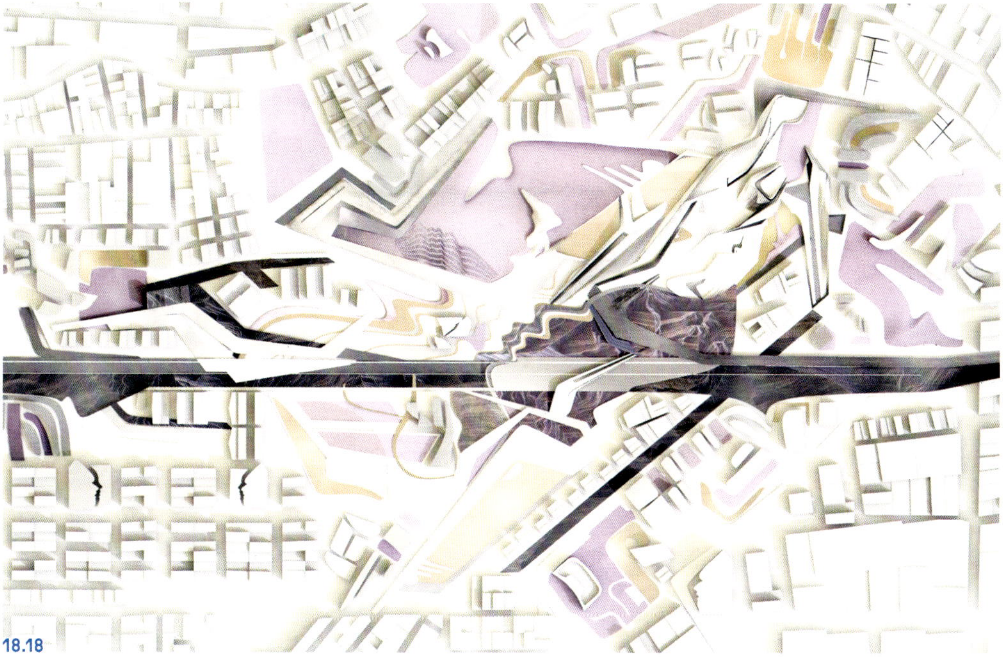
18.18

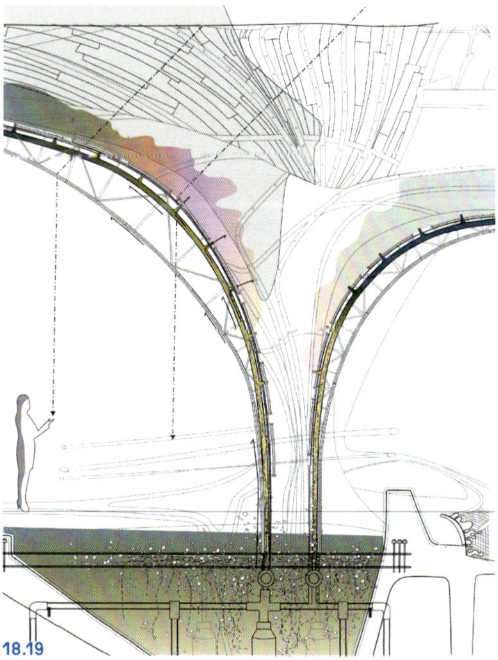
18.19

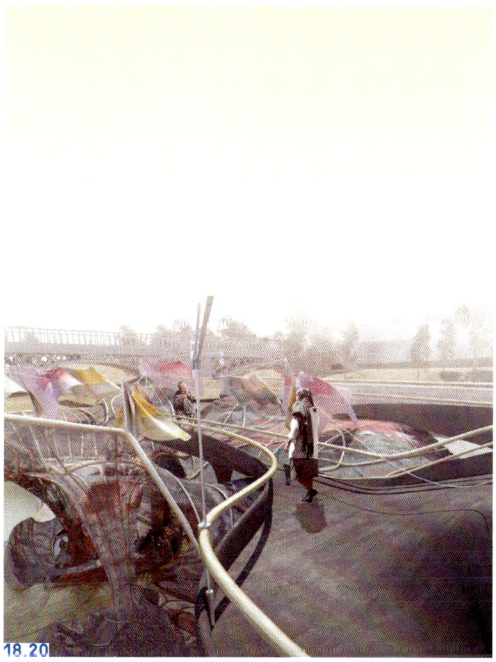
18.20

Figs. 18.19 – 18.20. Chan Sze (Maisie) Yan Y5 'Trace and Marking'. Water system canopy utilising polluted water from the Rimac river in Lima, together with natural oxidation processes, in order to create colourful textile products, based on native symbolic tones. The concrete structure acts as an extension of the existing promenade, while the lightweight transparent canopy emerges from the base of the river below. They blend with each other in order to create a participatory public building, where users engage with both pollution awareness and upcycling of those pollutants into consumer-friendly textiles.

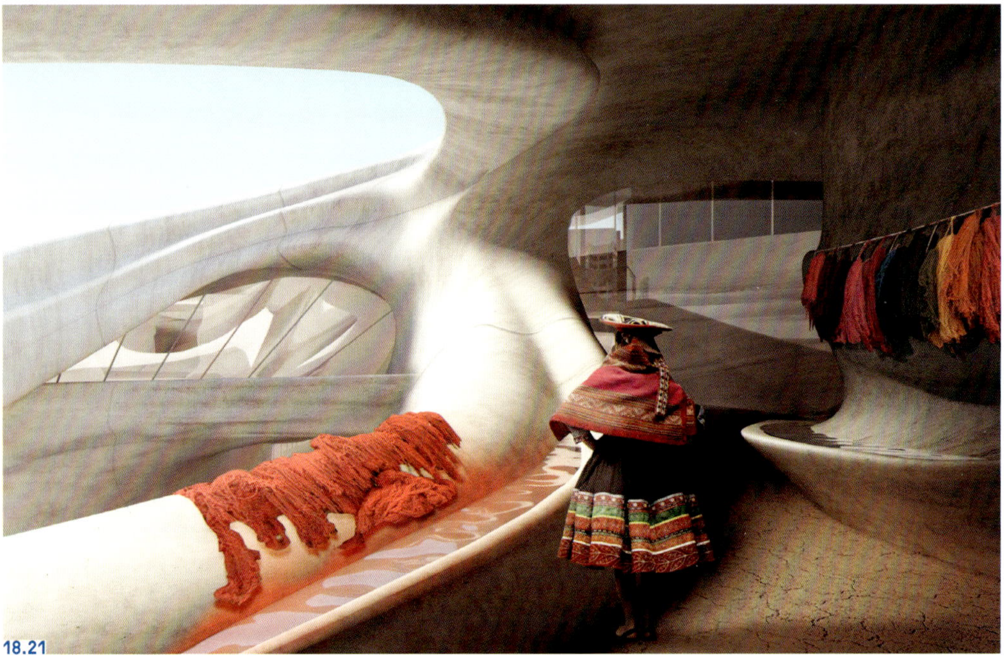

18.21

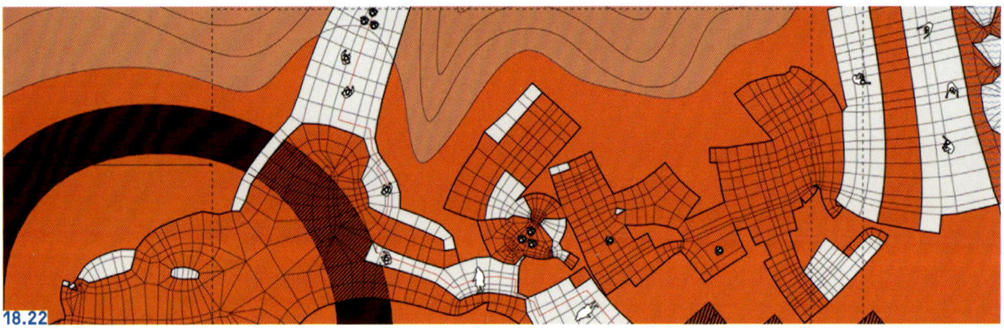

18.22

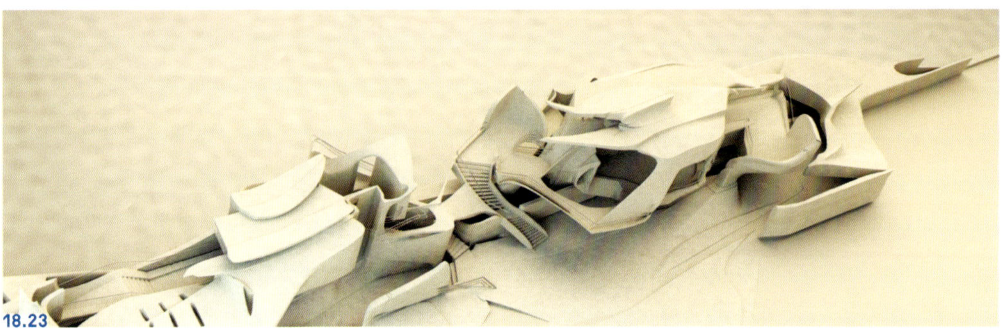

18.23

Fig. 18.21 Ren Yang Tan Y4, 'Woven Futures'. The project is a proposition for an Urban Andean Weaving workshop to revitalise an abandoned civic plot adjacent to the museum of art in the Exposition Palace Park of Lima. This will create an independent enterprise zone for textile art production and education. **Fig. 18.22 Anjie Gu** Y5, 'Unfolding Maps – Civic Centre for Cusco'. Drawing inspired by ancient Andean water vessels and their unique form of mapping the environment. Between the plan and the unfolded 3D model, the drawing maps Cusco's key features in order to create a spatial arrangement system for the internal spaces of the civic centre proposal. **Fig. 18.23 Arti Braudi** Y5, 'Syncretic City'. Between a building and a semi-enclosed landscape, the project explores hybrid identities in postcolonial Lima.

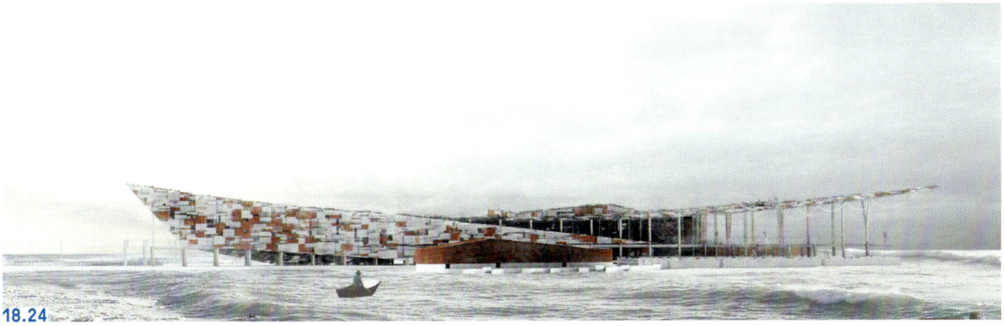

18.24

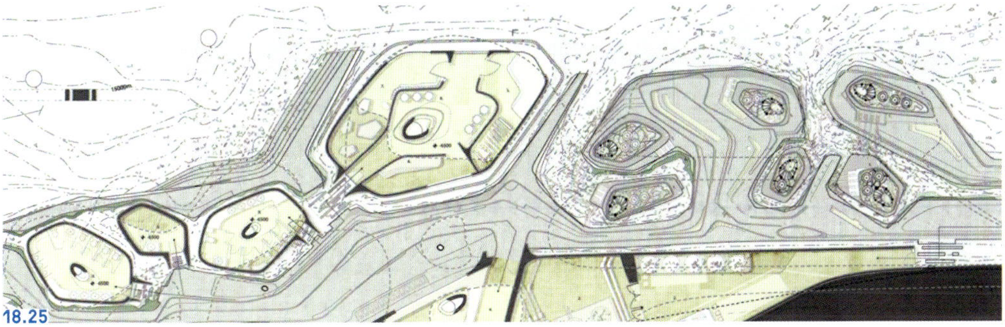

18.25

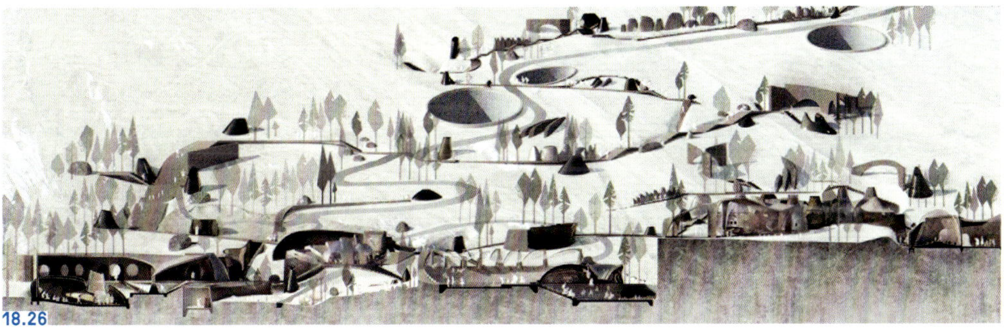

18.26

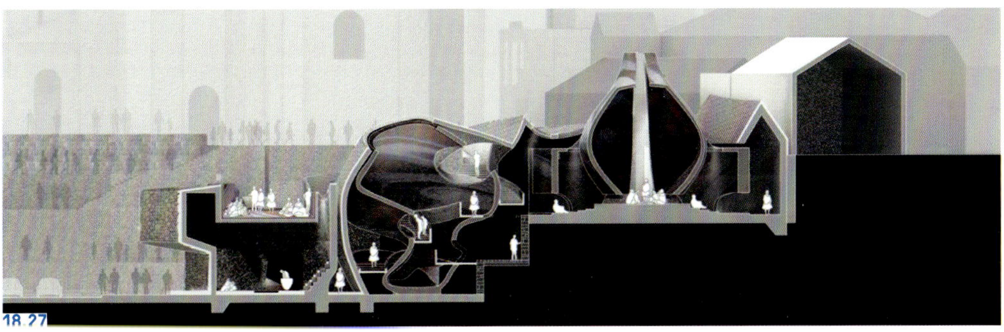

18.27

Fig. 18.24 Matthew James Rogers Y4, 'Floating Fishery'. Proposal for a floating fishery, bridging sea and land. **Fig. 18.25 Chan Sze (Maisie) Yan** Y5, 'Trace and Marking'. Plan organising making activities and visitor areas. Positioned along the Rimac river in Lima, Peru, the design reacts to water levels and pollution in a dynamic sequence of floating hubs and unifying canopies. **Fig. 18.26 Man Jia** Y5, 'Land Speaks Identity'. Section through the landscape, Quechua Language School. By designing a rule set for the position, forms, openings and materials of the schools, a journey of discovery ensues. Allowing Quechua language, identity and landscape to encounter each other within a steep mountainous topography. **Fig. 18.27 Anjie Gu** Y5, 'Unfolding Maps – Civic Centre for Cusco'. Section through exhibition spaces and open public areas above. The project explores how Andean culture would perceive the natural and built environment in today's urban context, so as to deliver an architectural map which is about both exhibition and usage, but also functions as a chamber of experiences.

Unit 19 Architecture Made of Parts

Mollie Claypool, Manuel Jimenez García, Gilles Retsin

Year 4
Elliot Bishop, Alya El-Chiati, Sara Martinez, Milot Pireva, Jevgenij Rodionov, Liangjie Wu, Hui Ye, Michael Zieja

Year 5
Tzoulia Baltsavia, Gintare Stonkute, Ivo Tedbury, Oscar Walheim

Thank you to our consultants and critics: Jakub Klaska, Harald Trapp, Mario Carpo, Lei Zheng, Nils Fischer, Moa Carlsson, Patrik Schumacher, Sofia Krimizi, Jeroen van Ameijde, Brendon Carlin, Isaïe Bloch, Elliot Mayer, Julian Siravo, Vicente Soler, Alessandro Bava, Effie Kostantinou, Claire McAndrew, Antón García Abril, Aldo Sollazo

Set in post-crisis Avila, Spain, Unit 19 looked into digital production and mass housing. The unit understands digital fabrication technologies not just as tools for mere formal differentiation, but first and foremost as a new mode of production containing a much more subversive agency for political and social change. The unit fundamentally questioned the approach of architects to both digital design and digital production, developing strategies for fully automated, distributed and discrete manufacturing of housing. Students engaged with a range of questions, from contemporary domesticity to the digital economy, robotics and post-capitalism. At the same time, the unit was also deeply invested in design issues such as part-to-whole relations, composition, differentiation and algorithmic design.

——This year's research started with case studies looking into modes of production of housing – looking at historic precedents such as Jean Prouvé's Maison Tropicale and Buckminster Fuller's Dymaxion House, as well as contemporary work by Antón García Abril and the WikiHouse Foundation. The unit attempted to understand the complexities of the housing crisis, both in Spain and London. We debated contemporary forms of domesticity, such as Airbnb, micro-dwellings and self-build initiatives. This initial research was combined with readings by Neil Gerschenfeld, Christopher Alexander and Jeremy Rifkin, as well as computational workshops with Processing and Unity.

——Students were then asked to develop a set of parts, in relation to a specific digital fabrication technology. These parts were defined as open-ended, universal and versatile building blocks, with a digital connectivity logic. This discrete method advances a theoretical argument about the nature of digital design as fundamentally discrete, and also responds to ideas coming from open-source, distributed modes of production, typical for a digitised economy.

——By questioning and designing the system of production behind their building blocks, students developed provocative social and political scenarios intrinsic to their design projects. These scenarios range from micro-housing projects built out of folded sheet-metal (Alya El-Chiati, Year 4), to large collective housing projects based on technologies such as 3D printing or robotic foam-cutting (Tzoulia Baltsavia, Gintare Stonkute, Year 5, Jevgenij Rodionov, Year 4). Other projects are based on discrete robotic assembly (Ivo Tedbury, Year 5) or investigate an entire set of building typologies based on a sophisticated discrete syntax (Oscar Walheim, Year 5). Social scenarios such as youth unemployment in Spain are addressed (Sara Martinez, Year 4), giving rise to new building typologies for mass housing (Liangjie Wu, Milot Pireva, Michael Zieja, Year 4). Projects also took on board questions of a post-scarcity society, resulting in new shared living typologies (Elliot Bishop, Hui Ye, Year 4).

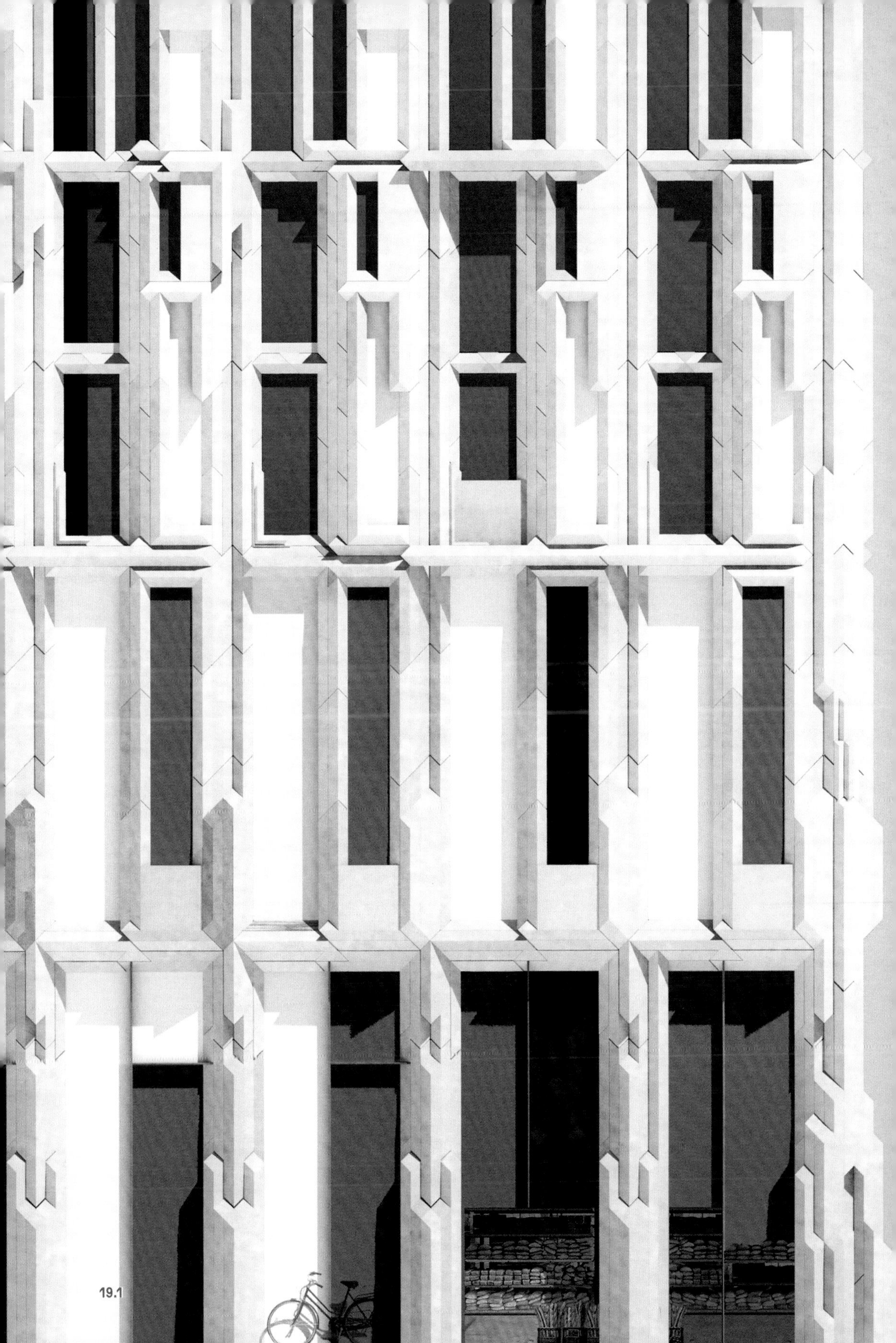
19.1

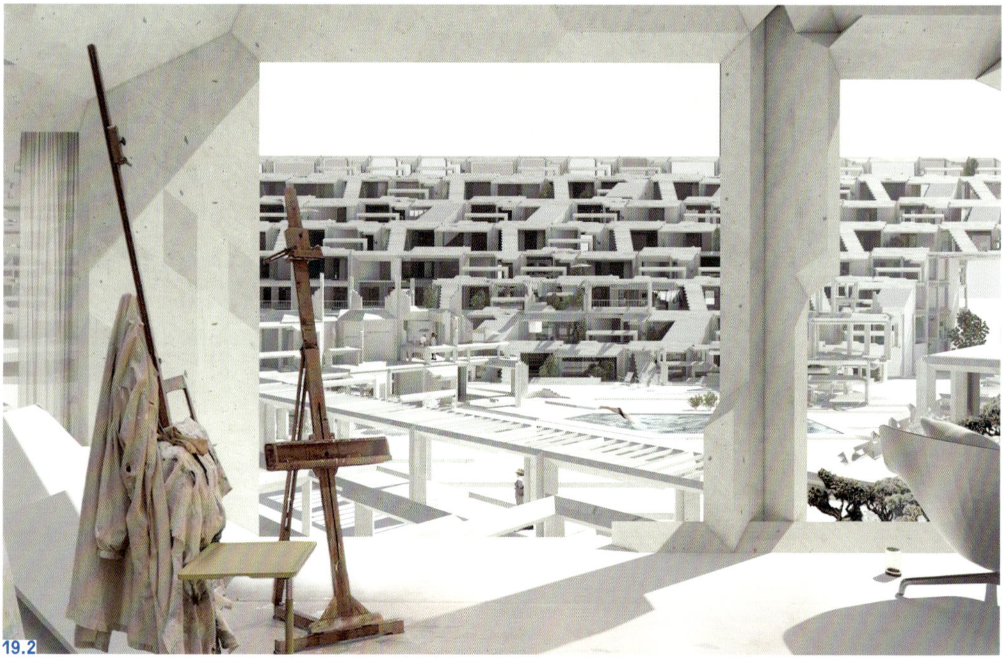

19.2

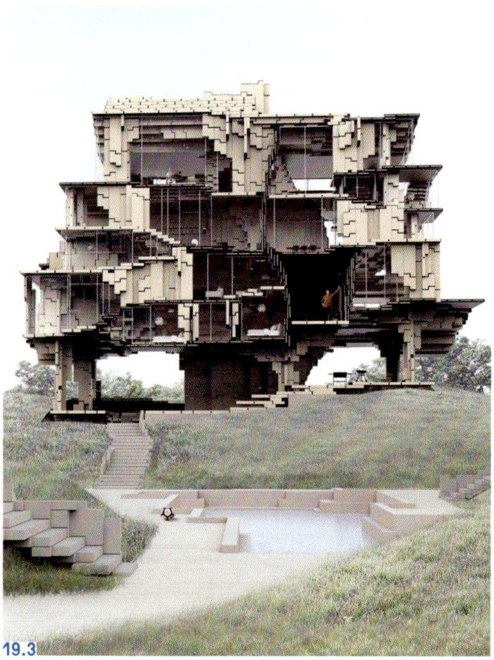

19.3

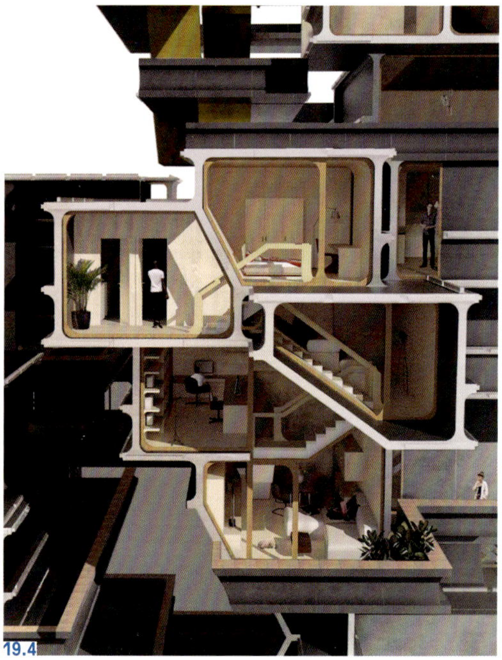

19.4

Figs. 19.1 – 19.2 Oscar Walheim Y5, 'Avila Automatic'. This project develops a new construction ecology – a self-replicating, recombinant architecture. Deploying vacuum-forming as a simple, intuitive and fundamental process, Avila Automatic explores the potential of discrete digital formwork in the generation of precast architectural elements. The recombinatory techniques facilitated by the process result in a new kind of construction ecology. Developing a multitude of typologies, the project explores the formal syntax and modes of inhabitation resulting from this new mode of production. **Fig. 19.3 Hui Ye** Y4, 'Free-Form Assembly'. Thin timber sheet material is combined into box-like building elements, with a male-female connection system. The elements establish differentiated interior conditions, characterised by undulating, stepped surfaces. Different structural and architectural conditions are emergent properties of the continuous recombination of parts, rather than predefined types. The resultant typology is a multi-family house, where the ground floor is left open as a communal space, connected to a green public space. **Figs. 19.4 – 19.5 Tzoulia Baltsavia** Y5, 'I-Architecture'. The project proposes an open-source system based on a kit of parts that can be fabricated using robotic hot-wire cutting. These elements allow for rapid and efficient deployment of an open-ended and adaptive housing product. The discreteness of the kit of parts allows for scalability, something current approaches to open-source architecture often lack.

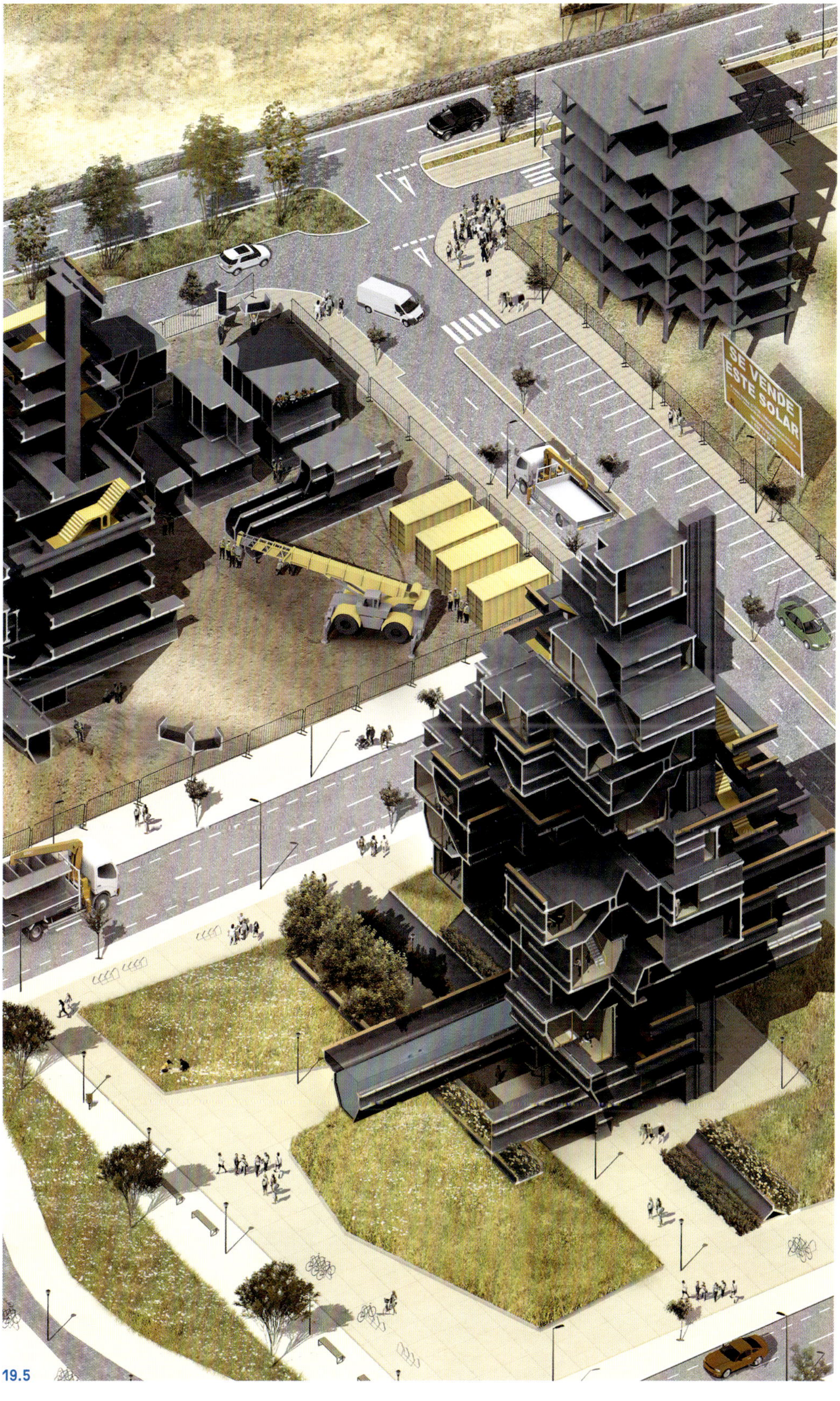

19.5

19.6

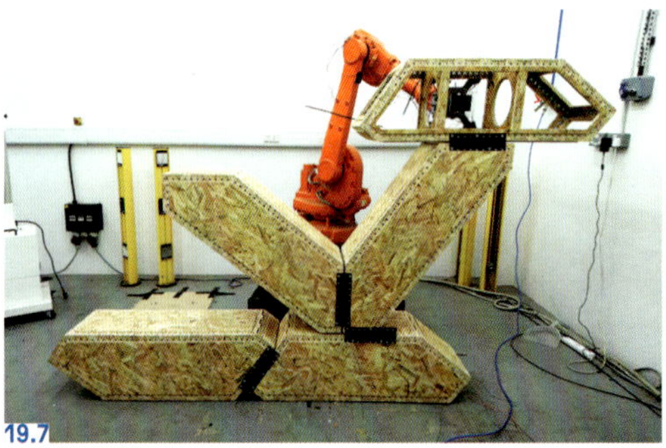

19.7

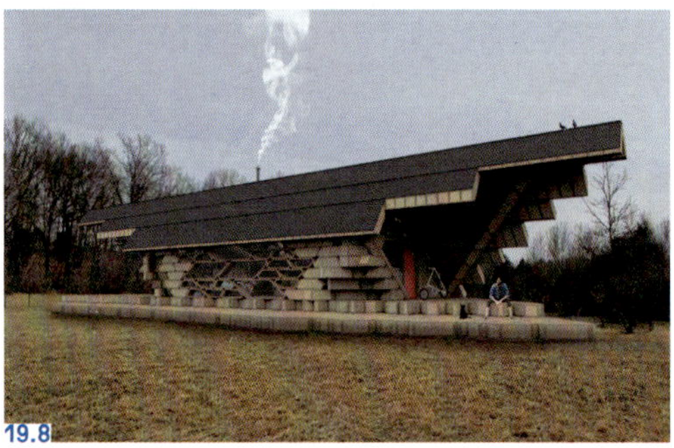

19.8

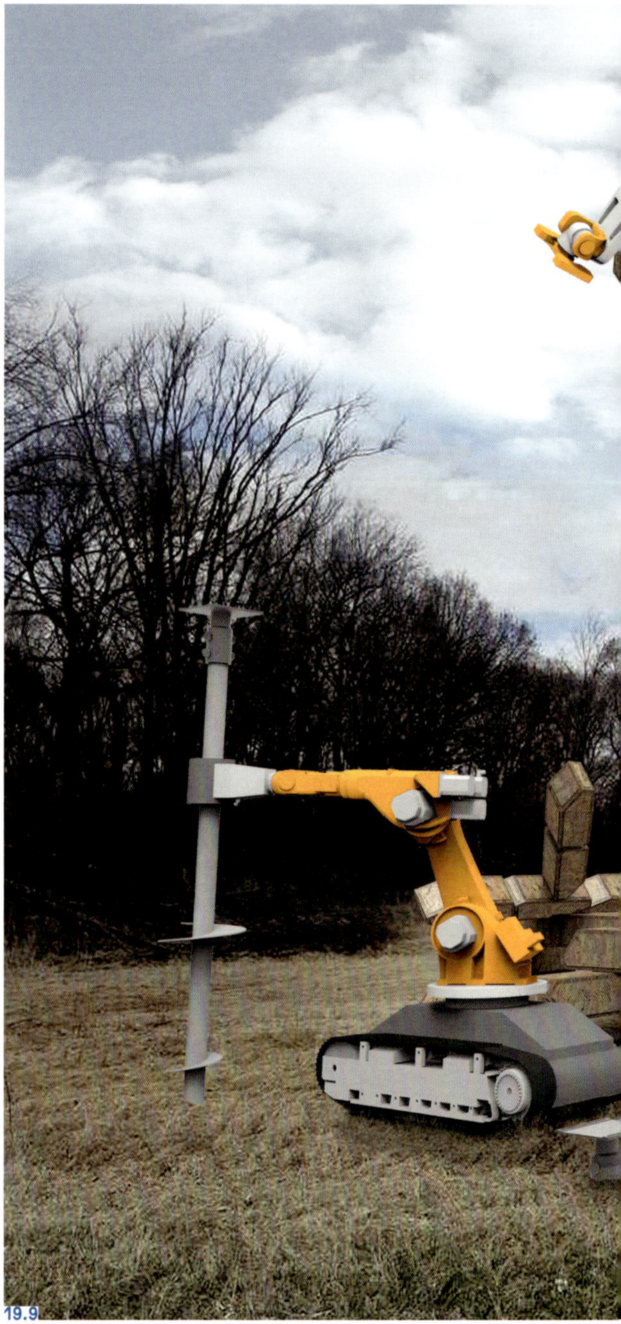

19.9

Fig. 19.6 Gintare Stonkute Y5, 'Print My Village'. The project combines 3D printing technology with prefabricated mass housing. Instead of using large and expensive 3D printers, which would have to be larger than the building itself, the project uses small machines to fabricate a set of universal parts. These parts can then be assembled into larger housing blocks, allowing for a shorter production chain and more flexibility. **Figs. 19.7 – 19.8 Ivo Tedbury** Y5, 'Semblr'. Semblr is a construction platform that enables the automated production of dwellings and other structures. It uses discrete timber bricks and distributed robots which move relative to the structures they assemble. The project states that the use of robots to construct buildings and other structures should lead to shared prosperity in society. This requires an open-source syntax, common to both robotic systems and to the design of the assembled product. An example scenario shows the platform as tool to house people made redundant because of job automation. Leaving behind the capital-based static housing of labour culture, they begin their new post-work lives in Semblr dwellings automatically assembled at a location of their choosing. The physical and temporal flexibility of the system, and the fact that it operates at near-zero financial and environmental cost, means both quasi-nomadic and quasi-luxury living is possible. **Fig. 19.9 Ivo Tedbury** Y5, 'Semblr'. The system's technical foundation is a single syntax for cross-discipline coordination in the form of connection point object-oriented programming (OOP) 'objects' on the edges of the bricks, integrated systems and the robot end

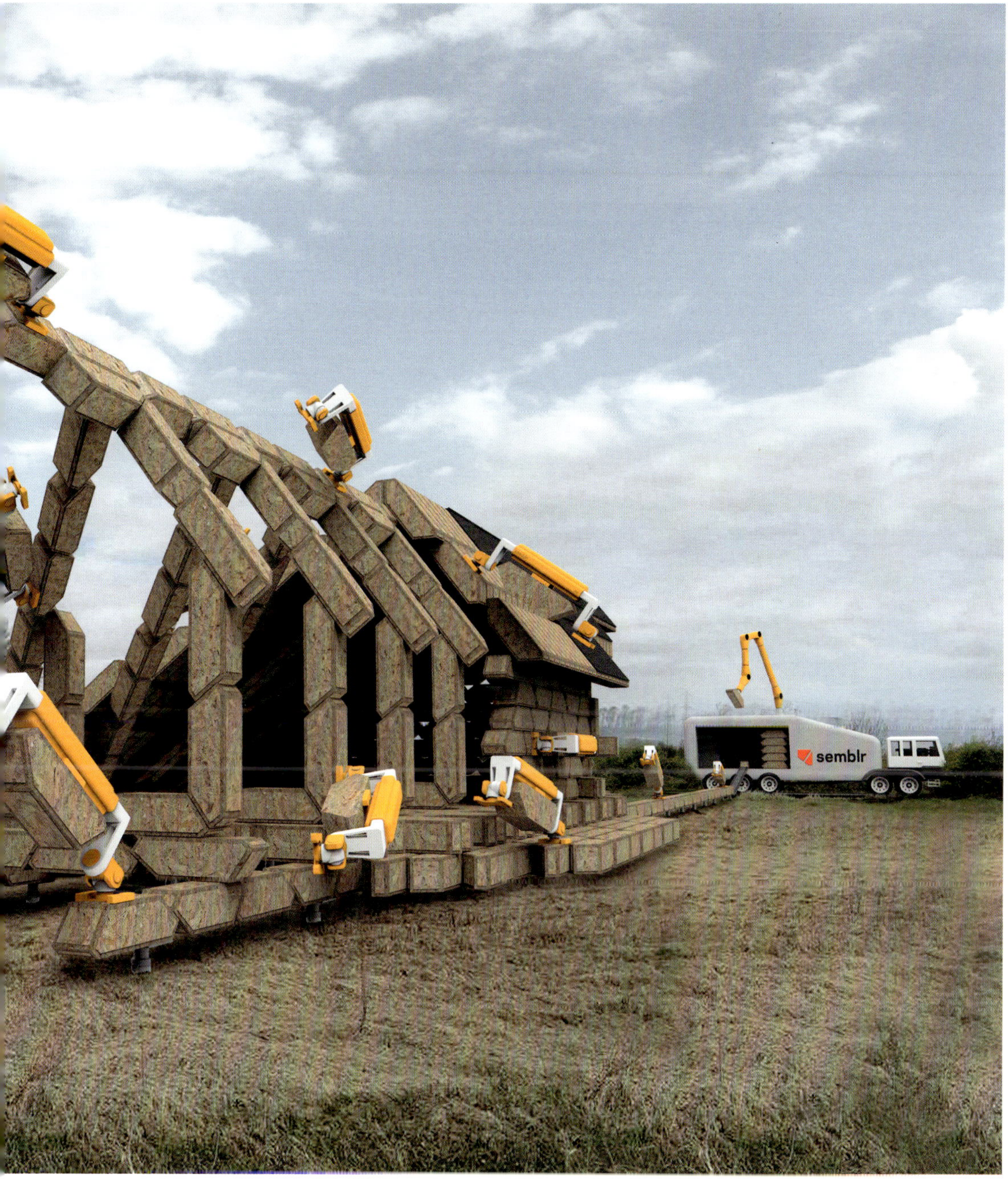

effectors. This shared DNA between brick and robot allows fluid digital and physical interactions, and radically expands the remit of BIM modelling to include robotic assembly and changes to the building over time.

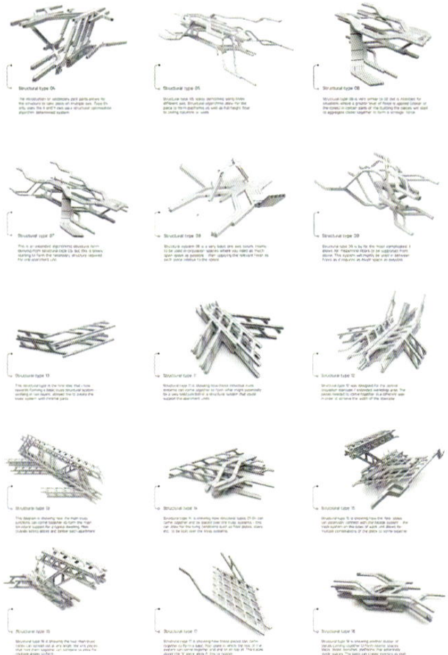

19.10

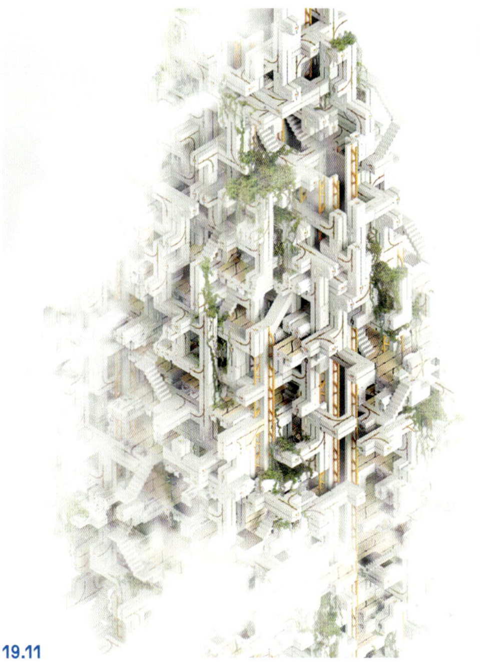

19.11

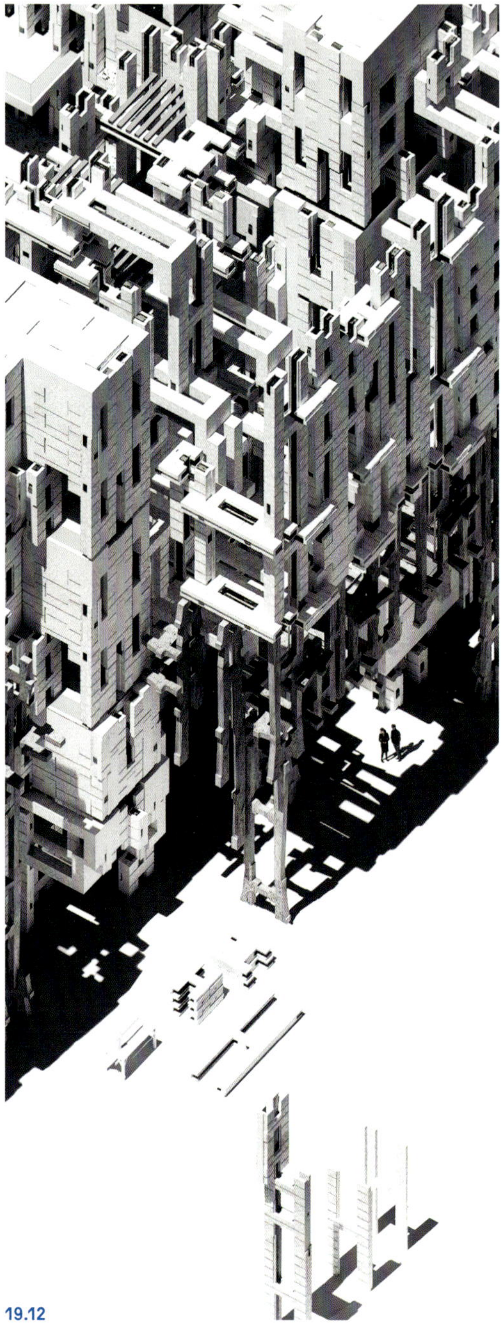

19.12

Fig. 19.10 Milot Pireva Y4, 'Hands-On Living'. A limited but open-ended set of composite steel/timber elements can be used to construct a variety of spaces and structures. The construction system makes use of affordable materials and widely available CNC machines. This set of parts is deployed on a porous, longitudinal housing block that combines communal production spaces with apartment units. **Fig. 19.11 Jevgenij Rodionov** Y4, 'Universal Housing Block'. Universal Housing Block is a contemporary take on the social housing production models prominent in Britain. The project proposes a digitally driven system which aims to democratise the production of housing by making design and production methods accessible to the public. **Fig. 19.12 Sara Martinez** Y4, 'H-ome'. The project proposes a new collective housing typology for the so-called 'Ni estudia, Ni trabaja' (not studying, not working) generation in Spain. The project aims to provide an affordable method of construction, provided in this case by local authorities as part of a defined government plan, which will allow the 'NiNis' to enter the housing market and move out of their parents' homes. **Fig. 19.13 Ayla El-Chiati** Y4, 'Tiny Living London'. Using a set of folded steel sheets, this project organises sixteen micro-apartments on the plot of Victorian House. Structural ribs and folds increase the strength of the steel sheets. The thin steel construction elements reduce the thickness of floors and allow a greater density of units.

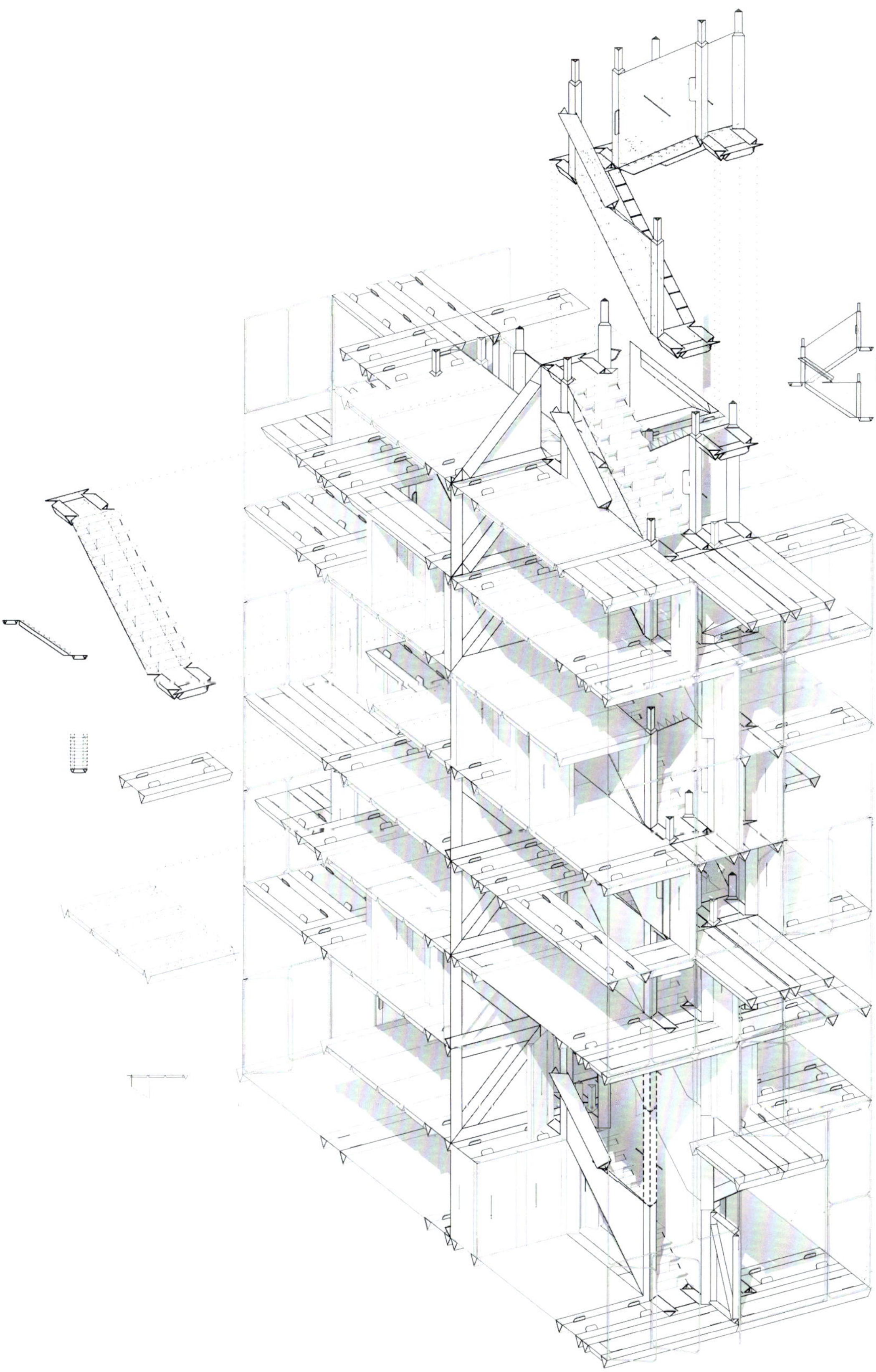

19.13

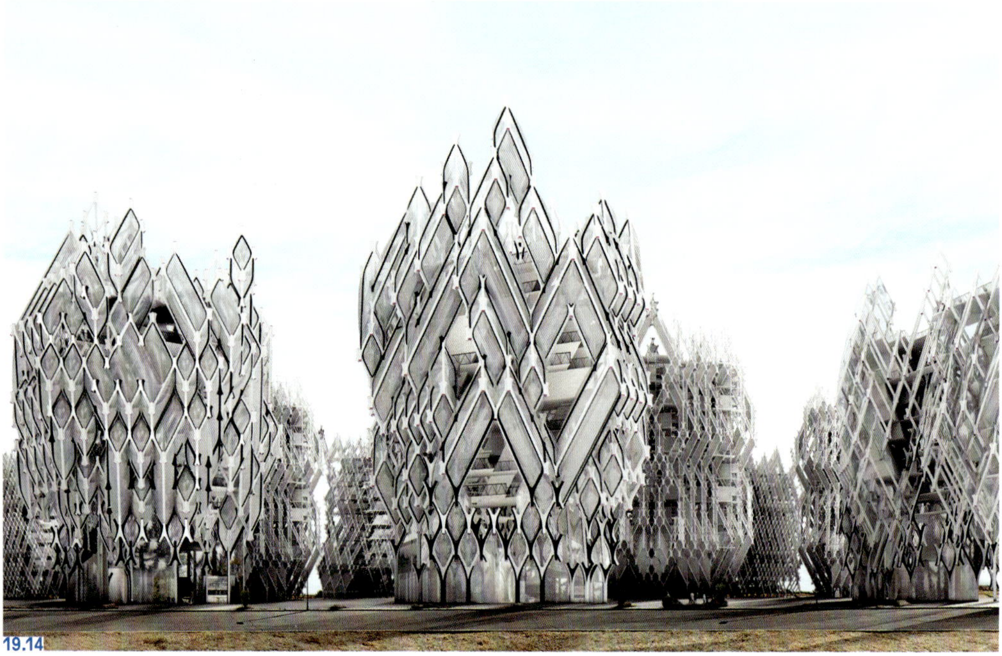

19.14

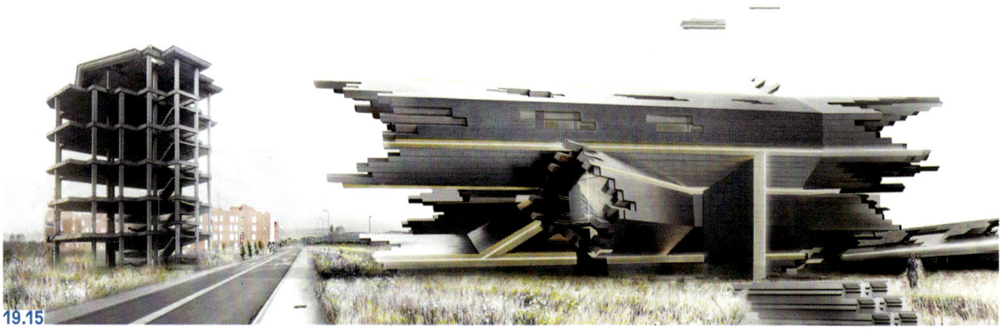

19.15

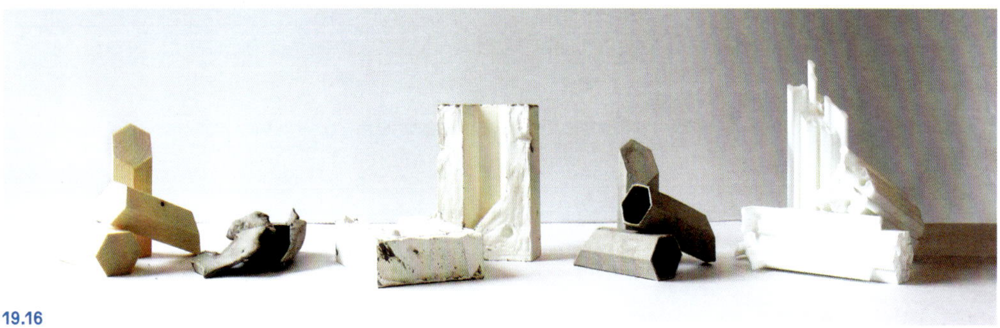

19.16

Fig. 19.14 Lianjie Wu Y4, 'Branch Part System'. The project develops a high-rise housing typology based on a space frame structure. This frame can be constructed from standardised timber elements and a set of nodes, which use curve-folded thin steel sheet formwork. **Fig. 19.15 Elliott Bishop** Y4, 'Foam Town'. This proposal theorises a building system that maximises the automation of building production and construction for the social commons. Engaging with new forms of production and reproduction through the process of CNC hot-wire cutting, and automated drone construction assembly, the project actively rethinks traditional construction techniques. **Fig. 19.16 Michael Zieja** Y4, 'HEX'. Current building techniques are inefficient and rely heavily on manual labour and a skilled workforce. HEX v.3 proposes a redefined building method, relying on a kit of parts that is inherently digital. Therefore, by providing users with an intuitive dataset or alphabet of parts for how the system can be best adapted to suit different uses, it gives people the ability to influence their future through direct action and join a community of HEX v.3 developers. **Fig. 19.17 Gintare Stonkute** Y5, 'Print My Village'. This axonometric drawing shows the construction process of 3D-printed mass housing units in Avila. Building blocks are printed on the site using a farm of small-scale 3D printers. The elements are then assembled into larger structures, establishing a porous, cloud-like building with gradients of density.

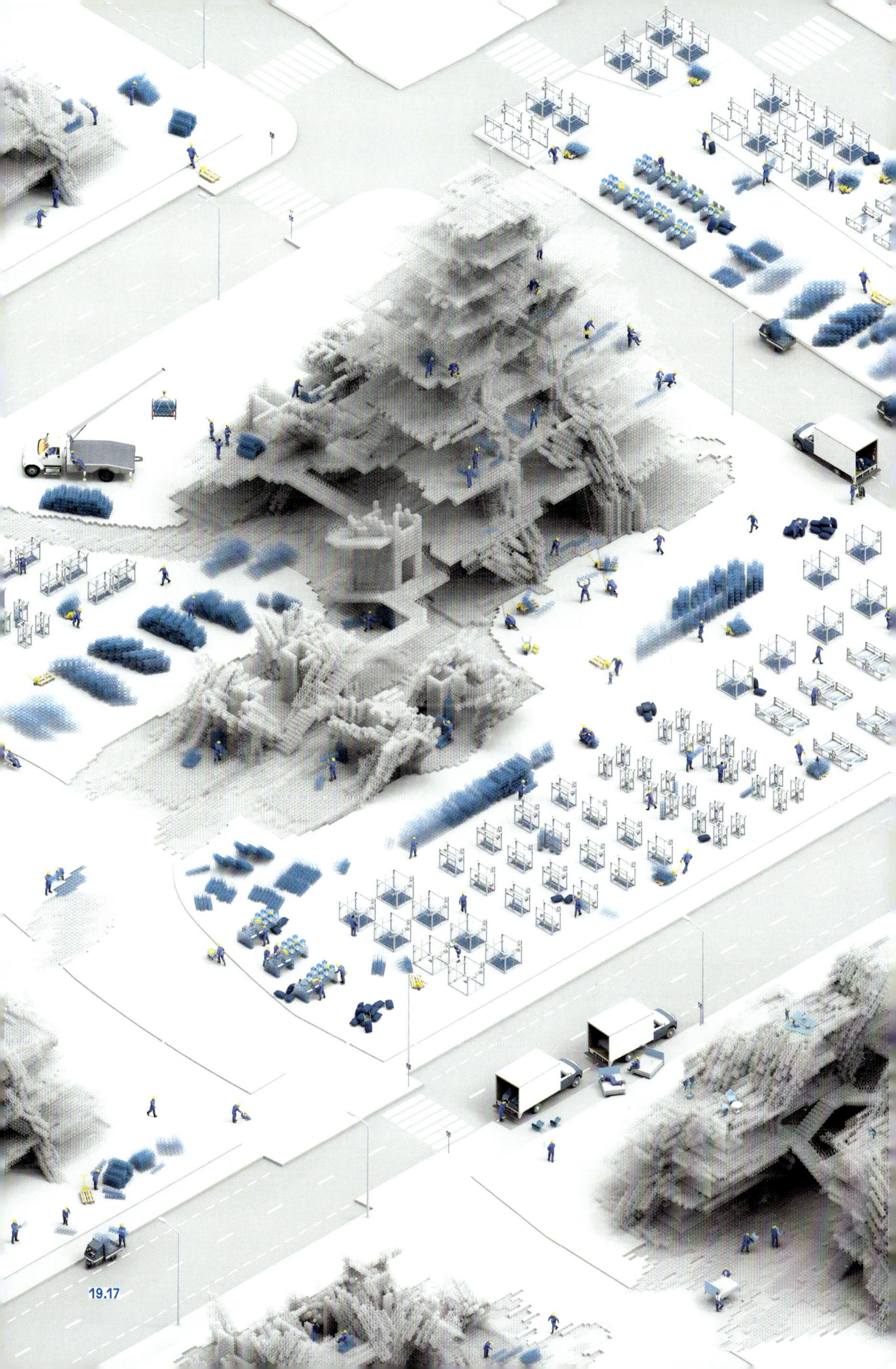

19.17

Unit 20 High-Tech + Low-Tech Composites

Marjan Colletti, Marcos Cruz, Javier Ruiz Rodriguez

Year 4
Yulia Amaral, Daryl Brown, Yinghua (Will) Chen, Fadhil Fadhil, Yi Ki Liong, Cristina Manta, Shi Qi (Kiki) Tu, Alexis Udegbe

Year 5
Thomas Bush, Mon Thi Han, Patrick Mawson, Matthew Pratt, Helen Oi Yee Siu, Jessica Wang, Ching Yiu (Tommy) Wong, Man Chung (Tom) Wong

Thank you to our Design Realisation tutors Justin Nicholls and Maria Eugenia Villafañe, and to our critics

In a time of increasing demand for sustainable solutions in technology and design, there has been much debate around the increasingly important relationship between low-tech procedures within high-tech environments. The main premise this year has been to engage with the composite conditions that make both advanced technological systems, and traditional ones, part of contemporary life. This has been a hugely significant step towards reducing the use of resource-hungry technologies and materials that have been overused in the 20th century.

——Contemporary society has acknowledged that long-established techniques have been successful in the past and are often simpler, more environmental friendly and more 'human' than excessively synthetic procedures. However, the great advantage we have nowadays is that it is not mandatory to revert to the basics of vernacular architecture. We are currently witnessing the emergence of a new paradigm, in which an intensified use of new technology allows us to increase the precision of design and manufacturing and customised replication of components, and also helps us embrace a novel sense of materiality in architecture that can be both analogue and digital, conceptual and physical, hard and soft, technical and poetic, etc.

——Designers are able to predict form and performance prior to materialisation and at the same time rethink traditional techniques in an entirely new, post-digital way. Besides the great advantages in terms of design control that allows us to invent forms that have far higher levels of complexity and space than before, this insight opens up architecture to a truly multi-disciplinary and contextual approach: not only can we now participate in co-authoring novel material-material assemblages, we can also co-author material-urban and material-nature aggregations, as well as a plethora of other composites.

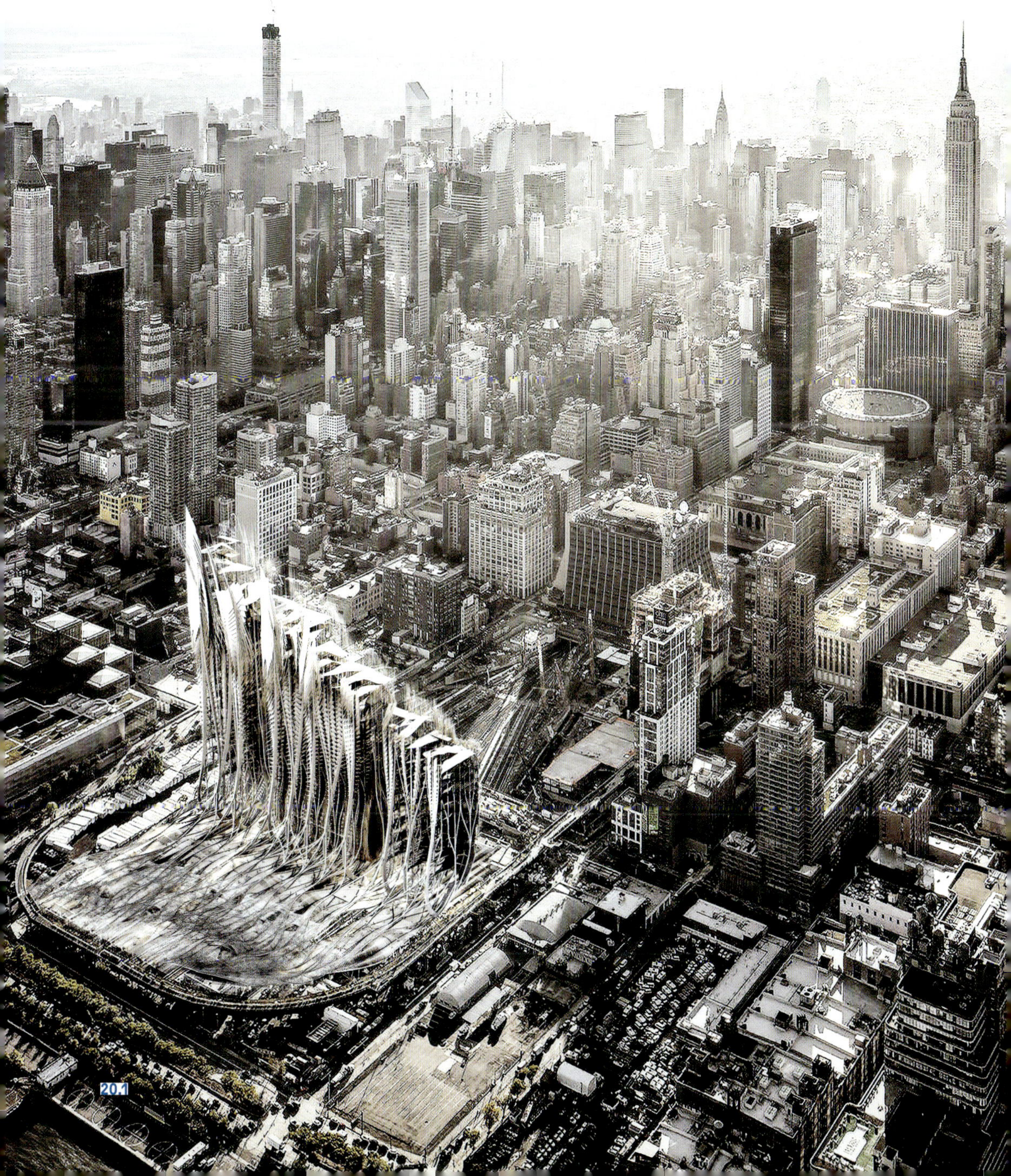

20.1

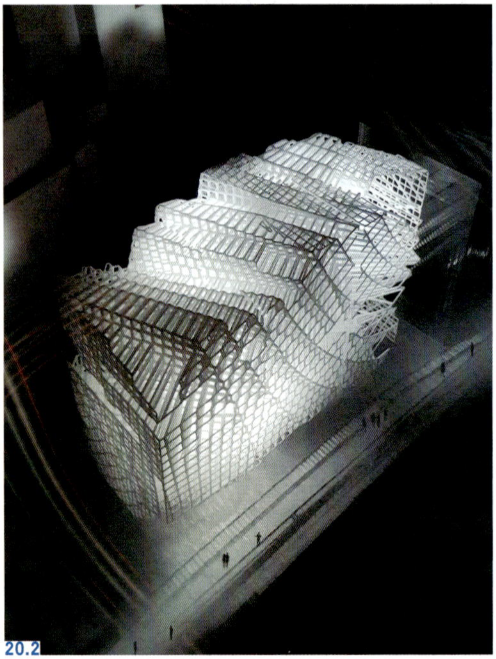

20.2

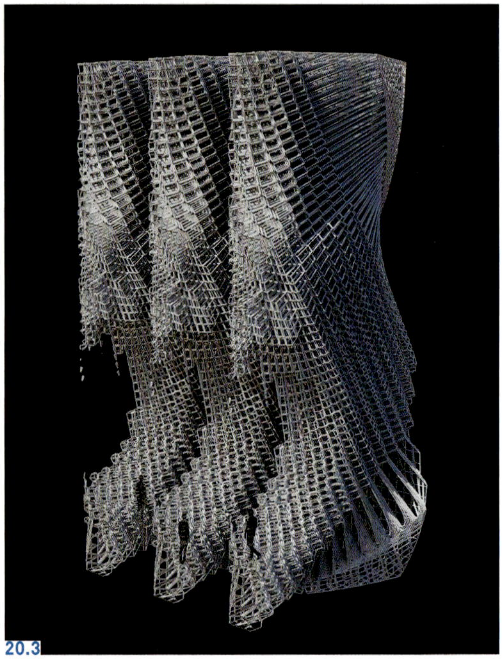

20.3

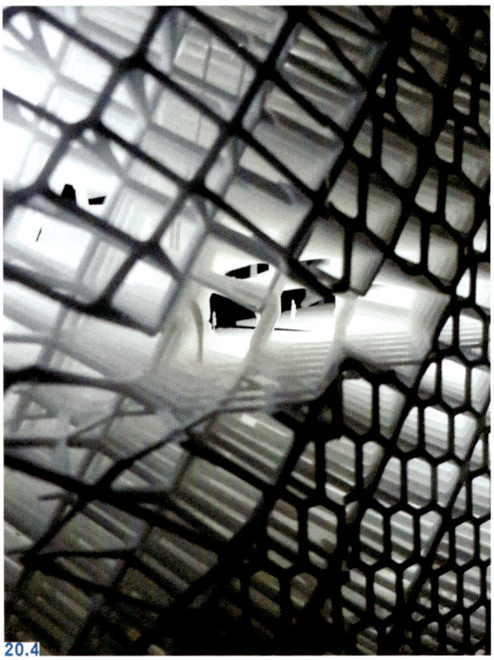

20.4

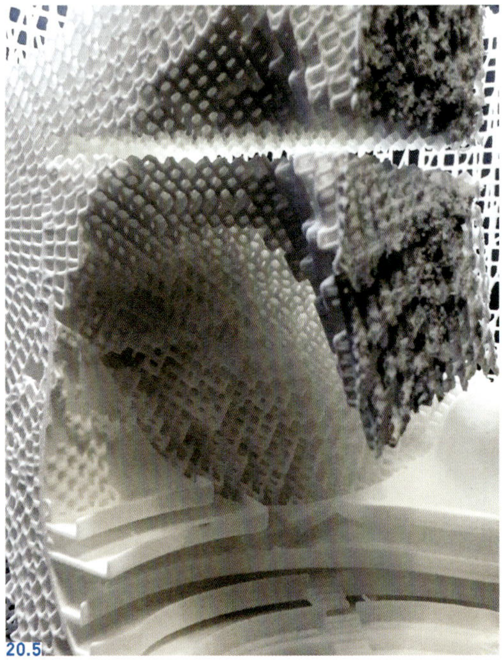

20.5

Fig. 20.1 Matthew Pratt Y5, 'Transitions of the Filigree'. Ideas of branching and connectivity influence the programme of the New York Forum to produce an architecture that transitions from micro- to macro-scale in its elements. Several investigations into origins of the filigree provide the basis for geometric, material and time-based studies into a transient architectural condition between one- and four-dimensionality, translated through contextual site responses to the Hudson Yards rail depot and surrounding High Line connection. **Figs. 20.2 – 20.5 Jessica Wang** Y5, 'Tessellated Acoustic Symbiosis – A Chamber Hall and Church Interface'. The project investigates the acoustic qualities in a chamber music hall and a Pentecostal church (gospel) and emphasises the translation of precise high-tech digital sound design into the low-tech fabrication of tessellated acoustic tiles which explore the possibilities for acoustical integration. The exoskeleton structure is bound within a rectangular form as an attempt to integrate into the New York cityscape. The interior is formed by Voronoi-inspired tiles that are intended to tessellate within an extravagant framework that simultaneously performs as acoustic control and enclosure. **Fig. 20.6 Helen Oi Yee Siu** Y5, 'Adaptive Patterning: Aqua Therapy and Spa Centre, New York'. The analogy of adaptive patterns is extended to an architectural scale. The patterned building skin acts as a filter for light, ventilation and a solar heat store. The building possesses the delicate, interlacing language of earlier knitted studies, whilst responding to external macroclimate and internal microclimate demands.

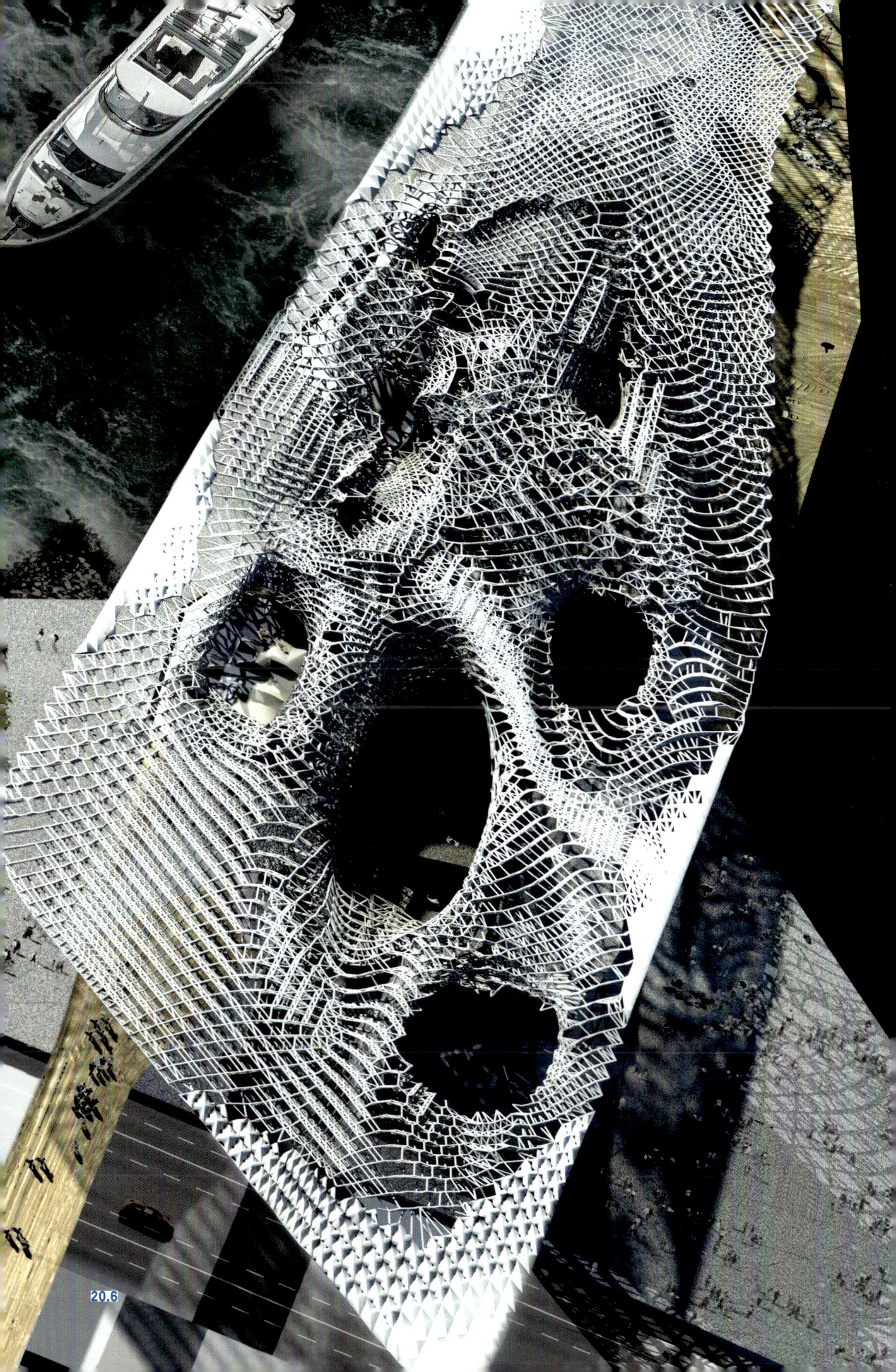
20.6

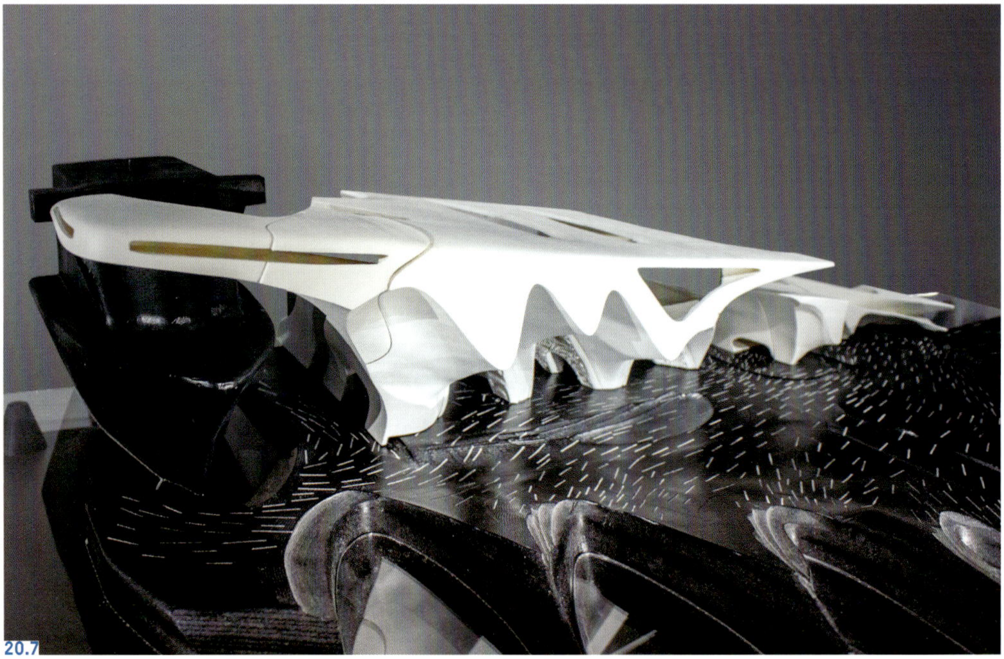

20.7

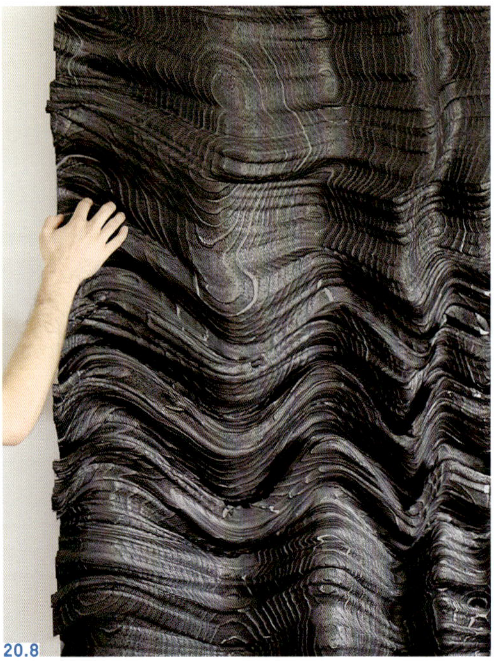

20.8

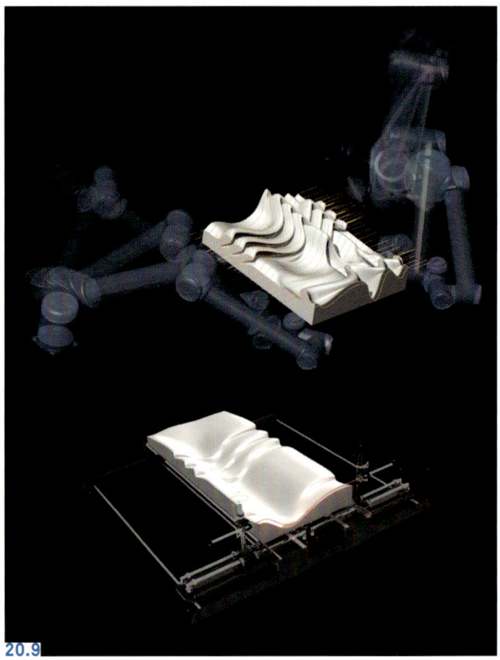

20.9

Figs. 20.7 – 20.9 Patrick Mawson Y5, 'Brooklyn Cruise and Logistics Terminal'. The project investigates the sensual relationship between architecture, its ecological context and user, and how, through the construction of 'sensuous cells', one can establish meteorological gradients for environmental comfort and functionality. Air flow simulations and programmatic functions determine the carving of space through a hierarchy of robotically controlled scoops and slashes, establishing space for international cruise liners, down to the human scale. **Fig. 20.10 Man Chung (Tom) Wong** Y5, 'Hair – Fibrous Invasion'. Inspired by the biological function of hair, this project explores thermal, structural and environmental potentials of fibrous systems in architecture. It proposes a Museum of Meteorology, which uses hair-inspired responsive environmental components that generate a series of climatically controlled zones, exhibiting various meteorological phenomena.

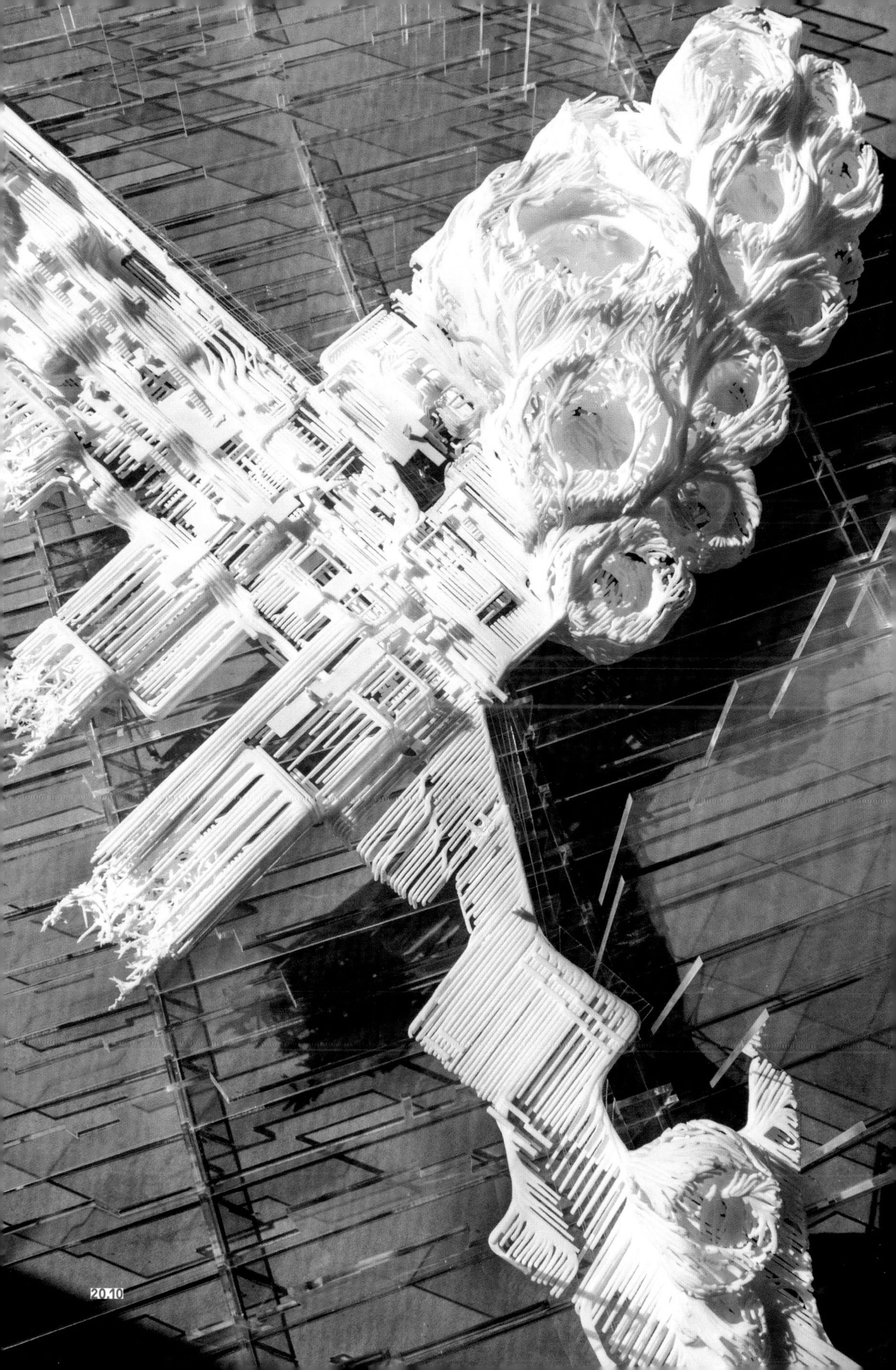
20.10

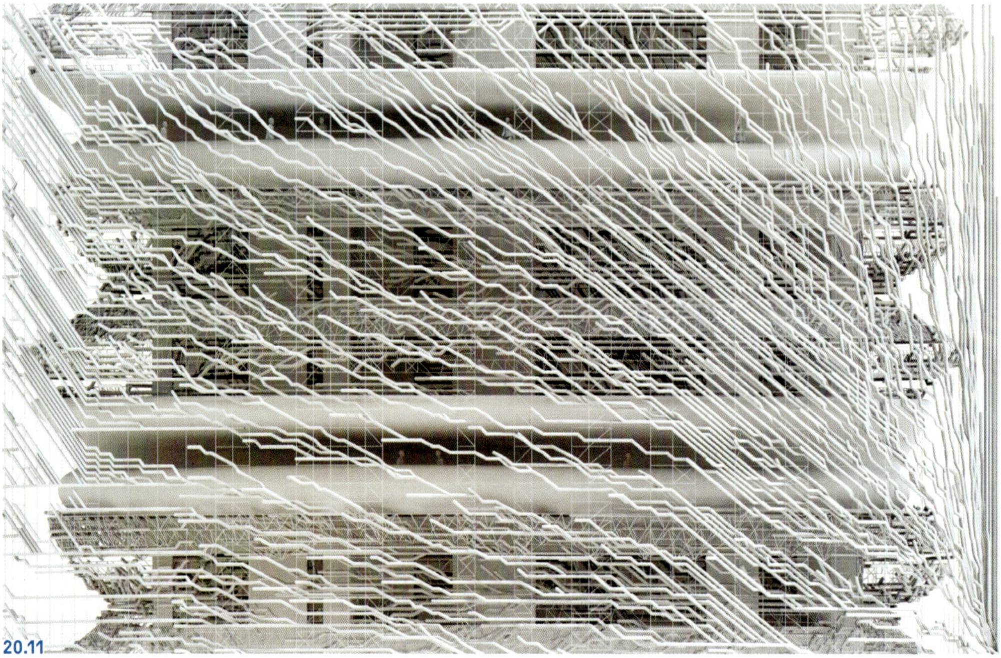

20.11

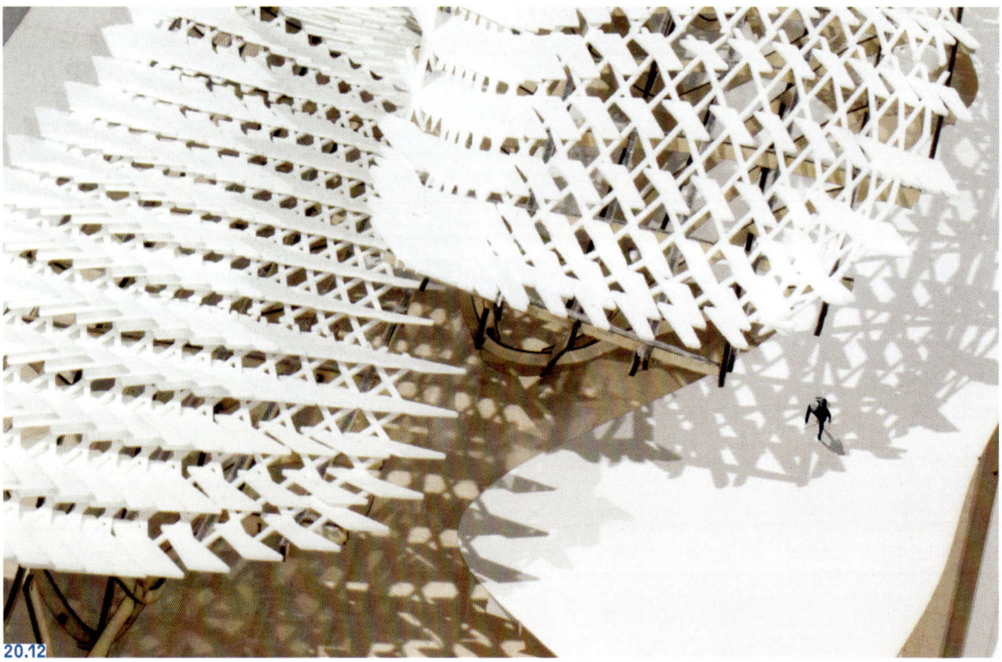

20.12

Fig. 20.11 Mon Thi Han Y5, 'Fluid Integrated Building Skins'. The proposal is a 400-metre environmental residential tower in Hudson Yards, New York. The project is a research and design exploration into the thermal regulating functions of the human blood vascular system. It questions conventional air-conditioning technologies ingrained in our building design culture. Through design research, the project's aim is to develop fluid integrated environmental building envelopes for regulation of thermal mass and temperature, and therefore it reduces cooling loads in buildings and significantly reduces energy consumption. **Fig. 20.12 Ching Yiu (Tommy) Wong** Y5, 'New Hudson Yards Market, New York'. The project is an investigation into plywood's bending properties as well as market typologies in New York City. Located at the end of the High Line Park, the proposal aims to be a new tourist attraction that acts as an extension and a connection to the Hudson Yards redevelopment. Key design concepts include spatial fluidity and a flexible skin made from plywood. **Fig. 20.13 Thomas Bush** Y5, 'Deforming Fibres'. Residential apartments with a public velodrome that integrates into the High Line in West Chelsea, NYC. The project investigates anisotropic deformations in analogue and digital methods, trying to create deformable enclosures that use fibrous materials. The dynamic moments are tuned to control light, through reflection and shading at various scales, from individual modules to apartments and the whole building scale.

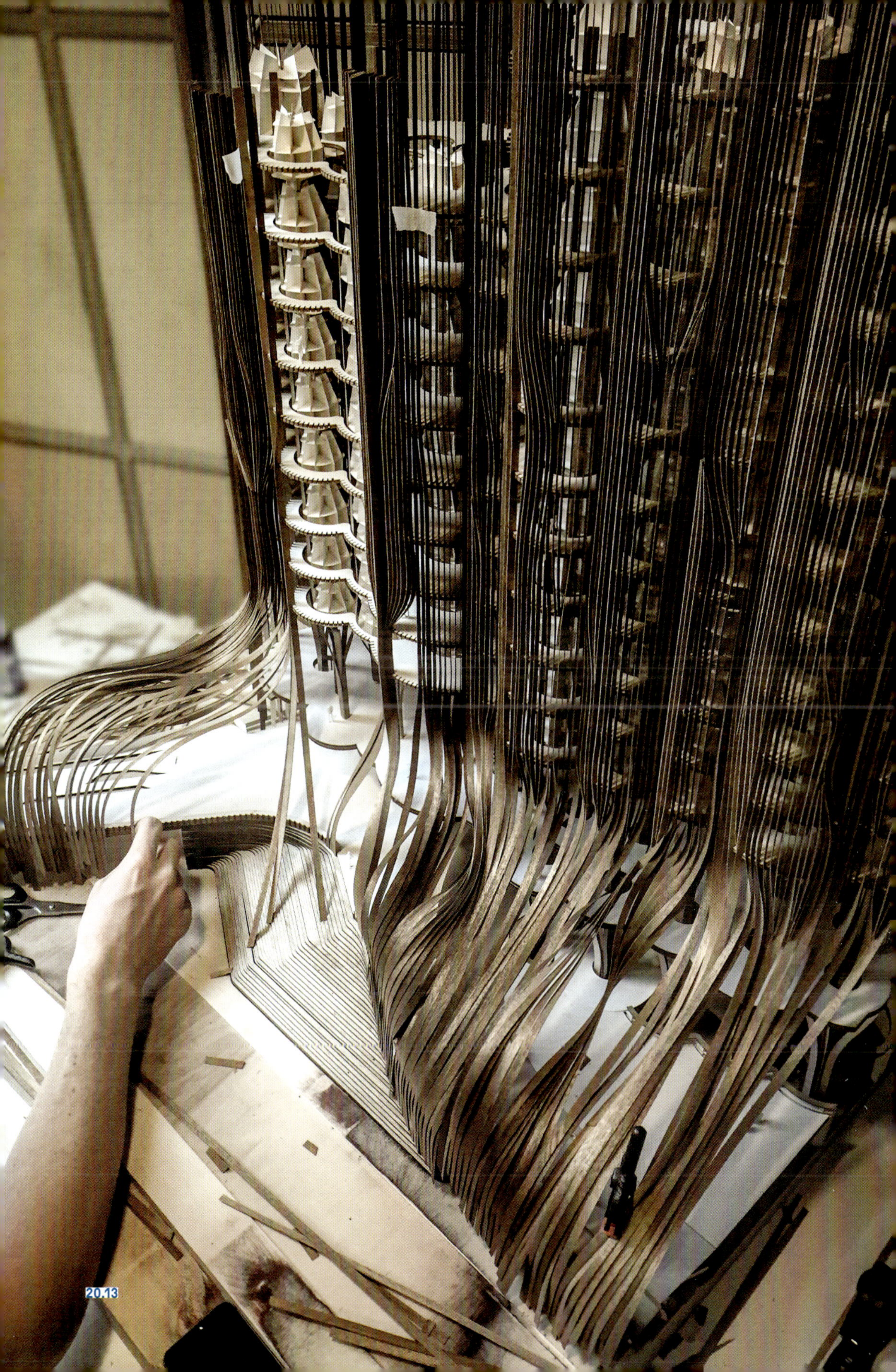

20.13

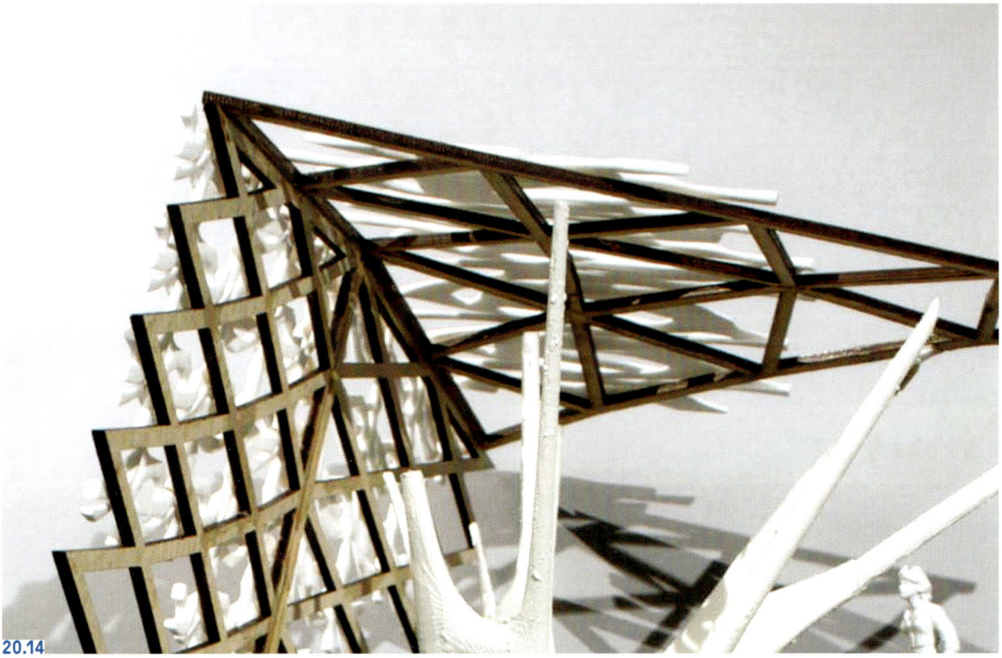

20.14

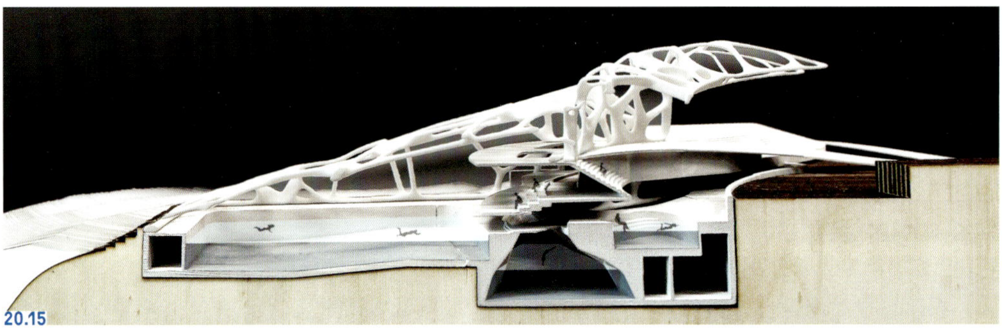

20.15

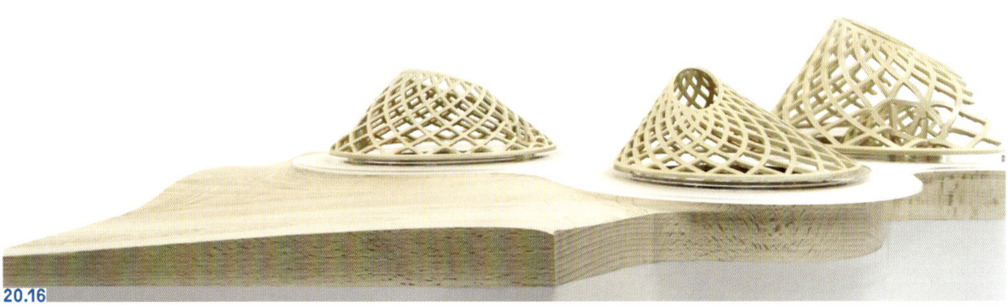

20.16

Fig. 20.14 Daryl Brown Y4, 'The Maverick Fiedler Forest School for the Performing Arts'. An exploration of hybridising concrete, designing its formations as well as its casting recipes. Linear bridging forms generated by fabric formwork casting are explored using tensile nylon fibres as an aggregate. Crafted structural concrete formations challenge the rigidity of the solid formwork casting readily used in modern engineering. **Fig. 20.15 Shi Qi (Kiki) Tu** Y4, 'The Maverick Aquatic Sports Centre'. The building design stems from geometrical and functional investigations of porosities. Fluid embedded within the structure of the building canopy regulates the building environment through a solar water heating and evaporative cooling system. **20.16 Yi Ki Liong** Y4, 'The Maverick Centre for the Research and Conservation of Native Aquatic Plants'. The brief envisions an educational facility that aims to revitalise the aquaculture of Boston Harbour. A series of biomes house regional aquatic plant species and an underground seed library, which encourages a diffusion of knowledge between in-house researchers and the public. The project challenges threshold boundaries between various environmental conditions within the building, and explores the use of a double-skinned system.

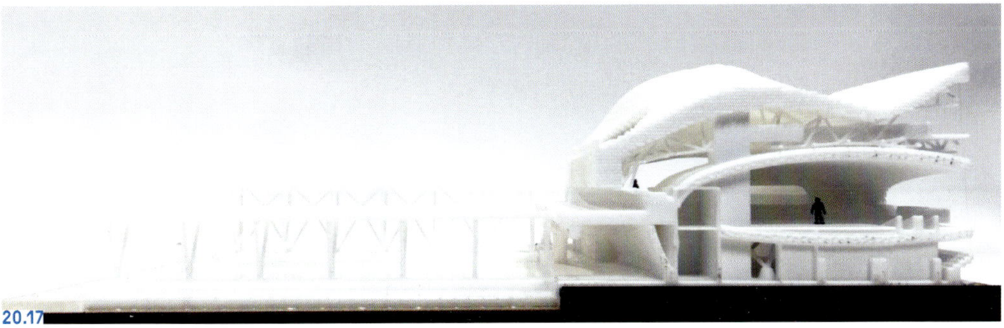

20.17

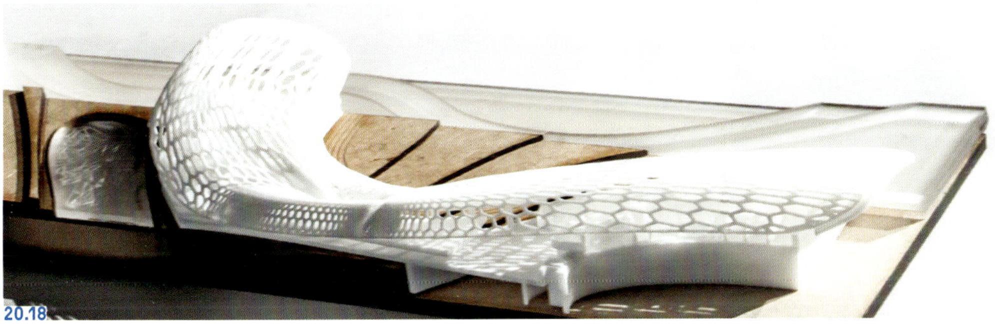

20.18

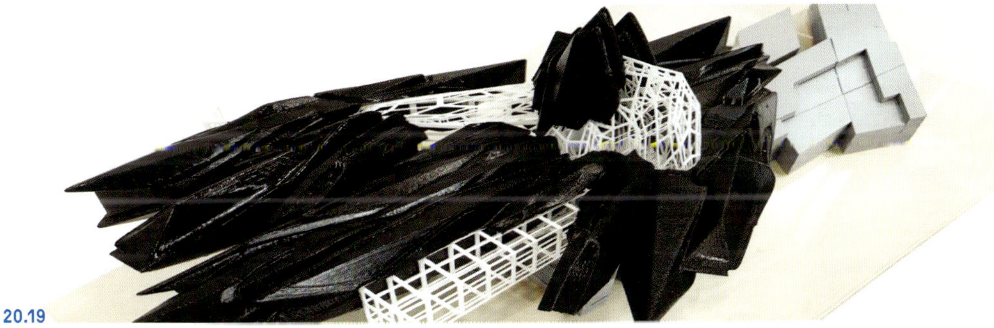

20.19

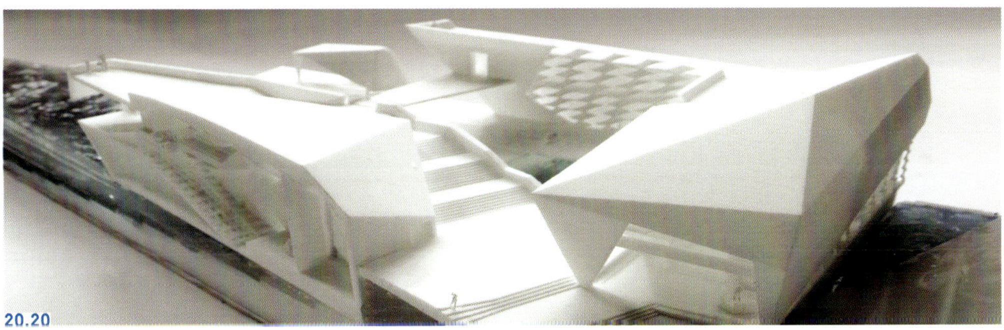

20.20

Fig. 20.17 **Yinghua (Will) Chen** Y4, 'The Maverick Ferry Terminal'. This project aims to improve the economic and urban cultural environment in response to the government's Maverick Revitalisation Plan. The proposal envisions a ferry terminal with a biological landscape as the skin of the building, with carbon fibre composites used as the main material for the building's framework. **Fig. 20.18** **Cristina Manta** Y4, 'The Maverick Student Centre & Food Market'. The project provides street food, local seafood and a fresh produce market integrated into student facilities and learning spaces. The central twisting column celebrates the simultaneous interconnection of activities and circulation patterns, resulting in a conceptual spatial composite. **Fig. 20.19** **Fadhil Fadhil** Y4, 'Naval Immersive Simulation Laboratories'. Subtractive Boolean methods and seaming techniques examine the insertion of one object into another, treating the interior space as an object existing inside an exterior object. **Fig. 20.20** **Yulia Amaral** Y4, 'Maverick Department of Artistic Expression'. The project is a public performance arts centre that aims to reinvigorate the local community of East Boston. The micro-environmental goals are achieved by a façade consisting of a waste product and titanium dioxide bio-composite, which aims to improve the surrounding air quality.

Unit 21

ö (Swedish) = 'Island'/'Refuge'

Abigail Ashton, Tom Holberton, Andrew Porter

Year 4
Jack Clay, Katie Cunningham, Ahmed Al Gamal, Steve Graves, Yasaman Mohsanizadeh, Joe Travers-Jones, Yun Wan, Feng Yang, Anqi Yu

Year 5
Paddi Benson, Jonathan Davies, Eleanor Downs, Eleanor Figueiredo, Aleks Kravchenko, Tom Savage, Katherine Scott, Alexia Souvaliotis, Sally Taylor, Aviva Wang, Camilla Wright

Thank you to our Practice Tutor, Tom Holberton and our Structural Engineer, Brian Eckersley, EOC

Thank you to our critics: Roberto Bottazzi, Mina Gospavic, Stephen Gage, Christine Hawley, Diony Kypraiou, Calum Macdonald, Luke Pearson, Charlotte Reynolds, Sayan Skandarajah, Tony Smart

Stockholm is Scandinavia's largest city, built over 14 islands with 50 bridges, on a greater archipelago of 20,000 islands, where Lake Mälaren meets the Baltic Sea. As one of Europe's fastest-growing urban economies, it has embraced investments in 'smart' city networks and open data to develop the world's second most prolific tech hub and become the startup capital of Europe. Yet this spirit of experimentalism is also made possible due to a certain Swedish isolationism, a position at the northern fringe of Europe, and the mindset of *Jantelagen*, which prioritises the collective over the individual. The 'city between the bridges' also comprises 30% water and 30% protected green space, culminating in a disaggregated city – not only geographically but socially, politically and financially.

——In an age where overwhelming quantities of 'big data' assert and drive the systems of top-down control and order, the unit considered the potential opportunities of the islands of small data we generate and carry ourselves through daily life in the city. We looked for how these personal digital traces and behaviours might translate to a unique architectural language that informs and alters behaviour.

——The year started with the Swedish 'Stuga' – this exploits the plentiful land to build simple sparse dwellings where Swedes will seek refuge in the summer months. Often located by water, they are built to a very basic standard where the ritualistic routines of survival – chopping wood, repairs and renovation – offer a counterpoint to the stress of urban life and provide a physical manifestation of the commitment to quality of life. Often passed from family to family, lent by friends or companies, they offer a place for solitude, quiet individualism, and time spent purposefully on self-development through communing with nature. The students were asked to design a personal retreat space. Taking any signal from their behaviour, movements, or activity, recorded through phones or any other digital and analogue means; they then test its translation into a personal spatial language through models and drawings. Projects were generated from the esoteric observations of routine, the glitches in data, or the disruptive cloud left behind.

——The students sited the main building project amongst the islands of Stockholm. They considered the political, legal and economic frameworks as sources of data. They drew on the social, human and environmental factors to explore new methods of forming space, controlling light and testing innovative materials. The unit was interested in the manifestation of these hybrids of immaterial and physical space into outcomes that were resolutely framed as design propositions. From the drawn or modelled language of the first project, they developed larger architectural proposals with detailed programmes, considering when their architecture acted as islands and when it acted as a bridge.

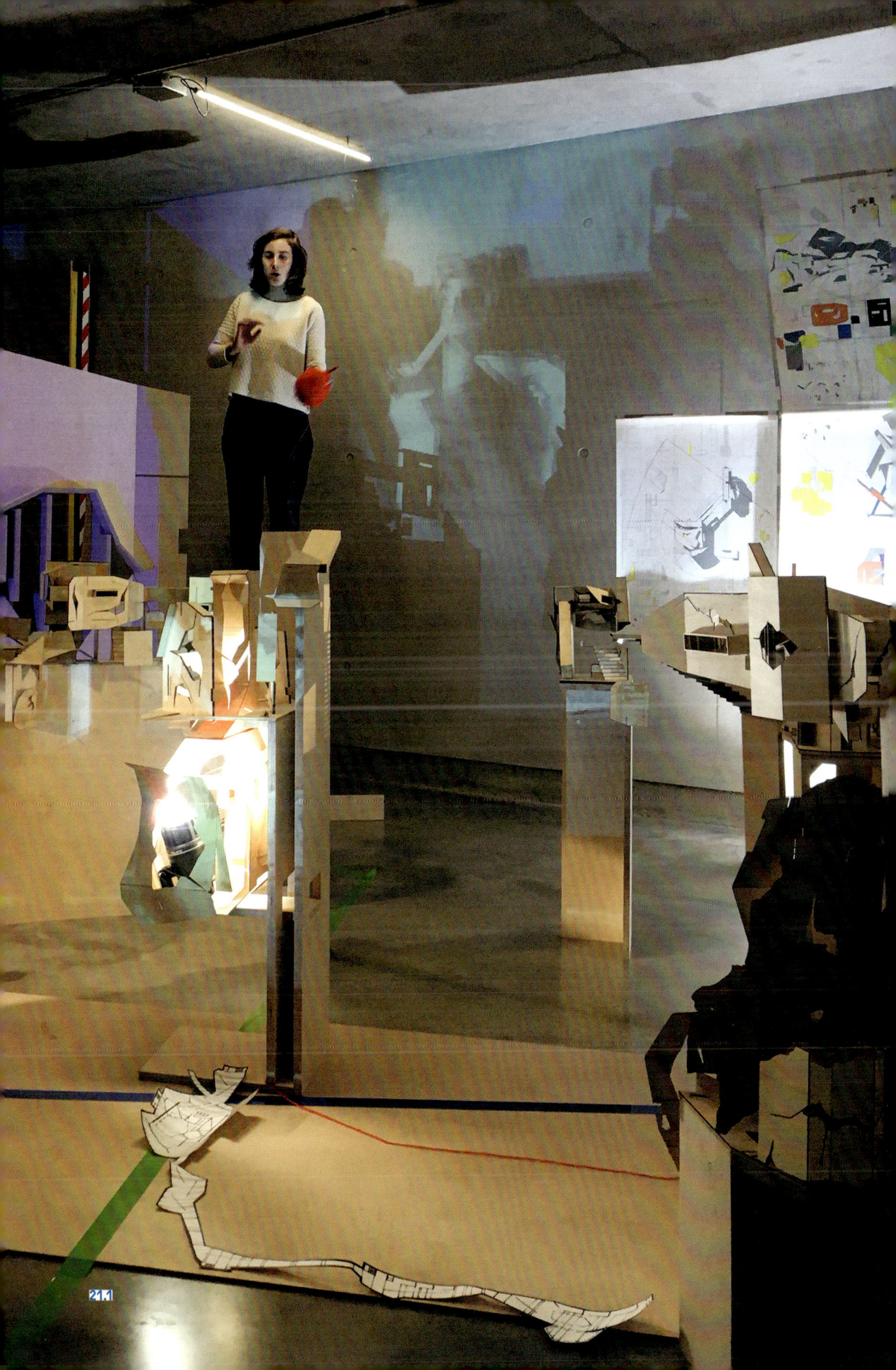

21.1

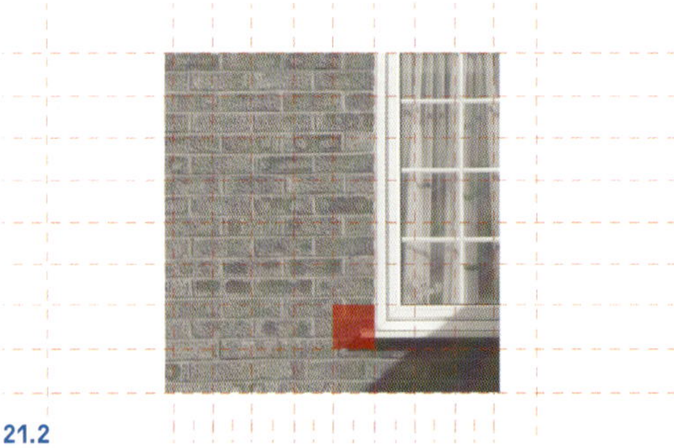

21.2

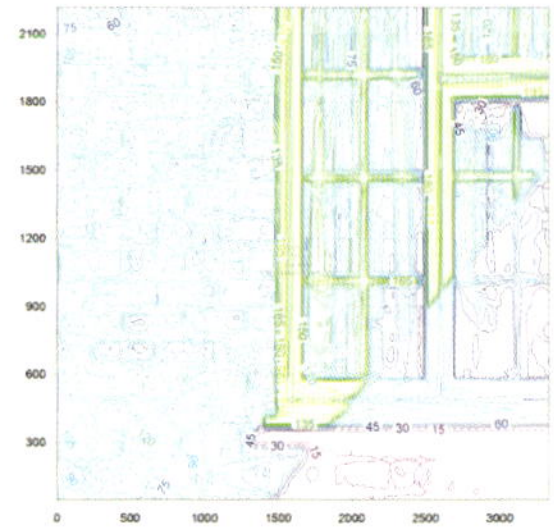

21.3

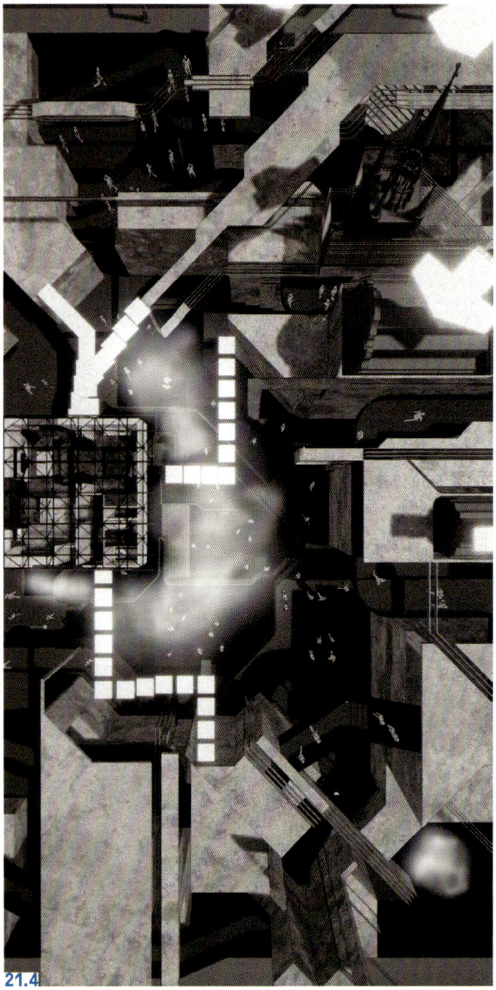

21.4

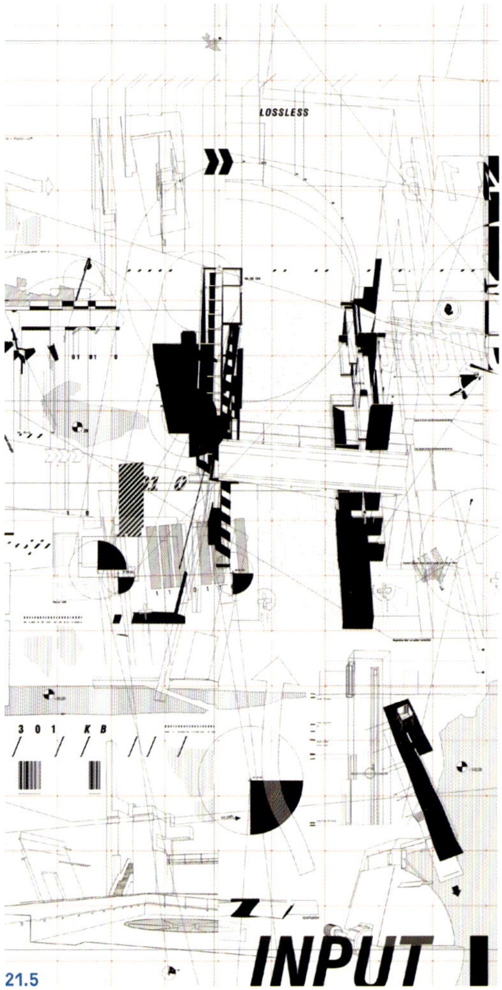

21.5

Fig. 21.1 Paddi Benson Y5, 'Lost [and Found] in Play'. The project constructs a playroom or real-space intervention within a Bartlett studio which relates to, and can stand in for, the remote site – the island of Långholmen in Stockholm. The reclaimed identities of Långholmen are then explored and examined through models of each of the interventions and their relationship to each other in the playroom. The project therefore inhabits two sites; the disused island of Långholmen and the constructed interactive space of play within the Bartlett studio. Each of the interventions is a transitional object within the playroom. Individually, they are informed by, and inform the purpose and identity, of their location. **Figs. 21.2 – 21.3 Alexia Souvaliotis** Y5, 'Stuga'. The 'Stuga' exploits the plentiful land to build simple sparse dwellings where Swedes seek refuge in the summer months. By looking at different images and how they make us feel depending on their colours/captured atmospheres, an architectural language will be developed by breaking down personal photographs of my house into their basic elements in order to create a physical and quantifiable data landscape. These data landscapes, which take the form of waterfall graphs, form an architectural toolkit to be used when designing each element of the Stuga, from the entire roof structure down to each individual floor tile. A set of virtual data is manipulated to become a tangible and physical environment for isolation and refuge. **Fig. 21.4 Tom Savage** Y5, 'Can a Video Game Change the Way Stockholmers View their City?' The city of Stockholm is in the grip of a housing crisis. A new social hierarchy has emerged based not on where one is

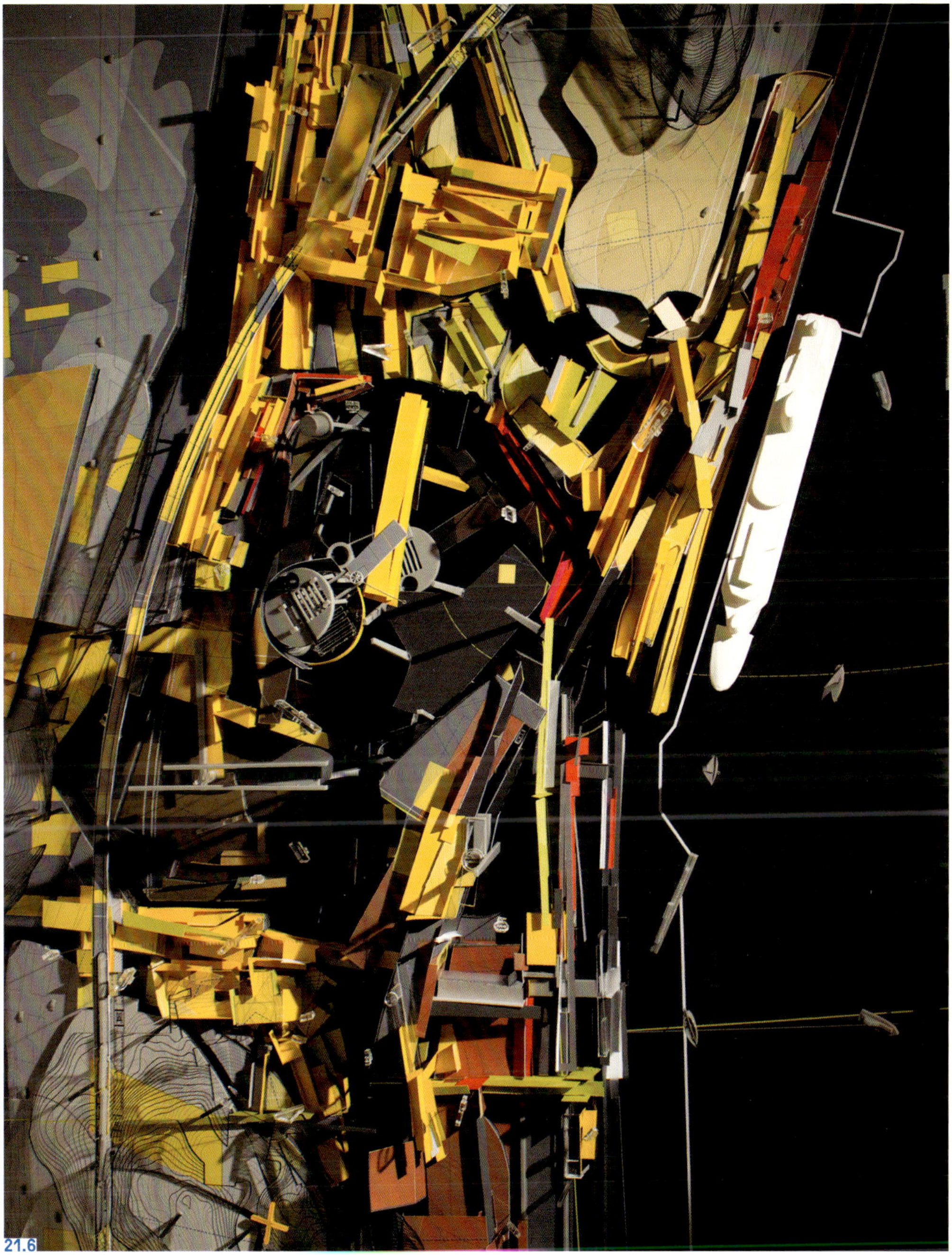

21.6

able to live, but rather how long they can live there for. Stockholm's inner city is gridlocked, with nowhere for new residents to go. Now Sweden's unique unitary housing model has a twenty-year waiting list for inner-city homes. A new simulation, made using a layered organisational strategy of time-based buildings and infrastructure, is proposed to change a player's social thinking from a location-based society to a time-based one. **Fig. 21.5 Camilla Wright** Y5, 'A (Wiki) Leaking Building'. The Data Institute is a private coding school, server bank and public campus. It seeks to inform the citizens of Stockholm about digital data and draw attention to WikiLeaks concerning Sweden. Using computational methods, WikiLeaks data is encoded within the form and programmatic function of the building such that it both generates and loses data during its lifespan. WikiLeaks manifest at all scales and materiality, from rock excavation to 'punch card' tickets. **Fig. 21.6 Katherine Scott** Y5, 'Archiving the Anthropocene: Architecture in the Age of Man'. 'The Anthropocene' has been proposed as a term that describes our current geological age. The masterplan proposed is a forward-facing archive, critiquing the role of architecture in the Anthropocene. The landscape is a Bergsonian simultaneity, with historic geometric traces of architecture on the site re-established as new buildings for the deep future. The built landscape is considered as a process, constantly evolving in the duration of time, with each piece of architecture acting as a piece of data itself. This creates an Anthropocenic archive of ruins for the future.

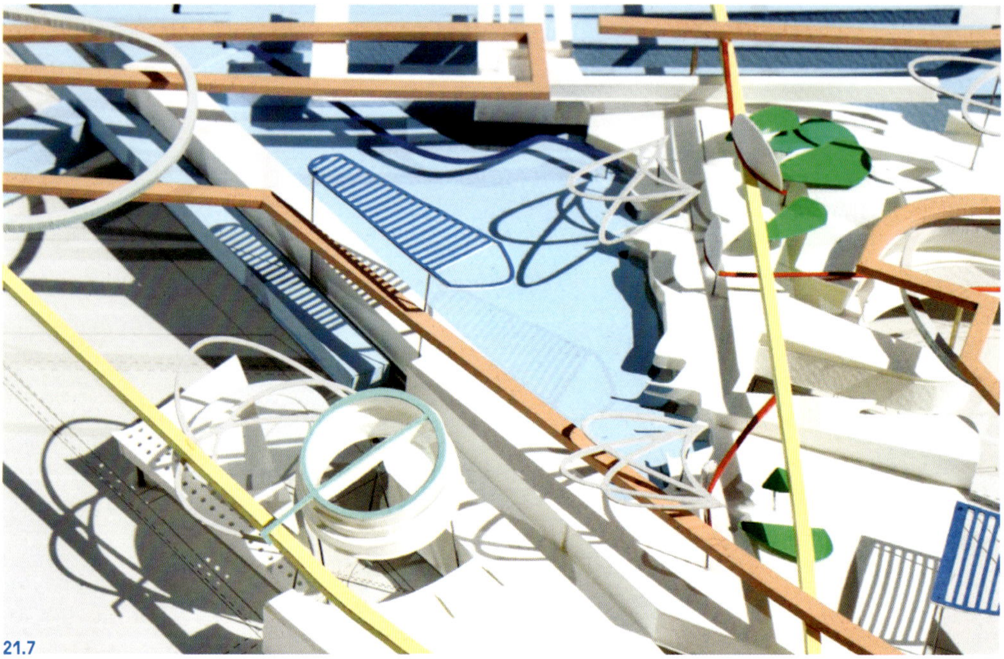

21.7

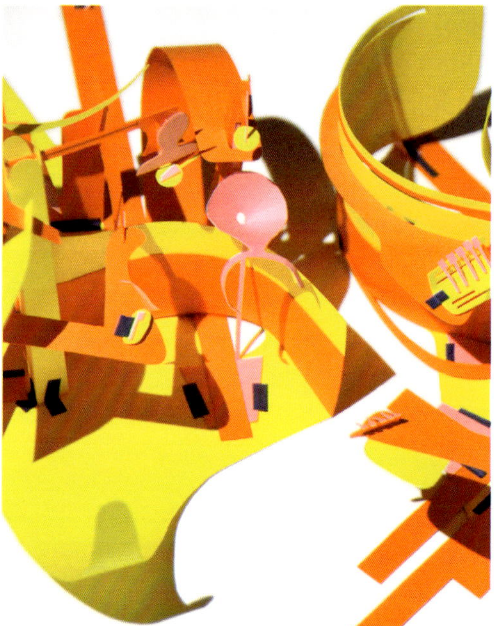

21.8

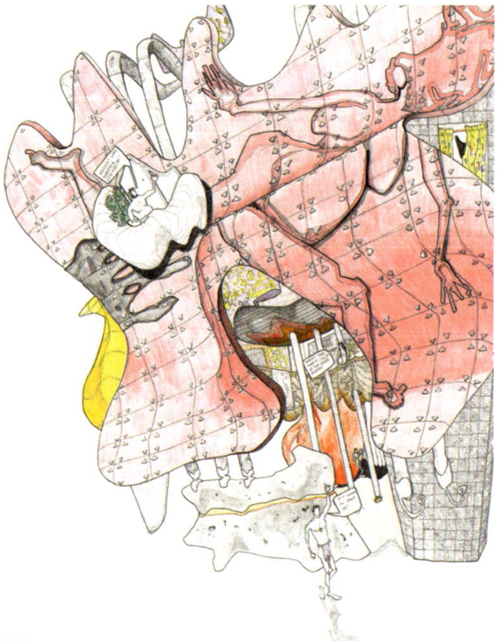

21.9

Fig. 21.7 Sally Taylor Y5, 'SAD in Stockholm'. Stockholm consists of a recreational island, Djurgården, known as the city's 'Green Lung'. This is where people who live in the city go to escape urban life. A clinic and retreat from the winter blues is proposed within a landscape setting for the high percentage of Swedes who suffer from SAD. Using shadow studies to develop the form, the proposed scheme extends out into the Djurgårdsbrunnsviken bay. The proposal includes three key zones: 'Dawn Clinic', 'Seasonal Gardens' and 'Winter Workout', all of which are intended to help reduce some of the common symptoms of SAD. **Fig. 21.8 Feng Yang** Y4, 'Teeth + Tea'. This project explored the spatial composition of rituals through model-making. **Fig. 21.9 Jack Clay** Y4, 'Frank's House'. A vessel to investigate the dialogue between freehand drawing and digital fabrication. **Fig. 21.10 Aviva Wang** Y5, 'Beautification Council's Beautiful Building'. This project aims to challenge the Stockholm Council of Beautification (Stockholm's Skönhetsrådet) which advises its city planning authority on all local proposals. The council has thirteen members from backgrounds which are mostly unconnected to architecture. Studying these council members as individuals of various ages and backgrounds enables the making of 'rules' for each member. These rules are applied to existing site buildings one after another as a metaphorical representation of their meeting, during which they take turns to give advice. The outcome of this process is a controlled yet unexpected piece, manifesting the Council's unique influence on Stockholm's urban form.

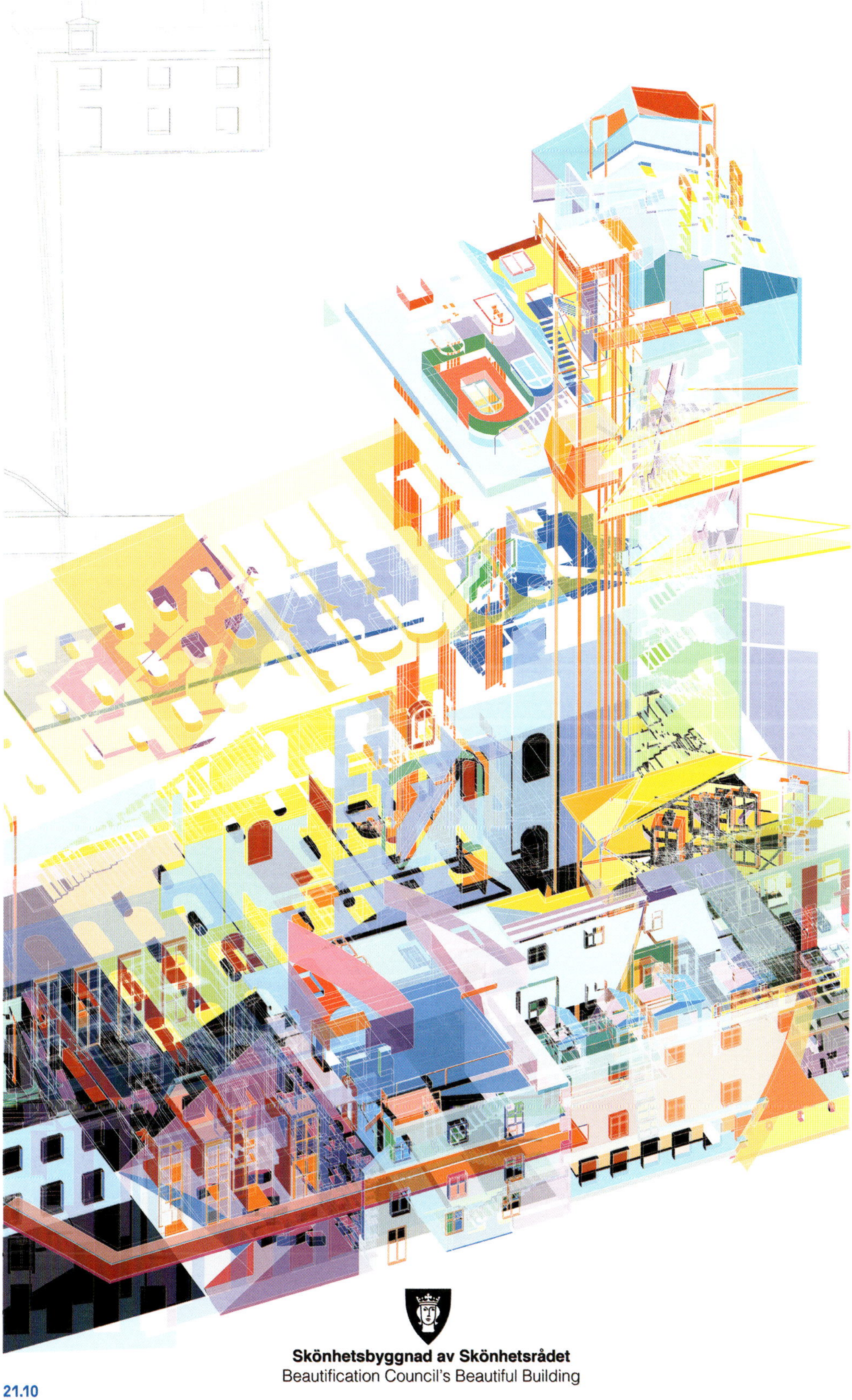
Skönhetsbyggnad av Skönhetsrådet
Beautification Council's Beautiful Building

21.10

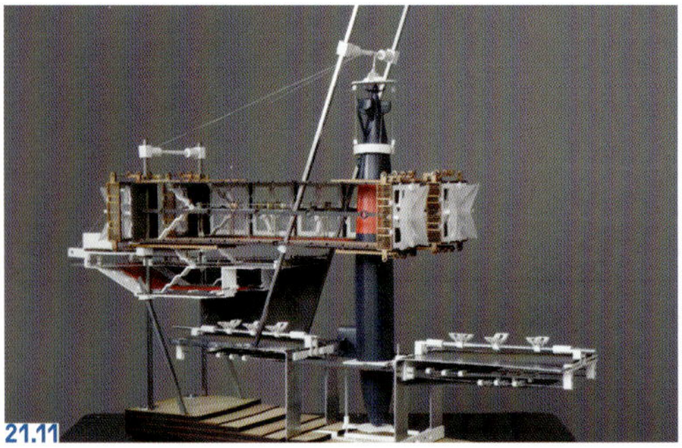

21.11

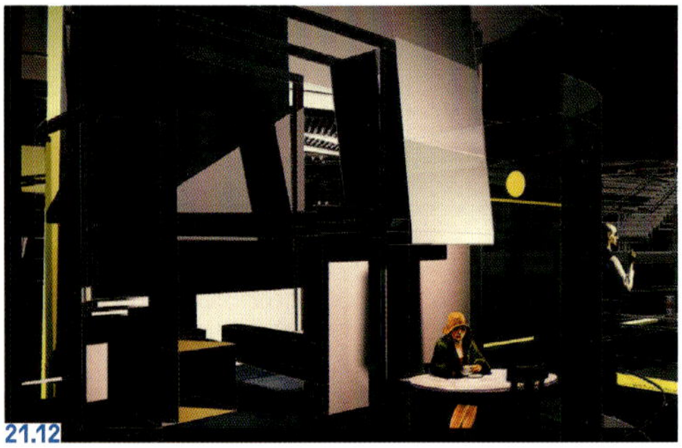

21.12

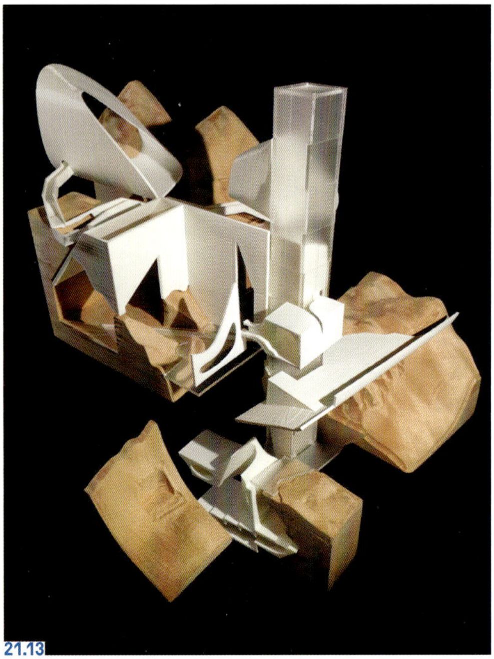

21.13

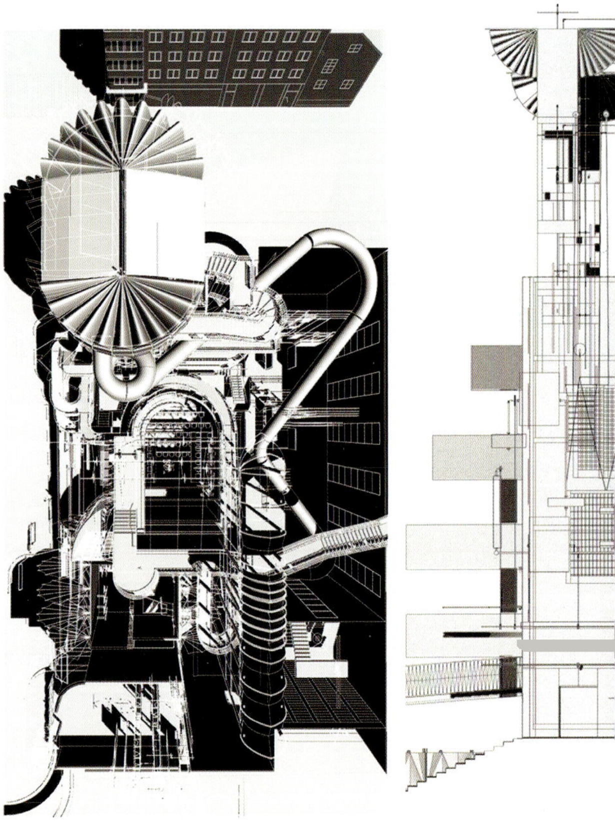

21.14

Fig. 21.11 Katie Cunningham Y4, 'Siaröfortet Submarine Attractions and Gotland's Submarine Dismantling Resort'. The theme of the projects is Sweden's worsening relationship with Russia and its vulnerable geographical and political position between Russia and NATO. With a weak military unable to put a stop to current Russian acts of aggression, public awareness is the strongest available deterrent. Siaröfortet Submarine Attractions are proposed cruise ship stops along the archipelago. These installations react to trespassing submarines, allowing the users to catch a better glimpse. The main project looks at the potential Russian decommissioned submarines' relationships to nuclear crisis. It proposes a dismantling facility which deals with the nuclear load, using the recycled material and unspent nuclear energy for leisure and educational amenities. Its position on the Baltic island of Gotland is of defensive interest to both NATO and Russia.
Fig. 21.12 Anqi Yu Y4, '24 Slussen', a re-masterplan of a disconnected and pedestrian-unfriendly waterfront area in Slussen, a run-down traffic interchange built in the 1930s. As an urban strategy, this project reconnects water back to the existing city fabric and makes the water frontage more accessible to pedestrians by proposing a series of descending terraces and a new facility. As an active public space, this project explores the transformation between physical space and its appearance at night with controlled lighting, through taking the Scandinavian darkness as a canvas and lights as paint. At night, such luminous moments form specific atmospheres, which fit in with the wider night lighting context

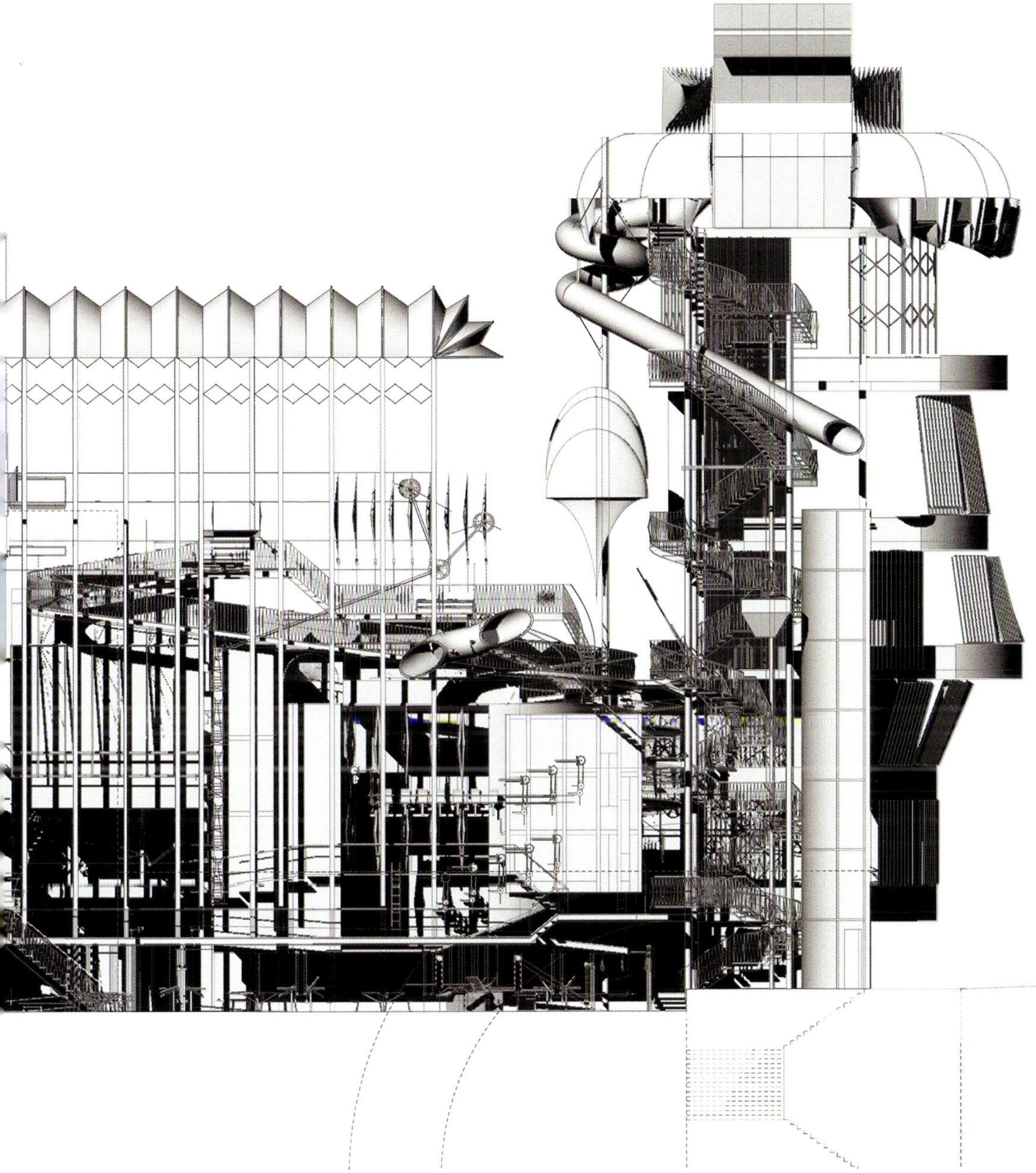

in Stockholm. **Fig. 21.13 Aleks Kravchenko** Y5, 'Huset på SÖDER'. Influenced by the sociopolitical differences between Kungsholmen and Södermalm (often shortened to 'Söder'), the project aims to create a new type of town hall to represent Söder. Located on Skinnarviksberget, the design aims to redefine the conservative relationship with the ground. Whilst the space uses in the town hall follow its precedent across the water, the spaces themselves are reimagined. 'Huset på Söder' investigates the thresholds between the existing and the man-made. The project has developed to explore the way building and model-making methods create design constraints. Materiality of the project is articulated through the methods of construction, further reflected through model-making method choices.

Fig. 21.14 Eleanor Downs Y5, 'LET'S PARTICIPATE!'. Participation and the right to the city is investigated through the lens of tracking physical activity and measuring collective engagement. A new civic hall in the centre of Stockholm is proposed as a testing site for a physical manifestation of this investigation. The architectural proposal takes the form of a mechanised building requiring energetic input from participants. How can successful participation be defined and measured? What is a 'right to the city' in today's terms? The new Medborgarhuset is a frenzy of participation, an exploration into the joy of effort. It demonstrates the noble aim of 'Allborgarratten' (right to the city) yet hints at more complicated, and perhaps sinister, undertones.

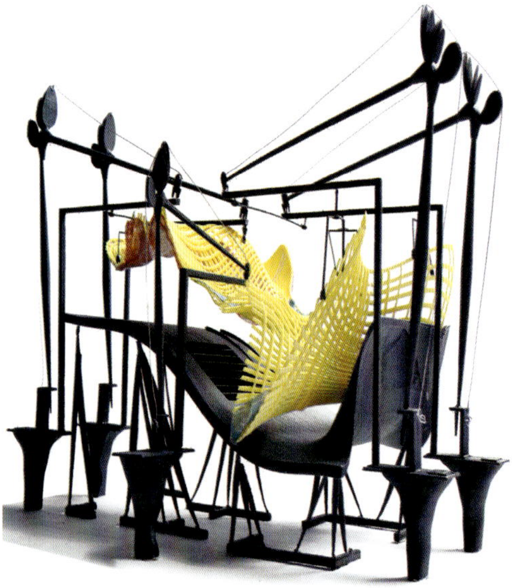

21.15

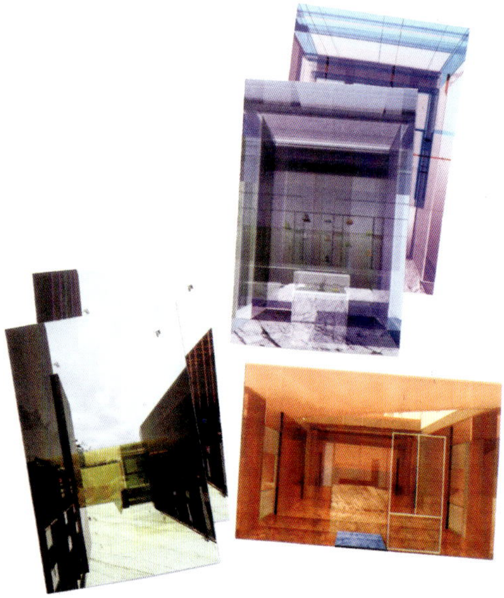

21.16

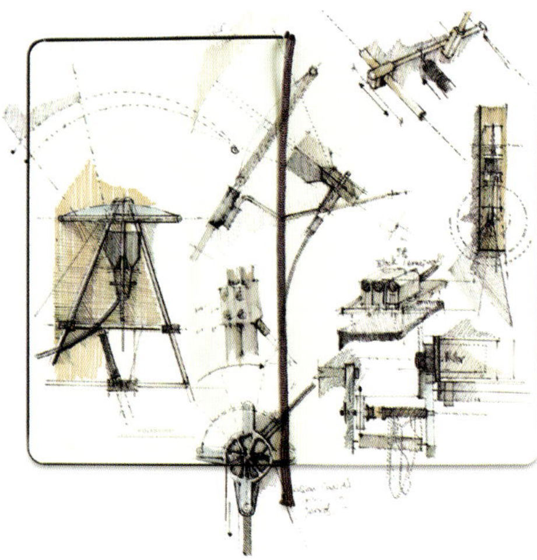

21.17

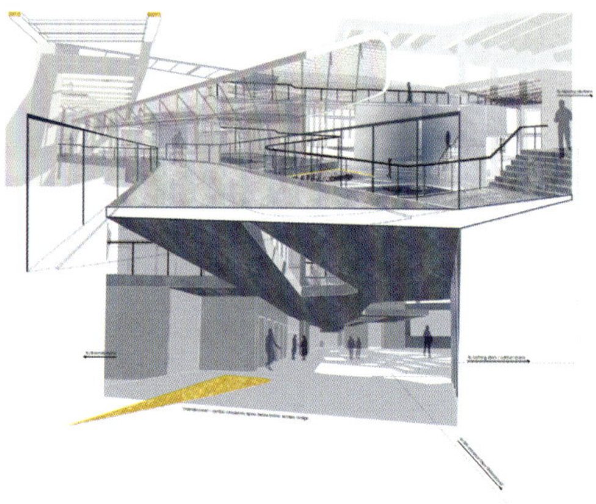

21.18

21.15 Yasaman Mohsanizadeh Y4, 'The Unicorn Incubator'. **Fig. 21.16 Joe Travers-Jones** Y4, 'Return to Sender'. **Fig. 21.17 Steve Graves** Y4, 'Maritime Graveyard'. **Fig. 21.18 Eleanor Figueiredo** Y5, 'Glasbruksholmen'. This project seeks to reinstate a lost island in the Stockholm archipelago. The project addresses the paradoxical Swedish desire for both isolation and escape, and permanent connectivity through digital technologies: an environment is created whereby individuals can retain autonomy and find sanctuary within Stockholm's urban fabric, whilst avoiding state surveillance. The island/enclave forms a reinvention of the bathhouse, providing a base for civic assembly in the heart of the city. It explores how architectural and spatial parameters are interpreted and/or distorted through transparency, reflection and refraction. **Fig. 21.19 Jonathan Davies** Y5, 'Sea Level: A Thousand Plateaus'. This project is a paradoxical attempt to design without autonomy – a proposal and a critique. A series of algorithms provide the framework upon which an urbanism is grown. Set within the Stockholm archipelago, the proposals explore the relationship between design and auto-generation. Raw material is fed through an adaptive system within the dry-dock and ejected into the Baltic Sea, territorialising it as Deleuzian 'smooth space'. This is gradually punctuated through occupation as the landscape is augmented to provide utility – the process of 'striation'. The interplay between these two conceptions of space develops a networked urbanism that fosters multiplicity and dynamism.

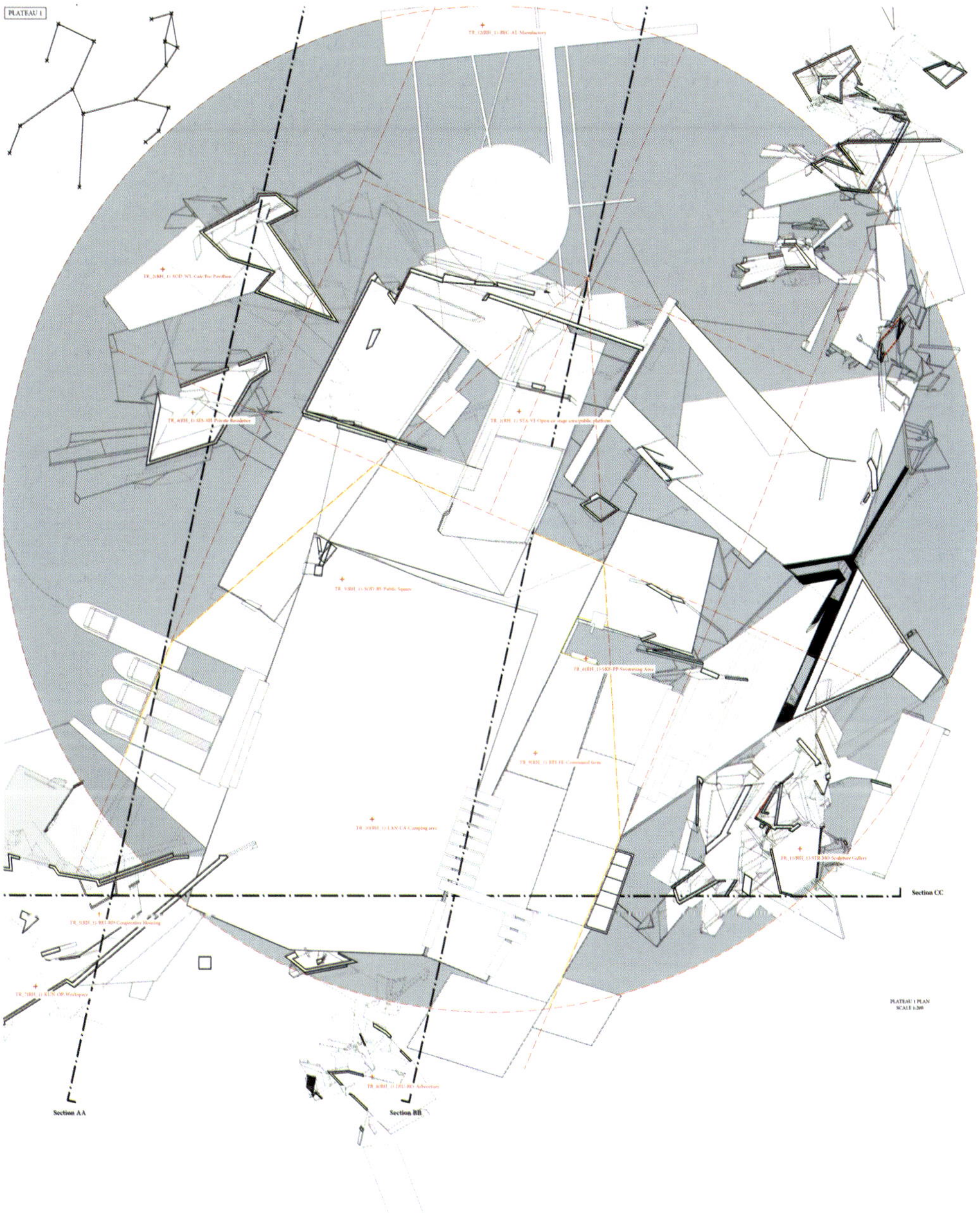

PLATEAU 1
Section CC
PLATEAU 1 PLAN
SCALE 1:200
Section AA
Section BB

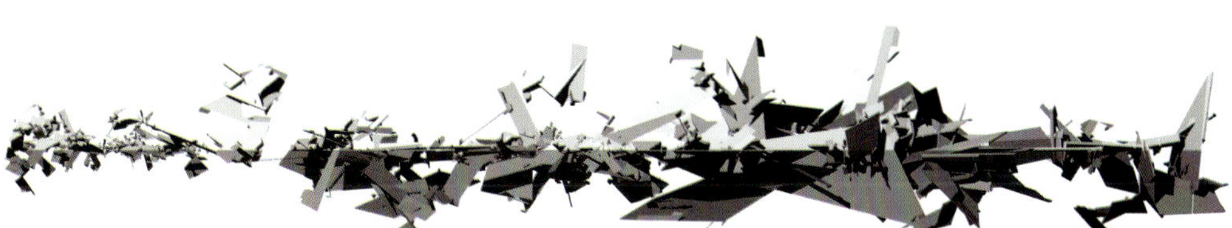

21.19

Unit 22

The Post-Millennial Revolution

Izaskun Chinchilla, Carlos Jiménez Cenamor

Year 4
Alex Anderson, Isabelle Tung, Laurence Flint, Rufus Edmondson, Timmy Whitehouse, Xin Zhan

Year 5
Georgina Halabi, Hei Tung (Whitney) Wong, Huma Mohyuddin, Jack Sargent, Kuba Tomaszczyk, Laura Young, Supichaya Chaisiriroj and Yuen Nam (Elaine) Tsang

Thank you to:
Pedro Gil, Practice Tutor, Edward Hoare, Structural Consultant, and our magnificent crit panels during the whole academic year: Fany Kostourou, Kristina Causer, Marcela Araguez, Sol Pérez Martínez, Sabine Storp, Lara Lesmes, Fredrik Hellberg, Manolis Stavrakakis, Adriana Cabello, Cristina Traba, Eduardo Camarena, Bruce Irwin, Paolo Zaide, Sean Griffiths

Thank you to our field trip workshop students and tutors from UDEM, Monterrey: Francisco Javier Serrano Alanís, Ana Teresa Furber Rodríguez, Sergio Gustavo Parroquin Sansores, Daniela Martínez Chapa, Rodrigo Gastélum Garza, Hilda Marcela Cabrales Arzola, Ana Paula Treviño Martínez, Alejandra Acuña Verano, María Catalina Gómez Elizondo, Lorena Guadalupe Cavazos Muñoz. Tutors: Arne Riekstins, Abril Denise Balbuena, Carlos García González (Dean Art, Architecture and Design)

Thank you to our sponsors: Luis Vidal + Architects and UDEM (Universidad de Monterrey, Mexico)

Those born between 1982-1996 ('millennials'), and the generations born after this, are predicted to radically reform education and working systems not only via the massive resources of online activity and new relationships they engender, but also via a more qualitative aspiration: the search for new educational and working systems that also fulfil their potential. Millennials are the first generation that no longer require an authority figure to access information – they may enjoy external stimuli 24/7, be in social contact at all times, and learn more from a portable device than from a seminar. Unit 22 has explored how this will change the spaces in which we will play, learn, work and live in the near future.

——Every year, we use our brief to break the tension between the traditional axes of architectural design, still experienced by many as a set of technical achievements, or the outcome of an aesthetic manifesto, and understood generally as the core of the creative enterprise of the architect, or as a linear solution applied to a local problem. We aim to introduce a fourth dimension to our students' work: people, and more specifically, people who are connected both to each other and to their environment. The first stage in our four-dimensional architecture is to understand all stakeholders involved in a given situation, and then to devise ways to represent their points of view and practices, and finally, to design on these grounds.

——Today, there is a pipeline of information available to everyone. The skills for making decisions have become dynamic. Co-working, for example, is the spatial translation of distributed decision-making. Our projects explore the political, spatial, urban and typological implication of such changes. Consequences in the architectural object have arisen: in most of the projects, the role of the furniture, soft materials and 'software' challenge the traditional role of structural elements. However, this has also allowed us to take a page from the analysis of power, as in the classic Bachrach and Baratz sense, and bring to the fore the relevance of non-decisions, in order to build isolated objects. We have discovered that transforming an existing building, offering the population better access to facilities, and providing services (perhaps not place-based) are sometimes much better solutions than a brand new building, in terms of reducing negative impact and creating benefits.

——A way to visualise this is to see the changing role of architects as part of the transition from an 'empty world' paradigm to that of a 'full world', a formulation which we borrow from Herman Daly, an ecological economist. This means that the tools, references, habits and criteria of excellence we use must be completely overhauled.

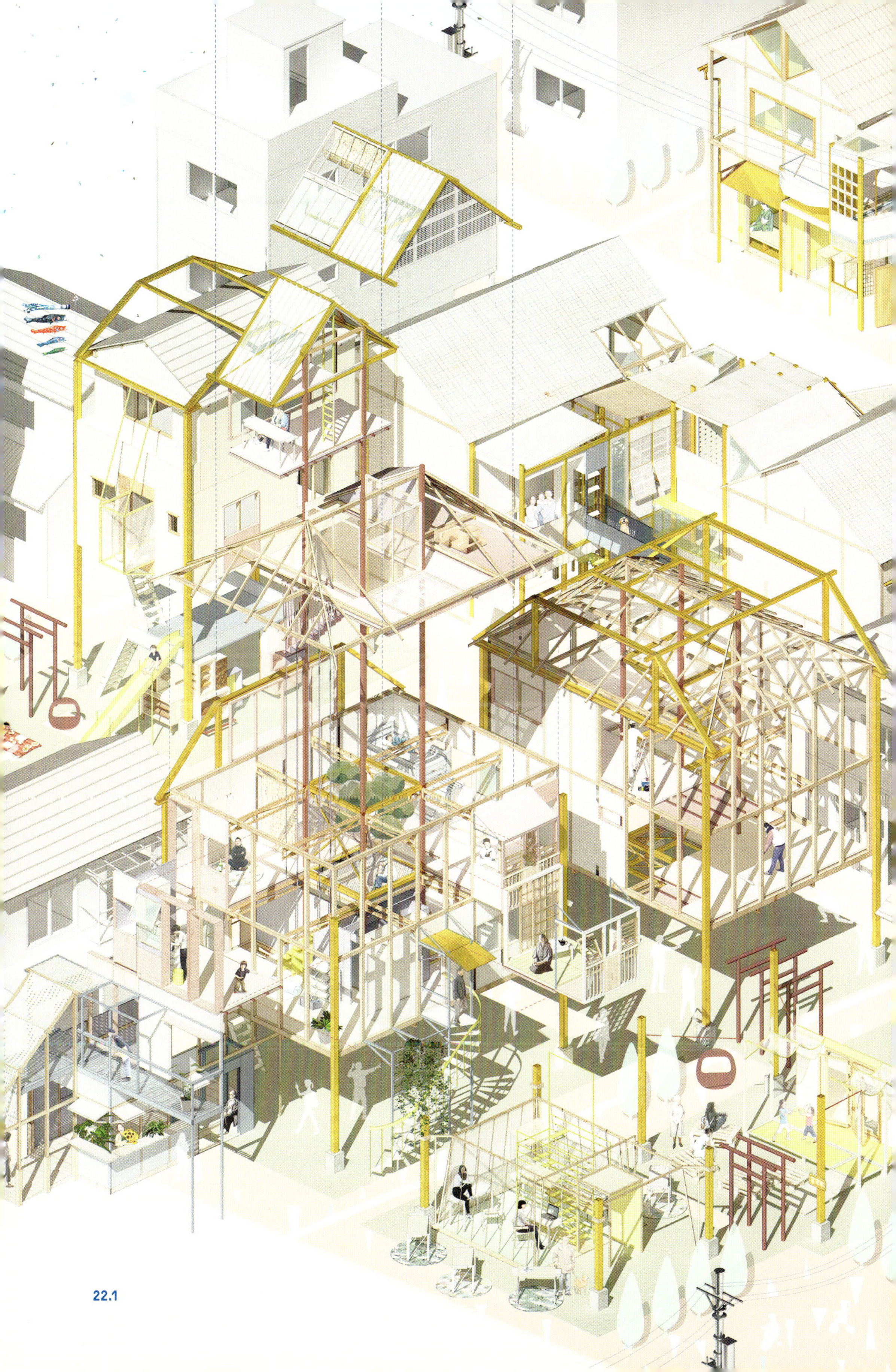

22.1

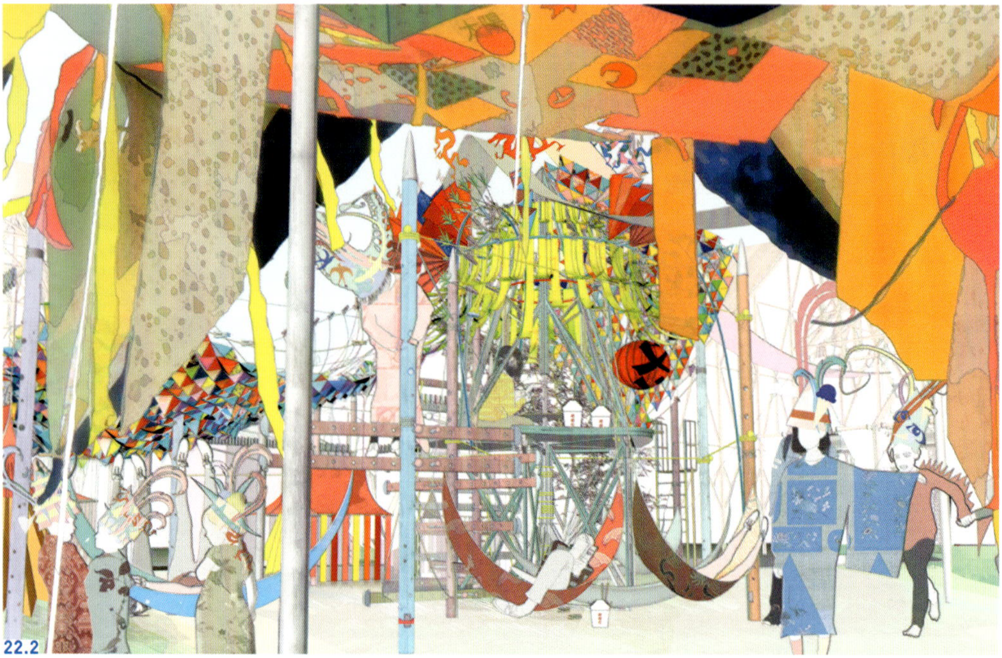

22.2

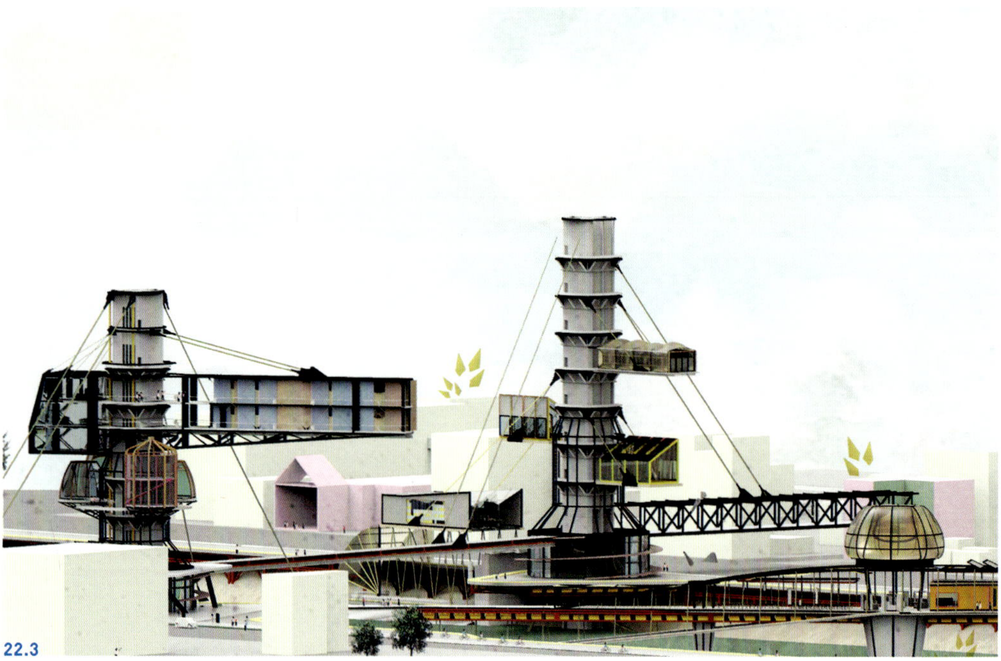

22.3

Fig. 22.1 **Yuen Nam (Elaine) Tsang** Y5, '2027: The Reclaimed Japanese House'. As a remedy for the rapid housing disposal cycle and an ageing society in Japan, the proposal explores alternative strategies to 'remake' Japanese houses for a co-living lifestyle for the next generation. Using reclaimed materials, via communal structures, and connecting ground-level shared pods, the project empowers people in a wider urban context. **Fig. 22.2** **Rufus Edmondson** Y4, 'Hackney-Exchange'. The Hackney-based school of culture uses empirical learning as a method of conservation in order to celebrate the world's most threatened cultural characteristics - language, craft and culinary heritage. Millennials from Hackney will transform spaces within the building and construct their own cultural pavilions, reflecting the changing identity of the borough. **Fig. 22.3** **Hei Tung (Whitney) Wong** Y5, 'University of Everywhere'. This project imagines how future education can be accessible without the constraint of time and location. Learning spaces become a community hub where learners, teachers, entrepreneurs, makers and designers all come together to work, learn and collaborate. The design of each spatial component reinforces the idea that learning can take place anywhere. **Fig. 22.4** **Alex Anderson** Y4, 'Bain Town Craft Quarter' is a pilot scheme that's part of the wider Bahamas Intangible Heritage Project. The design fosters community-based tourism, helping to decentralise the existing tourist market from a few large hotels to focus on smaller sustainable community initiatives.

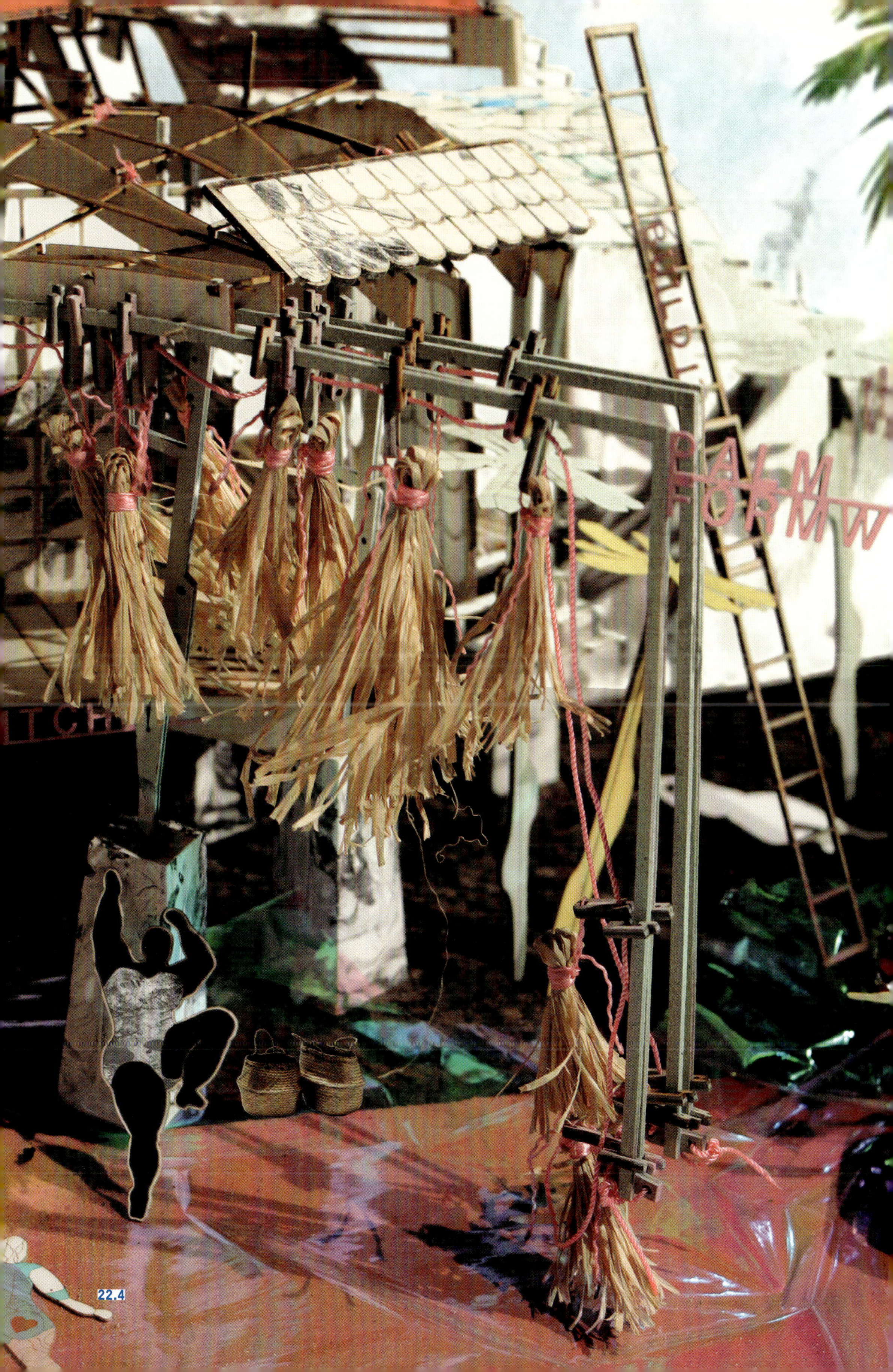

22.4

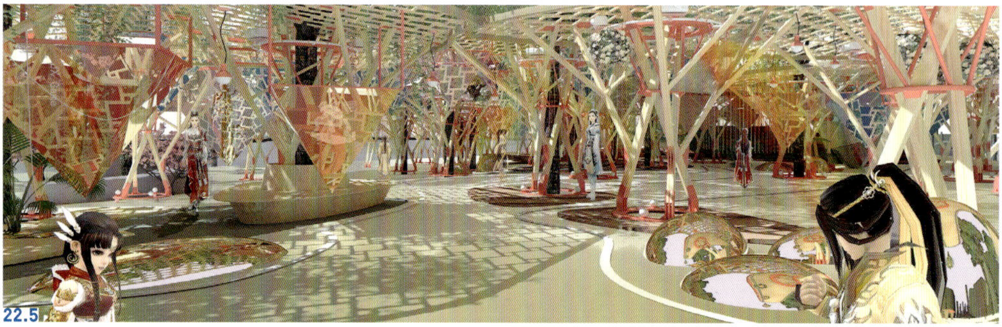

22.5

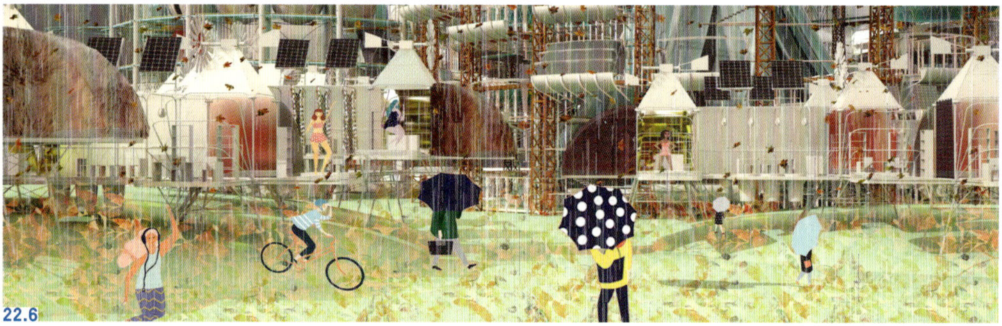

22.6

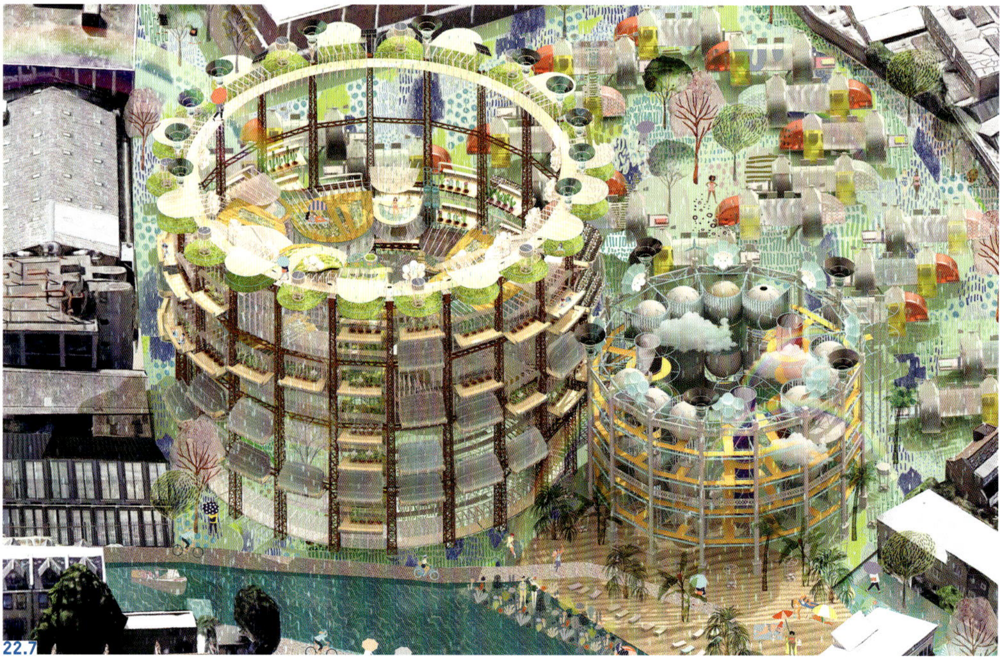

22.7

Fig. 22.5 Xin Zhan Y4, '2.5D Garden'. Based in Hangzhou, China, this project proposes an immersive learning experience via a 3D holographic projection combined with a 'cosplay' performance space. The bamboo reciprocal frame construction takes inspiration from traditional Chinese gardens, and when juxtaposed with fantastical projections, it blurs local and online experiences of the space. **Figs. 22.6 – 22.7 Georgina Halabi** Y5, 'Whatever the Weather'. The project re-inhabits Bethnal Green's historic gasholders with an interactive weather playground, a co-living community and a co-working hub designed for millennials. The programme reflects on our relationship with the outdoors and aims to recalibrate our comfort zone in the light of happiness felt from environmental conditions. Variable building skins choreograph comfort and thus temper internal environments according to user preference. Just as we change our clothes, the proposal aims to make the façades of the future more flexible. **Fig. 22.8 Laurence Flint** Y4, 'Yokosuka 2020'. The project proposes to use the energy of the Olympics to foster social ambition in response to Japan's vacant housing crisis, and Olympic shortcomings. The lightweight canopy system explores the potential of a shrinkable building to relate to the short- and long-term needs of residents within a shrinking city. By integrating a theatre school with topographic connections, the building provides for a variety of local present and future stakeholders.

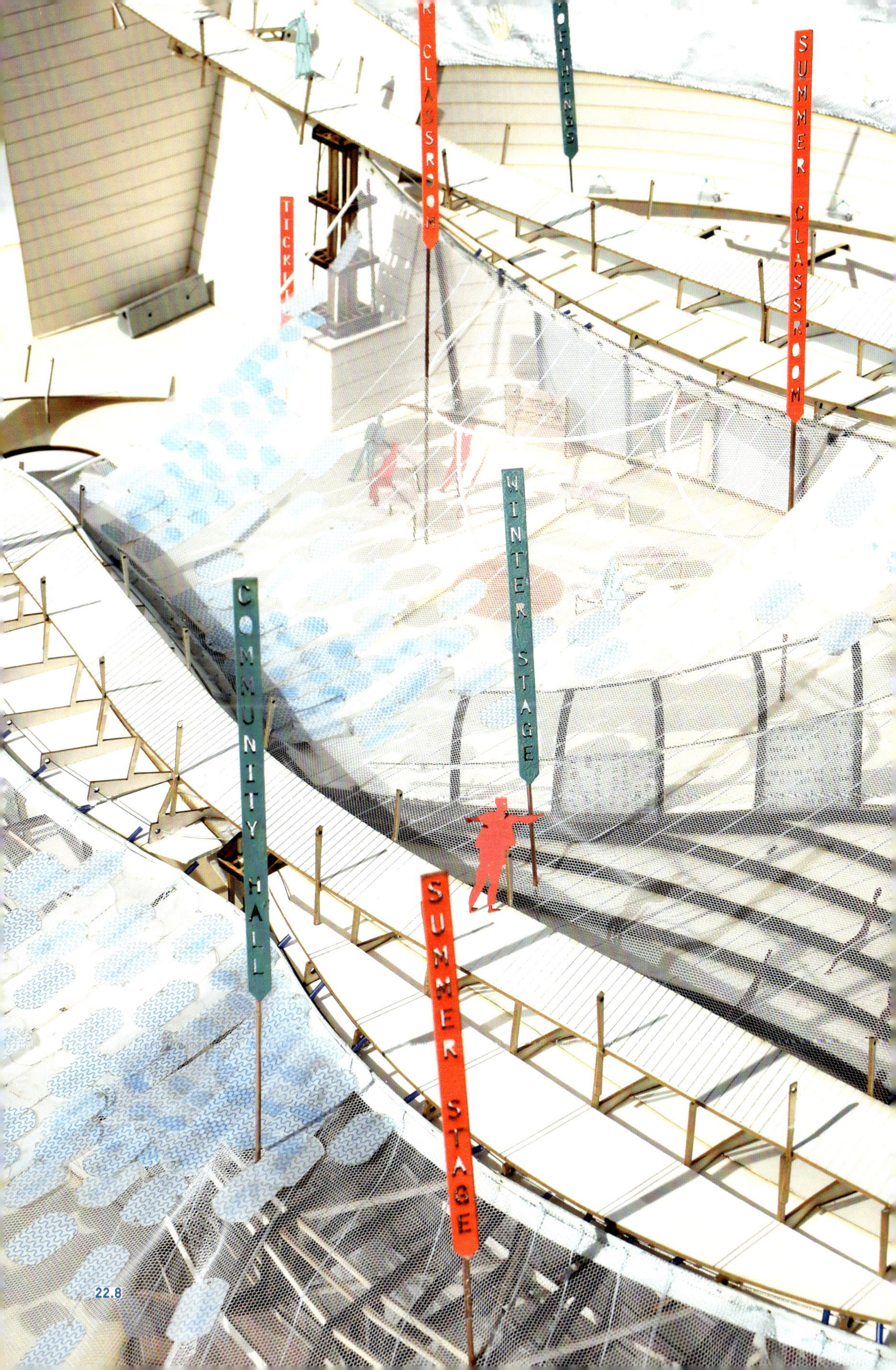
SUMMER CLASSROOM
WINTER STAGE
COMMUNITY HALL
SUMMER STAGE

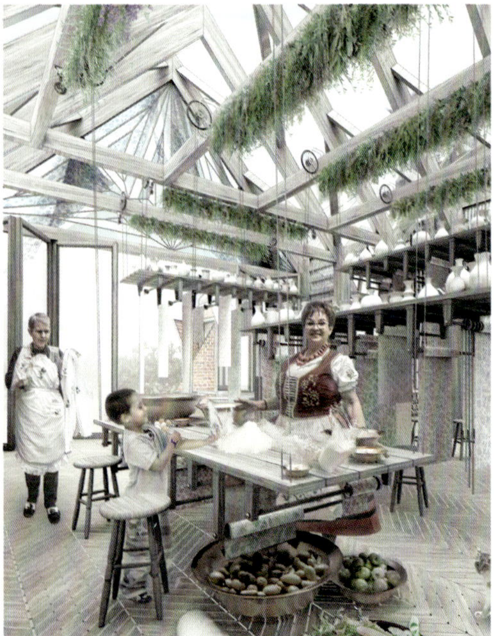

22.9

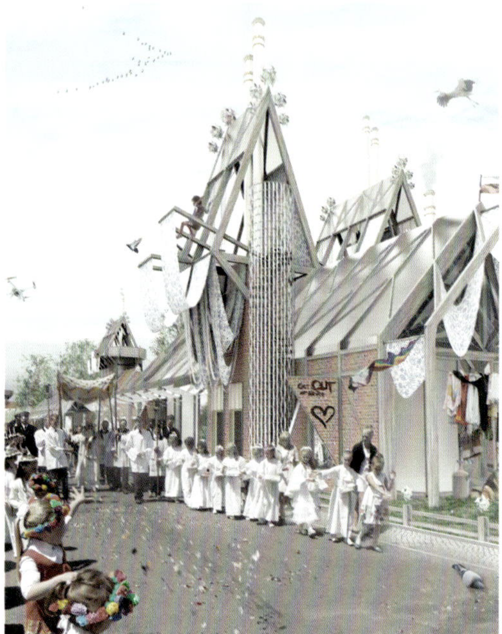

22.10

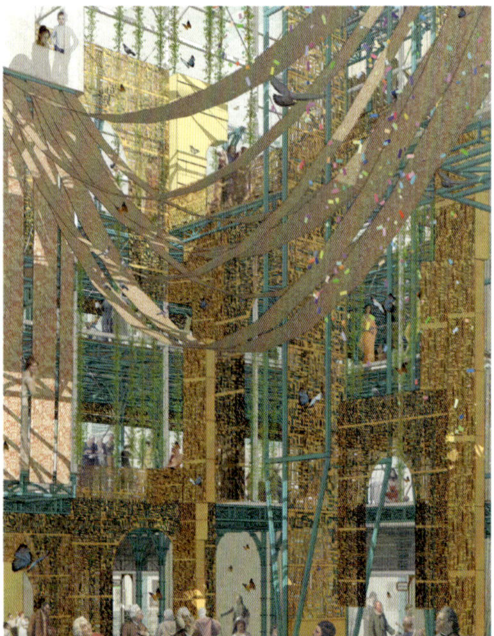

22.11

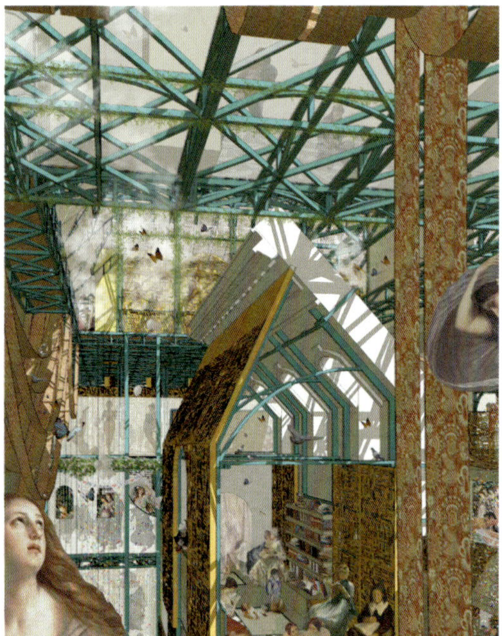

22.12

Figs. 22.9 – 22.10 Kuba Tomaszczyk Y5, 'In Search of Kashubia'. An architectural speculation on the future of one of the most dynamic indigenous ethnic groups in Europe. The project explores Kashubian life on a number of different scales: urban, building and furniture. The masterplan discreetly combines the spheres of co-living, co-learning and co-working that interweave in the construction and on the landscape of the rural site. An emphasis on the inter-generational transfer of knowledge informed a strategic neighbourhood plan and approach to design. **Figs. 22.11 – 22.12 Huma Mohyuddin** Y5, 'The New Women's Club in Mayfair'. The scheme redefines the representation of female empowerment. By proposing a New Women's Club, this project challenges the traditional values of a Gentleman's Club and Mayfair's brand of exclusivity. This new environment empowers women by focusing on their current needs and allows for people of different cultural, ethnic, economic, educational and religious backgrounds to form a space with their own personal identity. **Fig. 22.13 Timmy Whitehouse** Y4, 'Poly-hack Park'. An adaptive space for learning, play and production hacked by refugees, which cuts through an existing car park in downtown Athens. Multiple procurement strategies explore the potential of a 'hacked architecture' by re-appropriating the car park, and allowing refugees and city users to hack their own spaces.

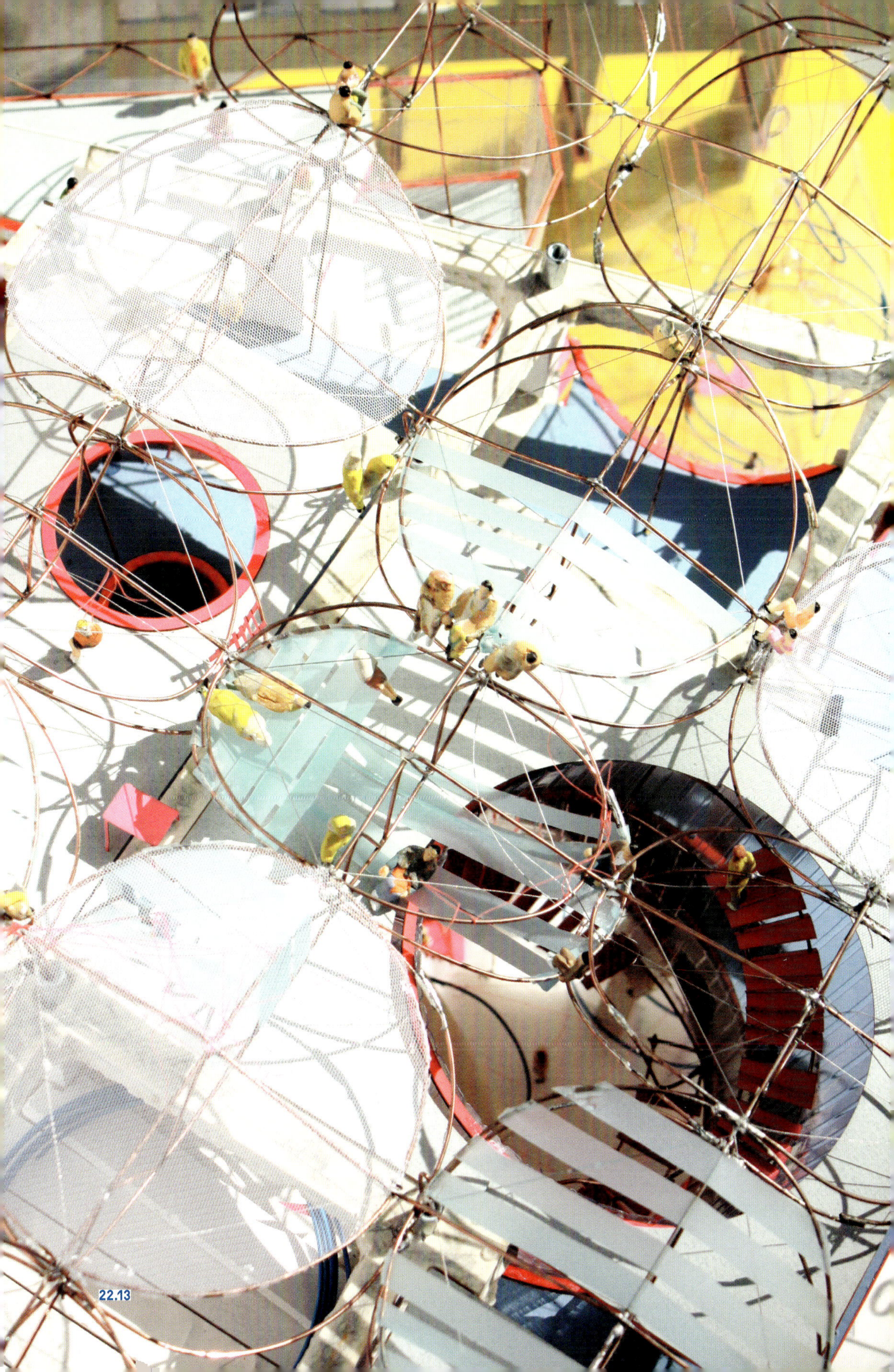
22.13

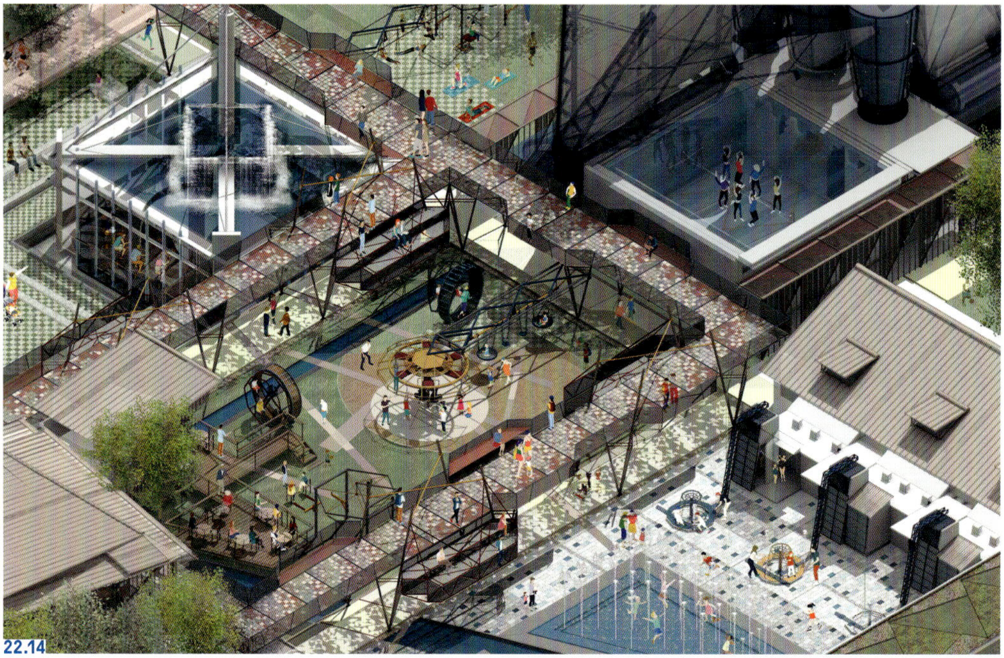

22.14

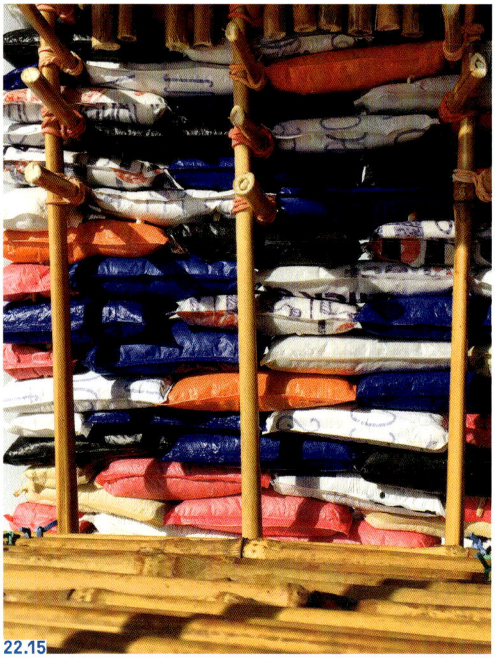

22.15

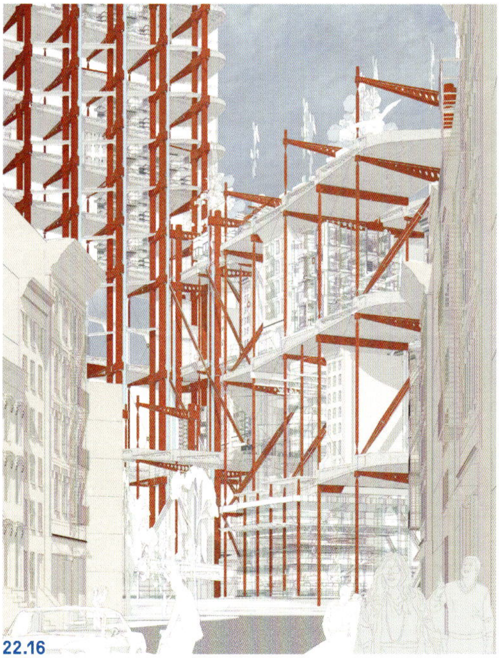

22.16

Fig. 22.14 Supichaya Chaisiriroj Y5, 'Lumphini Fitness Academy and Lifestyle Centre'. The project imagines an extension to an urban park in Bangkok, Thailand. The centre offers exercise-oriented facilities to the ever-increasing users of Lumphini Park. The programmatic design investigates how buildings could reduce heat gains by way of passive systems powered by the exercising public. **Fig. 22.15 Isabelle Tung** Y4, 'Homegrown City'. The proposed masterplan and up-cycling education centre within the Kamala Nehru informal settlement in Patna, India, aims to encourage settlers to turn plastic bag waste into beautiful daily objects. The project explores the idea of using plastic bags as a construction material, whilst creating flexible housing typologies aimed at improving the living conditions of current and future settlers.

Figs. 22.16 – 22.17 Jack Sargent Y5, 'The Broadway Super Triangle'. Forming a physical manifestation of the internet age, this scheme proposes a cross-programmatic, super-urban scaled intervention that aims to facilitate inter-community engagement in Brooklyn, New York.

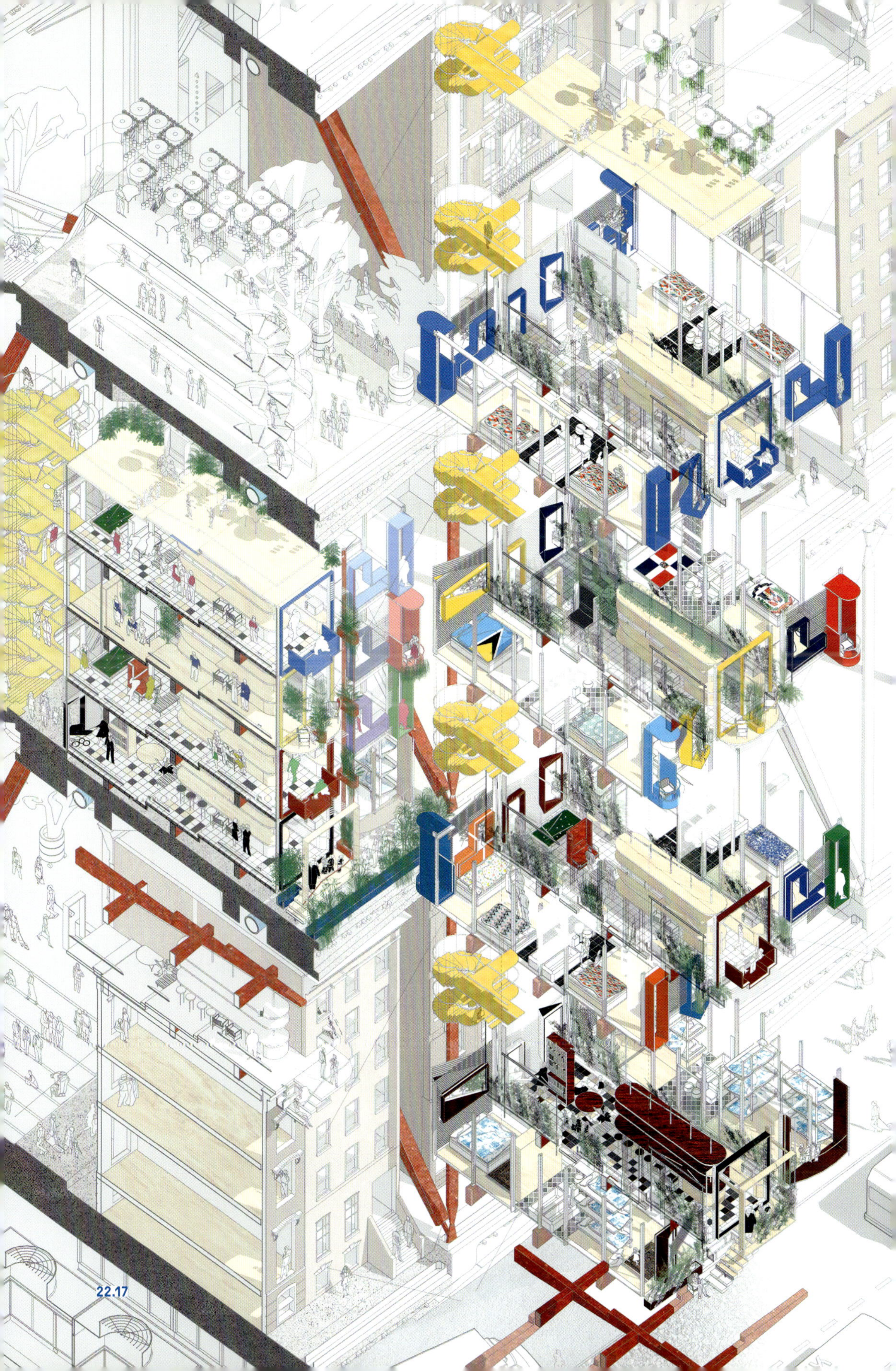
22.17

Unit 24 Make-Believe

Penelope Haralambidou, Michael Tite

Year 4
John Cruwys, Tom James, Matei Mitrache, Masahiro Nakamura, Rose Shaw, Paula Strunden, Stefania Tsigkouni

Year 5
Sabina Berariu, Thomas Brown, Clare Dallimore, Matthew Lucraft, Martyna Marciniak, Gergana Popova, Nick Shackleton, Jasper Stevens

Special thanks for digital film, animation and interactive media teaching to Keiichi Matsuda

Workshops:
Angeliki Vasileiou, Kevin Pollard, Neutral Digital, Shed-Works, Studio Archetype

Thank you to:
Jack Holmes, Sergio Irigoyen, Rashed Khandker, Greg Kythreotis, Brook Lin, Sam McGill, Dan Scoulding, Ben Shetерline

Thank you to our critics:
Ollie Alsop, Anna Ulrikke Andersen, Nat Chard, Patrick Chen, Daniel Cotton, Nico Czyz, Max Dewdney, Stephen Gage, Tamsin Hanke, Colin Herperger, Ifigeneia Liangi, Chris Pierce, Merijn Royaards, Sayan Skandarajah, Henrietta Williams

Unit 24 is a group of architectural storytellers employing film, animation, drawing, VR/AR and physical modelling in pursuit of spatial propositions that harness the potential of time-based media. We nurture freethinkers who investigate ideas and techniques in collaboration with other like-minded experts. We find inspiration in the dialogue between film and architecture and their intertwined histories; film has the power to construct the psyche of a city while architectural ideas are changing the way that film is generated and understood.

——This year we turned our attention to the growing frictions between urban bubbles of overabundance and post-urban pockets of debilitating scarcity. We asked whether a cinematic architecture of 'make-believe' can address this dichotomy with proposals that marry fact and fiction.

——In November, in the immediate aftermath of the US Presidential Election, we explored the contrasting territories of LA and Arizona, tracing a path across the underlying geographic, social and fictional fault lines that separate these neighbouring, yet deeply diverse regions. Since it first swelled out of the Californian desert in the late 1800s, the growth of LA has been inextricably linked to the business of making moving images and storytelling. Conversely, the cinematic landscapes of Arizona have provided the outward gaze for America to reflect upon its history. This sense of emptiness breeds the mythical and surreal, triggering sightings of unexpected objects and the birth of conspiracy theories.

——Within these febrile territories, we searched for new kinds of make-believe that blur the boundaries between truth and reality. We explored the fictionalised urban landscapes of LA, the sun-baked world in and around the Salk Institute and discovered the desert-inspired utopias of Taliesin West, Arcosanti and Biosphere 2, where architecture playfully imagines an alternative make-believe future.

——Upon our return, we interpreted our findings into the local climate of the post-Brexit maelstrom. We conjured new visions for these towns with proud, yet long-lost pasts: from Great Yarmouth to Rugeley, from Stratford to Port Stanley. Our students propose speculative new narratives for half-forgotten towns like these, creating stories that might beggar belief, but which are so hair-brained that they might just work.

——Year 5 projects build on last year's investigations, creating architectural 'essay films' that explore wild new frontiers and states of speculative magic. A series of workshops with games designers, visualisers, VR developers and sound technologists supported the work along with access to Oculus Rift and HTC Vive Developer Kits.

——Throughout the year, Unit 24 has evolved into a band of virtual storytellers, snaggletoothed mythmakers, digital hoaxers and political yarn-spinners, who aim to make believers out of anyone who might care to listen.

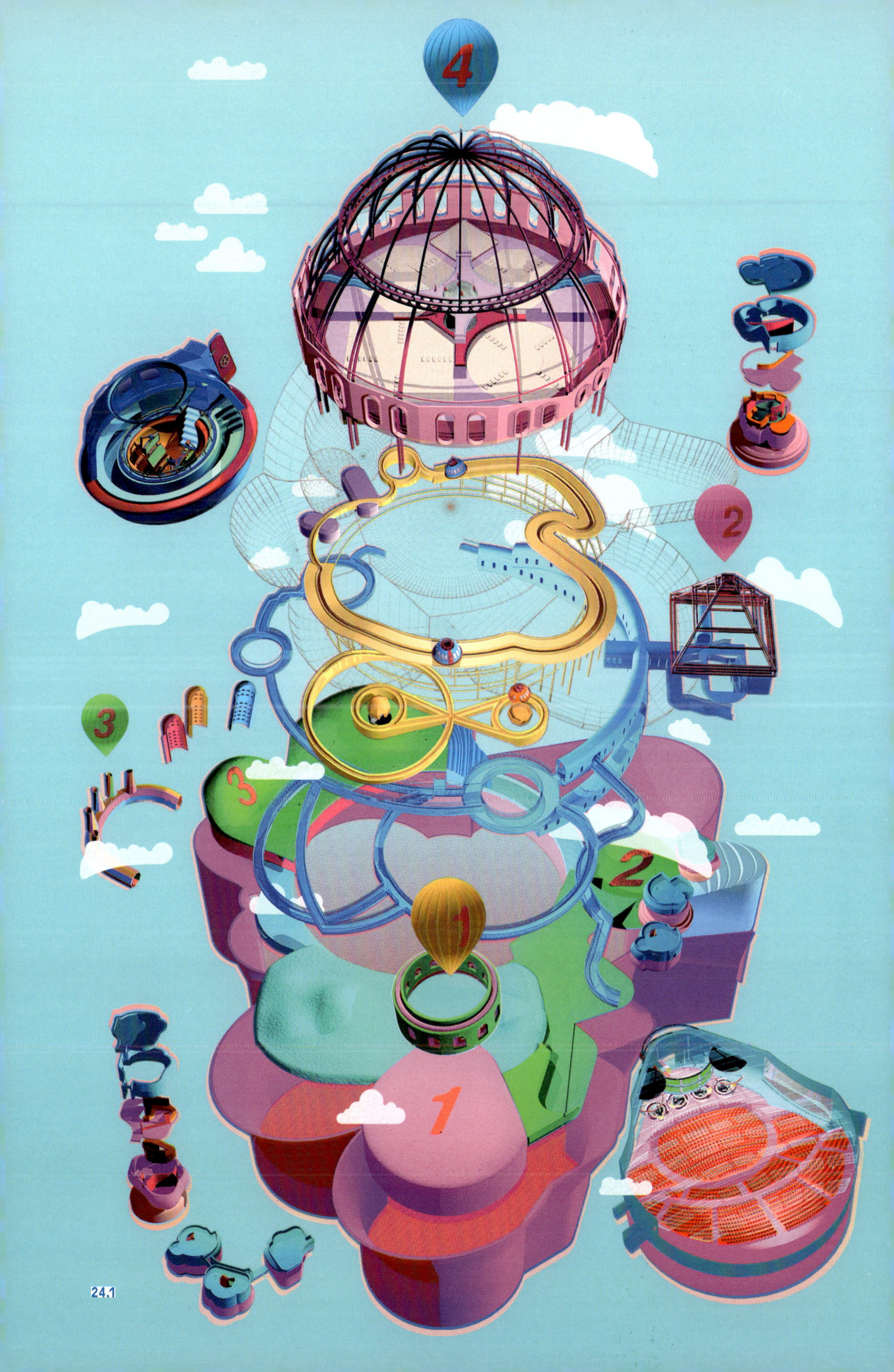

24.1

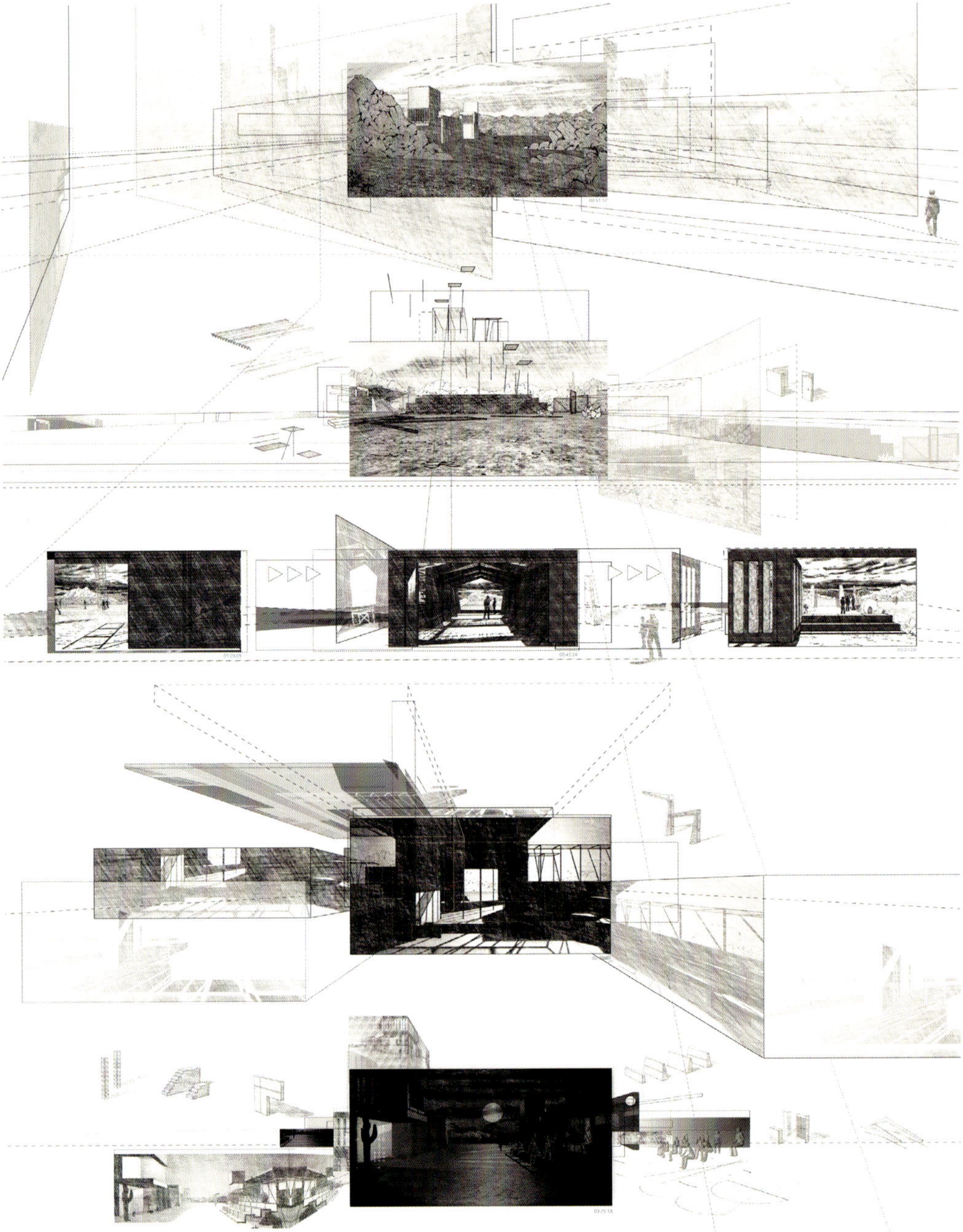

24.2

Fig. 24.1 Nick Shackleton Y5, 'Let's Live'. 'Let's Live!' is not a utopia, but a community of online gaming performers, where work has been substituted by a desire to play. Players/performers lay bare their everyday lives to the millions of online spectators that consume content. The architecture derives directly from the game-space, where brick and mortar merge with the digital world of gaming. A highly choreographed sequence of rituals merge play with everyday life, and the settlement provides a backdrop for the broadcasting that blurs the physical with the digital. **Fig. 24.2 Clare Dallimore** Y5, 'Drawing in Time: Desert Filmscape'. Set in Arizona's interior upland, the project acts as a rebellion against Hollywood cinema. Exploring themes of frontier, utopian living and cinema, the project proposes a new environment for independent filmmakers working and living outside of the urban sprawl of nearby Phoenix, which culminates in an annual Independent Film Festival. Two-dimensional drawings are transformed into the three-dimensional filmic space, grafting the crafted nature of the hand-drawn elements into a digital form, set in space and time. **Fig. 24.3 Gergana Popova** Y5, 'City as Stage'. The project revisits a period in the history of London, where theatre and city were constructing each other. Sited in Smithfield Market, the New Museum of London opposes the contemporary desire for the object, explores the intangible part of our heritage and celebrates traces of forgotten history. Inspired by the site's long history of co-existence between a market and a funfair, 'City as Stage' merges theatre, market and museum.

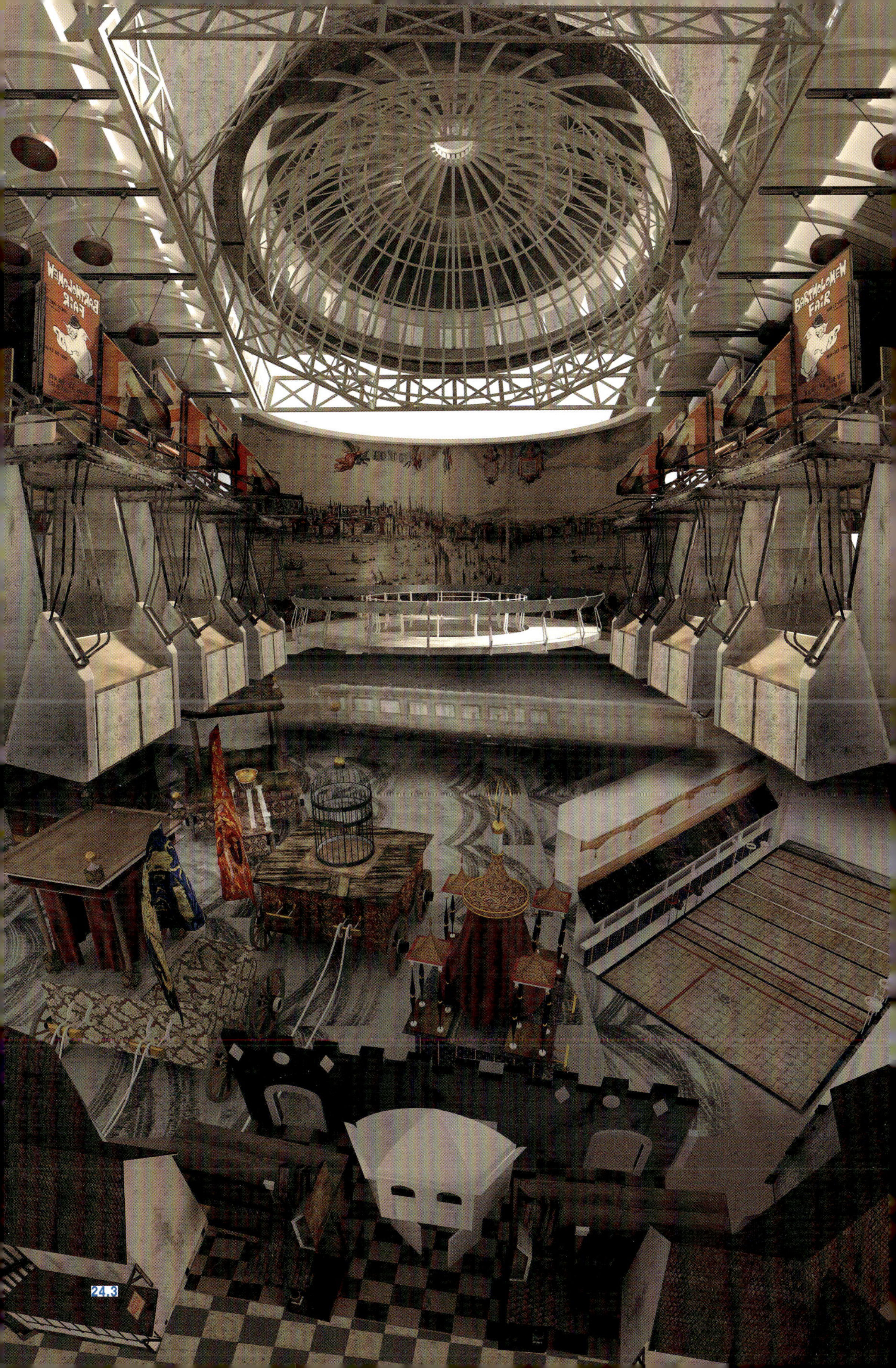
BARTHOLOMEW FAIR
BARTHOLOMEW FAIR
24.3

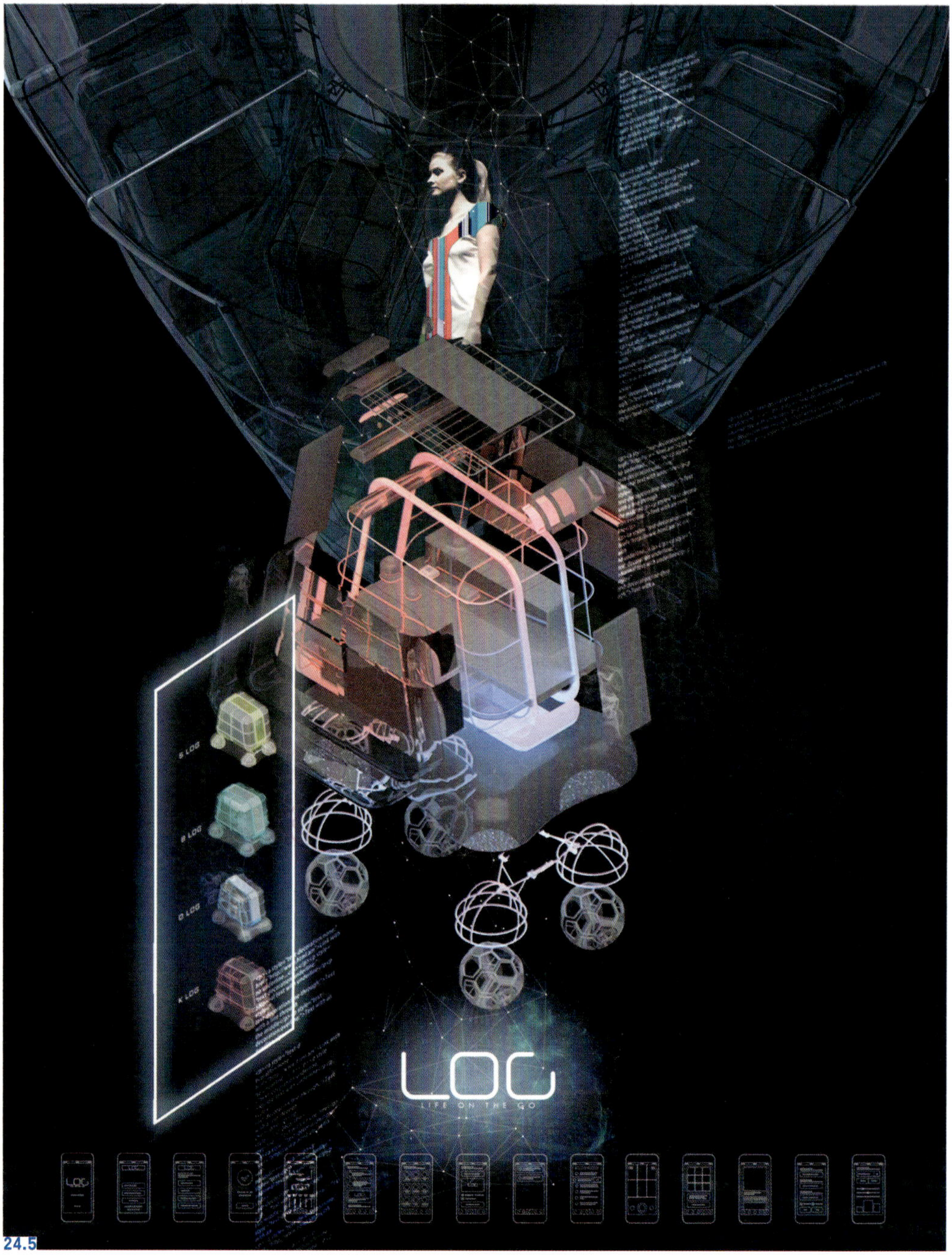

24.5

Fig. 24.4 **Sabina Berariu** Y5, 'LOG | Deconstructed domesticity'. We are witnessing a spilling of the home at urban scale, where old bonds break, spatial linkages dissolve and new types of domestic urban composition emerge. This project is grounded in the digital nomadic movement, paired with the shifting nature of domestic environments and the possibility of integrating technology into everyday objects which respond to the biochemical composition of the human body. On a micro-level, the project addresses the fundamental biochemical composition of the nomad, while on a macro-level, the design assumes that old paradigms of property ownership and social status are superseded. LOG, 'Life on the Go', a high-end branded line of home-mobile products, controlled through wearable technology, is proposed as an alternative to current domestic architectures. **Fig. 24.5** **Thomas Brown** Y5, 'Resorting to Canvey'. Resorting To Canvey is a speculative framework for a new environmentally responsible holiday resort. The project addresses one of the most pressing challenges facing not only Canvey's tourism industry, but much of the built environment situated along the Thames Estuary including London: vulnerability to severe flooding due to sea-level rise. The film presents a case of positive flooding of the future holiday resort through the narrative of an unassuming protagonist, Bert Vandewiele. Bert is the caretaker at Thorney Bay Village, and is faced with many challenges whilst keeping the environmental flooding station-cum-holiday resort running smoothly for the holidaymakers.

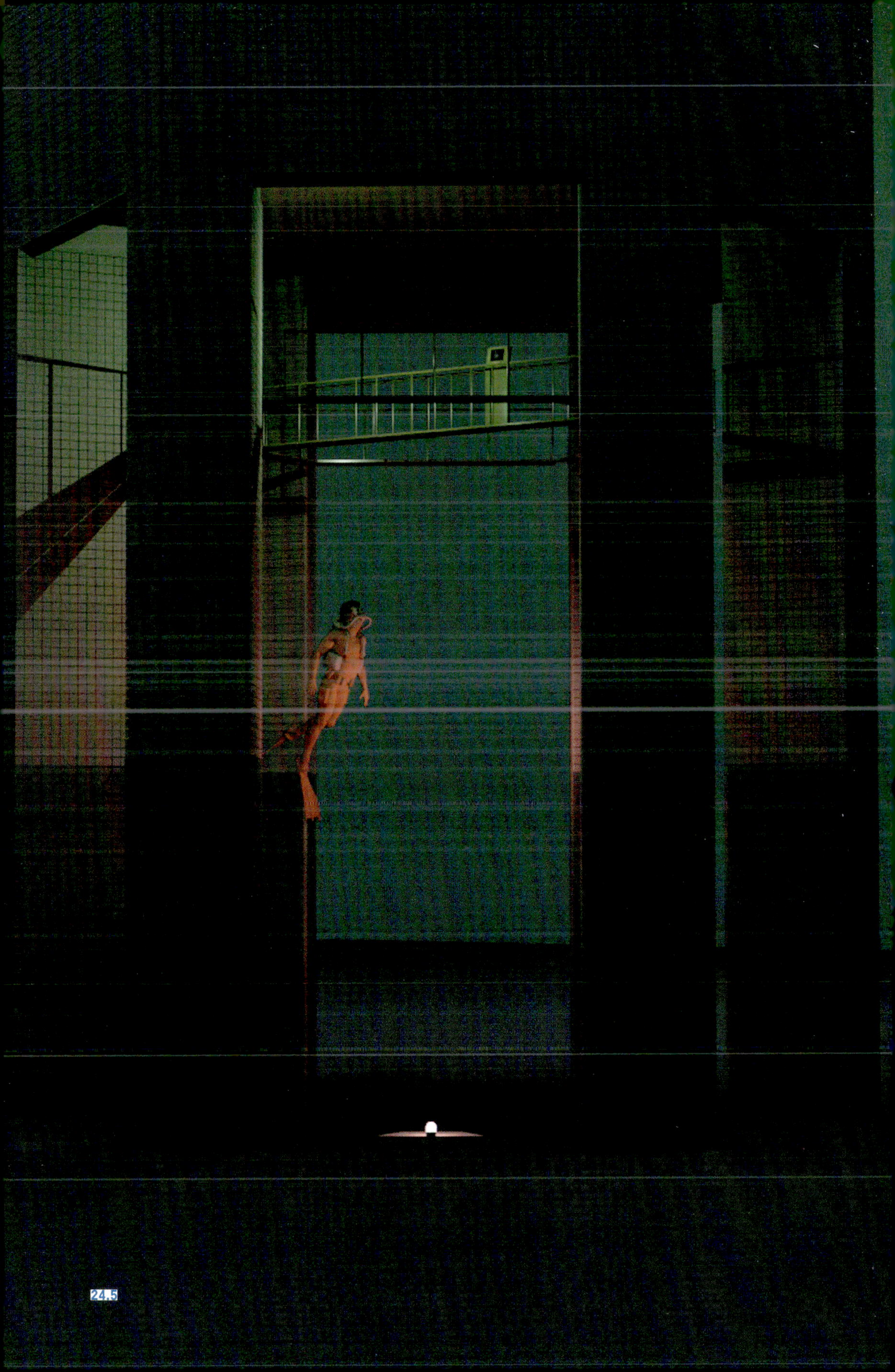

24.5

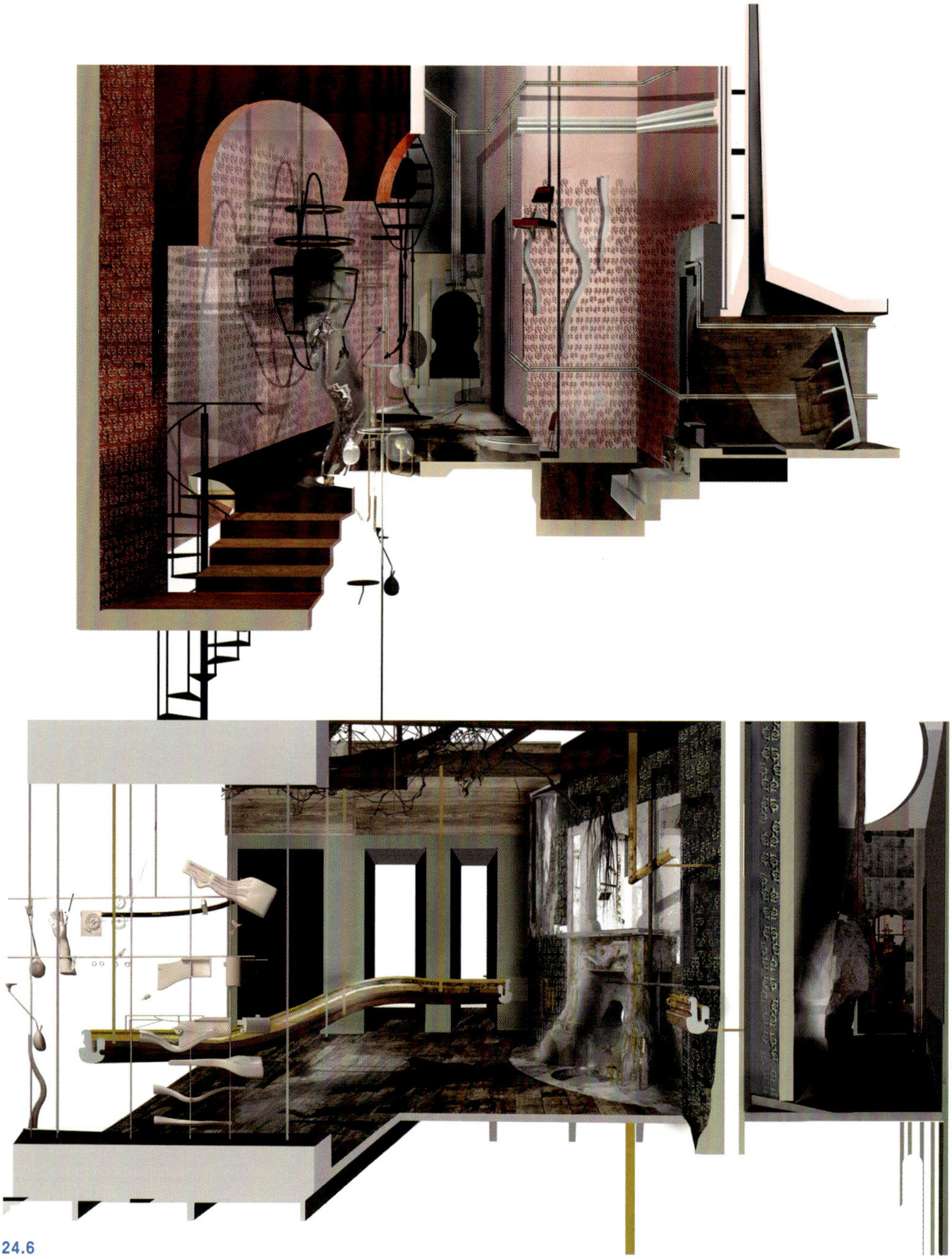

24.6

Fig. 24.6 Martyna Marciniak Y5, 'Paul E. Phylo's Palace'. A revival of the Enlightenment idea of architecture that has the potential to inspire desire and love. The Palace is a character that leads its visitors on a courtship journey from the lounge of anticipation, through the hall of indifference, the dining-room of awakening, to the boudoir of ultimate excitement. Similar to a living organism, the building reacts to the visitor's presence – it uncovers its secret passages, blushes, grows and decomposes. **Fig. 24.7 Jasper Stevens** Y5, 'The London NOTEL'. Part cinema, part immersive theatre, part hotel, the London NOTEL is a hybrid that merges VR with physical architecture. The building is only there to be touched, existing as haptic infrastructure designed to guide visitors through immersive cinematic narratives. But, there are rumours that some guests have never returned, lost inside the building's multiple realities. A Private Investigator has been hired to investigate. Provided with only a map of the building, he arrives on a rainy Saturday night... **Fig. 24.8 Matthew Lucraft** Y5, 'A Monument to Outlast Humanity'. Emerging from the abandoned suburbs of the Sonoran Desert, the North Surprise Community Settlement is an experiment in idealised future living without paid labour. A group of ageing RVers pioneer an earthen, handmade architecture, an embodiment of a community voice and a lasting relic of their existence. Over time, a network of radially planned micro-communities spreads across the desert; the 'streets' undulate above and below the ground, forming an evolving artificial landscape intimately connected with the site's fascinating past.

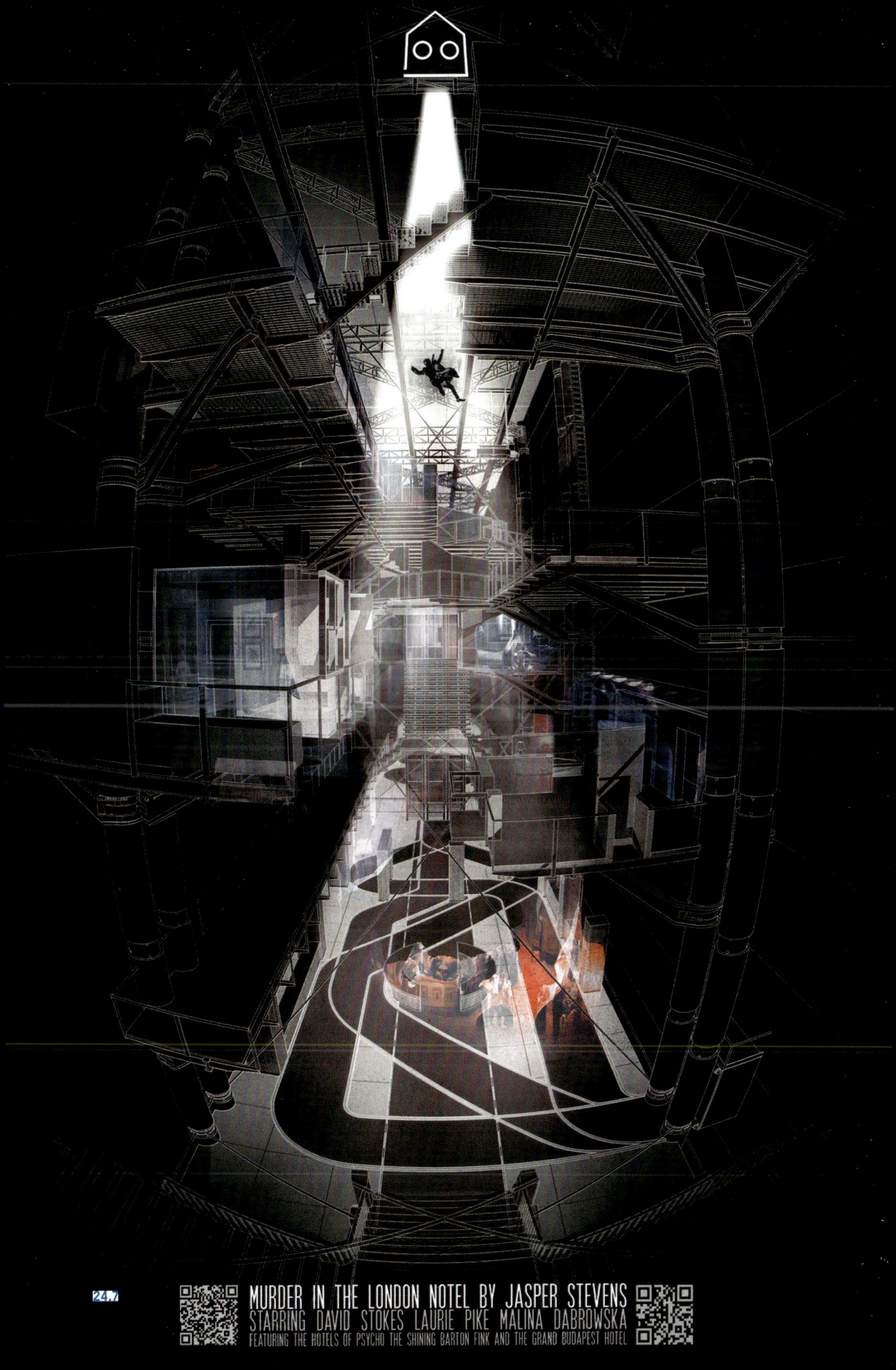
MURDER IN THE LONDON NOTEL BY JASPER STEVENS
STARRING DAVID STOKES LAURIE PIKE MALINA DABROWSKA
FEATURING THE HOTELS OF PSYCHO THE SHINING BARTON FINK AND THE GRAND BUDAPEST HOTEL

24.7

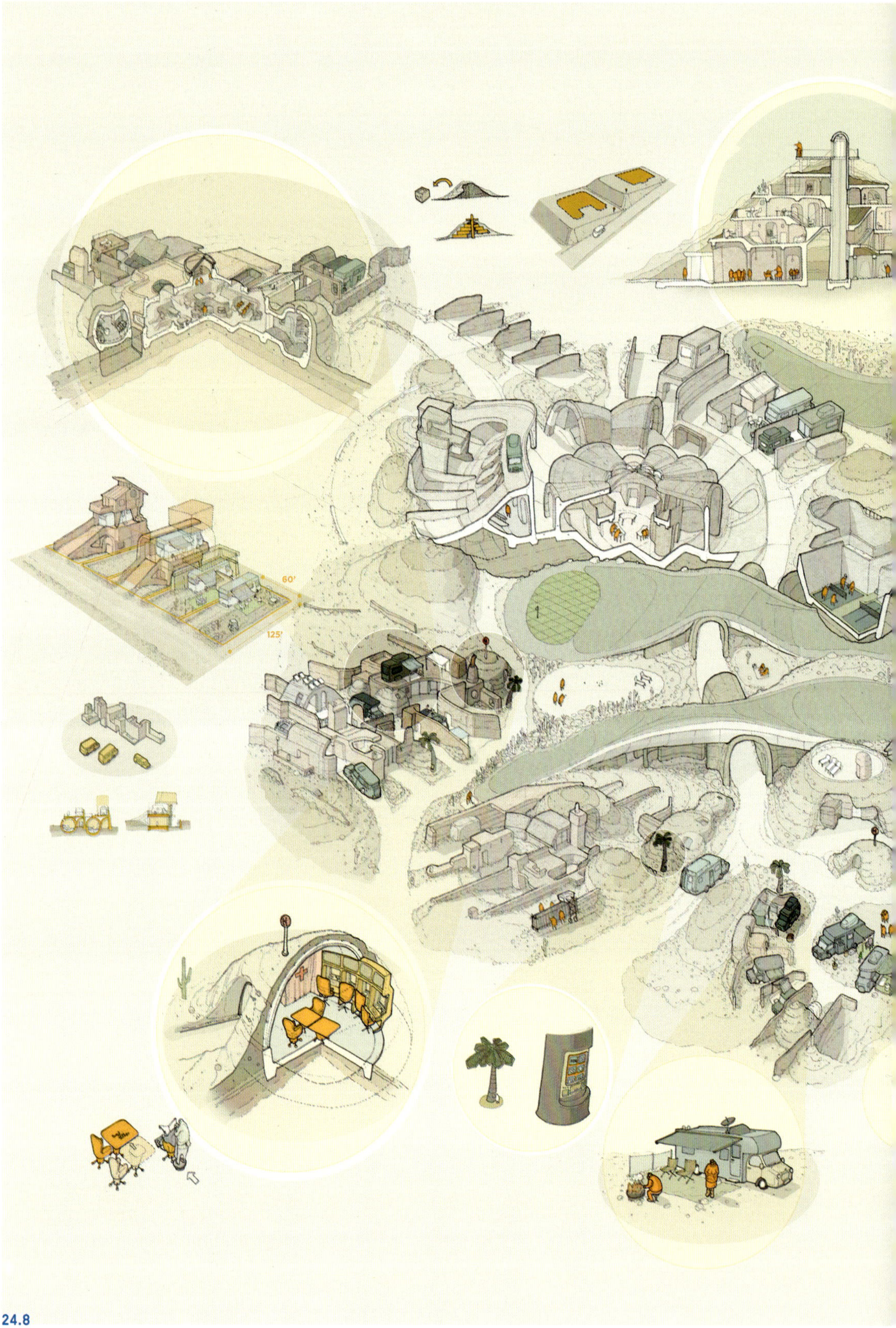

24.8

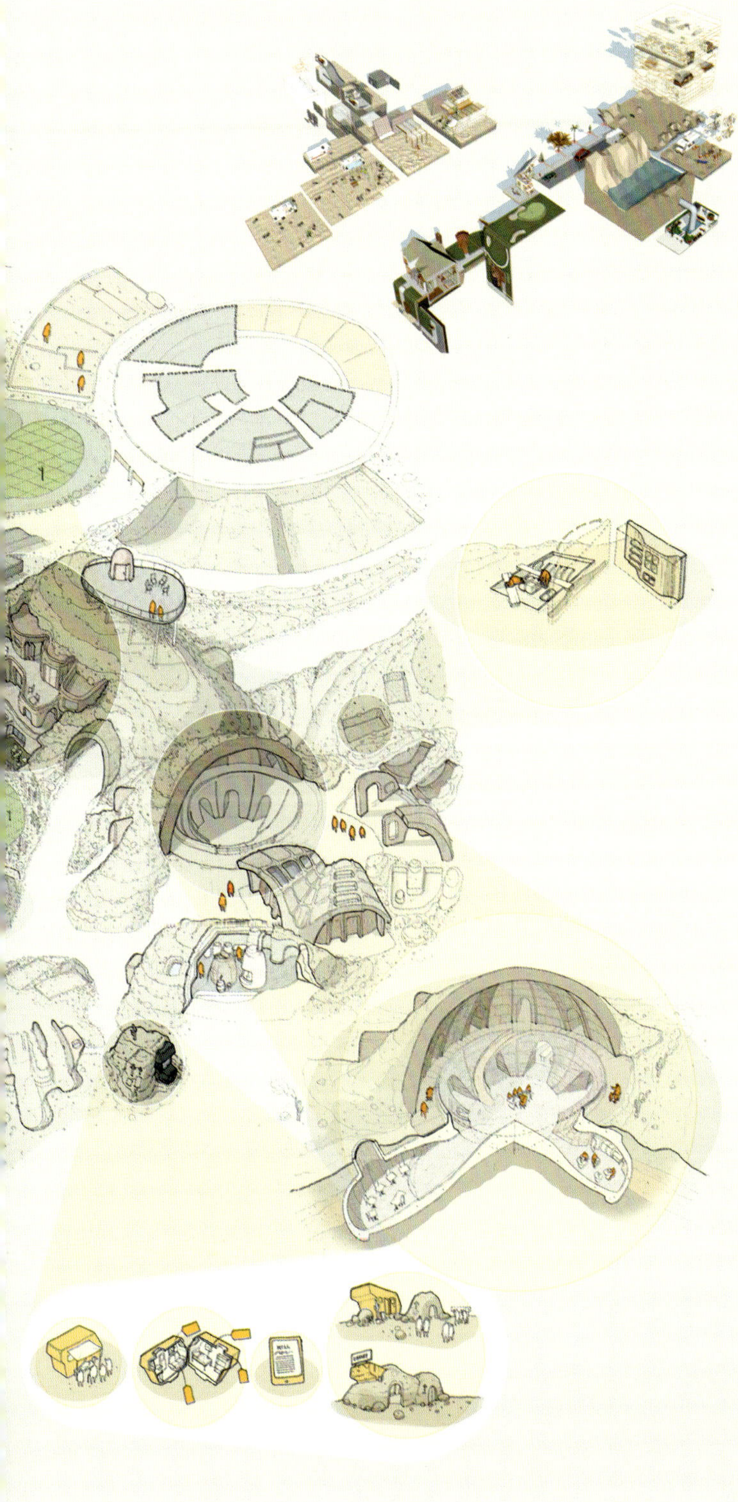

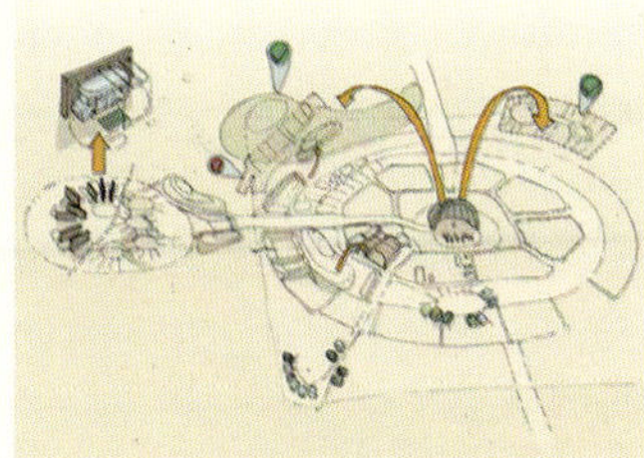

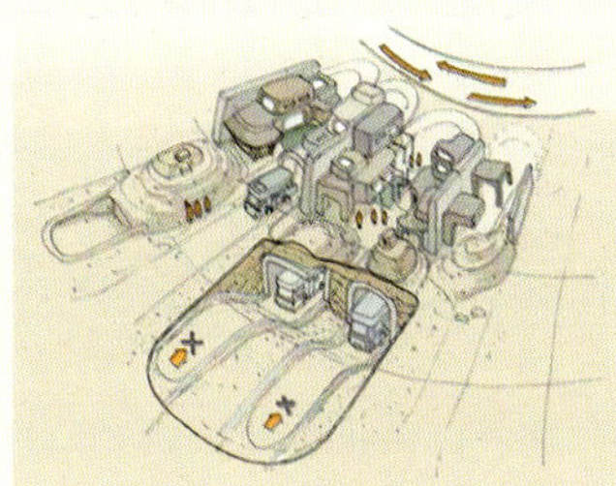

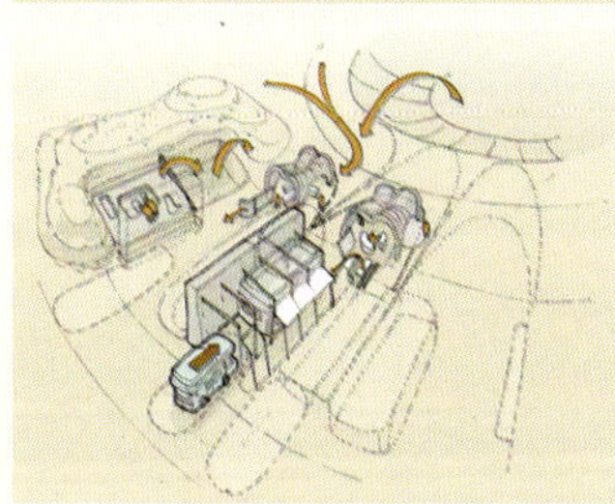

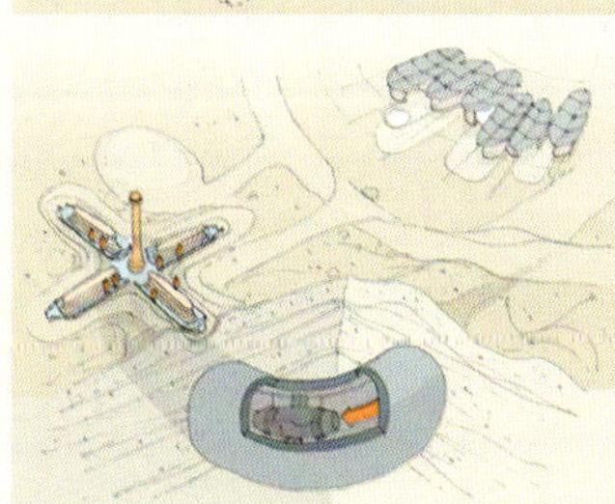

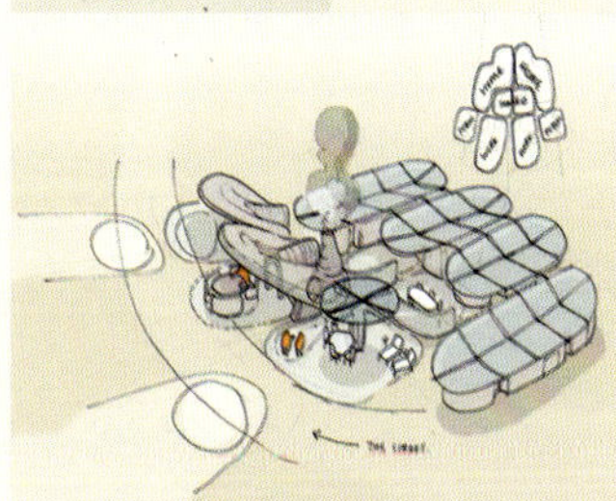

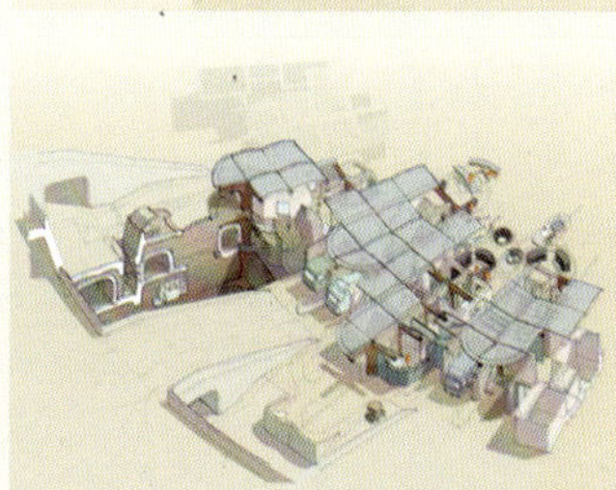

Unit 25 Negotiating the Seam

Nat Chard, Emma-Kate Matthews

Year 4
Callum Campbell, Vlad Daraban, Declan Harvey, Demetris Ktorides, Isaac Leung, Arwen Liu, Vita Rossi, Dougal Sadler

Year 5
George Bolwell, Simona Fratila, Andrea Rocco Matta, Kirsty McMullan, Thomas Parker, Daniel Van Der Poll, Peter West

Thank you to our Design Realisation tutor, Jerry Tate

Thank you to our critics: Penelope Haralambidou, Colin Fournier, Birgir Orn Jonsson, Neil Spiller, Mar Fer Saez, Mark Morris, Eva Ravenborg, Shaun Murray, Ifigeneia Liangi, Simon Withers, Phuong-Trâm Nguyen, Emmanuel Vercruysse, Rebecca Loewen, Mark Ruthven, Frederik Petersen, Thomas Pearce, Matthew Butcher, Carlos Jiménez Cenamor, Bob Sheil

Thank you to our sponsors: RIAA Barker Gillette, Helix Architecture, Tate Harmer, Studio Mark Ruthven

Unit 25 is interested in experimental architectural practices, both as a means of proposing architecture and as an educational method. We concentrate on ways of thinking through the drawings and constructions we make, where the act of drawing or making might tease out possibilities beyond our immediate imagination.

——This year, we have been looking at equivocal conditions. We started out by comparing Bertillon's criminology laboratory (where the apparatus was constructed with a specificity to the programme) and Freud's study, where apart from his chair, almost everything that is active in his practice of psychoanalysis pre-dates his invention of the discipline. Antique artefacts and furniture are appropriated for his purpose yet the room appears as instrumental and specific as Bertillon's laboratory. We considered the realm between specificity and appropriation.

——We also looked at Gio Ponte's 'chair chair', a chair he said had no adjectives and was only about being a chair, yet at the same time he named it to describe its lack of weight – he also made it about lightness. He wanted it to be at once the essence of a chair and yet specifically about one thing beyond being a chair.

——More generally, we looked at the ambiguity between realities and representation, spending time in Vienna and around Munich looking at conditions in the Baroque and Rococo periods, where the seams between representations and realities were blurred, especially at the Wurtzburg Residenz.

——We started by examining equivocal conditions and then, from this exploration, each student went on to develop their own particular path of study.

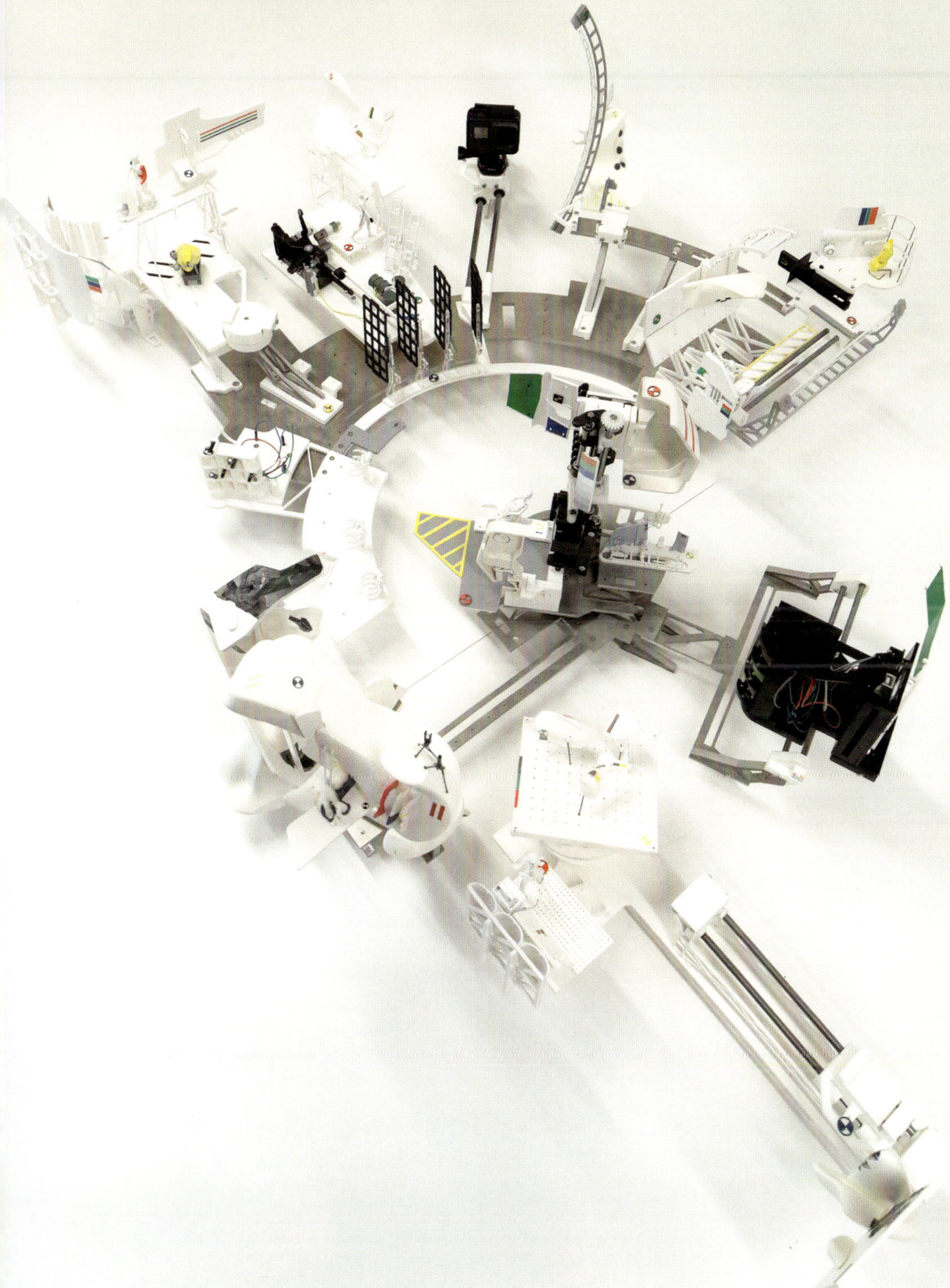

25.1

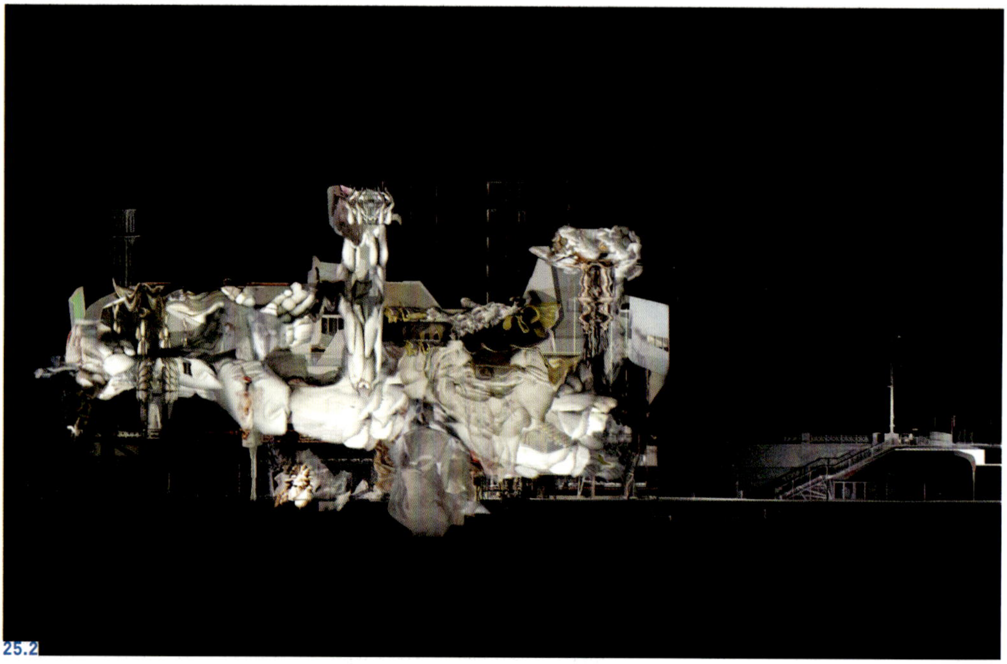

25.2

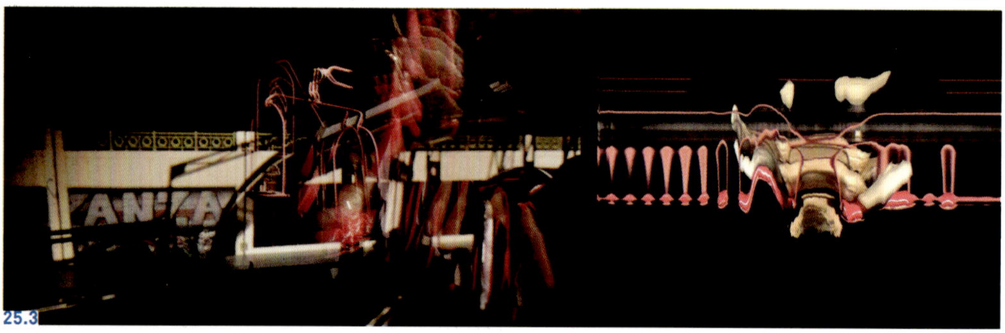

25.3

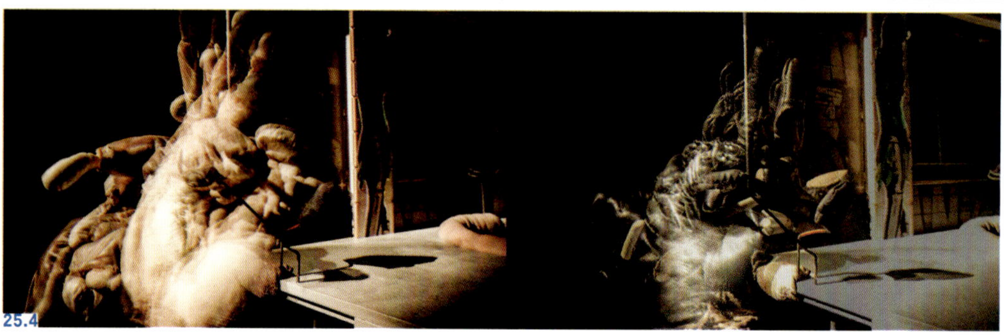

25.4

Fig. 25.1 **Thomas Parker** Y5, 'An Architecture of Lumetric Causality'. Generative Model. Film and photographs of the model are translated digitally by a programme to open up possibilities beyond the imagination. The translations are selected for a physical collage which is then translated (mostly by hand) into a set of architectural drawings. **Fig. 25.2** **Kirsty McMullan** Y5, 'Simultaneous Narratives'. View from the Donaukanal. The building is designed through a series of gestures captured through various photographic processes. Each part of the project has a dedicated model as a set to locate the gestures that are played out with specially designed (and tailored) gloves. **Fig. 25.3** **Kirsty McMullan** Y5, 'Simultaneous Narratives'. One of many studies to work out the parts of the building. The tailors prepare garments for the many social occasions in Vienna. The building adapts to these events and acts in anticipation of the city's events. **Fig. 25.4** **Kirsty McMullan** Y5, 'Simultaneous Narratives'. Two studies using different gloves. Note the wire choreographic registers that programme what is known in advance so work can be done as intuitively as possible on the things that the gloves can design. **Fig. 25.5** **Peter West** Y5, 'City of Desire'. A fragment of a fragmented hostel that is dispersed around Vienna. The cuts in the grey walls allow phosphorescent paint to be sprayed onto the stretched fabric screens, casting shadows of passing travellers while also fleetingly showing decaying projections.

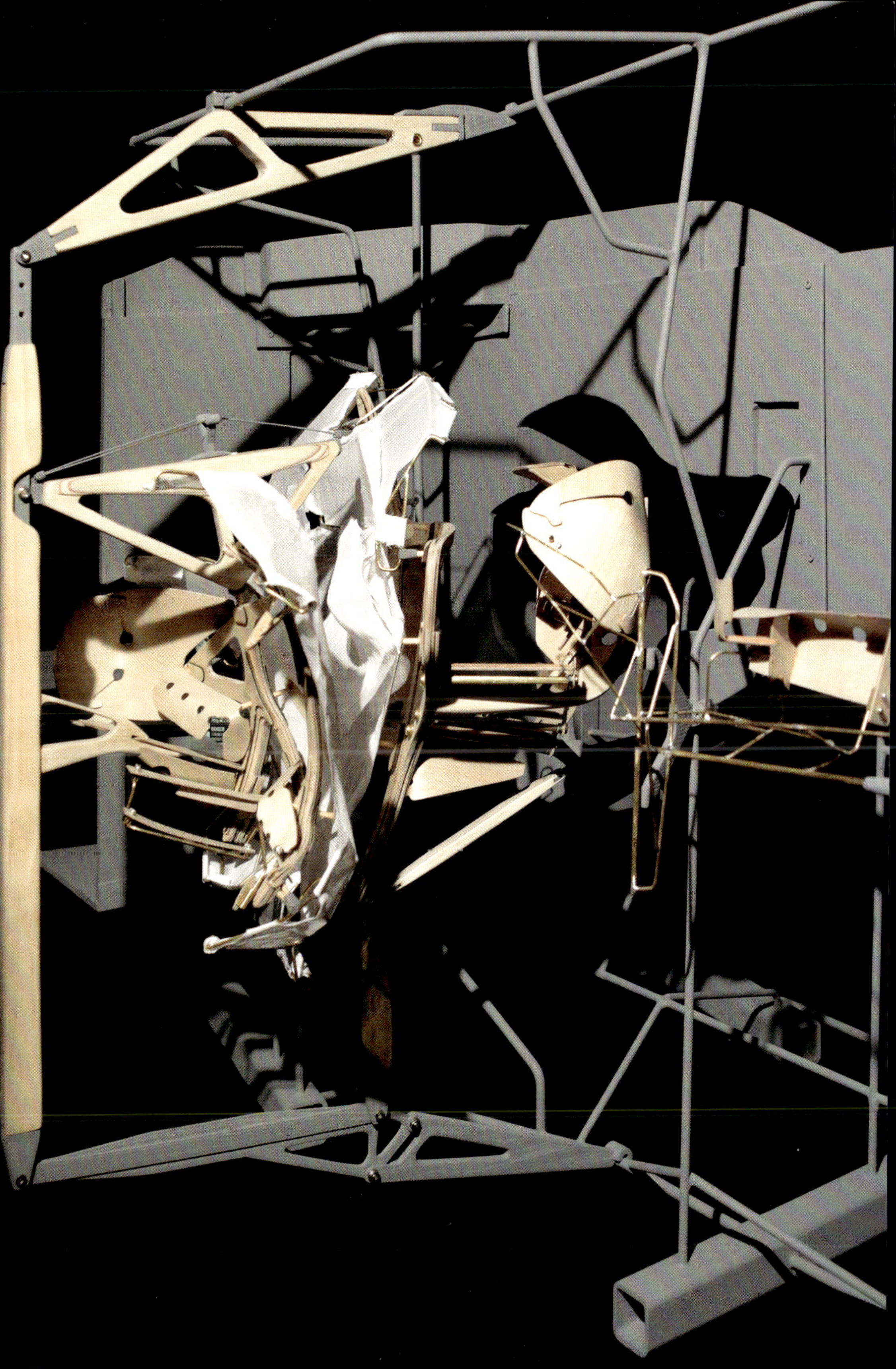

25.5

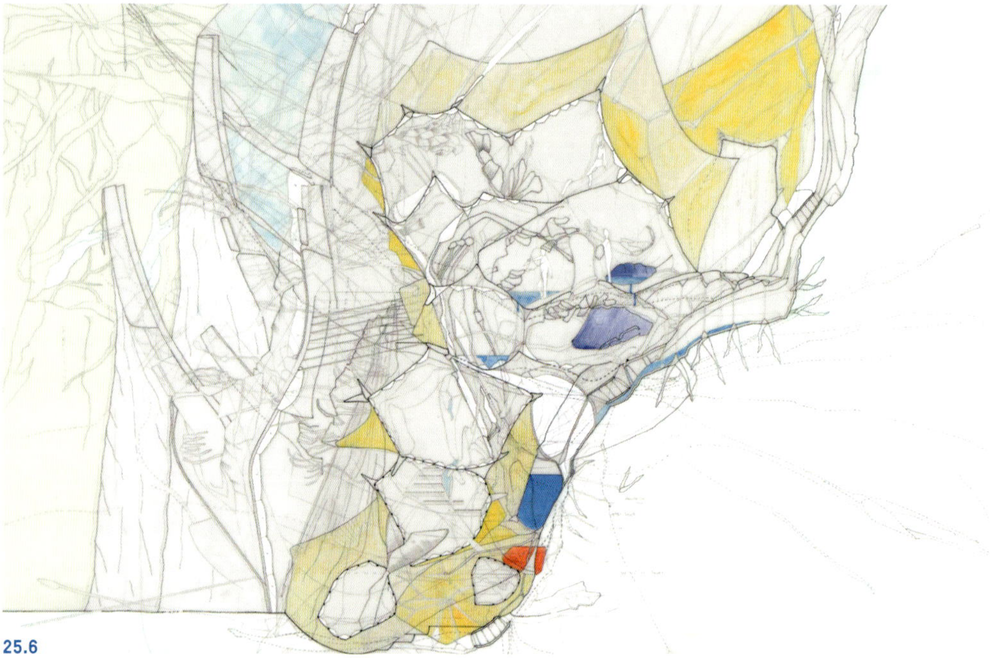

25.6

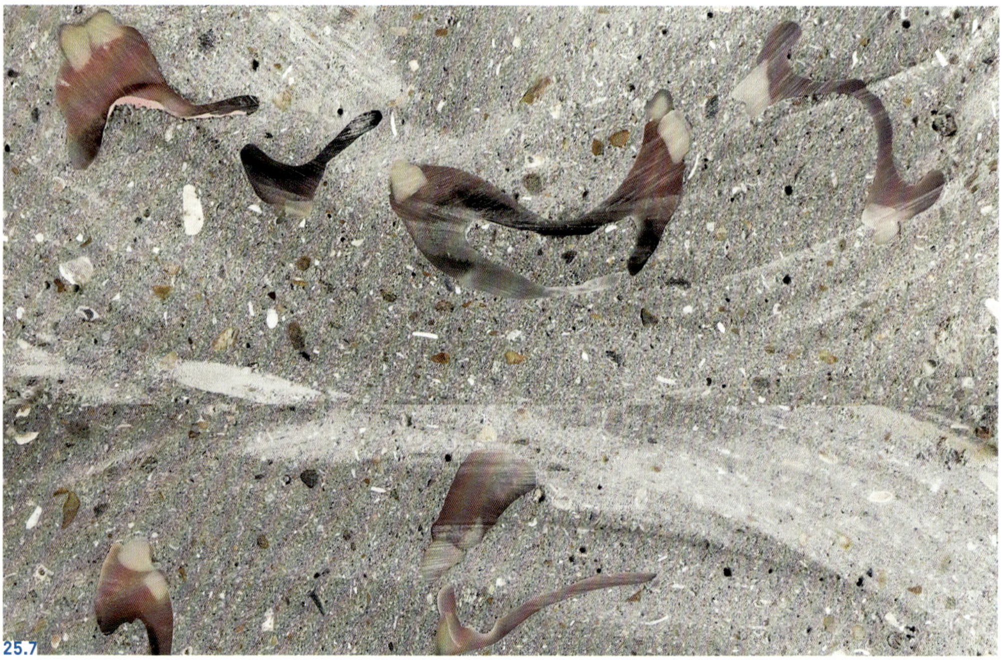

25.7

Fig. 25.6 George Bolwell Y5, 'Thicket Bathhouse'. Bodies, undergrowth and the parts that make up a bathhouse are melded together in a building that explores spatial thickness on the hills above Graz. **Fig. 25.7 Vita Rossi** Y4, 'Lost Property Office'. In a building that teases out many ways to understand a lost property office, building materials are themselves created out of unclaimed lost property. **Fig. 25.8 Vlad Daraban** Y4, 'Occupying the Glitch'. A selective scan of a building in Vienna reveals only the parts it wishes to give away – one of a number of surveillance techniques used to probe this café and archive. **Fig. 25.9 Arwen Liu** Y4, 'Purposeless Place'. This project looks at how to occupy a city without the compulsion to be purposeful, providing a sequence of ambiguous distractions next to the canal in Vienna.

25.8

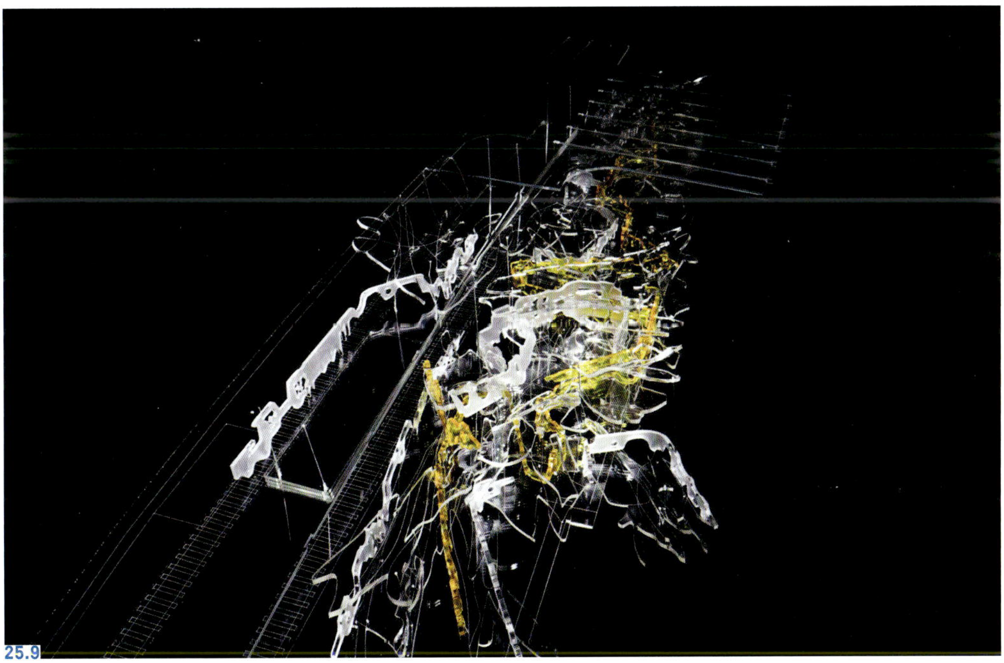
25.9

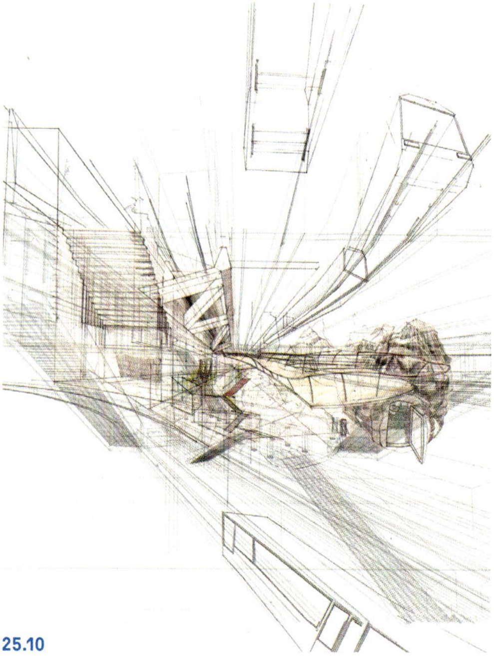

25.10

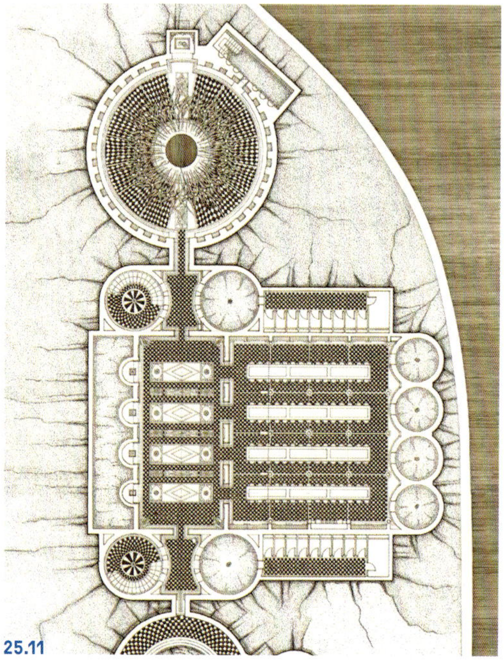

25.11

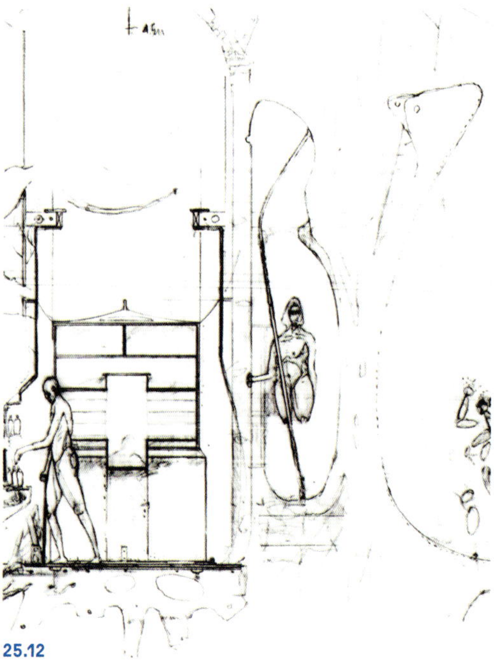

25.12

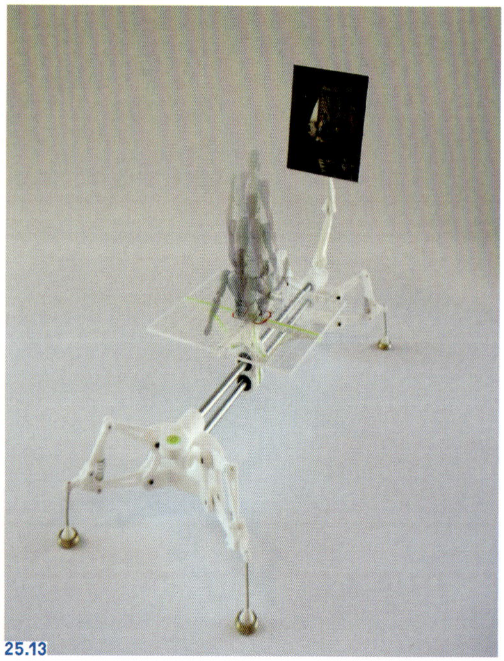

25.13

Fig. 25.10 Dougal Sadler Y4, 'Folded City'. A series of folded paper studies which emerge through games of chance inform a proposal for a new entrance to a Viennese subway station that leads its passengers astray. **Fig. 25.11 Simona Fratila** Y5, 'Alien Archive'. A number of archives in capital cities register the stories of immigrants. These archives are similar but take on small but dislocating differences due to the cultural differences of their host city. **Fig. 25.12 Demetris Ktorides** Y4, 'Between the Frame and the Picture'. Seducing unsuspecting travellers on the Vienna subway into a lush and perplexing labyrinth. **Fig. 25.13 Callum Campbell** Y4, 'A Gallery for One Painting'. **Fig. 25.14 Andrea Rocco Matta** Y5, 'The Manufacture of Memories'. A collection of suggestive small buildings made out of folded rectangles tease out unspecified memories.

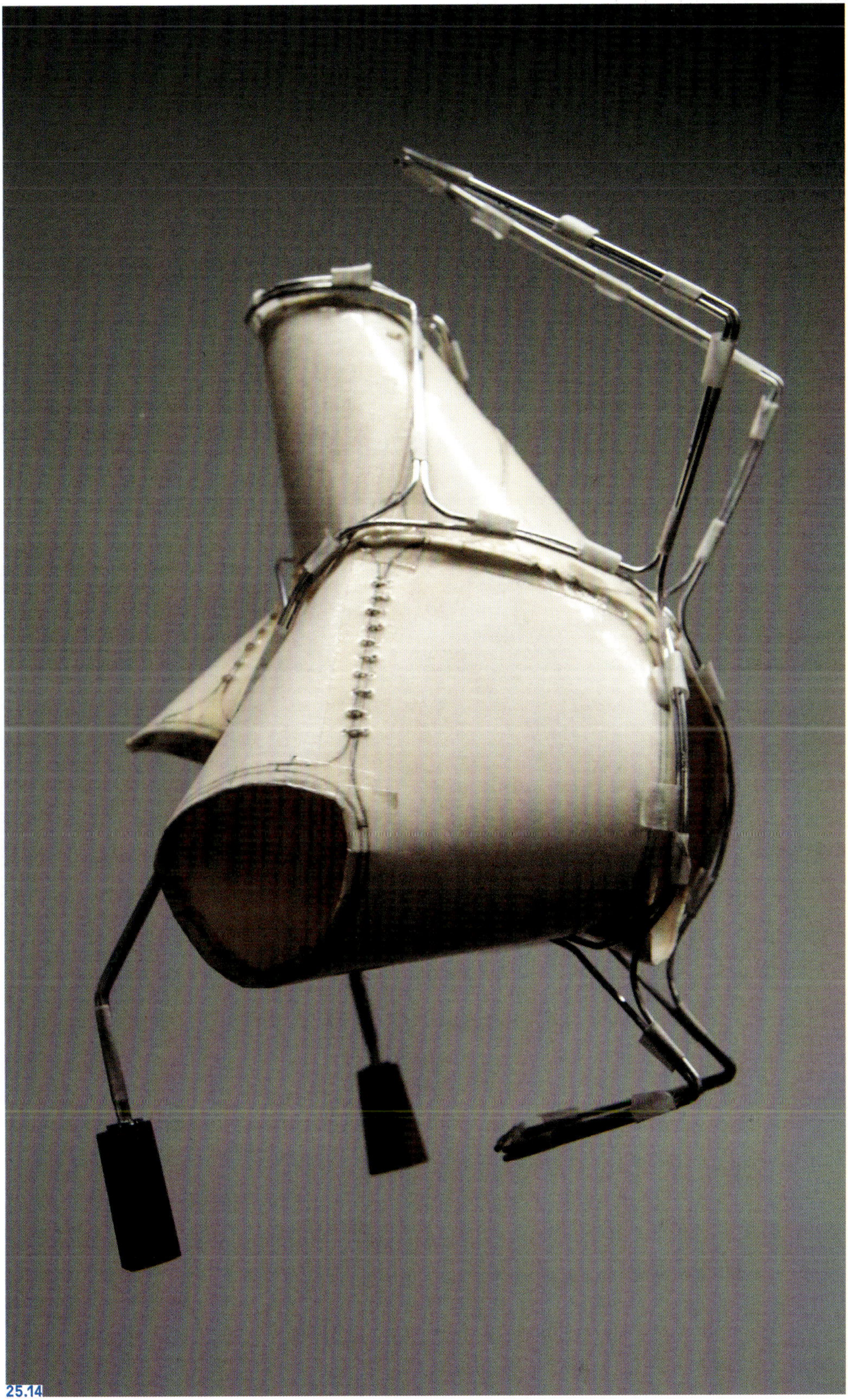

25.14

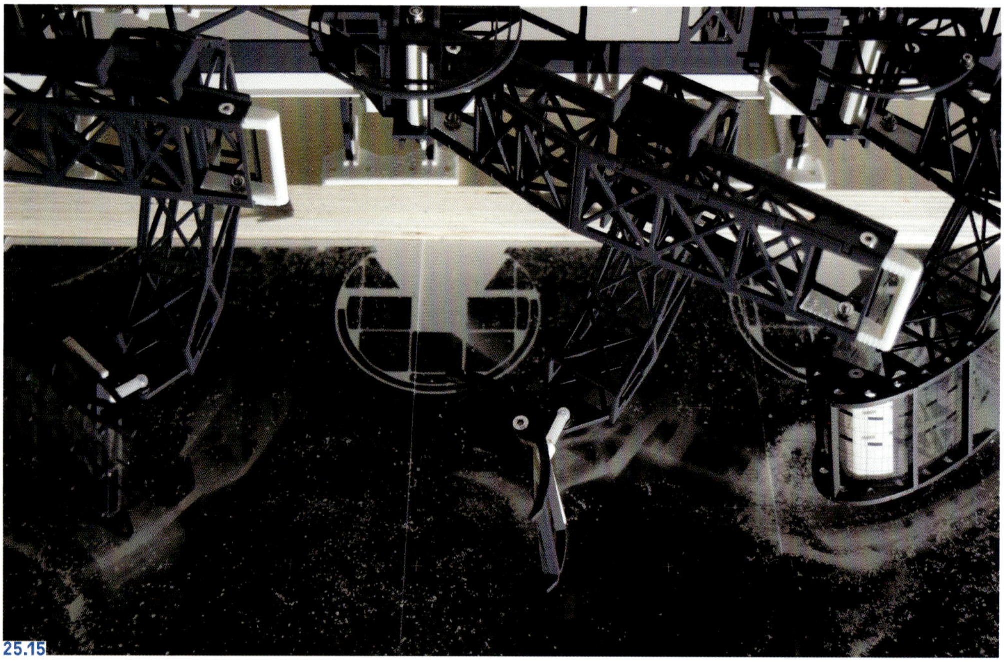

25.15

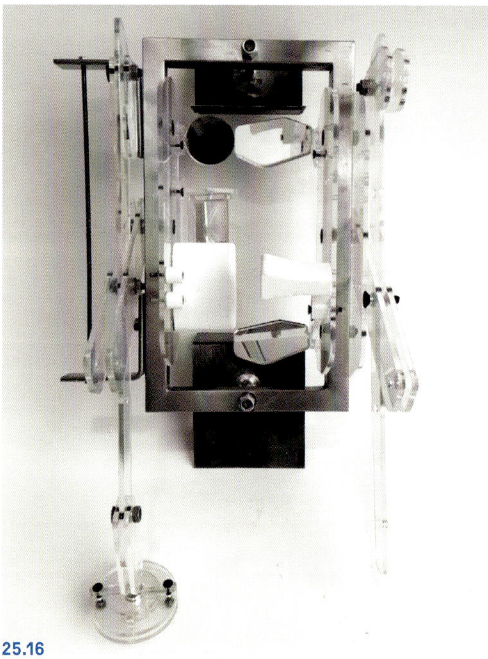

25.16

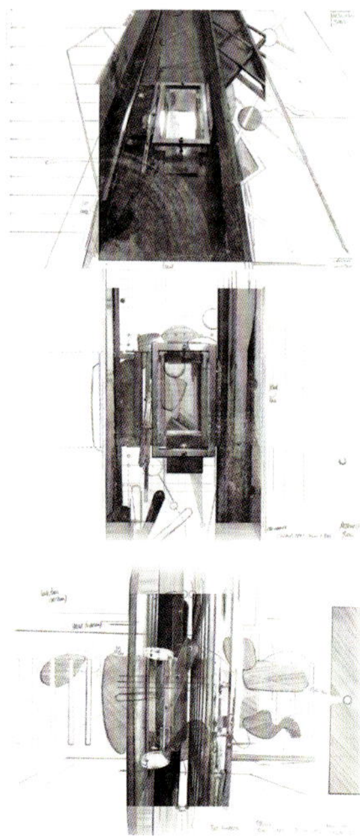

25.17

Fig. 25.15 Declan Harvey Y4, 'Hydrological Research Centre in Munich'. Under the cover of scientific research into the flow of the river Isar, the project investigates its potential level of threat to the city. **Figs. 25.16 – 25.17 Isaac Leung** Y4, 'Framing Theatricality'. As a rehearsal for designing a performance centre in a Baroque palace in Graz, a small proscenium is installed for a lift, allowing visitors to anticipate what might colour one's expectations of what might lie beyond. **Fig. 25.18 Daniel Van Der Poll** Y5, 'Illuminated City – a Tourist Information Centre in Graz'. This project began by using models together with an overhead projector, where the glowing model related to its projection. It then became a tourist centre that discusses the immediate underbelly of the city.

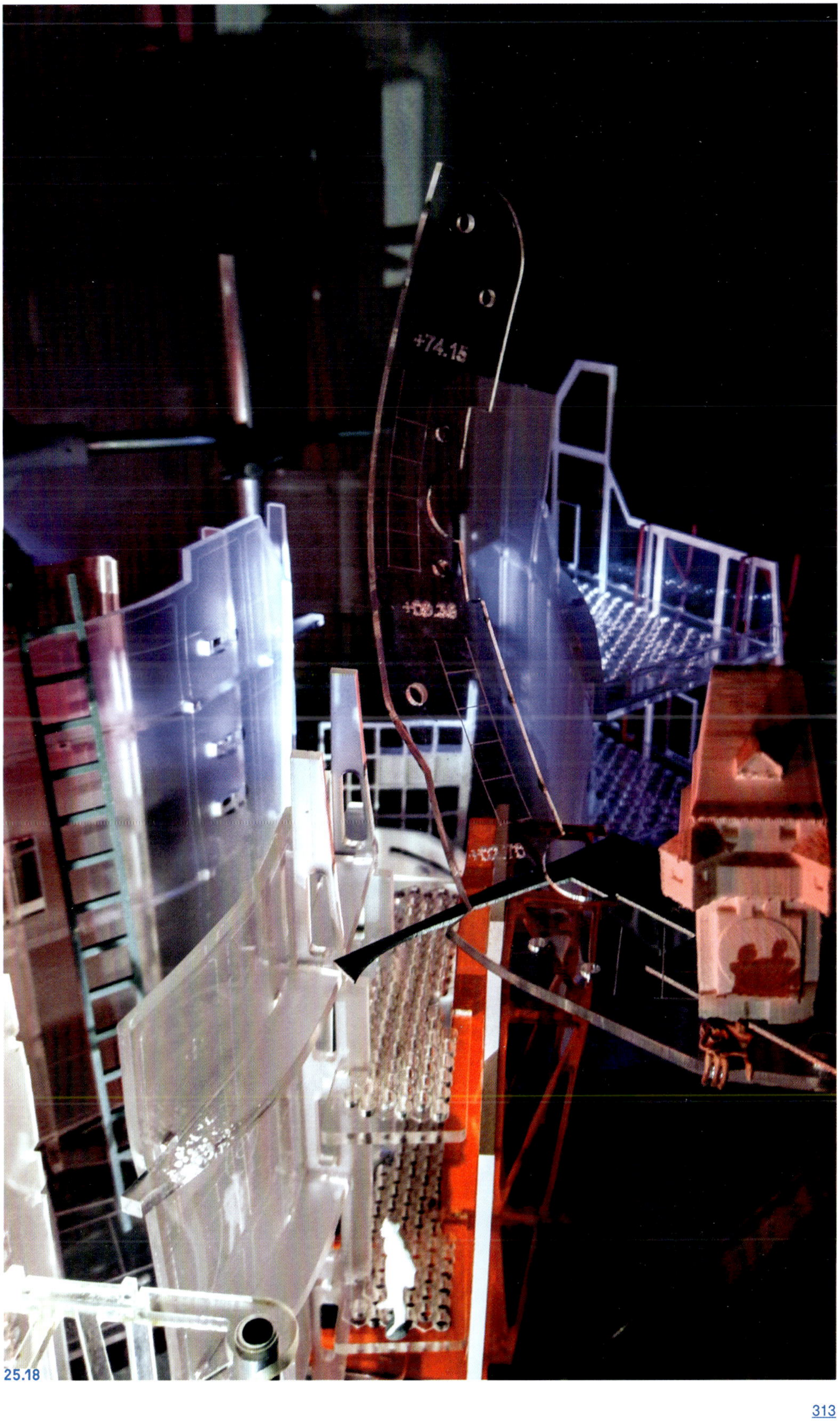

25.18

Unit 26 Hyper-Architectures of Play

Simon Kennedy, Gabby Shawcross

Year 4
Juan Escudero Pablos, Ezer Han, Ivan Hung, Clara Lee, Yiran Ma, Miten Mistry, Henrik Pihlveus, Hannah Sargeant, Carina Tran, Songyang Zhou

Year 5
Cui (Bob) Chang, Qidan Chen, Grace Quah, Dionysis Toumazis

Thank you to our collaborators Jason Bruges and Adam Heslop of Jason Bruges Studio, film composer Kevin Pollard, screenwriter Andrew Gow of Raindog Films, designer and filmmaker Keiichi Matsuda, Kevin Haley of Aberrant Architecture

Thank you to Tim Sloan of Levitate Architects for Design Realisation support, and to Aran Chadwick of Atelier One for structural engineering consultations.

Thank you to:
Pau Bajet, Jason Bruges (Jason Bruges Studio), Aran Chadwick (Atelier One), Hal Currey (HAL Architects), William Firebrace, Professor Stephen Gage, Alexis Germanos (3X Architects), Andrew Gow (Raindog Films), Kevin Haley (Aberrant Architects), Stephen Harty (Harty and Harty), Adam Heslop (Jason Bruges Studio), Ifigeneia Liangi, J-J Lorraine (Morrow Lorraine Architects), Keiichi Matsuda, Ana Monrabal-Cook (Roz Barr Architects), Kevin Pollard, Tim Sloan (Levitate Architects), Graeme Williamson (NORD)

Play

This year the unit investigated *play*: the interplay between architecture and occupant, play in architecture and architecture in play.

——We looked to play and games as culturally significant activities – spatial, relational human practices that can inform the design and production of architecture. We probed logic, interface, interaction, tactics and strategies to discover architectural potential in the ambiguity, modality, atmosphere and delight of games and play. Light and sound, colour, texture and temperature were brought into play. Dynamic structures reconfigured while digital surfaces observed and responded to our every move. The unit played their designs and designed ludic structures for their players.

Hyper-Architectures

We proposed 'Hyper-Architectures': those that were intensified, and those that responded to and created a reality above and beyond the present. Hybrid, combining the real and projected, they were time-based, energising the transitory, ephemeral and the emergent, actuating the dynamic, volatile and the variable. Interactive virtual technologies represent an as-yet ill-defined new cultural layer, which architects must use to their advantage. Intensification could occur in both physical and virtual planes, separately and/or simultaneously. Synthetic spaces are the present! (and the future!).

New Forms of Practice

Unit 26 is a film unit. Our aim is to explore the potential of the moving image to develop new forms of architectural practice. We create filmic architectures and architectural films that explore animated and augmented relationships between people and place. Predicated on the belief that architecture is experiential and time-based, we use cinematic techniques to investigate, simulate and speculate.

Our techniques include storyboards, stop-motion, hand-drawing, four-dimensional drawing, hyper-lapse, motion-matching, models and interactive mock-ups.

Workshops, Talks and Visits

Unit 26 benefits from a broad network of associated professionals, whose contributions serve as a counterpoint to the conceptual and theoretical discourse within the unit, as well as providing inspiration and practical guidance.

This year, workshops introduced students to filmmaking principles and innovative techniques. Studio visits connected students to inspiring practitioners in the worlds of interactive art, architecture, film and gaming.

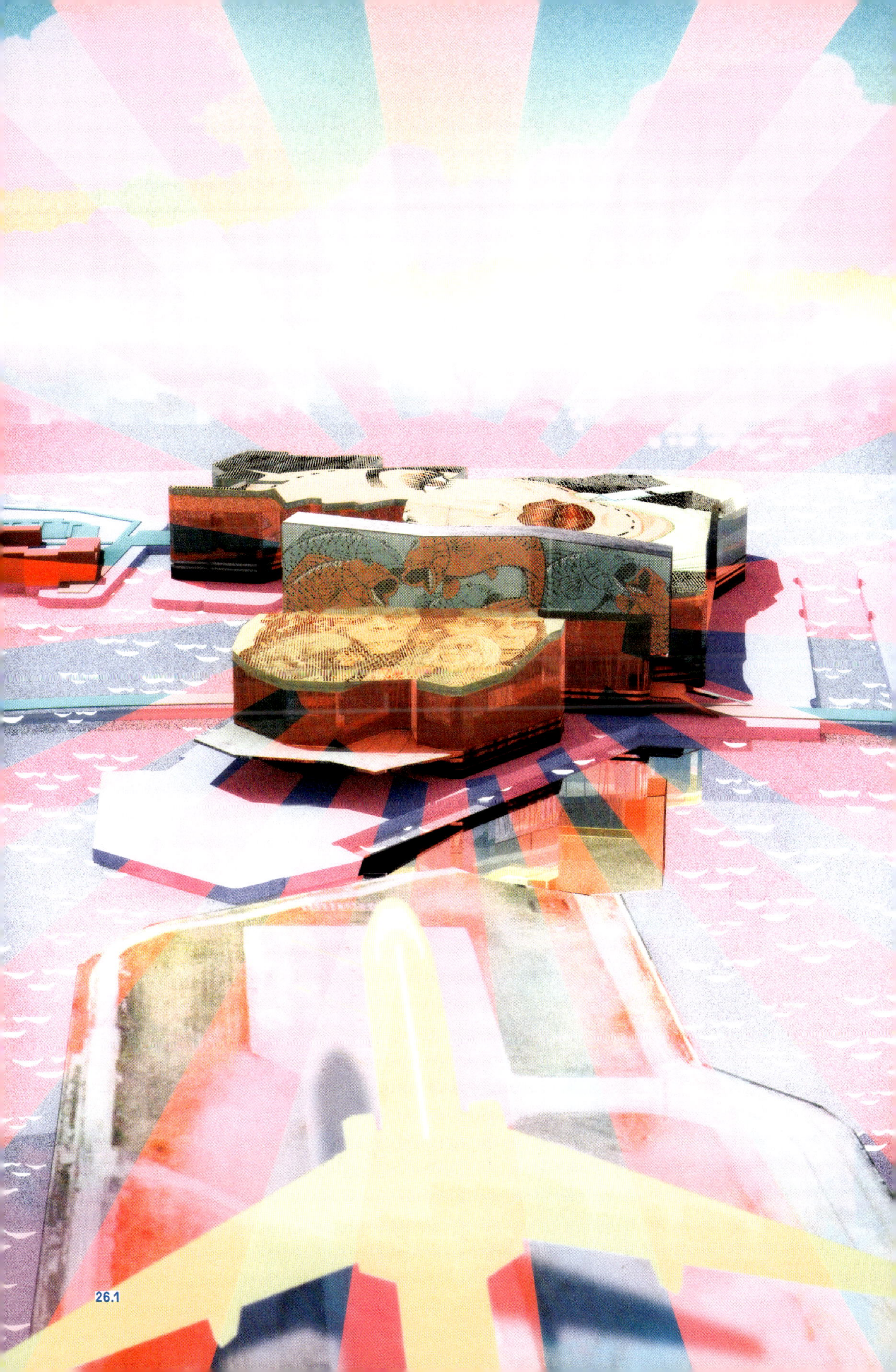

26.1

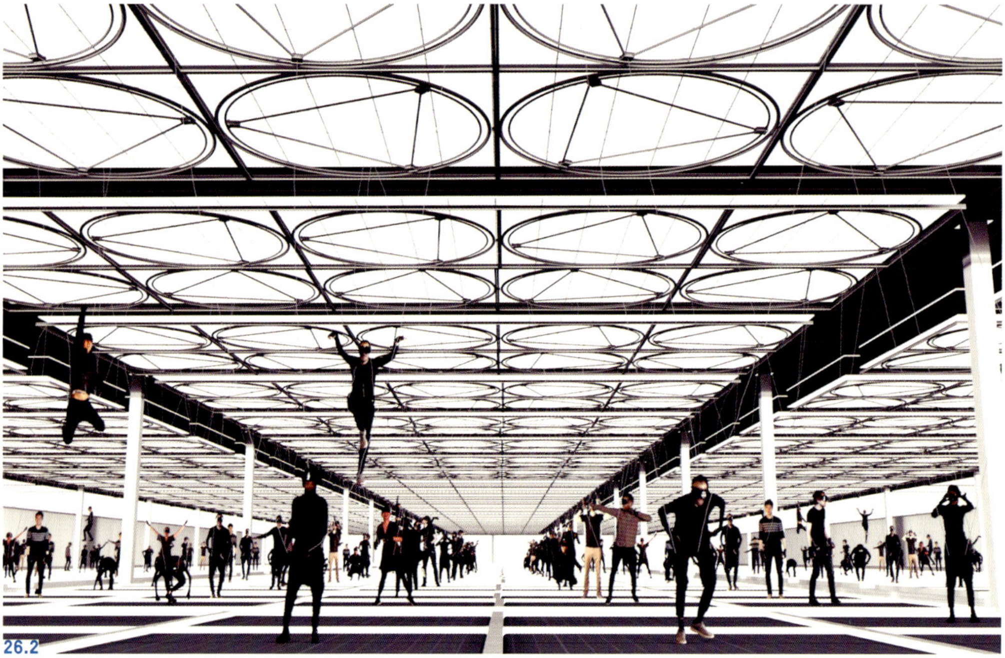
26.2

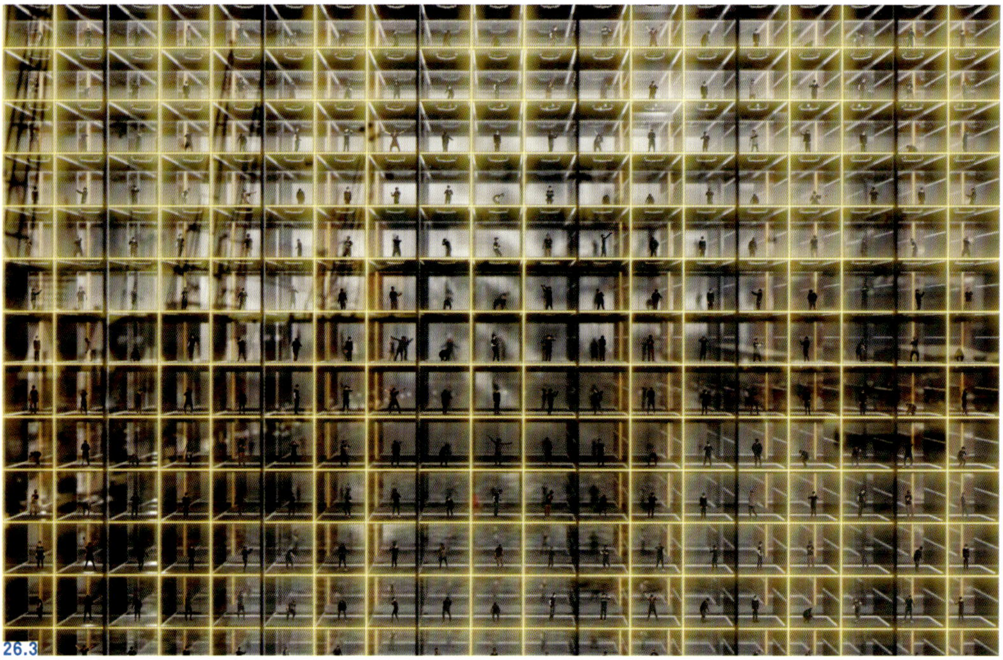
26.3

Fig. 26.1 **Juan Escudero Pablos** Y4, 'Cockaigne Island'. Recognising that shopping is (almost) all that is left of public space in the 21st century, Cockaigne Island is a new, aspirational super-mall. Offering an extreme vision of consumerism where everything that can be experienced is for sale, visitors are invited not only to spend, spend, spend but also to change their appearance, even their bodies. Retail units manifest as ever-changing exhibits that are constantly rebuilt and replaced in a theatrical spectacle of continuous profit. **Figs. 26.2 – 26.3** **Dionysis Toumazis** Y5, 'Interreality'. Set in a transitional period between contemporary work culture and a post-work, post-scarcity near-future, the project proposes a new typology for housing virtual reality activities. Faced with vocational obsolescence, visitors to the building seek meaning and change in their lives by digitally sampling other realities. The 'Interreality' experience places users in an interactive feedback loop between virtual and physical worlds, transforming their attitudes and behavioural patterns for the better. **Figs. 26.4 – 26.5** **Yiran Ma** Y4, 'The Museum Of Disappearing Landscapes'. The museum stores and curates digital data collected from endangered and rapidly changing sites around the globe. Using water spray projection, arrays of lasers and other holographic techniques, the museum translates the data into sophisticated new spatial journeys. Situated opposite the Royal Victoria Dock, the museum uses water from the Thames to create mist projections at a vast urban scale.

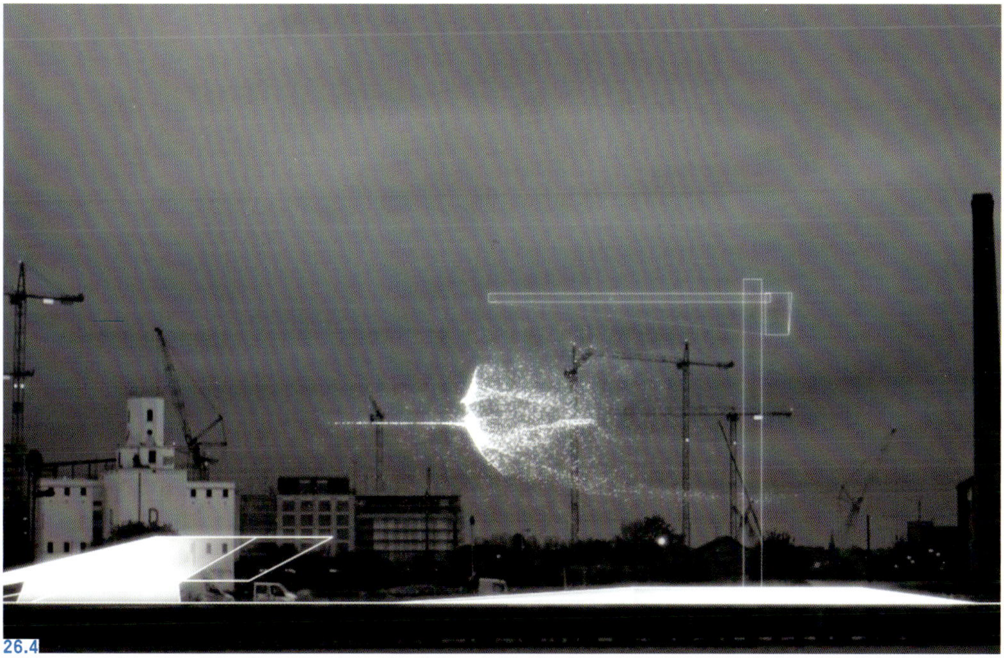

26.4

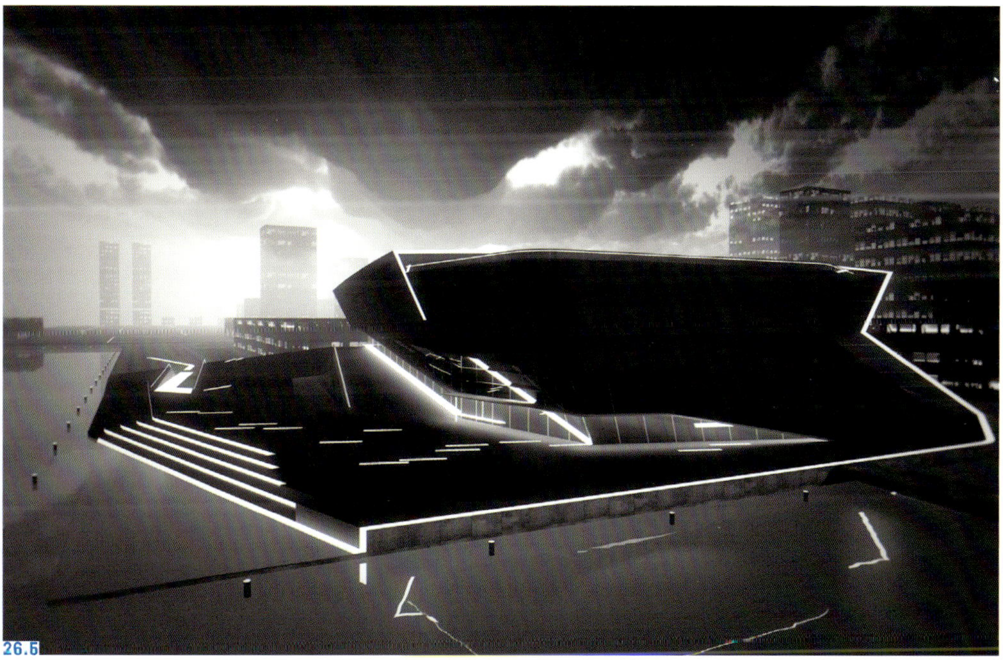

26.5

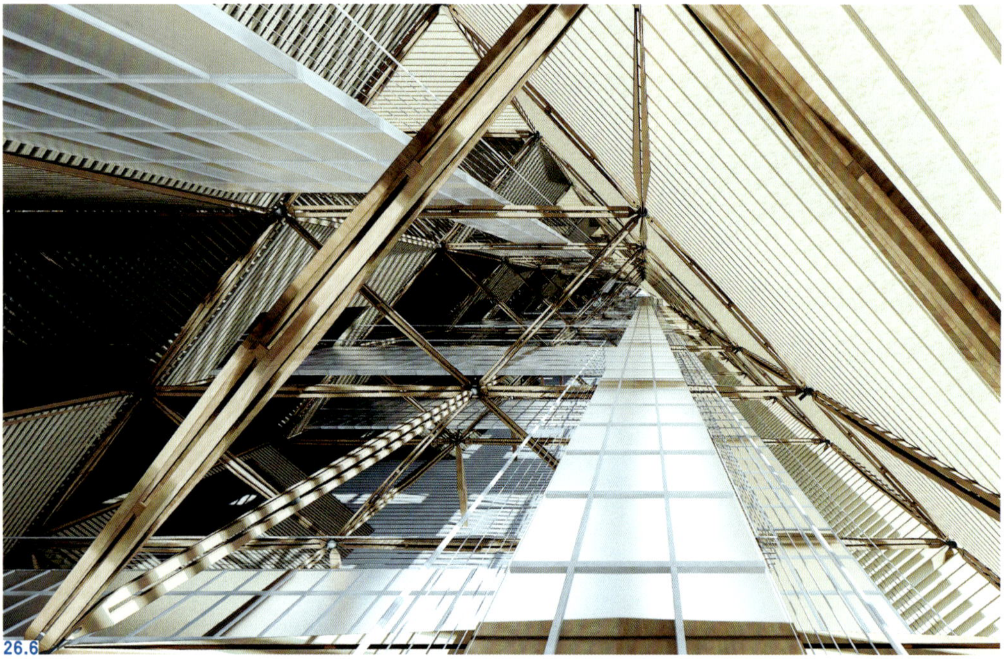

26.6

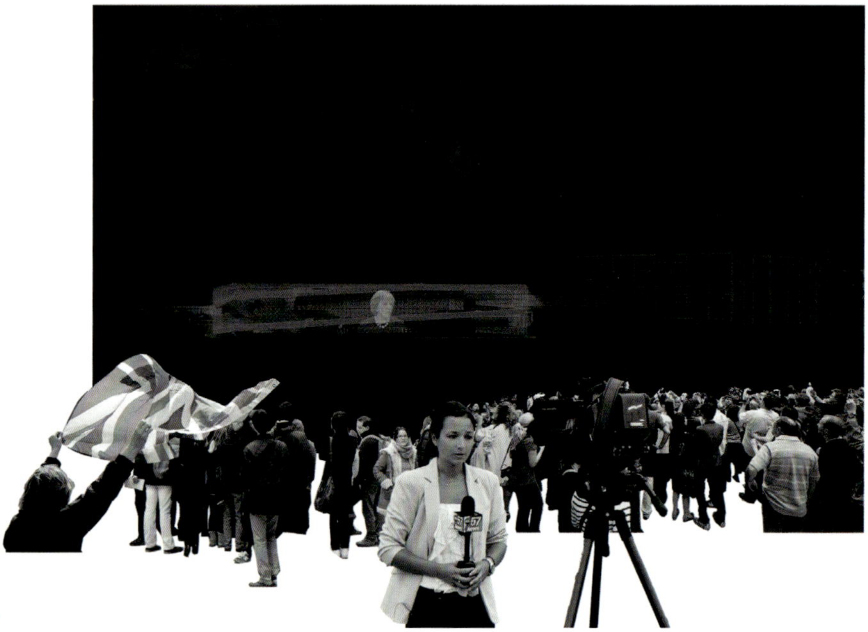

26.7

Fig. 26.6 **Ivan Hung** Y4, 'Publicised Peace'. The project proposes the relocation of the UN Security Council to a busy site in Silvertown. Containing housing for the representatives, a Council chamber and library/archive, the scheme consists of a vividly transparent building. The structure publicises the internal activities on a vast, exterior digital display, presenting an iconic view to aircraft passing overhead, and allowing the public to move freely through the lower levels without compromising the security of its occupants. **Fig. 26.7** **Clara Lee** Y4, 'Brexit Negotiation Chamber'. The project proposes a floating structure, constructed at minimum cost and at furious pace, to house the ongoing Brexit negotiations. Featuring a debating chamber with public viewing platforms and broadcast facilities, maze-like forests secrete tiny, darkened meeting rooms where the real negotiations take place. Constructed and initially located in Silvertown, the building can be towed anywhere in the world. **Figs. 26.8 – 26.9** **Songyang Zhou** Y4, 'Mirror'. Floating in the water next to the Excel Centre, the project recognises the power and increasing ubiquity of virtual reality devices, and proposes a new type of conference centre capable of bringing together occupants from all over the world. Remote users manifest as 'avatars' – floating drones that display facial characteristics of the remote user in real-time. The building creates new types of space that accommodate humans and avatars equally.

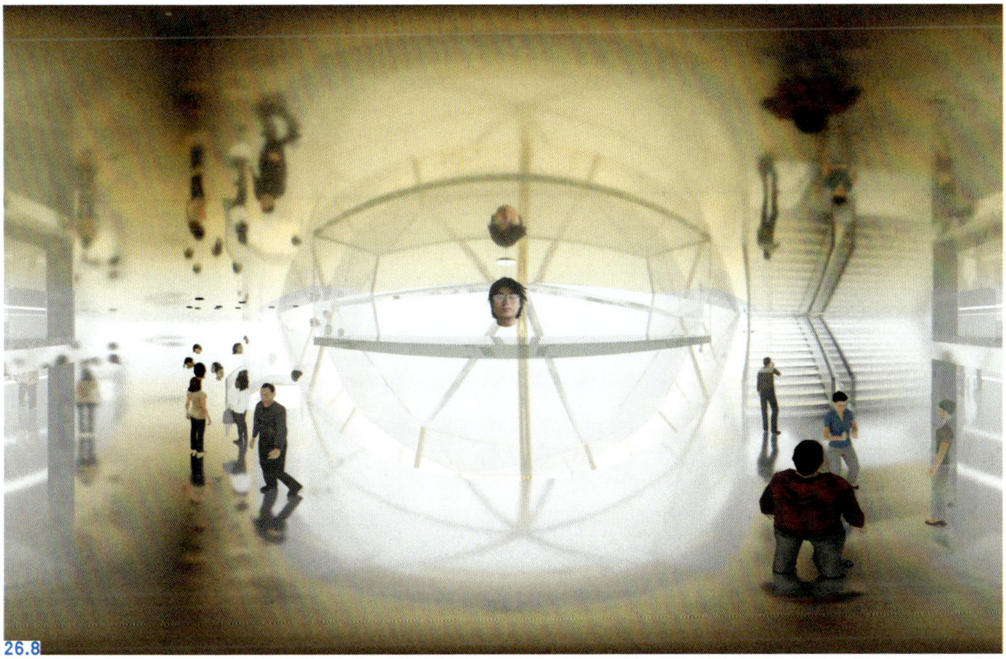

26.8

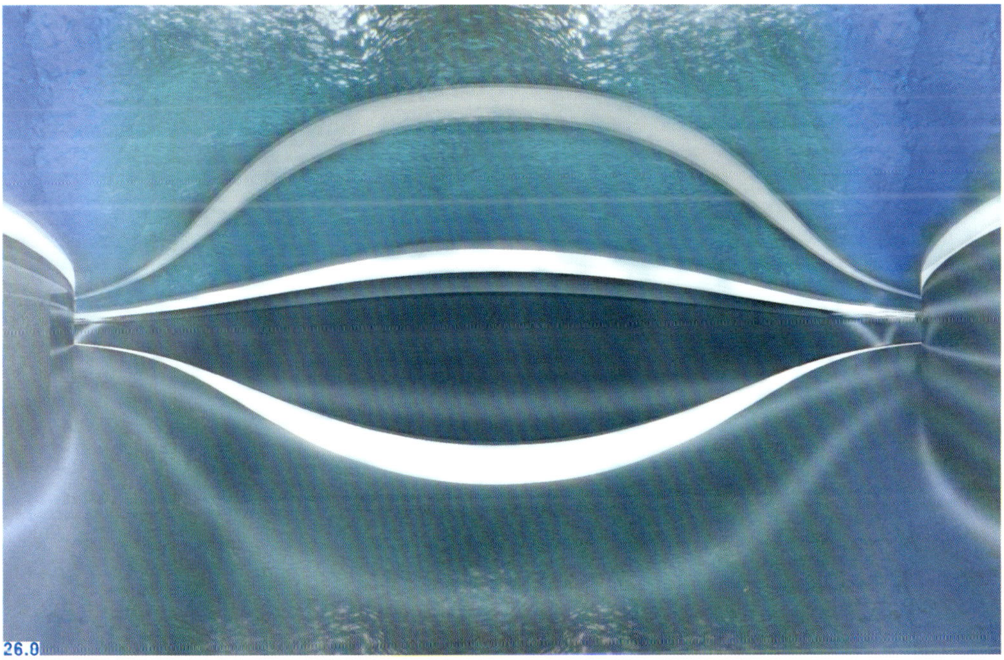

26.9

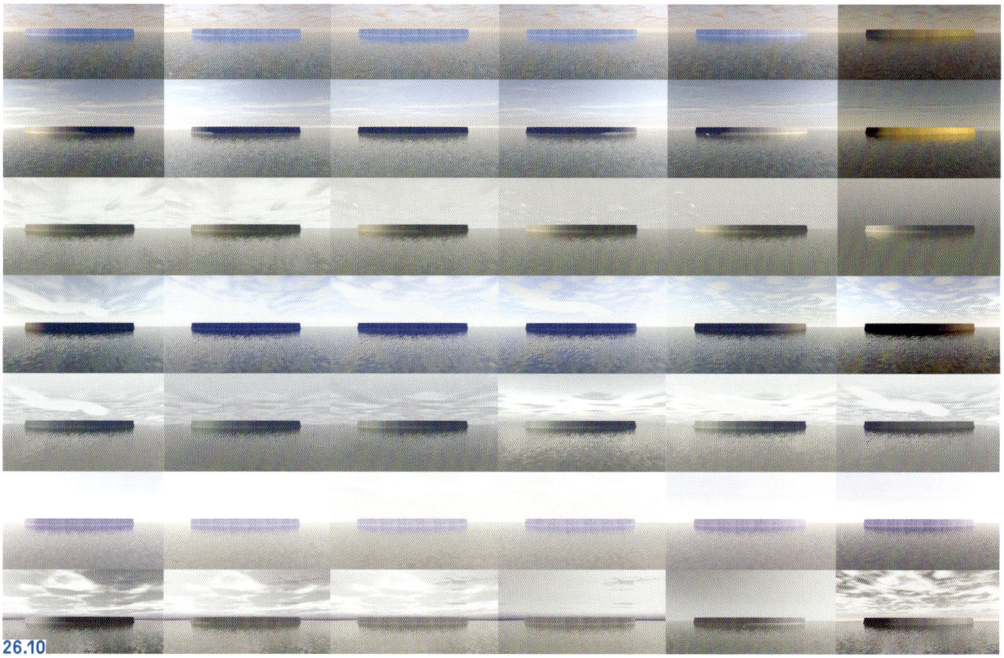

26.10

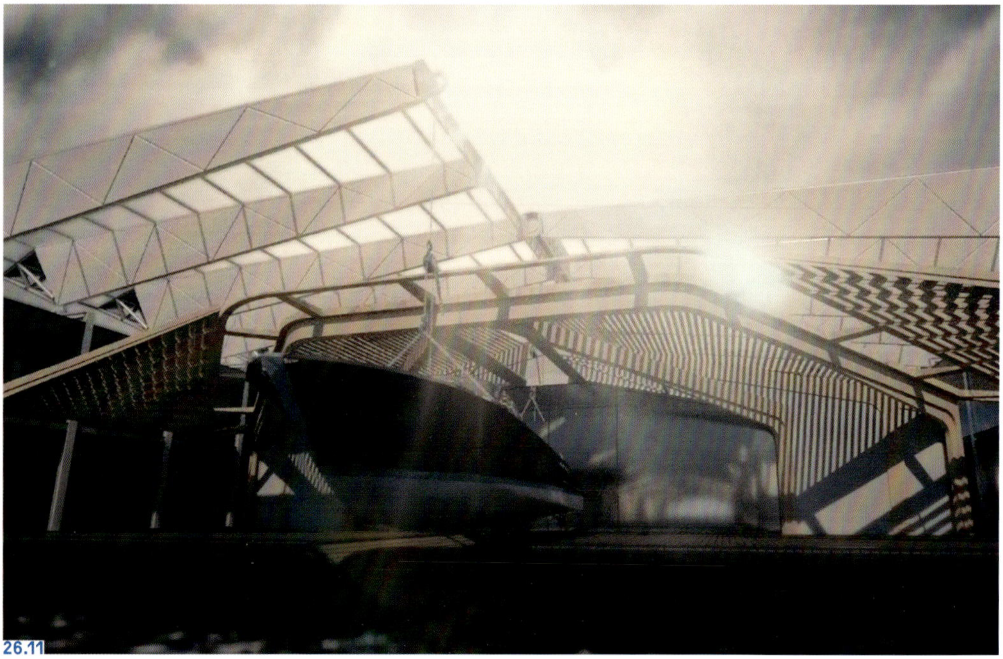

26.11

Fig. 26.10 Carina Tran Y4, 'Escape From London'. A yoga retreat situated in the water near the Thames Barrier, the project contains a series of carefully sequenced spaces and walkways. Progression from one part of the structure to another takes time, hopefully engendering a sense of calm in the user. The building has an intimate relationship with the site and its tidal variations, sometimes allowing the water to flood the structure, causing parts to be submerged entirely, and cutting users off from the bank and the rest of the building. **Fig. 26.11 Henrick Pihlveus** Y4, 'Made In Silvertown'. Responding to the history of the site and seeking to reinvigorate a declining industry, the project proposes a boat building factory where professionals and unskilled members of the public can collaborate in the production of sophisticated industrial objects. Film is specifically used as a tool to test the project, supported by time-based drawings. **Fig. 26.12 Cui (Bob) Chang** Y5, 'CESDS'. The physical world is on the brink of a major technological breakthrough that will revolutionise the way architects conceive of space, closing the gap between the digital and the physical. The project imagines a near-future spatial design school merging the disciplines of architecture, game design and film effects, using the immersive technologies of augmented reality, virtual reality and holographic projection. These technologies are not only employed to develop and test designs, but are also used to display the designs to the general public, via an urban scale mixed-reality park and huge installation towers.

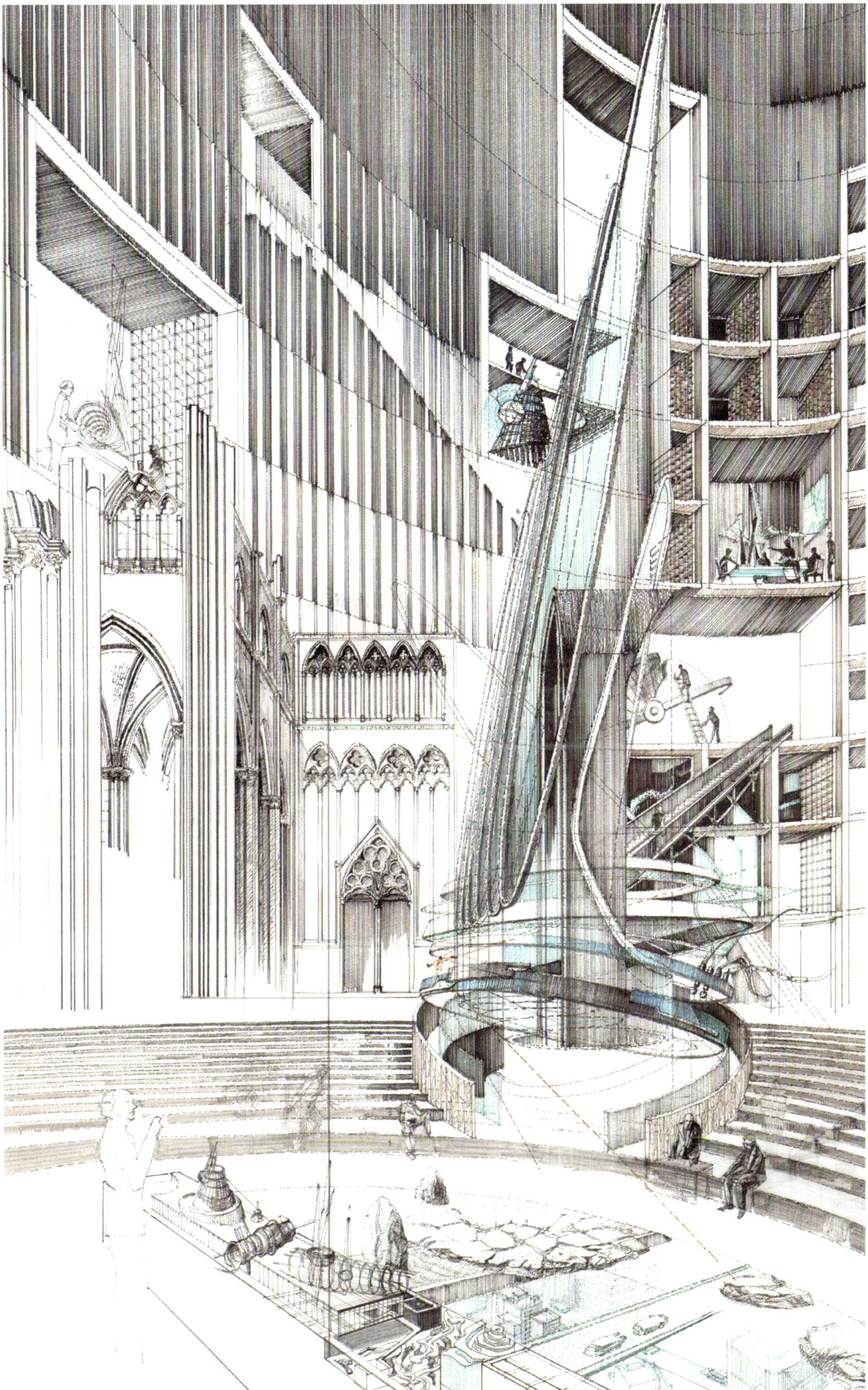

26.12

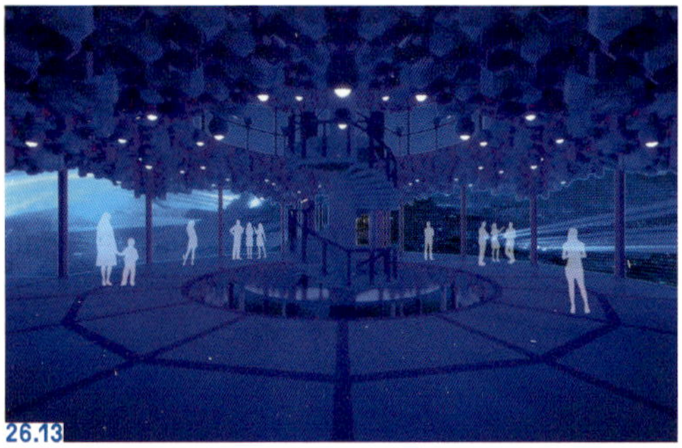
26.13

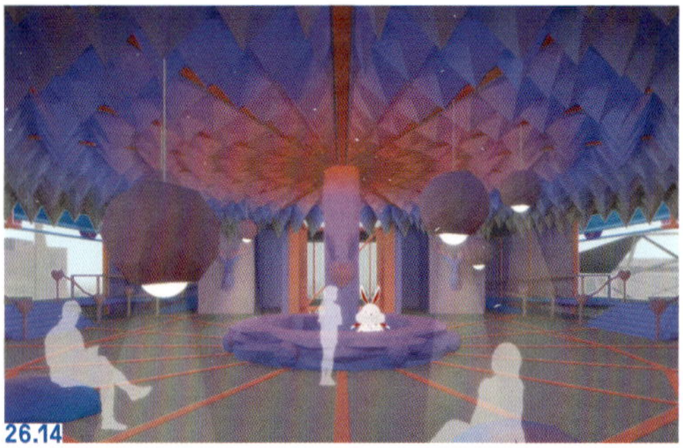
26.14

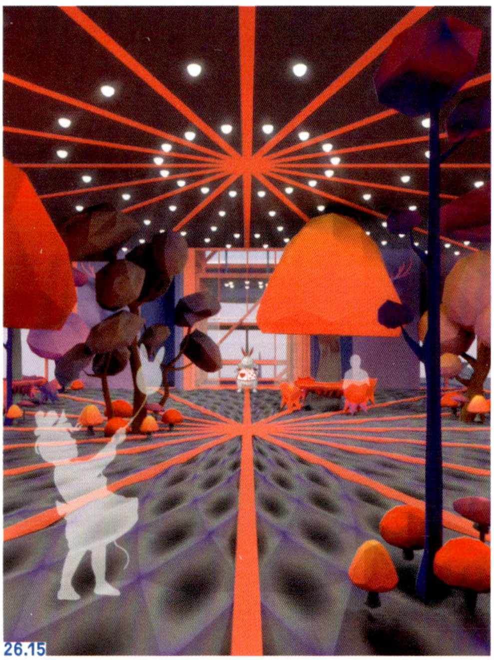
26.15

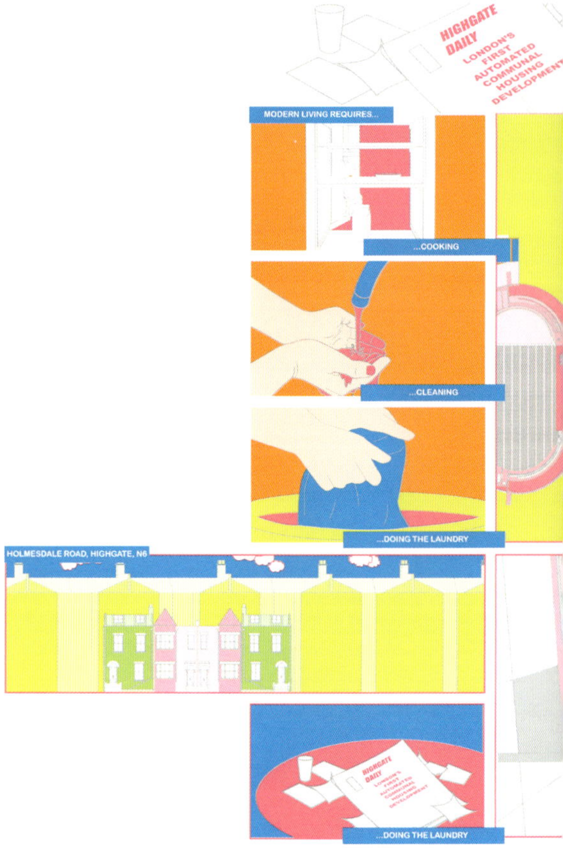

26.16

Figs. 26.13 – 26.15 Qidan Chen Y5, 'Wonderland'. Inspired by 'Alice's Adventures in Wonderland' and its various interpretations in films and theme parks, the project proposes an inhabited bridge structure that spans the Royal Victoria Dock. Providing space for players of multiple game types, from croquet and tabletop games to video games and underwater chess, the building itself is experienced as a type of game, with access to lower, more complex levels only granted when players are successful in upper arenas. **Fig. 26.16 Grace Quah** Y5, 'Silvertown Plug-In'. The project investigates the gendered division of domestic labour by exploring the spatial possibilities of automation. The design addresses the site of Silvertown as a remnant of industrialisation, examining the impact of labour on urban forms and the amount of work still undertaken in the home. Capitalising on the untapped £1.1 trillion value of domestic labour to the UK economy, the project is a communal housing scheme that performs all necessary housework. Housing modules 'plug in' to an infrastructure of automated dishwashing, cooking and cleaning facilities as a critique of the role of technology in the design of the modern home. Through film, the building embodies mechanical as well as human-like qualities. As the traditional gendered sphere of 'invisible' work becomes visible, domestic chores become an urban, spatial performance.

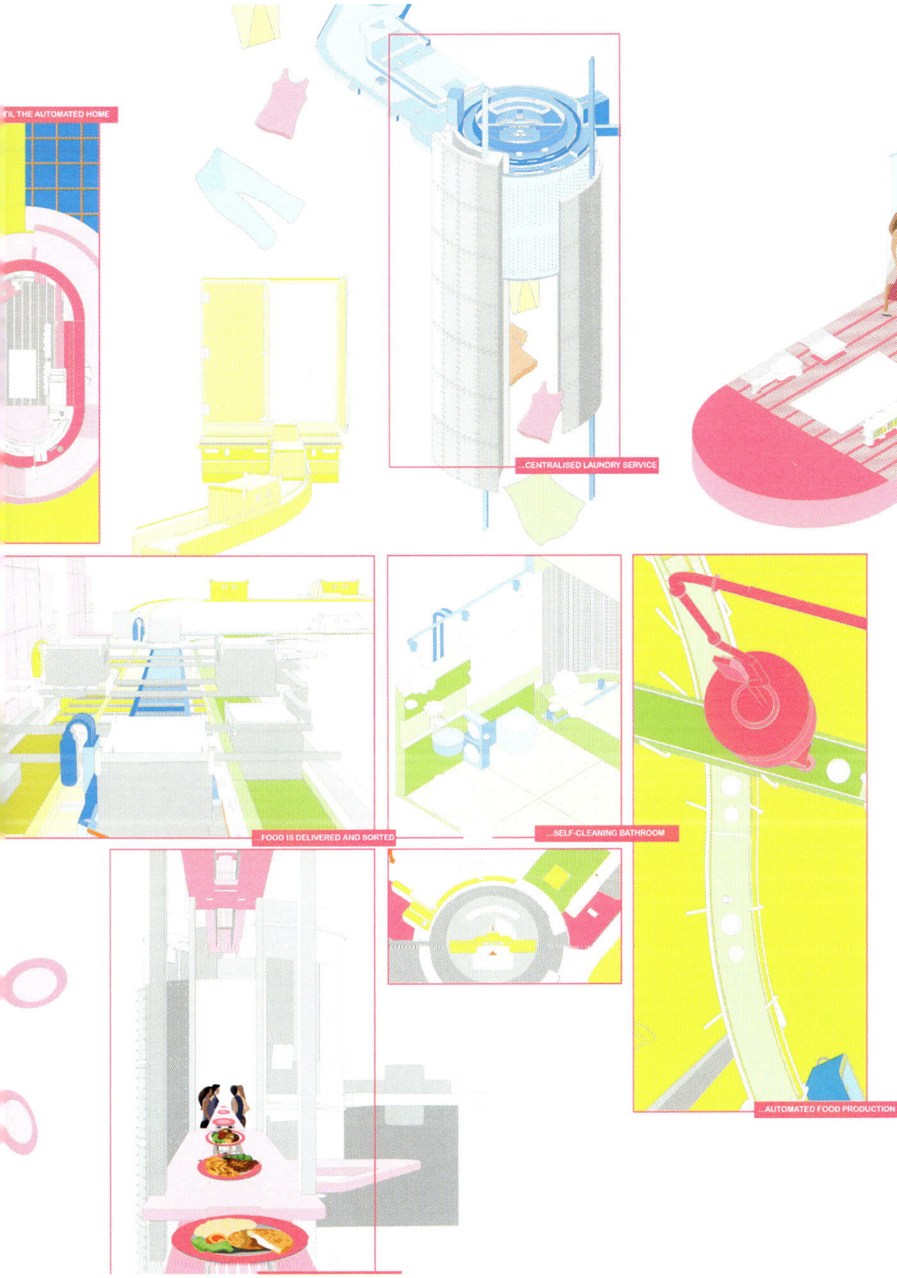
TIL THE AUTOMATED HOME
...CENTRALISED LAUNDRY SERVICE
LEISURE
...FOOD IS DELIVERED AND SORTED
...SELF-CLEANING BATHROOM
...AUTOMATED FOOD PRODUCTION

Year 4

MArch Design Realisation

Module Coordinators: James O'Leary, Dirk Krolikowski

Thanks to all the structural consultants who have worked with individual students to realise their projects, and to Max Fordham, environmental consultants to all units

Thanks to Saint-Gobain for sponsoring the Design Realisation Saint-Gobain Innovation Award 2017

Lecturers
Damian Eley (ARUP Structures), Joanna Pencakowski (RSHP), Mario Pirwitz (JSWD), Hareth Pochee (Max Fordham), Evan Greenberg (AA/UCL), Jan Guell (NIKKEN SEKEI), Sara Klomps (Zaha Hadid Architects), Laura Hannigan (AKT II), Xavier de Kestelier (Foster + Partners), Ho-Yin Ng (AL_A), Tim Lucas (Price & Myers), James O'Leary (The Bartlett), Dirk Krolikowski (The Bartlett/ DKFS Architects)

Practice Tutors
Unit 10 Jon Kaminsky (Hawkins\Brown), **Unit 11** Rhys Cannon (Gruff Ltd), **Unit 12** James Hampton (Periscope), **Unit 14** Dirk Krolikowski (The Bartlett/ DKFS Architects), **Unit 15** Max Arrocet, Raffael Petrovic and Ho-Yin Ng (AL_A), **Unit 16** Ralph Parker (HONEY), **Unit 17** James Daykin (Daykin Marshall) and Simon Tonks (RSHP), **Unit 18** Anna Woodeson & Robert Haworth (LTS Architects), **Unit 19** Jakub Klaska (Zaha Hadid Architects), **Unit 20** Justin Nicholls (Fathom Architects), **Unit 21** Tom Holberton (Rick Mather Architects), **Unit 22** Pedro Gil (Studio Gil Architects), **Unit 24** Michael Tite (Michael Tite Architecture Ltd.), **Unit 25** Jerry Tate (Tate Harmer), **Unit 26**: Tim Sloan (Levitate)

The Design Realisation (DR) course provides the opportunity for all Year 4 Masters students to consider how buildings are designed, constructed and delivered. Students are asked to reflect upon their relationship with technology, the environment and the profession. This is explored through an iterative critical examination of the major building design project taught within the context of individual design units in Year 4. Students are supported by an extensive lecture series, seminars and cross-unit crits. The course bridges the worlds of academia and practice, engaging with many renowned design practices and consultancies. A dedicated practice-based architect, structural engineer and environmental engineer support each design unit, working individually with students to develop their work throughout the duration of the programme.

——This year, we have seen some excellent work in DR across a wide variety of media, scales of practice and diversity of approach. This has made it exceptionally difficult to select the winner of the DR Innovation award, kindly sponsored again by Saint-Gobain. This year the prize is shared between five exceptional students, whose response to DR has been genuinely innovative and packed with wonderful design ideas. This year's Design Realisation Innovation Award goes to: Patrick Horne, Unit 11; Ryan Blackford, Unit 14; George Courtauld, Unit 14; Laurence Blackwell-Thale, Unit 11; and Eleanor Sampson, Unit 11.

——Patrick Horne's project outlines a series of interventions into the existing fabric of a traditional Venetian canalside palazzo. Each of the key programmatic functions benefits from the exploration and understanding of the pre-existing construction of the building. Inventive adaptations of existing 'temporary works' technology are utilised to create permanent inhabitable propositions.

——Ryan Blackford's proposal 'hacks' the Stephansdom in central Vienna and weaves a sophisticated narrative around foreign powers manipulating European politics via cyber warfare. The observations and deductions are precise, inventive and unexpected. They surprise through the thoroughness and quality of documentation that materialises the boundary between virtual and physical politics.

——George Courtauld's DR work synthesises the notion of music as a communal act of sharing experiences with advanced airship technology. In a time when we are losing cultural infrastructure, this project aims to tap into the democratisation of music, culture and our city streets through technology. It reinvents the opera as a semi-fictional tale that could change the way we cherish European culture.

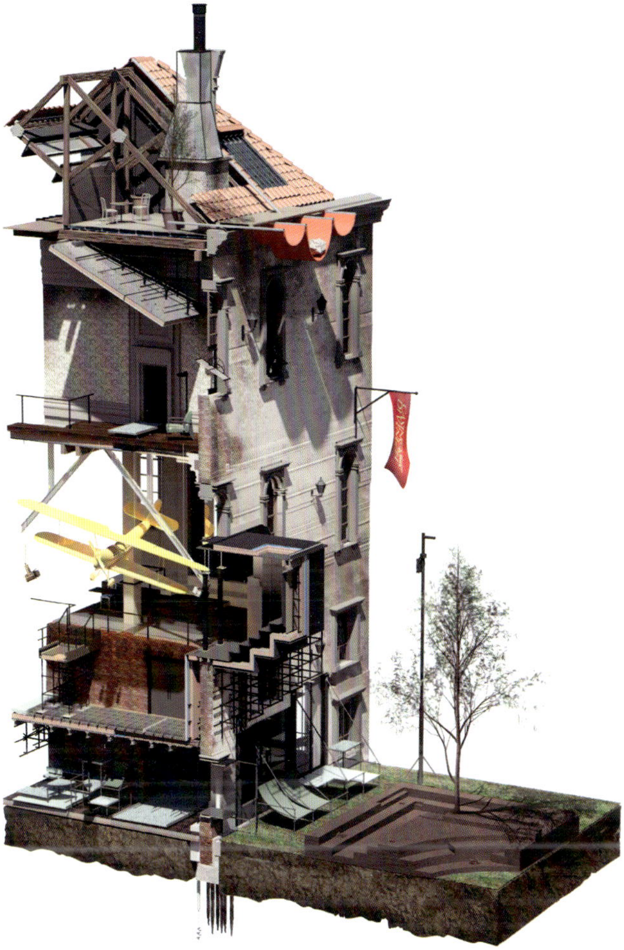

——Laurence Blackwell-Thale's project is packed with original ideas, each of which has been rigorously explored to create incredible spatial experiences at Miniatur Wunderland. There is some wonderfully innovative integration of the building services with the building fabric and (most importantly) the sets within, which through this synthesis become part of the building fabric.

——Eleanor Sampson's work is a thorough investigation into the tectonics of a new building in Venice, which is designed to actively fail and potentially collapse around its occupants. The building design is focused on the central tower element and its very slow 'collapse' as it sinks into the Venetian mud. There are some beautifully coordinated details for harnessing water/drainage in order to accelerate the weathering processes. The building service strategy and its multiple outer-skin system is considered both in relationship to the comfort of the visitors and to the structural fabric and its erosion.

——Well done to all for an outstanding effort that has stretched the parameters of the possible in Design Realisation.

Image: Patrick Horne, Unit 11, 'The Post-Internet Town Hall': Renovating Ca' Vendramin Calergi Palace

Advanced Architectural Studies

Module Coordinator: Dr Tania Sengupta
Teaching Assistant: Marcela Araguez

Seminars
Flexible Bodies, Flexible Selves
Tijana Stevanovic
Hidden Histories and Multiple Modernities
Edward Denison
U-topographics: Utopic Journeys into Postmodern Culture
Robin Wilson
Architecture & The People: unpicking the politics of how places are made (and what that means for practice)
Daisy Froud
Criticism & the History of the Architectural Magazine
Anne Hultzsch
Senses and the City
Jacob Paskins
An Ecology of Mind – revisiting Gregory Bateson's 1976 seminar in the era of World Systems
Jon Goodbun
Type: Culture, Meaning, Practice, Politics
Tania Sengupta
Architecture, Art & the City
Eva Branscome
Ornament: Barbaric Splendour or Architectural Sophistication?
Oliver Domeisen
Architecture and the Image of Decay
Paul Dobraszczyk
Gothic Designs, Gothic Desires
Jeffrey Miller

The Advanced Architectural Studies module, in the first year of the two-year professional Masters programme, focuses on architectural histories and theories. Here, we reflect on architecture within a broader, critical, intellectual and contextual field, simultaneously producing and being produced by it. We look at architecture's interfaces with other disciplinary and knowledge fields – from the scientific and technological to the social sciences and the humanities. We straddle empirical and theoretical knowledge, design and history, the iconic and the everyday.

——Depending on individual interest, the course helps students engage with architectural history and theory as a critical approach to augment design, as a parallel domain to test out design approaches or as a discrete or autonomous domain of architectural engagement. It focuses on three key types of academic development: first, a reflective, critical and analytical approach; second, research instinct and investigative methods, and third, skills of synthesis, writing and articulation. The module also acts as foundational ground for the Masters thesis that students undertake in the final year of the MArch programme.

——The course consists of a set of lectures followed by the core of the module – six tutor-led seminars on a diverse range of themes. These span the architectural histories of various global contexts, and, thematically, issues such as buildings, urbanism, typology, ecology, politics, technology, production, public participation, urban regeneration, phenomenology, historiography and representation (see list of seminars). The lectures are on the architectural, urban and spatial histories of sequential moments of the nineteenth and twentieth centuries, but rendered through the individual conceptual and methodological frameworks of each of the seminar tutors. At the end, based on their learning from the lectures and seminars, the students formulate a critical enquiry around a topic of their choice and produce a 4,000-word essay.

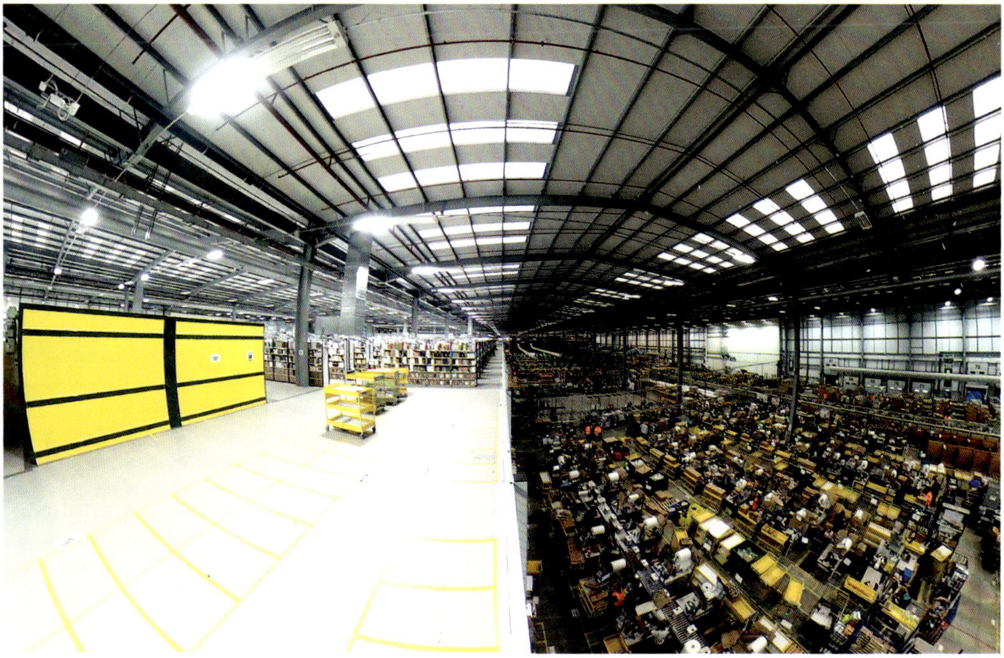

John Cruwys
Walkin' in a Heterotopic Wonderland: Utopia and the Amazon Fulfilment Centre
Tutor: Robin Wilson

To the delight of children across the globe, Father Christmas has yet again successfully completed his 36-hour journey around the world, where he travelled at a speed of over 1,500mph to deliver 2.2 billion presents, and managed to consume 137 million glasses of milk and 46 million bottles of sherry. Presumably, Father Christmas, his wife, and his elves retire to their home/workshop – the utopian commune that has achieved total toy production perfection (where time is immaterial so no order is ever too big) – and take a well-earned rest. Fortunately, in Rugeley, Staffordshire, the BHX1 Amazon Fulfilment Centre acts as Santa's Workshop by proxy. Sited within the fenced-off Towers Business Park, the fulfilment centre offers a spatial product that is a world unto itself, presenting an image of anonymity while providing a service that, less than two decades ago, only existed in the minds of infants. If Santa's workshop exists as a utopian space, the Amazon Fulfilment Centre seeks to be an approximation of this utopia.

——Inherently utopic, 'fulfilment' ideates a space where desire is realised and so eradicated. The Fulfilment Centre claims to provide outright customer satisfaction. Its aspiration is a place that is utterly self-regulated and harmonious, while also authoritarian, hierarchical and restrictive – a space that is, as Elizabeth Grosz writes, "conceivable only in the temporal dimension", the embodiment of which is often problematic. Can a utopia imaginably be contained within a warehouse just off the A51?

——In 1984, Michel Foucault proposed the term 'heterotopia' to better describe such antithetical spaces which approach the boundaries of utopia while also being absolutely different from the utopia of which they speak. A decade later, Marc Augé discussed the proliferation of 'non places' – isolated organisations that fail to contain organic society and abstract interactions within them. However, Foucault's and Augé's writings are no longer considered contemporary works, and the idea of heterotopia has since settled and evolved along with the non-places that famously contained them. Through this essay I will seek to define the Amazon Fulfilment Centre as a new type of heterotopia – a kind of hybrid spatial successor bred of super-convenience, taking the form of pervasive light-industrial enclaves that are capable of appearing simultaneously mythic and mundane. This essay performs a nuanced spatial study of the fulfilment centre – an ambiguous by-product of our present-day built environment – in order to challenge and update the idea of the heterotopia.

Image: Inside the BHX1 Amazon Fulfilment Centre, Rugeley.

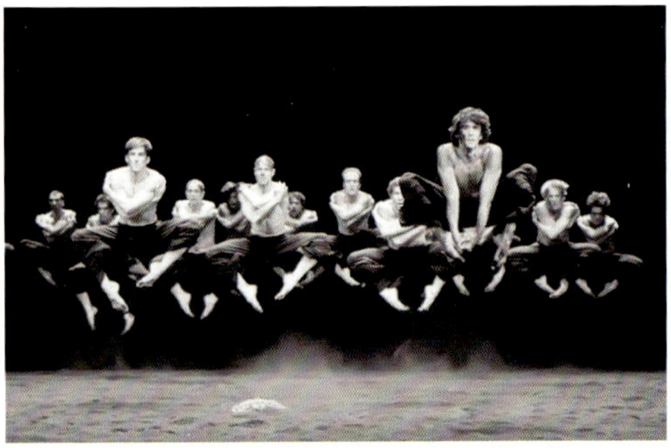

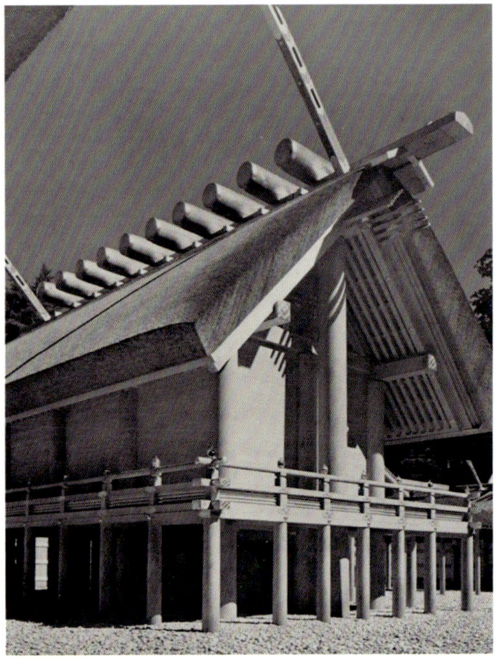

Esha Thapar

"A history that performs" – Shikinensengū: Vicennial ritual renewal of the Grand Ise Shrine as a form of 'round-dance'

Tutor: Edward Denison

"Every artistic creation, every artistic pleasure presupposes a certain carnival spirit. Or, to express myself in a modern way – the haze of carnival candles is the true atmosphere of art."
Gottfried Semper, 2004

This study was framed around the notion of the 'round-dance' as expressed by Heidegger and mirrored by the Shikinensengū – a ritual of re-creation repeated every twenty years by followers of the Japanese Shinto religion. Choreographed around the three main themes of Tanztheater – choreutics, rituals of repetition and re-enactment – this essay aims to unify the two principle themes of dance and architecture through a critical investigation of the Grand Ise Shrine using the lens of dance theory (as seen in the dance forms of Rudolf Laban and Pina Bausch), casting this world-famous site as 'an architecture of performance'.

——The study draws new and perceptive insights, such as the parallels between the Meiji Restoration and Bausch's choreography in relation to didactics and the significance achieved from 'performing the doing'. Other examples include choreutics and the notion of a chorus in both Bausch's work and the opening act in preparing the materials for the construction of the Ise Shrine, the importance of time as highlighted in Laban's definition of 'effort' and in the choreography of the Shikinensengū, and the creation of a sense of intimacy at a large scale by collective participation. Repetition is another example, demonstrated by the process of falling, where parallels can be drawn between the preparatory contemplation of the carpenters and Bausch's performers of the falling dance, where in both instances, the accentuated impact is created by the minimisation of initial movement.

——The essay raises questions about the disciplinary boundaries of architecture and the potential for other forms of artistic and bodily expression to reveal new ways of understanding architectural sites, processes and meanings. The conclusion is that architectural thinking and dance practice share resonance with each other through their philosophies, theories and perceptions of space and time, relative to our body and sensory experiences. Questions such as 'Could Tanztheater be viewed as the architecture of performance?' or conversely, 'Could the architecture of performance be portrayed as a branch of Tanztheater?' open up new territories and possibilities for thinking about relationships between architecture and other human experiences.

Image: The beauty of practice and repetition display final outcomes of a similar visual impact. Left: Performance from Wim Wenders' production 'Pina'. Right: Grand Ise Shrine (Inner)

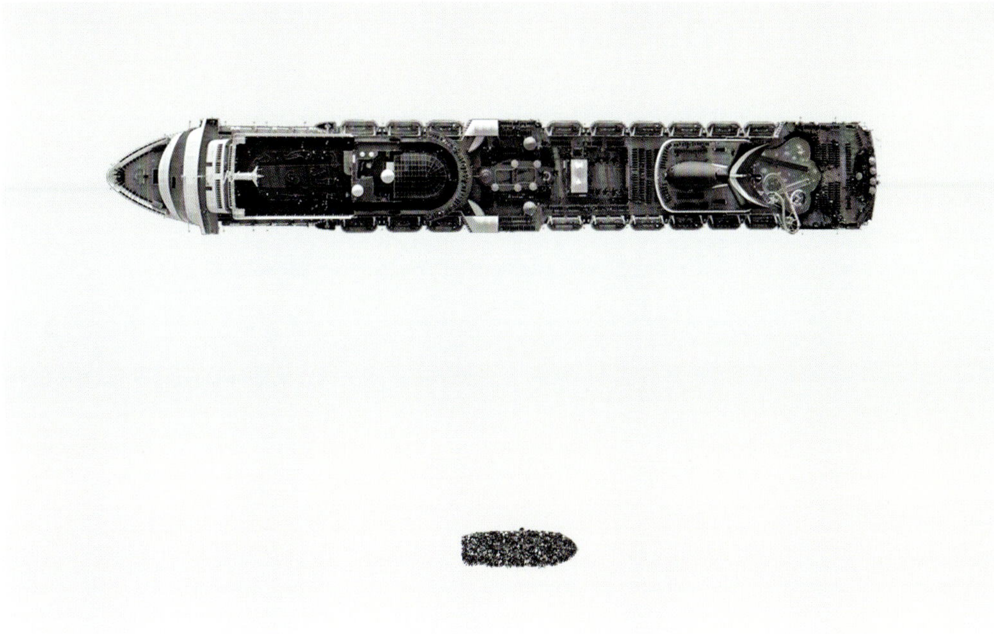

Joseph Roberts
Venice: A 'Real Abstraction'
Tutor: Jon Goodbun

It is not hard to picture Venice in your mind: romantic images of Baroque, Gothic and Renaissance architecture, frozen in time upon an isolated island. It is far harder to visualise the sum of its economic and social transactions: the proliferation of tourists; the movement patterns of illegal street vendors; the spike and flux of real estate prices; the corruption of public infrastructure funding; the emigration of the Venetian population; the 'hands-tied' reliance on global advertising for restoration work; and its imports and exports of products and people.

——This more obscure side of Venice demonstrates a characteristic consequence of global capitalism whereby things foreign to one another are bizarrely juxtaposed, their connections not legible outright. Venice is ruled by interactions of this kind, which take place on subterranean layers, are difficult to visualise and even harder to make sense of. The immateriality and invisibility of such a web of relations fundamentally underpins Venice's society and life, rendering them abstract.

——This essay explores Venice through the narrative of two protagonists – a migrant and a tourist – to interrogate potential routes through such 'abstractions'. Through a discussion of their interaction with various Venetian commodities (coffee, Gucci handbags and cultural knick-knacks), the metaphysical pulls and pushes that lead both the migrant and the tourist to Venice can be traced back to a common antagonist: the social relations of capital.

——These social relations dictate how capital is circulated in Venice and have an assertive impact on its urban space. A cheap cultural souvenir, for example, has a string of relations that lead back to the factories of China, where the product is created. Its 'value' can then only be realised on the tourist strip of Venice. These souvenir stalls have pushed local produce like glassblowing to the peripheral islands. Tracing such webs of relations expose the tourist-dominated market of central Venice as a place solely for the exchange of value. Since a crucial condition for realising value is that a market be found, the city becomes de facto an organised and orchestrated marketplace. Historic buildings are used as the backdrop to legitimise illegitimate objects at the point of sale; every ground floor, back room and storage cupboard is evaluated for its sales potential; churches form frames from which gigantic advertising boards can hang; the pizza is replaced by the Big Mac and public space transforms into the arena of the spectacle.

Image: Cruise ship/Migrant boat

Year 5 Thesis

Dr Edward Denison, Dr Robin Wilson, Oliver Wilton

The Thesis enables Year 5 students to research, develop and define the basis for their work, addressing architecture and relevant related disciplines such as the visual arts, humanities, cultural theory, anthropology, computation, physical or social sciences, engineering, manufacturing, environmental design and urbanism.

——Students undertake the work in depth, supported by specialist tutors who are individually allocated to them based on their stated areas of interest, in consultation with their Design Unit Tutors. The result is a study of 9,000 words, or equivalent, that documents relevant research activities and outcomes and typically includes one or more propositional elements that may include the development of an argument or hypothesis, the development of a design strategy, or the development and testing of a series of design components in relation to a specific line of inquiry or interest.

——The Thesis is an inventive, critical and directed research activity that augments the work students undertake in the design studio. The symbiotic relationship between thesis and design varies from being evident and explicit to being situated more broadly in a wider sphere of intellectual interest. We anticipate that a number of theses from this year's academic cohort will be developed into external publications.

Thesis Tutors
Hector Altamirano, Alessandro Ayuso, Andy Barnett, Matthew Barnett-Howland, Carolina Bartram, Paul Bavister, Jan Birksted, Camilo Boano, Iain Borden, Roberto Bottazzi, Jos Boys, Eva Branscome, Andrew Budgen, Brent Carnell, Mario Carpo, Simon Carter, Nat Chard, Amica Dall, Meredith Davey, Edward Denison, Paul Dobraszczyk, Oliver Domeisen, Stephen Gage, Stelios Giamarelos, Polly Gould, Gary Grant, Jane Hall, Francesca Hughes, Susanne Isa, Jan Kattein, Zoe Laughlin, Guan Lee, Chris Leung, Stephen Lorimer, Luke Lowings, Abel Maciel, Richard Martin, Euan Mills, Harry Parr, Jacob Paskins, Luke Pearson, Hareth Pochee, Alan Powers, Sophia Psarra, Rokia Raslan, David Roberts, David Rudlin, Tania Sengupta, Alistair Shaw, Bob Sheil, Neil Spiller, Nina Vollenbröker, Tim Waterman, William Whitby, Robin Wilson, Oliver Wilton, Simon Withers, Stamatis Zografos

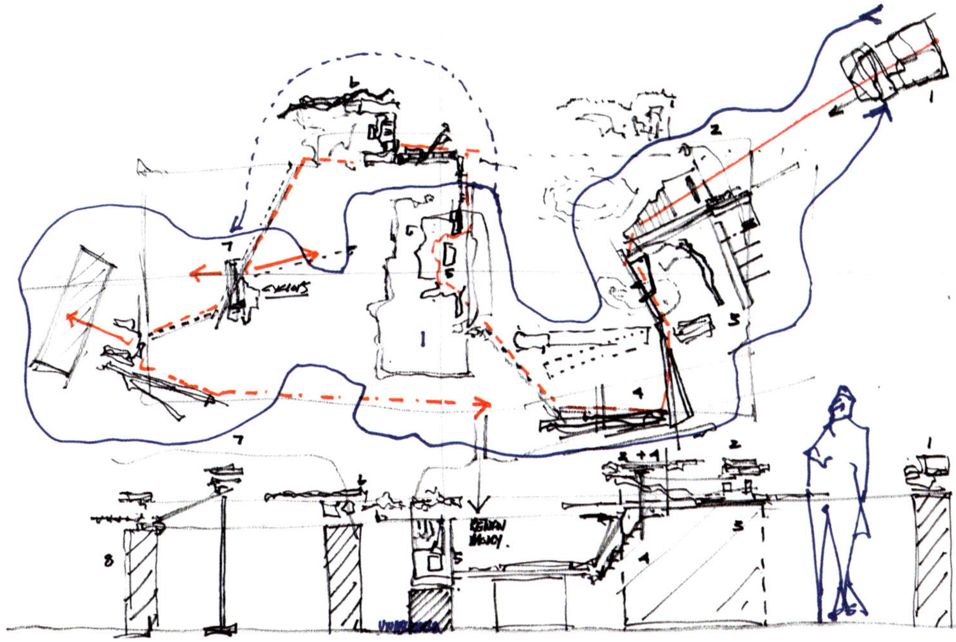

Paddi Benson
Lost [and Found] in Play
Thesis Tutor: Francesca Hughes

Donald Winnicott (1896-1971) is now regarded as one of the most significant post-war psychoanalytic practitioners and theoreticians. In his seminal lecture *Playing and Reality*, delivered in the early 1950s and published in 1971, he identified the 'potential space' which occurs at the moment when the infant begins separating the 'self' from the mother; the infant (together with the intuition of the mother) fills this space with 'creative play' and the imaginative transformation of first possessions – what Winnicott refers to as 'transitional objects'.[1] The space of cleavage that results from separation is colonised, tested and explored through play. Is play then essentially about the codifying or interrogation of new space? Winnicott understood that the use of these transitional objects belonged to an intermediate area between the 'subjective' interior of the infant and the perceived 'objective' exterior, and that such play/use of symbols is the foundation of all cultural experiment and life.[2] Importantly, Winnicott recognised that the architect inhabits an 'intermediate area', constructively interleaving imagined and real worlds. This imaginative domain of the architect is continuous with the 'play area' of the small child who is 'lost in play'.[3]

———Winnicott's framework allows us to understand more clearly the continuity of creativity through play (which links the individual to the wider world) and the nuanced distinction between creative artists who use language (Homer, Dante, Shakespeare, Joyce) and those using non-verbal, improvisatory communication (the pre-language infant but also the visual artist, composer and architect). The focus of this thesis is on this latter group who, without words, are able to communicate evocatively with an engaged audience and, on occasion, reclaim a distracted audience. Applying Winnicott's framework to the performance art of Stuart Brisley and the musical improvisation of Don Ellis, the thesis addresses the following questions: can play be viewed as an apparatus which engages the imagination to test and even transcend its own boundaries? What are the economies of play? What lessons can students of architecture draw from non-verbal creative practice, music and performance? How can this be instrumentalised in an architectural proposition?

1. Donald Winnicott, *Playing and Reality*, (London: Routledge, 2005), 135. Winnicott's convention of the 'mother' is used on the understanding that this can also refer to any parental carer regardless of gender.
2. Ibid., 107.
3. Ibid., 18. This 'intermediate area' is the site of Stuart Brisley's performance and the improvisation of Don Ellis, discussed in part 2 of the thesis, Bubble and Kernel.

Image: The Squiggle Map: a peregrination. Sketch by the author

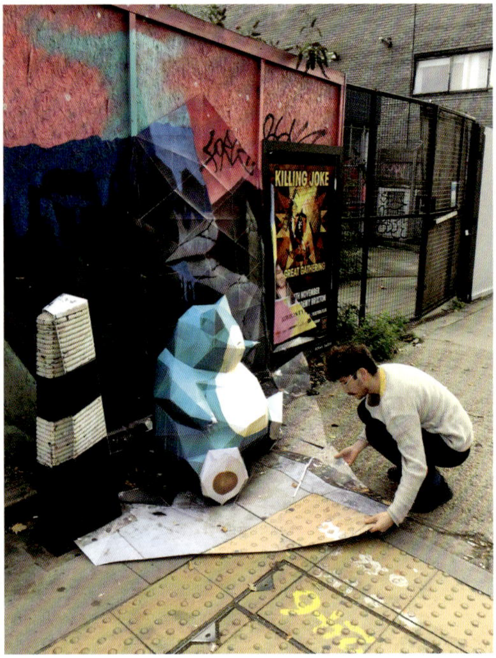

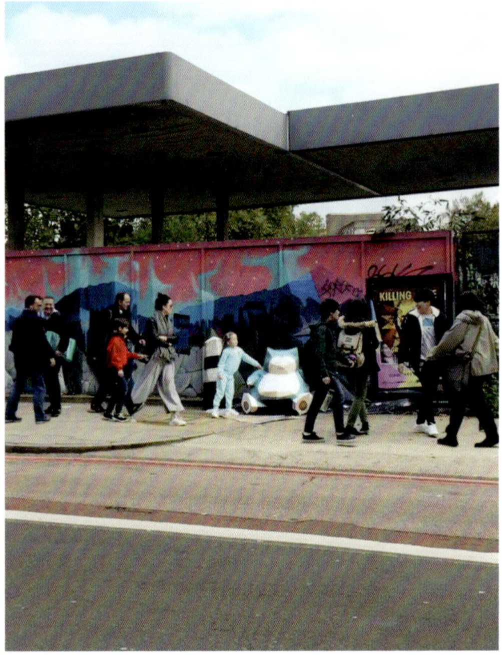

Agostino Nickl
Phygital Futures – Learning from Pokémon Go
Thesis Tutor: Luke Pearson

Using geolocations and a smartphone interface, Pokémon Go enforced a new layer of use on an urban scale – taking the self-contained game environment out of the equation. Virtual maps and physical terrain were joined, creating huge four-dimensional struggles.

——With the fad coming to a halt – by now plummeting trainer numbers have transformed urban hunting grounds into peaceful habitats for digital creatures – it is time to reassess. The process of stepping out into the augmented world – registering for an online account, orientating within the game map, making a first catch – serves as the backbone to a case study of Pokémon Go. Laying emphasis on the spatial nature of the game, the reader is taken for a fictive stroll through the city. This approach structures the discussion about the interfaces and game elements that are observed and scrutinised along the way. Bringing in current coverage retrieved from online magazines and blogs as well as contextualising these findings with notions taken from cultural history and philosophy, social sciences and game studies, this walk is augmented.

——Once woven into this broad framework, Pokémon Go is established as a relevant object of enquiry rather than being dismissed as a transient fad. This opens up spaces for a broader discussion about the technologies involved, the relationship between game space and 'real' space, and the societal implications. What can we, as architects and urban planners, take on from the 'phygital' (physical plus digital) world of Pokémon Go? How can new technologies such as Augmented Reality and gaming principles inform new design methodologies?

——To provoke discussion around these questions the author introduces his own design research, Realised Augmentity, a series of experiments conducted to investigate the possibility of Augmented Reality as a tool for delivery, and an attempt to formulate a compelling alternative to detached digital manufacturing processes such as robotic milling and 3D printing.

——Phygital Futures aims to shed light on how the introduction of a gamified urban layer challenges our relationship with data. What potentials lay bare in front of urban planners when maps and datasets become play and design resources of the future? And finally, will the notion of games as social constructs make game design an important societal tool that can be employed for participatory governance and design processes? This outlook will hopefully foster imagination as well as delineate new fields of research and enquiry.

Image: The Papercast technique enabled an augmented Snorlax to be transformed into a publicly tangible artefact. Photo by the author

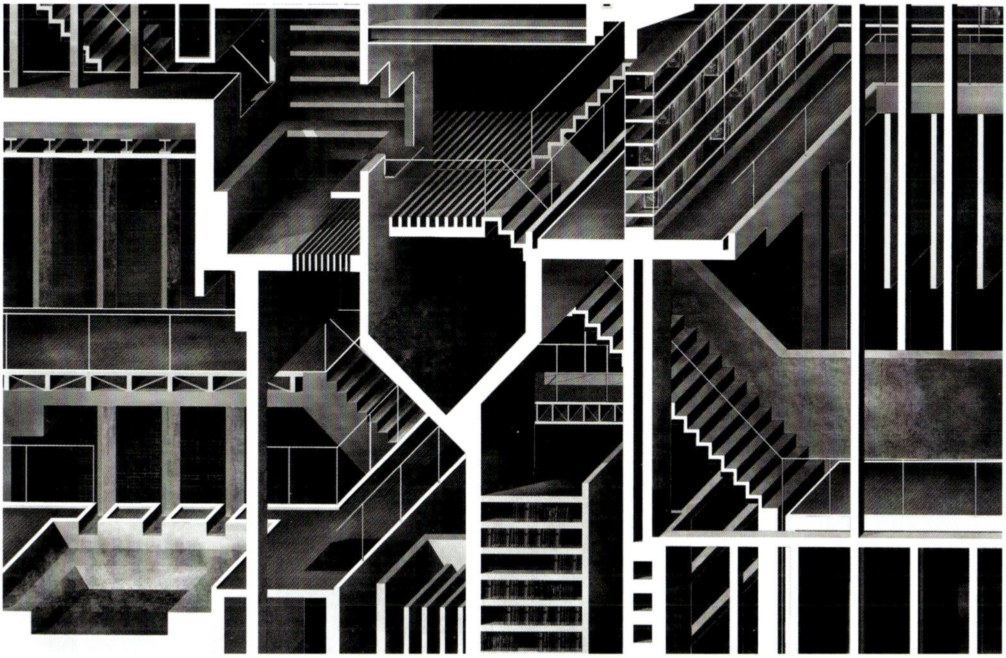

Kirsty McMullan

Spiralling Space-Time: Between Fiction and Reality in **The Museum of Innocence**

Thesis Tutor: Sophia Psarra

Architects design and realise future realities. As such, the majority of our work consists of testing the imaginary. However, as a profession dealing with real-world constraints, including the need to convince clients of our professional competence, we try to appear to have knowledge, and disguise the use of the imaginary. In doing so, we reject the 'unknowns' in favour of what we already know, leaving little room for the parts of the project where the imagination can thrive.

——This thesis seeks to examine the relationship between reality and fiction as a site for activating the imagination. This is relevant to architecture within the context of intellectual engagement for both author and audience, architect and occupant, process and result. It is also of larger political significance in terms of the city, which holds both the individual and collective memories of its people. Fiction can make one think more critically about the real, and motivate people to claim their right to the imagination, often through physical places and objects.

——The question of this relationship between reality and fiction is explored in the context of *The Museum of Innocence* in Istanbul, a project by world-renowned Turkish author Orhan Pamuk. This case study was selected because, as both a novel and a museum conceived simultaneously, it is a venture that flourishes in the space between reality and the imaginary. Traversing literature and architecture, it also interrogates the translation of ideas between the conceptual world and the physical realm, with particular relevance to Istanbul's current political climate. The thesis examines the novel and the museum through diagrams to help visualise Pamuk's techniques and effects, before synthesizing the two in relation to the city. Whilst both are disparate forms of representation, they share elements that are intrinsic to architecture – space and time. It is, therefore, through raising the notion of space-time specifically, that a clearer theoretical understanding of this interaction might be realised with generative implications for architecture.

——The thesis argues that *The Museum of Innocence* achieves the sensation of being suspended in space-time, using a spiral structure to create a position from which we can pause to consider our relationship with the city's past, present and future. It proposes that in order to design places with a deep connection to the city and intellectual engagement with the occupant, the imaginary must be taken seriously as a testing-ground.

Image: Inside The Museum of Innocence, photo by the author

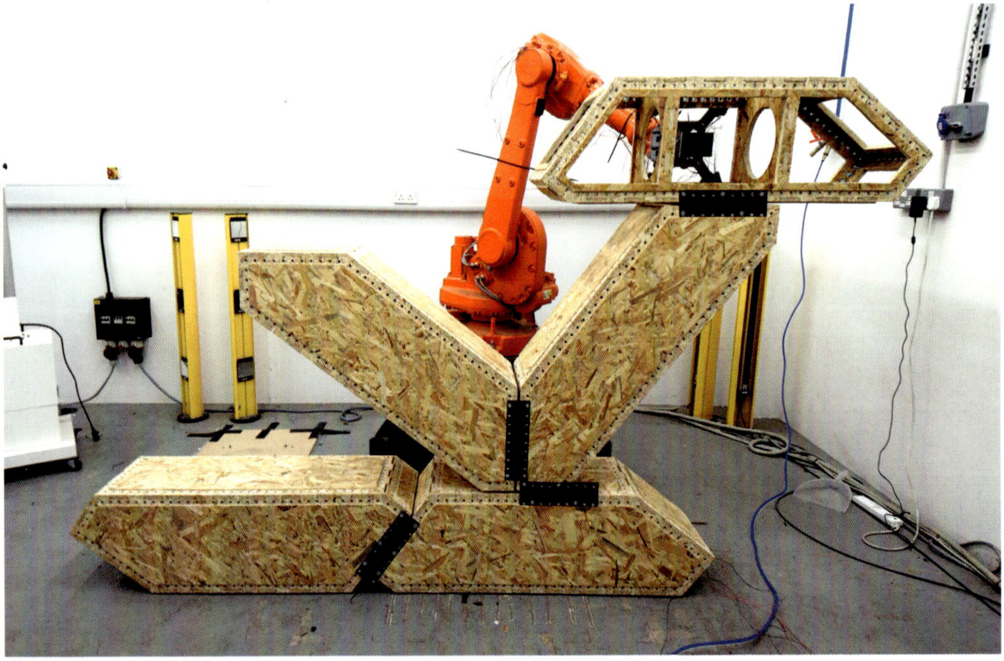

Ivo Tedbury
SEMBLR Construction Platform – using open-source RobOBIM as a development framework to facilitate and safeguard the automation of building construction
Thesis Tutor: Oliver Wilton

The use of robots to construct buildings and other structures has the potential to lead to shared prosperity, if the technology is developed through a suitable platform. This could be enabled by an open-source syntax, common to both robotic systems and the design of the assembled product: Robot-oriented Building Information Modelling (RobOBIM). This design research, developing and testing the SEMBLR system, addresses both technical and social-political considerations and seeks to investigate the feasibility of the RobOBIM approach.

——For automated robotic assembly of building-scale structures, a relative robot system (where the robot moves relative to the object it is assembling) has the key advantage of circumventing external infrastructure constraints to allow unlimited form and size. For the SEMBLR system, aggregations of composite timber 'bricks' are both the desired construction objective and the assembler robot's locomotion infrastructure. An unconventional design approach is needed, given that 'these robots, plus the materials they assemble, are best viewed as a combined system'[1].

——To this end, SEMBLR uses a single syntax, which augments traditional Building Information Modelling (BIM) to include the integration of robotic assembly systems. The proposed system is developed and tested physically at 1:1 scale using a bespoke end-effector mounted on an industrial robot, and digitally using custom robot simulation scripts.

——This field of investigation links to the ever-evolving labour movement – robots could build normal structures without the need for human labour or vast capital expenditure. Making construction labour unnecessary could be good for humanity, but the required tools must be developed from within our existing capitalist society in such a way that the citizens retain the right to choose how they are used. Thus, a sociopolitical conceptual framework is proposed, outlining how automated construction systems could be developed and implemented to socially progressive effect, addressing matters including open intellectual property, distributed production, environmental sustainability, public ownership, a collaborative platform and phased system development. Overall, the research anticipates a new field of technical exploration, entwined with an evolving sociopolitical outlook for the emerging design and building processes.

1. Gershenfeld, N. et al. (2015). Macrofabrication with Digital Materials: Robotic Assembly. *Architectural Design*, 85(5), pp. 122-127.

Image: Five SEMBLR bricks, reversibly assembled using a custom end-effector and industrial robot, driven by RobOBIM data-structure of the bricks.

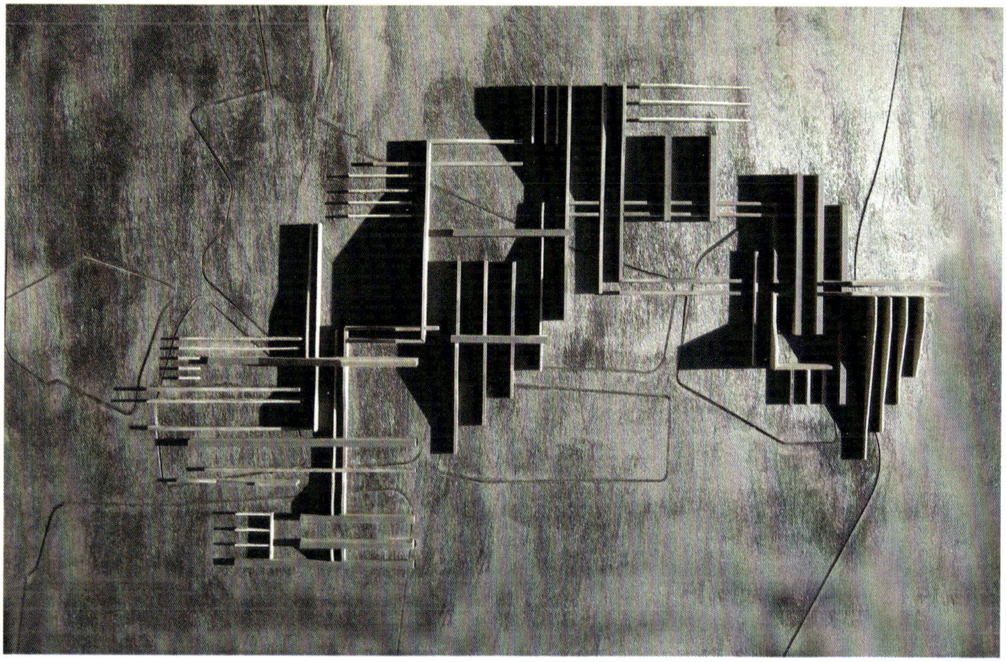

Ozan Toksoz-Blauel

Between Organic and Cosmic Architecture: A Historical Re-evaluation of Hans Scharoun

Thesis Tutor: Jan Birksted

This thesis questions the accepted view, posed by architectural historian Peter Blundell-Jones, that Hans Scharoun was an 'Organic' Architect. The term 'Organic' was first used by Frank Lloyd Wright to describe site-specific architecture that had spatial fluidity from the outside to the inside. From the analysis of Scharoun's original written and drawn material, housed in the AdK Archives in Berlin, a second impression of the architect is revealed. Scharoun often referred to the theory of 'Cosmic' architecture in his work, a vision that was developed during his involvement with the expressionists in the early 1920s.

——The term 'Cosmic' was used in Germany during the interwar years to describe the ideal society and it was believed that Cosmic Architecture, as the highest form of art, would act as the main agent to aid in the development of a utopian society. After the Second World War in 1951, Scharoun won a competition to build a school in the heavily bombed city of Darmstadt. Within this campus design, one can find a room that he named 'The Cosmic Room'. Scharoun's unrealised design for The Cosmic Room exposes many facets of his belief in the theory of Cosmic architecture.

——Contrary to the site-specific characteristics of Organic architecture, Cosmic architecture used natural symbolism to translate intellectual thought through physical form. Scharoun projected the natural seasonal sunlight changes within the space of the Cosmic Room to symbolise the passing of time and the cycle of life. It was believed that the use of natural symbolism in The Cosmic Room would allow the students of the school to gain a higher level of consciousness. Scharoun's interest in human consciousness and the development of society can be traced back to his interest in the work of philosophers such as Kant or Heidegger, whom he frequently quoted in his speeches.

——It is mainly within Scharoun's drawings that one can find evidence of his Cosmic interests, yet subtle references of his constant preoccupation with Cosmic architecture is noticeable in his built work.

——Unlike Bundell-Jones' argument that Scharoun's early involvement with the German Expressionists was merely a stepping stone to what we now perceive as his 'Organic' style, this thesis argues that Organic architecture lacks the spiritual, utopian quality of Cosmic belief that was nurtured through a prolonged period of unrest in Germany throughout Scharoun's professional career.

Image: A sculpted landscape over time. The sculpture was designed in conjunction with the research on Hans Scharoun's Cosmic design approach of symbolising the meaning of time through nature and seasonal changes. Image by the author

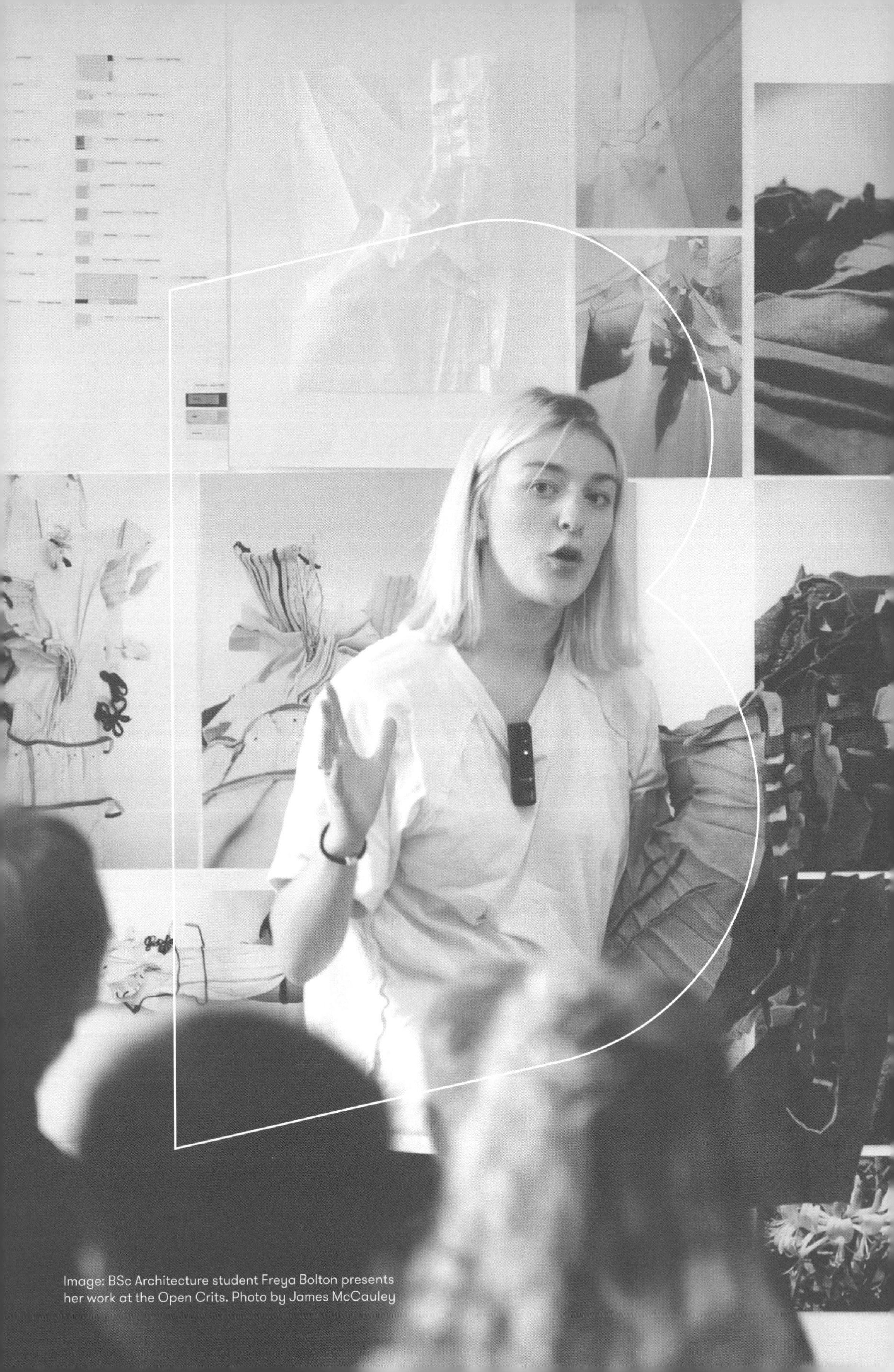

Image: BSc Architecture student Freya Bolton presents her work at the Open Crits. Photo by James McCauley

MEng Engineering & Architectural Design

Programme Director: Luke Olsen

Affiliated practices and institutes
AKT II, Arup, BuroHappold, Feilden Clegg Bradley Studios, Foster + Partners, Hoare Lea Consulting Engineers, Laing O'Rourke, Max Fordham, Price & Myers, CIBSE (Chartered Institution of Building Services Engineers), EI (Energy Institute), JBM (Joint Board of Moderators), ICE (Institution of Civil Engineers), IStructE (Institution of Structural Engineers), ARB (Architects Registration Board) and the RIBA (Royal Institute of British Architects)

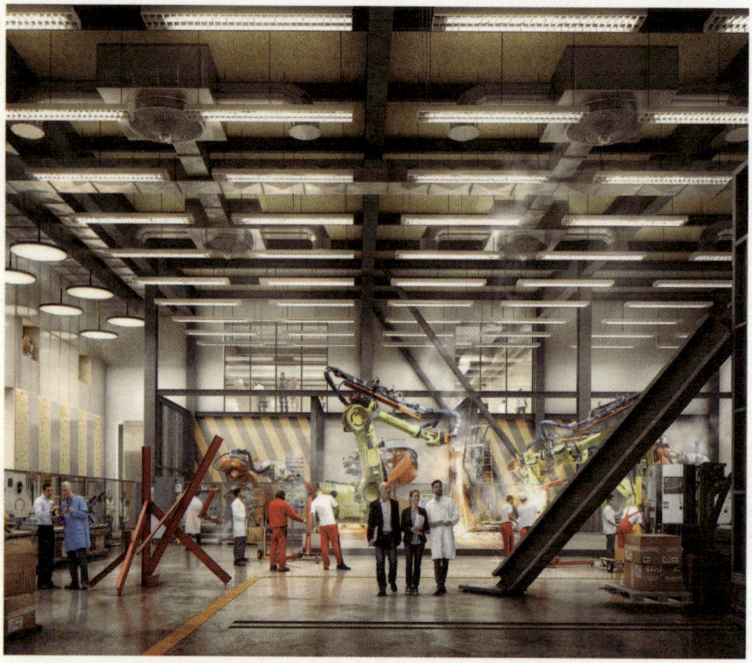

This new pioneering four-year integrated Masters in Engineering and Architectural Design challenges students to develop a critical, independent, experimental and technically rigorous approach to the design of the built environment. The programme is delivered by leading experts drawn from The Bartlett School of Architecture, the Institute for Environmental Design and Engineering [IEDE] and Civil Environmental and Geomatic Engineering [CEGE], all at UCL.

——Placing creativity, innovation and design at the centre of engineering education, the programme pushes beyond conventional models, providing students with the opportunity to understand and develop advanced design methodologies while acquiring expertise on how to augment, communicate and resolve visionary designs through engineering knowledge. Students will learn how to imagine, conceptualise and deliver resilient buildings that incorporate lifelong environmental, structural and societal responsibilities.

——Graduates will be equipped with the knowledge and expertise to undertake a project from inception and brief development through to detail design and post-occupancy evaluation. As advocates for their designs, students will engage in robust, informed interdisciplinary discussion to enhance the design of the built environment. Our MEng Engineering & Architectural Design graduates will be the future leaders of a collaborative and organisationally complex industry.

Image: Here East Hawkins\Brown Architects. Visualisation-Pixel Flakes

MArch Architectural Design (B-Pro)

Programme Director: Gilles Retsin

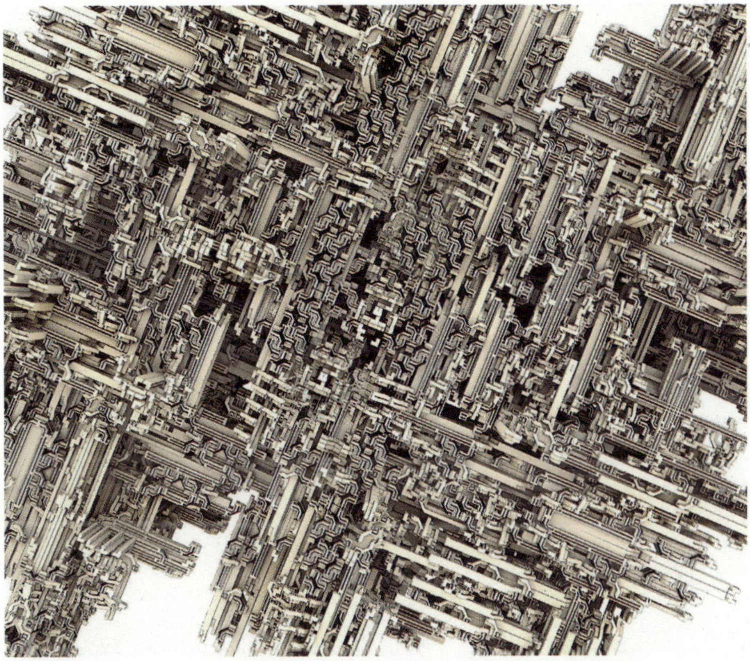

The MArch Architectural Design is a 12-month full-time post-professional course. It is part of B-Pro, the umbrella structure for post-professional Masters programmes at The Bartlett School of Architecture, directed by Professor Frédéric Migayrou. Composed of an international body of experts and students, it is designed to deliver diverse yet focused strands of speculative research, emphasising the key role computation plays within complex design synthesis.

——With access to B-made, one of the most advanced fabrication workshops in Europe, our students are introduced to highly advanced coding, fabrication and robotic skills, aimed at computational and technological fluency. Simultaneously, students are exposed to larger theoretical underpinnings specifically tailored to their enquiries. Next academic year will see MArch Architectural Design collaborate closely with MSc/MRes Architectural Computing to bring students together, sharing lectures, workshops and cross-disciplinary events relating to computational design, such as Bartlett Plexus.

——The course is organised into Labs and Research Clusters, offering students the chance to choose a distinct field of enquiry. We explore the latest approaches to robotics and AI, CNC fabrication, 3D printing, supercomputing, simulation, generative design, interactivity, advanced algorithms, extensive material prototyping and links to material science.

Labs

Design Computation Lab
Mollie Claypool, Manuel Jiménez García, Gilles Retsin and Vicente Soler

BiotA Lab
Marcos Cruz and Richard Beckett

Material Lab
Daniel Widrig and Guan Lee

Research Clusters

RC1
Daghan Cam, Andy Lomas

RC2
Maj Plemenitas

RC3
Ruairi Glynn, Jessica In, Matt Jacob, Yuri Suzuki

RC4
Manuel Jiménez García, Gilles Retsin, Vicente Soler

RC5
Adam Holloway, Guan Lee

RC6
Daniel Widrig, Stefan Bassing, Soomeen Hahm

RC7
Marcos Cruz, Richard Beckett, Chris Leung, Javier Ruiz

RC8
Daniel Kohler

Report Coordinator
Stephen Gage

Image: RC4, INT, Discrete Robotic Assembly (Qianyi Li, Zoey Tan, Claudia Tanskanen, Xiaolin Yin)

MArch Urban Design (B-Pro)

Programme Director: Professor Mark Smout

Research Clusters
RC11
Sabine Storp and Patrick Weber with Rae Whittow-Williams
RC12
Luke Pearson and Sandra Youkhana with David Roberts
RC13
Eddie Blake and Sam Jacob with Amica Dall
RC14
Roberto Botazzi and Kostas Grigoriadis with Annarita Papeschi
RC16/Urban Morphogenesis Lab
Tommaso Casucci, Filippo Nassetti and Claudia Pasquero with Emmanouil Zaroukas
RC18
Enriqueta Llabres Valls and Zachary Fluker with Nuria Alvarez Lombardero

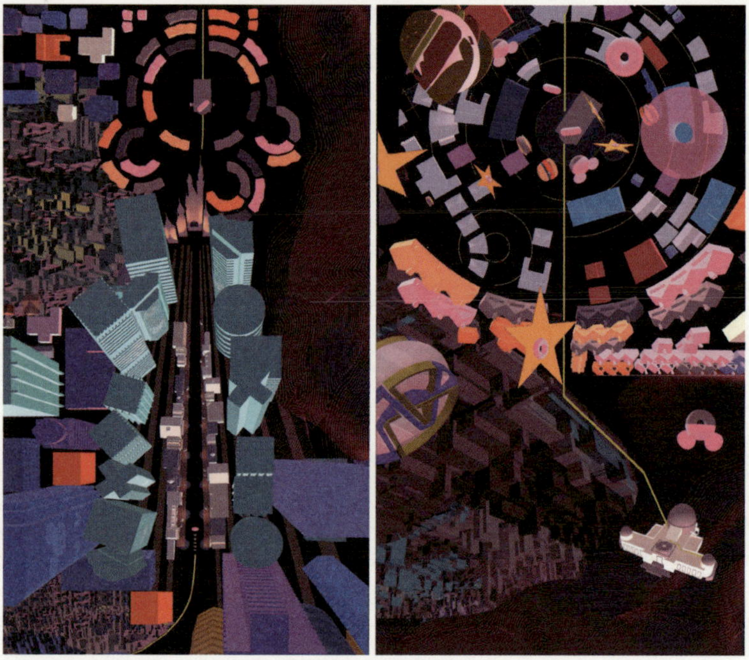

Image: 'RC12 Plays LA: Temples of Consumption'. As part of the cluster's research into urbanism through videogames made in Unity3D, we explore Los Angeles through the representations of itself

The MArch Urban Design is a 12-month studio-based programme that brings together a new generation of designers and thinkers from across the world. The course provides a rich and stimulating environment for long-term research on the challenges of global urbanisation and the creative potential of speculative design. It is part of B-Pro, the umbrella structure for post-professional Masters programmes at The Bartlett School of Architecture, directed by Professor Frédéric Migayrou.

——Urban design is a particular form of enquiry into the nature of the city, its form and function. It seeks to understand the city as a place of human coexistence and to devise strategies and projects to guide its future development and evolution. Throughout the course, students are encouraged to innovate and explore new ideas in design and theory. They are introduced to design skills, critical enquiry and related technologies. They use this experience to shape polemic interventions, and develop speculative projects on a variety of scales. Students are encouraged to explore and understand their host city, London, one of the most richly diverse cities in the world.

MA Architectural History

Programme Director: Professor Peg Rawes

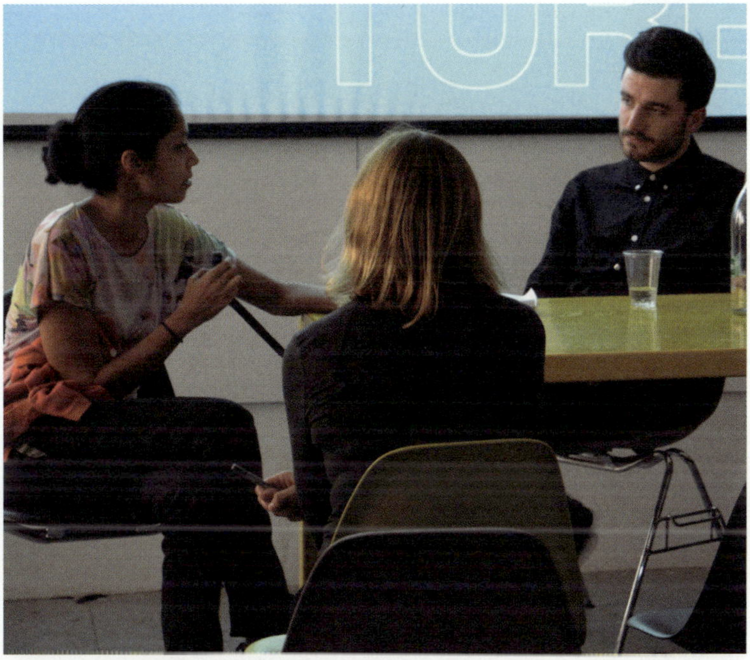

Architecture consists not only of buildings and projects, but also of the life that takes place within them, and the ideas and discussions that they give rise to. MA Architectural History actively explores what history can do for architecture. Over twelve months, students develop skills for interrogating, extending or reframing the discipline and its phenomena, often by situating architecture within broader debates about culture, history and politics.

——These 'situated histories' show us the active roles that architectural history has today: how it can transform and innovate our understandings of the built environment; how it can change our modes of engagement with cities and buildings; how different materialisations of history have different powers and effects and how different modes of verbal and visual expression can produce different audiences. Frequently, the work brings in ideas from different fields to re-situate architecture within the discipline and beyond – for example, in relation to ecological, feminist, digital or postcolonial theory; film, conceptual art or literary criticism; urban ethnography or activist politics. Each final project is an experiment in which a specific architectural phenomenon is examined in the light of a particular theory or set of ideas, to see how our view of it might change – or, alternatively, how a theory might need to be refreshed.

——The programme's Situating Architecture Symposium published work by the cohort in 'Disputed Architectures' (October 2016); visit The Bartlett School of Architecture on issuu.com to read it online.

Teaching Staff
Iain Borden, Eva Branscome, Ben Campkin, Mario Carpo, Edward Denison, Murray Fraser, Peter Guillery, Polly Gould, Michal Murawski, Jacob Paskins, Barbara Penner, Jane Rendell, David Roberts, Tania Sengupta, Michael Short, Robin Wilson

Image: 'Disputed Architectures', MA Architectural History Symposium, October 2016

MA Architecture & Historic Urban Environments

Programme Director: Dr Edward Denison

Teaching staff
Eva Branscome, Hannah Corlett, Edward Denison, Peter Guillery, Helen Jones, Aileen Reid, Andrew Saint, Philip Temple, Colin Thom

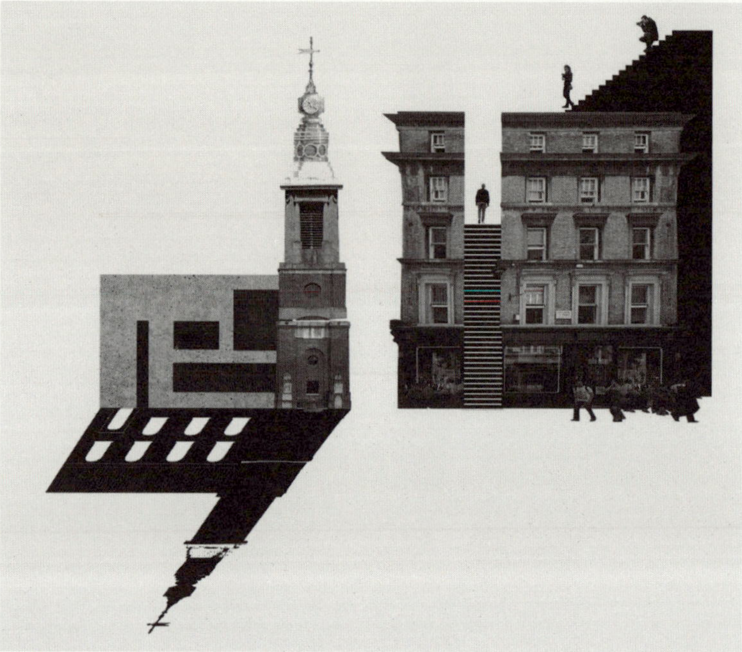

Image: 'Soho, Urban Colonisation'. Design Research: Julen Aguinagalde, Martina Reichenbach, Tasos Theodorakakis

Our MA Architecture & Historic Urban Environments pioneers the development of a more diverse and creative approach to the reinterpretation and reuse of historical environments in cities around the world. It does this through imaginative architectural designs and urban strategies, informed by issues of cultural heritage.

——This 12-month programme is exceptional in linking the core research challenge of innovative design with in-depth processes of urban surveying, recording, mapping and analysis. As such, the programme has a strong international component, viewing cities around the world as fascinating laboratories for investigations into architectural and historic urban environments, with London being the prime example.

——The programme is delivered through a combination of lectures, seminars, practical workshops, fieldwork visits and individual and group tutorials. Assessment is through project critique reviews, project portfolios, coursework essays, individual and group presentations, a dissertation/major project and a viva examination with an external examiner. Core modules include: Design Practice for Historic Environments; Design Research Methods for Historic Environments; Issues in Historic Urban Environments; Surveying and Recording of Cities; and Urban Regeneration and Cultural Heritage.

MRes Architecture & Digital Theory

Programme Directors: Professor Mario Carpo, Professor Frédéric Migayrou

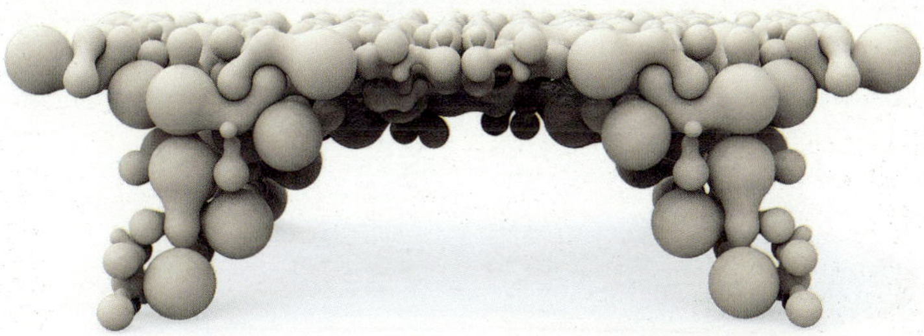

MRes Architecture & Digital Theory is dedicated to the theory, history and criticism of digital design and digital fabrication. This rigorous 12-month programme provides a grounding in research for students either trained in the design professions, or with a primary background in digital technology or the digital humanities, who are looking to further their understanding of digital innovation. The programme focuses in particular on the challenge of complexity in computational design and on its aesthetic, technological, economic and epistemological implications.

——Research topics include: agent-based conception; the new sciences of simulation, optimisation and form-finding; the transdisciplinary scalability of computational models; robotics and the engineering and modelisation of new materials and of variable property materials; and the history of digital notations and the demise of notational processes in the current data-driven computational environment.

——Digital design and digital conception are also considered from epistemological and historical perspectives, from cybernetics through to the most innovative experiments in various disciplines. This critical dimension, emerging from an exhaustive archaeology of these discourses, is related to global sociopolitical contexts, in order to redefine the mutations, status and efficiency of design in the digital world.

Image: MArch Architectural Design, RC4, Mickey Matter, 'MetaBall-ism'

MSc/MRes Architectural Computation (B-Pro)

Programme Director: Manuel Jiménez García

Teaching Staff
Sean Hanna, Christopher Leung, Ava Fatah, Sam Griffiths, Martin Zaltz-Austwick, Martha Tsigkari, Angelos Chroni

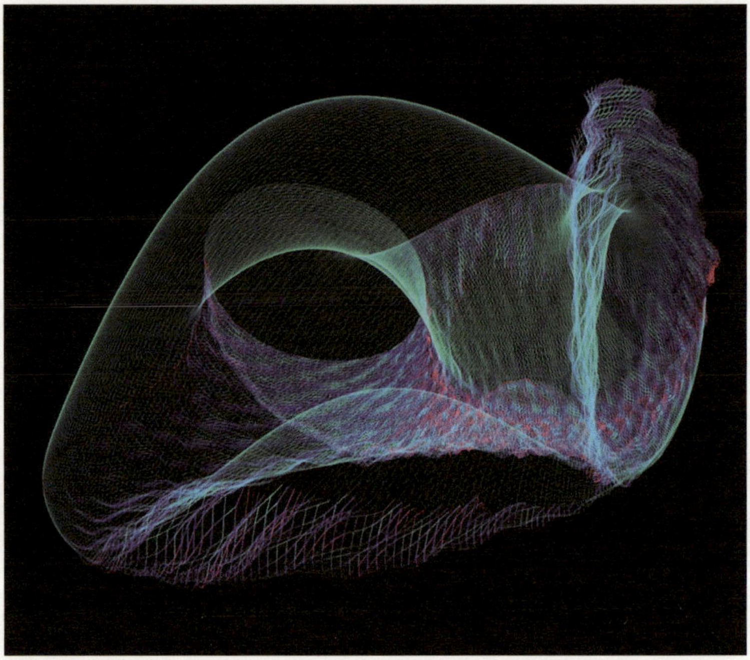

Our MSc/MRes Architectural Computation programmes engage and advance the main technologies by which tomorrow's architecture will be designed and constructed. From parametric design to 'big data' analytics, computation is increasingly important in the built environment. Our courses provide students with the depth of understanding to exploit computation fully in the context of world-leading design, research and industry. We also see computation as a technology driving fundamental shifts in industry, society and, most radically, the way we think.

——The learning of technical knowledge, such as computer coding, plays a stronger role than in many comparable courses, not only as a skill, but as a framework for thought. This technical knowledge is supported by a broad theoretical understanding of algorithms and philosophies of artificial intelligence and related domains.

——Students apply this knowledge in active design or scientific research projects which frequently make internationally recognised contributions to the field. Thesis work may take the form of exhibitions in venues such as the Royal Academy of Arts, London and the Centre Georges Pompidou, Paris; open source software for design or CADCAM; and internationally peer-reviewed publications.

——In 2017/18 the programme will collaborate closely with MArch Architectural Design, sharing lectures, workshops and cross-disciplinary events about computational design, such as Bartlett Plexus.

Image: A Creative Evolutionary Design System by Fabio Galicia

MSc/MRes Spatial Design: Architecture & Cities

Programme Directors: Dr Kayvan Karimi, Dr Sophia Psarra

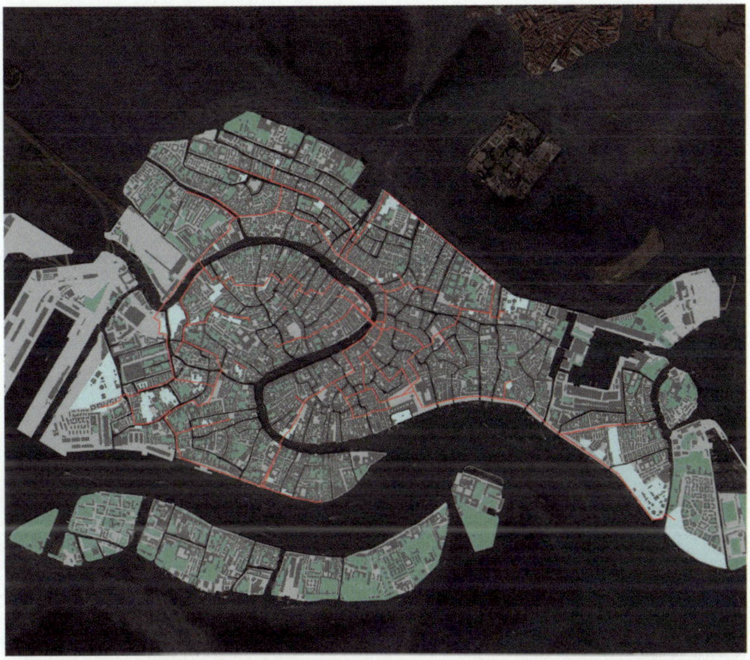

Teaching Staff
Kinda Al-Sayed, Sam Griffiths, Kayvan Karimi, Alan Penn, Sophia Psarra, Kerstin Sailer, Laura Vaughan

The MSc/MRes Spatial Design: Architecture & Cities centres on furthering students' understanding of architecture and urban design as instruments in the development of society. It offers a self-directed route of study that concentrates on research skills, enabling students either to take their existing architecture and urban design experience to a higher level, or set them up for a PhD. Using the theoretical and analytical framework of space syntax, it involves the study of architecture from the scale of individual buildings to small-scale urban design through to planning entire cities.

——Students develop in-depth theoretical and practical knowledge of the built environment and its functions considered as spatial, physical and human systems. They acquire a high level of skill in the research and analysis of buildings and cities as patterns of space inhabited by individuals, communities and organisations, in support of better and more humane design. Instead of confining architecture to the role of designing iconic buildings, the course takes a combined theoretical and analytical approach to architecture, urban design and planning, in the service of constructing a better built environment for society, as well as an improved public realm.

Image: Floating Life: Productive Community in Venice by Mian Ji

MA Situated Practice

Programme Director: James O'Leary

Teaching staff
James O'Leary, Jane Rendell plus visiting tutors and academics

Affiliated centres and institutions
UCL Urban Laboratory, The Slade School of Fine Art, Folkestone Triennial, Goldsmiths Fine Art Research Programme

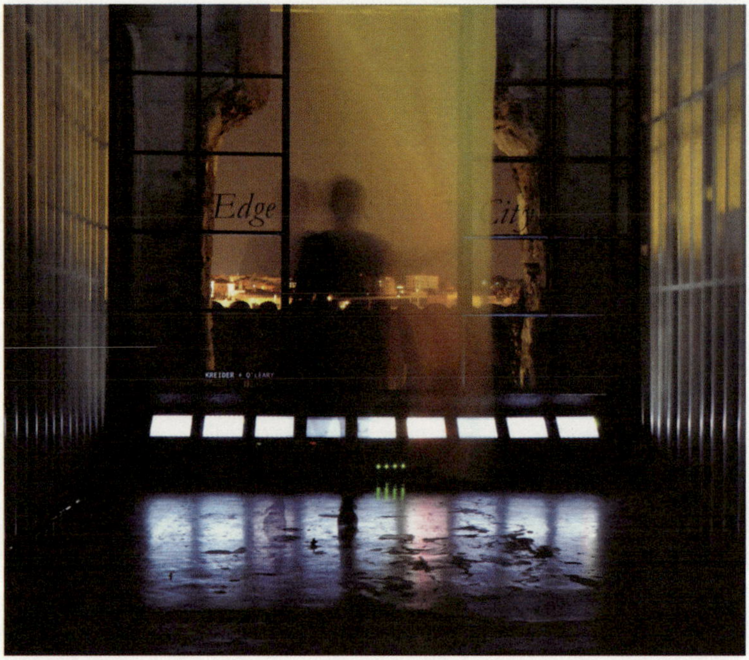

Recent shifts in contemporary culture have produced an increasing overlap of practices, methods and approaches from the worlds of art and design. We are interested in exploring new forms of practice within this evolving terrain, particularly work that is situated physically and engages with contemporary social, cultural and political conditions.

——This new 15-month course examines the fertile territories where the discipline of architecture cross-pollinates with other creative arts. Outcomes will combine media – comprising site-specific and performative installations, interventions, designs and events – that engage with their contexts and particular publics.

——MA Situated Practice is designed for creative individuals from across disciplinary boundaries who want to define their own forms of practice. Students will be taught the principles and skills of situated practice in relation to spatial theories in art, architecture, performativity, urbanism and writing, developing a strong understanding of appropriate research methodologies in art and design practice-led research. They will also make projects that are site-related – from physical installations and digital interventions to site writings.

——Graduates from MA Situated Practice will be highly equipped to pioneer new forms of hybrid practice between art and architecture in the domains of spatial practice, urban design, event design, critical and theoretical writing, performance and craft.

Image: Kreider + O'Leary, Edge City, Lisbon Architecture Triennale, Portugal (2013) © Kreider + O'Leary

MArch Design for Performance & Interaction

Programme Director: Ruairi Glynn

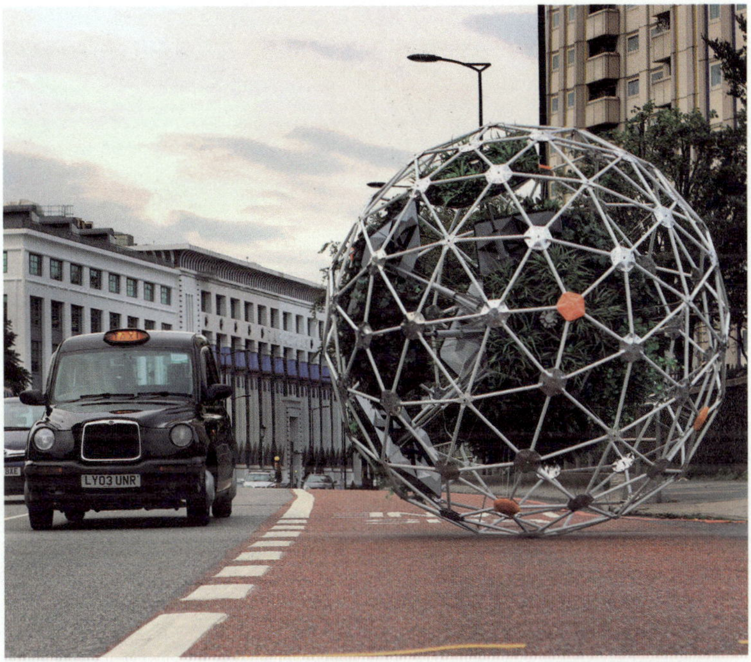

Affiliated practices and groups
Arup, Bompas & Parr, Ciminod Studio, Jason Bruges Studio, Intel, Marshmallow Laser Feast, onedotzero, Rose Bruford College of Theatre and Performance, Royal Central School of Speech and Drama, ScanLAB Projects, Shobana Jeyasingh Dance Company, Stufish, Troika, Twitter, Soundform, Umbrellium

This new 15-month Masters teaches design in four dimensions. Students will design the performance and interaction of objects, environments and people using the latest fabrication, sensing, computation, networked and responsive technologies. Emphasis is placed on prototyping, from interactive objects and installations to staged events and performance architecture. The course attracts students globally from a wide range of artistic and technical backgrounds and enjoys unrivalled access to cross-disciplinary enterprise, provided by both The Bartlett and UCL.

——At the core of the programme is the belief that the creation of spaces for performance, and the creation of performances within them, are symbiotic design activities. Design using interactive technologies enables us to consider objects, space, people and systems as potential performers, and our new studio facilities at Here East will offer unprecedented opportunities for groundbreaking work.

——MArch Design for Performance & Interaction has relevance across spatial and urban design, interface and systems design, auditorium and scenographic design, lighting and sound installation, performance and event design and virtual and physical environments that draw people together. We believe this provides an unprecedented opportunity for informed, skilled and transdisciplinary designers to define, and also deliver, spaces and systems for performance and interaction in the 21st century.

Image: Hortum Machina B, William Victor Camilleri and Danilo Sampaio, Interactive Architecture Lab

MArch Design for Manufacture

Programme Director: Professor Bob Sheil

Affiliated practices and institutes
Arup, BuroHappold, Foster + Partners, Laing O'Rourke, Price & Myers, ScanLAB Projects, UCL Civil, Environmental and Geomatic Engineering (CEGE), UCL Institute for Environmental Design and Engineering (IEDE)

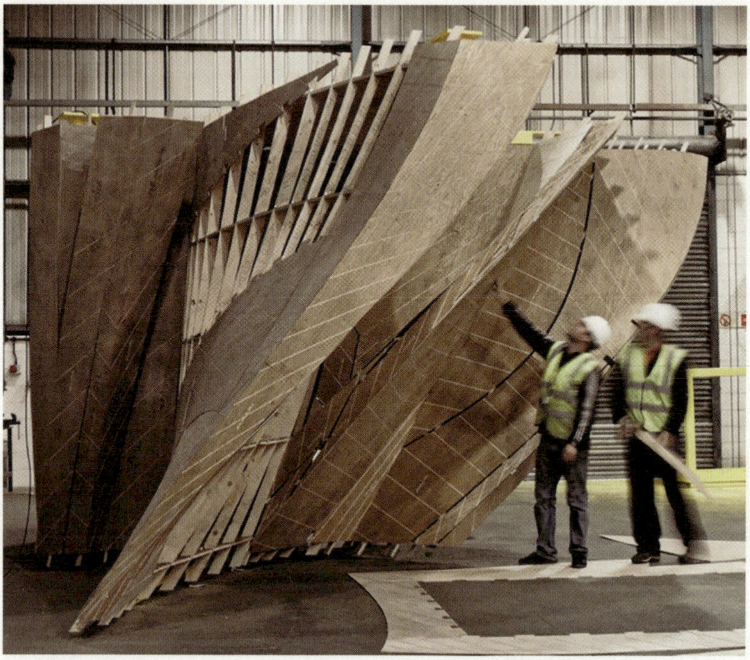

This 15-month Masters teaches students how to place their design skills in the context of pioneering developments in construction, fabrication, assembly and automation, including robotics.

——There is an abundance of advanced design and engineering tools in the UK that an elite workforce develop and deploy to export their expertise worldwide. Yet there is currently a shortage of skilled workers at the point of production tasked with delivering increasingly sophisticated and challenging projects by clients, in line with rising expectations on quality and regulation. This unique Masters prepares a new professional workforce of highly skilled, creative and adaptable experts with knowledge in design, engineering, material behaviour, analogue and digital craft, and advanced systems operations. Students will be exposed to and inspired by new forms of advanced design and engineering methodologies – such as robotics and 3D scanning – that are currently reinventing core approaches to shaping, making and refitting the built and manufactured environment.

Image: Tim Lucas, Price & Myers and Bartlett School of Architecture Lecturer in Structural Design. Photo by Maarten Kleinhout

Pg Dip in Professional Practice & Management in Architecture (ARB/RIBA Part 3)

Programme Director: Professor Susan Ware

The Professional Studies team aim to educate and equip a generation of architects to practice in an increasingly diverse and challenging environment. We do this by providing teaching and learning that encourage students to develop skills beyond those required by basic professional criteria through reflection, appraisal, critical enquiry and research. We ask students to examine the role of the architect in the changing global construction industry to examine the effect of politics and economics on the design and procurement of the built environment in future practice. In addition, we encourage students to explore an entrepreneurial approach to using their practice and business management skills in an increasingly competitive professional environment.

——The programme provides the students with the skills, knowledge, ability, judgment and integrity to be competent to practice and register as an architect through ARB and obtain Chartered Membership of the RIBA. The RIBA and ARB professional criteria are used as a basis to establish evidence of candidates' fitness to practice, threshold of competence (in terms of knowledge and ability) and professionalism (in terms of conduct and responsibility). However, the demanding programme aims to extend the students' learning well beyond the minimum required for professional registration. The school draws extensively from longstanding connections with practice and the construction industry to deliver teaching and learning at the forefront of current practice

——The flexible programme can be taken over 12, 18 or 24 months and in addition it is anticipated that in 2018 we will be offering a six-month fast track option. The programme, which commences in January, is delivered through a comprehensive series of 55 lectures given by experts from practice and from within the Faculty. The structure allows for a diversity of delivery and assessment methods replicating real-life scenarios, roles and responsibilities from practice. The final submission comprises the case study, personal evaluation and professional experience record, and is supported by a team of tutors through a series of one-to-one tutorials.

——In addition, the professional studies team provide a Year Out Programme and range of CPD short courses and other practice/registration-orientated courses.

MPhil/PhD Architectural Design

Acting Programme Director: Dr Penelope Haralambidou
Programme Coordinator: Dr Nina Vollenbröker

The MPhil/PhD Architectural Design allows exceptional and reflective designers to undertake research within The Bartlett School of Architecture's speculative and experimental ethos. The first to be established in the UK, our MPhil/PhD Architectural Design is internationally recognised as one of the most influential doctoral programmes dedicated to architectural design.

——The programme draws on the strengths of design teaching and doctoral research at The Bartlett, encouraging the development of architectural research through the interaction of drawing and writing. An architectural design doctoral thesis has two interrelated elements of equal importance – a project and a text – that share a research theme and a productive relationship. The project may be drawn, filmed, built, or use whatever medium is appropriate.

——UCL's multidisciplinary environment offers a stimulating and varied research culture that connects research by architectural design to developments in other disciplines such as anthropology, art, digital media, engineering, geography and medicine. The PhD Architectural Design programme is intended for graduates of architecture and other disciplines who wish to pursue research by architectural design, with over 60 students currently enrolled from around the world.

——The MPhil/PhD Architectural Design and MPhil/PhD Architectural History & Theory programmes organise a number of annual events. PhD Research Projects, an exhibition and conference with presentations and work by current PhD students, is held in Term 2. Invited critics in 2017 were Professor Marcos Cruz, The Bartlett School of Architecture; Professor Sylvia Lavin, University of California, Los Angeles; Dr Tarsha Finney, University of Technology Sydney; Professor Frédéric Migayrou, The Bartlett School of Architecture; Professor François Penz, University of Cambridge; and Dr Neil Wenman, Hauser & Wirth London. Throughout the year, PhD Research Conversations seminars provide the opportunity for doctoral candidates to present work in progress.

Current Students

Yota Adilenidou, Ava Aghakouchak, Bihter Almac, Luisa Silva Alpalhão, Nicola Antaki, Nerea Elorduy Amoros, Anna Andersen, Paul Bavister, Richard Beckett, Katy Beinart, Giulio Brugnaro, Matthew Butcher, Armando Caroca Fernandez, Niccolo Casas, Ines Dantas Ribeiro Bernardes, Bernadette Devilat, Ting Ding, Killian Doherty, Daniyal Farhani, Judit Ferencz, Pavlos Fereos, Susan Fitzgerald, Ruairi Glynn, Isabel Gutierrez Sanchez, Colin Herperger, Bill Hodgson, Sander Holsgens, Christiana Ioannou, Nahed Jawad, Tae Young Kim, Paul King, Dionysia Kypraiou, Hina Lad, Felipe Lanuza, Ifigeneia Liangi, Tea Lim, Rebecca Loewen, Thandiwe Loewenson, Shneel Malik, Samar Maqusi, Matthew McDonald, Matteo Melioli, Phuong-Trâm Nguyen, Ollie Palmer, Christos Papastergiou, Annarita Papeschi, Thomas Pearce, Luke Pearson, Mariana Pestana, Arthur Prior, Sarah Riviere, Felix Robbins, Natalia Romik, Merijn Royaards, Sayan Sakandarajah, Alexandru Senciuc, Wiltrud Simbuerger, Eva Sopeoglou, Camila Sotomayor, Ro Spankie, Dimitrie Stefanescu, Quynh Vantu, Cindy Walters, Daniel Wilkinson, Henrietta Williams, Seda Zirek, Fiona Zisch

Graduating Students

Popi Iacovou, Felipe Lanuza, Jane Madsen, David Roberts, Theodore Spyropoulos

Current Supervisors

Alisa Andrasek, Professor Peter Bishop, Dr Camillo Boano, Professor Iain Borden, Professor Victor Buchli, Professor Mario Carpo, Dr Ben Campkin, Professor Nat Chard, Professor Marjan Colletti, Professor Sir Peter Cook, Professor Marcos Cruz, Dr Edward Denison, Professor Murray Fraser, Professor Colin Fournier, Professor Stephen Gage, Dr François Guesnet, Dr Sean Hanna, Dr Penelope Haralambidou, Professor Christine Hawley, Professor Jonathan Hill, Dr Jan Kattein, Dr Chris Leung, Professor CJ Lim, Dr Yeoryia Manolopoulou, Professor Mark Miodownik, Professor Raf Orlowski, Professor Sebastien Ourselin, Professor Alan Penn, Dr Barbara Penner, Dr Sophia Psarra, Professor Peg Rawes, Professor Jane Rendell, Professor Bob Sheil, Professor Mark Smout, Professor Philip Steadman, Dr Hugo Spiers, Professor Neil Spiller, Professor Michael Stewart, Professor Philip Tabor, Dr Claire Thomson

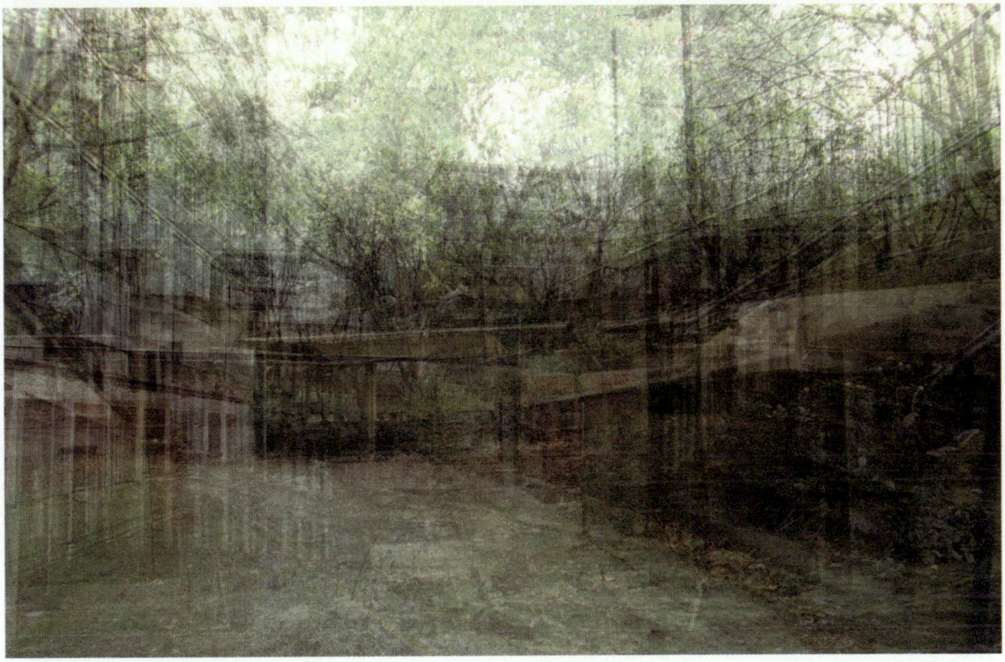

Graduating Students

Dr Popi Iacovou
Performing Casa Malaparte: Architecture as a Living Portrait
Principal supervisor: Dr Yeoryia Manolopoulou
Subsidiary supervisor: Professor Jonathan Hill

Dr Felipe Lanuza
Absence through Layering: From Experiencing Urban Leftovers to Reimagining Sites
Principal supervisor: Dr Barbara Penner
Subsidiary supervisor: Dr Ben Campkin

Dr Jane Madsen
Kleist and the Space of Collapse
Principal supervisor: Professor Peg Rawes
Subsidiary supervisor: Jayne Parker

Dr David Roberts
Make Public: Performing Public Housing in Regenerating East London
Principal supervisor: Professor Jane Rendell
Subsidiary supervisor: Dr Ben Campkin

Dr Theodore Spyropoulos
Constructing Participatory Environments: A Behavioural Model for Design
Principal supervisors: Dr Ranulph Glanville, Professor Stephen Gage
Subsidiary supervisor: Professor Alan Penn

Image: Felipe Lanuza, Heygate Estate, 2012

MPhil/PhD Architectural History & Theory

Programme Director: Dr Barbara Penner
Programme Coordinator: Dr Nina Vollenbröker

Current Students
Wesley Aelbrecht, Tilo Amhoff, Sabina Andron, Vasileios Aronidis, Gregorio Astengo, Tal Bar, Ruth Bernatek, Thomas Callan, Chin-Wei Chang, Mollie Claypool, Miranda Critchley, Sally Cummings, Sevcan Ercan, Marcela Araguez Escobar, Pol Esteve, Nadia Gobova, Irene Kelly, Jeong Hye Kim, Claudio Leoni, Kieran Mahon, Carlo Menon, Soledad Perez Martinez, Matthew Poulter, Sophie Read, Ryan Ross, Ozayr Saloojee, Amy Smith, Lina Sun, Huda Tayob, Claire Tunnacliffe, Adam Walls, Freya Wigzell

Graduating Students
Pinar Aykaç, Stylianos Giamarelos, Dragan Pavlovic, Regner Ramos

Our MPhil/PhD Architectural History & Theory programme allows students to conduct an exhaustive piece of research into an area of their own selection and definition. Great importance is placed on the originality of information uncovered, the creativity of the interpretations made and the rigour of the methodological procedures adopted.

——Approximately 25-30 students from around the world are enrolled at any one time for MPhil/PhD research in this field. The range of research topics undertaken is broad, but most explore the history and theory of architecture and cities from c.1800 to the present day, with an emphasis on the critical reading of these subjects from cultural, political and experiential viewpoints.

——The programme draws on the expertise and experience of The Bartlett School of Architecture's team of architectural historians and theorists, who are recognised internationally for their contributions to the field. The programme itself is highly dynamic, with an active series of talks, seminars and conferences which students are expected to attend. In keeping with UCL's multidisciplinary ethos, connections between architectural research and other fields are encouraged, and there are active collaborations with the Departments of Anthropology, Fine Art and Geography, and with UCL Urban Lab.

Current Supervisors
Dr Jan Birksted, Professor Peter Bishop, Dr Camillo Boano, Professor Iain Borden, Dr Victor Buchli, Professor Mario Carpo, Dr Ben Campkin, Dr Edward Denison, Professor Adrian Forty, Professor Murray Fraser, Professor Jonathan Hill, Dr Barbara Penner, Dr Sophia Psarra, Dr Peg Rawes, Professor Jane Rendell, Dr Stephanie Schwartz, Dr Tania Sengupta

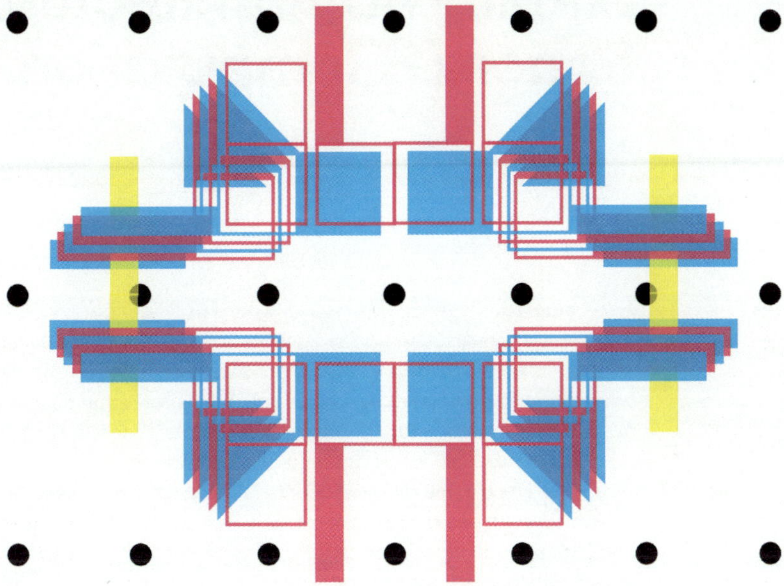

Graduating Students

Dr Pinar Aykaç
Musealisation as an Urban Process: The Transformation of the Sultanahmet District in Istanbul's Historic Peninsula
Principal supervisor: Professor Murray Fraser
Subsidiary supervisor: Dr Sophia Psarra

Dr Stelios Giamarelos
The Postmodern Ferment: The Reconsideration of the Modern, the Regional and the Critical in the Architectural Practice of Suzana and Dimitris Antonakakis, c.1980
Principal supervisor: Professor Peg Rawes
Subsidiary supervisor: Professor Iain Borden

Dr Dragan Pavlovic
The Architectural History of London Fashion Week and its Role in the Production of London as a Global City
Principal supervisor: Dr Ben Campkin
Subsidiary supervisor: Dr Barbara Penner

Dr Regner Ramos
Spatial Practices/Digital Traces: Embodiment and Reconfigurations of Urban Spaces Through GPS Mobile Applications
Principal supervisor: Dr Ben Campkin
Subsidiary supervisor: Professor Peg Rawes

Image: Dr Regner Ramos, *Spatial Practices/Digital Traces: Embodiment and Reconfigurations of Urban Spaces Through GPS Mobile Applications*

MPhil/PhD Architectural Space & Computation

Programme Director: Dr Sean Hanna

Current Students
Andre Afonso, Moritz Behrens, Deborah Do Rosario Benros, Tom Bolton, Giulio Brugnaro, Frosso (Efrosini) Charalambous, Blerta Dino, Ahmed Tarek (Zaki) Fouad, Francesca Froy, Paul Goodship, Evan Greenberg, Emma Gribble, Abril Herrera Chavez, Fani Kostourou, Petros Koutsolampros, Kimon-Vincent Krenz, Stephen Law, Nazila Maghzian, Velina Mirincheva, Nurulhuda Mohammad Isa, Rosica Pachilova, Stamatios Psarras, Dimitrie Stefanescu, Markus Urban

Graduating Students
John Bingham-Hall, Pheereeya Boonchaiyapruek, Cauê Capillé, Athina Lazaridou, Frederik Weissenborn, Yao Shen

The Bartlett's MPhil/PhD Architectural Space and Computation is associated with the world-renowned Space Syntax Laboratory, which offers an ideal intellectual environment to develop interdisciplinary research from an architectural perspective, seeking to advance knowledge by studying the relations between spatial patterns and social outcomes, and between architectural design knowledge and computation.

——The programme allows students to conduct a piece of independent research in one of two principal streams. In Space and Society in Buildings and Cities, students use space syntax theories and methods to study the effects of spatial design on aspects of social, organisational and economic performance of buildings and urban areas. In Architectural Computation, students apply technology to research into the built environment, bringing innovative computational analytical methods to the heart of the design process.

——Whilst the programme is intended primarily for students from an architectural or urban design background wishing to pursue a programme that involves empirical research, many of our students hold degrees from other disciplines, such as geography, philosophy, anthropology, urban history, crime science, physics or computer science.

——Students pursue independent research projects supervised by a principal and subsidiary supervisor, culminating in a doctoral thesis. Student topics are aligned to staff members' research interests, which include media architecture and design interaction, architectural computation, urban form and society, workplace design and organisational behaviour, spatial narratives, space syntax and evidence-based design, urban design, spatial cultures and urban spatial history.

——Research supervision is complemented by a programme of fortnightly seminars throughout the academic year – some student-led, others led by leading experts from UCL and around the world. In their first year, students will commonly audit selected modules from the lab's two postgraduate programmes: MSc/MRes Space Syntax or MSc/MRes Architectural Computation, benefiting from the rigorous training in theories and methods that these provide. The programme is also associated with the InnoChain European research network and the Engineering Doctorate in Virtual Environments, Imaging & Visualisation. Students on these programmes will typically take some of their taught modules jointly.

Current Supervisors
Dr Martin Zaltz Austwick (Centre for Advanced Spatial Analysis), Dr Jeff Bezemer (UCL Institute of Education), Dr Duncan Brumby (UCL Interaction Centre), Ava Fatah, Jorge Fiori (Development and Planning Unit), Professor Murray Fraser, Dr Sam Griffiths, Dr Sean Hanna, Dr Kayvan Karimi, Dr Liora Malki-Epshtein (Department of Civil, Environmental & Geomatic Engineering), Dr Paul Marshall (UCL Interaction Centre), Peter McLellan (Bartlett Real Estate Institute), Dr Anna Mavrogianni (Bartlett Institute for Environmental Design and Engineering), Professor Alan Penn, Dr Sophia Psarra, Dr Kerstin Sailer, Professor Bob Sheil, Dr Tasos Varoudis, Professor Laura Vaughan, Dr Katharine Willis (Plymouth University)

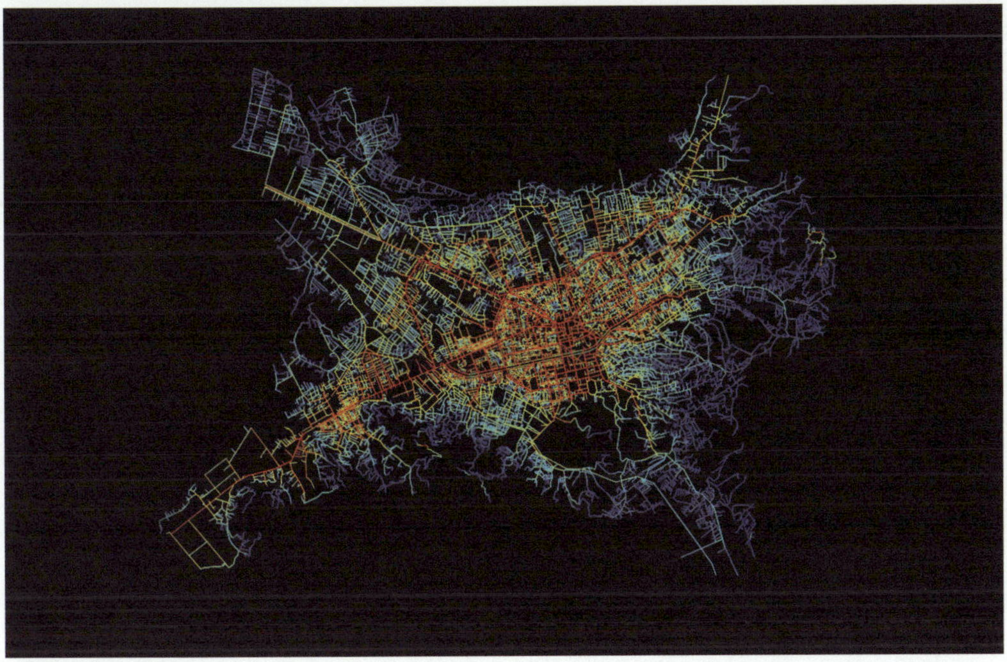

Graduating Students

John Bingham-Hall
The blog and the territory: placing hyperlocal media and its publics in a London neighbourhood
Principal Supervisor: Ava Fatah
Subsidiary Supervisor: Professor Laura Vaughan

Pheereeya Boonchaiyapruek
Spatial culture and spatial capital in Bangkok: a study of adaptability and diversity in the urban transformation process
Principal Supervisor: Dr Sam Griffiths
Subsidiary Supervisor: Professor Laura Vaughan

Cauê Capillé
Spatial cultures of public libraries: The interrelation of architecture, collective use and political agendas in Medellín's Library-Parks
Principal Supervisor: Dr Sophia Psarra
Subsidiary Supervisor: Professor Alan Penn

Athina Lazaridou
Three-dimensional spatial navigation in real and virtual museums
Principal Supervisor: Dr Sophia Psarra
Subsidiary Supervisor: Dr Sean Hanna

Yao Shen
Understanding Functional Urban Centrality: Spatio-Functional Interaction and its Socio-economic Impact in Central Shanghai
Principal Supervisor: Dr Kayvan Karimi
Subsidiary Supervisor: Professor Laura Vaughan

Frederik Weissenborn
What is urban materialism? Deconstructing the 'image of the city' in Marxist geography, space syntax and SIRN
Principal Supervisor: Professor Alan Penn
Subsidiary Supervisor: Dr Sam Griffiths

Image: Space syntax analysis of urban growth in Tirana, 1921-2016 © Blerta Dino, 2017

MPhil/PhD Architecture & Digital Theory

Programme Directors: Professor Mario Carpo, Professor Frédéric Migayrou

Computational tools for design and fabrication are inspiring contemporary architecture, reshaping the global building and construction industry, and upending the definition and roles of the design professions as we have known them in the West since the Renaissance. Since the early 1990s, schools of architecture have been at the forefront of digital innovation, and many ideas and technologies that were originally born or developed in design studios have already gone mainstream, prompting and driving global trends. Politicians and decision-makers studying the global implications of digital technologies often refer to the pioneering work of architects and architectural theoreticians, and critical categories that were first introduced and developed by the design professions and by the architectural avant-garde have been largely adopted by industrialists, sociologists and philosophers trying to come to terms with the new paradigms of a post-mechanical society.

——The Bartlett's MPhil/PhD Architecture and Digital Theory allows students to research a scholarly subject of their choosing, at the intersection of design, theory, history, and criticism, allowing them to draw from the unequalled resources of the thriving digital design community at the School, under the supervision of Professors Migayrou or Carpo. This doctoral programme is meant in particular for students who are preparing for an academic or curatorial career, regardless of their respective backgrounds or training.

Research areas

Digital design and fabrication: notational languages and design-to-production integration, from spline modellers to discretisation. History and criticism of design and fabrication software and of digital styles: from parametricism to computation. Designing with Big Data and the challenge of complexity: generative, agent-based design and cellular automata. Image theory and theories of digital replications. From pixel to voxel: 3D scanning, 3D printing and voxelisation. Material computation and structural design: granularity, variable properties materials, bio-technologies and bio-computing. From Finite Element Analysis to the 'new science' of simulation and optimisation.

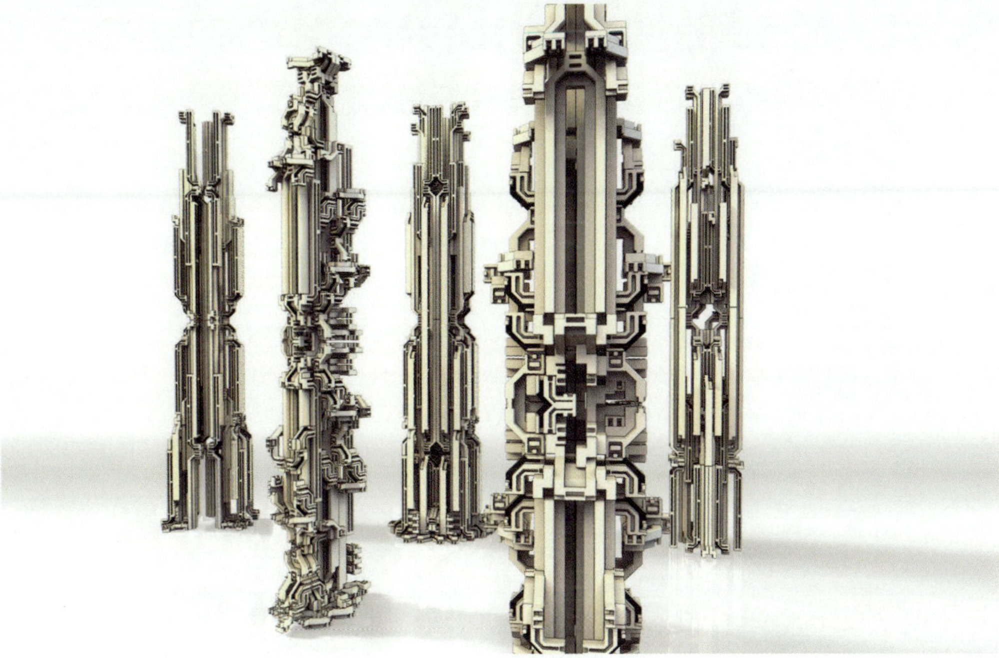

——From machine to body: the new body-machine interfaces and prosthetic apparata; scanning, sensing, virtual and augmented reality, immersive and interactive environments, from wearables to the domestic, urban and territorial scales.

——From bodies to collective intelligence: datascapes, real-time mapping, GIS and sociopolitical geography, landscapes and biotech control, history and theory of space syntax and technologies of simulation for urbanism and planning. Geospatial cyberinfrastructure.

——Cognitive aspects of design computing systems. Intelligent Support in design and in the built environment.

——The new political economy of digitally driven environments: from non-linearity and Object-Oriented Ontology to the new markets, pricing, and business models of digital econometrics.

——History of digital tools for notation and fabrication, from manual to mechanical to electrical to electronic; from Alberti's geometrical and number-based replication machines to early CAD-CAM in the 20th century. History of quantification in design and of design processes as cultural technologies: geometry and projections, numeracy and the rise of formalisation in early modern architectural theory. The modern analytic approach to structural design, from Galileo to F.E.A.

Image: MArch Architectural Design, RC4, INT, 'Versatile'

Bartlett Short Courses

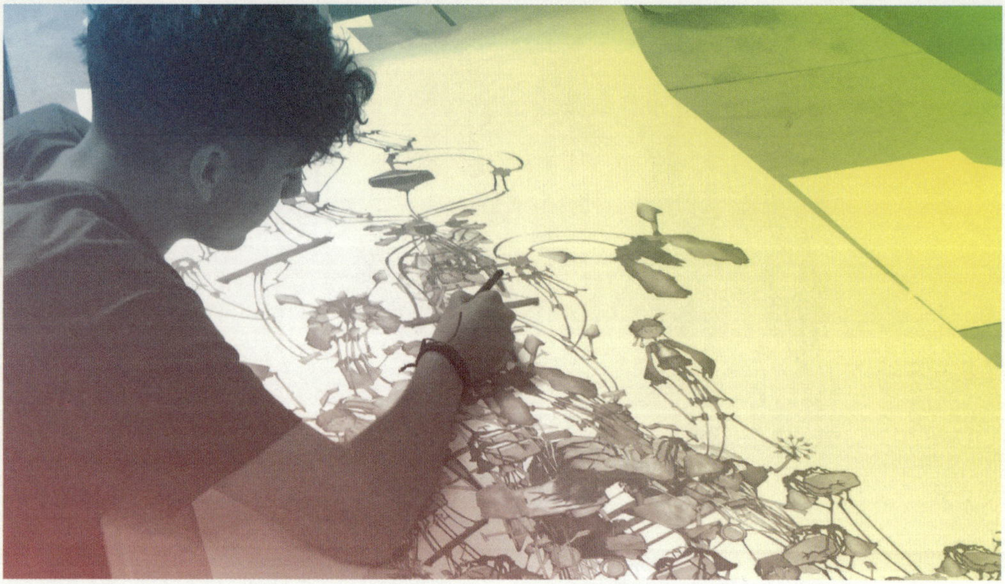

Every year, we welcome hundreds of students from around the world to experience The Bartlett School of Architecture through our range of short courses. As a world-leading architecture school in the heart of London, we are proud to offer courses for students at all stages of their education and career.

Summer School

Our Summer School is a unique opportunity for 16- to 18-year-olds to explore imaginative thinking, drawing, speculation and construction for the first time, using The Bartlett's outstanding workshops and facilities over a period of two or four weeks.

——You will be joining students from all over the world to produce drawings, objects, models and larger installations, in groups and individually, under the guidance of The Bartlett's skilled and experienced tutors.

Summer Studio

Ideal for students already studying architecture or a related discipline at university, our Summer Studio is an academic and architectural adventure, enabling students to build their design skills and conceptual and critical thinking within a playful atmosphere of experimentation and fabrication.

——With two- and four-week options, there's also the opportunity to prepare a substantial portfolio during this course.

Summer Skill-ups

The Summer Skill-ups are intensive five-day courses offering computer and portfolio training to hone existing skills and develop new ones. These can be taken in conjunction with the four-week Summer School or Summer Studio.

Pop-Up Collaboration

A series of tailor-made programmes offered to schools and universities wanting to gain an insight into the design approaches taught at The Bartlett School of Architecture.

UCL Pre-Masters Certificate in Architecture

A six-month course beginning in January 2018 for students holding a conditional offer for The Bartlett's MArch Architecture (ARB/RIBA Part 2).

Postgraduate Certificate in Advanced Architectural Research (pgCAAR)

This programme enables postgraduate students to take their work to a higher level of design and theoretical development in preparation for further study.

Search **Bartlett short courses** online to find out more.

Image: Daniel Wilkinson

Open Crits

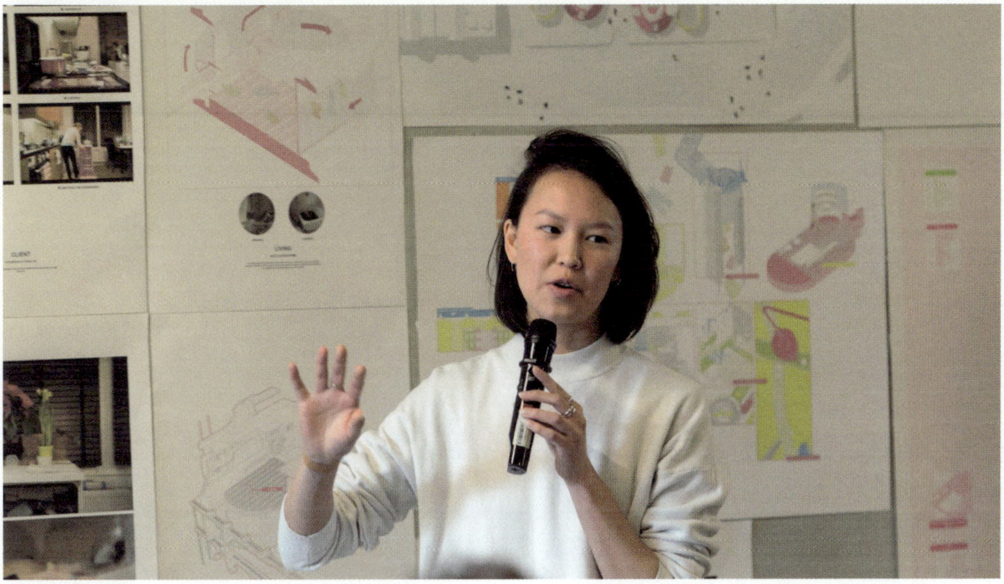

The Open Crits are a chance for distinguished external critics to critique the work of our BSc Architecture Year 3 and MArch Architecture Year 5 students. Each year, the Open Crits yield a fascinating, exploratory dialogue with students, showcasing The Bartlett's diversity at its best.

Critics

Will Alsop, aLL Design
David Bickle, V&A
Barbara-Ann Campbell-Lange
Izaskun Chincilla, The Bartlett
Nigel Coates, nigelcoates
Peter Cook, CRAB Studio
Colin Fournier, The Bartlett
Simon Herron, University of Greenwich
Christine Hawley, The Bartlett
Catherine Ince, V&A
Susanna Isa, University of Greenwich
Amanda Levete, AL_A
Niall McLaughlin, The Bartlett
Josep Mias, The Bartlett
Paul Monaghan, Allford Hall Monaghan Morris
Rory Olcayto, Open-City
Wolf Prix, COOP HIMMELB(L)AU
Yael Reisner, Yael Reisner Studio
Catherine Slessor
Maria Smith, Interrobang
Brett Steele, AA School
Emmanuel Vercruysse, The Bartlett
Suzie Zuber, Open-City

Participating Students

Gabriel Beard, Freya Bolton, Thomas Bush, Jun Hao Chan, Hohgun Choi, Justin Chow, Peter Davies, Emma de Haan, Christopher Delahunt, Georgina Halabi, Juwhan Han, Georgia May Jaeckle, Man Jia, Ziyu Jiang , Hannah Lewis, Isabel Li, Matt Lucraft, Rory Noble-Turner, Edie Parfitt, Thomas Parker, Bethany Penman, Dan Pope, Matthew Pratt, Grace Quah, Cassidy Reid, Sarmad Suhail, Ivo Tedbury, Joshua Toh, Peter West, Ke Yang

Image: Grace Quah (Unit 26) presents her project at Open Crits 2017. Photo by James McCauley

Bartlett Lectures

The Bartlett International Lecture Series

Attracting guests from across the capital, our International Lecture Series has featured over 500 distinguished speakers since its inception in 1996. Lectures in this series are open to the public, free to attend and are extremely popular. Moreover, they are all available online via the School's Vimeo channel.

This year's speakers have included:

Nigel Coates
Peggy Deamer
Odile Decq
Yvonne Farrell + Shelby McNamara
Murray Fraser
Simon Herron + Suzanne Isa
Dan Hill + Joseph Grima
Jonathan Hill
Charles Holland
Louisa Hutton
Sylvia Lavin
Lesley Lokko
Thom Mayne
Nicholas de Monchaux
Farshid Moussavi
Eva Prats
Wolf D. Prix
Jose Sanchez
Felicity Scott
Kjetil Traedal-Thorsen
Bernard Tschumi

The Bartlett International Lecture Series is generously supported by the Fletcher Priest Trust.

A range of smaller lecture series attracted a wide range of speakers. These included:

Bartlett Plexus

The Plexus Project is an open-to-all initiative that brings together the creative talent of different disciplines to share techniques, solve problems and build networks.

Recent speakers have included:
Jeroen van Ameijde, Guilio Brugnaro, Dagham Cam, Jan Dierckx, Moritz Doerstelmann, Jelle Feringa, Mathias Gmachl, Alvaro Lopez, Josef Musil, Casey Rehm, Luis Rodil-Fernandez, Roland Snooks, Aldo Sollazzo, Dimitrie Stefanescu, Satoru Sugihara, Claudia Tanskanen, Daniel Widrig

Situating Architecture

Situating Architecture is an architectural history lecture series, affiliated with our renowned MA Architectural History programme and designed for both current students and members of the public alike.

Recent speakers have included:
Dr Kuba Szreder, Dr Polly Gould, Professor Mark Swenarton, Dr Jacob Paskins, Dr Michal Murawski, Dr Karen Burns, Dr Shahed Saleem, Dr David Roberts

What's next for The Bartlett?

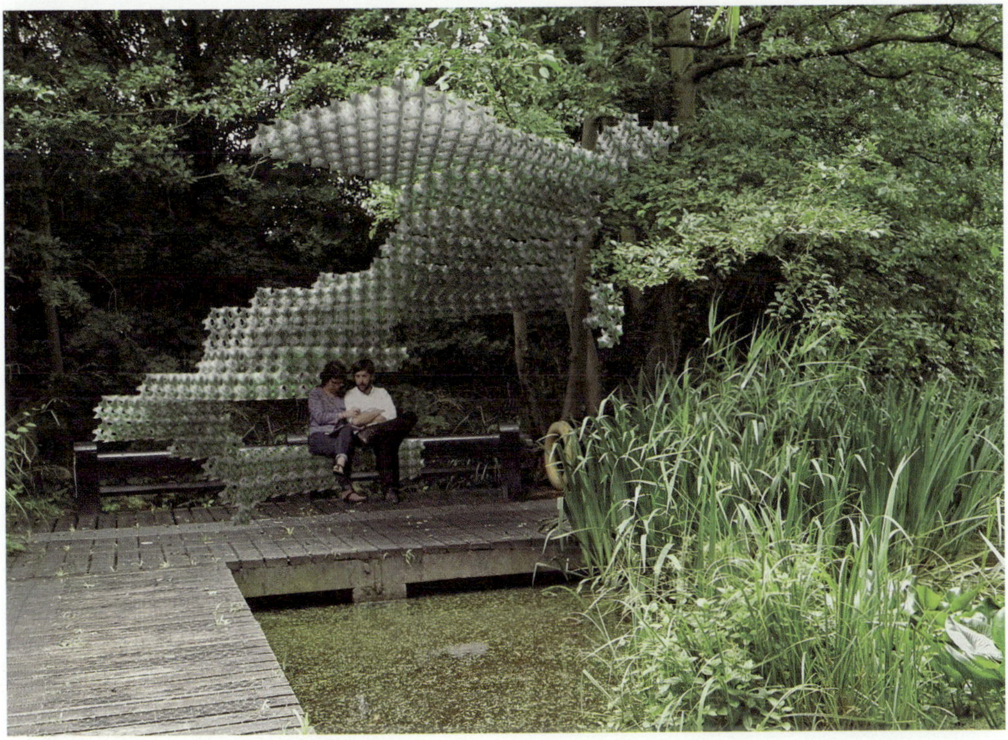

In 2018, we'll be launching a number of new programmes at The Bartlett School of Architecture, including an MArch and MSc Biointegrated Design and MLA and MA Landscape Architecture (subject to approval).

——Our Biointegrated Design (BioID) programmes explore a radically new and interdisciplinary area and are unique to The Bartlett. The programmes offer two separate study routes with distinct career paths – an MArch for design students and an MSc (run together with UCL's Biochemical Engineering Department) for science students.

——The work of BioID at The Bartlett will be shared between design studios, science laboratories and fabrication workshops. Material testing, speciation and in-vitro propagation will be carried out in parallel to the use of analytical modelling and self-generative tools. These provide feedback and data for the planning, fabrication and growth of small and large-scale biodigital prototypes. The project outcomes will vary from grown objects and bioreactors to components and/or spaces, all of which will emerge from the complex relationship between the environment, specific sociocultural contexts and programmes, and the interfacial properties of materials and organisms.

——Our upcoming MLA and MA Landscape Architecture programmes will approach landscape design with a similar studio model to that used by our world-leading MArch Architecture (RIBA/ARB Part 2). In addition to design modules, these programmes feature an environment module that complements the design studio, addressing aspects of strategy and detail, as well as modules that situate the discipline and the work of the landscape architect both within theory and practice.

Image: BiotA Lab. Environmentally responsive canopy with algae growth for Camley Street Nature Park, London
Students: Julie Hagopian, Sanika Mohite, Qian Huang, Xinyi Zhou

22 Gordon Street

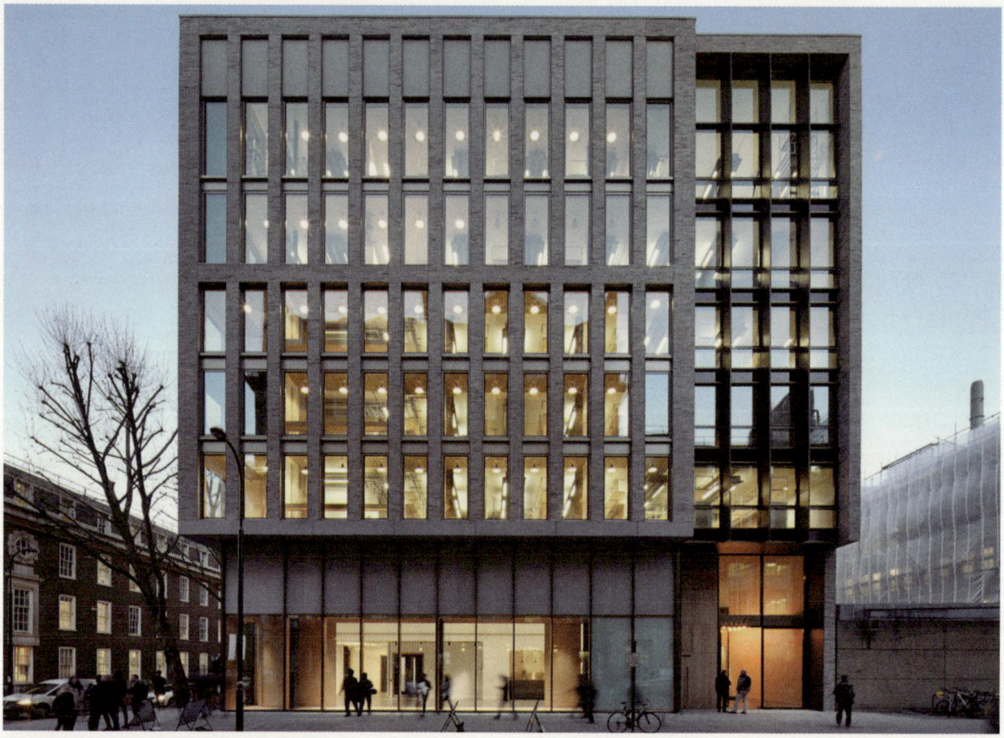

In early 2017, we moved back into our transformed home at 22 Gordon Street (formerly Wates House) on UCL's Bloomsbury Campus. The £30 million refurbishment and extension, carried out by architects Hawkins\Brown as part of UCL's Bloomsbury Campus Refurbishments project, provides additional space and an entirely new environment for the School.

——The new building has additional floors and an expansion to the south that includes an exquisitely crafted black steel stair. It contains superb new studios, new social and café areas, a contemporary exhibition space and expanded workshops.

——In line with UCL's sustainability and environmental strategy, the concrete structure of the original Wates House – home of the School since the 1970s – has been retained. This has helped significantly reduce carbon emissions and landfill waste associated with the construction project. It has also allowed the building's rich history to remain visible through a number of subtle features, such as the original blue and red handrails of the internal staircases.

——Alan Penn, Dean of the UCL Bartlett Faculty of the Built Environment, has described how four years of hard work have resulted in a "prized building for UCL," which "introduces a new generation of staff and students to the possibility of what can happen through effective collaboration". Meanwhile, Euan Macdonald, partner at Hawkins\Brown, has spoken of how "as an institution, it has become better integrated into its context – more outward-looking and welcoming to the public".

——The building has proved popular not only with students and staff, but also with the wider architectural community. It has already won a prestigious 2017 RIBA London Region Award, and has been shortlisted for the coveted 2017 AJ Building of the Year award.

——With its atmosphere of openness, spontaneity and collaboration, the new building is transforming how the School of Architecture works as cohesive body of over 900 students and 200 staff. This became apparent during the Open Crits in March 2017, which took full advantage of the new shared spaces to show off the exceptional quality of student work in a context of lively engagement and debate.

Architect: Hawkins\Brown
Contractor: Gilbert Ash

Image: 22 Gordon Street. Photo by Jack Hobhouse

Here East

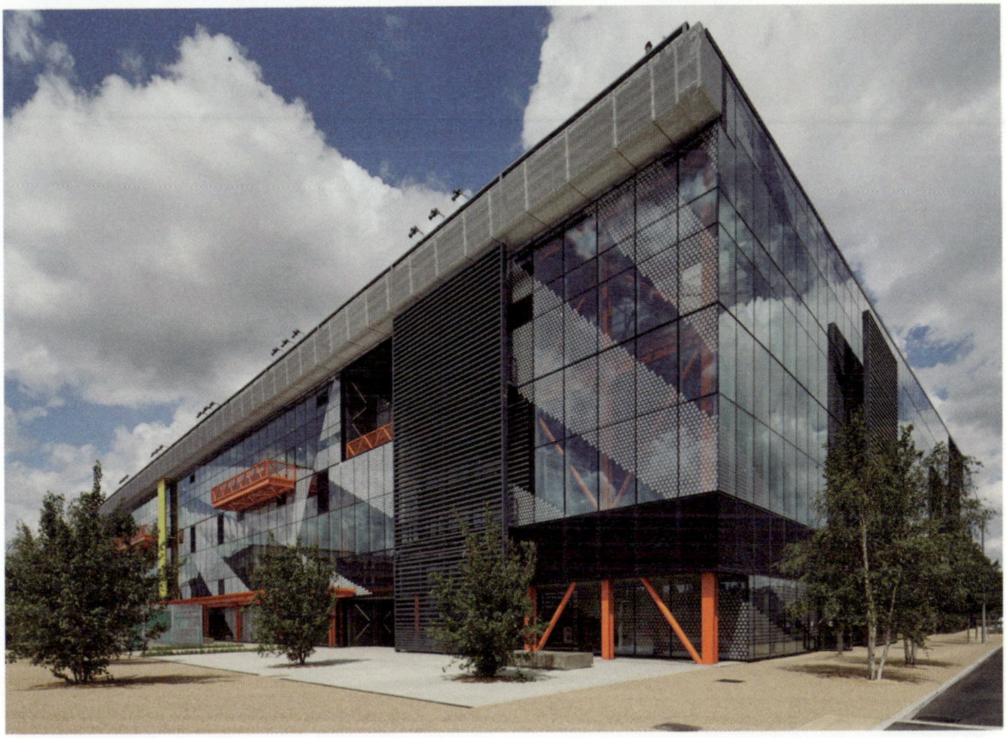

Occupying over 1.2 million square foot in London's Queen Elizabeth Olympic Park, Here East is one of London's most exciting new developments. A home for individuals and companies ranging from start-ups to some of the best-known companies both in the UK and globally, Here East offers unparalleled infrastructure for innovation and excellence.

——In 2016, UCL took over 3,000 square metres of studio space at Here East, which will be used to undertake groundbreaking research in areas that include architecture, infrastructure, transport, robotics, healthcare, manufacturing and environmental measurement. The Bartlett, UCL's Faculty of the Built Environment, and UCL Engineering will be expanding into these premises in late 2017 with teaching across four new programmes: MEng Engineering and Architectural Design, MA Situated Practice, MArch Design for Performance & Interaction and MArch Design for Manufacturing.

——The scale of The Bartlett at Here East will enable UCL to strengthen its interdisciplinary research and teaching, as well as promote greater engagement with the local community, in advance of the opening of UCL East at Queen Elizabeth Olympic Park in the 2020/21 academic year.

Image: Here East, Hawkins\Brown Architects

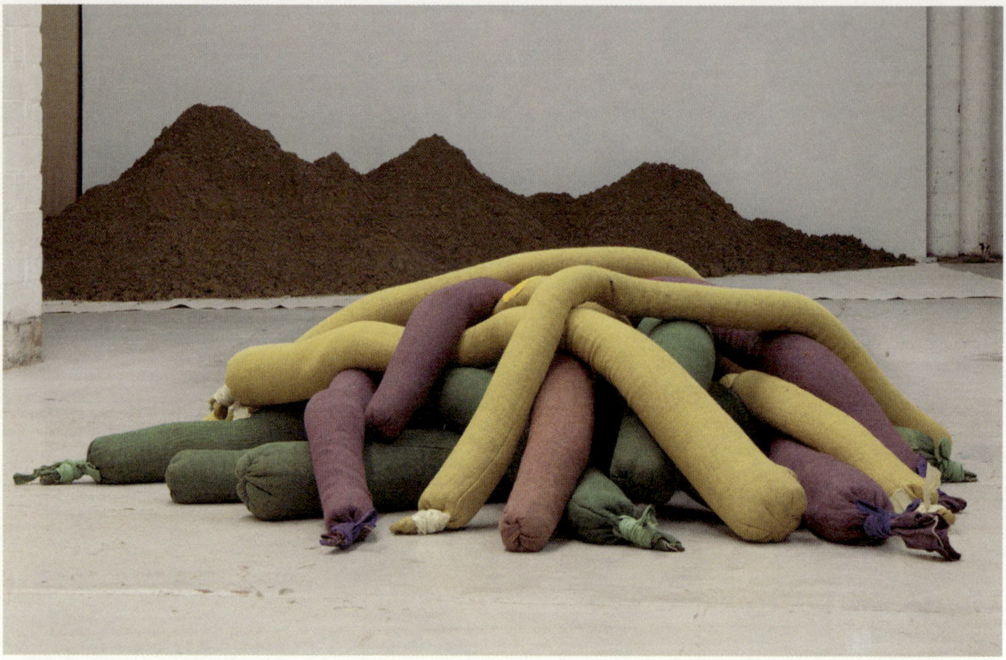

ThinkSpace

Launched in February 2016, ThinkSpace is a forum for cross-disciplinary discussion and debate at UCL curated by Jeremy Melvin, a renowned architectural historian, curator, writer and journalist (and now a Visiting Professor at The Bartlett School of Architecture).

Events are free and open to members of the public, and have attracted audiences well beyond the bounds of The Bartlett and UCL. Over the last twelve months, discussions have centred on wide-ranging and topical themes – most recently, for example, the idea of 'post-truth'. Contributors have included a diverse range of experts from academia, the law and medicine as well as the worlds of art, architecture and design.

Speakers are encouraged to draw on their often considerable experience and expertise, with subjects explored in an original and thought-provoking way. Each event includes an opportunity for questions from the audience followed by in-depth answers from the panel, leading to some impassioned and enlightening debate.

Themes and speakers from 2016–17:

Mazes and Labyrinths – Parts 1 and 2
Katy Soar
Sam McElhinney
Richard Sennett
Matthew Gandy
Simon Faithfull
MaryAnne Stevens

Corruption – Parts 1 and 2
Anita Berlin
Greg Dart
Richard Wentworth
Geoffrey Bindman
Jason File

Truth, post-truth and culture
Adrian Forty
Jo Melvin
Peg Rawes

Image: one-ton corner piece '67 (1967) and heap 3' 67 (1967) installed in Cullinan Richards, Vyner Street, 2015, © The Estate of Barry Flanagan, courtesy of Plubronze Ltd. From 'Thinkspace: truth, post-truth and culture'

EDGE
SITUATED PRACTICE IN ART, ARCHITECTURE AND URBANISM

14 SEPT
7 OCT
4 NOV

´GATEWAY, ˈPERIPHERY, ˉBORDER

EDGE
SITUATED PRACTICE
IN ART, ARCHITECTURE
AND URBANISM

is organised by the UCL Urban Laboratory and Folkestone Triennial 2017, with additional support from the Slade School of Fine Art, UCL and The Bartlett School of Architecture, UCL.

EDGE.SITUATED-PRACTICE.NET

EDGE
Where an area that is known or privileged meets another that is unknown or ignored; a point of balance between contrary or diverse phenomena; a place of connectivity and interaction.

This trio of day-long symposia, presented as part of Folkestone Triennial 2017, explores the concept of situated practice in contemporary art, architecture and urbanism. The events bring together practitioners and thinkers at three 'edge' locations connected by the High Speed 1 railway, which acts as a geographical link and embodies ideas associated with community, connectivity and escapism.

Each of the three events invites participants to respond to its specific location, investigating the sensory, social and environmental impact of their individual approaches, and together generating a narrative exploration of the creative use of interstitial spaces.

All are welcome to participate in this interdisciplinary adventure. The audience is invited to follow from one event to the next, engaging with each place as a creative asset and manifestation of a particular kind of 'edge':

GATEWAY (14 SEPT)
UCL BLOOMSBURY, LONDON
The Gower Street campus of UCL, originally planned and built on the urban/rural edge of London, acts as a 'learning gateway' for its students, as well as a transport gateway via the King's Cross development. Speakers will draw on perspectives offered by art, architecture, anthropology and pedagogy.

PERIPHERY (7 OCT)
HERE EAST, QUEEN ELIZABETH OLYMPIC PARK
Investment for the 2012 Olympic Games brought rapid development to the previously neglected Stratford area. It will shortly become the home of Here East, a cluster of institutions including the Bartlett School of Architecture. Speakers will look at the challenges of creative place-making from the perspective of architecture, urbanism and planning; some contributions will be 'performed' rather than spoken.

BORDER (4 NOV)
QUARTERHOUSE, FOLKESTONE
At the littoral edge of southeast England, Folkestone and its urbanism connect equally with water and land. From 1842 to 1992 it was the main pivot for passenger transport between France and England, and with the more recent construction of HS1, Folkestone has been gifted the status of dormitory suburb to the Capital. On the final day, the focus will again be on art-led urbanism, especially the contribution of the 'local international' and the 'social practice' of artists, architects and critics.

Full list of speakers announced in July 2017.

urbanlab · Creative Foundation · Folkestone Triennial · UCL Slade School of Fine Art · The Bartlett School of Architecture · Supported using public funding by ARTS COUNCIL ENGLAND

Staff, Visitors & Consultants

A
Thomas Abbs
Wes Aelbrecht
Visiting Prof Robert Aish
Prof Laura Allen
Kit Allsopp
Dr Kinda Al-Sayed
Alisa Andrasek
Sabina Andron
Marcela Aragüez Escobar
Max Arrocet
Abigail Ashton
Gregorio Astengo
Edwina Attlee

B
Julia Backhaus
Edward Baggs
Stefan Bassing
Paul Bavister
Richard Beckett
Johan Berglund
Prof Peter Bishop
Izzy Blackburn
Eddie Blake
Isaie Bloch
William Bondin
Prof Iain Borden
Dr Roberto Bottazzi
Visiting Prof Andy Bow
Matthew Bowles
Eva Branscome
Pascal Bronner
Giulio Brugnaro
Mark Burgess
Bim Burton
Matthew Butcher

C
Joel Cady
Dr Graham Cairns
Dağhan Cam
Blanche Cameron
William Camilleri
Barbara-Ann Campbell-Lange
Dr Ben Campkin
Moa Carlsson
Dr Brent Carnell
Prof Mario Carpo
Martyn Carter
Tommaso Casucci
Eray Cayli
Megha Chand Inglis
Prof Nat Chard
Laura Cherry
Izaskun Chinchilla Moreno
Dr Evengelia Chrysikou
Mollie Claypool
Prof Marjan Colletti
Fenella Collingridge
Emeritus Prof Peter Cook
Hannah Corlett
Paul Crudge
Prof Marcos Cruz
James Curwen

D
Christina Dahdaleh
Amica Dall
Xavier de Kestelier
Ricardo Carvalho de Ostos
Dr Edward Denison
Bernadette Devilat
Dr Ashley Dhanani
Simon Dickens
Alice Dietsch
Paul Dobraszczyk
Inigo Dodd
Oliver Domeisen
Elizabeth Dow

E
Gary Edwards
Sevcan Ercan
Ruth Evison
Dr Eve Eylers

F
Ava Fatah
Marco Ferrari
Zachary Fluker
Emma Flynn
Prof Adrian Forty
Visiting Prof John Fraser
Prof Murray Fraser
Daisy Froud

G
Prof Stephen Gage
Octavian Gheorghiu
Stelios Giamarelos
Jorge Gil
Emer Girling
Ruairi Glynn
Dr Jon Goodbun
Aleema Gray
Kevin Green
Evan Greenberg
Dr Sam Griffiths
Kostas Grigoriadis
Visiting Prof Joseph Grima
Visiting Prof Nicholas Grimshaw
Peter Guillery

H
Michael Hadi
Soomeen Hahm
Tamsin Hanke
Dr Sean Hanna
Dr Penelope Haralambidou
Colin Herperger
Prof Jonathan Hill
Visiting Prof Dan Hill
Prof Bill Hillier
Thomas Hillier
Bill Hodgson
Tom Holberton
Adam Holloway
Oliver Houchell
Vincent Hughe
Francesca Hughes
Dr Anne Hultzsch
Maxwell Hutchinson
Vincent Huyghe
Johan Hybschmann

I
Jessica In

J
Sam Jacob
Matt Jakob
JunHa Jang Jang
Carlos Jiménez Cenamor
Manuel Jiménez Garcia
Steve Johnson
Helen Jones

K
Mara-Sophia Kanthak
Dr Kayvan Karimi
Dr Jan Kattein
Jonathan Kendall
Simon Kennedy
Honorary Visiting Prof David Kirsh
Daniel Kohler
Fani Kostourou
Sofia Krimizi
Dirk Krolikowski
Dionysia Kypraiou

L
Jonathan Ladd
Chee-Kit Lai

Ruby Law
Eli Lee
Dr Guan Lee
Stefan Lengen
Lucy Leonard
Dr Christopher Leung
Amanda Levete
Ifigeneia Liangi
Prof CJ Lim
Enriqueta Llabres
Rebecca Loewen
Thandi Loewenson
Andy Lomas
Nuria Alvarez Lombardero
Alvaro Lopez
Tim Lucas

M

Shneel Malik
Arthur Mamou-Mani
Dr Yeoryia Manolopoulou
Jonathan Martin
Adriana Massidda
Emma-Kate Matthews
Alexander McCann
Prof Niall McLaughlin
Visiting Professor Jeremy Melvin
Visiting Professor Josep Mias
Stoll Michael
Bartlett Prof Frederic Migayrou
Jeffrey Miller
Sarah Milne
Tom Mole
Ana Monrabal-Cook
Ana Moutinho

N

Filippo Nassetti
Ho-Yin Ng
Thi-Phuong Nguyen
Hikaru Nissanke
Tim Norman

O

Jamie O'Brien
James O'Leary
Brian O'Reilly
Bernie Ococ
Luke Olsen
Jakub Owczarek

P

Mattia Pagura
Dr Garyfalia Palaiologou
Annarita Papeschi
Salumeh Parekh
Jacob Paskins
Claudia Pasquero
Thomas Pearce
Luke Pearson
Prof Alan Penn
Dr Barbara Penner
Mads Peterson
Frosso Pimenides
Maj Plemenitas
Andrew Porter
Arthur Prior
Dr Sophia Psarra

R

Caroline Rabourdin
Robert Randall
Prof Peg Rawes
Sophie Read
Luis Rego
Dr Aileen Reid
Prof Jane Rendell
Gilles Retsin
Arturo Revilla
Charlotte Reynolds
Harriet Richardson
Kimberly Riley
Aleksandrina Rizova
Dr David Roberts
Gavin Robotham
Jonathan Rock
Indigo Rohrer
Dr Jonathan Rokem
Javier Ruiz

S

Dr Kerstin Sailer
Prof Andrew Saint
Dr Sahed Saleem
Joanna Saxon
Carina Schneider
Peter Scully
Dr Tania Sengupta
Dr Miguel Serra
Sara Shafiei
Anthony Shawcross
Prof Bob Sheil
Naz Siddique
Sayan Skandarajah
Amy Smith
Paul Smoothy
Prof Mark Smout
Vicente Soler
Eloy Solis
Matthew Springett
Brian Stater
Emmanouil Stavrakakis
John Steadman
Dr Kimberley Steed-German
Dimitri Stefanescu
Tijana Stevanovic
Rachel Stevenson
Sabine Storp
Greg Storrar
Michiko Sumi
Yuri Suzuki

T

Martin Tang
Dr Lusine Tarkhanyan
Huda Tayob
Philip Temple
Colin Thom
Michael Tite
Freddy Tuppen
Tomas Tvarijonas

V

Melis Van Den Berg
Kim van Poeteren
Dr Tasos Varoudis
Prof Laura Vaughan
Emmanuel Vercruysse
Viktoria Viktorija
Dr Nina Vollenbroker

W

Prof Susan Ware
Bill Watts
Patrick Weber
Nick Westby
Alice Whewell
Visiting Prof Mark Whitby
Andrew Whiting
Rae Whittow-Williams
Daniel Widrig
Graeme Williamson
Dr Robin Wilson
Oliver Wilton
Nicholas Winnard
Katy Wood

Y

Umut Yamac
Sandra Youkhana
Michelle Young

Z

Paolo Zaide
Emmanouil Zaroukas
Fiona Zisch
Stamtios Zografos

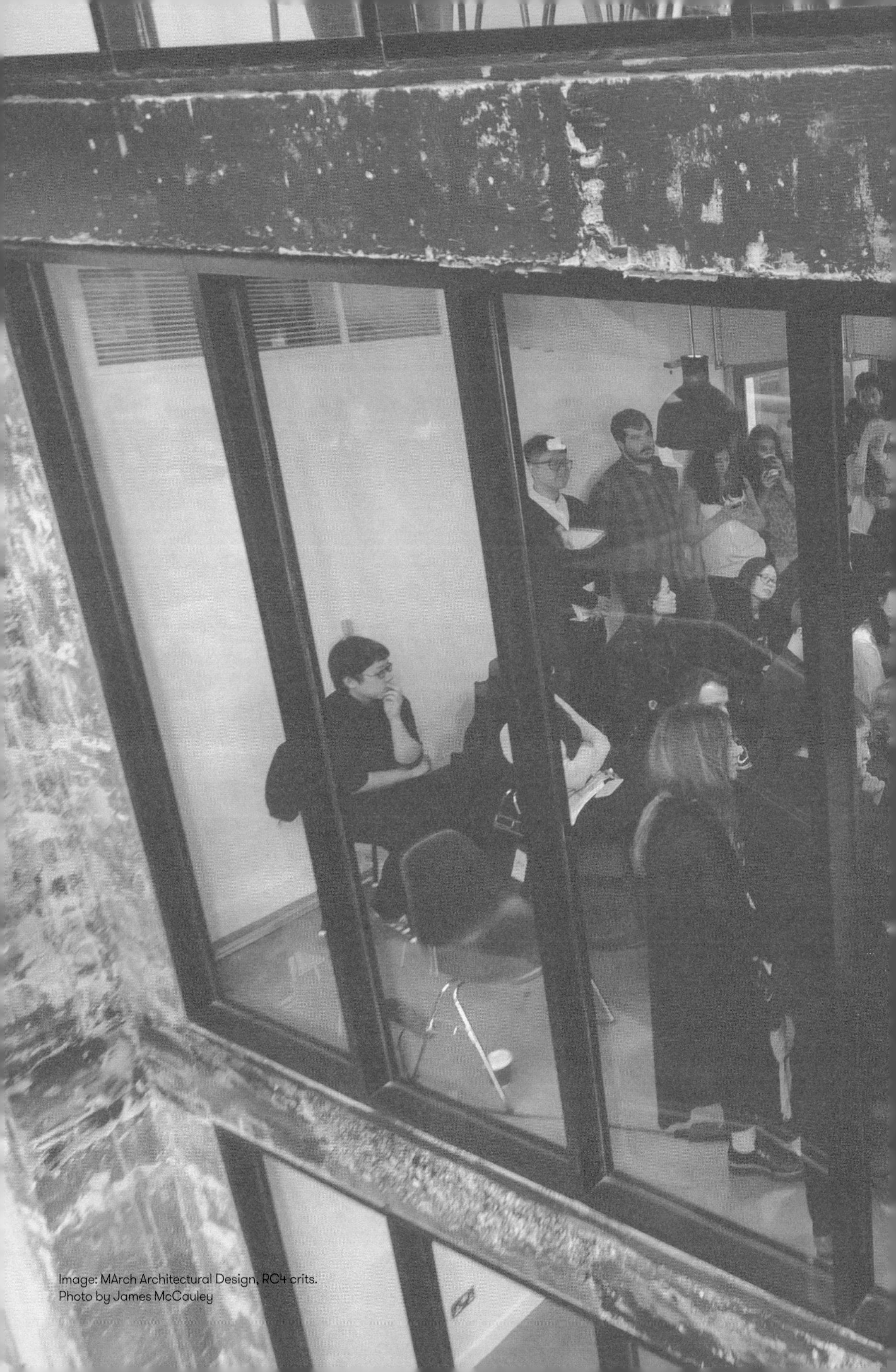

Image: MArch Architectural Design, RC4 crits.
Photo by James McCauley

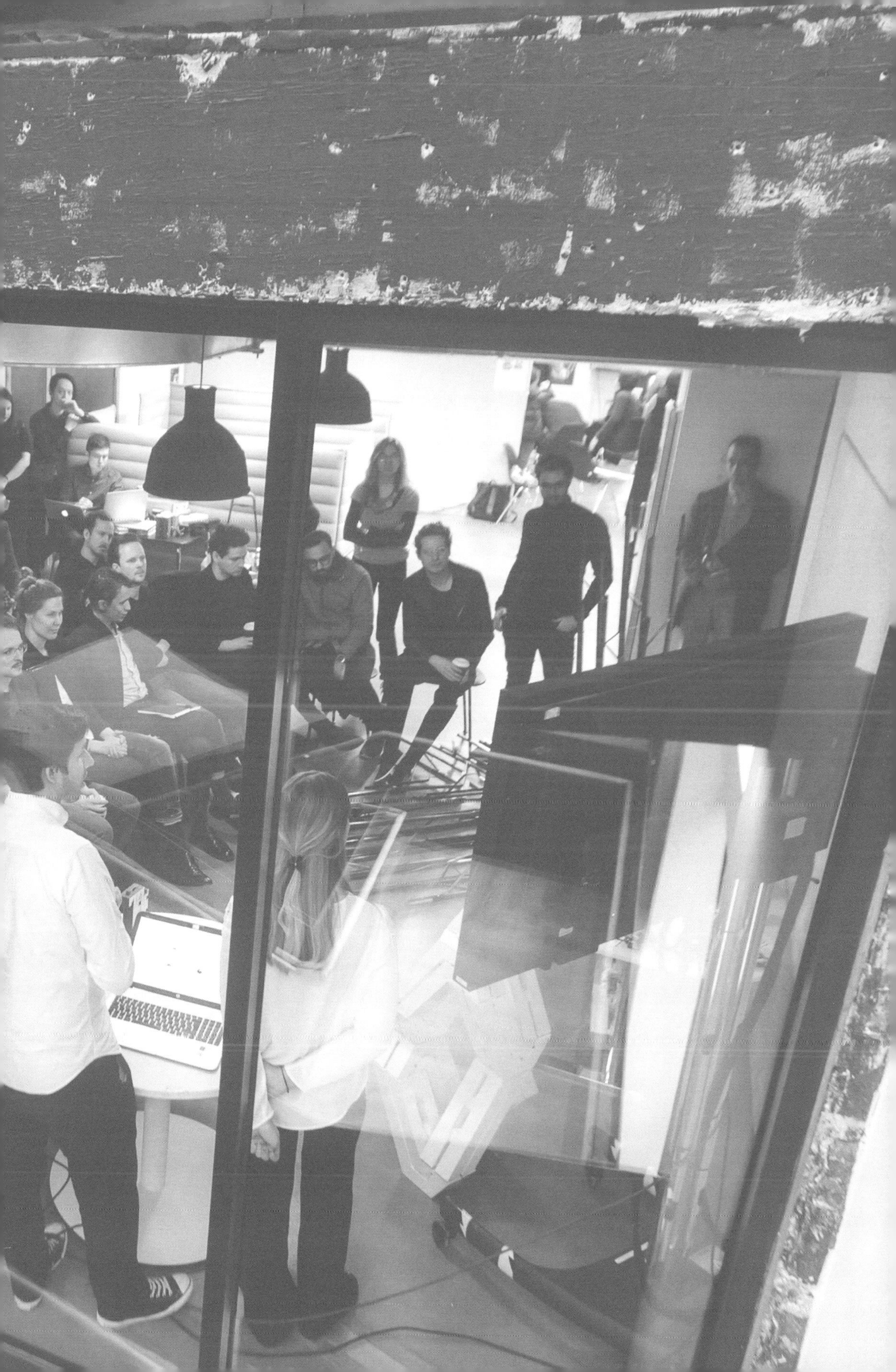

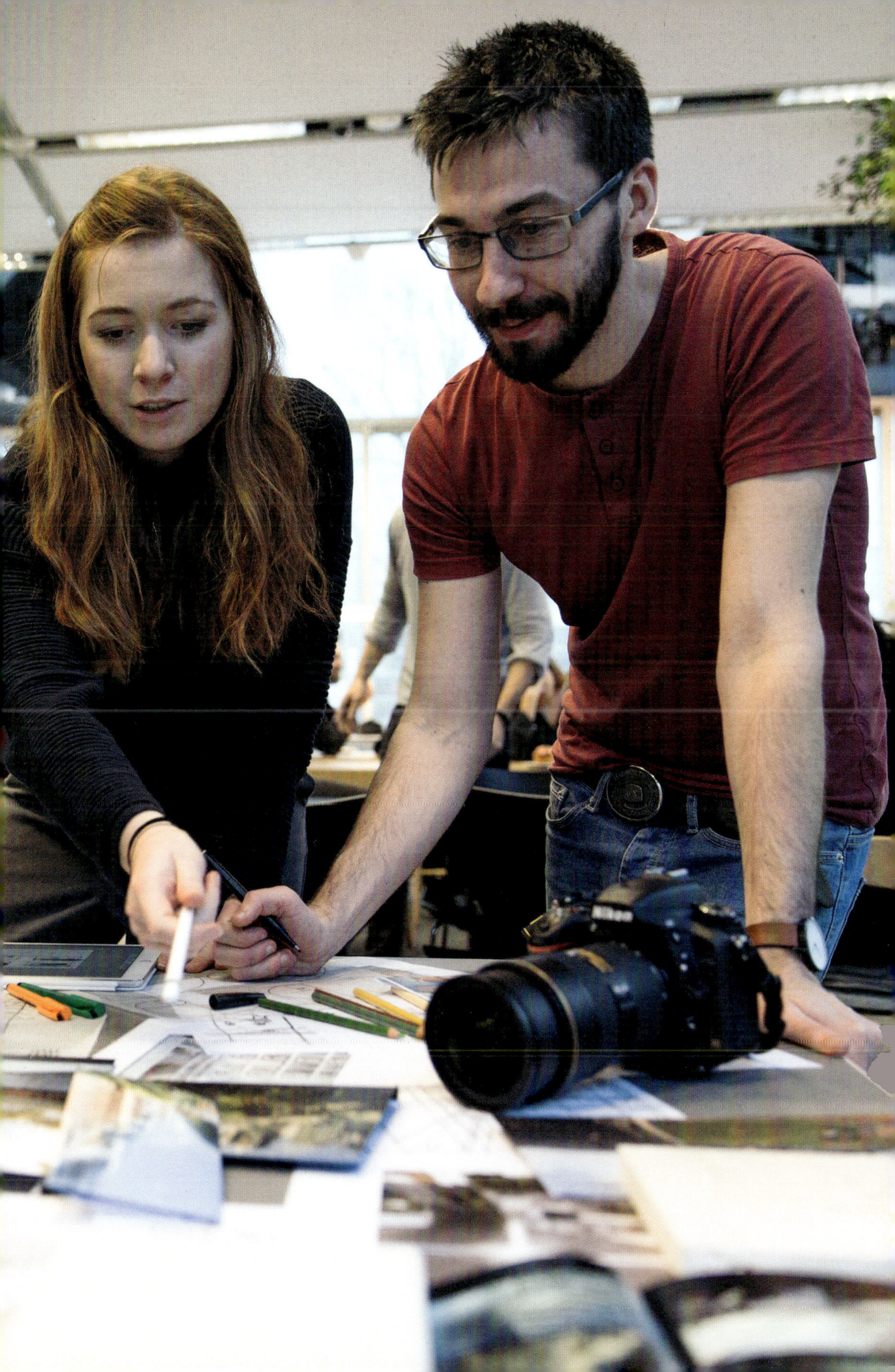

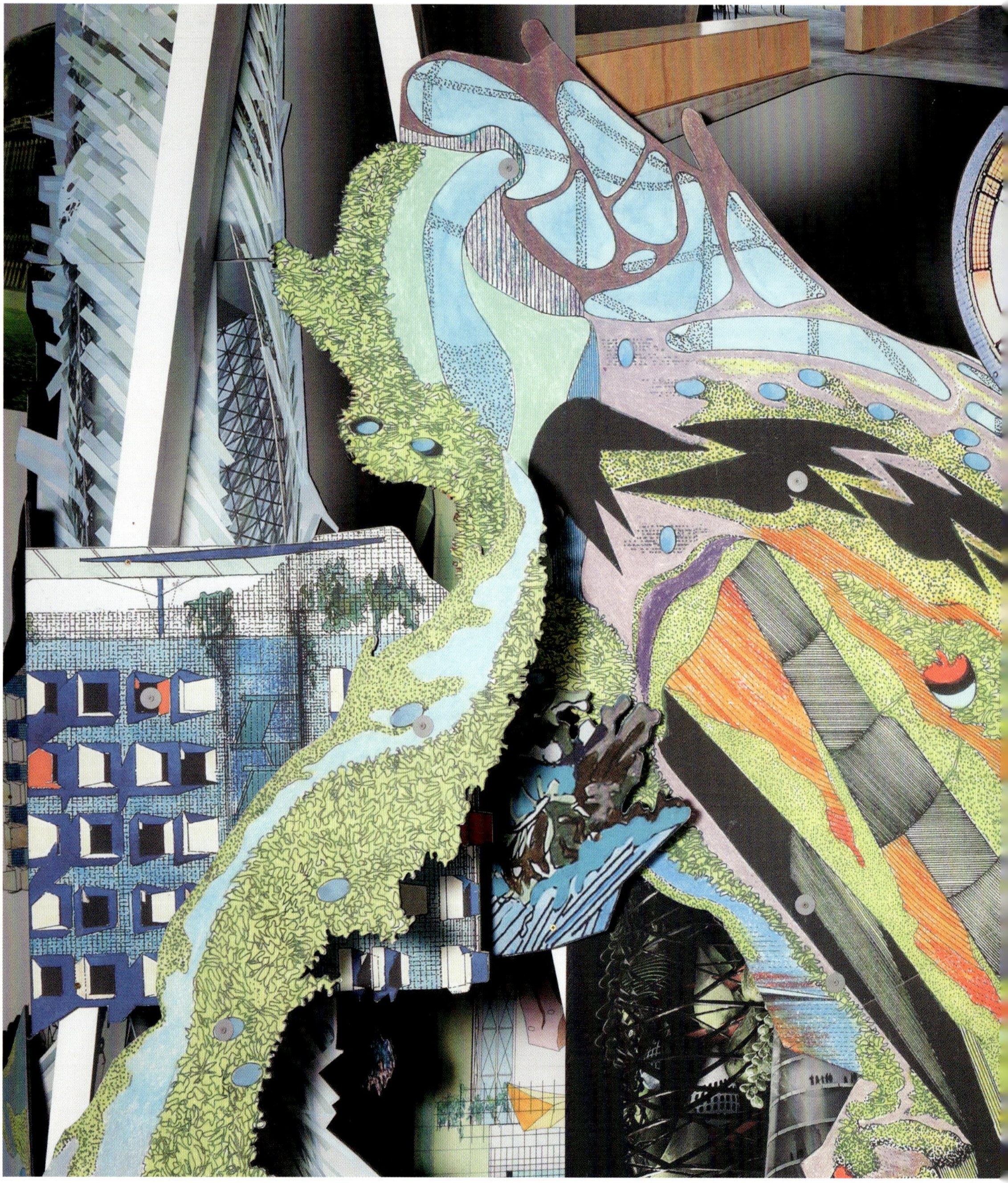

With many thanks to our 'Sir Peter Cook: 80 Years, 80 Ideas' sponsors, ABB, Lathams and the Student Print Club.

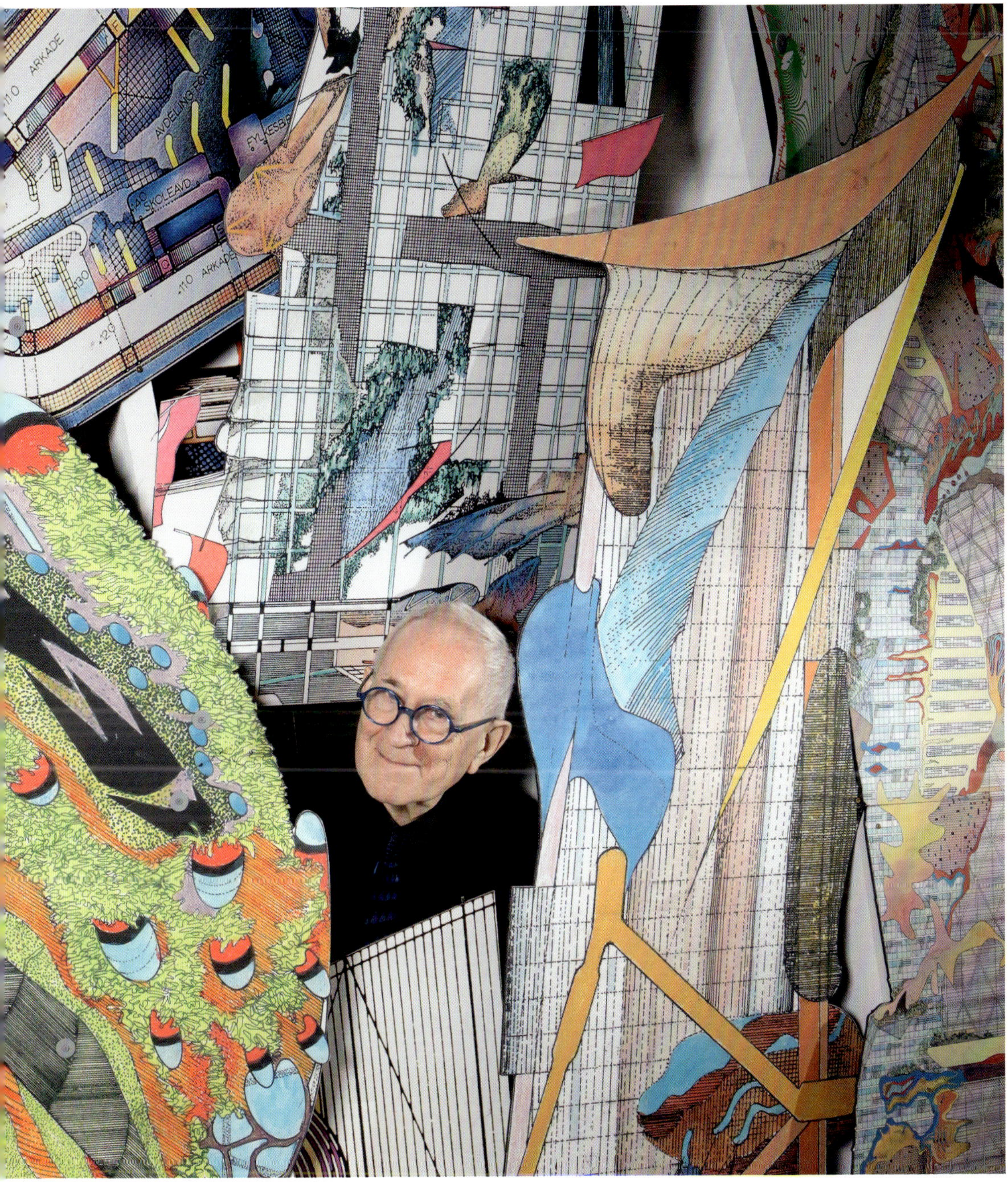

The Bartlett School of Architecture's new exhibition space was launched in February 2017 with 'Sir Peter Cook: 80 Years, 80 Ideas', the largest and most comprehensive exhibition of Sir Peter Cook's visionary architectural work to date.

We look forward to welcoming you to future exhibitions, and please do get in touch with us if you are interested in sponsoring one.

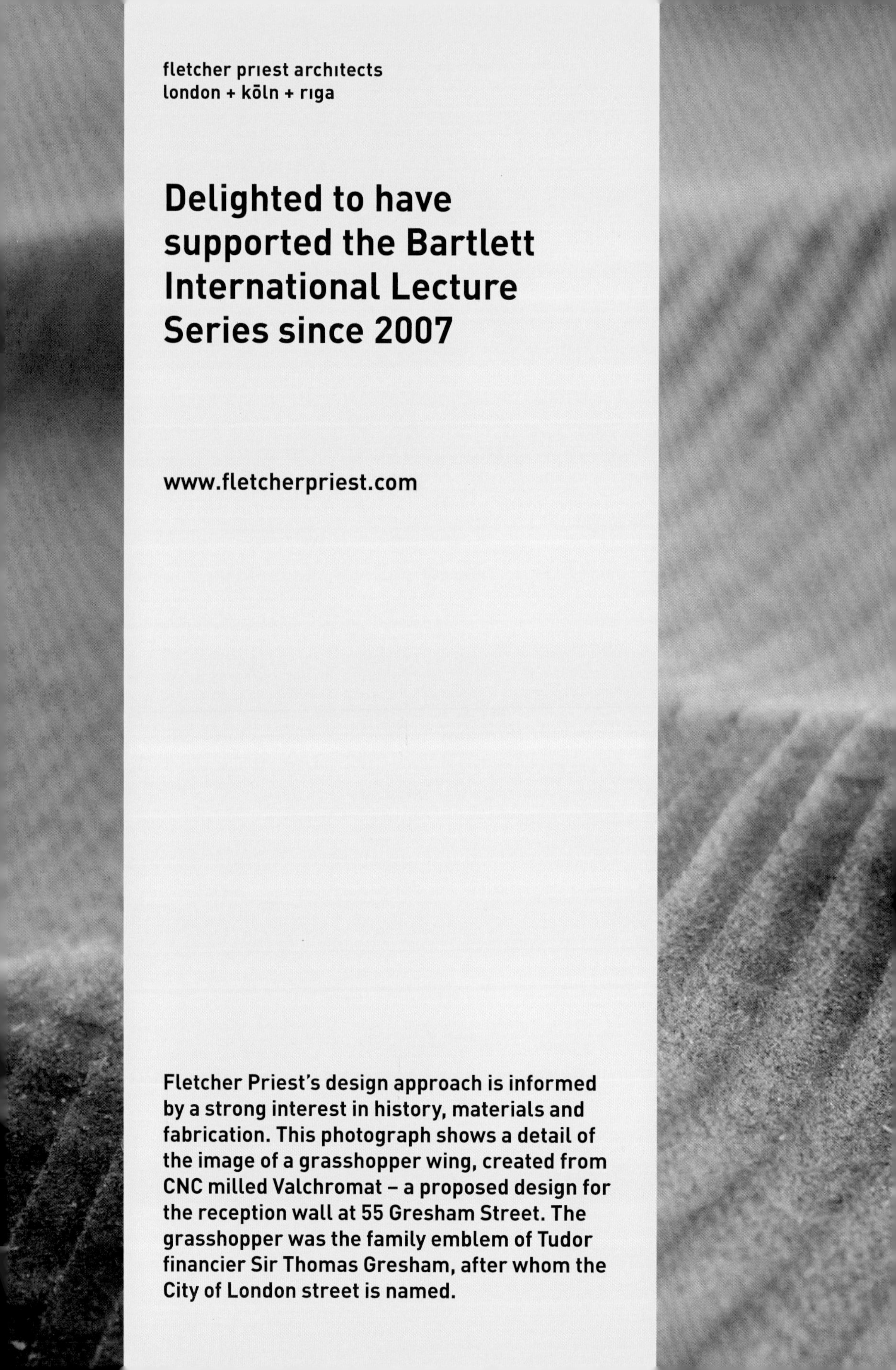

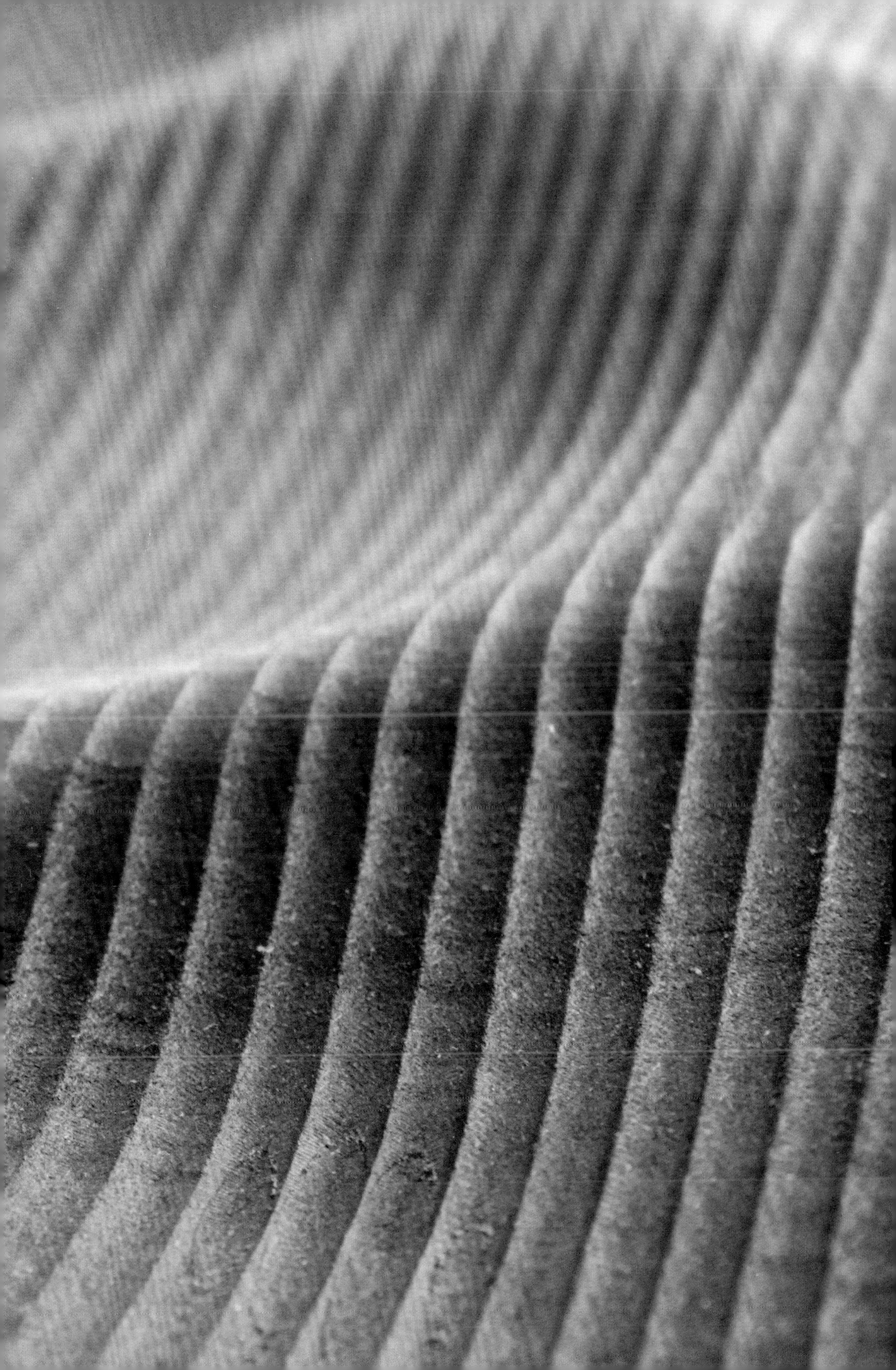

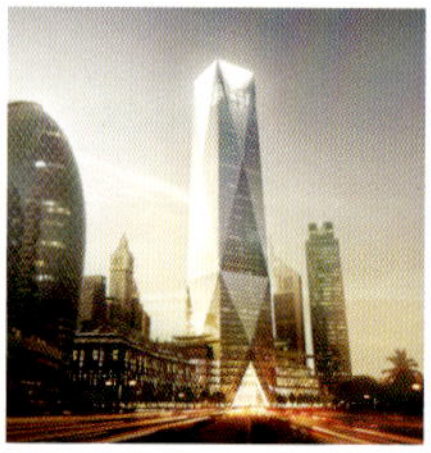

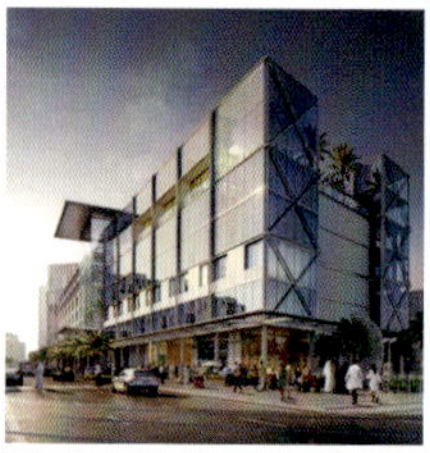

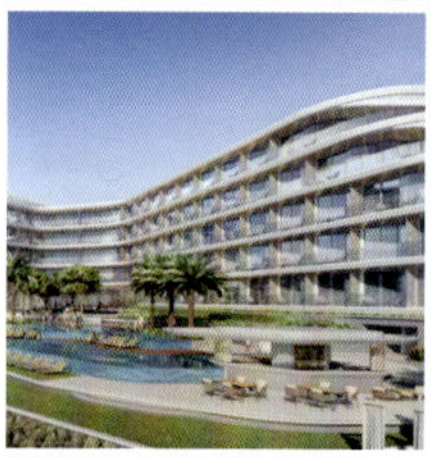

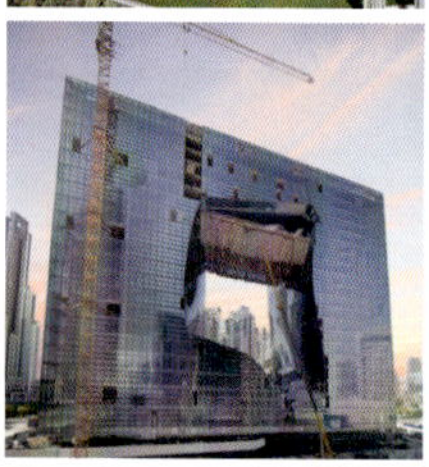

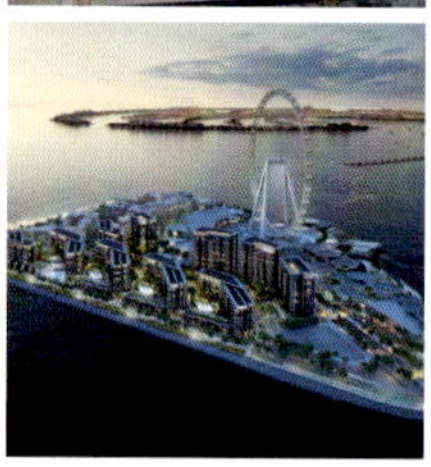

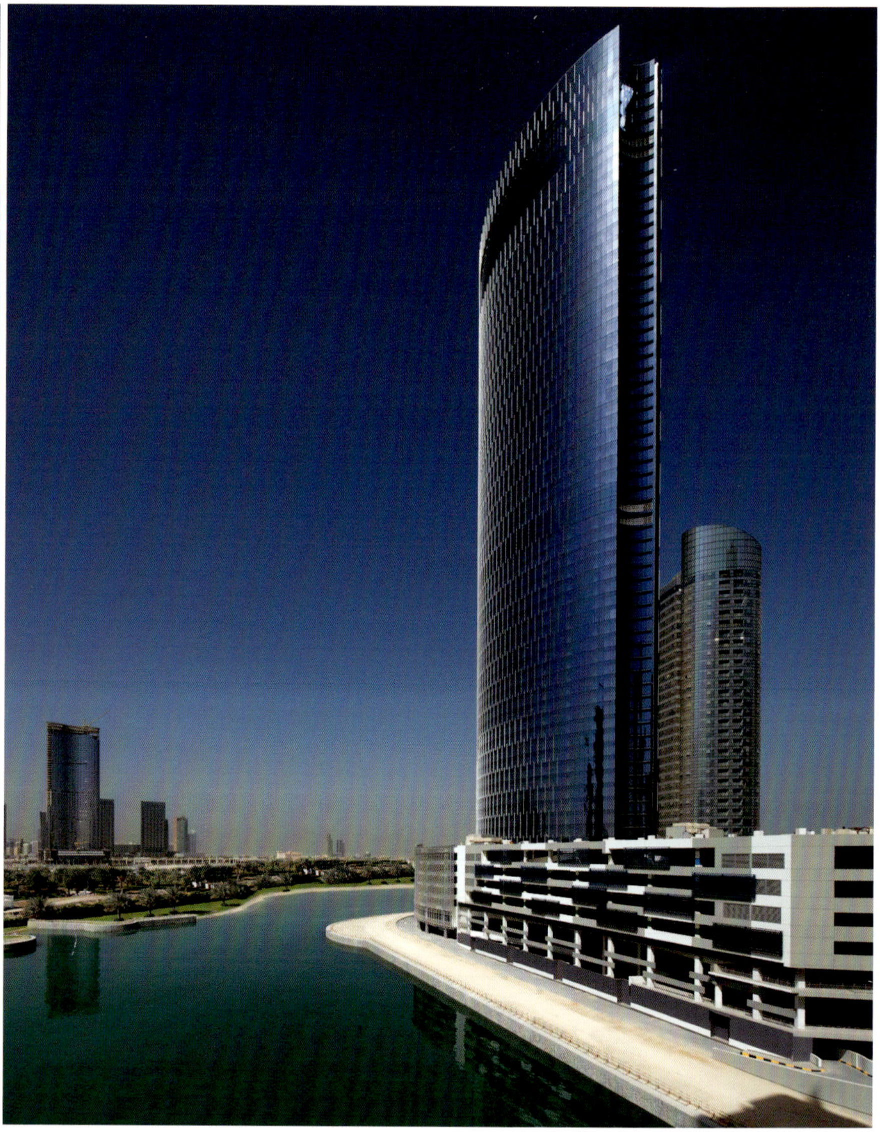

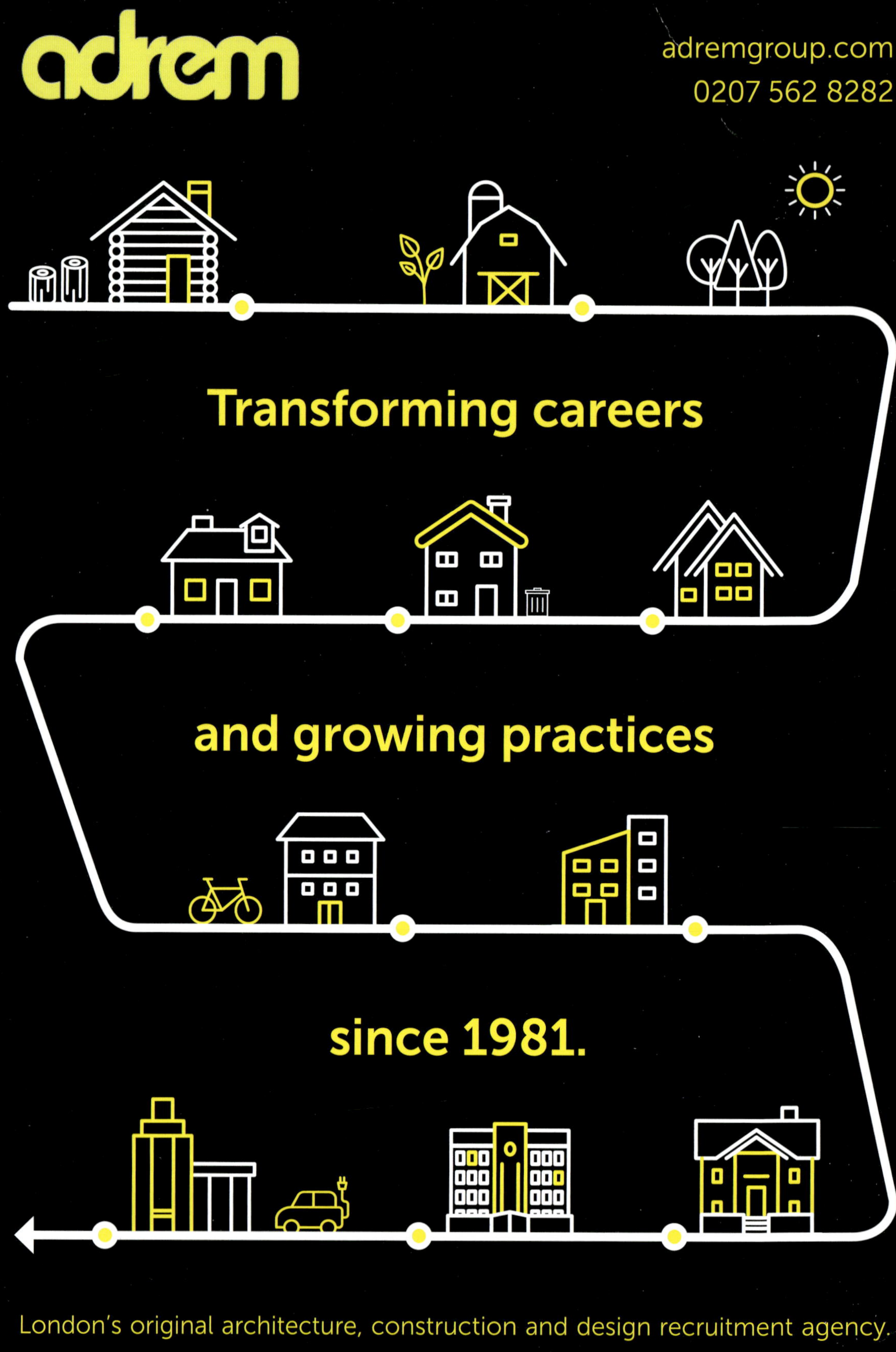
adrem
adremgroup.com
0207 562 8282
Transforming careers
and growing practices
since 1981.
London's original architecture, construction and design recruitment agency.

Supporters

We are grateful to our generous supporters:

Summer Show Main Title Supporter 2017
Allford Hall Monaghan Morris

Summer Show Sponsor
Foster + Partners
Brewer Smith Brewer Gulf

Summer Show Opener's Prize
Wilkinson Eyre

Bartlett International Lecture Series
Fletcher Priest Trust

Architecture Prizes
Saint-Gobain
Max Fordham

MArch Architecture Bursaries
Wes Lunn Design Education Trust
Kohn Pedersen Fox Associates
Rogers Stirk Harbour + Partners
Hawkins\Brown
Imagination Academy

VIP Reception
Adrem
Haines Watts

ALLFORD HALL MONAGHAN MORRIS

Foster + Partners

fletcher priest architects
london + köln + riga

BSBG

WilkinsonEyre

adrem

Haines Watts
Local Matters. National Strength.

bartlett.ucl.ac.uk/architecture

Publisher
The Bartlett School of Architecture, UCL

Editor
Eli Lee

Editorial Team
Ruth Evison, James Curwen

Graphic Design
Patrick Morrissey, Unlimited
weareunlimited.co.uk

Executive Editor
Laura Allen

ISBN 978-0-9954819-7-8

For more information on all the programmes and modules at The Bartlett Faculty of the Built Environment, UCL, visit ucl.ac.uk/bartlett

The Bartlett School of Architecture, UCL
22 Gordon Street
London WC1H 0QB

+44 (0)20 3108 9646
architecture@ucl.ac.uk

Twitter: @BartlettArchUCL
facebook.com/BartlettArchitectureUCL
Instagram: bartlettarchucl
vimeo.com/bartlettarchucl

The Bartlett School of Architecture

UCL